encyclopedia of
pentecostal and charismatic christianity

ROUTLEDGE ENCYCLOPEDIAS OF RELIGION AND SOCIETY

David Levinson, *Series Editor*

The Encyclopedia of Millennialism and Millennial Movements

Richard A. Landes, *Editor*

The Encyclopedia of African and African-American Religions

Stephen D. Glazier, *Editor*

The Encyclopedia of Fundamentalism

Brenda E. Brasher, *Editor*

The Encyclopedia of Religious Freedom

Catharine Cookson, *Editor*

The Encyclopedia of Religion and War

Gabriel Palmer-Fernandez, *Editor*

The Encyclopedia of Religious Rites, Rituals, and Festivals

Frank A. Salamone, *Editor*

The Encyclopedia of Pentecostal and Charismatic Christianity

Stanley M. Burgess, *Editor*

encyclopedia of
pentecostal and charismatic christianity

Stanley M. Burgess, Editor

Religion & Society
A Berkshire Reference Work

Routledge
Taylor & Francis Group
New York London

Published in 2006 by
Routledge
Taylor & Francis Group
270 Madison Avenue
New York, NY 10016

Published in Great Britain by
Routledge
Taylor & Francis Group
2 Park Square
Milton Park, Abingdon
Oxon OX14 4RN

Printed in the United States of America on acid-free paper
10 9 8 7 6 5 4 3 2 1

International Standard Book Number-10: 0-415-96966-2 (Hardcover)
International Standard Book Number-13: 978-0-415-96966-6 (Hardcover)
Library of Congress Card Number 2005037111

Library of Congress Cataloging-in-Publication Data

Encyclopedia of Pentecostal and charismatic Christianity / Stanley M. Burgess, editor.
    p. cm. -- (Religion and society)
    "A Berkshire Reference Work."
  Includes bibliographical references and index.
  ISBN 0-415-96966-2
  1. Pentecostalism--Encyclopedias. I. Burgess, Stanley M., 1937- II. Series: Routledge encyclopedias of religion and society. III. Series.

BR1644.E63 2006
270.8'203--dc22
                                         2005037111

Taylor & Francis Group is the Academic Division of Informa plc.

Visit the Taylor & Francis Web site at
http://www.taylorandfrancis.com

and the Routledge Web site at
http://www.routledge-ny.com

Contents

Editorial Advisory Board

List of Entries

List of Entries

List of Abbreviations

KJV	King James Version
NAB	New American Bible
NASB	New American Standard Bible
NIV	New International Version
NJB	New Jerusalem Bible
NRSV	New Revised Standard Version
OEB	Oxford English Bible
RSV	Revised Standard Version

Introduction

Christianity has experienced frequent periods of renewal. It is fair to say that Christian renewal has been both "transtemporal" (reappearing throughout the past two millennia), and "transspatial" (in all regions where the followers of Jesus have spread his message). Recent scholarship has demonstrated that renewal has often been associated with "peoples of the Spirit," despite opposition and marginalization of such groups by the ecclesiastical forces that have resisted enthusiasm in any form. The countless waves of renewal that followed the first century have been punctuated by prophetic voices, together with miracles, signs and wonders, and other evidences of what we now broadly call Pentecostalism.

This volume concentrates on modern Pentecostalism (since 1901), which differs from earlier versions in its scope and influence. Perhaps most surprising to both insiders and outsiders, this branch of Christianity now is second in size to the Roman Catholic Church. In 2000, 27 percent of all Christians (approximately 537 million) were part of the renewal, with classical Pentecostals numbering 66 million, charismatics 176 million, and neocharismatics 295 million. The combined movements are growing at the rate of 9 million per year, with the total at approximately 571 million in mid-2004.

Classical Pentecostals usually mark their origins on 1 January 1901, at Charles Parham's Bethel Bible School in Topeka, Kansas, when Agnes Ozman spoke in tongues (glossolalia). We now are aware that this was not the first post-apostolic incidence of such glossolalia. In reality, the real significance of this date was that Pentecostals for the first time linked the "initial physical evidence of Spirit Baptism" with tongues speech. This has remained the common distinctive claimed by most classical Pentecostal denominations.

The Charismatic movement emerged in already existing Christian denominations from 1959 onwards. On 3 October 1960, Dennis Bennett, an Episcopal rector in Van Nuys, California, announced to his congregation that in November 1959 he had been baptized with the Holy Spirit and had spoken in tongues. By the early 1960s people in virtually every major Protestant tradition had similar experiences. In February 1967 the Charismatic movement spread to the Roman Catholic Church, beginning simultaneously at Duquesne University in Pittsburgh, Pennsylvania, and in Bogota, Columbia. All charismatics emphasize a "life in the Spirit" and the importance of extraordinary gifts of the Spirit, including but not limited to glossolalia, both in private prayer and in public worship.

By far the largest group within modern Pentecostalism is the neocharismatics. This is a catchall category that comprises nearly nineteen thousand independent, indigenous, nondenominational and postdenominational groups that cannot be classified as either classical Pentecostal or charismatic. They share with classical Pentecostals and charismatics a common emphasis on exuberant worship, the Holy Spirit, spiritual gifts, Pentecostal-like experiences (*not* Pentecostal terminology), signs and wonders, and power encounters. In virtually every other way, however, they are as diverse as the world's cultures they represent.

The purpose of this volume is to introduce the reader to these vast worldwide Christian renewal movements. Contributors represent both "insider" and "outsider" perspectives. Treatment is necessarily uneven because academic scholarship of classical Pentecostal and Charismatic movements is just now flowering, and the independent and indigenous churches and groups included in the neo-charismatic fold have only been episodically studied by social scientists.

The volume contains 135 articles covering four broad topics—Concepts, History and Study of Pentecostalism, Practices and Institutions, and Regional Surveys. The Concepts articles cover particular beliefs, doctrines, or theological approaches central to Pentecostalism. These articles describe and explain the concepts from the viewpoint of Pentecostalism in a way that will be clear to the uniformed reader. The History and Study articles cover paradigms, methods, approaches, or institutions that have been used or involved in the study of Pentecostalism. The Practices and Institutions articles focus on movements or institutions within Pentecostalism, and related movements or institutions, or general sets of practices within Pentecostalism that pertain to the relationship between Pentecostalism and society in general. The Regions articles survey Pentecostalism in a particular geographical area or a nation. The articles are supplemented by dozens of photos and sidebars and an extensive index.

Because it transcends space and culture and is growing so rapidly, especially in the "three-quarters world," the Pentecostal-Charismatic renewal is increasingly difficult to define in traditional terms. To borrow a Durkheimian (1912) expression, it might be more appropriate to call these movements the emerging "collective effervescence" of the Christian world.

Acknowledgments

I wish to acknowledge David Levinson and his outstanding Berkshire Publishing Group staff for their ongoing assistance in the development of this volume. David provided encouragement and necessary guidance, but always allowed me complete freedom in areas of content and emphasis. Staff members Emily Colangelo, Joseph DiStefano, Jessica LaPointe, Courtney Linehan, and Marcy Ross were most helpful in editorial and production coordination. I am grateful as well to Marie-Claire Antoine of Routledge for her encouragement in the early stages of this project. Thanks also to my editorial board, William Wedenoja, Jerry Shepperd, and Martyn Percy, for their wise counsel.

I have benefited from the support of both Missouri State University and Regent University. Special thanks to my colleagues, deans, and staffs in both institutions for their continued assistance. To all contributors, many of whom are former colleagues and students—friends of long-standing—I am deeply indebted. Numerous archives were opened to me, most notably the Flower Pentecostal Archives in Springfield, Missouri, where Wayne Warner and Glenn Gohr were always available to answer questions and to provide necessary details. My graduate assistant, Eric Newberg at Regent, has lightened my load on many occasions.

Finally, I thank my wife, Dr. Ruth Vassar Burgess, a scholar in her own right, for providing ideas, and just the appropriate combination of spur and salve needed to complete *The Encyclopedia of Pentecostal and Charismatic Christianity.*

STANLEY M. BURGESS

Further Reading

Barrett, D., & Johnson, T. (2004). Annual statistical table on global mission: 2004. *International Bulletin of Missionary Research*, 28(25).

Barrett, D., & Johnson, T. (2002). Global statistics. In S. Burgess, *New International Dictionary of Pentecostal and Charismatic Movements* (pp. 286–287). Grand Rapids, MI: Zondervan.

Durkheim, E. (1995). *Elementary forms of religious life*. New York: Simon and Schuster. (Original work published 1912)

Africa, East

East Africa was originally considered to include Kenya, Uganda, and Tanzania (called Tanganyika prior to 1964 and German East Africa prior to around 1920). In colonial times, this region fell under the jurisdiction of British and German administration, although it became an exclusively British colonial domain after World War I. The historiography of East African Christianity has long focused on mission Christianity in the late nineteenth and early twentieth centuries. This changed around the 1960s, when there was an outgrowth of independent and charismatic churches, founded by African prophets and based on biblical beliefs, African religiosity, and the manifestation of charismatic gifts. This religious creativity based in local agency and drawing on African religious concerns and practices helped to root Christianity firmly in the East African environment. The East African revival movement and the activities of Pentecostal missionaries provided the ground from which Charismatic and Neo-Pentecostal Christianity later emerged in East Africa.

East African Revival

In 1927, the East African Revival—known as the *Balokole* in Luganda and as the *Ahonoki* in Kikuyu (two languages of the region)—started within missionary churches in Rwanda and spread to Uganda, Tanganyika, and Kenya. The revival evolved as a response to the perceived lethargy of missionary Christianity. It was a spontaneous mass movement initiated and sustained mainly by indigenous agency, predominantly African laity. It embraced the Charismatic movement in the Anglican Church of Uganda and made room for schismatic movements among the Luo people, such as the Church of Christ in Africa, which began as an Anglican revival movement called *Johera* (People of Love) in 1952 but separated from the Anglican Church in 1957, and Mario Legio of Africa, a split from Roman Catholicism. These offshoots place doctrinal emphasis on salvation in the form of a personal encounter with Jesus and stress mutual confession of sins as well as the primacy of visions and dreams, prophecy, speaking in tongues, prayers, hymn singing, and dancing. The participation of local and foreign evangelists and the enthusiasm of school- and college-aged participants have contributed to the revival's flourishing. The revivalists were challenged to form local self-supporting evangelical groups, which led in the 1960s and 1970s to the proliferation of local evangelical teams.

Roho Movements

One manifestation of African struggles for self-determination in the religious sphere was the emergence of prophets and prophetesses, who, seized by the Holy Spirit, acquired charismatic gifts leading to the establishment of spiritual churches. During the late 1920s and early 1930s, Luo and Kikuyu lands witnessed a high proliferation of African-instituted churches (AICs; also called African Initiated Churches). The emergence of *Roho* (the Holy Spirit) movements among the Luo is traced to 1912, the year in which Roho was believed to have made its initial appearance in the Ruwe region of present-day Tanzania. Most *arathi* (prophets or seers) use Roho to designate themselves as a community in the power of the Holy Spirit.

1

With headquarters in Nyanza province, the Masanda Holy Ghost Church of East Africa, Cross Church of East Africa, and Ruwe Holy Ghost Church of East Africa share common historical traits. They view themselves as custodians of the Spirit, and all trace their origin to the ecstatic Roho movement. The last of these, the Ruwe Church, crystallized under the leadership of Alfayo Odongo Mango of Masanda in the 1930s.

The historiography of the *Joroho* (People of the Spirit) is centered on Mango. He was involved with the Anglican Church and was even appointed deacon of a large, predominantly Luo area in 1927. Following a traumatic mystical experience, he began to preach to his people. Imbued with the Holy Spirit, he was able to heal people, foresee the future, and assert the need for an African-led church in the face of foreign domination. Mango is portrayed by followers as both a temporal and spiritual liberator. His life and violent martyr's death have great significance for them, and he is frequently mentioned during ritual services as members recount episodes in Roho ecclesial history. The Joroho converge annually on Ruwe and Masanda for the Sikunuu mar Raper (Celebration of Remembrance) to worship and celebrate the bravery of Mango and their other martyrs, who died in 1934. These sacred sites are also their "New Jerusalem" and "new home."

The Wakorino represents several Kikuyu AICs that trace their origin to the same period. The Agikuyu spirit churches emerged in Central Kenya during the religious and political upheavals of the 1920s; members were also variously called *arathi*, *watu wa Mungu* (people of God), *aroti* (dreamers), or *akurinu* (roaring prophets), because of their spiritual quest for possession of the Holy Spirit. Joseph Ng'ang'a was one of the most famous *arathi* charismatic figures. He had a spiritual experience in 1926, in which God called him to an active spiritual life. Ng'ang'a went into spiritual seclusion for three years, devoting himself to prayer, meditation, fasting, and intensive Bible study. Emerging out from this spiritual retreat, he began preaching in the villages near his home.

From the 1930s, *arathi* and Roho churches faced criticism from both mission churches and the colonial government. Both *arathi* and Roho churches emphasized millennial deliverance and opposed the occupation of their lands by Europeans and the missions' denunciation of polygymy and clitoridectomy. They rejected foreign currency, amenities, and food, and spoke against certain Western and local beliefs and practices. *Arathi* gave up Western clothes and took to wearing *kanzu* (a long white gown) and a white turban. Drawing upon the vernacular Kikuyu Bible, *arathi* rooted their beliefs in God and the Holy Spirit, their election by God as a chosen people, their concepts of purity and impurity; and their faith in dreams, prophecy, and healing.

Meanwhile, colonial officials and missionary authorities considered Mango's activities among the Luo subversive and troubling, and thus were carefully watching him. His political activities heightened when he joined the campaign for the recovery of land traditionally claimed by the Wanga people. Mango's involvement in the Luo-Wanga land disputes as well as his religious activity led to his murder in 1934. Although most of the AICs faced harsh repression on both the political and religious fronts, most survived and gradually acquired legitimacy in the postindependence era.

Missionary Pentecostals

The earliest missionary Pentecostals to come to East Africa were relatively late on the scene compared with the Anglicans and Moravians, who had arrived in the 1860s and 1890s respectively. Many Europeans, particularly Britons, moved to East Africa after World War I, but one of the earliest Pentecostal missionaries, Emil Danielsson, came from Finland to Kenya even earlier, in 1912. Other early arrivals were Clarence Grothaus and Karl and Marion Wittick, who arrived in 1913 and worked as missionaries first in German East Africa and later in Kenya. A second group of missionaries, led by George Bowie of the Bethel Pentecostal Assembly (out of Newark, New Jersey) arrived in German East Africa in 1914. Scandinavian (Swedish and Norwegian) missionaries arrived in Tanganyika in 1921. In the 1930s, Paul and Evelyn Derr, U.S. Pentecostal missionaries, went to Tanzania. Meanwhile, in Kenya, the Canadian Otto Keller continued the work started by Karl Wittick. On land purchased in Nyang'ori (western Kenya), Keller established a church, school, workshop, student dormitories, and a home for missionaries. This Kenya Mission sought affiliation with the Pentecostal Assemblies of Canada (PAOC).

PAOC Legacy

In 1924, PAOC accepted Kenya as one of its mission fields, with Nyang'ori becoming the center of its missions outreach. A great revival broke out at the mission stations in 1929, and many people from many ethnic groups were converted and filled with the Holy Spirit. This conversion necessitated the recruitment of Kenyans to further the mission work. Educational programs were started to instruct new converts. A number of earlier PAOC missionaries became involved in educational work. Although Germany lost their East African colony to Britain after World War I, German-speaking Pentecostal missions continued to be involved in evangelization there. The PAOC, under the Canadian evangelist Willard Cantelon, forged links with the German Volksmission (German People's Mission). Since 1956, the two groups have collaborated in missionary work in East Africa. Schools were seen as a means of evangelism, and so churches and schools were erected side by side. Both men and women were involved in education, medical work, and church building.

The PAOC's Pentecostal influences spread to Uganda through individual Ugandans' contacts with Kenyans. Ugandans who attended programs in Kenya were baptized and became filled with the Holy Spirit. When they returned to Uganda, they started to build churches and spread the message. These religious trends grew stronger in 1944 with the visit of Vernon Morrison, at that time PAOC's field director for East Africa. Other missionaries, including William and Viola Brown (in 1956), Arn and Elsie Bowler (in the 1960s), and Alex Strong (in 1970), joined in missionary work and in the building of churches.

The PAOC work in Kenya, Uganda, and Tanzania was originally united under the Pentecostal Assemblies of East Africa until the break-up of the East African Federation. As a consequence of the break-up, each country took up the name Pentecostal Assemblies of God (PAG). The missionary body expanded after World War II, but was drastically reduced in the 1970s.

In 1968, the PAG in Uganda obtained its official registration through the efforts of Robert Earnes. Prior to the erection of the first Bible School at Mbale, Uganda, Ugandan PAG pastors all received training at Nyang'ori in Kenya. Sadly, all PAOC missionaries were forced to leave Uganda during the political upheaval instigated by Uganda's president Idi Amin in the 1970s.

PAG work in Tanzania started when Kenyan Pentecostals moved to Tanzania, partly in search of land. The Mau Mau movement that preceded Kenyan independence had immense impact on these missionary activities. The uprising, which revolved around the Kikuyu, Embu, and Meru peoples, was aimed at wresting political power from the British. From 1965, most churches erected by the PAOC turned over control of the church to Kenyan national leaders such as Charles Gungu, Richard Odongo, and Richard Odeng. In Uganda, national leaders of the earliest Pentecostal formations included Gideon Okakaali and John Ekanyu.

Other Pentecostal Missionary Groups

Other Pentecostal bodies that established missions in East Africa include the Finnish Free Foreign Mission, which founded the Full Gospel Churches of Kenya in 1949, and the Swedish Free Mission and Pentecostal Foreign Mission of Norway, which, in a 1984 merger, created the Free Pentecostal Fellowship in Kenya. The Kenyan Assemblies of God was founded in 1969 by Dale Brown, an independent Pentecostal missionary.

The Swedish Free Mission first became involved in missionary work in Tanganyika in 1932. The Finnish Free Foreign Mission joined them in a collaborative work in 1934. In 1986, the Swedish Free Mission in Tanzania metamorphosed into Umoja wa Makanisa ya Pentekoste Katika Tanzania (Pentecostal Churches Association in Tanzania).

In Uganda, Gary and Marilyn Skinner pioneered the Kampala Pentecostal Church, a large English-speaking Pentecostal church. The Elim Pentecostal Fellowship Uganda (from the Elim Fellowship of Lima, New York) began working in Uganda in 1962. Norwegian and Finnish Pentecostal missionaries followed in 1963.

Recent Developments

Charismatic and Pentecostal churches have proliferated from the 1980s onwards. Some have been founded by indigenous East Africans and others by foreign evangelists. One of the largest Pentecostal churches in Nairobi is the PAG-owned Valley Road Pentecostal Church. This church was formerly led by a number of foreign missionaries but is now headed by indigenous leadership. The Pentecostal Evangelistic Fellowship of Africa, established by the Elim Fellowship of Lima, New York, through Bud Sickler, is today an independent, self-supporting association led by Erastus Otteno. Independent Pentecostal churches founded and led by Kenyans include the Redeemed Gospel Church, founded by Arthur Gitonga; the Christ Pentecostal Church, founded by Gabriel Otieno; and several others. The Full Gospel Bible Fellowship, which originated in Nigeria, was introduced into Tanzania in the late 1980s. That church, led by Zacharia Kakobe, is today one of the fastest-growing churches in Tanzania.

African evangelists and church founders have played a crucial role in the vernacularization of Christianity in East Africa. They have been instrumental in translating the scriptures, interpreting the Christian message, and conveying it to others. African evangelists have understood the relevance of the Christian message to their own lives and the lives of local people, and thus could communicate in a way that makes for more understanding and a greater contextualization of Christianity.

AFE ADOGAME

See also African Initiated Churches; Contextualization; Globalization of Pentecostalism

Further Reading

Anderson, W. B. (1977). *The church in East Africa 1840–1974.* Nairobi, Kenya: Uzima Press.

Droz, Y. (2001). The local roots of the Kenyan Pentecostal revival: Conversion, healing, social and political mobility. *IFRA: Les Cahiers, 20,* 23–44.

Githieya, F. K. (1997). *The freedom of the spirit: African indigenous churches in Kenya.* Atlanta, GA: Scholars Press.

Hoehler-Fatton, C. (1996). *Women of fire and spirit: Faith and gender in Roho religion in western Kenya.* Oxford, UK: Oxford University Press.

Kenyatta, J. (1962). *Facing Mount Kenya.* London: Vintage. (Original work published 1938)

Murray, J. (1974). The Kikuyu spirit churches. *Journal of Religion in Africa, 5*(3), 198–234.

Rasmussen, A. B. (1996). *Modern African spirituality: The independent Holy Spirit churches in East Africa, 1902–1976.* London: British Academic Press.

Spear, T., & Kimambo, I. N. (Eds.). (1999). *East African expressions of Christianity.* Oxford, UK: James Curry.

Welbourn, F. B. (1961). *East African rebels: A study of some independent churches.* London: SCM.

Welbourn, F. B., & Ogot, B. A. (1966). *A place to feel at home: A study of independent churches in western Kenya.* London: Oxford University Press.

Africa, North (and the Middle East)

The purpose of this article is to give the reader an overview of the Pentecostal, charismatic, and neo-charismatic communities (also known as renewal churches) of this vast region. Such an overview will require noting a number of the difficulties that these communities experience. Not every member experiences persecution. In most societies Christians are left alone, provided they stay within the bounds of both societal laws and demands of local customs. In villages throughout the region that traditionally have both Christian and Muslim populations, most coexist peacefully, can form friendships, and even participate in feasts in the other's communities. Still, Western standards of freedom of worship and expression do not prevail throughout the region.

The area encompassed by this article is vast, stretching some five thousand miles from Morocco to Afghanistan, and more than thirty-five hundred miles from Kazakhstan to Sudan, containing a population in excess of a half a billion. Because of the enormity of the area, the regions will be briefly introduced in this work, with selected countries covered in more detail.

Area-Wide Issues

The problems faced by the renewal peoples of the region come in a number of guises. These involve issues surrounding the status of apostasy, *dhimmitude,* neocolonialism, and Islamic Fundamentalism. These issues are introduced here and will be expanded upon in the discussion of individual subregions and individual countries.

Apostasy

The subject of apostasy from Islam is a severe problem for these communities of faith. Proselytizing is illegal in virtually every country. Likewise, conversion (especially from Islam) is illegal. The penalty for conversion or proselytizing can be death. More often, the penalty consists of negative sanctions from family, kin, and neighbors in an effort to persuade the convert to return to Islam.

One cannot openly witness in most of these societies, apart from suffering some sort of legal repercussions. Foreign missionaries rarely approach strangers. However, one is generally allowed latitude to discuss religion if one is asked about it by a Muslim. Even Saudi Arabian law (which is the most restrictive of all in regard to non-Muslims) allows foreign workers to respond to questions about religion from local Muslims. Even when foreigners are identified by the government as likely clandestine missionaries, they are tolerated until a complaint is filed. The complaint will be acted upon, and generally at the very least the foreigner's visa will not be renewed. Oftentimes, the charges filed will include charges that go beyond proselytizing, including such charges as espionage, consuming alcohol, sodomy, and the like. Foreigners also cannot possess evangelistic materials for distribution in most countries in the region.

The response to converts varies widely from society to society. Generally governments do not violently intervene in the case of apostasy, but local responses can include beatings unto death. In other areas, the response is more accepting.

Dhimmitude

Dhimmitude denotes the legal status of certain non-Muslims dwelling under Muslim political control. Those who fall under this category are those who are known as the "People of the Book"—those religions that have a written collection of Scriptures. Initially, this rubric was aimed at Jews and Christians, though the category broadened, as Muslim rule extended, to include Zoroastrians and Hindus. *Dhimmis* are granted freedom of religion, legal system autonomy (except when Muslims are involved; further, they can choose to be governed by Islamic law rather than their own tradition), and local political autonomy in exchange for a special tax (known as the *jizya*). *Dhimmis* are under the military protection of their Muslim overlords as well (which in turn prevents *dhimmis* from needing weapons). This status was once nearly universal in the Muslim world, though the tax and most formal laws (e.g., differing clothing for *dhimmis*) have disappeared throughout the region. However, many of the distinctive marks of status have passed into culture (e.g. clothing), as well as lowered social ranking. Legal distinctions between Muslims and non-Muslims still exist as well.

Neocolonialism

Another problem faced by both converts and missionaries is the reaction against former Western colonial powers as North African and Middle Eastern nations become more disentangled from the ties of their former Western overlords. The normal economic abuse inherent in a colonial relationship is not forgotten by any of the countries in the region. Conversion to Christianity in general is viewed not only as apostasy from Islam, but also as an act of subversion, of abandoning one's culture for the West. Perhaps this thought is best illustrated by Article 10 of the Cairo Declaration on Human Rights in Islam (1990): "It is prohibited to exercise any form of compulsion on man or to exploit his poverty or ignorance in order to convert him to another religion or atheism." Another example would be the prohibition one finds in the Constitution of Pakistan, which prohibits an educational facility from forcing students to worship or engage in ceremonies or learn about religions other than their own. Clearly, the concern in these examples is forced cultural domination by the West.

Distrust is focused not merely upon missionaries, but also aid workers, contractors, and upon businesspersons from the West. The materialism and moral laxity viewed on satellite channels beaming episodes of American productions such as *Baywatch*, soap operas, and MTV are considered to be agents of corruption by most sincere Muslims, both of spiritual values (e.g., lusts of the flesh) and of societal ethics (e.g., emphasis on individual desires and upon materialism at the exclusion of concern for others). Individuality, so celebrated by the West, is understood to be anti-Islam and anti-Arab.

Neocolonialism is still alive, as money from Western nations in the form of loans, grants, and trade agreements exerts pressure upon these nations to conform to Western standards of individual freedoms. The United States is the prime mover in this process.

Fundamentalism

Islamic Fundamentalism is a response to Western materialism and moral laxity. Fundamentalism's appeal of spiritual power is quite attractive to those who lack economic and political power. Among the many targets of Fundamentalists are Christians, who in addition to being non-Muslim, embody the values of the West (at least according to the Fundamentalists).

Successes

Despite these obstacles, renewal churches are growing throughout the region, in some cases at a rapid rate. Most of the successes are attributed to the supernatural aspects of these traditions. Healings are a common avenue of conversion. Jesus (or in Arabic, Isa) is the greatest prophet in Islam aside from Muhammad. Many of the hadiths (oral traditions traced to Muhammad or to followers who knew him) concerning Jesus paint him as a great healer. Thus, associating Jesus with this act does not require much of a leap. However, the hadith accounts paint him as more of a physician and tend to downplay his compassion. Islam rejects both his divinity and his atoning death, holding that humans are not inherently sinful (and the prophets—including among others in Christian tradition, Adam, Abraham, Moses, and Jesus—were all sinless), and there was no need for atonement. Visions and dreams are also commonly reported as playing a role in conversion.

The miraculous does not appeal to one particular class of Muslims, namely the Sufis. The Sufis practice an ecstatic religion, which is filled with the same types of experiences as renewal believers. Sufis can be Sunnis or Shiites. In some areas, Sufis are themselves oppressed.

The bulk of missionary work occurs on a one-on-one basis. One is rarely successful in confronting Muslims head-on, and even more rarely is one successful in approaching a stranger. The distribution of pamphlets, Bibles, and other literature occurs, as well as the distribution of a widely successful film entitled *The Jesus Film*, and cassette tapes. Also, Christians are allowed to have Muslims attend church in most countries (Saudi Arabia is a notable exception), provided they did not in any way coerce their appearance. However, it is the interaction with believers, including accounts of the miraculous, that ultimately wins the bulk of converts. Theological, philosophical, and other approaches pale to experiential.

Subregions

The following is an examination of individual countries within the regions of central Asia, the Middle East, the Arabian peninsula, and North Africa that illustrates the interaction between the dominant cultures (and governments) and the local Christian populations.

Central Asia (Azerbaijan, Kazakhstan, Kyrgyzstan, Tajikistan, and Uzbekistan)

These nations were all formerly members of the Soviet Union. They inherited an apparatus for controlling religions, which they all still employ to some degree against religions the government is suspicious of. The prime method of restricting churches is by means of bureaucracy, by not issuing permits for meetings, denying requests to build churches, and voiding leases with church bodies. For example, one Pentecostal church in Kyrgyzstan was shut down for failing to meet building code requirements, as were its two affiliate churches elsewhere in the country. The government later revoked the church's tax-exempt status, in an effort to slow the growth of this denomination, which has nearly ten thousand adherents.

Unregistered activity of any sort is suspect and liable to criminal prosecution. A new law in Turkmenistan, for instance, declares that any illegal religious gathering will result in a sentence of a year of "corrective labor." Only Sunni Muslims and Russian Orthodox are recognized religions that can obtain permits to legally gather, as the government does not recognize any other religious body as possessing the required minimum of five hundred adherents. A presidential decree nullifying the law goes unacknowledged for the most part.

Uzbekistan Uzbekistan often goes beyond bureaucratic oppression to imprisoning individuals. Imprisonment was the lot of a number of pastors, including a number of Pentecostals. Consistent international pressure has reduced sentences, although steep fines (often one hundred times the average monthly wage, totaling about $600) are still assessed for activities the government finds displeasing. Another Pentecostal pastor was told to return (again and again) for a permit that has yet (after two years) to be issued. After a confession that the local government did not want Christianity spread in their locale and threats including prosecution, the pastor sought asylum outside (as have many other Protestants—only the Russian Orthodox Church claims that neither they nor converts encounter substantive hostility in Uzbekistan). In another example of government hostility, two Pentecostals were arrested while reading the Bible in the home of one. Private worship is legally allowed, but the police arrested them on the grounds that they were preaching to each other (and thus proselytizing rather than worshipping). They were beaten before being released.

Western South Asia (Afghanistan, Pakistan)

Afghanistan is likely the least evangelized country in the entire region. Approximately three thousand or so are Christian, roughly half of them Pentecostal. Pakistan has the greatest number of neocharismatics in the region (perhaps more than half a million), and the greatest number of combined renewal churches in the region (as well as having nearly twice the total population of any other country in the region). Life is precarious in much of the country, as Pakistan's loose hold on tribal regions has fostered a haven for Fundamentalist groups. The government walks an uneasy line between shari'ah (Muslim traditional laws) and efforts to court Western money (and the demands for minority rights that come with it). Freedom of worship varies from area to area within the country.

Middle East (Iran, Iraq, Israel, Jordan, Lebanon, Palestine, Syria)

Lebanon and Syria have the highest concentrations of Christians in the subregion, though their numbers of renewal churches are not correspondingly high. These churches are growing very slowly in Lebanon, due in part to animosity lingering from the civil war that ended in 1992. This circumstance may change soon, given a presidential decree allowing a wide range of educational, worship, and aid projects to be undertaken by the Evangelical Assemblies of God. Christians are treated comparatively well in Syria and Jordan, though conversion is not accepted. The war in Iraq has left the analysis of the future of the renewal churches there in limbo for the present. The same can be said of Christians in Palestine.

Iran Iran's government is among the most recalcitrant regarding Christians in the region. Apostasy is among the five offenses that merit capital punishment, in accord with the Shiite concept of shari'ah. Five Assembly of God pastors have been murdered since 1990. A number of Pentecostals have been arrested, imprisoned, and beaten for holding unauthorized meetings. The most notable recent example (in 2004) was that of the arrest of more than eighty during the General Council meeting of the Iranian Assembly of God. Ultimately, all but one were released. Despite the intense pressures in a land where apostasy often means death, there are more than fifteen thousand Pentecostals and charismatics in Iran.

Israel Israel allows proselytism, at least for the present—there have been a number of bills presented to the Knesset to change this practice. More than five thousand Pentecostals live in Israel, and it is the fastest growing Protestant group in the nation. Most government interference comes in the form of rejecting building permits or arresting believers in the course of public confrontation (even if they were assaulted), or deporting missionaries who are considered to be much too public. Violence is rarely employed by either the government or individuals.

Arabian Peninsula (Bahrain, Kuwait, Oman, Qatar, Saudi Arabia, United Arab Emirates, Yemen)

This area contains societies that are among the least tolerant of Christianity and foreigners in general (including Muslim workers from other Arab countries). Saudi Arabia and Yemen would certainly fit into this category. However, one also has the counter examples of Bahrain and Oman, in which churches can build without government interference and meet with relative freedom (though proselytizing is still illegal). Most missionary activity throughout the peninsula is carried on by foreign workers, who try to reach fellow workers.

Saudi Arabia Saudi Arabia is the most repressive regime toward all forms of Christianity, spurred by the fact that it is the birthplace of Islam, and it contains the two holiest sites in the Muslim world. Islam is the only reli-

gion officially allowed to exist in the country. One is not compelled to be Muslim and is allowed to practice religion privately, according to the legal code. However, home gatherings are still subject to raids by the Muttawa, the religious police. A Filipino Pentecostal worker and pastor was arrested and sentenced to be beheaded after months of torture and solitary confinement for operating a home church. A worldwide campaign spearheaded by Amnesty International managed to secure his deportation on the day he was to be executed. Due to enormous political pressure (much of it fallout from the events of September 11, 2001), the Saudi government now rarely imprisons or beats foreigners, instead pressuring their employers to deport them. Despite the extreme danger faced by converts, missionaries in the region estimate the numbers to be in the tens of thousands.

North Africa (Algeria, Egypt, Libya, Morocco, Sudan, Tunisia)

The Magrib (literally "west"), the lands of North Africa west of Egypt, have always been resistant to Christianity. The presence of aggressive Fundamentalists in Algeria makes life especially precarious.

Egypt Egypt has the highest number of Christians in the Muslim world. Officially 10 percent of the population is Christian (many think that number is too low). The Coptic church dominates numerically, and a Charismatic movement has started within the tradition. Renewal members perhaps number 100,000. The government allows missionaries to enter the country. However, they are subject to approval by recognized churches. For example, most Pentecostal missionaries are subject to the approval of the Assemblies of God council in Egypt. Islamic Fundamentalism is a serious threat, especially in the south, where the bulk of the Christian population resides. The treatment of the government towards converts is comparable to the government treatment of those who are legally dead. Apostates cannot marry, inherit, access bank accounts, or have their identification cards changed to "Christian," among other civil rights forfeited. Arrest and imprisonment can occur as well.

Sudan Sudan also has a significant Christian and Pentecostal population, Christians numbering perhaps 10 million, and Pentecostals in the thousands. The current head of state has overseen the issuance of fatwas (religious commands from noted clerics) that promote the killing of Christians and animists. Since 1989, 2 million have been murdered by groups with government backing, and approximately 5 million made homeless, many of these becoming enslaved.

Future

The future for the region ultimately holds promise, as the processes of nationhood and globalization are furthered in the region. Both of these Western concepts stress individual rights and tolerance. Economic pressure from the West will ensure that this process toward complete freedom will continue to move forward. However, in some regions, this process will not be accomplished without continued hindrances and suffering for a lengthy period of time.

MARK ANTHONY PHELPS

See also Globalization of Pentecostalism; Islam, Relationship to

Further Reading

Bailey, B. & Bailey, J. M. (2003). *Who are the Christians in the Middle East?* Grand Rapids, MI: Eerdmans.

Bat Ye'or. (2002). *Islam and dhimmitude* (M. Kochan & D. Littman, Trans.). Madison, NJ: Fairleigh Dickenson.

Cox, H. (1995). *Fire from heaven: The rise of Pentecostal spirituality and the reshaping of religion in the twenty-first century.* Reading, MA: Addison-Wesley.

Gleason, G. (1997). *The Central Asia states: Discovering independence.* Boulder, CO: Westview.

Held, C. (2001). *Middle East patterns: Places, peoples, and politics* (3rd ed.). Boulder, CO: Westview.

Jones, C. E. (1995). *The Charismatic movement: A guide to the study of neo-Pentecostalism with emphasis on Anglo-American Sources* (2 vols.). Metuchen, NJ: Scarecrow.

Khalidi, T. (2001). *The Muslim Jesus: Sayings and stories in Islamic literature.* Cambridge, MA: Harvard.

Nydell, M. (2003). *Understanding the Arabs: A guide for Westerners* (3rd ed.). Yarmouth, ME: Intercultural.

Waines, D. (1995). *An Introduction to Islam.* New York: Cambridge.

Africa, South

South Africa was one of the first countries in the world in which the Pentecostal movement took root. The 2001 government census reveals that it has a high proportion (8 percent) of Pentecostal and neocharismatic followers. The number of charismatics in traditional churches, however, is difficult to establish. It may also be the country with one of the widest arrays of Pentecostal and charismatic diversity.

A Country Well Prepared

The cradle for Pentecostalism in South Africa was prepared during the last decades of the nineteenth century and the beginning of the twentieth century. The global prayer revival around 1860 had a remarkable impact on South Africa's dominant church of that time, the Dutch Reformed Church (DRC). The renowned Dr. Andrew Murray, a leader of the Holiness movement, belonged to the DRC. He was a prominent figure in the revival.

In South Africa as in many other parts of the globe, the Zionist church of John Alexander Dowie prepared the hearts of many people for the advent of the Pentecostal movement. His three main proponents in South Africa were Johannes Büchler, Daniel Bryant, and P. L. le Roux; le Roux subsequently became South Africa's first indigenous Pentecostal leader. The Zionist church began in South Africa as a purely white movement, but today is an exclusively black movement. It is the largest and fastest-growing segment of both Christianity and of non-Christian movements in South Africa.

The Second Anglo-Boer War (1899–1902) left a rent in South Africa's social fabric and left a great many South Africans in dire poverty and spiritual need. Afrikaners were especially hard hit. Strange as it might sound, these conditions created fertile soil for the birthing of the Pentecostal movement.

Major Pentecostal Groups and Offshoots

There are four major Pentecostal denominations in South Africa. These are the Apostolic Faith Mission of South Africa (AFM), the Assemblies of God (AG), the Full Gospel Church of God (FGC), and the Pentecostal Protestant Church (PPC). Additionally, in 1985 several neocharismatic churches joined to form the International Federation of Christian Churches (IFCC).

The Apostolic Faith Mission of South Africa

Two U.S. missionaries, John G. Lake and Thomas Hezmalhalch, came to South Africa in April 1908, shortly after embracing Pentecostalism in the United States. Lake had served for a time under John Alexander Dowie in Zion City, Illinois, and the two men were also well known at the Azusa Street, Los Angeles mission of William Seymour. They thought South Africa a wild, uncivilized, and heathen country.

During the first few years of the twentieth century people in different parts of South Africa had similar spiritual experiences, accompanied with the speaking in tongues, independently of one another. Lake and Hezmalhalch experienced a Pentecostal revival in Johannesburg; they were instrumental in linking many of these groups, spurring a movement that had started spontaneously in different places.

The remarkable apostolic ministry of Lake continued until 1913, when he returned to the United States, leaving behind an established movement: the Apostolic Faith Mission of South Africa. This movement was characterized by a strong evangelistic zeal and emphasis on divine healing. The AFM set out as an integrated church. It was only after Lake had left that a slow but sure process of racial segregation evolved.

In addition to Lake, who went on to become a respected pioneer of the worldwide Pentecostal movement, another son of the AFM became one of the world's best-known Pentecostals. Called "Mr. Pentecost," David du Plessis, general secretary of the AFM from 1936 to 1947, became the personification of the Pentecostal movement for Protestants and Roman Catholics alike.

The AFM remained divided along racial lines until 3 April 1996, when it became the first segregated church in South Africa to unite and structurally integrate its black, white, colored, and Asian sections. Today the AFM has about 1,400 congregations, 2,000 pastors and 1.15 million members. It is also established in twenty-four countries in addition to South Africa. Many independent and neocharismatic churches have a direct or indirect link with the AFM, as many of their founders, leaders, and members have AFM roots.

The Assemblies of God (AG)

In 1908 the Canadian Charles Chawner and the American Henry Turney began working as missionaries in South Africa. After the AG came into being in the United States in 1914, Turney applied for membership. He was approved and in 1917 he registered the AG in South Africa.

Over the years a number of overseas missionaries worked in autonomous groups under the banner of the AG. James Mullan and the well-known Nicholaas Benghu, one of the most influential indigenous Pentecostal leaders, started their own groups in 1944 and 1945, respectively. These groups eventually eclipsed the other groups in numbers and influence. Eventually strife led to two serious splits (in 1964 and 1981),

resulting in more than one AG in South Africa. After a process of more than a decade, reconciliation was eventually reached in November 2002. The AG is today a strong indigenous church with about sixteen hundred assemblies in South Africa.

The Full Gospel Church of God (FGC)

In April 1910, George Bowie came from a small U.S. church, Bethel Pentecostal Assembly, to do mission work in South Africa. Soon other overseas missionaries joined him, and a new autonomous work, Pentecostal Mission, was formed. Although one or two prominent members of the AFM joined later on, this church cannot be seen as a breakaway from the AFM.

There was a split in 1916, but the groups were reconciled in 1920 and the reunited church became known as the Full Gospel Church. After two years of negotiations, the FGC amalgamated with the Church of God of Cleveland, Tennessee, in 1951, bringing the FGC into the international Pentecostal arena. A further milestone was the unification of the different race groups in October 1997. The FGC today has around 1,000 congregations and 400,000 adherents.

The Pentecostal Protestant Church (PPC)

The PPC came into being after a split from the AFM in October 1958. There were two main reasons for the split. Some felt that the AFM had lost some of its original Pentecostal fervor and was too much bent on becoming a recognized church. The second reason was politics. The deputy president of the AFM at the time, G. R. Wessels, was appointed senator. Some found the involvement of a pastor in party politics to be unpalatable. Originally only 11 pastors and 1,755 members broke away; later more left, while others returned. The PPC has 220 congregations.

The International Federation of Christian Churches (IFCC)

After three years as a loose fellowship of independent neocharismatic churches, the IFCC was formed in 1985. It developed into an established Pentecostal-neocharismatic denomination, mainly due to its pastoral success, media exposure, and the political influence of one of its founders and leader, Ray McCauley, who has the largest local church in South Africa.

The IFCC split in 1996. A minority group felt its original intention to be a loose fellowship of independent churches was being betrayed by the increasingly

John Lake, the pioneer of the Pentecostal movement in South Africa. *Courtesy of Isak Burger.*

structured nature of the federation. There are about 300 IFCC churches in the country.

Black Pentecostals

Pentecostalism is booming among the black people of South Africa, just as it is in other parts of the African continent. In many cases black adherents do not call themselves Pentecostals, but prefer names such as People of the Spirit, Born-agains, and Bazalwane (a Zulu word for "Brethren"), which express a particular relationship of likeminded, saved people. There are three main groupings of black Pentecostal churches: Pentecostal mission churches that comprise black Pentecostal churches, and which originated from (predominantly white) Pentecostal mission churches such as those described in the previous section; Independent African Pentecostal churches that are younger Pentecostal and neocharismatic churches founded and governed by blacks independent of white control; and Indigenous (independent) Pentecostal-type churches that are churches with historical and theological connections with the Pentecostal churches and are founded, governed and propagated exclusively by blacks.

Although some classical Pentecostals have problems accepting the independent Zionist (which has nothing to do with Jewish Zionism) Pentecostal-type churches as truly Pentecostal, and despite many significant and sometimes striking differences, these churches still have much in common with classical Pentecostal churches. As the scholar Allan Anderson has observed, "All have a marked emphasis on the working of the Holy Spirit in the church with supernatural 'gifts of the Spirit', especially healing, exorcism, speaking in tongues and prophesying—although there are sometimes pronounced differences in the practice of these gifts. All

these churches also practice adults 'believers' baptism by either single or triune immersion. It is these factors which distinguish them from most other Christian groups" (Anderson and Otwang 1993, 5).

Growth of the Pentecostal Movement

The growth of Pentecostal and charismatic churches in South Africa, especially the indigenous and Pentecostal-type churches, is remarkable. Since the last quarter of the twentieth century, this style of church has grown "to such an extent that it has become *the* major force to be reckoned with in South African Christianity" (Anderson and Otwang, 1993, 138).

This growth can be explained first by its success in contextualizing and indigenizing Christianity in Africa. African Pentecostalism has proven itself able to adapt and fulfill the religious aspirations and expression of Africans in a remarkable way. Africans have "found in Pentecostalism a place to 'be at home'. African Pentecostalism has Africanised Christian liturgy in a free and spontaneous way that does not betray its essential Christian character, and has liberated it from the foreignness of European forms…They proclaim a holistic salvation that embraces the whole person" (Anderson and Otwang 1993, 139).

Zion Christian Church

There are hundreds of these black, independent, Spirit-oriented churches. They are usually built around a person with special leadership and charismatic gifts. In addition to originating in South Africa, they are all exclusively black. The largest denomination in South Africa today is one of these Pentecostal-type churches, called Zion Christian Church. It has about 5 million members and is led by Bishop Barnabas Lekghanyane. Its annual Easter gathering is attended by about 2 million people. Lekghanyane himself is a mysterious figure who seldom appears in public. The ZCC is easily identifiable by the Zionist badge and special colored garments worn by its members. It is interesting that the Zionist church movement in South Africa started as a purely white movement that flowed into the Pentecostal movement, while today it is an exclusively black movement. Many Zionist churches have *Apostolic* or *Zion* in their names.

Smaller Pentecostal and Neocharismatic Churches

Over the years a number of smaller indigenous churches have started in South Africa, sometimes as a result of splits from existing Pentecostal churches. Among these are the Members in Christ, Five-Fold Ministries International, Assemblies of Christ, International Pentecost Church, His People Christian Ministries, and Christian Family Church.

International Pentecostal Churches

Apart from those already mentioned, many of the major Pentecostal and neocharismatic churches in the United States have over the years found their way to South Africa. They include the International Four Square Gospel Church, the Church of God in Christ, the Pentecostal Holiness, the United Pentecostal Church and the Association of Vineyard Churches.

General Remarks

The leveling of the religious playing field since the advent of democracy in 1994 contributed Pentecostal and neocharismatic churches becoming more involved in social, political, and national affairs as well as in their developing increasingly good ecumenical relationships.

Since the announcement that South Africa was to host the Twentieth World Pentecostal Conference in September 2004, remarkable cooperation between the different Pentecostal and neocharismatic churches has taken place. Twenty-six of these churches form the National Host Committee. South Africa is also the first country to host this conference with the backing not only of the Pentecostal churches but also of the neocharismatic churches.

As is the case in many African countries, South Africa is experiencing unknown Pentecostal and charismatic growth. While the First World section of the country tends to move slowly in the direction of its European counterparts, the African and colored part of the population is experiencing an above-average religious growth, especially in the Pentecostal context.

ISAK BURGER

Further Reading

Anderson, A. H. (1991). *Moya: The Holy Spirit in an African context*. Pretoria: University of South Africa.
Anderson, A. H. (1992). *Bazalwane: African Pentecostals in South Africa*. Pretoria: University of South Africa.
Anderson, A. H., & Otwang, S. (1993). *Tumelo: The faith of African Pentecostals in South Africa*. Pretoria: University of South Africa.
Burger, I. vd M. (1987). *Geskiedenis van die Apostoliese Geloofsending van Suid-Afrika, 1908–1958* [History of the Apostolic Faith Mission of South Africa, 1908–1958]. Braamfontein, South Africa: Evangelie Uitgewers.
du Plessis, D. J. (1963). *The Spirit bade me go*. Oakland, CA: Author.
du Plessis, I. G. L. (1994). *Pinkster-Panorama: 'n Geskiedenis van die Volle Evangelie Kerk van God in Suidelike Afrika, 1910–1983* [Pentecostal Panorama: A history of the Full Gospel Church of God in southern Africa, 1910–1983]. Irene, South Africa: Die Volle Evangelie Kerk van God.
du Plessis, J. (1919). *The life of Andrew Murray of South Africa*. London: Marshall Brothers.
Lindsay, G. (1952). *Sketches from the life and ministry of John G. Lake*. Shreveport, LA: Voice of Healing Publishing Co.
Lindsay, G. (1972). *John G. Lake: Apostle to Africa*. Dallas, TX: Christ for the Nations.
Reidt, W. H. (1981). *John G. Lake: Adventure in God*. Tulsa, OK: Harrison House.
Slosser, B. (1977). *A man called Mr. Pentecost: The story of David du Plessis*. Plainfield, NJ: Logos International.
Sundkler B. G. M. (1961). *Bantu prophets in South Africa*. London: Oxford University Press.
Sundkler, B. G. M. (1976). *Zulu Zion and some Swazi Zionists*. London: Oxford University Press.
Venter, E. A. (1983). *Ons Geskiedenisalbum* [Our History Album]. Potchefstroom, South Africa: Author.

Africa, West

There was a time when missionaries sailing for Africa bought a one-way ticket with no thought of returning to their country of origin. It was as if the early missionaries in the beginning of the nineteenth century carried their coffins in their belongings. Malaria and other dangerous diseases were awaiting them on the African continent. Thus, their journey was a trip of faith. They were ready to lay down their lives for the sake of the Kingdom, and many did so.

The outpouring of the Holy Spirit at the beginning of the twentieth century, known as the Pentecostal Revival, stirred a burning desire among its participants to reach people for Christ. Those who were filled with the Holy Spirit felt "empowered" for missionary work, many times without specifically knowing where they would be going. These missionary pioneers made the sacrifice of leaving everything behind, to obey the divine call, not knowing the immense legacy they would be leaving for future generations. Many did indeed die on the mission fields where their bodies wait for the resurrection of the saints. Nonetheless, churches were planted, and they are continuing to grow, albeit in a manner that the Western missionaries would not have anticipated.

Today most observers and scholars of world religion agree that the center of Christianity is shifting "southward." Andrew Walls (2002) clearly states:

It is widely recognized that there has occurred within the present century a demographic shift in the center of gravity of the Christian world, which means that more than half of the world's Christians live in Africa, Asia, Latin America or the Pacific, and that the proportion doing so grows annually. This means that we have to regard African Christianity as potential[ly] the representative Christianity of the twenty-first century.

If it is true that the African church is growing so rapidly, then the church of Africa will have an important role to play in the Christian world of the future, and is thus worthy of study. The topic of the West African missionary movement is massive, thus the following account can only touch on key aspects. The author hopes that the following survey will shed light on our understanding of the expansion of Christianity in Africa.

A West African Missionary Church

A few years ago, a seminary student remarked that the time had come for the African church to send missionaries to the West. One's initial response might be, "how can this be possible?" Today, however, the African churches are playing an important role in sending missionaries to other parts of the world. In an article published in the *International Bulletin of Missionary Research* (2001), Wilbert Shenk writes:

The past decade had proved to be pivotal in geopolitical terms. Along with the end of the cold war and the globalization of the world economy, a sea of change in the locus of Christian initiative has taken place. Churches in Asia, Africa and Latin America are now sending thousands of missionaries to other regions and countries, while the decline and disorientation of the churches in the West is a matter of mounting concern. Today the West presents a demanding missiological challenge.

The Pentecostal experience of the Holy Spirit is an integral aspect in the African theology of missions. Most contemporary theologies of missions neglect the very important and necessary role of the Holy Spirit. Relatively little has been written in the West or in Africa on the crucial significance of the Holy Spirit in

connection with the missionary witness. The African church, however, was born out of a missionary vision because God was and still is a missionary God. Thus an important question needs to be asked: How did the churches of the third world or developing countries assume a leading role in the Christian missionary movement? Could it be because of the emphasis on the power of the Holy Spirit? One might say that Africa in some sense owes the West a debt. The Western missionaries brought the Gospel to Africa. Now the time has come to return the favor and take the Gospel back to their parts of the world, in which the church is in decline. The African church must respond in gratitude to God first, and secondly to those who were willing to risk their lives to bring the Gospel overseas.

New Understanding of Missions

The African church is becoming a powerful missionary force. Looking at the biblical example, it is clear that if the church wants to grow, it must put missions first. The Father sent Jesus who, in turn, sent His disciples. For Africans, if the missionary task can no longer be effectively accomplished in the "Western way," it will have to be done in the African way. The African church's finances and vision will necessitate a distinctly African strategy for missions. Currently, the African church/mission projects do not have as much financial backing as Western-based missions. The African mission will be dependent on African provision. It is time however, for those who brought the Gospel to listen to the emerging voices of Africa, in order to empower the worldwide Church of Jesus Christ to participate in the *missio Dei*.

For decades, when discussing missions planning, the main focus was on looking to the West for leadership. Now, as the African missionary movement develops, it will devise its own rules for playing the game. Today, the ascendancy of missions is clearly apparent in the curriculum of the Bible schools and the missions boards formed by national churches across the continent. The example of the Assemblies of God in Burkina Faso is a good illustration. Although situated in one of the poorest countries in the world, the church in Burkina Faso is leading the way in West Africa by sending missionaries out of the country. In a bold move the first missionaries from Burkina Faso were sent to Benin in 1987 and started a missionary outreach in the city of Ouidah, known for being the world center of voodoo. The first missionaries sent from Burkina Faso to Ghana were supported collaboratively with the U.S. Assemblies of God. Other missionaries have followed to the extent that the Burkina Faso church now has missionaries in Togo, Senegal, Mali, Niger, Guinea, Côte-D'Ivoire, Belgium, Switzerland and Ghana. Other churches in West Africa have followed the Burkina Faso model. While the missionaries from Burkina Faso are not riding four-wheelers as the better-equipped Western missionaries do, nevertheless they are reaching the world for Christ. The Bible does not say, "how beautiful are the four-wheelers of those who bring good news!" Instead, it says, "How beautiful are the feet of those who bring good news!" (Romans 10:15, NIV).

Perhaps it was the simplicity of Burkina Faso missionaries that gained the attention of Justin Long, a leading researcher of *Charisma Magazine*, who ranked the church of Burkina third among the world's fastest growing churches. The primary reasons for the success of the African church can be seen in its vibrant enthusiasm for missionary work, the renewed interest in the power of the Holy Spirit and education at the grassroots level. Leaders are teaching churches to support missions and to pray for the missionaries they are sending. The Assemblies of God of Burkina Faso, under the aegis of the Vision Missionnaire des Assemblées de Dieu du Burkina (Visionary Mission of the Assemblies of God of Burkina) is currently supporting approximately one hundred missionaries working out of country in Africa and Europe, with an additional five hundred home missionaries sent to unreached people groups. Their mission department produces a monthly missionary bulletin, distributed to supporting churches and individuals. The strength of African missions is found mostly in their autonomous principles favoring indigenous leadership, self-support and propagation. Other independent churches such as the Deeper Life, the Winner Chapel, etc. are sending missionaries all over the continent and overseas.

Church planting must be central to any missionary work. Most churches in Africa were planted through the vision and hard work of missionaries. The missionary vision of the worldwide church is to reach the entire Earth with the Christian message. This necessitates the crossing of cultural borders to take the message beyond the local community. Planting indigenous churches is the primary key to accomplishing this worldwide mission of God. The planting of indigenous churches requires the power of the Holy Spirit to succeed. Jesus told His disciples to wait until they were empowered by the Holy Spirit and then they would be His witnesses in Jerusalem, and in all Judea and Samaria, and to the ends of the Earth (Acts 1:8). Jesus also stated that the Gospel of the Kingdom would be preached to the whole world as a testimony to all nations and then the end will come (Matthew 24:14).

Partnerships in Missions

The goal of reaching the entire world with the Gospel message will not be possible without transnational networks and partnerships in missions. The first Pentecostal missionaries to West Africa opened mission stations everywhere they went. However, most of these early missionaries established a paternalistic relationship with the African nationals instead of empowering the indigenous church to do church planting on its own. Because of the early missionary's paternalistic strategy and the oppression of colonial powers, Africans began seeking their independence from colonial oppression. Anti-white feelings arose in many African countries. In some cases, missionaries abandoned the field without having adequately trained the indigenous church leadership.

In parts of Africa, anti-colonial movements sometimes took an anti-Christian stance as well. Nationalist leaders accused white missionaries of telling Africans to pray and then stealing their land while their heads were bowed. Jomo Keneyatta, Kenya's first President, accused missionaries of trying to destroy African culture. Political independence on the continent had in some cases brought with it a mortal threat to Western missionaries, as Africans associated white missionaries with colonial rule. Not only foreigners were mistreated. African prophetic leaders also were arrested and jailed.

With the independence of the African nations, missionary church leaders were obliged to relinquish control and establish partnerships between the missionary churches and the mother churches. Yet these partnerships were far from an ideal situation. An African proverb says: "the hand which receives is always under the one giving." Author Ronald Allen in his book, *Missionary Methods: St. Paul or Ours?* (1987) makes this assertion:

> The wealthier church can tie so many strings to its share of the partnership that the African church operates like a puppet. African churches must sometimes choose between buckling under pressure from Euro-American church[es] and standing on their rights as partners and pushing against the hands that tie the strings. On the other hand, African churches sometimes exercise their part of partnership in ways disappointing to their partners. Will the churches regard one another with suspicion? Or will they acknowledge the uncertainties and

ambiguities of this period and trust that, fumbling and faltering, they can walk together into a new era of genuinely cooperative witness?

In the partnership strategy, there are uncertainties and ambiguities but this must not stop the cooperation between the partners. Being partners means sharing equal responsibilities and recognizing the need for the African church to free herself from dependency. It might be appropriate here to think in terms of equality, both in service and responsibility.

The emergence of new Pentecostal-Charismatic churches in Africa, Europe and America in the beginning of the twenty-first century presents an opportunity for a review of the partnership strategy and its unresolved issues. These issues include the relationship between the Western missionaries and national leaders, as well as issues relating to finances and management. Despite these challenges, the African Church has made incredible advances and is continuing to grow and take the lead in worldwide missions. Jesus made this promise: "I will build my church and the gates of hell will not prevail against it" (Matthew 16:18).

Future Challenges

The incredible growth in the African Church should not be regarded as a cry of triumphalism, but rather a signal that new changes and challenges are in store for the worldwide church. The history of the church in Africa indicates clearly that despite the human tragedies of hunger, diseases, poverty, plagues, tribal wars, genocides, and drought, Jesus is building His Church through national leaders and expatriates who are called to labor hand in hand. The independence and autonomy of African churches are now a reality. In some instances, this autonomy came as a result of government pressure requiring mission properties and church control to be turned over to national leadership. In others, it came as cultural necessity following the political independence. Generally speaking, mission agencies were quick to relinquish control. The African Independent Churches (AICs) have provided one of the most significant missionary outreaches in Africa. They have become truly independent and self-reliant. These are indigenous churches unrelated to Western missionary agencies and have become an incredible force in Africa. AICs have recognized their common identity with worldwide Christianity yet have been able to maintain their indigenous characteristics.

The ultimate goal of the church, namely to reach the world for Christ, is not without future obstacles.

The unfinished task of world evangelism lies ahead. Perhaps the greatest challenge facing the African church is the competition of Islam. Muslims have proven to be highly resistant to the Christian message. Although the church is growing in Africa, Islam is also gaining ground all over the African continent. Islamic countries today send missionaries not just to Africa but all over the world. While the church in West Africa is growing, this is not the case in the northern part of Africa, where missionary activity is generally not welcomed. Uniting the African church in their efforts to win the continent for Christ is another challenge the church is currently facing. One way to meet these challenges is through interdenominational networks and transnational cooperation. Stronger churches can assist others in reaching their full potential.

Outlook

Africa is blessed with vibrant spirituality and an abundance of natural resources. The contribution of African spirituality is of great importance to the effective proclamation of the Gospel. The African church must continue to rely on the Holy Spirit to empower church growth. Africa's style of worship, especially spontaneous prayer and dance, is a vivid illustration of freedom in the contextualization of Christianity. This contextual Christianity meets the needs of the people more substantively than the sterile forms of worship imposed from outside in the past. Just as the African Church has contextualized its worship and liturgical styles, there is also a need for a contextualized theology of the church—an ecclesiology that will be christological and pneumatological. The contextualized approach must be without compromise in letting indigenous Christianity find its way, by writing local hymnology and using local dialects, idioms and concepts to express its own faith. The pneumatic experiences of the Pentecostal churches of Africa are shaping the face of Christianity. Despite the difficulties the African continent is facing, African Christianity is ready to play an important role in the world Christian movement. The African Church is pregnant with new ideas and potentialities that will astonish the world. The African church has opened a new page and chapter in the history of world missions.

JEAN-BAPTISTE ROAMBA

See also Africa, East; African Initiated Churches; Africa, North (and the Middle East); Africa, South; Islam, Relationship to

Further Reading

Allen, R. (1987). *Missionary Methods: St. Paul or ours?* Grand Rapids, MI: Eerdmans.

Bediako, K. (1995). *Christianity in Africa: The renewal of a non-Western religion.* Edinburgh, UK: Edinburgh University Press Ltd.

Bosch, D. J. (2004). *Transforming mission: Paradigm shift in theology of mission.* New York: Orbis Books.

Brandt-Bessire, D. (1986). *Aux sources de la spiritualite pentecôtiste.* Geneva, Switzerland: Labor et Fides.

Larbi, K. E. (2001). *Pentecostalism: The eddies of Ghanaian Christianity.* Accra, Ghana: Blessed Publications.

Omenyo, C. N. (2000). Essential aspects of African ecclesiology: The case of the African Independent Churches. *Pneuma: The Journal of the Society of Pentecostal Studies, 22*(2).

Pobee, J. S. (1979). *Toward an African theology.* Nashville, TN: Parthenon Press.

Pomerville, P. A. (1985). *The third force in missions.* Peabody, MA: Hendrickson Publishers.

Sanneh, L. (1983). *West African Christianity: The religious impact.* New York: Orbis Books.

Sanneh, L. (1997). *The crown and the turban: Muslims and West African pluralism.* Boulder, CO: Westview Press.

Shenk, W. (2001, July). Out of Africa: Non-theology of mission. *International Bulletin of Missionary Research.*

Walls, A. F. (1996). *The missionary movement in Christian history: Studies in the transmission of faith.* New York: Orbis Books.

Walls, A. F. (2002). *The cross-cultural process in Christian history.* New York: Orbis Books.

African Initiated Churches

The transformation of Christianity in Africa continues to present fascinating stories and compelling case studies. African Christianity is remarkably protean, always changing and always in a process of renewal. The independence movements that swept through Africa in the late nineteenth century also had lasting influences within the religious sphere. African prophets and charismatic leaders established their own religious movements as a valid protest against foreign missionaries, whom the African religious leaders portrayed as self-serving sanctimonious soul seekers. There is no gainsaying the fact that nationalistic fervor and the paucity of indigenous ethos and worldview in missionary Christianity contributed to the emergence of African Initiated Churches. The emergence of these churches showed how important it was to make the Christian message relevant to the African milieu and condition. Western missionary agents and the religious institutions they established were often regarded as unsympathetic to African culture and religious aspirations: African Initiated Churches were one answer to the hegemonic structures and attitudes of those Western institutions. The genius of African Initiated Churches relates to the creative ways they have contextualized the good news within African societies. They have created religious institutions that have enabled African Christians to feel at home with Christianity and to express themselves spiritually in a Christian context. Their interpretation of the Bible, unique worship styles, charismatic fervor, and focus on the Holy Spirit are enduring contributions to the story of world Christianity. It is also quite common to refer to these churches as African Instituted Churches, African Indigenous Churches, or African Independent Churches.

Gifts of the Holy Spirit

One of the spiritual elements that African Initiated Churches have inherited from the Pentecostal and Charismatic movements is the emphasis on the baptism of the Holy Spirit. The reception of the Holy Spirit is accompanied by glossolalia (speaking in tongues). The Holy Spirit is also the powerful force for healing and exorcism. The emphases on healing and human wholeness are in harmony with both biblical tradition and African traditional culture. The orientation toward the Holy Spirit in these indigenous congregations undergirds a holistic spirituality. They believe that for spirituality to be authentic and relevant it must connect with all of life, and the Spirit of the Lord must empower all aspects of life. The Spirit is the veritable fire from heaven that devours all the machinations of the devil and all malevolent forces. The concept of Spirit in the belief system of African Christians is inextricably connected with the concept of power. The Holy Spirit is the enabling power that gives people control over a situation that would otherwise be beyond human capacity to handle. African Initiated Churches emphasize the conscious experience of receiving the Holy Spirit and its concomitant power and authority. Power is essential in the relationship between human beings and the Ultimate Reality.

African Initiated Churches also stress healing and exorcism. These churches are concerned with this-worldly or proximate salvation. Africans have traditionally worshipped God to obtain concrete benefits—more children, healing, avoidance of calamities, success in trade, or a

A Pentecostal church in rural Ghana. *Courtesy of istockphoto.com/srodgers.*

big harvest. One of the intentions of African Initiated Churches is to provide the religious structures that can ensure such concrete benefits. In Africa, human liberation is conceived in both spiritual and material terms.

History of African Initiated Churches

The earliest fervor for independence and prophetism in Africa began around 1888–1917. This was the period when independent churches of the Ethiopian type were established in South Africa by prophets such as Mangena Mokone, P. J. Mzimba, Timothy Cekwane, and Isaiah Shembe. About the same time, independent churches were established in Nigeria by Mojola Agbebi, Garrick Braide, and Joseph B. Shadare. The spirit of religious freedom engendered during this period spread all over the African continent like wildfire well into the twentieth century. Although these charismatic churches started as small groups, with time some of them developed into powerful and significant religious movements.

African Initiated Churches Today

African Initiated Churches now participate in ecumenical deliberations and consultations. For instance, four churches from the African Initiated Church tradition now belong to the World Council of Churches. These churches are the African Church of the Holy Spirit (from Kenya); the African Israel Nineveh Church (also from Kenya); the Church of the Lord, Aladura (from Nigeria); and Eglise de Jesus Christ sur la Terre par le prophète Simon Kimbangu, or EJCSK (The Church of Jesus Christ on Earth through the Prophet Simon Kimbangu; from the Congo). Their presence in the World Council of Churches underlines the fact that this ecumenical body is no longer an insular organization. The *oikos* (Greek: house) of God is a fellowship of churches with different worship styles, ethos, spirituality, and theology.

The unprecedented growth of African Initiated Churches is a bold affirmation that it is possible to be African and Christian at the same time. These churches have enabled Africans to think theologically and to feel at home with Christianity. Members of these churches have the freedom to dance, sing, clap, speak in tongues, jump around with joy, and celebrate the good news of Jesus Christ with gusto. Africans may worship in their own language and use many resources from their culture for their theological reflections. African Initiated Churches are providing the tools through which an authentic church can be realized in Africa. The rise of the African Initiated Church movement is an appropriate challenge to a Christianity that so often gives the appearance of lackluster antiquarianism that is out of touch with people's existential concerns. It is a protest against the verbal and cerebral form of Western Christianity, and it represents a cultural renaissance in response to the cultural imperialism undertaken by the missionary representatives of the historic mission churches in Africa.

The African Initiated Church movement highlights Africa's indelible stamp on world Christianity. This Charismatic movement is also a ringing testimony to the fact that Africans have not been merely passive recipients of the gospel. Africans have made concerted efforts to make the Christian message relevant to the African worldview and culture. One of the implications of the demographic shift in world Christianity in the twenty-first century is that people from diverse cultures have redefined Christianity on their own terms and within their own local framework. Christianity has become a multicultural world religion, blossoming in many cultures, unencumbered by any subversive hegemonic control, and galvanized by many indigenous initiatives.

AKINTUNDE E. AKINADE

See also Africa, East; Indigenous Churches

Further Reading

Isichei, E. (1995). *A history of Christianity in Africa.* Grand Rapids, MI: Eerdmans.

Martey, E. (1993). *African theology: Inculturation and liberation.* Maryknoll, NY: Orbis Books.

Omoyajowo, J. A. (1982). *Cherubim and seraphim: The history of an African independent church.* New York: Nok Publishers International.

Peel, J. D. Y. (1968). *Aladura: A religious movement among the Yoruba.* Oxford, UK: Oxford University Press.

Turner, H. W. (1967). *African independent church.* Oxford, UK: Oxford University Press.

Webster, J. B. (1964). *The African churches among the Yoruba.* Oxford, UK: Oxford University Press.

Welbourn, F. (1962). *East African rebels.* London: SCM Press.

America, Latin

Pentecostalism has emerged in the decades since World War II as the most culturally sensitive and dynamic form of Christianity in Latin America. Although the first Pentecostal groups appeared in the region early in the twentieth century, virtually at the same time as they appeared in North America and Europe, the Latin American movements were largely ignored until they began to flourish in the years following World War II. The backdrop to this growth was the convulsive social change produced by rapidly growing populations and demographic shifts, the rise of large industrial cities, improved communications and transportation, better educational systems, the dislocation of peasants with the modernization of agriculture, and the disruption of paternalistic labor relations. Moreover, populist politicians brought peasants and the urban proletariat increasingly into national life, giving women and, in some countries, illiterates, the vote. In this uncertain climate people's religious loyalties were seriously challenged. According to most estimates, Pentecostals and charismatics account for at least three-quarters of all new converts found in the rapidly growing Latin American Protestant community since 1945 and now represent at least two-thirds of all non-Roman Catholic Christians in the region.

While Pentecostals as a community generally remain a religious minority within Latin American nations, in several—notably Chile, Brazil, Guatemala, and El Salvador—Pentecostal churches have found a recognized place in national life, as reflected in the churches' educational and social service programs and the public's generally altered perceptions of adherents.

Initially Latin American Pentecostal movements were generally considered to be products of North American religious proselytism, but studies that appeared in the 1990s by the scholars David Stoll, David Martin, and Harvey Cox, among others, clearly identified these movements as growing out of Latin America's own religious impulses. Moreover, studies indicate that in several countries European Pentecostals have influenced these groups as much as have North American Pentecostals. Scholars generally conclude that while Pentecostals have the potential to bring about needed social reforms, their primary impact has been the renewed fervor they have brought to Latin American religious life. In all Latin American countries Pentecostals and charismatics make up the largest Evangelical (Protestant) grouping and in all but three or four countries a Pentecostal organization is the largest reported Protestant denomination. In addition, the Pentecostals' experiential theology and popular styles have influenced both the historic Protestant groups and Roman Catholics, such that both traditions have to some degree adopted Pentecostal styles and emphases. Worldwide, Latin American Pentecostals by some estimates may account for as much as 40 percent of all classical Pentecostals.

Composition

A feature of Pentecostal movements is their religious autonomy, which enables them to develop independently within each national society among populations that are especially susceptible to the Pentecostals' emphases and infectious enthusiasm. The sociologist David Martin has emphasized the effectiveness of these groups in addressing the concerns and aspirations of the masses and mobilizing them for action. Pentecostals differ from socially oriented populist political groups in being notoriously independent and inclined to initiating their own programs. But increasingly observers recognize that the "classical" Pentecostals have been joined (and in some cases apparently superseded) by energetic charismatic groups that possess many of the same characteristics but whose progressive methods have greater appeal for the emerging middle class. In the nomenclature of Latin America religious groups, Pentecostals are those of the classical variety, whether identified with a North American or European denomination or mission or entirely autonomous and "indigenous" in style. Protestant charismatics are usually referred to as Neo-Pentecostals, while Catholic Pentecostals are regularly referred to simply as charismatics (carismáticos).

The classical Pentecostals in large part have been drawn from marginal sectors of society that typically have formed closely knit, familial congregations in modest facilities that reflect their humble social origins. Their pastors—sometimes women and often young people in their twenties—are usually persons endowed with natural leadership gifts but who usually lack much formal training. These groups typically have observed rigid standards of conduct, and their warm, often spontaneous meetings feature lay participation, noisy prayer, converts' testimonies, emphasis on physical healing, and emotional responses to intense, motivational sermons.

By comparison, the Neo-Pentecostal groups tend to meet in hotels or their own spacious facilities for celebrative meetings that feature upbeat music in contemporary styles. Their congregations, whose dress and conduct standards are usually more relaxed than those of the Pentecostals, are more likely to include business and professional people who more often arrive in cars than by public transportation. While the Pentecostals emphasize dedication and commitment, Neo-Pentecostal groups more often stress the resolution of personal problems and promises of prosperity. While the classical Pentecostals typically have avoided compromising political affiliations, the Neo-Pentecostals and independents frequently have been identified with political figures. Although numerically the Pentecostals in most countries far outnumber the other classifications, much of the growth in recent decades has come from the Neo-Pentecostals and new independent churches usually led by

charismatic pastors who make effective use of radio and television, and it is these groups that have attracted the most scholarly and journalistic interest. Catholic charismatics, who are found in many dioceses, operate under the scrutiny of the Catholic hierarchy. The gulf between Catholic charismatics and classical Pentecostals in most countries is especially pronounced, despite many similarities in emphases and styles. At root these stem from the issue of authority: Pentecostals find their spiritual and institutional bases in the Reformed doctrines of *sola scriptura*, salvation by grace alone, and the priesthood of the believer, and reject the Catholic doctrine of Petrine authority, while Catholics cannot validate any movement outside the confines of the church, the sole custodian of salvation. Nevertheless, since both groups often use the same worship choruses and theological language, their radio and television programs are sometimes almost indistinguishable.

Following this taxonomy, the largest movements in the region are those identified either as classical Pentecostals or as Neo-Pentecostals. In the former category are the Assembleias de Deus (Brazil) and Asambleas de Dios (in all of the Spanish-speaking countries) with an estimated combined total of 15–20 million adherents. Other theologically similar groups are the Iglesia de Dios (affiliates of the Church of God, Cleveland, Tennessee), Iglesia Cuadrangular (affiliates of the International Church of the Foursquare Gospel, United States), Iglesia Pentecostal Unida (loosely affiliated with the United Pentecostal Church, United States), and Iglesia Apostólica de la Fe en Cristo Jesús (Apostolic Church of Faith in Christ Jesus, strongest in Mexico with sister organizations in the United States and other countries).

Prominent Neo-Pentecostals (corresponding to conventional definitions of charismatics) include three Brazilian churches, the Igreja Universal do Reino de Dios (Universal Church of the Kingdom of God), Deus e Amor (God Is Love), and Brasil Para Cristo (Brazil for Christ). Guatemala has produced a number of similar high-profile movements, including the Fraternidad Cristiana de Guatemala (the Christian Brotherhood of Guatemala), Misión Cristiana Elim (Elim Christian Mission), and the Iglesia Evangélica Cristiana Calvario (Calvary Evangelical Christian Church). Several of these groups have built large, showcase auditoriums for their central churches.

Shared Characteristics

Despite the differences in the composition of these groups, their appeals and functions are similar. A non-Pentecostal writer, Argentine Baptist pastor Pablo

Deiros, characterizes Latin American Pentecostals as part of the evangelical wing of the historic Protestant churches. He emphasizes that these groups are growing because converts readily share their faith with family members, friends, and neighbors. Latin American Pentecostals share with their non-Pentecostal evangelical counterparts the same doctrinal and ethical convictions and, more important, the abiding sense of the meaning and necessity of a personal experience of redemption. Deiros characterizes Pentecostal worship as joyful, enthusiastic, and filled with hope. Whereas Roman Catholicism emphasizes the work of the Holy Spirit through the priests and the sacraments and other Protestant denominations see the manifestations of the Spirit primarily through the understanding and exposition of the Scriptures, Pentecostals see the Spirit working directly, in the personal experiences of believers. Most, but not all, Pentecostals expect that baptism in the Holy Spirit will be accompanied by glossolalia (speaking in tongues), but physical healing is an even more widely recognized indication of divine presence.

Although the generic properties of Pentecostalism are so universally experienced that they partially obscure pronounced denominational differences, these churches are notoriously fragmented. In Chile alone, it is estimated that the original Pentecostal group that began as an insurgency within the Methodist mission of Willis Hoover (1856–1936) in 1909 has produced more than thirty separate organizations. The versatility of Pentecostal groups has made them particularly compatible with ethnic and social class movements. Entire indigenous communities in Argentina, Guatemala, Mexico, and the Andean countries have converted to Pentecostal Christianity. In cultures that already embrace supernaturalism, the Pentecostals' emphasis on spirits and divine intervention is not extraordinary.

Country-by-Country Development

It is difficult to understand the appeal of these groups without reference to their idiosyncrasies, the unique conditions, the forceful or inspiring leaders, and the particular issues surrounding their origins.

Brazil

Brazilian Pentecostalism began virtually at the same time at the two extremes of the national territory under the auspices of two different evangelists. In the northern state of Para, Swedish Baptist missionaries who had encountered Pentecostalism in Chicago during their brief residence in the United States proselytized members of a local Baptist congregation to establish what eventually became the largest denominational group, the Assembleias de Deus. Through the developmental years from 1910 to the 1930s the prevalent influences among the Brazilians were Swedish, although from the beginning the Brazilians were clearly in control of their own movement and borrowed or developed styles compatible with their own tastes and values. The denominational name itself had little to do with the North American Assemblies of God, whose influence was strategic but negligible in respect to the volume of churches established during the first half of the twentieth century. Unlike their North American counterparts, the polity (ecclesiastical organization) of these groups is episcopal, with regional *pastores presidentes* in dictatorial control of the churches.

In the meantime, in the city of Sao Paulo an Italian convert to the movement, who also encountered Pentecostalism in Chicago, introduced the faith to expatriate Italians. After only a brief residence, Luigi Francescon (1866–1936) left an organized congregation that developed into the Congregaçao Cristã (Christian Congregation), a group that grew large largely within the Italian community and retained its own idiosyncratic forms. While other denominational groups made a contribution to the spread of the movement, Neo-Pentecostal groups such as Deus e Amor and Brasil para Cristo were in large measure spin-offs from the existing denominations. It is hard not to see in Brazilian Pentecostalism traits and orientations that are decidedly Brazilian, so that Pentecostalism appears to have built on existing religious proclivities (like spirit possession and authoritarianism even while traditional forms of these practices are emphatically repudiated). The fact that the classical Pentecostal groups, especially, have developed strong aversions to common practices appears to be an effort on the part of these converts to create easily distinguishable social boundaries. Thus, churches separate their members legalistically not only from drinking, gambling, and sexual indulgence, but from commercial entertainment, participation in some civic activities, and provocative dress (practices that even now draw considerable respect because they are often considered ideal behavior). Even now, in many churches outside large cities, men and women typically occupy different sides of the auditorium and dress, especially for women, is rigidly regulated.

Argentina

In Argentina, in contrast, Protestantism has traditionally been largely a concern of immigrant populations, especially English and German communities for whom Protestantism was part of their national culture. When after years of slow growth Pentecostal churches did begin to gain widespread recognition in the 1980s, the revivals occurred just after the Falklands (Malvinas) war (April 1982), when the general population was devastated by the humiliating defeat of the Argentine forces and, apparently, sought a more engaging faith. Several dynamic leaders emerged at the head of large Pentecostal churches, surprising themselves with the windfall of converts that their previously much less effective efforts had produced.

Chile

In Chile, a country characterized by relative isolation, progressive, democratic traditions, and early development of an urban, industrial economy, rural migrants settled in sprawling urban slums where political radicalism flourished. In this environment Pentecostalism, introduced by Willis Hoover, gained a large following among the marginal working class, which European sociologist Christian Lalive d'Pinay suggested displayed the values of traditional rural workers accustomed to paternalistic, autocratic landowners. Although the Pentecostals began to fragment after Hoover's death in 1936, the two largest groups make up about 80 percent of all Chilean Pentecostals and constitute in the aggregate about 25 percent of all Chileans.

Guatemala and El Salvador

Next to Brazil and Chile, the countries with the largest proportion of Pentecostals are the countries of Central America, especially Guatemala and El Salvador. In Guatemala, Protestants benefited from the long tradition of anticlericalism begun by the nineteenth-century president Justo Rufino Barrios. During Barrios's lengthy dictatorship (1871–1885), the Catholic Church was deprived of its benefits, clerical dress was prohibited, and Church lands were confiscated. Historians have concurred that the Guatemalan Catholic Church never recovered from this attack. As part of his policies, Barrios encouraged Protestant immigration. The various missions continued to grow for a century, so that by the 1980s sectarian Protestantism was an established feature of the Guatemalan religious landscape, giving that country a kind of religious pluralism infrequently found in Latin America.

Against this backdrop, the first Pentecostals established a foothold in the departments bordering El Salvador and then moved into the highlands, where many of their converts were Mayas whose traditions were entwined with their religious practices. Although several major Pentecostal groups emerged, all of them adapted readily to the cultural milieu of the rural and urban poor. By 1976, after a devastating earthquake that brought many Protestant relief agencies into the country, the evangelical churches were identified with relief and reconstruction programs. As the Protestant groups acquired visibility in national life, the increasing proportion of Pentecostals in the Protestant community resulted in their recognition and greater acceptance. These groups acquired greater status as groups of charismatics, many of them within the established denominations and the more progressive classical Pentecostal groups, moved into prominence. Today several Neo-Pentecostal megachurches dominate the Guatemalan religious scene, despite the fact that the Roman Catholic Church and Mayan traditional religions remain numerically stronger.

Similarly, Pentecostals in neighboring El Salvador established networks of congregations among the rural working class that eventually made these groups a major force in the country as the rural migration swelled the population of the cities. At present the Asambleas de Dios de El Salvador is the largest evangelical church in the country, followed by other large Pentecostal groups, the Iglesia de Dios and the Príncipe de Paz (Prince of Peace). Apart from the various Catholic schools that in the aggregate are larger, the Liceo Cristiano, founded by a Pentecostal pastor, is the largest private school in the country.

Puerto Rico

Pentecostals have also found a strong following in Puerto Rico, culturally a part of Latin America despite its status as a commonwealth within the jurisdiction of the United Sates. It is estimated that approximately 25 percent of the population of the island are Pentecostals, compared with 8 percent in Mexico, 6 percent in Cuba, 10 percent in Colombia, and 15 percent in Peru.

The Future

There is good reason to assume that Pentecostal-Charismatic groups will not simply fade away. In fact, as has often been pointed out, despite substantial attrition, these groups continue to show a substantial net growth. Rather than trail off any time soon, one may rather expect that with social mobility, increased interaction with the mainstream of national life, and generational changes, Pentecostals will remain a force in

Latin American religious life, albeit with altered forms and functions.

EVERETT WILSON

See also Brazil; Catholic Charismatic Movement; Catholicism, Roman; Hispanic Pentecostalism

Further Reading

Boudewijnse, B., Droogers, A., & Kamteeg, F. (Eds.). (1998). *More than opium: An anthropological approach to Latin American and Caribbean Pentecostal praxis.* Lanham, MD: Scarecrow Press.

Cleary, E. L., & Stewart-Gambino, H. W. (Eds.). (1997). *Power, politics, and Pentecostals in Latin America.* Boulder, CO: Westview Press.

Cox, H. (1995). *Fire from heaven: The rise of Pentecostal spirituality and the reshaping of religion in the twenty-first century.* Reading, MA: Addison Wesley.

Garrard-Burnett, V., & Stoll, D. (Eds.). (1993). *Rethinking Protestantism in Latin America.* Philadelphia: Temple University Press.

Jenkins, P. (2002). *The next Christendom: The coming of global Christianity.* New York: Oxford University Press.

Martin, D. (1990). *Tongues of fire: The explosion of Protestantism in Latin America.* Oxford, UK: Basil Blackwell.

Stoll, D. (1990). *Is Latin America turning Protestant? The politics of evangelical growth.* Berkeley and Los Angeles: University of California Press.

America, North

The Pentecostal movement, the largest religious movement to originate in the United States, has become a global force and the fastest growing Christian movement in the world. With over 550 million followers after only a century from its founding in 1901, the Pentecostal movement is now represented in more than 120 nations and has penetrated all the other Christian traditions through the Charismatic movement, which began in 1960. Moreover, the founding of thousands of newer Neocharismatic movements in the developing world has caused some scholars to call Pentecostalism the religion of choice in the Third World.

With roots in the Holiness movement, which grew out of the Holiness wing of American Methodism, the Pentecostal movement appeared in Topeka, Kansas, in January 1901 under the ministry of Charles Fox Parham (1873–1929), a former Methodist preacher. When students in his Bible school began to speak in tongues while seeking a baptism in the Holy Spirit, Parham concluded that tongues were the Bible evidence of the Pentecostal baptism which came as a third blessing after the experiences of justification (forgiveness of sins) and sanctification (transformation from sinner to saint). His first impulse was to see tongues as miraculous languages for missionaries that would do away with the need for language study. Evidential tongues became the cardinal and central doctrine of the Pentecostal revivals that were affected by Parham's teaching.

William J. Seymour and Azusa Street

The man who made the Pentecostal movement a worldwide phenomenon was a black Holiness preacher, William Joseph Seymour (1870–1922), who opened a revival center on Azusa Street in Los Angeles in April 1906. Thousands of people flocked to Los Angeles to receive their baptism in the Holy Spirit in services that were deeply rooted in black Holiness worship styles. From Azusa Street, the story of the new Pentecost spread across North America. Prominent leaders in the United States included Gaston B. Cashwell from North Carolina, Charles Harrison Mason from Memphis, Tennessee, Ambrose J. Tomlinson from eastern Tennessee, and William H. Durham from Chicago. The movement reached Canada in 1906 through the influence of Durham. Early Canadian leaders were Andrew H. Argue of Winnipeg and James and Ellen Hebden of Toronto. The movement reached Mexico in 1914 under the leadership of Romana de Valenzuela, who had been in Azusa Street in 1906.

Pentecostalism first took root as a mass movement in the southern United States, mainly in several small Holiness churches that had been organized in the late 1890s. These included the Church of God in Christ (Memphis, Tennessee) led by Mason, the Pentecostal Holiness Church (North Carolina) led by Abner B. Crumpler, the Fire Baptized Holiness Church (Georgia) led by Joseph H. King, and the Church of God (Cleveland, Tennessee) led by Tomlinson.

In a short time, the movement spread from North America to many parts of the world. The first missionaries were greatly influenced by the Azusa Street meetings and acknowledged the leadership of Seymour. Early apostles of the movement included Thomas B. Barrett (Norway and Europe, 1907), Alexander A. Boddy (England, 1907), Thomas J. McIntosh (China, 1907), Alfred G. Garr (India, 1907), John G. Lake (South Africa, 1908), Luigi Francecon (Italy and Latin America, 1909), Daniel Berg and

Pentecostalism and Cuban Miami

As elsewhere in the world, Pentecostalism has been one of the fastest-growing religions in the Cuban community in Miami. As the extract below indicates, it is displacing both Roman Catholicism and other denominations of Protestantism.

The early 1970s saw an increase in the work of newer (non-historic) denominations, such as the Pentecostals, Nazarenes and charismatic-oriented groups. In 1990, it could be said that Pentecostals and Baptists have the largest number of faithful among all Protestant groups. The Pentecostals are distributed among various denominations and independent congregations. Although they may now outnumber Southern Baptists, the latter still represents the single denomination, with the most members and congregations among Cubans in South Florida.

Meanwhile, the number of independent and charismatic (or Pentecostal) congregations continues to grow. There is a new congregation almost every month. Some of these churches have more members than even the main Baptist congregations or the large churches in other historic denominations. (The largest of the new Pentecostal-charismatic congregations in South Florida may be the People's Cathedral, La Catedral del Pueblo.) The first Spanish-language Pentecostal church in Miami was the Primera Iglesia de la Biblia Abierta, a predominantly Puerto Rican congregation with a few Cuban members organized before the Cuban exodus. Roberto Dominguez, the first pastor of the church, is Puerto Rican. In 1961, Gabriel Caride, a well-known Cuban Pentecostal pastor affiliated to the Assemblies of God, started a congregation and refugee center on Flagler Street. Later, another Cuban Assemblies of God pastor, Andrés Román, started a Bible Institute. In 1990, the Assemblies of God stood as the largest Pentecostal group among Cubans in South Florida, with about 20 Spanish congregations.

Other denominations with at least several predominantly Cuban churches are the Cleveland, Tennessee-based Church of God, several other denominations also called the Church of God, the Church of God of Prophesy, the Open Bible, the Elim Missionary Assemblies and the Pentecostal Church of God. (The latter is a Puerto Rican-based denomination, and most of its Miami churches are Puerto Rican.) Several independent congregations also work among Cubans in the Miami area, and some are quite large, such as Fe para Miami, Cristo rompe las cadenas, and Alfa y Omega, among others.

Source: Ramos, M. A., & Román, A. A. (1991). The Cubans, religion and south Florida. In A. Jorge, J. Suchlicki, & A. Leyva de Varona (Eds.), *Cuban exiles in Florida: their presence and contribution* (pp. 130–131). Miami, FL: University of Miami, North-South Center Publications for the Research Institute for Cuban Studies.

Gunnar Vingren (Brazil, 1910), and Ivan Voronaev (Russia and Eastern Europe, 1920).

Internal Controversies

After its initial successes, the North American movement was torn by two major controversies that were to divide the movement into three distinct theological camps. The first concerned the question of entire sanctification as a second and perfecting work of grace, a doctrine that had been received from the Methodist Holiness tradition. In 1911 William Durham of Chicago began teaching what he called the "finished work of Calvary," a theology that discarded the idea of sanctification as a definite work of grace. Opposing him were the founders of the movement, Parham and Seymour, as well as the southern Pentecostal churches that had been formed before 1900. In 1914 Durham's followers organized the Assemblies of God in the city of Hot Springs, Arkansas. This church was destined to become the largest Pentecostal denomination in the world by the end of the century. The founding of the Assemblies of God also opened up a racial divide in the movement, since most of the white founders of the new church separated themselves from the black members of the organization after having been ordained under Charles

H. Mason and the predominately black Church of God in Christ.

A second major division occurred in the Assemblies of God in 1916 when some ministers espoused what was then called the "new issue" concerning the doctrine of the Trinity. The new "Oneness" or "Jesus' Name" movement began in 1911 in a camp meeting near Los Angeles when a Bible study caused some ministers to teach that rather than a trinity of Father, Son, and Holy Spirit, there was only one person in the Godhead, Jesus Christ. Furthermore, the only valid form of water baptism was in Jesus' name rather than the traditional Trinitarian formula. Also, tongues were seen as not only an evidence of being baptized in the Holy Spirit, but as being necessary to salvation. After the Assemblies of God excommunicated the Oneness minister from the church, two major Oneness denominations developed. The first was the Pentecostal Assemblies of the World, a church that was totally integrated racially. By 1945, however, most of the white ministers had left the church to join in creating the United Pentecostal Church in St. Louis, Missouri.

Interracial Beginnings

Although Pentecostalism began under Parham and Seymour with interracial leadership, the movement in the United States gradually joined in the system of segregated and separate black and white churches. At Azusa Street, the pastor was a black man, William Seymour, who was admired by both blacks and whites. One of the miracles of the Azusa Street meetings was the free and relaxed mixing of the races. In the beginning, most of the Azusa worshippers were poor blacks—laborers, maids, and washerwomen. The appeal of the meetings was so great, however, that soon people of all races and ethnic backgrounds were filling the building. At times the majority of the worshippers were white with a mixture of Mexicans and Asians joining in. At the height of the meetings, Frank Bartleman, a white observer, said of Azusa Street, "the color line was washed away in the Blood" (1980, 54).

From 1901 to 1924, the U.S. Pentecostal movement constituted a notable exception to the religious segregation that dominated U.S. church life. But one by one, most of the Pentecostal denominations separated on the basis of race. Racial separations occurred in the Fire-Baptized Holiness Church in 1908, in the Pentecostal Holiness Church in 1913, and in the Church of God in Christ in 1914. The Church of God (Cleveland, Tennessee) was the only denomination that never separated on racial lines.

In contrast, there seems to have been no racial separations of the churches in Canada or Mexico. Most of the Canadian and Mexican Pentecostal churches were planted by Americans who also were affected by Azusa Street.

Pentecostals and Society

While American society and the mainline churches were unaware of the divisions within the movement, they soon became aware of a new and growing religious force that not only challenged the established Protestant and Catholic Churches, but questioned the prevailing social order as well. The Holiness code of the Pentecostals led them to criticize mainline church members for using tobacco, for drinking alcoholic beverages, for attending movies and theaters, for using makeup, and for dressing extravagantly or immodestly. Some Pentecostals were pacifists and were persecuted for not supporting World War I. One leader, Charles H. Mason, was investigated by the FBI and jailed for his pacifist sermons and speeches.

Pentecostals also differed from mainstream norms in their acceptance of women preachers. Since the Pentecostals believed that the Second Coming of Christ was at the door, everyone was recruited to win the world before it was too late. The most famous Pentecostal woman preacher was Canadian-born Aimee Semple McPherson (1890–1944), who began as a traveling evangelist and ended as the founder of a new denomination, the International Church of the Foursquare Gospel, headquartered in Los Angeles. This was organized from her massive Angelus Temple, which seated 5,000 persons and boasted 25,000 members. Other Pentecostal women ministers of note were Maria Woodworth-Etter and Kathryn Kuhlman.

As the movement grew, it attracted the attention of critics in the church world as well as the scientific community. In the earliest days violent persecution was not uncommon. Added to this were the lurid and racist comments of the nation's newspapers and magazines. Many religious periodicals lampooned the expressive worship styles of the Pentecostals. The most vocal critics were those among the Holiness people who rejected speaking in tongues, and those among the Fundamentalists who held that tongues and other miracles had ceased. Early Holiness critics included Alma White, who wrote a book in 1912 titled *Demons and Tongues*. Fundamentalist rejection was most extreme in Benjamin Warfield's 1918 book *Counterfeit Miracles*, which held that not one miracle had occurred since the death of the last apostle.

The academic community offered deprivation and mental instability theories to account for what was seen as bizarre behavior on the part of Pentecostals. Typical of this genre was Yale University professor George Bernard Cutten's 1927 book titled *The Gift of Tongues: A study in pathological aspects of Christianity*. Since most Pentecostals were poor and uneducated, it was assumed that they were also ignorant and confused. Despite the stereotypes, there were some well-educated Pentecostals who ably defended their faith through books and magazines produced by the movement. Other Pentecostals used their spiritual gifts and entrepreneurial skills to build large churches and to lead dramatic and successful healing crusades that began to attract multitudes of curious visitors.

The movement grew slowly in the United States in the decades before World War II. In the U.S. census of 1936 the larger Pentecostal denominations reported the following membership figures:

The Assemblies of God	47,950
The Church of God in Christ	30,263
The Church of God (Cleveland, Tennessee)	23,247
The Pentecostal Holiness Church	8,096

Pentecostalism also spread from Azusa Street to Canada through the influence of A. H. Argue and James and Ellen Hebden of Toronto. The earliest Mexican Pentecostal mission was led by a woman, Romana de Valenzuela, who was at Azusa Street. Later missionaries from the United States included Henry Ball of the Assemblies of God and J. H. Ingram of the Church of God.

Post–World War II Growth

After World War II the growth and development of the Pentecostal churches in North America suddenly began to make an impression on the public. There were many reasons for the rise of the Pentecostals after 1945. One was postwar prosperity. Since Pentecostals shared in the economic prosperity that followed the war, they began to build large and impressive church buildings in many cities. As they prospered, many earned college degrees and entered middle-class professions, becoming teachers, lawyers, and businessmen. This led to a lessening of persecution and more integration into surrounding communities. As with other new religious groups, the stages of Pentecostals' relationship to society at large progressed from persecution to toleration and finally to acceptance.

Another reason for the postwar growth was the appearance of the healing crusade movement that began in 1948 under the leadership of such evangelists as Oral Roberts, William Branham, and Jack Coe. In a few years these preachers were attracting enormous crowds to their tent crusades. Roberts, in particular, caught the fancy of the public with dramatic services under his "tent cathedral." By the 1950s he was drawing attention and crowds that rivaled those of Billy Graham. In 1953 Roberts created the televangelist genre when he brought his television healing crusades into the living rooms of television watchers. This created an intense interest in Pentecostalism among people of all denominations.

Adding to this interest was the ministry of the Full Gospel Business Men's Fellowship International (FGBMFI) organized by Demos Shakarian in 1952. Well-to-do Pentecostals gathered in restaurants and hotels to provide an arena for mainstream people who might never enter a Pentecostal church. These "ballroom saints" added an aura of middle-class and financial success to the movement. At the same time, David du Plessis (1905–1987), a South African Pentecostal who had moved to the United States, began to make contact with the National and World Council of Churches as an unofficial spokesman for the Pentecostal movement. His later work as an observer at Vatican II gave Pentecostals a voice to the Roman Catholic world.

Protestant Neo-Pentecostals

By the 1960s Pentecostalism began to make inroads into the mainstream Protestant churches, spurred by the pioneering efforts of an Episcopal priest, Dennis Bennett, from Van Nuys, California, who spoke in tongues in 1960 and, although controversial, was able to remain in the Episcopal Church. This sparked a new movement whose first leaders were known as Neo-Pentecostals. By the 1970s the movement spread to practically all the Protestant churches in North America and around the world. Other leaders included Gerald Derstine (Mennonite), Larry Christenson (Lutheran), Howard Irvin (Baptist), Brick Bradford (Presbyterian), Tommy Tyson (Methodist), and Vernon Stoop (United Church of Christ). By 1965 these movements had adopted the name *charismatic* and had become highly organized renewal forces in the mainline churches.

Catholic Charismatics

The most surprising event was the beginning of the Catholic Charismatic movement, which began among graduate students in Duquesne University in Pittsburgh, Pennsylvania, in 1967. Initially the movement

A Pentecostal church in Seminole, Texas. *Courtesy of istockphoto.com/empath.*

spread among students and faculty in other campuses, such as Notre Dame and the University of Michigan. In a short time, the movement began to spread to the parish level, as thousands of charismatic prayer groups sprang up across the nation. As the Catholic movement spread to over 120 nations, it gained the approval of the Vatican and eventually the belated approval of the major Pentecostal denominations in the United States.

From the beginnings of the movement, and despite early opposition and even persecution, the Pentecostals remained essentially an ecumenical movement with hopes of reaching all churches with what they termed the "full Gospel." After the appearance of the Charismatic movement in the mainstream churches, the Pentecostals joined in several mass ecumenical conferences that brought all the various elements of the renewal together as a witness to the church world. The first of these was a massive conference in Kansas City in 1977, which drew some fifty thousand persons to Arrowhead Stadium. Led by a Catholic, Kevin Ranaghan, the conference delegates were evenly divided between Protestants and Catholics. Other massive conferences in New Orleans, Louisiana (1987), Indianapolis, Indiana (1990), Orlando, Florida (1995), and St. Louis, Missouri (2000), were led by Pentecostal ecumenist Vinson Synan. Large charismatic conferences were also held in Mexico and Canada, the largest of which were led by members of the Catholic Charismatic Renewal.

Throughout these years the Pentecostals (now dubbed Classical Pentecostals, to distinguish them from the Neo-Pentecostals and charismatics) continued to grow rapidly in the United States and around the world. In a 1979 survey conducted by George Gallup and *Christianity Today Magazine*, 19 percent of the U.S. public identified themselves as Pentecostal or charismatic. This amounted to 29 million people eighteen or older. In general, the poll reported that about 20 percent of the members of mainline Protestant and Catholic Churches self-identified as charismatics. By the end of the century, the fastest growing megachurches in the United States were Pentecostal congregations or independent charismatic churches. The same held true in Mexico and Canada. Beyond the borders of the United States, explosive Pentecostal growth in Latin America, Africa, and East Asia marked Pentecostalism as a major religious force in the Third World. In fact, by the year 2000, after only a century of existence, the Pentecostal-Charismatic movement constituted the second largest family of Christians in the world, outnumbered only by the Roman Catholic Church.

In the first decade of the twenty-first century, the prospects for future growth seem to be unlimited. Providing direction for this burgeoning movement was a new generation of renewal colleges and universities, including Oral Roberts University (founded in 1965 in Tulsa, Oklahoma) and Regent University in Virginia

Beach, Virginia, (founded in 1978 by televangelist Pat Robertson). With greater theological depth and the resources of such American missionary churches as the Assemblies of God, the Church of God, the Church of the Foursquare Gospel, and the Pentecostal Holiness Church, the movement seems poised to become an even greater force in the spiritual landscape of the world.

Vinson Synan

See also Antecedents of Pentecostalism; Catholic Charismatic Movement; Oneness Theology; Pentecostalism, Classical; Race Relations

Further Reading

Anderson, R. (1979). *Vision of the disinherited: The making of American Pentecostalism.* New York: Oxford University Press.

Bartleman, F., & Synan, V. (Eds.). (1980). *Azusa Street: The roots of modern day Pentecost.* Plainfield, NJ: Bridge Publishing Company.

Blumhofer, E. (1993). *Restoring the faith: The Assemblies of God, Pentecostalism and American culture.* Urbana: The University of Illinois Press.

Clemmons, I. (1996). *Bishop C. H. Mason and the roots of the Church of God in Christ.* Bakersfield, CA: Pneumalife Publishers.

Cox, H. (1994). *Fire from heaven: The rise of Pentecostal spirituality and the reshaping of Christianity in the twenty-first century.* Reading, MA: Addison-Wesley.

Dayton, D. (1987). *The theological roots of Pentecostalism.* Metuchen, NJ: Scarecrow Press.

Dieter, M. (1996). *The Holiness movement of the nineteenth century* (2nd ed.). Metuchen, NJ: Scarecrow Press.

Goff, J. (1988). *Fields white unto harvest: Charles Fox Parham and the missionary origins of Pentecostalism.* Fayetteville: University of Arkansas Press.

Harrell, E. (1975). *All things are possible: The healing and Charismatic revivals in modern America.* Bloomington: Indiana University Press.

Jones, C. (1983). *Guide to the study of the Pentecostal movement.* Metuchen, NJ: Scarecrow Press.

Synan, V. (1997). *The Holiness-Pentecostal tradition: Charismatic movements in the twentieth century.* Grand Rapids, MI: William B. Eerdmans.

Synan, V. (2001). *Century of the Holy Spirit: 100 years of Pentecostal and Charismatic renewal.* Nashville, TN: Thomas Nelson.

Wacker, G. (2001). *Heaven below: Early Pentecostals and American culture.* Cambridge, MA: Harvard University Press.

Animism

One belief of Pentecostals is that God has unlimited power and that this power is released to meet the needs of His people in the form of healing and blessing. This distinctive theological belief provides Pentecostals with a unique opportunity to approach animists who share similar beliefs. The majority of non-Westerners have an animistic orientation. Religions such as Buddhism, Hinduism, and Confucianism are affected by and contain animistic beliefs and practices in one way or another. This religious context becomes fertile ground for receiving Pentecostal beliefs in God's power.

Defining Animism

Animism is a belief in personal spirits and impersonal spiritual forces. Animists perceive that unseen spirits and forces have power over human affairs. People who have experienced such spiritual power and influence seek its help with such human needs and desires as healing, success, and decisions for the future. They attempt to manipulate the power of the spirits for a favorable future.

An animistic understanding of the world includes organic spirit beings such as gods, ancestor spirits, ghosts, nature spirits, and demons. Spiritual forces are impersonal powers manifested in various forms, such as in magic, sorcery, astrology, witchcraft, and the evil eye. Both organic spirit beings and other spiritual forces interact, according to animistic belief, with people in their daily lives. The power of the spirits and spiritual forces can bring evil as well as good.

Animism and Pentecostalism

Both animism and Pentecostalism believe that the visible world is connected with the invisible and that there is an interaction between the divine and human beings. In times of need, animists would seek the help of religious practitioners whom they believe have access to the spirit world and who communicate with the spirits to determine the spirits' desire. Through the help of these practitioners, animists believe that the power of the spirits can be released to prevent or undo any misfortune that an evil spirit may bring into their lives or to influence a spirit to bring fortune. Pentecostals, for their part, also believe that evil spirits can cause sickness and misfortune, while God's power through the Holy Spirit is available to help Christians ward off those evil spirits. God's power, according to Pentecostals, is greater than any other spiritual force. Like animists, Pentecostals acknowledge people who have spiritual gifts and seek their help for healing, wisdom, advice, and guidance.

Both belief systems also focus on the issue of power. Animists recognize the power that ancestor spirits have over their living descendents, the power of witchcraft to harm newborn babies and the harvest, the power of magic over human affairs, the power of spirit forces to bring sickness, and the power of sorcerers to work for revenge. This recognition easily leads to fear of spiritual forces. On the other hand, the animists also believe in benevolent spiritual forces, including the power of priests to bring blessings, a good spirit's power to counter malevolent spiritual forces, ancestor spirits' ability to reveal the causes of misfortune, and the power of spirit forces to bring healing.

To appropriate such spiritual forces, the animistic religious specialists employ various methods of divination such as omens, astrology, ordeals, and dreams. Pentecostals throughout history have demonstrated that they experience the power of the Holy Spirit in worship, prayer, and preaching. It is a regular feature of Pentecostal belief all over the world to pray for healing and to expect God to meet believers' various needs through the power of the Holy Spirit, manifested in miracles. Equally unique is the Pentecostal belief in and experience of a "power encounter"—a confrontation between Satan's power and God's power. It is readily admitted that the power of Satan is much stronger than that of humans; thus, human power alone cannot counter, fight, or conquer the strong force and power of evil spirits. However, according to Pentecostal belief, God's people are empowered by God through the experience that Pentecostals call the baptism in the Holy Spirit. This experience is different from the "born again" experience, and its empowerment is for Christian witness (Acts 1:8).

God's power can be manifested through various spiritual gifts, such as healing, miracles, words of wisdom or knowledge, prophecy, tongues or interpretation of tongues (1 Corinthians 12:8–11), or through God's direct intervention in human situations. Pentecostals believe that God is both transcendental and immanent to help them. Their belief is power oriented, and God's power is a very important element in their lives.

Animists and Pentecostals also share an emphasis on experiences. The animists' main motif in their religious involvement is the experience of spirits' power in their lives, be it through healing, blessing, divination, or the warding off of misfortunes caused by evil spirits, achieved through the help of other spirits. Similarly,

the Pentecostal theology of power is no mere abstraction but is tangible in daily life. However, the source of their experience is quite different. The animists believe in ancestor spirits and impersonal forces, whereas Pentecostals believe in the supreme but personal God and His Spirit, who created the universe and humankind.

This brief comparison of animism and Pentecostalism reveals similarities in their worldviews and religious beliefs, in spite of fundamental differences in the source of their experiences. These similarities may be the primary cause of the explosive growth of the Pentecostal movement in the non-Western world, where animism is the foundation of their religiosity and culture. Pentecostalism, unlike other Christian traditions, has been able to provide functional substitutes for those areas' animistic religiosity, rather than simply dismissing their religious expectations as superstition. These shared religious instincts open up the possibility of Pentecostal syncretism when the appropriation of supernatural power becomes the focus of the religious orientation. Unfortunately, this syncretistic tendency seems to have appeared in many Pentecostal-like religious groups in the non-Western world.

Julie C. Ma

See also Asia, East; Demon Possession, Casting out Demons

Further Reading

Burnett, D. (1992). *Unearthly powers.* Nashville, TN: Thomas Nelson Publishers.

Ma, J. C. (2000). *When Spirit meets the spirits.* Frankfurt am Main, Germany: Peter Lang.

Rheenen, G. V. (1991). *Communicating Christ in animistic contexts.* Grand Rapids, MI: Baker.

Anoint, Anointing

Pentecostals and charismatics believe that anointing enables believers to trust in the saving power of Jesus and empowers them to a level of ministry performance not otherwise possible. The importance of Holy Spirit anointing can be seen in both the Old and New Testaments.

Old Testament Usage

In the Old Testament, anointing signified either being set apart or the presence of God. It took place in a variety of

Table 1. Overview of Greek Words for "Anoint"

	Aleipho	*Chirō*
Definition	The process of smearing or pouring soft fat or oil over a person or thing.	To touch the surface lightly, anoint, to paint.
OT Usage	For the care of the body: Ruth 3:3; 2 Chronicles 28:15; Daniel 10:3; Judges 16:8	The coronation of kings: Judges 9:8, 15; 1 Samuel 9:16; 10:11; 15:1,17; 16:3, 12ff; 1 Kings 1:39; 2 Kings 9:3; 11:12; 19:3
	Omitted during mourning: 2 Samuel 14:2	Bestowing of authority: Psalm 45:7
	Care of a guest: Psalm 23:5	Coupled with the gift of God's spirit and protection: 1 Samuel 16:13; 24:6–11; 26:9–23; 2 Samuel 1:14ff; 19:21f; 23:1ff; Isaiah 11:2
	Symbolic sense: Genesis 31:13; Exodus 40:15; Numbers 3:3	Anointing of priest: Exodus 28:41; 29:1–7, 29; 40:13–15; Leviticus 4:3
		Anointing of objects: Exodus 29:26; 30:26; 40:9–10; Leviticus 8:10; Numbers 7:1
		Symbolic sense: Isaiah 61:1; Ezekiel 16:9
NT Usage	For the care of the body: Matthew 6:17	The exclusive use of this verb form in the New Testament is to signify "the bestowal of the Holy Spirit, special power, or a divine commission" (Müller 1975, 122).
	To honor a guest: Luke 7:38, 46; John 11:2; 12:3	The anointing of Jesus by God: Luke 4:18; Acts 4:27; 10:38; Hebrews 1:9
	Prepare the dead: Mark 16:1	The anointing of Christians: 2 Corinthians 1:21–22; 1 John 2:20, 27
	Heal the sick: Mark 6:13; James 5:14	

Source: Müller (1975, 119–124).

settings. (See table 1.) The first appearance of the word anoint (*aleipho*) is in Genesis 31:13 and refers to an action that took place in Genesis 28:18—the "anointing" or the "pouring of oil" on a pillar by Jacob. Jacob's purpose in anointing the pillar was to seal the vision he had in a dream, now known as "Jacob's Ladder," in which God promised him the land upon which he lay. In Exodus, the priesthood of Aaron is established: "And you shall anoint them and ordain them and consecrate them that they may serve Me as priests" (Exodus 28:41, NASB).

Judges 9:8 describes the anointing of kings, a ritual that culminates in the anointing of David: "The Spirit of the Lord came mightily upon David from that day forward" (1 Samuel 16:12ff). Up to this point, anointing, whether it was of an object, a priest, or a king, carried with it the idea of being set apart for a special purpose. Now anointing carried with it the presence of God in the form of His Spirit, His authority, and perhaps His healing touch.

New Testament Usage

In the New Testament, anointing falls upon the living Body of Christ, the Church. At first, the references to anointing are applied only to Jesus. At His baptism, the Spirit fills Him, enabling Him to carry out His messianic mission (Luke 3:21–22). After He is tempted by the devil, Jesus announces the anointing His ministry would carry by claiming the applicability of Isaiah 61:1

to Himself (Luke 4:17ff.). But this anointing does not remain with Jesus alone.

In Matthew 16:18–19, following Peter's confession of Jesus as the Christ, Jesus says that He will build His church and to that body He will give authority. In Luke 10:1ff, the seventy are sent out with authority over demons and with the power of healing. In John 15:26–27, the disciples are told that they will be able to testify to the truth because they will be anointed with the Spirit just as He had been. In Mark 13:11 and Luke 21:12–19, the disciples are told specifically not to worry about what they will say because they will be given anointed speech. When Peter arose and addressed the crowd at Pentecost (Acts 2:1ff), he did so under the anointing of the Holy Spirit. Finally, this anointing is promised to all those who believe in Jesus as the only Son of God: "As for you, the anointing which you received from Him abides in you, and you have no need for anyone to teach you; but as His anointing teaches you about all things, and is true and is not a lie, and just as it has taught you, you abide in Him" (1 John 2:27).

Metamorphosis of Anointing

According to the *New Bible Dictionary*:

Fundamentally, the anointing was an act of God (1 Samuel 10:1), and the word 'anointed' was used metaphorically to mean the bestowal of divine favour

(Psalms 23:5; 92:10) or appointment to a special place or function in the purpose of God (Psalm 105:15; Isaiah 45:1). Further, the anointing symbolized equipment for service, and is associated with the outpouring of the Spirit of God (1 Samuel 10:1, 9; 16:13; Isaiah 61:1; Zechariah 4:1–14). (Wood and Marshall 1996, 49)

Jack W. Hayford, a Pentecostal-Charismatic leader, has explained that God does not give someone His Spirit only for a sensory experience and that this has been true for millennia, not only for believers but also for God's Son.

The Anointing of Jesus

Kenneth Wuest, a Biblical scholar, describes the anointing of Jesus, which enabled Him to do battle with and ultimately defeat the devil, in the following words:

In Acts 10:38 the verb is in the active voice. The subject, "God," does the acting, and the Holy Spirit, designated by the instrumental case, even though Himself a Person, is here looked upon as a means that is impersonal so far as any activity in the premises is concerned. That means that the element which God used in anointing the Man Christ Jesus was the Holy Spirit. The Holy Spirit did not do the anointing. He is that with which Jesus was anointed…. Thus, in the case of our Lord, the anointing with the Spirit refers to the Person of the Holy Spirit coming upon Him, this position of the Holy Spirit providing the potential equipment for ministry of which our Lord was to avail Himself. (*Untranslatable Riches* in Wuest 1997, 79)

Consistent with the Old Testament sense of the concept, the anointing of Jesus is seen as a mantle laid upon Him. This was a kind of anointing that could and would from time to time be removed, as was the case with Saul (1 Samuel 16:14). The New Testament concept of anointing, however, was to be different: "The reception of the Holy Spirit allows the believer to share in the messianic anointing of Jesus. The designation 'Christian' connotes a member of the community of the 'Anointed One'"(Powell 2002, 318).

The Anointing of Jesus' Followers

The anointing that believers receive upon placing their trust in Christ is described in 1 John 2:27. The Greek word *chiro* is used here but not as a verb. Wuest writes:

We have here the noun form of *chrio*, which is *chrisma*, and is translated 'anointing'. In the case of our Lord, the Holy Spirit rested *upon* Him, for that was the order in the dispensation of law (Numbers 11:29). In the case of the believer during this Age of Grace, the Holy Spirit is placed *within* him (John 14:17). His ministry in the believer today is not only for service as was the case in Old Testament times, but also for sanctification. [Wuest concludes,] "The baptism by the Spirit is for the introduction of the believer into the Body of Christ, the anointing with the Spirit is His coming to dwell in the Christian, and the fullness of the Spirit is for power for service. (*Treasures from the Greek New Testament* in Wuest 1997, 125)

Therefore, from the perspective of Pentecostal-Charismatic believers, anointing is best understood as the Spirit's action upon people in a way that enables them to receive the work of the Spirit in their lives. However, Pentecostal-Charismatic believers also speak of the necessity of cooperating with the presence of the Spirit within in order to derive its full benefit. Wuest sums up anointing this way:

The Spirit was sent to the believer's heart to make His home there. That means that the Christian must make Him feel at home. He can do that by giving the Holy Spirit absolute liberty of action in his heart, the home in which He lives. This means that the believer is to yield himself, all of himself, to the Spirit's control, depend upon the Spirit for guidance, teaching, strength. (*Untranslatable Riches* in Wuest 1997, 83)

A Three-Fold Ministry

When Pentecostal-Charismatic believers put their trust in the power of the Spirit within, the purpose of New Testament anointment comes to fruition: "When the anointing of God rests on human flesh, it makes everything flow better"(Tenney 1998, 41). That purpose can be summed up as a three-fold ministry:

1. The anointing of the Spirit helps the believer to understand the Scripture to a depth not possible without the full measure of anointing.

2. The anointing of the Spirit helps the believer to pray in a way that engages the spiritual realm in the dimension of deliverance, protection, provision, healing, intercession, and spiritual warfare not otherwise possible without the full measure of anointing.

3. The anointing of the Spirit helps the believer to proclaim the Gospel both inspirationally and apologetically in a way not otherwise possible without the full measure of anointing.

Hence, the Pentecostal-Charismatic movement invites all believers to live a fully anointed life. This invitation from God is clear and significant.

John E. Dooley

See also Oil, Anointing with

Further Reading

Bloesch, D. (2000). *The Holy Spirit*. Downers Grove, IL: InterVarsity Press.

Christenson, L. (1981). *The renewed mind*. Minneapolis, MN: Bethany House.

Christenson, L. (2000). *Ride the river*. Bloomington, MN: Bethany House.

Hayford, J. (1996). *The beauty of spiritual language*. Nashville, TN: Thomas Nelson.

Land, S. J. (1997). *Pentecostal spirituality*. Sheffield, UK: Sheffield Academic Press.

Martos, J. (1983). Anointing. In A. Richardson & J. Bowden (Eds.), *The Westminster dictionary of Christian theology* (p. 22). Philadelphia: Westminster Press.

Müller, D. (1975). Anoint. In C. Brown (Ed.), *New International Dictionary of New Testament Theology* (Vol. 1, pp. 119–124). Grand Rapids, MI: Zondervan.

New American Standard Bible. (1995). LaHabra, CA: Lockman Foundation.

Otis, G., Jr. (1999). *Informed intercession*. Ventura, CA: Renew Books.

Pinnock, C. (1996). *Flame of love*. Downers Grove, IL: InterVarsity Press.

Powell, T. (2002). Anointing with oil. In S. M. Burgess & E. M. Van Derr Maas (Eds.), *New International dictionary of Pentecostal and Charismatic movements* (p. 318). Grand Rapids, MI: Zondervan.

Sziksszai, S. (1982). Anoint. In G. A. Buttrick (Ed.), *The interpreter's dictionary of the Bible* (Vol. 1, pp. 138–139). Nashville, TN: Abingdon Press.

Tenny, T. (1998). *The God chasers*. Shippenburg, PA: Destiny Image.

Wood, D. R. W., & Marshall, I. H. (1996). *New Bible dictionary* (3rd ed.). Downers Grove, IL: InterVarsity Press.

Wuest, K. S. (1997). *Wuest's word studies from the Greek New Testament: For the English reader*. Grand Rapids, MI: Eerdmans.

Yoder, B. (2001). *The breaker anointing*. Colorado Springs, CO: Wagner Publications.

Antecedents of Pentecostalism

Classical Pentecostals have assumed the uniqueness of their movement. They argue that Pentecostalism had its origins in the first century of the Christian era, and that these early Pentecostal characteristics waned after 100 CE, only to reappear on 1 January 1901 with the spiritual outpouring at Charles F. Parham's Bethel Bible School at Topeka, Kansas. This they understood to be the fulfillment of the prophecy in Joel 2 of an "early rain" and a "latter rain." In short, classical Pentecostals have assumed that the Holy Spirit had deistic tendencies, appearing with power in the first century church and evidenced by signs and wonders—equivalent to a "first cause"—and then remaining largely detached from the church, withholding such spiritual evidences until the modern Pentecostal outpourings.

Much of this understanding of Christian history was based on the Pentecostal interpretation of Joel 2:23, which speaks of a "former rain" of spiritual blessing, followed eventually by a "latter rain," or the visitation of the Spirit. Clearly, this assumed eighteen hundred years of spiritual drought, devoid of Pentecostal manifestations.

In their insistence that the church had suffered from a long-term absence of spectacular spiritual giftings, Pentecostals unwittingly tended to side with certain Protestant cessationists, such as the late nineteenth-century Princeton theologian B. B. Warfield. Unlike early Pentecostals, however, Warfield argued that miracles, signs, wonders, and other spiritual gifts were unnecessary once the apostolic church had been founded and the canon had been written. Pentecostals instead insisted that the church was famished from a lack of divine visitation and was awaiting a second great outpouring, which they assumed to be their own movement.

Perhaps because of the early attachment of early-twentieth-century Pentecostals to Darby's dispensationalism—which in the form of the Scofield Reference Bible was more the basis for most of their early schooling than a study of church history—and because of their perceived uniqueness, Pentecostals at first failed to recognize the appearance of people of the Spirit in every era of Christian history and in all locations, both East and West, where Christianity took root. The Church of Rome and all Eastern Christian churches long have recorded the work of the divine Spirit among them, only recently pausing to reflect on their hagiographic abuses.

Ancient Churches (100–600 CE)

At the end of the first century, both Bishop Clement of Rome and Bishop Ignatius of Antioch document the

Symeon the New Theologian (949–1022 CE) on Divine Spirit

From on high give me Your grace, give me Your Divine Spirit!

Give me Your Paraclete, Savior, send Him as You promised.

Send Him even now upon me as I sit in the Upper Chamber.

O Master, completely transcending every earthly care beyond the whole world,

and seeking You as I wait to receive Your Spirit.

Source: Maloney, G. A. (Trans.). (1976). *Hymns of Divine Love by St. Symeon the New Theologian, 41* (p. 208). Denville, NJ: Dimension Books.

continuation of prophetic gifts. Other first-century writers find it necessary to distinguish between true and false prophets because of their continued presence in the church.

In the second century, Justin Martyr documents a continuation of the gifts of prophecy and miracles. Irenaeus of Lyon describes gifts of prophecy, discernment of spirits, and exorcism in his Gallic church. He even mentions that individuals have been raised from the dead. Hippolytus of Rome suggests there is no need to lay hands on laity who already exercise gifts of healing. Tertullian reports exorcisms, healings, and revelations among Carthaginian Christians.

By the third century, Tertullian joins temporarily with the "New Prophets" (Montanists), whom he insists are instruments in revealing the full provision of the Holy Spirit. Origen of Alexandria indicates that healings, exorcisms, and validating signs and wonders continue to draw unbelievers into the Christian fold. Gregory Thaumaturgus ("the wonder-worker") prophesies, heals the sick, and takes dominion over demons, among numerous other signs and wonders that add credibility to his ministry. Athanasius' life of Antony of the Desert is the first important biography of the charismatic desert saints, who prophesy, heal the sick, and discern spirits.

In the fourth century, Augustine of Hippo reports divine healings and other miracles that lead to the conversion of pagans. Meanwhile, the heretical Messalians of Syria (c. 360–800) practice the laying on of hands for Spirit baptism. They teach that every person, including Christ, was possessed from birth by a personal demon. Through unceasing fervent prayer and other ascetic exercises, and the baptism of the Holy Spirit, the evil forces could be driven out.

In the sixth century, Gregory the Great (Pope Gregory I), in his biographies of contemporary saints, provides the documentation through eyewitness accounts of a range of miracles, including healings, raising of the dead, exorcisms, foretelling of the future, and deliverance from dangers. He directly correlates miracles with the missionary enterprise of Augustine of Canterbury and his companions to the Anglo-Saxons.

Medieval Churches

In the tenth and eleventh centuries, Symeon the New Theologian, perhaps the most famous Eastern charismatic Christian, reports his intimate spiritual experiences. These include a "baptism of the Holy Spirit" accompanied by gifts of copious tears, compunction, and visions of God as light.

In the twelfth century, Hildegard of Bingen experiences ecstatic visions (which she later paints) and gifts of tears and compunction, wisdom, knowledge, and prophecy. Numerous miracles are attributed to her. She also is reported to have sung "concerts" in the Spirit, and to have written entire books in unknown languages. Apocalyptic writers such as Rupert of Deutz (c. 1075–1129/30) and Joachim of Fiore (c. 1132–1202) exercise a wide variety of spiritual gifts.

The sermons of Francis of Assisi (1181–1226) are accompanied by miracles of great power, including casting out devils, healing the sick, and prophecy. Similarly, the homilies of Thomas Aquinas (1224–1274) are frequently confirmed by miracles, and he experiences ecstasies, especially in the last months of his life. Vincent Ferrer (1350–1419), a Spirit-filled Dominican missionary, draws huge crowds when he preaches. Everywhere his ministry is accompanied by remarkable miracles, including healings and raising the dead.

In the East, Gregory Palamas (1296–1359) emphasizes the laying on of hands for receiving the gifts of healing, miracles, foreknowledge, irrefutable wisdom,

An Excerpt from *On the Spiritual Life*, a treatise by St. Vincent Ferrer

As the extract below illustrates, St. Vincent Ferrer (1350–1412) combined a deeply spiritual approach with the practicalities of how best to reach his listeners.

In sermons and talks, use simple language and a homely conversational style to explain each particular point. As far as you can, give plenty of examples; then, whoever has committed that particular sin will have his conscience pricked, as though you were preaching to him alone. But it must be done in such a way that your words do not appear to come from a soul full of pride or scorn. Speak rather out of the depths of love and fatherly care, like a father suffering for his sinful children, as if they were gravely ill, or trapped in a deep pit, whom he is trying to draw out and set free, and look after like a mother. You must be like one who delights in their progress, and in the glory in heaven that they are hoping for.

Such a style usually has a good effect on a congregation. For, to speak of virtues and vices in general terms evokes little response from listeners.

Similarly in confession, whether you are gently comforting the timid, or more sternly putting the fear of God into the hardened sinner, you must always show the deepest love, so that the sinner always feels that your words come out of pure love. In this way, your words of sweetness and love will have a more penetrating effect.

But in your desire to be of use to the souls of your neighbours, you must first of all have recourse to God with your whole heart, and simply make this request of him. Ask him in his goodness to pour into you that love in which is the sum of all virtues, through which you may be able to achieve what you desire

Source: St. Vincent Ferrer. (n.d.). *On the spiritual life.* Retrieved September 20, 2004, from http://www.vatican.va/spirit/documents/spirit_20010405_vincenzo-ferrer_en.html

---

diverse tongues, and interpretation of tongues. He also reports personal ecstasies and visions of divine light.

The radical dualists known as Messalians (or "praying people"), originating in East Syria, continue to play a fringe role in the early Middle Ages. The Messalians deny the value of existing orthodox sacraments and priesthood, declaring that they had been made perfect and superior by the reception of the divine Spirit. For this they are persecuted and eliminated in the area. But radical dualism breaks out again in Asia Minor, Armenia, and the Balkans with the emergence of the Paulicians, who also declare themselves baptized in the Holy Spirit. They are decimated and dispersed in the tenth century. But radical dualism reemerges shortly thereafter with the Bogomils ("beloved of God") who claim to be made perfect by the infilling of the Holy Spirit. By the thirteenth and fourteenth centuries, Bogomilism actually becomes the national religion of Bosnia. It is wiped out in the fifteenth century.

Probably growing out of Balkan Bogomilism, Catharism (known in France as Albigensianism) is the most powerful heresy in the medieval West. The Cathars replace Roman Catholic sacraments with the *consolamentum*, baptism with fire and the Holy Ghost, performed by the imposition of hands. After receiving the *consolamentum*, Cathar *perfecti* face a lifetime of rigid asceticism so as to remain pure. This form of radical dualism lasts until the fourteenth century, when it finally succumbs to intense persecution (the so-called "Albigensian Crusade").

Sixteenth Century

Radical reformer Thomas Müntzer emphasizes the "inner word" of the Spirit, Holy Spirit possession and guidance, and direct revelation in visions and dreams. He insists that Christians are to experience the Holy Spirit as powerfully in the sixteenth century as in the time of the prophets and apostles. He holds to the necessity of a baptism of the Holy Spirit, whereby the elect can discern spirits and unlock biblical mysteries.

Ignatius Loyola, founder of the Society of Jesus (the Jesuits), frequently receives divine communications. He personally experiences the gift of tears—often in such abundance that he cannot control himself—and the gift of *loquela*, which a few modern scholars associate with today's charismatic phenomenon of sung glossolalia (tongues).

Seventeenth Century

The central doctrine of the Religious Society of Friends (the Quakers) is the "inner light/word," with the Holy Spirit speaking directly to the human mind. Early Quakers record visions, healings, and prophecies, which they liken to the Day of Pentecost. There even is evidence of tongues speech among them.

The prophets of the Cevennes (the Camisards), French Protestant resistance fighters against royalist Catholic forces, claim to be directly inspired by the divine Spirit. Their children prophesy at very early ages. The Camisards are seized by ecstatic inspiration, during which they utter strange and often amazing things and speak in languages of which they have no knowledge.

Jansenists, a radical Augustinian movement in the Roman Catholic Church from 1640 to 1801, were known for their signs and wonders, spiritual dancing, healings, and prophetic utterances—including speaking in unknown tongues and understanding foreign languages of which they have no knowledge.

Eighteenth Century

The Awakened, a Lutheran revivalistic movement in Finland, begins in 1796 with a sudden outpouring of the Holy Spirit, accompanied by such observable signs as visions and glossolalia. This renewal continues into the twentieth century.

Seraphim of Sarov (1759–1833), the Russian Orthodox charismatic leader, asserts that the goal of the Christian life is the reception of the Holy Spirit. His "evidence" for a baptism of the Holy Spirit is a transfiguration experience—being transformed, while still in the flesh, into divine light. Seraphim is also remembered for a gift of healing.

Nineteenth Century

Presbyterian pastor Edward Irving (1792–1834) proposes a return to the apostolic pattern, with the fivefold offices of apostles, prophets, evangelists, pastors, and teachers. His followers, the Irvingites, seek a new outpouring of the Holy Spirit. They begin to experience charismata, especially glossolalia. Ironically, Irving is himself relegated to a minor role in his congregation because he receives no charismata. Notwithstanding,

he continues to argue for the necessity of miracles. Irving also is credited with founding the West of Scotland revival (1830), led by laity and featuring a variety of spiritual giftings, including prophesy, healings, glossolalia, and interpretation of tongues.

Pentecostal phenomena, including glossolalia, are experienced by South Indian Christians in Travancore (Kerala) and Madras State (Tamil Nadu) in the 1860s and 1870s. It also is reported that by the end of the nineteenth century, approximately 900,000 in African Initiated Churches have experienced Pentecostal-like phenomena.

Some radical evangelicals propose that, according to Jesus' promise in Mark 16:17, God would bestow intelligible human languages on missionaries. This would enable them to bypass formal language study to begin preaching immediately after arriving on their fields, since little time remained for evangelism. Mary Campbell, a member of the charismatic movement in Scotland, reports that she received the Turkish language and the language of the Palau island group in the Pacific Ocean to equip her to preach to these peoples. However, the teaching that the gift of diverse tongues is given for missions activity is abandoned by early twentieth-century classical Pentecostals when their anticipated gifting is not realized.

Lessons

Far from being unique in Christian history, modern classical Pentecostals must come to recognize their movement as among the latest chapters in a long history of peoples of the Spirit. Classical Pentecostals *are* unique in their insistence that glossolalia (tongues) is the initial physical evidence of the Baptism of the Holy Spirit.

STANLEY M. BURGESS

See also Azusa Street Revival; Pentecostal Theology; Pentecostalism, Classical; Protestantism

Further Reading

Armstrong, C. (2002, October 7). Timeline of the Spirit-gifted. *Christianity Today.*

Ash, J. L. (1976). The decline of ecstatic prophecy in the early Church. *Theological Studies, 35.*

Bouyer, L. (1974). Charismatic movements in history within the Church. *One in Christ, 10*(2), 148–161.

Bresson, B. L. (1966). *Studies in ecstasy.* New York: Vantage Press.

Burgess, S. M. (1984). *The Holy Spirit: Ancient Christian traditions.* Peabody, MA: Hendrickson.

Burgess, S. M. (1989). *The Holy Spirit: Eastern Christian traditions*. Peabody, MA: Hendrickson.

Burgess, S. M. (1997). *The Holy Spirit: Medieval Roman Catholic and Reformation traditions*. Peabody, MA: Hendrickson.

Knox, R. A. (1950). *Enthusiasm: A chapter in the history of religion*. London: Oxford University Press.

O'Carroll, M. (1987). *Trinitas: A theological encyclopedia of the Holy Trinity*. Wilmington, DE: Michael Glazier.

O'Carroll, M. (1990). *Veni Creator Spiritus: A theological encyclopedia of the Holy Spirit*. Collegeville, MN: Glazier/Liturgical.

Tsirpanlis, C. N. (1978). Pneumatology in the Eastern Church. *Diakonia, 13*(1).

Williams, G., & Waldvogel, E. (1975). A history of speaking in tongues and related gifts. In M. P. Hamilton (Ed.), *The Charismatic movement* (pp. 61–113). Grand Rapids, MI: Eerdmans.

Anthropology (Theology of Humans)

Anthropology is the study of humankind. The academic discipline of anthropology studies human origins, human nature, and human diversity in an empirical manner. Pentecostals have very different, theological, ideas on human origins and human nature. They also have beliefs about the destiny of humankind that are central to their faith.

Human Origins

Pentecostals adhere to fundamentalist teachings on the issue of creation and reject the idea of evolution. Following the book of Genesis in the Bible, they believe that there was a being called God who created the heavens and the earth and all living things, including Adam and Eve, the first humans, who were fashioned in His image. Unlike anthropologists, Pentecostals believe that humans are a separate creation, set apart from other creatures, and the climax of creation. They preach that only humans have free will and an immortal soul and believe that God gave humans the power to rule over the earth.

According to Pentecostals, God created woman so that man might have company, making Eve from Adam's rib. This provides a foundation for the idea that men and women are meant to be together as monogamous couples, as well as for a belief in the superiority of men. According to Pentecostals, Adam and Eve were created without sin. It was God's plan for them to dwell in Paradise forever, but they disobeyed God and tasted good and evil from the tree of knowledge. God then punished Adam and Eve by casting them out of the Garden of Eden and condemning them and their descendants to suffering and death. Because of this Fall, men know the burden of labor and women the pain of childbirth and the duty of submitting to their husbands. Both have the burden of choosing right from wrong.

Human Nature

Pentecostals believe that every individual is made lovingly by God and is therefore a divine creation. Because God is responsible for the abilities they enjoy and the disabilities they have to bear, they believe that both should be cherished as parts of His divine plan. In the Pentecostal worldview, God determines the destiny of every individual, although He does not often reveal His reasons. Taking a life, even one's own, is sinful, because it interferes with God's plan.

Reproduction is also part of God's plan. The Assemblies of God, for example, says that sexuality is a "God-given desire." On the other hand, Pentecostals are opposed to homosexuality, believing it to be unnatural or contrary to God's plan. Also, according to Pentecostal teaching, life begins at conception; therefore, abortion is murder and a sin.

Although they see themselves as God's creations, Pentecostals believe that they come into the world tainted with the sin of Adam and Eve. Because sin is a fundamental part of human nature, humans are destined to suffer. But the purpose of suffering, as Pentecostals see it, is to bring people to God, who provided them with the gift of healing to relieve suffering.

Pentecostals believe that, because of the fall of Adam and Eve, they are born into a world of temptation and sin. The world as they know it is not the one that God created, but a man-made world under the rule of Satan, who surrounds them with temptations to make them sin and offend God. The world they live in is therefore a challenge. Pentecostals preach that Jesus came to earth to bear their sins for them, asking only that they accept Him as their savior.

Pentecostals believe they are called to "holiness" by God—that is, to live life according to "the Word," which is the Bible. They believe that God also gave them His Holy Spirit to guide the way. The Holy Spirit is said to dwell inside everyone who accepts Christ as their savior. The Spirit serves as a guide to living a moral life in an immoral world. The Spirit may bring the fruits of love, joy, peace, patience, kindness, goodness, faithfulness, gentleness, and self-control as well as the gifts of wisdom, knowledge, faith, healing, prophecy, speaking in tongues, and interpretation of tongues.

Pentecostals consider the body to be the temple of the Holy Spirit and say that it should be kept clean and pure because the Spirit will not dwell in an impure body. Likewise, the demons of the world cannot dwell in a spiritually clean body. Pentecostals believe that in order to maintain purity, they should abstain from alcohol, tobacco, narcotics, and the use of profanity.

Pentecostals place special emphasis on sexuality, which they believe has a place only in reproduction. Sin and sexuality are virtually synonymous in the Pentecostal world, and sermons often dwell on fornication and adultery. Social dancing and gambling are discouraged and sometimes prohibited because they take place in "sinful" surroundings, and cosmetics, jewelry, and fancy hairdos and clothes are discouraged because they call too much attention to the physical self. Pentecostals are family-centered and place a high value on raising children. They believe the two-parent nuclear family is a key part of God's plan for humanity.

Pentecostals see their lives as a constant struggle to choose between sin and holiness, Satan and God, and eternal damnation and salvation. They say that those who choose to become Christian must accept Jesus as their personal savior and live in a Christ-like manner. Christians turn their backs on the past and are born again as new, changed people, kind, loving, humble, and obedient people, pure in thought and deed. This experience of spiritual rebirth not only erases past sins, it also changes the nature of the reborn person. A saved person is a "saint" who has a personal relationship with God.

Being a Christian is a constant struggle because Christians have to face the devil and the temptations of the world, and they are naturally inclined to sinful pursuits. A Christian needs to pray, study the Bible, follow the Holy Spirit, avoid the world, and seek the fellowship and support of other Christians to stay on the path of salvation. Salvation is based solely on faith in Jesus and not on good works.

Human Destiny

Pentecostals believe that death is God's punishment for the sin of Adam and Eve, but that it is God's plan to put an end to death itself and restore the initial state of immortality in Paradise. Pentecostals are premillennial—that is, they believe they are living in the Last Days before the end of the world. In the Last Days, it is prophesied, there will be a decline in morality and

"signs and wonders" or miraculous events (the "Latter Rain") signaling the imminent Rapture of the Living Saints, when Christians will be taken to heaven. Pentecostals therefore interpret social decay as a sign of impending glory.

They believe that the Rapture will be followed by a period called the Tribulation, when the world will be ruled by the Antichrist. It will begin with prosperity and end in plagues. After seven years, Jesus will return (known as the Second Coming) and vanquish Satan in the Battle of Armageddon, casting him into the Bottomless Pit. Christians will enjoy a thousand-year period of perfection on earth they call the Millennium. Satan will then be released from the Bottomless Pit as a final test. The living and the dead will be judged by God, and those who are saved will live for eternity in the Holy City of New Jerusalem, while those who are not will be cast with Satan into the Lake of Fire, to burn in Hell forever.

WILLIAM WEDENOJA

See also Anti-intellectualism; Creation, Re-creation

Further Reading

Anderson, R. M. (1979). The Pentecostal message. In *Visions of the disinherited: The making of American Pentecostalism* (pp. 79–97). New York: Oxford University Press.

Brodwin, P. (2003). Pentecostalism in translation: Religion and the production of community in the Haitian diaspora. *American Ethnologist 30*(1), 85–101.

Faupel, D. W. (1996). *The everlasting gospel: The significance of eschatology in the development of Pentecostal thought.* Sheffield, UK: Sheffield Academic Press.

Anti-intellectualism

Anti-intellectualism is the inclination to emphasize feelings and emotions rather than the intellect and logic. Even though the term did not become popular until the 1950s, Pentecostal and charismatic Christianity have long stressed the workings of the Holy Spirit more than reason and the mind. Critics of Pentecostalism classify the movement as anti-intellectual, whereas modern defenders of the faith maintain that its distinctive emphasis on the spiritual, rather than the cerebral, is purposeful. Richard Hofstradter, in his renowned *Anti-Intellectualism in the American Life*, argued that Evangelicalism, including Pentecostalism, was one of the prominent reasons for the presence of anti-intellectualism in the United States.

Anti-intellectual Roots of Pentecostalism

Pentecostalism, a form of Evangelical Protestantism that stresses salvation, baptism in the Spirit, divine healings, and the imminent Second Coming of Christ, has long been wary of the intellect. Present in each of the four distinctive traits of Pentecostalism listed above is a lack of concern with the matters of the mind. Ever since the birth of modern Pentecostalism in early twentieth-century North America, the Pentecostal message has included the quintessential belief that the Holy Spirit falls upon the faithful and causes them to engage in various ecstatic practices with the body, most notably speaking in tongues (glossolalia). While Darwinism, the social gospel, ecumenism, and biblical criticism were all gaining support in mainline Protestant churches during the nineteenth and twentieth centuries, the Holiness and Pentecostal movements took a more conservative approach. Condemning the so-called intellectual advances as false doctrines, early Pentecostals advocated living a life "in the Spirit" without concentrating upon the intellectual foundations of their faith.

The Reverend Charles Fox Parham (1873–1929), a former Methodist minister sometimes referred to as the "father of Pentecostalism," taught that glossolalia served as the initial evidence of one's baptism in the Spirit. With a zeal for the Holy Spirit and the Bible as his only textbook, Parham's teaching career was short-lived at the small Bethel Bible College in Topeka, Kansas. Parham's background included some college experience, but he never earned a degree. On 1 January 1901, Agnes Ozman (1870–1937), one of Parham's students, became the first to speak in tongues; that event traditionally marks the beginning of Pentecostalism's first wave. Ozman reportedly started speaking in Chinese; her initial evidence of the Holy Spirit supported Parham's teaching that one did not need to learn foreign languages for world missionary efforts, which contributed to anti-intellectualism. Parham taught that the Spirit would give missionaries the words they needed to say through a phenomenon known as xenolalia, or speaking in a recognized foreign language.

In 1906 a major revival occurred at Azusa Street in Los Angeles. This outpouring of the Spirit was experienced by a variety of people—men and women, clergy and laity, black and white. The leader of this phenomenon was William Joseph Seymour (1870–1922), an African-American who once had to sit outside Parham's classroom because of segregation. Through his writings in the *Apostolic Faith*, Seymour was responsible for developing an early Holiness-Pentecostal theology. This new theology highlighted subjective spiritual experiences rather than the pursuit of intellectual knowledge.

With the precedent of Ozman and Azusa Street, later Pentecostal devotees did not feel the need for intellectual foundations explaining their faith. Pentecostals managed to grow through proselytizing their own racial and socioeconomic groups. With its stance against materialism and modernism, early Pentecostals attracted new devotees from the lower social strata in North American society. Most of the early Pentecostals were from the working class and had no time for or interest in intellectual speculation. In fact, many Pentecostals adopted the view that faith and reason are binary opposites, opposed to one another. Pentecostals have always insisted that faith in Jesus Christ is the only prerequisite for receiving the Holy Spirit. Pentecostal scholars, nevertheless, insist there is a healthy balance between faith and reason, and that reason deserves a place in the life of a Pentecostal Christian.

Anti-intellectualism in Education

Early Pentecostals were not well educated and were therefore frequently the subjects of much criticism by outsiders. Stereotyped as illiterate folk, county bumpkins, and "Holy Rollers," early Pentecostals experienced persecution for their ecstatic practices. As Pentecostalism grew worldwide in number of adherents and in terms of acceptance by the general public, early Pentecostals saw no problems with their lack of formally trained pastors and leaders; on the contrary, many Pentecostals, since they too were largely uneducated, were convinced that formal education was not necessary. Pentecostal populism, or the wisdom of common people, was responsible for this attitude. The social scientist Os Guinness notes that "populism rejected educated leadership and put a boundless trust in the common person" (Guinness 1994, 46). One reason an academic degree was not required or even recommended was that Pentecostalism emphasized the imminent return of Jesus Christ.

Despite the rhetoric of some Pentecostal extremists, who held that knowledge was "of the devil," the evidence best suggests that early Pentecostals feared secular, formal education, but not all forms of education. Early Pentecostals feared any form of education that excluded the role of the Holy Spirit, but they did not fear the acquisition of knowledge itself. Many churches and missions served as a means to train pastors during the movement's formative years. Later, in order to provide adequate training for its ministers, Pentecostals began opening their own training institutions. The Southern California Bible College, which was the first institution sponsored by the Assemblies of God to offer a four-year degree program, opened in the late 1930s; it was followed by Pentecostal Bible schools and Bible colleges that opened after World War II, which in turn paved the way for the opening of Pentecostal liberal arts colleges, seminaries, and universities. At first Pentecostal institutions had difficulties in finding qualified instructors; today, however, many of their professors are trained at respected institutions around the world.

Pentecostal Otherworldliness

Originally, the Holiness movement in general and Pentecostalism in particular advocated cultural separatism, that is, these movements taught that one should not conform to the ideas, beliefs, and practices of the world. Citing Paul's injunction, "Do not conform any longer to the pattern of this world, but be transformed by the renewing of your mind" (Romans 12:2, NIV), many early Pentecostals viewed the world with suspicion. One tendency toward anti-intellectualism came from viewing the secular world as dangerous to one's mind instead of enlightening. Pentecostalism advocates that believers should submit their minds to God for development.

Early Pentecostalism had strongly otherworldly priorities, to the degree that many early Pentecostals considered Christians who participated in intellectualism and rationalism to be apostates. Believing that the end of days was at hand and that Christ's return was imminent, Pentecostal pioneers saw no virtue in thinking too much.

Premillennialism's Influence

Due to the popularity of the Scofield Reference Bible (1909), dispensationalism became an influential factor in Pentecostal theology. Many dispensationalists believe in seven distinct dispensations, or sets, of time. Dispensationalism's eschatological influence on Pentecostal theology can be seen at the very birth of the Pentecostal movement: Charles Fox Parham was an advocate of premillennialism—the belief that the Second Coming of Christ will occur before the millennium. However, early Pentecostalists disagreed with the dispensationalists' claim that "sign gifts"—that is, the sorts of gifts of the Spirit that Pentecostals

manifested—were for the first-century church only and should be taboo in the modern era.

Pentecostals believe that the arrival of sign gifts means that the Second Coming is near. Because of this, Pentecostals have historically focused their attention and energy on missionary projects rather than on establishing research institutions. Even though Pentecostal scholars are moving away from dispensationalism, there remains a sense of urgency concerning the Second Coming.

Differences from Fundamentalism

Despite the fact that the general public mistakenly considers Pentecostals to be Christian Fundamentalists, the two movements are separate streams in Protestantism. Apart from their differences over present-day miracles (which Pentecostals accept and Fundamentalists do not), most Pentecostals during the 1920s and 1930s considered themselves Fundamentalists. Soon afterwards, however, two substantial breaks occurred between Pentecostalism and Fundamentalism that would forever separate them. The first happened in 1928 when the World's Christian Fundamentals Association determined that Pentecostals were not to be considered in fellowship with Fundamentalists due to Pentecostals' emphasis on signs and miracles. Another separation between the two groups occurred in 1943 when some moderate Fundamentalists were put off by the display of signs made by a group headed by Carl McIntire, the founder of American Council of Christian Churches (ACCC).

Whereas one may clearly see antimodernist thought and tendencies in Fundamentalism, Pentecostalism has remained more fluid and diverse in its theology. Early Fundamentalists were skeptical of Pentecostal religious experiences, while early Pentecostals viewed Fundamentalists negatively because they were not baptized in the Spirit. Despite this, Pentecostals, like Fundamentalists, believe that Bible is the inspired word of God. Fundamentalists rely on strictly literal interpretations of the Bible as a means of knowing God. Pentecostals, on the other hand, believe that God can and does communicate directly through a variety of means other than the Bible. Even though Pentecostals have been considered anti-intellectual, one scholar notes that "Pentecostals emerged without the deep anti-intellectual bias that distinguished much of conservative Protestantism after 1925" (Synan 1997, 207). On the one hand, Fundamentalism emphasizes the anti-intellectual traits of isolationism and separatism as a response to competing worldviews. On the other hand, Pentecostalism and the charismatic movement worldwide tend to emphasize ecumenism within a variety of diverse, global traditions.

The Intellect and Biblical Interpretation

Modern-day Pentecostal scholarship reflects a more progressive approach towards biblical interpretation than was present in early Pentecostalism. Early Pentecostals strove for a "plain" reading of the biblical text, and most of the early Pentecostal leaders steered away from biblical criticism. Today, however, higher forms of biblical criticism are being used by many Pentecostal Bible scholars, though many Pentecostals may not be aware of this. Walter J. Hollenweger laments, "While we [Bible scholars] are trained in the details of critical theology, our church members still discuss whether or not Adam and Eve, Noah, and Methuselah, were historical persons" (Hollenweger 1997, 323). Today's Pentecostal Bible scholars draw on Jesus' paraphrase of Deuteronomy 6:5, in which Jesus said, "Love the Lord your God with all your heart and with all your soul and with all your mind" (Matthew 22:37; Mark 12:30; Luke 10:27, NIV), to argue that the mind should be an integral part of one's relationship with God.

Future of the Intellect in Pentecostalism

Evangelical scholars began speaking out against anti-intellectualism quite vociferously during the last years of the twentieth century. Os Guinness' *Fit Bodies Fat Minds* and Mark Noll's *The Scandal of the Evangelical Mind* have demonstrated the pervasiveness of anti-intellectualism in Evangelicalism in general and in Pentecostalism in particular. The Pentecostal scholar James K. A. Smith admits that "Pentecostal faith and practice is strongly opposed to any intellectualizing of the faith," but in response to Noll, questions Noll's "failure to define what he means by theology" (Smith 226, 231). Today, many Pentecostal scholars are striving for a balanced relationship between faith and reason.

Pentecostal educators are now weighing academic goals with spiritual aspects in the classroom. At the collegiate level, modern Pentecostal scholars are accustomed to and comfortable with performing high-level academic research. As the popularity of Pentecostal Bible colleges increases, debates between those Pentecostals who advocate a traditional approach to Pentecostal education and those who want to include secular majors at the Bible colleges grow more heated. Nevertheless, Pentecostal and charismatic Christianity, so long as it retains its unique perspectives, will remain a "religion of the heart" that is defined by its emotionally charged worship and emphasis on ecstatic religious experiences. Where once anti-intellectual rhetoric abounded, Pentecostals are now making a conscious effort to ignore the intellect no longer—but they do not want to risk an intellectualizing of the faith. Critics continue to maintain that Pentecostalism is an emotionally charged faith that harbors an anti-intellectual attitude; Pentecostals, for their part, cherish the role of the supernatural and the life of the Spirit in their faith.

JOHN R. KENNEDY

See also Education; Experience, Theology of; Fundamentalism; Philosophy and Theology; Society, Pentecostal Attitudes toward

Further Reading

Dayton, D. W. (1987). *Theological roots of Pentecostalism.* Metuchen, NJ: The Scarecrow Press.

Erickson, M. J. (1993). *The Evangelical mind and heart: Perspectives on theological and practical issues.* Grand Rapids, MI: Baker Books.

Guinness, O. (1994). *Fit bodies fat minds: Why Evangelicals don't think and what to do about it.* Grand Rapids, MI: Baker Books.

Hittenberger, J. S. (2001). Toward a Pentecostal philosophy of education. *Pneuma, 23*(2), 217–244.

Hofstadter, R. (1962). *Anti-intellectualism in American life.* New York: Vintage.

Hollenweger, W. J. (1997). *Pentecostalism: Origins and developments worldwide.* Peabody, MA: Hendrickson Publishers.

Horton, S. (1967). *The promise of His coming.* Springfield, MO: Gospel Publishing House.

McKinney, E. L. (2000). Some spiritual aspects of Pentecostal education: A personal journey. *Asian Journal of Pentecostal Studies, 3*(2), 253–279.

Noll, M. A. (1994). *The scandal of the Evangelical mind.* Grand Rapids, MI: William B. Eerdmans Publishing.

Smith, J. K. A. (1997). Scandalizing theology: A Pentecostal response to Noll's *Scandal. Pneuma, 19*(2), 225–238.

Synan, V. (1997). *The holiness-Pentecostal tradition: Charismatic movements in the twentieth century* (2nd ed). Grand Rapids, MI: William B. Eerdmans Publishing.

Tarr, D. (1997). Transcendence, immanence, and the emerging Pentecostal academy. In W. Ma & R. Menzies (Eds.), *Pentecostalism in context: Essay in honor of William W. Menzies* (192–222). Sheffield, UK: Sheffield Academic Press.

Wacker, G. (2001). *Heaven below.* Cambridge, MA: Harvard University Press.

Walker, A. (1997). Thoroughly modern: Sociological reflections on the Charismatic movement from the end of the twentieth century. In S. Hunt & M. B. Hamilton (Eds.), *Charismatic Christianity* (pp. 17–42). New York: St. Martin's Press.

Wilson, L. F. (2002). Bible institutes, colleges, and university. In S. Burgess (Ed.), *The new international dictionary of Pentecostal and Charismatic movements* (pp. 372–380). Grand Rapids, MI: Zondervan.

Apostle, Apostolic

The office of apostle (Greek *apostolos*, from *apostellein*, "to send forth") has been controversial among Pentecostals throughout the history of the movement. Soon after Pentecostalism emerged at the beginning of the twentieth century, most of the developing organizations adopted a cessationist interpretation of the apostolic office (believing that the apostolic period ended early in Christian history), while some small groups and independents insisted on both the existence of and need for modern-day apostles. More recently, some Pentecostals have developed a hermeneutic that distinguishes between two kinds of apostles: those directly appointed and sent by Christ—particularly the original twelve and Paul (called foundational apostles or apostles of the Lamb)—and those commissioned indirectly by the church. This latter use of the word *apostle*, however, is understood by many Pentecostal scholars to indicate merely a messenger. They argue, therefore, that these messengers should be distinguished from the original commissioned eyewitnesses of Christ, and thus should not be identified technically as apostles.

Nevertheless, since the rise of the Charismatic movement in the 1960s, belief in and expectation of modern-day apostles has increased. Indeed, the twentieth century closed with an enthusiastic push by many advocates of modern-day apostles to recognize and reinstate the office of apostle in the church. As a result, the concept of modern-day apostles has begun to penetrate some mainstream evangelical churches and even the historic sacramental traditions.

In the mid-1990s the "new apostolic reformation" was inaugurated, reviving historic controversies and creating a multiplicity of new interpretations. It has forced Christians to answer again several old questions: What are the marks and qualifications of an apostle? And, if the office is relevant today, what are the differences between the original twelve apostles, other New Testament apostles, and modern-day apostles? Is there a distinction between *office* and *function*? If so, can one function as an apostle without holding the office?

What does apostolic succession mean from a Pentecostal perspective? These and other questions have in turn revived discussions on the nature, structure, and unity of the church itself. Thus, many Pentecostal ecumenists believe that some form of the apostolic office may hold the key to ecclesial identity in the twenty-first century and the hope for ecumenical fulfillment.

Restorationist Impulse

Pentecostalism emerged from an impulse to restore apostolic Christianity. This prophetic expectation of the "restitution of all things" (Acts 3:21, KJV) was the heart-throb of men like B. H. Irwin, Frank W. Sandford, A. B. Simpson, C. F. Parham, W. J. Seymour, C. H. Mason, and A. J. Tomlinson. Thus Parham and his followers named their movement "Apostolic Faith." Most first-generation Pentecostals, like Tomlinson (a former Quaker), looked initially for the reemergence of apostles to complete the restoration of the "last-days church." This expectation, however, soon gave way to the prevailing Protestant view that held the purpose of the apostolic office to have been fulfilled in the first century. Accordingly, the post-apostolic church has since been ruled by elders or overseers (*presbuteroi*), particularly bishops (*episcopoi*) and deacons (*diakonoi*). Hence, most Pentecostal pioneers identified with apostolic faith but not with an ecclesiastical office positioned at the apex of an ascending hierarchy.

Nevertheless, the Latter Rain movement, which emerged within Pentecostalism beginning in the 1940s, spawned several independent churches and small associations that organized themselves around an apostle or a band of apostles. Typical of these groups was the one led by Grady R. Kent beginning in the 1950s. Kent pulled out of the Church of God of Prophecy in 1957 and established The Church of God (Jerusalem Acres) centered in Cleveland, Tennessee. He reinstated the office of apostle and reestablished the government of the church based on what he considered to be the apostolic model in the New Testament. Kent himself took the title of chief bishop and exercised final authority over the entire body of his followers, including twelve latter-day apostles. Most of the groups like Kent's emerged with strong restoration impulses and tended to develop exclusive ecclesiologies.

New Apostolic Reformation

Since the mid-1990s, C. Peter Wagner, the president of Global Harvest Ministries, has maintained that the church is in the midst of a new apostolic reformation, in which the very foundation of the church is being restored to its original apostolic model in the New Testament. His influence as a professor at Fuller Theological Seminary, and his books—*Churchquake!*; *Apostles of the City*; *The New Apostolic Churches*; and *Apostles and Prophets*—have made a major impact on many Pentecostal and charismatic churches. Wagner, who believes himself to be an apostle, defines *apostle* as one who is charismatically gifted with "unusual" authority to govern the church and to convey a vision of its future. For him, the apostle is appointed directly by God; the church merely recognizes the apostle's divine call and office. According to Wagner, the apostle is further identified as one who has extraordinary character that has been tried by God.

Wagner's view of modern-day apostles has been influenced by Great Britain's Roger Mitchell, a pastor and codirector of the International Strategic Prayer Network for Europe. Mitchell sees two kinds of apostles in the New Testament, namely, vertical and horizontal. Wagner determined that vertical apostles have a certain sphere of authority within a limited number of churches and among a limited number of other vertical apostles. He cites Paul, Timothy, Titus, and Epaphroditus as being vertical apostles, with Paul serving as the "apostolic team leader." Horizontal apostles, on the other hand, are divinely anointed and empowered with broader, if not universal, authority. Wagner cites James, the Lord's brother, as an example of a horizontal apostle. He bases this on the fact that James presided over the council of Jerusalem (Acts 15), and apparently had authority to call other apostles and elders together for this meeting. Moreover, Wagner sees in James's statement "Therefore my judgment is" (Acts 15:19) evidence of a unilateral authority to make decrees for the whole church. Wagner has come to the conclusion that he is himself a horizontal apostle.

In his book *First Apostles, Last Apostles*, Peter Lyne identifies apostles by their ability (or giftedness) to organize and grow churches. He distinguishes between ordinary ministers and apostles, the latter proving their apostleship by fruitful and successful efforts in missionary work and church organization. His rationale for modern-day apostles is that as the Father sent the Son, and the Son sent the twelve apostles, so now the Holy Spirit anoints and sends multitudes of apostles into the world to reap the harvest and establish churches.

One of Wagner's disciples, John Wimber, carried the idea of apostle into the so-called "third wave" of Pentecostalism in the 1980s. Wimber, the founder of the Vineyard Christian Fellowship, began in 1975 to teach with Wagner at Fuller Theological Seminary. His controversial course—"Signs, Wonders, and Church Growth"—in the Fuller School of World Mission emphasized especially the gift of healing but advocated also the restoration of apostles. This course has had a profound effect on many charismatic as well as noncharismatic groups throughout the United States and the world.

Classical Pentecostal View

Notwithstanding the influence of Wagner and the prophets of the new apostolic reformation, most Pentecostals have remained in the camp of the cessationists in regard to apostles. They believe the apostolic office was necessary only in order to lay a historical foundation for the church, upon which future generations would continue to build. They thus interpret Paul's statement in Ephesians 2:20 ("built upon the foundation of apostles and prophets") in a historical context, seeing it as having been completed in the New Testament. Once the church was founded, there was no need for more founders. They see the situation as being analogous to that of the historical Jesus, whose earthly life and ministry provided the basis for the Gospel. Indeed, Christ is the cornerstone in the same foundation that was formed and completed by the apostles in the New Testament.

Most of these Pentecostals have thus resisted the hermeneutic of theologians like Jon Ruthven (*On the Cessation of the Charismata*), who insists that Ephesians 2:20 necessitates the continuation of apostles and prophets in the church today. If correct, Ruthven's hermeneutic would mean that the foundation of the church is more or less fluid, and dependent upon the inspiration and revelation of modern-day apostles rather than on the eyewitness accounts of New Testament apostles and their inspired writings. Ruthven's interpretation, therefore, opens the door for the notion that the biblical canon is open ended—that authoritative revelation for the church is still unfolding. For the majority of Pentecostals, this notion is unthinkable, if not heretical.

Most classical Pentecostals simply do not believe that advocates for modern-day apostles have made their case, hermeneutically and theologically. Thus, no major classical Pentecostal fellowship—Church of God, Church of God in Christ, International Pentecostal Holiness Church, Assembly of God, or any of the others—has modified its form of government and polity to include apostles. This may reveal, however, not merely the hermeneutical method of classical Pentecostals in regard to the office of apostle, but a reluctance to open themselves up again to the embarrassment occasioned by some in their ranks becoming exalted through messianic delusions and various forms of megalomania.

Ongoing Debate

The task facing those who advocate modern-day apostles is the construction of a convincing set of identifying marks that are different from those of the original twelve apostles. This may prove to be especially difficult, if not impossible, for those who have conceded that the twelve apostles bore special marks and qualifications that cannot be repeated: namely, personal appointments received directly from the historical Christ and eyewitness experiences of His life and resurrection. Indeed, it may be argued that the marks and qualifications set forth by advocates of modern-day apostles are no more than what is seen in any number of gifted pastors and evangelists in the church.

On the other hand, those who deny the existence and relevance of modern-day apostles and prophets must reconcile passages such as 1 Corinthians 12:28 and Ephesians 4:11 with their hermeneutic of cessation. This may be a challenge for Pentecostals who otherwise zealously proclaim and defend spiritual and charismatic gifts, such as those listed in Romans 12, 1 Corinthians 12, and Ephesians 4. In any case, it is not likely that these differences in interpretation among Pentecostals will be resolved any time soon.

Apostolic Nature of the Church

Notwithstanding the fact that Pentecostals have disagreed over the nature, purpose, and relevance of the office of apostle, they have been united in opinion from the beginning in regard to the apostolic nature of the church. In fact, Pentecostal spirituality and apostolicity have been considered nearly synonymous in meaning. Pentecostals believe that the very essence of apostolicity flows out of the indwelling power of the Spirit. Through the dynamic of the Spirit—particularly the baptism in the Spirit—the whole church becomes apostolic; that is to say, the whole church under the ecstatic power of the Spirit is filled with apostolic power and is sent forth to witness.

Thus, unlike the Roman Catholic and Eastern Orthodox traditions that see the apostolate now embodied in a college of bishops, Pentecostals believe apostolic succession is embodied in the whole body of Spirit-baptized believers. The theologian Roger Stronstad argues in his *Prophethood of All Believers* that the whole Pentecostal church now exists and functions in the ec-

static gift of prophecy. In fulfillment of Joel's prophecy (Joel 2:28–30), the Spirit is poured out indiscriminately upon "all flesh" (Acts 2). The church is thus no longer limited to a handful of prophets who come on the scene at particular intervals (particularly in times of spiritual crises) to denounce sin and warn of impending judgment; rather, the entire body of Spirit-baptized believers now prophesy with power and give ecstatic witness of the full Gospel—and they continue also "steadfastly in the apostles' doctrine" (Acts 2:42).

Following this line of thought, some Pentecostals argue for the idea of an apostlehood of believers. For them, the apostolic gift is essentially resident in the Holy Spirit, who since the day of Pentecost anoints and permeates the whole church with ecstatic power and authority. Thus, through the Spirit of the ascended Christ, who descended on the day of Pentecost, all Spirit-baptized believers are empowered and charismatically gifted. In this manner, the whole body of Christ partakes of Christ's apostleship. Hence, the whole church is now sent into the world as a witness. All believers can now proclaim the Resurrection of Christ with power, and with the promise that miraculous signs and wonders shall follow those that believe.

Notwithstanding the Spirit's anointing for witness, the theologian Cecil M. Robeck, Jr., stresses the fact that genuine apostolicity must join together life and witness. He thus encourages sacramental traditions to seek for experiential holiness to authenticate their claims of apostolicity. The Church of God theologian Steven Land, in his *Pentecostal Spirituality*, emphasizes the indispensable need to have "right affections" with God. According to Land, spiritual power flows out of hearts that have been cleansed by the sanctifying grace of the Spirit. Pentecostals universally agree with Land in this regard, affirming that holiness of life is a necessary qualification for genuine apostolicity.

Wade H. Phillips

See also Cessationism; Latter Rain

Further Reading

Cannistraci, D. (1996). *Apostles and the emerging apostolic movement: A biblical look at apostleship and how God is using it to bless his church today.* Ventura, CA: Renew Books.

Karkkainen, V-M. (2001). Pentecostalism and the claim for apostolicity: An essay in ecumenical ecclesiology. *Evangelical Review of Theology, 25*(4), 323–336.

Land, S. J. (1993). *Pentecostal spirituality.* Sheffield, UK: Sheffield Academic Press.

Lyne, P. (1999). *First apostles, last apostles.* Kent, UK: Sovereign World Ltd.

Ruthven, J. (1993). *On the cessation of the charismata.* Sheffield, UK: Sheffield Academic Press.

Stronstad, R. (1999). *The prophethood of all believers.* Sheffield, UK: Sheffield Academic Press.

Tomlinson, A. J. (1913). *The last great conflict.* Cleveland, TN: The Press of Walter E. Rogers.

Wagner, P. C. (1999). *Churchquake!* Ventura, CA: Gospel Light Publications.

Wagner, P. C. (1998). *The new apostolic churches.* Ventura, CA: Gospel Light Publications.

Wagner, P. C. (2000). *Apostles and prophets: The foundation of the church.* Ventura, CA: Regal Books.

Wagner, P. C. (2000). *Apostles of the City.* Colorado Springs, CO: Wagner Publications.

Art

Like their forebears in the Holiness movement, Pentecostals created a spiritual world with words rather than pictures, and their beliefs evolved through the use of imagination rather than sight. The climax for many worshippers in the Pentecostal tradition is to be still before the Lord—overwhelmed with the felt presence of God, eyes closed, shut off from the world.

The paucity of external stimuli in the architectural styles of the buildings used for worship also encourages worshippers to use their imaginations. In the period between 1908 and 1960, Pentecostals normally gathered in plain mission halls or in ex-Wesleyan chapels that were devoid of pictorial images. There would have been a text emblazoned on the wall in Gothic type behind the pulpit, declaring such encouragements as "The Lord is near" or "Behold I come quickly." Although current Pentecostal and Charismatic churches have often moved into buildings full of technological hardware, the predominant architectural style is still functional: large spaces that allow the congregation to gather in large numbers. Decoration may be confined to national flags that declare the geographical spread of the congregation or to banners that have illustrated texts rather than uninterpreted artistic representations. The size of these buildings declares the success of the Pentecostal message.

Pentecostal Spirituality

The word dominates because Pentecostals stress obedience to the uninterpreted truths of Scripture. Pentecostal spirituality relies on direction, destiny, and predetermined progress; it is not a ramble but a spiritual journey with clear signposts along a straight road. Truths have to be immediately accessible and clear and applicable to everyday life, rather than hidden in the uncertainties of interpretation. There is no room for the vagueness of art, which is by definition open to individual interpretation. Pentecostalism is distinctly utilitarian and pragmatic. Each element of spirituality has to have a clear purpose that will lead to renewed obedience to Christ.

Pentecostalism is also based on an oral tradition. Pentecostals are more interested in testimonies of God's provision and salvation than in exegeses of scriptural texts. They marvel at God's goodness but portray this in life, not in art. Finally, Pentecostal spirituality is communal. It insists on horizontal relationships in the church because it believes that it is partially through these relationships that a vertical relationship with the Lord is mediated. Therefore, Pentecostals prefer to gather in groups to experience the Spirit rather than remain in the more solitary position of artists and art lovers.

However, some visual images have been incorporated into Pentecostal spirituality. On the whole, these have been used to encourage individuals to "walk" with God. Word pictures have fed the imagination in many ways. For instance, the oratorical skills of the best preachers recreate biblical worlds and create spiritual expectations; services may use contemporary songs to repeat images of rivers, fire, and light; people testify to heavenly visions; people using the gifts of the Spirit sometimes claim that they can "see" ailments or blockages to spiritual progress.

Visions

One of the spiritual experiences valued by Pentecostals is the prophetic word. This has often been a catalyst for action, development, or decision making for both individuals and churches. One standard way that the prophetic word is delivered is by drawing from a fund of standardized images: clouds bringing the "rain of revival," growing plants representing individual Christian growth, or waves on a seashore bringing blessings to recipients are recognizable leitmotifs within Pentecostalism.

Rarely have whole groups of Pentecostals claimed to see the same image, although this famously happened in 1914 in a small Mission Hall named Island Place in Llanelli, South Wales. Stephen Jeffreys, an evangelist with mystical leanings used to receiving vivid visions, was preaching when people claimed that they could see a lamb's head on the wall behind him. After a quarter of an hour, this transformed into the face of Jesus, which remained on the wall for six hours. Jeffreys described the image as the living face of Jesus with "a Roman nose and Jewish features. His hair was like wool, parted in the middle, with a curl on each temple over his eyes and ears. His head was slightly leaning to the left and His expression was pitiful"…it looked as though his hair was streaked with white such as a middle-aged man in grief" (Adams 1926,14). The First World War broke out two weeks later, and Jeffreys always believed that the vision had been a warning of the carnage.

When the story was told, in Adams's book and in a 1916 article, hundreds claimed to have seen the vision and lists of individuals with their addresses were drawn up in an attempt to verify the vision. Although Pentecostals were convinced that this was a real vision of their Lord, the story was seen as a one-off event and no Pentecostal tradition regarding corporate visions emerged from it. It simply remained in the collective memory to highlight the compassion they believed Jesus had toward victims of the war. The vision was interpreted at length and deemed to be pictorial didacticism; it was not appreciated for its own sake.

Art and Preaching

The use of art for teaching was a dramatic part of the ministry of Aimee Semple McPherson. This most exotic and flamboyant of all Pentecostal evangelists constructed elaborate tableaux to preach against. She used live camels to show the impossibility of the animal going through the eye of a needle, or wore a Little Bo Peep costume to dramatize the parable of the lost sheep. Her inventiveness was always used to persuade people to receive Christ. It was music hall entertainment transformed into Pentecostal preaching. Her innovative and exciting visual approach attracted thousands to her meetings and over time enabled her to establish one of the largest Pentecostal denominations.

Other evangelists would use art in a subtler way to attract crowds. For instance, Willard Cantelon, a Canadian evangelist with a worldwide ministry, painted while he preached. This engaged people's interest and was copied by preachers. But this too was not creating art with intrinsic value.

Simon Coleman, a British anthropologist, studied the link between the theology and the aesthetic consciousness of the Word of Life Church in Uppsala, Sweden. He highlighted the fact that the church, in common with Pentecostal and charismatic groups, avoided pictorial displays of Christ. In the Word of Life complex, there was only one picture of Christ—a picture of Christ as a bodybuilder. The muscular Jesus is presumably communicating the message that those who respond to Christ can avail themselves of the same positive, optimistic spiritual (and physical) strength. However, this is the exception rather than the rule because while Pentecostals delight in privatized visions, they do not expect to see these visions relayed on canvas.

One of the main reasons for this is that Pentecostals have been solely concerned to see the "full Gospel" proclaimed. Because they believed that the Lord's return was imminent, the earliest generations of Pentecostals did not feel that they had time to engage in the arts. Their concern was to preach the Gospel and to persuade people to accept the truth of Christ. When allied with their ability to communicate to the working classes, who were less inclined to pursue the arts, there was neither the need nor the opportunity for Pentecostals to develop their aesthetic tendencies.

Pentecostal Artists

In the light of this it is clear to see why Pentecostalism has not bred artists. In the early days of British Pentecostalism, those with artistic leanings had to either renounce them or subsume them in the greater cause of the Gospel. One such artist, William Burton (1886–1971), missionary to the Congo, enjoyed painting and drawing at the encouragement of his mother, but he was regularly criticized by some Pentecostals for spending time painting. However, Burton sold as many paintings as he could and used the money to fund his mission work.

As a young man, Howard Carter (1891–1971), chairman of the British Assemblies of God, attended art college. His brother, John Carter, illustrates the attitude of many Pentecostals to this:

> He [Howard] had lived for art. It was his meat and drink, his breath, his soul, his life-blood. . . . He tried for a time to serve two master[s] but all in vain. He knew he couldn't share his love: it was Christ or art: and after an awesome struggle, Christ won the victory. . . . One day, a never to-be-forgotten day, Howard walked out of the art school leaving everything behind—paints, brushes, palette, canvasses, modeling tools—everything, and never went back. Christ had triumphed gloriously. (Carter, 1971, 15)

However, there was a Welsh artist named Nicholas Evans (1907–2004) who was able to follow both "masters": one commentator calls him a "rare, possibly unique, example of a Pentecostal who had achieved an international reputation as an artist" (Harvey, 1997, 111). Evans was born in Aberdare, South Wales, in the aftermath of the Welsh Revival. After leaving school at fourteen, he spent two years employed in the coal mines, after which he progressed to working on the railways for the rest of his working life. A lay preacher with the Apostolic Church, he didn't discover his artistic abilities until he retired. Although he received no formal training, he quickly came to be noticed by art critics.

His pictures revolve around themes relating to mining and reflect his Pentecostal faith. He claimed that the paintings were the result of his being led by the Spirit, in the same way as preachers claim to be inspired as they speak. His paintings are exhibited in various galleries in Wales and bear titles such as *Ashes to Ashes, Dust to Dust*; *The Trumpet shall Sound—Resurrection*; and *Entombed—Jesus in the Midst*. The oil paintings are dark and sometimes bleak representations of miners working in dangerous cramped conditions underground. His faith is clear, though, in each of the works. Christ is the one who is incarnate in the mine, alongside the miners (*Entombed*) and the Resurrection is clearly happening in the Welsh village (*The Trumpet shall Sound*). Though nationally recognized as a significant artist, it is pertinent that most Pentecostals do not know his work.

Pentecostalism, rooted in the breathless, frenetic activity of revivalism, has not paused to see what art its own ranks produced. The faith and response to their lives as Pentecostals, and the artistic expressions of those responses, are likely to continue to emerge in music, words, and communal activity rather than in the artist's studio or the quiet of an art gallery.

NEIL HUDSON

See also Media (Television, Radio, Internet); Music; Visions and Dreams

Further Reading

Adams, W. J. (1926). *Miracles of today*. Stockholm, Sweden: W. J. Adams.

Boddy, A. (1916). The face of Christ—A miraculous appearance. *Confidence*, July, 113–114.

Blumhofer, E. (1993). *Aimee Semple McPherson: Everybody's sister*. Grand Rapids, MI: Eerdmans.

Carter, J. (1971). *Howard Carter—Man of the spirit*. Nottingham, UK: Assemblies of God Publishing House.

Coleman, S. (2000). *The globalisation of charismatic Christianity*. Cambridge, UK: Cambridge University Press.

Epstein, D. M. (1993). *Sister Aimee*. San Diego, CA: Harcourt Brace.

Harvey, J. (1997). Images of God: Artistic inspiration and Pentecostal theology (A case study). *Journal of Pentecostal Theology, 10*, 111–124.

Harvey, J. (1999). *Image of the invisible*. Cardiff, UK: University of Wales.

Wacker, G. (2001). *Heaven below*. Cambridge, MA: Harvard University Press.

Whittaker, C. (1983). *Seven Pentecostal pioneers*. Basingstoke, UK: Marshalls.

Womersley, H. (1973). *W.F.P. Burton Congo pioneer*. Eastbourne, UK: Victory Press.

Asceticism

Asceticism is the practice of exercising self-denial, or, more appropriately, the training of the body to avoid pleasures and comfort in order to attain a spiritual goal. Asceticism assumes that this exercise will aid in the training of the soul, thereby aiding the attainment of greater virtue or spiritual development.

Asceticism is found in virtually all religions. Its practice varies but it has common features by which it can be identified. The outstanding common denominator is practitioners' desire to move to a higher level of accomplishment physically, mentally, morally, and spiritually. It is hoped that through training and discipline the higher level can be achieved.

As in other world religions, there were many operative factors behind the rise and cultivation of asceticism in early Christianity. These included the belief that spirituality was best preserved by simplifying one's mode of life, a perception of the ephemeral nature of earthly life, which prompted believers to anchor their hope in otherworldliness, the belief that people must be in a state of ritual purity before entering into communion with the supernatural, the belief that it was possible to earn the attention, pity, and compassion of the divine through one's suffering in ascetic practices, and the belief that ascetic practices were a means to gain supernatural powers.

Ascetic Practices in Christianity

There have been many different ascetic practices in Christianity. The most common ascetic practices focus on sexual relations, abstinence from food, and renunciation of material goods. These self-restraints are seen as acts of devotion and morality. They are aimed especially at controlling the lower appetites and cultivating virtues and spiritual perfection.

In many ascetic movements celibacy has been regarded as the first commandment. The words of the Lord Jesus in Matthew 19:12 (about spiritual eunuchs who prefer the celibate state because of their intense interest in the affairs of the kingdom of heaven) as well as the injunction of St. Paul in I Corinthians 7 (that by reason of the present distress those who were not married should not enter into marriage) were construed by some early Christians to imply absolute abstinence from marriage. And so in early Christianity the practice of chastity and celibacy emerged in some communities. Most ascetics also considered sex as an evil that was to be avoided. Cohabitation was regarded as producing ceremonial uncleanliness, while ritual purity was considered a necessary condition for approaching the divine.

Endure hardship with us like a good soldier of Christ Jesus.

2 Timothy 2:3 (New International Version)

Rejecting the ownership of material goods is another fundamental principle in asceticism, and some early Christians gave themselves up to poverty, while some monks lived on alms they received but ensured that these gifts did not accumulate. Christians from early times observed forty days of fasting during the Lenten period. This fasting cycle did not satisfy the needs of some ascetics, however, who went ahead to establish the tradition of controlling the types and amount of food that should be taken. Some resorted to eating a meager diet of stale bread with water once or twice a day. Abstinence from such delicacies as meat, fish, eggs, and milk was one of the most common ascetic practices found among the early Christian monks.

Asceticism is often observed in conjunction with spiritual exercise such as meditation and contemplative prayer. Some early ascetics denied themselves of sleep, using all kinds of methods to keep themselves awake in order to devote more time to prayer. Some ascetics confined themselves to desolate locations such as the wilderness, the desert's edge, mountains, or cliffs, while some went so far as to live atop very tall pillars.

Some ascetics tried to inflict both psychological and physical pain on themselves. Most pain-producing asceticism was done for the purpose of penance, especially when devotees found themselves being tempted by the earthly pleasures that they were trying to forgo. It was said, for example, that one monk burned away almost all his fingers and the thumbs of both hands in order to rid himself of lust. Some ascetics also rejected personal hygiene; they bathed only occasionally or not at all, and they left their hair unkempt. They hoped in this way to liberate their spiritual element from the defilement of the body and physical living.

Asceticism Among Pentecostals

The rise of Pentecostalism in the early twentieth century was a revival of deep spirituality. While earlier forms of Pentecostalism were based on holiness and a life of devotion, the unique characteristic of modern twentieth-century Pentecostalism was its emphasis on the baptism of the Holy Spirit, with the initial evidence of speaking in tongues. Modern Pentecostalism has come to be identified with a pragmatic faith in signs and miracles as answers to sincere prayers to God. Pentecostals believe that the power of the Holy Spirit manifests itself in the lives of believers in the form of the gifts of the Holy Spirit, which include, for example, the ability to heal the sick and to perform other miracles. Pentecostals believe these gifts of the Holy Spirit are as operative today as they were in the early Church. Because miracles, signs, and wonders are clear evidence of the resident power of God, many Pentecostal ministers embark on some of the ascetic practices of the early and medieval churches in order to attain the gifts that will produce those signs and wonders. Therefore ascetic practices of some form seem to be part and parcel of Pentecostal faith and practices today.

Celibacy

Celibacy as an ascetic practice is rarely found among Pentecostals, as the idea of a dichotomous separation of body and spirit and the attendant belief that the body is evil and must be suppressed for the good of the spirit is not commonly held. While alert to heed to the injunction of the Bible not to dabble in the works of the flesh, Pentecostals emphasize the virtues of fidelity in marriage and not committing fornication.

Prayer and Fasting

The most common ascetic practice among African Pentecostals is contemplative praying or meditation in secluded places called prayer mountains. Here, after the strain of climbing the mountain, devotees and suppliants engage in prayer with marathon fasting to seek spiritual power in order to perform miracles or to have victory over whatever physical or spiritual problems they have. Sometimes the prayer mountains are not physical mountaintops or hills; the real essence is seclusion. Suppliants are enjoined to attend retreats, conventions, and camp meetings where rigorous feats such as standing for hours while praying or meditating on the words of God are encouraged. Married couples who retreat together to the secluded places are expected not to engage in sexual intercourse.

Fasting with prayer is also observed among African Pentecostals. Even though some Pentecostal movements do not observe the traditional Christian Lent, they do encourage their members to fast now and then. Fasting is encouraged in order to curb excessive appetite for food and thereby cultivate a vibrant spiritual vitality and devotion to God. At the beginning of the year members may be encouraged to pray and fast for prescribed days—usually three, seven, twenty-one, or forty days. Apart from the general fasting prescribed for the whole congregation, occasionally suppliants who need a miracle or special favor will be asked to fast. Also, a group known as the prayer warriors may gather when the need arises to pray and fast on some issue affecting the members or the Church as a whole. Additionally, most Pentecostals virtually in all regions forbid drinking, the serving of alcoholic beverages, and the sale of alcohol or products made with it.

Rejection of Worldly Goods and Ways

Opposition to worldliness and spiritual pollution is strong among the classical Pentecostals, especially in Africa. In order to guard against spiritual laxity and corrupt worldly practices, certain ethical rules and regulations are prescribed for ministers and members. Male and female members are forbidden to have close interaction. In church, men and women sit separately: Men sit at the right side, while women sit on the left. In strict compliance with St. Paul's injunction in I Corinthians 11:5, women are expected to cover their heads when praying. Young girls are enjoined to dress modestly, in a way that will not attract undue attention. They are not to follow worldly fads in hair adornment or clothing.

The Neo-Pentecostal and Charismatic movements are more relaxed with regard to clothing; indeed, members are reminded that they are free to put on earrings, bangles, bracelets, and necklaces to glorify the Lord, who owns silver and gold. While classical Pentecostal-

ism deplores materialism and admonishes members to shun any marks of worldliness, Neo-Pentecostals hold that prosperity is a sign of divine favor. Similarly, members of classical Pentecostal churches are admonished not to go to cinemas, operas, dance halls, and the like, because Christians are believed to have been set apart from the world as royal priests. Neo-Pentecostals, however, do not have such rigid restrictions.

Apparently, in order to entice young students, and accommodate professionals, businessmen and women, Neo-Pentecostals oblige a variety of sports, amusements and current fashions. Unlike the Holiness movements, they allow women to expose their hair and have it "jerry-curled" or "permed." They hardly frown at women putting on expensive jewelry and gorgeous adornment. They declare that "grace gives license for all things," and that "to the pure all things are pure."

Outlook

Evidently, Neo-Pentecostals have less interest in asceticism as a tool for achieving the gifts of the Holy Spirit. Most Neo-Pentecostal ministers believe and teach that it is by the grace of God, and not through works (ascetic practices) that God endows his servants with the ability to perform miracles. In spite of this position, some of the ascetic practices will continue to remain as part of Christianity especially in African Indigenous Churches and the Roman Catholic Church.

Deji Isaac Ayegboyin

See also African Initiated Churches; Ethics (Social, Sexual); Society, Pentecostal Attitudes toward

Further Reading

Cairns, E. E. (1996). *Christianity through the centuries*. Grand Rapids, MI: Zondervan.

Ericsson, M. J. (1985). *Christian theology*. Grand Rapids, MI: Baker Book House.

Levi, S. J. (1966). *Religion in practice*. New York: Harper & Row.

Smith, M. A. (1990). *Lion handbook history of Christianity*. Oxford, UK: Lion Publishers.

Asia, East

In this study, East Asia refers to two large geographical and cultural blocks: Northeast Asia and Southeast Asia. The former includes Mongolia, Korea, Japan, and

The Yoido Full Gospel Church in Seoul, Korea, the largest church in the Christian world with nearly 800,000 members. *Courtesy of Stanley Burgess.*

China, including Taiwan and Hong Kong. The latter covers Indonesia, the Philippines, Vietnam, Laos, Cambodia, Malaysia, Singapore, Thailand, and Myanmar (Burma). In cultural-religious terms, the area may be loosely divided into three subareas: a Chinese cultural sphere, including China, Taiwan and other states with substantial Chinese populations (such as Singapore and Malaysia), and countries with a long history of receiving Chinese cultural influences (Korea, Japan, Mongolia); Malay states, marked by Islamic influences (such as the Philippines, Malaysia, and Indonesia); and an Indochinese sphere, with a strong Buddhist influence (Vietnam, Laos, Cambodia, Thailand, Myanmar, Nepal).

This region represents around 2 billion people, or 33 percent of the world's entire population. Diversity in culture, religion, politics, and economy is so vast that it is almost impossible to generalize about the region in any meaningful way. Economically, Japan represents the second-largest world economy, and the four so-called economic tigers of Asia (Taiwan, Hong Kong, South Korea, and Singapore) are here. But North Korea, Laos, and Cambodia represent some of the poorest economies in the world. Political systems in the region display the same diversity: North Korea remains a Stalinist state; China, Vietnam, and several other states

maintain a Communist-socialist ideology but have moved toward market economies. The Philippines, Japan, Korea, and Thailand, on the other hand, emulate Western democratic politics to a greater or lesser degree. As for the religious scene, there are state-sanctioned religions in Japan (Shinto), Indonesia and Malaysia (Islam), and Nepal, Thailand, and Myanmar (Buddhism), but there are other states with complete religious freedom, such as Korea and the Philippines, as well as countries where religion is simply not allowed or religious freedom is very restricted (such as North Korea). In terms of cultural diversity, most northeast Asian countries display heavy Chinese influence, as do Singapore and parts of Malaysia, while the Philippines has a strongly Spanish Catholic culture and many Southeast Asian countries are heavily influenced by Malay traditions.

Nonetheless, the nations of the region display several important common characteristics. First, all but Thailand and Japan were at one time or another ruled by colonial powers. The colonizers and the length of their rules varied, but the experience of a colonial past has shaped the values, worldviews, and cultures of these countries. Second, regardless of current religious orientations, the foundational religious layer is animism.

There are many "folk" religions even within the traditional established religions. This animistic worldview includes a holistic view of life and the world that allows the natural and supernatural to exist together. Third, many nations in East Asia experienced drastic changes in the twentieth century. Often these include a colonial period, achievement of independence, nation building (which includes identity building), and conflicts over religious, political, and ethnic issues. Pentecostalism was introduced to the region in the midst of these struggles.

Current Demographics

Currently, based on recent estimate by the scholar David Barrett, the total world Pentecostal population is 524 million (8.7 percent of the total world population). The same source notes that the growth rate has been 2.1 percent per annum. Assuming this growth continues, the Pentecostal community in Asia as a whole is expected to number 811.6 million by 2025.

However, this impressive development is not shared equally by all the nations in the region. Some countries have recorded a disproportionate share of the impressive growth of this Christian denomination. South Korea is an example; it now claims 7.8 million Pentecostal-Charismatic believers (16.2 percent of Korea's total population). Explosive growth has been reported in the Philippines, where there are now 20 million believers (26.4 percent of the Philippine population), and in Indonesia (9.45 million; 4.5 percent of the population), Singapore (150,000 believers; 4.1 percent of the total population), Malaysia (540,000 thousand; 2.4 percent), and Myanmar (960,000; 2.1 percent).

On the other hand, in several countries Pentecostalism (and Christianity in general) has experienced a great difficulty in taking root. Japan's 1.8 million believers represent just 1.4 percent of the population, and numbers are also low for Taiwan (359,000 believers; 1.6 percent of the population), Thailand (800,000 believers; 1.4 percent of the population), Vietnam (800,000; 1 percent), Laos (50,000; 0.9 percent), Cambodia (56,000; 0.5 percent), and North Korea (no reasonable estimate is possible). In several places emerging churches have new potential. China, with its fast-growing house church network (now estimated to comprise 54.3 million believers, or 4.3 percent of China's 1.3 billion total population) falls into this category. In Mongolia, which only became open to the outside world in the early 1990s, there has also been much Pentecostal activity and emerging new national leaders, although total numbers are still small

(9,900, or 0.4 percent of Mongolia's total population). Nepal, which opened itself to the outside world in the 1900s, now has 500,000 Pentecostal-Charismatic believers (2.1 percent of its total population).

Characteristics

The unique features of Pentecostalism in the region can be discussed in terms of the movement's socioeconomic, religious, political, and experiential aspects interacting with the Asian context.

Socioeconomic Aspect

Pentecostalism flourishes among the socially marginalized poor, providing a meaningful place for them. In many places, such as Korea, upward social mobility has taken place among the Pentecostals. Preaching of God's blessing in terms of prosperity and healing has brought this social upliftment, as in Latin America. This aspect of the Pentecostal message is often criticized as an Asian variety of the problematic Western "prosperity gospel."

Religious Aspect

Pentecostalism has a policy of nonengagement with other religions. Unlike their Western counterparts, most Asian Pentecostals have come from non-Christian religions, and often at a great cost. Persecution is their regular experience. Thus, their attitude toward other religions is rather negative, and they consider practitioners of other religions as targets of evangelism. More open interreligious confrontation is found in certain parts of the region, such as Indonesia. On the other hand, Pentecostalism's emphasis on spiritual experiences has led several scholars to conclude that there are similarities between animism and Pentecostalism, although Pentecostal leaders in Korea greatly object to this comparison.

Social Aspect

Recently Pentecostal-Charismatic believers have begun to recognize their ability to influence society through social and political involvement. For instance, El Shaddai, a charismatic Catholic group in the Philippines that claims some 7 to 8 million supporters in the country and another million outside of the Philippines, supported the candidacy of Joseph Estrada for president in 1998 and has shown support for other candidates in more recent years.

Indonesian Pentecostal-Charismatics are also encouraged to be involved in politics.

Experiential Aspect

Pentecostalism has brought an affective dimension to Christian life. Regions of East Asia in which Chinese cultural influence has been strong have tended to develop a more cerebral type of Christianity, often setting aside the experiential dimension of religious life and depriving it of its affective elements. Affective experience and expression in religious life are critical for Asians, which may explain why Pentecostalism has thrived there. Pentecostalism's lively music, testimonies (which anyone can offer), participatory worship, lively preaching, audience response in the form of altar calls, and prayers for healing and miracles have been powerful attractive forces. In fact, many non-Pentecostal Christian denominations have been forced to adopt Pentecostal-style worship in response to the demands of their members (particularly young members). It is noted that the majority of Asian Pentecostals are still young.

Toward the Future

Asian Pentecostalism will continue to grow exponentially, particularly in China as many house church movements exhibit Pentecostal characteristics. Given Asia's sheer size of population, if the number of Asians who embrace Pentecostalism reaches the same proportion of the total population as it has in Africa, Asian Pentecostals will number 811.6 million by 2025, and more than 80 percent of the world's Pentecostals would be found in the East Asian countries. As megacities mushroom in Asia, so will Pentecostal megachurches. Pentecostalism's missionary activities are expected to grow as well (as exemplified by the Chinese "Back to Jerusalem" movement). Growing Pentecostal scholarship will also provide useful theological reflections not only for Asian Pentecostals, but also for Pentecostals in general. Asian Pentecostalism can be a potential powerhouse on the global religious scene.

However, there are also significant challenges. Some Pentecostal churches—for example, in Korea—are now facing the slowing of church growth. This coincides with the economic achievement of the society. How will this religion of the poor provide dynamism and spiritual attraction to the no-longer poor? Western Pentecostal churches do not seem to provide helpful models. Also, the rise of all types of religious fundamentalism may bring non-Christian Fundamentalists into conflict with Pentecostals, who might be considered a Fundamentalist wing of Christianity. Whether or not the rise of Pentecostal scholarship in Asia will suffocate spiritual dynamism, as early Pentecostals feared, will most likely be tested in Asia. No one doubts, however, that Asian Pentecostalism will be a powerful religious force that will affect the course of many Asian societies, positively as well as negatively. The world will continue to watch it closely.

WONSUK MA

See also Animism; China; Korea; Philippines

Further Reading

Anderson, A., & Tang, E. (Eds.). (2004). *Asian and Pentecostal: The charismatic faces of Christianity in Asia.* Oxford, UK: Regnum Books.

Barrett, D., Kurian, G. T., & Johnson, T. M. (Eds.). (2001). *World Christian encyclopaedia: A comparative survey of churches and religions in the modern world: Vol 1. The world by countries: Religionists, churches, ministries* (2nd ed.). Oxford, UK: Oxford University Press.

Hosack, J. (2001). The arrival of Pentecostals and charismatics in Thailand. *Asian Journal of Pentecostal Studies, 4*(1), 109–117.

Seleky, T. (2001). A history of the Pentecostal movement in Indonesia. *Asian Journal of Pentecostal Studies, 4*(1), 131–148.

Sharma, B. K. (2001). A history of the Pentecostal movement in Nepal. *Asian Journal of Pentecostal Studies, 4*(2), 295–305.

Wiyono, G. (2001). Timor revival: A historical study of the great twentieth-century revival in Indonesia. *Asian Journal of Pentecostal Studies, 4*(2), 269–293.

Azusa Street Revival

The origin of the Pentecostal movement can be traced to the Holiness wing of American Methodism at the beginning of the twentieth century. On 1 January 1901, former Methodist preacher (and founder of the Apostolic Faith movement) Charles Fox Parham (1873–1929) laid hands upon Agnes Ozman to initiate the baptism in the Holy Spirit at his bible school in Topeka, Kansas. When Ozman began to speak in tongues, Parham concluded that tongues (glossolalia) was the Bible evidence of the Pentecostal baptism, which came as a third blessing after the experiences of justification (forgiveness of sins) and sanctification (transformation from

Excerpt of a Sermon by William J. Seymour

The extract below is from a sermon titled "River of Living Water," preached by William J. Seymour at the Azusa Street Mission in the fall of 1906.

In the fourth chapter of John, the words come, "Jesus answered and said unto her, If thou knewest the gift of God and who it is that saith to thee Give me to drink, thou wouldest have asked of Him and He would have given thee living water." Praise God for the living waters today that flow freely, for it comes from God to every hungry and thirsty heart. Jesus said, "He that believeth on me, as the scripture hath said, out of his inmost being shall flow rivers of living waters." Then we are able to go in the mighty name of Jesus to the ends of the earth and water dry places, deserts and solitary places until these parched, sad, lonely hearts are made to rejoice in the God of their salvation. We want the rivers today. Hallelujah! Glory to God in the highest!

In Jesus Christ we get forgiveness of sin, and we get sanctification of our spirit, soul and body, and upon that we get the gift of the Holy Ghost that Jesus promised to His disciples, the promise of the Father. All this we get through the atonement. Hallelujah!

Source: Seymour, W. J. (1906). *Azusa Street Sermons*. LaCygne, KS: River of Revival Ministries.

sinner to saint). The baptism of the Holy Spirit had already been recognized by many in the Holiness movement as the third stage in a Christian's development; however, Parham was the first to insist on tongues as evidence of Spirit baptism. Evidential tongues became the cardinal and central doctrine of the Pentecostal revivals that were affected by Parham's teaching.

In 1905 Parham took his theology to Houston, Texas and opened a second Bible school. Here an African-American preacher named William Joseph Seymour (1870–1922) absorbed Parham's third-blessing theology, with its distinctive emphasis on tongues as the "Bible evidence" of the baptism of the Holy Spirit. Seymour took this doctrine to the West Coast in 1906, having been invited to pastor a small Holiness mission in Los Angeles.

During Seymour's first sermon he taught that speaking in tongues is the initial, physical evidence of the baptism in the Holy Spirit. His belief that those who had not spoken in tongues had not actually received the baptism of the Holy Spirit offended many church members, some of whom had claimed Spirit baptism for most of their lives. Seymour argued that they had only experienced sanctification, and that another spiritual "experience" awaited them. When he returned for the night service, he found the door securely padlocked—he was locked out in the cold. Having nowhere else to go, he was given shelter by Edward Lee, a member of the church who was somewhat sympathetic toward his ministry, but unsure of his peculiar doctrine of initial evidence.

It was in the living room of Lee's home on Bonnie Brae Street that Seymour began holding prayer meetings that soon mushroomed into revival meetings that had to be moved out onto the porch. On 9 April 1906, an eight-year-old boy was apparently the first among his congregation to experience the baptism of the Holy Spirit evidenced by glossolalia. Soon the gatherings grew so large that the porch collapsed during one of the meetings. No one was injured, and Seymour (who was joined by two other students from Parham's school, Lucy Farrow and J. A. Warren) moved the revival into a vacant building located at 312 Azusa Street on 14 April 1906.

As he preached and prayed his novel message, fervent revival broke out, marked by powerful spiritual experiences, including ecstatic singing, dancing, and prophecy, as well as speaking in tongues. News spread quickly (particularly via Seymour's publication *The Apostolic Faith*), and Parham's theology of a "third blessing" of the baptism in the Holy Spirit evidenced by speaking in other tongues penetrated the Christian community.

The Power of Revival

The public received news of the happening from a *Los Angeles Times* story on 18 April 1906, which was also the day of the great San Francisco earthquake. The newspaper caption read "Weird Babble of Tongues/ New Sect of Fanatics is Breaking Loose." However derogatory, this coverage gave free publicity to the revival, and soon the serious and the curious were making their way to Azusa Street.

Thousands flocked to the Azusa Street mission so that they too might receive their baptism of the Spirit. Worship services continued seven days a week, from morning until night, for three and half years (1906–1909), in a ramshackle Los Angeles building that had once served as a horse stable. Improvised pews were made from rough planks set on nail kegs, and the pulpit from two empty wooden crates set on end. Proponents and detractors alike acknowledged the revival's astonishing power. The first issue of the *Apostolic Faith* newsletter in September 1906 reported: "Proud, well-dressed preachers come in to 'investigate.' Soon their high looks are replaced with wonder, then conviction comes, and very often you will find them in a short time wallowing on the dirty floor, asking God to forgive them and make them as little children." People would rush to the altars to repent of sin and to seek the face of God spontaneously, and would often fall to the floor throughout the congregation as the power of God rushed upon them.

The success of Seymour's revival in terms of numbers was phenomenal. Crowds of people began to flock to the Azusa Street Mission, attracted, in part, by sensationalistic newspaper accounts. By late summer an estimated twelve hundred people could be found attending a prayer meeting at the site. The San Francisco earthquake, which occurred on 18 April 1906, also contributed to the revival's success. Frank Bartleman, a local Holiness evangelist who had participated in Seymour's prayer meetings even before he moved to Azusa Street, publicized the idea that the devastating quake signaled the imminence of the apocalypse and encouraged readers of his tracts to join the revival while there was still time.

Spread of Third-Blessing Theology

As Holiness churches were caught up in this distinctive revivalistic stream, they frequently felt compelled to follow Parham and Seymour in revising their views to distinguish the second blessing of sanctification from the baptism of the Holy Spirit. Indeed, Seymour dedicated much energy in *The Apostolic Faith* from 1906 to 1909 to providing theological justification for this distinction to the larger Holiness community of which he perceived himself to be a part.

Dissention

Pentecostalism's nascent theology soon faced a challenge that involved a return to a revised "two-blessing" conception of Christian experience. William H. Durham (1873–1912), who had received his Pentecostal experience at Azusa Street in 1906, returned there in 1911 preaching that sanctification was a "finished work" that occurred at conversion. Thus, the baptism of the Holy Spirit with speaking in tongues rather than sanctification was the second experience Christians should seek following justification. Seymour barred Durham from Azusa Street, but Durham's reductionism gained increasing momentum among Pentecostals, especially those that had entered the movement from outside the Holiness tradition. The eruption in 1914 of further struggles over biblically correct water-baptismal formulas and the nature of the Trinity resulted in the formation of the Oneness branch of Pentecostalism in which baptism of the Holy Spirit and tongues speech were seen as taking place concurrently with conversion.

The Gift of Tongues

The earliest Pentecostals believed that they spoke with xenolalic, rather than glossolalic tongues. For example, when Agnes Ozman spoke in tongues on 1 January 1901, she was reported as having been enabled by the Holy Spirit to speak in Chinese. This was going to open the door for successful evangelism in China.

When the xenolalia theory did not pan out, Pentecostals redefined their tongues experience as glossolalia. But they retained the theology implicit in the previous claim. If the baptism in the Holy Spirit can empower a person to preach the gospel in a language previously unknown, then the baptism in the Holy Spirit is the only criteria for qualification to preach the Gospel. Since all members of the body of Christ are eligible to receive the baptism in the Holy Spirit, all members of the body of Christ can be qualified in this way to preach the Gospel and participate in the mission of the church.

Race Relations in the Revival

A distinctive feature of the early Azusa Street Revival was its interracial, intercultural, and gender-crossing character, involving blacks, whites, Latinos, and foreigners, and women as well as men in key leadership roles. Although Jim Crow legislation, racial injustice, and even lynching were rampant in America at this time, the revival in Los Angeles in its early phases exhibited racial harmony. Group photos of the original leaders portray blacks and whites, and men and women, in poses suggesting a genuine partnership in ministry. Whites acknowledged the leadership of a black man, William Seymour. Seymour regarded this breaking down of social barriers as an even more distinctive mark of the Holy Spirit than speaking in tongues.

Gaston B. Cashwell, a white southerner, came to Los Angeles to seek spiritual fullness and was at first dismayed by the interracial worship. Yet he soon repented of his racism and received the baptism of the Holy Spirit by the laying on of hands by a teenage black man. He returned to North Carolina and became the Pentecostal apostle to the southeastern United States.

Yet not all responded as Cashwell did. Seymour's teacher Parham—who had sponsored Seymour's trip to California, and thus indirectly spawned the Azusa Street Revival—arrived in Los Angeles and was horrified to see the informality of black-white relations there (and especially contact between black men and white women). He reacted with unprintable racial slurs and denunciations, and the episode created an irreparable breach with Seymour. Parham attempted to set up a counter-revival at another location in Los Angeles, and yet the revival's epicenter remained on Azusa Street. Parham's reputation was later tarnished by charges of sexual impropriety, and he ultimately had little influence in the Pentecostal movement he had helped to establish. When he unsuccessfully tried to assert his influence in the Azusa movement, Parham opened the door to the development of Pentecostal groups to rival his Apostolic Faith organization. These groups eventually included the Church of God in Christ, the Apostolic Overcoming Holy Church of God, Triumph the Church, and Kingdom of God in Christ—all African-American denominations. However, the influence of the revival on Azusa Street in Los Angeles also contributed to the emergence of many white-oriented Pentecostal groups such as the Assemblies of God and the United Pentecostal Church.

The leaders at Azusa Street also had a falling out along racial lines, triggered by Seymour's decision to marry an African-American woman. Two white women—influenced perhaps by romantic disappointment—objected to the marriage and then absconded with the only copies of the mailing list for the *Apostolic Faith* newsletter, which promptly ceased publication. Changes in racial attitudes led Seymour to implement a new policy according to which the head of the Azusa Street mission had to be a person of color. Despite these setbacks, the Azusa Street Revival entered a second peak period in 1911 and exerted a far-ranging influence in world Pentecostalism.

JESS LAPOINTE, WITH MATERIAL FROM VINSON SYNAN, ROBBIE KAGARISE, BENJAMIN ROBINSON, AND MICHAEL MCCLYMOND

See also America, North; Experience, Theology of; Glossolalia; Initial Evidence; Neocharismatic Movements; Pentecostalism, Classical; Race Relations

B

Baptism in the Holy Spirit

The noun phrase "baptism in the Holy Spirit" does not exist in the New Testament. In verb form, it is a term used by John the Baptist in all four Gospels (Matthew 3:11; Mark 1:8; Luke 3:16; John 1:33) and quoted affirmatively by Jesus in Acts 1:5 and 8 to describe the post-resurrection ministry of Jesus as the giver of the Spirit. In these texts, John contrasts his own ministry of repentance through water baptism with Jesus' role as the One who will usher in the new era of the Spirit. In this contrast, John is clear that Jesus as the One who bestows the Spirit is superior, since He is the source of new life. John is not the source of new life, but rather the one who prepares the way for Jesus and bears witness to His arrival (John 1:6–13). Christ as the Baptizer in the Spirit and the Giver of life will judge and restore according to the Gospel witnesses, for the "winnowing fork is in His hand to clear His threshing floor" (Luke 3:17, NIV).

Spirit Baptism as Charismatic Experience

To say that Christ is the Baptizer in the Spirit, however, does not tell us much about the precise nature of this action. Modern Holiness and Pentecostal movements sought to revive the notion of "baptism in the Holy Spirit" to describe revival experiences among Christians. In this cluster of theologies, Christ baptizes in the Spirit to deepen or to renew the Christian life. The term came to prominence in the nineteenth-century Holiness movement as a way of describing a sanctification experience for those who were already converted. Whether or not John Wesley, the one to whom the Holiness

movement claimed allegiance, ever recognized the validity of a Spirit baptism for believers is debatable. Spirit baptism also came to be understood as an empowerment of the Christian life by participants in the nineteenth-century revivals that took place at Keswick, England. This understanding must be combined with the expectation among some late nineteenth-century Holiness folk of a latter rain of the Spirit, which would bring with it a restoration of apostolic signs and wonders like those in the book of Acts following the bestowal of the Spirit at Pentecost (Acts 2:4; 3:6–8; 4:30–31; 5:12; 8:7; 9:40–42; 10:46; 14:8–10; 19:6, 11; 20:9–12). From the soil of such influences at the turn of the twentieth century sprang the use of Spirit baptism among Pentecostals as the central metaphor for describing an experience of power for witness, involving various gifts of the Holy Spirit, especially the more extraordinary gifts of inspired speech and divine healing.

Early Pentecostals were divided over how to define the experience of sanctification in relation to one's initial conversion to Christ. Holiness Pentecostals, following the Holiness movement's doctrine of sanctification discussed above, distinguished between conversion and sanctification, viewing the empowerment of the Spirit in Spirit baptism as a third stage. Pentecostals from more Reformed backgrounds integrated conversion and sanctification into one, advocating a two-stage entry into the abundant life of the Spirit (conversion/sanctification and Spirit baptism). Both sides supported the doctrine of "subsequence," which viewed Spirit baptism as subsequent to the salvific categories of conversion and sanctification. However, not all Pentecostal groups came to support this subsequence doctrine. For example, the Oneness Pentecostals (known as such for their unitarian view of God) took an integrated understanding of Spirit baptism as the bestowal of the Spirit connected inseparably to conversion and water baptism in an initiation complex. The ecumenical influence of their doctrine was hindered by their insistence that baptism be in Jesus' name only and evidenced specifically by speaking in tongues. But a large enough majority of the Pentecostal movement embraced the doctrine of subsequence to make it distinctively classical Pentecostal, despite recent signs of waning support for it in the Pentecostal mainstream.

---

[1]When the day of Pentecost came,
they were all together in one place.

[2]Suddenly a sound like the blowing of a violent wind came from heaven and filled the whole house where they were sitting.

[3]They saw what seemed to be tongues of fire that separated and came to rest on each of them.

[4]All of them were filled with the Holy Spirit and began to speak in other tongues as the Spirit enabled them.

Acts 2: 1–4 (New International Version)

The doctrine of subsequence was symptomatic of the tendency, typical of revivalism, to view the onset of the Christian life as a series of breakthroughs in the Spirit. In accenting new beginnings, this spirituality tended to lose sight at times of the continuity of the Christian life. Thus, the doctrine of subsequence has led in the view of certain Wesleyans and Pentecostals to an unfortunate bifurcation of purity (sanctification) and power (charismatic empowerment for witness) among Pentecostals. However, the doctrine of subsequence in Pentecostal theology does not imply, as some assume it does, that Christians who have not been Spirit baptized do not possess the Holy Spirit—only that they have not experienced the enhanced power and openness to extraordinary gifts of the Spirit indicative for Pentecostals of Spirit baptism.

Some have charged that the typically classical Pentecostal understanding of baptism in the Holy Spirit turns a divine act of universal Christian initiation into an auxiliary spiritual experience that is the elite privilege of certain Christians only. Most Pentecostals who accept subsequence would disavow any intention of elitism, characterizing their theology of Spirit baptism as a renewal experience for all Christians. However, some find the charge of elitism difficult to avoid leveling at Pentecostals who regard speaking in tongues as the *necessary*

sign of Spirit baptism. This is because spiritual renewal or power tends with this doctrine to be confined to tongues-speakers (or Pentecostals and charismatics). Some Pentecostal leaders and scholars have come out against this tendency toward exclusivity. For example, a prominent Pentecostal preacher, Jack Hayford, values the experience of tongues as a "heavenly language" while rejecting the necessity of tongues as the sign of Spirit baptism. Spirit baptism for Hayford merely opens up the possibility or privilege of speaking in tongues, implying that many may not wish to take advantage of it. Such a doctrine of tongues as a common but not necessary evidence of Spirit baptism opens up spiritual renewal to a much broader ecumenical audience. Pentecostals in the United States are divided over Hayford's proposal.

Historically, there have been various ways of defining the relationship between Spirit baptism and speaking in tongues among Pentecostals. The Pentecostal pioneer William J. Seymour saw in tongues evidence that Spirit baptism was uniting Christians across racial, class, and linguistic boundaries. Some even felt that tongues allowed one to preach miraculously in unlearned foreign languages (*xenolalia*). But this idea soon waned, giving way to the dominant understanding of tongues as a heavenly language or as unintelligible utterances that symbolize the inadequacy of rational speech to express the divine mystery. On a global scale, speaking in tongues has a prominent place in Pentecostal spirituality, but the doctrine of tongues as the initial and necessary evidence of baptism in the Holy Spirit is not universally followed among Pentecostals, and tends to be most popular among classical Pentecostals in the United States.

Acts 8 is the classic text used by most Pentecostals to support their understanding of Spirit baptism as an experience of empowerment subsequent to conversion to Christ. In this chapter, the Samaritans accept the Gospel and are baptized in Jesus' name but do not yet have the Spirit (8:14–16); they receive it later at the hands of the apostles Peter and John. Pentecostal New Testament Scholar Robert Menzies notes that the possibility of believers being baptized in Jesus' name but not yet having the Spirit would have been unimaginable to Paul (Romans 8:9). This fact implies for Menzies a fundamental difference between Lukan and Pauline pneumatologies. For Menzies, Luke is indebted to a typically Jewish pneumatology that understands the reception of the Spirit as an empowerment or charismatic enrichment (referring to gifts of the Spirit, or *charismata*). Paul, however, goes deeper, connecting the work of the Spirit to one's initiation to Christ by faith.

Menzies thus accuses those who see Spirit baptism in Acts as salvific of reading a Pauline pneumatology into Luke. Menzies then uses this charismatic understanding of Spirit baptism in Luke to explain the Pentecostal doctrine of Spirit baptism as a charismatic experience subsequent to conversion. He regards this more theological hermeneutic as superior to the older Pentecostal tendency to argue from a perceived pattern in Acts separating the bestowal of the Spirit from faith and repentance (as well as water baptism). Menzies is aware of the fact that his position does little more than open up the *possibility* of viewing Spirit baptism as a post-conversion charismatic empowerment. Even if one grants his nonsalvific understanding of Luke's use of the verb to "baptize" in the Spirit, one could still integrate Luke's pneumatology with Paul's in a way that avoids separating the charismatic and salvific elements of Spirit baptism. This is the option suggested by the Reformed and sacramental understandings of Spirit baptism.

The Reformed Perspective

Spirit baptism among Reformed or Evangelical Christians has been defined as regeneration or new birth, an experience had by all Christians by virtue of their conversion to Christ through faith (Romans 8:9). Spirit baptism is thus "repentance unto life" (Acts 11:18) or a figurative "baptism" into Christ by faith (1 Corinthians 12:13) and not some separate stage of spiritual renewal or power. Prominent New Testament scholar James Dunn has argued that Spirit baptism is the bestowal of the Spirit that functions as God's culminating act of regeneration. Our vital responses to God in repentance or water baptism are thus not most important to our conversion to Christ. Christian identity is sealed instead by the bestowal of the Spirit, which is referred to in Scripture as a being "baptized" in the Spirit. Though critical of Pentecostal theology, Dunn gives credence to the Pentecostal movement by regarding Spirit baptism as profoundly experiential and charismatic for the Christian life (at least eventually), and he criticizes the mainline churches for reducing the experience of the Spirit to sacramental or psychological categories. Nevertheless, Spirit baptism is for Dunn a divine act that occurs at the moment of true faith in Christ. Dunn's assumption that Spirit baptism is connected to faith in Christ alone has made him critical of both the Pentecostal and the sacramental views of Spirit baptism.

The Sacramental Perspective

Those from sacramental traditions, such as Kilian McDonnell and George Montague, have sought to understand Spirit baptism as universally experienced among Christians through the sacramental rites of initiation (baptism/confirmation and the Eucharist). Jesus' reception of the Spirit at His baptism thus becomes paradigmatic of the connection between baptism and the reception of the Spirit among Christians (Acts 2:38; 19:5–6; and 1 Corinthians 12:13, which is understood literally as "water baptism"). In disagreement with Dunn, sacramental theologians would connect the reception of the Spirit to the sacramental rites of initiation and not to faith alone. There is but "one baptism" in water and Spirit (Ephesians 4:5). But, like Dunn, McDonnell and Montague grant validity to the Pentecostal movement by regarding Spirit baptism as linked in the New Testament and the writings of the Church Fathers to charismatic experience. In the view of McDonnell and Montague, sacramental grace in us will eventually (either at the moment of initiation or later) burst forth in experiences of charismatic power. Though Pentecostals in their view have a faulty *theology* of Spirit baptism by detaching it from sacramental initiation, Pentecostals do validly call the church to the *experience* of Spirit baptism in life This is the view of Spirit baptism that became prominent among charismatic Catholics, Lutherans, and Anglicans in the 1970s and later. It became common for them to refer to Spirit baptism as a release of the Spirit received at sacramental initiation.

There are Pentecostals who have been attracted to this doctrine of Spirit baptism as a release in life of the charismatic implications of the reception of the Spirit in Christian initiation. Other Pentecostals fear that Spirit baptism as a release or breakthrough of the Spirit in life precludes the need to seek a definite reception of the Spirit for empowered witness. The Catholic theologian Francis Sullivan shares this concern, and has quoted persuasively from Thomas Aquinas in favor of a new endowment of the Spirit that is subsequent to sacramental initiation and is not to be viewed as merely the outworking of sacramental grace. However, unlike the Pentecostal view of Spirit baptism as a one-time event after conversion to Christ, Sullivan views every breakthrough or filling of the Spirit as a fresh Spirit baptism. This whole discussion raises the question of how one understands continuity in the Christian life in relation to new beginnings.

Spirit Baptism in Theological Reflection

Is Spirit baptism connected to faith alone or is it fulfilled in the sacramental rites of initiation? Is it necessarily evidenced by speaking in tongues or does it merely open up the possibility of tongues speech and other miraculous gifts? Is it a release of the Spirit received in Christian conversion/initiation or is it a new reception of the Spirit? There is no unified Pentecostal answer to these questions, although Spirit baptism still has vast appeal among Pentecostals as an entry, at least in part, to power and charismatic involvement. Interestingly, recent Pentecostal theologians have not paid much attention to the doctrine of baptism in the Spirit. A Pentecostal theological reflection on Spirit baptism has not been written since Harold Hunter's and Howard Irvin's extensive defenses of the doctrine of subsequence in the 1980s.

This lack of attention to a theology of Spirit baptism among classical Pentecostal theologians is due in part to the impressive historical scholarship that has shown Pentecostal theology to have been more complex from the beginning than a mere belief in Spirit baptism and speaking in tongues. This insight has caused Pentecostal theologians to pursue other ways of construing what is distinctive about Pentecostal theology than a mere reflection on the baptism and gifts of the Spirit. And churches around the globe with Pentecostal-like worship but with little connection to classical Pentecostal theology are proliferating, making Pentecostalism an ever more complex phenomenon. Moreover, some Pentecostal theologians and exegetes feel that the doctrine of subsequence is weak exegetically and theologically or ecumenically unfruitful, despite the challenging arguments of Menzies. The tendency has been to reflect on the ecumenical implications of the Pentecostal stress on pneumatology, eschatological fervor, missionary zeal, or experience of God (understood especially as *pathos*, involving the sanctification of the affections in the light of the Kingdom of God to come).

In conversation with this more ecumenical direction in Pentecostal theology, the Methodist (ex-Pentecostal) theologian Lyle Dabney suggests that Spirit baptism can function as an overarching category that describes the total role of Christ as the Giver of life and the Inaugurator of the new creation. Placing the new creation under the category of Spirit baptism will grant pneumatology a more robust role in Christian theology as a whole. If Spirit baptism is to capture the imaginations of Pentecostal theologians in the future, it will most likely take such an ecumenically broad direction but without neglecting the need for a definite moment in life when weary or complacent Christians become charismatically aware and empowered.

FRANK D. MACCHIA

See also Baptism, Water; Initiation Rites; Sanctification

Further Reading

Chan, S. (1999). Evidential glossolalia and the doctrine of subsequence. *Asian Journal of Pentecostal Studies, 2*(2), 195–211.

Dabney, L. (2001). Justified in the Spirit: Soteriological reflections on the Resurrection. *International Journal of Systematic Theology, 3*(1), 46–68.

Dunn, J. D. G. (1970). *Baptism in the Holy Spirit: A re-examination of the New Testament teaching on the gift of the Spirit in relation to Pentecostalism today*. Naperville, IL: A. R. Allenson.

Lederle, H. (1988). *Treasures old and new: Interpretations of Spirit baptism in the charismatic renewal movement*. Peabody, MA: Hendrickson.

McDonnell, K., & Montague, G. (1990). *Christian initiation and baptism in the Holy Spirit: Evidence from the first eight centuries*. Wilmington, DE: Michael Glazier Books.

Menzies, R. (1995). *Empowered for witness: The Spirit in Luke-Acts*. Sheffield, UK: Sheffield Academic Press.

Sullivan, F. A. (1982). *Charisms and charismatic renewal: A biblical and theological study*. Ann Arbor, MI: Servant Books.

Baptism, Water

Water baptism within Pentecostal and charismatic Christianity has taken a variety of forms depending upon the particular branch of the movement being examined. The three main areas of variance are believer's baptism versus paedobaptism, immersion versus sprinkling or pouring, and baptismal formulas. Of particular note for Pentecostals and charismatics is research that indicates a connection between baptism in the Holy Spirit and water baptism in the practice of the early church.

Believer's Baptism Versus Paedobaptism

Believer's baptism refers to the practice of baptizing only those who have made a conscious profession of personal faith in Jesus Christ. This would necessarily exclude infants and children who are too young to be able to express such faith. This view sees water baptism as an outward expression of a personal faith that actually precedes baptism. Usually the baptism itself is not seen as accomplishing regeneration (rebirth or salvation), but it may still be considered, by some who hold to this view, to contain some sacramental aspect (a means of grace) that makes it more than simply an outward symbol, but a means of connecting by faith with

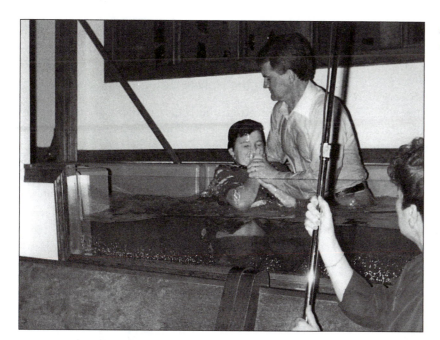

A young convert is baptized by the pastor.
Courtesy of Benjamin Johnson.

the greater spiritual reality that it represents, namely an identification with the death and resurrection of Christ and a passing through judgment, which results in rebirth and newness of life for the believer. Since baptism is considered a public proclamation of the individual's choice to accept and follow Jesus Christ, the maturity to make such a choice is seen as essential. Most of the major Pentecostal denominations and independent charismatic churches hold to some form of believer's water baptism.

Paedobaptism, on the other hand, is the practice of baptizing infants and children who have not made a personal profession of faith. In this view, baptism is identified with the Old Testament practice of circumcision, in that it is seen as an induction into the covenantal community. As in the Old Testament, the parents of the infant are already members of the community and their faith is seen as influencing the life and destiny of the child. In some traditions, water baptism is seen as the means for actual rebirth or salvation. This is known as baptismal regeneration. In this view, salvation itself is transmitted to the recipient of water baptism by means of the virtue of the sacrament of baptism, even apart from faith. It is the sacramental act itself that saves. This view, however, is rare in Pentecostal-Charismatic circles. More often, those who practice paedobaptism see it as an inclusion in the Christian community that holds the promise of a future individual confirmation of personal faith by the child once he or she has reached an age at which understanding and personal decision are possible. This view is held most often by charismatics who are found in more liturgical communities, such as Presbyterian, Episcopalian/Anglican, and Roman Catholic traditions.

Immersion Versus Sprinkling/Pouring

The question of how an individual is baptized is largely dependent upon the particular Pentecostal or charismatic tradition of which the person is a part. Pentecostals and most independent charismatic churches tend to practice baptism by immersion (complete submersion of the individual in water), while more liturgical traditions either prefer sprinkling or pouring of water over the head to the exclusion of immersion or as an alternative to immersion. From a practical standpoint, those traditions that practice paedobaptism are most likely to also practice sprinkling and/or pouring. It is noteworthy that some traditions that practice baptismal immersion do not consider baptisms performed through sprinkling or pouring to be valid.

Baptismal Formulas

The question of baptismal formula (the words that are spoken over an individual who is being baptized) has been an issue of contention, particularly within the Pentecostal tradition. Pentecostals and charismatics who hold to the doctrine of the Holy Trinity tend to baptize "in the name of the Father, and of the Son, and of the Holy Spirit," in keeping with the formula prescribed by Jesus in Matthew 28:19 (NIV).

However, Oneness Pentecostals prefer to baptize "in the name of Jesus Christ," in keeping with the practice of the apostle Peter as seen in Acts 2:38 and 10:48. Oneness Pentecostals usually consider baptism using the Trinitarian formula as invalid and are therefore often referred to as "Jesus Only" Pentecostals. The Oneness tradition sees the practice of the church in Acts of baptizing in the name of Jesus as the practical fulfillment of the formula used by Jesus in Matthew 28. In short, when the apostles obeyed the command of Jesus to baptize in the name of the Father, and of the Son, and of the Holy Spirit, they baptized in the name of Jesus Christ, which, for Oneness Pentecostals, indicates their understanding that the name of Jesus Christ is the name of the Father, and the Son, and the Holy Spirit.

And when Jesus was baptized, he went up immediately from the water, and behold, the heavens were opened and he saw the Spirit of God descending like a dove, and alighting on him.

Matthew 3:16 (Revised Standard Version)

In an attempt to resolve this difference or at least, out of pastoral concern, to remove the possibility of a believer questioning the validity of his or her baptism at some future time, some Trinitarian Pentecostals and charismatics have adjusted their baptismal formula to include the wording presented in Acts. As such, they baptize "in the name of the Father, and of the Son—our Lord Jesus Christ, and of the Holy Spirit." While this may appear to resolve the *practical* disagreement, the resolution is only apparent as it does not resolve the underlying tension, which is one of differing *theological* understandings.

In order to understand the full structure behind this argument, it is necessary to recognize that underlying the reluctance of Oneness Pentecostalism to accept the Trinitarian baptismal formula is a much more profound rejection of the doctrine of the Trinity itself (Oneness Pentecostalism denies Trinitarianism, seeing it as a form of tritheism). It is this belief that is the primary motivation for Oneness Pentecostalism's rejection of the Trinitarian baptismal formula, rather than an arbitrary preference for the account of Acts over that of the Gospels. Thus, simply adding the words "our Lord Jesus Christ" to the Trinitarian baptismal formula did not truly resolve the doctrinal issue, since this did not address the theological concern of Oneness Pente-

costalism. (Oneness Pentecostalism also sees water baptism as an essential prerequisite to salvation.)

Baptism in the Holy Spirit

While Pentecostals and charismatics have historically almost exclusively called upon the New Testament to support their claim for the importance of baptism in the Holy Spirit for Christian life and practice, seeing the contemporary charismatic renewal as a rediscovery of a practice that disappeared after the New Testament period, historical studies have now demonstrated that the practice of calling down the Holy Spirit, with the expectation of charismatic endowments upon the new believer as part of the initiatory rite of water baptism was practiced by the early church for centuries afterward.

As in Tertullian, and Hilary, so also in Cyril, one finds the elements in the rites of Christian initiation which the contemporary charismatic renewal identifies as belonging to the baptism in the Spirit: either imposition of hands or anointing, praying for the descent of the Spirit, expectation that the charisms will be manifested. Two contemporaries of Cyril, Basil of Caesarea and Gregory Nazianzus, place charisms in relation to baptism. (McDonnell and Montague 1990, 224–225)

This has given additional support to the Pentecostal and charismatic practice of baptism in the Holy Spirit and served to further enrich their understanding of Christian initiation, and water baptism, in particular.

Twenty-First Century Outlook

Water baptism has an important place in the faith and practice of Pentecostals and charismatics. The differences in practice and understanding, while at times sources of controversy, are also evidences of the broad spectrum of traditions through which the influence of the renewal movement has stretched. As scholars continue to explore the connection between Christian initiation practices, including water baptism and the baptism in the Holy Spirit, Pentecostal and charismatic Christians may anticipate new opportunities for constructive dialogue with those outside the renewal movement.

DAVID J. MASSEY

See also Baptism in the Holy Spirit; Initiation Rites; Oneness Theology; Trinitarianism

Further Reading

Bernard, D. K. (1983). *The oneness of God*. Hazelwood, MO: Word Aflame Press.

Boyd, G. A. (1992). *Oneness Pentecostals and the Trinity*. Grand Rapids, MI: Baker Book House.

Bundy, D. (1993). The genre of systematic theology in Pentecostalism. *Pneuma: The Journal of the Society for Pentecostal Studies, 15*(1), 89–107.

Clanton, A. L., & Clanton, C. (1995). *United we stand*. Hazelwood, MO: Pentecostal Publishing House.

Dunn, J. D. G. (1970). *Baptism in the Holy Spirit: A re-examination of the New Testament teaching on the gift of the Spirit in relation to Pentecostalism today*. Philadelphia: The Westminster Press.

Macchia, F. D. (2002). Salvation and Spirit baptism: Another look at James Dunn's classic. *Pneuma: The Journal of the Society for Pentecostal Studies, 24*(1), 1–6.

McDonnell, K. (n.d.). *Response to Martin Parmentier on baptism and Spirit baptism in the church fathers*. Retrieved June 3, 2004, from http://www.fullnet.net/np/archives/cyberj/kilian.html

McDonnell, K., & Montague, G. T. (1990). *Christian initiation and baptism in the Holy Spirit: Evidence from the first eight centuries*. Collegeville, MN: The Liturgical Press.

Menzies, W. M. (1971). *Anointed to serve: The story of the Assemblies of God*. Springfield, MO: Gospel Publishing House.

Menzies, W. W., & Horton, S. M. (1999). *Bible doctrines: A Pentecostal perspective*. Springfield, MO: Logion Press.

Parmentier, M. (n.d.). *Water baptism and Spirit baptism in the church fathers*. Retrieved June 3, 2004, from http://www.pctii.org/cyberj/cyberj3/martin.html

Porter, S. E., & Cross, A. R. (2002). *Dimensions of baptism: Biblical and theological studies*. New York: Sheffield Academic Press.

Binding and Loosing

In Pentecostal and charismatic movements, *binding and loosing* usually refers to the casting out of demons (or one aspect of such an act) and the consequent liberation of persons or places from demonic subjugation. The definitive reference to binding and loosing comes from Jesus' words to Peter in Matthew 16:19 (NIV), giving Peter the "keys of the kingdom of heaven," so that whatever is "bound on earth shall be bound in heaven" and whatever is "loosed on earth shall be loosed in heaven" (cf. Matthew 18:18, which is directed to a broader audience). The end result is that the gates of hell will not withstand the mission of the church (Matthew 16:18), implying for many Pentecostals that the binding and loosing relates to the overcoming of dark powers that oppose the purposes of God.

This Pentecostal interpretation of binding and loosing in Matthew 16:19 and 18:18 as exorcism has been called into question on exegetical or theological grounds. From the second century onward, the rise of episcopal authority in the church influenced the interpretation of this text as an endorsement of apostolic authority in applying church discipline and preserving proper doctrine. In the context of this apostolic authority of Peter and the other disciples, binding and loosing would relate to the interpretation of the truth or the enforcement of loyalty to the truth in the church through discipline. Research into Jewish rabbinic sources has supported this understanding of binding and loosing, as well as the related need to bind one to, or release one from, a vow. A connection with John 20:23 might indicate as well an interpretation of binding and loosing in the context of proclaiming or withholding the forgiveness of sins.

Many Pentecostals and charismatics, however, stand by their interpretation of Matthew 16:19 and 18:18 as a reference to the subjugation and exorcism of demons. Their assumption has received scholarly support from an important article on this topic written by Richard H. Heirs in the *Journal of Biblical Literature* (1985). Heirs notes that scholarship on this text in Matthew tends to neglect evidence from Jewish intertestamental literature and elsewhere in the New Testament that refers to the subjugation and exorcism of demonic powers as a "binding" and the resulting liberation of people as a "loosing." The key New Testament text here is Mark 3:27, where Jesus characterized his own ministry as binding the strong man (Satan) in order to spoil his goods or hinder and destroy his works. To be loosed is also to be freed from demonic influence (Luke 13:16; Mark 7:34–35).

The "keys" of 16:19 are mentioned elsewhere in the New Testament as symbolic of the authority to subjugate demonic forces—and even death itself—over which the devil had authority (Revelations 1:18, 20:1–3; Hebrews 2:14–15). The reference in Matthew 16:18 to the "gates of hell" as not being able to withstand such divinely-given authority further supports this connection between the keys and the subjugation of demonic forces and the forces of death. The commission to preach, heal, and cast out demons is indeed given by Jesus to the disciples (Mark 3:14–16, 6:7; Luke 10:18–19). Heirs concludes, "Conceivably, Matthew intended the saying of 16:19 to mean that Peter was given the power over [and] against both Satan and death"

(Heirs 1985, 247). Heirs concedes, however, that the binding and loosing may have been meant to have a broader application as well, touching on *any* matter threatening Christians in ministry (Matthew 18:19).

Binding and loosing probably had a broader application for Matthew than the subjugation of the forces of darkness, causing the church through the ministry of the Gospel to resist the forces of death and destruction wherever they may be and whatever their cause. This insight calls into question the exclusive focus on the demonic among Pentecostals who define their ministry by Matthew 16:19 and 18:18, especially leaders of "deliverance" ministries who have even claimed that their entire gift is to bind demons by taking authority over them in order to remove them from places or the lives of individuals. Some have questioned whether demons should receive such attention by any Gospel ministry, in light of the near silence about them in the Old Testament. Critics have charged that the worldview implied by some of these deliverance ministries seems closer to the universe filled with threatening spirits assumed by the Near Eastern religions surrounding ancient Israel than to the universe determined and dominated by the word of Yahweh proclaimed by the Jewish faith. Even though the subjugation of demonic forces received greater attention in the Gospels, Jesus placed a greater emphasis on the fact that our names are written in heaven (Luke 10:20). The New Testament exhorts Christians to withstand the weapons of dark forces (Ephesians 6:11) or to resist their influence (James 4:7), but there are no explicit instructions for binding and loosing demons, and especially not for the elaborate practices present among some groups for naming, cataloging, and binding territorial spirits.

Regarding whether binding and loosing the forces of darkness have a place in Pentecostal and charismatic ministry today, some would agree with the demythologizing hermeneutic of Rudolf Bultmann that attention to the demonic is a throwback to an outdated mythological worldview and a distraction from the human and social sources of destructive power. Others, such as Walter Wink, find in the biblical texts concerning the subjugation of the dark powers an important insight into the fact that there is a spiritual dynamic at work in social structures, mores, and institutions, as well as in individual lives, that must be confronted and overcome in efforts to minister the Gospel to the world in a way that does not neglect concrete powers of resistance.

To confront such challenges, many turn to the fact that Jesus commissioned a wide circle of disciples to preach and to heal (Luke 10), implying for Pentecostals that binding and loosing is the right of all Christians, at least those prepared for such spiritual warfare. They thus tend to resist restricting the application of Matthew 16:19 to Peter and apostolic privilege. Pentecostals tend instead to emphasize lay participation in the ministerial commission handed down from Jesus to the Apostles. Indeed, the preaching of the Gospel with signs and wonders of deliverance supported in the narrative of Acts is based on the anointing of Jesus to "heal all those who were in the grip of the devil" (Acts 10:38) and was not restricted to Apostles (Acts 8:9–13). Jesus' casting out of demons by the Spirit of God was one of the principal means by which the Kingdom of God came upon people (Matthew 12:28). The Spirit poured out upon the people of God in Acts 2 empowered the church to participate in the ministry of Jesus to activate the Gospel in people's lives through redemption and liberation. Paul preached the Gospel with the demonstration of the power of the Spirit so that the faith of Christians would rest on the power of God's grace and not on the power of human wisdom and rhetoric (1 Corinthians 2:4–5).

For many, the demonic is not to dominate people's attention in this ministry, but neither are they to ignore it. It may even be the gift of certain healers in the church to remind people of this fact. It was the mid-nineteenth century Reformed pastor Johann Blumhardt who reminded people through his victorious prayers for the deliverance of Gottlieben Dittus from demonic spirits that the Kingdom of God is not just an abstract principle of divine sovereignty over history, but also a power of deliverance in the concrete, bodily existence of persons in the here and now.

Frank D. Macchia

See also Demon Possession, Casting Out Demons; Exorcism

Further Reading

Heirs, R. H. (1985). "Binding and loosing": The Matthean authorizations. *Journal of Biblical Literature, 104*(2), 233–250.

MacNutt, F. (1995). *Deliverance from evil spirits: A practical manual.* Grand Rapids, MI: Chosen Books.

Wink, W. (1998). *The powers that be: Theology for a new millennium.* New York: Doubleday.

Black Pentecostalism

While Pentecostalism is the fastest growing branch of Protestantism, few people are aware of the unique contributions of African-Americans to the movement's growth in the twentieth century. Black Pentecostalism shares with the rest of the movement an orthodox Christian theology, including a code of strict moral standards and the belief that the last period of revelation has begun and the return of the Lord is imminent; however, it also incorporates elements unique to African-American culture, including a progressive social agenda that is less common in the rest of Pentecostal and charismatic Christianity. From its affinities with slave religion in the antebellum South and traditional black Christian worship, to what some refer to as Neo-Pentecostalism, black Pentecostalism has played a vibrant role in the African-American experience.

Holiness Roots

Like other branches of Pentecostalism, the African-American variant has origins in the Holiness movement, which started in 1867 when a group of Methodists organized the National Camp Meeting Association for the Promotion of Holiness. The modern Pentecostal movement in America dates from 1906 at the Azusa Street revival in California, but its roots go back as far as the eighteenth century, to John Wesley and the birth of Methodism. In fact, Pentecostalism has been called "primitive Methodism's extended incarnation" (Brunner 1970, 37).

Just as Holiness originated in the 1840s and 1850s as a reform movement within the Methodist Church, so Pentecostalism originally emerged as a reformation of the traditional black church, which by the late nineteenth century had begun trending away from strict doctrinal orthodoxy and toward Darwinism and the Social Gospel movement. The antiliberal reformation was also a reaction to a perceived move toward the formalism of the established sacramental churches.

What distinguished African-American Pentecostalism from other segments of Pentecostalism was that it held on to its interracial nature. The Holiness movement involved both blacks and whites, at a time when racism was a powerful force in American culture. One historian of Pentecostalism, Vinson Synan, has written, "In an age of Social Darwinism, Jim Crowism, and general white supremacy, the fact that Pentecostal blacks and whites worshipped together in virtual equality was a significant exception to the prevailing attitudes and practices" (1997, 167). In fact, the central figure in the Azusa Street Revival was an African-American pastor named William J. Seymour.

The interracial nature of the modern Pentecostal movement, however, was not to continue. By 1924 all of the Pentecostal movements in the United States had fallen prey to the prevailing racial attitudes and prac-

tices of their day. The miracle of Azusa Street faded away as denominations began to dominate the Pentecostal landscape. Not until the so-called Memphis Miracle, which took place in 1994 in Memphis, Tennessee, would there be a symbolic return to the inclusive nature of the modern Pentecostal movement. At this historic meeting a new racially inclusive organization was formed, called the Pentecostal-Charismatic Churches of North America, bridging the racial divisions that had characterized North American Pentecostalism.

Traditional Black Worship

Pentecostal and charismatic worship is in many ways not too different from other forms of black Christian worship that would not necessarily be characterized as such. The distinctive element of black Pentecostal worship is primarily the practice of speaking in tongues, but the religious ecstasy and joy that dominate the worship in Pentecostal music, prayers, and preaching is common to all of what is deemed "black worship." Congregations that retreat from a style of worship paralleling that of mainline white churches are often said to be either returning to a traditional black worship or becoming Pentecostal-Charismatic, depending on whether the gifts of the Spirit such as tongues are in operation or not.

Such a shift in worship style is usually marked by several elements. Worship that was once staid and stoic becomes lively and enthusiastic. During worship, people are caught up in ecstatic moments of praise. Some are speaking in tongues; others are dancing in the Spirit, while still others are resting on the floor. Music once dominated by anthems and hymns written by white Europeans is now supplanted by contemporary gospel and praise choruses. In church after church, grand pianos and pipe organs or their electronic clones are replaced by Hammond organs, electronic keyboards and synthesizers, bass and rhythm guitars, bongos, congas, and various other types of percussion. Worship services that used to be predictable in their length and composition become more capricious. In recent years, such changes have come so fast and furious that many black Christians are left wondering who took "their church."

Is this phenomenon Neo-Pentecostalism, or the restoration of traditional African-American worship? The answer lies in both Pentecostalism and traditional black worship. There is a distinct difference between the recent renewal in African-American congregations and in congregations of other ethnicities. The songs sung and the freedoms to embrace the Holy Spirit are common elements of Pentecostal or charismatic renewal, but the manner in which they are presented and manifested in black churches are at times radically different. Adrienne Gaines, news editor for *Charisma Magazine*, tends to argue that this phenomenon is Neo-Pentecostalism, while Cheryl Townsend Gilkes, a professor of sociology and African-American studies at Colby College, disagrees. Gilkes maintains that the renewal being experienced "is simply a revitalization of traditional 'black worship,' which has always been more experiential than traditional white churches, but was rejected for a time by the better educated black middle class" (quoted in Gaines 2003, 38).

Slave Religious Experience

There is a strong cultural heritage that makes worship from a Eurocentric perspective incongruous for most African-Americans. A look back to the days of slavery and how Christian worship and lingering Africanisms coexisted shows that "organized white churches did not encompass the religious life of the Southern Negro," but that "the Negro developed a religious life of his own" (Raboteau 1978, x). The slaves traded to the Americas brought with them their tribal rituals, customs, and religion. Historians doubt there were many, if any, Christians among the slaves. In all cases, slaves were forbidden to practice their tribal beliefs. Instead, where worship was allowed, they were introduced to Christianity. The Christianity to which they were introduced, however, was designed to keep them obedient and docile.

But converted slaves held their own religious services, and those services often developed a very different character from those of their masters. Referred to in recent scholarship (Raboteau 1978) as an "invisible institution," slave worship services were held clandestinely in brush arbors hastily built in the fields and woods or in various dwellings, the participants always taking care to muffle any noise that might draw the attention of the masters. These services were often characterized by preaching, singing, prayer, communal support, and "feeling the spirit." The religious beliefs of the slaves' African heritage influenced the expression of their newfound faith: just as vibrant singing, dancing, and drumming played an important role in the rituals of their ancestral religions, so too found a place in their Christian worship.

As segregation took hold across the country following the Civil War, freedmen were kept out of the churches of their former masters. It was agreed in the Presbyterian Church, to take one example, to send missionaries to the freedmen to help them develop their own congregations under the strict oversight of white preachers. One such Presbyterian missionary recorded his impressions of a large black worship meeting in Texas:

> Whatever [the preacher] says is of but little note, but the wild gestures, the intonation of voice, the singsong, long rolling words, the wild climaxes, the hundreds of responses from old and young, male and female, is like a gathering storm, and when the singing commences, and the shouting, stamping, and clapping hands, laughing, crying, falling down, etc., all mingle in its choruses. The scene is like chaos, a Babel of confusion, and grows louder until miles around you can hear shrieks and yells, like an army rushing to battle, and this continues often till daylight, and night after night for weeks, until their converts are numbered by hundreds. (Quoted in Thompson 1963, 312–313)

Their sensibilities offended by the wild and unrestrained nature of the former slaves' worship, the missionaries built secondary schools and colleges to educate them out of their own cultural expressions and instill in them in a Eurocentric understanding of the faith. The freedmen's customs and art forms, including their music, were considered illegitimate at worst or quaint "folk music" at best. Black congregations that more closely followed white forms of worship were therefore held in higher regard by the dominant culture than traditional black worship. For decades, exuberant worship—which came to be characterized, often negatively, as Holiness, then Pentecostalism—would be frowned upon and seen as nothing more than the anguished outpourings of troubled souls that could be corrected through education.

Neo-Pentecostalism

The attitude in the African-American community has undergone a dramatic shift in recent decades. Younger people are, in some instances, radically interested in reclaiming their traditional culture. No longer are many willing to accept what their parents and grandparents accepted. Among many young blacks, braids and twists in the hair are supplanting Eurocentric styles, and the traditional garments of various African nations are replacing Western clothing. Individual tastes in music have also changed: gospel music is not exclusive to Sunday, but has become a truly popular genre as gospel radio stations grow and CD sales soar. Together, these trends create an environment ripe for the spiritual manifestations that often accompany true renewal.

Lawrence H. Mamiya, an associate professor of religion and African studies at Vassar College, is credited with coining the term *Neo-Pentecostal* to describe the phenomenon of charismatic or Pentecostal renewal in the African-American congregations of the late twentieth century. However, in the context of growing worldwide movements this term does not adequately describe the phenomenon, any more than does identifying it with traditional black worship. Both designations—Neo-Pentecostalism and traditional black worship—have connotations that black Pentecostalism today eschews.

In addition to its religious characteristics, the traditional African-American church has also been socially and politically active, but only in the sense of demanding political rights for blacks as a group. Some, such as those in the Black Muslim movement, have therefore accused the black Christian church of ignoring the needs of the individual. The black Christian focus on issues of equality and civil rights while overlooking the perceived needs of the individual afforded an opportunity to the Muslim community to forge a strong presence in the African-American community. On the other side, the broader Pentecostal community was notorious for focusing on worship at the expense of social activism. The charismatic church, like the Evangelical church, was known for being ultraconservative in its political beliefs at the expense of the interests of minorities. Therefore, the Neo-Pentecostal designation for black Christian renewal was accurate only as it referred to ecstatic moments of worship. Having won full political and social rights, blacks in the late twentieth century were unwilling to accept any longer the givens of either designation.

Black Pentecostalism embraces all of the ecstatic elements of the modern Pentecostal movement, as well as the social activism of the traditional black church. But it also introduces a new element that speaks to blacks in the post-civil rights era: African-American Pentecostal churches today are incubators for entrepreneurs. They sponsor schools, operate church-based businesses, develop land for housing, and redevelop whole communities. These congregations are extremely proactive about empowering families and individuals; they are full-service churches that minister to the total person. They are acutely aware of their heritage, but they have given their Pentecostal designation a new dimension.

Outlook for the Future

Vinson Synan writes, "Although over the decades black Pentecostalism has experienced changes in its theological perspectives, worship style, class orientation, and political views, it has retained its strong commitment to Scripture, conversion, Spirit baptism, evangelism, healing, prayer, and its African heritage" (2001, 290). Pentecostalism has experienced explosive growth worldwide, including among African-Americans. "Megachurches" are on the rise, and denominational allegiances are giving way to Pentecostal and charismatic volunteer associations and fellowships presided over by spiritual bishops. This growth is not expected to abate, but to continue its escalation. Furthermore, the burgeoning growth of independent movements is being challenged by Pentecostal and charismatic renewal in mainline sacramental churches. If this renewal proves to be a long-term trend rather than a passing phenomenon, the Pentecostal-Charismatic movement stands to become the dominant expression of Christianity among African-Americans.

JAMES H. LOGAN, JR.

See also African Initiated Churches; Azusa Street Revival; Memphis Miracle; Race Relations; Slavery

Further Reading

Adefila, J. A. (1975). *Slave religion in the antebellum South: A study of the role of Africanisms in the black response to Christianity*. Doctoral dissertation, Brandeis University.

Asante, M. K. (1987). *The Afrocentric idea*. Philadelphia: Temple University Press.

Boles, J. (Ed.). (1988). *Master and slaves in the house of the Lord: Race and religion in the American South, 1740–1870*. Lexington: University Press of Kentucky.

Brunner, F. D. (1970). *A theology of the Holy Spirit: The Pentecostal experience and the New Testament witness*. Grand Rapids, MI: Eerdmans.

Creel, M. W. (1988). *A peculiar people: Slave religion and community culture among the Gullahs*. New York: New York University Press.

Fountain, D. L. (1999). *Long on religion, short on Christianity: Slave religion 1830–1870*. Doctoral dissertation, University of Mississippi.

Gaines, A. (2003, May). Revive us, precious Lord. *Charisma Magazine*, 37–44.

Gaustad, E. S. (Ed.). (1982). *A documentary history of religion in America to the Civil War*. Grand Rapids, MI: Eerdmans.

Holloway, J. E. (Ed.). (1991). *Africanisms in American culture*. Bloomington: Indiana University Press.

Johnson, P. E. (Ed.). (1994). *African American Christianity: Essays in history*. Berkeley, CA: University Press.

Jones, C. (1983). *Guide to the study of the Pentecostal movement*. Metuchen, NJ: Scarecrow Press.

Jones, C. (1987). *Black holiness: A guide to the study of black participation in Wesleyan perfectionistic and glossolalic Pentecostal movements*. Metuchen, NJ: Scarecrow Press.

Lincoln, C. E., & Mamiya, L. H. (1990). *The black church in the African American experience*. Durham, NC: Duke University Press.

Melton, J. G., & Ward, G. (Eds.). (1993). *Encyclopedia of African American religions*. New York: Garland Reference Library of Social Science.

Raboteau, A. (1978). *Slave religion: The "invisible institution" in the antebellum South*. New York: Oxford University Press.

Sernett, M. C. (2001). *African American religious history: A documentary witness* (2nd ed.). Durham, NC: Duke University Press.

Smith, T. (1978). Religion and ethnicity in America. *American Historical Review, 83*(5), 1155–1185.

Sobel, M. (1979). *Travelin' on: The slave journey to an Afro-Baptist faith*. Princeton, NJ: Princeton University Press.

Synan, V. (1997). *The Holiness-Pentecostal tradition: Charismatic movements in the twentieth century*. Grand Rapids, MI: Eerdmans.

Synan, V. (2001). *The century of the Holy Spirit: 100 years of Pentecostal and charismatic renewal*. Nashville, TN: Nelson Reference.

Taylor, J. V. (1963). *The primal vision: Christian presence amid African religion*. London: SCM Press Ltd.

Thompson, E. T. (1963). *Presbyterians in the South: Vol. 2. 1861–1890*. Richmond, VA: John Knox Press.

Walker, W. T. (1979). *Somebody's calling my name: Black sacred music and social change*. Valley Forge, PA: Judson Press.

Young, A. L. (1996). Archaeological evidence of African-style ritual and healing practices in the upland South. *Tennessee Anthropologist, 21*(2), 139–155.

Blessing

According to *The Strongest Strong's Exhaustive Concordance of the Bible* (2001), the word *bless* occurs 127 times in the King James Bible. *Blessing* occurs 67 times, *blessings* 12 times, and *blessed* 302 times. *Bless* is a verb denoting the act of consecration by a religious rite or word. It also means to invoke divine care. The noun *blessing* refers to a thing received from God or from other people that satisfies a need or makes one happy. *Blessed* (pronounced BLES-id) is an adjective describing great happiness as a result of the blessing.

Thus, because of the preponderance of Scriptures relating to blessedness, can we assume that the blessings are less important than their effect on the blessed?

No, but we can assume that a few blessings can result in a life full of happiness. Simply stated, God blesses with blessings, and people are blessed as a result. The greatest and most puzzling of the blessings can be found in the beatitudes recorded in Matthew 5:1–12. They are puzzling because the state of being blessed results in the blessing rather then the other way around, as in, "Blessed are the poor in spirit for theirs is the kingdom of heaven" (NIV).

In the Old Testament, for the most part, God was blessing His children. However, many references involve people either blessing God or blessing other people. For example, they sent people off with a blessing or a specific prayer for God's special favor (Genesis 24:60). For the children of Israel, it was good to begin with a blessing and end with a blessing, to pronounce blessing in coming and going (Genesis 31:55).

In the New Testament, the blessing involved people's resultant behavior and, in some cases, their specific behavior toward those who would seek to curse, persecute, or revile (Matthew 5:44; Luke 6:28; Romans 12:14; 1 Corinthians 4:12). People's behavior as a result of repentance, as well as of being filled with the Holy Spirit, is paramount in the New Testament. The emphasis appears to be on the quality of the relationship between people as well as with God.

Spirit-filled Christians use the term "bless God" (followed by bending the knee in homage or adoration) in worship. "God bless you" spoken to another person invites divine care on him or her. "You are a blessing" means what you have done on my behalf makes me content and happy.

Benny Hinn, a healing evangelist known worldwide for extraordinary manifestations of the Spirit in his services, says many scriptural references show God's willingness and earnest desire to bless His children—both in the natural realm and the spiritual (Psalms 112:1–2; Psalms 133:1–3; Proverbs 10:22; Isaiah 44:3).

Basis and Development

After creating all living creatures in the air, on the land, and in the waters on the fifth day of creation, God said it was good and He blessed it (Genesis 1:22). Then, after creating Adam and forming Eve from Adam's rib on the sixth day, God blessed them and told them to be fruitful and replenish the earth (Genesis 1:28; 5:1–2). For human beings, there was no blessing more fundamental than the ability to reproduce.

However, no blessing was given to the inanimate objects (day and night, heaven and earth, land and sea, plant life, sun, moon, stars, etc.) created in the first four

Matthew 5: 1–12 (King James Version)

[1]And seeing the multitudes, he went up into a mountain: and when he was set, his disciples came unto him:

[2]And he opened his mouth, and taught them, saying,

[3]Blessed are the poor in spirit: for theirs is the kingdom of heaven.

[4]Blessed are they that mourn: for they shall be comforted.

[5]Blessed are the meek: for they shall inherit the earth.

[6]Blessed are they which do hunger and thirst after righteousness: for they shall be filled.

[7]Blessed are the merciful: for they shall obtain mercy.

[8]Blessed are the pure in heart: for they shall see God.

[9]Blessed are the peacemakers: for they shall be called the children of God.

[10]Blessed are they which are persecuted for righteousness' sake: for theirs is the kingdom of heaven.

[11]Blessed are ye, when men shall revile you, and persecute you, and shall say all manner of evil against you falsely, for my sake.

[12]Rejoice, and be exceeding glad: for great is your reward in heaven: for so persecuted they the prophets which were before you.

days of creation. Some authorities say that when God blessed His creation, the emphasis was on the life-infusing power of the divine Word. Thus, God's blessing is His formative, empowering word, often with overtones of appointing destiny.

After the blessing on all living creatures, God rested on the seventh day, following all the work He had made (Genesis 2:2), and then He blessed the seventh day. Not only did God bless the seventh day, He emphasized its divinely designated purpose by sanctifying it, setting it apart for the service of God (Genesis 2:3; Exodus 20:11).

Many generations after Adam and Eve, one of the earliest precedents for blessing by mankind occurs in Genesis 27, when Isaac, thinking he was blessing his eldest son, Esau, blessed Jacob instead. Through deceit, Jacob obtained the birthright of the eldest son; and along with it came the blessing, since both the birthright and the blessing were part of the inheritance of the firstborn.

Numbers 6:22–27 records the priestly blessing God gave Moses along with instructions to give Aaron and his sons, saying, "This is how you are to bless the Israelites.... The Lord bless you and keep you; the Lord make his face shine upon you and be gracious to you; the Lord turn his face toward you and give you peace." Many pastors quote this blessing at the close of their services.

Just before His ascension into heaven, Christ led the disciples out to Bethany, where He lifted up His hands and blessed them. While He was blessing them, He was taken up into heaven (Luke 24:50).

The Apostle Paul bids farewell to the brethren at Corinth and pronounces a blessing upon them (2 Corinthians 13:14). This blessing invokes the grace of the Lord Jesus, the love of God, and the fellowship of the Holy Spirit. To the church at Philippi, Paul writes, "The grace of the Lord Jesus Christ be with your spirit. Amen" (Philippians 4:23). Paul also closes his second letter to the church at Thessalonica with a blessing: "Now may the Lord of peace himself give you peace at all times and in every way. The Lord be with all of you. The grace of our Lord Jesus Christ be with you all" (2 Thessalonians 3:16–17).

The unknown writer of the book of Hebrews closed his letter with a blessing closely resembling Paul's. In many of his blessings Paul used the word "peace" and "grace." Hebrews 13:20–21 and 25 shows that the blessing begins with "May the God of peace..." and closes with "grace be with you all."

Conditions for Receiving Blessings

The primary condition for receiving blessings from God is obedience (Exodus 19:5; Deuteronomy 11:26, l5:4, and 28:1–14; Job 36:11; Proverbs 3:1; John 10:27). Blessings do not have to be pursued; they are set in motion by obedience and will overtake those who meet God's conditions. "And it shall come to pass, if thou shalt hearken diligently unto the voice of the Lord thy God, to observe and do all his commandments...all these blessings shall come on thee, and overtake thee" (Deuteronomy 28:1–14, KJV).

According to one writer, John P. Milton, "The condition for experiencing and being a blessing in the sense of the covenant with Abraham is obedience" (1965, 97). Christ Himself became obedient to the will of God even until his death (Philippians 2:8).

Praise be to the God and Father of our Lord Jesus Christ, who has blessed us in the heavenly realms with every spiritual blessing in Christ.

Ephesians 1:3 (New International Version)

Other conditions for receiving God's blessings include: rebuking wickedness (Proverbs 24:25); keeping His ways (Psalms 84:5 and 12; Proverbs 8:32); being faithful (Proverbs 28:20); being unselfish (Proverbs 11:26); being compassionate (1 Peter 3:8–9); fearing but delighting in His commandments (Psalms 112:1); and paying tithes (Malachi 3:10).

Hinn writes, "When we live according to God's principles and meet the conditions outlined in the Word of God, God promises to pour out blessings to such a degree that we cannot contain them" (1997, 27). Milton also states, "We cannot take the promise of blessing as, in any sense whatsoever, a *word of God* and fail to see that the blessing must involve a sense of relationship to God as the giver, an acknowledgment of dependence on Him, an experience of fellowship with Him" (1965, 106).

Types of Blessings

Many scriptural references point to God's willingness and desire to bless His children in every area, in both the natural and the spiritual realm. The promise to Abraham and his seed in Genesis 12:1–3 has a temporal (material) aspect as well as a spiritual aspect. Both aspects can be traced in Genesis, chapters 12 through 50. In this connection, Milton writes, "It is unlikely that the Patriarchs separated sharply between the two; for to them religion was not something *apart from life*, but *a part of life*" (1965, 73). The intended result of God's blessing on Abraham is that Abraham should, in turn, himself be a blessing (Genesis 12:2). This blessing of Abraham is imparted to the Gentiles through Jesus Christ (Galatians 3:14).

Different types of blessings include: exaltation, health, reproductivness, prosperity, victory, and God's

favor. Deuteronomy 28 lists the following types of blessings: blessed no matter where you are (verse 3), children, crops, and animals (verse 4), food (verse 5), when traveling (verse 6), enemies will flee (verse 7), food and provisions (verse 8), and when working (verse 8).

Innumerable blessings come with the exercise of spiritual gifts recorded in I Corinthians 12:4–10. However, speaking in tongues, interpretation of tongues and divine healing are distinct characteristics of the Pentecostal-Charismatic community. The manifestation of the fruit of the Spirit (Galatians 5:22) particularly involves one's influence on and involvement with other people.

Special Blessings

Various religious groups place great emphasis on formal, ritualistic blessings; others shy away from such formality. However, the New Testament gives several examples of special ritualistic blessings that Spirit-filled Christians use. Among them are Holy Communion (Matthew 26:17–30; Mark 14:12–26; Luke 22:7–31), and water baptism by immersion based on the accounts of Christ's baptism by John the Baptist (Matthew 3:13–17; Mark 1:9–11; Luke 3:21–22, John 1:29–33) and the injunction by Christ Himself in Matthew 28:19. Often the difference between Pentecostal-Charismatics and other Christians is the method used, e.g., baptism by immersion rather than sprinkling.

However, Pentecostals, charismatics and other Christian communities share some standard blessings. Some may be spoken infrequently, however, such as new home dedications. Blessing a new baby is based upon the account in Mark 10:13–16, as well as the other Gospels, where Jesus took the children up in his arms, put his hands upon them, and blessed them. Elaborating on this, the authors Smalley and Trent write, "A family blessing begins with meaningful touching. It continues with a spoken message of high value, a message that pictures a special future for the individual being blessed, and one that is based on an active commitment to see the blessing come to pass" (1986, 24).

Blessings are spoken at meals, marriage ceremonies, new home dedications, and church dedications. Pastors often dismiss their congregations with a special blessing such as those Paul wrote to the various churches in Asia. Special blessings are primarily reserved for special occasions and commend the individual or event to God, recognizing that God is the source of all blessings.

When people "bless" God, it is an act of homage expressed in an act of praise. The Psalmist David blesses

God in Psalms 103:1 (KJV), beginning with "Bless the Lord, O my soul: and all that is within me, bless his holy name." When God blesses people, it represents an attitude of favor expressed actively in the bestowal of good gifts. The Apostle Paul prayed that the church at Ephesus would be "filled with all the fullness of God" (Ephesians 3:19). Solomon declared, "The blessing of the Lord, it maketh rich, and he addeth no sorrow with it" (Proverbs 10:22).

ELEANOR G. SYLER

See also Anoint, Anointing; Gifts of the Spirit; Praise

Further Reading

Basham, D. (1977). *Beyond blessing to obedience.* Fort Lauderdale, FL: CGM.

Hayford, J. W. (1994). *Power and blessings: Celebrating the disciplines of Spirit-filled living.* Wheaton, IL: Victor Books.

Hinn, B. (1997). *Biblical road to blessing.* Nashville, TN: Thomas Nelson.

Koenig, J. (1992). *Rediscovering New Testament prayer: Boldness and blessing in the name of Jesus.* San Francisco: Harper.

Milton, J. P. (1965). *God's covenant of blessing.* Madison, WI: Straus.

Prince, D. (1990). *Blessing or curse: You can choose.* Old Tappan, NJ: Chosen Books.

Smalley, G., & Trent, J. (1986). *The blessing.* Nashville, TN: Thomas Nelson.

Smalley, G., & Trent, J. (1993). *The gift of blessing.* Nashville, TN: Thomas Nelson.

Strong, J. (2001). *The strongest Strong's exhaustive concordance of the Bible.* Grand Rapids, MI: Zondervan.

Westermann, C. (1978). *Blessing in the Bible and the life of the church.* (K. Crim, Trans.). Philadelphia: Fortress Press.

White, E. G. (1958). *Love unlimited.* Mountain View, CA: Pacific Press Publishing Association.

Born Again

The term *born again* characterizes one of the more recent distinguishing traits of Christianity. It refers to a spiritual experience that effects a radical change in personality and character; a gift from God received by faith, resulting in joy, forgiveness of sins, and a new outlook on life. In the twentieth century, Jimmy Carter, president of the United States from 1977 to 1981 and a Southern Baptist, popularized it. In 2004, Barna Research Online stated that 38 percent of the adult population in the United States belongs to some Christian group that embraces the born-again experience. "Born again" pertains to adults, according to this survey, who have made a personal commitment to Christ as their savior, who say that he is important in their lives, and who believe they will experience eternal salvation because they have confessed their sins.

However, this concept has also become a point of contention in modern discussions among Pentecostal, Evangelical, and Roman Catholic Christians. With the increased interest in Spirit baptism in the twentieth century, a debate has emerged over the relationship between being baptized in the Spirit and the born-again experience and image, specifically over whether or not Spirit baptism describes the rebirth itself or whether the baptism follows the experience of being born again.

Old Testament Background

The image of being "born again" appears repeatedly in the Old Testament, taken from the natural relationship that existed between the father and mother in ancient Near East family life. Israel's writers used this imagery when describing the beginning of Israel as a nation.

Formation of the Nation of Israel

Birthing imagery is not only rooted in the ancient Near East, but is often used in the religious thought of ancient Israel. Deuteronomy 32 contains abundant imagery of God giving birth to Israel, appearing in a variety of ways in a lengthy song, the poetic form of which makes it a rich depository of metaphorical language. Scholars call this chapter "The Song of Moses," set just before Moses' death at the end of the Israelites' forty years of wandering in the wilderness before entering the Promised Land. According to Deuteronomy 31:19, Moses wrote down this song at the direction of God and led all the people in singing it. It contains instructions and warnings about the Israelites' unfaithfulness when they entered the land. In the song's warnings, Israel's existence and journey is likened to an infant who is born and raised carefully, and who then rejects its parents. Metaphorical language of salvation is used in terms of God as the Israelites' father, who caused them to be born.

Two verses in particular, Deuteronomy 32:6 and 18 focus on this image. Both verses appear in Hebrew parallel verse form, repeating and wrapping together in a metaphorical manner the various words to describe this image. Verse 6 (NRSV) appears like this:

Do you thus repay the LORD,

O foolish and senseless people?

Is not he your *father*,

who *created* you,

who *made* you

and *established* you? (emphasis added)

The image of *father* is expanded to include three activities—creating, making, and establishing—all related to the idea of coming into being. Though the specific verb *born* does not occur, the related concept of *father* suggests its presence is intended, assisting the interpreter to know how to understand the verbs that follow.

Verse 18 (NRSV) specifically expresses the idea of bringing Israel into existence in terms of being born:

You were unmindful of the *Rock* that *bore* you;

you forgot the *God* who *gave* you *birth* (emphasis added)

This verse also adds another metaphor, that of God as a rock This metaphor also appears in Deuteronomy 32:15, along with God as the "Savior" who "made" Israel, conveying both the idea of coming into being and achieving salvation. The word for *made* in verse 15 is the same word, both in Hebrew and Greek, as the one that appears in verse 18.

The Song of Moses, then, clearly establishes the image of being born, along with a number of related words, in describing Israel's beginning as salvation and creation.

New Exodus and the Future of Israel

Another place where birthing imagery appears is in the book of Isaiah, which covers the time from about 750 BCE to about 540 BCE. The language of creation and birthing occurs in particular in this prophetic book, because it is here that the prophet preaches God's judgment against those who have rejected Him. Both Israel and Judah (the nation divided under King Solomon in 933 BCE) together come under the judgment of God and His promises of salvation. The North, as Israel is called, was exiled in 721 BCE, while the South, or Judah, went into captivity in 586 BCE These catastrophic judgmental events were known as the Exile. When Isaiah preached concerning Judah in Babylon after 586, he spoke about God's promise of deliverance in terms of the first exodus of the nation from Egypt Since the model of salvation is based on the first exo-

dus, similar language is reused (see especially Isaiah 42:14 and 43:1–7, 15–21).

Isaiah, especially from chapters 40 through 53, speaks of creating a new people using similar language, imagery, and metaphors for the salvation of people who are under judgment and in need of forgiveness and deliverance. Quite a few terms or images refer to God's salvation of His people in these Old Testament contexts. Birth imagery and language, while expressing part of the larger concept of salvation, stands alone in some cases as a synonym for salvation.

Creative Breath in Ezekiel

The prophet Ezekiel, writing from around 593 BCE to 586 BCE or later, spoke to the Judeans, whom the Babylonians had deported. In visions, God shows Ezekiel (especially in chapters 8 through 11) the spiritual condition of His people. Because of their sinfulness, God will severely judge them, and then later save them. In Ezekiel 37, the hand of the Lord brings the prophet to a valley full of dry bones, where the Spirit breathes life into these bones. The language here echoes that of Genesis 2:7, the creation/salvation of the nation in the first exodus, and Isaiah's promise of creating Israel in the new exodus. Similarly in Ezekiel 47, when the plan of the new temple is finished, water gushes out from the altar, flowing eastward toward the Dead Sea, giving life to everything in its wake. Both chapters echo the arrival of salvation as birth from death by way of the Spirit's activity.

Concluding Observations

Birthing language is rooted in ancient Near Eastern metaphor, and Israelite prophets pick up the imagery and apply it to God's creation of the nation of Israel. Creation language then becomes a common image for salvation, both in the first exodus and in the next one.

New Testament Imagery

A wide range of images and metaphors for the concept of salvation appears in the New Testament. For instance, in 2 Corinthians 5:17 and Galatians 6:15, the Apostle Paul describes the person in Christ as a new creation. Similar usages appear in Ephesians 2:10 and 4:24. James 1:18 speaks of God as both having given birth to Christians and as having created them. Titus 3:5, while containing a different Greek word from the one for *born again*, conveys the same meaning, and adds the term *renewing*; as in John 3:5, Titus associates

John 3:1-3 (New International Version)

[1]Now there was a man of the Pharisees named Nicodemus, a member of the Jewish ruling council.
[2]He came to Jesus at night and said, "Rabbi, we know you are a teacher who has come from God. For no one could perform the miraculous signs you are doing if God were not with him."
[3]In reply Jesus declared, "I tell you the truth, no one can see the kingdom of God unless he is born again."

the rebirth image with *water* and *Spirit*. Other words in the New Testament, such as *regeneration* and *conversion*, convey the idea of a radical transformation in a person's nature from an old way of living to a new way.

The corporate perception of salvation, birthing, and creation also appears in the New Testament. Matthew in particular is clear that the new people of God are constituted in Jesus. Matthew 2:15 explains the exodus route of Jesus and His parents with reference to Hosea 11:1, in which *son* is used to refer to Israel; but in Matthew, Jesus is the son—the new Israel. The corporate concept is also implied in the Pauline description of the believer as "being in Christ," giving rise to the use of the metaphors of building and body to describe the corporate idea of many individuals being one.

Further, the prominence of the work of the Spirit in the new creation/exodus/birthing as demonstrated in the prophets receives full recognition in the New Testament. When John the Baptist preaches about a greater One who will baptize with the Spirit, he means Jesus will work through the Spirit. Thus, His kingdom will be spiritual. The work of the Spirit in salvation finds full expression in Paul's epistles and John's Gospel in particular.

The new exodus theme dominates many areas of the New Testament, such as in the words of John the Baptist and elsewhere in the Gospels and Acts. The book of Hebrews also is filled with exodus and wilderness language. All of these things are connected to the "born again" imagery.

John's Gospel and 1 Peter

The new exodus theme appears throughout the content and structure of the Gospel of John, not only with John the Baptist but also with the signs that so characterize the Gospel. Being born again, emphasized in this Gospel, is a major image used in describing salvation. The Greek version of the Old Testament at Deuteronomy 32:18 uses the same verb as the one in John 3:3, 5,

and 7. The work of the Spirit and Jesus' atonement serve as the form and substance of this theology and experience. "Born again" in the Greek actually occurs only twice: in John 3:3 and 7. Various translations use a variety of terms to translate the Greek, usually *born again, born anew,* or born *from above.* The verb in John 3:5 occurs with a different modifier, born "by water and Spirit," but it parallels the saying in verse 3.

Born again in English translation occurs also in 1 Peter 1:23, but the Greek word is different from the one in John 3:3, 5, and 7. First, it does not have an accompanying modifier such as *again.* Second, the verb stem is different, though both are from the same root. First Peter has the prefix that means *again,* like the English prefix *re-.* The Greek word at 1 Peter 1:23 also occurs in 1:3, where many translations have "has given us new birth."

Primitive and Medieval Church Eras

While theological development was dynamic and expansive in the era after the completion of the canon, and the imagery of being born again was swallowed up in this movement, a definite trend can be observed: With some frequency, John 3:3 and 3:5 were conflated during this time; verse 5, with "born of water and Spirit," was interpreted in combination with the "born again" of verse 3, either through citation or theological expression. Water, now identified with baptism, became the means by which the Spirit gives new birth. For Irenaeus (c. 120–200 CE) *water* became *sacred water,* and a bit earlier, Justin Martyr states that the process of "rebirth" involves believing in Christ, fasting and praying, entreating God for the remission of sins, and receiving remission of sins and regeneration through the baptismal water. In the fourth century, Gregory Nazianzen explicitly notes that water baptism purifies from sins, remits trespasses, and causes renovation and regeneration. Putting John 3:3 and 5 together, he further says that the Spirit alone is not sufficient, but that

Titus 3:3-7 (New International Version)

[3]At one time we too were foolish, disobedient, deceived and enslaved by all kinds of passions and pleasures. We lived in malice and envy, being hated and hating one another.

[4]But when the kindness and love of God our Savior appeared,

[5]he saved us, not because of righteous things we had done, but because of his mercy. He saved us through the washing of rebirth and renewal by the Holy Spirit,

[6]whom he poured out on us generously through Jesus Christ our Savior,

[7]so that, having been justified by his grace, we might become heirs having the hope of eternal life.

baptism is necessary. In this view, the body and the soul are two entities, the inward and outward; the body needs the external cleansing of water. Similarly, Augustine (354–430) believed that water baptism has efficacy to bring about life and salvation (connecting this with John 3:5 ff.). By the time of John of Damascus, in the eighth century, holy baptism equals birth by water and Spirit.

However, others from the fourth century forward focused more on the role of the Spirit. For instance, Basil the Great (c. 330–379) notes that the old life is cut at conversion and that this is only accomplished when one is born again; regeneration, the beginning of the second life, then begins. This comes through imitating the burial of Jesus through water baptism. Water baptism is a symbol signifying the putting off of the works of the flesh. Philoxenus, the Bishop of Mabbogh (440–523), believed that mere baptism was not enough for salvation, though he believed in its sacramental character of efficacy and grace. The person must live as one set on fire by the Holy Spirit. Being born again in this case is a process, in which one must go through a series of symbolic rebirths and baptisms.

This view of being born again helps to explain the emergence of infant baptism. Baptism of infants—receiving the Spirit and maturing—was like a seed sown at rebirth that then grew. The theology for this begins in the second and third centuries with the likes of Irenaeus, Origen, and Hippolytus. The Church eventually split in the ninth century over the use of icons, into the Roman Catholic (West) and the Greek Orthodox (East) churches. Both appeal to the same early Church Fathers for their traditions. Before and after the division, the Church practiced baptismal regeneration. The Greek Orthodox view is quite similar to that expressed by Philoxenus on the maturing process of children.

This period, then, can be summarized in this fashion: Left behind was the connection with the new exodus imagery that framed the New Testament idea of salvation and new birth. Creation is still part of this conceptualization, though in different ways—now more in respect to the old "man," "man of flesh," "inner man," the soul. "Born again" imagery is submerged and understood within larger theological systems, especially taking on a sacramental character. It is now understood more as a process.

The Reformation

Many forces were at work in the Reformation that began in 1517, all of which would have an impact through the centuries. One of these driving forces, Martin Luther, continued to embrace infant baptism and baptismal regeneration but reacted to doctrine of salvation by works that had emerged in the Catholic Church. Like his contemporary John Calvin, Luther placed the work of salvation totally in God's power. He spoke against the rationalism of Erasmus in the event of being born again and of the powerlessness of the flesh in the exercise of the will because of the sinful nature of all people. Luther, though, would not look upon the event as an experience. This would be a work, and works were preceded by *becoming* followed by *being,* through faith and grace. It later is articulated in this manner: In baptism, God gives abundant grace, called *new birth*, which removes the guilt of original sin, though original sin remains in nature itself.

The Anabaptist movement, which began around 1525, was more radical than Luther. The Anabaptists were called so because they did not believe in infant baptism or baptismal regeneration. All who had been baptized as infants had to be baptized again as adults.

Anabaptists taught that one must believe and repent to be born again. Baptism followed these.

The various theologies that developed in Church history around the imagery of being born again focused on several aspects: the source of rebirth (God, human effort, or a combination of the two); the means (water and Spirit in some related manner, or Spirit alone); and the sequence of events leading to salvation (faith, repentance, and baptism).

Modern Times to the Present

Two movements serve to illustrate the further development of this imagery into the present. On the one hand, Anabaptists believed, as they still do, that to be born again is the same as Spirit baptism. Acts 2 in this instance is connected with John 3:3 and given the same interpretation. On the other hand, John Wesley (1703–1791) is credited with beginning the other development: To be born again is the first experience and the subsequent one is to be Spirit baptized.

With the emergence of Pentecostalism at the beginning of the twentieth century, especially from experiences in Topeka, Kansas, and Azusa Street in Los Angeles, debate began anew over the sequence of events related to being born again. Evangelicals from various denominations believed that the born-again experience and Spirit baptism described the same event. But with the arrival of a new experience known as speaking in tongues, there emerged among Pentecostals language to describe Spirit baptism apart from being born again. Spirit baptism was an additional experience of the Spirit given particularly to witness for Christ with power.

J. D. G. Dunn argues forcefully that Acts 2, the major text for the Pentecostal experience, speaks of regeneration. Acts, then, addresses the fact that the people who were converted had not yet received the Spirit and were not real Christians. Dunn used and popularized the term *conversion-initiation* to describe what Evangelicals had believed all along. He argued, however, that Evangelicals did lack the power that came from being born again as described in Acts. Charismatics, many of whom are Evangelical (as are the Pentecostals), have received Spirit baptism and note its distinctive contributions, but do not necessarily believe it is as distinct as Pentecostals think.

Some Roman Catholics have participated in the charismatic renewal and, because of charismatics' association with Pentecostals and Evangelicals, have had to adjust to the "born again" terminology so prominent among Evangelical and Pentecostal believers. They have for centuries believed that salvation, including the work of the Spirit, was a process, and the specific term *born again* as an event had been lost in liturgy and practice if not in theology. They are attempting to come to grips with this popular terminology and to make room for it without changing substantially their theology and practice.

BENNY C. AKER

See also Baptism in the Holy Spirit; Baptism, Water; Sanctification

Further Reading

Canales, A. D. (2002). A rebirth of being "born again": Theological, sacramental and pastoral reflections from a Roman Catholic perspective. *Journal of Pentecostal Theology, 11*(1), 98–119.

Christensen, D. L. (2002). *Word biblical commentary: Vol. 6B. Deuteronomy 21:10–34:12.* Dallas, TX: Word, Inc.

Dunn, J. D. G. (1970). *Baptism in the Holy Spirit.* London: SCM.

Duggan, M. (1985). The cross and the Holy Spirit in Paul: Implications for baptism in the Holy Spirit. *Pneuma: The Journal of the Society for Pentecostal Studies, 7*(2), 135–146.

Fee, G. D. (1985). Baptism in the Holy Spirit: The issue of separability and subsequence. *Pneuma: The Journal of the Society for Pentecostal Studies, 7*(2), 87–99.

Hodges, M. L. (1972). A distinct experience. *Paraclete, 6*(2), 22–28.

Hocken, P. (1985). The meaning and purpose of baptism in the Holy Spirit. *Pneuma: The Journal of the Society for Pentecostal Studies, 7*(2), 125–133.

Lovelace, R. (1985). Baptism in the Holy Spirit and the Evangelical tradition. *Pneuma: The Journal of the Society for Pentecostal Studies, 7*(2), 101–123.

Menzies, R. P. (1991). *The development of early Christian pneumatology with special reference to Luke-Acts.* Sheffield, UK: JSOT Press.

Mergal, A. M. (Ed.). (1957). Evangelical Catholicism as represented by Juan de Valdés. In *The Library of Christian Classics* (Vol. 25). Philadelphia: Westminster Press.

Orchard, R. E. (1972). The Holy Spirit and resurrection. *Paraclete, 6*(2), 3–7.

Pauck, W. (Ed. & Trans.). (1961). Luther: Lectures on Romans. In *The Library of Christian Classics* (Vol. 15). Philadelphia: Westminster Press.

Pribble, S. (2004). Do you know the truth about being born again? Retrieved May 11, 2004, from http://www.reformed.com/pub/bornagai/htm

Robeck, C. M., Jr. (1985). Baptism in the Holy Spirit: Its purpose(s). *Pneuma: The Journal of the Society for Pentecostal Studies, 7*(2), 83–86.

Roberts, A., Donaldson, J., & Coxe, A. C. (Eds.). (1997). Fragments from the lost writings of Irenaeus. In *The Ante-Nicene Fathers: Vol. 1. The Apostolic Fathers with Justin Martyr and Irenaeus*. Oak Harbor, WA: Logos Research Systems.

Roberts, A., Donaldson, J., & Coxe, A. C. (Eds.). (1997). The first apology of Justin. In *The Ante-Nicene Fathers: Vol. 1. The Apostolic Fathers with Justin Martyr and Irenaeus*. Oak Harbor, WA: Logos Research Systems.

Rupp, E. G., & Marlow, A. N. (Trans.). (1969). Luther and Erasmus: Free will and salvation. *The Library of Christian Classics* (Vol. 17). Philadelphia: Westminster Press.

Schaff, P. (Ed.). (1997). *The Nicene and post-Nicene Fathers* (Vols. 4 & 12). Oak Harbor, WA: Logos Research Systems.

Schaff, P. (Ed.). (1997). *The Nicene and post-Nicene Fathers, second series* (Vols. 4, 5, 9, & 13). Oak Harbor, WA: Logos Research Systems.

Turner, M. (1996). *Power from on high: The Spirit in Israel's restoration and witness in Luke-Acts*. Sheffield, UK: Sheffield Academic Press.

Williams, G. H. (Ed.). (1957). Spiritual and Anabaptist writers: Documents illustrative of the radical Reformation. In *The Library of Christian Classics* (Vol. 25). Philadelphia, Westminster Press.

Brazil

Brazil is culturally and religiously unique. With a population of about 175 million, the country reports an estimated 20 million Pentecostals, Roman Catholic charismatics, and Neo-Pentecostals. Yet, while Brazilians account for half of all Latin Americans in these categories, Brazil remains the largest Roman Catholic country in the world, and the practitioners of the enormously popular Afro-Brazilian religions probably far exceed the number of Pentecostals and charismatics.

The distinctiveness of Brazilian Pentecostalism undoubtedly is to some extent a result of its cultural background. These groups usually have organizational structures that reflect the authoritarian styles found in Brazilian society and politics, and their norms of conduct have been attributed to prevailing cultural features. For example, Pentecostals, as a marginal group, have often taken to the streets carrying the Brazilian flag to demonstrate their legitimacy within the national system, and their prohibitions against some common practices (like rigid standards of modesty in women's dress) apparently have been an exaggerated attempt to emphasize clear lines of demarcation between themselves and the larger society.

Pentecostalism and Brazilian Spirituality

Although Brazilian Pentecostals repudiate the various forms of popular spiritualism—which hold that spirits of the dead communicate with the living through mediums—these religious movements provide a useful backdrop for understanding the affinity of Brazilians generally for the transcendental. For example, as many as 5 percent of all Brazilians are considered disciples of Alan Kardec, a French spiritualist whose ideas were introduced in the country in the nineteenth century. In addition to these "high spiritists" found among the middle classes, many Brazilians identify with a "low" or syncretic spiritism that has incorporated many Catholic and African elements. The wide diversity among them has resulted in some scholars' denying that a generic Afro-Brazilian religion exists. While some groups retain African terminology in their liturgies, the largest Brazilian spiritist movement, Umbanda, uses Portuguese to invoke spirits and has borrowed from Brazilian Catholicism, so that the spirits called on may be either African deities or Catholic saints. Although Catholic leaders have often denounced Umbanda, opposing it is difficult, because there is no Umbanda hierarchy and each Umbanda center is autonomous.

Pentecostalism was introduced into Brazil in 1909, fewer than four years after the movement came to prominence with the Azusa Street Revival in Los Angeles, by lay ministers only recently acquainted with the movement's doctrinal emphases. At that time Pentecostals had not organized denominationally, and generally, like the Holiness movement from which they were largely derived, they were averse to organizing along the lines of the established denominations. Accordingly, the Brazilian Pentecostals did not develop as extensions of North American religious institutions. The group that presently bears the name Assembleias de Deus was organized five years before the organization of its North American putative namesake, the General Council of the Assemblies of God, and originally called itself A Fe Apostolica (the Apostolic Faith).

From the beginning these churches were strongly influenced by European missionaries: The first two widely successful Brazilian Pentecostal groups were the Congregaçao Cristã (Christian Congregation) started by Italian evangelists who became acquainted with the Pentecostal movement in Chicago, and the Assembleius de Deus, founded by two Swedish immigrants to the United States, Einar Vingren and Daniel

Berg. Both the Swedish and the Italian missionaries left indelible marks on the Brazilian churches they founded, notably in their doctrinal emphases, their ecclesiastical polities, and their styles of worship. Yet also from the beginning, the initiative for evangelizing the country, founding new churches, and organizing and sustaining congregations was undertaken by Brazilians themselves. Already by the 1940s there was a Brazilian Pentecostal community of 100,000.

While Pentecostalism was taking root institutionally, with churches in place across the country by World War II, Brazil was undergoing rapid change that appears to have accelerated the movement's spread. Nationalism intensified during the war years and during the regime of Getulio Vargas (1930–1945 and 1950–1954), which gave impetus to economic development and popular political organization. U.S. assistance in exploiting the nation's extensive iron reserves and the construction of automobile assembly plants in the 1950s gave promise of significant economic development. The rise of the industrial South Central region, job opportunities in the coffee zone in Paraná State, and burgeoning cities offering employment in construction brought massive demographic changes. Meanwhile, traditional rural life was revolutionized by the rise of corporate farming and the opening of new markets for Brazilian agricultural products. With the breakdown of traditional rural labor and land-use patterns, many peasants (caboclos) left the drought-plagued land to find work in the cities of the northern states. When there was no work in the northern cities, many migrants joined the stream of men and families seeking work in metropolitan areas to the south.

While the growth of Pentecostal groups is not merely a function of instability in a society, the social disintegration accompanying a rapidly modernizing economy like Brazil's contributes to the appeal of Pentecostalism. The Brazilian Evangelical churches, in large part made up of Pentecostal congregations, have often functioned as surrogate families for men and women separated from their extended families and communities, providing social, emotional, and spiritual support. The churches warmly welcome newcomers and, with their human and material resources, are in a position to help stabilize the lives of the individuals otherwise left to struggle on their own.

Leading Pentecostal Denominations

Although the two original Pentecostal groups have continued to play important roles—the Assembleias de Deus is listed in religious censuses as having more than

10 million adherents—the rapid growth of several Neo-Pentecostal organizations has dominated most recent considerations of Brazilian Pentecostalism. The Igreja Evangelica Pentecostal Brazil para Cristo (Pentecostal Evangelical Church Brazil for Christ) was founded in 1955 by Manoel de Melo, a charismatic leader who emphasized social programs and was involved in politics; other groups followed. Brazil para Cristo is believed to have about 5,000 congregations, with 2 million adherents and 1 million formal members. Even larger is the Igreja Pentecostal Deus e Amor (God is Love Pentecostal Church), with 3,200 congregations, many of them large and urban, and a combined total of 3 million adherents. The largest of the Neo-Pentecostal churches is the Igreja Universal do Reino de Deus (Universal Church of the Kingdom of God), founded by Bishop Edir Macedo and claiming an estimated 10,000 congregations, 2 million adult members, and 4 million adherents.

While each of these organizations exhibits its own approach, a feature common to all of them is that they have attracted business and professional people on a greater scale than the traditional Pentecostals. They are more clearly urban and progressive than the classical Pentecostals, whose traditional values have made them appear rigid and legalistic and outside the more progressive streams of Brazilian life. These groups generally (and the Universal Church of the Kingdom of God in particular), have involved themselves in business ventures and in civic affairs, and they have gained a national presence through effective use of television and radio in some of the largest Brazilian communications markets.

Pentecostalism's Appeal

Why do Brazilians, the vast majority of whom were baptized as Catholics, opt for the Evangelical faith, especially in its Pentecostal form? Sociologist Cecilia Mariz's comparisons of progressive Catholic congregations, spiritists, and Pentecostals found that Pentecostalism had a less secular orientation than the groups, called Base Ecumenical Communities or CEBs (from the Portuguese), organized by progressive priests in Catholic parishes in the 1980s. The CEBs represented a sharp break with folk religions, because they attempted through a process of raising awareness to redefine the relationship between religion and culture. Pentecostals, on the other hand, have been able to identify more closely with traditional popular thinking by reinforcing many popular assumptions about the supernatural.

From the other direction, Pentecostals also offer a plausible alternative to the widespread Afro-Brazilian movements. John Burdick has found that some individuals originally associated with spiritism became disenchanted with the costly therapy sometimes offered as a remedy for their problems. The Pentecostal church, according to Burdick, is attractive for its faith healing and what he calls the church's "cult of affliction."

> The bond of suffering among petitioners permits a temporary suspension of social roles and status, forging an arena unencumbered by social sensitivity. [One] pastor explained that people brought their problems to him because he was separated from the world where their problems come up. "In the Catholic Church you are not leaving society. This is a refuge." Since the Pentecostal pastor explained domestic discord as the work of the devil, people are freed from a sense of personal responsibility for their problems. (Burdick 1993, 101, 102)

Catholic Charismatics

The Catholic charismatics emerged in the 1970s, an era dominated by liberation theology, a progressive movement in the Catholic Church that called for greater social action based on a correct reading of the Bible and Christian theology. Accordingly, much of the energy for reform among Catholics was directed toward social activism rather than to the inward-looking spirituality of the Charismatic movement. Nevertheless, charismatic cells were established in many parishes, and they continued after the decline of liberation theology, which was opposed in its most insistent forms by Pope John Paul II.

Neither of these somewhat opposed Catholic groups, however, had as much success in Brazil as Pentecostalism. Some observers believe this is because, unlike Protestant Pentecostalism, the Catholic Charismatic and liberation theology movements were to some degree formed from the top down, under the aegis of high-ranking church leaders, rather than being Brazilian grassroots initiatives as Pentecostalism was.

Pentecostals in Civic Life

One indication of the Pentecostals' impact on Brazilian national life has been their entry into politics. In 2004, of the six hundred members of the National Congress, sixty-one (fifty eight deputies and three senators) are evangelicals. Although Pentecostals in the past were underrepresented among the evangelicals, the increasing involvement of Pentecostals and Neo-Pentecostals in public life has been credited with recent rapid gains in representation. Socially conservative, the Pentecostal voting bloc in Brazil resembles the religious right in the United States on issues like abortion, gay marriage, and legalization of drugs. In 2003 Brazilian evangelical lawmakers helped obstruct a proposal to clone human embryos to harvest stem cells for research.

On issues of both domestic spending and foreign policy, however, the Brazilian Pentecostals appear to borrow planks from the liberal platform: They support public health measures, public education, and a higher minimum wage. Far from hawkish, Pentecostals are staunchly opposed to the U.S. engagement in Iraq. However, Brazil's Evangelical contingent in the legislature frequently fails to stand together. The members span the political spectrum and often oppose one another on specific issues. Pentecostal pastors often encourage their parishioners to vote and recommend specific candidates and issues, strategize for campaigns, and support some candidates who have added titles like "Bishop" or "Pastor" to their official ballot designations. Brazil's current president, Luiz Inacio Lula, courted Evangelical leaders in his successful 2002 campaign and had to overcome the opposition of an avowedly Evangelical opponent in order to win the runoff election. Presently, an estimated 27 million Brazilians—15 percent of the nation—are considered Evangelicals, and as many as two-thirds of them are Pentecostals or charismatics.

The pervasiveness of Pentecostalism in Brazil gives it a significant presence in national life. Moreover, for world Pentecostalism, Brazil has become one of its largest and most structured movements. The performance of these groups may well indicate the future course of Pentecostalism—whether it finds an ongoing, constructive role in revitalizing the social and spiritual life of nations where it has taken root, or whether it will be found inadequate to meet the demands of complex societies facing enormous social challenges.

EVERETT A. WILSON

See also America, Latin; Catholic Charismatic Movement

Further Reading

Boudewijnse, B., Droogers, A., & Kamsteeg, F. (Eds.). (1998). *More than opium: An anthropological approach to Latin*

American and Caribbean Pentecostal praxis. Lanham, MD: Scarecrow Press.

Burdick, J. (1993). *Looking for God in Brazil: The progressive Catholic Church in urban Brazil's religious arena*. Berkeley: University of California Press.

Chestnut, R. A. (1997). *Born again in Brazil: The Pentecostal boom and the pathogens of poverty*. New Brunswick, NJ: Rutgers University Press.

Chu, H. (2004, June 7). Moved by the spirit to govern. *The Los Angeles Times*, pp. A1, A5.

Ireland, R. (1991). *Kingdoms come: Religion and politics in Brazil*. Pittsburgh, PA: University of Pittsburgh Press.

Mariz, C. (1994). *Coping with poverty: Pentecostals and Christian base communities in Brazil*. Philadelphia: Temple University Press.

C

Capitalism

Capitalism is a system of economic relations in which private individuals or corporations own and operate the means of production of goods that are then sold in a free market. Workers in this system make a living by exchanging labor for wages. Business owners make a living by trying to sell their goods for more than they cost to produce. To maximize profits, businesses seek cheap resources and inexpensive labor.

The rise of modern capitalism is associated with the eighteenth- and nineteenth-century industrial revolutions in Western Europe and the United States, which introduced large-scale machine-driven manufacturing. By the end of the twentieth century, the focus of the free-market economies had shifted to service and information technology. In response to the appalling working conditions of nineteenth-century industrial capitalism, socialist or state-controlled economies were brought to power by force in the twentieth century in the Union of Soviet Socialist Republics (USSR) and countries aligned with it. With the dismantling of the USSR in 1991 and the introduction of democratic reforms in the Soviet bloc countries, capitalism emerged as the dominant global economic system.

The Protestant Work Ethic

From the sixteenth century, the development of capitalism was compatible with the rise of Protestantism and its call to morality, hard work, efficiency, and stewardship—an attitude identified by the German so-ciologist and economist Max Weber as the "Protestant work ethic." In his now-classic *The Protestant Ethic and the Spirit of Capitalism,* first published in 1904, Weber explained the rise of capitalism in various European nations as the result of a religiously inspired willingness to shift from agrarian to industrial economies. Whereas the tradition among common people in Europe had been to work just hard enough to satisfy their daily needs, Protestantism admonished believers to demonstrate their election to the company of the saved through hard work, frugality, responsible management of goods, and the subsequent accumulation of wealth. Protestantism, the "religion of the heart," gave individuals faith in their ability to undertake ventures that might previously have seemed impossible. And, forbidden to engage in excessive consumption, successful Protestants invested their profits in further wealth-generating ventures.

The nineteenth-century political philosopher Karl Marx built his theory of socialism around the notion that material conditions, not ideas, drive social change (and will ultimately be the undoing of capitalism), but Weber and others since have argued effectively that Protestant theology and early capitalist economics were mutually reinforcing developments.

The Pentecostal variant of Protestantism developed in the United States in the early twentieth century. It has roots in the Methodist Holiness movement of the nineteenth century, and is characterized by the revivalist tradition, a belief in divine healing, and premillennialist anticipation of the imminent return of Christ. In North American Pentecostalism, working-class congregants embraced the Holiness ascetic practice of denying the physical self, while embracing the tenets of labor: discipline, efficiency, and cleanliness.

Global Expansion

For most people living in developing nations in the twenty-first century, the globalization of capitalism has not improved their lives, and in many cases their condition has worsened. Growing proportions of national budgets are being allocated for debt repayment, forcing diminishing support for social welfare programs such as education, health care, and housing. Ties to traditional local practices are weakened by the promise of financial gain and social mobility. In the southern hemisphere, government-approved manufacturing zones welcome businesses seeking inexpensive labor and resources and minimal government regulation. Workers forced out of their rural agrarian communities migrate to cities, flooding the urban labor market and driving wages down and unemployment up.

These transformations in developing nations have been accompanied by an extraordinary growth of Pentecostalism. Pentecostalism eases the shift from rural to urban life, acknowledging spiritual beliefs associated with rural traditions and offering the emotional release of glossolalia. It addresses the spiritual needs of the working class by teaching the traditional Protestant values of obedience, honesty, hard work, thrift, self-denial, and sobriety. And the apolitical attitude of most Pentecostals has made them valued laborers and loyal citizens. Thus, Pentecostalism can serve to defuse radical critiques of society, promoting instead acceptance and conformity.

Capitalism and Poverty

The early twentieth-century rise of Pentecostalism among the lower class in the United States is being replicated in South America. Pentecostal writer Grant Wacker's (1995) identification of primitivism (a return to the most basic aspects of life) and pragmatism (awareness of the realities of existence) as fundamental components of Pentecostalism helps to explain its exponential growth among those excluded from the benefits of capitalist expansion into developing nations.

People who are destitute can justify their situation by arguing that worldly goods are of no value, or they can devise a means for acquiring those goods. Over time, Pentecostals have done both. Early Pentecostals coming from the impoverished and working classes understood their spare existence to be evidence of a life committed to Bible-based holiness, whereas contemporary Pentecostals are inspired by the message of faith-based accumulation of wealth. Such teachings are well suited to a Western capitalist ideological framework, making material goods evidence of God's blessing.

Pentecostalism's clear ethical injunction against participating in the "sins of worldliness" prepares indigenous people for their roles in highly bureaucratized, impersonal, and homogeneous market structures. Its emphasis on a personal relationship with God through Christ and its strict enforcement of individual behavioral norms enables the impoverished to cope with and even accept their straitened circumstances. When faith-based prosperity is preached by Pentecostal ministers, financial need becomes evidence of a lack of faith in God.

As a global phenomenon addressing sin and salvation, sickness and healing, and economic marginalization, Pentecostalism finds a ready niche in developing nations where global capitalism operates as an extra-local authority, leaving no obvious person or entity individuals can hold accountable for how their lives are organized. Moneyed control of production in these areas is complete, leaving only family, religion, and education to be managed locally; and growing inequality and economic dislocation increase people's reliance on religion to explain structural social problems. Finally, the threat of terrorism, nuclear instability, and other global dangers all boost people's inclination to adopt an apocalyptic view of the future.

As capitalism advances, rates of absolute poverty in developing nations have grown, in some cases to levels exceeding 50 percent. But while the working poor are a key constituency of Pentecostalism, only a small percentage actually become Pentecostal. What distinguishes those who convert? Chance is one factor: Many people experience a personal crisis at one time or another, but few meet a Pentecostal who can introduce them to the faith during this key period. Most people who convert bring a background of embracing the supernatural. For these, Pentecostalism offers a prophetic explanation of problems both personal and global.

Religion and Economy

Explanatory theories abound regarding the correlation between the growth of both capitalism and Pentecostalism in developing nations. Popular, but disregarded by serious thinkers, are conspiratorial claims of direct cooperation between multinational

Extract from Max Weber's
The Protestant Ethic and the Spirit of Capitalism

We may hence quote here a passage from John Wesley himself which might well serve as a motto for everything which has been said above. For it shows that the leaders of these ascetic movements understood the seemingly paradoxical relationships which we have here analysed perfectly well, and in the same sense that we have given them. He wrote:

"I fear, wherever riches have increased, the essence of religion has decreased in the same proportion. Therefore I do not see how it is possible, in the nature of things, for any revival of true religion to continue long. For religion must necessarily produce both industry and frugality, and these cannot but produce riches. But as riches increase, so will pride, anger, and love of the world in all its branches. How then is it possible that Methodism, that is, a religion of the heart, though it flourishes now as a green bay tree, should continue in this state? For the Methodists in every place grow diligent and frugal; consequently they increase in goods. Hence they proportionately increase in pride, in anger, in the desire of the flesh, the desire of the eyes, and the pride of life. So, although the form of religion remains, the spirit is swiftly vanishing away. Is there no way to prevent this-this continual decay of pure religion? We ought not to prevent people from being diligent and frugal; we must exhort all Christians to gain all they can, and to save all they can; that is, in effect, to grow rich."

Source: Weber, M. (1930). *The Protestant ethic and the spirit of capitalism* (Chap. 5). Boston: Unwin Hyman.

corporations and missionaries in working to modernize locals by divesting them of their traditions distancing them from the social activism of liberation theology. A related theory identifies Pentecostal leaders as the actual entrepreneurs riding the capitalist wave of expansion. Lending plausibility to these theories is the success of Christian satellite television networks. Global satellite systems link believers and nonbelievers alike with twenty-four-hour, seven-days-a-week Christian programming. Relying on generous donations from viewers, these not-for-profit networks erase the line between content and advertising.

The most widely accepted theory compares the impact of Methodist Holiness on the U.S. industrial revolution with that of Pentecostalism on the global industrial wave. However, some have noted that the global transformation from agriculture to manufacturing is happening much faster, is directed by multinational corporations, and because of high technology does not require the same personal values transmitted to laborers by Puritan asceticism and Methodist Holiness. Pentecostal tolerance of the local beliefs and practices of indigenous peoples builds an affinity supporting a rapid transition from traditional to Christian attitudes, among them the Protestant ethic of industriousness. Meanwhile, the asceticism of the Puritans, no longer regarded as necessary in a prosperous consumer economy, has been replaced by charismatic emotional expression that serves to counterbalance a highly rationalized society.

There is little evidence of significant economic gains by Pentecostals in developing nations. Instead, as with other fundamentalist movements, Pentecostalism offers hope for survival to those uprooted and dehumanized by industrial capitalism. Some observers credit Pentecostalism with dissuading the poor from revolting against the conditions brought about by global capitalism, making them instead willing participants in the creation of wealth in which they have so far not shared. In Pentecostalism, the economically oppressed find fellowship and hope for a better future despite the losses of the present.

The ardent spirituality affirmed and promoted by Pentecostalism and its strict code of moral conduct offers values missing in capitalism and its singular focus on commercial matters. The faith functions as a Christian spiritual haven from the ravages of capitalism, while preserving an emotional connection with some of the spirit of traditional religious practices;

this explains the exponential growth of Pentecostalism among those most negatively affected by global marketplace capitalism.

Late Capitalism

The Pentecostal movement began in the United States partly in reaction to the rise of science and political liberalism, both of which seemed to threaten traditional values. Pentecostals and other Fundamentalist Christians therefore sought to reinforce or reclaim their control over the primary agents of socialization: family, church, and school.

In the twenty-first century the Pentecostal-Charismatic movement brings its traditional, socially conservative message to developing nations experiencing the extraordinary impoverishment accompanying the shift from agricultural to manufacturing. The Protestant work ethic it teaches creates an industrious but quiescent labor force, while the increasing strength of community of Pentecostal congregations counters the human suffering engendered by economic change; charismatic worship allows emotional release from the oppression of poverty in daily life. To deal with the loss of traditional society and persistent poverty, Pentecostalism offers an identity, a purpose, and hope for the future. With its belief in a living God present in the world in the form of the Holy Spirit performing miracles of healing and rescue from the violence of global capitalism, Pentecostalism restores community life lost with the demise of traditional societies.

ELAINE R. CLEETON

See also Prosperity Theology; Rich and Riches

Further Reading

Anderson, R. M. (1979). *Vision of the disinherited: The making of American Pentecostalism*. New York: Oxford University Press.

Brouwer, S., Gifford, P., & Rose, S. (1996). *Exporting the American gospel: Global Christian fundamentalism*. New York: Routledge.

Cox, H. (1995). *Fire from heaven: The rise of Pentecostal spirituality and the reshaping of religion in the twenty-first century*. Reading, MA: Addison-Wesley.

Fukuyama, F. (1996). *Trust: The social virtues and the creation of prosperity*. New York: The Free Press.

Horn, J. (1989). *From rags to riches: An analysis of the faith movement and its relation to the classical Pentecostal movement*. Pretoria: University of South Africa.

Martin, D. (2002). *Pentecostalism: The world their parish*. Malden, MA: Blackwell.

Maxwell, D. (1999). Historicizing Christian independency: The southern African Pentecostal movement c. 1908–60. *The Journal of African History, 40*, 243–276.

Poloma, M. M. (1989). *The Assemblies of God at the crossroads: Charisma and institutional dilemmas*. Knoxville: University of Tennessee Press.

Robertons, R. (1992). *Globalization: Social theory and global culture*. London: Sage.

Smith, D. (1999). *Writing the social*. Toronto, Canada: University of Toronto Press.

Wacker, G. (1995). Searching for Eden with a satellite dish. In R. T. Hughes (Ed.), *The primitive church in the modern world* (pp. 139–166). Urbana: University of Illinois Press.

Wacker, G. (2001). *Heaven below: Early Pentecostals and American culture*. Cambridge, MA: Harvard University Press.

Weber, M. (1976). *The Protestant ethic and the spirit of capitalism*. New York: Charles Scribner's Sons.

Catholic Charismatic Movement

Since 1967 the Catholic Charismatic Renewal has changed the lives of millions of Catholics all over the world. It has been accepted and encouraged by the church authorities, and is today seen as one of the most effective instruments for evangelization and mission. As such it will play an increasingly important part in the development of the Catholic Church in the years ahead.

Preparation

In 1962 Pope John XXIII launched the Catholic Church into the Second Vatican Council with a prayer that began with these words: "Divine Spirit, renew your wonders in this our age, as in a new Pentecost." The aim of the Council was to review every part of the life of the Catholic Church, and to make it better able to present the Gospel to the world of the twentieth and subsequent centuries; for this to happen, Pope John knew there would have to be a great outpouring of the Holy Spirit. His prayer was answered, and there was a profound sense of the presence of the Holy Spirit throughout the deliberations of the Cardinals and Bishops assembled in Rome. At the opening of the Council there was an emphasis on the renewing power of the Holy Spirit, and this theme is repeated throughout the documents of Vatican II, never more so than when the question of the charisms, or gifts of the Holy

Spirit, are discussed. Taking the view that the charisms were the prerogative of every Christian by virtue of their baptism, the Council included the following in the written Constitution on the Church, *Lumen Gentium*:

> It is not only through the sacraments and the ministrations of the Church that the Holy Spirit makes holy the People and enriches them with his virtues. Allotting his gifts according as he wills (1 Corinthians 12:11), he also distributes special graces among the faithful of every rank. By these gifts he makes them fit and ready to undertake various tasks and offices for the renewal and building up of the Church, as it is written, "the manifestation of the Spirit is given to everyone for profit" (1 Corinthians 12:7). Whether these charisms be very remarkable or the more simple and widely diffused, they are to be received with thanksgiving and consolation, since they are fitting and useful for the needs of the Church. (Flannery 1975, paragraph 12)

This paragraph showed an openness among the Catholic hierarchy to manifestations of the supernatural power of the Spirit among ordinary lay men and women, and it prepared the ground for what was to happen at the "Duquesne Weekend" a few years later. This recognition of the important role of the laity in the life of the Church was an important theme of the Second Vatican Council, as was the recognition of Christians of other denominations as brothers and sisters in Christ, in whom the Spirit was at work. All these things were preparation for what was about to happen.

Beginnings

At a spiritual retreat in February 1967 a group of Catholic college students at Duquesne University in Pittsburgh, Pennsylvania, were baptized in the Holy Spirit, thereby beginning the Catholic Charismatic Renewal. This Renewal can today be found in 235 countries. However, while the "Duquesne Weekend," as it became known, is generally regarded as the beginning, it was not an isolated event—the Spirit was already at work in individual men and women. The weekend was planned by a small group, which included two professors of theology at Duquesne University, under the title "The Acts of the Apostles: or how to become Christians." Both men had recently read *The Cross and the Switchblade* by David Wilkerson and *They speak with Other Tongues* by John Sherrill, and as preparation for the weekend they asked their students to read the Wilkerson book as well as the early chapters of the Book of Acts.

Both men had also recently attended a Protestant charismatic prayer meeting at Chapel Hill in Pittsburgh, and through a remarkable Presbyterian woman, Flo Dodge, had received the baptism in the Holy Spirit. It was this experience that they brought to the Duquesne Weekend, and while Flo Dodge and her companions fasted and prayed for the Lord to move in power, many of the twenty-five students attending were baptized in the Holy Spirit, experiencing the gift of tongues and other supernatural manifestations of the Spirit's presence. The New Pentecost for which Pope John XXIII had prayed had arrived among ordinary Catholic men and women.

Spread

The Catholic Charismatic Renewal (CCR) spread rapidly through campuses in the United States and from there into the wider Catholic Church, and press reports began to appear in national Catholic publications in the United States in April and May of 1967. No grassroots movement had ever traveled as fast or as far as this one. In the beginning the CCR spread through existing links among students, parishes, and friends, resulting in a widespread network of local prayer groups and charismatic communities. Soon there were large conferences and renewal gatherings, which gave the CCR a sense of unity and purpose, as well as bringing it greater prominence in the life of the Church. According to the *World Christian Encyclopedia*, by 1969 charismatic prayer groups had begun in 13 countries, by 1970 in 25, by 1975 in 93, and by 2000 in 235 countries. By the year 2000 almost 120 million Catholics had opened their lives to this outpouring of the Holy Spirit. A breakdown by region finds 8,711,000 in Africa, 16,422,000 in Asia, 11,021,000 in Europe, 73,604,000 in Latin America, 9,742,000 in North America, and in Oceania 350,000. To these 120 million living charismatics must be added the 20 million who have died since 1967, bringing the total number of Catholics who have been baptized in the Holy Spirit to 140 million.

Nature

Under the word "renewal," the *Oxford English Dictionary* gives this definition: "Among charismatic Christians, the state or process of being renewed in the Holy Spirit." It is a process that usually begins with an event in which God touches the life of an individual by the power of His Holy Spirit and changes him or her. In Catholic understanding, there are no special, superior people called "charismatics," but there are millions of ordinary men and women whose lives have been renewed "charismatically"—in other words, by an action of the Holy Spirit. Through the grace of renewal, a subnormal or "inherited" Christianity is changed into a full and active life of faith lived in the power of the Holy Spirit. This experience is called "baptism in the Holy Spirit" by Catholics in most English-speaking countries and elsewhere. It is also called "the release of the Holy Spirit" or "the out-pouring (effusion) of the Holy Spirit."

The CCR has remained unlike any other movement in the Catholic Church, for there is no inspired human founder and there are no universal programs of initiation or formation. It is simply, powerfully, and uniquely a sovereign work of God through His Holy Spirit. In the words of Cardinal Leon-Josef Suenens:

> We should not see in this renewal just one more movement to be set alongside many others in the church today. Rather than a movement, charismatic renewal is a moving of the holy spirit which can reach all Christians, lay or cleric. It is comparable to a high voltage current of grace which is coursing through the church. (Suenens 1977, chapter VI)

Aims

An early document of the International Council of the CCR stated that the aims of the Catholic Charismatic Renewal were the same as the objectives of the Church—that is, the conversion, salvation, and sanctification of every human being. Its distinctive characteristic was the understanding that the role of the Holy Spirit in this work had not changed since the day of Pentecost, so that that every Christian could experience His presence and His outpouring of power and gifts in the same way they were experienced by the first Christians. The proof of the authenticity of all this depends primarily on a study of its effects on people's lives, for the aim is not to provide religious experiences but to help people to live renewed and effective Christian lives, and to serve the mission of the Church. While emphasizing the essential role of the Holy Spirit, the CCR remains Trinitarian. It also emphasizes the relationship with God the Father and is Christ-centered, clearly proclaiming Jesus as Savior and Lord of all, and teaching that to know Him is the only path to true peace and fulfillment.

Forms and Structures

The most common expressions are prayer meetings, covenant communities, mission teams, discipleship schools, and communities or groups with a special ministry or service to offer to the wider church. In the Preamble to the first Statutes of the International Council, the CCR was described in these words:

> It is a highly diverse collection of individuals, groups, ministries and activities, often quite independent of one another, in different stages and modes of development, and with differing emphases. One of the characteristics is the enormous variety of expressions and ministries, all inspired by the Holy Spirit and carried out in his power, which have found a home under its umbrella. Whilst majoring on relationships and networks rather than on structures, those involved all share the same fundamental experience of the empowering presence of the Holy Spirit. These patterns of informal relationships are to be found at local, diocesan, national, and international levels. They are very often characterized by free association, dialogue, and co-operation, rather than by formal structures either locally or nationally.

The CCR does not see itself as existing to build up a big organization, but to encourage others into a renewed spiritual life. Some structure has been found necessary to facilitate the working of the Spirit, so there are local, national, regional, and international teams of leaders formed into service committees to help advise, offer leadership training, and organize conferences and other gatherings of participants. These service committees are usually recognized either formally or informally by the diocesan bishop or by national bishops' conferences. At the international level, the Vatican officially recognized the International Catholic Charismatic Renewal Council in 1993 as a body for the promotion of the CCR throughout the world; in 1990 it had granted similar recognition to the Catholic Fraternity of Charismatic Covenant Communities. All these structures exist solely to facilitate the work of the Holy Spirit and not to exercise authority over the CCR or to build their own kingdoms. Authority remains in the hands of the bishops.

Attitude of the Hierarchy

From the early days, in spite of the hostility of some local clergy and laity, the Catholic hierarchy have looked upon the CCR as a positive development in the life of the Church. In 1975 Pope Paul VI famously referred to it as "a chance for the Church and for the world" (*Then Peter stood up. . .* 2000, 18). Pope John Paul II regularly commended the ministry of the CCR and held regular meetings with its national and international leaders. On 14 March 1992, at a meeting to mark the twenty-fifth anniversary of the CCR he said this: "I willingly join you in giving praise to God for the many fruits which the CCR has borne in the life of the Church. The emergence of the Renewal following the Second Vatican Council was a particular gift of the Holy Spirit to the Church" (*Then Peter stood up. . .* 2000, 55).

On October 30, 1998, Pope John Paul II addressed the Ninth International Leaders' Conference, and included these words:

> The Catholic Charismatic Renewal has helped many Christians to rediscover the presence and power of the Holy Spirit in their lives, in the life of the Church and in the world; and this rediscovery has awakened in them a faith in Christ filled with joy, a great love of the Church, and a generous dedication to her evangelizing mission. (*Then Peter stood up. . .* 2000, 71)

On the eve of Pentecost in 1998 outside St. Peter's in Rome, Pope John Paul reminded the whole Church:

> The institutional and charismatic aspects are co-essential as it were to the Church's constitution. They contribute, although differently, to the life, renewal and sanctification of God's people. It is from this providential rediscovery of the Church's charismatic dimension that, before and after the Council, a remarkable pattern of growth has been established for ecclesial movements and new communities. (*Then Peter stood up. . .* 2000, 91)

Ecumenical Inspirations

The Catholic Charismatic Renewal owes much to the inspiration, example, and encouragement of Christians in many Protestant and Pentecostal churches who had already experienced the same grace in their own lives. While the context and the working out may differ for Catholics, the grace is the same, and the introduction of the baptism in the Holy Spirit took place in many countries with the welcome participation of Christian men and women from other traditions. But it was to be expected that the Charismatic Renewal would also find its own place and identity in the life of the Catholic Church, bringing with it the call to seek a continuing outpouring of the Holy Spirit and a radical personal conversion to Jesus Christ. This in no way diminishes the close relationships, fellowship, and cooperation that exist with mainline Pentecostal denominations within Protestantism, with Anglican and Orthodox

charismatics, and with many of the 260 million independent neocharismatics worldwide. Catholics and Protestants who are baptized in the Spirit hold many things in common in their expressions of faith and their practice of the charisms.

Catholic Characteristics

Catholic charismatics see a definite continuity in the work of the Spirit since the day of Pentecost. Kilian McDonnell and George Montague, two theological researchers, have revealed that early Christian writers understood baptism in the Holy Spirit and the impartation of charisms as an integral part of Christian initiation. They therefore claim that they belong to public liturgy, not just to private piety. For Catholic charismatics, accepting baptism in the Spirit does not mean joining a movement—it means embracing the fullness of Christian initiation. In this initiation through baptism and confirmation, the gift of the Holy Spirit is received, but the effects can only be limited unless there is also the conscious and deliberate cooperation of the individual. Many church members have been inadequately evangelized, have received little spiritual formation after confirmation, and very few have been properly discipled.

The primary call of the CCR is seen as a call for a mature, personal conversion to Jesus Christ as Lord and Savior, to a new receptivity to the person and gifts of the Holy Spirit, and to a desire for Christian formation and discipleship. This calls not only for a release of the baptismal graces already received, but also for new outpourings of the power and charismatic gifts of the Holy Spirit. A Catholic understanding of the charisms is that they are much more numerous than those listed by St. Paul, and that speaking in tongues is not the essential sign of baptism in the Holy Spirit.

The Future

Today the Catholic Charismatic Renewal stands at the heart of the Catholic Church. The numbers involved are static in Europe and North America, but increasing dramatically in Africa, Asia, and Latin America. In 2000 *The World Christian Encyclopedia* predicted that there would be 240 million living Catholic charismatics in 2025, to which must be added the 70 million who will have died since 1967, making a total of 310 million baptized in the Holy Spirit. Acceptance by the hierarchy is total, and the influence on the life of the Catholic Church of 240 million committed, gifted, and active charismatics will be enormous. But challenges lie ahead.

For example, there is a temptation to try to be more acceptable to others in the Catholic Church by speaking less about the things they find uncomfortable—tongues, prophecy, healing, and baptism in the Holy Spirit—and good leadership will be needed to ensure that this temptation is resisted. There is also the danger of competition and division. It will be important to remember that there is no competition between the institutional and charismatic dimensions of the life of the church—they are both essential for a healthy body.

The CCR has brought a new emphasis to the importance of daily listening to the voice and guidance of the Spirit, of doing everything in his strength and not in our own, of giving the control back to God. One Scripture verse encapsulates the essential message of the Catholic Charismatic Renewal Movement: "Not by might, not by power, but by my Spirit, says the Lord" (Zechariah 4:6).

J. CHARLES WHITEHEAD

See also Baptism in the Holy Spirit

Further Reading

Barrett, D. B., & Johnson, T. M. (Eds.). (2000). *World Christian encyclopedia* (2nd ed.). Oxford, UK: Oxford University Press.

Collins, P. (1991). *Maturing in the spirit*. Dublin, Ireland: The Columba Press.

Cooper, K. (2001). *The Catholic charismatic renewal*. London, UK: The Catholic Truth Society.

Cordes, P. (1997). *Call to holiness*. Collegeville, MN: The Liturgical Press.

Flannery, A. (Ed.). (1975). *Lumen Gentium. The conciliar and post conciliar documents of Vatican II*. Dublin, Ireland: Dominican Publications.

Gallagher, M. P. (1992). *As by a new Pentecost*. Steubenville, OH: Franciscan University Press.

Heron, B. (1989). *Praying for healing*. Darton, UK: Longman and Todd.

Hocken, P. (2001). *Blazing the trail*. Stoke-on-Trent, UK: Bible Alive Ltd.

McDonnell, K., & Montague, G. T. (1991). *Christian initiation and baptism in the Holy Spirit*. Collegeville, MN: The Liturgical Press.

Petit, I. (2004). *The God who speaks; & You will receive power*. Luton, UK: New Life Publishing.

Ranaghan, D., & Ranaghan, K. (1971). *Catholic Pentecostals today*. South Bend, IN: Charismatic Renewal Services.

Smith, B., & Commadeur, A. (2000). *Streams of living water*. Melbourne, Australia: Comsoda Communications.

Statutes of ICCRS. Vatican City: The Pontifical Council for the Laity.

Suenens, L. J. (1977). *A new Pentecost?* London: Fount Paperbacks.

Then Peter stood up... (2000). Rome: International Catholic Charismatic Renewal Services.

Whitehead, C. (1993). *Pentecost is for living*. Darton, UK, Longman and Todd.

Whitehead, C. (2003). *The nature of the Catholic charismatic renewal*. Luton, UK: Goodnews Books.

Wilkerson, D. (1967). *The cross and the switchblade*. London: Lakeland.

Cessationism

Cessationism is a doctrine that denies the spiritual gifts forming the distinctive core of the Pentecostal and charismatic tradition. Cessationism claims that because miracles and other extraordinary spiritual gifts either served only as a temporary aid to establish the church or to accredit its doctrines, these gifts did not continue long after the apostolic period.

History

Cessationism originated in intramural Jewish polemics, but was adopted by the early Church to account for the apparent decline of spiritual gifts in the first few Christian centuries. Several Church Fathers, among them Chrysostom and Origen, taught cessationism while at other times serving up accounts of spiritual gifts such as prophecies, healings, and especially exorcisms. Augustine began his career as a cessationist, but explicitly reversed his position in his *The City of God against the Pagans*.

It was the Protestant Reformers, however, who used cessationism as a major weapon aimed at undercutting Roman Catholic claims to evolving doctrines and the apostolic authority of the Pope. John Calvin complained, "In demanding miracles from us [the Protestants], they [Catholics] act dishonestly; for we have not coined some new gospel, but retain the very one the truth of which is confirmed by all the miracles which Christ and the apostles ever wrought" (*Institutes of the Christian Religion*).

In the early twentieth century, a Princeton Calvinist, Benjamin Warfield, in his *Counterfeit Miracles* (1918), attacked the growing religious diversity in America—marked by the spread of Catholicism, Christian Science, theological liberalism, early healing evangelists, and proto-Pentecostalism (in the Irvingites)—by denying their shared belief in continuing spiritual gifts,

I Corinthians 13: 8-10 (King James Version)

[8]Charity never faileth: but whether there be prophecies, they shall fail; whether there be tongues, they shall cease; whether there be knowledge, it shall vanish away.

[9]For we know in part, and we prophesy in part.

[10]But when that which is perfect is come, then that which is in part shall be done away.

particularly divine healing. Pentecostals and charismatics have criticized Warfield, who is considered the most prominent exponent of cessationism, for what they call his philosophically naïve and extrabiblical notion of miracle, his selective and hypercritical treatment of the historical evidence for continuing spiritual gifts, and, in view of his use of cessationism to protect the authority of Scripture, his surprising lack of biblical arguments for his position.

Contemporary Cessationism

More recent cessationists have appealed more to Scripture to support their position. Some argue that Ephesians 2:20 (RSV) shows that the Church is built on the "foundation of the apostles and prophets," indicating such gifts existed only in the foundational first generation of the Church. Hebrews 2:4 appears to place the confirmation function of spiritual gifts and miracles in the past. But a number of Pentecostal and charismatic scholars maintain that these Scriptures actually invalidate cessationism. The most common Scripture once used by cessationists, 1 Corinthians 13:8–10, has been largely abandoned, or co-opted by their opponents. The passage asserts that spiritual gifts such as prophecy, tongues, and knowledge will be done away with at the appearance of "the perfect," a term that cessationists traditionally applied to the completed canon of the New Testament. The consensus of biblical commentators, however, following all extant early Church Fathers, have understood "the perfect" to mean the end of the age or the Second Coming of Christ—a reading that would precisely contradict cessationism.

An influential and moving article by Daniel Wallace called "Who's Afraid of the Holy Spirit?" (*Christianity Today*, 1994) reflects a growing openness toward contemporary expressions of God's revelation and power, even among self-described cessationists. In a recent Gallup poll, 89 percent of Americans agreed with the statement, "Even today miracles are performed by the

power of God." Cessationism, then, is a doctrine in decline, defended mostly by extreme conservatives among Baptist, Presbyterian, and Church of Christ denominations in North America.

Modern Responses to Cessationism

Pentecostals and charismatics have only recently mounted a more serious biblical, as opposed to experiential, defense of their distinctive doctrines of continuing spiritual gifts and miracles. For example, Jack Deere, the author of *Surprised by the Power of the Spirit* (1994) and *Surprised by the Voice of God* (1996), has suggested that no one who had not been exposed to cessationism beforehand would ever derive such a doctrine from a reading of the New Testament itself. These scholars point out a number of Scriptures that deny cessationism. Romans 11:29 explicitly states a universal principle: "The *charismata* [spiritual gifts] and calling of God are not withdrawn." Another Pauline principle is that no person with one kind of spiritual gift may say to another who is differently gifted, "I have no need of you" (1 Corinthians 12:21). Cessationism says exactly that. The Apostle requires that his readers "eagerly desire spiritual gifts, especially the gift of prophecy" (1 Corinthians 14:1). He also instructs, "my brothers, be eager to prophesy, and do not forbid speaking in tongues" (1 Corinthians 14:39; 1 Thessalonians 5:19–20). Cessationism denies the modern relevance of these clear biblical commands.

The Pentecostal-Charismatic response to cessationism may have far-reaching implications, asserting as it does that the essence of Christianity is not the Protestant "message" or "word," but of Christ's presence in power. It asserts that the miracles of Jesus and his followers are not proofs of the Gospel, but the Gospel itself; that salvation is not only rescue from hell, but a deliverance from the sin, sickness, and accursedness of the present age. The very essence of the "new covenant" inaugurated by the Spirit-bearing Messiah is that all Israel will become prophets (Numbers 11:29; cf.

Isaiah 59:21; Jeremiah 31:33–34; Joel 2:28–30), resulting not only in the priesthood of all believers, but also the prophethood of all believers (John 14:16, 26; 1 Thessalonians 5:19–20; 1 Peter 4:10–11; Revelation 19:10, 22:9). Numerous other passages of the New Testament also deny cessationism.

Prospects

Arguably, cessationism has distorted a number of traditional Protestant doctrines—such as those of the Kingdom of God, the Holy Spirit, covenant, faith, salvation, the Church, discipleship, prayer, mission, and eschatology—which, if their adherents followed the emphases of the New Testament, would emerge more prominently or would display a notable charismatic dimension. A Pentecostal or charismatic theology shaped by biblical emphases rather than Protestant tradition is yet to be written.

Jon Mark Ruthven

See also Antecedents of Pentecostalism; Charismata; Fruit of the Spirit; Gifts of the Spirit

Further Reading

Augustine. (1998). *The city of God against the Pagans* (R. W. Dyson, Ed. & Trans.). New York: Cambridge University Press. (Original work published 427 CE)

Calvin, J. (1986). *Institutes of the Christian religion* (J. T. McNeill, Ed., & F. L. Battles, Trans.). Grand Rapids, MI: Eerdmans. (Original work published 1559)

Deere, J. (1994). *Surprised by the power of the Spirit*. Grand Rapids, MI: Zondervan.

Deere, J. (1996). *Surprised by the voice of God*. Grand Rapids, MI: Zondervan.

Farnell, F. D. (1993). When will the gift of prophecy cease? *Bibliotheca Sacra 598*(150), 186–191.

Gaffin, R. (1979). *Perspectives on Pentecost: Studies in New Testament teachings on the gifts of the Holy Spirit*. Grand Rapids, MI: Baker.

Green, G. L. (2001). "As for prophecies, they will come to an end": 2 Peter, Paul and Plutarch on "The obsolescence of oracles." *Journal for the Study of the New Testament, 82*, 107–122.

Greig, G. S., & Springer, K. (Eds.). (1993). *The kingdom and the power*. Ventura, CA: Gospel Light.

Grudem, W., & Gaffin, R. (Eds.). (1996). *Are miraculous gifts for today? Four views*. Grand Rapids, MI: Zondervan.

Horton, M. (Ed.). (1993). *Power religion: The selling out of the Evangelical church?* Chicago: Moody.

Houghton, M. J. (1996). A reexamination of 1 Corinthians 13:8–13. *Bibliotheca Sacra, 153*, 344–356.

Poythress, V. (1996). Modern spiritual gifts as analogous to apostolic gifts. *Journal of the Evangelical Theological Society, 39*, 71–101.

Ruthven, J. (1993). *On the cessation of the charismata: The Protestant polemic on postbiblical miracles*. Sheffield, UK: Sheffield Academic Press.

Ruthven, J. (2002). Ephesians 2:20 and the "foundational" gifts. *Journal of Pentecostal Theology, 10*, 28–43.

Shogren, G. S. (1999). How did they suppose "the perfect" would come? 1 Corinthians 13:8–12 in patristic exegesis. *Journal of Pentecostal Theology, 15*, 99–121.

Smith, D. R. (2001). The Scottish Presbyterians and Covenanters: A continuationist experience in a cessationist theology. *Westminster Theological Journal, 63*, 39–63.

Wallace, D. B. (1994). Who's afraid of the Holy Spirit? The uneasy conscience of a non-charismatic evangelical. *Christianity Today, 38*, 34–38.

Warfield, B. B. (1918). *Counterfeit miracles*. New York: Charles Scribners Sons.

White, R. F. (1992). Gaffin and Grudem on Eph 2:20: In defense of Gaffin's cessationist exegesis. *Westminster Theological Journal, 54*, 303–320.

White, R. F. (1993). Richard Gaffin and Wayne Grudem on 1 Cor 13:10: A comparison of cessationist and noncessationist argumentation. *Journal of the Evangelical Theological Society, 35*, 173–181.

Charismata

Charisma (plural *charismata*) is a Greek word meaning "gracious gifts," or "gifts of grace." It is popularly used to refer to a number of practices known as "spiritual gifts." It is used this way in the New Testament as well, but with a wider range of meaning. The English word *charisma*, borrowed from the Greek, has become a largely secular term referring to a personal magnetism or quality of leadership, a "capacity to inspire devotion and enthusiasm" (*New Shorter Oxford Dictionary*, 1993 ed.). As such, it has no proper plural, and is perhaps slightly closer in meaning to the Greek word *charis*, or "grace." The more exact English equivalent to *charismata* is *charism(s)*. The adjective *charismatic* can be used either in a secular way, to describe any dynamic leader, or as a religious term alluding to the exercise of the spiritual gifts mentioned in the New Testament.

Paul's Spiritual Charisma

The Greek word *charisma*, according to James Dunn in his commentary on Romans (1988, 30), is a term that "Christian (and sociological!) vocabulary owes almost entirely to Paul; prior to his taking it over and giving it significance it had only a minimal currency. Paul could use the term for God's intervention in his own life, delivering him from death and despair (2 Corinthians 1:11), but more typically in his letters it refers to something offered to his readers. Dunn points out "a characteristic of a spiritual gift for Paul is that it is not for oneself, but for sharing" (1988, 30). As Paul tells the Christian believers at Rome, "I desire to see you, that I might share with you some spiritual gift of grace to strengthen you" (Romans 1:11).

The phrase "spiritual gift of grace" is striking, for it combines two of Paul's characteristic terms for the "gifts of the Spirit" (see 1 Corinthians 12:1, 4, 31, and 14:1) in an almost redundant manner. That is, if charisma is already a spiritual gift, then what is a "spiritual charisma"? In effect, as Dunn says, Paul is "adding emphasis—a *truly* spiritual gift" (1988, 30; emphasis added). At this point in Romans it is unclear what he has in mind, especially when he goes on to explain it rather vaguely as being "mutually encouraged by each other's faith" (1:12). Some find his promised "spiritual gift of grace" in the letter itself, whether as a whole or in those parts that constitute his own personal contribution to the Christian message ("my gospel," Romans 16:25), in contrast to the message he and his readers had received in common.

The difficulty with both options is that Paul seems to say that in order to impart this "spiritual gift of grace," he must visit Rome in person (see Romans 1:10–11, "that now at last by the will of God I might come to you. For I desire to see you.") Near the end of Romans he reiterates, "I have desired for many years to come to you," promising to do so on his way to Spain (15:23–24, 28). "I know that when I come to you," he continues, "I will come in the fullness of the blessing of Christ" (Romans 15:29), so that "when I come to you with joy I might be refreshed together with you" (15:32). This "fullness of the blessing of Christ" appears to correspond to the "spiritual gift of grace" promised fourteen chapters earlier (Romans 1:11), while the mutual refreshment he hopes to enjoy with the Roman believers echoes the mutual "encouragement" he had hoped for earlier in almost the same breath (1:12).

Still, the question remains, What exactly *was* this "fullness of blessing" or "spiritual charisma"? In the body of his letter to the Romans, Paul contrasts God's free "gift of grace" with human sin ("the transgression," Romans 5:15), with divine retribution ("the judgment," Romans 5:16), and above all with death, "the wages of sin," so as to identify it finally with "eternal life in Jesus Christ our Lord" (Romans 6:23). But his focus in chap-

ters 1 and 15 is on his own role in God's plan of salvation, specifically his completion of a Gentile mission "from Jerusalem all the way around to Illyricum" (Romans 15:19) and his return to Jerusalem to present the collection for "the poor among the saints" to the Jewish believers there (15:25–27, 31). To him, that material "gracious gift" from Gentile to Jewish Christians signaled the "fullness" of the Gentiles that would, in the plan of God, soon yield a corresponding "fullness" of the people of Israel (see Romans 11:12, 25–26). This evidently is the "fullness of the blessing of Christ" (Romans 15:29), or "my gospel" (16:25), a "spiritual gift of grace" indeed to the Christians at Rome (and everywhere), something in which they and Paul could rejoice together.

Israel's Charismata

Paul makes it clear that the charismata did not begin with the coming of "eternal life in Jesus Christ our Lord" (Romans 6:23). He bolsters his assertion of Israel's future salvation with the claim that "the gifts of grace and the call of God are irrevocable" (Romans 11:29). These are Israel's charismata given long ago, and Paul has enumerated them already: "first, that the oracles of God were entrusted to them" (Romans 3:2), and further, that "theirs is the adoption, and the glory, and the covenants, and the legal system, and worship, and the promises; theirs are the patriarchs, and from them came the Christ, humanly speaking, who is God over all, blessed forever. Amen." (Romans 9:4–5).

All these are charismata, irrevocable "gifts of grace," Paul is saying, for God's gifts are given unconditionally, never to be taken away. They belong to Israel's "calling," or election as the people of God, a calling now shared by Paul individually as apostle (Romans 1:1), and corporately by the Gentile Christians at Rome and throughout the world (1:6–7, 8:29–30). In Christ, most of Israel's charismata belong to Gentile Christians as well, for theirs too are the Jewish Scriptures, the adoption as God's children (see Romans 8:15, 23), and the glory that goes with it (8:18, 21, 30), and the true worship of God (see 12:1). Theirs too are the patriarchs (notably Abraham, Romans 4:9–12), the covenants made with them, and the accompanying promises (see Romans 4:13–25, 15:8), above all those centered on "the Christ," or Messiah, Son of David and Son of God (see Romans 1:3–4).

Christian Charismata

If true "worship" (Romans 9:4) is one of Israel's gifts from God now made available to Gentile Christian believers, Paul wants to help define the form it takes in the Christian congregations he founded, such as the one at Corinth, and even those he did not establish, such as that in Rome. The "mercies of God" (Romans 12:1), on the basis of which Paul makes his appeal to the believers at Rome, are nothing other than these irrevocable charismata reserved for Jew and Gentile alike. They are the foundation of the "rational worship" that Paul envisions for the Christian community. This "sacrificial" system, he claims, is based not on animal sacrifices in a temple, but (in the tradition of the Jewish prophets) on obedience. The "living sacrifice" of which he speaks (Romans 12:1) consists of the "bodies" of Christian believers incorporated into a single "body" (Romans 12:4), or charismatic congregation representing Christ in the world.

Before he even begins to list the charismata he sees operating in the congregation, Paul emphasizes humility, and by implication love, as the key to the exercise of these "gracious gifts." Building on what he had said to Gentile Christians in the preceding chapter (see Romans 11:20, "Don't be proud"), he warns his readers not to "think of yourself more highly than you ought to think" (Romans 12:3) and to "get along with each other; don't be proud, but associate with the lowly, and don't be conceited" (12:16). Paul speaks here out of "the grace [charis] given me" (Romans 12:3) to all who "have gracious gifts [charismata] differing according to the grace [charis] given us" (12:6). These "gracious gifts" he enumerates as prophesy, ministry, teaching, preaching, sharing with others, caring for others, and showing mercy (Romans 12:6–8). None of them, with the possible exception of prophesy, were distinctly supernatural or miraculous gifts.

Paul is almost certainly writing to Rome from Corinth, and in his first letter to Corinth he had expressed his pleasure that "you are not lacking in any gracious gift [charisma] as you await the revelation of our Lord Jesus Christ" (1 Corinthians 1:7). He had also used charismata as one of several terms for spiritual gifts—either as a general designation for all gifts (1 Corinthians 12:31), or specifically with "healings" (1 Corinthians 12:9, 28, 30), or in conjunction with "the Spirit" (12:4), just as ministries was used in conjunction with Jesus as "Lord," and workings in conjunction with "God who works them all in everyone" (see 1 Corinthians 12:4–6). Several of the most conspicuous gifts of the Spirit at Corinth—speaking in tongues, the interpretation of tongues, miracles, gifts of healing, and distinguishing between spirits—are conspicuous in Romans only by their absence. Paul may have felt that there was no need to export Corinth's problems with the more

spectacular charismata to another city. Yet common to both letters is a rather broad use of the term to refer to all of God's spiritual gifts, whether in worship or in everyday life. Even a person's marital status is God's "gracious gift" or charisma, whether it be marriage or celibacy (see 1 Corinthians 7:7). Central to both Romans and 1 Corinthians is a concern that the charismata be exercised with humility (Romans 12:3, 16) and love (Romans 12:9–10 and 13:8–10; 1 Corinthians 13), to "build up" and not tear down or divide the Christian community (1 Corinthians 14:3–5, 12, 26).

The same is true in 1 Peter, a letter probably originating from the same congregation or congregations in Rome to which Paul's letter to the Romans had been sent. There, centering more on "God" and "Jesus Christ" than on "the Spirit," the author writes, "Whatever gracious gift [charisma], each has received, use it in ministry to each other as good managers of the diversified grace [charis] of God; if any speak, as oracles of God, if any minister, as out of the strength that God supplies, so that in everything God may be glorified through Jesus Christ, to whom is the glory and the power forever and ever. Amen." (1 Peter 4:10–11).

Timothy's Charisma

The only individual other than Paul singled out in the New Testament as having received a specific charisma from God is Timothy. In each of his letters to Timothy, Paul mentions a "gracious gift," or charisma, which Timothy is said to have been given, whether "through a prophesy, with the laying on of the hands of the presbytery" (1 Timothy 4:14), or "through the laying on of my hands" (2 Timothy 1:6). The first instance recalls the author's obscure reference to "the prophecies made earlier about you" (1 Timothy 1:18), and makes it more explicit. Timothy's gift seems to involve the reading of Scripture, preaching, and especially teaching (1 Timothy 4:13, 16). Paul urges him not to neglect it (1 Timothy 4:14), but to rekindle it (2 Timothy 1:6), for like the faith he inherited from his mother and grandmother, it is "within" him (2 Timothy 1:5, 6), part of his very being, an expression of the "grace" given in principle to all believers "before the ages began" (1 Timothy 1:9).

Here we see the beginning of something close to the later practice of ordination, in which the charismata are placed to some degree under the jurisdiction of the Christian community. First, the charisma of prophesy is used to call attention to others who are gifted in the congregation, and then their gifts are recognized and ratified by the laying on of hands, whether by the elders of the congregation, or by the Apostle, or both (for a similar procedure, see Acts 13:1–3). While scholars are not in agreement as to whether Paul actually wrote 1 and 2 Timothy, the principle that emerges there agrees broadly with Paul's conviction that the gifts of God are for the people of God, not the reverse; or, in Paul's own words, "the spirits of the prophets are subject to the prophets" (1 Corinthians 14:32).

J. RAMSEY MICHAELS

See also Gifts of the Spirit

Further Reading

Bittlinger, A. (1967). *Gifts and graces: A commentary on 1 Corinthians 12–14.* London: Hodder and Stoughton.

Conzelmann, H. (1974). Charis, charisma. In *Theological dictionary of the New Testament* (Vol. 9, pp. 391–406). Grand Rapids, MI: Eerdmans.

Dunn, J. D. G. (1988). *Word biblical commentary: Vol. 38A Romans 1–8.* Nashville, TN: Thomas Nelson

Fee, G. D. (1987). *The first epistle to the Corinthians.* Grand Rapids, MI: Eerdmans.

Fee, G. D. (1993). Gifts of the Spirit. In *Dictionary of Paul and his letters* (pp. 339–347) Downers Grove, IL: InterVarsity Press.

Fee, G. D. (1994) *God's empowering presence: The Holy Spirit in the letters of Paul.* Peabody, MA: Hendrickson.

Fitzmyer, J. A. (1993). *Romans: A new translation with introduction and commentary* New York: Doubleday.

Koenig, J. (1978). *Charismata: God's gift for God's people.* Philadelphia: Westminster Press.

Longenecker, R. N. (1999). The focus of Romans: The central role of 5:1–8:39 in the argument of the letter. In S. K. Soderlund & N. T. Wright (Eds.), *Romans and the people of God* (pp. 49–69). Grand Rapids, MI: Eerdmans.

Luter, A. B., Jr. (1993). Grace. In *Dictionary of Paul and his letters* (pp. 372–374) Downers Grove, IL: InterVarsity Press.

Moffatt, J. (1931). *Grace in the New Testament.* London: Hodder and Stoughton.

Moo, D. J. (1996). *The epistle to the Romans.* Grand Rapids, MI: Eerdmans.

Mounce, W. D. (2000). *Word biblical commentary: Vol. 46. Pastoral epistles.* Nashville, TN: Thomas Nelson

Nardoni, E. (1993). The concept of charism in Paul. *Catholic Biblical Quarterly, 55,* 68–80.

Stevens, R. P. (1999). "The full blessing of Christ" (Romans 15:29): A sermon. In S. K. Soderlund & N. T. Wright (Eds.), *Romans and the people of God* (pp. 295–303). Grand Rapids, MI: Eerdmans.

Charismatic Movement

The Charismatic movement is one of the most significant religious developments in recent church history. It emerged in a dramatic and unexpected fashion. In *The Century of the Holy Spirit*, Vinson Synan writes, "One of the surprises of the renewal was that it came first to the more sacramental and traditional Protestant churches rather than the more evangelical and fundamentalist denominations" (2001, 177). The Charismatic movement consists primarily of the Charismatic Renewal in the historic Anglican, Catholic, Orthodox, and Protestant Churches. It also includes the independent Pentecostal ministries that transcended the classical Pentecostal denominations. As we will see below, there was a good deal of intermingling between the two.

A Renewal Movement

Charismatics are those who attest to an experience of spiritual renewal through the power of the Holy Spirit. The term "charismatic" relates to the spiritual gifts of the Christian Scriptures. It comes from the Greek word *charismata*, which is derived from *charis*, meaning "grace" or "unmerited favor," conveying the notion of a gift. Hence, charismatics are so named because they put special emphasis on spiritual gifts, including speaking in tongues, prophecy, healing, and exorcism.

The Charismatic movement is similar to Pentecostalism in its emphasis on spiritual gifts, but it is dissimilar in that it is not sectarian, given that its origins were in the historic churches. All dissimilarities aside, the Charismatic movement should be seen as a constituent part of the Pentecostal-Charismatic movements, known in the parlance of insiders as "the renewal movement."

According to the prevailing classification of Barrett, Kurian, and Johnson, the renewal movement is thought to consist of three waves. The first wave is classical Pentecostalism; the second is the Charismatic Renewal; and the third is the neocharismatics. There are differing opinions over whether these waves have been successive or simultaneous. As of 2002, the renewal movement is estimated to number about 523 million people, making up 27.7 percent of organized global Christianity, of which 65 million are Pentecostals, 175 million are charismatics, and 295 million are neocharismatics. Pentecostals have proliferated into 740 denominations operating in 225 countries; charismatics have organized 6,530 denominations in 235 countries; and neocharismatics have spawned

18,810 denominations in 225 countries. It is an astounding fact that while 79 million renewal adherents live in North America, the vast majority reside in Latin America (141 million), Asia (134 million), and Africa (126 million).

In describing the Charismatic movement one should proceed with circumspection. Given the preponderance of non-Western peoples in the renewal movement, Stanley M. Burgess urges historians to be wary of what he calls "Amerocentric historiographic assumptions," which are grounded in the view that America is the home base of the renewal movement (2001, 86). Burgess questions the traditional claim that the global Pentecostal movement stemmed from a central point of origin in Topeka or Los Angeles. In a similar vein, David D. Bundy writes, "Certainly no theory that makes the American experience paradigmatic can explain the global realities of Pentecostalism" (in Burgess and van der Maas 2002, 417).

Beginning of the Movement

The origin of the Charismatic movement is commonly associated with Dennis Bennett, an American Episcopalian vicar. On 3 April 1960, Bennett announced to his Van Nuys, California, parish that he had spoken in tongues. He then resigned on the spot rather than foment a church split. One of Bennett's sympathizers, Jean Stone, circulated Bennett's testimony in a periodical called *Voice*. She also contacted *Newsweek* and *Time*, both of which published articles in the summer of 1960. The next year she established the Blessed Trinity Society and began publishing *Trinity*, a quarterly periodical. In the meantime Bennett moved on to St. Luke's Episcopal in Seattle, which was soon transformed from a church in decline to a thriving vortex of charismatic vitality and power. A few years after Bennett's first wife died of cancer in 1963, he was remarried to Rita Marie Reed, with whom he founded the Christian Renewal Association in 1968. They collaborated in a transdenominational ministry. Dennis and Rita Bennett's influence was widely felt by means of their worldwide speaking ministry and the publication of their books, beginning with Dennis's *Nine O'Clock in the Morning* (1970), which recounts his personal story.

A second benchmark of the origins of the Charismatic movement was the outbreak of tongues-speaking among American Roman Catholics, which started in 1967 when a group of teachers at Duquesne University read two books—*The Cross and the Switchblade* (1963) by David Wilkerson and *They Speak with Other Tongues* (1964) by John Sherrill. Soon thereafter they experienced the baptism of the Holy Spirit and then led a retreat at which a group of thirty graduate students spontaneously entered into the same experience. Two recent graduates of Notre Dame, Ralph Martin and Stephen Clark, went to Duquesne to see what was going on, and they too were baptized in the Spirit. Swiftly the Catholic Charismatic Renewal spread to Michigan State, Iowa State, and other universities. The religious press caught wind of the renewal when a group of one hundred students gathered at Notre Dame in April 1967, for a weekend of prayer and reflection. In the fall of that year Martin and Clark began a ministry at the University of Michigan that would develop into the Word of God Community and play a leading role in the dispersion of the Catholic Charismatic Renewal. Those who participated in the inception of the Catholic Charismatic Renewal in 1967 regarded these remarkable events as an answer to Pope John XXIII's opening prayer at Vatican II for a "New Pentecost."

Early Leaders

The above events signaled the official beginning of the Charismatic movement, but in reality there were earlier stirrings. Several pastors of mainline denominations had been baptized in the Holy Spirit. Some notable examples are Harald Bredesen (Lutheran) in 1946, Tommy Tyson (Methodist) in 1951, Don Basham (Disciples of Christ) in 1953, James Brown (Presbyterian) in 1956, Pat Roberston (Southern Baptist) in 1956, Larry Christenson (American Lutheran) in 1961, Donald Pfotenshauer (Lutheran-Missouri Synod) in 1964, J. Rodman Williams (Presbyterian) in 1967, Nelson Litwiller (Mennonite) in 1970, and Eusebuius Stephanou (Greek Orthodox) in 1972. As an outgrowth, many renewal ministries were launched by mainline charismatics to revitalize their denominations from within, including Charismatic Renewal Services, Lutheran Charismatic Renewal Services, the American Baptist Charismatic Fellowship, Anglican Renewal Ministries, Parish Renewal Council, Logos Ministry for Orthodox Renewal, and the Renewal Fellowship.

Of those who experienced the baptism of the Holy Spirit prior to the "official" beginning of the Charismatic Renewal, two deserve special mention. The first is Agnes Sanford, author of the classic work on inner healing, *The Healing Light* (1947). After experiencing the baptism of the Holy Spirit and speaking in tongues, Sanford and her husband established the School of Pastoral Care in 1955, offering retreats on healing prayer, at which she taught and demonstrated the healing power of the Holy Spirit. The second is Pat Robertson, who held ordination with the Southern Baptist Convention until he ran for president in 1988. After serving as an associate of the Lutheran charismatic Harald Bredesen, in 1959 Robertson purchased a defunct UHF television station and in 1966 created the Christian Broadcasting Network. Robertson is the creator and host of the highly regarded *The 700 Club*. In 1977 Robertson founded CBN University, now Regent University, on the CBN campus, which has graduate schools in business, communication and arts, counseling, divinity, education, law, and leadership studies.

At the same time certain Pentecostals were broadening their appeal beyond the classical Pentecostal denominations. Foremost among them was Oral Roberts, who in 1947 launched his healing ministry. In 1955 he started a weekly television broadcast that exposed the American public to his healing crusades, which by 1968 numbered more than three hundred. Roberts established Oral Roberts University in 1965, which became a major academic institution with graduate schools in business, dentistry, education, law, medicine, nursing, and theology. In 1968 Roberts affiliated with the United Methodist Church. For thirty years his Sunday morning television station was the top syndicated religious program in America. By the 1980s his monthly column was featured in 674 newspapers and more than 15 million copies of his 88 books were in circulation. Another ministry that propelled the charismatic message beyond the confines of organized Pentecostalism was the Full Gospel Business Men's Fellowship International founded by businessman Demos Shakarian in 1951. Shakarian's vision was to establish a nonsectarian fellowship. His strategy was to gather businessmen at breakfast meetings to hear charismatic speakers. The speaker at the first meeting was Oral Roberts. Shakarian's ministry grew at an explosive rate, from a membership of 100,000 in the 1960s to 300,000 in 1972, and contributed to the success of many independent Pentecostals, including Kenneth Hagin and Kenneth Copland.

David du Plessis Of all the nonsectarian Pentecostals, David du Plessis did the most to build bridges between Pentecostals and the mainline denominations. The inspiration for du Plessis' ecumenical endeavors originated with a prophecy in 1936 from British Pentecostal evangelist Smith Wigglesworth, who declared that du Plessis would give witness to the remote parts of the world if he would remain faithful to the Lord. In 1952 du Plessis dropped by the offices of the World Council of Churches and was invited by John Macay to the 1952 meeting of the International Missionary Council. Du Plessis attended six Assemblies of the World Council between 1954 and 1983 and lectured at major theological seminaries, including Princeton, Yale, and Union. He was personally received by three popes, was an invited guest at the third session of Vatican II, and played a major role in the Roman Catholic-Pentecostal Dialogue. For his efforts on behalf of ecumenism, he was known affectionately as Mr. Pentecost. However, his own denomination, the Assemblies of God, rewarded him by revoking his ministerial credentials in 1962. In 1980 he was reinstated after his denomination belatedly developed an appreciation for his contribution to ecumenical dialogue. It is safe to say that the ministry of du Plessis contributed significantly to the wide impact of the Charismatic movement.

Rapid Growth

In the 1970s there was an explosion of independent charismatic church growth. The new churches were nondenominational. They were charismatic in that they regarded the baptism of the Holy Spirit as normative, yet did not insist that Spirit baptism had to be evidenced by speaking in tongues. They practiced believer's baptism and organized their leadership according to the five-fold ministry of Ephesians 4:11.

Two significant developments were associated with the independent charismatic churches. The first was the shepherding movement, which began under the aegis of Christian Growth Ministries, led by five popular charismatic Bible teachers—Don Basham, Ern Baxter, Bob Mumford, Derek Prince, and Charles Simpson. Their objective was to preserve doctrinal and moral purity by means of accountability relationships, that is, shepherding. Their distinctive teachings were authority, submission, pastoral care, and discipleship. When the shepherding movement was widely criticized for spiritual abuses, it fell into disrepute and waned swiftly. The second development was the formation of inter-church associations. The new charismatic churches wanted to maintain their nondenominational status, yet they also desired to enter into fellowship with like-minded bodies. Many affiliated with the National Leadership Conference, formed in 1979. Other similar networks were the People of Destiny International, founded by Larry Tomczak and C. J. Mahaney in 1982, and the Fellowship of Covenant Ministers and Conferences, formed by Howard Simpson in 1987.

Worldwide Expansion

The Charismatic Renewal also impacted the Orthodox Church, mainly in the West, but also in Egypt, Lebanon, Kenya, Tanzania, and Uganda. The greatest renewal activity was in the Greek Orthodox Church. The focal points of renewal were the journals *Logos* and *Theosis*. The most prominent leaders of Orthodox Renewal in America were Boris Zabrodsky, Athanasius Emmert, and Eusebius Stephanou, each of whom was censured by Orthodox officials. Stephanou was canonically suspended and almost defrocked. Rather than be muzzled, Emmert switched over to the Melkite Church in 1987. Not dissuaded, in 1989 Stephanou established the Brotherhood of St. Symeon, opened an Orthodox Renewal Center in Florida, and began publishing *The Orthodox Evangelist*. Interest in the Orthodox Church among charismatics was sparked when Michael Harper, perhaps the most prominent leader of the Anglican Renewal, converted to the Orthodox Church in 1995 and published the story of his pilgrimage in *The True Light* (1997).

Europe

Karla Poewe locates the roots of the global culture of charismatic Christianity in the Pietist movement of eighteenth-century Germany. She finds an historical antecedent in August Hermann Francke's comprehensive vision for the renewal of the individual, church, state, and education. She identifies several features of Francke's Pietism reflected in the discourse and practice of contemporary charismatics, specifically:

> a practical spirituality equally comfortable with visions and service; a sensitivity to cultural relations; an emphasis on science, literature and education generally; and the founding of various institutions, including orphanages, houses to reclaim prostitutes, schools, colleges, missions, hospitals, even a system of banking for the poor. (Poewe 1994, 7)

More recent charismatic manifestations have occurred in Europe since 1945. Some notable examples are Basilea Schlink and the Mary Sisters in Darmstadt, Germany, the London Healing Mission and the Evangelical Divine Healing Fellowship in England, and Wim Verhoef and his "Fire" Group ministry among Dutch students. The Charismatic movement in America had a definite impact in Europe. The news of Dennis Bennett's famous announcement in America sparked strong interest. Larry Christenson addressed the Enkenbach conference in August 1963. David du Plessis visited England, Holland, and Switzerland in the fall of 1963 and spent a month in Britain in 1964. Possibly the most influential leaders were Michael Harper of England and Arnold Bittlinger of West Germany. The former established the Fountain Trust, which sponsored renewal

conferences, and the latter, affiliated with the World Council of Churches, published *The Church Is Charismatic* (1981).

Africa

Outbreaks of the Charismatic movement were not limited to Europe and North America. In Africa the occasion for the emergence of the Anglican Charismatic movement in Nigeria, Kenya, and Uganda was the global influenza pandemic of 1918. As people in these countries gathered for prayer, large numbers of black Anglicans were filled with the Holy Spirit and later formed charismatic prayer groups within Anglican parishes. The majority, however, were soon evicted; only a minority (10 percent) remained within Anglicanism, resulting in what later became known as the "Anglican Charismatic Renewal" (Barrett, Kurian, and Johnson 2001, 290). But where did the rest go? Some in Kenya may have later joined the African Israel Church Nineveh, which was an expression of the Charismatic movement, according to Henry Asige Ajega. This church was formed in 1921 through an outpouring of the Holy Spirit. The testimony of its founder, M. P. D. Kwuti, is indicative of the kind of events that led to the formation of African Indigenous Churches. He reports that one night "I began to speak in tongues like the apostles of the New Testament." He quit his job as a teacher and began preaching from village to village, discovering that God had given him the gift of healing prayer. Soon he ran into resistance. As he tells it, "The Kellers (white missionaries) supported me, but many members of the Pentecostal church disliked me because I urged them to confess their sins. They wouldn't let me preach in their churches" (Martin and Mullen 1984, 217–218).

The African Indigenous Churches are sometimes regarded as syncretistic for their allegedly occult practices. One example is the case of the Musama Disco Christo Church of Ghana, founded in the 1920s. Its founder, Joseph William Egyanka Appiah, was dismissed from the Methodist Church for the use of secret medicines and special drugs, as well as for performing miracles of healing by prayer. He then gathered a group of followers, who prayed for and received the baptism of the Holy Spirit, and organized the Musama Disco Christo Church, which put a high premium on dreams, visions and trances, healing power, and spiritual warfare. While polygamy was not considered a mortal sin, fetishes and charms were rejected. At a prayer meeting, the leader said, "We are all in this Church because we have found healing here. But for this Church the great majority of us here assembled would not be alive today. That is the reason why we are here: Is this not so?" To that question came from the congregation the response, a unanimous and most decided "Yes!" (Pobee 1986, 127). The reader may decide where to the draw the line between contextualization and syncretism.

Latin America

In Latin America the countries most affected by the Charismatic movement within the historical denominations were Argentina, Brazil, Chile, and Colombia. In the 1950s the baptism of the Holy Spirit swept through Baptist, Methodist, Presbyterian, and Seventh-Day Adventist denominations. During the 1960s these denominations responded by expelling their charismatics, who then organized independent fellowships dedicated to renewal. The Catholic Renewal in Latin America began later. The first international consultation of Latin American leaders of the Catholic Renewal occurred in 1973 in Bogota, Colombia, with twenty-three leaders representing eight countries. According to Peter Hocken, the Catholic Renewal in Latin America is a grassroots populist movement. It has contributed significantly to ecumenical cooperation between Protestant and Catholic charismatics. During the 1970s many Christians experienced the baptism of the Holy Spirit through the Evangelical Association of Bible Churches in San Jose, Costa Rica. Many Catholics and Protestants were drawn together by the shared ministry of Argentinian pastors Juan Carlos Ortiz and Alberto Motessi and American Catholics Francis MacNutt and Barbara Shlemon.

Asia

In Asia, the countries most impacted by the Charismatic movement are India, Indonesia, China, and Korea. The antecedents of the Charismatic movement in India reach back into the nineteenth century with John Christian Arroolappen and Pandita Ramabai and Sadhu Sundar Singh in the twentieth century. The Catholic Charismatic Renewal came to India in 1972. The first charismatic prayer groups were organized in Bombay and grew rapidly. The movement spread throughout India. The first National Charismatic Conference was held in Bombay in 1974–1975. The leader is Matthew Naickomparambil, who was baptized in the Spirit in the early 1970s.

China It is truly amazing, in view of the harsh persecution of Christians during the Cultural Revolution, that today the number of charismatics in China is only exceeded by Brazil and the United States. This is due to the House Church movement, which has provided an informal setting conducive to the outpouring of the Holy Spirit. Especially since the death of Mao Tse-tung, the house churches have taken advantage of greater freedom to proclaim the Gospel. From 1970 to 1995 the Chinese church grew from about 1.5 million to over 78 million, of which 65 percent are charismatic in orientation.

Korea Several of the world's largest churches are located in Korea. It is of interest that they are mostly charismatic in orientation. The well-known all-night prayer meetings, exorcisms, prayer mountains, and healing services in Korea did not appear out of nowhere. In traditional Korean society, the shaman (*mudang*) served as a link between ordinary people and the spirit world, which was thought to be populated by numerous gods, ancestors, and spirits. The shaman was relied upon to transform malevolent spirits into protective spirits by means of healings and exorcisms. Mark Mullins argues that, whether regarded as syncretism or contextualization, it is undeniable that shamanistic religion has permeated Korean churches. He asserts that Paul Yonggi Cho's doctrine of the "three-fold blessing of salvation" is a synthesis of Korean shamanism, Robert Schuller's positive thinking, and the pragmatism of the Fuller church growth school of missiology. In Korea these three touchstones are widely accepted as the "triple meter faith" (Mullins 1994, 91–92).

Accomplishments

By the year 2000 the Charismatic Renewal had spread to all of the 250 distinct ecclesiastical confessions, traditions, and families in Christianity. Charismatics had grown from 3.3 million in 1970 to 175 million in 2000. Over one hundred new Charismatic mission agencies have recently been formed in the Western world and over three hundred in the Third World. Given the prodigious growth of the Charismatic movement, its impact is worthy of acknowledgement. The Charismatic movement can be credited with four major accomplishments.

First, although one surely regrets the divisions in many denominations due to the Charismatic movement, one must still acknowledge the ecumenical impulse present among charismatics. This impulse was demonstrated by two important events. The first was the Kansas City Conference of 1977, attended by fifty thousand charismatics of every stripe. This well-planned gathering combined the annual conferences of denominational Charismatic Renewal groups with general workshops in the afternoons and plenary sessions in the evenings. A memorable spontaneous prophecy at one of the evening sessions declared, "Mourn and weep, for the body of my Son is broken." The prevailing theme was a call for reconciliation of the churches. Synan's assessment is that the Kansas City Conference "was the greatest and most visible sign of unity" in the Pentecostal-Charismatic movements (2001, 130). The second event was the Roman Catholic-Pentecostal Dialogue. The credit for initiating the dialogue belongs largely to David du Plessis, who moderated the opening rounds along with Kilian McDonnell. The Pentecostal team included both Pentecostals and charismatics. The format was the presentation, discussion, and publication of scholarly papers. To this point, the dialogue has completed five rounds, addressing such topics as the scriptural basis for the baptism of the Spirit, speaking in tongues, Mary, the role of the Holy Spirit in Christian initiation, the sacraments, ecclesiology, hermeneutics, mission, evangelization, social justice, prayer, healing, and worship. Perhaps the best outcome of the dialogue is that in spite of their differences Pentecostals and Roman Catholics are growing in mutual acceptance, understanding and respect.

Second, by means of the diffusion of charismatic innovations, the church has been reinvented. A new shape of global Christianity has emerged. Throughout Christian history, when renewal movements come into being, they form their own culture. The Charismatic movement has developed its own forms of doctrine, worship, spiritual phenomena, organization, and outreach. What is truly remarkable is that the physiognomy of the Charismatic movement has penetrated and been assimilated into the wider church. One can observe charismatic influences in the prevalence of praise music, cell groups, prayer marches, spiritual mapping, worship evangelism, and innovative uses of mass media. Those who have made pilgrimages to the charismatic meccas all over the world, whether in Seattle, Ann Arbor, Kansas City, Toronto, Pensacola, San Jose, Bogota, Bombay, Jakarta, Nairobi, Accra, or Seoul, have come away renewed in the Holy Spirit and inspired to continue the renewal from within their own churches back home. Truly, something of great magnitude has occurred with the emergence and dispersion of the global charismatic religious culture.

Third, in a certain respect, the Charismatic movement is socially transformative. An illustrative example comes from South Africa. During the Charismatic Renewal of the 1970s, racial barriers were dismantled. The Archbishop of Cape Town writes, "The Spirit destroys barriers between people whether these are created by different church traditions or by ideologies and fears and resentments. He sets Whites free from fear and Blacks from the imprisonment of resentments so that they have a new freedom to communicate" (Bittlinger 1981, 178). In the aftermath charismatics were accused of racism because of their refusal to affiliate with the African National Congress. Field research found that they were not racists, but were strongly opposed to political violence and corruption. In fact, the patterns of interaction in the charismatic churches of South Africa were found to be cross-ethnic, cross-racial and cross-national.

Finally, the fourth accomplishment is in the area of scholarship. Certain historians and sociologists have argued that Pentecostalism ameliorated the deprivations of its adherents, who supposedly came from the lower echelons of society. According to the deprivation paradigm, the sectarianism, spiritual elitism, millenarianism, and legalism of Pentecostalism is seen as attractive to the poor, the disinherited, and socially marginalized. Pentecostalism supplied a religious status denied in the mainstream society and infused its members with identity, significance, and hope for a better world with the anticipated Second Coming of Christ. However, the Charismatic movement challenged the deprivation paradigm. Walter Hollenweger writes, "The prayer meetings of the Catholic Pentecostals shattered the 'economic deprivation' theory that had routinely been set forth as an 'explanation' of the older, classical Pentecostalism" (Hollenweger 1972, 8). There were enough upwardly mobile or better-situated charismatics to refute deprivation and other social explanations as the primary reason for the attractiveness of the renewal movement. Sociologists of religion now generally agree that the tie between Pentecostalism and social dislocation remains unproven. Far from rejecting the dominant values of American society, charismatics, even more than Pentecostals, cherished the values of activity and work, achievement and success, moral orientation, external conformity, nationalism, and patriotism. The Prosperity Gospel, which gained wide acceptance in Pentecostal-Charismatic circles, played down sacrifice and poverty and uplifted the goal of overcoming adverse circumstances by means of acquiring prosperity and wealth.

Eric N. Newberg

See also Catholic Charismatic Movement; Dialogues, Catholic and Pentecostal; Orthodoxy, Eastern; Prosperity

Theology; Shepherding and Discipleship Movement; Social Transformation

Further Reading

Barrett, D. B., & Johnson, T. M. (2002). Global statistics. In S. M. Burgess and E. van der Maas (Eds.), *The new international dictionary of Pentecostal and Charismatic movements* (pp. 284–301). Grand Rapids, MI: Zondervan.

Barrett, D. B., Kurian, G. T., & Johnson, T. M. (2001). *World Christian encyclopedia* (Vol. 1). Oxford, UK: Oxford University Press.

Bittlinger, A. (Ed.). (1981). *The church is charismatic*. Geneva, Switzerland: World Council of Churches.

Burgess, S. M. (2001). Pentecostalism in India: An overview. *Asian Journal of Pentecostal Studies*, 4(1), 85–98.

Burgess, S. M., & van der Maas, E. (Eds.). (2002). *The new international dictionary of Pentecostal and Charismatic movements*. Grand Rapids, MI: Zondervan.

Harrell, D. E., Jr. (1975). *All things are possible*. Bloomington: University of Indiana Press.

Hexham, I., & Poewe, K. (1994). Charismatic churches in South Africa: A critique of criticisms and problems of bias. In K. Poewe (Ed.), *Charismatic Christianity as a global culture* (pp 50–69). Columbia: University of South Carolina Press.

Hocken, P. (2002). *Holy Spirit movements of modern times*. Unpublished manuscript, Free University of Amsterdam.

Hollenweger, W. (1972). *The Pentecostals*. Minneapolis, MN: Augsburg Publishing House.

Hunt, S. J. (2002). Deprivation and Western Pentecostalism revisited: Neo-Pentecostalism. *PentecoStudies, Online journal for the interdisciplinary study of Pentecostalism and Charismatic Movements*, 1(2), 1–29.

Jung, H. (2003). Endued with power: The Pentecostal-Charismatic renewal and the Asian churches in the twenty-first century. *Asian Journal of Pentecostal Studies*, 6(1), 63–82.

Martin, D., & Mullen, P. (Eds.) (1984). *Strange gifts? A guide to Charismatic Renewal*. Oxford, UK: Basil Blackwell.

McGuire, M. B. (1982). *Pentecostal Catholics*. Philadelphia: Temple University Press.

Mullins, M. R. (1994). The Empire strikes back: Korean Pentecostal mission to Japan. In K. Poewe (Ed.), *Charismatic Christianity as a global culture*. Columbia: University of South Carolina Press.

Neitz, M. J. (1987). *Charisma and community*. New Brunswick, NJ: Transaction.

Poewe, K. (Ed.). (1994). *Charismatic Christianity as a global culture*. Columbia: University of South Carolina Press.

Pobee, J. S. (1986). I will lift up my eyes to Mozano. *International Review of Mission*, 75(298), 123–128.

Poloma, M. M. (1982). *The Charismatic movement*. Boston: Twayne.

Synan, V. (2001). *The century of the Holy Spirit*. Nashville, TN: Thomas Nelson Publishers.

Synan, V. (2001). *In the latter days*. Fairfax, VA: Xulon Press.

China

The Pentecostal movement in China evolved in the wake of the Boxer Rebellion (1900), in which more than two hundred missionaries and more than thirty thousand Chinese Christians were killed. The uprising was simultaneously anti-Christian and anti-Western, a fact that influenced the indigenization of Christianity, which in turn had a strong impact on the Pentecostal movement in China.

1907–1949: Early Pentecostal Missionaries

The earliest known foothold of Pentecostalism in China was gained in Hong Kong in August 1907, when Mr. and Mrs. T. J. McIntosh of North Carolina arrived. Whereas most of the early missionaries who came to China were influenced by the Azusa Street Revival, the McIntoshes were not. Soon after their arrival, in 1908, an early Chinese convert to Pentecostalism, Mok Lai Chi, helped spearhead the Pentecostal Chinese newspaper *Pentecostal Truths*. Also in early 1908, there was a Pentecostal mission established in Zhengding, Hebei. For several years this was the major Pentecostal center in North China. In 1912 a cofounder of this mission, Bernt Berntsen, established another early Pentecostal Chinese newspaper, *Popular Gospel Truth*. From 1907 to 1910 many other Pentecostal missionaries settled in Shandong province, Shanghai, and Hong Kong.

From 1907 to 1915, traditional missions agencies like the China Inland Mission and the Christian and Missionary Alliance had major disputes concerning the role of Spirit baptism and speaking in tongues within their missionary bodies. Due to the strong stances that developed, several missionaries left to join the Pentecostal ranks. Many of these missionaries joined the Assemblies of God (or USA AG, established in the United States in 1914) or the Pentecostal Missionary Union (established in the United Kingdom in 1909), which later merged with other groups in 1926 to form the AG of Great Britain and Ireland. By 1915, missionaries who had left their missions boards to join Pentecostal agencies, together with new Pentecostal missionaries, numbered about 150 at nearly thirty sites throughout China.

From 1915 to 1949, the largest Pentecostal missionary bodies within China were the USA AG, the AG of Great Britain and Ireland, and the Pentecostal Assemblies of Canada. By the mid-1930s, there were still about 150 missionaries. They emphasized evangelism, but only a small percentage of Chinese Christians were Pentecostal converts. During the 1940s the mission field experienced great difficulties due to the war with Japan and the Chinese civil war, both of which at various times caused many missionaries to evacuate or relocate. By 1948, the largest national Pentecostal group was the AG of China, with nine districts, 150 churches, about twelve thousand adherents and six representative Bible schools around the country.

1907–1949: Indigenous Pentecostal Groups

As a result of the indigenization of Christianity in general in China, several indigenous Pentecostal denominations developed, most notably the True Jesus Church and the Jesus Family. Although strongly Pentecostal, these groups were especially nationalist and did not work with the missions agencies.

The True Jesus Church was established in 1917 by Paul Wei, Zhang Lingshen, and Barnabas Zhang, with their first church in Tianjin. They espoused the "Jesus only" baptismal formula and emphasized speaking in tongues and healings, but they were adamant about worshipping only on the Sabbath and were likewise exclusivist in that members had to renounce ties to any other Christian groups. After Paul Wei's death in 1919, the True Jesus Church quickly expanded into Shandong, Hebei, Henan, and throughout the central part of China. By the late 1940s, this church was the largest of the independent denominations. After 1949, they relocated their international headquarters to Taiwan, and have been a strong movement among Chinese worldwide since then.

The Jesus Family was founded in 1922 in rural Shandong by Jing Dianying. This group was organized according to a communal lifestyle: They lived and worked together and owned property in common. While being thoroughly Pentecostal in their spiritual gifts and their worship style, they also strongly emphasized the certain and immediate return of Christ.

Another Pentecostal group, the Spiritual Gifts church, was established in Shandong province in the early 1930s. They were tied to the "Shandong Revivals," but were more a movement than a stable organized entity. Another influential indigenous group was the Little Flock, founded by Ni Duosheng (Watchman Nee). Although their understanding of the Holy Spirit was closer to that of the Holiness movement than the Pentecostal,

Nee and the Little Flock's influence was felt throughout Pentecostal China.

Pentecostalism since 1949

Since the Communist takeover of China in 1949, Pentecostalism has gone through traumatic upheavals. In the 1950s Pentecostals were allowed to meet as part of a government-sanctioned combined Protestant church called the Three Self Patriotic Movement (TSPM). Due to Pentecostal missions theory and practice, which emphasized quick basic Bible training and then sending out to minister, very few Pentecostal Chinese ever received advanced theological training with the respective degrees. As such, when the TSPM was formed, very few if any Pentecostals were to be found in the leadership structure, even on the provincial level.

In the early 1950s, the mainland China branches of the True Jesus Church, the Jesus Family, and the Little Flock were all disbanded by the government and many of their leaders imprisoned. The Pentecostal church in China was thereafter comparatively small, but since the traumatic period of the Cultural Revolution (1966–1976), the church has seen phenomenal growth. Some estimates chart the growth from about 1.5 million believers around 1970 to 80 million by 2000, of which about 65 percent are considered Pentecostal or charismatic. This group may not subscribe to all the traditional Pentecostal beliefs, but they do emphasize the work of the Holy Spirit, the miraculous, and spiritual gifts such as speaking in tongues. Furthermore, besides the resurrected True Jesus Church and the Jesus Family, many newer Pentecostal groups have appeared, including the Disciples Faith church, the New Testament church, and Fangcheng Pai, among others. In addition to these indigenous entities, the traditional Pentecostal missions agencies have been actively working in Hong Kong, Macao, and Taiwan, while also working in various ways to assist the Pentecostal renewal of China.

PAUL W. LEWIS

See also Asia, East

Further Reading

Bays, D. (1993). Christian revival in China, 1900–1937. In E. Blumhofer & R. Balmer (Eds.), *Modern Christian revivals* (pp. 161–179). Urbana: University of Illinois Press.

Bays, D. (1994). Indigenous Protestant churches in China, 1900–1937: A Pentecostal case study. In S. Kaplan (Ed.), *Indigenous responses to Western Christianity* (pp. 124–143). New York: New York University Press.

Bays, D. (1996). The growth of independent Christianity in China, 1900–1937. In D. Bays (Ed.), *Christianity in China*. Stanford, CA: Stanford University Press.

Bays, D. (1999). The Protestant missionary establishment and the Pentecostal movement. In E. Blumhofer, R. Spittler, & G. Wacker (Eds.), *Pentecostal currents in American Protestantism* (pp. 50–67). Urbana: University of Illinois Press.

Bays, D., & Johnson, T. M. (2002). China. In S. Burgess (Ed.), *International dictionary of Pentecostal and Charismatic movements* (pp. 58–64). Grand Rapids, MI: Zondervan.

Deng, Z. (2001). Indigenous Chinese Pentecostal denominations. *China Study Journal, 16*(3), 5–22.

Hunter, A., & Chan, K-K. 1993. *Protestantism in contemporary China*. New York: Cambridge University Press.

Lambert, T. (1994). *The resurrection of the Chinese church*. Wheaton, IL: OMF.

Lambert, T. (1999). *China's Christian millions*. London: OMF/Monarch Books.

Oblau, G. (2001). Pentecostal by default? Reflections on contemporary Christianity in China. *China Study Journal 16*(3), 23–37.

Sumiko, Y. (2000). *History of Protestantism in China: The indigenization of Christianity*. Tokyo: The Toho Gakkai.

Tang, E. (2002). "Yellers" and healers—Pentecostalism and the study of grassroots Christianity in China. *China Study Journal, 17*(3), 19–29.

Wesley, L. (2004). Is the Chinese church predominantly Pentecostal? *Asian Journal of Pentecostal Studies, 7*(1), 225–254.

Christology

The term "Christology" refers to the study of the person of Jesus Christ. While much of the historical debate in Christendom centers on the express Christian claim of Jesus' union of the divine and human natures, recent christological inquiries are beginning to extend the boundaries to include His work and purpose (soteriology, the doctrine of salvation). The growth of Pentecostal theology exhibits both consistency with historic Christianity as well as the development of particular emphases that integrate the person, work, and purpose of Jesus. These Pentecostal models offer a variety of christological expressions not unlike those of the New Testament writers in the first century world. The existence of the four Gospels—Matthew, Mark, Luke, and John—as well as the distinctive pictures painted by Paul and other New Testament writers provide a reminder of the christological diversity within the Christian canon. As contemporary Pentecostals work diligently to give adequate expression to the common core of the person and work of Jesus Christ, a similar plurality of expression serves as a constant reminder that fresh christological perspectives continue to emerge for needy contexts.

Pentecostals and Historic Christianity

From the earliest days of Christianity, various emphases concerning Christ begin to emerge. The brief life of Jesus of Nazareth on Earth, his suffering and death, and his subsequent resurrection and ascension form the foundation for Christian theology in general and Christology in particular. Volker Küster proposes theological representations of the life of Jesus fundamental to the three historic traditions of Christianity, specifically, Catholicism, Protestantism, and Orthodoxy. First, the Christology of early Catholicism focuses on the incarnation of the pre-existent Son of God in the form of Jesus of Nazareth (John 1:14, RSV, "The Word became flesh and dwelt among us"). Belief in the incarnation of God in Jesus Christ also exalts Mary as "the mother of God," with the child Jesus as the symbol of Catholic piety. From this central perspective of the incarnation, death is the necessary consequence, and the Resurrection completes the cycle. Second, the Protestant theology of the cross does not downplay the idea of incarnation, but shifts the focus to Jesus' suffering and death on the cross where He is condemned for our sins and for our justification. Martin Luther's "theology of the cross," serves as the dominating principle of his whole theology, maintaining that God can be found only through the shame and suffering of the cross. Third, the piety of the Eastern Orthodox tradition, primarily focusing on icons and liturgy, looks heavenward, where the resurrected Christ sits at the right hand of the Father. The longing for immortality provides the driving force of Orthodox Christology with its concept of salvation as divinization. In the liturgy of the church, the incarnation and the cross begin the way of salvation, which culminates in glorious victory over death.

The participation of Pentecostal-Charismatic believers within these three major streams of Christendom generally displays christological continuity with the basic tenets of the specific tradition. However, to these three major approaches, Finnish Pentecostal Veli-Matti Kärkkäinen adds a new and controversial fourth model, namely, the empowerment Christology of Pentecostalism and the Charismatic movement. He argues that Pentecostals do not neglect the incarnation, cross, and Resurrection, but look to Christ especially as the miracle worker and baptizer with the Holy Spirit as the source of empowerment. Whether for physical healing, freedom from evil powers, or charismatic gifts, Pentecostals look to Jesus as the model of spirit-filled Christianity. This concept offers an important corrective to criticisms often pointed at the movement by critics who argue that Pentecostals are centered more on the Holy Spirit than on Jesus Christ. While Pentecostal theology and praxis is often inclined toward pneumacentric emphases, the ideal paradigm is always found in the person and ministry of Jesus. The principle may be expressed as follows: the more of the Spirit pervading total experience, the greater the adoption of Jesus as the object of adoration and imitation.

Early Developments—"The Full Gospel"

The infancy of the Pentecostal movement in comparison to the other great traditions of faith makes the distillation of a simple and straightforward Christology difficult. Early Pentecostalism was primarily oral because for the first half-century and more, Pentecostals, untrained in academic environments, did not generally engage formal Christology or even lives of Jesus. And when they did, what was written down in tract form, evangelistic booklets, or sermons was almost always—except for denominational statements of faith—appropriated through personal and altar-like responses. However, this non-academic development does not necessarily preclude Pentecostals from conducting sound exegetical discipline and reflection; Pentecostals delight in advancing their pragmatic views of Jesus. Further, while the creeds are not generally taught in order to facilitate proper interpretation of Jesus, Pentecostals tend to rely on the Holy Spirit to reveal the Christ of the Scriptures. Ironically, while downplaying these formulaic articles of the Christian faith, a keynote begins to materialize. A. B. Simpson (1843–1919), founder of the Christian and Missionary Alliance, advances the four-fold role of Christ as "Our Saviour, Sanctifier, Healer, and Soon Coming King" to which the Pentecostals would insert a fifth task, "Christ our Baptizer in the Holy Spirit." These great works of Jesus are known as the "full gospel" and divide the movement into two doctrinal directions. The first simply adds Christ as baptizer to the four-fold role and kept all five roles distinct (Church of God in Christ, Church of God [Cleveland, TN]), while a second formation based on William Durham's teaching on the "Finished Work of Christ" merges the role of Jesus as savior with that of sanctifier (International Church of the Foursquare Gospel and Assemblies of God).

Each of the five- or four-fold Gospel components contributes to a Pentecostal Christology. For Pentecostals, Jesus' role as the agent of salvation extends beyond the hope of eternal life and freedom from the guilt of sin to include a salvific effect upon the immediate life, namely, through sanctification. Despite disagreement on the reception of this sanctifying work, agreement persists in keeping with an empowerment Christology, whereby Pentecostals focus on the ability to break away from the cycle of sin and live after the pattern of Jesus (Romans 6, 7; 1 John 3:16). Jesus as the agent of healing flows from a rich nineteenth-century heritage that claims to return to the teaching of the New Testament (see Matthew 8:16–17 in light of Isaiah 53). If Jesus was active as a healer during his ministry on Earth, and if he is still active in the present world, contemporary evidence of His healing power will abound. Jesus as the baptizer in the Holy Spirit offers an elevated encounter of the living Jesus with lordship implications. For Pentecostals, Spirit baptism is an experience emblematic of total surrender to the person of Jesus. This surrender moves beyond mere justification to include power to live like Jesus and to represent Him to the world (Luke 24:29; Acts 1:8). The final component of the "full gospel" is the hope of a glorious return of the living Christ. The returning Christ will raise the dead unto eternal life, transform this present world, and judge humanity.

Oneness Debate

Oneness Pentecostals, originally called the "New Issue" or "Jesus Only," took on organizational form in 1917 as a result of expulsion from the recently chartered Assemblies of God (1914). As a form of modalism, proponents preserve the radical monarchy of God and affirm simultaneous triune revelation in the one divine being revealed as Father in the Son and as Spirit through the Son. These origins are found in the early tendency of Pentecostals to discover repeatable biblical patterns, especially in the book of Acts. At a 1913 Pentecostal camp meeting in Los Angeles, Canadian evangelist R. E. McAlister posits that the early apostles only baptized converts in Jesus' name and not in a Trinitarian formula. Shortly thereafter Frank Ewart concludes that the Trinitarian designations of Father, Son, and Holy Spirit are simply functional descriptions of the self-disclosure of the one God in the human person of Jesus.

This idea is summed up in Colossians 2:9, a favorite passage of Oneness theologians: "For in him the whole fullness of deity dwells bodily." As a challenge to Trinitarians, it is argued that if only one Person of the

Godhead becomes incarnate, then Jesus is neither the full revelation of deity nor the revelation of the full deity. David Bernard, noted Oneness Pentecostal theologian, states: "There is no possibility of separating God and Jesus, and there is no God visible outside of Jesus" (1983, 29). As participants in Pentecostalism, Oneness proponents emerge to reject the classical Christian contention for the Trinity, while keeping distinctive Pentecostal doctrine, specifically a pneumatological Christology in which Jesus of Nazareth functions as the incarnate presence of the Father's self-disclosure through the dynamic work of the Spirit. As Oneness and Trinitarian Pentecostals continue to engage each other, it will be important for both sides to listen attentively. Trinitarian Pentecostals must wrestle with the Oneness movement as a substantial presence within Pentecostalism, while Oneness Pentecostals must address christological positions that stand not only outside of traditional Pentecostal theology but also broader Christendom.

Pentecostals and the Paradigmatic Jesus

A fruitful contribution by Pentecostals to christological discussions concerns the work and purpose of Jesus as a model for spiritual experience and mission. Understanding this offers further tempering of the common criticism against Pentecostals for an apparent overemphasis on the Holy Spirit to the detriment of Jesus. While this may in part be true as demonstrated by the plethora of literature on the work of the Holy Spirit, the criticism is likely overstated. If it is true that Pentecostals are pneumacentric, the paradigm for the life of the Spirit is found first and foremost in the person of Jesus. Jesus is an example not only for first century believers (John 13:15; 1 Corinthians 4:17; 11:1; 1 Peter 2:21), but also the contemporary prototype for those wanting to live in the power of the Spirit (Romans 8:29). In the same way that the Spirit working in Jesus empowered him to carry out his divine mission, so disciples of every generation are empowered by the Holy Spirit to live as people of God. Further, Jesus whom the Spirit anointed and to whom the Spirit bears witness is "the same, yesterday, today, and forever" (Hebrews 13:8).

This concept may be expressed through the dual examples of Jesus the miracle worker and Jesus the exorcist. Both roles follow the ideal of Jesus as healer. Thus, just as the miracle-working Jesus did many extraordinary acts while on Earth, so also contemporary Pentecostals expect to perform similar signs. And since the Gospels are filled with accounts of the power of Jesus over demons, Pentecostals and charismatics see the ministry of Jesus as the biblical paradigm for the practice of exorcisms. Further, since precedent for this is found in the book of Acts, where the apostolic church follows in the tradition of Jesus the exorcist, so also the contemporary Pentecostal continues in the tradition of Jesus. While it is worth noting that the diversity of opinion as to whether these events should be deemed exorcisms, the act of expelling evil spirits through the name of Jesus Christ, or healing that is from natural or psychological causes, is ongoing, agreement is realized in the recognition of both as a continuation of the ministry of Jesus (Acts 1:1).

Future Directions in Global Pentecostalism

As the Pentecostalism of the global north moves into its second century, once oral and local traditions are becoming increasingly systematized. However, in the emerging global south, a mosaic of theological and specifically christological contexts are starting to address varying needs and desires while also possessing the potential to influence the classical views of the north. First, a current and future direction for Christian theology is located in the encounter between Christianity and other faiths. While some Pentecostals view this in negative terms, a missiological movement ought to rejoice at the opportunities at the frontiers of the next phase of Christian history. Second, this challenge will increasingly call for a greater relationship between an ontological Christology (the person of Christ) and a functional Christology (what Christ has done for humanity). For example, while Jesus as healer, miracle worker, and exorcist is often paradigmatic for the life of the Pentecostal believer, a developing lacuna may include the exemplary suffering of Jesus. The global north, often desirous of God's blessings coupled with health and prosperity, finds it difficult to identify with the cross of Christ. This must also be contrasted with the emergence of a Pentecostalism, especially in the global south, where believers undoubtedly identify strongly with Christ as liberator and reconciler. Finally, ongoing christological awareness will be increasingly global, intercultural and eclectic thereby transcending current ecclesiastical and theological boundaries. Like the Gospel writers of the first century, Pentecostals and charismatics of the twenty-first century are well positioned to address this rich range of voices, and strive for meaningful christological foci.

MARTIN WILLIAM MITTELSTADT

See also Globalization of Pentecostalism; Holy Spirit; Oneness Theology; Trinitarianism

Further Reading

Aulén, G. (1950). *Christus victor*. London: SPCK.

Bernard, D. (1983). *The oneness of God*. Hazelwood, MO: Pentecostal Publishing House.

Del Colle, R. (1993). Spirit-Christology: Dogmatic foundations for Pentecostal-Charismatic spirituality. *Journal of Pentecostal Theology, 3*, 91–112.

Dunn, J. D. G. (1990). *Unity and diversity in the New Testament* (2nd ed.). Harrisville, PA: Trinity Press International.

Dunn, J. D. G. (2003). *Jesus remembered: Christianity in the making, 1*. Grand Rapids, MI: Eerdmans.

Erickson, M. *Christian theology* (2nd ed.). Grand Rapids, MI: Baker Book House.

Hunter, H. D. (1992). The resurgence of spirit Christology. *Journal of the European Theological Association, 10*, 50–57.

Kärkkäinen, V.-M. (2003). *Christology: A global introduction: An ecumenical, international, and contextual perspective*. Grand Rapids, MI: Baker Academic.

Küster, V. (2001). *The many faces of Jesus Christ: Intercultural Christology*. Maryknoll, NY: Orbis.

Jenkins, P. (2002). *The next Christendom: The coming of global Christianity*. New York: Oxford.

Johnson, L. T. (1998). *Living Jesus: Learning the heart of the gospel*. San Francisco: Harper.

Moltmann, J. (1972). *The crucified God: The cross of Christ as the foundation and criticism of Christian theology*. New York: Harper.

Reed, D. (1997). Oneness Pentecostalism: Problems and possibilities for Pentecostal theology. *Journal of Pentecostal Theology, 11*, 73–93.

Simpson, A. B. (1887). *The fourfold gospel*. Harrisburg, PA: Christian Publications.

Smail, T. (1994). The cross and the spirit. *The love of power or the power of love*. Minneapolis, MN: Bethany House.

Twelftree, G. H. (1993). *Jesus the exorcist: A contribution to the study of the historical Jesus*. Tübingen: Mohr-Siebeck.

Wacker, G. (2001). *Heaven below: Early Pentecostals and American culture*. Cambridge, MA: Harvard University Press.

Church Growth

The term "church growth" developed out of the desire to see why some churches grow. Initially, it referred primarily to the study of the growth of a corporate church (e.g., the church of Korea or the church of Nigeria) or a local church (e.g., the Yoido Full Gospel Church in Seoul, Korea). In the 1950s to 1970s, the term "church growth" became more commonly used to mean the study of why some churches grow, and what principles can be extracted to use in other churches elsewhere. The church growth movement had an early interest in Pentecostal churches, both in their dynamic growth and in why they were growing. Since the 1970s, there has been a stronger appreciation and focus among Pentecostals themselves to look critically at themselves with "church growth" eyes.

Background

The father of the church growth movement is considered to be Donald A. McGavran. McGavran developed his ideas while a missionary in India with the United Christian Missionary Society (affiliated with the Disciples of Christ). In his tenure in India, while under the influence of John Mott (of the Student Volunteer Movement) and Bishop J. Waskom Pickett (Methodist), McGavran reevaluated traditional missionary practices (i.e., the "mission station" approach) focusing on the Indian "people movement." This missionary experience during the 1920s and 1930s set the groundwork for his book *The Bridges of God: A Study in the Strategy of Missions* in 1955. It was McGavran himself who used the term "church growth" for this new endeavor, and this book is considered to be the beginning of the church growth movement. In 1960, he founded the Institute of Church Growth in Eugene, Oregon, which commenced operations in 1961. Here he was joined by Australian anthropologist Alan Tippett. In 1964, McGavran established the journal *Church Growth Bulletin* and was its director until 1980. This journal was an important outlet for spreading church growth ideals and concepts. In 1965, the institute became part of the School of World Mission at Fuller Theological Seminary in Pasadena, California, and McGavran became the founding dean of that school. With Donald McGavran's monumental work, *Understanding Church Growth* (originally published in 1970), the church growth movement as envisioned by McGavran grew into prominence.

In the early 1970s, with McGavran's consistent focus on the missiological context, there was no strong voice for American church growth until C. Peter Wagner emerged in this capacity with such books as *Our Kind of People: The Ethical Dimensions of Church Growth in America* (1979). Up to the 1970s, the movement had a strong missiological connection—McGavran (India), Wagner (Bolivia), Ralph D. Winter (Guatemala), Arthur Glasser (China), Charles Kraft (Nigeria), and others having served previously as missionaries. After the 1970s many of the main articulators were from pastoral or evangelistic backgrounds—Winfield Arn, Carl F.

The first graduating class of the Southern California Bible School in 1925. *Courtesy of Vanguard University.*

George, George Hunter III, and Elmer Towns. From the early 1980s, another facet became emphasized within the church growth movement, namely "signs and wonders." This emphasis started with the course taught by John Wimber at Fuller in 1981 entitled "Signs, Wonders, and Church Growth," followed by "The Miraculous and Church Growth" (1982–1985); numerous works by Wimber and Wagner highlighted this aspect of church growth.

During the 1980s and into the early 1990s, numerous church growth associations and societies were established, such as the American Society of Church Growth in Pasadena, California (1984), the British Church Growth Association originally in London (1981), and the Institute of Church Growth tied to Yoido Full Gospel Church, Seoul, Korea (1993). Further, several journals pertaining to church growth were also established. Whereas since the mid-1990s the church growth movement has somewhat diminished in importance in theological institutions within the United States in deference to "leadership" and the "seeker-sensitive" movement, this movement is still a dominant force internationally.

Basic Tenets

The focus of the church growth movement is to identify those characteristics, methods, and techniques that help churches grow or impede others churches' growth. The movement was not just interested in recording the growth of churches or their historical developments, but rather the emphasis was on the principles as to why and how the churches grew. One of the key principles espoused by this movement is the "homogeneous unit principle," which emphasizes the desire of people to be brought to church and stay in a church with others of like race, language, and social background. Further, people tend to reach out to those like themselves, especially to family, friends, and coworkers. So, there is an emphasis on "building bridges" in order to bring others to faith in Jesus Christ. There are also some church growth strategists who study the death of churches and why these churches died in order to find principles that will help other churches to become or remain vital growing churches. Several other key principles espoused by those within the church growth movement are the foundation of biblical principles, an emphasis on evangelism, developing discipleship groups, lay leadership involvement and training, and structuring for growth. Those within the movement also have redefined "discipleship" to mean taking nonbelievers from that stage to maturity in Christ.

Since McGavran, the tools used by the church growth experts have been the tools used in the behavioral and social sciences, most notably demographics. In demographics, there is an endeavor to map out an area by using census and related material to target the various groups of an area. Further, there is a conscious decision as to which "homogeneous unit" to focus on and which group will be most receptive to the message presented.

The church growth movement has also had some criticisms concerning the philosophy or the excesses of the movement. For one, some have pointed to the apparent "result" orientation of the movement, that the only sign of successful growth is numerical growth. Second, some have questioned the foundations of both McGavran and Wagner as being more pragmatic, or social sciences oriented, and not adequately grounded in the Bible. Critics have felt that the Bible was being used to support their preconceived ideas and not as the foundation for their philosophy. Further, some have accused those who used "church growth" principles of growth by transfer (i.e., sheep stealing) rather than growth by evangelism. Several church growth advocates have answered these accusations extensively; yet, these are common and ongoing charges.

Church Growth Movement and Pentecostalism

In reference to Pentecostalism, the church growth movement has had two main facets. First, initially there were studies on the growth of Pentecostal churches by non-Pentecostals from within the church growth movement, frequently within broader works such as the studies on the churches in Mexico (McGavran, Huegel, and Taylor 1963), Brazil (Read 1965), the Philippines (Montgomery 1975), and Latin America as a whole (Read, Monterroso, and Johnson 1969). Further, McGavran's article "What Makes Pentecostal Churches Grow?" in the journal *Global Church Growth* (January 1977), various other articles in the *Church Growth Bulletin* (later *Global Church Growth*), and Wagner's book *Look Out! The Pentecostals are Coming* (1973) were strong endorsements of Pentecostal churches and Pentecostalism as a whole. An example of Pentecostal church growth principles is Wagner's "church growth" analysis of Pentecostalism in the *Dictionary of*

Pentecostal and Charismatic Movements (Burgess, McGee, and Alexander 1988). Wagner noted several factors that have led to Pentecostal growth: biblical triumphalism (God will do great things); targeting the poor and oppressed; multiple tracks to ordination (there is not a minimal academic requirement); high local-church autonomy; the apostolic model of church planting; and schism (which allows for two churches or groups to reach out instead of the original one). Wagner also notes that the local churches tend to be conservative Evangelicals, have related Bible training of the constituents, and have strong pastoral leadership. Further, Pentecostal churches have strong emphasis on the work of the Holy Spirit and a real emphasis on prayer, worship, and lay participation. Furthermore, financial support is voluntary yet abundant.

The second major facet was that early on there were Pentecostal scholars from within the church growth movement who wrote on church growth within Pentecostalism (e.g., May 1990; Thomas 1978; Womack 1977). Several of these graduated from Fuller's School of World Mission and wrote their dissertations concerning their respective Pentecostal denominations and/or geographical areas. Further, many of these students were in denominational leadership and/or became teachers in Pentecostal schools such as the Assemblies of God Theological Seminary (Springfield, Missouri), Church of God Theological Seminary (Cleveland, Tennessee), Gospel Theological Seminary (Daejeon, Korea), Hansei University (Kyunggi-do, Korea), International Correspondence Institute University (now Global University), Oral Roberts University (Tulsa, Oklahoma), and Vanguard University (Costa Mesa, California). These prominent Pentecostal Fuller graduates (and the year of graduation) include Collin Crago (Assemblies of God, Australia, 1991), Terrance Lewis (Assemblies of God United States, 1980), Flavius J. May (Church of God, Cleveland, Tennessee, 1989), L. Grant McClung (Church of God, 1985), Myung Sung-hoon (Yoido Full Gospel Church, Seoul, Korea, 1990), Benjamin Shinde (Assemblies of God, India, 1974), and Chris Thomas (Assemblies of God, Malaysia, 1976). These and other Pentecostals' dissertations, although in most cases unpublished, were the foundation for many articles that were published in denominational journals, were the basis for courses taught within the Pentecostal schools, and were frequently the foundation for denominational leadership decisions. While these authors and others later were the key instigators and teachers of church growth within Pentecostal schools, there were also prominent Pentecostal pastors who exerted a strong influence on the perception and propagation of the church growth movement, such as Tommy Barnett, David Cho Yonggi, Prince Guneratham, and Jack Hayford. Whereas the church growth analysis and usage of these Pentecostals differ little from other Evangelical church leaders, Pentecostal church growth analysis had a strong emphasis on the Holy Spirit and the miraculous within the workings and growth of the church. This was especially true prior to the "Signs, Wonders, and Church Growth" course and the advent of the "third wave" instigated by Wimber and Wagner.

Although the church growth movement within Pentecostal circles is still strong internationally, this is especially true in Korea, where the Yoido Full Gospel Church and its Senior Pastor David Yonggi Cho have actively pursued the ongoing development of the church growth movement. This focus was propagated by the numerous works by Pastor Cho himself or about his church growth techniques (Ma, Menzies, and Bae 2004; Myung and Hong 2003) and his establishment of the Institute of Church Growth. This institute has overseen the annual Church Growth International conferences, numerous church growth publications like the *Church Growth Manual* (1986–), and the magazine *Church Growth*, which is distributed to over 125 countries around the world.

In reference to church growth, Pentecostals (especially in the United States) have tended to evolve through three stages. Early Pentecostal churches (1900s–1950s) grew but they did not know why, except to state that the reason for the growth was spiritual. They emphasized the "Spirit-led" dynamic that resulted in the growth of the churches. The second stage was the identifying of certain principles and methods that led to the growth of the Pentecostal churches. Some of this analysis, especially by missionaries like Melvin Hodges, happened in the early years of the church growth movement. However, with the blossoming of the movement, the purposeful endeavor to seek out growth principles became more commonplace, as exemplified by Pentecostal denominational church growth conferences. The emphasized growth principles tended to be both spiritual, such as the need for prayer and the miraculous, and social, such as the emphasis on music and the "homogeneous" small groups. The third stage is the contemporary bifurcation between the traditional forms and foci of early Pentecostalism and the contemporary, "seeker-sensitive" charismatic forms of the church. Both emphasize the need for the miraculous but they are divided on the liturgical formulations of the churches. So whereas many agree with the same principles, they see the practices as divergent. Furthermore, the traditional Pentecostal churches suggest that the charismatic

churches' practices deviate from "true Pentecostalism" or are, at worst, syncretistic with the world. Interestingly, all three stages can still be found within Pentecostalism today.

PAUL W. LEWIS

See also African Initiated Churches; America, Latin; Brazil; China; Korea; Philippines

Further Reading

Cho, P. Y. (1984). *More than numbers.* Waco, TX: Word Books.

Green, H. (1972). *Why churches die.* Minneapolis, MN: Bethany Fellowship.

Hodges, M. (1965a). Administering for church growth. In D. McGavran (Ed.), *Church growth and Christian mission* (pp. 214–227). New York: Harper & Row.

Hodges, M. (1965b). Creating climate for church growth. In D. McGavran (Ed.), *Church growth and Christian mission* (pp. 27–39). New York: Harper & Row.

Hong, Y. (2000). Revisiting church growth in Korean Protestantism: A theological reflection. *International Review of Mission*, 89(353), 190–202.

Kang, C. (2004). Resources for studies of David Yonggi Cho. In W. Ma, W. Menzies, & H. Bae (Eds.), *David Yonggi Cho: A close look at his theology and ministry.* Baguio, Philippines: APTS Press.

Ma, W., Menzies, W., & Bae, H. (Eds.). (2004). *David Yonggi Cho: A close look at his theology and ministry.* Baguio, Philippines: APTS Press.

May, F. J. (1990). *The Book of Acts and church growth.* Cleveland, TN: Pathway Press.

McClung, L. G. (1986). *Azusa Street and beyond: Pentecostal missions and church growth in the twentieth century.* South Plainfield, NJ: Logos.

McGavran, D. (1955). *The bridges of God.* New York: Friendship Press.

McGavran, D. (1970). *Understanding church growth.* Grand Rapids, MI: Eerdmans.

McGavran, D., Huegel, J., & Taylor, J. (1963). *Church growth in Mexico.* Grand Rapids, MI: Eerdmans.

Montgomery, J. (1975). *Fire in the Philippines* (Rev. ed.). Carol Stream, IL: Creation House.

Myung, S.-H., & Hong, Y.-G. (Eds.). (2003). *Charis and Charisma: David Yonggi Cho and the Growth of Yoido Full Gospel Church.* London: Regnum.

Rainer, T. S. (1998). Evangelism and church growth. In D. Dockery (Ed.), *New dimensions in evangelical thought* (pp. 411–426). Downers Grove, IL: InterVarsity Press.

Read, W. (1965). *New patterns of church growth in Brazil.* Grand Rapids, MI: Eerdmans.

Read, W., Monterrosso, V., & Johnson, H. (1969). *Latin American church growth.* Grand Rapids, MI: Eerdmans.

Thomas, C. (1978). *Diaspora Indians: Church growth among Indians in West Malaysia*. Penang, Malaysia: Malaysia Indian Evangelism Council.

Tippett, A. (Ed.). (1973). *God, man, and church growth: A Festschrift in honor of Donald Anderson McGavran*. Grand Rapids, MI: Eerdmans.

Wagner, C. P. (1979). *Look out! The Pentecostals are coming*. Carol Stream, IL: Creation House.

Wagner, C. P. (1979). *Our kind of people: The ethical dimensions of church growth in America*. Philadelphia: John Knox.

Wagner, C. P. (1988). Church Growth. In S. Burgess, G. McGee, & P. Alexander (Eds.), *Dictionary of Pentecostal and Charismatic Movements* (pp. 180–195). Grand Rapids, MI: Zondervan.

Womack, D. (1977). *The pyramid principle of church growth*. Minneapolis, MN: Bethany Fellowship.

Church, Theology of the

The church is the church of God, the work fundamentally of God's salvific grace. The term *ekklesia* in the New Testament refers to the gathering together of the assembly of Christians by God. The fact that the church is the *ekklesia* of God (e.g., Acts 20:28; cf. Psalm 74:2) distinguishes this assembly from secular forms of *ekklesia* in the ancient world. The church recognizes its connection with the people of God in the Old Testament, since there is one olive tree created by God to be God's people (Romans 11:13–14). Christ fulfills Israel's election and the mystery of God's plan from the time of Abraham for the people of God to reach all nations (Genesis 17:3–4), causing the church to find its own election "in Christ" (Ephesians 1:4). Thus, the church is also the *ekklesia* of the Lord, for Christ is its foundation (1 Corinthians 3:11). The church abides in Christ (John 4:4) and gathers in his name (Matthew 18:20).

The church is also the new creation of the Spirit, who was breathed upon the disciples by Christ after His Resurrection (John 20:22; 1 Corinthians 15:45) and poured out upon the post-Easter assembly in Jerusalem on the Day of Pentecost after the ascension (Acts 2). It is by the Spirit that the church confesses Jesus as Lord to the glory of the Father and is graced to build itself up in love through multiple gifts as the body of Christ on Earth (Ephesians 4; 1 Corinthians 12). The church is also empowered by the Spirit to proclaim the gospel and to bear witness to Christ in the world (Acts 1:8). The church depends on the intercessory ministry of Christ for its grace (Hebrews 4), interceding also by the Spirit for a suffering world (Romans 8:26). The church, as a pilgrim people, lives "between the times" from the down payment of the Spirit while waiting in hope for the fulfillment of the Kingdom of God (Ephesians 1:13–14).

There are various metaphors of the church in the New Testament, such as the branches of the vine (which is Christ; John 15), the body of Christ (1 Corinthians 12), the bride of Christ (Revelation 22:17), the army of God (Ephesians 6:10–11), the temple of God (Ephesians 2:21–22), and an olive tree (Romans 11:13–14). This metaphorical language is highly suggestive of what the church is, leaving room for varying theological interpretations. For example, the metaphor "body of Christ" suggests an organic model of the church in which the people of God are by nature the "extension" of Christ in the world. An overemphasis on this model can lead to a theology of the church that lacks sufficient stress on the church's responsibility to become the church ever anew through ongoing reformation and faithfulness. The church as the "bride of Christ" with its emphasis on the church's covenant relationship with Christ and consequent commitment to ongoing faithfulness can provide balance.

Both baptism and the Eucharist characterized the church of the New Testament as participant in the death and Resurrection of Christ and as the reconciled/reconciling community in which "there is no longer Jew or Greek, there is no longer slave or free, there is no longer male or female, for all…are one in Christ" (Galatians 3:28,). The church thus lives from the *koinonia* of God as Father, Son, and Spirit, devoting itself "to the apostles' teaching and fellowship, to the breaking of bread and prayers" (Acts 2:42). Paul placed great value on the foundational witnesses having seen the risen Christ and having been entrusted with the tradition of the gospel to hand down to others (1 Corinthians 15). This tradition itself bore witness to the redemptive power of God to redeem and liberate humanity by the Kingdom of God experienced through Jesus as God's anointed Messiah (Matthew 12:28). The church finds its nature in the New Testament as the body of Christ's disciples, seeking to fulfill the will of the Father by the power of the Spirit so as to embody and to further the redemption, reconciliation, and justice of the Kingdom of God in the world. The church has developed classic "marks" (*notae*), to which we now turn.

The Marks of the Church

The Nicene-Constantinople Creed affirmed the church as one, holy, catholic, and apostolic. These marks gain their substance and direction in the fact that the church is the church of God, elect of the Father, redeemed by the Son, and sanctified/gifted/empowered by the Spirit (1 Peter 1:2).

One

The unity of the church is thus "of the Spirit" in the "one Lord" and the "one God and Father of all" (Ephesians 4:3–6). This unity of diversely gifted members is also spoken of as by "the same Spirit," "the same Lord," and "the same God who activates all of them" (1 Corinthians 12:4–6). Jesus prayed that the company of disciples who would follow him be one, stating, "As you, Father, are in me and I am in you, may they also be in us, so that the world may believe that you have sent me" (John 17:21). This unity is based in the *koinonia* of God and is thus active, vibrant, and visible or able to serve the church's witness to the gospel. It is also a goal worthy of intentional prayer and action (Ephesians 4:3), although there is in God already a united people as a gift of God in the world (Ephesians 4:4). The unity that is a gift is also a task and is to be made visible on the local level, but also more universally among every family on earth that bears the name of the Father (Ephesians 3:15). This is not to be a monolithic "world church." The most widely accepted model of unity in the ecumenical movement has been inspired by the Anglican communion, namely, a unity in *diversity*. The church can have many various branches though one stem. Those who hold this view of the church's unity realize that it is a uniquely Protestant vision not shared by the Catholic and Orthodox communions. For these communions, divisions do not exist *in* the church, only *from* it. The church is already visibly one, even though there are communities of genuine faith that are divided from it and have gifts to share with the mother church. Vatican II purposely regarded the catholicity of the church as "subsisting in" the Roman Catholic communion in order to allow for elements of catholicity to exist in divided communities of Christian faith outside of the visible church.

Holy

The holiness of the church is rooted in Christ, who set himself apart to fulfill the will of the Father in order that his followers be sanctified in God's Word and truth (John 17:17–19). As such, the church is to be in the world but not of it, because it remains faithful to the Word of life as it witnesses of this to others (John 17:14–16). The church is baptized into Christ's death so that it may rise to newness of life in the power of His Resurrection (Romans 6:4; Philippians 3:10). It is also

"sanctified by his Spirit" (1 Peter 1:2), who is the "Holy" Spirit of God, in order that it would follow Christ in the world and obey His commandments, the chief of which is love. The church is thus able to bear fruit that glorifies the Father (John 15:1–17). Holiness is love that does not compromise with evil and injustice but seeks in all things to rejoice in truth and in the hope for the fulfillment of God's will on Earth (1 Corinthians 13:6–7).

Catholic

The term "catholic" has historically taken on both qualitative and quantitative implications. Qualitatively, the term can denote the fullness of grace, truth, and spiritual gifts. Quantitatively, the church is "catholic" as the people of God spread throughout the world. Cyril of Jerusalem combined the qualitative and quantitative by stating that the Catholic Church "is called catholic because it is spread throughout the world" and because "it teaches universally and completely all doctrines," "subjects to right worship all humankind," and "possesses in itself every conceivable virtue, whether in deeds, words or in spiritual gifts of every kind" (*Catechetical Lectures*, 18.23). Catholicity is an ecumenical issue, especially as it relates to the unity of the church and the church's eschatological orientation toward the fullness of redemption yet to come.

Apostolic

The term "apostle" literally meant "sent one." The apostolicity of the church is rooted in the nature of Christ and the Spirit as sent of God to bring about redemption in all of creation. The apostles were "sent" as well to represent Christ in the power of the Spirit (John 20:21–22). The inner circle of the apostles saw the risen Christ and were directly commissioned by Him to guard and spread the Gospel. Paul claimed to belong to this circle, granting him equal authority to the pillars of the church (Galatians 1–2). The entire church is apostolic in a derivative sense, however, since it is sent to be the witness of Christ in the power of the Spirit as well. The apostolicity of the church involves remaining true to the original legacy that the apostles received from Christ. This legacy involves the vibrant experience of the Spirit, faithfulness to the Word of God, the missionary task, and episcopal succession, both its nature and role in history.

Free churches, which resist any connection to the state and define the church as a fellowship of believers, have not much explicit sense of apostolic succession in history, nor of continuous tradition. Even if some of these churches should have bishops or apostles, their stress is not on continuity of oversight and tradition in history but rather on the need to constantly restore and renew the church to its original calling under the ongoing threat of discontinuity from it. The World Council of Churches Faith and Order document, *Baptism, Eucharist, Ministry* (Lima, Peru, 1982), affirmed episcopal succession as instrumental in maintaining the continuity of the church and its tradition in history. It also sought, however, to affirm those who seem in the view of the framers to implicitly honor apostolic succession by having some sort of regard for current episcopal oversight in the church.

Is the office of the bishop that provides overseers in the church essential to the church? Catholic, Orthodox, and Anglican traditions regard the office of the bishop as essential (*esse*) to the church, whereas other communions would regard only Christ as essential to the church. The bishops are in this case for the "good" (*bene esse*) of the church. In those communions that make the bishop essential to the church, too much emphasis can be placed on the uniqueness of their role in overseeing the church, conceiving of this in highly juridical ways that tend to alienate the office from the many gifts and ministries inspired by the Spirit among the laity in the church. Official Catholic ecclesiology regards the office of the bishop as qualitatively different from the gifted ministries of the laity because of its nature and calling to represent Christ in continuity with the pope as overseers in the church. This position produces a hierarchical ecclesiology. Free-church traditions may want to grant the overseers or leaders of the church special authority in Christ but would tend to see these as spiritual gifts essentially no different in nature than other gifted ministries. This free-church view thus tends toward an ecclesiology that stresses mutual responsibility and partnership in ministry. Despite these differences, many across the lines of the various communions, even among those who view the office of the bishop as qualitatively different from the spiritual gifts in the church, still want to highlight the office of the bishop as a gift (*charism*) in the church as well, though one that is unique. The role of the Spirit uses various gifts to enhance the *koinonia* or communion of the people of God.

Nature and Boundaries of the Church

What is the church? Ecclesiologies within various communions are complex and tend to overlap in ecumenical sensitivity to one another. For example, the Catholic theologian Hans Küng in his classic ecclesiology, *The Church* (1976), attempted to offset the heavily hierarchical and juridical notions of the church featured in Catholic ecclesiologies with an emphasis on the charismatic structure of the church. Vatican II as well included a notion of the church as the pilgrim people headed toward eschatological perfection, a focus welcomed by Protestants. On the other hand, Miroslav Volf (1997) wrote a free-church ecclesiology in which he attempted to reveal the shortcomings of viewing the church as merely an association of believers (a weakness of free-church ecclesiologies). He based the church more deeply in the *koinonia* (communion) of God as Father, Son, and Spirit, which gave his ecclesiology appeal beyond free-church contexts.

But there are unique emphases within various communions that will tend to be prominent when answering the question concerning the nature of the church and its boundaries. For example, those of the Catholic Church will tend to focus on the church as a world body in communion with the pope and participating in the Eucharist. Communities of faith outside of the church will contain valuable elements of catholicity though they are divided from the mother church (the exception is the Eastern Orthodox churches, which the Vatican has come to regard as "sister" churches). Eastern Orthodox Christians will call attention to the church as a local church (consisting of churches within a diocese) that participates in the Eucharist under the supervision of a local bishop. Those in the Anglican communion would most likely call attention to the church as a diverse body (*corpus per mixtum*) containing many branches. Those from Anabaptist roots will be likely to highlight the church as a community of disciples of Jesus, who are called to provide a witness to the peace and justice of the Kingdom of God in their devotion to Christ. Those of the magisterial Reformation will tend to see the church as the creation of the Word of God (*creatura verba*), called to be the church ever and again through faithful proclamation and participation in the principal sacraments of the church: baptism and Eucharist. Pentecostals are likely to call attention to the charismatic structure of the church as well as to "anointed" preaching "with signs following." Those of other free-church traditions will highlight the church as a fellowship of believers.

Different emphases call attention to potentially valuable aspects of the nature and boundaries of the church, but they also give rise to thorny ecumenical challenges. For example, free-church missionaries evangelize in countries heavily populated by Catholic or Orthodox Christians among folks baptized as infants but not yet having come to a personal faith in Christ. Since these missionaries see the church as a fellowship of believers, they would see the folk they evangelize as unbelievers having no legitimate connection to the church. Catholic or Orthodox church leaders, however, will view these infant-baptized folk as involved in a sacramental journey within their churches that is sustained by the faith of the church and that should not be interrupted by free-church proselytism. In the light of such tense issues, ecumenical discussions on the nature and boundaries of the church must continue in search of greater common understanding.

Koinonia: The Ecumenical Consensus

Comparative ecclesiology is the method whereby representatives from various church bodies develop a greater understanding of their different traditions and seek a richer sense of commonality within diversity. It seems that comparative ecclesiology and other forms of ecumenical work on the nature of the church have recently served to sensitize Christians to the ecclesiological issues that divide them. The renewed appreciation for the church as a *koinonia* or communion with the life of God has especially done much to inspire the insight that our divisions, no matter how serious or scandalous, do not "reach to heaven" and that it is still possible to arrive at certain common understandings of the nature and purpose of the church in the midst of our differences. Communion ecclesiology, which focuses on the church as *koinonia*, has also gained popularity in response to this development.

The communion that is already realized in the church and is the future goal of the church has its source in the very being of God as Father, Son, and Holy Spirit. Thus, the communion of the church is fundamentally drawn from the Trinitarian life of God. There is in the New Testament a "Trinitarian structure" to comments about the church's life, unity, and mission, although nothing in the context of these texts requires it (Ephesians 4:1–6; 1 Corinthians 12:4–6). The implication is that the church draws its nature centrally from the *koinonia* of God. The *koinonia* of God, however, has taken humanity and creation into itself by way of a salvation history featuring the mutual redemptive work of Christ and the Spirit as the "left and right hands of God" (Irenaeus).

Of course, in ecumenical documents, the church is also pictured as the gift of the Word of God, a mystery or sacrament of God's love or real, saving presence in the world, a pilgrim people on the way toward completion, or a prophetic sign of the Kingdom of God in the world as it seeks to proclaim the good news and be an instrument of justice and peace in the world. These descriptions imply that the church is also involved in *kerygma* (proclamation), *diakonia* (service), and *liturgia* (worship and sacraments).

Postscript

Some believe that the church is being reconfigured in the twenty-first century toward a kind of grassroots ecumenism. Megachurches have arisen drawing congregants from a variety of church backgrounds. Some have even begun to speculate that we are approaching a post-denominational era of the church in which people will attend a church with little thought given to denominational loyalties. Furthermore, Pentecostal and charismatic styles of worship and types of ministry are having a vast influence among the churches across denominational lines, especially in places like Asia, Africa, and Central America. Meanwhile, free-church congregations are coming into being in the United States and abroad that are seeking to rediscover ancient liturgical forms of worship. The churches in the world are involved in an interesting kind of mutual transformation that might serve in the long run to bring us all closer together.

Frank D. Macchia

See also Apostle, Apostolic; Doctrine, Development of; Ecumenism and Ecumenical Movement

Further Reading

Kärkkäinen, V.-M. (2002). *An introduction to ecclesiology: Ecumenical, historical, and global perspectives.* Downers Grove, IL: InterVarsity.

Küng, H. (1976). *The church.* New York: Doubleday.

Volf, M. (1997). *After our likeness: The church as the image of the Trinity.* Grand Rapids, MI: Eerdmans.

Baptism, Eucharist, ministry: Report of the World Council of Churches Faith and Order Commission, Lima Peru, 1982. (1984). In H. Meyer & L. Vischer (Eds.), *Growth in agreement: Reports and agreed statements of ecumenical conversations on a world level* (pp. 465–503). New York: Paulist Press.

Communion (Eucharist)

Churches stemming from the Reformation, in general, present a variety of theologies and practices concerning "sacraments"; the term itself is not intended in a unique way, some confessional traditions preferring the term "ordinances." The Orthodox and the Catholic Churches' traditions are comfortable with the use of the terms "mystery" (translated into Latin as "*sacramentum*") and "sacramentality," which frame their views concerning the sacraments and the role of the church over them.

Christians have always believed that the sacrifice of Christ is and remains a unique event; his command: "Do this in remembrance of me" (1 Corinthians 11:23–25), however, has been interpreted differently by the different churches throughout the centuries. Therefore, Pentecostals and charismatics have followed their respective confessional backgrounds about the Eucharist, the role and significance of which still constitutes one of the main differences among them. It is possible to identify a unifying element—as well as a contribution to the theological debate—in the role of the Holy Spirit, for his signs and wonders are strongly oriented to worship, in which the celebration of the Eucharist takes place.

Biblical Roots

It is a central Christian belief that God has freely created human beings so that they can share His divine life and enjoy communion with the Trinity (1 Corinthians 1:9). This sharing is also a gift in which the believers participate in their earthly pilgrimage (2 Corinthians 13:13). The Eucharist has always signified the kind of communion between God and His people as is expressed in various Old Testament (Exodus 16:4; 24:8–11; Psalm 23:5; Proverbs 9:1–6; Isaiah 65:13) and New Testament (Luke 13:29; 14:15; Matthew 8:11; Mark 6:30–44; 8:1–10) images of God's care for his creatures and of a foretaste of the heavenly meal in the kingdom. The New Testament texts describing the call of Christians to partake in God's life are often also accounts of the Christian communities' celebration of the Eucharist in obedience to Christ's command, as appears in the self-understanding of the first communities: "The cup of blessing that we bless, is it not a sharing in the blood of Christ? The bread that we break, is it not a sharing in the body of Christ? Because there is one bread, we who are many are one body, for we all partake of the one bread" (1 Corinthians 10:16–17; see also the texts of the Lord's Supper: Matthew 26:26–30; Mark 14:22–26; Luke 22:14–22; John 6:22–59). In the Acts of the Apostles the practice of breaking the bread is always associated with common prayer, fraternal gatherings, sharing and consolation, and mission (Acts 2:42–46; 20:7–12; 27:35) and in two contexts with the reception of the Holy Spirit's gifts (Acts 2:37–42; 13:2–3). Some exegetes are willing to consider the Emmaus episode (Luke 24:13–35) as a

Eucharistic text because of the link it establishes between the breaking of the bread and the Resurrection of Christ, thus enlarging the understanding of the Eucharist from the notion of sacrifice to one of a meal of joy with the risen Lord.

All biblical contexts related to communion and the Eucharist reveal a descriptive as well as a normative relationship between the Word, the Eucharist, and the Christian community.

Pentecostal and Charismatic Perspective

The Pentecostals' understanding of Eucharist is based on the various positions in Protestant theological debate about Eucharist. For Martin Luther (1483–1546) the Eucharistic communion is a sign of personal incorporation into Christ and his saints in blessings and sufferings; such deeply ecclesial "being-in-Christ" is a mystical union with him through the eating and drinking of the consecrated bread and wine. Luther's later theology conceives the Eucharist as something for Christians to receive (not to do), a sacrifice of prayer, praise, and thanksgiving: consequently, the presence of Christ is a spiritual one, and it is reached by faith. Ulrich Zwingli (1484–1531) held that "eating Christ" means "believing in Christ" and "belonging to His Body," and that the value of the Eucharist is mainly in its being a memorial, thus, for those who participate in it, a grace-given (not a grace-giving) event. John Calvin (1509–1564) asserted that the Eucharist is our thanksgiving to God for his unceasing grace, and for this reason he called humankind a Eucharistic people by nature. Calvin stresses the role of the Word and the Spirit, and considers the sacraments as the visible representation of the Word preached and imparted; the Lord's Supper is oriented to deepening the bond between the Word and baptism.

The Pentecostals' understanding of the Eucharist—although there is no uniform vision—follows primarily a Reformed/Zwinglian theology. They conceive it as an ordinance given by the Lord, to be celebrated in memory of the salvific event of his sacrifice on the cross, which made it possible for humankind to be set free from sin and to be born to eternal life, as was prefigured in the Old Testament Passover. There is no real presence of Christ in the Eucharist, which does not affect what it represents, but it is a visible sign of receiving God's grace in faith.

Pentecostals emphasize the mandate to evangelize as springing from the Eucharist. This is true of the dimension of service as well, to the extent that foot washing (John 13:4–20) is considered by some groups to be as mandatory as the Eucharist.

As far as the celebration praxis is concerned, Pentecostals have no uniform pattern in frequency or structure. Though not considered a necessary element, bread (either unleavened or not) is used in their celebrations, while the use of wine is usually avoided, the rejection of alcohol being strictly normative for most groups.

Charismatics follow the classical Catholic sacramental theology according to which the church—being the sacrament of salvation—celebrates the salvific acts of Christ, which are efficacious signs of grace, inasmuch as they realize what they signify. Accordingly, the Eucharist actualizes the sacrifice of Christ, through the power of the Holy Spirit, who is invoked during the celebration: "Through Him, in Him, with Him in the unity of the Holy Spirit" (Roman Canon 1974, 509). Beside the theological focus on the epiclesis (prayer addressed to the Father to send the Holy Spirit upon the bread and wine to transform them into the Body and Blood of Christ), charismatic celebrations present the typical characteristics of a Spirit-centered spirituality, emphasizing the aspect of praise (constitutive of the Eucharist, whose etymological meaning is "thanksgiving"), as well as the aspect of intercession (more emphasized by Catholics, the Eucharist being the sacrifice offered by the community of the believers). Praying, praising, and speaking in tongues are integral parts of joyful Pentecostal-Charismatic worship.

Theologically speaking, the Catholic trend—especially after Vatican II—is focused on the unitarian dynamism of the sacraments of initiation (baptism, Eucharist, confirmation), which fully incorporate into the body of Christ: such theological orientation will certainly enrich, and at the same time be enriched by, the charismatic viewpoint and experience.

Further Theological Developments

Late twentieth-century theological reflection has brought decisive contributions in ecclesiology, which have indicated new directions for further discussion.

The first direction concerns "sacramentality." The action of the Holy Spirit is characterized by immediacy, while the action of Christ is mediated by the incarnation: this very circumstance should not be misleading. Immediacy of the Holy Spirit does not imply lack of any "mediation": in fact, there will always be limitations and constraints in the fleshly existence of the human being receiving those gifts. Such mediation can be interpreted along the lines of visibility, implied in the notion of sacramentality. Now, while it is possible to recognize a sacramental dimension in Pentecostal glossolalia, because of the speaking and listening involved, and though many Pentecostals are uncomfortable with the use of the term "sacrament," they may agree on "sacramentality" taken in an "analogous" or "broad" sense. Nonetheless, theological differences between Catholics' and Pentecostals' concept of "sacramentality" still remain, for Catholics develop their theology in the context of the institutional embodiment of the risen Christ (underemphasizing the open work of the Spirit), while Pentecostals stress the aspect of the work of the Spirit as a "theophany" (underemphasizing the incarnational aspect of the economy of salvation).

A second direction regards pneumatological dynamics. Inspiration and institution—to which are commonly associated respectively charisms and ministry—are the two modes of the divine presence and action among us. Institutions are places for the encounter of the faithful with Christ; inspiration is the living part of the institutions and the ultimate purpose for which institutions are established. The relationship between ministry and charism is, however, difficult to define, at times conflicting, especially when approached with one-sided attitudes. A challenging question, in this perspective, concerns baptism in the Spirit in its relation to belonging to the church: Baptism in the Spirit, in fact, does not happen only to believers fully participating in the Christian embodiment in Christ through baptism in water. Unbaptized people (or even atheists) may receive the Spirit so that they repent, pray, and listen to the Spirit's promptings. Nonetheless, the bond between charismatic endowment, sacramental worship, and Eucharistic community seems oriented to full incorporation in Christ (as witnessed in Acts 10:30–47, where unbaptized Cornelius, upon receiving baptism in the Spirit, is immediately baptized in the water).

A third direction concerns ecumenical dialogue. The ecumenical movement, born in the twentieth century and aiming at restoring visible unity among separated Christian churches through spiritual sharing, theological dialogue, and common witness, has been developing a theological reflection on ecclesiology since the 1960s and early 1970s. Through a comparative as well as Christologically centered methodology, the churches have been asked to reflect on their respective theology and praxis concerning the sacraments. Such reflection has produced, besides several bilateral dialogues, a remarkable document, the "BEM" (*Baptism, Eucharist, and Ministry*), published in 1982 by the Faith and Order Commission of the World Council of Churches. The document expresses biblical and theological convergence among the churches about the meaning and the practice of the three sacraments.

Pentecostal churches have always been reluctant to engage in ecumenical dialogue in search of visible unity, stressing the spiritual invisible bond of unity the Holy Spirit creates among believers. Thus they hardly participate in ecumenical meetings and structures. Nevertheless, some Pentecostals have been involved in the BEM reflection and response process, expressing appreciation for the emphasis on the uniqueness of Jesus' sacrifice, its pneumatic and eschatological dimension, and the consequent missionary and ethical demands for believers. Critical remarks concerned the emphasis on "sacraments" at the expense of a more Word-centered perspective.

Converging Perspectives

A fruitful reflection regards *koinonia* as a key concept for understanding and describing the mystery of the church, in which unity and diversity are harmonized. *Koinonia* is a powerful ecclesiological pattern, since it is biblically rooted and it expresses the Trinitarian communion believers are called to share and to be images of, which is the communion the first Christians experienced. Most Christian churches recognize baptism in water as the bond of communion that incorporates a person into the body of Christ, and therefore into the Una Sancta, the undivided church in a real—though incomplete—*koinonia* in Christ. Pentecostals do not commonly recognize baptism in water as a salvific sacrament incorporating a person into the church, but as an external sign of the regeneration in Christ received by the believer. Such regeneration expresses a *koinonia* intended by Pentecostals, as the spiritual bond among Christians, while the term refers also to visible unity among other denominations (e.g., the Catholic and the Orthodox Church). Along the same lines, Eucharist is the spiritual *koinonia*-creating meal for believers.

Despite all the difficulties, *koinonia* is an efficacious conceptual framework for contextualizing future dialogue on the Eucharist, both when considered sacramentally as the heart of the community's life, and eschatologically as the foretaste of eternal life.

TERESA FRANCESCA ROSSI

See also Ordinances and Sacraments

Further Reading

Chan, S. (2000). Mother church: Towards a Pentecostal ecclesiology. *Pneuma*, 22(2), 177–208.

Cocksworth, C. J. (1993). *Evangelical eucharistic thought in the church of England*. Cambridge, UK: Cambridge University Press.

Commission on Faith and Order of the World Council of Churches. (1982). *Baptism, Eucharist, and ministry*. Geneva, Switzerland: WCC Publications.

Cummings, O. F. (1997). The reformers and eucharistic ecclesiology. *One in Christ, 33*(1), 47–54.

Durasoff, S. (1973). *Bright wind of the Spirit: Pentecostalism today*. London: Hodder & Stoughton.

Gelpi, D. L. (1971). *Pentecostalism: A theological viewpoint*. New York: Paulist.

Gros, J. (2003). A pilgrimage in the spirit: Pentecostal testimony in the faith and order movement. *Pneuma, 25*(1), 29–53.

Hocken, P. (1996). *The strategy of the spirit?* Guildford, UK: Eagle.

Hunter, H. D. (2003). Two movements of the Holy Spirit in the 20th century? A closer look at global Pentecostalism and ecumenism. *One in Christ, 38*(1), 31–39.

Kärkkäinen, V.-M. (2000). Spirit church and Christ: An ecumenical inquiry into pneumatological ecclesiology. *One in Christ, 36*(4), 338–353.

Macchia, F. D. (1993). Tongues as a sign: Towards a sacramental understanding of Pentecostal experience. *Pneuma, 15*(1), 61–76.

Macchia, F. D. (2001). Spirit, word and kingdom: Theological reflections on the Reformed/Pentecostal dialogue. *Ecumenical Trends, 30*(3), 1–7.

O'Connor, E. (1973). Institution and inspiration: Two modes of Jesus' presence in the church. In N. L. Wogen (Ed.), *Jesus, where are you taking us? Messages from the first international Lutheran conference on the Holy Spirit* (pp. 189–203). Carol Stream, IL: Creation House.

Reumann, J. (1985). *The supper of the Lord: The New Testament, ecumenical dialogues, and faith and order on Eucharist*. Philadelphia: Fortress.

Robeck, C. M. (1995). A Pentecostal look at the World Council of Churches. *The Ecumenical Review, 47*(1), 60–69.

Robeck, C. M. (1998). A Pentecostal assessment of "Towards a common understanding and vision" of the WCC. *Mid-Stream, 37*(1), 1–36.

Roman Canon. (1974). *Eucharistic Prayer 1: The Sacramentary* (pp. 509). Collegeville, MN: The Liturgical Press.

Schrotenboer, P. (Ed.) (1992). *An evangelical response to baptism, eucharist, and ministry*. Carlisle, UK: Paternoster.

Stevenson, K. W. (1986). *Eucharist and offering*. New York: Pueblo.

Tugwell, S., Every, G., Orme Mills, J., & Hocken, P. (1976). *New heaven? New earth? An encounter with Pentecostalism*. London: Darton, Longman & Todd.

Wainwright, G. (2002). *Eucharist and eschatology.* Akron, OH: OSL Publications.

Wogen, N. L. (Ed.). *Jesus, where are you taking us? Messages from the first international Lutheran conference on the Holy Spirit.* Carol Stream, IL: Creation House.

Contextualization

The specific Christian use of the term *contextualization* refers to the attempt to understand and apply the unchanging words and principles of Scripture in particular cultural situations and settings. This simple statement, however, belies a complex and controversial topic. Contextualization is a term that emerged in literary circles, was appropriated by theologians, and is pursued in practice by pastors and missionaries of all stripes across the world.

Linguistic Origins

The term *contextualization* was coined by linguists in the twentieth century to assert that the meanings of words, sentences, and paragraphs of any culture's literature were alone not sufficient to understand a text. The circumstances of the writing needed to be considered in interpretation, but more importantly, the impact of the words in the context of their reading was seen to be essential to the overall understanding of the writing. This situation-based understanding of text came to be known as contextualization.

Christian Appropriation

It is often noted that the first Christian use of the term *contextualization* was within the mainline Christian report *Ministry in Context: The Third Mandate Programme of the Theological Education Fund (1970–1977)*, commissioned by the World Council of Churches, which was convinced that previous models of biblical interpretation were no longer relevant and was seeking a new existential model of biblical application. The authors of the report intended to propose an approach to Scripture that did not start with its inspiration and authority, but with the application of a particular text within a particular setting. The historicity of the text was subjugated to modern perception, and biblical texts began to be evaluated as more or less useful than others. Absent any sense of absoluteness regarding the Scriptures, the culture and language of the people to whom the gospel was to be communicated began to be taken as normative. Thus the first Christian theological usage of the term *contextualization* was a recommendation by mainline theologians to put less emphasis on the original meaning of a text and much more on its potential usage in a given culture. While evangelical thinkers rejected this approach to understanding and communicating Scripture, the term *contextualization* seemed to fit a concept that had long been recognized as vital in the process of promoting and expanding Christianity. Evangelicals were passionate about the idea that to communicate ideas from one time and culture to another is an exceedingly complex process, in which consideration has to be given to the worldviews, cognitive processes, linguistic forms, behavioral patterns, communication media, social structures, and motivational sources of the culture in which the message was originally delivered and the one to whom it is to be applied.

Eugene Nida noted in his hugely influential work *Message and Mission: The Community of Christian Faith* that for accurate and appropriate communication of truth, a "three culture model" must be noted for effective contextualization. Nida said that the cultures of not only the originators of a text and the ultimate receivers of the text should be considered in communicating ancient truths to modern ears, but the culture of modern Christianity as well, since effective communication can be hampered by modern presuppositions and expectations. These emphases on "truth" and "accuracy" and "communication" motivated evangelicals to embrace the concept and the term *contextualization*.

Mainline Christianity has sometimes included in the term the notion that appropriate application of biblical truths is often hampered by contemporary cultural or conservative theological norms, and thus Western, male, imperialist biases must be sniffed out and eliminated in order to come to appropriate understandings of any text. Feminist and liberation theologies tend to use and promote this understanding of the term *contextualization*. In this line of thinking, the truthfulness of any text is established largely by the perceived existential impact that text has in its application to a contemporary issue or idea.

Evangelical Particulars

Evangelical Christians believe that the Bible as it exists today represents the inspired words of God and that each section of it was written with one necessary meaning within that text, which is best understood by examining the culture and setting of the circumstances of the text's original reading. By considering these factors, an inherent meaning with a variety of doctrinal and practical implications is derived, which then must be communicated in such a way as to convey the same meaning and implications in culturally relevant and appropriate ways. David Hesselgrave comments, "The adequacy of an attempted contextualization must be measured by the degree to which it faithfully reflects the meaning of the biblical text." He continues on to note that "This is not to imply that biblical content *becomes* true. Rather, because it *is* true, it can, if properly understood, be repeatedly applied to specific contexts in an ever changing, multicultural world" (Hesselgrave 1995, 115–116).

For instance, Paul's ongoing discussions regarding eating meat sacrificed to idols in 1 Corinthians must be understood in the light of the religious, economic, and social attributes of Greek society in the first century, and his conclusions understood in that setting, but then those ideas must be interpreted in such a way as to have relevance and impact to the topic of chewing betel nuts in Africa or drinking alcohol in Indonesia.

Hesselgrave notes that the Christian Scriptures were written in a particular context, but have been contextualized by each succeeding generation of Christians to be meaningful in their own settings. Therefore, modern Christians must decontextualize, or strip away inferences and presuppositions to get back to the original kernel of truth, then recontextualize that thought in order to communicate it effectively to a target culture.

Both sides of this interpretive process—what the text meant in its original setting and what it means in a contemporary context—are essential to contextualization. If an attempt is made simply to apply an ancient text to a contemporary setting without due attention to the world of the text's origin, the result is what Anthony Thiselton calls "routinization." Routinization results from a desire to use a text to address a modern issue with the words of Scripture without first thoroughly exegeting its primary initial implication. Thiselton also indicates that when what might appear to be contextualization has no depth in its historical understanding, then routinization often provides the apologetic for a deeply held and generally unquestioned belief to remain unchallenged.

Perhaps the term *contextualization* is most often adopted and used by those involved in missionary endeavors. Especially during the last half of the twentieth century, Evangelical missionaries intensely sought to separate their evangelism from any hint of westernization. Especially in the latter half of the twentieth century, *indigenous* was the buzzword, as Western missionaries

sought to establish self-governed, self-supporting, and self-propagating mission endeavors, but those missionary products were still often seen to be primarily Western in culture. In seeking appropriate means to produce culturally relevant indigenous churches, communicating the heart of the gospel effectively to disparate cultures became a passionate pursuit.

Pentecostal Uniquenesses

Pentecostal Christianity tends to accept the Evangelical model of contextualization, with one huge addition—they stress more the direct intervention and guidance of the Holy Spirit in the communication, application, and expression of the gospel. Whether within the Western church or in barely literate developing countries, Pentecostals believe that the Spirit works to make God known in culturally appropriate ways. In Western, rational contexts this may take the form of special understanding (among other wonders), whereas in supernaturally inclined spiritistic cultures, they hold that the Spirit works through supernatural manifestations that demonstrate the superiority of God's power to the other powers of that particular people group. For example, in many cultures, Pentecostalism's emphasis on healing has provided quick verification of the authenticity of Christianity. The University of Birmingham's Allan Anderson has observed:

> In these cultures, the religious specialist or "person of God" has power to heal the sick and ward off evil spirits and sorcery. This holistic function, which does not separate "physical" from "spiritual," is restored in Pentecostalism, and people see it as a "powerful" religion to meet human needs. (Anderson 2003, 4)

Further, Anderson asserts that traditional tribal worldviews tend to focus on health and protection, and thus do not relate well to a modernistic form of Christianity that focuses on rational doctrines more than action and intervention in the supernatural realm. But in that same modern context, Pentecostalism's affirmation of the biblical world's presuppositions about the proximity and influence of the supernatural realm becomes a much more relevant and meaningful version of Christianity. Within Pentecostalism, the distance between the ancient and modern worlds does not seem so far.

Beyond Textual Contextualization

Of course there is more to Christianity than textual exegesis, as the preceding paragraphs have indicated.

Some definitions of contextualization focus on theological systems more than hermeneutics. Within this understanding, text is just one means of knowing, communicating, and applying truth.

David Hesselgrave offers a succinct evangelical definition of contextualization that goes beyond mere hermeneutics:

> From this point of view Christian contextualization can be thought of as the attempt to communicate the message of the person, works, Word, and will of God in a way that is faithful to God's revelation, especially as it is put forth in the teachings of Holy Scripture, and that it is meaningful to respondents in their respective cultural and existential contexts. Contextualization is both verbal and nonverbal and has to do with theologizing, Bible translation, interpretation and application, incarnational lifestyle, evangelism, Christian instruction, church planting and growth, church organization, worship style—indeed with all of those activities involved in carrying out the Great Commission. (Hesselgrave 1995, 115)

To Hesselgrave and others, not only do the texts of Christianity need to be interpreted so that they are meaningful to those of a different era, but so do all the "lived truths" of Christianity, including fellowship, service, outreach, and even worship, not to mention "hard teachings" of the Bible about slaves and masters and obedience to evil dictators, among others.

Since Pentecostalism is very willing to expand its understanding of God's will beyond mere interpretation of text, Pentecostalism is eager to contextualize its particular way of life. Allan Anderson recognizes Pentecostal contextualization within tribal cultures in the "spontaneous liturgy" of Pentecostal worship, which encourages ecstatic utterances, clapping, loud and simultaneous prayer, and dancing and which fits easily into contexts in which "a sense of divine immediacy is taken for granted." Indeed, "a sympathetic approach to local life and culture and the retention of certain indigenous religious practices are undoubtedly major reasons for their attraction (to Pentecostal Christianity)" (Anderson 2003, 9,10,12).

Implications

Within Christianity, mainline and Evangelical Christians take dramatically different approaches to the concept of contextualization. Mainline theology tends to seek a very basic original meaning for the original text, as free as possible from any hint of supernaturalist bias, then attempts to apply that streamlined text to a con-

temporary idea or issue, letting the modern context supply a modern theological and practical application for those particular words.

Evangelical contextualization ideally goes to great lengths of language, cultural, and ancient religious study to determine as closely as possible the original meaning and implications of a particular text, then strives to find appropriate contemporary applications, in which the first-century (or earlier) principles can be understood and practiced in the modern realm.

Pentecostal contextualization adds the dimension of the present active work of the Holy Spirit in understanding Scripture and in speaking prophetically to the world. Thus, contextualization is the intersection of biblical exegesis, cultural application, and the Holy Spirit's enlightenment of spiritual truths. Within Pentecostalism, the Holy Spirit is sometimes regarded as doing the "heavy lifting" of understanding and application.

Though many articles note that *contextualization* seemed to be a buzzword during the last few decades of the twentieth century, all affirm that the concept of accurately connecting biblical truth with modern people of any culture in a way they can perceive and receive it is a vital Christian concept. Without contextualization, the truths of Scripture remain locked away in a cage of time and culture, essentially meaningless and useless to the modern realm.

David E. Embree

See also Globalization of Pentecostalism; Indigenous Churches

Further Reading

Anderson, A. (2003, January). *Towards a Pentecostal missiology for the majority world*. Paper presented at the International Symposium on Pentecostal Missiology, Asia-Pacific Theological Seminary, Baguio City, Philippines.

Bosch, D. (1991). *Transforming mission: Paradigm shifts in the theology of mission*. Maryknoll, NY: Orbis.

Eerdmans, S. L., Prevignano, C. L., & Thibault, P. J. (Eds.). (2003). *Language and interaction: Discussions with John J. Gumperz*. Amsterdam: John Benjamins.

Glasser, A., & McGavran, D. (1993). *Contemporary theologies of mission*. Grand Rapids, MI: Baker.

Hesselgrave, D. J. (1995). Contextualization that is authentic and relevant. *International Journal of Frontier Missions, 12*(3), 116.

Long, J. D. (1997) *Westernization vs. contextualization: What's your picture of a Christianized people?* South Hamilton, MA: Gordon Conwell Seminary Center for the Study of Global Christianity.

Moreau, S., & O'Rear, M. (n.d.). Annotated bibliography on contextualization. Retrieved September 8, 2004, from http://www.mislinks.org/biblio/query.php

Nida, E. (1960). *Message and mission: The community of Christian faith*. New York: Harper & Row.

Tate, R. (2005). Contextualization. *A handbook to biblical literature: Interpretational methods and terms*. Peabody, MA: Hendrickson Publishers.

Coe, S. (1972). *Ministry in context: The third mandate programme of the Theological Education Fund (1970–1977)* (p. 20). Bromely, UK: World Council of Churches.

Thiselton, A. (1992). *New horizons in hermeneutics*. Grand Rapids, MI: Zondervan.

Covenant

The theme of "covenant" has emerged recently as a key concept in Pentecostal-Charismatic theology. Traditional theology has neglected the Spirit of God and the correlated gifts of revelation and prophecy as a significant, if not dominant, element of the new covenant promised in the Old Testament. In contrast to traditional Protestantism, then, a Pentecostal-Charismatic theology could claim that the Spirit of prophecy (and related gifts) are as much a part of the new covenant promises as the forgiveness of sin.

Traditional Views

From at least the time of the Reformation, the central focus of Christian theology, both Catholic and Protestant, was "salvation" in the forensic sense of the forgiveness of sins and attaining heaven. The nature and means of salvation came to be explained by means of the covenant theme, particularly the contrast of the old and new covenants described in Scripture. The covenant became a particularly strong motif in the Reformed theology of Calvin, and later in Roman Catholic theology. Since Pentecostalism and its derivative, the Charismatic movement in both its Catholic and mainstream Protestant expressions, have been, until recently, remarkably uncritical of their respective theological roots, then it is no surprise that they all inherited their concepts of covenant unchanged and largely ignored. Two exceptions to this conformity to tradition appear in the use of covenant theme in Pentecostal "faith teaching" and in newer explorations of the new covenant as involving the outpouring of spiritual gifts as well as providing benefits of "salvation" as traditionally understood.

The traditional portrayal of covenant focuses on the means of atonement for sin. Calvin is the first Protestant theologian to develop the covenant concept as a major expression of his soteriology. According to Calvin, those of faith within the Old Testament era (the old covenant) received God's grace for salvation, which anticipated and was to be realized fully in Christ as the mediator of the new covenant. The essential benefit of this new covenant is "eternal life," a result of the promised relationship: "'I will be your God, and you shall be my people' [Lev 26:12]. The prophets also commonly explained that life and salvation and the whole concept of blessedness are embraced in these words" (Calvin 1986, 2:10). This relationship results in the remission of sins, renovation of the heart (particularly for a righteous life), and illumination of the mind. Biblically, the latter two suggest operations of spiritual gifts, but Protestants cast them within traditional soteriology as themes of piety, ethics, as well as heightened awareness and appreciation for salvation and Scripture. Hendrik Berkhof (1979) is perhaps the best modern expression of this tradition.

The Reformed tradition of covenant focused on its provisions for salvation from sin, though its central Old Testament proof text was the new covenant promise of Jeremiah 31:31. Jesus declares himself as the final sacrifice and the priestly mediator of "the new covenant in my blood" (Luke 22:20, NRSV; see also 1 Corinthians 11:25; Hebrews 9:15; 12:24).

Pentecostal and Charismatic Traditions

A derivative of the Reformed covenant theology was dispensationalism, which listed seven covenants, rather than the traditional two. Earlier Pentecostalism (c. 1920s–1970s), which then had identified closely with American Fundamentalism, adopted the dispensationalist scheme of the extremely popular *Scofield Reference Bible* (1909). C. I. Scofield, following J. N. Darby, taught that history was divided into seven covenant periods of progressive and cumulative revelation, each expressing a different test against which man would be judged. Pentecostals were usually undeterred by dispensationalism's teaching that tongues and other "sign gifts" (e.g., prophecy, healing, and miracles) ceased with the appearance of the New Testament canon of writings. This cessationist doctrine appeared odd to Pentecostals, since it required an additional dispensation of God's revelatory "test" for mankind: a "church age" subdivided into pre– and post–New Testament canon eras. Seven (God's perfect number) dispensations should have been sufficient.

The covenant in faith teaching, particularly in evangelist Kenneth Copeland, involves the Christian's appropriation of the blessings of Abraham (Genesis 17) and of Israel (Deuteronomy 28), based on the death of Christ, who transfers the believer from the curses of the law into its blessings. Some see this as a justification for the so-called "prosperity gospel," which sees material blessings and good health as evidence of one's true faith.

Recent Pentecostal-Charismatic thinking on the covenant involves a recovery of major biblical themes neglected in the traditional theology of the New Covenant, for example: the explicit promise of the charismatic Spirit of God for the "new Israel of God," the church; the relevance of this theme to the central mission of Jesus; the Kingdom of God and its expression in power; and finally, the commissioning of the church to replicate that new highly charismatic mission in the ministry of each and every participant of the new covenant.

First Covenant with Israel

According to Eiben (1999) the central purpose for the rescue of Israel from bondage and her creation as a new nation was that they would be "separated" for Yahweh to be commissioned as a "kingdom of priests" (Exodus 19:5–6; compare the identical commission for New Testament believers in 1 Peter 2:5, 9). Today we think of priests as administering sacraments leading to the forgiveness of sins. However, while Old Testament priests were similarly commissioned to perform the sacrificial offerings, they also had an important function in discerning and articulating revelation from God (Judges 17:5; 18:5; 1 Samuel 14:36–42) to any who "inquired of the Lord" (Judges 20:26–28; 1 Samuel 23:2–6).

God initiated the nation-creating covenant by the command that "*all* the people"—the Kingdom of God— are to be commissioned as prophetic priests both by hearing (Exodus 19:9) and by seeing him (19:11). The Israelites wilted under the intensity of this experience, opting instead (as is a universal human characteristic) to avoid personally experiencing God's presence and power in favor someone who would represent them instead: Moses (Exodus 20:18–19): "You! You speak to us! We will listen, but let not God speak to us, or we will die!" (author's translation). Later, God made a second attempt to spread more widely the commission to be prophetic priests when he poured out his Spirit on seventy (or seventy-two) additional representatives of Israel (Numbers 11:26–28). Again, the human resistance to the outpouring of God's graces broadly is expressed in Joshua, Moses' assistant, who wants to limit claims to God's power to one leader. Moses, however, understands God's true intent: "I wish that *all* the Lord's people were *prophets*," (author's translation) a term that indicated an ongoing functioning of the gift. A clear echo of Moses' sentiment for the universality of God's prophetic Spirit appears in the New Testament (1 Corinthians 14:5a).

Prophecies of a New Covenant

The Old Testament prophets foresaw that God would raise up a new covenant Kingdom of God comprised of priestly prophets, inaugurated by a "prophet like Moses"—the Messiah. Overwhelmingly, however, the message of the Old Testament prophets was a message of Israel's failure to reach the covenant ideal of becoming a priestly "light to the nations," that is, in receiving and proclaiming God's oracles to the world. By obeying the covenant, Israel would have been at the head of the nations, an example and proof of God's blessings (Leviticus 26:6–9; Deuteronomy 28:1). Instead, Israel continually broke her covenant with God, until she was consumed by her enemies in judgment (Leviticus 26:14–46; Deuteronomy 28:15–68). Israel also lost her anointing for prophetic ministry: "We do not see our signs; there is no longer any prophet" (author's translation, Psalm 74:9).

Nevertheless, the prophets foresaw a new Kingdom of God, a new Israel, when the Spirit of prophecy would be poured out, not only on them (Ezekiel 36:26; 39:29), but on "all flesh" (Joel 2:26–28). Specifically, the covenant with the new Israel would include the provision of a "new heart," which is the center of spiritual discernment and perception of divinely revealed wisdom (Jeremiah 31:31; 32:40; Ezekiel 11:19; 36:26). The new covenant of prophecy appears in a passage rarely cited in traditional covenant theology (Isaiah 59:20–21), but which has great significance both to New Testament theology and to that of Pentecostals and charismatics:

> The Redeemer will come to Zion. . . ." Says the Lord. . . . "[T]his is My covenant with them: My Spirit who is upon you, and My words which I have put in your mouth, shall not depart from your mouth, nor from the mouth of your descendants, nor from the mouth of your descendants' descendants," says the Lord, "from this time and forevermore." (Author's translation)

This "Redeemer" is often identified with the "servant" of the Lord in Isaiah who will be given to the new Israel as a "new covenant" to be a "light to the nations," to "open blind eyes," and to deliver "prisoners" (Isaiah 42:6–7; 61:1). This promise comes from the Lord, who gives his Spirit to those who walk the earth (Isaiah 42:5; see also Isaiah 49:6). According to the Old Testament prophets, "the bestowal of the Spirit is the primary characteristic of the [new covenant] age of final redemption" (Lampe 1955, 162).

Jesus' Inauguration of the New Covenant

The doctrine of the new covenant in the New Testament has traditionally focused on the means of the forgiveness of sins. However, unlike their Protestant interpreters, New Testament writers see the fulfillment of the servant of God theme in Isaiah (42:1–7; 49:1–11; 50:4–9; 52:13–53:12) as much in Jesus' prophetic ministry and miracles as in his program for "salvation" (Matthew 8:17; 12:18–21; 26:67; Isaiah 61:1–3; John 12:37–41). This servant was offered as the new covenant (Luke 22:20; 1 Corinthians 11:25) both as savior and as example to the new Israel of charismatic ministry. Accordingly, Jesus also came as the prophet like Moses (Deuteronomy 18:15–17), who not only introduced the new law (the Sermon on the Mount, Matthew 5–7), but also a new covenant in the power of signs and wonders and prophecy. In the Johannine Passover sections, the promise of the new covenant (Jeremiah 31:33–34, NRSV: "But this is the covenant that I will make with the house of Israel after those days.... No longer shall they teach one another, or say to each other, 'Know the LORD'") is fulfilled in the promise that the Holy Spirit who will "teach you all things" (John 14:26 NIV; 1 John 2:27; similarly Matthew 23:8–10; 1 Corinthians 2:13; Galatians 1:12; 1 Thessalonians 4:9). The new covenant, then, involves the intentions of God ("the law") being written "on the heart"—that is, perceived spiritually or prophetically—rather than being learned from other people. This promised Holy Spirit, echoing the Jeremiah 31 prophecy, is offered in the context of Jesus inaugurating the new covenant (John 14:15–17, 26; 15:26–27; 16:7–11, 13–14).

Just as Moses and Jesus were the archetypes for the ideal Israel, Christians were to model on this archetype, thereby reconstituting themselves as the new Israel of God (Titus 1:1; James 1:1), as a "royal priesthood, a holy nation" (1 Peter 2:9, NRSV), or as the new temple where God's charismatic Spirit dwells (1 Corinthians 3:16; 2 Corinthians 6:16; Ephesians 2:21; Revelation 3:12). Similarly, the Kingdom of God, Jesus' central message, included the idea of a "holy nation" of a new covenant people, who were to express themselves not only in "separateness/holiness," but in charismatic power ("The Kingdom of God does not consist of talk, but of power," 1 Corinthians 4:20 NIV; Matthew 12:28; Luke 11:20). The

new Kingdom derives significance from the twelve, the seventy (or seventy-two), and the one hundred twenty, at Pentecost, numbers that all point to the twelve tribes or representative leadership of the new Israel, who were to express the new covenant of the "servant."

The mission of the new covenant/Kingdom of God is explicit in the commissioning accounts to the twelve (Matthew 10; Mark 3:1; Luke 9), the seventy (or seventy-two; Luke 10), and later to the one hundred twenty at Pentecost (Acts 1:8). The disciples (the prototypes of the New Israel) were to present the kingdom in power—in healing, exorcism, and repentance; they were commanded to "heal the sick, and say to them, 'The Kingdom of God has come to you'" (Luke 10:9, NIV). Pentecost, of course, represented the fulfillment of the new covenant of the Spirit being poured out on all flesh (Joel 2:28–31). Second Corinthians 3:1–18 develops these themes more thoroughly, where the promises of Jeremiah 31:31–34 and Ezekiel 36:24–28 are shown to be fulfilled in the new covenant experience of the charismatic and intimacy-creating Spirit of God.

A Pentecostal-Charismatic exposition of the biblical covenant theme, then, can stand as an important corrective, supplementing the traditional focus, by an understanding of the new covenant as also the promise of the Spirit and his charismatic power.

JON MARK RUTHVEN

See also Church, Theology of the; Scripture, Holy

Further Reading

Berkhof, H. (1979). *Christian faith*. Grand Rapids, MI: Eerdmans.

Calvin, J. (1986). *Institutes of the Christian Religion* (F. L. Battles, Ed. & Trans.). Grand Rapids, MI: Eerdmans.

Eiben, R. (1999). *This promise is for all: Revelation in the believer as a central characteristic of the new covenant*. Unpublished master's thesis, Regent University, Virginia Beach, VA.

Fee, G. (1994). *God's empowering presence: The Holy Spirit in the letters of Paul*. Peabody, MA: Hendrickson.

Gräbe, P. (2001). *Der neue Bund in der frühchristlichen Literatur unter Berücksichtigung der alttestamentlich-jüdischen Voraussetzungen* (Forschung zur Bibel 96). Würtzburg, Germany: Echter Verlag.

Hafemann, S. (1996). The "temple of the Spirit" as the inaugural fulfillment of the new covenant within the Corinthian correspondence. *Ex Auditu, 12*, 29–42.

Helm, P. (1983). Calvin and the covenant: Unity and continuity. *Evangelical Quarterly, 55*(2), 65–81.

Kaiser, W. (2000). *Mission in the Old Testament: Israel as a light to the nations*. Grand Rapids, MI: Baker.

Lampe, G. W. H. (1955). The HS in the Writings of St Luke. In D. E. Nineham (Ed.), *Studies in the Gospels: Essays in memory of R. H. Lightfoot.* Oxford, UK: Blackwell.

Lillback, P. (2001). *The binding of God: Calvin's role in the development of covenant theology.* Grand Rapids, MI: Baker.

Meeks, W. (1967). *The prophet-king: Moses traditions and the Johannine Christology.* Leiden, Netherlands: E. J. Brill.

Mendenhall, G., & Herion, G. (1992). Covenant. In D. N. Freedman (Ed.), *The Anchor Bible Dictionary* (Vol. 1, pp. 1179–1202). New York: Doubleday.

Myland, D. (1910). *The latter rain covenant and Pentecostal power.* Chicago: Evangel Publishing House.

O'Toole, R. (1983). Acts 2:30 and the Davidic covenant of Pentecost. *Journal of Biblical Literature, 102,* 245–258.

Pettegrew, L. (2001). *The new covenant ministry of the Holy Spirit.* Grand Rapids, MI: Kregel.

Quell, G., & Behm, J. (1964). *Diatithemi, diatheke.* In G. Kittel (Ed.), *The Theological Dictionary of the New Testament* (Vol. 2, pp. 104–134; G. Bomiley, Trans.). Grand Rapids, MI: Eerdmans.

Ruthven, J. (1993). *On the cessation of the charismata: The Protestant polemic on post-biblical miracles.* New York: Continuum.

Ruthven, J. (2000). The "imitation of Christ" in Christian tradition: Its missing charismatic emphasis. *Journal of Pentecostal Theology, 16*(1), 60–77.

Schatzmann, S. (1987). *A Pauline theology of charismata.* Peabody, MA: Hendrickson.

Stronstad, R. (2003). *The prophethood of all believers: A study in Luke's charismatic theology.* Sheffield, UK: University of Sheffield Academic Press.

Thorsell, P. (1998). The spirit in the present age: Preliminary fulfillment of the predicted new covenant according to Paul. *Journal of the Evangelical Theological Society, 41*(3), 397–413.

Twelftree, G. (1999). *Jesus: The miracle worker.* Downers Grove, IL: InterVarsity.

Weinfeld, M. (1975). Berit. In G. J. Botterweck & H. Ringgren (Eds.), *Theological Dictionary of the Old Testament* (Vol. 2, pp. 253–279). Grand Rapids, MI: Eerdmans.

Creation, Re-creation

Pentecostal-Charismatic theology is sometimes referred to as "renewal" theology—a designation that clearly suggests the theme of creation/re-creation. It is possible that this theme will emerge as *the* distinctive contribution of Pentecostal-Charismatic theology to Christian theology as a whole. Implicit within this trajectory of understanding are new readings of Christology, soteriology, pneumatology, and ecclesiology that expand tra-

ditional Protestant thought in ways that are congruent with both the ancient wisdom of Eastern Orthodoxy and the relatively modern Pentecostal interpretation of life in the Spirit. As we shall see, for example, envisioning the key concept of "justification" as a re-creating work of the Spirit rather than just as a forensic act of pardon yields rich Trinitarian implications. Additional ramifications follow in areas such as spirituality, healing, the church, ecology, and social justice. Theological innovations such as these hold great promise for helping the church better define what it means to be Christian in a post-Christian, postmodern world.

Creation from a Biblical Perspective

The theme of creation/re-creation is integral to both the Hebrew and Christian understandings of who God is and what God does. Hebrew monotheism gave us the first fully nuanced vision of God as the singular Creator. Prior cosmogonies envisioned the cosmos as uncreated, eternal, and cyclic. Various deities shaped preexisting matter to make, rather than create, the world and its inhabitants. Time consisted of sequences of world cycles in which eternal recurrence, rather than novelty or significant freedom, predominated. History, so to speak, went nowhere.

In contradistinction, the Hebrews proclaimed a God who was unique (Isaiah 46:9) and transcendent (Psalm 90:2; Nehemiah 9:6), and who spoke creation into existence (Genesis 1:3; Psalms 33:9; 148:5) rather than "creating" through heavenly warfare, as did the gods of the Mesopotamian and Babylonian myth cycles. The striking idea that God created ex nihilo became explicit before the closing of the Old Testament canon (2 Maccabees 7:28; Hebrews 11:3).

Unlike pagan mythologies that portrayed creation as tragically marred by the battles and character flaws of the gods, the Hebrew Scriptures declare that God's creation is "very good" (Genesis 1:31) and celebrate its diversity, richness, and infinite novelty (Psalm 104). The Hebrew and Christian God is therefore paradigmatically "Creator of heaven and earth" (Genesis 14:19, 22). God's character as "father" (Deuteronomy 32:6) and "king" (Isaiah 43:15) are rooted in His status as Creator. Indeed, humanity's refusal to recognize and acknowledge God as Creator lies at the root of human sin and alienation (Romans 1:20–25; Revelation 4:11).

Correlation of Creation and Salvation History

The idea of "progressive history," as opposed to eternal recurrence, was born along with the revelation of a transcendent Creator for two reasons. First, God created free beings in His own image (Genesis 1:27) and charged them to exercise dominion and reflect His holiness (Genesis 1:28; Leviticus 11:45). Human creativity and responsible action are thus dignified in Judeo-Christian anthropology. Part of what it means to bear the image of God is that we, like God, are able to create. Our choices matter to God in the scheme of things. Existentially speaking, we not only *can* act creatively, we *must*; for we cannot avoid moral decision making and action.

The solemn message of Genesis 3 is that the freedom to create is also the freedom to destroy. Humankind uses our freedom to turn against our Creator, incurring alienation, suffering, and shame. But God was neither daunted nor taken unaware by the fall, and here we see the second and most fundamental foundation for the revolutionary new understanding of history as progressive. In creating ex nihilo, God initiated a world in which time was an arrow, not a circle. Creation is unfolding toward a divinely ordained telos or goal (Isaiah 46:9–11). While sin may have broken and marred God's creation, the Creator—by virtue of His status *as* creator—is equal to the task of redeeming creation's brokenness via divine *re*-creation (Isaiah 43:1; 65:17).

From the biblical perspective then, the marrow of history is *salvation history*: the covenant-centered action of the covenant-initiating God. Karl Barth expresses well the critical insight that the doctrine of redemption flows directly from the doctrine of creation in describing creation as "the external basis of the covenant," and covenant, conversely, as "the internal basis of creation" (Barth 1958, 94, 329). Scripture sheds marvelous light on the nature of God's superintending faithfulness toward His creation in revealing that Christ is the Lamb slain "from the foundation of the world" (Revelation 13:8; 1 Peter 1:20; Matthew 25:34; Ephesians 1:4).

God's Redeeming Activity

Though not often clearly recognized, re-creation is the primary mode of God's saving action, both in individual spiritual regeneration and in the wider sweep of cosmic eschatology. For example, David prays: "Create in me a pure heart, O God, and renew a steadfast spirit within me" in Psalm 51:10 (NIV). The same Hebrew term used here for "create," bara, is used in Genesis 1:1 to describe God's initial creative act. The repentant psalmist thus suggests that regaining a right standing with God requires a divinely effected "re-creation" of His sin-distorted heart/spirit. Pauline theology speaks

in exactly the same vein: "If anyone is in Christ, he is a new creation; the old has gone, the new has come! (2 Corinthians 5:17, NIV; also John 3:3; Romans 12:2; Galatians 6:15; Colossians 3:10).

We must, however, avoid interpreting "new creation" purely in terms of personal *metanoia* (change of mind, conversion). The ultimate focus of God's salvific intent is one with that of His creative intent: creation itself. A "new heaven and a new earth, the home of righteousness" (2 Peter 3:13; Isaiah 65:17; 66:22; Revelation 21:1) is the aim of the eschatological promise of both testaments. Jesus spoke of this coming restoration of the world in Matthew 19:28 (see also Matthew 17:11), as did Peter in his first sermon (Acts 3:19, 21). Paul expresses the creation-centered implications of this eschatological expectation with great clarity in Romans 8:19–21, which climaxes: "the creation itself will be liberated from its bondage to decay and brought into the glorious freedom of the children of God" (see also 2 Maccabees 7:9).

Intelligence remains absolutely faithful to itself in recognizing the existence in the soul of a faculty superior to itself and leading thought above itself. This faculty is supernatural love.

Simone Weil (1909–1943)

The paradigmatic expression of God's eschatological intent for both His saints and His creation is found in the physical resurrection of the human Jesus. The resurrected Jesus represents a new order of reality: one that is both continuous and discontinuous with the present order. While he possessed a "spiritual *body*" it was not simply a body of "flesh and blood" but rather a "life-giving spirit" (1 Corinthians 15). From the Greek perspective, eternity and time, spirit and matter, were incommensurable. From the biblical perspective, however, the boundary between them will be overcome in the fullness of God's redemptive activity. God intends to resurrect not only His saints, but also His creation; to redeem them not simply "above" history, but from "within" history. Only then will we be able to know creation—including ourselves—in its true form (1 John 3:2).

Creation, Re-creation, and the Holy Spirit

In looking at the grand sweep of creation and re-creation biblically we are quickly brought face-to-face with the central role of the Spirit in both activities. The Spirit hovers over the primeval waters, bringing cosmos out of chaos (Genesis 1:2; Psalm 33:6). He is the Creator of physical life (Genesis 2:7, Job 12:10; 33:4; 34:14–15, Psalm 104:30) and spiritual life (John 6:63). Spirit is the key to the resuscitation of creation and the renewal of God's people (Isaiah 32:15; Ezekiel 36:26–27; Joel 2:28). Spirit is, finally, the power through which the dead can be raised (Ezekiel 37:1–6).

So closely linked are the Spirit and creation/re-creation that Killian McDonnell has observed, "to do pneumatology is to do eschatology" (McDonnell 2003, 33). We can illustrate the truth of this statement by looking at the role of the Spirit in Jesus' career. Jesus' ministry was one sustained manifestation of realized eschatological power. His words, acts, and very being witnessed to the reality that "the kingdom of God has come" (Matthew 12:28, NIV). Indeed, the Spirit undergirded every aspect of Jesus' activity. The very name "Christ" connotes Spirit anointing. Scripture informs us that the Spirit was the medium of Jesus' conception (Luke 1:35). Jesus is baptized in the Spirit (Luke 3:21–22), commissioned by the Spirit (Luke 4:18), empowered by the Spirit (John 3:34; Acts 10:38), directed by the Spirit (Luke 4:1–2), enabled by the Spirit to offer Himself as a sacrifice (Hebrews 9:14), and, climactically, raised from the dead by the Spirit (Romans 1:4; 8:11a).

Renewal theologians like Clark Pinnock (Pinnock 1996, 79–111) suggest constructing a "Spirit Christology" consistent with the Bible's own pneumatic emphasis (Matthew 12:32). A key implication suggested by such a construct is that Jesus' incarnation, baptism, Spirit-directed activity, death, and resurrection *taken together* paradigmatically recapitulate the history of unfaithful Israel and failed humanity in such a way as to release salvific power into the human situation. The life of Christ was a "Spirit event" that plays itself out in us as God's adopted children as the Spirit saves, sustains, sanctifies, and brings eschatological renewal to us (Romans 8:11b, 18; 1 Corinthians 6:14). As Paul put it, we are "saved through [Christ's] *life*" (Romans 5:10, NIV; emphasis added), not simply through His death—though by far the largest emphasis in Protestant theology is on the cross.

Spirit Christology complements traditional Logos Christology. It makes good sense of scriptural analogies such as Paul's description of Christ as the New Adam (1 Corinthians 15:49). It envisions Jesus' life as a Spirit-empowered matrix of God's re-creative power, which thereafter becomes accessible to humanity via Pentecost. In this light, the Spirit-Christ event is, in Karl Rahner's words, as "the irreversible beginning of the

coming of God as the absolute future of the world" (Pinnock 1996, 101).

Justification and Re-creation

Luther rightly identified justification as the doctrine upon which the church stands or falls. In an interesting contemporary development, many leading renewal theologians are declaring the importance of reinterpreting this doctrine in a way that does fuller justice to the re-creating activity of the Spirit.

Reformed theology has tended to interpret justification forensically as unmerited favor imparted by Christ to satisfy the wrath of an impartial judge (the Father). However, it is arguable that this approach, which traces to Anselm, is more reflective of secular Roman distributive justice than of the biblical paradigm of justification, which is not primarily punitive, but redemptive (Deuteronomy 24:12–13; Psalms 33:18–22; 112:4–6; Isaiah 11:4; Jeremiah 22:15–16). The Old Testament promise of the "new covenant," particularly, was a promise that God would "justify" His broken creation by acting unilaterally to deliver it from sin and death (Jeremiah 31:31–34; Romans 3:26; 2 Corinthians 3:6; Hebrews 12:24; 1 John 1:9).

Contra the Reformed emphasis that we are justified by Christ's death, Romans 4:25 suggests that Christ was "*raised* . . . for our justification" (NIV; emphasis added; see also 8:11; 1 Corinthians 15:17; 1 Timothy 3:16). Frank D. Macchia concludes that "righteousness is 'reckoned' to us in faith (Romans 4:23–24) not because Christ's 'merits' have been transferred to us, but because the new creation to be experienced in the resurrection has already laid claim to us in our present state through the presence of the Spirit and our corresponding response of faith" (Macchia 2001, 212). Renewal theology thus envisions salvation history being enacted as the Spirit manifests Godself in the risen Christ, renewing creation and "establishing justice" for it eschatologically. It also resonates with the Hebrew emphasis that God as "justifier" calls His people to care for the social and physical welfare of His created order and all persons.

Theosis: The Ultimate Renewal

One of the most interesting and fruitful veins of research underway currently is the dialogue that leading Pentecostal and charismatic scholars are having with Eastern Orthodoxy. Eastern Orthodoxy's anthropology is synergistic and optimistic—closer to the Arminianism of Wesleyanism and Pentecostalism than to the

Calvinism of the Reformers. It is also experiential, mystical and, like classical Pentecostalism, concerned with sanctification, transformation, and the "higher life." But it is in Eastern Orthodoxy's pneumatology that the greatest riches lie for Pentecostal-Charismatics. It may be argued that Eastern Orthodox theology is pneumatic theology par excellence. The Spirit is everywhere active in Orthodox theology, for the Spirit's Trinitarian economy is seen as being equal with, but never disconnected from, that of the Son (unlike in Western theology, where the addition of the *filioque* to the Nicene Creed arguably led to the subordination of the Spirit to the Son).

Theosis refers to the process of deification or divinization that is the eschatological terminus of salvation. Tuomo Mannermaa has summarized the doctrine thus: "Divine life has manifested itself in Christ. In the church as the body of Christ, man has a share in the life. Man partakes thereby of 'the divine nature' (2 Peter 1:4). This 'nature,' or divine life, permeates the being of man like a leaven in order to restore it to its original condition as *imago Dei*" (quoted in Kärkkäinen 2002, 28–29; see also Exodus 7:1; 34:30; Psalm 82:6; John 17:21; 2 Corinthians 3:18; 8:9). Of course, *theosis* is a graced divination, not the ontological divinity that belongs to the Trinity alone.

Pentecostal theologian Veli Matti Kärkkäinen's research reveals that deification was accepted and incorporated by both the Reformers and the radical reformers, including the Anabaptists, from whom the Pentecostals inherited much of their theology. It was spoken of by Wesley, who drew from Eastern Orthodox sources in his theologizing. Recent scholarship has located explicit references to deification in Luther's sermons, and convergent ideas in the theologies of Pentecostals William J. Seymour, Minnie Abrahams, and Thomas Barrett.

The Church Fathers found in *theosis* a remarkable synopsis of God's plan of salvation in Christ. Irenaeus summarized: "Because of his limitless love [Christ] became what we are in order to make us what even he himself is." Athanasius said similarly, "Christ became human that humans might become divine." The Orthodox vision of *theosis* invites us to understand Christ's self-emptying (Philippians 2:5–11) not merely as a matter of God *descending* and becoming human, but equally of God *raising up* our humanity and divinizing it in Christ. Clearly, the concept of *theosis* represents the most profound act of re-creation imaginable. It is surely rife with prolific implications for further theological investigation.

Implications

Karl Barth predicted that one day a theology of the Spirit would become the future of Christian theology. Similarly, Karl Rahner speculated that pneumatology would become the fundamental point of departure for Western theology. It may be that the emerging consensus of renewal theology will fulfill these predictions. Central to this consensus is the motif of the Holy Spirit acting together with the Son as the "two hands of the Father" (Irenaeus) in creation and in re-creation. As Pentecostal-Charismatic Christianity continues to emerge as the dominant form of Christianity globally, the theme of pneumatic creation and re-creation will assume a central role in twenty-first-century theology.

H. S. HORTON-PARKER

See also Church, Theology of the; Covenant; Orthodoxy, Eastern

Further Reading

Barth, K. (1958). *Church dogmatics* (Vol. 3). Edinburgh, UK: T & T Clark.

Clendenin, D. B. (Ed.). (2003). *Eastern Orthodox theology.* Grand Rapids, MI: Baker Academic.

Dabney, D. L. (2001). Justified by the Spirit: Soteriological reflections on the resurrection. *International Journal of Systematic Theology, 3*(1), 46–68.

Dabney, D. L. (2001). Saul's armor: The problem and promise of Pentecostal theology today. *Pneuma, 23*(1), 115–146.

Frankfort, H. (1972). *Before philosophy.* Baltimore: Penguin.

Heidel, A. (1951). *The Babylonian genesis.* Chicago: University of Chicago Press.

Kärkkäinen, V.-M. (2002). The Holy Spirit and justification: The ecumenical significance of Luther's doctrine of salvation. *Pneuma, 24*(1), 26–39.

Kärkkäinen, V.-M. (2002). *Toward a pneumatological theology: Pentecostal and ecumenical perspectives on ecclesiology, soteriology, and theology of mission.* Lanham, MD: University Press of America.

Long, C. H. (1965). *Alpha: The myths of creation.* Toronto, Canada: Collier.

Lossky, V. (1976). *The mystical theology of the Eastern Church.* Crestwood, NY: St. Vladimir's Seminary Press.

Macchia, F. D. (1992). Sighs too deep for words: Toward a theology of glossolalia. *Journal of Pentecostal Theology, 1*(1), 47–73.

Macchia, F. D. (2001). Justification through new creation. *Theology Today, 58,* 202–217.

Macchia, F. D. (in press). *Baptized in the Spirit: Toward a global Pentecostal theology*. Grand Rapids, MI: Zondervan.

McDonnell, K. (2003). *The other hand of God: The Holy Spirit as the universal touch and goal*. Collegeville, MN: Liturgical.

Moltmann, J. (1985). *God in creation: A new theology of creation and the spirit of God*. San Francisco: Harper & Row.

Pinnock, C. H. (1996). *Flame of love: A theology of the Holy Spirit*. Downers Grove, IL: InterVarsity.

Studebaker, S. (2003). Pentecostal soteriology and pneumatology. *Journal of Pentecostal Theology, 11*(2), 248–270.

von Rad, G. (1962). *Old Testament theology* (Vol. 1). New York: Harper & Row.

von Rad, G. (1972). *Genesis.* London: SCM.

D

Deliverance

Deliverance refers to setting individuals free from the control, bondage, or influence of evil spirits, or demons. This is commonly done by prayer and using the name of Jesus in commanding the demon(s) to exit the tormented person. In this article, "deliverance" is used differently than "exorcism." Exorcism refers to the expulsion of demons from an individual whom the spirits fully control. Deliverance here refers to the breaking of spiritual bondage or influence in an individual who is not under total control by evil spirits.

Deliverance can be a controversial subject. The suggestion that Christians could need help in overcoming behavioral or doctrinal bondage—fostered by evil spirits—is actively opposed by Pentecostal thinkers with the exception of Derek Prince (1915–2003). At the same time, Pentecostal authors seem to admit that one who is a Christian might incur spiritual bondage through disobedience. While this article seeks to be cautious, some statements may seem bold because, while there seems to be a great deal of uniformity in the language and thinking of Pentecostal writers, the author sees a considerable hedging of terms in places where qualifying statements in one section of a work would appear to modify stronger statements in another section. This may occur without any inference drawn by the author of the work itself.

There are two issues that make the discussion of "deliverance" and "exorcism" more relevant. The first is the Pentecostal encounter with non-Western shamanistic cultures in the third world and the relationship of Pentecostals with indigenous Christian movements found in such cultures. Such movements have been ac-cused of shamanistic practices themselves. The second issue has to do with the reaction of Pentecostal denominations to the charismatic approach to deliverance and inner healing.

Biblical View of Evil Spirits

The origin of demonic spirits is beyond the scope of this article, but their existence seems to be confirmed in a number of scriptural texts. The Scriptures are not dominated by a concern with demonic forces, nor are they dualistic in the sense that humans are torn between equally powerful forces of darkness and light. Rather, the Scriptures focus on God, His sovereign reign and saving grace. The Bible seems to treat the existence and activity of evil spirits in a balanced manner. Not every illness or trouble is ascribed to the demonic. At the same time many cases of demonic oppression are recorded, especially in the New Testament.

Some modern scholars see all references to the supernatural as the product of culturally determined "myths." This view appears simplistic, and "leaves one completely unable to explain or to cope with the depth of despair implied in human madness and evil" (Macchia 1995, 205). Nor is a naturalistic worldview able to adequately describe or interpret human experience. Experience in third-world mission fields seems to confirm the idea that demons are real, personal, and evil entities that seek to harm humans.

The Bible speaks of "unclean spirits" (Matthew 10:1; 12:43; Mark 3:11; Luke 8:29; Acts 5:16; and Revelation 16:13) or "evil spirits" (Matthew 12:45; Luke 7:21; 8:2; 11:26; Acts 19:12–16) who can torment those outside of a covenant relationship with God, oppose God's reign, and seek to trouble God's own covenant people. At times the New Testament identifies evil spirits by their function, such as a seducing spirit (1 Timothy 4:1) or a spirit of divination (Acts 16:16). Missionary W. Duane Collins notes that demons exploit or oppress (*katadunasteuo*, Acts 10:38), trouble (*ochleo* Acts 5:16), or overtake people and "seize them with hostile intent" (*katalambano*, Mark 9:18) (Collins 1993, 27). The activities of demons include tempting and opposing believers (Ephesians 6:12; 1 Thessalonians 2:18; 3:5), encouraging idol worship (1 Corinthians 8:4; 10:19–21), and possessing, deceiving, and ensnaring the wicked (Luke 22:3; 2 Corinthians 4:4; 1 Timothy 3:7).

"Demonization" and the Christian

The biblical term *daimonizomai* is often translated in English versions as "possessed" by a demon, when the actual meaning may be closer to "afflicted," "troubled," or "oppressed" by a demon. This causes some confusion in Pentecostal discussions of deliverance or exorcism. Since the idea of "possession" implies ownership and control, Pentecostals uniformly reject the idea that a (true) Christian—a believer—can be "possessed" by a demon (the exception would be Derek Prince). Theologian Guy P. Duffield cites Luke 11:21, 22; Acts 26:18; Colossians 1:13; 1 John 5:18; and 2 Timothy 2:25, 26 to say that it is not considered possible for a Christian to have a demon dwelling in him or her. "Can a demon and the Holy Spirit dwell in the same house?" (Duffield and Van Cleave 1983, 494). The believer is secure from possession by Satan (Luke 8:2; 11:22, 24, 19–21). In this, Pentecostals seem little different from Evangelical authors such as Merrill F. Unger or C. Fred Dickason, who are often referenced by Pentecostal scholars.

While this seems to say that any "Christian" who is experiencing demonic intrusion was never or is no longer saved, Pentecostals do not assert that the believer is totally immune from Satan's power. We have deliverance from Satan as long as we enter into spiritual warfare (as in resisting the devil) and live by faith and in obedience to Christ. The Christian must continually enter into Christ's victory. "[Satan's] power has been broken for *those who are faithful to Christ* by the redemption which He has achieved" (Pearlman 1981, 91; emphasis added). Bondage comes and is maintained by human disobedience, seen as the yielding of the will to Satan, which is most often spoken in terms of moral transgression. The sense is that a major moral lapse or a series of smaller lapses allow one to fall under the power of the enemy. "Possession" signals that the (former) believer is no longer a child of God.

Another important issue is that of occult involvement. Such passages as 1 Corinthians 10:7, 14–22 warn Christians against participating in the occult or the worship of pagan gods, for such will bring them into "participation" (*koinonia*) with demonic forces (compare Galatians 4:8, 9) in a way similar to the participation experienced in communion. Such practices as fortune telling, telepathy, clairvoyance, charms, magic healing, or any attempted contact with the dead are seen by Pentecostals not as "innocent parlor tricks" but as very dangerous practices.

Deliverance Defined

In light of the above, "deliverance" is defined as helping others find freedom in Christ from some bondage, such as self-destructive beliefs or behavior patterns, which seems to go beyond issues of Christian discipline, indicating the activity of a demonic agent. Note that "beliefs" here would also include intuitional or emotional beliefs that derive from teaching, trauma, or other reactions to life's experiences. One's beliefs about God are often formed more from experience than from scriptural exposition. Christ is the center of deliverance. Any "deliverance" by means of another power than Christ Himself is a false hope, and will open those who trust in it to further domination by evil forces.

This assumes that Christian disciplines such as prayer, worship, and Bible reading may prove insufficient for gaining freedom from demonic bondage for some sufferers. This idea is not easily seen in Pentecostal theologies. Until the 1970s, when such writers as Derek Prince, Don Basham, and Francis MacNutt became widely read, Pentecostal theologians appear to have considered the "classic" mode of confession of sin, Bible study, and fervent prayer to be sufficient for any situation of spiritual warfare in much the same way as non-Pentecostal Evangelicals such as Edward N. Gross or David Powlinson. The exception to this was bodily afflictions or diseases that were caused by demonic affliction.

During the last quarter of the twentieth century some Pentecostals have distinguished between deliverance for the "oppressed" by demons and exorcism for those possessed. "Oppression" is here considered to come from outside the afflicted personality (thus not dwelling in the same "house" as the Holy Spirit). Possession is then thought to occur "inside" the personality, the demon often being seen as dominating the physical body from within the soul. Few writers would use the term "exorcism" except to refer to the expulsion of demons from unbelievers, although Evangelist

George Canty discusses possible degrees of "satanic interference" ranging from "total" or "occasional" control to various forms of influence or interference (Canty 1976, 247–248).

Discerning the Need for Deliverance

The need for deliverance can be signaled by certain "symptoms." Such "symptoms" may include persistent evil or destructive behaviors or emotions; extreme mood fluctuations; superstitions, idolatry or "unnatural asceticism"; resorting to charms, divinations, or sorcery; enslaving habits; and an antipathy to the power of the Holy Spirit.

However, merely evaluating such symptoms cannot give one certainty regarding whether or not an evil spirit is at work. Because such symptoms can have other causes than the intrusion or bondage of an evil spirit, it is also necessary to gain discernment in order to distinguish between demonic possession and pathological conditions caused by physical or psychiatric illnesses. Such discernment, as a strong sense or conviction of evil spirits at work in a person (or of their absence), must be gained either through the gift of discerning spirits (1 Corinthians 12:10), through some revelation by the Holy Spirit, or through persistent prayer. One should be very cautious about administering deliverance until such discernment is gained.

Methods of Deliverance

No office of exorcist is recognized in Pentecostal churches. Any Spirit-filled believer is qualified to bring deliverance to a sufferer. In practice, however, the harder exorcisms are usually left to the pastor or to one who has a "deliverance ministry."

Some pastors or "deliverance ministers" have developed elaborate "binding" practices resembling the rituals of first-century exorcists, liturgies involving prayer and "anointing oil," or speculations about the organization and characteristics of demons. However, in the absence of instructions for dealing with foul spirits in the New Testament, the manner in which Christ and the apostles acted must guide us. Pentecostals tend to shun "conversing" with demons and do not feel that learning the "name" of the spirit is important to deliverance.

The primary method of deliverance is the name of Jesus, used with a sense of authority to abjure the demon to release the person. However, even this formula may not always be necessary. The Christian carries authority over the spirits by virtue of being who she or he is in Christ. "Christ has given us a certain 'power of attorney' to act in his behalf, or 'in his name,' without necessarily quoting the name constantly" (Duffield and Van Cleave 1983, 490).

Toward the Future

Since the 1980s, many Pentecostal congregations have adopted the charismatic practices of deliverance taught by such writers as Don Basham or Neil Anderson. These practices emphasize confession of sins, receiving and giving forgiveness, and renouncing the evil spirit and/or the cause of its entry into the sufferer's life, as well as "aftercare" involving ongoing counseling and discipleship. These methods are seen as strengthening one's relationship to God, which Pentecostals have long seen as key to our victory.

This may represent that Pentecostal thought regarding deliverance is in process toward a more balanced view between "the idea that the child of God is totally immune to all Satanic power...and the opposite view that the Christian is vulnerable at all times to legions of devils which must be constantly dealt with" (Canty 1976, 248). Pentecostal scholars would do well to investigate this approach, as well as the whole subject of "inner healing."

As witchcraft, necromancy, and other occult practices become more and more widespread and accepted in Western societies, Pentecostals will find that the demonic becomes commonplace. One example is the introduction of many Western people to "spirit guides" through Spiritist churches or indigenous religions. When the demonic nature of such guides becomes apparent, these people often turn to Pentecostal churches for help. If the church is seen as the continuation of the Spirit-anointed ministry of Jesus Christ, then the church must wrestle with the question of how Jesus' ministry to those oppressed by demons can be applied to Christians who find themselves trapped by demonic bondage.

JAMES M. HENDERSON

See also Binding and Loosing; Exorcism

Further Reading

Anderson, N. T. (1990). *Victory over the darkness: Realizing the power of your identity in Christ*. Ventura, CA: Regal.

Anderson, N. T. (1993). *The bondage breaker*. Eugene, OR: Harvest House.

Anderson, N. T. (1995). *Helping others find freedom in Christ*. Ventura, CA: Regal.

Anderson, N. T., & Warner, T. M. (2000). *The beginner's guide to spiritual warfare*. Ann Arbor, MI: Vine/Servant.

Basham, D. (1972). *Deliver us from evil*. Washington Depot, CT: Chosen.

Basham, D. (1974). *A manual for spiritual warfare*. Greensburg, PA: Manna.

Brewster, P. S. (1976). *Pentecostal doctrine*. Cheltenham, UK: Grenehurst Press.

Canty, G. (1976). Demons and casting out demons. In P. S. Brewster (Ed.), *Pentecostal doctrine* (pp. 241–257). Cheltenham, UK: Grenehurst Press.

Collins, W. D. (1993). An Assemblies of God perspective on demonology. Part I. *Paraclete 27*(4), 26.

Dickason, C. F. (1987). *Demon possession and the Christian*. Westchester, IL: Crossway.

Duffield, G. P., & Van Cleave, N. M. (1983). *Foundations of Pentecostal theology*. Los Angeles: L.I.F.E. Bible College.

Gross, E. N. (1990). *Miracles, demons, and spiritual warfare: An urgent call for discernment*. Grand Rapids, MI: Baker.

Hagin, K. E. (1984). *Ministry to the oppressed*. Tulsa, OK: Faith Library Publications.

Harper, M. (1970). *Spiritual warfare*. Plainfield, NJ: Logos International.

Hogan, J. P. (1983). Spiritual warfare. In G. Jones (Ed.), *Conference on the Holy Spirit digest: A condensation of plenary session and seminars of the Conference on the Holy Spirit in Springfield, Missouri, August 16–18, 1982* (Vol. 2, pp. 28–31). Springfield, MO: Gospel Publishing House.

Kraiss, W. E. (1983). Anointing with oil and laying on of hands. In G. Jones (Ed.), *Conference on the Holy Spirit digest: A condensation of plenary sessions and seminars of the Conference on the Holy Spirit in Springfield, Missouri, August 16–18, 1982* (Vol. 2, pp. 281–285). Springfield, MO: Gospel Publishing House.

Lagerwerf, L. (1985). Witchcraft, sorcery, and spirit possession—pastoral responses in Africa. *Exchange—Bulletin of Third World Christian Literature, 14*, 1–62.

Lowe, C. (1998). *Territorial spirits and world evangelization: A biblical, historical, and missiological critique of strategic-level spiritual warfare*. Sevenoak, UK: Overseas Missionary Fellowship.

Macchia, F. D. (1995). Repudiating the enemy: Satan and demons. In S. M. Horton (Ed.), *Systematic theology* (pp. 194–213). Springfield, MO: Logion.

MacNutt, F. (1999). *Healing*. Notre Dame, IN: Ave Maria.

Morino, B. R. (1995). The origin, nature, and consequences of sin. In S. M. Horton (Ed.), *Systematic theology* (pp. 255–290). Springfield, MO: Logion.

Pearlman, M. (1981). *Knowing the doctrines of the Bible*. Springfield, MO: Gospel.

Powlinson, D. (1995). *Power encounters: Reclaiming spiritual warfare*. Grand Rapids, MI: Baker.

Prince, D. (1998). *They shall expel demons: What you need to know about demons—your invisible enemies*. Grand Rapids, MI: Chosen Books.

Prince, D. (n.d.). *Expelling demons: An introduction into practical demonology*. Fort Lauderdale, FL: Author.

Scanlan, M., & Cirner, R. J. (1980). *Deliverance from evil spirits: A weapon for spiritual warfare*. Ann Arbor, MI: Servant.

Twelftree, G. H. (1986). The place of exorcism in contemporary ministry. *St. Mark's Review, 127*, 25–39.

Twelftree, G. H. (1993). *Jesus the exorcist*. Tubingen, Germany: Mohr.

Twelftree, G. H. (1999). *Jesus the miracle worker: A historical and theological study*. Downers Grove, IL: InterVarsity Press.

Unger, M. F. (1971). *Demons in the world today: A study of occultism in the light of God's word*. Wheaton, IL: Tyndale House.

Unger, M. F. (1977). *What demons can do to saints*. Chicago: Moody.

Warner, T. M. (1991). *Spiritual warfare*. Wheaton, IL: Crossway.

Demon Possession, Casting out Demons

Since the Pentecostal and charismatic traditions have accepted the reality of a spiritual world, including a hostile and personal enemy, it is important to look at the terms related to demon possession and the practice of exorcising individuals who have been demonized.

Terms

The term "demon" (*daimon*) was used in Greek culture to refer to a god or minor deity in the context of animistic beliefs as a type of intermediary being between God and humanity, who could exercise some sort of supervision over the cosmos. These "demons" were sometimes regarded in a positive light. The translators of the Septuagint and writers of the New Testament preferred the term "demon" (*daimonion*) to designate an "evil spirit." The normal term "demon" (*daimonion*; *daimon* in Matthew 8:31; Mark 5:12; Luke 8:29) refers to an "evil spirit" and is used "of independent beings, who occupy a position somewhere between the human and divine" (Bauer, Arndt, and Gingrich 1969, 168). The term is used in the Gospel narratives to refer to the spiritual beings who wreak havoc upon people in a wide variety of destructive ways. The spiritual being is sometimes described as an "evil spirit" (*ponaron pneuma*—Luke 7:21; 8:2) or "unclean spirit" (*akathartos pneuma*—Matthew 12:43). Further, in several of the passages, there is a curious alternation between the singular and plural numbers referring to the demonized person; in one instance, the name "Legion" may refer to the plurality of demons or the name "Legion" may represent an evasive answer from the demon(s) who does not wish to disclose its identity (Mark 5:9; Luke 8:30). The demons are obedient to Satan and are intent upon harming people in their bodies, emotions, minds, spirits, and will; they often spontaneously manifest their presence by a violent response to Jesus' person and speak through the tormented person. They can cause self-injury, debilitation, impairment of bodily health, and torment and can enter animals and take control over them as well.

The verb that signifies the demon's control over a person is *daimonizomai*, and has been translated as "possessed by a demon" (Mark 5:18) or with an adverb, "cruelly tormented by a demon" (*kakos daimonizetai*—Matthew 15:22). We also find the construction "to have a demon" (*daimonion echein*—Mark 5:15). The verb "to be possessed by a demon" may be more aptly translated by the term "to be demonized," a state in which a person can be controlled in various way by demon powers. An unfortunate man in Capernaum is physically present in the synagogue, but nevertheless belongs to another sphere, "in an unclean spirit" (Mark 1:23), and is not in control of his own life. The Gerasene demoniac (Mark 5:2–5; Matthew 8:28—two demoniacs) is in a desperate condition. Mark provides three verses, which highlight the grievous condition of the man: he lives a solitary existence in the sphere of the unclean (tombs), possesses a superhuman strength, shouts, cuts himself with stones, and is incapable of being restrained through chains. In Mark 9:17–18, details abound concerning the pitiful state of the epileptic son: he is robbed of speech and experiences violent seizures, being thrown to the ground, foaming at the mouth, gnashing his teeth, and becoming rigid and self-destructive (thrown into the fire or water to kill him). The deformed woman has been bound by Satan for eighteen years (Luke 13:11, 16) and unable to stand erect. A Syro-Phoenician woman comes to Jesus on behalf of her demonized daughter, who is in a needy condition (Mark 7:24–30). Although no specific details are provided, presumably the daughter is in a condition serious enough that she cannot make the trip with her mother; we have no details in the text as to the extent to which she or her mother were subject to ridicule and embarrassment. Within these narra-tives, the demonization of various individuals suggests various levels of demonic control. Not all are as severe as the Gerasene demoniac.

Significance of Demonization and Exorcism

The Gospels are full of narratives in which a colossal war is being waged between God and Satan, between life and death, between freedom and bondage, health and disease, between liberation and demonic control. In His own personal life and subsequent ministry, Jesus' conflict with Satan and evil spirits is no casual, incidental, or secondary purpose or activity. Following Jesus' initial conflict with Satan and demons (beasts) in the Temptation narrative (Mark 1:12–13), one of Jesus' first public appearances in the Capernaum synagogue issues in a dramatic encounter with a possessed man. Jesus' very presence evokes a violent and aggressive response. Throughout His ministry, through narrative, teaching, and response to people, Jesus assumes an aggressive posture with respect to Satan and demon powers and their role in demonization, wrong human attitudes and choices, disease and death. The primary culprit for the deadly intent is the devil, who fosters hostility to the point of actual murder as well as confusion, doubt, and lying accusation.

In the Fourth Gospel, Jesus says the devil is the father of the murderous Jews; the devil causes murderous purpose to be carried out and lies to be spoken against Jesus, the ultimate embodiment of truth (John 8:44). He fathers murderous purpose and fathers lies, and both aims express his nature—both in the context of religious judgment by those who "appear," i.e., the self-assured religious critics. Their self-assurance is voiced in the expressions "Abraham is our father" (8:39, NIV), and "The only Father we have is God himself" (8:41). In this same paragraph, Jesus consistently speaks of the truth (8:40, 44, 45, 46), to which the leaders are closed. They have "bought into" the devil's lie and the devil's perversion of the truth. The devil chooses and uses religious people, feeds their false self-assurance, fosters confusion and lying, and furthers hostility and murder—all in the name of religious "rightness." The deceitful and murderous purpose is actualized, when the devil puts it into the heart of Judas to betray Jesus (John 13:2). In this regard, Judas is called "a devil"(John 6:70). In the moment of the Crucifixion, the forces of darkness and the forces of life are positioned in a cataclysmic confrontation.

Death, disease, and possession are clear and observable symbols of the disorder that has broken in upon the world—all traceable to human sin. The healing of bodies, the exorcisms of demonized individuals, the forgiveness of sins, and the raising from the dead are symbols of the divine life that has invaded the broken world. The healing of disease and the exorcism of demonized persons are signs of God's redemptive grace and God's victory over the forces of evil. This victory has been won in a climactic way in Jesus Christ's victory over sin and death on the cross.

Two Perspectives

In the various Gospel stories, Jesus' conflict with Satan and evil spirits can be looked at from a cosmological and a personal perspective. From a cosmological perspective, Jesus is the stronger one who has invaded the strong man's house and bound him, and thus is able to plunder his "furniture/possessions," i.e., set free those who are in bondage to the enemy. From a personal perspective, Jesus frees individuals whose wills are controlled by a hostile, alien, and destructive power. He frees and grants new life and health to those who have been possessed by demons.

The Disciples and Exorcism

The initial call of the disciples (Mark 1:16–20) is formalized into their appointment as "apostles" with a threefold purpose: (1) to be with Him, (2) to be sent out to preach, (3) to have authority over unclean spirits (3:14). The first purpose is significant; it is a call to relationship—they must be with Him, learn from Him by word, example, and relationship before they could be sent out in mission (6:6b–13). Their work is similar to the work of Jesus: ministry of the word and manifestation of authority in exorcism. The miraculous activity, including exorcism, is paired with the proclamation of the kingdom's advent. In 6:7, the Twelve are given authority over unclean spirits and therefore to cast out demons—which they do (6:13). Such victory over unclean spirits is accompanied by the declaration "the Kingdom of God has come upon you" (Mark 1:13–14; compare Luke 10:9). In Matthew 12:28, the coming of the Kingdom of God is associated with three things: (1) the messianic person of Jesus, "But if I . . . "; (2) the activity of the Spirit of God, "by the Spirit of God"; (3) exorcism, "cast out demons." In addition, the disciples also "heal" (Mark 6:13) and "teach" (6:30). The first purpose of the formal appointment was to "be with Jesus," which is then realized after the return of the disciples from their mission trip; they return to be with him again (6:30). Jesus serves as a participating mentor

to the Twelve. He is always personally involved in doing the work of His unique mission, yet He is ever so conscious of teaching the disciples who would "do and teach" (Mark 6:30) what He had done and taught. Such "doing and teaching" includes their conflict with evil spirits. The three blocks of material in Mark are bound together in a clear fashion and in a sequential manner. These are the "high points" that connect the other narratives, as the disciples are observers and participants in His ministry. The close manner in which exorcism is paired with declaration of the kingdom's presence removes the exorcisms from the notion of incantation and magic. Just as Jesus came to "destroy the works of the devil" (1 John 3:8, NRSV), so the disciples are charged with the same purpose and granted the same authority; their exorcisms will signify the presence of the kingdom in their Sender.

In Luke 10:17–20, there is a revealing interchange between Jesus and the seventy-two, following their short-term missions trip. The disciples had been sent out in pairs to preach the kingdom's presence and to heal. Although exorcism is not mentioned in the charge (10:1–12), it certainly can be implied by virtue of the disciples' report after their trip of the subjection of demons to them. It is noteworthy that the seventy-two are flushed with the excitement and joy over the subjection of demons to them in Jesus' name (10:17). Jesus responds with a jubilant cry, expressed in four clauses: I was beholding Satan falling from heaven like lightning. I have given you authority to trample on snakes and scorpions, and to overcome all the power of the enemy; nothing will harm you (10:18, author's translation).

In this context, Satan's fall like lightning from heaven is the immediate effect of the disciples' success in casting out demons; the exorcisms done in Jesus' name signify the breaking-in of the kingdom of God into the world (compare Matthew 12:28 and Luke 11:20). C. K. Barrett notes, "The defeat of subordinate members of the Kingdom of evil is a proof of the sovereign activity of God, that is, of the defeat of Satan" (1947, 64). The overcoming of the lesser demons is a sign of the overthrow of their chief. Mention made of Satan in heaven is aligned with the Old Testament passages where Satan is a member of the heavenly court, from whence he can fall (Isaiah 14:12–15). Although the disciples are prepared for rejection in their mission trip, Jesus nonetheless assures them of their ultimate security and protection (Luke 10:20).

The disciples are destined for the unending bliss of the coming kingdom. Their joy is based upon their successful exorcisms. Jesus says that their joy is not to be based on exorcisms (activity) but rather in their saving position (sphere and position). It is a position of incredible privilege and not a cause for superficial triumph. The exorcisms "are no doubt a sign of the approaching salvation, but they are necessarily of less import than the fact that the disciples are elect participants in the salvation itself" (Barrett 1947, 64). Exorcisms are not the "end-all" but signs of the end, that is, the final subjugation of the force(s) of evil.

During this intermediate period of the church, the activity of the enemy will continue to increase. Not only did Jesus hold this view, but the early church held it as well. In fact, the church believed that demonism would attain its greatest manifestation before the final crisis (2 Thessalonians 2). Jesus sensed that the activity of Satan would increase not only in clear-cut demonic responses, but in the lack of receptivity on the part of the people, including a hostility that would bring about His death. Ultimately, Satan's triumph would mean his undoing (John 12:31–32; 16:11).

Accordingly, it was only through Jesus' death that the enemy's power over the people of God could be broken. It was to be an incredible paradox that He, who was stronger than the strong man, should apparently be found in the power of the strong man. He is the object of temptation and trial, and yet it is He who speaks with and casts out demons with authority. We see a real balance between the active and passive elements in the life of Jesus. His strength lies in His submission to the will of His Father even in His apparent failure.

The people of God within the Pentecostal and charismatic traditions have been especially alert to the reality of Satan's destructive power and sensitive to the way in which they could cooperate with the Spirit of God to bring new life to those individuals who are possessed. On the cosmological level, there is a life and death struggle that has been waged and continues to be fought, since the people of God live in two ages, "the already but not yet." On the personal level, the church has been alert to persons who are in need of deliverance, freedom, and relief. The fact that Jesus entrusted His disciples with a mission similar to His (Mark 3:15) and that the early church continued with a ministry of exorcism (Acts 5:16) confirms the role of the church in delivering people from the power of the strong one. Paul clearly affirms the rise of demonism in the "last days" when he warns the church against those who "abandon the faith and follow deceiving spirits and doctrines of demons" (1 Timothy 4:1, NIV). Those individuals of the church gifted with discernment are enabled to recognize the alien forces that take up resi-dence within people. Through a ministry of exorcism, the church can help to create wholeness and freedom that signifies the presence of the Kingdom of God.

J. Lyle Story

See also Binding and Loosing; Deliverance; Exorcism

Further Reading

Barrett, C. K. (1947). *The Holy Spirit and the gospel tradition.* London: SPCK.

Bauer, W., Arndt, W. F., & Gingrich, W. (1969). *A Greek-English lexicon of the New Testament and other early Christian literature.* Chicago: University of Chicago Press.

Boyd, G. A. (1992). *Satan and the problem of evil.* Downers Grove, IL: InterVarsity.

Erickson, M. J. (1998). *Christian theology.* Grand Rapids, MI: Baker.

Foerster, W. (1964). Daimon. In G. Kittel (Ed.), *Theological dictionary of the New Testament* (Vol. 2). Grand Rapids, MI: Eerdmans.

Gaster, T. H. (1962). Demon. In K. R. Krim & G. A. Buttrick (Eds.), *The interpreter's dictionary of the Bible* (Vol. A–D). Nashville, TN: Abingdon.

Major, H. D. A., Manson, T. W, & Wright, C. J. (1956). *The mission and message of Jesus.* New York: E. P. Dutton.

McClelland, S. E. (2001). Demon, Demonization. In W. A. Elwell (Ed.), *Evangelical dictionary of theology.* Grand Rapids, MI: Baker.

Twelftree, G. H. (1992). Demon, devil, Satan. In J. B. Green, S. McKnight, & I. H. Marshall (Eds.), *Dictionary of Jesus and the gospels.* Downers Grove, IL: InterVarsity.

Williams, J. R. (1992). *Renewal theology* (Vol. 2). Grand Rapids, MI: Zondervan.

Dialogues, Catholic and Pentecostal

One of the most unlikely ecumenical developments of the twentieth century, and yet with some of the farthest-reaching implications, has been the emergence and continuation of official international conversation between Pentecostals and the Vatican. From their revivalistic beginnings in the early 1900s, Pentecostal churches faced rejection and isolation from more established churches worldwide, and they responded in kind by spending decades promoting Christian fellowship almost exclusively amongst themselves. By the 1940s, Pentecostals began to find it acceptable to build relationship with Evangelicals through associations such as the World Evangelical Fellowship and, in the

United States, the National Association of Evangelicals. But it was considered inappropriate for most Pentecostals to pursue relationship with churches considered to be theologically liberal, especially those affiliated with the World Council of Churches. And dialogue with the Roman Catholic Church was out of the question, since many Pentecostals believed that Rome was the apostate church referred to in the book of Revelation. On the Catholic side, Pentecostals were considered a cult and were not recognized as a legitimate ecclesial body until after the Second Vatican Council.

Roman Catholic–Pentecostal Dialogue

The ongoing international dialogue between the Roman Catholic Church and classical Pentecostals emerged due largely to three specific influences: the Vatican II commitment to ecumenism, the charismatic renewal, and the ecumenical vision of the South African Pentecostal, David du Plessis. Du Plessis was among the first Pentecostals to show interest in the work of the World Council of Churches (WCC) in the 1950s, and he visited Rome in 1961. While there he was received by Augustin Cardinal Bea, the president of the Vatican's Secretariat for Promoting Christian Unity (SPCU). As a result of that meeting Bea invited du Plessis to attend the third session of Vatican II as an observer in 1964. Du Plessis later attended the Fourth Assembly of the WCC in Uppsala, Sweden, in 1968, and while there became acquainted with Father Kilian McDonnell, OSB, a Catholic theologian who became a scholar and friend of the charismatic renewal. The friendship between du Plessis and McDonnell was a key factor which facilitated the beginning of the dialogue.

Over the next four years du Plessis engaged in communications with the office of the SPCU. The new SPCU president was Cardinal Jan Willebrands, and du Plessis had read remarks made in a speech by Willebrands that there was a need to establish ecumenical contact with non-Catholic churches who did not belong to any of the ecclesial communities formed out of the sixteenth-century Protestant Reformation, including Pentecostals. Du Plessis wrote Willebrands in June 1970, requesting that a dialogue be established, and Willebrands agreed to assemble an initial meeting. After further meetings and the establishing of a steering committee, a commitment to dialogue was made by both sides, and cochairpersons were named: Father Kilian McDonnell for the Catholics, and David du Plessis for the Pentecostals. It was agreed that teams of nine from each side (with the Pentecostal team made up of both classical Pentecostals and charismatics from

mainline Protestant churches) would meet for five years, one week each year. Theologians from each side would present papers on themes decided by the steering committee. An agreed account would be produced each year, and a press release would be prepared.

The steering committee prepared a report outlining their priorities in starting the dialogue. They indicated that prayer, spirituality, and theological reflection would be emphasized, along with the significance of the life and fullness of the Holy Spirit for the church. Their intention was to explore ways in which sharing truth would enable Catholics and Pentecostal-Charismatic churches to grow together. A specific distinction was made between this dialogue and others, in that for these conversations structural union was not to be a goal, but rather unity in prayer and common witness.

First Quinquennium (1972–1976)

The first five years of dialogue focused on themes of significance to those involved in the charismatic renewal, which was at the height of its influence at that time. Most dialogue participants from the Pentecostal side were from mainline churches involved in the renewal who were in relationship with David du Plessis. Topics dealt with included prayer and worship, evangelism, common witness, the relationship of baptism in the Holy Spirit to Christian initiation, the scriptural basis for the Spirit-filled life, spiritual gifts in the mystical tradition, and the charismatic dimensions of sacramental and ecclesial life. The findings of the five years were outlined in a final report, although it was made clear that none of the traditions represented at the dialogue were bound to the theological positions presented. Rather, participants were encouraged to make the report available to their constituents and church leaders around the world for consideration. Suggestions for further study were made, most of which were taken up by the dialogue in later years.

For a scholarly treatment of the historical background to the dialogue and with special focus on the issues raised during the first quinquennium, see Arnold Bittlinger's *Papst und Pfingstler: Der romisch katholisch-Pfingstliche Dialog und seine okumenische Relevanz* (1978).

Second Quinquennium (1977–1982)

Cardinal Willebrands authorized a second round of discussions in 1976. With the beginning of this second session a major shift in participation was established. Whereas the first quinquennium's Pentecostal participants were both classical Pentecostals and members of the Charismatic movement who were in historic churches (Lutheran, Orthodox, Presbyterian, and others), starting in 1976 those in dialogue with Catholics were restricted to members of classical Pentecostal denominations. This was decided for three reasons: Pentecostals wanted more of their denominations involved, Catholics already were in official dialogue with most of the historic churches from which the charismatic participants came, and, probably most important, the Vatican's leadership wanted the format of this dialogue to be consistent with their other bilateral dialogues. Catholics wished to dialogue specifically with another church or ecclesial group rather than with representatives of many church groups; in this case, they wished to dialogue with members of those Pentecostal churches that emerged from the early twentieth-century revival.

Two important changes to the dialogue process were introduced by the cochairs. David du Plessis successfully argued for the inclusion of "observers" to the annual sessions. His hope was to expose as many Pentecostals as possible to the dialogue, thus engendering more support for it among leaders and churches. A maximum of six Pentecostal observers per year would be permitted, but they were not to speak during the formal dialogue sessions. In addition, Kilian McDonnell introduced the concept of "hard questions," a process that included the posing of particular questions on key issues by each side, followed by the presentation of oral and written responses to those questions after each side met in caucus. This process enabled the discussions to more specifically pinpoint key issues needing clarification, often leading to acknowledgment of convergence between the sides.

The dialogue during the second phase was widely understood to have gone well, though not without challenges. One challenge was the wide range of topics presented by scholars; there were sixteen different papers during the second phase, including experience, speaking in tongues, hermeneutics, Mary, healing, tradition, and the church as communion. Later reflection on this phase would lead the steering committee in future years to keep the range of topics more focused.

Another issue that challenged Pentecostals was the personal price paid for participation in the dialogue. Some Pentecostals declined to participate due either to prohibitions by their denominational leadership, or negative publicity and public pressure; one Pentecostal attended as an observer only on the condition that he not be included in official pictures or press releases. One Pentecostal, Jerry L. Sandidge, was given the ultimatum to either cease participation in the dialogue or face being recalled as a missionary; he eventually de-

cided to return to the United States and continue his work in the dialogue.

An exhaustive study on the second phase of the dialogue was published by Sandidge, who served on the steering committee as secretary for the Pentecostal side. His work is entitled *The Roman Catholic-Pentecostal Dialogue (1977–1982): A Study in Developing Ecumenism* (1987).

Third Quinquennium (1985–1989)

Before the beginning of the third quinquennium, the steering committee accepted the resignation of an aging David du Plessis, whose position of Pentecostal cochair was taken up by his younger brother Justus. Kilian McDonnell had also resigned, but was persuaded to continue on as Catholic cochair. Justus du Plessis had been a dialogue participant since 1974 and had served on the steering committee. He was at the time the ecumenical liaison of the Apostolic Faith Mission of South Africa, and his leadership would provide continuity in the carrying out of his older brother's vision. A new team of Pentecostals were invited, a combination of theologians, pastors, and denominational leaders. The Catholic side assembled a new team to participate as well.

Pentecostal denominations were encouraged to send official delegates to the third phase, and a number of churches were officially represented: the Church of God (Cleveland, Tennessee), Church of God of Prophecy, International Church of the Foursquare Gospel, Independent Assemblies of God International, International Evangelical Church, Apostolic Faith Mission of South Africa, and Apostolic Church of the Faith in Jesus Christ (Mexico). Other Pentecostals (from Great Britain, the Netherlands, and Sweden) attended with the blessing of their denominational leadership, though not in an official capacity of representation.

The work of this phase of dialogue received more publicity and scholarly attention than did the previous sessions. In addition to wider coverage in Pentecostal newsletters and magazines, the final report (along with the previous two final reports) was published in *Pneuma: The Journal of the Society for Pentecostal Studies* in 1990. Two scholarly dissertations were written on the work of the third quinquennium. Paul D. Lee published *Pentecostal Ecclesiology in Roman Catholic–Pentecostal Dialogue: A Catholic Reading of the Third Quinquennium (1985–1989)* in 1994. His work was complemented by the Finnish Pentecostal Veli-Matti Kärkkäinen's *Spiritus ubi vult spirat: Pneumatology in Roman Catholic–Pentecostal Dialogue (1972–1989)*.

The theme for the third quinquennium was *koinonia*, a useful vehicle for ecumenical dialogue in many circles during those years. Annual topics around this theme included the communion of saints (1985); the Holy Spirit and the New Testament vision of *koinonia* (1986); *koinonia*, church, and sacrament" (1987); and *koinonia* and baptism (1989). A final report was drafted during the 1990 session.

Fourth Phase (1990–1997)

The theme chosen for this series of discussions was evangelization, proselytism, and common witness. After years of study on *koinonia* during the third quinquennium, the dialogue partners concluded that indeed "a real though imperfect *koinonia*" was shared between the two sides (Final Report 1990, 128). A natural next focus was how these two groups treated each other. Discussions began in 1990 centered on the history of mission and evangelization among the two traditions. In 1991 the topic was the biblical and systematic foundations for evangelization, in 1992 the relationship between evangelization and culture, in 1993 evangelization and social justice, in 1994 evangelization and proselytism, and in 1995 the two sides discussed the possibilities for common witness. 1996 and 1997 were spent preparing a final report.

During this phase of the dialogue several key changes in leadership took place. Both cosecretaries of the dialogue, Jerry L. Sandidge for the Pentecostals and Heinz-Albert Raem for the Catholics, fell victim to illness and died. Justis du Plessis resigned in 1991, and was replaced as Pentecostal cochair by Cecil M. Robeck Jr., who had served on the steering committee since 1985.

Upon the conclusion of their work the members of the dialogue were granted an audience with Pope John Paul II on 31 July 1997 in commemoration of the twenty-fifth anniversary of the dialogue. Robeck represented both sides in commending to him the findings of their work together on evangelization, proselytism, and common witness. The final report has been published by the Vatican, in *Pneuma*, and by the *Asian Journal for Pentecostal Studies*. It has appeared in English, French, and Spanish. It was also the subject of a scholarly review by Veli-Matti Kärkkäinen published in 1999 entitled *Ad ultimum terrae: Evangelization, Proselytism, and Common Witness in Roman Catholic–Pentecostal Dialogue 1990–1997*.

Fifth Phase (1998–2004)

The issues raised in the fourth phase over the distinctions between evangelization and proselytism pointed to key unresolved issues between the dialogue partners. Who was a Christian and thus did not need to be evangelized? What does it mean to call oneself a Christian? These and related questions led to the establishment of topics for the fifth phase around the theme of becoming a Christian, with special focus on biblical and patristic sources. Papers were presented on Christian initiation and the baptism in the Holy Spirit (1998), faith and Christian initiation (1999), conversion and Christian initiation (2000), Christian experience in community (2001), and catechesis and formation in community (2002). The years 2003 and 2004 were devoted to preparing a report on the findings of this phase, which was expected to be ready for publication in 2005.

Assessment and Future Prospects

An important gauge for measuring the significance of any ecumenical dialogue is the reception its work receives from its constituents. The four published final reports from each completed dialogue phase through 1997 have successively been received with more favor and on a wider scope, culminating in the critical acclaim enjoyed by the dialogue regarding its work on the 1997 report on evangelization and proselytism. Pentecostal, Catholic, and Protestant scholars are increasingly interacting with the dialogue and its work.

One of the indicators of reception of the international dialogue in general is growth in conversation and relationship at regional and local levels. A few examples of such success in the United States can be cited. One is a local dialogue between the St. Louis Archdiocese and various Assemblies of God pastors and theologians in Springfield, Missouri, the denomination's international headquarters, which was begun with encouragement from the late Jerry L. Sandidge as an outgrowth of the international dialogue and has continued since the mid-1980s. Begun in 1996 and continuing each year since is an annual Pentecostal-Catholic dialogue held in conjunction with the annual meeting of the Society for Pentecostal Studies. In addition, Pentecostals are active participants in discussions between Catholics and Evangelicals. At the local level is a Los Angeles conversation cosponsored by that archdiocese and Fuller Theological Seminary that has been ongoing since 1987; also, in 2003 a national Evangelical-Catholic dialogue was established, cosponsored by the National Conference of Catholic Bishops. Both of these Evangelical dialogue teams include several Pentecostal participants. A common methodology of these local, regional, and national conversations is to evaluate and extend the work that has been accomplished at the international level.

Granted these and other successes of the dialogue, significant challenges lie ahead if it is to have greater visibility and impact. The Pentecostal churches in particular have struggled to generate widespread interest in the dialogue or its findings among its denominational leaders and members. While several Pentecostal denominations have sent official delegates to represent them over the years (including those mentioned above and others who have since done so), notably absent are some of the largest U.S. Pentecostal groups such as the Assemblies of God and the Church of God in Christ, as well as Pentecostal churches from the two-thirds world. Some of these churches have continuing negative views of the Roman Catholic Church, and others see little value in ongoing theological dialogue with non-Pentecostals. Another barrier has been lack of funding that would allow for more diversified Pentecostal representation, through either subsidizing the travel expense of participants or holding the annual sessions in southern hemisphere locations. The level of academic and scholarly sophistication of the process and its documents alienates Pentecostals (and Catholics) from embracing the dialogue on a more popular level, so consideration of methodological adjustment is in order. Nevertheless, this unique conversation between the largest church in the world and the world's fastest-growing Christian movement has great relevance and holds promise in influencing the direction of the twenty-first-century church.

DAVID L. COLE

See also Catholic Charismatic Movement; Ecumenism and Ecumenical Movement

Further Reading

Bittlinger, A. (1978). *Papst und Pfingstler: Der romisch katholisch-Pfingstler Dialog und seine okumenische Relevanz.* Frankfurt am Main, Germany: Peter Lang.

Cole, D. L. (1998). *Pentecostal koinonia: An emerging ecumenical ecclesiology among Pentecostals.* Unpublished doctoral dissertation, Fuller Theological Seminary, Pasadena, CA.

Crowe, T. R. (1993). *Pentecostal unity: Recurring frustration and enduring hopes.* Chicago: Loyola Press.

Del Colle, R. (2003). Roman Catholic/Pentecostal dialogue: Theological suggestions for consideration. *Pneuma: The Journal of the Society for Pentecostal Studies, 25*(1), 93–96.

Evangelization, proselytism, and common witness: The report from the fourth phase of the international dialogue (1990–1997) between the Roman Catholic Church and some Pentecostal churches and leaders. (1999). *Pneuma: The Journal of the Society for Pentecostal Studies, 21*(1), 11–51.

Final report of the dialogue between the secretariat for promoting Christian unity of the Roman Catholic Church and leaders of some Pentecostal churches and participants in the charismatic movement within Protestant and Anglican churches, 1972–1976. *Pneuma: The Journal of the Society for Pentecostal Studies, 12*(2), 85–95.

Final report of the dialogue between the secretariat for promoting Christian unity of the Roman Catholic Church and some classical Pentecostals, 1977–1982. (1984). *Information Service, 55*(2–3), 72–80.

Hocken, P. D. (1988). Dialogue extraordinary. *One in Christ, 24*(3), 212–213.

Hollenweger, W. J. (1997). *Pentecostalism: Origins and developments worldwide.* Peabody, MA: Hendrickson.

Hollenweger, W. J. (1999). Roman Catholics and Pentecostals in dialogue. *Ecumenical Review, 51*(2), 147–159.

Kärkkäinen, V.-M. (1998). *Spiritus ubi vult spirat: Pneumatology in Roman Catholic–Pentecostal dialogue (1972–1989).* Helsinki, Finland: Luther Agricola Society.

Kärkkäinen, V.-M. (1999). *Ad ultimum terrae: Evangelization, proselytism, and common witness in the Roman Catholic–Pentecostal dialogue 1990–1997.* Frankfurt am Main, Germany: Peter Lang.

Lee, P. D. (1994). *Pentecostal ecclesiology in the Roman Catholic–Pentecostal dialogue: A Catholic reading of the third quinquennium (1985–1989).* Rome: Pontificia Studiorum Universitas A S. Thoma Aq. in Urbe.

McDonnell, K. (1995). Five defining issues: The international classical Pentecostal–Roman Catholic dialogue. *Pneuma: The Journal of the Society for Pentecostal Studies, 17*(2), 175–188.

McDonnell, K. (1995). Improbable conversations: The International classical Pentecostal–Roman Catholic dialogue. *Pneuma: The Journal of the Society for Pentecostal Studies, 17*(2), 163–174.

Perspectives on *koinonia*: The report from the third quinquennium of the dialogue between the Pontifical Council for Promoting Christian Unity of the Roman Catholic Church and some classical Pentecostal churches and leaders 1985–1989. (1990) *Pneuma: The Journal of the Society for Pentecostal Studies, 12*(2), 117–142.

Radano, J. (1992). The Pentecostal–Roman Catholic international dialogue, 1972–1991. *Mid-Stream, 31*(1), 26–31.

Rausch, T. P. (2000). Catholic-Evangelical relations: Signs of progress. In T. P. Rausch (Ed.), *Catholics and evangelicals: Do they share a common future?* (pp. 37–55). Mahwah, NJ: Paulist.

Robeck, C. M., Jr. (1990). Specks and logs, Catholics and Pentecostals. *Pneuma: The Journal of the Society for Pentecostal Studies, 12*(2), 77–83.

Robeck, C. M., Jr. (1997). Evangelicals and Catholics together. *One in Christ, 33*(2), 138–160.

Robeck, C. M., Jr. (1999). Do "good fences make good neighbors"? Evangelization, proselytism, and common witness. *Asian Journal of Pentecostal Studies, 2*(1) 87–103.

Robeck, C. M., Jr. (1999). When being a "martyr" is not enough: Catholics and Pentecostals. *Pneuma: The Journal of the Society for Pentecostal Studies, 21*(1), 3–10.

Robeck, C. M., Jr., & Sandidge, J. L. (2002). Dialogue, Catholic and Pentecostal. In S. M. Burgess & E. Van Der Maas (Eds.), *New international dictionary of Pentecostal and Charismatic movements* (pp. 576–582). Grand Rapids, MI: Zondervan.

Sandidge, J. L. (1987). *The Roman Catholic–Pentecostal dialogue (1977–1982): A study in developing ecumenism* (Vols. 1–2). Frankfurt am Main, Germany: Peter Lang.

Discernment, Spiritual

Spiritual discernment is the charismatic gift and cognitive ability to recognize, judge, and distinguish the correlation of the inner spirit to its concrete physical manifestation. It is crucial for the church to determine what spirit is inspiring any spiritual manifestation it may encounter. The role of spiritual discernment, therefore, is vital for the edification, unity, and protection of the community of faith, as well as empowering the church in its mission. This article will seek to (1) define the term *spiritual discernment*, (2) examine the role of discernment in the life and ministry of the church, (3) explain how spiritual discernment empowers the church in its mission, and (4) discuss the implications for the church in the twenty-first century.

Defining Spiritual Discernment

What is spiritual discernment? What is being discerned: is it the Holy Spirit, a demonic spirit, or the spirit of humanity? Is discernment a natural ability or is it a charism of the Spirit? The answer to these queries can best be facilitated by an examination of the terms.

Amos Yong has defined the spirit of anything as "the complex of habits, tendencies, and laws that shape, guide, and in some way manifest and/or determine its phenomenal or concrete behavior" (Yong 2003, 130). For example, the fruit of the Spirit (Galatians 5:22–23) is manifested in the life of an individual or an institution as the Holy Spirit guides and shapes its character and tendencies. Although Simon the sorcerer of Samaria believed the preaching of Philip and was baptized, Peter discerned that he was motivated by bitterness and iniquity (Acts 8:9–23). The truculent self-destructive habits of a person possessed of a demon are manifested in a man of the Gerasenes (Mark 5:1–5). On the other hand, demonic activity or the motivation of an individual may not be easily perceived; perhaps they are intentionally hidden from view in order to deceive (Acts 16:16–18). Likewise, the spiritual power enabling a ruler, government, or an institution can be good or evil, and it may or may not be easily recognized (Daniel 10:20–21). Discerning what spirit is at work, therefore, is crucial to the life and ministry of the church.

The Old Testament teaches that discernment is both a natural ability that is acquired and refined through experience as well as a charismatic endowment of the Holy Spirit. An examination of the various Hebrew words that mean discernment—*nakar, yada, biyn,* and *shama*—as they are used in the context of Scripture will help us define this term. The Hebrew Bible depicts discernment as recognition (*nakar*) intimately connected to the physical senses of sight (Genesis 31:32; 38:25; 1 Kings 20:41), hearing (Ezra 3:13), and touch (Genesis 27:23). Discernment, therefore, is knowledge (*yada*) gained through sensory perception (*nakar*) and the Scripture (2 Samuel 19:35; Ezekiel 44:23; Jonah 4:11, Ecclesiastes 8:5). The exercise of this knowledge (*yada*) develops discernment as an understanding (*biyn*) of good and evil (Proverbs 7:7; Job 6:30). Thus, the wise are discerning as they learn to listen (*shama*) intently (1 Kings 3:11; 2 Samuel 14:12–17) in order to make sound judgments. Although discernment can be gained through experience, Solomon recognized the great responsibility bequeathed to him as king; hence, he requested that God would charismatically endow him with the gift of *shama* (discernment) that he may *biyn* (discern) between good and evil (1 Kings 3:9–12).

The New Testament, also, teaches that discernment—depicted in Greek as *diakrisis* and *diakrino*—is both a natural ability and a charismatic gift. The mature Christians have trained their senses to enable them to discern (*diakrisis*) both good and evil (Hebrews 5:14). Jesus, however, charged the religious leaders of his day with hypocrisy because they had the natural ability to discern (*diakrino*) the weather patterns but lacked spiritual discernment (Matthew 16:3; Luke 12:56). Discernment as natural ability is limited, therefore, because it is man's wisdom gained through comparing natural things. In fact, a person using natural discernment often does not understand the manifestations of the Holy Spirit because they are discerned (*diakrino*) spiritually (1 Corinthians 2:14). Furthermore, spiritual discernment is given and developed by the Holy Spirit, by comparing spiritual things (2:13), so that we may understand the deep things of God (2:9–12). Clearly, the New Testament teaches that a depth exists in certain spiritual manifestations that natural ability is unable to discern; thus, God bestows the charismatic gift of discerning of spirits upon individuals in the church (12:10).

To sum up this section, spiritual things are manifested through physical realities. The term *spiritual discernment,* therefore, can best be defined as the ability to recognize, judge, and distinguish the correlation of the inner spirit to its concrete physical manifestation: the motivating force behind an individual, government, or institution. Because of the limitations of natural discernment, the charismatic gift of discerning of spirits is vital to the life and ministry of the church.

Spiritual Discernment in the Church

It is crucial for the church to determine what spirit is inspiring any spiritual manifestation it may encounter. The role of spiritual discernment, therefore, is vital for the edification, unity, and protection of the community of faith, as well as empowering the church in its mission.

The gifts of the Spirit are given to individuals to edify the community of faith (1 Corinthians 14:26). There is an inherent danger among believers of exalting the more flamboyant gifts and neglecting the less dynamic manifestations. The diversity of spiritual gifts, therefore, "must not be seen in terms of natural abilities, but in terms of their spiritual gifts. Since God gives all spiritual gifts, who are we to value some and devalue others?" (Arrington 2003, 250). Thus, charismatic endowments are not innate talents or abilities, but they are manifestations of the Spirit's presence and power (1 Corinthians 12:7). The body of Christ is arranged in an interdependent manner so that its edification depends upon the proper function of each member's gift. So the charismatic endowment of discerning of spirits edifies the community of faith by maintaining unity among its members.

Paul uses an analogy of the human body to illustrate the interdependence of its various members (1 Corinthians 12:12–17). God has placed great diversity in the community of faith so that the body would not lack any necessary gift and would function at its optimal potential. However, the very gifts that God has bequeathed to the church to maintain its unity and care for one another (12:25) are often the sources of many divisions in

the church and partings of the way. When the pride of spiritual gifts and conceit of natural talent and abilities motivate an elitist tendency in the church, the gift of discernment can perceive the depth of the situation. Some individuals perform many good works to gain power and prestige, in order to cause schism in the church. Those who discern only by natural ability will understand these to be exceptionally good people. The spiritually discerning person, nevertheless, will recognize them for what they are: wolves that have come in the midst of the flock with selfish hidden agendas. Spiritual discernment, then, is crucial in recognizing what spirit is working through an individual or group so that unity can be maintained and the body protected.

Spiritual discernment also protects the church by recognizing, judging, and distinguishing what spirit is at work in the manifestation of other spiritual gifts. Apparently the early church did not consider spiritual gifts to be infallible and understood the need to determine their origin and purpose. For example, prophetic utterances were not to be accepted until they were judged (*diakrino*) by the community of faith (1 Corinthians 14:29). In fact, discerning of spirits seems to be the companion gift to prophecy as the gift of interpretation is the companion gift to the gift of tongues. In other words, for the church to be properly edified the gift of tongues should be accompanied by the gift of interpretation (14:27–28); correspondingly, when the gift of discerning of spirits is conjoined to the manifestation of the prophetic gift, the church is edified and protected from false prophets. Manifestations that are not inspired by the Holy Spirit will fail the necessary criteria of discernment: the edification of the body; the exaltation of Christ; its motivation should be an act of love; new revelations are compared to past revealed truth; and the person must be willing to allow their words and deeds to be judged (discerned) by the community of faith. Of course, discerning of spirits is not limited to judging prophecy, but discernment includes recognizing, distinguishing, and judging all gifts of the spirit, as well as other spiritual manifestations. Spiritual discernment, therefore, extends to a much broader area than manifestations in the local church. The church has a mission of global evangelization, and spiritual discernment fills a definite role in empowering the church in its mission.

How Spiritual Discernment Empowers the Church

To fulfill its mission the church will contact various cultures, institutions, and religions; consequently, the role of spiritual discernment is to determine what spirit is at work in these entities.

Enlightenment reason, with its closed system of thinking, has influenced the thought process of the Western world. The church must fulfill its mission in a society that attributes sin to social injustice and the environment of one's rearing. The question of evil is often diagnosed as a different formation of the brain in certain individuals; for example, the brain of a serial killer operates in a different fashion than that of most normal people. For the Spirit-filled discerning believer, these generalities are not sufficient to explicate what spirit is at work in and through evil people. According to Scripture, all humanity is culpable of sin and in need of redemption; hence, the mission of the church is to translate the gospel to this culture. What determines if someone is in need of social ministry, counseling, or deliverance from evil? This is not an easy task, but this dilemma accentuates the need of divine enablement for the church to fulfill its mission. Spiritual discernment can enable the church to distinguish (discern) what spirit is at work—the fallen human spirit, the demonic, or the Holy Spirit—in an individual or an institution.

The question of institutional evil is even more perplexing and challenging. What spirit is working in an institution that promotes slavery, racism, poverty, violence, and gender subordination? Clearly, the Spirit of Christ is not the force motivating such institutions. What are not so apparent are the political connections these institutions—which are deemed evil—have with a free society. Often there is a direct correlation between the prosperity of the free society and the empowerment of these institutions of evil. Have the lines of institutional, national, and Christian identity been blurred? The Pentecostal-Charismatic movement is a global outpouring of the Holy Spirit that transcends all national, denominational, and cultural boundaries; hence, this issue cannot be avoided. Spiritual discernment, therefore, is crucial to distinguishing between what is good and evil in the various institutions, cultures, and religions it encounters.

As the church fulfills its mission of global evangelization, it encounters the religions of other cultures. What spirit is at work in these other religions? The response that all other religions are motivated and inspired by evil spirits is simplistic, and it does not perceive the depth of the question. Although Jesus Christ is the ultimate and definitive revelation of God, the Holy Spirit is the Spirit of Life who fills and vivifies all of creation and directs it toward its teleological goal of re-creation (Psalms 33:6; 104:29–30). Could the Holy Spirit have bestowed a limited inspiration and revela-

tion upon these religions? Is there any prevenient grace evident among these other religions that can serve as talking points of evangelism? Amos Yong has helped to move this discussion forward by developing a "criteriology for discerning the Spirit(s)—the Holy Spirit and whatever other spiritual realities there may be—in the religions. This will lead to the discussion of comparative religion and comparative theology" (Yong 2003, 163). Spiritual discernment, therefore, is crucial for the church to fulfill its mission of evangelization among the other religions of the world in the twenty-first century.

Implications in the Twenty-First Century

The contemporary query concerning God is not "Is God dead?" Rather the more pressing question is "Who is the real and true God?" The world in the twenty-first century has become a global community; consequently, the church is confronted today with a return to spirituality influenced by many religions. The Pentecostal-Charismatic-Neocharismatic movement has prospered from its humble position at the beginning of the twentieth century to become the second largest Christian movement in the world. This unprecedented growth occurred during the reign of Enlightenment reason, modernism, and postmodernism while traditional churches were in decline. The success of Pentecostalism can largely be attributed to its spirituality. The spiritual life is a salvific journey with God, and it is a journey in God. It is a life lived in the Spirit; thus, a spiritual person lives responsively to the Spirit. The church is called, therefore, to faithfully remember with discerning reflection how the Spirit has been encountered by the community of faith, and to live in the present informed, protected, and empowered with spiritual discernment to fulfill its mission. Surely, the church stands poised to reap the greatest harvest of souls in history as it reveals Jesus Christ—the definitive revelation of the true God—to the world.

HERSHEL ODELL BRYANT

See also Charismata; Evil, Problem of; Fruit of the Spirit; Gifts of the Spirit

Further Reading

Arrington, F. L. (1978). *Divine order in the church.* Cleveland, OH: Pathway.

Arrington, F. L. (2003). *Encountering the Holy Spirit: Paths of Christian growth and service.* Cleveland, OH: Pathway.

Arrington, F. L., & Stronstad, R. (1999). *Full life Bible commentary to the New Testament: An international commentary for Spirit-filled Christians*. Grand Rapids, MI: Zondervan.

Bittlinger, A. (1973). *Gifts and ministries*. Grand Rapids, MI: Eerdmans.

Bushel, H. M. F. (1999). Krites, kriterion, kritikos, anakrino, anakrivo, apokrima, apokrisis, diakrivo. In G. Kittel (Ed.), *Theological dictionary of the New Testament* (Vol. 3, pp. 943–950). Grand Rapids, MI: Eerdmans.

Delling, G. (1999). Aisthanomai, aisthesis, aistheterion. In G. Kittel (Ed.), *Theological dictionary of the New Testament* (Vol. 1, pp. 178–188). Grand Rapids, MI: Eerdmans.

Dunn, J. D. G. (1998). Discernment of Spirits—A Neglected Gift. *The Christ and the spirit: Collected essays of James D.G. Dunn* (Vol. 2, pp. 311–328). Grand Rapids, MI: Eerdmans.

Fee, G. D. (1987). *The first epistle to the Corinthians*. Grand Rapids, MI: Eerdmans.

Horton, H. L. C. (1971). *The gifts of the Spirit* (10th ed.). London: Assemblies of God Publishing House.

Horton, S. M. (1976). *What the Bible says about the Holy Spirit*. Springfield, MO: Gospel.

Koenig, J. (1978). *Charismata: God's gifts for God's people*. Philadelphia: Westminster.

Ruthven, J. M. (1993). *On the cessation of charismata: The Protestant polemic on post-biblical miracles*. Sheffield, UK: Sheffield Academic.

Stackhouse, J. G. (2001). *No other gods before me? Evangelicals and the challenge of world religions*. Grand Rapids, MI: Baker Academic.

Yong, A. (2000). *Discerning the Spirit(s): A Pentecostal-Charismatic contribution to Christian theology of religions*. Sheffield, UK: Sheffield Academic.

Yong, A. (2002). *Spirit-word-community: Theological hermeneutics in Trinitarian perspective*. Aldershot, UK: Ashgate.

Yong, A. (2003). *Beyond the impasse: Toward a pneumatological theology of religions*. Grand Rapids, MI: Baker Academic.

Dispensationalism

Dispensationalism is a Bible-based comprehensive view of interpreting prophecy, particularly that of the so-called "End Times." Part of Bible prophecy speaks of the end of the world, the Second Coming of Jesus Christ, and the restoration of Israel and of God's rule on the earth. These prophecies about the End Times are the subject of a section of theology called eschatology (Greek *eschaton*—last things).

Dispensationalism, then, was an attempt by John Nelson Darby to clarify which prophecies were to come before which, trying to figure out how and when the Lord Jesus Christ would come back. It is based on a literal reading of the Bible.

Dispensationalism, as a definition, means a period of time of stewardship during which God tests man. It was used to describe different time periods and sort them into a sequence of God's dealing with men all through the Bible. The dispensationalist writers imagined that they had discovered seven of these time periods, or economies, introduced by a different covenant with God each time. They also saw a distinction between God's plan for Israel and for the church.

John Nelson Darby

As mentioned, foremost among these dispensationalist writers was John Nelson Darby (1800–1882). Darby was an Irishman who had become an Anglican priest in the Church of Ireland. Early in his career, he became extremely dissatisfied with the established church and left in 1831, joining a new denomination in England called the Plymouth Brethren. Appalled at the state of belief among the Anglican clergy, and convinced that the whole Christian church needed reforming, he set about studying and writing about ecclesiology (the study of the church itself) and Bible prophecy (eschatology). He wrote many books, including *Synopsis of the Books of the Bible* and *A New Translation of the Old and New Testaments*.

Cyrus Scofield and the Scofield Bible

For all of that, Darby would probably be virtually unknown today if his writings had not been discovered by another man, Cyrus Scofield (1843–1921), an American veteran of the Civil War. Scofield, a legislator, was taken with Darby's central thesis in his writings: namely, that Scriptures referring to Israel really were to Israel alone, not the church, as John Calvin, the Presbyterian founder had taught. This meant that Israel was to be reconstituted as a nation in the future (at this point in history the Jews were still scattered throughout the world, and Turkey ruled the Holy Land. It seemed fantastic that the Jews would ever get their land back, let alone that there could be an Israel again).

Scofield incorporated Darby's ideas into the *Scofield Reference Bible*, teaching the future return of the Jews to Israel, the Second Coming, the Seven Dispensations of Time, the Gap Theory of Creation (a view of creation which says that God created the universe billions of years ago, that this universe was ruined by Satan's fall, and that God then remade it a few thousand years ago, creating Adam and Eve as new human beings).

Scofield took the difficult concepts of Darby, rewriting them as easy-to-read captions and sidebars in his King James Version Bible. It was an immediate success. Upon its release in 1909, the Scofield Bible was a best seller. Millions of copies were sold (and still are being sold). By the mid-twentieth century, it was widely used by Fundamentalists, Baptists, Evangelicals, and Pentecostals. In fact, in many Bible colleges, it was the textbook of the school, the only Bible used.

Darby's dispensationalist influence, then, was distributed almost accidentally by the Scofield Bible's immense popularity. Many are not aware that, in studying the Scofield Bible's notes, they are also reading Darby's interpretations.

Darby's influence became so strong in the nineteenth century that evangelists such as Dwight L. Moody (1837–1899), founder of Moody Bible Institute, became a dispensationalist preacher. Through Scofield, in the twentieth century, so did Lewis Sperry Chafer (1871–1952), founding president of Dallas Theological Seminary. He incorporated Darby's and Scofield's dispensationalist ideas into his systematic-theology volumes, studied by most Fundamentalist pastors in America and Canada until the 1970s. Darby and Scofield, then, had an immense outreach into North American Fundamentalism, Evangelicalism, and even Pentecostalism. Although both Darby and Scofield did not make a place in these dispensations for the outpouring of the Holy Spirit, as believed by Pentecostals, the latter movement widely used the Scofield Bible in their Bible institutes and colleges well into the 1970s. Thus, dispensationalism directly influenced both Fundamentalism and Pentecostalism, even though these movements were diametrically opposed to one another.

Famous Users of Dispensationalist Ideas

Other well-known evangelists using Darby/Scofield prophecy ideas were Aimee Semple McPherson (1890–1944), founder of the Foursquare Church; Smith Wigglesworth (1859–1947); Evan Roberts of the Welsh Revival; Bob A. Jones (1883–1968), founder of Bob Jones University; A. W. Tozer (1897–1963); Harry Ironside (1876–1951); and Billy Graham (1917–), who regularly preached a second-coming-of-Christ sermon in his crusades. Other modern Fundamentalist writers and preachers still using the Darby/Scofield notes and Bible system are Hal Lindsey (*The Late Great Planet Earth*); Jack Van Impe; Jimmy Swaggart; Pat Robertson (although he seems to have backed away from some of this system's emphasis); Jerry Falwell; John Hagee; and Oral Roberts. The books and films based on Tim La-

Haye's *Left Behind* series were also influenced by the Darby/Scofield ideas.

Dispensationalism and Protestant Fundamentalism

Although already mentioned, it must be made clear that dispensationalism was a founding influence of American Protestant Fundamentalism. "The eschatological vision of the Fundamentalists is informed by the literal reading of dispensationalist materials" (Barr 1977, 13–14). By believing in the imminent Coming of Christ as laid out in dispensationalist prophecy charts, books, films, videos, and cassette-tape messages, the Fundamentalist Christian is given virtually no other interpretation of Bible prophecy. Since eschatology and prophecy inform the whole of the Fundamentalist system, they may be said to be the linchpin of Fundamentalism. This cannot be overstated: Dispensationalism as invented by John Nelson Darby, popularized by Cyrus Scofield, and disseminated through books, Bibles, and television created and continues to feed the Christian Fundamentalist mind-set and movement.

As dispensationalism continued to grow and be widely disseminated by such nineteenth-century evangelists as D. L. Moody and twentieth-century evangelists such as Reuben Torrey, liberalism and criticism of the Bible was also invading American culture and even the seminaries. Thus, dispensationalists, with their view of the imminent Coming of Christ and the consequent belief in the degradation of the culture, launched efforts to try to save the Presbyterian Church, at least, from loss of faith in the Bible. Seeing liberalism as an attack on the Bible, Torrey in 1910 assembled other evangelists and prominent laymen and launched a project called *The Fundamentals*. This was the writing, printing, and dissemination of up to twelve paperback books of about 70 pages each to every pastor and missionary in North America and the world. Sixty-eight of the best Bible-believing authors were selected, some of them extremely well educated, such as J. Gresham Machen and Benjamin B. Warfield, both of Princeton Theological Seminary. These writers were set to work writing the series of books dealing with various aspects of Protestant Christian faith, such as "The Virgin Birth of Christ" (Christ was born without sin, of the Virgin Mary), "The Veracity and Infallibility of the Bible," and "The Resurrection of Christ." When this project was finished, it was called "The Fundamentals." They were sent out free, without cost to the recipient, with the request that they be read and preached on by the receiving minister or missionary. Several million volumes were sent out. They were extremely influential and, of course, incorporated some dispensational ideas also.

In spite of these efforts, American Protestantism did not turn to "The Fundamentals." The main-line denominations became more and more liberal in their approach to the Bible. So those who accepted "The Fundamentals" of the faith, influenced by Darby and by the Scofield Bible, a best seller since 1909, formed an interdenominational movement called Fundamentalism. Machen and Warfield left Princeton Seminary and founded Westminster Seminary in Philadelphia. Other seminaries were later also founded, such as Gordon-Conwell in Massachusetts, Fuller in California, Trinity in Chicago, and Dallas Theological Seminary in Texas. Dispensationalism gave the belief system and Fundamentalism became the vehicle to propel the belief throughout North America and, through Fundamentalist missions, to the whole world. It also influenced worldwide Pentecostalism, since the early movement adopted the Scofield Bible for its Bible schools. Since Pentecostalism and its close relative, the Charismatic movement, currently number over 500 million adherents, Darby and Scofield now influence a large part of humanity and a very large part of Protestantism. Even those Protestants who prefer to be called conservative Evangelicals show characteristics that in another frame of reference would be Fundamentalist, at least in the original sense, but the word "fundamentalist" is now so negative a term that most Fundamental believers prefer to be called Evangelicals instead.

Dispensational Doctrine and Its Distribution

The Bible has a profound influence over all these movements. Dispensationalism gained such power because it seemed to explain how the Bible was put together and how to interpret Scripture. Thus, the Bible is the final judge of all truth. Since Scofield reassembled the ideas of Darby and inserted them into the texts, as well as in the footnotes, of the Bible itself, people reading Scofield's Bible are actually unaware that when they think they are reading Scripture, they are actually reading Scofield's notes instead. Darby's Seven Dispensations and Seven Covenants are interspersed in Scripture in such a way that, to the casual reader, they seem to be part of the Bible. The Bible reading is supplemented by conferences, prophecy studies, television programs such as those of Jack Van Impe and John Hagee, cassette tapes, videos, CDs and DVDs. There are also a whole series of studies as commentaries to back up the Scofield Bible. Since the Bible is of extreme importance to Christians, a Scofield Bible, laden with notes, prophetic charts, and interpretations, can end up being the dominant influence on the reader. People may begin to interpret Bible prophecy in such a way as to live their whole lives based on it.

Various best-selling books by Hal Lindsey, such as *The Late Great Planet Earth* are clearly based on the Scofield Bible. The book and film series *Left Behind* is based on this same system of belief. Looking at world events, the dispensationalist interprets modern-day events in light of the prophetic charts obtained from dispensationalist teachers. This can lead to naming a modern-day dictator as the Antichrist or believing that the end of the world is rapidly approaching. Thus, dispensational teaching attempts to inform the believer of his or her place in the prophetic scheme of things.

What Exactly Did Darby and Scofield Teach?

First, it must again be noted that Scofield's notes, as well as his footnotes, are placed in the text of the Bible chapters themselves. This cannot have been by accident. Although the style of printing (that is, the font) is different for Scofield's notes, the reader still has a tendency to read the notes as if they were the Bible itself and not simply Scofield's notes. Thus, the reader imbibes the doctrine of dispensationalism perhaps without being aware of it.

Second, Scofield taught that a panorama of the Bible is needed, with a key to interpret it. This panorama was needed because the Bible, "the most widely circulated of books, at once provokes and baffles study" (Scofield 1909, 9). This means that with Darby's studies and Scofield's panorama of the Bible, each Scripture could be fitted into its proper prophetic setting. "It is found in the fact that no particular portion of Scripture is to be intelligently comprehended apart from some conception of its place in the whole, for the Bible story and message is like a picture wrought out in mosaics: each book, chapter, verse and word forms a necessary part, and has its own appointed place" (Scofield 1909, 9).

These are the unifying features Darby and Scofield saw in the Bible using the number seven as much as possible:

1. One God from Genesis to Revelation

2. One continuous story of humanity and God

3. One prophecy related to the redemption of many, even though many prophecies are given

4. One unfolding truth

5. One redemption—by the blood of animals first, then by Jesus Christ

6. One great theme—Jesus the Christ

7. One harmony in doctrine

"These proofs, to every candid mind, give the unanswerable proof of the divine inspiration of the Bible" (Scofield 1909, 9).

The dispensational scheme divides the Bible up into five parts:

1. The Old Testament—the preparation for the coming of Christ

2. The Gospels—the manifestation of Christ

3. The Acts of the Apostles—the propagation of the message of Christ

4. The Epistles—the explanation of the Gospel

5. The Revelation—the consummation

These divisions are then divided into seven separate covenants and dispensations of time. The seven are the following:

1. Innocence—Adam and Eve in their original sinless state

2. Conscience—Adam and Eve, aware of sinning, leave the garden of paradise

3. Human government—Noah, after the flood

4. Promise—Abraham's call out of Ur of Chaldea (modern Iraq)

5. Law—Moses and the Ten Commandments

6. Church—foundation of the Body of Christ

7. Kingdom—New Heavens, New Earth

Sometimes the "Tribulation" is added as number 7 and the "Kingdom" as 8.

Notice that in this scheme there is no mention of Jesus Christ. This seems to be because these dispensations are periods of testing time for humankind with respect to obedience to the will of God. Notice also that in this dispensational scheme there are three covenantal periods in Genesis and not one for Jesus Christ in the New Testament. Jesus is included in the Church Age (number 6), however. Scofield writes, "The cumulative revelation of the previous dispensations combines with this (dispensation) to emphasize the utter sinfulness of man and the adequacy of the historically completed work of Christ to save by grace through faith all who come to God by Jesus" (Scofield 1909, 18). The Church Age, also being a failure, is characterized in Scofield by increasing spiritual corruption, opposition to the Gospel and apostasy from the faith.

Thus, the Kingdom Age (number 8) comes in. The other six dispensations have been failures; only the Kingdom Age, which is future, after the Church Age, will succeed. This means that when someone reads the rest of Scripture, aside from the future Kingdom, he or she is reading about failure. This Church Age's ending occurs when the "Rapture" of the church happens. The Rapture is a belief never known or taught by the church, but popularized by Darby at the Powers Court Conference in 1831 and then later by Scofield. During the Rapture, the believers who have maintained their belief in Christ through the great Apostasy will be taken up into the air by Christ's secret Second Coming. They will stay with Him while the Antichrist rules on the earth for seven years, and then will return with Christ to Earth to destroy the Antichrist and Satan's power altogether. Christ will then establish his kingdom on Earth, and the believers will share in that reign of God. Evil will be destroyed, God through His Son will once again rule the Earth, and Satan will be chained for one thousand years of peace. After this, Satan will be loosed for a time and then be defeated completely by Christ and thrown into the lake of fire with his demonic angels and followers. This is the second death and the final defeat of evil.

So among the new ideas taught by dispensationalism was the "Rapture," the two-part Second Coming of Christ, the seven years of Tribulation, the seven-year reign of the Antichrist, the new idea of the millennium as being brought in after the Rapture and Tribulation, and the final defeat of Satan.

Since the dispensationalists are future-kingdom believers (i.e., the Kingdom has not yet come), they watch for modern events to usher in the Rapture and the reign of the Antichrist. This regularly results in various world leaders being assigned the title. Hitler and Mussolini were both believed to be the Antichrist at one time. Dispensationalists are also extremely suspicious of the United Nations, the World Council of Churches, and the Roman Catholic Church, whom they believe could easily turn out to be the Antichrist system of religion and commerce identified in the book of Revelation (Revelation 18:10–18). Dispensational belief also points to the reestablishment of Israel as a nation. It is therefore the duty and right of all Fundamentalist believers to pray for and support Israel. Even though the Arabs are children of Abraham, they are not members of this covenant.

In the dispensational scheme, Israel is like a prophetic time clock, ticking toward midnight, when Jesus will come back, be revealed to those who previously refused to believe in him, and reign forever over the whole world from Jerusalem.

Outlook of the Twenty-first Century

The advent of the Scofield Bible and television has immeasurably helped popularize what would have been just another Bible movement at the turn of the twentieth century. It is impossible to say where the dispensational movement will go next. It is certain, however, that it will continue to be influential in the Fundamentalist churches in the years to come.

PETER E. PROSSER

See also Eschatology; Scripture, Holy

Further Reading

Barr, J. (1977). *Fundamentalism.* London: SCM Press.

Erickson, M. (1982). *Contemporary options.* Grand Rapids, MI: Baker.

Gerstner, J. (1991). *Wrongly dividing the word of truth.* Brentwood, TN: Wolgemuth & Hyatt.

Lindsey, H. (1970). *The late great planet earth.* Grand Rapids, MI: Zondervan.

Marsden, G. (1980). *Fundamentalism in American culture.* Grand Rapids, MI: Eerdmans.

Marsden, G. (1987). *Reforming Fundamentalism.* Grand Rapids, MI: Eerdmans.

The Scofield Reference Bible. (1909). Oxford, UK: Oxford University Press.

Dissent

Dissent is one of the few qualities that characterize multiple Pentecostal movements, both past and future, particularly because it features prominently in the self-testimony of participants. Dissent has a highly nuanced function in Pentecostal and charismatic communities. Depending on how it is variably deployed within different communities, dissenting beliefs and practices reflect the specific characteristics of each community and its societal context. The Pentecostal and charismatic theological doctrines that help form and maintain a dissenting worldview are employed with varying levels of intentionality by the acting participants and in varying ways depending on the group with which Pentecostals and charismatics are contrasting themselves.

Theology of Dissent

Pentecostal eschatology was a strong influence in the initial stages of the Pentecostal movement and has continued to contribute to Pentecostal and charismatic worldviews. The imminent return of Christ and the heavenly order profoundly affected early Pentecostal interpretations of material capital and earthly concerns. Life on this Earth was only a temporary sojourn compared to eternal citizenship in the fast approaching "New Heaven" and "New Earth." This focus on the Second Coming of Christ continues to play a large role in Pentecostal self-testimony, though participants' experiences in the earthly realm have become more prominent in their own evaluations of daily practices.

Dualism has also played a critical role in the formation of Pentecostal and charismatic forms of dissent. The belief that lived experience is divided between the "Kingdom of God" or of "light" and the "Kingdom of Darkness" or of "Satan" seems to motivate many of the Pentecostal and charismatic interpretations of acceptable activity. The dualistic construction may also emphasize the things of the world versus the things of God. The way this dualistic worldview is employed—which activities and institutions are assigned to which side of the dualistic worldview—can create vastly different responses to other social groups.

One ramification of a dualistic perspective is the formation of conversion narratives and a theology of conversion. This tends to be most important for persons who leave their original religious, denominational, or atheistic allegiances to form or join a new community of Pentecostal-Charismatic believers. Conversion into such communities emphasizes the reinterpretation of the "old life" as traveling in the "ways of darkness" and the modern world as the domain of the devil or the ungodly. The narrative sets apart the activities of the community and the individual as following the "ways of God," a mandate for every Pentecostal-Charismatic believer. Of course, it is then not enough to fashion one's social, mental, and emotional habits after the ways of God but the participant must also fight the ways of darkness by direct assault through evangelism.

One final point on the theology of dissent must be mentioned. In addition to this dualistic identification of the world, Pentecostals also maintain an intense conviction that the divine is concerned about their welfare and events in their daily lives. Prayer becomes extremely important as a means to supplicate the deity for aid in the life of the individual, the community, and the world at large. Belief in the deity's interest in human affairs and human well-being can easily segue into support for "prosperity gospel" teaching, which emphasizes the extreme extent to which the deity advocates human material gain. It can also be used to support types of "liberation theology" which emphasize the deity's concern for human welfare and justice as well as the believers' imperative to actively reach for the realization of justice. The mixture of this theological tenet with the division of the world into heavenly and earthly realms creates vastly different political and social concerns throughout Pentecostal and charismatic communities. While a dualistic worldview may encourage apolitical perspectives or the refusal of material gain, the interaction between human and divine in matters of daily living may encourage quite the opposite responses or various mixtures of responses.

History of Dissent

The focus of any scholastic inquiry will define which activities throughout the history of the movement qualify as dissenting activities. Some activities that may be described as persecution or oppression when looking at society's responses to Pentecostals may look like dissent when considered from the Pentecostal point of view. Thus it is possible that while unjust and violent activities were perpetrated against early Pentecostals, of equal interest are the ways Pentecostals themselves made sense of these circumstances and integrated those activities into their own self-narratives.

It should be no surprise that Pentecostalism in its first three or four decades was marked by dissent from society at large, dissent from existing Christianity, and dissent from within. The forerunner to the Pentecostal movement, the Holiness movement, had its share of all three forms of dissent and fashioned such dissent into a litmus test for the true believer. Much of Pentecostalism's sense of social mores and understandings of broader Christianity stem directly from the Holiness movement, including prohibitions against Coca-Cola, chewing gum, tobacco, liquor, rings, bracelets, earrings, neckties, and country fairs. Eventually this list would include lodges, political parties, labor unions, life insurance, medicines, doctors, dance halls, theaters, movies, public swimming, professional sports, beauty parlors, church bazaars, makeup, pork, coffee, tea, caffeine, immodest dress,

circuses, and fireworks. In addition to these prohibitions, Pentecostal worship practices further distinguished Pentecostals, quite intentionally, from society and Christendom.

Pentecostal Relations with the Poor, Racial Minorities, and Women

Initially American Pentecostalism was marked by an acceptance of persons from lower socioeconomic levels, the involvement of multiple ethnicities side by side, and the quite public ministerial role played by women in early denominations. It is well known that the Azusa Street Revival incorporated many of the city's poor and destitute and that Pentecostal communities sprang up amongst the poor, particularly in the rural South. This was not to the exclusion of persons from more average socioeconomic locations, but to suggest that the movement had little difficulty incorporating persons of various socioeconomic standings and that this ran counter to the average American practice.

The fact that the founder, William Seymour, was himself an African-American has taken a prominent place in Pentecostal scholarship. Considering the racial climate of the early twentieth century, the fact that black and white Pentecostals seemed to worship together without distinction and that African-Americans were prominent leaders in the movement distinguished Pentecostalism from other forms of Christianity and from American society. Cooperation was relatively short-lived, however, and with the foundation of formal Pentecostal organizations, black and white believers were increasingly segregated into separate congregations or separate denominations. This process of accommodation to the larger society illustrates an important point about Pentecostal dissent: while Pentecostals fashioned a faith worldview based on their separation from the world at large, they still had to operate within the world.

Women also featured prominently in early Pentecostal communities, both as participants and as leaders, but it was their role in leadership capacities that distinguished Pentecostalism from other forms of Christianity in the early twentieth century. The movement supported female evangelists like Aimee Semple McPherson (1890–1944) and Maria Woodworth-Etter (1844–1924) who became important figures in Pentecostalism. Support for women in leadership rested on the interpretation of a prophecy in Joel that in the last days the Holy Spirit would fall on all believers, signified for Pentecostals by Spirit baptism. Thus the

Pentecostal leadership had something of an imperative to allow women to function in a leadership capacity. Yet, just as was true for African-Americans, practices and attitudes concerning women were likewise affected by societal norms and standards. McPherson had to leave the Assemblies of God and form the International Church of the Foursquare Gospel to allow her to function as a pastor and evangelist. In fact, the Assemblies of God and most Pentecostal communities frowned on the involvement of women as pastors or elders and excessively debated the right of women to vote on church business. This attitude came not only from males in leadership, but most females seemed to express similar beliefs and apprehensions.

Pentecostals and Politics

Political ideology and involvement has been very interesting throughout Pentecostal history. In the first two to three decades of Pentecostalism in America, Pentecostals were wary of and opposed to such institutions as the League of Nations and the United States government. This is not to say that Pentecostals did not have mental and emotional bonds to the United States, but that the operation of government and political parties fell under the realm of the "ways of the world" at best and "the Kingdom of Darkness" at worst. This did not initially lead Pentecostals into political involvement but away from it. There is little evidence that early Pentecostals were greatly interested in political affairs, that they ran for office or backed particular candidates, or that they actively voted or participated in governmental social reform. It seems that the governance of "the state" was outside the realm of appropriate Christian concerns.

More recently, though, social and political dissension within Pentecostalism seems to have changed drastically from its earlier years. In contrast to a largely apolitical perspective advanced by early Pentecostals, modern Pentecostals in America are often highly involved in political advocacy. With the rise of the Christian Coalition and right-wing politics in the 1970s and 1980s, Pentecostals became part of an actively voting demographic, regularly cultivated by political candidates. Some of those candidates are themselves Pentecostals, including candidates in high positions within the United States government. It would be wrong to assume, however, that all Pentecostals who have become political and social activists share the same political perspective. The Pentecostal Coalition for Human Rights, for example, began as a political-action organization that championed sexual minorities and presently works with homosexuals in therapeutic and ministerial contexts.

Pentecostals and Christendom

Though early Pentecostals wanted to differentiate themselves from society, they were even more concerned with differentiating themselves from the rest of Christendom. Time and time again Pentecostal leaders attacked other denominations for their social programs, and high society for their decadence and ungodliness. Of course, mainline Christian and Holiness denominations largely condemned Pentecostals, with accusations that Pentecostals were trying to lure in the community's children and destroy families. Many Holiness leaders accused Pentecostal worship services of being riddled with demonic activity and witchcraft. Pentecostals responded to criticism of their worship practices by interpreting such practices as signifying Pentecostalism's "chosen" status.

Pentecostals' early anxieties and denunciations of alternative forms of Christianity continued to influence the Pentecostal denominations as they were accepted by other Christian communities. Though still condemned by Fundamentalists, in the 1940s the National Association of Evangelicals recognized the Pentecostal denominations, an initial step toward more general acceptance. Yet, there was and is some question about how willing Pentecostals were to be accepted by these outside Christian groups, especially mainstream Protestants and Catholics. The extent to which Pentecostalism was still defining itself in terms of dissension was reflected in the serious doubts and misgivings many Pentecostals had about the charismatic renewal and the Catholic Charismatic movement.

Internal Dissent

Finally, there was dissent from within Pentecostalism very early in its American history. Within the first and second decades of the movement, there were very personal attacks exchanged between Pentecostal leaders. Much of the splintering occurred over two charged theological issues—"second work" versus "finished work" and "Trinitarian" versus "oneness" theology. In the case of finished work, the idea that sanctification began at salvation, not as a secondary experience after salvation, resulted in the formation of multiple denominations, including the Assemblies of God. The oneness Pentecostal controversy resulted not only in the formation of multiple denominations that believed in baptizing in the name of Jesus only, but created schisms in the leadership of denominations like the Assemblies of God.

From the beginning most Pentecostal denominations were fairly separatist, even from each other. Not until 1947 did Pentecostal denominations begin to join together with the formation of the World Pentecostal Fellowship. This separatist impulse was not only true for early Pentecostalism, however, as is evident in the way many Pentecostals feel about the Charismatic and Neocharismatic movements today. Some of the animosity may have arisen because many of the participants in these new movements came from other Christian, non-Pentecostal denominations and chose to stay within their old communities instead of removing themselves to Pentecostal churches. It became particularly problematic when multiple Catholics became charismatics and when the Catholic leadership embraced these believers. Of course, there were theological differences that militated against total Pentecostal acceptance of these charismatic believers. Many charismatics challenged the classical Pentecostal understanding of glossolalia as the initial and only evidence for Spirit baptism. Even given these theological differences it would be difficult to say that Pentecostal indignation did not arise from charismatics also rejecting the traditional conversion narrative operative in Pentecostalism, staying instead in their own church bodies—churches traditionally associated with the wrong side of the spiritually dualistic universe.

Worldwide Pentecostal Dissension

Many countries parallel the experiences of American Pentecostalism, experiencing multiple waves of Pentecostal converts that differ considerably from each other. In Latin America and Africa, as well as Russia and Europe, many early Pentecostal converts were from lower economic strata (though this may reflect the general economic position of their respective societies at the time) and accepted a faith narrative more critical of worldly possessions and societal status. Second- and third-wave Pentecostals have tended to come from higher economic classes, in Nigeria and Brazil for example, making it difficult to attribute the worldwide growth of Pentecostalism solely to socioeconomic dissent among poor citizens, as it does not account for growth amongst middle and upper classes or growth in capitalist societies.

Pentecostalism in much of the world still incorporates a dualistic worldview, particularly in conversion narratives, thus seeing the past and parts of the modern world as belonging to an earthly or evil domain. Pentecostalism allows for conversion from indigenous religions in Africa, Latin America, and the Caribbean through this conversion narrative, yet allows many participants to continue to believe in the reality of local deities, now turned into demons or angels. Here again both dissent and accommodation are functioning at the same time. Yet another benefit of conversion narratives is the focus on the individual trying to achieve "selfhood," often cutting converts off from previous social groups, including families. This could be either a way of dissenting from traditional social structures including the nation-state, or a way of coping with a globalized world that is destroying traditional social structures and thus traditional modes of identity creation.

In terms of political dissent, Pentecostalism takes few predictable turns. In Nigeria, Pentecostals can be highly politically active as can some congregations in Brazil, yet many Chilean communities in the 1970s and 1980s remained inactive against the Pinochet regime. Latin American Pentecostals also voted for political leaders from the communist and socialist parties, thus dissenting from the current political powers and from North American Pentecostal majority perspectives as well. Within the same country, for example, Guatemala, different groups of Pentecostals support or resist the nation-state in varying ways, depending on the influence of socioeconomic factors. Here, the neocharismatic aristocracy has supported political powers that promise to promote big business but that have also persecuted the poorer Pentecostals. It is possible that refusing to participate in political activity, as is the case in some Brazilian congregations, can itself lead to a systemic breakdown in post-populist Latin American politics. Thus it is not necessarily the case the participants have to intend to dissent for dissent to occur. It can occur as one system encounters another.

Yet another kind of political and religious dissent in Pentecostalism occurs in the Caribbean, where Pentecostalism was never part of the colonial mission to civilize the colonized. Mainline Protestant and Catholic communities participated to varying extents in the colonial project of education and enculturation in order to produce colonial citizens. Rejection of the types of Christianity that accompanied colonial power and acceptance of Pentecostalism that, in its recent manifestations, largely post-dates the colonial process may be a way of dissenting against both older forms of Christianity and the colonial regime. This does not mean that Pentecostalism in the Caribbean adopts an activist stance in relation to politics, but that there are ways in which it dissents without outright political activism.

Oppression or Dissent, Passivism or Activism

It is worth noting yet again, that whether an activity is oppression or dissent has to do with who is attributed power and agency—the dominant members of a relationship or the weaker members. There is much that might be said about oppression and abuse of Pentecostal Christians the world over, yet what is even more interesting is the way Pentecostals incorporate oppression into their theology of dissent as a group set apart unto their God. Even though dissent seems to be a major part of the Pentecostal experience, from worship style to social habit, there have been both synchronic and diachronic variances that make the various instantiations of Pentecostalism appear very different, even contradictory. For example, it is difficult to predict whether Pentecostalism will propagate an activist or pacifist political stance or how various participants will relate to the customs and material wealth of dominant society. Over time the same group may seem to change radically, as with American Pentecostalism in which more recent participants' political and social activism and relative acceptance of material gain seems to contrast with early Pentecostals' position on the same issues. The transnational character of the modern world exacerbates these variances. Many nations contain communities of native citizens as well as diasporic Pentecostal communities hailing from other nations, creating multiple political and social perspectives.

It is important to remember that Pentecostal dissent has never been a wholesale rejection of the world but a creative balancing act between dissent and accommodation. It is also important to realize that the self-testimonies of a political activist or political pacifist, of an upper-class business holder or a poverty-stricken urban migrant will all include dissent as a major component. The deployment of theologies of dissent may change as may the interpretations and evaluations of what is included in the "world of darkness" and the most appropriate way to confront it, thus allowing for varying levels of materialism and activism. While some scholars have tried to understand the appeal of Pentecostalism as that which allows the poor and down-of-heart to resist the powers that have oppressed them, others have seen Pentecostalism as a force that pacifies the downtrodden, lulling them into inactivity. While some scholars see Pentecostalism as a globalizing force that obliterates regional and national identities, others have seen it as a way to make sense of the socio-economic situation and to maintain or fashion new identities. Perhaps all of these explanations of dissent and accommodation are correct. Perhaps Pentecostalism has become popular on a global scale because of its unique ability to entertain both impulses, integrating them into daily life.

ERIN D. KUHNS

See also Catholic Charismatic Movement; Globalization of Pentecostalism; Liberation Theology; Prosperity Theology; Trinitarianism

Further Reading

A. Corten & R. Marshall-Fratani (Eds.). (2001). *Between Babel and Pentecost: Transnational Pentecostalism in Africa and Latin America*. Bloomington: Indiana University Press.

Anderson, A. (1999a). Introduction: World Pentecostalism at a crossroads. In A. H. Anderson & W. J. Hollenweger (Eds.), *Pentecostals after a century: Global perspectives on a movement in transition* (pp. 19–32). Sheffield: Sheffield Academic Press.

Anderson, A. (1999b). Global Pentecostalism in the new millennium. In A. H. Anderson & W. J. Hollenweger (Eds.), *Pentecostals after a century: Global perspectives on a movement in transition* (pp. 209–223). Sheffield: Sheffield Academic Press.

Gaxiola-Gaxiola, M. J. (1991). Latin American Pentecostalism: A mosaic within a mosaic. *Pneuma 13*(2), 107–129.

Robeck, Jr., C. M. (1987). Pentecostals and social ethics. *Pneuma 9*, 103–107.

Sepúlveda, J. (1999). Indigenous Pentecostalism and the Chilean experience. In A. H. Anderson & W. J. Hollenweger (Eds.), *Pentecostals after a century: Global perspectives on a movement in transition* (pp. 111–134). Sheffield: Sheffield Academic Press.

Smith, D. (1991). Coming of age: A reflection on Pentecostals, politics and popular religion in Guatemala. *Pneuma 13*(2), 131–139.

Synan, V. (1997). *The Holiness Pentecostal tradition: Charismatic movements in the twentieth century*. Grand Rapids, MI: Eerdmans.

Doctrine, Development of

The development of doctrine deals principally with the enfolding of doctrine in the history of the church, especially of dogma, or those doctrines essential to Christian faith and identity. The topic of the development of doctrine involves an examination of the apparent development of doctrine in the history of the church in relation to Scripture and of the enduring faith at the core of the church's ongoing identity in history.

Doctrinal development in the history of the church began with the Bible, which contains rudimentary doctrinal formulations. The development of doctrine from the Bible onward can be seen in the development of one of the church's central dogmas, namely, the doctrine of the Trinity. Though the Bible can be said to be implicitly Trinitarian in its confessions and teachings, nowhere in the Bible is the term "Trinity" used of God nor is a Trinitarian theology of God explained. There is no "one essence, three persons" anywhere in Scripture. Moreover, different understandings of the Trinity, which are difficult to negotiate solely on biblical grounds, have arisen in the history of the church.

Challenges to Doctrinal Development

Although doctrinal development is a fact, controversy has arisen over how to understand and evaluate it. In the first several centuries of the church's history, the episcopal authority of bishops, canon, and creed were used to formulate the orthodox confession of the church, called "the rule of faith." The term *development* usually has a positive connotation, but one wing of the Protestant movement, Pentecostalism, tends to look upon episcopal authority and creeds in the history of the church with a certain amount of suspicion, mainly because of their role in institutionalizing the life of the Spirit.

While Pentecostals always assumed the value of sound doctrine, they tended to highlight the experience of the Spirit or the proclamation of the Gospel rather than the development of doctrine when discussing the presence of a faithful people throughout history. Stressing the unity of Christians from various church backgrounds through spiritual renewal and mission, Pentecostals were wary in the first two decades of the movement about writing creeds or doctrinal formulations, though as individuals they were certainly not shy about their beliefs.

Pentecostals have not been the only ones to place their emphasis on the development of the church's experience and life over its doctrinal development. Critical of Protestant orthodoxy, eighteenth- and nineteenth-century Pietism stressed experience and life over doctrine, seeking to expand Reformation identity by an understanding of evangelical faith primarily as heartfelt trust and devotion. Friedrich Schleiermacher, widely regarded as the progenitor of Liberal theology, also stressed the ongoing consciousness of God shared and celebrated by the church at the core of its ongoing faith. Doctrinal formulations, which had their value in the Liberal Protestant tradition only as symbolic expressions of Christian experience, were replaceable by significantly different formulations that were more relevant to cultural needs.

To criticize this view of the relationship of experience to doctrine, the Lutheran theologian George Lindbeck argued that doctrine is part of a larger framework of symbols in the life of the church that actually shape and nourish Christian experience. He argues that doctrine can function as the "grammar" of the language of faith, helping to guide the general language of worship and witness. Lindbeck's work has made it difficult if not impossible to conceive of Christian experience without doctrine, although the relationship between experience in worship and witness and doctrine may be more reciprocal than he allows. Doctrine helps to shape experience and experience influences the rise of doctrine. The two aspects of the life of faith are inseparable and mutually influential. As the historian Jaroslav Pelikan notes, doctrine involves "what the church believes, teaches, and confesses as it prays and suffers, serves and obeys, celebrates and awaits the coming of the Kingdom of God" (Pelikan 1969, 143). Doctrinal development comes not only through juridical decisions by church governing bodies but also through the *sensus fidei* (the active consent of all the people of God in their faithful witness to Christ in the power of the Spirit).

The deepest challenge within Pentecostalism to the doctrinal heritage of the church came from the Oneness controversy within the Assemblies of God, a young Pentecostal denomination. Oneness Pentecostals rejected the belief that God is three in essence, denying that the development of the church's Trinitarian faith is faithful to Scripture. Yet Oneness Pentecostals affirm the deity of Christ and glorify the Father through Christ in the power of the Spirit, which raises the question of whether they may be implicitly Trinitarian in faith though they reject the explicit affirmation of personal relations within the being of God. The debate over the Trinity made it impossible for Pentecostals to ignore the issue of the development of doctrine in history, although they had stated originally that they would establish no creed but would stress instead living Christianity. The Assemblies of God found itself drawn by the Oneness Pentecostals in its midst into a debate on the legitimacy of the dogma of the Trinity. The result was the formulation of a *Statement of Fundamental Truths* that defined the denomination as Trinitarian. Creeds were necessary after all.

It has become fashionable for those who delight in criticizing the mainstream Christian churches to assume that the formulation of Trinitarian orthodoxy in the early centuries of the church was essentially political, created to lock out certain voices, such as those of the Gnostics (or proto-Gnostics), which were allegedly flourishing as part of the ancient diversity of Christian faith. Increasingly popular are books like the *Da Vinci Code*, which base their plots on conspiracy theories concerning the early development of orthodoxy in the history of the church. However, theologies of the development of doctrine in history take issue with such a political reductionism of the enfolding of the faith in history. These theologies assume a divine design for the history of the church's faith and its doctrinal expressions as faith seeks understanding, in spite of the political realities involved in the establishment of orthodox doctrine. But how this divine design is understood in relation to the biblical witness and the vicissitudes of history is a difficult issue on which Christians across confessional lines are by no means in unanimous agreement.

Doctrinal Development and *Sola Scriptura*

Does the Protestant *sola scriptura* (Scripture alone) mean that nothing other than what is explicitly taught in Scripture is to be believed? Such an extreme biblicism would absolutize the initial faith of the church and fail to heed the ongoing guidance of the Spirit of Christ in history to help the church meet its new challenges with a fresh voice. The canon of the church is to provide the church with guidance for its doctrinal formulations, not to prevent the church from speaking in other than the language of Scripture. And even if the church should attempt to speak in only the language of Scripture (which is impossible), its language in new settings would still carry meanings beyond those between the biblical authors and the audiences original to their writing.

Such naive biblicism is a Protestant danger, though not many Protestants actually hold to it. The more realistic danger comes from the more refined Protestant view of doctrinal development as the history of the interpretation of Scripture or the history of the illumination of the meaning of the scriptural witness for history. But even here, an unrealistic amount of doctrinal freight can be loaded onto the biblical witness and the illusion created that the entire history of the church's doctrinal consensus is somehow explicitly present in the biblical witness only to be discovered at key moments in the church's history.

On the other hand, no one can claim the freedom to formulate radically novel expressions of faith that have no clear connection with the scriptural witness. Certainly the church does not have license in the name of

the Holy Spirit to sail such uncharted waters. The danger here is to Catholics as well as to Liberal Protestants, though not many would express the doctrinal history of the church in such terms. The more refined view is the real challenge, namely, what John Henry Newman, the Anglican theologian who turned Catholic, referred to in his classic nineteenth-century essay, *An Essay on the Development of Doctrine*, as "early anticipation." Elaborated later by the Catholic theologian Karl Rahner, the concept of anticipation holds that while there is genuine development of doctrinal truth in history, this development simply enfolds the implications of the original self-disclosure of God in Scripture, especially in Christ.

Not that doctrine merely discovers what is already in Scripture, but that the development of doctrine makes explicit what was only implicit in biblical revelation. The closure of revelation with the witness of the Apostles is actually a dis-closure of the living God to a dynamically receptive church. As such, the dynamism of the development of doctrine that sets that development in motion and sustains it is already built into the original revelation. The subsequent development is real but does not surpass the eschatologically final self-disclosure in Christ to which the biblical witness points. Rahner argues that the scriptural teachings have implications and a logic that are developed in the church's doctrinal history.

Anticipation is a useful concept, although extreme caution must be exercised. There are Protestants who would be quick to point out the danger of formulating a dogma based on a long history of church worship and tradition, only to read back from this into the scriptural witness an implication or a logic not sufficiently present there to support it. For example, is the bodily ascension of Mary to heaven clearly anticipated in what the Bible says about her? Not many Protestants would think so. They would be quick to note that something proclaimed as dogma should have clearer support from the biblical witness than what can be found for the exalted role granted Mary in Catholic tradition. On the other hand, there is no excuse for the scant attention afforded by most Protestants to the one through whose body and faithfulness God became flesh in Jesus as the faithful servant.

Since doctrine is mainly an ecclesiastical and not simply an individual affair, the development of doctrine calls for the preservation of the one faith (Ephesians 4:5 NIV) that was once and for all time delivered to the saints as a witness to the truth of the gospel (Jude 3). That the faith "once and for all" delivered can still "develop" is at the core of any notion of the development of dogma. It is an issue about which both Protestants and Catholics have something important to say. It is also an issue that divides the two sides from each other. Part of the difference lies in how the relationship between Scripture and tradition is construed.

Doctrine, Scripture, and Tradition

Pentecostals have not been very interested in tradition, although the Bible implies in places that behind the biblical witness is a tradition faithfully handed down (for example, 1 Corinthians 15:3–4). Though Protestants have a respect for tradition (for example, historic confessions), they have emphasized the Bible as the supreme standard that looms over the history of tradition as its judge (what may be termed the "otherness" of Scripture). Catholics, on the other hand, cherish the Bible as the primary guide to faith but see it as part of the church's overall developing tradition, helping the church discern truth in continuity with it. Commenting on the historic *lex orandi lex credendi* (rule of prayer, rule of faith), the British theologian Geoffrey Wainwright noted that Protestants have emphasized the correction of Scripture over the church's ongoing worship and tradition while Catholics have stressed the role of worship and tradition in shaping the church's understanding of truth, with Scripture viewed as a fundamental part of that tradition.

In defending the continuity of doctrinal tradition in history, one must be careful not to assume that the inner laws of development built within the flow of revelation necessitate the doctrinal development that actually occurred historically in the way in which it occurred (this is a standard criticism of John Henry Newman's theory of doctrinal development). There is certainly room in the actual development of doctrine for extraordinary leaps forward or an unfortunate halting of development. More to the point, the tradition of the Gospel is couched historically in various traditions, as the French Dominican Yves Congar saw so clearly. Though as theologian Metropolitan Emilianos noted, Protestants must be cautious not to detach Scripture from the broader matrix of the church's worship and witness; the role of Scripture in discerning truth in the midst of error remains for many an indispensable aspect of any understanding of the development of doctrine.

Doctrinal Development and Corruption

Catholicism in general, however, has stressed the continuity of truth in history through its diverse elaborations in changing times rather than the significant breaks and recovery of truth in history assumed by Protestants. Although doctrinal development is not beyond critical questioning and discussion, it does assume that the church has never radically broken with the faith once delivered to the saints. It believes that the one faith of the church endured as it found new and diverse expressions historically. The endurance of the one faith in history means that the development of doctrine, no matter how revolutionary and diverse in expression from generation to generation, cannot represent a radical break with the faith delivered originally to the saints. If it did, the church would be viewed as defecting from the faith and the truth of the faith would be regarded as lost to history.

Jesus promised to never leave or forsake his church (Matthew 28:20), which implies for many that the Spirit of Christ will keep such a radical defection of the church from taking place. Confidence in God's faithfulness (through the presence of the Spirit of Christ) with the church in history to preserve the faith is not to deny that the development of doctrine will experience weak and limited expression requiring elaboration and even correction. Catholic theologian Hans Küng noted rightly in his reflections on the Second Vatican Council that the history of doctrine can lead to a certain petrification of faith and thus stands in constant need of correction. The same letter from Paul that defended the original kerygma as taught from the Holy Spirit (1 Corinthians 2:13) also confessed that those who proclaim and teach it "see through a glass dimly" (1 Corinthians 13:12).

Protestants have shared different notions of the fall and restoration of the church in history, ranging from the alleged spiritual slumber of the church directly after the generation of the apostles (held among some Pietists and, later, most Pentecostals) to the onset of the Constantinian wedding of the church and politics in the fourth century (highlighted by many in the Anabaptist stream of the history of the church), to the medieval eclipsing of salvation by grace alone (stressed by Martin Luther and many mainstream Protestants). Some Pentecostals held to an expanding light theory after the church grew spiritually cold in the post-Apostolic age, involving salvation by grace (Martin Luther), sanctification (John Wesley), healing (Charles Cullis), and Spirit baptism with signs (Pentecostalism).

Despite such fall and recovery theories, few Protestants would be as radical as the Church of Latter Day Saints (Mormons) in assuming a total break of the church with its original faith. Protestant versions of the development of doctrine in history assume some sense of continuity of the church in history, even if, in addition to affirming the Nicene-Constantinopolitan Creed, their understanding favors the distinctive doctrinal or spiritual accents of those involved in describing the precise nature of this continuity. Doctrinal development contains the scars and limitations of fallibility, even disobedience to the scriptural witness, but it recognizes a genuine witness to the revelation of God that comes through Scripture.

Doctrinal Challenges

The basic challenge in any understanding of the development of doctrine is to discern the one faith within the developing formulations of faith in the history of the church. The one faith has a central core but a wonderfully diverse expression over time and throughout a variety of places. Such is the colorful bouquet of the truth that seeks to give glory to God and to bear witness to the divine self-disclosure that ultimately surpasses understanding.

FRANK D. MACCHIA

See also Church, Theology of the; Scripture, Holy

Further Reading

Emilianos, M. (1980). Consensus in the formulation of doctrine. *Greek Orthodox Theological Review, 25*(1), 21–35.

Newman, J. H. (1973). *An essay on the development of Christian doctrine*. New York: Penguin Books, Ltd.

Pelikan, J. (1969). *Development of Christian doctrine: Some historical prolegomena*. New Haven, CT: Yale University Press.

Rahner, K. (1982). Considerations on the development of dogma. *Theological Investigations* (pp. 3–35, Vol. 4). (K. Smyth, Trans.). New York: Crossroad.

Ecstasy

As a religious term, "ecstasy" refers to a wide variety of spiritual experiences by mystics from many different religious traditions. The word is derived from the Greek *ekstasis*, meaning "to stand or be placed outside of oneself" and in its strictest sense refers to a mystical state in which one becomes disassociated from sensory input while enraptured by divinity. There are different degrees of ecstasy and some mystics distinguish between different kinds of ecstatic experiences such as "union," "rapture," "trance," and "flight." In more extreme ecstatic states, mystics may become unresponsive to stimuli for extended periods. In the modern era these states have frequently been referred to as "altered states of consciousness." These exalted or transcendent states are considered spiritually beneficial, but can occasionally be psychopathic, producing an imbalanced psychological condition.

In its milder sense "ecstasy" can refer to any spiritual experience from which one derives intense joy or delight. This seems to be the sense in which some existentialists use the term as they describe the ecstasy of the I-Thou encounter or the ecstasy of ultimate concern. It is ecstasy in this milder sense that we most often find in the Protestant, Christian tradition, although Pentecostals and charismatics have testified to experiencing ecstasy in both senses.

Ecstasy in World Religions

Ecstatic experience is not unique to Christianity. It is commonly known within shamanism, Hinduism, Buddhism, Sufism, and kabbalism. Within these traditions ecstasy is induced by methods including meditation, ritual dance, drug use, and asceticism. Mystics in theistic and animistic religions often consider themselves possessed by a divine spirit when in an ecstatic condition. In pantheistic traditions it is common for ecstasy to blur any distinction between the individual and the divine as one is absorbed into the divine.

In the Hellenistic world in which the New Testament authors lived, ecstasy is reported among those who participated in the Mystery Religions. Worshipers in the cults of Cybele and Dionysus danced in wild, uncontrolled frenzies, and ecstatic speech commonly resulted. Though some scholars have compared this speech with Christian glossolalia, the ecstatic speech of the Mystery Religions was much more frequently prophetic in the native tongue than it was unintelligible speech in other languages. Attempts to find parallels between Christian tongues-speaking and the musings of the Oracle at Delphi also seem misguided. Christopher Forbes points out that the Oracle occasionally seemed unintelligible due only to the highly poetic and ambiguous nature of the prophecies that were delivered in understandable language.

Ecstasy in the Bible

It would be a mistake to conclude from the above that all ecstatic experiences are non-Christian or syncretistic in nature. While there are differences between Christian and non-Christian ecstasy, ecstatic experiences are recorded in both the Old and New Testaments. In Genesis 15:12 (NIV), we are told "Abram fell into a deep sleep, and a thick and dreadful darkness came over him...." This God-induced state deprived

Abram of external, sensory input so God could communicate with him more clearly and unmistakably. On two occasions (1 Samuel 10:5–12 and 1 Samuel 19:23, 24) Saul was overwhelmed by the Holy Spirit who caused him to break forth into ecstatic prophecy. Old Testament prophets such as Ezekiel, Daniel, and Zechariah were given transcendent experiences as they lost touch with their physical environment during the communication of prophetic visions.

There are instances of ecstasy in the New Testament as well. In Acts 10:10 Peter is said to fall "into a trance [*ekstasis*]" as he received a vision. Paul likewise tells of falling into an *ekstasis* in Acts 22:17 and he describes an ecstatic experience in 2 Corinthians 12:1, 2, saying that as he was translated into "the third heaven" he did not know "whether it was in the body or out of the body." John also witnesses to having ecstatic experiences "in the Spirit" as the Revelation is given to him (Revelation 1:10, 4:2, 17:3). In Acts, Luke calls ecstasy in its milder sense being "filled with the Spirit" (Acts 4:8; 31:9, 17; 13:9).

The above Scripture passages show that while Judeo-Christian ecstasy is not unique, it is distinctive. Rather than being possessed by or absorbed into the divine, these mystics maintained their own identity and possession of their faculties as they enjoyed fellowship with God. The degree to which this is so is seen in Paul's insistence in 1 Corinthians 14:32 that Christian prophecy and tongues-speech are subject to the speaker's control.

Christian Mystics

Throughout church history mystically inclined people have sought dynamic encounters with God, devoting much time to intense prayer and contemplation. In the transcendent experiences that resulted they felt a joyful union with God that defied explanation and which frequently disassociated them from sensory input. Notable Christian mystics who enjoyed periods of ecstasy include Catherine of Siena, Teresa of Avila, and John of the Cross.

While most of these mystics described their experiences in distinctly Christian terms, some of them did blend unorthodox elements in their teaching and practices. Meister Eckhart, for example, was charged with heresy for speaking in terms that seemed Gnostic and pantheistic. Madame Jeanne Guyon, a seventeenth-century mystic who has been highly lauded in our time, was condemned by a theological commission in 1695 for teachings such as the uselessness of petitionary prayer. Guyon also made statements that were imprudent for someone who did not want to appear pantheistic. While ecstasy has a biblical and historical

place in Christian experience, Christians who have embraced ecstatic phenomena have sometimes failed to preserve distinctive Christian characteristics.

Pentecostal and Charismatic Ecstasy

Pentecostals and charismatics tend to emphasize spiritual experience. Russell Spittler observes that "By far the most pervasive [Pentecostal and charismatic value] is the worth accorded to individual *experience*. Included are not only religious feeling and emotions of joy, or sorrow, but Pentecostals consider personal experience the arena of true religion" (Spittler 2002, 1097). Pentecostal and charismatic testimonies abound with references to "the anointing," "the glory," "the presence," "the power," and "outpourings." They speak of being "blessed," "filled," "touched," and even "zapped." Ecstasy in its milder sense is common among Pentecostals and charismatics.

Ecstasy is also reported among them in its stricter and more mystical sense. It occurred, for example, with some frequency among believers affected by the Mukti mission revival in India at the beginning of the twentieth century. American Pentecostals also testified to ecstatic experiences in this sense. William Durham, an influential early Pentecostal leader in Chicago, on one occasion lay conscious but helpless on the floor for two hours as he received revelations from God. This ecstasy that follows believers' "falling under the power" is usually called "being slain in the Spirit" or "resting in the Spirit."

The degree of ecstasy in this condition seems to vary widely. While some Pentecostals and charismatics such as William Durham have testified to fully cataleptic states, many of the "slain" seem to be ecstatic in the milder sense, as evidenced by the fact that some charismatic ministers will have those lying prostrate picked up by assistants so they might be ministered to more personally. It is especially difficult to determine the nature of the experience of the "slain" who have been encouraged by worship leaders or ministers to "do carpet time" and to remain on the floor in order to "soak."

Question of Tongues as Ecstatic Speech

There has been much debate among scholars as to whether speaking in tongues should be considered ecstatic speech. Five views have been espoused on this matter: (1) All tongues are ecstatic speech in either the strict or milder sense; (2) all tongues are ecstatic in the milder sense; (3) tongues with language content (as described in Acts) are not ecstatic, while "unintelligible" tongues (as described in the Pauline epistles) are ecstatic; (4) due to the connotation of "ecstatic" as "uncontrolled," no tongues-speech should be considered ecstatic; and (5) because the term "ecstatic" is so ambiguous, it is too confusing to use the word in relation to tongues-speech. D. A. Carson expresses this last view saying, "By and large, however, 'ecstasy' has become such a slippery term that it is probably better left out of the discussion unless it is thoroughly qualified and all sides in the debate know what is meant" (Carson 1987, 78–79).

Pentecostals and charismatics believe in and seek ecstatic spiritual experiences. In doing so they have generally, though not always, preserved the Christian distinctive of fellowship with as opposed to possession by or absorption into God. Though some seekers may embrace artificial or aberrant elements in their quest for mystical experience, biblical Christian ecstasy is nevertheless an indispensable part of Pentecostal and charismatic identity.

DAVID KOWALSKI

See also Baptism in the Holy Spirit; Enthusiasm; Experience, Theology of; Glossolalia

Further Reading

Bach, M. (1969). *The inner ecstasy.* New York: Abingdon Press.

Carson, D. A. (1987). *Showing the spirit: A theological exposition of 1 Corinthians 12–14.* Grand Rapids, MI: Baker Book House.

Cartledge, M. J. (2002). *Charismatic glossolalia: An empirical-theological study.* Burlington, VT: Ashgate Publishing Company.

Fee, G. (1987). *The First Epistle to the Corinthians.* Grand Rapids, MI: Eerdmans Publishing Company.

Forbes, C. (1997). *Prophecy and inspired speech.* Peabody, MA: Hendrickson Publishers.

Furse, M. L. (1977). *Mysticism, window on a world view.* Nashville, TN: Abingdon Press.

Guyon, M. J. (1981). *Union with God.* Goleta, CA: Christian Books.

Holm, N. G. (Ed.). (1981). *Religious ecstasy.* Stockholm, Sweden: Almqvist & Wiksell International.

Lawson, J. G. (1972). *Deeper experiences of famous Christians.* Anderson, IN: The Warner Press.

Oropeza, B. J. (1995). *A time to laugh: The holy laughter phenomenon examined.* Peabody, MA: Hendrickson Publishers.

Shelton, J. B. (1988). "Filled with the Holy Spirit" and "Full of the Holy Spirit": Lucan redactional phrases. In P. Elbert (Ed.), *Faces of renewal.* Peabody, MA: Hendrickson Publishers.

Spittler, R. (2002). Spirituality, Pentecostal and Charismatic. In S. Burgess (Ed.), *The new international dictionary of Pentecostal and Charismatic movements.* Grand Rapids, MI: Zondervan Publishing House.

Teresa of Avila. (1979). *The interior castle* (K. Kavanaugh & O. Rodriguez, Trans.). New York: Paulist Press.

Underhill, E. (1961). *Mysticism.* New York: E. P. Dutton & Co.

Underhill, E. (1964). *The mystics of the church.* New York: Schocken Books.

Wacker, G. (2001). *Heaven below: Early Pentecostals and American culture.* Cambridge, MA: Harvard University Press.

Williams, J. R. (1990). *Renewal theology* (Vol. 2). Grand Rapids, MI: Zondervan Publishing House.

Ecumenism and Ecumenical Movement

The first decade of the twentieth century saw the birth of two movements that ultimately changed the face and direction of the global church, perhaps as much as any other influences, for the duration of the century: the Pentecostal movement and the modern ecumenical movement. The movements arguably began with similar aspirations: the unity of believers around the Lordship of Jesus Christ and worldwide cooperation in the work of spreading the Gospel. Although the movements spent half a century ignorant of and estranged from one another, in the 1950s a process of rapprochement began. By the end of the century, Pentecostals showed signs of accepting responsibility for an ecumenical vision, while leaders from among the World Council of Churches and the post-Vatican II Roman Catholic Church realized that the growing Pentecostal movement was too significant to be ignored.

Obstacles to Ecumenical Progress

While the first several decades of the Pentecostal movement were generally characterized by isolationism and an anti-ecumenical outlook, Walter Hollenweger, Dale Irvin, and other scholars have argued that an "ecumenical root" was present at Azusa Street from the very beginning, and that the movement was expected to bring about reconciliation between different Christian denominations. Some of the same impulses that have driven the ecumenical movement were present at Azusa Street, particularly a challenge to the divisions among Christian churches of the world and a call for the unity of people across boundaries of race, gender, class, and language. The revival, led by William J. Seymour, was interracial and international in character, and included women in prominent leadership roles.

Efforts at international Pentecostal cooperation were made during the first decades following Azusa Street. Many conferences in Europe prepared the way for the Pentecostal World Conference (PWC). These include Alexander A. Boddy's Sunderland Conference (begun in 1908), the 1908 Hamburg Conference, and conferences in Mulheim, Zurich, and Amsterdam, all before World War I. After the war, G. R. Polman organized the 1921 International Pentecostal Conference in Amsterdam and attracted delegates and missionaries from thirteen nations. The 1939 European Pentecostal Conference in Stockholm, organized by Donald Gee and Lewi Pethrus, was the most significant other antecedent to the 1947 PWC in Zurich, with delegates from nearly twenty countries.

In North America, while the revival associated with Azusa Street carried the potential to be a force for unity, within a few years a spirit of independence led to the proliferation of splinter groups, churches, and denominations. This schismatic period among Pentecostals began before the Azusa Street Revival subsided and ran well into the 1920s, caused by doctrinal disputes, personality clashes, and questions of ecclesiology. This internal upheaval was compounded by the rejection that Pentecostals experienced from non-Pentecostal churches during the same time period over perceived fanaticisms, the presence of women in ministry, and emphases on holiness and healing. After this season of rejection and schism, the remainder of the 1920s and the 1930s were less volatile, as organizations gradually stabilized through the founding of Bible colleges and the promotion of overseas missions. But most of these churches adopted a practice of isolation, not interdenominational cooperation with one another, much less with non-Pentecostal churches.

Strategic Alliances

During the 1940s and 1950s, Pentecostals moved away from their predominantly sectarian ecclesial posture, within certain limitations. While still dealing with estrangement from nearly all established churches, they began to seek compatible partners for fellowship, as exemplified by Pentecostal identification with Evangelicals in North America during the formation of the National Association of Evangelicals (NAE) in the 1940s. This alliance developed while Pentecostals and Evangelicals found agreement in opposition to the mainstream ecumenical organizations that eventually became the World Council of Churches (WCC) and the National Council of Churches of Christ, USA (NCCC). Early NAE documents articulate why the Federal Council of Churches (FCCCA, later the NCCC) was no longer a fit vehicle for Evangelical cooperation. Among the stated reasons were references to liberalism, the idea of a Super-Church, and the FCCCA's relation to the Greek Orthodox churches and attitude toward the Roman Catholic Church, which were a perceived threat to the distinctive testimony of Protestantism. The original NAE Statement of Faith was publicly supported by several prominent Pentecostal denominational leaders in the aftermath of early NAE conventions, many of whom maintained powerful leadership profiles in their denominations for the next several decades, influencing Pentecostalism in its anti-ecumenical posture while promoting NAE cooperation.

Within five years of the initial Pentecostal commitments to the NAE, both the PWC and the Pentecostal Fellowship of North America (PFNA—disbanded in 1994 with the formation of the Pentecostal and Charismatic Churches of North America, or PCCNA) were in the process of formation. The first PWC was held in Zurich, Switzerland, in 1947, promoting spiritual fellowship (but opposed to structural union) and in the hopes of coordinating missions and evangelistic activities worldwide. These efforts at cooperation were only mildly successful, due largely to the inability to organize fiercely independent (mostly American) Pentecostals. After the 1947 PWC, North American Pentecostals followed suit and formally organized in 1948. Within two years the PFNA represented fourteen groups, over ten thousand churches and about 1 million Pentecostals in North America. Among those conspicuously absent from the fellowship were African-American Pentecostal churches, oneness Pentecostal groups, the Tomlinson branches of the Church of God, and the Pentecostal Church of God. In short, the PFNA represented mainstream white, orthodox Pentecostalism in North America.

Both the PWC and the PFNA demonstrated a capacity for visible, ecumenical cooperation with fellow Pentecostals over the years. The PWC's stated founding purposes included encouraging fellowship and cooperation among Pentecostals, demonstrating the essential unity of Spirit-baptized believers, cooperation in fulfilling the Great Commission, promoting courtesy and mutual understanding, providing assistance to needy Pentecostal bodies, promoting scriptural purity, and upholding Pentecostal truths. The PFNA limited its focus to the spiritual unity and fellowship of Pentecostal believers, promising complete autonomy for individual churches for the sake of independent Pentecostal leaders who were fearful of co-operative organizations. These fellowships demonstrated an appreciation for visible unity, while remaining committed to the Evangelical consensus of the NAE, sharing fully the anticommunism, anti-Catholicism, and anti-ecumenism of other NAE members.

Ecumenical Pioneers

With all due respect to individual ecumenical efforts among early Pentecostals (Seymour and W. F. Carothers in the United States, Polman in Europe, and others), Pentecostal ecumenism emerged in earnest beginning in the 1950s through the ministry of "Mr. Pentecost," David du Plessis. Du Plessis became an ambassador to mainline Protestants and Orthodox and Catholic Christians on behalf of Pentecostals, although they often didn't solicit or appreciate his work. He conversely challenged Pentecostals to build bridges of relationship with the other major streams of Christendom. His ecumenical trail-blazing until his death in 1987 was significant, particularly his presence at WCC General Assemblies, at Vatican II, and his role in the establishing of international dialogue between Catholics and Pentecostals.

Two contemporaries of du Plessis deserve mention as well. Donald Gee was a quiet force for ecumenism in comparison to the pronounced style of du Plessis. But beginning with his presence at the 1921 International Pentecostal Conference in Amsterdam through his chronicling of WCC and other ecumenical activity from 1947–1966 as editor of the PWC's publication *Pentecost* (perhaps the most significant ecumenical contribution of the PWC), Gee educated generations of Pentecostals concerning his passions, which were unity among Pentecostals and expressions of unity in the larger church. The other figure from the 1960s, who has continued to be a voice for and concerning Pentecostals, is the scholar Walter Hollenweger. Hollenweger first introduced Pentecostals to the WCC and argued for their large-scale inclusion (there had been a few small Pentecostal groups involved in the WCC by then) at the ecumenical table during his role as WCC secretary for evangelism from 1965–1971. He has been both an advocate and a harsh critic of Pentecostals ever since, but he challenged the church to take the global phenomenon of Pentecostalism seriously long before it became obvious to do so.

In more recent decades two Pentecostals in particular led by example in the ecumenical arena. Jerry Sandidge was an Assemblies of God scholar and missionary whose involvement in Faith and Order, WCC, and NCCC consultations, as well as the international Catholic-Pentecostal dialogue, was a model of responsible Pentecostal ecumenism. Sandidge, like du Plessis before him, was willing to pay the price of criticism and discipline by fellow Pentecostals who were unwilling to grasp his vision of Pentecostal participation in the expressed unity of the church. His friend and contemporary, Cecil M. Robeck Jr., joined Sandidge in many ecumenical ventures around the world, and has used his platforms of leadership (at Fuller Theological Seminary, in the Society for Pentecostal Studies, and elsewhere) to promote the valid and necessary cause of ecumenical engagement by Pentecostals. Robeck in recent years has from a more scholarly perspective carried the mantle of du Plessis, being sought after as a representative Pentecostal in ecumenical conversations in Geneva, Rome, and around the globe. Following the painstaking examples set by Sandidge (who passed away in 1992) and Robeck, other Pentecostals have begun to engage the world church responsibly in the last two decades, including Harold Hunter, Cheryl Bridges-Johns, Frank Macchia, Veli-Matti Kärkkäinen, David Daniels, and Amos Yong.

Conciliar Ecumenism in Recent Decades

Since the 1961 joining of the WCC by the Iglesia Pentecostal de Chile and the Mision Iglesia Pentecostal, Pentecostals have officially been represented in Geneva. However, the vast majority of Pentecostals worldwide have historically either ignored or opposed conciliar ecumenism. The best example of this is the ongoing position of the Assemblies of God, which has since 1965 affirmed a resolution at its General Council disapproving mainstream ecumenical activity in general, and in particular forbidding official Assemblies of God participation in such. However, in recent decades more Pentecostals have responded to the challenge of ecumenical engagement. For instance, six Pentecostals were present and active participants in 1993 at the Fifth World Conference on Faith and Order in Santiago de Compostela, Spain, a significant increase in Pentecostal representation at such gatherings. From a scholarly perspective Hunter and Robeck began to engage in direct dialogue with the WCC concerning its strategic ecumenical initiatives. Examples include Hunter's 1992 published Pentecostal responses to the major WCC programs "Towards a Common Expression of the Apostolic Faith Today," which eventually produced both *Baptism, Eucharist, and Ministry* (*BEM*) and *Confessing the One Faith* (*COF*), and Robeck's interaction with "Towards a Common Understanding and Vision" of the World Council of Churches (*CUV*).

155

Pentecostals also engaged in consultation with WCC member churches in 1994, 1996, and 1997. These consultations were brought about through the initiative of the WCC, which responded to a challenge at the 1991 WCC General Assembly in Canberra to engage in dialogue with nonmember churches, particularly Independent, Evangelical, and Pentecostal churches. In November 1994, WCC representatives met with over thirty Pentecostals (of mostly nonmember churches) in Lima, Peru, to explore ways to build bridges among and to Pentecostals in Latin America. Recommendations generated by the Lima consultation included a call for North-South Pentecostal dialogue, and also the opening up of a forum for dialogue between Pentecostals and representatives of the Catholic Church with the help of the WCC and the Latin American Council of Churches. The recommendation for a North-South dialogue among Pentecostals also helped to propel the WCC in its efforts to engage in consultation with U.S. Pentecostals. WCC member churches sent representatives to Costa Rica in June 1996, where they engaged in discussions with Pentecostals from both Latin America and the United States. This gathering doubled as an intra-Pentecostal ecumenical encounter, helping Pentecostals to speak to one another and recognize their own diversity, thus informing their attempts to clarify their identity and grow in unity.

The Pentecostal-WCC consultations were a precursor to a WCC-Pentecostal Joint Consultative Group (JCG) that was commissioned in 1998 at the WCC General Assembly in Harare, Zimbabwe. Twenty-nine classical Pentecostals participated in the Harare General Assembly in various capacities, and the JCG was formed for the purpose of furthering dialogue with Pentecostals who are not members of the WCC. Since its commissioning, the JCG, composed of theologians and church leaders from several nations, has met in various locations around the world, discussing convergences and divergences among their respective churches. The gatherings were designed to lead to a final report to be presented to the WCC.

In the United States, Pentecostal involvement with the NCCC was minimal until the 1980s. Those who pioneered the cooperation from the Pentecostal side were Sandidge and Robeck. They participated together in a four-year Working Group on Faith and Order under NCCC auspices on the subjects of ecclesiology and pneumatology, a study that grew out of a larger study on the apostolic faith in the North American context. Out of this emerged a consultation between the Faith and Order Commission of the NCCC and Pentecostal scholars that continued through the 1990s.

The most recent multilateral effort in the United States involving Pentecostals has been the newly formed association called Christian Churches Together in the USA (CCTUSA). It was conceived in the hopes of bridging the divide between churches historically connected to the NCCC and churches not so aligned. The latter include churches involved in the NAE and/or PCCNA, and Roman Catholics. In seeking to be more inclusive than either the NCCC or the NAE, CCTUSA insists that a mandate for existence be demonstrated through significant participation from five different Christian families: Evangelicals and Pentecostals, Orthodox, Roman Catholic, historic Protestants, and racial and ethnic churches. Organizational meetings began in 2001 and continued as churches across the United States studied the proposal, and by late 2004 several Evangelical and Pentecostal churches had made formal commitments to become CCTUSA participants, including two Pentecostal churches (Open Bible Churches and International Pentecostal Holiness Church), whose overseers became CCTUSA steering committee members. Thus Pentecostals have the potential to offer ecumenical participation and leadership in ways not seen before in the United States, should CCTUSA succeed in becoming a truly inclusive ecumenical force.

An international effort paralleling the CCTUSA initiative is the series of discussions aimed at establishing a Global Christian Forum (GCF) that would include a wide spectrum of churches and organizations. A meeting in September 2000 in Pasadena, California, included thirty representatives from around the world representing Orthodox, Roman Catholic, Anglican, Reformation Protestant, Pentecostal, and Evangelical churches, as well as Christian networks and parachurch organizations. Similar to the CCTUSA's aspirations, the GCF proposes a new approach, moving beyond the present ecumenical structures, enabling churches from a wider range of traditions to have places at a common table in order to discuss issues of mutual concern.

Bilateral Dialogues

Pentecostals have been involved in a number of bilateral dialogues at the international level since the early 1970s. The longest running, and most significant, international bilateral dialogue to date involving Pentecostals has been the international Pentecostal-Catholic dialogue. Shortly after the conclusion of the Vatican II council, conversations took place between Cardinal Jan Willebrands of the Vatican's Secretariat for Promoting Christian Unity and du Plessis that led to the beginning of dialogue discussions in 1972. Since that time, five series of formal conversations of five or more years in length have taken place. Four final reports from each round of discussion have been published, with a fifth focusing on the discussions since 1998 anticipated in 2005. Conversations have dealt with difficult but critical issues facing the dialogue partners, including evangelization and proselytism, *koinonia*, sacraments, the role of Mary and the saints, Christian initiation, and the charismata.

Another international dialogue of significance is that between Pentecostals and the World Alliance of Reformed Churches (WARC). It was initiated by a 1989 vote at the WARC general council in Korea to investigate the possibility of dialogue with Pentecostals. After WARC made an unsuccessful attempt to enlist Pentecostal partners through the PWC, with the assistance of Robeck, a Pentecostal team was assembled and discussions began in 1996. The first five-year round of conversations ending in 2000 centered on the theme "Word and Spirit, Church and World." Topics included spirituality, missions, the role of the Holy Spirit in the Church, the charismata, and eschatology. The second five-year session began in 2002 on the theme "Experience in Christian Faith and Life," including the topics of discipleship, discernment, and discipline in Christian life and practice.

Future Prospects

After over half a century of isolated attempts to shape church and culture, the ecumenical and Pentecostal movements are experiencing convergence in the fulfilling of their compatible missions. In a search for new life and relevance, conciliar ecumenical entities are respectfully courting participation and leadership from Pentecostal churches and individuals. And increasingly, Pentecostals are awakening to the challenge and opportunity of ecumenical participation. Future Pentecostal ecumenicity must approach ecumenical engagement from a broad range of levels and vantage points representative of the diversity within the Pentecostal movement. Pentecostals have successfully contributed to the ecumenical endeavor through multilateral and bilateral dialogues and will continue to do so, but the most fruitful and consistent area of ecumenical engagement at a sophisticated level has been and will continue to be the free exchange of ideas and relationships at annual academic society meetings—the U.S.-based Society for Pentecostal Studies, and sister societies in Europe, Asia, Africa, and Latin America. For Pentecostals to truly fulfill their ecumenical re-

sponsibilities, local ecumenism at the grass roots must be complimented by courageous stances taken by church and denominational leaders as Pentecostals assume a public role in caring for the whole church. Ongoing participation in new cooperative efforts such as the GCF and CCTUSA initiatives will demonstrate that Pentecostal churches indeed accept the ecumenical challenge before them.

DAVID L. COLE

See also Dialogues, Catholic and Pentecostal

Further Reading

Barr, W., & Yocum, R. (Eds.). (1994). *The church in the movement of the spirit*. Grand Rapids, MI: Eerdmans.

Blumhofer, E. (1993). *Restoring the faith: The Assemblies of God, Pentecostalism, and American culture*. Chicago: University of Illinois Press.

Carpenter, J. (Ed.). (1988). Evangelical action! And united we stand. In *A new Evangelical coalition: Early documents of the National Association of Evangelical*. New York: Garland.

Cole, D. (1998). *Pentecostal koinonia: An emerging ecumenical ecclesiology among Pentecostals*. Unpublished doctoral dissertation, Fuller Theological Seminary, Pasadena, California.

Gros, J. (1995). Toward a dialogue of conversion: The Pentecostal, evangelical and conciliar movements. *Pneuma: The Journal of the Society for Pentecostal Studies 17*(2), 189–201.

Gros, J. (1999). Pentecostal engagement in the wider Christian community. *Mid-Stream: The Ecumenical Movement Today, 38*(4), 26–49.

Gros, J. (2003). A pilgrimage in the spirit: Pentecostal testimony in the faith and order movement. *Pneuma: The Journal of the Society for Pentecostal Studies, 23*(1), 29–53.

Hollenweger, W. (1966). The Pentecostal movement and the world council of churches. *Ecumenical Review, 18*(3), 310–320.

Hollenweger, W. (1997). *Pentecostalism: Origins and developments worldwide*. Peabody, MA: Hendrickson.

Hunter, H. (1992). Reflections by a Pentecostalist on aspects of BEM. *Journal of Ecumenical Studies, 29*(34), 317–345.

Hunter, H. (2003). Two movements of the Holy Spirit in the 20th century? A closer look at global Pentecostalism and ecumenism. *One in Christ, 38* (1), 31–39.

Irvin, D. (1995). "Drawing all together in one bond of love": The ecumenical vision of William J. Seymour and the Azusa Street Revival. *Journal of Pentecostal Theology, 6*, 25–53.

Macchia, F. (2000). Dialogue, reformed-Pentecostal. In S. Burgess & E. van der Maas (Eds.), *Dictionary of Pentecostal and Charismatic movements* (pp. 575–576). Grand Rapids, MI: Zondervan.

Murch, J. D. (1956). *Cooperation without compromise: A history of the national association of evangelicals.* Grand Rapids, MI: Eerdmans.

Rausch, T. (Ed.). (2000). *Catholics and evangelicals: Do they share a common future?* Mahwah, NJ: Paulist.

Robeck, C. M. Jr. (1987). Pentecostals and the apostolic faith: Implications for ecumenism. *Pneuma: The Journal of the Society for Pentecostal Studies, 9*(1), 61–84.

Robeck, C. M. Jr. (1997). The Assemblies of God and ecumenical cooperation: 1920–1965. In W. Ma & R. Menzies (Eds.), Pentecostalism in context: Essays in honor of William W. Menzies. *Journal of Pentecostal Theology,* (Suppl. 11), 107–150.

Robeck, C. M. Jr. (1998). A Pentecostal assessment of "towards a common understanding and vision" of the WCC. *Mid-Stream: the Ecumenical Movement Today, 37*(1), 1–36.

Robeck, C. M. Jr. (2000). Dialogue, Catholic and classical Pentecostal. In S. Burgess & E. van der Maas (Eds.), *Dictionary of Pentecostal and Charismatic movements* (pp. 576–582). Grand Rapids, MI: Zondervan.

Robeck, C. M. Jr. (2000). Pentecostal World Conference. In S. Burgess & E. van der Maas (Eds.), *Dictionary of Pentecostal and Charismatic movements* (pp. 707–708). Grand Rapids, MI: Zondervan.

Robeck, C. M. Jr. (2000). World Council of Churches. In S. Burgess & E. van der Maas (Eds.), *Dictionary of Pentecostal and Charismatic movements* (pp. 1213–1217). Grand Rapids, MI: Zondervan.

Sandidge, J. (1989). A consultation summary. In A consultation: Confessing the apostolic faith from the perspective of the Pentecostal churches. In J. Burgess & J. Gros (Eds.), *Building unity: Ecumenical documents with Roman Catholic participation in the United States* (pp. 484–486). New York: Paulist.

van Beek, H. (1996). *Consultation with Pentecostals in the Americas.* Geneva, Switzerland: WCC.

van der Laan, C. (1991). *Sectarian against his will: Gerrit Roelof Polman and the birth of Pentecostalism in the Netherlands.* Metuchen, NJ: Scarecrow Press.

Word and spirit, church and world: The final report of the international dialogue between representatives of the world alliance of reformed churches and some classical Pentecostal churches and leaders 1996–2000. (2001). *Asian Journal of Pentecostal Studies 4*(1), 41–72.

Yong, A. (2002). Pentecostalism and ecumenism: Past, present, and future. Part 5 of 5. *The Pneuma Review, 5*(1), 29–38.

Education

Over the past century Pentecostals have established hundreds of institutions of higher education (IHEs) worldwide. Initially focused exclusively on the training of ministers, they gradually expanded into liberal arts and now also include professional and graduate education. Pentecostals have also launched thousands of elementary and secondary schools, many of them initiated through missionary efforts, but now sustained by vibrant national Pentecostal churches. These formal education efforts have been complemented by energetic nonformal education through church-based Sunday schools throughout the world. This survey of Pentecostal education focuses on higher education efforts in the United States.

Roots of Pentecostal Education

Though they distrusted formal education systems, early Pentecostals were not opposed to education as a means to an end. The twentieth-century Pentecostal revival in the United States began in a short-term Bible school in Topeka, Kansas, in 1901. The revival produced and was then sustained by many short-term Bible schools that functioned as training centers for Pentecostal church workers. Bible training during the day was often complemented by evangelistic services in the evening and the sending out of participants in evangelism groups.

The first permanent Pentecostal Bible schools were established in 1909 and at least ten Pentecostal Bible schools were functioning by 1914, the year in which the Assemblies of God (AG) was established. The organizational meeting that launched the AG included the following as one of its five purposes: "We may also have a proposition to lay before the body for a general Bible Training School with a literary department for our people." Two institutions were explicitly endorsed by this initial General Council of the AG. One, T. K. Leonard's Gospel School, was specifically created for ministerial training. E. N. Bell and J. R. Flower, the first chairman and secretary of the General Council, both served on the faculty of the Gospel School. The other endorsed school, R. B. Chisolm's Neshoba Holiness School, was a "literary school," offering primary, secondary, and collegiate courses in a variety of subjects.

Assemblies of God Higher Education

The development of higher education in the AG is illustrative of overall patterns in the Pentecostal movement. Bible training centers for ministerial preparation were established in San Francisco in 1919 and in Los Angeles the following year: Glad Tiding Bible Institute and Southern California Bible School (which eventually became Bethany College in Scotts Valley and Vanguard University in Costa Mesa). Central Bible Institute was established by the AG in Springfield, Missouri, in 1922. Spanish language Bible institutes were launched in California and Texas in 1926.

Five additional Bible institutes were launched in the 1930s that today exist as Christian colleges or universities affiliated with the AG. A department of education was authorized by the AG in 1937. The AG and other Pentecostals established links with evangelicals during the 1940s and helped to establish the Accrediting Association of Bible Institutes and Bible Colleges (AABIBC) in 1947. By 1951, all the AG schools were accredited by AABIBC at either the institute or collegiate level.

In 1955, the denomination launched its first college of arts and sciences, Evangel College. In 1959, Southern California Bible College became Southern California College (SCC), and in 1964 SCC became the first regionally accredited college in the AG. Others soon followed. In 1973, the AG launched its first seminary (now known as the Assemblies of God Theological Seminary). In the 1990s, four AG colleges changed their name and status to "university." Six other Pentecostal IHEs also have university status.

Pentecostal Schools

Pentecostal IHEs may be classified as follows:

- Type 1: Residential Bible schools and church-based Bible institutes (CBBIs) focus on hands-on ministry training.

- Type 2: Bible colleges with theological accreditation (in the United States and Canada, from the Association for Biblical Higher Education, (formerly AABIBC)), offer two-, three-, or four-year training programs for pastors, evangelists, and missionaries.

- Type 3: Christian colleges with regional accreditation from one of the six regional accrediting bodies in the United States offer an array of courses and majors in fields other than church ministry or theology.

- Type 4: Regionally accredited seminaries offer graduate degree programs.

- Type 5: Regionally accredited universities offer undergraduate degrees in a variety of majors and graduate programs in various professional fields.

Type 1 institutions dominated the early years of the Pentecostal movement. These were practical for ministry purposes, providing leaders for an exploding revival movement, and they were the least expensive, most flexible, and easiest to staff. A pastor and his associates could use their time during the week to teach classes and then engage their students in ministry during evenings and on weekends. Type 1 institutions include both residential Bible schools or institutes with relatively more formal academic standards, on the one hand, and CBBIs or schools of ministry, which usually accept less formal academic preparation.

Most CBBIs were and are proto-IHEs rather than postsecondary institutions of higher education, in that they often do not require a student to have completed secondary education in order to be admitted, do not award academic degrees, and do not have a permanent faculty. Many, however, seek articulation agreements with accredited institutions that will award transfer credits for their courses. The creation of such institutions is a testament to the dynamism of a grassroots religious movement in which participants take the entrepreneurial initiative to provide the training needed for effective church leadership and outreach. Within the AG, for example, the proliferation of "Master's Commission" programs and other CBBIs continues to be a sign of vitality at the local level (while presenting challenges to enrollments at residential Bible colleges). Likewise, newer movements such as Calvary Chapel and the Vineyard are creating many Bible institutes and ministry schools at the local level.

Hundreds of Type 1 institutions exist within the Pentecostal and Charismatic movement in the United States. Among the notable residential Bible institutes associated with the classical Pentecostal denominations are the Latin American Bible Institutes in California and Texas (AG), Elim Bible Institute (Elim Fellowship), and Holmes Bible College (Pentecostal Holiness). Outside the classical Pentecostal denominations are Type 1 institutions such as the Vineyard Leadership Institute, Christ for the Nations Institute, and Rhema Bible Training Center.

Type 2 institutions emerged in the second generation of the Pentecostal movement and often patterned themselves after Wesleyan and Evangelical institutions like Nyack and Moody Bible Institutes. The creation of the AABIBC linked Pentecostals with other Evangelicals in the creation of an accrediting body meant to standardize and assure the academic soundness of Bible colleges. Many institutions that once held AABIBC accreditation have since become regionally accredited, but many Pentecostal and charismatic IHEs still see their mission as best fulfilled within the context of a Bible college identity. These institutions exist to educate pastors, evangelists, and missionaries. They offer longer-term degree programs and provide instruction in the Bible, theology, and church ministries of many kinds. They are genuinely postsecondary institutions in that they require a high school diploma or its equivalent.

A survey of the membership of the Pentecostal and Charismatic Churches of North America (PCCNA), the fellowship of classical Pentecostal denominations, including those that are historically African-American and some of the newer movements, like the Association of Vineyard Churches, yielded the following list of Type 2 institutions presently active in American Pentecostalism: Beulah Heights Bible College (International Pentecostal Church of Christ); Central Bible College (AG); Eugene Bible College (Open Bible Churches); Heritage Bible College (Pentecostal Free Will Baptist); King's College and Seminary (Church on the Way (Foursquare)); International Bible College (Church of God, Cleveland, TN); Messenger College (Pentecostal Church of God); Zion Bible Institute (AG).

Type 3 institutions began to emerge in the 1960s as Bible colleges expanded their course offerings, sought regional accreditation, and changed their names to "Christian college" or simply "college," dropping "Bible." These colleges continue to offer Biblical studies or religion majors and to require an array of Bible courses. The models for these schools were often Evangelical IHEs, like Wheaton College, and most embrace an educational philosophy that integrates faith and learning and encourages a Christian calling to vocations outside of the church ministry as well as inside. A number of these Pentecostal institutions are members of the Evangelical grouping known as the Council of Christian Colleges and Universities (CCCU). Several of these have now gone on to become Type 5 institutions, but a survey of PCCNA members yielded the following list of Type 3 institutions: American Indian College (AG); Bethany College (AG); Emmanuel College (Pentecostal Holiness Church); Life Pacific College (International Church of the Foursquare Gospel); Southeastern College (AG); Trinity Bible College (AG); Valley Forge Christian College (AG).

Type 4 institutions emerged when Pentecostalism adopted the notion of seminary training for its ministers. While early Pentecostals had likened seminaries to cemeteries and rejected any attempt to require an academic degree as a criterion for ordination, Pentecostal leaders in the 1950s and 1960s began to recognize the need for post baccalaureate institutions that would prepare Pentecostal ministers in Pentecostal settings. Only

three such stand-alone institutions were identified by a search of PCCNA members, though others, such as the School of Divinity at Regent University and the School of Theology and Missions at Oral Roberts University, function within the framework of a Type 5 Pentecostal university. These three institutions are the Assemblies of God Theological Seminary (AG); Charles H. Mason Theological Seminary (Church of God in Christ); and the Church of God Theological Seminary (Church of God, Cleveland, TN).

The most recent type of Pentecostal IHE to emerge is also the most rapidly proliferating type: the Pentecostal university. Oral Roberts University (ORU), though not associated with the PCCNA, established the precedent when it was chartered in 1963. ORU now has approximately five thousand students, making it the largest of all the Pentecostal and charismatic universities. Regent University, which was established as CBN University in 1978, now has more than three thousand students. Lee University, affiliated with the Church of God in Cleveland, Tennessee, moved to university status in 1997 and now has close to four thousand students. The Type 5 Pentecostal and charismatic universities in the United States are the following: Evangel University (AG); Lee University (Church of God, Cleveland, TN); North Central University (AG); Northwest University (AG); Oral Roberts University (Independent); Patten University (Church of God, Cleveland, TN); Regent University (Independent); Southwest Assemblies of God University (AG); Southwestern Christian University (International Pentecostal Holiness Church); Vanguard University (AG).

The AG endorses nineteen IHEs in the United States, and hundreds of other AG and Pentecostal IHEs operate outside North America. Many of them follow the patterns of development outlined above.

Enrollment Changes

Enrollment growth in AG IHEs has been consistent. Between 1955 and 1978, nine or ten IHEs were endorsed by the AG and enrollment climbed by more than 300 percent, from 2,571 students to 8,283 students. From 1978 to 2003, the number of endorsed IHEs climbed to nineteen and total enrollment increased to 15,249, almost doubling in that twenty-five-year period. While undergraduate enrollment increased by approximately 30 percent during that period, graduate enrollment grew from 200 students in 1978 (all at the seminary) to over 950 students in 2003. Likewise, nontraditional student enrollment (defined as enrollment for credit in one or more of the following: extension sites, degree completion programs, distance education, correspondence courses, or study centers) increased from 0 in 1978 to 3,416 in 2003.

The following tables compare enrollment trends among the types of institutions currently endorsed by the AG. (Only institutions that were endorsed in 1994 and continue to be endorsed in 2003 are included and they are grouped by their current type and not by their type in 1994).

Table 1 suggests that the growth in undergraduate and graduate education within AG is occurring in Type 3, 4, and 5 institutions, all of which offer regionally accredited degrees and, with the exception of the seminary, a range of programs in a variety of fields. (The most prominent Type 2 institution in the AG, Central Bible College, has recently decided to pursue regional accreditation.)

Table 2 for nontraditional students displays a similar pattern, although the number of nontraditional students at Type 3 institutions has dropped along with those at Type 1 and 2 institutions.

This pattern of a growth in liberal arts colleges, seminaries, and universities accompanied by a declining enrollment in resident Bible institutes and Bible colleges can be found in other Pentecostal denominations as well. During the 1990s, three Bible colleges associated with the Church of God in Cleveland, Tennessee, closed their doors, while Patten University in California and Lee University in Tennessee, both regionally accredited, continue to function.

The following list shows the overall enrollment growth of AG-endorsed institutions along with other clusters of IHEs during the past decade (it should be noted that the 20 percent growth rate of AG IHEs exceeded the 15 percent growth rate of AG church attendance): CCCU-member IHEs (67 percent); Concordia University (Affiliated with Lutheran Church-Missouri Synod) (41 percent); AG Type 5 universities (40 percent); AG-endorsed institutions (20 percent); other private institutions (12 percent); public institutions (–0.7 percent).

Continuing Vitality

Over the past century, education has been a vital dimension of the Pentecostal movement in the United States and around the world. Beginning with short-term Bible schools, Pentecostal education has expanded into a fully orbed enterprise including nonformal Sunday Schools, formal elementary and secondary schools, Bible colleges, liberal arts colleges, seminaries, and universities. This pattern of educational development in the United States is also evident in nations around the world as Pentecostal churches seek to integrate dynamic Christian experience with all facets of life and learning.

JEFFREY S. HITTENBERGER

See also Philosophy and Theology

Table 1. Traditional Undergraduate and Graduate Enrollment, 1994 and 2003

Type of Institution	Number of Institutions	1994 Enrollment	2003 Enrollment	Gain or Loss	% Gain or Loss
1	3	325	241	-84	-26%
2	1	991	821	-170	-17%
3	5	2,728	3,243	+515	+19%
4	1	212	368	+156	+74%
5	5	5,538	6,739	+1,201	+22%

Table 2. Nontraditional Undergraduate and Graduate Enrollment, 1994 and 2003

Type of Institution	Number of Institutions	1994 Enrollment	2003 Enrollment	Gain or Loss	% Gain or Loss
1	3	233	0	-233	-100%
2	1	91	65	-26	-29%
3	5	1,868	299	-1,569	-84%
4	1	116	124	+8	+7%
5	5	292	1,429	+1,137	+389%
Global	1	581	1,499	+918	+158%

Further Reading

Blumhofer, E. (1989a). *The Assemblies of God, Volume 1-To 1941.* Springfield, MO: Gospel Publishing House.

Blumhofer, E. (1989b). *The Assemblies of God, Volume 2-Since 1941.* Springfield, MO: Gospel Publishing House.

Carpenter, J. (2002). *New Evangelical universities: Cogs in a world system, or players in a new game?* Retrieved August 1, 2003 from www.cccu.org/resourcecenter/

Corey, B. (1992). *Pentecostalism and the collegiate institution: A study in the decision to found Evangel College.* Unpublished doctoral dissertation, Boston College, Boston.

Corey, B. (1994, March). *Pentecostalism and the collegiate institution: A history and analysis of this strained alliance.* Paper presented for the Society of Pentecostal Studies annual conference.

Dempster, M. W., Klaus, B. D., & Petersen, D. (Eds.). (1999). *The globalization of Pentecostalism: A religion made to travel.* Irvine, CA: Regnum.

Hittenberger, J. (2001). Toward a Pentecostal Philosophy of Education. *Pneuma, 23, 2.*

Hittenberger, J. (2004). Globalization, Marketization, and the Mission of Pentecostal Higher Education in Africa. *Pneuma, 26, 2.*

Jenkins, P. (2001). *The next Christendom: The coming of global Christianity.* Oxford, UK: Oxford University Press.

Johns, C. B. (1993). *Pentecostal formation: A pedagogy among the oppressed.* Sheffield, UK: Sheffield Academic Press.

Marsden, G. M. (1998). *The outrageous idea of Christian scholarship.* New York: Oxford University Press.

Marsden, G. M. (1994). *The soul of the American university: From Protestant establishment to established nonbelief.* Oxford, UK: Oxford University Press.

Menzies, W. (1971). *Anointed to serve.* Springfield, MO: Gospel Publishing House.

Palmer, M. D. (2001). Orienting our lives: The importance of a liberal education for Pentecostals in the 21st Century. In *Teaching to make disciples: Collected papers of the 30th annual meeting of the society for Pentecostal studies* (pp. 315–336). Tulsa, OK: Oral Roberts University.

Wilson, L. F. (1999). *A vine of his own planting.* Costa Mesa, CA: Vanguard University.

Enculturation

Enculturation is the process by which an individual or organization learns the traditional content of a culture and is influenced by co-cultures and by society both transtemporally and transspatially. Cultural traits and patterns materialize through an evolving ethnology: language and communication patterns, institutionalized protocols and activities, beliefs, and values.

Three levels of enculturation range from microinitiation rites and practices to macrosystemic changes. First, children experience an enculturation process as they progress through developmental sequences. Second, enculturation occurs when individuals join organizations, such as socioreligious groups. Finally, organizations evolve as they meet the expectations of those within and without.

While Pentecostals and charismatics share common characteristics, such as the desire for a Holy Spirit-driven life, several differences exist. Besides the time of origin difference between Pentecostals (1900s) and charismatics (1960s), context stability is a central issue. Initially, Pentecostals in the United States either chose to leave or were dismissed from mainline churches when the Pentecostal revivals came to town. Biological family and friendship ties were severed when the "saved" became "members of the true family of God." Long-held religious traditions and church associations were discontinued as the family was redefined. Whereas half a century later, when the charismatics received the blessings from Holy Spirit renewal, most remained in their mainline denominational contexts. Many Pentecostals felt the charismatics should join them, because they were God's chosen people of the Spirit. But differing enculturation processes produced a renewal of tolerance from the mainline denominations. No longer were "Spirit-filled" members encouraged to leave.

Reciprocity is a key concept in personal or organizational evolution. Holding the possibility for change or continuity, reciprocity provides the possibility of integration and synergy between co-cultures and society. Reciprocity can promote assimilation and subsequent accommodation of co-cultural practices, thus determining the balance between change and continuity of shared meanings, shared understandings, and shared sense making.

Changes in actual Pentecostal practices occurred as they moved from a minority, fringe, or borderline status to simulated business organizations with hierarchical structures, forgetting founding premises. Changes occurred in the mainline denominations as well. Near the end of the twentieth century, Euro-American mainline denominations selected some of the Pentecostal practices in their alternative services, such as worship leaders and popular music styles, as well as renewed mission-outreach programs.

Pentecostals Resist Societal Influence

As the "Spirit of God was poured out" on diverse people at the beginning of the twentieth century, each brought differing cultural experiences and expectations to the Pentecostal movement. With differences in understanding, soon there were several church groups or denominations, each advocating their position or interpretation as the "correct one." Differences rather than similarities were emphasized.

Early in the twentieth century, Pentecostals in the United States rejected many of the practices of mainline Christian denominations, contending that they were "formalistic and cold." While in a minority status, Pentecostals sought to create a fellowship of believers dedicated to serving God wholeheartedly as the Holy Spirit guided them.

Society was called "the world." Adherents were admonished to be "in the world, but not of the world." To be "worldly" was seen as sinful and those who engaged in worldly practices were judged as sinners needing forgiveness and redemption. A distinction was made between the lost and the backslider. The lost were those souls who had not heard or had heard and not accepted salvation. The backslidden, now returned to a lost condition, were those who had accepted Christ, but had not received sanctification and had drifted back into the ways of the world. All appearances of evil, relating to both the inner and outer man, were to be avoided. Examples of "inner man's sins" generally related to prohibitions in the Ten Commandments and not loving one's neighbor as oneself. "Outer man's sins" often related to social practices, such as smoking, drinking alcoholic beverages, gambling and card playing, wearing makeup, current hairstyles and clothes ("clothesline preachers" shouted against garments too short, too tight, too revealing, or too gaudy), public swimming, attending sporting events or pool halls, attending movies, owning and viewing televisions ("hellavisions"), cursing and using the Lord's name in vain, and missing church services. Classical Pentecostals were opposed to blues and rock and roll music, although their services were filled with similar rhythms and beats.

When the Baptism of the Holy Spirit fell on both women and men, Pentecostals relied on the book of Joel (2:28–29) to justify women as preachers, evangelists, and missionaries. However, early ordination papers permitted women to fulfill these functions only in the event that there were no men present to administer the ordinances or to "fill the pulpit." A woman's place was understood clearly. Violating a "woman's place" was

sinful, resulting in isolation by Pentecostal church folk. Evil or sinful nature carried different meaning for each gender. Women bore a heavier guilt load, because they were the daughters of Eve. Adam, a somewhat spineless man, had simply been beguiled by her feminine wiles.

Anti-intellectualism continued among most Pentecostals. Leaders denigrated public and higher education, assuming that advanced training actually draws people away from God. Indoctrination was promoted as leaders encouraged their interpretations of faith and life issues. Reason was discounted; emotion and experience was elevated.

As the twentieth century progressed, Pentecostals continued to define and redefine sin. Legalism was seen as confining. Some proclaimed that "we were now not under the laws of the Old Testament, but all things had became new in Christ Jesus" (2 Corinthians 5:17). Functionally this meant the separation from worldliness and societal practices was no longer significant. Pentecostals could be in the world and of the world and still maintain a safe haven in an upcoming world.

Reciprocity: Pentecostals and Societal Influences

As time passed Pentecostal outlook and practices gradually adapted to mainstream society. There was a greater influence of reformed theology in the late twentieth century; whereas earlier most of the Pentecostal churches had been Arminian in theology. In family relations, early Pentecostals insisted on nuclear families with no divorces permitted, whereas divorces and remarriages are now common and annulments can be obtained in some Pentecostal denominations.

Pentecostals began to recognize different temporal constraints. Formerly eschatology was a driving force. There were all-night prayer and Holy Ghost revival meetings. Recently there has been stricter adherence to church planning with fixed time schedules. There is less emphasis on the parousia (second coming of Christ).

The Pentecostal approach to education changed significantly from the early years. Early Pentecostals emphasized Spirit-led and faith-based Bible schools and Sunday schools. Now there are more church-sponsored preschools, parochial schools, and institutions of higher education, including college and seminary degrees. Mass media has become more acceptable as print, radio, television, and Internet service are used for public relations, fund-raising, and evangelism.

Early Pentecostals avoided politics and involvement in government and insisted on a strict separation of church and state. More recently, many seek funds for faith-based initiatives, support lobbyists, political parties, and candidates, and have moved from pacifism or noninvolvement to aggressive involvement in national and foreign policies.

Originally Pentecostals held a "faith-based" view of economics, with God providing "according to His riches in glory." Now financial planning for estates and investment advice is given by teams of attorneys. Missionaries still encourage emotionally based appeals, fly-in fund-raising conventions, and short-term foreign ministry opportunities. Missionaries raise large budgets and are required to donate for national denominational offices, which in turn mandate missionary policies and behavior. Internet appeals for financial assistance are currently in vogue.

Even health care is approached differently. Early Pentecostals placed strong emphasis on healing by anointing and laying on of hands. In today's Pentecostal churches, healing services occur less frequently. Now spectacular healing campaigns are televised. Currently it is appropriate to seek medical services. Some contemporary Pentecostals even have a relaxed attitude toward social drinking in moderation.

Acts of conviction, ecstatic worship services, tarrying services, all night prayer meetings, prayer warriors, mothers in Israel, dancing in the Spirit, slain in the Spirit, prayer hankies, breaking vinyl records over the Sunday school superintendents' or pastors' heads (to celebrate record attendance), and even reports of resurrections from the dead have disappeared. Still practiced in some locales are speaking in tongues and interpretation, prophecies, fellowship meetings, and words of wisdom. Snake handling is seldom practiced among late twentieth and twenty-first century Pentecostals. They are not as identifiable by their distinct clothing, lack of cosmetics, and hairstyles, as they were at the time the movement originated. Charismatic music has been adopted, rather than traditional hymns and choruses. Sensationalism may be used in the megachurches, such as bringing jungle animals on the platform for drama presentations. The idea of sacred space is seldom considered.

Early lists of prohibitions have all but disappeared. The Pentecostal church may sponsor community fireworks and Fourth of July celebrations, sponsor public school partnerships, donate to community food banks, and provide counseling.

Charismatic Renewal

With the Charismatic Renewal, Some Pentecostals felt they had lost their uniqueness. Others wondered why the Holy Spirit would be outpoured on those with theological errors and worldly ways. To add to this tension, Pentecostal attempts to invite charismatics into their groups were generally unsuccessful.

By the end of the twentieth century, virtually all of the mainline denominations had some congregants who experienced the infilling of the Holy Spirit. Their renewed dedication and enthusiasm for exuberant worship resulted in much disequilibrium. The ensuing changes in worship styles brought a restructuring of services, with praise and blended varieties added to the traditional. Learning from one another promoted reciprocity and church renewal. Whereas the Pentecostals left mainstream churches and society; the charismatics stayed within and sought changes. In turn, society and mainstream churches brought systemic changes among the Pentecostals, who first tended to be comfortably isolationist. Most of their founding beliefs and practices were altered or discarded and they steered their boat into the mainstream of American religious life.

Missionaries

The compelling conviction that Jesus Christ was soon to return for His own resulted in an evangelistic fervor that propelled Pentecostals to develop active missions programs, both at home and abroad. Most of these pioneer missionaries were indoctrinated in small Bible training schools, but were not prepared for the ethnic and cultural differences abroad. This lack of in-depth education continued throughout the twentieth century. While most early missionaries learned local languages, some believed the Holy Spirit would empower them with "local dialect tongues as of fire" (Garr 1907). When this anticipation was not realized, they either despondently returned to the United States or they began language study.

In the 1950s, some mission boards proposed an altered policy. Influenced by Anglophones and supported by United States foreign policy, leaders suggested that because people all over the world were learning English, missionaries now could evangelize in English to indigenous people. This religious imperialism resulted in new missionaries being dependent on English speakers and translators to give their interpretations of the Scriptures. Furthermore, this policy encouraged business opportunities for native Christianized entrepreneurs to gain access to foreign capital, to acquire lists of contributors back in the States, to purchase properties, to send their children and chosen others abroad for education, to set up kingdoms or municipalities built on Western funds, and eventually to immigrate to Commonwealth nations and the United States.

Missionaries tended to portray their cultural traditions as being God given, whereas the earlier Christian indigenous, mainline movements, or local religions were labeled as evil, incomplete, or satanic. If the local Christians had not received the Holy Spirit and spoken in unknown tongues, then a new work of grace was needed. This usually required a new water baptism and coming out from among family, friends, and acquaintances to become part of the true family of God.

Unexpectedly, Western missions empowered native Pentecostals to challenge the parent organization. For example, South American leaders challenged the Assemblies of God's use of the term "international headquarters" in Springfield, Missouri, when they had a much larger population "south of the border." Shortly thereafter, Asian Pentecostals judged American Pentecostals to be lax in their religious practices. They then began sending Asian missionaries to the United States.

Analysis

Societal systems and systematic practices of mainline denominations have had a substantial impact on Pentecostal denominations in the twentieth century, bringing them more into the mainstream. The charismatic phenomenon brought spiritual renewal, the possibility of sincere ecumenical dialogue, and the dream of "reconciliation in the body of Christ."

RUTH BURGESS

See also Anti-intellectualism; Education; Society, Pentecostal Attitudes toward; Women

Further Reading

Burgess, J. H. (1980). Sermon notes. Chesapeake, VA: Burgess Archives.

Cornwall, R. (2004). Unpublished sermon. Gatlingburg, TN.

Garr, A. G. (1907). Tongues, the biblical evidence. *Cloud of witnesses to Pentecost in India.* n.p.

Griffith, R. M. (1997). *God's daughters: Evangelical women and the power of submission.* Berkeley: University of California Press.

Shaefer, R. T. (1998). *Sociology: A brief introduction.* New York: McGraw-Hill.

Enthusiasm

The term "enthusiasm" has traditionally been used as a pejorative designation for the conduct of misguided Christians who suppose themselves to be divinely inspired—being carried away by fanciful imagination and frenzied emotional conduct that is erroneously attributed to the Holy Spirit—when they are not. Enthusiasts' strange, disorderly, and schismatic behavior is often considered harmful to the cause of the Gospel and spiritually harmful to enthusiasts themselves. Although enthusiasm is found throughout all of church history, the term itself acquired this religious connotation during the sixteenth and seventeenth centuries as early Protestants reacted to mystical movements including the Familists; the French Camisard prophets; and the more extreme Anabaptist sects such as the prophets of Zwickau. "Enthusiasm" continued to be used this way until it gradually gave way to the more secular and less pejorative meaning of "ardent zeal" in the late nineteenth and early twentieth centuries. We find, for example, that toward the end of the nineteenth century Charles Finney still occasionally used "enthusiasm" in its religious sense, but preferred to call enthusiastic behavior "religious excitement."

Different Opinions

While there has been almost universal agreement on the meaning of "enthusiasm," there has been much debate among Christians as to its application. Charles Chauncy and John Wesley both described enthusiasm as "religious madness" but disagreed sharply as to exactly what behavior evidenced this madness. The Great Awakening of the eighteenth century, during which both of these men lived and ministered, had a polarizing effect on ministers who took a more rationalist approach to Christian experience and the revivalists who were more mystically inclined.

Many of the more rationalistic, "Old Light" ministers rejected any revivalist claims to "immediate inspiration," by which they meant any felt, spiritual experience in which God was thought to personally communicate with the individual. These ministers insisted that God only communicates through the Scriptures to the rational faculties and does so in a reasonably dispassionate way. Consequently they labeled as enthusiastic all psycho-spiritual phenomena, observable bodily effects, and claims to revelations. Charles Chauncy was so afraid of emotionalism that in his influential work, *Seasonable Thoughts on the State of Religion in New England*, he rebuked revivalist Gilbert Tennant for speaking of salvation "with a smile in his countenance" (Chauncy 1975, 127). What seemed most disturbing to Chauncy and others was the schismatic effect of revival, which upset the established order. They disapproved of people leaving more traditional churches to participate in revivalism and they decried the revivalists' use of lay preachers and lively forms of worship.

Chauncy's *Seasonable Thoughts* was largely a response to two of Jonathan Edwards' prorevival works, *Distinguishing Marks of a Work of the Spirit of God* and *Thoughts on the Revival in New England*. Edwards insisted that psycho-spiritual phenomena such as weeping, and bodily effects such as falling, trembling, and jerking were not in themselves criteria for judging a work of God one way or another. The Holy Spirit could work without such phenomena and such phenomenon could be produced apart from the Spirit's influence. Where Edwards, Wesley, and others differed from the antirevivalists was that they believed such phenomena could be a genuine response to a powerful manifestation of God's presence, and these phenomena were common in the First and Second Great Awakenings.

Nevertheless, revival leaders in the First and Second Great Awakenings were some of the most outspoken critics of enthusiasm. Some extreme phenomena such as animal noises and hysterical laughter were generally rejected as fleshly or demonic in origin. While revival leaders allowed for immediate inspiration they did concede that many revival participants were guilty of, as Wesley expressed it, "a falsely imagined influence or inspiration from God" (Wesley 1978, 470). Charles Finney bemoaned the fact that "many excitements that have been supposed to be revivals of religion, have after all had but very little true religion in them" (Finney 1979, 59). Edwards and Wesley strongly cautioned against the proud spirit that inevitably accompanied enthusiasm. Wesley warned that the enthusiast's pride would make him less likely to discern his or her own errors, and Edwards noted that enthusiasts typically bond closely around their peculiar beliefs and practices in a feeling of superiority that makes them less receptive to correction.

Pentecostals and Enthusiasm

Every revival movement has had to respond to charges of enthusiasm from critics outside of the revival and cope with the enthusiastic tendencies of some adherents within the revival. The Pentecostal revival has been no exception to this. Both Charles Parham and William Seymour complained of inappropriate and even demonic manifestations at the Azusa Street mission. In the pioneering atmosphere of the time, it was not uncommon for early Pentecostals to have strange "revelations," embrace unscriptural doctrines, or behave in odd ways. A. J. Tomlinson, the first general overseer of

the Church of God (Cleveland, Tennessee), noted that at times men and women attending his meetings would pull each others clothes and hair. He recalled that on one occasion "A man was lying on his back on the straw, and a woman walked up to him and kicked him on the side several times. . . . A little later [she] struck him a hard blow on his head with her hand" (Wacker 2001, 53). This kind of frenzied emotionalism provided critics of Pentecostalism with plenty of ammunition for their invectives against the movement.

Pentecostal leaders have responded to these invectives by declaring that the movement should not be judged as a whole by the extreme or aberrant behavior of some of its adherents. In fact, as the twentieth century unfolded, many Pentecostal leaders boldly spoke out against enthusiasm in the ranks. The Latter Rain Movement, which began in 1948 in North Battleford, Saskatchewan, was officially denounced by the Assemblies of God in 1949 for its aberrant beliefs and practices. This movement taught several doctrines that were at odds with historical orthodoxy, such as a denial of blood atonement, a denial of eternal hell, a belief in the ultimate deification of the church, and a belief in the ultimate reconciliation of the devil (although not everyone in this movement believed all of these doctrines). It was, however, their practices that most drew the ire of Pentecostal leaders. E. S. Williams, who was the general superintendent of the Assemblies of God at the time, focused his attack on the Latter Rain Movement's practice of prophesying over individuals as they laid hands upon them. These prophecies frequently provided direction for the person prophesied over and obedience to these directives sometimes had disastrous consequences.

Recent Controversies

Toward the end of the twentieth century, new elements emerged within Pentecostal and charismatic ranks that brought charges of enthusiasm, with some critics even bringing the old meaning of the word into contemporary use. Those most often charged with enthusiasm were charismatics involved in the "Laughing Revival" associated with the Toronto Airport church pastored by John Arnott and with figures such as Rodney Howard-Browne. "Laughing Revival" leaders allowed and even encouraged participants to act inebriated, laugh hysterically, and make animal noises. The Kansas City Prophets, led by, among others, Paul Cain, Bob Jones, John Paul Jackson, and Mike Bickle, brought many of the controversial teachings and practices of the Latter Rain Movement back into the spotlight.

Many Pentecostal and charismatic leaders spoke and wrote against these movements, saying those in them had been carried away by fanciful imaginations and frenzied emotions that they mistakenly attributed to the Holy Spirit's influence. The "Holy Laughter" phenomenon and animal noises were variously attributed by critics to the flesh, the devil, emotional instability, mass hypnosis, and group hysteria. B. J. Oropeza offered the more benign explanation that those who act in this way are dramatically overreacting to the Holy Spirit: "Might it be that many in Holy Laughter are really sensing God's presence, but overreacting? Could they have created their own patterns of routines in response to the Spirit's presence?" (Oropeza 1995, 104).

The Bible and Enthusiasm

Scripture used to address enthusiasm usually includes references to the principles of edification, order, and self-control in public worship taught by the apostle Paul in 1 Corinthians 11–14. Paul's statement that "the spirits of prophets are subject to the control of prophets" (1 Corinthians 14:32, NIV) is often referred to as paradigmatic for all spiritual manifestations, thereby ruling out uncontrolled or hysterical conduct. Many believers also consider enthusiasm to be a violation of Paul's command that "everything should be done in a fitting and orderly way" (1 Corinthians 14:40), and bizarre behavior is seen to ignore Paul's concern that outsiders, when observing Christian worship, not think Christians are out of their mind (1 Corinthians 14:23). Scriptural support for falling under the Spirit's power is often found in 2 Chronicles 5:13–14, Matthew 28:1–4, and Acts 9:3–6. Many interpreters believe the Bible teaches that God's powerful presence can cause bodily effects such as jerking and trembling, citing passages such as Psalm 99:1, Daniel 10:7, Jeremiah 5:22, and Acts 7:32. Weeping is seen in 2 Chronicles 34:27, Ezra 10:1, and Isaiah 22:12. Those who defend more controversial worship practices such as animal noises and hysterical laughter have used passages such as Jeremiah 23:9, Hosea 11:10, Amos 3:8 and John 17:13; but most Pentecostals and charismatics have not found support in these passages for such practices.

Nearly all observers agree that enthusiasm has been and will always be an issue that must be dealt with in association with revival movements. Consequently, Pentecostals and charismatics can reasonably expect to face controversies related to enthusiasm in the future.

What remains to be seen is how those controversies will be responded to.

DAVID KOWALSKI

See also Ecstasy; Latter Rain; Laughter, Holy; Revival and Revivalism

Further Reading

Chauncy, C. (1975). *Seasonable thoughts on the state of religion in New England.* Hicksville, NY: The Regina Press. (Original work published 1743)

Edwards, J. (1974a). Distinguishing marks of a work of the Spirit of God. In *The works of Jonathan Edwards* (vol. 2). Carlisle, PA: Banner of Truth Trust.

Edwards, J. (1974b). Thoughts on the revival in New England. In *The works of Jonathan Edwards* (vol. 1). Carlisle, PA: Banner of Truth Trust.

Finney, C. (1979). *Reflections on revival* (D. Dayton, Ed.). Minneapolis, MN: Bethany Fellowship.

Gee, D. (1961). *Toward Pentecostal unity.* Springfield, MO. Gospel Publishing House.

Goff, J. R., Jr., & Wacker, G. (Eds.). *Portraits of a generation: Early Pentecostal leaders.* Fayetteville: The University of Arkansas Press.

Gunter, W. S. (1989). *The limits of "Love Divine."* Nashville, TN: Kingswood Books.

Knox, R. (1950). *Enthusiasm.* Oxford, UK: The Clarendon Press.

Lee, U. (1967). *The historical backgrounds of early Methodist enthusiasm.* New York: AMS Press.

Locke, J. (1959). *An essay concerning human understanding* (vol. 2). New York: Dover Publications.

Lovejoy, D. (1969). *Religious enthusiasm and the Great Awakening.* Englewood Cliffs, NJ: Prentice Hall.

Middlemiss, D. (1996). *Interpreting charismatic experience.* London: SCM Press.

Oropeza, B. J. (1995). *A time to laugh: The Holy Laughter phenomenon examined.* Peabody, MA: Hendrickson Publishers.

Tucker, S. (1972). *Enthusiasm: A study in semantic change.* London: Cambridge University Press.

Riss, R. M. (1987). *Latter Rain: The Latter Rain Movement of 1948 and the mid-twentieth century evangelical awakening.* Mississauga, Canada: Honeycomb Visual Productions.

Wacker, G. (2001). *Heaven below: Early Pentecostals and American culture.* Cambridge, MA: Harvard University Press.

Wesley, J. (1978). The nature of enthusiasm. In *Wesley's Works* (vol. 5). Grand Rapids, MI: Baker Book House.

White, E. (1972). *Puritan rhetoric: The issue of emotion in religion.* Carbondale: Southern Illinois University Press.

Williams, E. S. (1949, April 16). Are we Pentecostals? *Pentecostal Evangel, 1822.*

Entrepreneurs, Religious

Upon first glance at the makings of Pentecostal history, it may seem that Pentecostal entrepreneurs are a fairly recent phenomenon. Further consideration, however, reveals that entrepreneurs have been part of the Pentecostal movement since its beginnings in America. As the movement has developed both in America and overseas, members of the Pentecostal and charismatic communities have increasingly come from the middle and upper classes, either as adult converts or as long-standing Pentecostals whose socioeconomic status has elevated in society. As the number of businessmen and women has grown in Pentecostal and charismatic congregations, so has the role these people have played both as entrepreneurs who propagate Pentecostal Christianity and as entrepreneurs who market products for Pentecostal-Charismatic demographics. This latter trend has attempted to meet demand as the considerable market-force of Christian-centered culture has increased in strength. Finally, the church ministries and church denominations themselves have been and continue to be a type of entrepreneurial force.

Early Pentecostal Entrepreneurs

Though many early Pentecostals in America came from the lower economic strata of American society, Religion professor Grant Wacker has shown that, in fact, early Pentecostals reflected the average social matrix in society at large. Thus, there were many members who not only were living fairly comfortably for the time and in the context of the first three decades of the twentieth century, but many, including business owners, did quite well for themselves and their families.

If this was true of the average Pentecostal membership it was even more so for many of its leaders. For example, Joel Adams Wright, who organized the First Fruit Harvesters in northern New England in 1897, used his business successes as a land agent to buy real estate in New Hampshire for his group's headquarters. Through his finances, the group also ran an orphanage and a retirement home. He and his sons later owned and operated two luxury resorts on the Maine coast. Wacker also mentions Richard Spurling, a founder of the Church of God, who owned nearly 1,100 acres of land as well as William Doctor Gentry, a Los Angeles healing evangelist, whose stock option in 1921 stood at $100,000. This is not to say that all early Pentecostal entrepreneurs achieved the same fiscal success, but that the early movement was not without its entrepreneurs, nor did it eschew their funds or membership.

Entrepreneurs as Laypeople

A group of Pentecostal entrepreneurs called the Full Gospel Business Men's Fellowship International interacted with the faith community in interesting and broadening ways beginning the 1950s. The effects of the organization suggest that Pentecostal entrepreneurs may influence more than the funding of church projects or supplying of Pentecostal consumers. They have affected the balance between old-line Pentecostals and the Charismatic movement and the theology of Pentecostal movements.

In 1951–1952, Demos Shakarian, an Armenian Pentecostal businessman who prospered in the California dairy industry, founded the Full Gospel Business Men's Fellowship International. Supported by Oral Roberts, the goal of the fellowship was to spread the "Pentecostal experience" to people who would not ordinarily attend a Pentecostal church. After the first chapter meeting in 1951, Thomas R. Nickel contributed the service of a printing press and became editor of the *Full Gospel Business Men's Voice*, the organ by which the fellowship would reach people in multiple communities across the world. The year 1952 saw the opening of eight new chapters in the United States and the first convention in Los Angeles for which the list of speakers included Oral Roberts, Jack Coe, Gordon Lindsey, Raymond T. Richey, O. L. Jaggers, and Tommy Hicks. By the mid-1960s, there were more than 300 chapters with 100,000 total members; in 1972 membership totaled 300,000; and, by 1988, there were over 3,000 chapters in 87 countries.

These Pentecostal entrepreneurs made major waves in the movement at large. They brought the spirit of the tent revivals into their services in hotel convention centers, but with the insistence that all meetings be laymen-led and nondenominational. True to its purpose, hundreds of thousands of mainline Protestants and Catholics joined, many becoming major speakers. Not surprisingly, given the increasing tensions from old line Pentecostal leaders toward the Charismatic movement, many of these Pentecostal denominational pastors felt threatened by the success of the Full Gospel Business Men's Fellowship. Not only was the organization responsible for the participation of charismatics and neocharismatics in what was traditionally a Pentecostal denominational experience, but the fellowship embraced and supported the rise of faith healers like Kenneth Copeland and Kenneth E. Hagin Sr. As a result, the organization became associated with the rise of "prosperity gospel" teaching, emphasizing the connection between conversion/Spirit baptism and material prosperity.

Entrepreneurial Leaders

While laypeople began to make connections between their identity as entrepreneurs and as Pentecostals or charismatics, leaders, continuing in the line of older Pentecostals, created massive ministry empires. Perhaps this is most clear in the televangelists associated with Pentecostal and charismatic ministry. While leaders in the movement have always incorporated printing and communication industries into their ministry, these particular leaders are on the extreme end of ministry empire growth rates. By focusing on these examples, let us not suppose that their various business practices and ethics are representative of all entrepreneurial ministries but that, increasingly, ministry programs are capable of massive size and expansion.

Oral Granville Roberts (b. 1918), beginning in the 1940s and continuing today, created a vast empire of business ventures. His businesses include traditional enterprises such as publication of books, periodicals, and other media, and he has expanded the role of telecommunications to previously unheralded proportions. Roberts broadened this portfolio to include a university, Oral Roberts University in Tulsa, Oklahoma, in 1965, a retirement center in 1966, and the City of Faith Research and Medical Center in 1981.

Following in his footsteps, Marion Gordon "Pat" Robertson (b. 1930) built up CBN—Christian Broadcasting Network—and in 1977, founded CBN University, now Regent University, a fully accredited graduate institution. Jimmy Lee Swaggart (b. 1935), at the height of his prosperity, established radio and television ministries, a college, a monthly magazine, and owned several media properties. James Orson (b. 1940) and Tammy Faye (b. 1942) Bakker held the PTL Television Network, a television production studio, and Heritage Village, a Christian entertainment complex that included the Grand Hotel, Christian condominiums, a water amusement park and a home for handicapped children—an empire totaling $172 million.

Pentecostal Entrepreneurs Overseas

Again, much is made of the attraction of Pentecostal and Charismatic movements to the poor around the world, but in several cases it is not that demographic alone that participates in these communities. For example, Nigerian Pentecostals from the 1980s and later tend to be from the lower-middle and middle classes of society. According to author Ruth Marshall-Fratani, Nigerian Pentecostal ministries regularly produce written publications and audio/visual programming, both in live broadcast and in recordings. These products may be distributed freely, but they are typically sold in growing numbers of private Christian bookshops along with foreign booklets and tracts. Marshall-Fratani also documents a growing number of "born-again" video rental outfits.

Author André Corten, when discussing Latin American Pentecostalism, notes that in Brazil Pentecostal churches typically use commercial advertising and participate in multiple industries including music records, CDs, cassettes, Evangelical videos, and musical instruments. Most interestingly the Universal Church of the Kingdom of God in Brazil, founded in 1977 by Edir Macedo, is worth an estimated $400 million. According to authors Ari Pedro Oro and Pablo Semán, the properties of the Universal Church of the Kingdom of God include a television network, about thirty radio stations, publishers, recording studios, a bank, a travel agency, and a holding company administering church business.

These are just a few examples that demonstrate that while both persons and Pentecostal institutions outside the United States can come from the lower economic classes, this is not always the case. In many places both members of Pentecostal communities and the ministries themselves are actively engaging in entrepreneurial practices.

Christian Popular Culture

In a strict sense many Pentecostal and charismatic ministries in the United States and abroad are entrepreneurial—operating multiple business ventures simultaneously. As the media have grown to play larger roles in evangelism, the ability of ministries to manage business projects is increasingly important. Aside from evangelistic efforts, however, Pentecostals and charismatics make up a large section of Christians who are participating in the formation and propagation of a "Christian popular culture." This culture is represented in everything from Christian publishing companies to Christian breath mints. According to history professor Edith Blumhofer, participating in Christian popular culture is a prominent feature of the Assemblies of God, one of the largest and most established Pentecostal denominations in the United States and abroad.

While it is admittedly difficult to identify how many owners and operators of such businesses are themselves American Pentecostal or charismatic, one particular market clearly evidences their participation—the market and sale of "praise and worship" music, commonly used in Pentecostal and charismatic congregations. Most of these songs and their writers have traditionally hailed from Pentecostal and charismatic church communities.

The earliest names in this business include the Maranatha! Music and Integrity labels but the extent to which Pentecostals and charismatics have control has been a source of contention for much of the history of the Christian contemporary music business. On the other hand, the Vineyard Music Group represents a venture that seems to be controlled largely by neocharismatics from the top down. It is affiliated with the Association of Vineyard Churches and the songs are often produced, marketed, and performed by members of that movement. Not only are these songs performed in churches but "praise and worship" music is increasingly purchased for private listening as well, demonstrating how Pentecostal and charismatic entrepreneurs are intentionally or unintentionally participating in this growing phenomenon of Christian popular culture.

Institutions and Entrepreneurial Activity

It is often a matter of perspective whether one would describe Pentecostal and charismatic ministerial activities as "ministry" or "business." In this era of "megachurches," both in the United States and places like Korea or Brazil, it is common for large ministry organizations to interact at some level in business activity. Nor is this a new phenomenon; early Pentecostal denominations inherited the use of publishing from the Holiness movement.

This is not to downplay the interesting variances within the Pentecostal movement. As has often been recognized, in America and to some extent in other countries, the Charismatic and Neocharismatic movements have drawn upon converts of generally higher social class location, emerging primarily from the middle classes of societies. This may be one explanation for the massive expansion of business and marketing within recent Pentecostal and charismatic ministries and the increasing popularity of organizations like the Full Gospel Business Men's Fellowship as more and more businessmen from non-Pentecostal denominations enter into this community of Pentecostal laymen.

Ultimately, the level of entrepreneurial activity pursued by Pentecostal and charismatic laypeople, leaders, and institutions is not a complete break from what has come before. Just as the proportion of Pentecostal business persons and business activities in early American history did not considerably differ from society at large, so it has been suggested that charismatic and neocharismatic understandings of entrepreneurial activity and personal economic growth are means by which people in many nations interact with transnationalism or globalization. In both cases the activities of members reflect to some degree the socioeconomic standing of the society in which they are a part. This is not to forget, however, that the interpretations given to entrepreneurial activity may reflect people using Pentecostal and charismatic narratives to interact with, to adapt to, or to change existing socioeconomic realities.

Erin Kuhns

See also Capitalism; Prosperity Theology; Rich and Riches

Further Reading

Anderson, R. M. (1979). *Vision of the disinherited: The making of American Pentecostalism.* New York: Oxford University Press.

Blumhofer, E. L. (1993). *Restoring the faith: The Assemblies of God, Pentecostalism, and American culture.* Urbana: University of Illinois Press.

Corten, A. (2001). Transnationalised religious needs and political delegitimisation in Latin America. In A. Corten & R. Marshall-Fratani (Eds.), *Between Babel and Pentecost: Transnational Pentecostalism in Africa and Latin America* (pp. 106–123). Bloomington: Indiana University Press.

Cox, H. (1995). *Fire from heaven: The rise of Pentecostal spirituality and the reshaping of religion in the twenty-first century.* Reading, MA: Addison-Wesley.

Foberby, V. (2000). *The awakening giant: The miraculous story of the Full Gospel Business Men's Fellowship International.* London: Marshall Pickering.

Hollenweger, W. (1972). *The Pentecostals: The Charismatic movement in the churches.* Minneapolis, MN: Augsburg Press.

Marshall-Fratani, R. (2001). Mediating the global and local in Nigerian Pentecostalism. In A. Corten & R. Marshall-Fratani (Eds.), *Between Babel and Pentecost: Transnational Pentecostalism in Africa and Latin America* (pp. 80–105). Bloomington: Indiana University Press.

Oro, A. P., & Semán, P. (2001). Brazilian Pentecostalism crosses national borders. In A. Corten & R. Marshall-Fratani (Eds.), *Between Babel and Pentecost: Transnational Pentecostalism in Africa and Latin America* (pp. 182–195). Bloomington: Indiana University Press.

Rabey, S. (1999). The profits of praise. *Christianity Today, 43,* 32–33.

Shakarian, D. (1996). *The happiest people on earth*. London: Hodder & Stoughton.

Synan, V. (1992). *Under his banner: History of the Full Gospel Business Men's Fellowship International*. Costa Mesa, CA: Gift Publications.

Synan, V. (1997). *The Holiness Pentecostal tradition: Charismatic movements in the twentieth century*. Grand Rapids, MI: Eerdmans.

Wacker, G. (2001). *Heaven below: Early Pentecostals and American culture*. Cambridge, MA: Harvard University Press.

Eschatology

Eschatology is an area of theology that examines the doctrine of final things (Greek, *eschatos*) in the Bible. Thus, it endeavors to determine how Bible prophecy fits together and how the church should understand it. The study of eschatology has given birth to many movements, doctrines, and even cults.

Early Eschatology

The earliest indication of eschatological study or analysis is in the writings of St. Paul in his first letter to the Thessalonians. In this epistle, there is an indication that a group in the early church, right after Jesus' Resurrection, believed that the last resurrection of the dead had already happened and that the church of Thessalonica had been "left behind." Paul quickly informed them that this was not so, giving rise to perhaps the first book in the New Testament.

St. Augustine, an intellectual convert to Christianity around 375 CE, took a look at eschatology and tried to fit the concept of the Second Coming, the Millennium, and the End of the World together. In doing so, he invented amillennialism (no millennium). He later became bishop of Hippo in North Africa (today's Bone, in Algeria) and believed that the millennium had begun when Jesus' message was accepted by the Roman Empire in 312–313 CE. This is called the historicist doctrine, or amillennialism: that prophecy can be explained in the ongoing belief in the unfolding of church history.

Premillennialism

A later belief, and one that has taken hold deeply in Fundamentalism, Evangelicalism and Pentecostalism, is called dispensationalist premillennialism. Dispensationalism is a prophetic belief system put together by John Nelson Darby (1800–1882). This belief, also known as premillennialism, states that everything spoken of by Jesus and the apostles and the book of Revelation about the End Times is prophetically to be revealed in the future (as opposed to the amillennialist view, which states that these prophecies are not of the future). Hence, Darby saw the first three books of Revelation to be the present age (in other words, the time of the early church and the apostles) and the next eighteen chapters as future—that is, to be revealed in future times. Thus, the person known as Antichrist, his false prophet "and the whore of Babylon" were all future occurrences, not to be confused with the then-Roman Empire Nero. If the book of Revelation spoke of the Roman Empire at all, it was a prophecy of a future Roman system, tied in with a reunion of all European countries into a resurrected Roman Empire, centered in Rome and united with a religious system ruled by the Pope. Present-day dispensational premillennialists look at the rapidly unifying European community of nations (now twenty-five countries and more to come) and see the answer to this prophecy. Some see the World Council of Churches and the papacy and equate that to the Antichrist and the false prophet.

Premillennialism sees the seven-year great tribulation (first propounded by John Nelson Darby in the nineteenth century), and believes the Antichrist is near.

The premillennial belief system became prevalent especially between the World Wars. Spurred on by the publishing of *The Scofield Reference Bible* in 1909, the movement gained steam when Fundamentalism began between 1910–1917. The Great War of 1914–1918 killed millions. That war was followed by a huge influenza epidemic, which also killed millions. The Great Depression of 1929 then hit home, followed by World War II and the nuclear age. The specter of a nuclear war, together with the formation of the new state of Israel in 1948 and the World Council of Churches, also in 1948, convinced many Protestants that the End was near. These events of war, pestilence, famine, and death seemed to match the Four Horsemen of the apocalypse of the Book of Revelation in the Bible. The futurist premillennialist view took hold in the early 1920s and was the dominant belief system in Evangelical, Fundamental, and Pentecostal belief for the remainder of the twentieth century.

Sales of *The Scofield Reference Bible* soared into the millions. Popular paperback books, such as Hal Lindsey's *The Late Great Planet Earth* sold tens of millions of copies. Tapes, conferences, prophecy charts, videos, and books such as the *Left Behind* series also were distributed by the millions. All these media left their mark on

Protestantism, to the virtual exclusion of almost any other interpretation of eschatology. Many Christians are not aware that there are other ways to interpret prophecy.

How did this happen? John Nelson Darby's version of Bible eschatology was new in the nineteenth century. It was a departure from the amillennial view of St. Augustine and the Protestant reformers, such as Martin Luther and John Calvin. Darby's prophetic version was popularized by Cyrus E. Scofield (1843–1921), a congregational minister and Kansas legislator who adopted Darby's notes and incorporated them into his Bible of 1909.

Thus, three generations of church people who grew up in the Fundamentalist, Pentecostal, and Evangelical movements largely followed Darby/Scofield ideas of dispensationalism, ignoring or unaware of other ways of understanding eschatology.

Darby and the Brethren

John Nelson Darby (1800–1882) had been an ordained priest with the Anglican Church of Ireland. He became so dissatisfied with the ritual and seeming unbelief of that Church, that he resigned his ordination and founded the Exclusive Brethren, also known as the Plymouth Brethren, in 1831 in England. This denomination was the polar opposite of the ornate ritualistic liturgy of the Anglican Church. Incorporating his premillennial dispensational eschatology into the new church, Darby would not allow a paid clergy, no ordination for his men, and pursued an exclusiveness vis-à-vis other Evangelicals, which earned the Brethren the title "exclusive." His people were not allowed to take Holy Communion with believers of like-minds who were not exclusive Brethren like himself. To the Brethren, all denominationalism was at best unnecessary, and at worst ungodly. Eventually, some of the Brethren felt that Darby's ideas were far too isolationist and split off to form a similar group called the Open Brethren. These movements would probably not have gained importance if not for the widespread dissemination of their premillennialist ideas throughout Protestantism. The Brethren's ideas successfully inserted themselves on the mission fields and especially China. Chinese leaders, such as Watchman Nee and the Little Flock Movement of Shang Hai, and the Keswick Movement copied their doctrines.

Eschatology and the Pentecostal Revival

Evan Roberts, lay leader of the Welsh Revival, prayed for eleven years for a revival of Christianity in his homeland of Wales (part of the British Isles). Its Celtic culture has its own language dating back thousands of years. Suddenly in June 1904, revival broke out in a small chapel where Roberts was preaching. The movement quickly spread all over Wales and then news traveled around the world. One of the major doctrines to be emphasized was the imminent arrival of the Lord Jesus Christ

News of the Welsh Revival was of particular interest to a new movement in the United States: the New Pentecostal movement centered in Azusa Street in Los Angeles.

Charles Parham, whose original Bible school had been situated in Topeka, Kansas, at the beginning of the twentieth century, had come into contact with a black preacher named William Seymour, who took courses from Parham when he moved his Bible school to Houston, Texas. One of the subjects studied in Parham's Bible school was eschatology. When Seymour moved to Los Angeles, he took Parham's eschatological doctrines with him. Attendance at the revival services on Azusa Street skyrocketed, and the worldwide Pentecostal revival began. One of the keynote doctrines emphasized in the early literature was that "Pentecost" was the final outpouring of the Holy Spirit prior to the Lord's Second Coming. It was believed that his Second Coming was to be soon; hence, Christ had sent his power to Azusa to baptize believers with the Holy Spirit. It was seen as an endowment, an empowering to live a holy life of sanctification and to preach the Gospel to the heathen with Pentecostal signs following. Thus the gift of tongues was an eschatological sign pointing to Joel, the Old Testament prophet, and his prediction of the End-Times revival and harvest of souls into God's Kingdom before judgment would fall on the ungodly.

Early movements associated with Azusa Street were often called "Apostolic," to indicate the power and the origin of the movement, or "Pentecostal" again for the same reason. A great missionary movement was born that sent men and women out across the world, preaching an eschatological End-Times message of repentance, faith, healing, and baptism of the Spirit with the signs of tongues. From the small beginnings of Azusa, the Pentecostal movement gradually grew until the Great Depression of 1929. During the Depression, the movement exploded, increasing 200 percent in some cases, (e.g., the American Assemblies of God).

The greatest growth occurred in the United States, Brazil, Chile, Sweden, and South Africa. After World War II, fast growth occurred again. The onset of the Charismatic movement (as the Pentecostal movement within the mainline Protestant and Catholic Church was called) from 1950 onward and particularly in the Catholic Church after the Vatican II Council (1962–1965) put the Pentecostals on the front page. The Jesus movement of the mid-sixties was also largely premillennial. Israel won back Jerusalem and the West Bank of Jordan in 1967. The Soviet Empire collapsed, and China also began to open its closed doors after fifty years of isolation. This enabled eschatological ideas to invade the former communist block. By the year 2000 David Barrett, a world-renowned mission scholar estimated that Pentecostalism, including the similar Charismatic movement, had grown to over 500 million people in less than one century.

The impact of premillennial eschatology on the movement cannot be underestimated. It still remains the predominant belief in the Pentecostal movement.

PETER E PROSSER

See also Azusa Street Revival; Dispensationalism; Scripture, Holy

Further Reading

Erickson, M. (1982). *Contemporary options in eschatology.* Grand Rapids, MI: Baker House.

Gerstner, J. (1991). *Wrongly dividing the word of truth.* Brentwood, TN: Wolgemuth and Hyatt Publishers.

Synan, V. (2001). *The century of the Holy Spirit.* Nashville, TN: Thomas Nelson Inc.

Ethics (Social, Sexual)

Contemporary Pentecostals occupy diverse social environments around the world, each of which poses its own distinctive ethical challenges. In North America Pentecostalism has been confronted for a century or more by a variety of social and public policy issues, to which Pentecostals have chosen (or found themselves compelled) to respond—from issues of war and peace to dress and social conduct. A large number of Pentecostal groups and denominations have been of one mind about some of these issues, while others have developed a range of responses that have evolved over time.

Participation in War

At the beginning of the twentieth century, Pentecostals generally but not universally were pacifists, though they engaged in little formal theorizing on the issue. Just before the outbreak of World War I, American Pentecostals came to express their pacifist tendencies more openly; after the war started but before the United States entered it, most American Pentecostals strongly opposed U.S. involvement. When the United States finally entered the war in 1917, some became conscientious objectors. In the years between the world wars, however, the pacifist position steadily weakened among Pentecostals. By the outset of World War II some Pentecostals endorsed the idea of Christian participation in war and declared the pacifist position unbiblical, though during the war several Pentecostal denominations reiterated their traditional pacifism. At the same time, the official pacifist positions of organizations like the Assemblies of God (AG) and the Church of God, Cleveland, Tennessee, (COG) were commonly ignored by their own constituencies.

Following World War II, pacifist tendencies continued to erode among Pentecostals. The COG altered its official pacifist position in 1947 to allow its members "liberty of conscience." In 1967 the Assemblies of God altered its position, which dated back to 1917, so as to allow each member to decide in accordance with his or her own conscience. The AG General Council Bylaws stated that while the denomination "deplores war," it recognizes "the right of each member to choose for himself whether to declare his position as a combatant [one who willingly serves in positions of violence], a noncombatant [one who serves only in nonviolent ways], or a conscientious objector [one who refuses to participate in any form of military service because of personal convictions regarding war]." But the United Pentecostal Church International (UPCI) has retained its long-held pacifist position, stating in its 2004 manual:

> Therefore, we propose to fulfill all the obligations of loyal citizens, but are constrained to declare against participating in combatant service in war, armed insurrection, property destruction, aiding or abetting in or the actual destruction of human life.... We believe that we can be consistent in serving our Government in certain noncombatant capacities, but not in the bearing of arms.

Positions taken by individual members and congregations of the Pentecostal Assemblies of Canada (PAOC) reflect the diverse religious and ethnic heritage of the Canadian people. Pentecostals in southern Manitoba, a region primarily rural and settled by Mennonites, are predominantly pacifist, reflecting the continuing Mennonite influence. Pentecostals in other provinces not influenced by the Mennonite tradition have been less sympathetic to the pacifist position.

Race Relations

The history of race relations in classical Pentecostal circles is mixed but generally does not reflect well on Pentecostals. At the Azusa Street Revival in the early twentieth century (1906–1913), people of many races worshipped together without apparent racial discord. At the time of the revival, it was described by the press as a "colored" congregation that met in a "tumble-down shack." Yet according to the writer Cecil Robeck, "It was a church where whites, blacks, Hispanics, Asians, and others met together regularly and where from their own perspective the 'color-line' was virtually nonexistent." In the decades that followed, however, Pentecostals generally succumbed to mainstream views of race relations. Few churches were integrated; the vast majority consisted of single-race congregations.

Despite having its roots in the South, where racial discrimination and segregation were overt and widespread, the Church of God stands as something of an exception to the rule. Since 1909 the denomination has had a number of black ministers and congregations, and none of its official policies differentiated between black and white churches or ministers until after 1920. In 1926, at the request of black ministers (probably due to prevailing social attitudes of the time), congregations were officially segregated. But forty years later, in 1966, the denomination struck down all official barriers. The official resolution, called "Racism and Ethnic Disparity," represents one of the most forceful statements against racism in Pentecostal circles:

> We commit towards the elimination of racism and bigotry, corporately identifying racism and bigotry as sinful hindrances which prevent us from truly realizing brotherhood and Christian love within and outside the body of the international church and the many peoples and races which it reaches and encompasses.

If the number of racially mixed congregations and racial diversity among leaders is a sign of a denomination's commitment to racial integration, then the Church of God of Prophecy (CGP) is probably the most racially integrated Pentecostal denomination in the world. According to one observer, Harold Hunter, "The CGP may have been the first church to defy Jim Crow laws in their worship services, and they have long opposed the Ku Klux Klan." The CGP has not only been integrated virtually from its beginning, but its current

leadership structure at all levels, including the General Presbytery, is fully integrated, and its worldwide membership contains roughly equal representation from blacks, whites, and Hispanics.

The Assemblies of God, basically a white denomination, has struggled with racial issues, particularly relations between blacks and whites, in a somewhat different way from other Pentecostal denominations. On one hand, the AG has never banned blacks or formally segregated its congregations; on the other, it did impede blacks who sought ministerial credentials, and it contributed virtually nothing to the civil rights struggle of the 1960s. In the last quarter of the twentieth century, the denomination's Division of Home Missions (now called Assemblies of God U.S. Missions) devoted increasing attention to inner-city ministry opportunities, but the total number of African-American members and ministers remains small. Notably, the Hispanic population is the fastest growing ethnic group in the AG. However, most congregations with substantial Hispanic memberships are not racially or ethnically mixed, and the AG allows separate church leadership structures at the district level where Spanish- and English-speaking churches coexist in close geographical proximity. The church's official position expresses support for universal human rights for all people regardless of race and condemns prejudice against any person because of race. It also officially recognizes that racism continues to confront the church, and the denomination calls for repentance on the part of "all who have sinned against God by participating in racism through personal thought or action, through church and social structures, or through failure to address the evils of racism."

The Church of God in Christ (CGC) is the largest African-American Pentecostal denomination in North America. A popular belief—the so-called Sisterhood Myth—is that the Church of God in Christ is the black counterpart of the Assemblies of God. However, the doctrinal differences that differentiate the two denominations make this belief untenable. Despite the fact that the CGC experienced a major split in 1969, the church experienced phenomenal growth in the 1970s and 1980s. A notable contributing factor seems to have been the friendship the denomination's leadership extended to people in the Charismatic movement, a distinction no other African-American denomination can claim.

The most notable single event involving racial reconciliation in Pentecostal circles occurred in 1994 at an interracial convocation of Pentecostal leaders, ministers, and scholars in Memphis, Tennessee. At that time the all-white Pentecostal Fellowship of North America

(PFNA) was disbanded in favor of a racially inclusive association called the Pentecostal and Charismatic Churches of North America. During the session—called by some the "Memphis Miracle"—leaders of predominantly white Pentecostal denominations repented of the long-standing racial insensitivity and implicit racism in the denominations they represented. Unlike the all-white leadership structure of the disbanded PFNA, the leadership of the newly established PCCNA was racially balanced: six whites and six blacks, headed by Bishop Ithiel Clemmons of the Church of God in Christ, an African-American. Commenting on the convocation, Vinson Synan (1977) observed: "The high point of the historic gathering was the session where a white Assemblies of God pastor washed the feet of Bishop Clemmons while begging forgiveness for the sins of the past."

Beginning and End of Life Issues

Like most conservative Evangelicals, classical Pentecostals oppose the practice of abortion on demand. They came later to the public debate over abortion, however, than Roman Catholics, who also officially oppose abortion on demand. Whereas Catholics have a long-held and well-established stance against the practice of abortion on demand, Pentecostals did not generally begin to focus serious attention on the issue until long after the 1973 Supreme Court ruling in *Roe v. Wade*.

The United Pentecostal Churches International (UPCI) issued a one-sentence statement against abortion in 1974, but did not adopt a fuller document until 1988. The Church of God of Prophecy addressed the issue in its General Assembly of 1981 in a discussion that took account of the various theological and scientific arguments of the time. Although the Assembly went on record equating abortion with murder ("to willfully abort that life [of a fetus] constitutes murder"), it concluded its deliberations by adopting a relatively moderate statement merely "advising against abortions." The Assemblies of God adopted its official position on the subject, called "A Biblical Perspective on Abortion," as late as 1985. (By way of comparison, its position on biblical inerrancy was adopted fifteen years earlier, in 1970.) Its current position paper, called "Sanctity of Human Life Including Abortion and Euthanasia" (2002), describes abortion as "a morally unacceptable alternative for birth control, population control, sex selection, and elimination of the physically and mentally handicapped." At the same time it does not completely forbid the practice, allowing for exceptions in cases where the mother's life is threatened. "If responsible diagnoses confirm that childbirth is likely to result in the death of the mother, historic Christian faith usually has favored the life of the mother above that of the unborn child since the mother is a mature person with established family and societal relationships and responsibilities."

Although classical Pentecostals widely oppose euthanasia and assisted suicide, only two Pentecostal denominations have developed formal position papers on these and related topics. The Pentecostal Assemblies of Canada's 2001 position paper, called "Dignity of Human Life," does not specifically define euthanasia, but it does speak generally of all human attempts "to usurp God's prerogative of determining the limits of human life." Its conclusion is that "active involvement in the termination of life must not be an option." At the same time, the document devotes two substantial paragraphs to "the dignity of conscience" and "the gift of freedom," and seems to leave room for individual moral choices. However, the document is general and philosophical in tone and gives little specific guidance regarding the exercise of choice when it comes to making decisions about end-of-life issues. For example, it gives no direction as to whether it is morally permissible to withhold treatment for a patient judged to be in a persistent vegetative state.

The AG's 2002 "Sanctity of Human Life" document says, "The Assemblies of God condemns as immoral the killing of the weak, the physically challenged, the mentally ill, or the aged, whether by a deliberate act or by coercing or assisting a person to commit suicide." At the same time, the AG recognizes the right of individuals to decide for themselves whether it is ever morally acceptable to forego the use of life-sustaining efforts. "The Assemblies of God respects the conscience of individual believers," and "does not find a biblical mandate for indefinite and artificial perpetuation of life in cases of persistent vegetative state or the prolonged cessation of biological function."

To date, the AG is the only Pentecostal denomination in North America to formally discuss in a position paper such issues as contraception, in vitro fertilization, reproductive cloning, stem cell research, and genetic intervention. Its "Sanctity of Human Life" document finds "no clear scriptural mandate" on the matter of contraception; raises concerns about in vitro fertilization but does not in principle condemn the practice for infertile couples; and asserts that "reproductive cloning is immoral and a matter of grave concern." Regarding stem cell research, it cites concerns but draws no specific conclusions and provides no specific ethical guidelines beyond saying that "the practice of cultivating stem cells from the tissue of aborted fetuses perpetuates the evil of abortion and should be prohibited." The document does support "morally responsible genetic research and therapies," though it advances the belief that laws should be enacted to provide legal safeguards "to prevent intrusive genetic screening and resultant discrimination as well as misguided experimentation and termination of life."

Gender Issues

In the late nineteenth- and early twentieth-century origins of the classical Pentecostal movement, many women emerged in leadership roles, including pastoral, evangelistic, teaching, and other ministry roles. Women were among the important associates of early Pentecostal pioneers like Charles Parham and William Seymour; others headed important ministries in their own right. In general they enjoyed considerable freedom to preach and carry out other ministries in the earliest days of the movement. After 1920, however, women in leadership and public ministry roles declined dramatically and continued to do so until the Charismatic renewal in the mid-1960s when in some quarters the decline was reversed. The reasons for this decline are many and complex. A major one seems to have been the influence on Pentecostals of Fundamentalists, whose teachings about certain biblical passages on the role of women gained ascendancy in conservative Christian circles and eventually among Pentecostals.

The legitimacy of women in ministry continues to be a controversial issue in Pentecostal circles. In 1990 the AG adopted a position paper called "The Role of Women in Ministry as Described in Holy Scripture," which concludes, "We must continue to be open to the full use of women's gifts in ministry and spiritual leadership." This statement, like others in the document, recognizes the fact that women have held positions of ministry (including leadership roles) throughout the church's history. But the tone of the statement is apologetic. Indeed, most of the hermeneutical work in the document is defensive, asserting the need to maintain something that is threatened: "We do not find sufficient evidence in [the Greek word] *kephale* to deny leadership roles to women"; "We conclude that we cannot find convincing evidence that the ministry of women is restricted according to some sacred or immutable principle." At the beginning of the twenty-first century, the AG, which is the largest Pentecostal denomination, officially endorses women in ministry (including top leadership positions), but none of its top denominational leaders are women and some of its largest churches deny leadership roles to women. The same is true of the Church of God, where the twelve members of the governing Presidium are all men. Indeed, although all Pentecostal denominations have some form of ministry division that addresses the needs of women and provides leadership opportunities for talented women, men continue to dominate virtually all of the top leadership positions in all Pentecostal denominations in North America.

Compassion Ministries

From the late nineteenth century to the first decade of the twenty-first, a discernible shift has occurred among Pentecostals in their posture toward compassion ministries, or ministries that address the physical, psychological, and material needs of people without necessarily involving the explicit verbal proclamation of the Gospel. Until the late 1970s, most Pentecostal groups and denominations distinguished sharply between missions and evangelism (overt efforts to proselytize) on the one hand and the so-called social gospel on the other. The social gospel, which began as a movement about 1870, sought to eliminate poverty, ignorance, and other social ills by reforming society according to Christian principles. Mainline Protestants as well as Roman Catholics were said, somewhat disparagingly by Pentecostals, to be engaged in the social gospel and were criticized for devoting insufficient attention to the explicit verbal proclamation of the Gospel.

Since the 1980s, however, many Pentecostal organizations seem to have moved to a different position, broadening their view of ministry. Without abandoning their commitment to the task of verbally proclaiming the Gospel message through traditional missions and evangelism, they have with increasing energy and urgency begun to respond to a broad range of human needs. The AG, for example, has developed a worldwide healthcare ministry that offers not only medical and educational assistance for needy people (including AIDS education for patients) but also training and seminars for healthcare professionals who seek to provide services outside the United States. The COG has developed a program called Men and Women of Action (MWOA) that enlists volunteers to work with missionaries, pastors, and church leaders around the world with practical ministries such as construction projects. In a departure from the attempts of early Pentecostals to dissociate themselves from the social gospel, the COG now says, "Bricks, nails, mortar and hammers are simply construction tools to many people, but to the MWOA these are Mission Tools."

The PAOC has developed a humanitarian arm called Emergency Relief and Development Overseas (ERDO), a global ministry designed to respond to the needs of people "living with devastating poverty, natural disaster, civil strife, famine and disease."

Technology-Related Ethical Issues

Three technological and social phenomena of the post–World War II era affected Pentecostals profoundly and irrevocably: widespread access to automobiles, easy availability of hand-held transistor radios, and the rise of television. Automobiles afforded North American young people, including Pentecostals, the privilege of going places and being with people in ways not generally available to pre–World War II generations. As teen pregnancy increased in the general population, so it increased among teens from Pentecostal families, following their discovery of comfortable, private accommodations in the back seats of cars. Automobiles also provided convenient private places to experiment with alcohol and tobacco, products their parents had forbidden them to use. The widespread availability of inexpensive, hand-held transistor radios in the 1950s offered immediate access to popular secular music. The emergence of television in the late 1940s and its widespread acceptance in American life in the 1950s affected Pentecostal family and church life pervasively and profoundly. It was one thing for parents to forbid their children to attend movies; it was quite another to exercise control over an electronic device that occupied a central place in the home. The television, more than any other single technological invention, allowed Pentecostal families to compare themselves with the popular images of family life presented by corporate marketing agents and program producers.

Having gained widespread acceptance and use in the 1990s in homes, businesses, and educational institutions, the so-called new media—digital devices and computer-mediated communication technologies, including the Internet and the World Wide Web—have shown signs of posing an additional challenge, somewhat different from those posed by the automobile, the transistor radio, and the television. Paradoxically, although the Internet offers inexpensive, almost instantaneous access to cultures around the world that most people in earlier times either could not visit at all or paid large sums of money to experience first hand, the Internet's primary social and moral challenge derives from the isolation it imposes on the user. Extended periods of intense isolation associated with Internet use—called "cocooning"—challenge traditional Pentecostal

social values in at least two ways. The most obvious way is that during prolonged periods of private interactivity, users can be exposed to certain kinds of Web sites (e.g., pornographic) that directly undermine traditional Pentecostal moral values. This challenge is the one most often noted by parents and church leaders. For example, the 1998 UPCI position paper "Computers and the Internet" says, "This new innovation literally brings the entire spectrum of information available in the world into any computer screen. While much of this information is wholesome and useful, a great amount is lewd, pornographic or dangerous." The less obvious but perhaps more substantial challenge derives from the way the Internet, even more than television, militates against the kind of community-building that has traditionally characterized Pentecostal social relations.

Social Norms and Mores of Daily Life

To the extent that classical Pentecostals have roots in the Holiness movement, they have been deeply affected by the social norms and mores of that movement. For example, the AG and the COG, both historically indebted to the Holiness movement, established strong social norms (including, in many instances, standards of church membership) in their early formative years that reflected Holiness beliefs and social expectations. These included stringent proscriptions on alcohol and tobacco use, social dancing, movie attendance, use of cosmetics, and wearing jewelry. It also included distinctly conservative, even austere, standards for apparel and hairstyles. Most of these social norms and mores were justified on the grounds that while spiritual and moral maturity are matters of the inner life, outward appearance and behavior reflect one's spiritual condition.

Thus, for example, in its official statement of practical commitments, the COG cites scriptural references supporting the claim that the human body is the temple of the Holy Ghost, and speaks of "glorifying God in our body." It goes on to identify numerous types of behaviors and practices that degrade the human body and thus defile the believer's relationship with God. Several of the position statements developed by the UPCI speak to its longstanding and continuing concerns over social norms and mores. It advocates against "mixed bathing" (males swimming with females); gambling; watching films; women cutting their hair, using make-up, or wearing jewelry; watching or even owning a television; listening to "unwholesome" radio programs or music; and engaging in "worldly sports or amusements." The UPCI's position on attire appears in a tract called "The Scriptures Decree Modesty in Dress." The document sets forth certain principles, said to derive from the New Testament, governing how women should dress: "modesty, moderation in cost, inclination toward godliness (decency), avoidance of outward adornment, shamefacedness and sobriety, distinction between male and female." Although it finds no specific instructions for men's attire and appearance in the New Testament, it contends that the same principles should apply to men as well as women.

The AG has not formally gone to the same lengths as the UPCI, but it has adopted position papers regarding alcohol (complete abstinence) and gambling (whether legal or illegal, an evil to be avoided). It has also published a series of documents speaking to a broad range of issues of lifestyle and practice, including friendships, dating, sexual relations, entertainment, social dancing, astrology, and transcendental meditation. The documents themselves—collectively called "AG Perspectives"—do not express the formal positions of the denomination, but they do reflect its conservative theological heritage and have been endorsed by the church's Commission on Doctrinal Purity and the Executive Presbytery.

Outlook on the Twenty-First Century

Some Pentecostal churches remain among the most conservative of any churches in North America, trying more or less successfully to adhere to their own long-held but gradually changing codes of dress, conduct, and practice—the so-called holiness standards. For example, the UPCI, recognizing the power of the television, continues to publish an official position against owning televisions: "because of the display of all these evils on television, we disapprove of any of our people having television sets in their homes." However, increasingly large numbers of young Pentecostals are indistinguishable from their peers, either in personal appearance or in behavior, in matters once thought to be distinctive if not defining features of the Pentecostal lifestyle. One of the major social and moral questions facing Pentecostals in the twenty-first century is whether they will be able to successfully nurture in their young people the spiritual and moral habits of the "inner life" (the original intent of the old Holiness movement), without alienating them by clinging to codes of dress, conduct, and practice that are probably unrecoverable and widely viewed as quaint and outdated fashions of earlier generations.

MICHAEL D. PALMER

See also Azusa Street Revival; Memphis Miracle; Race Relations; Society, Pentecostal Attitudes toward; Women

Further Reading

Amos, B. M. (1996). Race, gender, and justice. *Pneuma: The Journal of the Society for Pentecostal Studies*, *18*, 132–135.

Clemmons, I. C. (1996). What price reconciliation: reflections on the 'Memphis Dialogue.' *Pneuma: The Journal of the Society for Pentecostal Studies*, *18*, 116–122.

Dyck, H. (1996). L'esprit du seigneur est sur moi?: A brief analysis of the social ethics of the Pentecostal Assemblies of Canada (PAOC). *Society for Pentecostal Studies Annual Papers*.

Hunter, H. D. (Ed.). (1983). *Pastoral problems in the Pentecostal-Charismatic movement*. Cleveland, TN: Church of God School of Theology.

Hunter, H. D. (2002). Church of God of prophecy. In S. M. Burgess & E. M. Van Der Mass (Eds.), *New international dictionary of Pentecostal and Charismatic movements* (pp. 539–542). Grand Rapids, MI: Zondervan.

Kraut, R., Patterson, M., Lundmark, V., Kiesler, S., Mukopadhyay, T., & Scherlis, W. (1998). Internet paradox: A social technology that reduces social involvement and psychosocial well-being? *American Psychologist*, *53*(9), 1017–1031.

Macchia, F. D. (1995). From Azusa to Memphis: Evaluating the racial reconciliation dialogue among pentecostals. *Pneuma: The Journal of the Society for Pentecostal Studies*, *17*, 203–218.

Palmer, M. (2004). Reading and critical thinking: Pentecostal traditions vis-á-vis new media. In C. Ess (Ed.), *Critical thinking and the Bible in the age of new media*. Lanham, MD: University Press of America.

Robeck, C. M., Jr. (1987). Pentecostals and social ethics. *Pneuma: The Journal of the Society for Pentecostal Studies*, *9*, 103107.

Robeck, C. M., Jr. (1992). Faith, hope, love, and the eschaton. *Pneuma: The Journal of the Society for Pentecostal Studies*, *14*, 1–5.

Robeck, C. M., Jr. (1996). Racial reconciliation at Memphis: Some personal reflections. *Pneuma: The Journal of the Society for Pentecostal Studies*, *18*, 135–140.

Robeck, C. M., Jr. (2002). Azusa street revival. In S. M. Burgess & E. M. Van Der Mass (Eds.), *New international dictionary of Pentecostal and Charismatic movements* (pp. 344–350). Grand Rapids, MI: Zondervan.

Synan, V. (1977). *The Holiness-Pentecostal tradition: Charismatic movements in the twentieth century*. Grand Rapids, MI: William B. Eerdmans.

Europe

European Pentecostalism developed in what is traditionally seen as a Christian heartland. But it developed on a continent that was ravaged by two world wars. After 1918, when the first war ended, Russia was in the hands of an atheist dictatorship and after 1945, when the second war ended, a large bloc of traditionally Christian countries such as Hungary, Czechoslovakia, and Romania were also under Soviet control.

Consequently the development of European Pentecostalism was disrupted by the agonies and inconveniences of war and subsequently repressed by government agencies behind the iron curtain. In the democratic and free western part of Europe, however, opposition arose from traditional churches, particularly in Germany, but also in the southern part of Europe, especially Spain and Italy, where Roman Catholic dominance appeared unassailable.

Moreover, partly because of the wars, Europe was steadily secularized so that an examination of church attendance figures shows a peak (at least in Britain) in about 1950. A combination of war, opposition from established churches, and secularization must explain the relative numerical weakness of European Pentecostalism compared with North and South America, Africa, and Asia.

Method

Roughly one hundred years have passed since the beginnings of European Pentecostalism and the first generation of people associated with the original move of the Holy Spirit have all died. We are dependent for accurate reconstructions of Pentecostal history on numerous magazines and early books written, of course, in a variety of European languages. But no integrated history of European Pentecostalism based upon primary sources has yet been achieved, and such a compendious work would probably now be beyond the competence of any individual scholar. One English source, the magazine *Pentecost*, edited and published by Donald Gee from September 1947 until his death in 1966, does contain contemporary reports of Pentecostal life and activity from all over the world, and often with a special section on Europe. Perhaps as a result of the European Conference of Pentecostals (1939) and World Conference (in London in 1952), global accounts of the history of Pentecostalism began to appear after about 1960 (Bloch-Hoell 1964; Gee 1967; Hollenweger 1972) and most recently Anderson (2004). After about the 1980s academic Pentecostals began to provide detailed accounts of developments in their own countries, and these were often published, at least in abbreviated form, in the *Journal of the European Pentecostal Association* or the first or second editions of the *Dictionary of the Pentecostal and Charismatic Movements*. So the materials for this article are drawn either from general overviews of Pentecostalism, or from *Pentecost*, or from the English translations of the work of national scholars.

Beginnings

Pentecostalism was most warmly received in countries with strong traditions of religious freedom. Such countries tended to contain independent churches that, in practice, were usually either Baptist or Methodist. Established churches (those supported by taxation or having strong links to the state) tended to oppose Pentecostalism. Independent churches were most strongly represented in Scandinavia and in the United Kingdom, although all countries that contained a mixture of Protestant and Catholic churches had learned to recognize the value of religious freedom.

T. B. Barratt (1862–1940), whose English father had immigrated to Norway, was originally a member of the Methodist Episcopal church. Barratt, while fundraising in the United States, heard about the Azusa Street Revival and prayed for the fullness of the Spirit. He spoke in tongues and returned to Oslo, where revival scenes accompanied his ministry. This was in the year 1906. The initial spread of European Pentecostalism can be attributed on the human level almost entirely to the ministry of Barratt. Over the next few years he traveled to the United Kingdom (1907), Denmark (1907), Finland (1911), Russia (1911), and Iceland (1920) and, in each case, held meetings where Pentecostal phenomena were manifested. Moreover, quite quickly, Barratt came to the opinion that Pentecostals would need to form their own churches if the revival were to prosper. In other words he was in favor of new Pentecostal denominations rather than seeing Pentecostalism as a renewal movement within existing church structures. Such a judgment was also made by Lewi Pethrus (1884–1974), the influential Swedish leader, after being expelled by the Swedish Baptist Convention in 1913. Pethrus had become Pentecostal in 1907 under Barratt's ministry.

Consolidation

The typical pattern for the development of the churches within European countries is centered on a bold originator who (a) convenes a Pentecostal conference (e.g.,

Alexander Boddy in the United Kingdom or Emil Humburg and Jonathan Paul in Germany) or (b) is expelled from an existing denomination and yet has the strength to found a large new Pentecostal congregation (e.g., Barratt or Pethrus) or (c) evangelizes with a signs-and-wonders ministry that results in a string of connected congregations (e.g., George Jeffreys in the United Kingdom or Douglas Scott in France).

In each case the path is slightly different. The convener of the conference may draw together Evangelical Christians and seek to draw them into Pentecostal experience. The founder of a big new Pentecostal congregation may plant out a network of new small churches or start a Bible school, newspaper, or radio station that carries the Pentecostal message out to the rest of the country. The evangelist is most likely to bring new congregations into existence in major cities but then has the difficulty of making the transition from evangelistic work to routine denominational organization.

In a given country these patterns will be established simultaneously or in succession. In the United Kingdom George Jeffreys was the signs-and-wonders evangelist who established the Elim Pentecostal denomination in 1915, whereas Alexander Boddy brought Evangelicals into the Pentecostal experience between 1907 and 1914, but then John Nelson Parr convened a meeting that resulted in the formation of the Assemblies of God in 1924. In some countries, leading Pentecostals tried to refresh existing churches and to avoid forming Pentecostal denominations (as Gerrit Polman in the Netherlands from 1908) and in others, like Italy, persecution gave Pentecostals no choice but to fight for their existence, as they did after 1929 when Mussolini's Concordat discriminated against all Italian Protestants.

Gradually by these means Pentecostalism spread across Europe. Global interconnections played their part in this process. Swedish Pentecostals went to Brazil in 1911 and some of their converts went back to Portugal to become evangelists in 1913. Similarly, successful evangelists in one country might be invited to preach in others—as was the case with George Jeffreys, whose ministry extended to the Netherlands and Switzerland. Equally, respected teachers like Donald Gee during the 1930s spoke at a Bible school in Danzig, a city that later became part of Poland.

After 1945

In the immediate aftermath of war, unemployment, hunger, lack of housing, and the flood of refugees in central Europe stimulated the compassion of Pentecostals in the wealthier countries, and this, in its turn,

led to other forms of cooperation. At the same time American Assemblies of God saw the value in sending missionaries to Europe. Among their priorities was ministerial training. By the 1990s Continental Theological Seminary in Brussels had become an important teaching base for Pentecostals in the whole of Europe but especially in the poorer east, and the same could be said of the British Assemblies of God college at Mattersey, United Kingdom.

In the democratic half of Europe Pentecostal growth was steady and sometimes spectacular. In 1949 an Assembly of God building was dedicated in Rome. By 1951 the assembly at Stockholm had a membership of over six thousand. A census showed that Norwegian Pentecostals increased in numbers by 400 percent between 1940 and 1950. In 1952 the BBC broadcast its first Pentecostal service. Large gatherings took place in Sweden and, once the healing evangelists such as T. L. Osborn and A. C. Valdez began to extend their ministries more widely than North America, there were campaigns in the United Kingdom, France, the Netherlands, and Germany that attracted attention and filled large halls. In 1956 more than five thousand attended an evangelistic rally in Paris at which Douglas Scott spoke.

From the 1960s

The 1960s saw the beginnings of the Charismatic movement, in which the Holy Spirit was poured out upon the mainline denominations. The Pentecostals expected that they would be direct beneficiaries of this fresh breath of the Spirit but it later became apparent that the renewed Anglicans, Lutherans, Methodists, Baptists, and others were not inclined immediately to rush to join the Pentecostal denominations. In many parts of Europe Pentecostal denominations were now showing signs of being old-fashioned, even if the spiritual fire in the better congregations continued to burn brightly. Consequently, the Charismatic movement diffused spiritual experience and Pentecostal doctrine without leading to sudden correlative Pentecostal growth.

The breakup of the Soviet empire and the fall the Berlin Wall in 1989 had a spiritual as well as a political impact. The Pentecostal believers who had suffered under Communism were able to resume free and active lives. Bit by bit Pentecostal denominations in the old Eastern Bloc countries were rejuvenated and resourced. Short-term missions, ministry trips, and financial aid (some of it ill judged) flowed eastward. As the European Union expanded its borders in 2004, the prognosis for these Pentecostal churches was good. They, like the other classical Pentecostal denominations, could expect to plant churches, evangelize, train ministers, produce educational materials, and begin to affect the life of the countries where they were situated.

By the 1990s, the Charismatic movement had transformed normative patterns of evangelical worship but, nevertheless, the more radical charismatics had left to form their own apostolic new churches. Such churches functioned within networks and were led by an apostolic figure whose own ministry was a source of unity. The apostolic figure usually had an authoritative role and the ability to make decisions relating to the network as a whole: the pattern was modeled on what was perceived as the New Testament ministry of an apostle. By and large Pentecostal groups had tended to govern themselves through constitutions and committee structures that were less flexible, more bureaucratic, and therefore less attractive than the apostolic networks. Doctrinally, however, Pentecostals and apostolic new churches were very similar.

So Pentecostalism in Europe may now be divided into three broad groups: the classical Pentecostals, who have attempted to reform themselves to remove the worst bureaucratic elements within their systems; the charismatics, who continue to form a substantial and lively part of the Christian presence within Europe and whose conferences, camps, and conventions continue to attract substantial numbers; and the apostolic new churches, which are more difficult to judge because of their dependence upon the faith and ministry of their founding apostle.

The statistics on Pentecostalism indicate that the largest classical Pentecostal group in Europe is in Romania (over 850,000) and the smallest is in Hungary (11,000) whereas the largest number of charismatics is to be found in the United Kingdom (around 4 million), Italy is second with 3 million, and the smallest number is found in Portugal with just over 250,000. Russia has the highest number of neocharismatics with 5.3 million, and the United Kingdom is second with 1.4 million. These figures need to be interpreted against the size of national populations to be fully meaningful. Although statistics in Eastern Europe are harder to obtain, the figures indicate a Pentecostal presence in all the main European countries. When the biggest four countries of the European Union (Germany, France, the United Kingdom, and Italy) are compared, the United Kingdom and Italy show the highest numbers. Presumably, the early opposition of German Evangelicals through the anti-Pentecostal Berlin Declaration of 1909 and the continuing secular/Roman Catholic ethos in France have restricted Pentecostal growth. In each country, though, it is the charismatics who are the largest

constituency—hardly surprising in that they are drawn from across the Christian spectrum.

Classical Pentecostals continue to support each other in pan-European gatherings (such as the European Pentecostal Theological Association and the Pentecostal European Fellowship, which in 2003 became a legal body) and they may need further mutual support if the constitution of the European Union becomes more secular and therefore more hostile to religion.

WILLIAM K. KAY

See also Charismatic Movement; Great Britain; Pentecostalism, Classical

Further Reading

Anderson, A. (2004). *An introduction to Pentecostalism*. Cambridge, UK: Cambridge University Press.

Bloch-Hoell, N. (1964). *The Pentecostal movement: Its origins, developments, and distinctive character*. London: Allen & Unwin.

Burgess, S. M., & van der Maas, E. M. (Eds.). (2002). *New international dictionary of Pentecostal and charismatic movements*. Grand Rapids, MI: Zondervan.

Gee, D. (1967). *Wind and flame*. Luton, UK: Heath.

Hollenweger, W. J. (1972). *The Pentecostals*. London: SCM.

Kay, W. K., & Dyer, A. E. (Eds.). (2004). *Pentecostal and charismatic studies: A reader*. London: SCM.

Evangelism

Evangelism has had a prominent role within Pentecostalism since the inception of the Modern Pentecostal Movement. Pentecostals have closely tied their understanding of their Spirit-filled life to the role of evangelism. As such, evangelism is not only seen as foundational to their understanding of the biblical commands, but also as fundamental to their theological self-identity.

Definition and Related Terms

The term *evangelism* stems from the Greek noun *euangelion*, which means "good news" and which occurs seventy-five times in the New Testament, and the Greek verb *euangelizomai*, which means "to announce or proclaim the good news" and which occurs fifty-four times in the New Testament. Other Greek terms used to express this concept are *martys*, "witness"; *martyreo*, "to bear witness"; and *martyria*, "witness, testimony," which occur thirty-five, seventy-six, and

Sharing the Gospel. *Courtesy of istockphoto.com/ pattersonminx.*

thirty-seven times respectively in the New Testament. The Greek words *katangello,* "to proclaim" (sixty-one times), and *kerysso,* "to announce or to preach" (eighteen times), among others, are also New Testament words used for this function.

Evangelism can be defined as proclamation of the good news of Jesus Christ, concerning His incarnation, life, death, and resurrection, which for those who put their trust in Him will bring salvation. This salvation will lead them into fellowship with others, called the church, culminating in eternal life with God.

The role of evangelism is more than the persuasion of nonbelievers to the acceptance of Jesus Christ. True evangelism is not just mental assent or rational agreement but rather a holistic reception of the news of the overwhelming and overcoming power of Christ available to those who believe. The certainty and total pervasiveness of sin and death are a constant problem with humanity, but Jesus has overcome sin and death, and those who believe (that is, fully trust) in Him "die" to the old self and live in Christ. Further, Satan and the demonic forces can be overcome by those who accept Christ's Lordship. Pentecostals emphasize that this conversion experience is a personal encounter with the risen Lord through the mediating work of the Holy Spirit in opposition to the world, the flesh, and the satanic dominion. From the moment of conversion, there will be a change that takes place within the new believer.

Evangelism works through the "proclamation" and "witness" of the believer to the nonbeliever, when the Holy Spirit anoints the Word proclaimed, and the nonbelieving recipient must either accept or reject the prompting of the Holy Spirit. This endeavor, then, includes the purposeful articulation of the good news about Jesus Christ in a way understandable to the recipient, the work of the Holy Spirit in "wooing" the recipient, and the active participation of the recipient to accept or reject the Spirit-anointed message.

Biblical Reasons for Evangelism

Pentecostals see redemption and salvation of the lost and dying world as central to the biblical message. The biblical theme, frequently called the *missio dei,* demonstrates the divine desire that none should die separated from Him and His grace (John 3:16; 1 Timothy 2:4; 2 Peter 3:9, KJV). As such, the divine purpose is for the reconciliation of the world to God.

Furthermore, Pentecostals have from the outset seen the role of evangelism as being more than just an extension of their social movement, but rather as biblically based and a matter of obedience to the divine mandate. As such, Pentecostals are in an active, participatory role as "Christ's Ambassadors" (2 Corinthians 5:20) in fulfilling God's purposes in the world—thus, the Great Commission (Matthew 28:18–20; Mark 16:15–18; Luke 24:46–49). Pentecostals emphasize the point that although God has the power to bring people to Himself in any way He chooses, it "pleased God" by the proclamation of the good news to bring salvation to the nonbelieving world (1 Corinthians 1:21)—God's followers are included in fulfilling His purposes on the earth. Thus, evangelism is the believer's responsibility to those who have not heard the "good news" everywhere on the globe. Ultimately, evangelism and missionary work are inseparably linked.

Not only do Pentecostals emphasize the following of the divine mandate, Acts 1:8, Luke 24:48–9, and Acts 2 points to the empowerment of those who follow this mandate. Pentecostals believe that they are to receive divine enablement through being "filled with the Spirit" (also called baptism in the Holy Spirit) in order to be witnesses. Therefore, evangelism should be the primary reason for and result of the baptism of the Holy Spirit and the gifts of the Spirit (*charismata*). This empowerment is for all believers to be "witnesses," but

Billy Graham on Evangelism and Politics

If I had it to do over again, I would also avoid any semblance of involvement in partisan politics. On the whole . . . my primary concern in my contacts with political leaders has been as a pastor and spiritual counselor, not as a political adviser. When a president of the United States, for example, wept in my presence, or knelt with me to pray, or privately unburdened his concerns about his family, I was not thinking about his political philosophy or his personality but about his need for God's help.

And yet there have been times when I undoubtedly stepped over the line between politics and my calling as an evangelist. An evangelist is called to do one thing, and one thing only: to proclaim the Gospel. Becoming involved in strictly political issues or partisan politics inevitably dilutes the evangelist's impact and compromises his message. It is a lesson I wish I had learned earlier.

Source: Graham, B. (1997). *Just as I am: The autobiography of Billy Graham* (p. 724). New York: HarperCollins Publishers.

not everyone has the spiritual gift or calling to be an evangelist.

Further, Pentecostals also emphasize the role of social concern with the evangelistic message. They are inseparable in the divine mandate. However, Hodges and others have been quick to state that social concern should not take precedence over or replace proclamation, which is the tendency. There must be a balance.

Evangelism for Pentecostals, as noted by McClung, has three major theological components concerning why a person should be involved in evangelism. First, the Great Commission emphasizes the need for all believers to "go" as a matter of divine obedience. Further, Jesus was obedient to God the Father even to death (Philippians 2:8), and as He was sent so He sends us into the world as recipients of His Spirit and proclaimers of His "good news" (John 20:21–22). So we are to be obedient to the Great Commission while following His model of obedience.

Second, Pentecostals have a strong commitment to the "lostness" of humanity. There will be a final judgment and those who are not reached with the good news are destined to a judgment of eternal punishment, which includes eternal separation from God (Luke 13:3–5; Romans 2:12; 3:23; 5:12; 6:23; 2 Thessalonians 1: 7–8; James 1:15; 2 Peter 3:9; Revelation 20:11–15). Pentecostals believe that those who actively follow God and put their trust in Him are destined to eternal life with Him, and those who do not follow Him, including those who have not had a chance to hear the good news, are destined for eternal death without Him. This is why there is a strong emphasis on going to the ends of the earth, and the strong commitment of Pentecostals to foreign missions.

Third, Pentecostals believe that these are the "last days" (Acts 2:16–21), so on the one hand there is an urgency to complete the task before the imminent return of Christ. On the other hand, Pentecostal faithfulness in evangelism can help "hasten the day" (2 Peter 3:12) of the return of Christ as Matthew 24:14 states, "And this gospel of the kingdom will be preached in the whole world as a testimony to all nations, and then the end will come." Thus for Pentecostals the outpouring of the Holy Spirit with the evidence of "speaking in tongues" was directly tied to evangelism and the imminent return of Christ.

Evangelistic Methods and Media

Pentecostals have used a wide variety of methods in the evangelistic cause. Pentecostals have evangelized people on a "confrontational" individual basis by talking to people about the "good news" without having prior relationships with them. In the early part of the twentieth century, this might have taken the form of a small group singing and preaching on a street corner to passersby or of a one-on-one or door-to-door evangelistic campaign. It was not unusual for new converts to participate in these by giving their testimony.

A second common method used from Pentecostalism's inception is the camp meeting or crusade. In the early twentieth century these tended to be in tents or brush arbors. In these meetings there would be a key speaker preaching an evangelistic message, and advertisements, word of mouth, and personal accompaniment were ways to bring the nonbelieving populace to the meeting.

A third type of evangelism has been emphasized in recent years—lifestyle evangelism. This type emphasizes not only the proclamation but also the life of the proclaimer. This is especially important since it has been noted that a vast majority of those who have responded to evangelism were friends or relatives of believers.

But you will receive power when the Holy Spirit comes on you; and you will be my witnesses in Jerusalem, and in all Judea and Samaria, and to the ends of the earth.

Acts 1:8 (New International Version)

For Pentecostals, evangelism uses a wide variety of media. One of the most prominent is evangelistic literature. From the very beginning of the modern Pentecostal movement, literature in the form of evangelistic tracts and pamphlets played an important role in evangelism. Frequently these were used in concert with one-on-one "confrontational" evangelistic endeavors.

As for electronic media, from the 1920s and 1930s through the latter part of the twentieth century, radio was another dominant medium for evangelism. Frequently, local church pastors or evangelists would have evangelistic programs broadcast to local audiences, which in turn would invite nonbelievers to "accept the Lord Jesus into their hearts" or at least to come to their church to experience God. Pentecostal preachers such as A. A. Allen and Oral Roberts had prominent radio programs from the late 1940s on, and Pentecostal denominations likewise sponsored evangelistic radio programs such as *Revivaltime* (Assemblies of God) and *Forward in Faith* (Church of God, Cleveland, Tennessee). The Pentecostal missions' efforts also emphasized the use of radio such as that by the Far East Broadcasting Company (FEBC). By the 1960s, the prominence of radio was giving way to the television in Western countries. However, even today radio (especially shortwave) stills plays a significant role in much of the world. This is also one of the main evangelistic tools used to reach those who live in closed countries.

From the 1960s on, as television became increasingly prominent, Pentecostal "televangelists" such as Kathryn Kuhlman, Oral Roberts, and more recently Benny Hinn, televised evangelistic and healing campaigns, broadcasting the Pentecostal evangelistic message into the homes of people worldwide. Other Pentecostals or charismatics like Pat Robertson with the Christian Broadcasting Network (CBN) and the *700 Club*, Jim Bakker with the Praise the Lord Network (PTL), Jimmy Swaggart's weekly telecasts, and Paul and Jan Crouch's Trinity Broadcasting Network (TBN) have made a substantive impact on the weekly television audience. Although Bakker and Swaggart stepped out of the television spotlight due to moral failures in the mid-1980s, CBN, TBN, and other networks and televangelists are active in bringing the Pentecostal evangelistic message through the television into the homes of people around the world.

Supernatural Evangelism

Pentecostals, because of their worldview of God's supernatural work in healing and miracles, see this miraculous activity of God in the world as evangelistic by nature. In other words, because God's central purpose is the redemption and reconciliation of the world to Himself, as Acts 3 demonstrates, He will show His power as a sign of His reality in order that people may believe. This sense of the reality of God in the midst of the Pentecostals' meetings plays an evangelistic role both in the Spirit-led worship and in the Spirit-anointed preaching. The whole worship service then focuses on the presence of God in the midst of His people and thereby demands the appropriate response—from the believer, a deeper relationship and walk; from the nonbeliever a positive response to the invitation to have a personal relationship with God.

The Evangelist

The term *euangelistes*—"one who evangelizes" or "evangelist"—is found just three times in the New Testament. Act 21:8 names Philip as an "evangelist" apparently in contrast to the apostles. In 2 Timothy 4:5, Timothy is told to do the work of the "evangelist." In Ephesians 4:11, "evangelists" were considered one of the offices of the church for its edification. The focus of an evangelist, as Philip's life demonstrates, was to "proclaim" to individuals, such as the Ethiopian eunuch (Acts 8:26–40), or to crowds and large gatherings, such as at Samaria (Acts 8:4–13). Although there are those evangelists within Pentecostalism today who operate in both roles, the tendency is to operate in one or the other capacity. Due to the nature of those who operate in the public forum, these individuals have more public prominence. The individual or small group evangelist, however, still has a dominant role within Pentecostalism. Many Pentecostal churches have those who are gifted or prefer the role of the "confrontational" one-on-one evangelism or the small-group Bible-study-type evangelist.

Usually when the term "evangelist" is used within the Pentecostal tradition, it refers to those who hold the public role. They travel from town to town proclaiming the Pentecostal message to nonbelievers in public meetings (crusades, church, revivals). Some of the prominent Pentecostal evangelists of the first three decades of the twentieth century were A. H. Argue, Alexander Boddy, Stephen and George Jeffries, Aimee Semple McPherson, C. H. Mason, Charles S. Price, A. J. Tomlinson, Smith Wigglesworth, and Maria Woodworth-Etter. From the 1940s to the 1960s, other evangelists took center stage, such as A. A. Allen, William Branham, Gordon Lindsay, David Nunn, T. L. Osborn, Oral Roberts, and W. V. Grant. Since the 1960s others have emerged, such as Carlos Annacondia, Reinhard Bonnke, Morris Cerullo, Benny Hinn, Kathryn Kuhlman, R. W. Schambach, Lester Sumerall, Jimmy Swaggart, and others connected to the Charismatic movement such as John Osteen and James Robison. Many of these evangelists were also pastors, whether because their evangelistic career gained prominence due to the growth of the church they pastored or because it was a result of the new church plant that was started by the evangelistic event. The common methodologies used by these evangelists in their mass crusades included powerful music, praying for the sick or those beset with demons, testimonies, simultaneous prayer support by believers, and various types of literature (booklets, books, pamphlets, tracts, and magazines). Some even became prominent "healing evangelists" (e.g., Benny Hinn, Kathryn Kuhlman, Oral Roberts); their prominence came from the role of healing or exorcisms in their crusades, but the healings were seen as a tool to emphasize the presence of God in order to demand a response.

The Future of Evangelism

As Pentecostal evangelism reaches into the twenty-first century, there are some emphases that are already at the forefront. Due to the rise of the Internet and related technologies, there is already a conscious effort to use the Internet for evangelistic purposes, whether by the direct interactive potential on a website or by downloadable evangelistic materials.

Further, major Pentecostal denominations encourage evangelists through sponsored organizations and by providing or supporting conferences that allow for the exchange of information and for training. Several of the international evangelist conferences have had numerous Pentecostal participants. However, due to the prominent

A Christian motif symbolizing "Evangelize the World." *Courtesy of istockphoto.com/dawnhudson.*

moral failures of the mid-1980s, there is also a shared understanding that the evangelist needs to pay more attention to accountability and integrity.

PAUL W. LEWIS

See also Media (Television, Radio, Internet); Preaching

Further Reading

Barclift, M. (1987). The Holy Spirit and missions. *Paraclete* 21(3), 10–13.

Biddle, A. A. (1976). The Holy Spirit prompting evangelism. In P. S. Brewster (Ed.), *Pentecostal doctrine* (pp. 307–317). Cheltenham, UK: Elim Pentecostal Church Headquarters.

Brown, J. (1968). The Holy Spirit's activity in evangelism. *Paraclete* 2(1), 6–11.

Dalaba, O. (1977). *That none be lost.* Springfield, MO: Gospel Publishing House.

Dempster, M. (1991). Evangelism, social concern, and the Kingdom of God. In M. Dempster, B. Klaus, & D. Petersen (Eds.), *Called & empowered: Global mission in Pentecostal perspective* (pp. 22–43). Peabody, MA: Hendrickson Publishers.

Ford, C. (1987). The revival of evangelism. *Paraclete* 21(1), 8–11.

Harrell, D. (1975). *All things are possible.* Bloomington: Indiana University Press.

Hodges, M. (1977). *A theology of the church and its mission: A pentecostal perspective.* Springfield, MO: Gospel Publishing House.

Hodges, M. (1977). What is the Spirit saying to the churches? *Paraclete 11*(3), 3–7.

Hodges, M. (1981). Pentecost and world evangelism. *Paraclete 15*(2), 19–22.

Hughes, R. (1989). *Church of God distinctives* (rev. ed.). Cleveland, TN: Pathway Press.

McClung, L. G. (1986). *Azusa Street and beyond: Pentecostal missions and church growth in the twentieth century.* South Plainfield, NJ: Logos.

McClung, L. G. (2002). Evangelism. In S. Burgess (Ed.), *International Dictionary of Pentecostal and Charismatic movements* (pp. 617–620). Grand Rapids, MI: Zondervan.

McClung, L. G. (2002). Evangelists. In S. Burgess (Ed.), *International Dictionary of Pentecostal and Charismatic movements* (pp.620–623). Grand Rapids, MI: Zondervan.

McClung, L. G. (1999). "Try To Get People Saved": Revisiting the paradigm of an urgent Pentecostal missiology. In M. Dempster, B. Klaus, & D. Petersen (Eds.), *The globalization of Pentecostalism* (pp. 30–51). Carlisle, UK: Regnum.

Riss, R. (1988). *A survey of 20th century revival movements in North America.* Peabody, MA: Hendrickson Publishers.

York, J. (2000). *Missions in the age of the spirit.* Springfield, MO: Logion Press.

Evil, Problem of

The problem of evil can be demonstrated in the following question: "If God is all-powerful and all-loving, then why does God allow evil to prevail in the world?" This philosophical problem, or inquiry, questions God's existence in relation to the reality of evil in the world. Historically Pentecostals have not reflected upon the traditional problem of evil from a philosophical perspective. In other words, no formal theology of the problem of evil exists from a Pentecostal perspective. Charismatics, on the other hand, have relied on denominational approaches and therefore represent a plurality of views. A survey of the three major positions on the problem of evil in Christianity will be briefly discussed as well as locating where Pentecostals, charismatics, and neocharismatics find themselves within these positions. Following the survey, however, a Pentecostal approach to the problem of evil will be examined and developed.

Philosophical Problem of Evil

The pain and suffering of humanity worldwide have caused many to question the belief in an all-powerful, all-loving God. In other words, if God is all-powerful and all-loving, then why does God allow evil to prevail in the world? This central inquiry questions the internal consistency of the belief in a God who is all-loving and all-powerful in his ability to eliminate the suffering of humanity. Since evil exists in the world, the argument follows that an all-powerful and all-loving God does not exist. Despite the outcome of the proposition (an all-loving, all-powerful God does not exist because of evil in the world), perhaps how God relates to the world will need to be redefined. Any successful solution to this problem of evil must cohere with logical consistency. Below is a brief explanation of the various positions by which many Pentecostals, charismatics, and neocharismatics find solutions to this philosophical problem.

Classical theism views God as providentially guiding all meticulous details in the world, even human choices. Although humans have free will, they only act according to their desires, which are determined. Any evil that occurs in the world is a result of humans acting upon their desires; these desires, moreover, are the product of the original sin of Adam. All humans are totally deprived of moral goodness as a result of Adam's sin, which is the essential cause of evil in the world. Critics of this position often claim that if God is controlling all meticulous details of the world, then God becomes the ultimate cause of evil. St. Augustine (354–430 CE), Thomas Aquinas (1225–1274 CE), and John Calvin (1509–1564 CE) have upheld this classic position historically in its various forms, and charismatics, especially within a Calvinistic tradition, subscribe to this view.

Free-will theism views God as being affected by the free-will choices of humans. In other words, God's actions, decisions, and plans are contingent upon human libertarian freedom, which is the ability to self-choose apart from being determined. God has chosen to honor human choices, although at times these choices are contrary to God's nature, but God deliberately works to bring about the good in evil choices. Although God has foreknowledge of all human decisions, he strategizes to ensure that his overarching plan is achieved for the world. Because of human free will, evil abounds, but God has chosen to honor human choices. For this reason, an all-loving, all-powerful God does not eliminate evil and suffering, because to do so would violate human free will. Critics of free-will theism point out that libertarian freedom is not possible. Another criticism of free-will theism is: since God has knowledge of the future, why does he not eliminate evil persons from the world (for example, Hitler)? Many of the early church fathers, the Eastern Church, the Arminians, John Wesley (1703–1791), and the Pentecostal tradition hold to this free-will position.

St. Augustine on Evil, an Extract from *The Confessions*

Hear, Lord, my prayer; let not my soul faint under Thy discipline, nor let me faint in confessing unto Thee all Thy mercies, whereby Thou hast drawn me out of all my most evil ways, that Thou mightest become a delight to me above all the allurements which I once pursued; that I may most entirely love Thee, and clasp Thy hand with all my affections, and Thou mayest yet rescue me from every temptation, even unto the end. For lo, O Lord, my King and my God, for Thy service be whatever useful thing my childhood learned; for Thy service, that I speak, write, read, reckon. For Thou didst grant me Thy discipline, while I was learning vanities; and my sin of delighting in those vanities Thou hast forgiven. In them, indeed, I learnt many a useful word, but these may as well be learned in things not vain; and that is the safe path for the steps of youth.

Source: St. Augustine. (n.d.) *The confessions* (E. B. Pusey, Trans.).
Retrieved September 20, 2004, from http://etext.library.adelaide.edu.au/a/augustine/a92c/a92c.html

A variant form of free-will theism, open theism, promotes God's inability to know the future. In other words, God is open to the future. According to Open theism, the future is not an actual event, nor can God transcend time; therefore knowing future human choices is not possible for God because real choices have not yet been determined. Therefore, since God does not know future choices, God cannot be responsible for those choices. As a result, God is not responsible for evil. Since God has not foreseen the moral consequences of human decisions, God is not responsible for *not* eliminating people of evil inclinations (Hitler, for example) based upon foreknowledge (often a criticism of free-will theism). However, it has been argued by critics of open theism that God's sovereignty is diminished when divine foreknowledge is forsaken, but openness theologians would respond by saying that God in his sovereignty has chosen to limit himself in this capacity. This, they conclude, does not diminish God's omnipotence but highlights his self-limitation (thus his sovereignty) and self-sacrifice (his love). This view became popular in the late twentieth century and continues to grow in popularity among neocharismatic and Wesleyan-Pentecostal circles today. Clark H. Pinnock, John Sanders, and Gregory Boyd are representatives of this view and have written extensively on the subject.

Existential Problem of Evil

Those influenced by Western philosophy typically rehearse the traditional problem of evil in their confrontation with Christians. However, the existential problem of evil confronts everyone in modern society and across the world. With the existence of suffering, sickness, and nihilism that confront people daily, evil is an existential reality in which justice and wholeness are craved. The reality of evil has always been a concern for Pentecostals, but they have not generally understood evil in a philosophical framework as outlined in the section "the philosophical problem of evil"; rather, they have understood evil in terms of spiritual power.

Pentecostalism is the fastest growing Christian expression in the world. More Pentecostal believers live in the third world than in North America, and those in the third world now represent two-thirds of the Pentecostal population worldwide. Pentecostals worldwide have experienced evil in the most severe forms, from the genocide programs of various leaders in recent history, to the AIDS epidemic in South Africa, to terrorism in the Middle East, to China's persecution of believers. North Americans have little to complain about compared to the atrocities that many experience worldwide. For these third-world Pentecostals, the atrocities of evil are not reduced to philosophical speculation about what God can or will not do. Rather, they envision a world influenced by spiritual powers, affecting human beings positively or negatively. In the West, with its Reformation heritage, evil is defined in terms of original sin. Evil is rather internalized in the West, portraying humanity as morally corrupt as a result of Adam's transgression. The West's answer to evil, therefore, is justification by faith in Christ's atoning death. Third-world Pentecostals, on the other hand, view the resurrected Christ through the power of the Holy Spirit as the answer for evil. Since evil is thought in terms of spiritual power, Christ has overcome these powers in the resurrection, thus enabling people to experience freedom from the struggles and atrocities of their existential evils. Despite the continued reality of evil in the world, Christ continues to subjugate these powers as a result of his victory at the cross and Resurrection. The worldview of these third-world Pentecostals is much closer to that of the New Testament writings, in which Christ's victory is experienced in terms of deliverance from illness and demons.

Western Pentecostalism, although influenced by a scientific worldview, has been keenly aware of evil as existing in spiritual powers. From the early twentieth century, Pentecostals, although in different degrees, have viewed suffering and sickness as caused by spiritual powers. Because of Pentecostalism's indebtedness to its Protestant forbears, evil is thought of not only in terms of spiritual beings, but also as a moral bankruptcy that originated with Adam's sin. Humans make moral choices, but these moral choices, as a result of original sin, do not guarantee right choices; therefore, humans are in need of justification (pardon from the penalty of sin) and sanctification (release from the plague of sin) so that they can be free to choose the right. The latter category recognizes the power of sin's grip upon humanity, to whom the Holy Spirit brings real change in the moral condition over time. The importance of the Holy Spirit in sanctification for the Pentecostal is to ensure that the human heart, which every evil intention is thought to inhabit, is transformed and freed from sin's power, thus enabling the believer to live according to the Spirit (holy/righteous behavior). Sanctification is not only about individualized holiness, but about social holiness as well. To be "sanctified" is to live out holiness toward others in acts of love. For Pentecostals, God's sanctifying grace in individual lives is a prelude to what God will do in all of creation at the end. Just as the Spirit delivers believers from the "plague" of sin through sanctification, God will one day deliver creation from its pain and suffering. In the meantime, however, Pentecostals see their involvement in the world as participating in God's grand mission of re-creation. As a result of being transformed in sanctification, Pentecostals see themselves as agents of renewal to society, renewing society by doing acts of holiness, confronting evil powers, and engaging social injustice through the Spirit. Evil, in other words, for the Pentecostal is an existential reality not only found in individual lives but manifested in institutions and social entities by way of racism, suffering, nihilism, and alienation; these evils, according to Pentecostals, need

justice through Christ's cross and renewal by the Spirit's power.

Future Research

The Pentecostal understanding of evil is largely thought of in terms of spiritual powers causing such atrocities as sickness and suffering in humanity. Evil, for Pentecostals, is not deduced into philosophical propositions, but is a reality in which humanity is embedded; therefore, deliverance from this evil is achieved by Christ's cross and resurrection, which are the necessary ingredients for any satisfaction of justice or wholeness. Because Pentecostals have viewed existential evil as something to overcome by spiritual warfare, they have not adequately formulized a theology of suffering. Also, a formal theology of the philosophical problem of evil from a Pentecostal perspective has yet to be written. Future research will need to highlight how a Pentecostal awareness of spiritual powers contributes to the traditional problem of evil by integrating it into formal philosophical thought. Such a study would prove promising for Pentecostals and Christians worldwide as we continue to understand and confront evil.

B. Scott Lewis

See also Discernment, Spiritual; Sanctification

Further Reading

Carson, D. A. (1990). *How long, o Lord? Reflections on suffering and evil*. Grand Rapids, MI: Baker.

Boyd, G. (1997). *God at war: The Bible and spiritual conflict*. Downers Grove, IL: InterVarsity.

Boyd, G. (2001). *Satan and the problem of evil*. Downers Grove, IL: InterVarsity.

Feinberg, J. S. (1994). *The many faces of evil: Theological systems and the problem of evil* (Rev. ed.). Grand Rapids, MI: Zondervan.

Hannah, V. A. (1983). Original sin and sanctification: A problem for Wesleyans. *Wesleyan Theological Journal, 18*(2), 47–53.

Johns, C. B. (2004). From strength to strength: Neglected role of crisis in Western and Pentecostal discipleship. *Wesleyan Theological Journal, 39*(1), 137–53.

Kärkkäinen, V.-M. (2002). "Evil, love, and the left hand of God": The contribution of Luther's theology of the cross to an evangelical theology of evil. *Evangelical Quarterly, 74*(3), 215–234.

Macchia, F. D. (1995). Repudiating the enemy: Satan and demons. In S. M. Horton (Ed.), *Systematic Theology* (Rev. ed.; pp 194–213). Springfield, MO: Logion.

Pinnock, C. H. (2001). *Most moved mover: A theology of God's openness*. Grand Rapids, MI: Baker.

Sanders, J. (1998). *The God who risks: A theology of providence*. Downers Grove, IL: InterVarsity.

Sanders, J. (2003). "Open Theism": A radical revision or miniscule modification of Arminianism? *Wesleyan Theological Journal, 38*(2), 69–102.

Thomas, J. C. (1998). *The Devil, disease, and deliverance: Origins of illness in New Testament thought*. Sheffield, UK: Sheffield Academic.

Tiessen, T. (2000). *Providence and prayer: How does God work in the world?* Downers Grove, IL: InterVarsity.

Truesdale, A. L. (1984). Christian holiness and the problem of systematic evil. *Wesleyan Theological Journal, 19*(1), 39–62.

Exorcism

Exorcism refers to the expulsion of an evil spirit or spirits (generally called "demons") out of the person who is "possessed" or tormented and controlled by the spirit(s) inside. Exorcism is also sometimes referred to as *deliverance*. While independent Pentecostal churches appear always to have practiced exorcism, Pentecostal denominations have downplayed the ministry of exorcism during most of the twentieth century. Perhaps this is because a focus on demons "tends to evade human responsibility and to denigrate the sovereignty of God" (Macchia 1995, 203). The exception to such reluctance to "give glory" to the devil would be in cases of physical disease or affliction, which are often seen as caused by demons. In the ministry of exorcism, the Christian is participating in the eschatological Kingdom of God. Jesus asserted that the Kingdom of God had broken into this age by His driving out demons by the power of God (Matthew 12:28). That kingdom is not yet manifested fully, but it is present now, particularly in the anointing given the believer by the authority of Christ—and the power of the Holy Spirit—to continue the ministry of Christ on earth.

Biblical Evidence of Demons

The Bible mentions "unclean spirits" (Matthew 10:1; 12:43; Mark 3:11; Luke 8:29; Acts 5:16; Revelation 16:13) and "evil spirits" (Matthew 12:45; Luke 7:21; 8:2; 11:26; Acts 19:12–16). These spirits can afflict those who lack a covenant relationship with God; they may also oppose God's sovereignty and seek to attack God's people. Some evil spirits are identified by their function, such as a seducing spirit (1 Timothy 4:1) or a spirit of divination (Acts 16:16). Their aim is to destroy human beings created in God's image (1 Peter 5:8; compare 2 Corinthians 2:11). The activities of demons include encouraging and empowering idol worship (1 Corinthians 8:4; 10:19–21), causing various physical ailments, hindering the gospel (Matthew 13:19; 2 Corinthians 4:4), and blinding, deceiving, and ensnaring unbelievers (Luke 22:3; 2 Corinthians 4:4; 1 Timothy 3:7; Revelation 20:7, 8). That people can be possessed is shown in the ministry of Jesus, who performed many exorcisms (Matthew 8:16; 9:32; compare 12:26–28; Mark 5:2–13), and in that of the early apostles (Acts 5:16; 8:6, 7; 19:13–18). The usual New Testament phrase for demonization is "to have" a demon.

Possession and "Demonization"

Though the biblical term *daimonizomai* is often translated in English versions as "possessed" by a demon, the actual meaning may be closer to "afflicted," "troubled," or "oppressed" by a demon. Since the idea of "possession" implies complete power over the afflicted, Pentecostals have difficulty dealing in any category of demonization that does not manifest itself as total control. Pentecostals do make a distinction between demonic possession and demonic influence. The former is considered to occur from "within," where the body is entered and a dominating control is gained over the personality. The latter is considered to occur from outside the victim, without dominating the personality. This warfare from without is carried on by suggestion, temptation, influence, and bodily affliction. Christians can be influenced or afflicted in body by demons, but may not be possessed.

Unbelievers are more vulnerable to spiritual attack. Little thought seems to be given to how much more, or to what causes or allows demonization in unbelievers. On this point ideas vary from the opinion of pastor and writer Kenneth Hagin, who sees all unbelievers as more or less controlled by Satan, to those who see demonic influence as widespread but full "possession" as rare. In all of this, the Pentecostal understanding seems little different than that of some Evangelical writers such as Merrill F. Unger and C. Fred Dickason.

"Symptoms" and Discernment

The symptoms of demonization vary according to the severity of the case. Such symptoms range from negative emotions to compulsive, destructive behaviors. Even when counseling reveals causes sufficient to explain such behaviors, if the sufferer cannot find relief after cooperating with the counselor a demonic agent may be what keeps the sufferer in bondage.

Other symptoms may be religious in nature, such as idolatry, occult practices, the use of charms, or compulsive and extreme asceticism. Different voices, astounding strength, and strong antipathy to the name of Jesus are considered especially strong symptoms of demonic possession. Having a "spirit guide," a spirit entity that promises special guidance and help in this life, is considered a form of demonization, although such persons often feel very positive about the "spirituality" of having such a guide and resist any negative view of their association. If not alienated beforehand, the sensitive and spiritually aware Christian may be able to help such a person when the "spirit guide" begins to be a problem.

The need for spiritual discernment is extremely important. Exorcism should never be attempted without a clear spiritual understanding or revelation by the Holy Spirit that the problem is indeed demonic. Merely evaluating such "symptoms" as those described above cannot give one certainty that an evil spirit is at work. All of these symptoms can be caused by something other than the intrusion of an evil spirit. Many psychoses have been "misdiagnosed" by overeager exorcists to the damage of the sufferer. The Bible distinguishes between illness and possession (Mark 3:10–12), and this will hold for mental illnesses as well. To distinguish whether symptoms derive from psychosis or possession is very difficult without honest, humble seeking for spiritual discernment in prayer. Like people today, people in the ancient world did not attribute all mental ailments to demons.

Causes of Demonization and Possession

Little thought has been given to the reasons why some unbelievers are possessed, while most are not. There must be some barrier to demonic possession operating in or for the unbeliever. Although evil spirits may influence everyone on occasion, few appear to have been "possessed" even in ancient times. Perhaps it is a matter of giving demons entrance or invitation into the person affected. Persistence in evil or malevolence, such as unforgiveness, vengeance, working to harm, or cursing others (in the sense of wishing harm to befall them) may well open one to demonic intrusion (see Ephesians 4:24).

Occult practices are seen by Pentecostals as an open door to demonization and eventual possession. Such practices range from involvement in many practices considered innocent by contemporary society. Such things as ouija boards, psychic readings, séances, water dowsing, and horoscopes are popular but not considered "serious" occult involvement in secular and liberal Christian circles. In contrast, Pentecostals see them as being as dangerous as witchcraft. Involvement with spirit guides, being introduced to one in a Spiritist church, or contacting spirits through ceremonies such as in séances or indigenous religions—which may be taken as angels or the spirits of dead ancestors—is considered extremely dangerous by Pentecostals.

In the latter half of the twentieth century, the idea of "generational curses" or ancestral sins has been proposed as one potential source of demonization. Even Evangelicals are suggesting that such issues should be dealt with at conversion.

Methods of Exorcism

Pentecostals reject the idea that only an ordained person has the authority to perform exorcism. Every Christian is endowed with authority (Greek *exousia*) because she or he has been sealed by the Holy Spirit and elevated in status to sit with Christ in the heavenlies (Ephesians 1:13; 2:6; compare Colossians 3:1–3). This is true whether or not the particular believer has experienced the infilling of power (Greek *dunamis*) through the baptism in the Holy Spirit. In practice, exorcisms are usually left to a pastor, elder, or one who is known to "have an anointing" (to be empowered) for exorcism. However, these do not hold an office of exorcist and are often not ordained. Pentecostals note that there is no gift of exorcisms listed in such texts as 1 Corinthians 12 or Romans 12. The only applicable gift would be that of "discerning of spirits" (1 Corinthians 12:10). This does, however, point up the necessity of gaining discernment in the case of each sufferer thought to be possibly "possessed."

Although some "deliverance ministries" have developed elaborate "binding" rituals, designed to render the inhabiting demon powerless and unable to remain in the sufferer, Pentecostals generally reject any such liturgies of exorcism. They see the mechanics of exorcism as simple, even if the procedure may be long and arduous. The two primary methods of deliverance among Pentecostals are prevailing prayer for and over the afflicted person and the name of Jesus, used with a sense of authority to command the demon to release the person. However, even this formula may not always be strictly necessary. Other methods include quoting Scriptures regarding the victory of Christ over spiritual powers (often spoken to the demonic presence) and enthusiastic praise and worship to God.

Pentecostal scholars have been very skeptical of such practices as commanding the demon to divulge its name and then using that name to expel it (after all, why would a deceiving spirit tell the truth?). They do not believe that "conversing" with evil spirits is healthy. In the last quarter of the twentieth century, however, many Pentecostal pastors and congregations have adopted charismatic deliverance practices such as those advocated by Don Basham or Neil Anderson. Such practices include discovering the name of the demon and whether that demon is the "strongman," or the most powerful demon presently inhabiting the afflicted person. Other practices focus on giving and receiving forgiveness (sometimes as a statement of absolution) and renouncing any occult practices or curses, even those engendered by parents, grandparents, or great-grandparents. It remains to be seen if Pentecostal denominations will continue to allow such practices, embrace them, or condemn them.

Toward the Future

Pentecostals are faced with two challenges. First, Pentecostal scholars and denominations must respond to the charismatic approach to deliverance as a species of healing or inner healing. Perhaps the question of the legitimacy of inner healing should be considered as well. Second, Pentecostals should develop an understanding of exorcism (and/or deliverance) that helps them engage unbelievers. Helping unbelievers to recognize and avoid the dangers of spirit guides, divination, and other encounters with the spirit world would lead toward effective evangelization of postmodern people in the West and of shamanistic cultures in the third world.

To do so, Pentecostals must revisit their perception of idolatry. The idea of "idolatry" is usually discussed as putting "things" or perhaps ambition ahead of God, rather than in terms of involvement in occult practices. Understanding the spirit world as active in and through the physical, even "secular," world will serve as a beginning.

A major aspect of the ministry of Jesus was casting out demons. This was perhaps the most startling demonstration to the first-century world that the kingdom and power of the Creator God was breaking into the world through Christ and his people. Such a demonstration is sorely wanted today, especially in the Western world.

JAMES M. HENDERSON

See also Binding and Loosing; Deliverance

Further Reading

Anderson, N. T., & Warner, T. M. (2000). *The beginner's guide to spiritual warfare.* Ann Arbor, MI: Vine/Servant.

Basham, D. (1972). *Deliver us from evil.* Washington Depot, CT: Chosen Books.

Basham, D. (1974). *A manual for spiritual warfare.* Greensburg, PA: Manna.

Canty, G. (1976). Demons and casting out demons. In P. S. Brewster (Ed.), *Pentecostal doctrine* (pp. 241–257). Cheltenham, UK: Grenehurst Press.

Collins, W. D. (1993). An Assemblies of God perspective on demonology. Part I. *Paraclete, 27*(4), 26.

Dickason, C. F. (1987). *Demon possession and the Christian.* Westchester, IL: Crossway.

Duffield, G. P., & Van Cleave, N. M. (1983). *Foundations of Pentecostal theology.* Los Angeles: L.I.F.E. Bible College.

Gross, E. N. (1990). *Miracles, demons, and spiritual warfare: An urgent call for discernment.* Grand Rapids, MI: Baker.

Hagin, K. E. (1984). *Ministry to the oppressed.* Tulsa, OK: Faith Library Publications.

Harper, M. (1970). *Spiritual warfare.* Plainfield, NJ: Logos International.

Hogan, J. P. (1983). Spiritual warfare. In G. Jones (Ed.), *Conference on the Holy Spirit digest: A condensation of plenary session and seminars of the Conference on the Holy Spirit in Springfield, Missouri, August 16–18, 1982* (Vol. 2, pp. 28–31). Springfield, MO: Gospel Publishing House.

Lagerwerf, L. (1985). Witchcraft, sorcery, and Spirit possession—pastoral responses in Africa. *Exchange—Bulletin of Third World Christian Literature, 14,* 1–62.

Macchia, F. D. (1995). Repudiating the enemy: Satan and demons. In S. M. Horton (Ed.), *Systematic theology* (pp. 194–213). Springfield, MO: Logion.

MacNutt, F. (1999). *Healing.* Notre Dame, IN: Ave Maria.

Pearlman, M. (1981). *Knowing the doctrines of the Bible.* Springfield, MO: Gospel.

Powlinson, D. (1995). *Power encounters: Reclaiming spiritual warfare.* Grand Rapids, MI: Baker.

Prince, D. (1998). *They shall expel demons: What you need to know about demons—your invisible enemies.* Grand Rapids, MI: Chosen Books.

Prince, D. (n.d.). *Expelling demons: An introduction into practical demonology.* Fort Lauderdale, FL: Author.

Scanlan, M., & Cirner, R. J. (1980). *Deliverance from evil spirits: A weapon for spiritual warfare.* Ann Arbor, MI: Servant.

Unger, M. F. (1971). *Demons in the world today: A study of occultism in the light of God's word.* Wheaton, IL: Tyndale House.

Unger, M. F. (1977). *What demons can do to saints.* Chicago: Moody.

Experience, Theology of

Classical Pentecostalism and the Charismatic and Neocharismatic movements stress the availability and even necessity of contemporary, ongoing encounter

Excerpt from Smith Wigglesworth's *Ever Increasing Faith*

I went to the Vicarage, and there in the library I said to Mrs. Boddy, "I cannot rest any longer, I must have these tongues." . . . She rose up and laid her hands on me and *the fire fell.* I said, *"The fire's falling."* Then came a persistent knock at the door, and she had to go out. That was the best thing that could have happened, for I was ALONE WITH GOD. Then He gave me a revelation. Oh, it was wonderful! He showed me an empty cross and Jesus glorified. . . . Then I saw that God had purified me. It seemed that God gave me a new vision, and I saw a perfect being wihin [sic] me with mouth open, saying, "Clean! Clean! Clean!" When I began to repeat it I found myself speaking in other tongues. The joy was so great that when I came to utter it my tongue failed, and I began to worship God in other tongues as the Spirit gave me utterance. . . . The experiences in the Holy Spirit will not end until you are in heaven—till you are right in the presence of God forever.

Source: Wigglesworth, S. (1971). *Ever increasing faith* (pp. 112–113). Springfield, MO: Gospel Publishing House. (Original work published 1924)

with and empowerment by God through the Holy Spirit. They maintain that New Testament manifestations of the Spirit such as speaking in tongues, prophecy, healing, and visions should mark Christian experience today no less than they did in the Church's first century. This emphasis is their essential and unifying distinctive characteristic and causes them to diverge from cessationist traditions within Christianity that see these types of experience as having phased out with the close of the apostolic period and the development of the canon of Scripture.

Experience in Pentecostalism

Classical Pentecostalism's understanding of spiritual experience cannot be properly discussed without reference to what the movement terms "the baptism of the Holy Spirit." The place of this experience within the movement's theology can only be appreciated in light of its historical background. The nineteenth-century Holiness movement in America promoted sanctification as a "second blessing" of grace available to Christians subsequent to their initial conversion to Christ. Penitents received justification, or pardon from sin, by faith at conversion. In the subsequent experience of sanctification the dominance of the sinful nature was broken through faith in the work of Christ. This experience of sanctification was also sometimes spoken of as a "baptism of the Holy Spirit." Some elements of the movement, however, began to reinterpret the accepted Holiness paradigm. As a result of a powerful postsanctification spiritual experience in 1895, Benjamin Hardin Irwin (b. 1854), founder of the Fire-Baptized Holiness Church, began to distin-

guish between sanctification as a second work of grace and a "third blessing" of a spiritually empowering "baptism with the Holy Ghost and fire."

Development of this distinction proved to be formative for Pentecostal origins and theology of experience. Irwin's departure from the traditional Holiness theological fusion of sanctification and Spirit baptism captured the attention of Holiness devotee Charles Fox Parham (1873–1929). Parham, however, remained less than satisfied that anyone, including Irwin and his followers, perceived the true nature of this third experience as described in the New Testament in such passages as Acts 2:1–4. He also became aware of past occurrences of speaking in tongues (glossolalia) among such groups as Edward Irving's (1729–1834) Catholic Apostolic Church in England. It is possible that by Parham's October 1900 launch of Bethel Bible School in Topeka, Kansas, he already hypothesized that speaking in other tongues was the true evidence that one had received the baptism of the Holy Spirit. Any prior suspicion he might have felt in this regard was confirmed when speaking in tongues broke out among the Bethel students during prayer for the baptism of the Holy Spirit on 1 January 1901. Thereafter Parham began preaching a three-fold experiential Christianity that included justification, sanctification, and baptism of the Holy Spirit marked by speaking in other tongues.

In 1905 Parham took his theology to Houston, Texas, and opened a second Bible school. Here William Joseph Seymour (1870–1922) imbibed Parham's third-blessing theology with its distinctive emphasis on tongues as the "Bible evidence" of the baptism of the Holy Spirit. Seymour traveled with this doctrine to Los Angeles in 1906.

As he preached and prayed his novel message first on Bonnie Brae Street and then at Azusa Street, fervent revival broke out, marked by powerful spiritual experiences, including speaking in tongues. News spread quickly (particularly via Seymour's publication *The Apostolic Faith*), and Parham's theology of a "third blessing" of the baptism in the Holy Spirit evidenced by speaking in other tongues penetrated the Christian community. Thousands flocked to the Azusa Street mission from 1906 to 1909 so that they too might receive their baptism of the Spirit. As Holiness churches were caught up in this distinctive revivalistic stream, they frequently felt compelled to follow Parham and Seymour in revising their views to distinguish the second blessing of sanctification from the baptism of the Holy Spirit. Indeed, Seymour dedicated much energy in *The Apostolic Faith* from 1906 to 1909 to providing theological justification for this distinction to the larger Holiness community of which he perceived himself to be a part.

Fledgling Pentecostalism's budding theology soon faced a challenge that involved a return to a revised "two-blessing" conception of Christian experience. William H. Durham (1873–1912), who had received his Pentecostal experience at Azusa Street in 1906, returned there in 1911 preaching that sanctification was a "finished work" that occurred at conversion. Thus, the baptism of the Holy Spirit with speaking in tongues rather than sanctification was the second experience Christians should seek following justification. Seymour barred Durham from Azusa Street, but Durham's reductionism gained increasing momentum among Pentecostals, especially those that had entered the movement from outside the Holiness tradition. The eruption in 1914 of further struggles over biblically correct water-baptismal formulas and the nature of the Trinity resulted in the formation of the Oneness branch of Pentecostalism in which baptism of the Holy Spirit and tongues speech were seen as taking place concurrently with conversion.

These beginnings have bequeathed twenty-first century Pentecostalism three main schools of thought concerning the baptism of the Holy Spirit. Several branches (e.g., Church of God, Cleveland; Pentecostal Holiness) hold that the baptism of the Spirit is the third initiatory experience important for Christian development. In this view, following conversion a believer must seek sanctification. Once this purifying experience has been secured, the believer is then encouraged to go on to seek the empowering baptism of the Holy Spirit with the accompanying evidence of speaking in tongues as promised to believers by Jesus in Acts 1:8 and granted for the first time in Acts 2:4. An individual who has received this empowerment evidences it by spontaneously speaking forth prayer and praise to God in a "tongue" (language) previously unknown to the recipient. This experience functions for the believer as a gateway to a deeper spiritual life and a more effective testimony to the gospel. The second widely held view (e.g., Assemblies of God) is that the baptism of the Holy Spirit is a second experience available to Christian believers subsequent to their conversion to Christianity. Those subscribing to this view do not discount the importance of sanctification, but they hold that this occurs forensically in conjunction with one's initial conversion experience and is then worked out practically in a progressive growth in holiness. The Oneness position (e.g., United Pentecostal Church) departs from both of the former views and regards the baptism of the Holy Spirit and speaking in tongues as the evidence of conversion itself.

Reckoning with the historical and theological issues surrounding the baptism of the Holy Spirit is essential to understanding Pentecostalism's theology of experience. However, to focus solely on the doctrinal developments concerning the baptism of the Holy Spirit or the often-sensationalized issue of speaking in tongues is to overlook the essence of the Pentecostal perspective on spiritual experience—encounter with God. For Pentecostals, their experience of the Spirit allows them to stand in spiritual continuity with the apostolic church of the first century. In their encounters with the Holy Spirit they believe themselves to participate in the same divine reality that gave rise to earliest Christianity. "Here and now, there and then are telescoped and traversed by the Spirit…" (Land 1993, 98). In the Spirit they drink not from an old river of tradition but from the same divine spring from which the founders of the faith quenched their own spiritual thirst. Their encounter with God through the Holy Spirit links them not only to the past but to the future as well. Manifestations of the Spirit's power appear in many forms (e.g., the spontaneous utterance of a prophecy through a member of the assembled believers, the miraculous "anointing" or inspiration of a preacher, or someone's sudden deliverance from a debilitating vice). But in every case the demonstration of the Holy Spirit's power heralds the future age of spiritual restoration in which Christ will reign supreme in millennial glory and put evil under His feet.

Experience and the Charismatic Movement

While it may be impossible to pinpoint the beginning of the Charismatic movement, Episcopalian clergyman Dennis Bennett's 3 April 1960 announcement to his Van Nuys, California, congregation that he had spoken in tongues brought wide public attention to the phenomenon. As the movement penetrated mainline denominations in the 1960s and 1970s, Christians from traditional and liturgical backgrounds experienced the baptism of the Holy Spirit, speaking in tongues, and other phenomena associated with Pentecostalism. Believers might be "slain in the Spirit," becoming aware of the Holy Spirit's immanent presence to such a degree that they would fall to the ground in an unconscious or trancelike state. They might be so suffused with joy at the presence of God that they would break into a spontaneous step described as "dancing in the Spirit." This overwhelming sense of the divine presence of God in the Spirit might produce "holy laughter" or "singing in the Spirit." The same encounter might produce intense joy for some and a deep sense of repentance for others.

The rise of this movement produced a fresh approach to theologizing concerning the baptism of the Holy Spirit. Classical Pentecostal interpretations viewed the baptism of the Holy Spirit as an empowering experience effected through a *reception* of the Spirit. As Christians from mainline denominational backgrounds and eventually Roman Catholicism flooded the ranks of those having experienced powerful encounters with the Holy Spirit, they reflected on their experiences from a theological perspective that instructed them that they had already received the Holy Spirit at the time of their confirmation or baptism in water. What then were they to make of this new reality of God's Spirit? The answer seemed to be that this new experience was a *release* or *actualization* of the Holy Spirit who was already present within their lives as Christian believers.

This approach reflected the movement's understanding of the larger significance of the Spirit-inspired experiences flourishing among its adherents. Tongues speech, prophecy, miracles, visions, and other occurrences reminiscent of apostolic and classical Pentecostal testimonies were taken by those in the Charismatic movement as renewing influences bringing new life and vigor to ecclesiastical structures that had grown dull and brittle. Many denominations, including Roman Catholicism, ultimately moved not to stamp out this vivifying stream but to incorporate it into their traditions. Neocharismatics share much with this perspective, accepting "pentecostal-like experiences" (Burgess 2002, 928) but not identifying themselves with classical Pentecostalism or its terminology.

Unifying Motif: Encounter with God

Pentecostals, charismatics, and neocharismatics, while all functioning within the sphere of Christian doctrine, have different ecclesiastical backgrounds. Yet they are all characterized by similar "pneumatic" experiences. Among these the baptism in the Holy Spirit and speaking in tongues have been defining issues in the rise and development of the Pentecostal and Charismatic movements. More than any others these experiences of the Spirit have represented for Pentecostals and charismatics the heart of a renewed faith in Christ not bound to move solely in the cognitive realm but unleashed to function in the spiritual, emotive, and even physical aspects of human life. Indeed, this emphasis on spiritual renewal has allowed for a wide variety of encounters understood to be capable of carrying worshippers beyond their natural abilities into a greater spiritual freedom. Within this diversity the fundamental continuity between these groups' theologies of experience rests not in any exact duplication of doctrines but in their common ethos of direct, personal encounter with God through the immanent presence of the Spirit. They take the biblical idea of "God with us" (Matthew 1:23) very seriously, understanding it to be literally true not only historically in the person of Jesus but presently through the person of the Spirit. Encounter with God may occur through sacrament, service, or printed text, but it is not limited to this. It is personal, and those in these movements regard their experiences and the visible effects of those experiences as previews of a coming eternal celebration in the presence of God.

ROBBY J. KAGARISE

See also Baptism in the Holy Spirit; Ecstasy; Sanctification

Further Reading

Anderson, R. M. (1979). *Vision of the disinherited: The making of American Pentecostalism*. Peabody, MA: Hendrickson.

Bennett, D. J. (1970). *Nine o'clock in the morning*. Plainfield, NJ: Logos International.

Burgess, S. M. (2002). Neocharismatics. In S. M. Burgess (Ed.), *New international dictionary of Pentecostal and Charismatic movements* (p. 928). Grand Rapids, MI: Zondervan.

Cox, H. G. (1995). *Fire from heaven: The rise of Pentecostal spirituality and the reshaping of religion in the twenty-first century*. Reading, MA: Addison-Wesley.

Dayton, D. W. (1987). *Theological roots of Pentecostalism*. Metuchen, NJ: Hendrickson.

Ervin, H. M. (1968). *These are not drunken as ye suppose (Acts 2:15)*. Plainfield, NJ: Logos International.

Land, S. J. (1993). *Pentecostal spirituality: A passion for the kingdom* (Vol. 1). Sheffield, UK: Sheffield Academic Press.

McDonnell, K. (1975). *The Holy Spirit and power: The Catholic charismatic renewal*. Garden City, NY: Doubleday & Company, Inc.

Nelson, P. C. (1981). *Bible doctrines*. Springfield, MO: Gospel Publishing House.

Ruthven, J. (1993). *On the cessation of the charismata: The Protestant polemic on postbiblical miracles* (Vol. 3). Sheffield, UK: Sheffield Academic Press.

Synan, V. (1997). *The Holiness-Pentecostal tradition: Charismatic movements in the twentieth century* (2nd ed.). Grand Rapids, MI: William B. Eerdmans.

Synan, V. (2001). *The century of the Holy Spirit: 100 years of Pentecostal and charismatic renewal, 1901–2001*. Nashville, TN: Thomas Nelson.

Synan, V. (2003). *Voices of Pentecost: Testimonies of lives touched by the Holy Spirit*. Ann Arbor, MI: Servant Publications.

Williams, J. R. (1996). *Renewal theology: Systematic theology from a renewal perspective*. Grand Rapids, MI: Zondervan.

Faith, Gift of

Traditional theology usually distinguishes between "ordinary" or "saving" faith and "extraordinary" or "miraculous" faith. The "gift of faith" is traditionally seen as miraculous, since it is listed with healing and miracles in 1 Corinthians 12:9. This distinction, however, is not based on an analysis of scripture, but on the sharp Protestant distinction between faith for salvation (available today) and faith for miracles (which died with the Apostles). Scripture knows no such distinction; it sees all faith as a revelatory gift from God. St. Paul's listing faith as a "spiritual gift" simply recognizes that fact: His intention is not to place the gift of faith in a wholly different and usually inaccessible category for the normal believer. How, then, do different church traditions describe faith?

Faith in Christian Traditions

In *Summa Theologica* Thomas Aquinas defined faith as "the act of the intellect when it assents to divine truth under the influence of the will moved by God through grace," but Aquinas's mechanical schematic gave way to a more dynamic sense of faith in the Reformation. Against human "works" as a means to salvation, Martin Luther insisted on "faith alone," which, while it produced good works, represented a strong spiritual recognition of God's grace. To the reformers, faith came in response to the preached "Word"—the message of the Gospel or scripture. The object of this faith was salvation, in the sense of being destined for heaven. Faith was a Spirit-empowered response to God's truth, a gift of God's grace. However, in their overzealous rejection of Roman Catholic claims to miracles, both Luther and John Calvin follow John Chrysostom in their negativity toward the gift of faith, ignoring its biblical purpose for building up the body of believers. They all note that Judas, the betrayer of Christ, had the gift of faith to do miracles, but did not possess "saving faith." Accordingly, the gift of faith (the miraculous, extraordinary work of the Spirit) was only worthy of brief notice as a historical artifact in Protestant theological works and commentaries.

In Pentecostal and charismatic traditions, faith has been understood in a variety of ways. The theological vacuum surrounding the gift of faith and divine healing before the beginning of the twentieth century appears to have been filled by the only available teaching on faith for healing at the time: Christian Science and related sects. Christian Science is notable for its revival of certain Gnostic themes—for example, the denial of evil, particularly sickness, and the emphasis on faith as willpower or human effort. Followers also believe that strenuous affirmations of "divine reality" rather than recognizing illness (or "error") will bring the physical into line with the "divine mind."

Many early healing evangelists insisted, accordingly, that the physical characteristics of sickness represented the unreal, "lying symptoms of the Devil." Faith then involved the denial of these "lying symptoms" by strenuously affirming the divine perspective in the form of God's promises in scripture (for example, "I am the Lord that healeth thee") until the lying symptoms fell into line with the promises or Word of God. A variation of this teaching was that faith represented the fusion of the *logos* Word (Scriptural promises) with the *rhema* Word (a revelation or assurance from God). On this model, faith came by affirming scriptural promises until the *rhema* assurance effected the solution. An oft-quoted verse "faith cometh by hearing and hearing by the Word of God" meant that faith comes (one feels the divine assurance) via an affirmation and application of God's biblical promises to a need ("hearing the Word").

Some even went so far as to teach that one should never pray, "if it be Thy will," because prayer denied the promises of God to heal all our diseases and therefore weakened the resolve and faith of the one praying. Similarly, many denied the validity of medicine or physicians, arguing that they demeaned a sick person's faith in God's power to heal. However, most healing practitioners, including the major Pentecostal denominations, were uncomfortable with such extreme statements.

The term, "faith healing," then, emphasized faith in God's power to heal, rather than, as some critics suggested, on divine healing, which focused on God's act of healing as He initiates faith. Despite its critics, this model of faith dominated the teaching and preaching of most of the famous faith healers in the mid-twentieth century: Oral Roberts, William Branham, A. A. Allen, Jack Coe, T. L. Osborne, and Gordon Lindsey. The more recent derivative, the "faith teaching" or "word of faith" movement, is more closely associated with faith healers Kenneth Hagin, Kenneth Copeland, and Robert Tilton. Traditional Pentecostal denominations, however, have mostly distanced themselves from this latter movement, though they were heavily influenced by the earlier faith-healing theology.

The onset of the Charismatic Renewal since the 1960s brought fresh thinking about faith. The widespread encounter with the Holy Spirit within what were formerly called mainline churches brought with it a level of intellectual sophistication and a Romantic worldview that shaped a renewed interest in spiritual gifts. The new practitioners of healing tended to see faith less as a breaking of the supernatural into the natural (a model that was rightly rejected as unbiblical) than as an inherent expression of the Spirit-resident. The new movement also resisted the tendency of having faith in one's faith, replacing it with a new appreciation for listening prayer. This concept, certainly, was not unusual in older Pentecostalism, but the new charismatics like Francis MacNutt and John Wimber were more careful to allow the prayer of faith to be shaped by the leading of the Spirit rather than by a dogmatic and inflexible application of biblical promises for healing or other needs. In fact, for charismatics the prayer "Thy will be done" had the effect of building faith rather than hindering it. The reason for this was

that they sought the divine assurance of faith immediately and directly from God rather than forcing the appearance of faith through a one-size-fits-all positive confession. In this the new charismatics moved toward a more biblical view of the gift of faith.

Gift of Faith in Scripture

Biblical faith consists of the discernment of God-revealed assurance and aggressive, joyous, tenacious obedience to it with the goal of expressing the character, life, and power of God—that is, realizing the fullest possible expression of the Kingdom of God on earth. In practical terms, many recent Pentecostal and charismatic teachers believe that biblical faith means discovering what God wills in a specific case and aligning ourselves with God's goal and doing what needs to be done via prayer or other action until the original perception of God's will is realized.

The gift of faith itself is described in Hebrews 11:1 as "the assurance (Greek *hupostasin*) of things hoped for, the conviction (Greek *elengchos*) of things not seen." The primary meaning of both these Greek words is "the thing itself" or "the actual material" and not the derived meanings of "assurance," "conviction," and "proof." One could read this passage, then, as "Faith is experiencing the 'thing-itself' of what we hope for; the actual manifestation of what is not seen." The "experiencing" and the "manifestation" not only reveal what God has given us, but are so real as to be the thing itself. This may be similar to a prophetic vision in which the prophet, via the Spirit, is experiencing the events he is predicting. Obviously, this is a strong experience of faith. But Hebrews 11 appears to be teaching that faith is a revealed experience of an event removed from us in space or time.

Prominence of the Gift of Faith

If the above description is accepted for the gift of faith, then scripture informs us to a much greater extent than if we are limited to word studies that can be translated as "faith." In this regard, a number of other words encompass the dynamics of faith in scripture—for instance, divine wisdom, assurance, boldness, Kingdom of God, and Holy Spirit ("God has not given us a spirit of fear, but of power, love and discipline" 1 Timothy). Indeed, since about 60 percent of both the Old Testament and the New Testament appears in narrative form, descriptions of behavior, as in Hebrews 11, as well as formal didactic instruction in, say, the New Testament epistles, are valuable modes of teaching about faith.

In either case, the enormous emphasis on faith in scripture is clear. Placed as prominently as possible in the key narratives—for example, Eve and Adam (Genesis 3), Abraham (Genesis 12), Jacob (Genesis 37:5), Moses (Exodus 3), the Covenant at Sinai (Exodus 19), and the commissionings of the prophets (1 Samuel 1; Isaiah 6; Jerome 1; Ezekiel 1–3). This prominence also occurs in the didactic teaching of the Bible (for example, 1 Corinthians 1–3; Romans 1; Galatians 3; Hebrews 11; and James 1:2, 5–8; 2:14–-26). The prominent location of this teaching in these books shows the centrality of revelation and action in the life of faith: The choice is between the revelatory knowledge and experience of God (the life of faith) and the alienation from God based on one's own desires and mental resources.

The crucial and determining temptation to both the first and second Adam (Genesis 3; Matthew 4; Luke 4) is a pattern for all mankind—the first denies the life of faith and the second affirms it. The temptation of Eve is essentially the same as that of Jesus, except that the temptation in the Gospels is more sophisticated. Here the Tempter tries to induce Jesus to preapply or misapply scriptures to himself without heeding the biblical wisdom of when and how these principles apply (Proverbs 26:7). In each temptation, Jesus is careful not to claim a promise on his own initiative without first receiving the appropriate assurance of faith from the Father that the scriptural principle applies in this case. The so-called name-it-and-claim-it faith teaching fails at exactly this point. Faith, then, involves hearing from God before responding (Romans 10:17; Galatians 3:2–5).

Faith as Response to Revelation

What people do in response to God or Jesus is as telling as what they say. The Bible offers many examples of aggressive, extreme responses to God's promises. Abraham, of course, appears as a positive example of faith (hearing and obeying) (Romans 4:12, 16; Galatians 3:7; Hebrews 11:8, 17) and a negative one (Genesis 16, 21). He surrendered his homeland and his only, long-awaited son in response to God's command. Moreover, when Elisha told King Joash to beat arrows on the ground (2 Kings 13:18–19) the king did so in a half-hearted way, showing he lacked aggressive faith to execute God's will. The long story of David's fleeing Saul yet being consistently obedient and clinging to God's promises showed David's great faith. A favorite Pentecostal biblical story is that of David's mighty men, all of who serve as examples of aggressive, tenacious faith (2 Samuel 23:8–21).

In the Gospel of Mark, major miracle stories, which occupy a large amount of the text, point the reader ex-

plicitly to an unusual, tradition-breaking, aggressive faith in the quest for wholeness—for instance, the outrageous act of tearing apart a neighbor's roof to get a paralyzed man to Jesus (2:1–12); the ruler of a synagogue who faced the loss of status by consulting Jesus (5:21–24, 35–43); the woman with a menstrual disorder who dared to defile Jesus by touching him for healing (5:25–34; 7:21–37; 8:14–29; 10:46–52). The Book of Hebrews catalogues the amazing difficulties overcome by those with aggressive, desperate faith (11:37–38; Matthew 11:12).

Results of Faith

While most Pentecostals and charismatics strongly promote the traditional view that faith results in salvation—that is, attaining heaven through the atoning work of Christ—they also affirm what the Reformers denied—that is, the legitimacy of faith for healing and miracles. In fact, in the Synoptic Gospels, faith "is used almost exclusively in relation to miracles" (France 1992, 223). Throughout the New Testament, 93 of 223 instances of the *pistis* family of words ("faith"), or over 40 percent, apply to healings and exorcisms. The gift of faith, then, is not an expendable appendage to theology but occupies the very center of Christian experience.

Jon Mark Ruthven

See also Charismata; Gifts of the Spirit; Healing, Gifts of; Miracles, Gifts of; Positive Confession Theology

Further Reading

Baker, K. (1997). Hebrews 11—The Promise of Faith. *Review and Expositor, 94,* 439–445.

Clark, G. (1983). *Faith and saving faith.* Jefferson, MD: Trinity Foundation.

Dulles, A. (1994). *The assurance of things hoped for: A theology of Christian faith.* New York: Oxford University Press.

Farah, C. (1979). *From the pinnacle of the temple.* Plainfield, NJ: Logos.

France, R. (1992). Faith. In J. B. Green, S. McKnight, & I. H. Marshall (Eds.), *Dictionary of Jesus and the Gospels.* Downers Grove, IL: InterVarsity Press.

Gossett, D., & Kenyon, E. W. (1981). *The power of positive confession of God's word.* Tulsa, OK: Custom Graphics.

Hagin, K. (1983). *How to turn your faith loose.* Tulsa, OK: Hagin Ministries.

Hagin, K. (1966). *What faith is.* Tulsa, OK: Hagin Ministries.

Hellwig, M. (1990). A history of the concept of faith. In J. Lee (Ed.), *Handbook of faith* (pp. 3–23). Birmingham, AL: Religious Education Press.

Marshall, C. (1989). *Faith as a theme in Mark's narrative.* New York: Cambridge University Press.

McKelway, A. (1990). The systematic theology of faith: A Protestant perspective. In J. Lee (Ed.), *Handbook of faith* (pp. 164–202). Birmingham, AL: Religious Education Press.

Michel, O. (1975). Faith. *New International Dictionary of New Testament Theology* (Vol. 1, pp. 587–606). Grand Rapids, MI: Zondervan.

Neuman, H. (1990). Cultic origins of word-faith theology within the charismatic movement. *Pneuma, 12,* 32–55.

O'Collins, G., & Kendall, D. (1992). The faith of Jesus. *Theological Studies, 53,* 403–423.

Price, F. (1979). *Faith, foolishness, or presumption?* Tulsa, OK: Harrison House.

Pullum, S. (1999). *'Foul demons, come out!' The rhetoric of twentieth century faith healing.* Westport, CT: Prager Press.

Reid, M. (2002). *Faith: It's god given.* Fairfax, VA: Xulon.

Schlatter, A. (1963). *Der Glaube im Neuen Testament.* Stuttgart, Germany: Calwer Verlag.

Tillich, P. (1957). *The dynamics of faith.* New York: Harper & Row.

Wagner, C. P. (1988). *The third wave of the Holy Spirit.* Ann Arbor, MI: Servant.

Warner, S. (2000). *Experiencing the knowing of faith: An epistemology of religious formation.* Lanham, MD: University Press of America.

Wigglesworth, S. (1971). *Ever-increasing faith.* Springfield, MO: Gospel Publishing House. (Original work published in 1924)

Yaconelli, M. (1998). *Dangerous wonder: The adventure of childlike faith.* Colorado Springs, CO: Zondervan.

Yeung, M. (2002). *Faith in Jesus and Paul: A comparison with special reference to 'Faith that can remove mountains' and 'Your faith has healed/saved you.'* Tübingen, Germany: Siebeck.

Feminism

Feminism is defined as a human rights movement seeking to remove restrictions against women and advocating the advancement and emancipation of women. Feminist theories emanate from a belief in the equality of the genders and apply to all aspects of society: religious, political, and socioeconomic. This article provides an overview of how two renewal movements, the Pentecostal and the Charismatic, have responded to feminism.

Early Pentecostals and Feminist Practices

At the beginning of the twentieth century, Pentecostal revivalists called for a restoration of apostolic Christianity and a separation from what they considered the cold and indifferent mainline churches. Feminism was generally not an issue to these restorationists. Their apparent feministic practices, such as the ordination of women ministers, evangelists, and missionaries, were based on selected proof texting and the literal interpretation of Joel 2:28, 29 (NIV) ("I will pour out my spirit upon all flesh and your sons and daughters shall prophesy.... And also upon the servants and upon the handmaids in those days will I pour out my spirit.") Furthermore, the priesthood of all believers and the "blessed hope" of the imminent return of Jesus to set up his earthly kingdom marshaled all Pentecostals to spread the gospel "to every living creature" (Titus 2:13; Mark 16:15). They were called to fulfill the Great Commission (Acts 1:8). Pentecostals believed this was possible because they had been sanctified, spoke in other tongues as the Spirit of God gave them utterance, prophesied, experienced both the gifts and the fruits of the Spirit. A divine calling and an anointing was a life calling. To comply with this "heavenly call," both women and men were welcomed to join the "latter day rain" and spread the gospel to all nations (Barfoot and Sheppard 1980, 4).

Max Weber (1968) proposed that "the religion of the disprivileged (or disinherited) classes...is characterized by a tendency to allot equality to women." He insists, however, that this practice does not continue beyond the first generation, or when the religious organization moves from the prophetic to the priestly stage. This theory seems to be validated by two Pentecostal denominations—the Apostolic Faith Mission (Portland, Oregon) and the International Church of the Foursquare Gospel (Los Angeles, California)—both begun by women, with the rite of succession falling to their sons.

Subsequently, as American Pentecostalism institutionalized into the "priestly stage," major leadership roles fell to males in all Pentecostal denominations. Women were allowed to serve as leaders in women's groups, curriculum development positions, and children's ministries. This change has been accompanied by a steady decline in the percentage (not necessarily numbers) of ordained women ministers and appointed missionaries. Most of the seminary teachers and senior pastors continue to be males.

Weber's argument describing early Pentecostals as disprivileged or disinherited is problematic at best. What distinguished these disprivileged, nonprivileged, and privileged classes? The first two terms are pejorative and assume a mass movement of lower socioeconomic peoples converting to an exuberant form of worship. If the privileged were the mainline,

Carol Wiseman's "Lament of the Daughters"

This poem by Carol Wiseman, Founder and Director of The Center for Faith Leadership and biblical feminist scholar, addresses the status of women within the Church and the oppression of women within the body of Christ. While men are most often the oppressors of God's daughters, this poem laments that in reality God's battle is waged between the seed of Eve and the enemy of God, Satan. Nonetheless, Wiseman believes the battle can be won when men become aware of the oppressive role they play. This poem describes the pain that exists while the army of God remains a partial army, because His daughters are not allowed to fulfill their God-ordained purpose in bringing about the Kingdom.

How long O God, how long?
How long must we travail without a covering?
How long will you leave us in bondage, in oppression?
Would we have been better off in Egypt?

How long will our cries for freedom
Be ignored, be silenced,
How long will they fall on deaf ears?
On defiant platforms?

We cry out for freedom
Freedom to be who you, our great Creator,
    created us to be
To fulfill our destiny in you,
To deposit into the kingdom, the priceless treasures
You endowed us with at the breathing of your Ruach
    into us, creating life.

Grant O Yahweh, that freedom might come,
That the bonds of Eden be loosed,
That we might again be favored daughters
walking in freedom with you
searching and seeking your Holy wisdom and knowledge

How Long O God will our voices be silent,
Our hands desolate to perform thy great works,
Our gifts be unopened, our healing hands prevented
Our prophetic words refused?

How long before the war has overcome our brothers
Who refuse to allow us to help heal?
How long Oh God of Eve, of Rachael, of Mary
Before this day's daughters might perform the miracles
You placed within them?
How Long?

Will you circumcise again?
Will you circumcise the hearts of men?
That the daughters today might birth
the gifts within them, as Sarah and Mary
birthed the miracle you placed within them?
The travail is so long, so hard, so painful.
It is not for ourselves we cry out, but for those
Oh God who keep us in bondage
For it is their freedom that we seek,
That they might know the joy of
The blessings of thine hand within the daughters
For here you have placed a healing balm
A prophetic word, a lament for the nations,
    and indeed for them

How long will Egypt stand, will oppression rule?
How long will sin abound that your grace might
    therefore more abound?
Forsake not the creation of thine hand,
    the other side of you,
The feminine side of you

How long must Rachael weep?
How long must we travail with your divine gifts
    pent up inside us?
How long will bondage remain?
Let this day be the end, Oh Mighty Creator of All
Let the hearts of the Fathers turn toward you
With right understanding that your daughters
were created at your hand; equal
Created as your partners and theirs.

His Needs, Her Needs

In *His Needs, Her Needs,* Willard F. Harley Jr.'s book on saving marriages (a popular guide used by Pentecostal couples), Dr. Harley notes the following:

A man's five most basic needs in marriage:

1. Sexual fulfillment
2. Recreational companionship
3. An attractive spouse
4. Domestic support
5. Admiration

A woman's five most basic needs in marriage:

1. Affection
2. Conversation
3. Honesty and openness
4. Financial support
5. Family commitment

Source: Harley, W. F., Jr. (1986). *His needs, her needs. Building an affair-proof marriage* (p. 10). Old Tappen, NJ: Fleming H. Revell.

middle-class denominations entrenched with traditional patriarchalism, then the fledgling Pentecostals should not be labeled disprivileged or nonprivileged. While many adherents were recent immigrants and laborers, most Pentecostals separated from these "privileged systems" when they felt the power and moving of the Holy Spirit. Often both nuclear and extended families were fragmented when a spouse, child, aunt, uncle, or grandparent began attending a Pentecostal brush arbor revival or storefront church. Historian Grant Wacker (2001) correctly proposes that Pentecostals were a "cross section of the American population." At the same time, David Martin (2002) continues the myth of religious classism when he describes American Pentecostals as "the uprising of . . . the damned of the earth in the form of the redeemed."

Outside North America, quite another demographic finding is reported. In Africa and China, Pentecostalism appeals to the best educated in urban areas. In Latin America, Pentecostalism brought significant changes in domestic relations, with wives allowed to take initiatives in extra-domestic activities. Pentecostal men are jeered for yielding to their wives, who also believe that they have the right and responsibility to call their husbands to account for their waywardness.

Pentecostal women also are allowed greater informal power in church affairs.

The greatest charismatic feminist of the twentieth century was Sarasvati (Pandita) Ramabai (1858–1922). Pandita was a compassionate Indian social reformer, scholar, diplomat, and pioneer in spiritual renewal. In January 1905 she issued a call to prayer among the widows housed at her ashram at Kedgaon (Mukti) and other Christian women in West Central India. By June a major outpouring of the Holy Spirit came to Mukti and lasted until 1907. Pandita Ramabai's work is understood by many scholars to be the beginnings of Pentecostalism in India.

Later Pentecostals and Feminist Practices

On 2 September 2003 Wendy McElroy of FOX News proclaimed the advent of a new movement known as "Christian Feminism." This is a "school within the broader feminist tradition that seeks to define woman's liberation and her equality with man through reference to the Christian religion." What McElroy described was not really new, however. Small groups of Christian women, including Pentecostals, began to meet as early as 1976, to read, discuss, and to share research findings. Their largest opposition came from women in Fundamentalist churches, who could not admit to the major changes occurring in society.

Interestingly, Christian feminists, including many Pentecostals, still seek justification of their basic religious foundations. Despite scholarly evidence that godly women have been written out of history and the church's traditional theology of womanhood has been poisoned with misogyny, many Pentecostal women fall prey to a birth gender guilt. Pentecostal women generally shy away from dialogues that address basic issues, such as what it means to be a woman on a personal level, what it means to be a culture bearer of heritage and traditions, and what it means to be a woman in a global society.

Charismatics and Feminist Practices

Despite greater openness among Pentecostals to women in ministry during the early twentieth-century prophetic period, in subsequent years Christian feminism has flourished more successfully among their charismatic sisters. Clearly, hostility to women's leadership has provoked a more widespread indignation among charismatic communities than among Pentecostal women. Sociologist Paula Nesbitt has shown that decades of activism among both women and men in mainline Protestant denominations have permitted women to achieve full ordination and to assume clerical leadership as they feel called. In contrast, Pentecostal women do not see church leadership as their most pressing issue, certainly not in comparison to saving souls.

To a greater degree, women in the charismatic churches accepted society's expanding roles and responsibilities of women in leadership and the workplace. Their voices reflect scholarship, advocacy, mentoring, and social justice. While Women's Aglow started as a Spirit-led organization, the impact of changing societal mores encouraged a shift to group counseling as women became more vocal regarding divorce, abuses, and isolation. Many women in the charismatic churches became empowered to influence their churches' worship styles and mission programs. They brought vitality and an expanded belief system.

Looking Forward

During the transition from the era of prophet or prophetess to male-dominated priestly administration, Pentecostals attempted to distance themselves from the twentieth-century feminist movements. As the early,

vibrant female prophetesses and leaders passed, younger generations of women were not encouraged to assume such positions. In many cases, women were not encouraged to become missionaries, to attain senior pastor status, or to become district or national overseers or superintendents. Rather, they were kept in subservient places through fear, isolation, neglect, and intimidation. Selected negative stories perpetuated the myth that women were responsible for the fall of men and therefore could not be trusted in leadership positions.

While the schism between secular and Christian feminism is large, there are more underlying commonalities than they like to admit. Their emphasis on differences and their lack of toleration for one another will strengthen only those who benefit from the schism among women. Feminism is not an evil or pejorative word. Feminism carries the message that social justice can be a reality, both with and without a biblical mind-set.

RUTH V. BURGESS

See also Women

Further Reading

Aikman, D. (2003). *Jesus in Beijing: How Christianity is transforming China and changing the global balance of power.* Washington, D.C.: Regnery Publishing.

Barfoot, C. H., & Sheppard, G. T. (1980). Prophetic vs. priestly Religion: The changing role of women clergy in classical Pentecostal churches. *Review of Religious Research 22,* 2–17.

Blumhofer, E. (1993). *Aimee Semple McPherson: Everybody's sister.* Grand Rapids, MI: William B. Eerdmans.

Cavaness, B. (1994). God calling: Women in Assemblies of God missions. *Pneuma 16(1),* 49–62.

Chestnut, A. (1997). *Born again in Brazil: The Pentecostal boom and the pathogens of poverty.* New Brunswick, NJ: Rutgers University Press.

Cleary, E., & Stewart-Gambino, H. W. (Eds.). (1998). *Power, politics, and Pentecostals in Latin America.* Boulder, CO: Westview Press.

Corten, A., & Marshall-Fratani, R. (Eds.). (2001). *Between Babel and Pentecost: Transnational Pentecostalism in Africa and Latin America.* Bloomington: Indiana University Press.

Edwards, T. B. (1991). Ministry is not a male call. *The Youth Leader,* Jan/Feb.

Elliott, E. (1975). Why I oppose the ordination of women. *Christianity Today 6,* 12–16.

Gill, D. (1995). The contemporary state of women in ministry in the Assemblies of God. *Pneuma 17(1),* 33–36.

Griffith, R. M. (1997). *God's daughters: Evangelical women and the power of submission.* Berkeley: University of California Press.

Ingersol, S. (1994). Holiness women: Recovering a tradition. *Christian Century*, 29 June–6 July, 632.

Jewett, P. K. (1975). Why I favor the ordination of women. *Christianity Today*, 6 June, 7–12.

Lawless, E. J. (1988). *God's peculiar people: Women's voices and folk tradition in a Pentecostal church.* Lexington: The University Press of Kentucky.

Martin, D. (2002). *Pentecostalism: The world their parish.* Oxford, UK: Blackwell.

Nesbitt, P. D. (1997). *Feminization of the clergy in American occupational and organizational perspectives.* Oxford, UK: Oxford University Press.

Spencer, J. D. (Ed.). (1986). *Black women in the church: Historical highlights and profiles.* Pittsburgh, PA: Magna Graphics.

Stephenson, J. W. (1987). Reflections on the ordination of women. *Eastern Journal of Practical Theology*, 6–18.

Tucker, R. (1988). *Guardians of the great commission: The story of women in modern missions.* Grand Rapids, MI: Zondervan.

Wacker, G. (2001). *Heaven below: Early Pentecostals and American culture.* Cambridge, MA: Harvard University Press.

Warner, W. E. (1993). *Kathryn Kuhlman: The woman behind the miracles.* Ann Arbor, MI: Servant Publications.

Weber, M. (1968). *The Protestant Ethic and the Spirit of Capitalism.* New York: Scribner's Press.

White, C. E. (1986). *The beauty of Holiness: Phoebe Palmer as theologian, revivalist, feminist, and humanitarian.* Grand Rapids, MI: Francis Asbury Press.

Filled with the Spirit

To be filled with the Spirit is a dynamic encounter with the living God that normally results in a charismatic endowment of the Holy Spirit to fulfill the church's purpose as an eschatological missionary community (Acts 1:8). This article seeks to demonstrate the development of this view through a brief examination of the biblical, historical, and contemporary evidence of Spirit fullness, as well as the implications for the twenty-first century.

Biblical Evidence of Spirit Fullness

It is generally recognized that the soteriological activity of the Spirit in both the old and new covenants stands in close relationship (Genesis 15:6, Romans 4:1–25). Pentecostals, however, closely associate the charismata (gifts of grace) with the New Testament baptism in the Spirit—"filled with the Spirit" and "baptized in the Spirit" are synonymous terms for most Pentecostals (Acts 1:4–5, 2:1–4). Hence, the charismatic bestowal of the Spirit upon an individual in the Old Testament is not normally accentuated. The Hebrew Bible, nevertheless, depicts the Holy Spirit filling individuals (Exodus 31:3, Micah 3:8) and bestowing the charismata upon certain persons, empowering them to fulfill their missions.

Old Testament Evidence

This divine enablement of the Spirit anointed judges to overthrow the enemies that had subordinated Israel (Judges 3:10, 6:34, 11:29, 13:25). Moses, Joshua, David, and Solomon were all called to lead Israel; thus, the gift of wisdom was given to establish their authority and enable them to govern Israel (Deuteronomy 34:9, 1 Samuel 16:13, 18:5, 1 Kings 3:5–14). It is evident that the prophetic gift, as well as the charism of working of miracles, characterized the ministries of Elijah and Elisha (2 Kings 2:9–14). In fact, charismatically inspired speech was not an uncommon activity of the Spirit in the Hebrew Bible (1 Chronicles 12:18, 2 Chronicles 20:14, 24:20). The major and minor writing prophets were all inspired by the Spirit to speak and record their prophecies. It is important to note, however, that the experience of being filled with the Spirit in the old covenant was limited and temporary. Normally, the Holy Spirit would fill only certain individuals (prophets, warriors, judges, and kings), empowering them to fulfill a particular mission, and then withdraw when the task was accomplished.

The promise of the old covenant, however, is a new age of the Spirit that will be inaugurated with the coming of the Messiah. Ezekiel 36:25–27 depicts this promise as a new covenant that will transform the hearts of the participants, purify their conscience from sins, and indwell them through the Spirit. The prophet Joel spoke of the promise as a day when the charismatic endowment of the Spirit would be available to all of God's people (Joel 2:28–29). To be filled with the Spirit in the new covenant, therefore, is to be indwelt and empowered by the Spirit.

New Testament Evidence

The Gospels represent John the Baptist as a prophet of transition, preparing the way for the Messiah, who would inaugurate the eschatological age of fulfillment;

Acts 10: 44-46 (New International Version)

⁴⁴**While Peter was still speaking these words, the Holy Spirit came on all who heard the message.**

⁴⁵**The circumcised believers who had come with Peter were astonished that the gift of the Holy Spirit had been poured out even on the Gentiles.**

⁴⁶**For they heard them speaking in tongues and praising God.**

consequently, John's message and baptism were proleptic of the messianic Spirit baptism (Matthew 3:11). In fact, Jesus is depicted as the bearer of the Spirit. The Spirit effected Jesus' birth (Matthew 1:18–25), and He was filled by the Spirit at the Jordan River so that He was introduced as the Messiah, as well as empowered to fulfill his mission (John 1:31–34, Luke 4:14–19). Furthermore, Luke wanted his readers to understand that Jesus' desire for his disciples was that they also would be filled with the Spirit (Luke 24:46–49, Acts 1:4–5).

Classical Pentecostals recognize John 20:19–23 as the high priestly work of the resurrected Christ mediating regeneration to His faithful disciples by imparting the Spirit, thus fulfilling Ezekiel 36:25–27. Acts 2:1–4, accordingly, is the prophetic fulfillment of Joel 2:28–29, charismatically endowing the church as an eschatological missionary community (Acts 2:16–18). The emphasis of the Book of Acts is that being filled with the Spirit occurred with perceptible signs of charismatic endowments (Acts 8:15–19, 10:44–47, 19:6). In fact, if these signs of charismata were missing among believers, it was doubtful that they had been filled with the Spirit (Acts 8:12, 19:1–6).

The biblical evidence has shown that being filled with the Spirit is a dynamic encounter with the living God that normally results in a charismatic endowment of the Holy Spirit. Throughout the history of the church, this evidence has been both affirmed and questioned.

Historical Evidence of Spirit Fullness

The *Didache* (101 CE) is an early second-century document that depicts the charismata active among certain individuals in the early church. At this time in the history of the church, the charismatically endowed itinerant prophets and teachers were accorded the same importance as the ordained ministry.

The emergence of the Montanist movement (160 CE), however, seriously challenged the growing ecclesiastical authority invested in bishops as heirs of the apostles. The Montanists claimed to possess the final revelation to mankind—the New Prophecy—which superseded the teachings of Jesus and the apostles. The Montanists, therefore, asserted that their charismatically endowed movement was the true church, and the institutional church of the bishops was apostate. The result of this controversy was that the Montanist movement has forever been stigmatized with the charge of heresy, and the charismata became institutionalized and sacramentally invested in the office of the bishop.

Sacramentalism

The sacramentalist teachings of both the Western and Eastern churches are similar. The Holy Spirit descends on the waters of the baptismal font, and the catechumen receives the Spirit and is united to Christ and the church. During the rite of *confirmation* in the West or *chrismation* in the East, the person is filled with the Spirit in a new or fuller way than initially received at baptism; also, the person can expect to receive the charismata identified in Isaiah 11:2. Both traditions understand being filled with the Spirit is evidenced by a life of holiness.

There is some disparity between the East and West in their understanding of confirmation/chrismation and being filled with the Spirit. The West allows a separation of time between baptism and confirmation so that confirmation is an event subsequent to baptism. At this time, according to the West, a new character is imprinted on the recipient. The East, however, performs the rites of baptism and chrismation at the same event. For the East, chrismation is an extension of Pentecost, so that through the charismata all of the recipients are prophets and members of the royal priesthood. Also, the East understands chrismation as the beginning of a participation in the divine life leading to deification.

Although sacramentalists recognize the demonstration of the charismatic gifts as evidence of Spirit fullness—primarily among those who are canonized as saints—as well as less demonstrative signs, they are not concerned with external evidences of being filled with the Spirit.

Pentecostal View of History

Classical Pentecostals posit a view of church history that understands the early church was founded by the apostles in the demonstration and power of the charismata, known as the early rain (James 5:7–8). According to this view of history, the church entered an epoch of apostasy and a lacuna of the Spirit—beginning with the rise of sacramentalism and Constantinianism—until the modern outpouring of the Spirit. During this time, God was working to reform and restore truth to the church through various fringe groups and individuals such as Martin Luther and John Wesley. Classical Pentecostals, therefore, see the contemporary outpouring of the Spirit as the latter rain restoring the church to a charismatically endowed eschatological missionary community.

Contemporary Evidence of Spirit Fullness

Like storm clouds gathering for a great deluge to inundate all humanity, the Holiness revivals and Keswick Higher Life Movement were preparatory for the latter rain. Significant in this preparation is what happened at Bethel Bible School in Topeka, Kansas. Charles Parham (1873–1929), the founder and instructor of the school, assigned his students the task of searching the Scriptures to determine the biblical evidence of being filled with the Spirit. This Scriptural inquiry yielded the conclusion that glossolalia (speaking in tongues) is the Scriptural evidence of Spirit baptism (Acts 2:4, 10:46, 19:6; 1 Corinthians 14:1–33). On 1 January 1901, Agnes Ozman (1870–1937), who was a student at the Bible School, was filled with the Spirit and spoke in tongues. Soon Parham, as well as others, had received this Pentecostal experience. Thus, Parham began to carry the message across America that glossolalia is the initial evidence of Spirit baptism; however, it was one of his students, a black man named William J. Seymour, who would make his message heard around the world.

Classical Pentecostals

Most Pentecostal historians delineate the Azusa Street Revival of 1906–1909, under Seymour's leadership, as the time the latter rain began to fall. In true prophetic fashion, the Spirit crossed all social, racial, gender, and denominational barriers as believers were filled with the Spirit. Accordingly, the Azusa Street Revival influenced all the major Pentecostal movements. Most classical Pentecostals, therefore, affirm glossolalia as the initial evidence of being filled with the Spirit and that it is an experience subsequent to regeneration. The emphasis of this revival, however, was more than a renewal of glossolalia. In fact, those who were filled with the Spirit understood that they had received power to overcome the works of darkness and carry the gospel to the ends of the earth before the Parousia (Second Coming of Christ).

Charismatics

Beginning in 1960 and continuing into the twenty-first century, there has been a transdenominational renewal of the Spirit. Protestants, Catholics, and Orthodox alike have been filled with the Spirit and emphasized the present work of the charismata. This charismatic renewal has flowed out of a desire to experience the dynamic power of the Spirit within their particular church tradition; consequently, these believers have remained in their various traditions. Charismatics affirm glossolalia but do not always accept it as the initial evidence of Spirit fullness. Those charismatics who are of the sacramentalist tradition do not understand being filled with the Spirit as an experience separated from baptism and confirmation: it is the actualization or fulfillment of the sacramental initiation. Hence, charismatic renewal within the universal church has brought pressure on classical Pentecostals to accept groups they once considered apostate.

Neocharismatics

By 1980 there was a renewal of the Spirit among Evangelicals, who were filled with the Spirit and experienced glossolalia but refused to be labeled as Pentecostal or charismatic—commonly known as the *third wave* of the Spirit. Recently, Stanley Burgess broadened the term "third wave" and relabeled it neocharismatic, "to include the vast numbers of independent and indigenous churches and groups that cannot be classified as either pentecostal or charismatic" (Burgess 2002, xvii–xviii), yet they share a common emphasis of being filled with the Spirit and demonstration of the charismata. Significant to note is that many of these indigenous churches predate the contemporary (latter rain) outpouring of the Spirit in America.

Implications for the Twenty-first Century

Two corollary issues concerning Spirit fullness remain to be addressed in the twenty-first century: the issue of elitism—not all Christians are filled with the Spirit, thus creating an elite class in the church—and how Spirit fullness should be schematized into soteriology. The issues depicted here ask the questions: Is it possible for Pentecostals to speak about being filled with the Spirit in a manner so that it overcomes its elitist tendencies? How can Pentecostals define the terms so that they may speak in symphony about the role of the Spirit in conversion-initiation? Of course, how Pentecostals define the terms and understand history will have implications for the future of Pentecostal pneumatology.

Although there is a diversity of opinion among Pentecostals, charismatics, and neocharismatics concerning the evidence of Spirit fullness, there seems to be a consensus that being filled with the Spirit is a dynamic encounter that normally demonstrates charismatic manifestations. In addition, there is a common vision of world evangelization; therefore, the church is an eschatological missionary community.

HERSHEL ODELL BRYANT

See also Baptism in the Holy Spirit; Charismata; Evangelism; Latter Rain

Further Reading

Arrington, F. L. (2003). *Encountering the Holy Spirit: Paths of Christian growth and service.* Cleveland, OH: Pathway.

Burgess, S. M. (1989). *The Holy Spirit: Eastern Christian traditions.* Peabody, MA: Hendrickson.

Burgess, S. M. (1997). *The Holy Spirit: Medieval Roman Catholic and reformation traditions (sixth–sixteenth centuries).* Peabody, MA: Hendrickson.

Burgess, S. M. (2002). *The Holy Spirit: Ancient Christian traditions.* Peabody, MA: Hendrickson.

Dunn, J. D. G. (1970). *Baptism in the Holy Spirit: A Re-examination of the New Testament teaching on the gift of the Spirit in relation to Pentecostalism today.* London: S. C. M.

Hildebrandt, W. (1994). *An Old Testament theology of the Spirit of God.* Peabody, MA: Hendrickson.

Horton, S. M. (1976). *What the Bible says about the Holy Spirit.* Springfield, MO: Gospel Publishing House.

Land, S. J. (1993). *Pentecostal spirituality: A passion for the kingdom.* Sheffield, UK: Sheffield Academic Press.

McDonnell, K., & Montague, G. T. (1990). *Christian initiation and baptism in the Holy Spirit: Evidence from the first eight centuries.* Collegeville, MN: Liturgical Press.

McGee, G. B. (1991). *Initial evidence: Historical and biblical perspectives on the Pentecostal doctrine of Spirit baptism.* Peabody, MA: Hendrickson.

McQueen, L. R. (1995). *Joel and the Spirit: The cry of a prophetic hermeneutic.* Sheffield, UK: Sheffield Academic Press.

Schweizer, E. (1999). Pneuma pneumatikos. *TDNT, 6,* 332–453.

Fruit of the Spirit

The imagery of fruit is used by a number of authors in the both the Old and New Testaments (see Proverbs 1:31; Jeremiah 17:10; Hosea 10:12–13; Matthew 7:15–20; Romans 7:4–5; John 15:1–4; 2 Peter 1:8; Jude 12). The Pauline usage, in Galatians 5:22–23, provides the most studied consideration largely due to its connection to the work of the Holy Spirit. This theme has been much discussed in Pentecostal-Charismatic circles. References throughout Scripture use the fruit imagery as reflective of human behavior. These actions can be either productive or destructive, but when fruit is a corollary with the work of the Spirit, divine activity not human effort is emphasized. The bearing of fruit is wholly the work of the Holy Spirit. Fruit borne by the work of the Spirit is ultimately expressed in human action and relationship that express the character of Christ in tangible observable human interaction.

Gifts of the Spirit and Fruit of the Spirit

Gifts and fruit are similar in that they are only possible by the work of the Holy Spirit. Both gifts and fruit have as their central purpose to build up the followers of Jesus worshiping in committed community. Gifts and fruit are both maturable dimensions of spiritual life. Continual development, over a protracted period of time, is part of the reasonable expectation that followers of Jesus will have a continuing maturity into the image of Jesus Christ (Romans 8:29).

Distinctions between gifts and fruit are several. The gifts are charismatic empowerments for ministry, while fruit is the ethical expression of the indwelling presence of the Holy Spirit. While the gifts of the Spirit are given by the sovereign work of the Spirit and their manifestation is also at the initiative of the Spirit, followers of Jesus must all demonstrate all of the fruit of the Spirit.

Corinth provides a case study of how gifts without fruit can result in competition rather mutual support and self-interest rather than congregational maturity.

Gifts and fruit are not in competition with one another. The "most excellent way" is the mediation of the gifts through the fruit of the Spirit, primarily through love.

Early Pentecostal Reflection on Gifts and Fruit

Early Pentecostal writings reflected a desire to describe what interrelationship existed between the many dimensions of the life of the Spirit. Concern was evident that differences should be identified between the newly experienced Pentecostal life and Christian life for every person regardless of tradition. Early twentieth-century Pentecostal writers differentiated between the fruit of the Spirit, the gifts of the Spirit, and God-given abilities and talents, viewing each as necessary for mature Christian life. The fruit of the Spirit was not the result of a divine crisis experience, but an expected part of maturation in Christian life that became more consistently visible and deeply rooted in the believers whose lives were dedicated wholly to following Jesus.

The gifts of the Spirit were seen as a considerably different dimension of spiritual life. Gifts were not natural human abilities or qualities of human character that all Christians should manifest; gifts were the new supernatural initiative of the Spirit that indicated a unique presence of God in the believers' lives. The plethora of spiritual gifts was only open to those persons who had received the baptism of the Spirit with evidence of speaking in tongues. Spirit baptism did not automatically bring with it access to gifts; these had to be sought after subsequent to receiving Spirit baptism.

Further evidence of early Pentecostal teaching to clarify the dimensions of the work of the Holy Spirit is observed with early Pentecostal efforts to correct a perceived danger that taught that the fruit of the Spirit was clear evidence of the baptism of the Spirit. Pentecostal leadership countered this teaching by using the analogy of a tree and differentiating between sign and evidence. They posited that the leaves/sign of tongues would have to appear before the fruit/evidence of the Spirit. This analogy gives insight into the intentions of early Pentecostal leadership to guide participants in this movement with clear theological reflection that acknowledges the experience of believers and seeks to root it in biblical directive.

While little is specifically written about the fruit of the Spirit in the compiled Apostolic Faith papers published by the Azusa Street Mission in Los Angeles, the few times it is mentioned it does indicate clear understanding of the fruit of the Spirit as a replacement for the "fruit of sin." The minimal references do indicate that the fruit of the Spirit is clearly the result of a spiritual transformation and the necessary preparation for the baptism of the Holy Spirit.

Mid-Twentieth-Century Pentecostal Reflection

The development of the Pentecostal movement through the twentieth century provides further insight into how Pentecostals understood the fruit of the Spirit. There continues to be juxtaposition between gifts and fruit of the Spirit in the writings of Pentecostals. This is an indication that the writings are inevitably pastoral responses to perceptions about the work of the Spirit among Pentecostal believers. There is deep concern over people who receive the baptism of the Spirit and exercise certain gifts of the Spirit and yet do not exhibit a semblance of the fruit of the Spirit. Writers during this period challenge those who have outward manifestations, yet exhibit no ethics of character. The rhetorical question is regularly offered: How can there be a baptism of the Spirit that yields giftedness and does not make people holy?

Clarification about the connection between the gifts of the Spirit and the fruit of the Spirit continues in this period. There is definitive separation, with the baptism of the Holy Spirit said to yield supernatural gifts and the fruit of the Spirit coming from the Spirit of Christ in one's heart. Both Johannine and Pauline references are discussed with the abiding presence of Christ in one's life resulting in the fruit of the Spirit. It is even acknowledged that people who are not baptized in the Spirit can have holy lives; this due to the fact that they are walking and talking with Jesus and His character is revealed in their lives. It is readily acknowledged that some who display the supernatural power of God in their lives do not clearly demonstrate the holiness in their lives that results from spiritual fruit being borne in a deep abiding relationship with Christ.

Pentecostal writers during this era continually warn that possession of spiritual gifts is not the guarantee that the possessor has a right spirit. A person may have numerous gifts and manifestation in their lives, but without the love of God that is permanent, lasting fruit cannot be borne. Using the John 15 metaphor of the vine and branches Stanley Frodsham asks, "What is the sap of this heavenly Vine which, flowing into us will enable us to bring forth much fruit? It is the blessed Holy Spirit, and that is why the fruit is called the fruit of the Spirit" (Frodsham n.d., 71).

There is clear indication that the inevitable conflict between free reign for spiritual manifestations and some semblance of modicum and balance in congregational meetings impacts the discussion of the fruit of the Spirit during this time. When writing about the fruit of the Spirit in his 1932 book *Pentecost*, British Pentecostal Donald Gee describes his entire discussion of the fruit of the Spirit under one rubric: temperance/self-control. He is clearly speaking in response to a perception that spiritual equilibrium in some pastoral contexts is lacking. Gee says, "When Jesus comes into the heart, His Spirit controlling within produces as final fruit—temperance in all things" (Gee 1932, 81–82).

Charismatic Perspective

Reflection on the fruit of the Spirit by charismatic writers has seen this theme as the comprehensive designation by which the indwelling of the Holy Spirit impacts the believer's relationships to God and other people. The fruit are not viewed as biblical themes with merely emotional expression; rather they are seen as a quality of existence in the Kingdom of God. The Galatians 5:22–23 reference is exegeted with reference to the theme of "freedom" in this chapter. This new life of freedom, to walk in the Spirit, gives the possibility of true holiness. Striving after righteous living is not by human effort, but by the Spirit's enablement to fulfill the righteousness being sought after. There is not bondage, but freedom. The result of this walk of the spirit in freedom is "fruit," which the law could never produce. While the yielding of fruit is a long time in production, the results considerably outdistance anything that the law could accomplish. The Spirit of freedom, referred to in Galatians 5, allows believers to express the fruit of the Spirit in a great variety of ways, as they interact with the community of believers. This strengthens the community and causes an increased flourishing of spiritual maturity in the individual believer's life.

Current Pentecostal Exegesis on Galatians 5:22–23

Paul is quite intentional in using the term "fruit." The Galatians 5 reference to the "works of the flesh" (acts of sinful nature) is in sharp contrast to the usage of "fruit." In short, vices are "works" and virtues are "fruit." Paul clearly is suggesting that the Spirit has effectively replaced Torah. Not only do people who walk by the Spirit avoid walking in the way of the flesh, but also the Spirit effectively produces in them the very

character of God. Paul clearly is showing that when freedom is properly used by serving one another, people are empowered to do so by the Spirit. Believers cannot be passive, but must walk and live their lives in conformity to the Spirit's work.

The list of fruit in the Galatians 5 passage is also an intentional statement by Paul as to the breadth of the Spirit's captivity in the lives of believers. The list of virtues covers a wide span of dimensions of Christian life, both individually and in the community, supporting Paul's understanding of the all-encompassing nature of the activity of the Spirit. Each term or its cognate appears someplace else in Paul's writing and in every case is used in an ethical sense. Paul's usage of these terms must not be limited merely to the internal life of an individual believer, but must be seen in relationship to their impact upon the community of believers where the Spirit is present and working.

The list of the fruit of the Spirit is sometimes compared to the list of the gifts of the Spirit in 1 Corinthians 12:8–10 because of the parallel number of items in each list (nine). This perspective reads into Paul's logic as if Paul wanted there to be some correlation. The fruit and gifts lists are not compared in the Galatians 5:22–23 passage precisely because Paul is intentionally using the theme of fruit in this context. The context and the central argument of Paul in this entire book must be the overarching idea that informs interpretation of Galatians 5:22–23. Paul's argument in the book of Galatians is that the work of Christ and the coming of the Spirit have practically removed Torah as a guiding principle from the lives of God's people. He concludes this argument by saying, "Against such things here is no Law" (Galatians 5:23b, NIV). Torah is irrelevant when the fruit of the Spirit has been borne in a person's life and demonstrated in the community of believers.

Future Directions

Pentecostals and charismatics have regularly discussed gifts and fruit of the Spirit in an integrative manner because of deeply pastoral concerns over the experience of the Holy Spirit in believers' lives. The two dimensions of the Spirit's work are usually seen as the prophetic/missiological and the ethical/soteriological. These dimensions are regularly experienced in believers' lives simultaneously, yet need not be. Further study that would be helpful would include considering the concept "co-relational," which describes a relationship between two things that are frequently found together, but do not have a necessary causal relationship. This may be a helpful concept to develop further studies about gifts and fruit of the Spirit.

Byron D. Klaus

See also Charismata; Gifts of the Spirit

Further Reading

Christenson, L. (Ed.). (1987). *Welcome, Holy Spirit: A study of charismatic renewal in the church.* Minneapolis, MN: Augsburg.

Dayton, D. W. (Ed.) (1985). *Three early Pentecostal tracts.* New York: Garland.

Fee, G. D. (1994). *God's empowering presence: The Holy Spirit in the letters of Paul.* Peabody, MA: Hendrickson.

Frodsham, S. H. (n.d.). *Rivers of living water.* Springfield, MO: Gospel.

Gee, D. (1932). *Pentecost.* Springfield, MO: Gospel.

Gee, D. (1945). *After Pentecost: A sequel to "Pentecost".* Springfield, MO: Gospel.

Horton, S. M. (1994). *Systematic theology.* Springfield, MO: Logion.

Jacobsen, D. (2003). *Thinking in the Spirit: Theologies of the early Pentecostal movement.* Bloomington & Indianapolis: Indiana University Press.

Land, S. (1993). *Pentecostal spirituality: A passion for the kingdom.* Sheffield, UK: Sheffield Academic.

Lloyd-Jones, M. (1984). *Joy unspeakable: Power and renewal of the Holy Spirit.* Wheaton, IL: Harold Shaw.

McDonnel, K. (Ed.). (1980). *Presence, power, praise: Documents on the charismatic renewal.* Collegeville, MN: Liturgical.

Menzies, W. W., & Menzies, R. P. (2000). *Spirit and power: Foundations of Pentecostal experience.* Grand Rapids, MI: Zondervan.

Palma, A. D. (2001). *The Holy Spirit: A Pentecostal perspective.* Springfield, MO: Gospel.

Riggs, R. M. (1949). *The Spirit himself.* Springfield, MO: Gospel.

Williams, J. R. (1990). *Renewal theology: Salvation, the Holy Spirit, and Christian living.* Grand Rapids, MI: Academie.

Fundamentalism

"Fundamentalism" is a term broadly used today to describe a variety of radical religious movements throughout the world characterized by their opposition to modernization, secularization, and more recently globalization. The term was originally used to designate a conservative Protestant movement in North America that emerged in militant opposition to "liberalism" and "modernism" during the first decades of the twentieth century, leading historian George Marsden to quip, "A fundamentalist is an evangelical who is angry about something" (1991, 1). While this oppositional stance is often highlighted in descriptions of Fundamentalism, Christian or otherwise, it does not exhaust the identity of such movements today.

The origin of the term is found in a series of pamphlets called *The Fundamentals, or Testimony to the Truth* that were published in the United States between 1910 and 1915. In them were essays on biblical and theological topics written by a number of respected conservative authors from various denominational traditions. Underwritten by two wealthy laymen, some three million copies were distributed free of charge to church leaders throughout the English-speaking world. When William Bell Riley and a group of other conservatives called an organizing conference in 1919 for a new national association of like-minded church leaders, they chose the name "World's Christian Fundamentals Association." Harry Emerson Fosdick's 1922 sermon, "Shall the Fundamentalists Win?" helped seal the use of the term for theological conservatives while sharpening the divide between "fundamentalists" and "liberals" in the major Protestant denominations.

The term became more widely (and often derisively) associated in the popular imagination in the United States with traditional cultural values after the 1925 Scopes "Monkey Trial" in Dayton, Tennessee. There, in a courthouse, William Jennings Bryan and Clarence Darrow waged battle over a literal reading of the Bible, including the Genesis account of creation, versus a modern scientific worldview that included the theory of evolution. The erroneous notion that Fundamentalism is to be equated with rural values or premodern ways of thinking became hard to dislodge following 1925. Yet, as a Christian theological movement, Fundamentalism was just as likely to find a home in large urban churches. More important, it has demonstrated in its intellectual formulations a significant degree of dependence upon key elements of the same modern rationality that it seemingly opposes. Adherents have been particularly adept at embracing aspects of modern technology in making the case for their position. In many ways Fundamentalism is a child of the same modern spirit that it so vigorously seems to oppose.

Among the central theological tenets of the movement, five in particular have often been identified as the "fundamentals." These are belief in (1) biblical inerrancy; (2) the deity of Jesus Christ; (3) the virgin birth;

(4) substitutionary atonement; and (5) the bodily Resurrection and physical return of Jesus Christ. Most Fundamentalists adhere strictly to the doctrine of plenary inspiration, which is the belief that the Bible is inspired in all of its parts, although some would add that this doctrine only extends to the original manuscripts or languages. Some go so far as to embrace a dictation theory, which holds that the biblical writers were little more than secretaries taking down verbatim words that God intended to be revealed. Almost all Christian Fundamentalists reject the central tenets and practices of higher biblical criticism and its underlying philosophical presuppositions that regard the Bible as a human book comparable to other great books. The other doctrines, which pertain to a proper understanding of Jesus Christ, appear to Fundamentalist believers to follow from an affirmation of the literal truth of the Bible.

Ernst Sandeen has traced the biblical commitments of the movement into two nineteenth-century developments. The first is the Princeton school of theology identified with Charles Hodge, B. B. Warfield, and others. The Princeton school did not invent the doctrine of biblical inerrancy, but it extended it in scholastic debate against the emerging schools of biblical criticism coming to the U.S. shores from Europe. The Princeton theologians argued that in their original autographs the biblical texts were free of error not only in matters of faith and doctrine, but in matters of empirical claims and historical facts. Defense of the Bible became synonymous with defense of historical Christian faith against the corrosive claims of modern liberalism.

Sandeen traced the other root of twentieth-century Fundamentalism to John Nelson Darby's dispensational theology. Dispensationism was decisively premillennial in character (premillennialism teaches Christ's visible return at the beginning of a literal thousand-year reign on earth). Like most premillennial theologies, dispensationalism offered a pessimistic view of history that foretold social degeneration culminating in a time of tribulation just prior to Christ's Second Coming. Darby's particular version, however, introduced the novel notion of a secret removal, or "Rapture," of all true Christians just prior to this end-time tribulation. By the first decades of the twentieth century the prophetic time lines that Fundamentalists and dispensationalists popularized indicated that the end of the world was imminent. Fundamentalists withdrew from arenas of Christian social responsibility and in most cases from cooperative ventures with other movements or institutions, including those that were identifiably Christian. "Fundamentalist" became virtually interchangeable with "separatist" during this period.

The belief that Christians were about to be physically removed from the arena of historical tribulation was a major factor in the movement's pessimistic attitude toward social responsibility. The publication of Carl Henry's *The Uneasy Conscience of Modern Fundamentalism* in 1948 marks a major watershed in this regard and is often cited as one of the key texts in the emergence of neoevangelicalism movement from Fundamentalism. By the beginning of the 1960s, Fundamentalism had shrunk to become a small, right-wing flank of a new and growing Evangelical theological movement. A number of conservative Protestants in the United States and elsewhere continue to call themselves Fundamentalists today, but in general they seek to distance themselves from the more widely embraced and inclusive term "Evangelical."

The relationship of Fundamentalism to Pentecostalism, and more recently to the charismatic renewal, is complex. On the one hand, many early twentieth-century Pentecostal leaders such as Aimee Semple McPherson readily identified themselves as Fundamentalists. On the other hand on a number of points classical Pentecostalism clearly differed with Fundamentalism. Pentecostalism had its roots in the nineteenth-century Holiness movement whose teachings had coalesced around the four-fold Gospel of Jesus Christ as savior, sanctifier, healer and coming king. While the four-fold Gospel does not necessarily contradict the five fundamentals that were identified above, neither can it be reduced to them. Many early Pentecostals shared with Fundamentalists a commitment to biblical authority, but Pentecostals generally read the Bible through an experiential hermeneutical lens shaped by testimonies, which in turn emphasized the narrative character of biblical revelation over the propositional truth that Fundamentalists generally preferred. Pentecostalism was radically eschatological in its orientation and many of its early adherents embraced aspects of the dispensationalism that was a central component of Fundamentalism. But Pentecostals tended to regard the in-breaking of God's new age in ways that were more radical than what dispensationalism allowed.

There were other differences between the two movements. Fundamentalism was almost entirely an Anglo-American phenomenon, while Pentecostalism from its inception had a more multicultural character and a more global consciousness. Pentecostals were far more open to mystical experience than Fundamentalists were, while Fundamentalists embraced a more rational form of theology. Pentecostalism was often ready to reopen basic tenets of historical orthodox Christianity, including even the doctrine of the Trinity, while

Fundamentalism for the most part did not. Pentecostalism, like the Holiness movement before it, provided opportunities for women in ministry while Fundamentalists adamantly opposed this as unbiblical.

The most important divide between classical Pentecostals and Protestant Fundamentalists was over the issue of tongues and various other manifestations of the Spirit in worship. Fundamentalism organized itself as a movement around the ideological defense of the Bible. Its leaders consistently claimed to practice literal interpretation of Scripture. But Fundamentalism tended on both counts to lean in rational directions and favor expository biblical practices. A number of Fundamentalists adhered to the doctrine of cessationism regarding certain apostolic gifts reported in the pages of the New Testament. Their argument was that extraordinary gifts such as tongues or prophecy had been given in the New Testament period as a means of revelation, but that with the close of the apostolic age or the completion of the New Testament canon such gifts had ceased. Pentecostals implicitly accepted the notion that these gifts had generally diminished or ceased, but that this was only for a time. For Pentecostals it was axiomatic that the gifts had now been restored in the last days as the "latter rains" had begun to fall. Most Fundamentalists rejected such doctrines, leaving them with no option but to regard tongues and other visible manifestations of the Spirit as being either a result of self-delusion or, worse, a result of demonic deception. The latter belief was infamously illustrated by the Fundamentalist biblical commentator G. Campbell Morgan's statement that Pentecostalism was "the last vomit of Satan" (Anderson, 142).

Given these differences between the two movements, the fact that Pentecostals in the United States often sought to identify themselves with Fundamentalism is even more ironic. It should be noted that this identification was almost entirely confined to "white" or "Anglo" streams of early Pentecostalism. Few African-American or Mexican-American Pentecostals aligned themselves with Fundamentalism in the United States during the first decades of the twentieth century, nor was such identification made by Pentecostals in other parts of the world. Where the alignment did take place, it tended for Pentecostals to be more of a matter of cobelligerency rather than a true alliance. Pentecostal leaders found common ground with Fundamentalism in their shared opposition to what they perceived to be the lukewarm spiritual commitments of modern Christianity and to a lesser extent to the dangers of modern rationalism and criticism in

theology. Most Pentecostals shared with Fundamentalists an aversion to modern theology and its tendency to dismiss the miraculous aspects of faith in favor of scientific explanation.

A far stronger case can be made for Pentecostalism being a central factor in the emergence of neoevangelicalism from Fundamentalism after 1945. The largest group of churches that were part of the nascent organization of the National Association of Evangelicals in the early 1940s was Pentecostal. Pentecostal influences merged with Evangelical commitments in a number of parachurch movements during the 1950s and helped birth the Neopentecostal or charismatic renewal of the 1960s. With the emergence of what is sometimes called the "Third Wave" in evangelicalism in the 1970s and 1980s, the convergence of Pentecostal and Evangelical spirituality would seem to be complete. Fundamentalists, on the other hand, continue to oppose both movements as being deficient in their commitments to biblical absolutes and separatism.

At the beginning of this article it was noted that the term "fundamentalism" has become widely used to describe radical religious movements globally today. The most notable influence in this direction has been "The Fundamentalism Project," a major policy study sponsored from 1987 to 1994 by the American Academy of Arts and Sciences and directed by Martin E. Marty and R. Scott Appleby. Looking at religious movements across the world, the project identified a number of constants that define Fundamentalists. Whether Islam, Hindu, or Christian, Fundamentalists are absolutists regarding the sources of their authority and separatists in relation to other movements, even those with whom they share a broader religious identity. They are concerned to draw sharp boundaries around the truth that they claim to represent in their teachings and think of themselves as an embattled minority or remnant of the "elect" who alone are the true believers. Apocalyptic symbolism appears regularly in the rhetoric Fundamentalists espouse. Their struggle is portrayed in cosmic dimensions, with pronounced messianic and millennial themes appearing in the discourse. This latter tendency often leads to a militancy toward the wider society that embraces violence and at times even terror as legitimate means for advancing their position.

Here it is instructive to contrast the global Pentecostal movement today with Fundamentalism, Christian or otherwise. Pentecostalism is often identified with conservative political movements, and in many cases Pentecostal or charismatic churches have publicly supported right-wing political forces. But Pentecostals have also been identified with political movements of the left and in many cases have embraced a more progressive or prophetic political stance. Many first-generation Pentecostals in North America were pacifists, for instance, and counseled their members to seek alternative military service as conscientious objectors. Globally Pentecostal and charismatic churches today defy easy political categorization, while Fundamentalists are overwhelmingly identified with extreme right-wing political forces. On cultural and theological grounds, where Fundamentalists are committed to erecting borders to separate themselves from those who are less than "true believers," Pentecostalism has tended to be more inclusive. The global Pentecostal movement is not only much larger than its Christian Fundamentalist counterpart in this regard but is far more diverse in its teachings and practices. Pentecostalism has offered a vision that is open to something radically new, while Fundamentalism has tended to be the last remaining holdout for a dying order. Hence, while Pentecostalism and Fundamentalism might both be cited as movements that have challenged the hegemony of a modern intellectual world that is heir to the European Enlightenment, the two movements have parted ways regarding the solution that they offer.

DALE T. IRVIN

See also Scriptures, Holy

Further Reading

Anderson, R. M. (1979). *Vision of the disinherited: The making of American Pentecostalism.* New York: Oxford University Press.

Carpenter, J. A. (1999). *Revive us again: The reawakening of American Fundamentalism.* New York: Oxford University Press.

Henry, C. F. H. (2003). *The uneasy conscience of modern Fundamentalism.* Grand Rapids, MI: Wm. B. Eerdmans.

Marsden, G. M. (1980). *Fundamentalism and American culture.* New York: Oxford University Press.

Marsden, G. M. (Ed.). (1991). *Understanding Fundamentalism and evangelicalism.* Grand Rapids, MI: Eerdmans.

Marty, M. E., & Appleby, R. S. (Eds.). (1991–1995). *The Fundamentalism project: A series from the University of Chicago Press, 1–5.* Chicago: University of Chicago Press.

Sandeen, E. R. (1970). *The roots of Fundamentalism: British and American millenarianism 1800–1930.* Chicago: University of Chicago Press.

G

Gifts of the Spirit

If *gift of the Spirit* (singular) simply refers to the Holy Spirit of God understood as a gift conferred on God's people (see Acts 2:38, 8:20, 10:45, 11:17), then *gifts of the Spirit* (plural) are talents or capabilities given *by* the Holy Spirit. The Spirit is not the Gift but the Giver, or to put it another way, God the Giver confers certain abilities, and consequently certain practices, on the people of God *through* the Holy Spirit.

These gifts of the Spirit are not recognized as such in the New Testament unless and until they are actually put into practice. The debate, therefore, over whether these are natural talents present from birth, or supernatural talents given by virtue of what Christians call the *new birth*, or *baptism in the Holy Spirit*, is largely beside the point. They may or may not have been present from birth, but they are not gifts of the Spirit until they are put to work in the Christian community, enabling the community to do what it exists to do—that is, represent God in the world by confronting the world with God's message of new life in Jesus Christ.

New Testament Vocabulary

The precise Greek phrase for "gifts of the Spirit" never occurs in the New Testament. The operative terms are "spiritual things" (*pneumatika*; see Romans 15:27; 1 Corinthians 2:13, 9:11, 12:1, 14:1; Ephesians 1:3, 5:19; Colossians 3:16); "gracious gifts" (*charismata*; see Romans 11:29, 12:6; 1 Corinthians 12:4, 9, 28, 30, 31; also 1 Peter 4:10); "gifts" (*domata*, Ephesians 4:8; also *dōrea*, "gift," in Ephesians 3:7 and 4:7); "workings" (*energēmata*, see 1 Corinthians 12:6, 10); and "ministries" (*diakoniai*, see Romans 12:7; 1 Corinthians 12:5)—whether of God, Jesus, the Lord, or the Spirit.

Diversity and Unity

All these terms are ways of getting at the plurality of the Spirit, or the diversity of the working of God in Christian communities. To moderns, especially entering the twenty-first century, diversity is a positive value in itself, something for which to strive. In the world of early Judaism and early Christianity, by contrast, diversity was a given—in some sense a problem to be overcome. God was One in the Hebrew Bible (see Deuteronomy 6:4), and the Spirit of God was One. Yet because the Spirit's activity was often seen in relation to individuals or specific groups, the diversity of the Spirit's power and presence was constantly in evidence. The Spirit could be viewed rhetorically as plural when an author wanted to dramatize different virtues, as in relation to the expected Messiah: "The Spirit of the Lord will rest on him—the Spirit of wisdom and of understanding, the Spirit of counsel and power, the Spirit of knowledge and of the fear of the Lord" (Isaiah 11:2; cf. 1 Peter 4:14). Even the word *spirit* (*pneuma* in Greek) was occasionally used in the plural, not only with reference to evil or unclean spirits (as in the Gospels), but also referring to the varied activities of the Spirit of God. John, for example, in the book of Revelation sends greetings to the seven churches of Asia from God and "the seven spirits before his throne" (Revelation 1:4, also 5:6). The author of 1 John warns his readers not to believe every spirit, but to "test the spirits to see whether they are from God, because many false prophets have gone out into the world. This is how you can recognize the Spirit of God: Every spirit that acknowledges that Jesus Christ has come in the flesh is from God, but every spirit that does not acknowledge Jesus is not from God" (1 John 4:1–3; cf. 4:6).

Gifts in 1 Corinthians 12

The Apostle Paul articulates much the same principle: "No one speaking in the Spirit of God says 'Jesus is anathema,' and no one can say 'Jesus is Lord' except in the Holy Spirit" (1 Corinthians 12:3). This pronouncement introduces the most detailed discussion of spiritual gifts anywhere in the New Testament, centering on this very issue of unity and diversity. "There are varieties of gracious gifts [*charismata*]," Paul writes, "but the same Spirit. There are varieties of ministries [*diakoniai*] but the same Lord. There are varieties of workings [*energēmata*] but the same God who works them all in everyone" (1 Corinthians 12:5–6). The diversity was clear for anyone to see; what Paul does is affirm unity within this diversity. From a list of specific examples (12:7–11) he concludes, "All these are the work of one and the same Spirit" (12:11). The varied "showings" or "manifestations" (*phanerōsis*, 12:7) of the one Spirit of God to which Paul appeals here include "a message of wisdom" or of "knowledge" (12:8), "faith," "gifts of healings" (12:9), "working miracles," "prophecy," "discerning of spirits," "different tongues," and "interpretation of tongues" (12:10).

There is no evidence that Paul intended his list to be systematic or exhaustive. Some items fall into pairs, such as "tongues" and "interpretation of tongues," "prophecy" and "discerning of spirits," "message of wisdom" and of "knowledge," and perhaps "gifts of healings" and "working miracles." Yet "prophecy" and messages of "wisdom" or "knowledge" seem to overlap, while "faith" or "faithfulness" shows no particular relationship to any other item on the list. Its presence is strange, given Paul's insistence elsewhere on faith in Christ as necessary for salvation, and therefore as something common to *everyone* in the Christian community. Most of the gifts listed are gifts of speech, yet at least two (healings and miracles) are gifts of action, and we may well suspect that there were others (see 1 Peter 4:11: "If anyone *speaks*, he should do it as one speaking the very words of God. If anyone *serves*, he should do it with the strength God provides" [emphasis added]). If Paul was similarly conscious of a distinction between gifts of speech and of action, the question again arises of where faith belongs. Is it a gift of speech (see James 2:14–17), or action? At this point in the chapter the question remains unanswered.

Paul next introduces the metaphor of the human body, crowning his emphasis on unity with the conclusion that "we were all baptized by *one* Spirit into *one* body—whether Jews or Greeks, slave or free—and we were all given *one* Spirit to drink" (1 Corinthians 12:13; emphasis added). Far from being in tension, unity and diversity reinforce each other in Paul's argument. Only the recognition of the Spirit's unity can legitimize for him the Spirit's diverse expressions. He introduces a kind of fable in 12:14–26, in which he imagines different parts of the human body talking about their relationship to other parts, or to the body as a whole (for example, "Because I am not a hand, I do not belong to the body," 12:15; "I don't need you!" 12:21). The application comes in verses 27 through 30, where he again speaks directly of gifts: "first of all apostles, second prophets, third teachers, then miracles, then gifts of healings, helpful deeds, acts of service, different tongues" (12:28). He asks rhetorically, "Are all apostles? Are all prophets? Are all teachers? All miracles? Do all have gifts of healings? Do all speak in tongues? Do all interpret?" (12:29–30). The rhetorical questions echo (in part) the list just preceding, which in turn invites comparison with Paul's list earlier in the chapter (12:7–11).

The most conspicuous difference between the lists in 1 Corinthians 12:7–11 and 12:28–30 is that the latter begins with three items that refer not to powers or activities but to persons of status in the ancient church: apostles, prophets, and teachers. These are set off from what follows by being numbered from one to three, giving the impression that Paul has deliberately combined two kinds of lists, one applicable to the Christian Church generally and the other adapted specifically to a local congregation such as the one in Corinth. Of the six remaining items after "apostles, prophets and teachers," four coincide with the list back in verses 7 through 11. The only new items introduced are references to "helpful deeds" (*antilēmpseis*) and "acts of service" (*kybernēseis*). These are also the only two items from verse 28 that are not repeated in verses 29 and 30. When Paul asks, "Are all apostles? Are all prophets?" and so on, the two gifts he does *not* ask about are helpful deeds and acts of service. The reason for this is not hard to find: Helpful deeds and acts of service were not the sort of gifts that made others in the congregation envious. They are evidently the least "charismatic" of all the gifts in 1 Corinthians 12 and may not even have been counted among the gifts of the Spirit by anyone but Paul. They recall not so much the list in verses 7 through 11 as Paul's reference just before that to "varieties of ministries but the same Lord" and "varieties of workings but the same God who works them all in everyone" (12:5–6). Possibly they are ministries arising out of the gift of faith or faithfulness, which seemed to stand by itself in the previous list (12:9), unrelated to other gifts.

Presumably those who contributed to the work of the congregation by helping and serving others were the ones most tempted to say, "Because I am not a hand, I do not belong to the body"—that is, "Because I do not prophesy or work miracles or speak in tongues, I do not really count in the life of the congregation." Paul's purpose is not to list all the varied gifts of the Spirit, much less to rank them, but to attribute them all to the same Holy Spirit and make sure that faithful acts of service were not overlooked in the congregation's zeal for miracles and inspired speech. This is probably the point of Paul's strange reference to the "less honorable" or "unpresentable" parts of the human body that are "indispensable" and consequently treated with "special honor" or "special modesty" (12:22–24). He appears to have had in mind the male and female sex organs, which (in contrast to the foot, hand, head, eye, and ear in 12:15–21) go unmentioned in his extended illustration.

To introduce a modern analogy, the "helpers" and "servers" in a Christian congregation are like the coaching staff of a talented basketball team, who, though they lack the speed and athleticism of their players, are indispensable to the team's success. Paul appears to be making a case for these apparently ungifted movers and shakers in the Corinthian congregation, so that their efforts too might be recognized and appreciated as gifts of the Spirit. Near the end of 1 Corinthians, Paul urges his readers to "know [i.e., recognize] the household of Stephanas . . . the first converts in Achaia" for having "devoted themselves to the service of the saints. I urge you, brothers, to submit to such as these and to everyone who joins in the work, and labors at it" (1 Corinthians 16:15–16; cf. 1 Thessalonians 5:12–13). In 1 Corinthians 12 as well, Paul probably has in mind people of this sort, and he wants to make clear that their labors too belong among the spiritual gifts.

This emphasis sets the stage for a celebration of love in 1 Corinthians 13. Obviously, love is not one of the spiritual gifts, for no one can excuse a failure to love on the ground that "I don't have that gift." Yet if love motivates those who help and serve in the congregation without attracting attention to themselves, then love must govern as well the exercise of *all* the spiritual gifts. When it does, the gifts of the Spirit will be used without jealousy or arrogance to unify and build up the congregation, not divide or destroy it. In a very subtle way, Paul makes room for the apparently ungifted in his lists of the spiritual gifts, to the extent that when he urges, "But strive for the greater gifts" (12:31), it is by no means clear which ones he regards as greater.

Some have read this concluding sentence as an observation rather than a command, and more specifically as a rebuke, directed at those who are inappropriately striving for supposedly greater gifts. This would comport well with the notion that Paul is emphasizing the "lesser" gifts (or even non-gifts) of helping and serving. But this interpretation does not work, because at the beginning of chapter 14, after his excursus on love, Paul repeats what is unmistakably a command: "Pursue love, but strive for the spiritual gifts, especially that you may prophesy" (1 Corinthians 14:1). Prophecy, he argues, is greater than speaking in tongues (14:5) because it communicates meaning and therefore has the possibility of "building up" the congregation. Tongues-speaking also has this possibility, but only if it is accompanied by interpretation; otherwise it divides the hearer from the speaker. Paul can say, "I thank God that I speak in tongues more than all of you," while adding almost in the same breath, "but in the church I would rather speak five intelligible words to instruct others than ten thousand words in a tongue" (14:18–19). Paul was a charismatic, whether by ancient standards or modern ones, and yet the thrust of his argument in 1 Corinthians is to channel the charismatic experiences of his readers in such a way as to make them better servants to each other in the body of Christ.

Gifts in Romans 12

Paul accents the less celebrated gifts of helping and serving even more in Romans than in 1 Corinthians, with not even a mention of tongues-speaking, healing, or miracles. "We have differing gifts, according to the grace given us," he writes. "If it is prophecy, [let it be] in proportion to one's faith; if ministry, [let it be] in ministry; if a teacher, in teaching; if a preacher, in preaching; if sharing with others, [do it] generously; if caring for others, diligently; if showing mercy, cheerfully" (Romans 12:6–8). Here the "sharing," "caring," and "showing mercy" seem to correspond to the "helpful deeds" and "acts of service" in 1 Corinthians 12. Paul then adds, in the spirit of 1 Corinthians 13, "Let love be sincere. Hate what is evil; cling to what is good. Be devoted to one another in brotherly love. Honor one another above yourselves" (Romans 12:9–10).

Gifts in Ephesians

Paul speaks of gifts in one other place, echoing the "apostles, prophets and teachers" of 1 Corinthians 12:28. In Ephesians 4:8–11, he cites a biblical passage to illustrate the point that "To each of us grace is given according to the measure of the gift of Christ" (4:7). The passage is Psalm 68:18, which he quotes as "Having ascended on high, he led captive a host of captives, he gave gifts [*domata*] to human beings." These gifts are not explicitly gifts of the Spirit, but gifts of Christ made possible by His ascension to heaven and His consequent presence among His gathered people, understood collectively as his "body." Paul enumerates these gifts as "apostles, prophets, evangelists, shepherds, and teachers" (cf. 1 Corinthians 12:28), given "to equip the people of God for the work of ministry, to build up the body of Christ" (Ephesians 4:12). As in 1 Corinthians, the goal is "building up," or edification, and as in 1 Corinthians and Romans, the operative metaphor is the body of Christ.

Toward a Broader Definition

What emerges from this brief survey is that the New Testament, and Paul's contribution in particular, defines the gifts of the Spirit very broadly, so as to encompass both the natural and the supernatural, both what believers are miraculously *enabled* to do by the Spirit and power of God and what they are *willing* to do out of love for Christ and each other. It is perhaps largely because of Paul's influence that spiritual gifts have been defined rather broadly in the later Church, to include such acts or virtues as intercessory prayer, attentive listening, encouragement of others, sometimes even to the point of overlapping with what Paul elsewhere calls the "fruit of the Spirit" (see Galatians 5:22–23). Behind them all is a broad principle first expressed by John the Baptist—"A person can receive nothing unless it is given from heaven" (John 3:27)—and repeated explicitly by Paul—"What do you have that you did not receive?" (1 Corinthians 4:7). While modern Pentecostal and Charismatic movements have highlighted the gifts of tongues and prophecy in particular, they have also called attention to the gifts of the Spirit more generally, and in so doing have become agents of renewal in the wider Christian community.

J. Ramsey Michaels

See also Charismata; Fruit of the Spirit

Further Reading

Bridge, D., & Phypers, D. (1973*). Spiritual gifts and the church.* Downers Grove, IL: InterVarsity Press.

Bruner, F. D. (1970). *A theology of the Holy Spirit.* Grand Rapids, MI: Eerdmans.

Dunn, J. D. G. (1970). *Baptism in the Holy Spirit.* London: S. C. M. Press.

Ellis, E. E. (1978). *Prophecy and hermeneutic in early Christianity.* Grand Rapids, MI: Eerdmans.

Fee, G. D. (1987). *The first epistle to the Corinthians.* Grand Rapids, MI: Eerdmans.

Fee, G. D. (1993). Gifts of the Spirit. In *Dictionary of Paul and his letters* (pp. 339–347) Downers Grove, IL: InterVarsity Press.

Fee, G. D. (1994). *God's empowering presence: The Holy Spirit in the letters of Paul.* Peabody, MA: Hendrickson.

Goldingay, J. (1972). *The church and the gifts of the Spirit: A practical exposition of I Corinthians 12–14.* Bramcote, UK: Grove Books

Grudem, W. A. (1982). *The gift of prophecy in 1 Corinthians.* Washington, DC: University Press of America.

Hemphill, K. S. (1988). *Spiritual gifts: Empowering the New Testament church.* Nashville, TN: Broadman Press.

McGee, G. B. (Ed.). (1991). *Initial evidence.* Peabody, MA: Hendrickson.

Martin, R. P. (1978). *The Spirit and the congregation: Studies in 1 Corinthians 12–15.* Grand Rapids, MI: Eerdmans.

Schatzmann, S. (1986). *A Pauline theology of charismata.* Peabody, MA: Hendrickson.

Smalley, S. (1968). Spiritual gifts and 1 Corinthians 12–16. *Journal of Biblical Literature, 88,* 427–433.

Volf, M. (1991). *Work in the Spirit: Toward a theology of work.* New York: Oxford University Press.

Globalization of Pentecostalism

Social scientists over the last decade have led the way in employing the concept of globalization as an appropriate and relevant contemporary category for describing the emergence of Pentecostalism as a global cultural movement. The global growth and impact of Pentecostalism has been significant enough "to justify claims of a new reformation" and to warrant identification as "perhaps the most successful social movement of the past century" (Jenkins 2002, 7–8).

The single most significant global cultural trend of our times is undoubtedly the phenomenon described as globalization. The term "globalization" describes the experience of growing interconnectedness giving rise to the emergence of a global society in which economic, political, environmental, and cultural events and developments in one part of the world are affected by and influence other parts of the world. Although most people continue to live as citizens of a single nation, they are culturally, materially, and psychologically engaged with the lives of people in other countries as never before. Globalization as we observe it today is not exclusively about Western culture, but a new form of culture that knows no boundaries and is spreading globally through multidirectional interconnectedness.

Religions such as Christianity and Islam that claim universal relevance have always been viewed as possessing globalizing tendencies. Thus, the goal of the Christian mission to extend the Kingdom of God clearly transcends national and cultural boundaries. The birth and rapid global expansion of the Pentecostal movement in the twentieth century has led to widespread recognition of Pentecostalism as a major force in the Christian globalization enterprise, and a significant subset within the broader globalization movement. Globalization is applied to Pentecostalism in two distinct, but related, senses. First, it refers to the geographical expansion of the movement. Studies from this perspective are concerned with mapping the rapid and widespread growth of Pentecostalism, identifying regions and communities that experience exceptional growth, and suggesting reasons for the universal popularity and success of Pentecostalism as a global movement.

The second application of the term arises as a consequence of the first. Under scrutiny here is the cultural influence of Pentecostalism as a global movement. Thus cultural analysis of global Pentecostalism raises questions such as: How do the internal features of Pentecostalism relate to external factors that control the surrounding cultural context? To what extent do the internal, transcendent beliefs and values of Pentecostalism shape its social expression and witness? On the other hand, how much does the success of Pentecostalism depend on its capitulating to the needs and demands of the dominant culture? A fundamental issue that needs to be addressed is the very notion of a Pentecostal global culture. How legitimate is the idea of a globalized Pentecostalism, given the rich and diverse local expressions of the movement?

Pentecostal Identity

A key prior issue that must be addressed in any attempt to describe the growth of Pentecostalism is that of identity: How is Pentecostalism to be defined? What criteria do we apply in determining whether a church or movement should be classified as Pentecostal? Pentecostalism does not represent uniform doctrine, cultural homogeneity, or organizational unity. It rather consists of multifarious streams and a wide variety of expressions across the globe. For instance, the African Initiated Church organizations of sub-Saharan Africa, constituting a significant segment of Christianity in several countries, prefer to be known as Zionist or apostolic rather than Pentecostal or charismatic. Also, some Pentecostal streams identifying closely with Western evangelicalism have difficulty including within their definition unorthodox indigenous movements that embrace some culturally syncretistic elements. The scholarly consensus, however, is toward recognition of the pluralism within global Pentecostalism, and acceptance of an inclusive and globalized definition of Pentecostalism.

How, then, do we identify authentic Pentecostalism? The essence of Pentecostalism has been defined in various ways: in terms of a unifying distinctive historical-theological gestalt or worldview, common internal religious or cultural features, or distinctive sociological characteristics as a movement organization. There is, however, broad agreement on what constitutes the single most distinguishing feature of Pentecostalism: the central place ascribed to a transforming experience of God the Holy Spirit. Pentecostalism is thus best understood as a family or network of global movements characterized by an immediate experience of the Holy Spirit that shapes their worldview definitively. Within this broad definition there are a wide variety of churches and movements, the fundamental categories being the classical Pentecostals, the Charismatic movement, and the neocharismatics.

Pentecostalism as a Global Movement

It is based on this broad understanding of Pentecostal identity that Pentecostalism has been recognized as a vast global movement and the second largest Christian grouping in the world. The growth of Pentecostalism to an estimated 500 million adherents within a century of its birth as a modern movement has provoked considerable scholarly discussion. While the most significant growth of Pentecostalism has occurred in Latin America, Africa, and Asia, Pentecostalism can be found today in almost every corner of the globe. Pentecostalism has experienced greatest receptivity among the poor and working classes all over the world, although

Worshippers at the Yoido Full Gospel Church in Seoul, Korea. *Courtesy of Stanley Burgess.*

the growth of the movement in Western nations is marginal compared to its exponential growth rate in the non-Western world.

While Pentecostals themselves normally explain their phenomenal growth in terms of supernatural, providential intervention, critics point to other factors that may also have contributed to the growth of the movement. Some of these help explain, to some degree, why the growth of the movement is slower in some parts than in others. One reason cited for the movement's success is the nature of Pentecostalism as a movement organization rather than a centralized, structured organization. It thus functions as an organism and fulfils its mission through existing social relationships of family, friendship, and community. A second explanation suggests that the supernatural religious experience offered within Pentecostalism provides a therapeutic release for the poor, socially marginalized, and dispossessed. Thus the widespread acceptance of Pentecostalism in the non-Western world is helped by the prevailing cultural openness to Pentecostal supernaturalism, whereas the influence of rationalistic materialism and

modernism is clearly a hindrance to the advance of Pentecostalism in the West.

Pentecostalism is attractive to the poor and powerless also because it offers open access to liberative empowerment by the Holy Spirit. In this regard some have drawn attention to the role of glossolalia as offering the basis for an egalitarian ethic in the equal voice or "sacred space" it provides for the weak and powerful alike. There is, moreover, a strong and urgent sense of missionary compulsion deriving from its experiential spirituality. Perhaps the most significant factor responsible for the effective global expansion of Pentecostalism, which we shall examine more closely, is its remarkable ability to readily adapt to indigenous cultures.

Pentecostalism and Indigenous Cultures

Although there are features of commonality, or family resemblances, that connect the various expressions of Pentecostalism around the world, there is an amazing degree of heterogeneity among the churches and movements that are identified with Pentecostalism.

This is largely due to its quality as "the quintessential indigenous religion," (Dempster, Klaus, and Peterson 1999, 127) its greatest strength being its cultural adaptability and its ability to be localized.

The wind of globalization encounters powerful countercurrents in the forces of localization wherever it goes. Consequently, when ideas from one corner of the globe arrive at a new destination, they are rarely imbibed as they are—they are adapted to fit the local situation. This interaction between the global and local is sometimes referred to as "glocalization"—a term that describes the effective assimilation of globalization forces within the framework of local traditions, aspirations, and interests. Thus, Pentecostalism rarely has a leveling effect on any new culture it encounters: its distinctive spirituality, worldview, and practice are normally always reshaped by the sociocultural context. For this reason it has sometimes been described as "a religion made to travel."

This raises important questions regarding the essential nature of Pentecostalism and its universal relevance. How do the controlling beliefs and values of Pentecostalism relate to those of the host culture? Pentecostalism is frequently viewed as static and dogmatic, with rigid boundaries, and to that extent seemingly culturally hegemonic. Empirical examination, however, demonstrates that, to the contrary, Pentecostalism is not culturally autonomous, but dynamic, flexible, and well able to adapt to new circumstances. It both submits and conforms to some aspects of the social order, and at the same time challenges and transforms other features of the cultural context.

There is, consequently, an amazing degree of diversity among Pentecostal churches and movements. First, there is historical diversity. While a significant stream of Pentecostalism has its roots in American classical Pentecostal and independent charismatic churches, the roots of most other streams are in spontaneous indigenous movements of the Spirit within local contexts, largely independent of Western influences. Second, social diversity: Pentecostalism adapts easily to the demands of a stratified social structure. It can function effectively in settings as diverse as a small village hamlet, upper-class neighborhood living room, a shack in an urban slum, five-star hotel ballroom, or a traditional cathedral. Political diversity is manifested in the way some groups display political neutrality, while others are actively socialist, pro-democracy, or antidictatorial.

The autochthonous character of Pentecostalism thus enables it to take on the culture of a particular people group. It is in that sense a regionalized movement with different features from one part of the globe to the next. This quality has contributed significantly to the globalization of Pentecostalism: "Pentecostal diversity has generally worked towards utilizing the opportunities offered by the globalization process. As a global movement, Pentecostalism can be said to have become part of religious globalization" (Droogers 2004, 29).

Pentecostalism as a Global Culture

The rapid and widespread global expansion of Pentecostalism aroused interest in its universal appeal. By the mid-1990s it began to be described as a global culture due to certain features that seemed to highlight its global relevance. Its emphasis on the freedom of the Spirit meant that it was not tied down to any one doctrine, organization, community, or region. Thus while regional differences are real, many view its common spirituality as constituting the basis for a global Pentecostal culture. The common elements include an emphasis on experiential spirituality, the exercise of spiritual gifts, fervent worship and prayer, a high view of the Bible, vocational empowerment, and participation of all believers in ministry and mission, and conservative morality. Furthermore, access to modern electronic media, communications, travel, and technology has facilitated networking between Pentecostal churches and movements across the globe resulting in a significant degree of interdependence and commonality.

However, to what extent can we speak legitimately of a global Pentecostal culture? The adaptability of Pentecostalism to local indigenous cultures resists any notion of a supracultural homogenizing global process that might be implied in the employment of the term "globalization" in some contexts. Thus "'Globalization' must not be construed to mean an overarching hegemony of an 'international culture' that neatly separates the 'global' from the 'local'" (Anderson 2004, 6). We have seen that factors within the indigenous culture clearly affect how globalization is appropriated within a local context. The common features of global Pentecostalism are filtered and reinterpreted through the framework of local social and cultural context before they are assimilated within Pentecostal belief and practice in the region.

Pentecostal movements in different parts of the world are dynamic syntheses of complex impulses and processes that shape their cultural identity. Thus we can only describe Pentecostalism as a "global culture" in a qualified sense that it emphasizes a common stream of spirituality that resources all expressions of the global movement, but stops short of imposing artificial homogeneity upon a phenomenon marked by richly nuanced cultural diversity.

Future of Global Pentecostalism

Its phenomenal expansion within the first century of its existence and projections that the movement will cross the one billion mark by 2025 or 2050 have continued to fuel the growing realization that Pentecostalism is already reshaping the religion of the twenty-first century. However, the extraordinary success of the Pentecostal movement globally makes a sober assessment of future challenges and opportunities a critical need.

One of the greatest points of vulnerability is the direct consequence of reports and convincing statistics of massive growth, which sometimes tends to foster a shallow triumphalism within Pentecostalism, with several attendant dangers. This attitude of superiority is unhealthy because it suggests that movements that are successful and fast-growing are thus automatically self-validated and above criticism. Such triumphalism can also seriously damage the cause of Christ in regions of the world with a history of colonialism and in which Christian mission has been perceived as closely allied with the Western imperialist enterprise.

In a world where religion is today often seen as the focus of ethnic strife and conflict, any form of Christian triumphalism will inevitably cause communal discord and invite severe opposition. The challenge for Pentecostalism is to find a way of riding the globalization wave in a spirit of Christian servanthood that builds community and furthers universal harmony.

A second major challenge for the global Pentecostal movement is also a by-product of one of its strengths. Pentecostal churches and movements may be found in different shapes and cultural expressions all over the world. Syncretism is thus a very real danger within a movement that sometimes exhibits an uncritical pragmatism in the manner in which it capitulates to the demands of the dominant culture. The prosperity gospel, the practice of animal sacrifice, serpent handling, and shamanism that characterize Pentecostal groups in some parts of the world are illustrations of the tendency toward what some might term unhealthy accommodation within Pentecostalism.

Harvard theologian Harvey Cox draws attention to the most serious pitfall in this regard. While lauding the benefits that the emergence of a global technological culture offers for the globalization of the Christian movement, Cox warns of the dangerous consequences of a lack of an adequate critical theology of culture. He

sees the emergence of a "global market culture" resulting from globalization, as a modern form of idolatry, and laments the fact that Pentecostals appear to be capitulating to its seductive power. He thus observes that: "Christianity is not against markets, but it is unalterably opposed to allowing The Market and its false ethic to dictate the meaning of life; and the gospel stands in dramatic opposition to the dominant values of the currently reigning global market culture" (Cox 1999, 394).

The relationship between Pentecostalism and globalization is one of mutual reinforcement. Pentecostalism benefits under the conditions that globalization creates and in turn facilitates the globalization process. The genius of Pentecostalism is clearly the remarkable capacity of Pentecostal movements to incarnate themselves in various indigenous cultures, producing rich cultural and theological diversity, even while these movements remain organically united based on a common tradition of spirituality and distinct family spiritual resemblances.

Ivan Morris Satyavrata

See also Nationalism; Society, Pentecostal Attitudes toward

Further Reading

Anderson, A. (2004). *The globalization of Pentecostalism.* Retrieved March 8, 2004, from http://www.geocities.com/ccom_ctbi/ccom_AGM_files/020913-15_CCOM_AGM_Allan_Anderson.htm

Beyer, P. (1994). *Religion and globalization.* London: Sage.

Cox, H. (1995). *Fire from heaven: The rise of Pentecostal spirituality and the re-shaping of religion in the 21st century.* Reading, MA: Addison Wesley Publishing Company.

Cox, H. (1999). Pentecostalism and global market culture: A response to issues facing Pentecostalism in a postmodern world. In *The globalization of Pentecostalism: A religion made to travel* (pp. 386–395). Carlisle, UK: Regnum Books.

Dayton, D. (1987). *Theological roots of Pentecostalism.* Grand Rapids, MI: Francis Asbury Press.

Dempster, M. W., Klaus, B. D., & Peterson, D. (Eds.). (1999). *The globalization of Pentecostalism: A religion made to travel.* Carlisle, UK: Regnum Books.

Droogers, A. (2004). *Globalization and Pentecostal success.* Retrieved June 30, 2004, from http://casnws.scw.vu.nl/publicaties/droogers-globpent.html

Hexham, I., & Poewe, K. (1997). *New religions as global cultures, making the human sacred.* Boulder, CO: Westview Press.

Hollenweger, W. J. (1997). *Pentecostalism: Origins and developments worldwide.* Peabody, MA: Hendrickson Publishers.

Jenkins, P. (2002). *The next Christendom: The coming of global Christianity.* New York: Oxford University Press.

Martin, D. (1990). *Tongues of fire: The explosion of Pentecostalism in Latin America.* Oxford, UK: Basil Blackwell.

Poewe, K. (Ed.). (1994). *Charismatic Christianity as a global culture.* Columbia: University of South Carolina Press.

Poloma, M. M. (August 11–13, 2000). *The spirit bade me go: Pentecostalism and global religion.* Washington, D.C: Association for the Sociology of Religious Annual Meetings. Unpublished Paper.

Shaull, R., & Cesar, W. (2000). *Pentecostalism and the future of Christian churches.* Grand Rapids, MI: Eerdmans Publishing.

Synan, V. (1997). *The Holiness-Pentecostal tradition: Charismatic movements in the 20th century.* Grand Rapids, MI: Eerdmans Publishing.

Wacker, G. (2001). *Heaven below: Early Pentecostalism and American culture.* Cambridge, MA: Harvard University Press.

Glossolalia

Glossolalia comes from the Greek terms used in the New Testament to refer to speaking in tongues (from *glossa*, or tongue, and *lalein*, to speak). *Speaking in tongues* refers to a language miracle whereby under the inspiration of the Holy Spirit one is able to speak in a language (either human or heavenly) unknown to the speaker. There is considerable theological debate concerning the nature of glossolalia in the New Testament, much of it centering around how to compare Acts 2 with 1 Corinthians 14.

Nature of Glossolalia

On the surface, it appears that the tongues of Acts 2 are understood by their hearers (Acts 2:5–11)—making them an example of the form of glossolalia known as *xenolalia,* or divinely inspired speech in an existing language of which the speaker had no previous knowledge. On the other hand, the tongues of 1 Corinthians 14 cannot be understood by anyone without the spiritual gift of interpretation (1 Corinthians 14:14–15)—implying that tongues are unintelligible speech. Some have tried to explain this difference by noting that the audience of Acts 2 was international, while the congregation in Corinth was more provincial. The difference in audience between the two texts might explain why the tongues in Acts 2 were comprehensible to some, while in 1 Corinthians 12–14 they required a spiritual interpretation imparted through a spiritual gift.

This explanation is not entirely convincing, however, since 1 Corinthians 12–14 gives no hint that tongues can be translated through a normal knowledge of language; rather they must be interpreted spiritually, through a spiritual gift (1 Corinthians 12:10). Furthermore, precedent exists in ancient religious contexts for inspired tongues that need spiritual interpretation, increasing the likelihood, in some scholars' estimation, that the glossolalia at Corinth was analogous in nature.

Most damaging to the proposition that the tongues at Corinth were foreign languages is Paul's assumption that they are meant for a divine rather than a human audience (1 Corinthians 14:2). In fact, tongues in 1 Corinthians 14 seem to have their primary function for Paul in private prayer, while prophecy is for the public (14:3–4). Tongues are for self-edification as one gives thanks to God "with the spirit" (14:4, 14–15). Tongues in any human language would seem to be intended for some human audience that can understand them, making interpretation as a spiritual gift unnecessary, at least for some people. But 1 Corinthians 14 prefers prophecy as the means to communicate something in intelligible language to others (14:4, 19, 23–25). Tongues are likened to foreign languages a number of times in the chapter, especially in verses 6 through 12, but the relationship may be one of analogy rather than equivalency: Just as foreign languages require translation, so glossolalia requires spiritual interpretation to benefit others.

It appears difficult to reconcile the tongues that appear as unintelligible speech in 1 Corinthians 14 with the ones spoken in Acts 2 that were understood by their hearers, namely Diaspora Jews from around the world (and therefore fluent in a variety of languages). However, material elsewhere in Acts complicates this apparent instance of xenolalia: At no other point where tongues appear in the book (Acts 10:46, 19:6) is there an indication that they are communicating anything to a human audience—which suggests that their character in Acts 2 may have been anomalous.

A Jewish tradition in the first century held that the law given through Moses was communicated in all of the languages of the world. It may be that Pentecost at the time of the Apostles was a celebration of the Sinai covenant, which would make it theologically symbolic if the glossolalia spoken under the inspiration of the Spirit by the early followers of Jesus were actually understood in the languages of the world as well.

Pentecost would in that case have been viewed as the fulfillment of the Sinai covenant, but through a gift of the Spirit rather than of the law. Some have questioned further whether what was spoken at Pentecost was actually xenolalia, noting that Acts 2:6 states that each "one" heard "them," possibly implying that each person in the audience, no matter what his or her native language, heard the entire band of Jesus' followers speaking in that particular language. This raises the possibility that the tongues of Pentecost were unintelligible glossolalia accompanied by a miracle of *hearing,* in which each person heard the entire band of early Christians speak in the hearer's own language.

Stories of xenolalia exist in history, especially in the Pentecostal movement, but to date, no known case has been scientifically verified, despite extensive research in this area. However, if the miracle of xenolalia occurs as much in the hearing as in the speaking, then no scientific instruments will ever be able to record and verify it.

Theology of Glossolalia

The authors of Acts and 1 Corinthians gave slightly different explanations of the role of tongues and their place in the faith. Luke, the author of Acts, seems to allow for tongues to have value as a public sign, a stance not emphasized by Paul in 1 Corinthians. For Luke, tongues were a sign of the global reach of the Spirit's witness to the God's acts of salvation, especially in the person and work of Jesus of Nazareth. In Acts 2, the God of Israel is revealed in the languages of the nations. Whatever kind of xenolalia the tongues in Acts 2 represent, the theological significance remains largely the same, namely, that the sacred language is heard in the tongues of the gentile nations. There is here a "profaning" of the divine self-disclosure in a vast plurality of expressions.

The audience of Diaspora Jews who heard and understood the tongues in Acts 2 had been scattered, but were brought back together by the power of the Spirit and the Spirit's witness to Christ. This return to a universal language implies a reversal of the story in Genesis 11 of the tower of Babel, in which God scattered the first dwellers of an ancient city through the diversification of their language. Acts 17 notes that God has determined the geographical dwellings of the various peoples so they would grope for and find God, an implicit reference to the grace involved in the scattering of Babel (17:26–27). The limitation of Acts 2, however, is that the scattered audience that had returned to God were all Jews; in Acts 10, the unity willed for humanity is extended to the Gentiles. The explicit reference to tongues at the Gentile reception of the Spirit (Acts 10:46) is significant: The inclusion of people from every nation and every walk of life among the people of God begins to move from abstraction to concrete fulfillment with the acceptance of the Gentiles into the fold. Luke's point is obvious: the Spirit has been poured out upon all flesh, not in some generic or abstract sense, but in a way that bridges divisions and fragmentation to bring about a unity of all humanity. This unity respects the diversity of expressions of the truth of Christ who was crucified and risen for the redemption of the world.

1 Corinthians 14 does not have Luke's global context. This chapter deals with the issue of tongues in the context of a potentially chaotic church worship service. It seems that many of the Corinthians favored public expressions of tongues and ecstatic behavior, which were sure to provoke confusion and ridicule from visitors unaccustomed to such things (14:23). Tongues were a sign for unbelievers for Paul (14:22) but not one they will understand (14:21–23). Paul responds by favoring the intelligible forms of inspired speech (i.e., prophecy) for the public service; the unintelligible forms of inspired speech (i.e., tongues) are directed to God alone and serve to edify the individual speaking (1 Corinthians 14:2–4, 22–25). Whereas Luke assumes a close relationship between tongues and prophecy (Acts 2:17–18, 19:6), Paul distinguishes between them sharply in order to separate intelligible from unintelligible forms of inspired speech and assign a role to each. Paul allows tongues to be expressed in public, but only if they are interpreted for the listeners, and the responsibility for doing this is laid squarely on the shoulders of the speaker (1 Corinthians 14:13–15). The chief purpose of exercising spiritual gifts in public is to serve the goal of love and the edification of the church (14:26). It may be that Paul comes close to Luke's theology of tongues as a global sign of the redemption yet to come in Romans 8:26, where unutterable sighs express a yearning for the coming liberation of the creation. In this case, tongues would be a sign of human weakness as well as God's strength in the time in between the first fruits of the Spirit and the new creation yet to come. There is no indication that Paul values tongues less than prophecy, any more than public witness is valued over private prayers.

A Contemporary Theology of Glossolalia

Tongues have an important place in Pentecostal spirituality; they are the "Bible evidence" of baptism in the Holy Spirit. Paul asserts in 1 Corinthians 12 that not all believers speak in tongues (12:30), and in Pentecostal theology, these tongues not shared by everyone have commonly been understood as the congregational gift of tongues, while tongues as a private prayer were viewed as potentially available to all. The idea of preaching in tongues was abandoned in the first several years of the Pentecostal movement, and tongues as a transcendent form of prayer soon became the dominant view.

The Pentecostal pioneer William J. Seymour viewed tongues as a sign that Spirit baptism was bringing people together across racial and class lines. There has been a range of opinion within the Pentecostal movement about precise nature of the relationship between tongues and Spirit baptism. The most rigid view holds that tongues are a defining feature of Spirit baptism, and only tongue-speakers are said to have the fullness of the Spirit. Other Pentecostal theologians have made the relationship less rigid and more theoretical, explaining tongues as a symbol of the creation of a new common language, a sign of the Spirit that reconciles divided peoples. According to this view, Spirit baptism leads to the spiritual capacity or privilege of praying in tongues, although many Christians may decide not to use it. Tongues have been characterized as a primal form of speech made necessary by the inability of rational language to express the divine mystery—a kind of antilanguage pointing mysteriously to God's presence in a way analogous to the sacraments. Tongues are also said to function as eschatological signs and wonders of the fullness of redemption yet to come, signaling a free, wondrous, or playful relationship with God in the here and now. They also imply for many an upsetting of the social privilege of those who seem to monopolize public discourse by virtue of education or social class, granting everyone equal access to the inspired speech that transforms lives. The theological meaning of tongues depends on their function in the prayers of people of faith and the contexts in which such prayers occur.

FRANK D. MACCHIA

See also Charismata; Interpretation of Tongues

Further Reading

Hovenden, G. (2002). *Speaking in tongues: The New Testament evidence in context.* Sheffield, UK: Sheffield Academic Press.

Macchia, F. D. (1992). Sighs too deep for words: Towards a theology of glossolalia. *Journal of Pentecostal Theology, 1*(1). 47–73.

Mills, W. (Ed.). (1998). *Speaking in tongues: A guide to research on glossolalia.* Grand Rapids, MI: Baker Book House.

Williams, C. (1981). *Tongues of the spirit: A study of Pentecostal glossolalia.* Cardiff, UK: University of Wales Press.

Great Britain

Great Britain played an important part in the global revivalist movement. Phenomena such as being "slain in the Spirit," which would feature in late twentieth-century Charismatic Renewal, were first reported at meetings in the late eighteenth century by John and Charles Wesley and George Whitfield. In the following century, several promoters of charismatic revivalism—Edward Irving, Jonathan Edwards, and Billy Bray, for example—enjoyed significant followings. The modern Pentecostal movement arose from two distinct developments: the Welsh Revival (1904–1905) and the influence of Alexander Boddy, an Anglican clergyman and Vicar of Monkwearmouth, Sunderland, from 1886 to 1922, who was indirectly influenced by the Azusa Street Revival.

Boddy's place in Pentecostal history demonstrates how much modern Pentecostalism owes to global networking. Whereas the Welsh Revival was confined to its locality, Boddy's promotion of British Pentecostalism had an international flavor from the beginning, mainly because of the influence of Thomas Ball Barratt, an Englishman from Cornwall. On a visit to the United States to raise funds for a Methodist mission in Oslo, Norway, Barratt had experienced baptism in the Holy Spirit and speaking in tongues at the Azusa Street Mission; he'd also been exposed to the teachings of William J. Seymour, Charles F. Parham, and W. F. Carothers. After meeting Barratt in 1907, Boddy returned to England to promote a similar Pentecostal awakening. The Pentecostal revival took root here.

The rapid spread of Pentecostalism in Britain was not eclipsed by the Great War or by the harsh economic realities of the 1920s and 1930s. New groupings of fellowships and churches emerged, and these groupings later matured into denominations such as the Assemblies of God, the Church of God in Christ, and the Church of the Foursquare Gospel. These churches, which sometimes developed their identity through ethnicity or were led by prominent figures such as West Yorkshire preacher Smith Wigglesworth (1860–1947), enjoyed considerable growth throughout the twentieth century.

Origins of the Charismatic Renewal

There is a direct link between the development of British Pentecostalism and the burgeoning of the Charismatic Renewal. In 1936, some ten years before his death, Wigglesworth met David du Plessis (1905–1992), a young South African Pentecostal minister, and imparted a prophecy to him. Wigglesworth correctly predicted that Pentecostal phenomena were about to become ecumenical and global and that du Plessis would have a major role in expanding the number of people who would join this revival.

The role of du Plessis in the global Charismatic Renewal is regarded as seminal, since he was responsible for developing Pentecost outside of Pentecostalism. A number of church leaders in the latter half of the twentieth century were prepared to welcome Pentecostalism as a form of Evangelical revivalism. These leaders understood Pentecostal phenomena in the same way that the Wesleys and Whitfield had, namely, as accompaniments to preaching, conviction, repentance, and conversion, but as otherwise relatively insignificant. However, this created a context in which Pentecostalism as a movement (or as a grouping of emergent denominations) was either rejected or held in check by historic denominations, while the phenomena of Pentecostalism were increasingly regarded as apposite signs of a renewed, energizing, and dynamic spirituality.

Du Plessis, through the ministry of other British Pentecostal leaders such as Donald Gee, became the first significant exponent for exporting Pentecostalism to mainstream churches in Britain. Du Plessis's autobiography reveals that he regarded the mainline denominations as dead and felt called by God to bring about their spiritual renewal. This process began with Protestant denominations but later included (to his surprise) Roman Catholicism. Thus, sociologically and ecclesiastically, du Plessis's ministry paved the way for the birth of the Charismatic Renewal (that is, the inclusion of Pentecostal-type phenomena in historic denominations), which in turn allowed individuals, groups, and established mainstream churches to experience Pentecostal phenomena, adopt them, and yet remain within their denominations.

This led to a series of dynamic developments that culminated in ecclesiastical and spiritual renewal. One such development was that those caught up in the movement experienced a significant moment of spiritual renewal or rebirth which was sometimes associated with speaking in tongues or a comparable experience of spiritual catharsis. Another development was that there was renewed interest in the ministry of healing, which took several forms. In its early development it was led by organizations such as the Fountain Trust, which looked to an Anglican priest for direction. A third development was that patterns and forms of worship changed. For example, traditional hymnody ceded space for new generations of songwriters, such as the Fisherfolk in the sixties and seventies, Graham Kendrick in the eighties and nineties, and Matt Redman beginning in the nineties. Hymns were quickly replaced by simpler choruses, the organ by modern instruments and "praise bands," and traditional liturgy with new innovations such as dance, drama, and "informal worship."

A fourth development was that the cadence and timbre of worship shifted almost imperceptibly from being a reflection of core didactic themes to being centered on the emotional and spiritual state of worshippers and their relationship with God. Some scholars of new religious movements regard this moment as a turn towards the self, but this does not do justice to the quiet revolution in worship that was ushered in by the Charismatic Renewal. The new modes of worship allowed for greater freedom of expression, such as raising hands and dancing. Indeed, the now commonplace practice of shaking hands or hugging during the Peace (in a conventional Eucharist in most mainline denominations) may be due to the influence of charismatic renewal.

The Charismatic Renewal depended on a number of leaders. David Watson, perhaps the most significant figure in British Charismatic Renewal in the 1980s, became a household name among Evangelicals seeking renewal, although he himself remained within the Church of England. Other prominent figures included Michael Green, John Gunstone, David Pytches (Vicar of St. Andrew's Chorleywood and a former Bishop of Chile), Sandy Millar (Vicar of Holy Trinity Brompton), Nicky Gumbel (founder of the Alpha Course), Barry Kissell (author of *Springtime in the Church*), and Colin Urquhart (author and conference speaker).

The British Charismatic Renewal began to cultivate its own culture, which was expressed in new events, products, and symbols. Its growing influence can be seen in events such as *Spring Harvest*, an annual showcase for Evangelical Charismatic Renewal that began in 1979 and now attracts hundreds of thousands of attendees. Magazines such as *Renewal*, *Christian Woman*, and *21st Century Christian* also testify to the growing influence of the Charismatic Renewal. Most of the major religious publishers in Britain report that the Christian book market is dominated by authors and titles influenced by the Charismatic Renewal.

Every major denomination in Britain has been profoundly influenced by the Charismatic Renewal. Baptists, Methodists, and Roman Catholics have a significant percentage of members who owe something of their spiritual development to the Charismatic Renewal, and no denominational collation of hymnody is now without a representative sample of choruses.

Rise of New Churches

Despite the significant success of the Charismatic Renewal in Great Britain, the spiritual roots of revivalism continued to flourish outside mainstream denominations. To some extent, these roots corresponded to the spiritual tradition that gave birth to the Welsh Revival. In some Brethren and other more independent Christian traditions, the impact of early Pentecostalism and Charismatic Renewal did not lead to a greater commitment to ecumenism, but rather to an intensification of an extant sectarian tradition. The most recognizable expression of this was in the distinctively British House Church Movement, which enjoyed prominence from the late 1960s through the early 1990s. The House Church Movement stood outside the mainstream Charismatic Renewal, arguing that God had finished with the historic denominations, that they were dead and no longer a significant part of God's purposes. Those within the House Church Movement urged Christians to leave their churches and join a new initiative—not a new church, but rather a restoration of God's kingdom.

These "Restorationists" were committed to a range of core beliefs and ecclesiastical practices. For instance, they shunned ecumenical or collaborative contact with other churches, and members were typically bound to tithe their income as a condition of membership. They practiced "shepherding"—a form of disciplinary oversight and intervention that deeply impacted every area of life for individuals, families, and congregations. Restorationists were typically separatist in their ethos but committed to evangelism and other forms of outreach. Ironically, their socio-ecclesiastic behavior resembled that of the early pre–du Plessis Pentecostal denominations.

In his 1998 study of the British House Church Movement, author Andrew Walker divides the movement into two distinct strands: Type One (R1) individuals are "pure" and include Restorationists who are predominantly conditioned by a sectarian Brethren background. Leadership is exclusively male, and the structures of authority are normally clear, unambiguous, and tightly controlled. Type Two (R2) individuals are more open and accommodating in their outlook; they may have relationships with other charismatic churches, and their style of leadership is likely to be less formal, more fluid, and more innovative.

Key leaders of the House Church Movement included Arthur Wallis and Bryn and Kerry Jones for the R1 churches, and Terry Virgo (New Frontiers Churches), Gerald Coates (Pioneer Churches), and Roger Forster (Ichthus Fellowship) for the R2 churches. Walker's subsequent research showed that those grouped under the R1 umbrella experienced a steep decline in numbers and influence in the 1990s. R2 churches, on the other hand, repositioned themselves in the British Evangelical-Charismatic marketplace as "new churches." And although they too experienced a numerical decline in the 1990s, they managed to consolidate their identity.

Part of the reason for this dramatic boom and bust in Restorationist fortunes probably lay with the resurgence in Charismatic Renewal that took place from 1980 to the mid-1990s. The most influential figure in this for Britain was John Wimber, a Californian evangelist and church-growth exponent. Wimber formed a strong alliance with David Watson, the leading figure in British Charismatic Renewal in the early 1980s. Through Watson's endorsement, Wimber's influence spread, culminating in a series of conferences and publications that helped the Charismatic Renewal reach new heights. Wimber not only drew ministers and attendees from mainline churches but also worked closely with leaders and churches that were R2 in orientation. After the death of Watson in 1986, Wimber's influence grew through association with David Pytches (Chorleywood), and Sandy Millar (Holy Trinity Brompton), and had a major impact on the development of the Charismatic Renewal. Wimber eventually extended his network of Vineyard Churches to Britain, although their numbers remained comparatively modest.

With Wimber's death in 1997, many British charismatics felt that the movement had begun to lose its direction and momentum. The initial Rapture that had greeted the Toronto Blessing gave way to division among charismatics concerning its importance and usefulness to their cause. Increasing diversification of spiritual and ecclesial practices among charismatics points towards a future in which the Charismatic Renewal movement will be seen as just one resource among many.

Future Growth

For proponents of Charismatic Renewal in Britain, the twenty-first century ushered in an era of both promise and uncertainty. While organizations such as the Fountain Trust and Anglicans for Renewal no longer exist, new expressions of Charismatic Renewal are much in evidence. The Jesus Army, under the leadership of Noel Stanton, combines several features of Pentecostalism and includes a distinctive brand of community living and new urban evangelization programs. The church of St. Thomas Crookes in Sheffield recently began its own religious order, with the vicar becoming the Superior. The Order of Mission is Protestant, charismatic, and Evangelical; it developed a system of tertiary association and encouraged full members of the Order to commit to a daily cycle of prayer and living in community.

The church also bought and developed a new complex—Philadelphia—to enable the evangelization of inner cities throughout northern England. Members of the new Order describe the Philadelphia complex as a "monastery in an urban setting, for the express purpose of mission." Meanwhile, the new Superior—synthesizing the global and the local—now divides his time between a project in Phoenix, Arizona, and helping to establish new cells of the Order across England's northern cities and urban conurbations.

For those who remain in the historic Pentecostal denominations, there has also been growth, but of a new kind. Immigration in postwar Britain initially gave rise to a number of ethnically based churches, which were, on the whole, constrained by their origins. But in the last two decades new black Pentecostal churches, influenced by practices and doctrines from West Africa that distinguish them from some of the older Pentecostal churches, have spread rapidly. For example, the Redeemed Christian Church of God (RCCG), which opened in Britain in 1985, has seen rapid congregational growth.

After a century of growth, British Pentecostalism can justly regard itself as a significant stakeholder within a wider ecumenism. Its future looks assured. However, the prospects for the Charismatic Renewal as a movement with a distinct identity are far less certain in Britain. Enthusiasm for creating an intense atmosphere of intimate praise and worship showed some signs of atrophy during the last decade of the twentieth century. Diverse trends are emerging: For example, there are more alternative services that make use of youth culture, and there is evidence of charismatic churches adopting liturgical practices and moving away from their Evangelical theological roots into the mainstream. Many who were once wholly devoted to the movement have slowly turned towards richer spiritual and ecclesial diets in which charismatic renewal is just one element. Those who were once consumed by the Charismatic Renewal have themselves become its consumers.

The dream of du Plessis, who promoted Pentecost outside Pentecostalism, has to a large extent been realized within the British Charismatic Renewal. Thanks to proponents of the "Third Wave" like Peter Wagner, John Wimber, and David Pytches, many Christians now enjoy the fruits of Pentecostalism without departing from their own denomination. As Britons might put it, "They are having their cake and eating it."

Martyn Percy

See also Charismatic Movement; Europe

Further Reading

Blumhofer, E. (1986). Alexander Boddy and the rise of Pentecostalism in Great Britain. *Pneuma, 8*(1), 31–40.

du Plessis, D. (1977). *A man called Mr. Pentecost.* Plainfield, NJ: Logos International.

Hocken, P. (1986). *Streams of renewal: The origins and early development of Charismatic Renewal in Great Britain.* Exeter, UK: Paternoster Press.

Hunt, S. (2000). The new black Pentecostal churches in Britain. *Occasional paper, Center for Studies on New Religions* (pp. 1–16). London: London School of Economics.

Percy, M. (1996). *Words, wonders and power: Understanding contemporary Christian fundamentalism and revivalism.* London: SPCK.

Walker, A. (1998). *Restoring the kingdom: The radical Christianity of the house church movement.* Guildford, UK: Eagle Press.

Hands, Laying on of

The laying on or imposition of hands is important not only to the Pentecostal and charismatic communities, but also to many denominations of the church. A brief contextual examination of the "hand(s)" in Scripture sheds light on the theological implications related to the practice of imposition as it continues to this day.

Contexts of Meaning

Several figurative and literal meanings for laying on of hands are found in the Old and New Testaments. In the thirteen hundred or more biblical references, the dominant representation of the hand demonstrates ownership, control, or power (e.g., Genesis 9:2; Isaiah 47:6; Matthew 26:50; Acts 4:3). While the hand may represent care or protection (see 1 Chronicles 21:13; Psalms 31:5; Matthew 4:6; Luke 23:46), in some cases it is associated with complicity in wickedness (see Psalms 144:8; Ecclesiastes 7:26; Matthew 5:30; Revelation 9:20–21). Some uses of the hand relate to innocence (see 2 Samuel 22:21–25; Psalms 24:4; James 4:8). While there are a few usages that relate to the placement of the hand to make oaths or covenants (see Genesis 24:2–9, 47:29; Exodus 32:1), literal use of the hand usually has to do with work (e.g., Genesis 5:29; Haggai 2:17; Luke 9:62; 1 Thessalonians 4:11). References to the divine hand always speak of God's ultimate power (see Deuteronomy 2:15; Judges 2:15; Luke 1:66; Hebrews 10:31).

Imposition of Divine and Human Hands

When the "hand of the Lord" is spoken of as being upon someone, this usually refers to God's blessing and empowerment. The declaration also in many cases precedes descriptions of divine prophetic encounters (2 Kings 3:14–20; Ezekial 1:1–3; Acts 11:20–24; Revelation 1:17). Those seeking to obey God often invite His abiding help, which comes by His hand (Ezra 7:28; Nehemiah 2:8–18; 1 Peter 5:5–7). In a few cases, imposition of the Lord's hand speaks of judgment (Ezekial 39:21; Acts 13:9–11; Hebrews 10:31).

A messianic passage describing the hand of the Lord acting through King David prophetically points toward Jesus' future work (Psalm 89:20–37). God's hand is established through David and his descendants so that divine power and governance are openly displayed in the earth. Correspondingly, Matthew underscores a controversy regarding Jesus' identity as the "Son of David" (among others, Matthew 1:1, 20; 9:27; 12:23; and see esp. 22:41–46). The spiritual inference becomes tangible as Jesus heals many with his touch.

Transference of Guilt, Sin, and Punishment

In order for Levitical priests and members of the nation of Israel to safely encounter the manifest presence of God, they must atone for their sins. By laying hands upon beasts destined for sacrifice there is transference of guilt and punishment (Exodus 29; Leviticus 1:2–4, etc.; Numbers 8:9–20). At times goats are driven out of the community after the laying on of hands and confession of sin (Leviticus 16:21).

Following conviction for heinous crimes, hands were pressed upon the guilty before they were put to death by stoning (Leviticus 24:14–15; Deuteronomy 17:2–7). The condemned would literally bear the weight or consequences of their sin (Deuteronomy 17:2–7;

Psalm 38:1–3). This practice leads to a prophetic understanding of Christ's atoning work. "Assemble and come, gather from every side to My sacrifice which I am going to sacrifice for you, as a great sacrifice on the mountains of Israel" (Ezekial 39:17b, NASB). And, "I shall set My glory among the nations; and all the nations will see My judgment which I have executed, and My hand which I have laid on them" (Ezekial 39:21). Herein, the sacrificial formula is reversed as Yahweh provides the sacrifice, pouring out the judgment deserved by the nations upon another.

There are two major purposes for the imposition of hands: transference of guilt or sin, and blessing. Jesus is the sacrificial lamb of God who takes away the sins of the world, and also the Anointed One—Christ, the Son of David, who brings healing and deliverance. His life is relevant for both purposes (Matthew 1:1, 22:42; John 7:42). While the reign of heaven is extended through the hands of Jesus, His sacrifice opens the door for the coming of the Spirit at Pentecost (Ezekial 39:17–29; John 12:23–24, 16:7–11).

Blessing

The first specific mention of the use of hands in blessing occurs when Israel (Jacob) lays hands on two of his grandchildren. Joseph objects to an obvious impropriety, as the patriarch crosses his hands, placing his right hand on the younger son Ephraim. The action implies Manasseh will serve the younger (Genesis 48). In the New Testament, children come to Jesus for blessing at His hand and by His prayer. The Lord defends the importance of their request, explaining that the kingdom of heaven belongs to ones like these (Matthew 19:13–15; Mark 10:13–16). Seekers may only enter God's reign if they come like children (Luke 18:17). It is implied that the laying on of hands and prayer, in some cases, opens people to new dimensions of God's reign extending through them.

Jesus later lifts his hands to impart a blessing, similar to Aaron's action over the congregation (Leviticus 9:22, Luke 24:49–51). Just as the hand of the Lord extends to bless those who seek and obey Him, the action of touch effects the purposes of God (1 Kings 8:42; 2 Chronicles 6:29–33). Intercessors also reach toward God's presence with expectancy throughout Scripture (1 Kings 8:22, 38, 42, 54; Ezra 9:5; Nehemiah 8:6; Psalm 28:2, 88:9, etc.; Isaiah 1:15–20; 1 Timothy 2:8).

Healing

2 Kings 5:10–11 records that Elisha lays his entire body over the corpse of a boy subsequent to his being raised from the dead. Naaman seeks Elisha, expecting to be healed of leprosy by the waving of the prophet's hand over him (2 Kings 5:10–11). Jesus heals the sick and raises the dead continually with touch (Matthew 8:3, 14–15, 9:18, 9:24–26, 27–31, Mark 1:30–31, 40–42, 3:1–5, 5:22–23, 40–42, 6:2–5, 7:32–35, 8:22–25, Luke 4:38–40, 5:12–13, 8:41–42, 49–55, 13:11–13, 22:50–51). In one case he touches just the coffin to achieve the miracle (7:12–16). The same ability to heal later comes through the hands of Jesus' followers (Mark 16:17–18). Many individuals in the first-century church and thereafter wield the same ability (Acts 3:2–9, 5:12, 9:10–14, etc.).

Other Forms of Healing Touch

Apart from the example of the hemorrhaging woman who touches Jesus' cloak to be healed (Matthew 9:20–22; Mark 5:24–34; Luke 8:43–48), there are instances where others attempt the same (Matthew 14:34–36; Mark 3:8–10, 6:56; Luke 6:17–20). Handkerchiefs and aprons are taken from Paul to the sick to bring healing (Acts 19:11–12). Some are even restored as Peter's shadow passes over them (Acts 5:15). At times, healing takes place through encounter with Jesus' words (Matthew 8:5–13, 16, 12:10–13; Luke 6:6–10; 7:2–10). Controversy exists in the church today as to whether hands should be laid upon those who are demon-possessed. Some argue that Jesus never touches such people, but instead delivers by the authority of His presence and by His command (Matthew 8:28–32; 9:32–33; 17:14–21; Mark 5:1–20, 9:14–29; Luke 4:33–37, 9:37–43).

Ordination and Commissioning

Moses publicly confirms his endorsement of Joshua as a new leader while laying hands on him (Numbers 27:18–19). Keith Mattingly emphasizes not only the bestowal of honor through the gesture, but also prophetic conferment of God's very presence. He translates Numbers 27:23: "Yahweh spoke through the hand of Moses" (Mattingly 2001, 194–195). With the understanding that Joshua is filled with the Spirit through this event, it is clear that God's word supplies more than mere information (Deuteronomy 34:9). Similar endowment of the Word is given to Jeremiah the prophet directly through the hand of God (Jeremiah 1:4–10).

New Testament leadership is confirmed in the same manner with Timothy and others in Jerusalem. This takes place before the congregation of the disciples and with the elders (Acts 6:2–6, 1 Timothy 4:12–14). Affirmation of leadership by the imposition of hands is not to be made without consideration of a potential leader's moral strength, lest the reputation of the church become tarnished (1 Timothy 5:22).

God's Spirit

Joshua, as well as seven upcoming leaders in the New Testament Church, share the quality of having good character. They are also described as being individuals in whom the Spirit dwells, before the laying on of hands (Numbers 27:18; Acts 6:3–5). In Joshua there is a new impartation of the Spirit (Deuteronomy 34:9). Stephen, one of the seven, also seems to demonstrate increasing grace and power after the event (Acts 6:8–10). Although no specific mention is made regarding outpouring of the Spirit during the ceremony confirmating the Seven, manifestation of such may not be realized until a later time of need (Acts 7:55). This is also the case with respect to Paul and Barnabas as they are sent off to mission, after prayer and fasting, having hands laid on them (Acts 12:24–13:4). Later miracles take place at the hands of Paul (Acts 13:9).

In Acts 9:17, the Spirit fills Saul (Paul) while also healing him of blindness through the laying on of Ananias' hands. The apostle becomes a similar conduit of the Spirit as he lays hands on others (Acts 19:1–7). At the same time, he receives charismatic gifts of prophecy and tongues. Paul baptizes people in the name of Jesus for the reception of the Spirit, although they had previously only known John's water baptism. Samarians who had previously been baptized in the name of Jesus nevertheless did not receive the Spirit until visiting leaders of the Jerusalem church later place hands upon them (Acts 8:14–17). At other times the Spirit fills people without the imposition of hands (Acts 2:1–4, 11:1–18). Jesus himself accomplishes the same by breathing on his followers (John 2:21–22). The variety of biblical depictions of pneumatic impartation should dissuade the church from developing formulistic prayers or absolutes in doctrine.

In one case an evil-minded magician, Elymas, attempts to purchase the ability to baptize others in the Spirit with his hands. Ironically, the hand of the Lord renders him blind for a period of time, as a judgment for his impudence (Acts 13:7–12).

Spiritual Gifts

God's gifts equip believers for their service to Him in the world (Acts 1:5–8; Ephesians 4:7–12). Two references are made regarding Timothy's reception of spiritual gifts by the laying on of hands (1 Timothy 4:14;

2 Timothy 1:6). J. K. Parratt contends that Paul's desire to impart charismatic gifts to the Roman believers would have come through the practice of laying on of his hands as well (Romans 1:11). The apostle ties the concept of charismatic endowment to his future visit with them.

Present Day Application

Although the practice of the laying on of hands has become controversial or nonexistent in various segments of the church, it was considered basic teaching in the first century (Hebrews 6:1–2) For some, the present-day absence of this convention is evidence that its spiritual significance has been forgotten.

Many Christians who continue in the practice insist that any believer may be used by the Lord through the various contexts of the laying on of hands. Biblical texts often emphasize the consonant importance of prayerful intercession. According to this view, participants in the laying on of hands must remember they are only instruments in what the Lord Himself is accomplishing (Acts 3:12, 4:30).

Kenneth Grayston notes the protective significance of the hand of the Lord upon John the Baptist and other followers of Christ (Luke 1:66; John 10:29). He comments that believers place themselves into the care of the Lord's hand by humbling themselves (Psalm 91; 1 Peter 5:6–10). This is a reminder of Jesus' admonition that believers can only enter the Kingdom of God if they come to him like children (Luke 18:17).

STEVEN R. SERVICE

See also Healing, Gifts of

Further Reading

Brug, J. F. (1995). Ordination and installation in the Scriptures. *Wisconsin Lutheran Quarterly*, 92(4), 263–270.

Chavasse, C. L. (1970). Laying on of hands. *Expository Times*, 81, 150.

Diephouse, D. J. (1991). Hands-on worship: Expanding our practice of laying on of hands. *Reformed Worship*, 19, 4–6.

Flusser, D. (1957). Healing through the laying-on of hands in a Dead Sea scroll. *Israel Exploration Journal*, 7(2), 107–108.

Grad, B. R. (1994). The laying on of hands: Some clinical and experimental concerns. *Journal of Religion and Psychical Research*, 17(4), 182–188.

Grayston, K. (1970). The significance of the Word hand in the New Testament. In A.-L. Descamps & A. de Halleux (Eds.), *Mélanges bibliques en hommage au R P Béda Rigaux*. Gembloux, Belgium: Duculot.

Hayes, N. (1977). *God's power through laying on of hands.* Houston, TX: Hunter Ministries.

Headley, C. (2002). The laying on of hands and anointing in ministry for wholeness and healing. *Grove Worship Series.* Cambridge, UK: Grove Books.

Mattingly, K. (2001). The significance of Joshua's reception of the laying on of hands in Numbers 27:12–23. *Andrews University Seminary Studies, 39*(2), 191–208.

Mattingly, K. (2002). Joshua's reception of the laying on of hands: Pt 2, Deuteronomy 34:7 and conclusion. *Andrews University Seminary Studies, 40*(1), 89–103.

Oulton, J. E. L. (1955). Holy Spirit, baptism, and laying on of hands in Acts. *Expository Times, 66,* 236–240.

Parratt, J. K. (1966). An early Baptist on the laying on of hands. *Baptist Quarterly, 21,* 325–327.

Parratt, J. K. (1968). Romans 1:11 and Galatians 3:5: Pauline evidence for the laying on of hands? *Expository Times, 79,* 151–152.

Parratt, J. K. (1969). Laying on of hands in the New Testament: A re-examination in the light of the Hebrew terminology. *Expository Times, 80,* 210–214.

Payne, E. A. (1954). Baptists and the laying on of hands. *Baptist Quarterly, 15,* 203–215.

Payne, E. A. (1975). Baptists and Christian initiation. *Baptist Quarterly, 26,* 147–157.

Porter, H. B. (1954). Laying hands on the sick: Ancient rite and prayer book formulae. *Anglican Theological Review, 36*(2), 83–89.

Sieh, L. L. (1999). Reclaiming the Church's healing ministry. *Chaplaincy Today, 15*(2), 17–22.

Healing, Gifts of

Classical Pentecostalism has always promoted divine healing as a central expression of the ministry of the Church, entrusted to it by Jesus and mediated through the power of the Holy Spirit. This belief rests on Old Testament (Exodus 15:26; Isaiah 53:4, 5) and New Testament texts (Matthew 4:23; Mark 16:15ff) and the example of Jesus in his healing ministry, and has been reinforced by occurrences of healings throughout the history of Pentecostalism.

Jesus, the Healing Paradigm

The view that Jesus is a paradigm in his healing ministry for contemporary believers is tenaciously maintained by many Pentecostals. As a result, there is often a limited appreciation of other reasons that motivated the healing ministry of Jesus. Furthermore, Pentecostals affirm that the healing authority of Jesus has been delegated to the Church, viewing the commission to the apostles as being to all believers. However, too often the expectation of healing anticipated by many is not fulfilled, and reasons have been offered for this lack of healing including personal sin, a lack of faith, or that believers are imperfect channels for such healing power in all cases.

These unresolved tensions are located among Pentecostals throughout their history and are testimony to their willingness to cling to beliefs that are viewed as being accurate biblical perceptions, rather than to accept that which reality dictates. This is a fundamental Pentecostal stance. Reality is not viewed as being the only legitimate arbiter; it is also determined by the believers' perception of faith and their interpretation of Scripture. Instead of considering the possibility that Jesus' healing ministry may have been unique, they prefer to believe that the healing authority of his followers and its implementation is of an inferior quality, thus, to a degree, undermining their belief that Jesus delegated his authority to believers.

Causes of Sickness

Pentecostals believe that sickness is intrinsically evil, resulting from the sin of Adam and Eve, and fundamentally, to Satan himself (Job 2:7; Acts 10:38). Because of the association of some sickness with demonic influence in the Gospels, it is also assumed that a similar relationship may occur today with regard to some sicknesses. In these cases, the demonic source needs to be first removed, as a result of which, healing is to be expected. The Biblical declaration that sickness may be a chastisement for sin (1 Corinthians 11:30) has resulted in Pentecostals maintaining the belief that, on occasions, sickness may be the result of personal sin and that confession of that sin will result in the sickness being removed (James 5:15).

Will of God and Healing

Throughout the history of Pentecostalism, there have been those who have stated that it is always God's will to heal. Thus, at times, the ministry of healing has taken place in a verbal context of claiming or commanding healing. Such insistence often leads to confusion, guilt, despair, and, worst of all, an imperfect perception of God who appears arbitrary and unfeeling in his dealings with people, especially when healing does not occur. However, reluctance to abandon the

Extract from Sinclair Lewis's *Elmer Gantry* (1927)

Sinclair Lewis's novel about a clergyman with dubious morals caused much controversy upon its publication in 1927. On his way to a more mainstream pulpit, the title character, Elmer Gantry, joins forces with Sharon Falconer, an evangelist who gains a reputation as a healer.

The woman screamed, "Glory to God, I've got my hearing back!"

There was a sensation in the tabernacle, and everybody itched with desire to be relieved of whatever ailed him. Elmer led the healed deaf woman aside and asked her name for the newspapers. It is true that she could not hear him, but he wrote out his questions, she wrote the answers, and he got an excellent story for the papers and an idea for their holy work.

Why, he put it to Sharon, shouldn't she make healing a regular feature?

"I don't know that I have any gift for it," considered Sharon.

"Sure you have! Aren't you psychic? You bet. Go to it. We might pull off some healing services. I bet the collections would bust all records, and we'll have a distinct understanding with the local committees that we get all over a certain amount, besides the collection the last day."

"Well, we might try one. Of course, the Lord may have blessed me with special gifts that way, and to him be all the credit, oh, let's stop in here and have an ice cream soda, I LOVE banana splits, I hope nobody sees me, I feel like dancing tonight, anyway we'll talk over the possibility of healing, I'm going to take a hot bath the minute we get home with losh bath salts—losh and losh and losh."

The success was immense.

She alienated many evangelical pastors by divine healing, but she won all the readers of books about will-power, and her daily miracles were reported in the newspapers. And, or so it was reported, some of the patients remained cured.

She murmured to Elmer, "You know, maybe there really is something to this healing, and I get an enormous thrill out of it—telling the lame to chuck their crutches. That man last night, that cripple—he did feel lots better."

They decorated the altar now with crutches and walking-sticks, all given by grateful patients—except such as Elmer had been compelled to buy to make the exhibit inspiring from the start.

Source: Lewis, S. (1954). *Elmer Gantry* (pp. 223–224). New York: Dell. (Original work published 1927)

---

belief that it is God's will to heal the sick still causes some tensions in Pentecostal belief and practice.

However, throughout the Pentecostal era, there have been others who have reacted to the suggestion that because Jesus healed all who came to him for healing, the same pattern exists today. The issue of the conditional nature of divine healing is one of the areas that have experienced a noticeable change within Pentecostalism, though tension still remains. Some have suggested that although God has the power to heal, he does not always choose to do so, and in the case of the latter it is due to his sovereign will, or because the sickness was allowed by God for a reason. Thus, although the official Statements of Faith of most Pentecostal denominations offer the potential of divine healing, most refrain from expressing it as a guarantee. However, it is believed that bringing a person to God in prayer presumes that a positive infusion of his grace will be received by the sufferer.

Although the biblical narrative indicates that supernatural healings were generally immediate, the notion of gradual healings is common in healing scenarios today. Thus, while healing is accepted as a benefit currently available to believers, it is accepted that the timing of healing is uncertain; it might not even occur until after death. However, this framework has led to confusion and disappointment because it is not coupled with careful theologies of suffering and dying.

Healing as a Repeatable Miracle

In this excerpt from his book *Possibility Living*, Dr. Robert A. Schuller notes that the gift of healing can be obtained by those with enough faith to put into Christian principles into practice.

Jesus was the greatest physician the world has ever seen. He healed thousands of people on a regular basis. The mistake we make in interpreting this history given in the Scriptures is to assume that his healing power was miraculous and therefore not repeatable.

John Wimber, founder of Vineyard Ministries, taught at Fuller Theological Seminary in the late 1970s and early 1980s. The only professor without the "proper" credentials, he taught the class "Signs and Wonders." His teaching, which became the premise of his more than one thousand churches, is that Jesus gave us the power to do "miraculous" things through his disciples. That means you and I—anyone who has enough faith to put the principles into practice—could perform the same miracles that Jesus shared with us.

Source: Schuller, R. A., & Di Siena, D. (2000). *Possibility living: Add years to your life and life to your years with God's health plan.* New York: HarperCollins.

There has been a significant development in perception concerning healing and the will of God, which is the result of a major paradigm shift in theological understanding and a recognition that although the Kingdom has been established by Jesus, not all its benefits may be experienced in this life. Personal experience and a reexamination of biblical principles concerning healing and an increased awareness of the issue of the will of God have been the major causes of this development.

Evangelism

Healing is recognized as serving a higher purpose than just the physical healing of individuals, namely the proclamation of the Gospel. As such, it formed a major part of Christ's ministry and that of the early church, functioning as a sign of the establishment of the Kingdom of God. The relationship between healing and evangelism has always been prominent in Pentecostalism, though now most ministry of healing is anticipated for the benefit of believers, rather than unbelievers in evangelistic settings. Any similarity to the ministry of Jesus, in which healings were significantly intended to function as stepping-stones to faith, is now to a large degree less frequent.

Similarly, the role of the healing evangelist has largely been replaced by a local church-based practice of prayer, often by the leadership, in the context of corporate prayer for those suffering, as reflected in James 5:14–16. This is often allied to the anointing of the sick person with oil and the laying on of hands, the latter element following the common practice of Jesus, Peter, and Paul. The laying on of hands acts neither as a formal rite nor as a conductor of supernatural power but as a sign of compassion for and relationship with the sufferer and also as a symbol of the healing hands of Jesus.

Faith

The issue of faith is of major importance in praying for those who are sick. However, it has been and still is a confusing issue to many, not least because of the variety of opinions reflected. In many Pentecostal writings the identity of the faith required is often not clarified, nor is it clear as to whether the sufferer or the one praying should be expressing faith. For many, faith is equated with belief in a promise that healing is the guaranteed right of believers. Thus, before God will heal, some assume that they have to believe that he is going to do so. Without this certainty, the healing is assumed to be unlikely. Although most Pentecostals would reject this view, the fear of an absence or insufficient amount of faith has resulted in many experiencing guilt and discouragement due to an unnecessary perception that one may have been a block to one's own healing or that of another. Because of this belief, some Pentecostals have advocated a refusal to undertake medical therapies or to ignore symptoms of sickness as a proof of one's faith. Instead, it has been recommended that one should thank God for one's healing even though it was not yet apparent. Although there have been few reflective assessments of these claims against the background of a limited number of healings, increasingly, such a view has been rejected.

Faith has been identified as best understood when placed in the context of a relationship with God where it is recognized as being given by God when his will is to be achieved. Thus, the prayer of faith (James 5:15) is to be understood as a prayer offered in recognition that one is being influenced by God in the way that the prayer is articulated, as a result of which faith is granted to believe that restoration will occur. Thus, the prayer of faith may be identified as a prayer that engages the members of the church in a process that seeks to identify and effect the will of God in the life of the suffering member. Such a prayer can be offered by one who has taken time to tap God's resource of wisdom and appropriate it to a particular situation.

Faith in God is to be equated with a confidence that God's will will be achieved and that his ways are best. Having accepted this basic premise, Pentecostals are encouraged to pray for the sick while being open to the possibility that God may direct their prayers to achieve a different outcome, as reflected in the prayers of Paul that his "thorn in the flesh" be removed, though God provided his grace to live with the problem rather than its removal.

Prayer

Pentecostals have always affirmed the necessity of prayer in the context of a request for healing. Similarly, the attitude in which the prayer is offered or its motivation is of importance. For some, persistence in prayer or fasting has also been regarded as being important. It is recognized increasingly that prayer is not to be understood simply as a formal procedure in which the sufferer is presented to God for restoration but as an opportunity to identify God's will as to how one should pray.

For Pentecostals, there is great significance in the use of the name of Jesus in prayer. Though some use the name of Jesus in prayer because of historical practice, most do so believing that there is power associated with it, as reflected in the promises of Jesus (John 14:13, 14; 16:24) and the practice of the apostles (Acts 3:6, 16). However, the suggestion that healing power is inevitably released is largely rejected. The reason for the inclusion of the name is a reminder that not only does

the response to a prayer depend on the one to whom the prayer is addressed but also that the response is approved by him (1 John 5:14, 15). Claiming healing "in the name of the Lord" is generally equated with presumption unless God has specifically assured the one concerned that such a claim is in accordance with his will.

Healing and the Atonement of Christ

A popular belief among many Pentecostals concerns the value of the death of Christ in healing. This is based on a particular reading of Matthew 8:17 that is viewed as indicating that physical healing has been procured by Jesus at his death in the same way that the forgiveness of sins has been achieved. Others prefer to understand this text as one of the occasions where the author illustrates that Jesus, in his healing ministry, was fulfilling the prophecy applied to Messiah. Thus, rather than relating to his death to come, it is viewed as relating to his healing mission. 1 Peter 2:24 is also used to support the link between healing and the death of Christ though the context is of suffering relating to persecution not sickness. While some Pentecostals have identified a central element in the death of Jesus as relating to the granting of physical healing, similar to the granting of the forgiveness of sins, others have provided a more nuanced response, viewing the death of Jesus as providing the basis for physical healing though this may not necessarily be achieved in this life.

Gifts of Healings

The term "gifts of healings" (1 Corinthians. 12:9, 28, 30) is contained in a lengthy passage in which Paul explores the variety of the gifts given by the Spirit to the church.

The term *charismata* (gifts), a distinctively Pauline term, prefaces *iamatōn* (healings), in a combination that only occurs in the Pauline literature with regard to this particular gift. It may be that Paul is seeking to distinguish healing as a gift of the Spirit rather than allow it to be too quickly associated with a healer who has the ability to heal. Thus, rather assuming that a believer may have a permanent ability to heal, one should view each healing as a gift of God manifested through an individual who functions as a mediator between God and the one receiving the gift of healing.

The fact that both terms are in the plural has resulted in a range of explanatory suggestions. It is possible that Paul has in mind that each occasion of healing is to be identified as a gift of healing; thus, the person who is healed receives a gift of healing. It may be that he is demonstrating the comprehensive power of the Spirit to provide restoration for many illnesses. It is possible that some believers are enabled by the Spirit to facilitate the healing of particular illnesses. Although some have claimed this to be a true reflection of their own healing ministries, it raises the question as to what one should do if the particular restorative capacity is not available in those hoping to respond to someone in need of ministry. It is also not reflected in the healing narratives in Acts nor in James 5:14–18.

It is most probable that it describes the purpose of the Spirit to provide a variety of healings through a diversity of believers. Although it need not be assumed that such ability necessarily resides in a believer permanently, Paul does assume the presence of healers in the church (1 Corinthians 12:28). Such a definition may be applied to those who function in this gift more than other people.

Medicine

Pentecostalism tends not to contrast medical healing and divine healing and the former is not viewed suspiciously or negatively, and the assumption that one can rely on God instead of available medical therapies is now significantly diminished. However, there was an earlier tradition that advocated an antimedical stance. Dialogue and integration with medical practices, though as yet inadequately developed within Pentecostalism, have resulted in the recognition that although divine healing and medical therapy should not be confused, the latter is a gift of God to humanity and therefore is appropriate for believers to access.

Implications

Although there are variations, a number of constants may be identified within Pentecostalism concerning healing, foremost of which is that the ministry of the Spirit through believers means that healing is available whenever it is in keeping with the will of God. As well as the development of a more coherent and uniform presentation of guidelines and praxis concerning contemporary healing ministry, a positive and constructive Pentecostal theology of suffering is to be anticipated.

KEITH WARRINGTON

See also Charismata; Gifts of the Spirit; Hands, Laying on of; Positive Confession Theology

Further Reading

Brown, M. L. (1995). *Israel's divine healer*. Carlisle, UK: Paternoster Press.

Dayton, D. W. (1982). The rise of the Evangelical healing movement in nineteenth century America. *Pneuma: The Journal of the Society for Pentecostal Studies, 4*(1), 1–18.

Gunstone, J. (1986). *The Lord is our healer*. London: Hodder and Stoughton.

Harper, M. (1986). *The healings of Jesus*. London: Hodder and Stoughton.

Harrell, D. E., Jr. (1975). *All things are possible: The healing and Charismatic revivals in modern America*. Bloomington: Indiana University Press.

Menzies, R. P. (2000). Healing in the atonement. In W. W. Menzies & R. P. Menzies (Eds.), *Spirit and power: Foundations of Pentecostal experience* (pp. 159–170). Grand Rapids, MI: Zondervan.

Synan, V. (2000). A healer in the house? A historical perspective on healing in the Pentecostal/Charismatic tradition. *Asian Journal of Pentecostal Studies, 3*(2), 189–201.

Thomas, J. C. (1998). *The devil, disease and deliverance*. Sheffield, UK: Sheffield Academic Press.

Twelftree, G. (1999). *Jesus the miracle worker*. Downers Grove, IL: InterVarsity Press.

Wimber, J., & Springer, K. (1986). *Power healing*. London: Hodder and Stoughton.

Woolmer, J. (1999). *Healing and deliverance*. London: Hodder and Stoughton.

Hispanic Pentecostalism

Hispanic Pentecostalism, the Spanish- and Portuguese-speaking segment of the global Pentecostal and Charismatic movements, exemplifies in the United States and in Latin America the twentieth-century phenomenon of Pentecostalism's transforming influence upon a people, society, and faith.

Broadly defined, the term *Pentecostalism* may be understood to include the following groups: classical Pentecostals, who belong to denominations like the Assemblies of God and the International Church of the Foursquare Gospel; charismatics, who belong to mainline Christian denominations like Roman Catholicism or Methodism but who have experienced baptism in the Holy Spirit while remaining in their traditions; and neocharismatics, a catch-all category for those not classified as Pentecostals or charismatics but who share a common emphasis on the Holy Spirit.

Pentecostalism's explosive growth to over 550 million adherents in just a century has made it the second-largest Christian group after the Roman Catholic Church. In the summer of 1906, Hispanics were among the first recipients of "the fullness of the Spirit" at the Azusa Street Mission in downtown Los Angeles, and the Hispanic community has proven to be fertile ground for the movement. After World War II and especially since the 1980s, Hispanic Pentecostalism has been a force for renewal in the Church. In 2001 the United States, Canada, and Puerto Rico recorded 6 million Hispanic Pentecostals. This number represents 20 percent of the Latino population in these countries. In the same year Latin America recorded over 140 million Pentecostals, of which 23 percent were classical Pentecostals, 52 percent charismatics, and 24 percent neocharismatics.

Hispanic Nomenclature

In 1978 the U.S. government clustered the nation's Spanish-speaking minority under the category of *Hispanic*, a term encompassing all individuals who come from the Caribbean, Central or South America, or other culture of Spanish origin, regardless of race. The label inadequately classifies persons of such diverse backgrounds and characteristics. Most Latin American immigrants and U.S.-born Hispanics identify themselves by their family's original nationality: "I am (Ecuadorian, Bolivian, Guatemalan, etc.)." Others choose a "hyphenated American" identification, such as *Mexican-American*. But many refuse these labels, regarding them as prescribed by the dominant culture; the term *Latino* is widely preferred because it is considered more inclusive. Latinos are people with roots in Latin America, yet with Native American, African, Portuguese, and/or Spanish blood genetically intermixed.

Although there is no consensus on an all-encompassing term, both *Hispanic* and *Latino* may be used interchangeably for U.S. persons of Hispanic descent, and the term *Latin American* is appropriate to use for those in Latin America. At the beginning of the third millennium, millions of Latinos and Latin Americans are being drawn into Pentecostalism's worldview.

Hispanic Pentecostals in the United States

Pentecostalism's ethnic sensitivity partially explains its global acceptance; the movement's adaptability and mobility within cultures of diverse ethnicity has offered its followers a contextualized faith. Hispanic theologians employ the historical term *mestizaje* (referring to the intermixing of European and indigenous peoples) to express their heterogeneous identity and eclectic reality. One writer on Hispanic Christianity defines *mestizaje* biologically, as "the mixture of human groups of different makeup determining the color and shape of the eyes, skin pigmentation, and makeup of the bone structure" (Bañuelas 1995, 9), although the term has broad cultural connotations as well.

Latin American history records that an ethnic fusion commenced in 1492 when Spanish conquistadors amalgamated their religion and culture with those of Amerindians and Africans in Central and South America. A *New World* was not discovered, as the Spaniards believed, but rather a *mestizo world* was born, characterized by the genetic mixing of European men and native women. At the same time, the oppression and struggle of a people began. In Latino theology, *mestizaje* also represents the Latino's fight in God's world for self-identity and self-determination. The mestizo world consist of today's Latin American: the Salvadorian, Argentine, or Dominican in Latin America; but also the *mestizaje* is represented by the Latino immigrants arriving in the United States and future generations of Hispanics in the country. Pentecostalism has granted U.S. Hispanics space to cultivate a faith representative of their kaleidoscopic cultural context.

Initially the Azusa Street Revival of 1906 embodied a *mestizaje* of cultures and nationalities: "There was a total absence of racial discrimination. Blacks, whites, Chinese, and even Jews attended…In a short while the majority of attendants were white, but always there was complete integration of the races in the services" (Synan 1997, 99). Early accounts place Hispanics among the ethnic entourage of the modern Pentecost. Consequently Latino communities were directly influenced by the Pentecostal experience as recipients, both Latinos and others, shared their new spiritual baptism and started missions of their own.

Hispanic Pentecostal churches emerged within a few years of the revival. In 1912, several California communities, such as San Diego, San Bernardino, and Los Angeles, had Mexican congregations. Eastward along the Mexican border, Pentecostalism took root in Texas soil, and by 1917 seventeen towns had been reached. Pentecostalism spread in regions and states where Latinos were populous. In the Southwest (e.g., Texas and California) the Pentecostal churches are predominantly Mexican, while in the Northeast (e.g., New York), Puerto Rican congregations abound. After 1959, Cuban Pentecostals were sheltered in Florida, and the 1980s influx of Central Americans added to the Pentecostal *mestizaje*. Today Hispanic Pentecostal churches proliferate across the nation.

Allocation of Hispanic Pentecostal churches falls into four categories: U.S.-based Pentecostal denominations, such as the Assemblies of God and the Church of

God (Cleveland, Tennessee); independent ethnic churches; groups associated with Latin American Pentecostal churches such as the Brazilian Iglesia Universal del Reino de Dios (Universal Church of the Kingdom of God); and indigenous churches (native groups birthed naturally in the region), such as the Iglesia Apostólica de la Fe en Cristo Jesus (Apostolic Church of the Faith in Jesus Christ) and churches belonging to associations of churches like the Latin American Council of Christian Churches (LACCC).

Francisco "The Great Aztec" Olazábal

Pentecostal pioneers among Hispanics, such as Henry Ball (1896–1989), Alice Luce (1873–1955), and Juan Lugo (1890–1984), laid a stable foundation for subsequent Latino Pentecostals; but foremost among the personalities of early Hispanic Pentecostalism was Francisco Olazábal (1886–1937). In 1900 Olazábal converted to Methodism under the mentoring of George and Carrie Judd Montgomery in San Francisco. He returned to his native Mexico with an inescapable call to prepare for the ministry. After brief pastorates, he returned to the United States and entered Moody Bible Institute. In 1917 he joined the Assemblies of God after receiving the Pentecostal experience as a result of reuniting with the Montgomerys following their move to Pentecostalism. Olazábal led many Latino preachers and lay people into the Assemblies of God; but by 1923, dissatisfied with the Anglo-dominated Pentecostal organization, he and other Hispanic leaders formed the Latin American Council of Christian Churches.

For the next fourteen years, Olazábal's Pentecostal preaching and leadership in California, Texas, the Midwest, and Puerto Rico helped establish a strong Hispanic following. A contemporary biographer called him the "Great Aztec" because of his imposing persona and leadership. In 1937, at the peak of his evangelistic career, he died unexpectedly in an automobile accident in Texas, leaving a legacy of over 150 churches and an LACCC membership of 50,000.

Pentecostalism's Magnetism

A brief profile of the movement's generative themes demonstrates Pentecostalism's appeal and continued development in Latin America: Latin American Pentecostalism is a popular movement, a power over marginality, a church with a participatory mission, and a twentieth-century phenomenal movement.

A minority of Latin Americans benefit from modernism's neoliberalism, modernization, and privatization, and most live lives of unbearable marginalization. Under the weight of social, economic, and political crises, the poor choose Pentecostalism. For example, when masses of rural dwellers transition to an urban life of unanticipated frustration, dislocation, and loss of identity, Pentecostalism provides an alternative to the uncertainties of urbanization—a community of acceptance and recognition. It is a popular movement mainly among the poor who claim it as their own, a church of the people.

A main attraction of Pentecostal churches is the accessibility of power over marginality. People espouse a personal faith centered on an experiential spirituality. The newfound power gained through baptism in the Spirit enables the formerly disenfranchised to overcome spiritual and social evils. Pentecostalism's haven provides marginalized people space for upward mobility in health, finances, and relationships, as well as spiritual authority over demonic forces. For Pentecostals, life is no longer a matter of mere survival, but a new life of hope, dignity, and power over marginality.

Enlivened, Spirit-filled, and empowered individuals are able to establish mission-minded communities. Lay participation and leadership in the Church and in evangelization are the force behind the movement's global growth, in Latin America in particular. A Reformation emphasis is being restored in Catholic lands as Pentecostals rich and poor serve in God's "priesthood of all believers." The Holy Spirit empowers the Latin American Church as a protagonist in society to "go and make disciples of all nations" (Matthew 28:19).

Pentecostalism's popularity, power, and participatory role have made it a twentieth-century phenomenal movement. In the early 1980s the movement recorded amazing growth: every hour, 400 Latin Americans converted to Pentecostalism. In 1995 Brazil counted 47 percent of the population Pentecostal, while Chile (36 percent), Colombia (30 percent), Puerto Rico (27 percent), El Salvador (24 percent), and Guatemala (22 percent) demonstrated phenomenal growth towards the end of the twentieth century. Although Catholicism is the predominant cultural and social force in Latin America, Pentecostal renewal is transforming the Latin American religious scene.

Future Challenges

If U.S. Latino and Latin American Pentecostals are to realize a bright future, they must face the challenges of the third millennium As the Pentecostal family continues to grow, U.S. Latino Pentecostals must address the generational divide of language and culture. Second and later generations have trouble identifying their biculturalism in only Spanish-speaking churches. Whose society and culture will they claim? Is a bilingual Hispanic Church an effective model? Latin American Pentecostals and their U.S. counterparts also see this divide in terms of education. Has professional advancement alienated some Pentecostals from their churches? Do younger Pentecostals have space to be youth in society? These questions must be answered if Hispanic Pentecostalism desires to keep later generations within the fold.

Elaborating a Pentecostal Christian thought is another crucial identity task for Hispanics and Latin Americans. Contributions of this nature will orient Hispanics and instruct the Church at large. The 1990s presented an emergent flow of reflections and writings from several Latino and Latin American Pentecostal theologians like Samuel Solivan, Eldin Villafañe, Juan Sepulveda, Bernardo Campos, and others. Although this is a good start, many questions still need development from a Pentecostal standpoint. Is there both an explicit and implicit Latino Pentecostal theology? What would a distinctively Hispanic Pentecostal "theology of life" or systematic theology look like? Further study and elucidation must come from the Hispanic Pentecostal community so that the Latino voice will be well represented.

Globalization, postmodernism, ecology, and secularization are other challenges Hispanic Pentecostalism is facing along with the rest of the movement The story of this particular sector of Pentecostalism demonstrates vigor and life among the Spanish- and Portuguese-speaking peoples of the United States and Latin America. The *mestizaje* of peoples is being embraced by Pentecostalism, and in return people are opting for the phenomenal movement of the twentieth century. At the dawn of the third millennium, Hispanics and Latin Americans are full participants in Pentecostalism, the new dominant force in Christendom.

ELOY H. NOLIVOS

See also America, Latin; Brazil; Race Relations

Further Reading

Bañuelas, A. J. (1995). *Mestizo Christianity: Theology from the Latino perspective*. Maryknoll, NY: Orbis Books.

Isasi-Diaz, A. M., & Segovia, F. F. (1996). *Hispanic/Latino theology: Challenge and promise*. Minneapolis, MN: Fortress Press.

Solivan, S. (1998). *The spirit, pathos and liberation: Toward an Hispanic Pentecostal theology*. Sheffield, UK: Sheffield Academic Press.

Synan, V. (1997). *The Holiness-Pentecostal tradition: Charismatic movements in the twentieth century*. Grand Rapids, MI: Eerdmans.

Synan, V. (2001). *The century of the Holy Spirit: 100 years of Pentecostal and Charismatic renewal*. Nashville, TN: Thomas Nelson.

Historiography

The study of the modern Pentecostal and Charismatic movements has blossomed in the last twenty-five years. Although Pentecostalism was once marginalized, its global character and remarkable growth have brought it to the forefront. Nowhere is this more apparent than in Pentecostal historiography (the study of how history is interpreted and written); the centennial of the 1906 Azusa Street Revival will spur even more studies of the origins and history of modern Pentecostalism.

Historians using different historiographical approaches have interpreted the movement from within and without. With a few exceptions, the wider academic community has given more weight to the works of historians outside the movement, who usually adopt modern, non-providential historiographic methods. This is not surprising given the hyperprovidential and nonacademic character of the early attempts to tell the story of Pentecostalism.

Significant today, however, is the increasing professionalism of the movements' own historians and theologians. Pentecostal and charismatic researchers are now producing more specialized and nuanced studies of their movements. Signaling this new era in research was the inauguration in 2003 of a Ph.D. in Renewal Studies offered by Regent University in Virginia, the first accredited doctoral program in the world to focus exclusively on the history and theology of the renewing work of the Holy Spirit. (The term "Renewal" refers to contemporary expressions of the Pentecostal and Charismatic movements, whether these expressions consciously identify with the movements or are simply Pentecostal-like in their emphasis on the Holy Spirit and charismatic gifts.)

Regent University, along with other Renewal teaching institutions like Church of God Theological Seminary, Oral Roberts University, Assemblies of God Theological Seminary, and Asian Pacific Theological Seminary, is cultivating a rich soil for the study of modern Pentecostalism from the perspective of participant-scholars. As the burgeoning worldwide Renewal's scholarship continues to mature, distinct Renewal historiographies shaped by the movement's own ethos will develop and give new direction to Christian historiography in the twenty-first century.

A Survey of Renewal Historiography

A good place to begin to understand the Renewal is *The New International Dictionary of the Pentecostal and Charismatic Movements (NIDPCM)*, which contains hundreds of survey articles on significant persons, places, events, and ideas of the movements; many articles are survey length and most include bibliographies. The *NIDPCM* also includes two of the most comprehensive analyses of the Pentecostal and charismatic historiography yet produced. Grant Wacker's and Augustus Cerillo's article, "Bibliography and Historiography of Pentecostalism in the United States," with over twenty-five thousand words, interprets the developing historiography of modern Pentecostalism over the last hundred years. Equally helpful for its global analysis and historiographic discussion on the contributions of Walter Hollenwegger and others is the *NIDPCM* article by David Bundy, "Bibliography and Historiography outside North America." Both articles provide excellent bibliographic discussion.

Charles E. Jones's *A Guide to the Study of the Pentecostal Movement*, and *The Charismatic Movement: A Guide to the Study of Neo-Pentecostalism, with an Emphasis on Anglo-American Sources* catalog a wealth of primary and secondary materials. Watson Mill's *Charismatic in Modern Research: A Bibliography* is also helpful.

As one would expect, the oldest historical materials of early-twentieth-century Pentecostalism were the testimonials, articles, and tracts composed to popularize and spread the movement. Because the movement was too busy coming into existence to devote much time to reflecting on its origins, the movement's practitioners and players saw Pentecostalism simply as "a providentially generated, end-time religious revival fundamentally discontinuous with 1,900 years of Christian history" (Burgess and van der Maas 2002). This providential and restorationistic perspective has continued as a core idea over the decades. Even as late as 1961 Carl Brumback's Assemblies of God history, *Suddenly… from Heaven*, reveals an ahistorical orientation in its very title.

It was not until the 1960s and 1970s that more objective, though still sympathetic, works on the movement's history emerged, led by Klaude Kendrick's *The Promise Fulfilled: The history of the modern Pentecostal Movement* (1961), John Nichol's *The Pentecostals* (1966),

and Vinson Synan's *The Holiness-Pentecostal Movement in the United States* (1971; revised in 1997 with the new title *The Holiness-Pentecostal Tradition*); all three books grew out of doctoral dissertations. These new views of Pentecostal origins emphasized the roots of the movement and its continuity with nineteenth-century religious and social movements; Synan, for example, argued that Pentecostalism had emerged out of nineteenth-century Holiness movements.

Swiss theologian Walter Hollenwegger has been a significant analyst of Pentecostalism since the 1960s and has emphasized the African roots of the movement and its orality. While most of his works are available only in German, his two English books *The Pentecostals* (1972) and *Pentecostalism* (1997) interpret Pentecostalism in global perspective.

Donald Dayton's *The Theological Roots of Pentecostalism* (1987) explicitly affirmed turn-of-the-century Pentecostalism's continuity with its nineteenth-century heritage, agreeing with Synan on the movement's Holiness roots. But Dayton also emphasized the movement's unique theological impulse, which he believed was anchored in glossolalia as biblical evidence of Spirit baptism. For Dayton this focus on glossolalia was an unexpected result of the currents flowing from the Christian milieu of the late nineteenth century.

Probably no work more strikingly marked the developing study of Pentecostalism than Robert Mapes Anderson's book *Vision of the Disinherited: The Making of American Pentecostalism* (1979). Anderson, not a participant in the Pentecostal and Charismatic movements, provided one of the first scholarly critiques of the movement's origins. Placing Pentecostal origins firmly within its early twentieth-century social context, Anderson asserts that Pentecostalism was a response to the changing time in which it emerged. Arising almost exclusively among the poor and disenfranchised, Pentecostalism provided a feeling of belonging and empowerment for the marginalized and culturally alienated. Anderson's methodological sophistication, Marxist sociological approach, and unapologetic embrace of modern historiography leave no room for a providential view of historical causation.

Another sign of the movement's increasing recognition is Harvard religion professor Harvey Cox's 1992 book, *Fire from Heaven*. Cox gives a cautious but favorable assessment of Pentecostalism's importance to the global religious landscape at the end of the twentieth century. Though far more sympathetic than Anderson, Cox analyzes the movement as a unique social and cultural phenomenon while not ignoring its passionate spirituality.

Reflecting an increasing awareness of modern Pentecostalism's historical continuity are Stanley Burgess's three volumes on the history of pneumatology: *The Holy Spirit: Ancient Christian Traditions* (1984); *The Holy Spirit: Eastern Church Tradition* (1989); and *The Holy Spirit: Medieval Roman Catholic and Reformation Traditions* (1997). Spanning two millennia of the Christian story, Burgess' trilogy demonstrates that renewal has been an ongoing dynamic in Christian history and helps to counterbalance ahistorical notions of the Renewal.

In the last fifteen years, several historians have written on early Pentecostal history and found new respectability in the academic community. Edith Blumhoffer's *Restoring the faith: Assemblies of God, Pentecostalism, and American Culture* (1993) tells the history of Pentecostalism using the Pentecostal denomination Assemblies of God as a lens with which to view the larger Pentecostal and charismatic tradition in its North American context. Blumhoffer's biography *Aimee Semple McPherson: Everybody's Sister* (1993) on the eccentric healing evangelist who founded the International Church of the Foursquare Gospel and James Goff's biography on one of Pentecostalism's fathers, *Fields White unto Harvest: Charles Fox Parham and the Missionary Origins of Pentecostalism* (1988) show the increasing sophistication of historical interpretations of early Pentecostalism. Grant Wacker's *Heaven Below: Early Pentecostalism and American Culture* (2001) provides a perceptive and fresh understanding of the early Pentecostal ethos against the backdrop of the early twentieth century. Generally sympathetic toward Pentecostalism, these scholars employ a historiography that Wheaton University's Mark Noll calls "ordinary history," and they explore the identity of Pentecostalism's founders without dismissing or legitimizing the early leaders' claims of God's supernatural and providential activity.

Two theological works on early Pentecostalism are valuable for their historical perspective on the movement's developing self-understanding, *Pentecostal Spirituality: A Passion for the Kingdom* (1993) by Steven J. Land, and *Thinking in the Spirit: Theologies of the Early Pentecostal Movement* (2003) by Douglas Jacobsen.

David E. Harrell's *All Things are Possible: The Healing and Charismatic Revivals in Modern America* (1979) is an insightful history of the healing movement of the 1940s and 1950s and a chronicle of the early Charismatic Renewal in the 1960s. Harrell's biography *Oral Roberts: An American Life* (1987) is a detailed critical study of the evangelist's life during the middle of the twentieth century.

While no comprehensive history has been written on the broad and amorphous Charismatic Renewal, many specific sources are available. Helpful for researchers is Catholic scholar Kilian McDonnell's *Presence, Power, Praise: Documents on the Charismatic Renewal* (1980), which contains a broad range of documents produced by various denominations for and against the Charismatic Renewal. Richard Quebedeaux's *The New Charismatics II* (1983) is a dated but helpful history and interpretation, as is Michael Harper's *Three Sisters* (1979). Peter Hocken's article "The Charismatic Movement" (*NIDPCM*) is the best up-to-date survey of the history of the Charismatic Renewal. S. David Moore's *The Shepherding Movement: Controversy and Charismatic Ecclesiology* (2003) follows the history of one of the most controversial and influential movements of the 1970s and gives a detailed account of the inner workings of the Charismatic Renewal in that decade. Synan's accessible *Holiness-Pentecostal Tradition* (1997) supplies a concise, updated overview of the Roman Catholic, mainline Protestant, and independent streams of the Charismatic Renewal. His popularly written *Century of the Holy Spirit: 100 years of Pentecostal and Charismatic Christianity* (2001) gives insight into the Charismatic Renewal and also contains chapters on Hispanic Pentecostalism, African-American Pentecostalism, and the place of women in the Renewal.

In recent years researchers are focusing on the missional character and worldwide expressions of Pentecostalism. Notably are two books edited by Murray Dempster, Byron D. Klaus, and Douglas Peterson: *Called and empowered: Global mission in Pentecostal Perspective* (1991) and *The Globalization of Pentecostalism* (1999). Allan Anderson's *An Introduction to Pentecostalism: Global Charismatic Christianity* is another example.

Since its initial publication in 1979, *Pneuma: The Journal of the Society for Pentecostal Studies* has regularly featured historically focused essays and book reviews. The Society for Pentecostal Studies' quarterly newsletter provides bibliographies of newly published books, journal articles, and dissertations covering all areas of Renewal history and theology. Though not as focused on history, *The Journal of Pentecostal Theology* deserves mention. Its monograph supplement series has given many Renewal scholars the opportunity to publish their work. *The Asian Journal of Pentecostal Studies* is an example of growing Pentecostal scholarship outside the West.

The Shape of Renewal Historiography

Although there is a new acceptance in the academic world of well-crafted evaluations of the Pentecostal and Charismatic movements, this acceptance is in part due to their methodological approach, which mirrors secular approaches to historical studies. God's involvement in history is seen as beyond the realm of scholarly inquiry and judgment.

Because Renewal teaching institutions have only recently begun to provide advanced degrees, most Pentecostal and charismatic historians received their training outside the movement and adopted the assumptions of modern historiographers. This is at least in part why no informed academic articulations of distinctly Pentecostal and charismatic historiographies have yet been produced that reflect the Renewal's belief in the providential activity of Holy Spirit in history and its embrace of miracles and spiritual gifts. Given the scientific and rational orientation of contemporary historiography, this is understandable. Crafting histories that cohere with core ideology of the Renewal will not be easy. While remaining committed to the sound methodologies essential to historical study, any authentically Pentecostal and charismatic historiography will need to express the fiduciary, experiential, and contextual character of understanding that is embedded in the Renewal's belief and practice. Combining faith and experience with historical investigation flies in the face of the commonly accepted canons of historical inquiry, which continue to value dispassionate objectivity. Notwithstanding this, Renewal historians must forge historiographies that acknowledge both the cognitive and transcognitive dimensions of a Pentecostal and charismatic epistemology.

The Renewal movement's global dimensions and its diversity require varied historiographies. And since the largest expression of Pentecostal and charismatic Christianity is in the developing world, approaches to historical understanding will not necessarily share many of the assumptions of the Anglo-European academy.

Whatever their differences, Pentecostals and charismatics are both primitivistic and providential in how they interpret the Christian past. Their perspectives are embedded in a passion to experience today the same dynamic encounter with the Holy Spirit described in the New Testament. At the center of Pentecostal understanding is the conviction that God moved in his power and presence historically, interacting cooperatively with humankind, to influence and bring about his purposes in time and space. Any historiography that fails to embrace or at least respect this providential perspective will be rejected by the Renewal.

In the practice and piety of the movement, the true and most influential interpreters of Pentecostalism's history and theology are not academicians but pastors,

church leaders, and evangelists, because the movement's masses listen to them. Instead of addressing only other historians and theologians, professional scholars and Renewal researchers will need to make their work accessible and understandable to pastors and other workers in the field. Given its egalitarian character and grassroots orientation, the Renewal may be able to avoid the dichotomization between scholars and practitioners that so frequently follows the professionalizing of scholarship.

Constructing Renewal historiographies will probably entail confronting the arrogance that often surrounds modern scientific historiography. Fortunately, the emergence of postmodernity, while presenting its own challenges, has fostered a new recognition of the validity of diverse cultural perspectives and presuppositions that contrast with Western intellectual tradition. At the dawn of the twenty-first century, the dominance of Enlightenment-influenced epistemologies is fading and appreciation for the validity of differing worldviews is growing. This new openness, though often criticized, seems to be an open door through which Renewal historians can insert an informed, providential historiography.

A carefully crafted renewal historiography will encompass both the modern methodologies essential to historical study and a mindset that confesses a God intimately involved in His creation. It will also be sensitive to the nonprofessional forms of historical understanding characteristic of the worldwide Renewal: testimonies, songs, folklore, and accounts of amateurs. The antinomy between divine sovereignty and human responsibility inherent in Pentecostal and charismatic thought will have to be addressed. Thus the work of Renewal historiography will be to plausibly present its own history, which displays God at work in the world, but a God who by his Spirit empowers humans to accomplish His redemptive purposes.

Just how the Pentecostal and charismatic interpretation of historiography will be received in the broader contemporary academic world remains to be seen. Will Renewal historiographies gain a fair hearing given their full identification with a movement often perceived—and sometimes justly so—as anti-intellectual? Will attempts to embrace the transcognitive dimensions of learning only reinforce the stereotype of biased scholarship? Current shifts in the academy suggest that Renewal historiographies may find a new respect.

S. DAVID MOORE

See also Antecedents of Pentecostalism; Renewal, Church

Further Reading

Bundy, D. (2002). Bibliography and historiography outside North America. In S. Burgess & E. M. van der Maas (Eds.), *The new international dictionary of the Pentecostal and Charismatic movements*. Grand Rapids, MI: Zondervan.

Burgess, S., & van der Maas, E. M. (Eds.). (2002). *The new international dictionary of the Pentecostal and Charismatic movements*. Grand Rapids, MI: Zondervan.

Jones, C. E. (1983). *A guide to the study of the Pentecostal movement* (2 vols.). Metuchen, NJ: The Scarecrow Press, Inc.

Jones, C. E. (1995). *The Charismatic movement: A guide to the study of Neo-Pentecostalism, with an emphasis on Anglo-American sources* (2 vols.). Philadelphia: Scarecrow Press.

Mills, W. E. (1985). *Charismatic religion in modern research: A bibliography*. Macon, GA: Mercer University Press.

Wacker, G., & Cerillo, A. (2002). Bibliography and historiography of Pentecostalism in the United States. In S. Burgess & E. M. van der Maas (Eds.), *The new international dictionary of the Pentecostal and Charismatic movements*. Grand Rapids, MI: Zondervan.

Holy Spirit

The Third Person of the Trinity, the Holy Spirit, is of prime importance for modern Pentecostals and charismatics, who claim to be Spirit-gifted and Spirit-led. Modern peoples of the Spirit liken themselves to first-century apostolic Christians, who either were present on the day of Pentecost, or experienced that first outpouring of the divine Spirit. Pentecostals tend to view the work of the Spirit in the ensuing eighteen hundred years as less vital—indeed, as a spiritual wasteland. Given this understanding, they find identity in the uniqueness of a life in the Spirit shared with the first-century church.

Apostolic Church

It is true that the apostolic church's vital experience of the Holy Spirit waned significantly from the second century onward, in part because of a diminishing of both prophetic ministry and ecclesiastical emphasis on spiritual gifts. Prophets and priests failed to find common goals for the church, which suffered from prophetic abuse and an institutional process in which Spirit charismata came to be localized in the office of the bishop.

At the same time, theological understanding of the Person and work of the Holy Spirit grew slowly, as the church attempted to address significant Christological questions while expending most of its energies on survival in a hostile Roman world. The writings of Tertullian, a late second- and early third-century North African Father, give expression to the distinctive Personhood and work of the divine Spirit, and to a Trinitarian understanding of God as "three in One," a concept that would eventually be adopted by the larger church in the Nicene Creed.

The writings of the early Fathers also provide further definition of the salvific role of the Holy Spirit in baptism, and of the Spirit's reception in baptism, chrismation (in the East), and confirmation (in the West). At the same time, the reaction against early heresies such as Gnosticism and Montanism led mainline Christians to fear anyone who claimed special knowledge or revelation; this in turn led to a diminishing of the place of the prophet and a corresponding increase in the stature of the priest. For instance, Cyprian, bishop of Carthage from 248 to 258 CE, contends that spiritual gifts are vested in the bishop, who has the sole ability to exercise the charismata. The tension between prophecy and order in the church had emerged.

Post-Apostolic Church

There is strong evidence, however, for an ongoing exercise of spiritual gifts in the post-apostolic church. Irenaeus, Tertullian, and Origen provide specific examples outside the episcopate of second- and third-century charismata that served to validate the church's message and vitality.

With the end of widespread persecution (303 CE in the West, 324 in the East), Christians were free to focus on theological controversies and form creedal statements. Chief among the issues at hand was the conflict over the relationship among the Persons in the Trinity. The Council of Nicea in 325 issued a creedal statement declaring the Son coeternal and equal in substance with the Father. The place of the Holy Spirit was not agreed upon until the Second Ecumenical Council in 381 at Constantinople, when the council declared the Spirit to be "the Lord and Giver-of-Life, who proceedeth from the Father, who with the Father and the Son together is worshiped and glorified, who spake by the prophets."

This formulation did not settle the issue of the Spirit's relationship to the Son. Following Augustine of Hippo's assertion that the Spirit proceeded from the Father *and* the Son (a formula known as the *filioque*, Latin for "and the son"), and a similar interpolation in the Nicene-Constantinople creed by the Third Council of Toledo (589), the Western Church separated (formally in

1054) from the East, which retained the original formulation of the Spirit proceeding from the Father only. Even today, the issue of the *filioque* remains the primary theological difference between the Eastern and Western Churches.

At the Council of Ephesus (431), the Virgin Mary was declared to be *theotokos,* or "bearer of God," rather than *Christotokos,* or bearer of the human Jesus. From this time onward, the Holy Spirit was gradually replaced in popular piety by the Virgin Mary, and the divine Spirit was no longer referred to as feminine in Eastern writings. But the Spirit remained then, as it still is today, an object of piety in Eastern Churches, while in the West, with only a few exceptions, the divine Spirit was never again to be as important for piety for the vast majority of Christians.

Eastern Church Theologians

Most important among the fathers of Eastern Christianity for developing the doctrine of the Holy Spirit were the three Cappadocians (Basil the Great, Gregory of Nyssa, and Gregory of Nazianzen), Ephrem of Syria, Isaac of Ninevah, Symeon the New Theologian, and Gregory Palamas. Of these, Basil of Cappadocia and Symeon the New Theologian have particular significance for students of the history of Pentecostalism.

Basil (c. 330–379) came to be known as a champion of the Spirit (and eventually, "Doctor of the Holy Spirit") for his rejection of any suggestion that the Spirit was a created being, and for his insights into the relationship between the Spirit and the church. Basil's grasp of the divine Spirit's work in the life of the Christian is perhaps the most exceptional in the ancient world. As the Spirit is the conductor of the symphony of creation, He also is the creator of the church, which sanctifies all of creation through the work of the Spirit. Basil became known as a *pneumatophor*—an active receptacle, carrier, and distributor of the Holy Spirit and His gifts. To Basil, life in the Spirit involved more than withdrawal from the world and personal asceticism. It also included active involvement in providing relief to Christians, pagans, and Jews alike. Accordingly, Basil founded an entire community devoted to social relief in Cappadocia (in what is today central Turkey), calling it "New Town." Later this complex came to be called the Basilead in his honor.

Symeon the New Theologian (949–1022) argued that anyone could experience God in the same manner as first-century Christians. Such intense awareness of the divine presence, according to Symeon, begins when a person is baptized in the Holy Spirit, an experience subsequent to water baptism. Baptism in the Spirit is evidenced by the gift of tears and compunction (increased awareness of and sorrow for sins), and a greatly intensified awareness of the divine Trinity as a light dwelling within. The fruit of the Spirit (mentioned in Galatians 5) and other ascetic virtues would accompany the presence of the Holy Spirit, for these also are His gifts. In brief, Symeon, perhaps more than any other voice between the first and the nineteenth centuries, calls on Christians to return to a radical living of the Gospel, to the charismatic and prophetic life of the primitive church.

Certainly the greatest theologian of the ancient Western Church was Augustine, bishop of Hippo (354–430). Unlike the Eastern fathers, who begin with the three divine Persons and then proceed to the unity of God, Augustine begins with the unity of God and proceeds to the Persons. For Augustine, the Holy Spirit is consubstantial and coeternal with the Father and the Son. He is the Spirit of both the Father and of the Son; indeed, He is the communion of divine love between the other two divine Persons—a concept that remained central to Western Catholic pneumatology from that time onward. Because the Holy Spirit is the Spirit of both the Father and the Son, it follows that he proceeds from both. Augustine's formulation of Western Trinitarian dogma marks him as one of the most important pneumatological thinkers in Christian history, exerting great influence not only on the Roman Catholic Church, but also on evangelical Protestantism and classical Pentecostalism.

Dualist Variations

The subject of the Holy Spirit has often been pushed to the side by Christians who have been more interested in soteriology (doctrine of salvation) and eschatology (doctrine of "last things"). On the fringes of the Christian Church, and often openly declared heretical, have been a succession of radical dualist sects. Radical dualism teaches that the individual is controlled by cosmic forces of good and evil, and it accords little, if any, role to free will or individual responsibility. Such dualists have existed from before the birth of the church, and during the Christian era include among their number such groups as the Messalians, the Paulicians, the Bogomils, and the Cathars (sometimes called the Albigenses). All dualists believed that certain chosen individuals (a kind of "elect") had received special divine knowledge from the Holy Spirit. Other, less gifted individuals either acquiesced or were condemned by the intolerantly exclusive dualists. In all cases, radical

The Holy Spirit Expressed in Song

The Holy Spirit is the theme of many "old-time" Pentecostal songs, as is evident in the following choruses (compiled by Ruth and Stan Burgess) from three different songs:

I

Sweet Holy Spirit. Sweet heavenly dove.

Stay right here with us, filling us, thrilling us with your love.

And for each blessing we lift our hearts in praise.

Without a doubt we know that we have been redeemed.

II

Let go and let God have His wonderful way,

Let go and let God have His way,

Your sorrows will vanish, your night turn to day.

Let go and let God have His way.

III

Let it fall on me, Let it fall on me,

Let the pow'r of God, Now fall on me,

Let it fall on me, Let it fall on me,

Let the Breath of God, Now fall on me.

---

dualists purported to exercise gifts of the Spirit and emphasized a baptism in or with the Holy Spirit; they claimed to understand divine purposes. For most Christians (those outside the dualist sects) the charismata were for all believers, not simply for an elect few. Thus, radical dualists reject or minimize established order.

Each group of radical dualists had unique characteristics. For example, the Messalians taught that every individual has a personal demon or evil spirit that must be driven out by the reception of the Spirit of God (for them a separate and distinct baptism). The Cathars specifically replaced all sacraments with the *consolamentum*, a baptism of the Holy Ghost and fire, performed by the imposition of hands. Having received the Spirit, they were expected to live a perfect life. Any breach of the group's precepts resulted in a loss of the *consolamentum*

Women in the West

In the West, religious women also operated on the fringe, not because they were heretical like the radical dualists, but because they were women. Notwithstanding, they had enormous influence. Unable to administer the sacraments, hear confessions, grant absolution, or, in most cases, preach, their role was to pray for the salvation of souls in the Christian community. However, their powerful role as prophets, mediators, and healers, together with their writings, in which they claimed to be under the inspiration of the divine Spirit, had an enormous influence. One writer in 1158 expressed it well: "In these days God made manifest his power through the frail sex, in these handmaidens whom he filled with the prophetic spirit" (*Annales palidenses* [*Monumenta Germaniae historica, scriptorum tomus* 16], in Pertz 1859, 90).

Among these virtuous women, perhaps Hildegard of Bingen (1098–1179) is most impressive, both for her range of spiritual gifts and for the incredible influence she exercised over those around her, even popes. In one of her visions, which she later painted, she received the Holy Spirit and was crowned by parted tongues of fire. She wrote hymns under Spirit inspiration (seventy-seven are still extant), a history of the universe, a book on medicine, numerous theological commentaries, and a book on natural history. She also is remembered for her "concerts" in the Spirit, her ecstatic visions and resulting prophecies, and her numerous miracles. Perhaps most important, she exhibited a transparency with which she openly portrays her own spiritual experiences through artistic and written media.

The best remembered prophetic figure of the medieval church, Joachim of Fiore (c. 1130–1202), taught that human history could be divided into three overlapping time periods: the age of the Father (from creation to Christ), the age of the Son (from the ninth or seventh centuries BCE to 1260 CE), and the age of the Spirit (from about 500 CE to the end of the world). He predicted that during the age of the Spirit, humankind and the church would be perfected, and the world would be evangelized. But Joachim's positive visions of the future, like Montanus' before him, never materialized.

Protestant Reformers

The best known magisterial reformers of the sixteenth century shifted attention to the relationship of Holy Spirit and the Scriptures. Martin Luther (1483–1546) taught that the Spirit gives ratifying testimony of conversion to the believer. The Holy Spirit must come to Christians through the Scriptures and the sacraments, according to Luther, not through internal experiences as leading radical Reformers advocated. John Calvin agreed, adding that the church is created through the activity of the Spirit in fallen humans, electing them to salvation, giving them faith, and enabling them to persevere in it. To Calvin, prophecy is *forthtelling* (Spirit-motivated preaching) rather than foretelling.

Radical Reformers like Thomas Müntzer (c. 1489–1525) emphasized the "inner word" of the Spirit (as opposed to the "outer word" of Scripture), direct revelations in visions and dreams, Holy Spirit possession and guidance, and a belief in the millennium. Müntzer understood the apparent outpouring of the Spirit on himself and others as confirmation of the prophecy in Joel 2:27–32. He taught that Christians are to experience the Holy Spirit as powerfully in postbiblical times as they did at the time of the prophets and apostles. He insisted on the necessity of a baptism of the Holy Spirit.

While Müntzer's teachings led to civil violence, the Radical Reformation was saved from extinction by the leadership and teachings of Menno Simons (c. 1496–1561), who taught Christian pacifism. He emphasized the Spirit's role in *sanctification,* or being conformed to Christ's nature.

Catholic reformers gave more credence to the Spirit's giftings. In his *Spiritual Diary,* Ignatius of Loyola reports mystical tears, Trinitarian visions, various kinds of locutions (God speaking to the soul), profound mystical joys, and *loquela* (heavenly speech or music). Ignatius, the founder of the Society of Jesus (the Jesuits), explicitly states that the Holy Spirit will communicate God's will to the devout seeker.

Several important groups claiming to be led by the divine Spirit appeared in the seventeenth century. These included the Religious Society of Friends, or Quakers, who emphasized the "inner word or light," with the Spirit speaking directly to the human mind. The Prophets of the Cevennes (the Camisards), French Protestant resistance fighters, claimed to be directly inspired by the Holy Spirit. They are remembered for the prophecies of young children and for speaking in languages of which they had no prior knowledge (a phenomenon known as *xenolalia*). The Jansenists, a radical Augustinian movement in the Roman Catholic Church from 1640 to 1801, were known for their signs and wonders, spiritual dancings, healings, and prophetic utterances, including glossolalia.

Pentecostal Predecessors

During the eighteenth century, John Wesley's descendents, the early Methodists, introduced into Protestantism an awareness of the Holy Spirit's operation in all of human experience. Their influence was primary in the emergence of the nineteenth-century Holiness movement in the United States, which in turn birthed twentieth-century classical Pentecostals.

In 1796, the Awakened, a Lutheran revivalistic movement in Finland, experienced a sudden outpouring of the Holy Spirit, featuring visions and glossolalia. In Russia, Seraphim of Sarov (1759–1833), a Russian Orthodox charismatic leader, asserted that the goal of the Christian life is the reception of the Holy Spirit. He saw evidence of Spirit reception in a transfiguration experience—being transformed, while still in the flesh, into divine light.

Throughout the nineteenth century, many people of the Spirit emerged, including Edward Irving (1792–1834), the founder of the Irvingites, participants in the West of Scotland revival (1830), tongues-speaking South Indians (1860s and 1870s), and the emerging evangelical movement (A. B. Simpson, A. J. Gordon, Carrie Judd Montgomery, and John Alexander Dowie). By 1900, the stage had been set for the twentieth-century classical Pentecostal and Charismatic movements, which have dwarfed all predecessors in both their explosive growth and their global impact on Christianity.

STANLEY M. BURGESS

See also Apostle, Apostolic; Baptism in the Holy Spirit; Charismata

Further Reading

Bouyer, L. (1974). Charismatic movements in history within the church. *One in Christ*, *10*(2).

Burgess, S. (1984). *The Holy Spirit: Ancient Christian traditions* (original title *The Spirit and the church: Antiquity*). Peabody, MA: Hendrickson.

Burgess, S. (1989). *The Holy Spirit: Eastern Christian traditions.* Peabody, MA: Hendrickson.

Burgess, S. (1997). *The Holy Spirit: Medieval Roman Catholic and reformed traditions.* Peabody, MA: Hendrickson.

Congar, Y. M.-J. (1983). *I believe in the Holy Spirit* (3 vols.). New York: Seabury Press.

Hendry, G. S. (1956). *The Holy Spirit in Christian theology.* Philadelphia: Westminster.

Lewis, W. (1978). *Witnesses to the Spirit: An anthology.* Valley Forge, PA: Judson Press.

O'Carroll, M. (1987). *Trinitas: A theological encyclopedia of the Holy Trinity.* Wilmington, DE: Michael Glazier.

O'Carroll, M. (1990). *Veni Creator Spiritus: A theological encyclopedia of the Holy Spirit.* Collegeville, MN: Glazier/Liturgical.

Pertz, G. H. (1859). *Annales Palidenses. Monumenta Germaniae historica, scriptorum tomus* 16 (pp. 48–98). Hannover, Germany: n.p.

Hymnology

See Music

India

At the beginning of the twentieth century, news of a worldwide revival spreading among Evangelical circles caught the keen attention of Pandita Ramabai, a Marathi Brahman convert who led a missionary and charity organization called Mukti Mission in Kedgaon in Central India. Mukti Mission was backed by foreign help, and many Western missionaries took part in its work. Ramabai started a special prayer circle in 1905 that led to a remarkable revival at Mukti Mission, and in the years 1906–1907 the revival included various manifestations such as speaking in tongues. Some Americans, who worked for the mission and had heard about Azusa Street, started similarly speaking in tongues and interpreted the Mukti Mission as further proof for a worldwide Pentecostal end-time revival. The revival at Mukti Mission became another vital link from India for the global Pentecostal network that was to be established, as, for instance, two American missionaries who also became Pentecostals in India influenced the movement in other parts of the world: Minnie Abrams in Chile and Alice E. Luce in Mexico and among Hispanic Americans. But Mukti Mission also helped create Pentecostalism within India, although other events were similarly important, such as the arrival of active participants from Azusa Street in India (e.g., Alfred and Lillian Garr in 1907, and T. B. Barratt and George E. Berg in 1908). Within a very short time, a widespread and diffuse network was established that could be called the beginning of Pentecostalism in India. This initial Indian network led to different initiatives that brought about a Pentecostal movement on the subcontinent.

South India

While a number of American missionaries parlayed their experience and their contacts to establish congregations in South India, Indian leaders soon began to assert their power and form indigenous, Indian-led churches.

Kerala

In 1908, George E. Berg, a former Indian missionary and active participant from Azusa Street, came to India and won quite a few Indian adherents in what is currently called Kerala through his old contacts in the Brethren congregations there, including some indigenous leaders mainly from the Brethren background, but also from Mar Thoma Church and the Anderson Church of God. In 1913, Berg was joined by Robert F. Cook, another American Pentecostal missionary from Azusa Street, who continued the work when Berg left India a year later after a serious quarrel with Cook. In the 1920s many Indian evangelists and leaders, mainly from a Brethren or Holiness background, joined the Pentecostal faith (e.g., K. E. Abraham and A. J. John in 1923, and K. C. Cherian and P. V. John in 1924). Nevertheless, Cook, who permanently moved to Kerala in 1922, exercised a great deal of control over the emerging movement as he gave financial support to Indian evangelists and bought land to build churches (the first at Thuyavur in 1919). In the 1920s, funds became more easily available, because Cook had joined the Assemblies of God and other missionaries of that organization came to Kerala (Mary Chapman in 1921, John H. Burgess in 1927, and Martha Kucera in 1928). Nevertheless, the Indians, with their speaker K. E. Abraham, were very critical about attempts to combine financial support with organizational control, especially after the regional Council of Assemblies of God for South India and Ceylon was formed in 1929. During the late 1920s and early 1930s, Indian Pentecostal leaders were in serious conflict with Cook and among themselves about questions of leadership positions, financial matters, affiliation to Western missionary societies, and so on. In the 1930s, at the end of these quite turbulent conflicts, four larger Pentecostal churches came into being in Kerala, two with direct links to Western missions (Assemblies of God, Church of God) and two quite different independent organizations, though not completely without Western partners (Ceylon Pentecostal Mission, Indian Pentecostal Church of God).

These four Pentecostal organizations maintained a leading position in Kerala, but with their growth, they had to contend time and again with internal quarrels and stagnating tendencies. Hence, they were not in a position to offer an adequate framework for integrating younger leading personalities with new ideas. That led to the founding of new churches. As a result, Sharon Fellowship (founder P. J. Thomas, 1953) was born as a direct reaction to the quarrels within the Indian Pentecostal Church of God. Also the New India Church of God (founder V. A. Thamby, ca. 1973) developed itself in the course of its history as a reservoir for many who were dissatisfied with the Pentecostal church to which they once belonged. The leaders of the New India Bible Church (Thomas Philip, Abraham Philip, 1972) did not want their church to be identified outside distinctly as a Pentecostal church and therefore established an independent organization. Gospel for Asia (founder K. P. Yohannan, 1978) was first founded only as a mission work and began later (1993) to establish its own church structures as a result of its dissatisfaction with the missing missionary dynamic of the existing Pentecostal churches. A common characteristic of all churches mentioned above is that their leadership is in the hands of Syrian Christians. But since the 1940s, new Pentecostal churches were founded in Kerala that were not led by Syrian Christians, but by people groups that were considered much lower on the religio-social ladder: so-called Dalits or untouchables (and in some cases by Nadars and Ezhavas who normally would not come under the term Dalit). The inability of the churches led by Syrian Christians to integrate Dalit or Nadar leaders

was the primary reason for this division. The foundation of the World Missionary Evangelism in Kerala (founder C. S. Mathew, 1962) is a good example. An extreme case of the caste-compartmentalization within the Pentecostal movement in Kerala was the establishment of the "Kerala Division" of the Church of God (K. J. Chacko, first "State Overseer," 1972), which demonstrates the exclusion of Dalit participation in a Church of God dominated by Syrian Christians. While the churches dominated by Syrian Christians foster comparatively closer contact among themselves, they seldom have a close relationship with churches led by Dalits or Nadars.

Tamil Nadu

Despite a previous series of missionary activities, the Pentecostal movement could strike roots in present-day Tamil Nadu only after World War II. After the end of the World War II, indigenous Pentecostal churches proliferated in Tamil Nadu. The Indian Pentecostal Church of God achieved a few missionary successes coming from their stations in Andhra Pradesh. The Ceylon Pentecostal Mission, which attained new missionary strength under the chief pastor Alwin R. De Alwis also played an important role. At the same time, however, several experienced Tamil pastors left the Ceylon Pentecostal Mission and founded their own independent churches (John Rose, Full Gospel Pentecostal Church; S. B. Daniel and S. Ponraj, Pentecostal Church of India; G. Sunderam, Apostolic Christian Assembly). Because most of these pastors had lived together for some time in Malaysia, they had close contact with each other and a strong feeling of togetherness, though each of them led independent churches. Several other independent churches were also formed in that period, for example, in the southernmost part of Tamil Nadu where Sadhu Yesudhason became highly respected as the leader of a very influential indigenous church called Kirubasanam.

A second phase began in the 1960s; the foreign mission organizations changed, one after the other, to indigenous leadership, and it became increasingly possible for the indigenous churches to win international partners. The result of that convergent development led to the formation of new indigenous churches, which expanded rapidly beginning in the 1980s and were strongly anchored in the global Pentecostal movement through their foreign partners. Since the 1980s, the Pentecostal movement has also taken deep root in big cities like Madurai, Coimbatore, and Chennai. Chennai in particular experienced growth and became the most important center of the movement in southern India. Apart from the especially strong representation of the Assemblies of God, the scene was increasingly marked by many independent regional churches in this city. At the beginning of the twenty-first century, the Tamil-speaking south is arguably the most vibrant center of Indian Pentecostalism.

Karnataka and Andhra Pradesh

The Pentecostal movement in present-day Karnataka remains numerically weak in membership. It is limited almost entirely to migrants from Tamil Nadu, Kerala, and Andhra Pradesh, and it has scarcely touched the native Kannada-speaking population. There are no large centers of the Pentecostal movement in Karnataka, with the important exception of Bangalore and to some extent also the neighbouring Kolar Gold Fields.

In Andhra Pradesh, the Indian Pentecostal Church of God started missionary work from Kerala in the 1930s. In the second half of the 1940s, its Kerala missionaries (who all belonged to the Syrian Christian community) and their new Pentecostal recruits from Andhra Pradesh set up strong local and relatively independent centers, with financial assistance from overseas (e.g., P. M. Samuel, Vijayawada; P. T. Chacko, Secunderabad; P. L. Paramjothi, Antarvedipalam; K. R. David, Rajamundry; K. S. Joseph, Narasapur). It proved to be of special significance that the missionaries from Kerala (especially P. M. Samuel and P. T. Chacko) had far more overseas contacts than their colleagues from Andhra Pradesh. So, in the Indian Pentecostal Church of God, unfair distribution of financial support went along with the establishment of local centers, thus preparing the ground for recruitment campaigns by the Dallas-based World Missionary Evangelism (founder John E. Douglas Sr.) in the 1960s. As a result, with the exception of P. L. Paramjothi, almost all the important Telugu leaders in the Indian Pentecostal Church of God moved to World Missionary Evangelism, which suddenly became the biggest Pentecostal church in Andhra Pradesh. This was a severe setback for the Indian Pentecostal Church of God, but it consolidated its position relatively quickly and remains one of the bigger Pentecostal churches in Andhra Pradesh. Quite different was the situation of World Missionary Evangelism, which was shaken by repeated internal crises, especially in 1977 and 1988–1990, and never stabilized.

Since the 1970s, Indians who had lived for years in the United States were returning to Andhra Pradesh to begin their own missions with the backing of foreign sponsors they had found while overseas (e.g., in 1971, Ernest Komanapalli, Manna/Rock Church; in 1982, P. J. Titus, New Testament Church). The fact that they were well acquainted with Indian as well as American culture was quite an advantage for numerical success in membership. In addition, churches in the big cities with a regional emphasis proved their potential for growth and developed their own style (e.g., in Vizag, M. A. Paul's Christ's Church, 1973; Krupa Rao's Jesus Christ Prayer and Evangelistic Ministries, 1985). It is a peculiar characteristic of Andhra Pradesh that, in comparison, the missionary success of the classical Pentecostal churches proved to be comparatively modest, and the Assemblies of God, for instance, while successful elsewhere in South India, has scarcely gained a footing here.

North and Northeast India

Pentecostalism in North India started early with missionaries like Christian Schoonmaker. Schoonmaker originally came to India with the Christian and Missionary Alliance, then became Pentecostal under the decisive influence of the Mukti Mission and began to work for the Assemblies of God in North India in 1917. In the North, the Assemblies of God concentrated with some success on social work (orphanages, schools, dispensaries), with the "Mission of Mercy" started by Mark Buntain at Calcutta in 1953 as its best-known part. However, most Pentecostals in North India are South Indian migrants. Whereas some of them had already been members of Pentecostal churches in the South, others came into contact with the Pentecostal spirituality through one of the many missionary outreaches of South Indian Pentecostal churches to North India. In that way, a considerable Pentecostal presence has been reached among South Indian migrants that is quite noticeable in big cities like Delhi and Bombay, although, in regards to membership, Pentecostalism in North India remains very small like all other forms of Christianity there.

Since Indian independence, Pentecostalism has also made inroads into the Northeast, a Christian-dominated part of India. The Oneness United Pentecostal Church of God had a remarkable success in Mizoram in the 1960s and 1970s, and the Assemblies of God slowly became also an established force. However, recently the Pentecostal movement has seen greater momentum in the Northeast, and it seems that this area will soon become another center of Pentecostalism in India.

Catholic Charismatic Movement

Whereas among the Protestant mainline churches there is hardly any institutionalized Charismatic movement worth mentioning, the Catholic Church has a very strong one. It started in Bombay in 1972 where it continues to be the center of the movement. Influenced by the worldwide Catholic Charismatic movement, charismatic prayer groups were formed in India. Three priests, Fio Mascarenhas, S. J., James D'Souza, and Rufus Pereira shaped the character of the new movement. They organized frequent retreats through which laypeople were reached. Since 1974, it has published its own journal *Charisindia*. In the 1980s the Catholic Charismatic College was opened in Bombay, offering two-month Bible courses. In Kerala, charismatic healing services experienced massive growth at the end of the 1980s. Especially successful was the Vincentian Matthew Naickomparambil, whose retreats, comparable to Pentecostal healing rallies, are sometimes crowded by over 100,000 people. However, the active kernel of the movement was estimated by Rufus Pereira in 1995 as 50,000 only. There are hardly any ecumenical relations with the Pentecostal movement, and since the sensational conversion of one of its prominent members, the Tamil priest S. J. Berchmans, to the Pentecostal movement on 1991, relations have become even worse. However, some Pentecostals from Kerala have studied in Catholic theological institutions.

Outlook

The vast majority of the members of Indian Pentecostalism come from other, mostly Protestant, churches, and at the beginning of the twentieth-first century more than 20 percent of Indian Protestants are estimated to already belong to Pentecostal churches, and that percentage seems to be increasing. Indian Pentecostalism consists of many different churches that are independent of one another, but on fundamental doctrinal issues there is widespread agreement. There is a common Pentecostal identity, and the difference between Pentecostal and charismatic churches does not play much of a role in practical church life. The Indian Pentecostal movement is no simple copy of Western models, but Western origin and international relations are often strongly emphasized by the movement itself and seen as a major attraction to many Indians. A similar message goes out from the numerous Western guest preachers. They are not, it seems, an irritating foreign body but make an important contribution to missionary success, because they indicate that Pentecostal spirituality is firmly set in modern Western culture and so might serve as a gateway to the scientific-technical age with Western culture as its guarantor. At the same time, Indian Pentecostalism shows many contextual approximations to elements of Hindu and Indian Christian popular spirituality. Its orientation to experience and its ecstatic elements have much in common with the specific Indian and Hindu context and so do its healing practices. But theological views show that specific Indian influences are to a large extent shared orally and mediated less through books, taking place rather in Bible hours, prayer meetings, and conventions. If one looks into them, Indian Pentecostalism shows itself as a very Indian version of Pentecostal Christianity.

MICHAEL BERGUNDER

See also Church Growth; Indigenous Churches

Further Reading

Anderson, A., & Tang, E. (Eds.). (2004). *Asian and Pentecostal: The charismatic face of Christianity in Asia.* Oxford, UK: Regnum.

Bergunder, M. (2001). Miracle healing and exorcism: The South Indian Pentecostal movement in the context of popular Hinduism. *International Review of Mission, 90,* 103–112.

Bergunder, M. (2003). From Pentecostal healing evangelist to Kalki Avatar. The remarkable life of Paulaseer Lawrie alias Shree Lahari Krishna (1921–1989). In R. E. Frykenberg (Ed.), *Christians and missionaries in India: Cross-cultural communication since 1500* (pp. 357–375). London: Curzon.

Bergunder, M. (in press). *The South Indian Pentecostal movement in the 20th century.* Grand Rapids, MI: Eerdmans.

Burgess, S. M. (2001). Pentecostalism in India. *Asian Journal of Pentecostal Studies, 4,* 85–98.

Caplan, L. (1987). *Class and culture in urban India. Fundamentalism in a Christian community.* Oxford, UK: Clarendon Press.

Caplan, L. (1989). *Religion and power. Essays on the Christian community in Madras.* Madras, India: Christian Literature Society.

George, A. C. (2001). Pentecostal beginnings in Travancore, South India. *Asian Journal of Pentecostal Studies, 4,* 215–237.

Hedlund, R. E. (Ed.) (2000). *Christianity is Indian. The emergence of an indigenous community.* New Delhi, India: ISPCK.

McGee, G. B. (1999). "Latter rain" falling in the East. Early-twentieth-century Pentecostalism in India and the debate over speaking in tongues. *Church History, 68,* 648–665.

Saju. (1994). *Kerala Pentekosthu Charithram.* Kottayam, India: Good News Publications.

Satyavrata, I. M. (1999). Contextual perspectives on Pentecostalism as a global culture. A South Asian view. In M. W. Dempster & B. D. Klaus (Eds.), *The globalization of Pentecostalism. A religion made to travel.* Oxford, UK: Regnum Books International.

Stephen, M. (1999). *Towards a Pentecostal theology and ethics.* Kottayam, India: Chraisthava Bodhi Publications.

Indigenous Churches

Independent Christianity experienced explosive growth in Asia, Latin America, and Africa throughout the twentieth century. Global Christianity today is centered in these three regions. This rapidly spreading Christianity is indigenous to Asia, Africa, and Latin America. It is a vibrant faith, much of it Pentecostal or charismatic, with considerable appeal to the poor and the marginalized.

India

At an early time Christianity came to South Asia, where it adapted itself to the prevailing culture. A notable example is the Thomas Christianity of India. According to tradition, the apostle Thomas preached, died, and was buried in South India, and the community of Thomas Christians originated in the mission of St. Thomas in India. Thus historically, indigenous Christianity has a two-thousand-year tradition in South Asia. Cult and culture combined to preserve a Christian community that is authentically Christian as well as thoroughly Indian. The Thomas Christians have been an integral part of the social and religious fabric of the region for nearly two thousand years. It also appears that ancient Christianity once existed in the larger region of what is now Pakistan and Afghanistan prior to the advent of Islam.

Ancient South Asian Christianity has experienced countless rebirths. Attempts were made in Tamil Nadu (by R. de Nobili, Vedanayagam Shastri, and Krishna Pillai), in Bengal (by Keshub Chunder Sen), and in Maharashtra (by Narayan Vaman Tillak) to express historic Christianity through Indian cultural forms. Others who in various ways appropriated the gospel in an Indian mode included Sadhu Sundar Singh, R. C. Das at Varanasi, Subba Rao in Andhra, Devadas of the Bible Mission at Guntur, Brother Bakht Singh, and countless others. Pandita Ramabai is another notable example.

In Maharashtra, Pandita Ramabai (1858–1922) was a social activist and radical advocate of women's rights and egalitarianism. A Marathi Chitpavan Brahmin convert to Christianity, and an articulate spokesperson on behalf of suppressed Hindu women, her advocacy has earned her a place of honor in modern Indian history. In her conversion Ramabai neither rejected her own cultural background nor identified with Western customs. Mukti Church at Kedgaon emerged as an indigenous creation, distinct from "missionary" Christianity, an early expression of women's ministry and leadership.

In 1897 Ramabai invited Minnie Abrams, a Methodist "Holiness" missionary from America, to minister at Kedgaon. In 1905 a spiritual revival at Mukti was to reverberate far beyond Kedgaon. It has been suggested that Pentecostalism in India has roots in Maharashtra at the Ramabai Mukti Mission, Kedgaon. The revival spread as the Mukti bands carried the message throughout the Maratha country. Characterized by emotional phenomena, the impact of the awakening was long lasting in terms of conversions and changed lives. Ramabai channeled the enthusiasm of the believing community into famine relief work as well as social rehabilitation.

Mukti Church continues its legacy of ministry to needy women and children today. Mukti Church bears the Ramabai imprint of social vision combined with spiritual fervor. India has many more examples.

The Indigenous Churches of India (the official name of the assemblies associated with Brother Bakht Singh) must be mentioned, as well as numerous independent local assemblies and several breakaway denominations in Andhra Pradesh. At Madras the Laymen's Evangelical Fellowship is an example of a significant Holiness revival movement. Similar new churches are found in other parts of India. The largest cluster consists of numerous indigenous Pentecostal fellowships. Some are offshoots of the Indian Pentecostal Church of God (IPC) based in Kerala, while others have emerged from the more exclusive Ceylon Pentecostal Mission (CPM). At Bombay the charismatic New Life Fellowship is an indigenous house church movement that owns no property but has thousands of members functioning through cell churches throughout the city. Many of India's Christians are from humble backgrounds. Numbers of Dalits, tribals, and the poor are finding dignity and hope in a new identity as disciples of Jesus Christ.

Sri Lanka

Indigenous Sri Lankan Christianity has affinity to that of India as is illustrated by the history of Pentecostalism in Sri Lanka. The Ceylon Pentecostal Mission began as a breakaway from the Assemblies of God led by Alwin R. de Alwis and Pastor Paul in 1923. The

Literature used by indigenous Pentecostal churches in India.

CPM espoused an ascetic approach to spirituality. Ministers were not to marry and should wear white. They disdained the use of medicine and gave central importance to the doctrine of the Second Coming of Christ. Testimonies of miraculous healing attracted Buddhists and Hindus, and the wearing of white was appropriate culturally in Sri Lanka where Buddhist devotees wore white to visit the temples. The CPM also instituted indigenous forms of worship.

The CPM laid the foundation for other Pentecostal ministries not only in Sri Lanka and India but beyond with branches today in several countries. While exact membership figures are not available, in 1998 there were 848 branches reported worldwide (including 708 in India) and nearly five thousand full-time ministers. In addition there are independent assemblies and movements that have severed connections with the CPM. Some of these are prominent, such as the Apostolic Christian Assembly in Tamil Nadu, founded by Pastor G. Sundram, led today by Pastor Sam Sundaram, and many more.

Nepal

Nepal is of particular note—Christianity in Nepal is only in its first century. The story of the church in Nepal is a record of efforts by Nepali Christians to reach their own people. Prior to 1950 there were no Nepali Christians resident in Nepal. Nepal was closed to the outside, but Nepali people managed to seep out into India, where a number of them were converted and became active evangelists. These Nepali Christians organized their own Gorkha Mission. Contacts developed along the border, and there were excursions into Nepal as well, but there was no place for Christians in Nepal.

Revolution in 1950 brought change and the first decade of the church in Nepal. St. Xavier's School was started by the Catholics in 1951. Christian worship began in Kathmandu in 1953. Three Mar Thoma missionaries founded the Christa Shanti Sangh Ashram and took up residence in Kathmandu in 1953. Secret believers eventually were baptized. In 1953 the Nepal Evangelist Band received permission to open a hospital at Pokhara. In 1954 the United Mission to Nepal received permission to begin medical work. Other agencies followed, but primarily the story of the church in Nepal is a record of Nepali Christians, many of them women, penetrating their country with the gospel.

The Nepali church from its inception has been indigenous in character and outlook with emphasis on local leadership development. Discipleship schools and Bible schools were organized during the 1970s and 1980s. Kathmandu today has numerous small Bible training institutes, one or two seminaries, and at least one fledgling Christian university. The Association for Theological Education in Nepal serves to provide resources to meet the need of the growing Christian movement for training.

In 1991 there were more than fifty thousand baptized believers in Nepal. The current number of Christians is not known, but in 1996 it was estimated at about 200,000 Christians in Nepal, and more recently more than 500,000 were reported, as well as response in the diaspora Nepali community in northern India, Bhutan, and other countries. The witness of the gospel has advanced despite persecution, imprisonment, and other hardships.

The indigenous Christianity of Nepal has been described as Pentecostal or charismatic in character from its very inception. Even before Nepal opened its doors in 1951, Pentecostal missionaries in India were active on the Nepal border. Some of the converts were trained at the North India Bible Institute of the Assemblies of God at Hardoi. In Nepal converts were exposed to Pentecostal teaching. Besides the Assemblies of God, the Agape Fellowship and many independent churches are Pentecostal or charismatic.

Healing and exorcism are important dimensions of Christian witness in the animistic context of Tantric Hinduism and Tibetan Buddhism. It must be remembered that Christianity in Nepal is a first-century church, completely indigenous in origin.

Taiwan

In East Asia the translation of the gospel proceeds in a vast plurality of cultures, languages, and competing ideologies in which the church inculturates itself. Several examples may be noted. In Taiwan, the True Jesus Church has a distinctive understanding of Christ, which is somewhat less than Trinitarian but which stresses the unity of God and the full deity of Christ and his unity with the Father. The church holds five cardinal doctrines: baptism by immersion, Holy Communion, feet washing, baptism of the Holy Spirit, and Sabbath (Saturday) as the day of worship. This church experienced rapid growth and has expanded into other countries. The denomination is highly organized with participation from every local church. The laity, not the professional clergy, is the foundation of the church. The church is fully self-supporting. The True Jesus Church is Taiwan's third largest denomination.

The Assembly Hall Church is the second largest Protestant denomination in Taiwan. Origins are shrouded in mystery, the history unwritten, but these believers are the followers of Watchman Nee and Witness Lee. Organization is simple with no synods, conventions, committees, or headquarters, in spite of which the Assembly Hall is more highly organized than most denominations. The local church is the center of it all. Great emphasis is placed on lay training for evangelism. There is no clergy-laity distinction. Theologically the Assembly is both millennarian and Trinitarian with its own distinctive interpretation of the Trinity. A strict millennial outlook tends to an otherworldly separatism.

In addition to these two indigenous denominations, Taiwan has a large number of independent "local" churches with no outside affiliation or mission relationships. These too are a significant part of the Christian expression in Taiwan.

Japan

Christianity remains a relatively insignificant minority faith in Japan, where its perceived "Westernness" has been its major roadblock to acceptance and growth. The story of Christianity in Japan is replete with rejection of transplanted churches perceived as manifestations of an alien faith. But a recent study of twelve Japanese indigenous churches tells a different story. The Christian message in Japanese garb is creatively appropriated in these indigenous Christian movements.

Concern for the ancestors is a central issue among the Japanese. Traditional Protestant Christianity, however, fails to address this question. Protestant missionary theology and practice represent a discontinuity with customary Japanese beliefs. Leaders of indigenous Japanese Christian movements take a different approach, which gives attention to questions of household salvation and the possibility of ministry to the spirit world. Functional alternatives are found to traditional religious observances such as ancestor veneration. Exorcism of malignant spirits, purification rituals, and vicarious baptism are further examples of Japanese inculturation of Christianity.

The Spirit of Jesus Church is one such Japanese Church that in less than twenty years in the postwar period grew to be the second largest Protestant church in Japan, stressing lay witness and house meetings. Perhaps the best known Japanese indigenous tradition is the Non-church Movement of Uchimura Kanzo. The Way, Christ Heart Church, the Holy Ecclesia of Jesus, and the Original Gospel Movement are among other indigenous Japanese Christian churches.

South Korea

In South Korea, Christianity entered the core of Korean culture, identified with nationalism, and has produced the world's largest Christian congregations. Korean Christianity is predominantly Presbyterian. Outwardly "Western" in ornate basilicas with pipe organs and vested choirs, Korean Christianity has its own distinctive indigenous forms including a proliferation of breakaway Presbyterian denominations and other local expressions.

Korean Christianity is a study not only in independence and indigeneity but also in Korean contextuality and leadership dynamics expressed in a succession of breakaway movements. Not surprising, one finds Korean Presbyterian Churches in other countries where Koreans have engaged in mission. Large Korean churches of various denominations are found in North

America, and Korean missionaries have been sent to several countries of Africa, Asia, Latin America, and the Pacific. Christianity in Korea appears distinctly Korean, and Korean Christianity is aggressively missionary.

China

The case of China is fascinating. Cut off and under persecution for forty years, the church in China became fully indigenous and has experienced explosive growth. The "Chinese-ness" of the church is visible, and they no longer have any foreign connections. In parts of China where Christians were few during the missionary era, today tens of thousands of Christians are reported. While the visible church disappeared under the Cultural Revolution, the Christian faith survived in small house-group meetings. House churches had also been characteristic of earlier, prerevolutionary indigenous movements such as the True Jesus Church, the Little Flock, the Independent Church, and the Jesus Family. Under repression, the house churches proved flexible and became the training ground for an emerging lay leadership of the indigenous Chinese church.

Latin America

Until recently the Latin American phenomenon was largely unrecognized. It consists of fully indigenous churches developed exclusively with Latin American leadership and funds, an autochthonous movement primarily from the poor. In the Roman Catholic context the base ecclesial communities are an indigenous Christian movement independent from church and state, not officially separated from the Catholic Church, often functioning without priests, and essentially self-governing. Among the Protestants, the "grassroots" churches that are the outcome of Latin American revival movements are more indigenous in ministry and style and are experiencing spontaneous growth among the urban poor. Pentecostal churches are the fastest growing. The Pentecostals are more contextual than other churches and actualize the genius and ideals of Protestantism among the marginalized. In Central America emphasis on the Holy Spirit is an important distinctive leading to indigeneity in Pentecostal and other evangelical churches. These grassroots churches are spontaneous Christian fellowships found in every Latin American country, churches arising through local initiative independent of traditional mission structures. Considerable diversity exists, but there is one common feature: they are Latino incarnations of the gospel of Christ.

Outlook

Indigenous expressions can be found in every region of the world where Christianity has taken firm root, including North America. The Baptist, Methodist, and Pentecostal denominations of North America are examples of culturally assimilated churches of the Great Tradition, whereas Jehovah's Witnesses, Christian Science, and the Latter Day Saints are prime species of heretical fringe sects of the Little Tradition. The Seventh Day Adventists are an interesting case of a quasimarginal American church moving into the mainstream of the Christian tradition. In North America the Great Tradition consists of Baptists, Mennonites, and Methodists as well as Catholics, Lutherans, and Presbyterians. Pentecostals, who originated in North America, were looked upon as sectarian, but have entered the mainstream of church life in North America and are in the process of doing so in South America and other regions of the world including Asia.

Indigenous Christianity has proven adaptable and resilient. Christian witness involves empowerment activities among slum dwellers and street children, liberation of backward communities and tribals, encouragement of women's movements and Christ *Bhaktas*, use of indigenous communication media, employment of local proverbs and sayings, as well as the more traditional roles of community development, Bible translation, village schools, and church planting.

Churches of indigenous origins (CIOs) tend to be grassroots expressions of a popular Christianity of the Little Tradition. Indigenous Christianity is an authentic signature of faith wherever the gospel has taken root. From Jerusalem outward the gospel has continued to translate itself into local cultures. The phenomenon was true of what are now the established Christian traditions of North America and Europe, and is true as well of the emerging Christianity of Asia, Africa, Latin America, and the Pacific region.

ROGER E. HEDLUND

See also Africa, East; Africa, North (and the Middle East); Africa, South; Africa, West; African Initiated Churches; America, Latin; Asia, East; China; India; Korea

Further Reading

Abrams, M. F. (1999). *The baptism of the Holy Ghost and fire.* Kedgaon, India: Pandita Ramabai Mukti Mission. (Original work published 1906)

Adeney, D. H. (1985). *China: The church's long march.* Ventura, CA: Regal.

Aikman, D. (2003). *Jesus in Beijing: How Christianity is transforming China*. Washington, DC: Regnery.

Anderson, A., & Hollenweger, W. (Eds.). (1999). *Pentecostals after a century*. Sheffield, UK: Sheffield Academic.

Berg, M., & Pretiz, P. (1996). *Spontaneous combustion: Grassroots Christianity, Latin American style*. Pasadena, CA: William Carey Library.

Mundadan, A. M. (1984). *History of Christianity in India* (Vol. 1). Bangalore, India: Theological Publications.

Hedlund, R. (2000). *Quest for identity: India's churches of indigenous origin*. Delhi & Chennai, India: ISPCK.

Hedlund, R. (Ed.). (2004). *Christianity is Indian*. Delhi & Chennai, India: ISPCK.

Lambert, T. (1994). *The resurrection of the Chinese church*. Wheaton, IL: Harold Shaw.

Mullins, M. R. (1998). *Christianity made in Japan: A study of indigenous movements*. Honolulu, HI: University of Hawaii Press.

Perry, C. (1989). *A biographical history of the church in Nepal*. Wheaton, IL: Wheaton Graduate School, Wheaton College.

Perry, C. (1997). *Nepali around the world*. Kathmandu, Nepal: Ekta.

Rooney, J. (1984). *Shadows in the dark: A history of Christianity in Pakistan up to the 10th century*. Rawalpindi, India: Christian Study Centre.

Sanneh, L. (1991). *Translating the message*. Maryknoll, NY: Orbis.

Somaratna, G. P. V. (1996). *Origins of the Pentecostal mission in Sri Lanka*. Nugegoda, Sri Lanka: Margaya Fellowship.

Tennent, T. C. (2000). *Building Christianity on Indian foundations*. Delhi, India: ISPCK.

Initial Evidence

Pentecostals and charismatics agree that there is some relation between the experience of Spirit Baptism and speaking in tongues. However, the exact nature of that relationship is the divide that separates Classical Pentecostalism from others who share a belief in and experience with the contemporary moving of the Holy Spirit. Classical Pentecostalism associates speaking in tongues very closely with the experience of Spirit Baptism and uses several descriptive phrases to name that association: *Bible evidence, initial gift, only evidence, first evidence, standing sign,* and *initial evidence.*

Historical Development

The history of the Christian Church is replete with evidence of outbreaks and manifestations of spiritual gifts, including speaking in tongues. Among the many who have documented this, Stanley M. Burgess stands apart because of his effort to demonstrate that spiritual expressions accompanied the growth of the church. Burgess concluded that while tongues speech did occur at various points in the history of the church, the conscious linking of that to the experience of Spirit baptism did not take place until the nineteenth century, in the ministry of Edward Irving.

Edward Irving (1792–1834), an Anglican pastor in London, preached against what he considered the docetism of his day, arguing that Jesus was fully human and thus empowered by the Spirit. His emphasis on the full humanity of Jesus allowed him to assert that the power through which Jesus accomplished his mission and work was that of the Holy Spirit. From this biblical/historical vantage point, it was a small move to also assert that the power of the Holy Spirit was available to enhance the lives and ministries of contemporary believers.

After a successful preaching tour in Scotland from 1828 to 1829, one of the believers from Irving's meetings, Mary Campbell, was healed of tuberculosis, Spirit baptized, and spoke in tongues (1830). Word reached Irving in London, and he connected his preaching of a Spirit-endowed Christ with this event. In April 1831 he opened his church in Regent Square for prayer meetings, and within three months manifestations of the Spirit were common. Irving was defrocked by the Presbytery on 2 May 1832. He founded the Catholic Apostolic Church, where Spirit baptisms with tongues occurred. There were also other manifestations of gifts in the worship of Irving's church.

Irving preferred to call tongues the "standing sign" of Spirit baptism, an experience that he saw as subsequent to salvation. While not using the term "evidence," Irving did anticipate that those who were Spirit baptized would speak in tongues, and until they did they could not be said to be baptized. He was clear, however, that the Spirit indwells from salvation, so the ones who had not yet spoken in tongues should not be discouraged, for they still belong to God. As Irving understood it, Spirit baptism was available to all believers and would enhance holiness. Tongues serve as a gift and as a sign. As a sign they signal Spirit baptism. As a gift they edify the believer through the heightening of their communication with God and opening and preparing them for further gifts of the Spirit—gifts that will edify the congregation of believers.

The American Holiness movement, influenced by John Wesley and his successor John Fletcher, taught that believers should anticipate another work of grace in their lives, sanctification. This second work could be, and often was, called the baptism in the Holy Spirit. There were those in the Reformed tradition who also saw a second work of grace, but typically understood it to provide power for Christian witness more than sanctification. Such persons were R. A. Torrey, superintendent of the Moody Bible Institute, A. J. Gordon, Baptist pastor, and A. B. Simpson, founder of the Christian and Missionary Alliance.

Pentecostalism followed in this line and added the concept of speaking in tongues as the evidence of this second work of God's grace in the life of the believer. Charles F. Parham is important to Pentecostalism because of his central role in establishing the doctrine of tongues as the evidence of Spirit baptism. "Parham theorized that tongues as xenolalia or xenoglossa (unlearned human languages, a form of glossolalia) was a key component in the divine plan to expedite missionary evangelism at the end of human history" (McGee 1991, 102). While this certainly was one of the approaches to speaking in tongues, it proved to be unsatisfactory when individuals traveled to foreign lands and by and large could not speak in the languages of the indigenous peoples. Parham moved his ministry to Topeka, Kansas in 1898, where he opened the Bethel Healing Home and Bethel Bible School for persons who were in need of physical healing and training in biblical studies.

He was influenced by the Holiness movement of the late nineteenth century that was calling for a second work in the believer's life, sometimes called Spirit baptism, which would produce sanctification. The work of Benjamin Hardin Irwin, who saw a third work, a Spirit baptism of fire, especially influenced him. He was also influenced by Frank W. Sanford's teaching about the restoration of a work of the Spirit to equip believers for a great end-time effort at evangelism also impacted Parham.

The early view of tongues as the gift of speaking foreign languages for the evangelism of the world soon became less tenable as individuals traveled to foreign lands and were not able to preach in the languages of the people. One such was Alfred G. Garr. Garr received the baptism in the Holy Spirit with the evidence of speaking in tongues, which, he felt, qualified him to speak the language of India. However, he reported "I supposed God would let us talk to the natives of India in their own tongues; but He did not. So far I have not seen anyone who is able to preach to the natives in their own tongues with the languages given with the Holy Ghost" (McGee 1991, 102–103). Garr chose to recast his understanding of tongues in relation to Spirit baptism, still seeing them as evidential of the experience, but allowing that their ongoing function is to be seen in the prayer life of the believer.

There were many in the early development of twentieth-century Pentecostalism who believed in speaking in tongues but did not understand them as the initial evidence of the Spirit baptism. One of those was Minnie F. Abrams, a missionary to India where she worked with the famed Pandita Ramabai's Mukti Mission. She argued that tongues usually accompanied Spirit baptism, but since they were the same as the Pauline gift of tongues, not all would necessarily speak in tongues when baptized. The real evidence of Spirit baptism was manifestation of the fruit of the Spirit, especially love.

Another challenge to seeing the speaking in tongues as the initial evidence of Spirit baptism came from Fred F. Bosworth. Bosworth, an early leader in the Assemblies of God, concluded that the initial evidence doctrine was in error and left the Assemblies of God in 1918. He argued that since tongues in Acts was the same as the tongues mentioned as a gift in 1 Corinthians, and since gifts are sovereignly given, tongues could not be said to be the only evidence of Spirit baptism. "He further challenged the hermeneutical presupposition of the pattern: (1) it was not supported by an explicit command in Scripture; and (2) it was simply 'assumed from the fact that in three instances recorded in the Acts they spoke in tongues as a result of the baptism'" (McGee 1991, 109–110). He also noted that major figures in evangelism and mission throughout the Church's history had operated quite successfully without the speaking in tongues.

The champion of the linking of tongues to Spirit baptism as the initial evidence in the conflict within the Assemblies of God was Daniel W. Kerr. Kerr, a former CMA pastor, strongly defended the doctrine of initial evidence at the 1918 General Council of the Assemblies of God against the attacks Bosworth. Kerr appealed to his understanding that Luke consciously chose to include materials to prove theological points. Based on this, he argued that the pattern of Acts, which included the speaking in tongues associated with Spirit baptism, was applicable to the contemporary church in its formulation of doctrine. In 1916 the AG, in its Statement of Fundamental Truths, called for the "initial sign of speaking in tongues." In the controversy of 1918 the statement was revised to call for "the initial physical sign of speaking with other tongues." It appears that by 1918 the Pentecostal movement had decided that tongues is the evidence of Spirit baptism.

Hermeneutical Support

Pentecostals have consistently used the book of Acts as their paradigm for asserting initial evidence of tongues. According to Pentecostals, Luke's recording of the "pattern" of Spirit baptism, with the accompaniment of speaking in tongues (Acts 2:4; 10:45–46; 19:6), not only depicted the experience of the early church, but also established a doctrinal and spiritual norm for all believers. They did this because they saw Luke as a theologian. This hermeneutical approach exalted the historical narratives to the same level of doctrinal authority as the didactic sections of the Bible. William F. Carothers, an associate of Parham, used the Acts' pattern, especially Acts 10:45-46, as the defense for the initial evidence doctrine. George F. Taylor and Joseph H. King, early leaders in the Pentecostal Holiness Church also defended the initial evidence doctrine on the basis of the pattern of the book of Acts.

Pentecostal hermeneutics are a brand of restorationism, the approach to biblical material that sees the present experiences as restoring those of biblical times. Though not the first group to see itself as restoring the realities of biblical paradigms, Pentecostalism has taken its place among those ranks. Examples of other restorationist groups are Anabaptists; Pietists; the Moravians; followers of John Wesley; and the American Holiness movement.

Another critical method employed by Pentecostals to defend the doctrine of initial evidence is redaction criticism. Redaction criticism asserts that the biblical writers chose to use material to convey some theological concern. They selected and molded their material for serious reasons. This would have also been true of the way narrative material was used.

Non-Classical Pentecostal Views

Most charismatics associate (renewal in or) being baptized in the Spirit with the manifestation of the charismata, which regularly includes speaking in tongues—usually in a prominent position. Few charismatics accept that glossolalia is the sine qua non for Spirit baptism. (Lederle 1991, 131–132)

The argument from charismatics against tongues as the initial evidence of Spirit baptism takes at least these forms: (1) The New Testament does not claim tongues as the only evidence of Spirit baptism; (2) The New Testament does not claim tongues as the first evidence of Spirit baptism; (3) The New Testament does not claim tongues to be the conclusive evidence of Spirit baptism. Charismatics do link tongues to Spirit baptism, but they do not consider it as a necessary condition to validate the experience.

JAMES RAILEY

See also Azusa Street Revival; Baptism in the Holy Spirit; Glossolalia; Penetcostalism, Classical; Sanctification; Second Work of Grace

Further Reading

Ervin, H. M. (1987). *Spirit baptism: A biblical investigation*. Peabody, MA: Hendrickson Publishers.

Goff, J. R., Jr. (1991). Initial tongues in the theology of Charles Fox Parham. In G. B. McGee (Ed.), *Initial evidence: Historical and biblical perspectives on the Pentecostal doctrine of Spirit baptism*, (57–71). Peabody, MA: Hendrickson Publishers.

Holdcroft, L. T. (1979). *The Holy Spirit: A Pentecostal interpretation*. Springfield, MO: Gospel Publishing House.

Horton, S. M. (1976). *What the Bible says about the Holy Spirit*. Springfield, MO: Gospel Publishing House.

Kerr, D. W. (1922, September 2). The basis of our distinctive testimony. *Pentecostal Evangel*.

Kerr, D. W. (1923, August 11). The Bible evidence of the baptism with the Holy Ghost. *Pentecostal Evangel*.

Lederle, H. I. (1991). Initial evidence and the charismatic movement: An ecumenical appraisal. In G. B. McGee (Ed.), *Initial evidence: Historical and biblical perspectives on the Pentecostal doctrine of Spirit baptism*, (131–141). Peabody, MA: Hendrickson Publishers.

McGee, G. B. (1991). *Initial evidence: Historical and biblical perspectives on the Pentecostal doctrine of Spirit baptism*. Peabody, MA: Hendrickson Publishers.

Palma, A. D. (2001). *The Holy Spirit: A Pentecostal perspective*. Springfield, MO: Gospel Publishing House.

Stronstad, R. (1988). Trends in Pentecostal hermeneutics. *Paraclete*, 22(3), 1–12.

Stronstad, R. (1989). The Holy Spirit in Luke-Acts: A synthesis of Luke's pneumatology. *Paraclete*, 23(2), 18–26.

Williams, J. R. (1990). *Renewal theology: Salvation, the Holy Spirit, and Christian living*. Grand Rapids, MI: Zondervan Publishing House.

Initiation Rites

Initiation rites have existed in societies much longer than has Christianity. In local cultures, these rites are utilized to provide for their peoples appropriate things to do whenever there is a transition from one stage of life to another. The intention is a safe passage and the ritual activity or ceremony supports that passage. In

A cross by the lake at a Christian youth camp.
Courtesy of istockphoto.com/ssuni.

the academic discipline of cultural (social) anthropology, these rites are known as *rites of passage* or *rites of intensification*, with the former focusing on the individual and the latter on the group. Van Gennep, in his classic work *Rites of Passage*, postulated that in crucial times in the life of a person and society such as birth, puberty, marriage, death, movement in status, and so on, there are elaborate rituals and ceremonies that celebrate and mark such events. Normally the initiate is removed from the society as a whole, isolated either individually or corporately for a certain period of time, and then reintroduced into the society in his or her new status. These rites or ceremonies not only define and clarify relationships but have great value as social events.

Historical Understanding

The term "initiation" is not found in Holy Scripture. It comes from the Latin *initiare*, which, together with the noun *initiatio*, is found in ancient sources on the mystery cults. Within Christianity, "sacrament" is often used as a synonym for "initiation rite." Some Protestant traditions prefer the term "ordinances" while others favor the use of "sacraments." In contemporary Roman Catholic Church documents (Second Vatican Council documents, the Rites of the Catholic Church, the Code of Canon Law, and the *Catechism of the Catholic Church*), there are many references to initiation, Sacraments of Initiation, and Christian Initiation.

Augustine, in the fourth century, concluded that baptism and the Eucharist were the only two rites that were sacramental and they convey grace *ex opere operato* (by virtue of the act itself). The validity and power of the sacrament/rite resides in the holiness of Christ and the administering priest functions only as an instrument of Christ's grace.

During the Scholastic Period (eleventh to thirteenth centuries), the list of sacraments, believed to have been instituted by Christ, was enlarged and identified as: Baptism, Confirmation, Eucharist, Reconciliation (or Penance), Anointing of the sick, marriage (or matrimony), and Holy Orders. These were and are considered as instrumental causes of grace, the means by which God chooses to sanctify humanity and unify the Church. Of the seven, Baptism, Confirmation, and Eucharist are presently considered as initiation rites.

The sacraments monopolized the public worship life of Christian laity by the sixteenth century. From cradle to grave, one's entire life was sustained by the sacraments. "They formed the basis of pastoral care and provided resources for each stage of life passages as well as for the day-in and day-out journey" (White 1999, 14).

Taking issue over the seven sacraments of the Roman Catholic Church, Martin Luther wrote *The Babylonian Captivity of the Church,* in which he reduced the sacraments to two: Baptism and Eucharist. This document "stands as the most important single treatise shaping all Protestant sacramental life" (White 1999, 17). His criteria for accepting a sacrament is that "the symbolic act must be instituted by God and combined with a promise. Sacramental character ultimately depends on the presence of a divine Word of promise" (Olson 1999, 392 n. 37).

Appealing again to concepts within cultural anthropology, the issue of "form and meaning" is very relevant to understanding the process that led to major disagreements regarding Luther's views on baptism and the Lord's Supper. It is through cultural forms that meanings are transmitted from one human being to another and "the same form in different societies will have at least some different meanings" (Kraft 1996, 140). As with cultural forms in a given society, ecclesiastical forms existed and do exist within the Church. The medieval Catholic Church had defined both the form and the meaning of the sacraments/rites before Luther's original protest at Wittenberg in 1517.

Luther's larger battle came from within Protestant ranks as other reformers interpreted the meaning of the sacraments (the forms) differently. The first generation of Protestants existed in four distinct branches: Lutheran, Reformed, Anabaptists, and Anglican. While each shared common beliefs, different interpretations of the sacraments (initiation rites) divided their theology and praxis.

Pentecostal Understanding

In various ways Pentecostals reflect the Reformation heritage on rites and sacraments. However, while the forms have been retained, the meanings have morphed into a pattern that resembles rites of passage as defined by cultural anthropologists. An inclusive list in a nonprogressive order includes conversion, water baptism, dedication of children, sanctification, The Lord's Supper, and the baptism in the Holy Spirit. Some of these steps could (but do not always) imply increased levels of spirituality as progress is made from initial conversion, sanctification, and the baptism in the Holy Spirit. Historically, Pentecostals coming from the Wesleyan tradition include sanctification as a distinct second work of grace while those of a Reformed background do not. Water baptism, dedication of children, and the Lord's Supper normally come under the rubric of "ordinances."

In contrast to the Sacramentalists, who regard water baptism as the focus of conversion-initiation in which forgiveness, the gift of the Spirit, and membership in Christ become the focus of the rite, Pentecostals consider conversion as the first step in the initiatory process. Conversion in the New Testament is intentionally referred to as the "new birth" ("Jesus declared, 'I tell you the truth, no one can see the kingdom of God unless he is born again'"; John 3:3, NIV), which is a metaphor for the first initiatory rite in anthropology, the birth of a child. In the normal spiritual maturation of a believer, converts are encouraged to receive the baptism in the Holy Spirit as the salient spiritual rite of initiation.

Interspersed somewhere among the believer's spiritual conversion-initiation rites are water baptism, dedication of children, and the Lord's Supper in nonsequential order. Because the majority of Pentecostals do not view these ordinances as salvific, the timing is not considered crucial. Some insist upon baptizing converts upon the initial act of repentance while others require a period of catechism. With few exceptions, Pentecostals do not baptize infants (paedobaptism) or small children and will either encourage or allow those who have undergone infant baptism to be "re-baptized" upon their confession of faith in Jesus Christ.

In lieu of infant baptism, Pentecostals and others practice the dedication of infants or small children in which the parents pledge to rear them in the faith. "All seem to sense the need for some form of public profession of faith when a child reaches sufficient age" (White 1999, 51). In the non-Western world, the discrete distinction between the dedication of children and paedobaptism is often blurred.

Incorporating a theology of the Lord's Supper that it is primarily symbolic in nature, most Pentecostals tend to be very casual about its observance. While they may adhere to a rigid weekly, monthly, or quarterly schedule, it is normally understood as a remembrance of the Lord's death and commemorates his saving act. Reconciliation to one's neighbors and to God is emphasized as a precondition. The Lord's Supper (Holy Communion) is not seen as a source of forgiveness of sins. Open communion is normally practiced and all believers are encouraged to partake regardless of church or denominational affiliation.

Implications

Pentecostal views of initiation rites are similar to most Evangelical views with the exception of their belief concerning the baptism in the Holy Spirit. This distinctive rite of initiation sets them apart. During the time of the Azusa Street Revival in Los Angeles (1906–1909), Pentecostals were considered an aberration to Christianity. However, time has been kind. Today they are just one of several "confessions" that make up the body of Christ. While clinging to their distinct rite of initiation, the baptism in the Holy Spirit, they are now accepted by many who once disavowed them.

WARREN NEWBERRY

See also Baptism in the Holy Spirit; Baptism, Water; Communion (Eucharist); Ordinances and Sacraments; Sanctification

Further Reading

Browning, R. L., & Reed, R. A. (1985). *The sacraments in religious education and liturgy.* Birmingham, AL: Religious Education Press.

Dunn, J. D. G. (1970). *Baptism in the Holy Spirit: A re-examination of the New Testament teaching on the gift of the Spirit in relation to Pentecostalism today.* London: SCM Press.

Ervin, H. M. (1984). *Conversion-Initiation and the baptism in the Holy Spirit: An engaging critique of James D.G. Dunn's baptism in the Holy Spirit*. Peabody, MA: Hendrickson Publishers.

Final report of the international Roman Catholic/Pentecostal dialogue (1972–1976). (1990). *Pneuma: The Journal of the Society for Pentecostal Studies*, 12(2), 85–95.

Kraft, C. H. (1996). *Anthropology for Christian witness*. Maryknoll, NY: Orbis Books.

Olson, R. E. (1999). *The story of Christian theology: Twenty centuries of tradition & reform*. Downers Grove, IL: InterVarsity Press.

Van Gennep, A. (1960). *Rites of passage*. Chicago: University of Chicago Press.

White, J. F. (1999). *The sacraments in Protestant practice and faith*. Nashville, TN: Abingdon Press.

Interpretation of Tongues

The interpretation of tongues is just as much a miracle as Speaking in Tongues. Both are from the mind of the Holy Spirit. The interpreter looks to God in faith with full dependence just as the speaker looks to God for the terms spoken in the unknown tongue. The goal of the interpreter is not to provide comparable terms in his own language for the supernatural words spoken but to convey their meaning.

Basis of Interpretation

Interpretation of Tongues, the final gift of the Holy Spirit listed by Paul, is rooted in Paul's pastoral advice for the riddance of untranslated tongues in the congregation. He encourages those who speak in tongues to remain silent if an interpreter is not present, and he makes it clear that the interpreter's gift, like prophecy, can inspire a whole assembly. He urges the congregation to pray for the ability to interpret and makes it clear that all do not have this gift (1 Corinthians 12:30, 14:13, NAS).

Historical Overview

At Christianity's inception Speaking in Tongues was heard by Jewish pilgrims in their own native language (Acts 2:6–8, 11). Because these devout Jews heard their dialects being spoken by the first Christians on the day of Pentecost, interpretation was not necessary. Furthermore, there is no mention of Interpretation of Tongues in Acts 10:46 or 19:6. "Interpretation" is used by Paul in the sense of a charismatic gift, whereas it is used by Luke only to indicate a translation from one language to another (Acts 9:36).

Charles Fox Parham, a leader of the early Pentecostal movement, believed that those who were truly baptized with the Holy Spirit could speak in tongues and that their unfamiliar syllables were actually a foreign language that could be used for overseas missionary ventures. Parham understood speaking in tongues to be God's way of equipping believers to go to the mission fields without having to learn the language of the inhabitants. Although contemporaries disagreed with Parham's rationale for tongues, he never abandoned this view of the purpose of glossolalia.

One contemporary who disagreed with Parham was William J. Seymour, leader of the Azusa Street Revival, which took place in Los Angeles, California, from 1906 to 1909. According to Seymour, knowing the language of tongues was not necessary and Christians were not to bother with trying to understand it. The Azusa leader was convinced that God did not promise Christians that they would know what language they were speaking, but only that they would be given the interpretation of what was spoken. Seymour admonished his adherents not to seek after tongues but to pursue the Holy Spirit who would give the tongues in accordance with His divine will. Although Seymour's stance on tongues and interpretation was simplistic, for most of the twentieth century, classical Pentecostal teachers developed some of its nuances.

Gift of Interpretation?

There are those who refer to this gift as "the gift of Interpretation." Pentecostal speaker Harold Horton argues that this abbreviation reduces Interpretation of Tongues to the natural plane. He believes that the purpose of the gift is not just to give a clear explanation of spiritual matters; it is also to demonstrate a miracle, because the believer speaks under the guidance of the Holy Spirit. The Bible does not list a "gift of Interpretation," but it does record the "gift of Interpretation of Tongues" (1 Corinthians 12:10).

Is Interpretation Translation?

A translation attempts to give the exact meaning of what is spoken, but an interpretation involves giving the meaning or sense of the message. Those who reject the idea of Interpretation of Tongues follow the path of the Fathers and Reformers who saw tongues narrowly as translation. Because the length of the original message

1 Corinthians 12, 6-10 (New International Version)

[6]There are different kinds of working, but the same God works all of them in all men.

[7]Now to each one the manifestation of the Spirit is given for the common good.

[8]To one there is given through the Spirit the message of wisdom, to another the message of knowledge by means of the same Spirit,

[9]to another faith by the same Spirit, to another gifts of healing by that one Spirit,

[10]to another miraculous powers, to another prophecy, to another distinguishing between spirits, to another speaking in different kinds of tongues, and to still another the interpretation of tongues.

spoken in tongues may not be the same as the length of the interpretation, many doubt that the translator was really endowed with the ability to interpret what was spoken.

However, although interpretation is not usually translation, interpretation can be translation. The Spirit may choose to translate word for word through a willing vessel. Worthy of note is an Old Testament prefigurement in the narrative of Daniel found in the handwriting on the wall of Nebuchadnezzar's palace—MENE, MENE, TEKEL, PARSIN—which literally meant "Numbered, numbered, weighed, divided." The prophet Daniel attempted to interpret it to discover its complete meaning (Daniel 5:25–28). If one agrees with the words of Joseph in Genesis 40:8 about interpretations belonging to God, then it is easy to surmise that the Almighty is not bound to any method of interpretation. With this in mind, interpretation is translation in the sense that the Holy Spirit is free to use individuals to give a verbatim translation of heavenly messages in tongues; it is not translation if translation is defined as a word for word rendering in the vernacular. It is often a summary of what has been presented through the supernatural manifestation of tongues.

Is Tongues Part of Prophecy?

It has been assumed that tongues plus interpretation equals prophecy. This assertion has lead to some controversy about the distinctiveness of the gifts. For instance, if tongues plus interpretation equals prophecy, what would be the need for the former two gifts? Why should one be concerned with tongues and interpretation when the gift of prophecy would accomplish the same purpose? Tongues and Interpretation of Tongues are distinct gifts of the Holy Spirit as much as prophecy is. Although tongues coupled with interpretation is similar to prophecy in the sense that it may contain a message, this does not mean that the results are identical. Prophecy is primarily associated with edification, exhortation, and consolation; tongues relate essentially to the praise of God, expressing mysteries in the Spirit and offering supplications. Therefore, although the Interpretation of Tongues may include certain elements of the three dimensions of prophecy (edification, exhortation, and consolation), it operates in a different context.

Who Should Interpret? In the order of Interpretation of Tongues, it is clear from Paul's writings that only one person is to interpret (1 Corinthians 14:27). However, Paul did not limit the task of Interpretation of Tongues only to those who were different from the original speaker. For instance, in 1 Corinthians 14:13 Paul encourages those who speak in tongues to pray for the power to interpret so that the congregation may be edified. Paul's statement in verse 13 also makes it clear that those who use the gift of tongues should also be able to interpret their own message. Although Scripture permits a person to interpret their own message, it appears to be the exception and not the general rule. The Apostle Paul gave specific instructions by admonishing the Corinthians to refrain from Speaking in Tongues aloud in the church unless an interpreter is in attendance. However, he did not discourage the speaker of tongues from speaking to himself or to God (1 Corinthians 14:28).

Using the Gift

The gift of tongues has been well documented by both church historians and theologians and continues to be studied more than Interpretation of Tongues. However, with nearly 600 million Pentecostal and charismatic Christians in the world today, it is important to investigate Interpretation of Tongues as well as other spiritual gifts. Although classical Pentecostal scholars may be divided over whether or not tongues plus interpretation equals prophecy, Interpretation of Tongues shares prophecy's ability to edify the church (1 Corinthians 14:5). Interpretation of Tongues may have been overlooked as an important gift in the past because it is listed last among the gifts of the Spirit and is dependent on another gift called "kinds of tongues" (1 Corinthians 12:10). However, without Interpretation of Tongues, there would be a silence of spiritual tongues in the Church. Interpretation of Tongues is essential for the community because it unlocks the utterances of God's people through the Spirit of God. Because Speaking in Tongues is a heavenly utterance, there is a vital need for rational comprehension that can provide edification for all who are present.

CHARLES R. FOX, JR.

See also Gifts of the Spirit; Glossolalia; Prophecy, Gift of

Further Reading

Basham, D. (1971). *A handbook on tongues interpretation & prophecy*. Mobile, AL: Whitaker.

Fee, G. D. (1987). *The new international commentary on the New Testament, The First Epistle to the Corinthians*. Grand Rapids, MI: Eerdmans.

Gee, D. (1963). *Spiritual gifts in the work of the ministry today*. Springfield, MO: Gospel Publishing.

Horton, H. (1934). *The gifts of the spirit*. Springfield, MO: Gospel Publishing.

Lindsay, G. (1963). *Gifts of the spirit* (Vol. 4). Dallas, TX: Christ for the Nations.

Noble, E. M. (Ed.). (1994). *Like as of fire: Newspapers from the Azusa Street world wide revival*. Washington, DC: Middle Atlantic Regional Press.

Pytches, D. (1985). *Spiritual gifts in the local church*. Minneapolis, MN: Bethany House.

Warrington, K. (Ed.). (1998). *Pentecostal perspectives*. Carlisle, UK: Paternoster Press.

Williams, E. S. (1953). *Systematic theology*. Springfield, MO: Gospel Publishing.

Williams, J. R. (1996). *Renewal theology*. Grand Rapids, MI: Zondervan.

Islam, Relationship to

Islam and Christianity share a history of both theological dialogue and encounters marred by misunderstandings and violence. Pentecostal-Charismatic engagement with Islam can be viewed in relation to points of convergence between Islamic and Pentecostal theologies, the uncertain history of the Pentecostal-Charismatic mission in Muslim contexts, and areas of tension, conflict, and promise in the relationship between Pentecostal-Charismatics and Muslims.

Points of Theological Convergence

As a theistic faith grounded in understandings shared with the Judeo-Christian tradition, Islam shares with Christianity a number of common beliefs, including the Unity of God, revelation, prophets, judgment, heaven and hell, and the importance of living out one's faith in the world and in the social life of the believing community. There are several points of convergence between Islam and Pentecostal-Charismatic theologies that provide possible bridges for engagement at the level of theology, praxis, and relationship.

First, the Islamic worldview is holistic and understands faith as all encompassing, rather than compartmentalized. The Pentecostal understanding of Jesus as savior, healer, baptizer in the Spirit, and coming King similarly engages the believer with a God who is Lord of this world and the next, who is concerned with the spiritual, social, and physical dimensions of life. There is no distinction between sacred and secular. In Islamic theology, all of creation is under the reign of *Allah* (the Arabic word for God, used by both Muslim and Christian Arabs and in the Arabic translation of the Bible). Human life has meaning, is infused with religion and religious symbols, and leads to an afterlife.

Second, for both Islam and Pentecostalism, the supernatural is a reality and meets the felt needs of people. For hundreds of millions of ordinary Muslims, Islam as a lived experience is marked by dreams, visions, healings, supernatural "signs," and encounters with the demonic. Sufism (Islamic mysticism), with its ideal of loving surrender to God, permeates Muslim traditions, poetry, and music. Felt needs like sickness; fear of death, evil spirits, divorce, or family disaster; and a desire for sons and for good luck impel Muslims, particularly women, to go for help to "holy men" (*pirs, marabouts*) who are believed to possess spiritual power (*baraka*, blessing) to heal particular ailments or to intercede with God on their behalf. Common Muslims believe in *jinn* and the evil eye, buy amulets, repeat spiritual formulas, drink holy water, and offer prayers at the tombs of departed Muslim saints. While Pentecostal-Charismatic orthopraxy eschews such practices, it shares the notion of experiential spirituality and the recognition that God's power can touch the poor, sick, and oppressed at their point of need.

In the 1990s a number of Pentecostal Christian leaders in Iran were imprisoned and murdered. At left is Bishop Haik Hovsepian-Mehr, an Armenian Assemblies of God pastor, who was murdered in January 1994. The Rev. Mehdi Dibaj (middle photo) was also slain in 1994. Pastor Mohammed Bajher Yusefi (known as "Ravanbaksh" or soul giver), pictured at left in a photo with his wife and sons, was killed in 1996. *Photos courtesy of Leonard Bartlotti.*

Third, like certain Pentecostal-Charismatics, particularly the "word of faith" school, Muslims believe in the insuperable power of the written and spoken Word of God. Many Muslim men, women, and children wear amulets containing "powerful" Qur'anic verses; other verses in elaborate calligraphy are displayed in homes and shops; the Qur'an is recited during the month of fasting (Ramadan); and some Muslims have memorized and can recite the entire Qur'an. The Qur'an says, "My word shall not be changed" (*Sura* 50:29), and to speak or breathe out *suras* (chapters) from the Qur'an imparts blessing.

Finally, both Islam and Pentecostalism have an intrinsic missionary impulse and theology. Muslims are engaged in missionary activity (*da'wa*, literally "call" to Islam) throughout Africa, Europe, and the Americas. It is the duty of every Muslim to "strive" (the root meaning of *jihad*) to spread Islam and bring all of life under the rule of God's law (*shari'a*). For Pentecostal-Charismatics global witness is central and is the consequence of the Holy Spirit's outpouring, a mission to proclaim the good news of forgiveness of sins through Jesus "to the ends of the earth" (Acts 1:8, NIV). The rule of God is marked not by law or religio-cultural constraints (Acts 15), but by the empowering presence and lordship of the Spirit of Jesus Christ.

Pentecostal-Charismatic Missions in Muslim Contexts

In early Pentecostalism, the baptism in the Holy Spirit and a sense of eschatological urgency were compelling forces for missions to the nations. Though Muslims were not a primary focus of early witness, a small number of Pentecostal missionaries pioneered in the Middle East (Palestine, Egypt, Syria, Lebanon, Persia), establishing schools and orphanages, distributing Gospel literature, visiting prisons, and bringing revival to traditional Christians.

Early Pioneers

Persian Pentecostals in America like John G. Warton, Andrew D. Urshan, and Philip Shabaz returned as missionaries to the land of their birth. G. S. Brelsford (1858–1912), H. E. Randall (d. 1938) and others brought the Pentecostal message to Egypt. Single Pentecostal women were especially notable, including Yumna G. Malick (1874–1966) in Lebanon and Syria; A. Elizabeth Brown (1866–1940) and Laura Radford (1869–1950) in Palestine; and Lillian Trasher (1887–1961), whose orphanage (est. 1911) in Asyut, Egypt, endures to this day.

Years of Neglect

In the fifty-year period after 1930, Pentecostals did very little about the Muslim world. There were exceptions, for example, missionaries like Howard (1911–1995) and Olive (b. 1919) Hawkes (Bangladesh); Philip (b. 1916) and Hazel (b. 1917) Crouch (Egypt); Calvin (1924–2000) and Marian (b. 1924) Olson (Bangladesh); David K. (1931–1984) and Deborah (b. 1931) Irwin (Egypt, Malawi); Mark (b. 1931) and Gladys (b. 1932) Bliss (Liberia, Iran, Bangladesh); as well as Swedish Pentecostals (Pakistan, Bangladesh, NW China), Dutch Pentecostals (Dutch East Indies), and a trickle of other workers in the Middle East and India. However, most efforts were focused on non-Muslims and Christian-background believers (e.g., Hawkes and Olson worked mostly with the Hindu-background church). Like other missions, Pentecostals assumed that a revival among a Christian minority would lead to Muslim evangelization. The approach overlooked barriers of prejudice and culture, yielded meager results, and generally failed to produce indigenous Muslim-background churches.

Surprisingly, in Algeria, the work of largely non-charismatic missionaries led to a strong charismatic church planting movement, particularly among the Kabyle (Berbers). Before Algeria's independence in 1962, a woman named Rahima came to Christ through the witness of a small French Pentecostal church. Today, the indigenous church movement among the Kabyle is overwhelmingly charismatic—over forty thousand Muslim followers of Jesus, and growing. This is partly due to Rahima's influence and partly due to the fact that Pentecostal-Charismatic spirituality "fit" well in the spirit-aware Algerian context.

In general, however, despite their successes with non-Muslims, Pentecostals were "ill equipped to evangelize Muslims and…certain national churches ignored them altogether" (McGee 1989, 228). McGee notes, "the lack of strategy…led to their clustering in metropolitan areas and neglecting outreach to isolated peoples" (1989, 226). Other impediments included the founding and maintenance of charitable institutions; the focus on Christian subcultures (e.g., through Bible institutes, correspondence programs, etc.); and the tendency to avoid unresponsive or hostile sectors of population. Reliance on traditional approaches (e.g., winning "converts" one by one rather than in families or groups; cultural extraction; reliance on "missionary" visas), and unbelief that Muslim-background churches could be established, were also barriers. In truth, Pentecostal attention was largely focused elsewhere, for example, on the burgeoning harvest in Latin America, rather than on perceived closed doors and pioneer sowing in the "hard soils" of the Muslim world.

Prominent mission leader, Greg Livingstone, lamented in 1982, "If you Pentecostals have so much 'power,' why are there so few of you in the Muslim world?" (personal communication with author). Phil Parshall, whose seminal 1980 book *New Paths in Muslim Evangelism* wrote the script for all subsequent debates about evangelical approaches to Muslim contextualization, appealed, "It is our responsibility as Christians to seek an anointing that we may be powerful instruments in the hand of God. Muslims must come to realize that our God is alive—and that He confirms His existence with tangible proofs" (1980, 155). However, in the September 1981 *Mountain Movers* magazine, Assemblies of God mission leader Charles E. Greenaway reported there were just four Assemblies of God missionary couples working full-time in Muslim evangelism.

Resurgence of Muslim Ministry

The over fifty-year period of relative Pentecostal neglect of the Muslim world was followed by an upsurge of interest, prayer, and missionary outreach by Pentecostal-Charismatics in the 1980s and 1990s. David Irwin's founding of the Center for Ministry to Muslims (CMM) in 1982 is a convenient marker of this turnaround. The cornerstone of CMM's ministry was the "*Jumaa* Prayer Fellowship," which enlisted Pentecostals to intercede for Muslims every Friday (*Jumaa*, the day for Muslim community prayer). Other CMM initiatives included a literature ministry; prayer bulletin; traveling display, *A Prayer Pilgrimage through the Muslim World*; training seminars for missionaries, national pastors and Bible schools; and efforts to help churches understand Islam.

The Pentecostal refocus on Islam was derivative and flowed from larger currents in Evangelical missions, particularly the new frontier mission paradigm centered on "unreached peoples" following the 1974 International Congress on World Evangelization in Lausanne, Switzerland. Missiologist Ralph D. Winter's founding of the U.S. Center for World Mission (1977); the Samuel Zwemer Institute (an outgrowth of the North American Conference on Muslim Evangelization, 1978); and international conferences (World Consultation on Frontier Missions, Edinburgh, 1980); outlined as never before the cultural dimensions of "the Unfinished Task"—including thousands of Muslim ethno-linguistic groups lacking a viable, indigenous church movement in their midst.

Pentecostal denominations have used a variety of approaches to reach Muslims including low-key friendship evangelism, literature, radio, Bible correspondence ministries (ICI, now Global University; the contextualized "Allah-u Akbar" course offered by the Center for Education in Malaga, Spain), and, more recently, Teen Challenge drug treatment programs. A characteristic of denominational strategies has been to work through national (non-Muslim background) churches where they exist. While Irwin argued for new contextualized approaches, the "people group" focus and notions of mono-ethnic or contextualized Muslim background churches remain contested concepts.

Neo-Pentecostal–Charismatic outreach to Muslims generally took the form of media ministries (e.g., CBN broadcasts to the Middle East), and, more commonly, large-scale "healing campaigns" and "miracle crusades" (despite the negative connotations of the term "crusade" for Muslims). The latter followed the pattern of the overseas tours of revivalists and healing evangelists of the 1940s and 1950s.

Reinhardt Bonnke's mass rallies in Africa over a thirty-year period since 1966 impacted Muslims of South Africa, Kenya, Tanzania, Northern Ghana, Nigeria and other West African countries, and often attracted huge audiences, with numbers exceeding 100,000. Morris Cerullo held campaigns in Indonesia and the Middle East, and Marilyn Hickey in Pakistan and elsewhere. These open-air meetings attracted largely non-Muslim audiences; however, Muslims also attended, many thousands heard the Gospel, and remarkable testimonies of healing followed. Generally, however, due to lack of follow-up or contextualized strategies, the campaigns resulted in little actual church growth among Muslims.

Some charismatic and Neo-Pentecostal approaches have been confrontational, condemnatory, and antagonistic toward Islam and Muslims. Bonnke considers Muslims as, by definition, part of Satan's empire: "We are even knocking on the gates of the Islamic fortresses …gripped by a holy determination to carry out the Great Commission of our Lord, which is a command to attack the strongholds of Satan" (quoted in Gifford 1992, 171). "Miracle crusades" have been cancelled in Nigeria and Mali because of fears of violence and the offense arising from his views. "To Muslims, Bonnke's aim is the elimination of every Mosque from Africa in the shortest possible time. This elimination is to be achieved through evangelisation and not through arson but in Muslim eyes the ultimate effect is the same, their cultural annihilation" (Gifford 1992, 171). Notwithstanding the broad seed sowing of healing campaigns, the absence of dialogue, the use of militant and polemical language (associated with a theology of spiritual warfare), and resultant communal tensions have raised questions about this overall approach to evangelizing Muslims.

Until the 1980s, charismatics lacked links to mission agencies (most Evangelical missions did not accept candidates who spoke in tongues). Today, however, charismatic workers are part of the warp and woof of ministries to Muslims and are at the forefront of developing creative strategies for culturally relevant (contextualized) church planting. Non-Western Pentecostal-Charismatics—Latin American, Nigerian, Korean, Indonesian, and Filipino—have emerged as a vibrant new force. As one veteran missionary to North Africa put it, "We wouldn't call ourselves charismatic, but I think that if you're going to plant churches in the Muslim context, you should expect that those churches are going to have a charismatic element to them" (personal communication with author).

Tension, Conflict and Promise

Christian-Muslim relations today are affected by international events, terrorism, and political and socioeconomic forces as much as religious considerations. There are tensions and conflicts, as well as promising signs, in the relationship between Pentecostal-Charismatics and the world of Islam.

Persecution and Church Growth

Rapid church growth has been associated with persecution and restrictions on religious freedom. The Iranian Assemblies of God may be the only example in the entire Muslim world where a majority Christian background church has become a majority Muslim background church. Prior to the 1979 Iranian Revolution, there were an estimated three thousand Evangelicals and five hundred Muslim-background believers in Christ in Iran. Currently, Iranian Evangelicals number twenty thousand to thirty thousand worldwide, the majority of them Muslim background. Transformation occurred in the 1960s as Spirit-filled Armenians opened their hearts and established churches that welcomed their Persian Muslim neighbors. Iranian Pentecostals have paid a price for their witness and have endured harassment, government oppression, intimidation, imprisonment, and death.

In Nigeria, Africa's most populous country, Christians (one-third of whom are Pentecostal-Charismatic, according to Patrick Johnstone, 2001, 489) have also suffered from outbreaks of religious violence. Since 1991, hundreds of churches have been destroyed by Muslim militias, and thousands of pastors and believers killed. Some Pentecostals have retaliated in kind. In contrast with Iran, the bloodshed in northern Nigeria is between Muslim and Christian citizens, fueled by militant Islamists, attempts to impose shari'a law in local states, ethnic and political enmities, and contestations over land. Nevertheless, church growth has been spectacular; Nigerian missionaries continue to be active among Nigeria's 46 million Muslims, who have become more receptive to the Gospel.

Israel and the Nations

Another area of tension with Islam is Pentecostal-Charismatic Zionism. Charismatic leaders' unquestioning support for the nation of Israel, based on a theology that equates biblical Israel with the modern nation-state, has alienated Muslims worldwide. Within that theology a failure to take seriously biblical injunctions regarding justice and equality before the law for both Jews and non-Jews (Leviticus 19:34; 24:22; Exodus 23:9; Deuteronomy 27:19) has exacerbated that alienation. Perceived Christian support for the continued military occupation of the West Bank and Gaza, and the violence and restrictions on freedom that have resulted, has caused outrage among Muslims and dismay among Arab Christians. One antidote to political partisanship is a new vision of Christ the Servant of all: "It is too small a thing for you to be my servant to restore the tribes of Jacob and bring back those of Israel I have kept. I will also make you a light for the Gentiles, that you may bring my salvation to the ends of the earth" (Isaiah 49:6).

Signs of Promise

Despite tensions, there is enormous potential for broad Pentecostal-Charismatic engagement with the Muslim world. Many Muslims have come to Christ through the stepping-stones of dreams, signs confirming the truth of the Gospel, and the power of prayer in the name of Jesus. A Jesus who meets needs, heals, performs the miraculous, answers prayer, and delivers from evil spirits, fear, loneliness and death, is a powerful attraction to Muslims.

At the same time, as Greg Livingstone (1993, 18) points out, we need to balance "a popular but mostly unexamined hypothesis that 'there won't be any breakthrough in the Muslim world except through signs and wonders'"—that apart from miraculous workings there is no point attempting to plant churches in Muslim cities; in actuality, the real problem is "quantitative"—"Where there is 'little sowing, there is little reaping' (2 Corinthians 9:6)." More research is needed to explore the role of methodologies that involve "power encounters" (Kraft 1989), the working of miracles, word of knowledge, physical and inner healing and exorcism in the process of conversion, discipleship, and church planting.

The world's 1.3 billion Muslims in over 3,100 distinct people groups are both a challenge and an opportunity for the Church. Pentecostal-Charismatic vitality, diversity, personnel, and global resources must be focused more purposefully on informed, long-term, incarnational service and church planting among Muslim peoples. Pentecostal-Charismatics have an opportunity to relate their dynamic faith to the felt needs of their Muslim neighbors, with a view to "waging peace on

Islam" (Mallouhi 2000) and "healing the broken family of Abraham" (McCurry 2001). For Muslims, the most credible proof of the Gospel's truth is a loving Christian. The Pentecostal anointing inspires eschatological hope: the vision of followers of Jesus within every Muslim "tribe and language and people and nation" (Revelation 5:9).

LEONARD N. BARTLOTTI

See also Africa, North (and the Middle East)

Further Reading

Bartlotti, L. N. (1985). *A prayer pilgrimage through the Muslim world*. Minneapolis, MN: CMM.

Chesworth, J. (2003). Fundamentalism and outreach strategies in East Africa: Christian Evangelism and Muslim Da'wa. In B. Soares (Ed.), *Proceedings of the third international colloquium Muslim/Christian encounters in Africa, 22–24 May 2003*. Institute for the Study of Islamic Thought in Africa (ISITA) Program of African Studies Northwestern University.

Dibaj, M. (1993). *The written defense of the Rev. Mehdi Dibaj delivered to the Sari Court of Justice, Sari, Iran, December 3, 1993*. Retrieved October 15, 2004 from http://www.farsinet.com/ici/dibaj/

Gifford, P. (1986). "Africa shall be saved": An appraisal of Reinhard Bonnke's Pan-African crusade. *Journal of Religion in Africa 17*(1), 63–92.

Gifford, P. (1992). Reinhard Bonnke's mission to Africa, and his 1991 Nairobi crusade. In P. Gifford (Ed.), *New dimensions in African Christianity* (pp. 157–182). Nairobi, Kenya: All Africa Conference of Churches.

Johnstone, P., & Mandryk, J. (2001). *Operation world: 21st century edition*. Waynesboro, GA: Paternoster Press.

Kraft, C. H. (1989). *Christianity with power: Your worldview and your experience of the supernatural*. Ann Arbor, MI: Servant Books.

Livingstone, G. (1993). *Planting churches in Muslim cities: A team approach*. Grand Rapids, MI: Baker Books.

Love, R. (2000). *Muslims, magic and the Kingdom of God: Church planting among folk Muslims*. Pasadena, CA: William Carey Library.

Mallouhi, C. A. (2000). *Waging peace on Islam*. London: Monarch Books.

McCurry, D. (2001). *Healing the broken family of Abraham: New life for Muslims*. Colorado Springs, CO: Ministries to Muslims.

McGee, G. B. (1989). *This Gospel shall be preached: A history and theology of Assemblies of God foreign missions since 1959*. Springfield, MO: Gospel Publishing House.

Musk, B. A. (2003). *The unseen face of Islam: Sharing the Gospel with ordinary Muslims at street level*. London: Monarch Books.

Parshall, P. (1980). *New paths in Muslim evangelism: Evangelical approaches to contextualization*. Grand Rapids, MI: Baker Book House.

Parshall, P. (1983). *Bridges to Islam: Christian perspectives on folk Islam*. Grand Rapids, MI: Baker Book House.

Stacey, V. (1986). *Christ Supreme over Satan: Spiritual warfare, folk religion and the occult*. Lahore, Pakistan: Masihi Isha'at Khana.

Woodberry, J. D. (Ed.). (1989). *Muslims and Christians on the Emmaus road*. Monrovia, CA: MARC.

Judaism, Relationship to

Pentecostals have an affinity to the Jews and the nation of Israel as a result of their distinctive view of God's work before the return of Jesus Christ. The relationship of charismatics and neocharismatics to Judaism more closely reflects standard Christian relationships to Judaism. The attitudes of charismatics are influenced by the stance of the denomination of which they are a part. Few things can thus be said that apply to all three groups. One common testimony is that the experience of the Holy Spirit brings new life to the believer's reading of the Bible. Since the Hebrew scriptures make up a majority of the Christian Bible and since nearly all the writers of the New Testament were Jews, those with a Pentecostal-Charismatic experience commonly find a fresh appreciation for the Jews. The fact that Jesus was the Jewish Messiah (Christ) and the fulfillment of all things Jewish, puts the Jews in a unique light. Understanding Jesus, then, means understanding the Jewish scriptures that Jesus interpreted and understanding the practices observed by devout Jews to this day.

Pentecostals

Love for the Bible was characteristic of the early Pentecostals. They often spoke in the style and vocabulary of their favorite translation, the King James Version, and were fonder of the Hebrew scriptures, the Christian Old Testament, than Christians in mainline denominations. This may have been in part because Pentecostals and the Jews in the Bible both thought of God in experiential terms and not in metaphysical terms. For the Israelites, God was He who delivered His people out of slavery in Egypt by His great power. Pentecostals thought of God as He who with the blood of His Son had delivered His people out of the slavery of sin by His Holy Spirit. Pentecostals have always been people of *testimony*, ready to share what God had done and was doing in their lives. Further, because the early Pentecostals were on the lower end of the social and economic scale, they related closely to the experience of oppression of the Israelites. This was even truer for black Pentecostals. Both black and white Pentecostals regularly sang songs that expressed the joy and blessing of the Holy Spirit in terms of the Scriptures, using images like Canaan, the Jordan, Zion, manna, the blood, and the pillar of fire.

Because Pentecostals believe the Bible is God's word, they find all parts of Scripture of matchless value. The details of the furniture and decoration of the Tabernacle, for example, are regarded by modern Christians as symbols of the holy lifestyle required by God. An increasingly popular phenomenon in Pentecostal churches in recent years is the presentation by Jewish Christians of the elements of the Passover observance; the Jewish ritual is interpreted through Christian eyes. But though Pentecostals have regularly derived Christian lessons from the Hebrew Scriptures, they have never abandoned the literal reading of the Bible. The churches they had abandoned had explained away the reality of the Bible's claims, but the God they experienced was the God of the miraculous; they found no reason not to take at face value the biblical claims that the Red Sea had parted at Moses' hand and that Jesus gave his disciples the power to cast out demons and heal the sick. Passages that referred to the Jews were usually taken literally: "Pray for the peace of Jerusalem"

271

(Psalms 122:6, NRSV), "I will bless those who bless you and curse those who curse you" (Genesis 12:3). According to Pentecostals, since God does not change and his word abides forever, such divine declarations remain in effect.

One of the basic characteristics of those involved in the early Pentecostal movement was a certainty that they were living in the last days before the return of Jesus Christ. The outpouring of the Holy Spirit was the means by which God was restoring the church to the purity and effectiveness of the New Testament Church. Pentecostals were alert, then, to recognize the "signs of the times" (Matthew 16:3) that Scripture guaranteed would precede the coming of the Lord. The *Apostolic Times* newspaper from the Azusa Street Revival mission cited the great earthquake that hit San Francisco within days of the outbreak of the revival as a fulfillment of the great signs in the earth foretold by Jesus in Matthew 24.

What was and still is decisive for the way Pentecostals relate to the Jews is their belief that the Bible prophesies that in the last days, in conjunction with the return of Jesus Christ, God would bring the Jews back to Israel and establish them there in peace. Ezekiel, for example, has a vision of a valley of dry bones that God gathers together and reinvigorates by his breath. God promises that He will in a similar way put His Spirit in His people and place them back in their own land (Ezekiel 37:14). For those who had dramatically experienced the power of God's Spirit, this was not difficult to believe. One of the early volumes of the *Apostolic Faith* newspaper, in a section entitled "Signs of His Coming," says that Jesus' parable of the fig tree (Luke 21:29–32) refers to the Jews, who for a time rejected their Messiah, but only "until the Gentile age should be fulfilled." This echoes a much-cited text in Paul's letter to the Romans (11:25–26), which speaks of a "blindness" upon Israel "until the fullness of Gentiles is completed, and so all Israel will be saved." This piece goes on to say that the Jews are "making all preparations to rebuild the temple at Jerusalem" (Seymour 1997, 35).

The same article concludes with a description of the "early and latter rains" that characterized the weather of Palestine, a popular theme of early Pentecostals and a key link between Jews and Pentecostals. The prophet Joel (Joel 2:23) promises that God will bestow the rains of spring and autumn on the "children of Zion" and their land. In this one article we find an example of the common double fulfillment of the "latter rain" in (a) the abundant (literal) rain that God was now showering on the land of Palestine with its returned Jews and (b) the (figurative) rain "upon the church, the baptism

with the Holy Ghost and fire," creating what one scholar terms a "fraternal identity" between Pentecostals and Israel (Gannon 2003, 242–248). This latter rain was the sign of and preparation for the harvest—figuratively, the end-time harvest of souls.

Over the years, Pentecostals increasingly assumed the eschatological framework of dispensationalism, an interpretational approach to the Bible that originated about 1850 and became popular in the United States in the twentieth century. Dispensationalism makes sharp distinctions in how God works among humans though history—it preaches, for example, that God related to Adam and Eve in the Garden in one way, to the Jews under the Mosaic Law in another way, and to Christians in the era of grace in yet another way. Many came to accept this approach because of the widespread use among Pentecostals of *The Scofield Reference Bible*. Dispensationalism, like early Pentecostalism, reads the Bible literally and maintains that God has not yet fulfilled his promises to Israel. One difference is that dispensationalism places the ultimate redemption of the Jews to the period after the church has completed its work and been taken to heaven, while early Pentecostals linked the end-time work of the Spirit with the church and Israel.

The intensity of attention given to Israel and the ingathering of the Jews was influenced by events in the Middle East. Expectations soared with the Balfour Declaration expressing Great Britain's support for a Jewish homeland that included Jerusalem in 1917. Many identified this as the close of the era of the Gentiles and thus the initiation of the salvation of all Israel (Romans 11:25). Another peak of prophetic speculation occurred with the founding of the modern state of Israel in 1948. For many, this surely was the final ingathering; some concluded in subsequent years that the Second Coming would have to occur within one generation, or forty years from this date. Prophetic shockwaves also shook the world with the seemingly miraculous events of the Six Day War in 1967. On the other hand, events have sometimes dampened enthusiasm, such as the early stages of the Yom Kippur War in 1971, when many were shocked at the vulnerability of Israel.

There is a nearly universal belief that the Jews in some sense continue to be God's chosen people, though there are differences on what exactly this means. Pentecostals have related to Jews over the last century in two important ways. Some have viewed the Jews as unique for their place in the past and future of God's plan; they see them as descendants of the patriarchs of the faith, and believe that they will constitute

God's people on earth again after the Rapture. The Gospel of Jesus as Savior must be shared with them as with all other unbelievers, yet evangelism of the Jews has the added dimension of preparing those who will themselves proclaim the Gospel when Christians are removed from the earth. Some emphasize that evangelism is still "to the Jew first" (Romans 1:16). Others focus on the divine aspect of the future ingathering of the Jews and understand the role of the church less as evangelists than as comforters of Israel (Isaiah 40:1) in a hostile world.

In various ways, Pentecostals have tried to demonstrate their solidarity with the Jews in the land that God gave them and to which God had brought them back. Since many Pentecostals now have disposable incomes, many joined trips to Israel to see the places where Jesus ministered. Such trips were at times explicitly associated with showing support for the nation. The Sixth Pentecostal World Conference met in Jerusalem in 1961, at a time when the city was divided and many nations had boycotted any international activity. The decision to meet in Jerusalem in such circumstances was a statement of support for Israel and was enthusiastically received as such by national and city leaders.

Pentecostals have also been active in groups such as the International Christian Embassy in Jerusalem, an organization that takes the biblical injunctions to bless and comfort the Jews as a contemporary Christian mandate. The Embassy devotes its efforts in Israel to meeting the needs of the poor, the sick, and recent immigrants. In the fall of 2004, it sponsored its twenty-fifth annual gathering during the Jewish festival of Tabernacles to demonstrate its love for and solidarity with the Jews as God's people. Both top executives of the Embassy at the time of this writing are ministers ordained with Pentecostal denominations.

However, the support for Israel on the part of Western Pentecostals has often been more romantic than real, and some Pentecostals have been anti-Semites. White Pentecostals sometimes harbored prejudice against Jews that reflected stereotypes common among the white population, and black Pentecostals often reflected the attitudes toward Jews held by the larger black community. It should also be noted that Zionism is characteristic only of churches in or directly influenced by Western Pentecostalism; in most parts of the world, the status and future of the Jews are issues that rarely arise.

The contemporary dialogue between some Christian and Jewish groups and the trend in scholarship toward mutual affirmation of the two faith traditions are not supported by Pentecostals. Christians in this modern dialogue are not interested in converting their Jewish colleagues, but in better understanding them; from this perspective, Jews are complete in their faith and do not need to be saved by becoming Christians. Pentecostals, however, insist that salvation is only possible by coming to faith in Jesus. Jews, then, are lost in sin and will be condemned to hell unless they repent and accept Jesus as their Messiah. Some Pentecostals, as a result, are reticent to celebrate the nation of Israel, because the Jews have not turned in faith to their Messiah; others rejoice because of their confidence that this national repentance will occur in God's time, after the church is removed at the Rapture.

Charismatics

Charismatics do not share Pentecostal eschatology; instead, they reflect the attitudes toward Jews that characterize their particular denomination. Both the Vatican and the World Council of Churches have taken positions that have not been received well by Israel—for example, they believe that Israel should withdraw from the occupied territories (the West Bank and East Jerusalem). The Vatican has also never recognized Israel diplomatically. Such positions reflect a concern for the interests and rights of all residents of the area, and are not driven by the Pentecostal belief that God has given Jews the land forever. The predominant biblical interpretation in these mainline denominations holds that God's ultimate work is the church, where Jew and Gentile are brought together into one body; all believers are the children of Abraham (Galatians 4:28–29). No physical restoration of national Israel should be expected in the future because Palestinians are as valuable in God's sight as Jews. Christian Zionists dub this perspective "replacement theology" (the church replaces Israel as God's people) and condemn it.

Messianic Judaism became a major component of the Charismatic renewal in the 1970s. The idea that Jews who accept Jesus as their Messiah could maintain Jewish practices and form congregations with distinctive worship styles was not new. After all, the earliest believers were Jews who did not assume a developed Christian culture when they accepted Jesus as the Messiah; they thought of themselves as Jews and their practices continued to reflect that identity. Messianic Judaism is the modern appearance of this earliest Christianity. Like its prototype, it is diverse; major variations exist on its observance of Torah, its attitudes toward Zionism, and whether services are conducted in Hebrew or occur on Saturday or Sunday. Having been influenced by the Jesus movement of the 1960s, most leaders in the Messianic movement are charismatic, and thus are open to the operation of the gifts of the Spirit. Services in Messianic congregations or synagogues are charismatic in worship style, incorporating enthusiastic participation in music and dance influenced by modern Israeli forms. But the actual manifestation of these gifts in services is less here than in standard charismatic gatherings, because of the intentional emphasis on the group being Jewish rather than charismatic.

There are hundreds of these congregations worldwide, most notably in North America and Israel. Many are affiliated with Pentecostal denominations, but tend to be aggressively independent in practice and minimize their association with Christian organizations. A significant portion—often a majority—of the membership in Messianic congregations in America are Gentiles.

Mainstream Judaism has adamantly rejected these congregations. Jews for Jesus, founded in 1975, has been the target of hostility because of its aggressive approach to evangelism. Jewish writers have sought to expose leaders of Messianic congregations as Christian missionaries, agents who seek to disguise themselves as Jews. Some mainline Christian representatives have also expressed opposition to the movement; it is an embarrassment to those involved in the contemporary Christian-Jewish dialogue.

Neocharismatics

Neocharismatics are more diverse than Pentecostals and charismatics. In North America they tend to be characterized by their view that the church replaces Israel as God's people, which some Pentecostals denounce as anti-Zionist. Like charismatics, neocharismatics do not share the Pentecostal conviction that the Jews remain God's people and that Israel has a unique role in God's agenda.

ROBERT A. BERG

See also Messianic Jews; Scripture, Holy

Further Reading

Anderson, R. M. (1979). *Vision of the disinherited. The making of American Pentecostalism.* New York: Oxford University Press.

Ariel, Y. (1991). *On behalf of Israel: American fundamentalist attitudes toward Jews, Judaism, and Zionism, 1865–1945.* Brooklyn, NY: Carlson.

Ariel, Y. (2000). *Evangelizing the chosen people. Missions to the Jews in America, 1880–2000.* Chapel Hill: University of North Carolina Press.

Arrington, F. L. (1994). *Christian doctrine. A Pentecostal perspective* (Vols. 1–3). Cleveland, TN: Pathway.

Dayton, D. W. (Ed.). (1985). *The sermons of Charles F. Parham.* New York: Garland.

Gannon, R. L. (2003). *The shifting romance with Israel: American Pentecostal ideology of Zionism and the Jewish state.* Unpublished doctoral dissertation, Hebrew University of Jerusalem, Israel.

Harris-Shapiro, C. (1999). *Messianic Judaism. A rabbi's journey through religious change in America.* Boston: Beacon Press.

Hocken, P. (1994). *The glory and the shame. Reflections on the 20th century outpouring of the Holy Spirit.* Guildford, UK: Eagle.

Myland, D. W. (1985). The latter rain covenant and Pentecostal power. In D. W. Dayton (Ed.), *Three early Pentecostal tracts.* New York: Garland.

Nicholls, W. (1995). *Christian antisemitism. A history of hate.* Northvale, NJ: Jason Aronson.

Rosen, M., & Proctor, W. (1974). *Jews for Jesus.* Old Tappan, NJ: Revell.

Seymour, W. J. (Ed.). (1997). *The Azusa Street papers.* Foley, AR: Together in the Harvest Publications. (Original work published 1906–1908)

Wasserman, J. S. (2000). *Messianic Jewish congregations. Who sold this business to the gentiles?* Lanham, MD: University Press of America.

Williams, J. (1992). *The Church, the kingdom, and last things* (Vol. 3). Grand Rapids, MI: Zondervan.

K

Knowledge, Word of

The word of knowledge, according to most current Pentecostal-Charismatic interpreters, is a gift of the Holy Spirit by which the recipient becomes aware of information through revelation from God rather than human communication or learning. That information can then be applied in the life of the recipient or shared with other members of the body of Christ for their edification. This definition, however, is not uncontested among Pentecostal and charismatic leaders.

Defining the Word of Knowledge

The phrase "word of knowledge" (*logos gnoseos*) occurs only one time in the New Testament, forming part of a list of nine charismatic gifts in 1 Corinthians 12:7–10: the word of wisdom, the word of knowledge, faith, gifts of healing, the working of miracles, prophecy, discerning of spirits, tongues, and the interpretation of tongues. Among virtually all interpreters, the word of wisdom and the word of knowledge are seen as seen as closely related.

Catholic and Orthodox interpreters have historically tended to define the word of knowledge in terms of verbal expressions of knowledge about the nature and purposes of God or the interpretation of Scripture. The function of the gift was thus seen as relating to the teaching function of the church. Evangelical Protestant interpretation, which focused strongly on the Bible as the principal (and sometimes exclusive) source of verbal revelation about God, followed in this same direction, stressing the relation of the gift to biblical interpretation and teaching. Early Pentecostal teaching represented a departure from the traditional reading of the phrase. Emphasizing the "supernatural" quality of the gifts of the Spirit, Pentecostals began to interpret this gift or manifestation of the Spirit as a work of miraculous, spontaneous revelation from God to the Spirit-filled believer of facts of a broader nature.

Pentecostals and charismatics have not, however, historically agreed about the exact nature of the word of knowledge. Differences in interpretation among Pentecostal and charismatic interpreters seem to fall along the lines of educational and ministerial backgrounds, with highly educated Pentecostal New Testament scholars taking one position and less educated, more pragmatic phenomenological interpreters taking another. The professional scholars, such as early Pentecostal Bible teacher Myer Pearlman, Stanley Horton, J. Rodman Williams, and Craig Keener, have tended to interpret the word *gnosis* (knowledge) using a hermeneutic guided by narrow textual context. They examine the Pauline usage of the word *gnosis* in other texts such as 2 Corinthians 4:6 ("the light of the knowledge of the glory of God," NRSV), 2 Corinthians 2:14 ("the heavenly fragrance of the knowledge God gives us in Christ"), and Ephesians 1:17 ("the spirit of wisdom and revelation in the knowledge of him"), and accordingly they interpret the word of knowledge as having to do with knowledge about God. It is thus interpreted in the traditional way—as the revelation of information about the person, nature, or purposes of God, or in other words, doctrinal knowledge.

In contrast to the interpretation of professional scholars, early Pentecostal theologians (such as Ralph Riggs and Frank Boyd) and perhaps most Pentecostal-Charismatic ministers (such as Harold Horton, L. Thomas

Holdcroft, and Pat Robertson) interpret the word of knowledge phenomenologically, relating the broader meaning of the English word "knowledge" to their own life contexts, in which they have experienced the miraculous revelation of otherwise unknown facts of quotidian life at particular moments that brought edification to themselves or other believers. This phenomenological interpretation is then carried back to the Scriptures in search of examples from narrative passages. Scriptural examples that are commonly adduced in support of this interpretation are Jesus' knowledge of Nathaniel's actions under the fig tree (John 1:48), Jesus' knowledge of the marital status of the woman at the well (John 4:17, 18), Peter's knowledge of the deception of Ananias and Sapphira (Acts 5:1–6), Paul's knowledge that a shipwreck was about to occur (Acts 27:10), and other cases.

The Inclusion of *Logos*

Both professional scholars and practicing ministers have insisted that the phrase "word of knowledge" is especially significant for the inclusion of the word *logos* ("word"). Along the same lines of difference that mark interpretations of the *gnosis* side of the phrase, interpreters have tended to argue that the inclusion of the word *logos* has special significance. The professional exegetes tend to argue that the word *logos* points to the public utterance of knowledge about God. The practitioners have argued that "word" refers to the revelation of a particular fact or bit of knowledge, and that it need not be uttered publicly to be effective.

Leading contemporary Pentecostal exegetes such as Anthony Palma and Craig Keener have noted either that the meaning of the phrase *logos gnoseos* remains uncertain or that both interpretations have biblical warrant, whether they define the word of knowledge or simply exemplify other revelatory operations of the Holy Spirit. In the end, the argument over the meaning of the phrase does not cancel out the fact that both interpretations—the revelation of truth about God or about facts relating to humans—are reported as part of Pentecostal and charismatic spiritual life. Defining the exact boundaries along a range of revelatory gifts—from prophecy to the word of wisdom, to discernment of spirits, to the word of knowledge or to other spiritual revelations proves to be difficult, even for Pentecostal scholars. What is common among them all is the belief that ongoing, divinely given revelation is a contemporary reality.

JOSEPH L. CASTLEBERRY

See also Wisdom, Word of

Further Reading

Fee, G. D. (1994). *God's empowering presence: The Holy Spirit in the letters of Paul.* Peabody, MA: Hendrickson.

Holdcroft, L. T. (1962). *The Holy Spirit: A Pentecostal interpretation.* Springfield, MO: Gospel.

Keener, C. S. (2001). *Gift and giver: The Holy Spirit for today.* Grand Rapids, MI: Baker.

Palma, A. D. (2001). *The Holy Spirit in Pentecostal perspective.* Springfield, MO: Logion.

Riggs, R. M. (1949). *The Spirit himself.* Springfield, MO: Gospel.

Korea

The modern history of Korea is a tragic one. Most of the first half of the twentieth century (1910–1945) was occupied by the brutal rule of Japan. Young Protestant Christianity, begun in 1885 with the arrival of the first two Protestant missionaries, grew in this harsh environment. However, Korea is one of the few Asian nations where Christianity did not come through the colonizing power, but suffered with the people under the colonizer's oppressive rule. This may be a major reason why Korean Christianity grew exponentially in the twentieth century. When the nation was finally liberated in 1945, it was quickly divided in two: communist north and democratic south. In 1950, the North invaded the South and the resulting three-year Korean War took five million lives and left most of the infrastructure destroyed. More importantly, Communists targeted Christian leaders and churches in every city and town they occupied. Christianity, which had survived harsh colonial rule, was trampled by the same Korean people. This war also brought many northern Christians and leaders to the South. In the postwar period, these determined Christian refugees began many strong churches including Youngnak Presbyterian Church and Choonghyun Presbyterian Church. During the four decades after the war, in the midst of economic and political difficulties, Korean Christianity flourished and was hailed as the success of the modern missionary movement. By the conclusion of this period, Korean Christianity claimed 27 percent of South Korea's total population of 46.8 million. During this period of Christian growth, Korean Pentecostalism also grew. To this date, Christianity in North Korea is considered minimal. Expert in global Christianity David Barrett estimates the number of Korean Pentecostals in 2025 to reach

9.5 million, or 41.7 percent of Korean Christians or 18 percent of the total population of South Korea.

History of Pentecostalism in Korea

Before the arrival of Pentecostal missionaries, the Korean church experienced Pentecost-like spiritual experiences. In the second half of the twentieth century, at least three types of Pentecostal Christianity are found in Korea.

Precursors

There is a debate as to whether the Pyungyang Great Revival (1907) should be considered "Pentecostal" or one of the precursors of the Korean Pentecostal movement. It may be reasonable to see this and other revivals as precursors, just as the Holiness movement in the nineteenth century is viewed in the same way as the modern Pentecostal movement, even if some beliefs (e.g., "healing"), terminology (e.g., "baptism in the Spirit") and practices (e.g., intense prayer, emphasis on holiness) are found in both movements.

The Pyungyang Revival movement was led by missionaries and national leaders (such as Sun-joo Kil). This spiritual renewal quickly spread throughout the nation, as people sought emotional and spiritual comfort from the oppressive Japanese annexation. The unique dawn prayer meeting began with this revival and, to this date, marks Korean Christian spirituality. As a result, a considerable church growth was recorded. It is also possible that the idea of a prayer mountain, another unique feature of Korean Christianity, may have started around this period, although organized prayer mountains appeared only after the liberation of the nation. This revival was characterized by the emphasis on repentance and concerted prayer as the entire congregation raises their voices in prayer for a lengthy period. This is another feature of the Korean Christian—and especially Pentecostal—tradition.

The following decades produced important revival leaders rather than a nationwide revival movement. Yong-do Lee (1901–1933), a Methodist minister, began to preach the spiritual union of believers with Christ. His mystical message brought not only a new wave of revival but also criticisms. His short life influenced the troubled nation as Japanese harsh rule intensified. Lee's message can be viewed as escapist as he emphasized the internal aspect of Christian spirituality. Another revivalist, Ik-doo Kim, is known for his open-air preaching on the Kingdom of God, as his message is condensed into two words, "Jesus, Heaven!" He is also

Pastor David Yonggi Cho of the Yoido Full Gospel Church in Seoul. *Courtesy of Stanley Burgess.*

credited with healing and exorcism, which drew large crowds to his meetings. His popularity is attested to by the fact that his Presbyterian denomination appointed a study committee to investigate the genuineness of Lee's miracles. The report affirmed his claim.

Pentecostal Denominations

The first Pentecostal missionary, Mary Rumsey, arrived in 1928. This single woman experienced the baptism in the Spirit with the evidence of speaking in tongues. Like many early Pentecostal missionaries, Rumsey left without any systematic support. Arriving in Japan in 1927, she prepared her ministry in Korea under C. F. Juergensen, another Pentecostal missionary in Japan. Her first contact was Hong Huh, a clerk in the Anglican office. Attracted to the new doctrine and Rumsey's commitment, Huh became the first Korean Pentecostal minister and in 1932 pioneered with her the very first Subinggo Pentecostal Church in Seoul. They were soon joined by T. M Parsons, E. H. Meredith, and L. Vessey, independent Pentecostal missionaries, as well as national workers Boo-keun Bae and Sung-san Park. Both studied in the Pentecostal Bible school in Japan. In 1937, Rumsey was forced to leave Korea as Japanese authorities expelled all foreign missionaries. By this time, there were six Pentecostal churches and 173 members with ten workers throughout the nation. The Chosun Pentecostal Church was organized in 1938. Under severe persecution, however, not only from the authorities, but also from other Christian denominations, the number of Pentecostal churches was reduced to four, with four ministers and eighty members by 1945, when the Japanese rule in Korea was over.

After the liberation, the remnants of the Chosun Pentecostal Church were reorganized in 1949 into Pentecostal Church, Soonchun, Korea. With the arrival of Arthur B. Chesnut in 1951, the first appointed missionary of the U.S. Assemblies of God, the Korean Assemblies of God was organized with the leaders of the Korean Christ Pentecostal Church in 1953 at Namboo Church in Seoul. Quickly, Full Gospel Bible Institute (now Hansei University) was established in 1953 and began to train workers. The history of the Korean Assemblies of God is primarily represented by David Yonggi Cho with the unprecedented success of his Yoido Full Gospel Church, which claimed to have 700,000 members by 1992, registering as the single largest congregation in the world. Currently this denomination, a sister organization of the worldwide Assemblies of God, has a combined membership of 1,338,008. It also boasts 2,128 ministers, 1,886 churches, 17 theological schools, and 383 cross-cultural missionaries in 116 countries.

Soon other major Pentecostal denominations followed the Assemblies of God in establishing their presence in Korea. The Church of God (Cleveland, Tennessee) had their first missionary, Richard A. Jackson, in 1963, and their Church of God Bible College (now Hanyoung University) was founded in 1970. Today, the denomination has 118 churches, 190 members, one training school, and four cross-cultural missionaries.

The Korean Foursquare Church was founded by Rev. Shin-ok Kim in Daejon City during the postwar era. Being an educator, Kim established Daesung Christian School Foundation with several middle and high schools to provide education for war-torn Korean society. During her study in the States, she made contact with the International Foursquare Church in California, and upon her return, the Korean Foursquare Church was formally organized in 1970, its Gospel Bible College in 1972, and Gospel Theological Seminary in 1990. Currently 54 churches, 102 ministers, two training institutions, and five cross-cultural missionaries are part of this Pentecostal body.

Also present in Korea are several groups split from the Assemblies of God. The most substantial one is Jesus Assemblies of God founded in 1981 as David Yonggi Cho and his group of churches and ministries began. After Cho rejoined the Assemblies of God, some churches and ministers have remained as Jesus Assemblies of God under the leadership of Yong-mok Cho, Yonggi Cho's younger brother. His Church of Grace and Truth has a dozen congregations scattered in the southern part of the Seoul metropolis with a combined membership of 450,000, making it the second largest church in the world. Currently Jesus Assemblies of God has about 300 churches, 450 ministers, one training school, and 20 cross-cultural missionaries.

There are several other Pentecostal groups, such as Church of God of Prophecy, United Pentecostal Church, and Holiness Pentecostal Church, but their presence and influence is almost minimal. (For Holiness Pentecostal denomination, see below.)

Indigenous Pentecostal Movement

What then happened to the old revival traditions that served as precursors for the modern Pentecostal movement in Korea? As much as they have influenced the overall Christian spirituality of Korean Christianity, several communities have developed them into an indigenous Pentecostal form apart from the established Pentecostal denominations. The most significant example is the Yongmun Prayer Mountain. Established by a Methodist elder, Woon-mong Nah, in 1945, this prayer mountain served as the haven for believers who desired and experienced Pentecostal faith. His publicized summer revival camp once attracted more than twenty thousand visitors from all over the country and had a dozen branch prayer mountains during its peak period. From here, the Pentecostal message (including healing, baptism in the Spirit with speaking in tongues) spread like wildfire. The prayer mountain provided a unique environment where such experiences were encouraged, while the majority of churches did not openly advocate such elements.

Nah also established two training institutions, Yongmun Mountain Bible School (1955) and Gideon Theological Seminary (1956), and the unprecedented Christian convent, Yongmun Mountain Convent (1956), in the prayer mountain. Every year, Bible school students were sent throughout the nation for evangelism. Their spiritual expressions such as clapping while singing, unison prayer, prayer for healing and Spirit baptism, at first harshly criticized, were gradually accepted, particularly by Pentecostal churches in the later years. Another unique feature of this indigenous Pentecostal group is the link between Christianity and patriotism. As the nation often experienced threats and sometimes armed confrontations, Nah launched a twenty-four-hour prayer altar for national security. He twice sent his Bible school students close to the demilitarized zone with the intention of crossing the heavily fortified border. His successful weekly newspaper, *Gospel Times*, first appeared in 1960 as a daily paper, then as a weekly. In 1979, Nah arranged with the U.S. Holiness Pentecostal denomination for an alliance, but this was short-lived because the arrangement was marred by several issues, including theological ones.

In recent years, as the lifestyle of average Koreans has changed due to economic development and, more important, several denominations questioned some of Nah's teaching as heretic, the operation of the Yongmun Prayer Mountain was gradually reduced, and so was its influence on the Korean church. Now his son, Soo-young Nah, is the director and still maintains annual summer revival camps. In spite of the decreasing presence and influence of this unique community, its significant contribution to the Korean Pentecostal movement cannot be ignored.

Charismatic Christianity

As previously observed, there has been a long spiritual tradition in the Korean church that overlapped the Pentecostal movement. The old Pentecost-like spirituality continued in various avenues including revival meetings (generally, every local church had at least one, or often two, annual week-long revival meetings.) This special occasion was marked by diligent study of the Bible and emphasis on a personal encounter with God. The latter included healing, personal crisis experiences, and baptism in the Spirit (often with speaking in tongues, although this terminology was not always employed). Many known revival speakers, regardless of their denominational affiliation, openly preached on speaking in tongues, healing, and miracles, among other topics.

With the powerful impact of the Pentecostal message primarily coming from Cho, this "Pentecostalization" trend accelerated. Greatly motivated by Cho's success in church growth, Korean Christianity, which was already open to the spiritual dynamic, began to adopt Pentecostal worship (including music), message, prayer (e.g., Friday overnight prayer meetings, prayer mountain) and programs (such as the cell system). Thus, it is almost a rule that in Korea such Pentecostal-like believers are found in every church tradition. The

Catholic Church is not an exception. Professor Y. S. Eim estimates that there are more than 700,000 Catholic Pentecostals in Korea.

The exact number of such believers is simply impossible to estimate in any degree of certainty. However, it would be a conservative estimate to suggest one-third of Korean Christianity (except Pentecostal denominations) falls in this category.

Characteristics

In addition to the typical Pentecostal characteristics, Korean Pentecostalism has developed the following unique contributions:

Church Growth

The explosive growth achieved by the Korean church in the 1970s and 1980s is generally credited to the leading role of Pentecostal churches, particularly by Yoido Full Gospel Church. Almost all the twelve megachurches in Korea exhibit a Pentecostal type of worship and message. The influence of a Pentecostal type of leadership, often labeled as "charismatic," has also become a widespread pattern that is linked to significant church growth. Throughout the country, many large churches were planted, and most of them were Cho's daughter churches.

Generalization of Pentecostalism

Related to the church growth phenomenon is the wide influence of Pentecostal-type worship, leadership, and preaching. Perhaps due to the Korean spiritual tradition, special meetings such as revival meetings in local churches generally preach on topics such as healing, "receiving grace" (often another expression for a personal spiritual encounter with God, including baptism in the Spirit), and even exorcism. The exponential growth of Yoido Full Gospel Church has been the sure proof of the validity of Pentecostal-type Christianity; thus, pastors and churches have adopted, to a varying degree, Pentecostal beliefs, practices, and styles.

Emphasis on Prayer and Fasting

The emphasis on prayer is a feature found in Korean spiritual tradition. However, Yongmun Prayer Mountain forcefully developed this feature. In 1973 as David Yonggi Cho and his mother-in-law, Jashil Choi, opened Osanni Fasting and Prayer Mountain (later renamed as Cho Jashil International Fasting Prayer Mountain), a strong emphasis on fasting was added to Korean Pentecostal spirituality. Choi not only preached on the benefit of fasting, but also wrote several books. Her passion was widespread and during the New Year holidays, thousands of Christians (regardless of church affiliation) come to spend several days in prayer and fasting. Fasting is believed to increase one's spiritual awareness and spiritual power to live a successful Christian life, to experience God's blessing such as healing, and to witness to others.

Theological Contributions

There are several important theological contributions that Korean Pentecostalism has brought. The first is the emphasis on a "good God." Understandably, traditional Christian groups that had gone through harsh historical realities developed a passive attitude toward the present life, and thus a martyr type of spirituality. Their orientation was extremely otherworldly, and suffering was often viewed as virtuous. However, with the rise of David Yonggi Cho and his Yoido Full Gospel Church, the message of a "good God" began to impact the Christian perspective toward their present life to become more positive, thus, more proactive. Although it is sometimes accused of being a Korean version of positive-thinking teaching, this theological emphasis has brought a significant theological shift in popular Christian thinking as well as in pulpit messages.

The second is the experiential dimension of Christian life. Primarily due to the Confucian moral values of Korea, the official side of Korean Christianity (e.g., Sunday worship, official theology) tended to be more intellectual and sober. This was further enhanced by the Reformed or Presbyterian dominance of Korean Christianity. This, however, did not provide more "primal" spiritual needs particularly coming from Korean Shamanistic religious orientation, that is, the emotional and experiential dimension of religious life.

The third is the utilization of laity for ministry. Cho decided to mobilize women for his radical cell system. In a male dominant culture, this move practically revolutionized the traditional perception of clergy-centered ministry. The women cell leadership was proven to be effective, as they were able to reach their neighborhoods through various social channels. This concept was soon expanded to male cell leadership and even children cell leaders.

Future Challenges

In the 1990s, the growth of the Korean church stagnated and eventually stopped. Suddenly the Pentecostal characteristics were challenged as Korea had achieved a substantial economic development. The following are some of the challenges that Korean Pentecostalism is facing in the twenty-first century.

Theological

The theological backbone of the Korean Pentecostal movement has been the "good God" and its consequential theology of blessing, which brought about church growth and social upward mobility. The "dark side" of this was the overly "this world" oriented focus, and more significantly self-centered Christianity, from which Shamanistic charges against Pentecostalism arose. As people now have experienced prosperity, the ultimate theological goal of the Pentecostal message has been questioned and challenged, although modern Pentecostalism found witnessing as the ultimate theological destiny of Spirit-filled Christians (Acts 1:8).

Pentecostal Identity

The generalization of Pentecostalism as a powerful phenomenon in spreading the Pentecostal message throughout Korean Christianity also has had an adverse effect in blurring the Pentecostal identity. Often the "Holy Spirit movement" is a popular expression of a series of revivals, and the historical and theological identity of Pentecostalism has frequently collapsed in this. For several decades, among Pentecostal churches, there was a strong move to align with Presbyterian worship. Pentecostal denominations and their academia are to establish their unique identity coming from theological traditions and historical development.

Church Growth

The slowdown of church growth has been general, including Pentecostal groups. The unique Pentecostal message and worship, once perceived as the main cause of church growth, is being questioned to see if the Korean church needs new strategies other than the Pentecostal ones. The megachurch approach to church growth has gradually shifted to church multiplication, and this is powerfully demonstrated by more than a dozen megachurches throughout the country that are daughter churches of Yoido Full Gospel Church. This appears to be the right reinterpretation of church growth that can exert a positive impact on other regions such as western Europe and North America.

Global Perspective

The Korean Pentecostal tradition, along with Korean Christianity in general, has a unique and challenging development in the context of social difficulties. Having achieved growth, economic development, and the timely missionary movement, Korean Pentecostal believers and churches are poised to share their theological experiences and spiritual heritage with other struggling third-world churches and assist them in the process. In order for this to take place, the entire church in Korea needs to have a radical shift in their ecclesiological understanding. Cho's life-long influence on world Christianity should continue even in the post-Cho era. In the same way, the "charismatic" and indigenous segment of the Korean Pentecostal movement should be diligently studied and shared with the world.

WONSUK MA

See also Asia, East; Church Growth

Further Reading

Eim, Y. (2002). South Korea. In S. Burgess & E. M. van der Maas (Eds.), *New international dictionary of Pentecostal and Charismatic movements.* Grand Rapids, MI: Zondervan.

Kennedy, N. L. (1980). *Dream your way to success: The story of Dr. Yonggi Cho and Korea.* Plainfield, NJ: Logos International.

Ma, W. (2001). The Korean Pentecostal movement: Retrospect and prospect for the new century. *Australasian Pentecostal Studies, 5–6,* 63–94.

Ma, W., Menzies, W. W., & Bae, H. (Eds.). (2004). *David Yonggi Cho: A close look at his theology and ministry.* Baguio, Philippines: APTS Press.

Yoo, B. (1988). *Korean Pentecostalism: Its history and theology.* Frankfurt am Main, Germany: Peter Lang.

Laity, Clergy

The Pentecostal-Charismatic movement represents such diverse constituencies that it is difficult to make any univocal statement about its nature, except to reaffirm precisely that which makes it Pentecostal-Charismatic: the attention given to the activity of the Holy Spirit in the church. This makes it difficult to arrive at a Pentecostal-Charismatic definition of the relationship between clergy and laity. In general, charismatic Catholics and charismatics from mainline denominations have continued to adhere to the definitions of clergy and laity characteristic of their affiliations. Therefore this article will focus on the Pentecostal movement, which is itself diverse. However, we can say that at its core the Pentecostal movement can be characterized as a return to the charismatic style of leadership attested to in the period of the judges and in the Pauline churches.

The tribal league of Israel, before the rise of the monarchy, had no hierarchical government, nor would its people have followed just anyone with a title. The people followed the one upon whom the Spirit of Yahweh rushed. Even the first kings of Israel were chosen by charisma rather than lineage or social standing. Likewise, what qualified men and women to speak in the Pauline churches was charisma rather than office, and the charisms of the Spirit were available to every member of the gathered community of worshippers (1 Corinthians 14:29–31).

Clergy and Laity in the New Testament

There are no two biblical terms that directly correspond to the popular contemporary understanding of clergy and laity. When we speak of clergy, we refer to those who have been recognized and appointed by an institutional church body as authorized administrators of the word of God and the sacraments specific to that institution. When we speak of laity, we refer to the members of the congregation who benefit from the ministry of the clergy.

Such a clear-cut definition is not found in the New Testament. Instead, the New Testament makes use of a wide range of leadership metaphors that underscore different dimensions of the role of the minister. David Bennett (1993, 62) emphasizes that more than half of the metaphors used by Jesus to describe the leadership role his disciples are to have in the church and in the world focus, not in the authority of the leader, but in the authority to which the leader must submit. The term "shepherd" (*poimen*), for example, refers to one who cares for a flock that belongs to someone else; an "apostle" (*apostolos*) is one who has been sent by another. These metaphors emphasize that, though the New Testament leader is one who has authority to lead, he or she is first and foremost one who has submitted to God's authority.

The teachings of Jesus also use metaphors that describe this submission to God as that which qualifies individuals for responsible leadership in the lives of others. For example, in Luke 12, Jesus speaks a parable about a "manager" (*oikonomos*), picturing the disciple as one who is given charge of others. Then in Luke 19:12–27, Jesus gives a parable about ten servants who were each given an amount of money to invest. Those who invested it wisely were afterwards given cities to govern. The point is that the one who is trusted to lead is the one who demonstrates commitment and devotion to his master.

It seems that the Pauline churches were entrusted to the leadership of "elders" (*presbyterous*) and "overseers" (*episkopous*) who were appointed to administrate. Acts 20:17, 28 and Titus 1:6–7 seem to suggest that the two terms are synonymous. The Pastoral Epistles contain the bulk of references to these offices.

Ephesians 4:11ff presents a five-fold structure to the leadership of the church: apostle, prophet, evangelist, pastor, and teacher. The purpose of this five-fold ministry is spelled out clearly in the verses that follow: "to prepare God's people for works of service, so that the body of Christ may be built up until we all reach unity in the faith and in the knowledge of the Son of God and become mature, attaining to the whole measure of the fullness of Christ" (Ephesians 4:12–13, NIV).

The New Testament pictures the offices of church leadership as offices of responsibility and authority. Leaders are not without authority—to the contrary, Paul exhorted Timothy to "encourage and rebuke with all authority" (2 Timothy 2:15)— but that authority exists only for the purpose of empowering the leader to fulfill his or her responsibility to bring the body of Christ to maturity and to equip each member for the work of the ministry.

The Azusa Street Movement

In 1906 William Seymour traveled to Los Angeles, California, from Topeka, Kansas, in response to an invitation to pastor a small Holiness mission. In Topeka, he studied under Charles Fox Parham, who on 1 January 1901 successfully laid hands upon Agnes Ozman for the baptism in the Holy Spirit with the evidence of speaking in tongues.

Upon arrival in Los Angeles, Seymour preached his first sermon at the little Methodist church during which he taught that speaking in tongues is the initial, physical evidence of the baptism in the Holy Spirit. When he returned for the night service, he found himself locked out in the cold, the door securely padlocked as a sure sign that he had worn out his welcome. Having nowhere else to go, he was given shelter by a member of the church, who was somewhat sympathetic toward his ministry, but unsure of his peculiar doctrine of initial evidence.

It was in the living room of this home—the home of a man by the name of Edward Lee—that Seymour began holding prayer meetings that soon mushroomed into revival meetings that had to be moved out onto the porch, and then (after the porch collapsed during one of the meetings) into a vacant building located at 312 Azusa Street.

As far as leadership was concerned, these early Pentecostals were primitivists and antistructuralists. They wanted to militate away from hierarchical forms of church government and reestablish the government of the Holy Spirit. Thus, during the early days at Azusa Street, the floor was given to anyone who felt the unction of the Spirit to testify, preach, or sing. In fact, early Pentecostals would be uncomfortable speaking of having leaders at all. Theirs was a type of ecclesiastical *docetism* in which those occupying leadership positions only *seemed* to lead. They felt that they were led by the Holy Spirit and univocally claimed to speak only what the Holy Spirit spoke and to do only what the Spirit was doing.

This sentiment emerged partly as a result of the unique way in which the Holy Spirit was believed to have governed the Azusa Street meetings. It was reported that people would stand and speak when the Holy Spirit anointed them to do so, and when the anointing would lift, conviction would descend and the person would sit down. People would rush to the altars to repent of sin and to seek the face of God spontaneously, and people would often fall to the floor throughout the congregation as the power of God rushed upon them.

The second reason for this had to do with the fact that the early Pentecostals were persecuted by denominational groups that saw the spiritual manifestations characteristic of their meetings as outlandish and inappropriate. As a result, Pentecostalism developed a disdain for denominationalism and an antistructuralist tendency that virtually erased the line between clergy and laity. In fact, Robert Owens rightly refers to glossolalia as the "ultimate antistructuralist phenomenon" and the "benchmark of the experience" of the Azusa Street renewal (Owens 2001). The early Pentecostals saw speaking in tongues as the quintessential act of human surrender to the Holy Spirit. In order to speak in tongues, one needed no theological education, no practical expertise, and no intellectual capacity. All one needed was to fully surrender to the Holy Spirit. This principle became the paradigm of the emerging Pentecostal movement.

The same principle applied to missions also. The earliest Pentecostals believed that they spoke with xenolalic, rather than glossolalic tongues. They believed that with the baptism in the Holy Spirit came the knowledge of what foreign language was being spoken. For example, when Agnes Ozman spoke in tongues on 1 January 1901, she was reported as having been enabled by the Holy Spirit to speak in Chinese. This was going to open the door for successful evangelism in China.

When the xenolalia theory did not pan out, Pentecostals redefined their tongues experience as glossolalia. But they retained the theology implicit in the previous claim. If the baptism in the Holy Spirit can empower a person to preach the gospel in a language previously unknown, then the baptism in the Holy Spirit is the only criteria for qualification to preach the Gospel. Since all members of the body of Christ are eligible to receive the baptism in the Holy Spirit, all members of the body of Christ can be qualified in this way to preach the Gospel and participate in the mission of the church.

Denominational Pentecostalism

As the Pentecostal movement developed from an ad hoc, interracial, cross gender, interdenominational renewal into a multifaceted, racially bifurcated, plethora of ecclesial structures, there were clear signs that emerging Pentecostal denominations were anxious to preserve the same openness to the Spirit that was found in the Azusa Street meetings. This "vision of leaderlessness," as Grant Wacker calls it (2001, 141), created a sense of equality between clergy and laity, while simultaneously creating an authoritarianism that in some senses was more pronounced than that of the denominational groups from whom the Pentecostals sought to diverge. Since the Holy Spirit was the leader, the saints were all brothers and sisters, and aptly referred to each other in this way. Yet, the claim of complete submission to the Spirit also implicitly contained the claim to a high level of spiritual authority.

As far as equality was concerned, Pentecostal clergy tended to claim no special standing with God, or even specific giftedness that transcended that of the average Christian. If used mightily by God, most Pentecostal leaders would attribute it to their being "yielded" to the Holy Spirit, and would claim that all believers in Jesus Christ are capable of ministering in the same way if only they would become yielded to the same degree.

Theologically, the doctrine of the baptism in the Holy Spirit as empowerment for service served to underscore the priesthood of all believers. Pentecostals believed that the baptism in the Holy Spirit was for all believers, thus all believers were to take part in the work of the ministry. The gifts of the Spirit, such as interpretation of tongues and prophecy, were seen as avenues through which all believers could minister to the body of Christ.

This theological conviction opened the door for those who were otherwise considered unsuitable for ministry to find fruitful places of service and impact.

Throughout the twentieth century, several notable women built magnificent ministries through which many confessed conversion experiences, were healed, and baptized in the Holy Spirit. Among them were Kathryn Kuhlman (1907–1976) and Aimee Semple McPherson (1890–1944). Many were attracted to their ministries, seeing them as living examples of the heart of the Pentecostal leadership conviction, that leadership is the work of the Spirit and subsequently the work of all of God's people. Seeing them flourish caused the world to awe, but also to hunger for the same dynamic Holy Ghost power that was the wind beneath their wings.

BENJAMIN ISRAEL ROBINSON

See also Apostle, Apostolic; Preaching

Further Reading

Bennett, D. (1993). *Metaphors of ministry*: Grand Rapids, MI: Baker Book House.

Owens, R. (2001). The Azusa Street Revival. In V. Synan (Ed.), *The century of the Holy Spirit*. Nashville, TN: Thomas Nelson Publishers.

Synan, V. (1997). *The Holiness-Pentecostal tradition*. Grand Rapids, MI: Eerdmans.

Wacker, G. (2001). *Heaven below*. Cambridge, MA: Harvard University Press.

Latter Rain

The Latter Rain movement is a mid-twentieth-century revival movement, mainly within North American Pentecostalism, that initially called for a renewal within established Pentecostal church organizations, and when coupled with the healing movement of the same era, provided a significant stimulus for the subsequent Charismatic movement. It is most commonly known as the New Order of the Latter Rain, especially by its opponents. It should be distinguished from early-twentieth-century Pentecostalism, which also used the idea of a "latter rain" as a central motif. The concept of the "latter rain" was thought by adherents to be rooted in the natural phenomenon of Palestine of an early and a latter rain. Proponents constructed a worldview built on an eschatological framework that suggested that the early church, that is, the church of the book of Acts, was symbolized by the "early rain" and the church of the end times would experience a new outpouring of the Spirit or a "latter rain."

The Latter Rain movement grew out of a concern that declension was occurring within North American Pentecostalism. By the 1940s, many classical Pentecostal organizations, those organizations who trace their roots to the Azusa Street Revival of 1906–1909, were experiencing two significant changes. First, modern Pentecostalism was birthed in an atmosphere of signs and wonders and there was a perception that this was waning. Second, Pentecostal organizations were reaching out for acceptance by the newly formed National Association of Evangelicals. Some Pentecostals looked upon this as indicative of a loss of spiritual vigor.

Beginnings

The Latter Rain movement traces its beginning to Sharon Orphanage and Schools in North Battleford, Saskatchewan, Canada. George Hawtin, a pastor in the Pentecostal Assemblies of Canada (PAOC), had founded a Bible school in Star City, Saskatchewan, which was later moved to Saskatoon. A series of disputes between Hawtin and the PAOC led to Hawtin's resignation, both from the school and from the PAOC. He and another member of the faculty, P. G. Hunt, along with George's brother Ern, joined Herrick Holt in North Battleford and opened Sharon Orphanage and Schools. On 12 February 1948, in North Battleford, the proponents reported that God had done a "new thing," referencing Isaiah 43:19 (KJV).

This "new thing" included visible demonstrations of the gifts of the Spirit, especially the gifts of healing. The *Sharon Star* publicized the events of 1948 and upcoming conventions and soon crowds were arriving in North Battleford from all over North America. This publicity gave rise to invitations for the leaders to speak at significant churches outside of Saskatchewan. One such invitation came from Reg Layzell of Glad Tidings Temple in Vancouver, British Columbia. One prominent visitor to the November 1948 Glad Tidings meeting was Myrtle Beall, pastor of Bethesda Missionary Temple, Detroit, Michigan. Beall, convinced of the reality of the revival, returned to Detroit to make Bethesda a center for the Latter Rain in the United States. A number of prominent leaders, including Ivan and Carlton Spencer from Elim Bible Institute in New York and Stanley Frodsham, longtime editor of the *Pentecostal Evangel*, the official publication of the Assemblies of God (AG), visited Bethesda and became participants in the movement. Swedish Pentecostal leader Lewi Pethrus and Thomas Wyatt, pastor of Wings of Heal-ing Temple in Portland, Oregon, were two other prominent sympathizers of the movement.

Opposition to the Movement

The major opponents of the movement came from the classical Pentecostal denominations. The PAOC, the AG, the Pentecostal Holiness Church, and the United Pentecostal Church all officially disapproved the beliefs and practices of the movement. Frodsham was forced to choose between his support for the Latter Rain movement and his editorship of *The Pentecostal Evangel*. He chose to retire as editor and return his credentials with the AG. The Pentecostal Fellowship of North America exerted pressure on members to disavow the movement. This opposition to the movement from Pentecostal denominations limited the reach of the revival within these denominations. However, select independent churches embraced the revival and with this support the movement continued for a limited time. Its lasting influence was on the soon-to-emerge Charismatic movement.

Significant Teachings of the Movement

The Latter Rain movement placed strong emphasis on the charismata. Some early proponents taught that the gifts of the Spirit were resident in the movement's leadership and were distributed by the laying on of hands of the presbytery. The gift of prophecy was more prominent in the Latter Rain movement than in the early Pentecostal revival. Accompanying this was an emphasis on charismatically chosen leadership, who were given significant spiritual authority. The Latter Rain looked for a restoration of the offices of the apostle and prophet.

George Warnock's *The Feast of Tabernacles* is thought to be the most representative publication of the movement. Warnock's thesis was that the Feast of Tabernacles, the last of three typological Old Testament feasts, was yet to happen. The Latter Rain would usher in this feast.

Much like the early Pentecostal movement, the Latter Rain movement was intentionally "undenominational." Local church autonomy was strongly stressed. Movement-wide leadership was charismatically chosen and, although apostles and prophets were recognized, this was not in the context of church organizational leadership.

Significance of the Latter Rain Movement

The New Order of the Latter Rain Movement flourished briefly in the mid-twentieth century. Today there is little left of the movement. However, the movement made a significant contribution to the wider Pentecostal-Charismatic movement in the twentieth century. Its major contribution was to the Charismatic movement. Coupled with the healing movement of the same time period, it formed one of the two streams that led to the formation of the Charismatic movement, particularly to the independent church movement within the broader Charismatic movement. For Pentecostal denominations, the Latter Rain movement served as a reminder that the Spirit can move on and attention must be given not only to denomination-building, but also to the leading of the Spirit.

ROBIN M. JOHNSTON

See also Charismata; Revival and Revivalism

Further Reading

Bernard, D. K. (1999). *A history of Christian doctrine* (Vol. 3). Hazelwood, MO: Word Aflame.

Faupel, D. W. (1980). The function of "model" in the interpretation of Pentecostal thought. *Pneuma, 2,* 50–71.

Holdcraft, T. (1980). The new order of the Latter Rain. *Pneuma, 2,* 46–60.

McGee, G. B. (2004). *People of the Spirit: The Assemblies of God.* Springfield, MO: Gospel.

Menzies, W. (1971). *Anointed to serve: The story of the Assemblies of God.* Springfield, MO: Gospel.

Riss, R. M. (1982). The Latter Rain movement of 1948. *Pneuma, 4,* 32–45.

Riss, R. M. (1988). *A survey of twentieth-century revival movements in North America.* Peabody, MA: Hendrickson.

Warnock, G. H. (1951). *The feast of tabernacles.* Cranbrook, Canada: Author.

Laughter, Holy

In 1418, the Second Council of Constance declared, "If any cleric or monk speaks jocular words, such as provoke laughter, let him be anathema." This classic example of organized religion taking itself too seriously illustrates why a revival of "holy laughter" at the end of the twentieth century attracted the widespread attention of religious and secular media alike.

Laughter in Church History

Of course this dramatic outbreak was not without historical precedent. "'Jubilation,' as it was sometimes called, has been evident throughout all of Church history, and included . . . drunkenness in the Spirit, and holy laughter" (Riss 1997, Introduction). For example, "Just prior to the Battle of Naseby in 1645 . . . Oliver Cromwell was drunken in the Spirit and filled with holy laughter" (Riss 1997, 17). *Fou rire*—"mad laughter," as it was called pejoratively—was ascribed to the French prophets of the Cevennes half a century later. John Wesley's *Journals* occasionally refer to uncontrollable laughter, as at Everton in 1758. One critic of such "enthusiasm" notes that Wesley mentions laughter "no less than four times as a characteristic index of 'consolation'" (Knox 1994, 528).

Pentecostal historian Vinson Synan reports that the "holy laugh" was one of many ecstatic spiritual manifestations characterizing the Cane Ridge Revival in Kentucky in 1801, and such laughter was frequently experienced during the 1906 Azusa Street Revival, which gave birth to worldwide Pentecostalism. Anglican A. A. Boddy wrote of his Azusa Street experience, "The Holy Ghost came in mighty power, causing me to laugh as I had never done in my life" (Riss 1997, 45). More recently, holy laughter at least occasionally accompanied evangelist Kathryn Kuhlman's ministry, and Dennis Balcombe, an American missionary in Hong Kong, videotaped Christians in secret house meetings in China in 1994 rolling around in uncontrollable Spirit-induced laughter.

Today's Laughing Revival

Colorful South African evangelist Rodney Howard-Browne is credited with instigating most contemporary experiences of holy laughter. Howard-Browne describes himself as "the Holy Ghost Bartender" serving up "the 'new wine' of the Holy Spirit" (Beverley 1995, 13–14), much to the consternation of critics like author Hank Hanegraaf. Though based in America since 1987, Howard-Browne remained largely unknown before a month of sensational meetings at the Carpenter's Home Assemblies of God in Lakeland, Florida, in 1993. There the Holy Spirit fell in power and brought wave after wave of uproarious laughter. That, in turn, brought the evangelist to the attention of the national media, and since then his ministry has been known as the "laughing revival." Those impacted in Lakeland included Richard Roberts, President of Oral Roberts University (ORU). When he and his famous father, Oral, invited Howard-Browne to the ORU campus in Tulsa, Oklahoma, the ensuing meetings reportedly impacted the student body so profoundly that classes were cancelled for two days as students were slain in the Spirit and laughed uncontrollably.

River of Renewal

Coverage of Howard-Browne's successes by *Charisma* magazine in August 1994 accelerated awareness of his laughing revival. But a year earlier, his ministry had already come to the attention of Randy Clark, pastor of St. Louis Vineyard in Missouri. Clark had been desperately "thirsty for more of God" and sought prayer from Howard-Browne to receive and be anointed to impart "the blessing." When Clark ministered back in his own church the next Sunday, many people fell under the power of the Holy Spirit. Clark shared his experience at a regional Vineyard pastors retreat, and the power of God fell mightily again. John Arnott, pastor of what became known as Toronto Airport Christian Fellowship after its ouster from the Vineyard in December 1995, heard what God was doing through Clark and invited him to speak at his church in Canada for a few days, beginning on 20 January 1994.

Arnott had also been relentlessly seeking more of God. He and his wife, Carol, had sought prayer and impartation from Argentine revival leader Claudio Friedzon in November 1993, and they had returned from Argentina with heightened expectancy. However, when the Spirit actually did begin to move in power as Clark ministered, no one was more surprised than Arnott himself. "This outpouring didn't look like we thought it would…our assumption was that we would see more people saved and healed…It never occurred to us that God would throw a massive party where people would laugh, roll, cry and become so empowered that emotional hurts from childhood were just lifted off them. The phenomena may be strange, but the fruit this is producing is extremely good" (Arnott 1995, 59).

The "Toronto Blessing"

What followed became a sustained outpouring of the Holy Spirit—dubbed "the Toronto Blessing" by the British press—in a revival that reportedly impacted over five thousand churches. The spiritually hungry flocked to Toronto by the tens of thousands and returned like firebrands to their own communities. Six years into the renewal, author Melinda Fish noted that "'the Toronto Blessing' has spread to the Body of Christ on every continent of the world and ignited other fires, including 'the Pensacola (FL) Outpouring'" (Fish 2001, 17). Theologian Frank Macchia highlighted the move-

ment's spiritual fruit: "Thousands are testifying to a changed life, to a new sense of missionary purpose, a greater love, holiness or faith, as a result of participating in a revival of holy laughter" (Macchia 1996, 4).

Laughter for the Twenty-First Century

Over 4 million visitors attended services in Toronto during the revival's first ten years. As the revival approached its tenth anniversary, sociologist Margaret Poloma released the first major study of the movement from a social-science perspective. Poloma found that the global Pentecostal-Charismatic movement—notwithstanding its accelerating numerical growth—had become somewhat "routinized." And Pentecostal historian Eddie Hyatt wrote that if "the Pentecostal and Charismatic churches truly valued and were, therefore, open to the manifest work of the Holy Spirit in their midst, there probably never would have been a Toronto Blessing" (Hyatt 1996, 210). He called the Toronto outpouring an "indictment on the rest of the churches"; Poloma pointed out that the revival brought deep spiritual revitalization and new energy to the whole Pentecostal-Charismatic movement.

Countless leaders have testified to a transforming personal encounter with the Holy Spirit in Toronto. And the movement worldwide is experiencing a notable increase in joy and effectiveness in ministry and missions as a direct result of the renewing power of holy laughter.

Donald R. Kantel

See also Ecstasy; Enthusiasm

Further Reading

Arnott, J. (1995). *The Father's blessing*. Orlando, FL: Creation House.

Arnott, J. (Ed.). (2000). *Experience the blessing: Testimonies from Toronto*. Ventura, CA: Renew Books.

Beverley, J. A. (1995). *Holy laughter and the Toronto Blessing: An investigative report*. Grand Rapids, MI: Zondervan.

Chevreau, G. (1994). *Catch the fire: The Toronto Blessing*. Toronto, Canada: Harper Collins.

Fish, M. (2001). *Keep coming, Holy Spirit: Living in the heart of revival*. Grand Rapids, MI: Chosen Books.

Hanegraaf, H. (1997). *Counterfeit revival*. Dallas, TX: Word.

Hyatt, E. L. (1996). *2000 years of charismatic Christianity*. Chicota, TX: Hyatt International Ministries.

Hunter, C., & Hunter, F. (1994). *Holy laughter*. Kingwood, TX: Hunter Books.

Knox, R. A. (1994). *Enthusiasm: A chapter in the history of religion*. Notre Dame, IN: University of Notre Dame Press.

Macchia, F. D. (1996). The 'Toronto Blessing': No laughing matter. *Journal of Pentecostal Theology, 8*, 3–6.

Oropeza, B. J. (1995). *A time to laugh: The holy laughter phenomenon examined*. Peabody, MA: Hendrickson.

Poloma, M. M. (2003). *Main street mystics: The Toronto Blessing and reviving Pentecostalism*. Walnut Creek, CA: Alta-Mira Press.

Riss, R., & Riss, K. (1997). *Images of revival: Another wave rolls in*. Shippensburg, PA: Revival Press.

Synan, V. (1997). *The Holiness-Pentecostal tradition: Charismatic movements in the twentieth century* (2nd ed.). Grand Rapids, MI: Eerdmans.

Liberalism

Liberalism refers to important, related movements within politics and religion in the modern period. Political liberalism is a Western Enlightenment philosophical tradition that holds commitments to individual liberty and equality. Religious liberalism is an accommodating approach to modernity that adopts Western methods of scholarship to examine sacred texts and adapts theology to modern ideals. Because the complex relationships between charismatics and liberalism are governed by the denominational climates to which they belong and thus lead too far afield, this article limits its focus to Pentecostals.

Political Liberalism

Political liberalism typically emphasizes the autonomous individual, civil liberties and rights, government by consent of the governed, the rule of law, private property, and tolerance of different views of the good life. Liberalism typically conceptualizes the state as a social contract among individuals; the purpose of the state is limited to its role as the remover of obstacles to liberty. Political liberalism had its beginnings in the Enlightenment challenge to the power of the monarch in Western Europe in the seventeenth and eighteenth centuries. Other crucial historical contexts were the American and French revolutions and the rise of capitalism in the late nineteenth century. Two distinct families of liberal political theory emerged from these contexts: a dominant group descended from John Locke (1632–1704), which privileges liberty and derives equalities from this commitment, and a later minority group descended from Georg Wilhelm Friedrich Hegel (1770–1831) that reverses the emphasis. Liberals occupy ground between libertarianism and communism, arguing that the former forgets equality, the latter liberty.

The Lockean family of liberalism is descended from Locke, Immanuel Kant (1724–1804), and John Stuart Mill (1806–1873). The early liberalism of Locke was framed to reject the concept of the divine right of kings by replacing it with a social contract that located rights in individuals. Kant later developed the essential idea of individual autonomy. Early liberal thought culminated in Mill, who emphasized that the liberty of the individual should be restricted only if his actions are injurious to others.

The second, smaller family of liberal thought is grounded mainly in the work of German philosopher Georg Wilhelm Friedrich Hegel. It emphasizes equality and social solidarity as a precondition for true liberty and holds a more positive view of political institutions. For Hegel, political institutions do not exist, as they do for Locke, in a negative sense to provide security of person and property, but they play a positive role as the framework in which persons experience true freedom.

Developments in Political Liberalism

The differences between the Lockean and Hegelian strands of liberalism are real but should not be overstated. The powerful economic upheavals of the industrial revolution pushed even Lockean liberals away from more laissez-faire notions of acquisition to egalitarian conceptions of redistribution via a welfare state supported by progressive taxes.

Contemporary political liberalism experienced a renaissance after John Rawls's (1921–2002) important book, *A Theory of Justice* (1971), where he held together commitments to individual liberty with an egalitarian concern for "the least advantaged." Following the Rawlsian revival, others have continued the egalitarian liberal project (Dworkin 2000) or developed more straightforwardly Lockean (Robert Nozick) or Hegelian (Jeffrey Stout, Charles Taylor, Michael Walzer) proposals.

Formal equality and freedom represented by the liberal tradition have become more or less accepted principles enshrined in law in the contemporary West. Liberalism also serves as the foundation for the United Nations Declaration on Human Rights; the division of rights into "Civil and Political Rights" and "Economic, Social, and Cultural Rights" largely echoes the Lockean and Hegelian strands respectively.

Liberalism is not without its critics. Some argue that the tensions between the commitments to liberty and

Liberalism

equality are in the end unmanageable. Others have criticized liberalism for its largely negative view of the state, and its promotion of a possessive individualism divorced from the common good (for example, the Roman Catholic Church in *Rerum Novarum*, 1891). Still others criticize its inability to attend to the importance of tradition, culture, and community (Alasdair MacIntyre). Religious critics of liberalism have criticized liberalism for restricting or excluding religious voices in public debate, and for separating "the right" and "the good" in a way that makes little sense to religious persons who seek to live morally and religiously integrated lives.

Theological Liberalism

Theological liberalism can be understood as a nineteenth- and twentieth-century theological affirmation of many of the Enlightenment ideals that engendered political liberalism. Theological liberalism should be seen as a primarily Protestant movement that is contemporaneous with, but broader than (sometimes incorporating socialism), its political cousin.

Theological liberalism attempted to reconstruct a modern Christianity by charting a middle way between "the authority-based orthodoxies of traditional Christianity and the spiritless materialism of modern atheism" (Dorrien 2001, xiii). This strategy has several general characteristics: the adoption of scholarly, critical methods to study biblical texts; the acceptance of the conclusions of modern science; a valuation of Scripture and church tradition as sources of theology rather than external authorities; a downplaying of the distinctiveness of Christian morality; and a conviction that the coming of the Kingdom of God demanded collective action aimed at structural changes in society rather than individual salvation. The effects of rapid industrialization and urban growth, especially unrestrained capitalism and violent labor disputes of the late nineteenth and early twentieth century, formed the crucial social context in which theological liberalism came into its own.

Varieties of Theological Liberalism

Grant Wacker has identified three variants of theological liberalism. Evangelical liberals follow Friedrich Schleiermacher (1768–1834), often called the father of modern theological liberalism. They practice a kind of avoidance strategy, emphasizing feeling and experience as the proper realm of religion and resigning claims that modernity has determined belong to science or morality. Modernist liberals engaged modernity more directly, considering the best of modern science and culture as normative for theology. The job of theologians of this school was to bring Christian theology into harmony with modernity, using methods such as process philosophy (Charles Hartshorne, 1897–2000) or correlational theology (Paul Tillich, 1886–1965). Naturalist liberals (John Dewey, 1859–1952), on the far left, sought to eliminate all supernatural elements from Christianity but argued that the biblical heritage still provided useful moral ideals.

The Social Gospel movement is representative of the pre–World War II golden age of theological liberalism. Under the leadership of Richard T. Ely (1854–1943), an economist, and Walter Rauschenbusch (1861–1918), a Baptist minister in one of the poorest urban areas in New York City, the Social Gospel movement emphasized the historical Jesus, who proclaimed the immanent Kingdom of God. It tapped socialism and the more Hegelian strands of political liberalism, emphasizing the social rather than individualistic aspects of sin and salvation, and addressing through law and social organizing the structural injustices arising from emerging industrial capitalism.

Although the Social Gospel movement declined, especially following the horrors of genocide in World War II, liberalism remained through the middle part of the twentieth century the dominant perspective in the top mainline Protestant divinity schools, such as Boston University School of Theology, the University of Chicago Divinity School, Union Theological Seminary, and Harvard Divinity School. The ecumenical movement, with the founding of the World Council of Churches in 1948 and the National Council of Churches (NCC) in 1950, was also a liberal project that assumed a common agenda of organizing against social injustice. Finally, the rise of standpoint theologies—feminist theology, black theology, and theologies from the developing world (Africa, Latin America, Asia)—have continued the liberal emphases on individual experience, the social nature of sin, and the importance of bringing about the Kingdom of God in history. The latter half of the twentieth century is notable for the sharp decline of the mainline liberal Protestant denominations and the radical growth of Pentecostal and other evangelical denominations.

Pentecostalism and Liberalism

Pentecostals inherited from the broader Protestant tradition several affinities with political liberalism, but they have given these their own unique stamp. First, and most generally, political liberalism's emphasis on

290

human equality and the authority of individual experience resonates with the general Protestant concept of individual salvation and sanctification; in fact, Louis Dumont has argued convincingly that the sixteenth-century Protestant concept may have paved the way for the Enlightenment developments. Pentecostals further emphasize that the experiences of all are valued; the spirit of God freely manifests itself among those on the underside of social hierarchies: the uneducated, women, even children. Second, political liberalism's debunking of tradition is also consistent with the Protestant *sola scriptura* rejection of much Catholic tradition and specifically with the Pentecostal sense of the coming of a new revolutionary "age of the spirit." Finally, like other Protestant sectarian movements, Pentecostalism was a direct beneficiary of political liberalism's notions of freedom of religion and tolerance. As Pentecostals have become more influential and less in need of direct protection, however, their explicit support of full religious liberty has been inconsistent.

North American Pentecostals and Liberalism

Pentecostalism is often described as a religion of the disinherited, which in theory aligns their class interest with liberal social concerns. Among North American Pentecostals, however, these harmonies were in the end disturbed by internal tensions with other aspects of liberalism and external affiliations with the wider evangelical movement.

Pentecostalism's relationship with the liberal Social Gospel movement illustrates both tendencies. At least three internal tensions are salient. First, the problems with which the social gospel was concerned were rooted in the industrial urban Northeast and therefore translated awkwardly in the rural Midwest and South. Second, liberalism was largely a movement among the powerful, educated classes in mainstream Protestant denominations; one could say it was a theology *for* the poor but not a theology *by* the poor. Unlike Pentecostal leaders who came from among the poor, liberal leaders were academically trained members of the middle class. Third, liberalism's aspirations of "Christianizing the social order" were optimistic and structural. Pentecostal theology, on the other hand, emphasized a more pessimistic view of human nature and individuals in need of salvation; such large-scale changes seemed unrealistic to the more rural, less socially influential Pentecostals.

Pentecostalism's external affiliation with Evangelicals, who denounced liberalism's compromises with modernity, also muted its early liberal tendencies.

Pentecostals were formally accepted by the National Association of Evangelicals (NAE) shortly after its formation in 1942. Because Evangelicals had already defined themselves largely in opposition to theological liberals—founding the NAE as the conservative rival to the NCC and *Christianity Today* as the counterweight to the *Christian Century*—affinities with the social gospel were prevented from developing into direct associations. For example, evangelicalism's premillennial theology of an imminent coming of the Kingdom of God finally trumped Pentecostalism's early Holiness movement heritage, transforming its concern for this-worldly social change into otherworldly individual salvation. Evangelism rather than social justice, individual conversions instead of structural changes became the hallmark of Pentecostal missions.

The story of Pentecostal growth, institutionalization, and upward mobility is paradigmatic of H. Richard Niebuhr's description of how radical sects experience growth and gradually come to look more like the hierarchical churches from which they sprang. For example, early Pentecostals were clearly among the disinherited; as early as the 1980s, however, a study of Assemblies of God members found them to be *more* likely than a national sample of Protestants to have higher-than-average earnings and to be college graduates. Early Pentecostals were also radically open to the movement of the Spirit across race and gender lines; the famous Azusa Street Mission was a racially mixed congregation, and prior to the 1920s there were numerous women ministers. Over time, however, the "color line" became evident in the Pentecostal movement, and the number of women ministers declined rapidly. Surveys have shown that Pentecostals continue to be less supportive of racial justice and more conservative regarding the role of women in society than Americans generally.

The most notable exception to this narrative is the recent influx and growth of Hispanic Pentecostals in North America. According to findings of a 2001 Pew Charitable Trust study, Hispanic Pentecostals in North America tend to be more liberal on social issues, sharing a social vision with other Hispanic Pentecostals in Latin America and with Roman Catholics.

Latin American Pentecostals

North American Pentecostals defined themselves in relation to Evangelicals and against theological liberals within a liberal democratic polity. In contrast, Latin American Pentecostals defined themselves in a more complex way in rivalry with Roman Catholic liberation theology in the context of colonialism and authoritarian or socialist governments.

Liberation theology, like the Social Gospel movement, can be considered part of "social Christianity," which holds this-worldly views of salvation achieved in and through human history. Liberation theology, however, differs from the Social Gospel movement in essential ways: its Marxist intellectual heritage, its colonial context of Third World economic exploitation, its more pessimistic view of human nature, its collectivist orientation, and its expectation of more drastic revolutionary change.

Pentecostals in Latin America have become the main rivals for adherents to liberation theology's base communities, and they claim to be closer to the poor in actuality than the Roman Catholic institutional church. They explain the phenomenal growth of Latin American Pentecostalism—the fastest growing religious group in the region today—by claiming, "Pentecostal churches do not opt for the poor because they are already a poor people's church, and that is why the poor are opting for them" (Mariz 1994, 138).

Recent studies have shown, however, that although both movements are active among the poor, there is no cause and effect relationship between the notable growth of Latin American Pentecostalism and the status of Roman Catholic base communities. Rather, they employ different strategies, providing diverse spaces that are attractive to the poor for different reasons. Pentecostalism emphasizes liberating the individual through conversion, encouraging austerity and sobriety, raising self-esteem through spiritual belonging, and the founding of mutual help groups. Thus, its goals are more about coping with poverty, and the paths it charts out of it are largely individual paths within present structures. In contrast, base communities emphasize the elevation of the community and work more systematically to oppose structural injustices, emphasizing basic rights for all. The dominance of the Catholic liberation theology model in the Latin American context, however, has on the whole led Latin American Pentecostals to be more theologically attuned to injustice and socially engaged than their North American counterparts.

The Future

Especially since the rise of the religious right in the 1980s, North American Pentecostals have followed Evangelicals even further from liberal concerns for social justice. As Pentecostalism continues to grow across the world, and as Pentecostals interact with charismatics in other denominations, negotiating the tensions between the more elite North American/Western European Pentecostals on the one hand and the less educated, less wealthy Pentecostals of Latin America, Africa, and Asia will be critical. It remains to be seen whether the more liberal third world Pentecostals develop a more thorough vision of social action akin to liberation theology, and whether such a vision will challenge the socially conservative stances of the first world elites or splinter into new sects. Furthermore, in countries such as Brazil, there is a burgeoning Pentecostal elite within the country, which may threaten the unity of the movement on a more local level.

ROBERT P. JONES

See also Ethics (Social, Sexual); Race Relations; Society, Pentecostal Attitudes toward; Women

Further Reading

Bergunder, M. (2001). The Pentecostal movement and basic ecclesial communities in Latin America: Sociological theories and theological debates. *International Review of Mission, 91*(361), 164–186.

Burdick, J. (1993). *Looking for God in Brazil: The progressive Catholic Church in urban Brazil's religious arena*. Berkeley: University of California Press.

Curtis, S. (2001). *A consuming faith: The social gospel and modern American culture*. Columbia: University of Missouri Press.

Dempster, M. W. (1987). Pentecostal social concern and the biblical mandate of social justice. *Pneuma, 9*(2), 129–154.

Dempster, M. W., Klaus, B. D., & Petersen, D. (1991). *Called and empowered: Global mission in Pentecostal perspective*. Peabody, MA: Hendrickson.

Dorrien, G. (2001). *The making of American liberal theology: Imagining progressive religion, 1805–1900*. Louisville, KY: Westminster John Knox.

Dorrien, G. (2003). *The making of American liberal theology: Idealism, realism, and modernity, 1900–1950*. Louisville, KY: Westminster John Knox.

Dumont, L. (1982). A modified view of our origins: The Christian beginnings of modern individualism. *Religion, 12*, 1–27.

Dworkin, R. (2000). *Sovereign virtue: The theory and practice of equality*. Cambridge, MA: Harvard University Press.

Finke, R., & Stark, R. (1992). *The churching of America, 1776–1990: Winners and losers in our religious economy*. New Brunswick, NJ: Rutgers University Press.

Gray, J. (1995). *Liberalism: Concepts in social thought* (2nd ed.). Minneapolis: University of Minnesota Press.

Gray, J. (2000). *Two faces of liberalism*. New York: New Press.

Gutiérrez, G. (1988). *A theology of liberation: History, politics, and salvation*. Maryknoll, NY: Orbis.

Hutchison, W. R. (1992). *The modernist impulse in American Protestantism*. Durham, NC: Duke University Press.

Ireland, R. (1997). Pentecostalism, conversions, and politics in Brazil. In E. L. Cleary & H. W. Stewart-Gambino (Eds.), *Power, politics, and Pentecostals in Latin America* (pp. 123–138). Boulder, CO: Westview.

Kärkkäinen, V. (2003). Spirituality as a resource for social justice: Reflections from the Catholic-Pentecostal dialogue. *Asian Journal of Pentecostal Studies, 6*(1), 83–96.

Kenyon, H. N. (1988). *An analysis of ethical issues in the history of the Assemblies of God*. Unpublished doctoral dissertation, Baylor University.

MacIntyre, A. C. (1985). *After virtue: A study in moral theory* (2nd ed.). London: Duckworth.

Manent, P. (1996). *An intellectual history of liberalism*. Princeton, NJ: Princeton University Press.

Mariz, C. L. (1994). *Coping with poverty: Pentecostals and Christian base communities in Brazil*. Philadelphia: Temple University Press.

Martins, A. D., & de Padua, L. P. (2002). The option for the poor and Pentecostalism in Brazil. *Exchange, 31*(2), 136–156.

Niebuhr, H. R. (1964). *The social sources of denominationalism*. Cleveland, OH: World.

Niebuhr, R. (1932). *Moral man and immoral society: A study in ethics and politics*. New York: C. Scribner's.

Nozick, R. (1974). *Anarchy, state, and utopia*. New York: Basic.

Petersen, D. (1996). *Not by might, nor by power: A Pentecostal theology of social concern in Latin America*. Oxford, UK: Regnum.

Poloma, M. M. (1989). *The Assemblies of God at the crossroads*. Knoxville: University of Tennessee Press.

Pope Leo XIII. (1992). *Rerum Novarum*: The condition of Labor. In S. O'Brien and T. Shannon, (Eds.), *Catholic social thought: The documentary heritage* (pp. 12–39). Maryknoll, NY: Orbis.

Rauschenbusch, W. (1997). *A theology for the social gospel*. Louisville, KY: Westminster John Knox.

Rawls, J. (1993). *Political liberalism*. New York: Columbia University Press.

Robeck, C. M., Jr. (1987). Pentecostals and social ethics. *Pneuma, 9*(2), 103–107.

Roof, W. C., & McKinney, W. (1987). *American mainline religion: Its changing shape and future*. New Brunswick, NJ: Rutgers University Press.

Sanks, T. H. (1980). Liberation theology and the social gospel: Variations on a theme. *Theological Studies, 41*, 668–682.

Stout, J. (2003). *Democracy and tradition*. Princeton, NJ: Princeton University Press.

Synan, V., & Society for Pentecostal Studies. (1975). *Aspects of Pentecostal-charismatic origins*. Plainfield, NJ: Logos.

Taylor, C. (1989). *Sources of the self: The making of the modern identity*. Cambridge, MA: Harvard University Press.

Wacker, G. (2001). *Heaven below: Early Pentecostals and American culture*. Cambridge, MA: Harvard University Press.

Walzer, M. (1983). *Spheres of justice: A defense of pluralism and equality*. New York: Basic Books.

Walzer, M. (2004). *Politics and passion: Toward a more egalitarian liberalism*. New Haven, CT: Yale University Press.

Weithman, P. (Ed.). (1997). *Religion and contemporary liberalism*. Notre Dame, IN: University of Notre Dame Press.

Liberation Theology

Many consider liberation theology (LT) the most forceful and original contribution made to twentieth-century theology. Unlike traditional theology, which tends to be speculative, rational, and detached, LT emphasizes the need for Christians to end poverty and oppression and bring the egalitarian Kingdom of God to the earth. Liberation theologians are quick to point out that truth is not something that is believed but something that is done. One of the founders of LT, the Peruvian Gustavo Gutiérrez (b.1928), defined LT as "a critical reflection on historical praxis in the light of the Word." According to liberation theologians, the Bible aims at the release of the oppressed and the marginalized from their historic sociocultural oppression.

Although LT was born in Latin America and is rooted in the resistance movements of the sixteenth-century colonial period and the theological reforms of the 1960s, it has had a worldwide impact. Many of the poor and oppressed who are now rising up and gaining a greater political voice in third world nations are Christians, and a large proportion of these Christians can be called Pentecostal or charismatic: The link between the liberation movement and Pentecostal and charismatic Christianity is significant and widespread.

Key Characteristics

The complexities of liberation theology make it difficult to define, but some key features are clear. First, LT views the poor as victims of the oppressive and even demonic economic structures of the modern capitalist world and demands a structural solution on a worldwide scale. In the words of Leonard Lovett, "Any proclamation that fails to deal with the structure of oppression (e.g. political and economic) is viewed as a preservation of the *status quo* and, therefore, opposed to liberation" (1987, 160). Liberation theologians contend that a true understanding of liberation does not come from sitting at a desk or in a seminary classroom but rather from interacting with the poor and being physically engaged in the human struggle. Liberation practices "compassion," or "suffering with" in order to understand and correct situations that debase and marginalize people.

Another important feature of LT is that it interprets Scripture in terms of the experiences of the poor. LT arose out of a conviction that the needs of the poor are not adequately addressed by traditional hermeneutical approaches; liberation theologians contend that traditional theologians aligned themselves with the social, economic, and political status quo of the greater secular society and that therefore their work was irrelevant to the needs of the poor. British theologian Christopher Rowland contends that the starting point for LT:

> ...is not detached reflection on Scripture and tradition but the present life of the shanty towns and the land struggles, the lack of basic amenities, the carelessness about the welfare of human persons, the death squads and the shattered lives of refugees. It is here in particular that its distinctiveness as compared with the theology of North American and European academies is most marked. (1999, 2–3)

In many instances, LT finds itself deeply imbedded within the official life and practice of the church. In Latin America, LT is closely associated with the Catholic Church, although the movement cannot be viewed solely in terms of this connection. LT is not simply a deviant popular movement, but rather a way of practicing Christianity that has been embraced not only by a large number of Latin American Catholic clergy but also by officials in many other denominations.

Hermeneutical and Biblical Roots

Perhaps the most influential pioneer in articulating the goals and strengths of LT is Gustavo Gutiérrez, a Catholic priest and theologian. Gutiérrez's 1968 address at a meeting of the National Office for Social Research in Peru ("Toward a Theology of Liberation") was a pivotal moment in the history of Christian theology because it allowed a worldwide audience to reflect upon LT. For Gutiérrez, liberation "means establishing the relationship that exists between human emancipation—in the social, political, and economic orders—and the kingdom of God" (1996, 26). He emphasizes "critical reflection on historical praxis" by asserting that LT

"is a theology which does not stop thinking about the world, but rather tries to be a moment in the process through which the world is transformed" (1996, 34).

The work of the brothers Leonardo and Clodovis Boff was also instrumental in bringing the tenets of LT to a wide audience of scholars and theologians. In response to the question "How are we to be Christians in a world of destitution and injustice?" the Boffs answered that "we can be followers of Jesus and true Christians only by making common cause with the poor and working out the gospel of liberation" (1998, 7). They believed that true liberation will occur only when individuals understand their situation and work to enact change in their society. Only when the oppressed come together to "claim everything that the existing system can give...[can they then] work toward the transformation of present society in the direction of a new society characterized by widespread participation, [and] a better and more just balance among social classes" (1998, 5).

A theological-liberative hermeneutic places a heavy emphasis on the enactment of its message above and beyond any academic explanation, and therefore all hermeneutical and theological reflections must be engaged with the real-world and ever-changing experiences of the poor. "What runs like a thread through all liberation theology is a commitment based on contemplation of God in the suffering Christ whose presence is hidden in the poor" (Rowland 1999, 12). Liberation theologians point to a dialectic between the poor and Scriptures, which they believe ensures the continuing relevance of biblical texts for the poor. They use the text to confront both the oppressed and the oppressors with a message from God.

The poor for whom liberation theologians advocate are those who find themselves on the brink of starvation, migrant and countryside workers, and workers who are generally unemployed and superfluous to the capitalist market system. They are not only living in economic poverty but are socially marginalized, politically outcast, racially oppressed, or excluded by predominantly male power structures. In her critique of the "lived reality" of LT, theologian Elina Vuola charges that "male liberation theologians, black and white, have not welcomed feminist critique with open arms, especially when it has been aimed at them. White, middle-class women from industrialized countries have been blind to the reality of the great majority of the world's women who are non-white and poor" (2002, 2). Feminist liberation theologians have also charged that males working in the liberation movement have relegated females to a gender role as mother or homemaker and failed to realize the full potential of female voices in the struggle for liberation.

Liberation theologians share the challenge of interpreting Scripture in the light of changing experiences and social concerns with Pentecostals and charismatics, who for over a century have sought to understand their new experience of the Holy Spirit in terms of changing church structures and varying social climates. While liberation theologians look to the poor and marginalized for the face of the suffering Christ, Pentecostals, recalling the initial meetings at Azusa Street, evoke images of the poor and oppressed who gathered together to receive the egalitarian "Spirit baptism." Pentecostals and charismatics may also find connections between the goals of LT regarding the treatment of women and minority groups and their own historical commitment to empowering women for ministry and the worldwide, multiethnic nature of their movements.

However, many Pentecostals and Evangelical charismatics are uncomfortable with the notion that the meaning of a sacred text may change with the fluctuations of modern realities and prefer instead to view the Bible as immune to the ebb and flow of human political and social conditions. Thus for some Pentecostals and charismatics the "hermeneutical circle" of LT is an evasion of the timeless and authoritative nature of the text, and the Scriptures are not speaking to the poor, to marginalized racial groups, or to either gender in any meaningful way.

As with any Christian movement, LT makes a greater use of some scriptural materials and themes than others. For example, liberation theologians frequently cite the Exodus as a model of God delivering his chosen people from a position of humiliation and slavery. They also find themes of social justice in passages like Isaiah 1:10–23 and Amos 5:21–24. The apocalyptic themes of the prophet Joel and the book of Revelation have provided hope both for the poor and for Pentecostals (who have historically been poor and marginalized). Jesus' social teachings in Matthew's Gospel allow liberation theologians to promise comfort to those who mourn, and Jesus' ministry among the poor and brokenhearted is viewed as a model for social change.

Pentecostal and Charismatic Reactions

There is, of course, no official or universally accepted Pentecostal or charismatic view of LT. Many charismatics and Pentecostals become wary when they believe that theology is being used as a servant of a purely secular ideology; Evangelicals (including charismatics and most Pentecostals) have generally viewed LT as "Marx-

ism garbed in theological language" (Petersen 1996, 193). Indeed, any association with the name "Marx" is quite enough to dissuade many Evangelical charismatics and Pentecostals from establishing a connection to LT or even tolerating it. For Pentecostals and charismatics who view liberation as a natural mandate of Scripture and church tradition, however, practicing LT does not imply a whole-hearted acceptance of Marxist principles. Rather than viewing the solution to humanity's problems through the lens of a purely secular political or economic revolution, Pentecostals are likely to demonstrate a need for spiritual salvation through Jesus Christ. As one Pentecostal scholar states, "It appears dubious that there can be authentic liberation into freedom apart from empowering Spiritual Presence. The root cause of our problem is a spiritual one" (Lovett 1987, 167).

Leading proponents of LT view salvation in terms of current material and spiritual realities while discounting Marx's atheism and his concept of historical materialism and choosing Christ as liberator. Although LT borrows some of its terminology and philosophy from the writings of Karl Marx, many liberation theologians vehemently deny any adherence to Marxist principles other than to use them as an instrument of liberation. They believe that the rise of Marxist liberation movements acting in the name of Christianity in the twentieth century shows that the very religion Marx ridiculed has become an effective vehicle not only for the expression of suffering but also for the effective change of oppressive social structures.

Some have charged that LT "rejected an easy cultural Christianity, only to introduce an easy countercultural Christianity," and argue that "the standard of its critique is not God's revealed will in his Word, but the political-cultural agenda of the left" (McGlasson 1994, 18–19). Indeed, many Pentecostals and charismatics may be uncomfortable with what they perceive as an overemphasis on the portions of Scripture that deal with the oppressed and the poor. Although few would deny the importance of these themes within the Scriptures, Pentecostals and Evangelical charismatics have traditionally been hesitant to accept the notion that social, political, and economic change should serve as a goal for life. Rather, they assert that Christians should be concerned with growing in the Spirit and preparing themselves on a spiritual level for the life to come in heaven.

Future of Liberation Theologies

Pentecostals and charismatics have often been charged with ignoring the physical needs of starving and oppressed human beings; they are frequently accused of providing medicine, food, shelter, and other basic needs only as a way of opening doors for evangelism and church planting. As one scholar noted:

> Very little serious theological work has been devoted to the development of a Pentecostal social ethic. As a consequence, current engagement in social ministry among Pentecostals seems to depend more on the individual conscience of influential leaders and the time-bound exigencies of politics and culture than on broadly shared theological agreements concerning the nature of the church and its moral mission in society. (Dempster 1987, 129)

However, within the last decade many charismatic and Pentecostal leaders have found value in incorporating the ideals of liberation into their existing view of God's plan for the church and the world. By viewing the appearance of the Spirit in Acts 2 as the initiation of a new religious, social, and political order, the distinctively Pentecostal doctrine of Sprit Baptism allows for charismatics and Pentecostals to strive for unity and social justice in what they see as a disjointed and broken world.

Whether or not LT will play a more significant role in Pentecostal or charismatic contexts remains to be seen. Many have noticed that LT, especially in its Latin American Catholic context, is dying out as a theological movement due to a lack of successors to the earlier generation of liberation scholars. Although society is severely fragmented between the rich and the poor, men and women, and various racial groups, Pentecostals and charismatics sympathetic to the goals of LT believe the unifying power of the Spirit can help the poor and oppressed to claim a right to spiritual and political equality.

BRIAN R. DOAK

See also America, Latin; Feminism; Marxism

Further Reading

Andelson, R. V., & Dawsey, J. M. (1992). *From wasteland to promised land: Liberation theology for a post-Marxist world.* Maryknoll, NY: Orbis Books.

Boff, L., & Boff, C. (1998). *Introducing liberation theology.* Maryknoll, NY: Orbis Books.

Dempster, M. W. (1987). Pentecostal social concern and the biblical mandate of social justice. *Pneuma: The Journal for the Society of Pentecostal Studies, 9*(2), 129–53.

Dempster, M. W., Klaus, B. D., & Petersen, D. (Eds.). (1999). *The globalization of Pentecostalism: A religion made to travel.* Oxford, UK: Regnum Books.

Gibellini, R. (1987). *The liberation theology debate.* Maryknoll, NY: Orbis Books.

Gutiérrez, G. (1988). *A theology of liberation: History, politics, and salvation.* C. Inda & J. Eagleson (Eds. & Trans.). Maryknoll, NY: Orbis Books.

Gutiérrez, G. (1996). *Gustavo Gutiérrez: Essential writings.* J. B. Nickoloff (Ed.). Maryknoll, NY: Orbis Books.

Hennelly, A. T (1990). *Liberation theology: A documentary history.* Maryknoll, NY: Orbis Books.

Kee, A. (1990). *Marx and the failure of liberation theology.* Philadelphia: Trinity International.

Lovett, L. (1987). Liberation: A dual-edged sword. *Pneuma: The Journal for the Society of Pentecostal Studies, 9*(2), 155–171.

McGlasson, P. C. (1994). *Another gospel: A confrontation with liberation theology.* Grand Rapids, MI: Baker Books.

Nessan, C. L. (1989). *Orthopraxis or heresy: The North American theological response to Latin American liberation theology.* Atlanta, GA: Scholars Press.

Petersen, D. (1996). *Not by might, nor by power: A Pentecostal theology of social concern in Latin America.* Oxford, UK: Regnum.

Pieris, A. (1988). *An Asian theology of liberation.* Maryknoll, NY: Orbis Books.

Rowland, C. (Ed.). (1999). *The Cambridge companion to liberation theology.* Cambridge, UK: Cambridge University Press.

Segundo, J. L. (1993). *Signs of the times: Theological reflections.* Maryknoll, NY: Orbis Books.

Smith, C. (1991). *The emergence of liberation theology: Radical religion and social movement theory.* Chicago: University of Chicago Press.

Sobrino, J. (1994). *The principle of mercy: Taking the crucified people from the cross.* Maryknoll, NY: Orbis Books.

Tombs, D. (2002). *Latin American liberation theology.* Boston: Brill Academic Publishers.

Vuola, E. (2002). *Limits of liberation theology: Feminist theology and the ethics of poverty and reproduction.* London: Sheffield Academic Press.

Marxism

Despite having an enormous amount of intellectual, political, and even commercial appeal, the term "Marxist" is resistant to a univocal definition and somewhat obscured by the variety of divergent interpretations that lay claim to the title of "true" Marxism. Broadly speaking, "Marxism" can refer to any form of idea that demonstrates its fidelity to the thought and influence of Karl Marx's literary-philosophical heritage. Put another way, a Marxist belief:

> is one held by anyone, academician or political stalwart, who thinks or can persuade others that the belief in question is in accordance with Marx's intellectual or political legacy...there is no Marxism that can be regarded as a straightforward exposition (let alone extension) of Marx's own views. (Carver 1997, 23–24)

Some prefer a rather strict interpretation of Marxism that refuses to allow for any perceived deviations from Marx's own writings (the term "Marxian" is sometimes used to designate ideas that can be traced back directly to Marx himself). However, much of what is known as Marxist today has been and will continue to be an amalgam of Frederick Engels's systematization of Marx's ideas over a century of critical theory. For our purposes, we will be content to use the term "Marxist" or "Marxism" to describe the general trajectory and impact of Marx's influence through his writings and his later interpreters, including those of Pentecostal and charismatic Christians.

Few thinkers in all of history have enjoyed the influence, polarizing appeal, and notoriety of Karl Marx.

Marxist thought has impacted every aspect of the social sciences, including religion, history, and politics, and permeated discussions of the individual and society for almost two hundred years. Important Marxist themes include "historical materialism" (the concept that events in history are driven by economic concerns and class conflict) and the dialectic between the bourgeoisie and the proletariat; in terms of religion, Marx wrote relatively little but is most famous for his statement characterizing religion as "the opiate of the people." Although Marx is less known for his views on religion (much less Pentecostal and charismatic Christianity) than other topics, the various tenets of Marxism have received mixed reviews from Pentecostals and charismatics and in some areas have played a significant role in Pentecostal and charismatic faith and practice.

Karl Marx: Background and Philosophy

Karl Marx was born in Trier, Germany in 1818 and encountered the philosophy of G. W. F. Hegel while studying at the University of Berlin. Later, Marx would claim that Hegel was "standing on his head," philosophically speaking, and Marx sought to stand Hegel on his feet by challenging some of Hegel's basic philosophical assumptions. Marx criticized Hegel's idealism, which for Hegel meant privileging the mind's ability to grasp the ephemeral direction of Absolute Spirit (*Geist*), and replaced Hegel's abstract philosophical idealism (and theology) with an embodied, historical materialism. Among Marx's most well-known and debated contributions is this notion of historical materialism, "a collection of empirical theses" that basically posits the economic structure of society as in fact the "real" basis of society. In other words it is the "growth of the productive forces [that] explains the general course of human history" (Bottomore 1997, 234–239), and, as the *Communist Manifesto* famously states, "the history of all hitherto existing society is the history of class struggles."

Marx observes the human species in terms of Darwinian evolution, asserting that humans are primarily "workers" (*homo faber*) who interact with their created tools in order to survive. For Marx, competition is not the natural state of being but rather an artificial byproduct of the capitalist system, thus producing an ongoing imbalance of materials and wealth. Within this very material struggle are the seeds of "class struggle"; certain individuals will inevitably elevate themselves above their fellow humans via their domination of the profit from their labor, creating an imbalance of power and the roots of discontent for those who are deprived of the surplus. The "privileged class" must therefore mold "consciousness itself" (i.e., human ideas about what is right/wrong or attractive/unattractive and what it is that humans should have and should want) in such a way as to benefit their unending pursuit of and mastery over surplus capital.

We should in no way assume that Marx presents us with a cohesive or systematic statement on religion or any one topic. Rather, Marx faced real historical and political struggles that prompted his writings. In fact, many of Marx's writings are occasional pieces, even newspaper articles, which he wrote for a New York paper in English. Classic Marxism's dissatisfaction with religion's ability to free humanity must be considered within Marx's historical context of mid-nineteenth-century European revolutions in France and Germany and the rise of capitalist economies; in 1844 Marx claims that "in Germany no form of bondage can be broken without breaking all forms of bondage. Germany, which is renowned for its thoroughness, cannot make a revolution unless it is a thorough one" (Raines 2002, 182). Therefore, Marx did not discriminate between what a Pentecostal or charismatic Christian might call "true Christianity" and what he saw as the oppressive and ideological treatment of the working classes by "Christian" elites during his lifetime.

Marx and Religion

It is interesting to note that although Marx's name is often invoked in discussions of religion's place in culture, Marx himself wrote no systematic statement on religion and did not offer any one volume dedicated solely to the topic of religion. Religion does appear from place to place as a brief focus in Marx's works, however, and through these appearances we have enough material to understand his general positions.

Marx's thought on religion in general is often solely characterized by his famous dictum asserting that religion "is the opiate of the people." However, his "Critique of Hegel's Philosophy of Right" contains a more nuanced treatment of religion's role than this short quip denouncing religion's validity. In this same essay Marx credits religion with serving to express the current realities of human suffering: "Religious suffering is at one and the same time the expression of real suffering and a protest against real suffering. Religion is the sigh of the oppressed creature, the heart of a heartless world and the soul of soulless conditions" (Raines 2002, 171). Nevertheless, Marx still sees religion's expression of suffering as merely providing an "illusory happiness," and the contentment that religion provides thus stands in the way of "real happiness." Marx criticizes religion's failure to deliver humans from their despondent conditions, calling for a "categorical imperative to overthrow all conditions in which man is a debased, enslaved, neglected, and contemptible being" (i.e., the conditions under which religion thrives) (Raines 2002, 177). For Marx, religion is simply one vestige of a failing and oppressive system in need of an overhaul.

Marx is quick to criticize what he views as the failures of Christianity in a mid-nineteenth-century European context. In a passage from his 1847 essay, "The Social Principles of Christianity," Marx states that Christianity's social principles "justified slavery in antiquity, glorified medieval serfdom, and, when necessary, [Christians] also know how to defend the oppression of the proletariat... preach the necessity of a ruling and an oppressed class, and for the latter they have only the pious wish that the former will be benevolent... declare all vile acts of the oppressors against the oppressed to be either just punishment for original sin and other sins." Furthermore, the social principles of Christianity "preach cowardice, self-contempt, abasement, submission, humility... [Christianity is] hypocritical, but the proletariat is revolutionary" (Raines 2002, 185–186).

Not all of Marx's writings, however, display such contempt for the beliefs and practices of Christians, however. In a letter written in 1881, two years before his death, Marx expresses admiration for early Christians who, by their "dream of the imminent destruction of the world" were inspired "in their struggle with the Roman world empire and [received] a certainty of victory" (Raines 2002, 239). The apocalyptic viewpoint of the early Christian communities served as the starting point for the eschatological focus of many early Pentecostals, who also found themselves struggling with what they considered to be an "empire" of dead and powerless Christianity in the early twentieth century.

Conflict and Dialogue

The "evangelical" Christian reaction to Marxist thought has often been quite hostile, and the majority of Pentecostals tend to share in this overall disdain for Marxist principles. Due to its popular association with Stalinist Russia, the former Soviet Union, and the policies of other self-proclaimed "Marxist" governments, "Marxism" is sometimes used as a buzzword to describe political or philosophical systems that are thought to be "undemocratic," "liberal," "extremist," "atheistic," "repressive," "violent," etc. However, it would be inadequate for us to assert that "Marxism" is an equivalent term to either "communism" or "socialism" as they have been practiced on the world scene in the twentieth and twenty-first centuries. (Communist political policies incorporate Marxist elements but are not synonymous with any one "Marxism.")

Some Pentecostal observers wish to see the rise of Pentecostalism as a direct indication of its superiority to certain forms of Marxist Communism: As one Pentecostal scholar puts it, "Communism…has disillusioned millions of its faithful followers and has lost its attraction for the modern youth and critical intelligentsia," whereas "Christianity, especially its Pentecostal branch, is experiencing phenomenal growth, permeating with the Gospel of Christ even the remotest cultures and language groups" (Kuzmic 1991, 145). In this sense, Christianity and Marxism are presented as rival religions, competing for the souls and allegiance of the poor and oppressed working class. However, in some situations Marxists may ally themselves with Pentecostals who are willing to fight for similar sociopolitical goals (such as fighting against injustice, poverty, and oppression).

Regarding the treatment of Pentecostals under established Marxist or Communist governments, many have suffered severe persecution. For example, the twentieth-century persecution of Christians in the former Soviet Union resulted in the emigration of thousands of Pentecostal Christians to countries like the United States and England. When Pentecostals have come under periods of intense persecution, they have often pursued what some have pejoratively called an "escapist" mentality, engaging in apocalyptic eschatology and opting to remain cut off from their surrounding communities. Despite the lack of accurate numbers, many missiologists assert that the Communist nation of China now contains the largest number of Christians of any country in the world, and many of the Christians in China's "underground" church are accurately characterized with the title "Pentecostal" or "charismatic." Thus China stands as an example of a nation whose government is influenced by Marxism but in which Pentecostal Christianity has not only survived but flourished, even though many of these Christians have been imprisoned or killed for spreading their faith.

Perhaps the most pervasive outworking of Marxist thought in Pentecostal and charismatic practice has come in the form of "Liberation Theology," a theological movement initiated in Latin America (where a high percentage of Christians are Pentecostal or charismatic) that seeks to replace traditional theological emphases on abstract intellectual theories with a real-world emphasis on the spiritual and material salvation of the marginalized and oppressed. Many liberation theologians borrow Marxian or Marxist ideas concerning the alienation of labor, class struggle, and the exploitation of the working class in relation to what is perceived as the inherent inequality and oppression generated by the capitalist market system. Generally speaking, Marxist themes are invoked by liberation theologians to dismiss what they view as the irrelevant stance of "traditional" religion and the unrighteous domination of the ruling class over the poor.

Outlook for the Twenty-first Century

Although relatively few Pentecostal or charismatic scholars have attempted to engage the philosophy of Karl Marx or various Marxist thinkers on a critical level, the increasingly sophisticated intellectual expressions of Pentecostal theology will inevitably continue to bump up against the challenge of Marx's philosophy. The fact that Pentecostal and charismatic movements are now spreading most rapidly among millions of individuals living in abject poverty who suffer as victims of the very class struggle Marx described ensures that for years to come Pentecostal and charismatic scholars and spiritual leaders will be forced to consider Marxist social critiques against the backdrop of their congregational needs.

BRIAN R. DOAK

See also Liberation Theology

Further Reading

Andelson, R. V., & Dawsey, J. M. (1992). *From wasteland to promised land: Liberation theology for a post-Marxist world*. Maryknoll, NY: Orbis Books.

Arnold, N. S. (1990). *Marx's radical critique of society: A reconstruction and critical evaluation*. Oxford, UK: Oxford University Press.

Berlin, I. (1939). *Karl Marx*. New York: Time, Inc.

Bottomore, T. (Ed.). (1997). *A dictionary of Marxist thought*. Oxford, UK: Blackwell.

Carver, T. (Ed.). (1997). *The Cambridge companion to Marx*. Cambridge, UK: Cambridge University Press.

Childress, J. F., & Macquarrie, J. (Eds.). (1986). *The Westminster dictionary of Christian ethics*. Philadelphia: The Westminster Press.

Dean, T. (1975). *Post theistic thinking: The Marxist-Christian dialogue in radical perspective*. Philadelphia: Temple University Press.

Kee, A. (1990). *Marx and the failure of liberation theology*. Philadelphia: Trinity Press International.

Kuzmic, P. (1991). Pentecostals respond to Marxism. In M. A. Dempster, et al. (Eds.), *Called and empowered: Pentecostal perspectives on global mission* (pp. 143–164). Peabody, MA: Hendrickson.

Marx, K., & Engels, F. (1964). *Karl Marx and Friedrich Engels on religion*. New York: Schocken Books.

Marx, K., & Engels, F. (1975). *Collected works*. New York: International Publishers.

McKown, D. B. (1975). *The classical Marxist critiques of religion: Marx, Engels, Lenin, Kautsky*. The Hague, Netherlands: Martinus Nijhoff.

McLellan, D. (1980). *Marxism after Marx: An introduction*. New York: HarperCollins.

Nessan, C. L. (1989). *Orthopraxis or heresy: The North American theological response to Latin American liberation theology*. Atlanta, GA: Scholars Press.

Pals, D. L. (1996). *Seven theories of religion*. Oxford, UK: Oxford University Press.

Raines, T. (Ed.). (2002). *Marx on religion*. Philadelphia: Temple University Press.

Tabb, W. K. (Ed.). (1986). *Churches in struggle: Liberation theologies and social change in North America*. New York: Monthly Review Press.

Turner, D. (1999). Marxism, liberation theology, and the way of religion. In C. Rowland (Ed.), *The Cambridge companion to liberation theology* (pp. 199–217). Cambridge, UK: Cambridge University Press.

Vree, D. (1982). Christian Marxists: A critique. In Q. L. Quade (Ed.), *The Pope and revolution: John Paul II confronts liberation theology* (pp. 37–45). Washington, DC: The Ethics and Public Policy Center.

Media (Television, Radio, Internet)

Televangelism and other forms of electronic media have played a vital part in the promotion of Pentecostalism. Even before the days of television, radio broadcasting by Pentecostal preachers was characterized by flamboyance and a high degree of artistic license. For example, there was Aimee Semple McPherson (1890–1944), the first woman in history to preach a radio sermon; with the opening of Foursquare Gospel-owned KFSG Radio Station in 1924, she also became the first woman to be granted a broadcast license by the Federal Broadcast Commission. After a number of years as an itinerant Pentecostal preacher (traveling about in a "gospel car"), she settled in Los Angeles, where she established the Angelus Temple in 1923. From here she broadcast her sermons, which unlike those of her contemporaries (such as Billy Sunday) emphasized the importance of works of charity and spiritual ecstasy.

McPherson's style prefigured the ostentatious and performative aspects of presentation that were later adopted by most major Pentecostal televangelists. She consciously capitalized upon a style that utilized low-key sex appeal to attract converts; she often preached wearing a white bridal gown, carrying a bouquet of flowers. McPherson also capitalized on the entertainment culture of Los Angeles and incorporated contemporary music and morality plays into her program of worship. She also wrote and produced some Christian operas.

Historical Background

Televangelism is a generic term that refers to a loose alliance of conservative Protestant Evangelicals and Pentecostals who practice their ministry through television programs and television channels. The advent of satellite and cable television has made the production of evangelistic programs comparatively inexpensive to produce and air. However, the phenomenon remains part of what media scholars call *narrowcasting* rather than of broadcasting. Televangelism is largely a product found within a conservative Protestant ghetto: It has little impact beyond its followers. But although it is mostly associated with North America, it now enjoys a modest global profile. Few countries in the world will be without access to a range of "God channels," even if the access is through cable and satellite rather than public broadcasting.

The history of televangelism belongs to a wider social and cultural chronicle, but several preliminary points need making before describing the phenomenon in more detail. First, televangelism is rooted in a broad historical milieu of radio preaching and other attempts by evangelists, Pentecostal preachers, and healers to reach the public through mass media. Arguably, televangelism belongs to the same tradition that prints tracts by the millions (which perhaps stretches back to the Reformation) and that now runs influential websites. Second, televangelism has developed in direct proportion to the rise of Evangelicalism and the "new right" in the United States; as the political, social, and economic power of Evangelicals has grown, so has the range of programs and the volume of channels.

Third, because of the decline of mainline denominations—which is also reflected in the amount of time given to religion in public-sector broadcasting—Evangelicals and Pentecostals have shown more willingness to invest both time and money in their own brand of television. Fourth, televangelism continues to elicit support from its (loyal) followers, who perceive it as a primary means of competing with secular alternatives in the media. Fifth, despite the narrow but ultimately intense support for televangelism, research continues to show that few outside the churches or the religion are persuaded or converted by the offerings of televangelists.

Sixth, although televangelism continues to thrive as a brand of narrowcasting within the world of television, it has yet to show that it can sustain interest in the highly competitive world of default viewing—that is, programs people watch, normally in public sector broadcasting, when they have not consciously chosen to view anything else. Seventh, televangelism is now an established American religious tradition, which has prompted a number of mainline denominations to launch their own programs on the airwaves, albeit with limited success.

Pentecostal Preachers and Television

Although preaching and evangelism through modern media has been a distinctive feature of Pentecostalism, it is North American Evangelicals who continue to lead the field in terms of output and influence. For example, the media output of Billy Graham (b. 1918), which typically reflects his core Evangelical beliefs, remains unrivalled. *Hour of Decision*, a weekly radio program, has been broadcast around the world for over fifty years; *Mission Television* specials are regularly broadcast in prime time in almost every market in the United States and Canada; a newspaper column, *My Answer*, is carried by newspapers across the United States; *Decision Magazine*, the official publication of the Billy Graham Association, continues to sell millions of copies a year; and World Wide Pictures has produced and distributed over 130 cinematographic productions. This prodigious output still dwarfs most Pentecostal leaders in the global Christian media market.

Similarly, the enduring appeal of the work of Robert H. Schuller (b. 1926) is best known through his weekly broadcast, *The Hour of Power*, which can be seen on cable and satellite television the world over. Strongly influenced by his mentor, Norman Vincent Peale, Schuller's teaching is focused on the positive aspects of the Gospel. His popularity is attributable to his conviction that individuals, by the power of positive thinking, can achieve anything they wish. Although he has been heavily criticized by church leaders of other denominations and by leading theologians, Schuller is nevertheless recognized as an extremely successful propagator of Christianity in an increasingly secular world.

In contrast, most Pentecostal preachers on the airwaves have met with less success than Evangelicals such as Graham and Schuller. However, a small but significant number have made their mark in North America during the last three decades—but not all for the right reasons. Jim Bakker (b. 1939) is best remembered for *The PTL Club* (*PTL* being an acronym for "Praise the Lord"). Bakker ministered on television with his wife, Tammy, until they divorced in 1992, following Bakker's term in jail for financial embezzlement and fraud, his affair with a prostitute, and his long-standing homosexual relationship with David Taggart, his assistant.

Similarly, Jimmy Swaggart (b. 1935) was a popular Pentecostal televangelist in the 1980s and a pioneer in that medium. However, while his own televangelism program was being taped in 1988, he confessed that he was guilty of an unspecified sin and that he would be temporarily leaving his ministry. Some time later, he was stopped for speeding and in the car with him was a prostitute. Swaggart's televangelism ministry never really recovered from this setback, although he retained his pastorate within his church.

Despite such spectacular and highly publicized failures, Pentecostalism spawned some household names in televangelism. Jerry Falwell (b. 1933), a fundamentalist Baptist, studied journalism at Lynchburg College before converting to Christianity. His best-known program, which has a considerable following, is *The Old Time Gospel Hour*. He also organized conservative lobby groups into a political action committee with millions of members dedicated to advocating conservative Christian beliefs (the Moral Majority), which was dissolved in 1989. More recently, Falwell attracted negative media coverage for a stream of divisive remarks: For example, he asserted that Tinky Winky, a character on the children's show *Tellytubbies*, was promoting homosexuality. Referring to the terrorist attacks on America on September 11, 2001, he said, "The pagans, and

301

Extract from a Sermon by Aimee Semple McPherson

Aimee Semple McPherson's gifts of persuasion are apparent in this excerpt from "This Is My Task," a sermon she delivered on 12 March 1939 at the Angelus Temple, Los Angeles, California.

By God's grace, if we can see our task and join hands and get together, we can spread the gospel around the world.

It's for your good! You have no business being sick—every one of you should get well and get up and go to work, huh? Get up and go to work and earn some money and help send the gospel out! Amen! If these dear students, bless their hearts, are called to struggle and strive and pinch pennies and make their way through school and go out and lay down their lives for Christ, then certainly it's no harder to ask us to get a good job and work at it, and not give a tenth, but give the whole business, except just what we need to keep ourselves alive. That's what they'll be doing out there—what's the difference? Am I right or wrong? I believe that I am! "Wist ye not I must be about my Father's business?!" THIS IS MY TASK!!

What is my task? To get the gospel around the world in the shortest possible time to every man and woman and boy and girl!

You say, "Well, Sister, you won't make much headway in Tibet, I'm afraid—that's kind of a closed country yet." Well, I don't know . . . by God's grace we're gonna back a short-wave radio station right up against their border and shoot her over—and get the men there to pick it up and to amplify it. I never saw any one of those people in those countries who didn't like to hear a phonograph, to play over and over and over and over and over, or like to hear a radio. You say, "Well, maybe the government won't let you!" Well, how 'bout letting the government broadcast the weather report and the things they want to do certain hours and then we have certain hours. I think there's a way that anything can be done. Oh—I just feel my task this morning!

Source: McPherson, A. S. (1939). *This is my task*. Retrieved September 21, 2004, from http://www.libertyharbor.org/sermon.htm

the abortionists, and the feminists, and the gays and the lesbians . . . I point the finger in their face and say 'you helped this happen.'"

Pat Robertson (b. 1930) hosts the popular prime time program *The 700 Club*. A fundamentalist Baptist who espouses a Pentecostal theology, he too initiated a powerful political action committee (the Christian Coalition) to lobby the federal government for conservative causes. Robertson established the Christian Broadcast Network in 1960, which is now seen in 180 countries and broadcast in 71 languages. In 1990 he founded International Family Entertainment; its main business was the Family Channel, which was sold to Fox Network in 1997.

Currently Jerry Falwell, Pat Robertson, and the conservative and quixotic Oral Roberts are probably the three best-known televangelists in the United States and they enjoy broad support among Pentecostal denominations. The Pentecostal televangelist firmament has also recently seen rising stars such as Benny Hinn

(b. 1953). Hinn became famous in the United States as host of the show *This Is Your Day*, transmitted by the Trinity Broadcasting Network, a Christian television network. On the show, Hinn practices faith healing and deliverance.

Context of Reception

The reputation of North American televangelism suffered considerably in the 1990s, following a series of high profile financial and personal scandals that engulfed some of its household names. Oral Roberts was widely ridiculed for locking himself away in the prayer tower he built in Oklahoma (a bizarre structure that resembles a cocktail shaker crossed with a Sputnik). Declaring that unless his followers gave more money to underwrite his television ministry, "God would call him home," he prayed and fasted for some weeks (he stopped when a local businessman and racehorse owner donated several million dollars). Jimmy Swaggart and

Jim Bakker had their reputations ruined by well-publicized stories of sexual impropriety, but both have since been partially rehabilitated as televangelists.

Despite the garish portrayal of televangelism in the secular media, it is important to recognize that the phenomenon operates on a number of levels. First, there are established programs that have been running for decades—such as *Old Fashioned Revival Hour* and *Old Time Gospel Hour*—which in their heyday drew audiences of more than 20 million people. These programs are folksy in their allure and clearly appeal to a constituency that enjoys the singing of hymns and a traditional talk or sermon that calls on them to be "born again."

Second, there are programs that are simply a televised extension of an existing ministry. The programs, uncomplicated in format and in technical production, are often simply a televised service or rally. Televangelists such as Benny Hinn, who are skillful performers and whose ministries depend to some extent on creating a divine dramaturgy, tend to suit this medium better than programs that utilize a studio audience.

Third, there are specific programs and channels that broadcast almost continually with a simple cycle or spiral of appeals: for converts (who may be casual viewers); for money from donors to carry on broadcasting, so there can be more converts; for more converts; for more money, so the televangelists can broadcast at more sociable hours so they can reach a wider public and make more converts; and so on. Such programs and channels have developed a range of unusual (or even notorious) practices that elevate the television set itself to a level of apotheosis, or at least confer a sacramental status upon it. Instances include viewers being encouraged to hold handkerchiefs, hands, wallets, and other items they may want blessed up against their television screen while a televangelist prays a "personal" prayer for each respondent. In this theological construction of reality, viewers are invited to believe that divine power flows from the televangelist through the television set into their home and personal life.

This is perhaps not quite as absurd as it may sound to some, when one considers the recent but explosive growth of interactive television. A number of the better-funded and more sophisticated channels that offer televangelism are now able to interact "live" on television with prayer partners, supporters, donors, and viewers. The possibility of viewer-televangelist conversations and real-time ministries has become a reality. With the advent of digital television, viewers can telephone, text message, or e-mail prayer requests during a broadcast and then invite others to join in these prayers. Instead of witnessing a religious program in isolation, the viewer can now become part of a larger network of active worshippers and indeed participate "live" with an act of worship or a large evangelistic rally.

Technology now makes active spiritual communion beyond spatial constraints possible. The television has been co-opted into armory of the Lord; it has become a divine instrument for defending the saints and attacking all kinds of foes and rebuking all manner of evil. The age of interactive armchair churchgoers has truly arrived. There is no collection plate, but there will be a free-phone credit-card hotline, which believers can use to pledge.

Outlook

Pentecostalism's use of the media has come a long way since the days of Billy Sunday and Aimee Semple McPherson. Televangelism has moved from being an expensive status symbol for a few well-funded expansive international itinerant ministries to being a medium of communication that is now within the grasp of most moderate-sized megachurches. The medium of videotape has been something that many Pentecostal ministries have been quick to exploit along with DVDs and CDs. Annually these sales run into billions of dollars. As media technology developed, Pentecostal churches found that they could afford to make and air programs with a dedicated regional appeal. They could in turn syndicate their distinctive style of televangelism through established Christian television channels the world over, which ensured that their audience was global as well as local. As television religion entered the third millennium, it adopted a mercurial role as an agent of globalization and interactive ministry.

The impact of these changes upon traditional televangelists has yet to be assessed. But it appears that the big names of televangelism over the last thirty years are slowly being squeezed out of a market that has not expanded in quite the way that many anticipated. Pat Robertson, Oral Roberts, and Jerry Falwell still vie for dominance in the televangelism firmament, but in truth the phenomenon is now prey to one of its own parents—choice. With more channels and media output to choose from, all religious broadcasters need to work harder and harder just to retain their market share. Were it not for the comparative fall in production costs, a number of televangelism networks would now be out of business.

The future of televangelism appears to be less with household-name televangelists and more with custom-made productions that provide a better fit for their target audiences. The days when developing nations imported the offerings of American televangelists wholesale are more or less gone. Now, at the beginning of the third millennium, African and Asian televangelists such as Dnakararn in India produce their own material for their own contexts. European Christian networks are now more commonplace, although they continue to rely on a diet that is supplemented by offerings from North America. The Internet continues to grow in influence, enabling immediacy and participation. Live webcasts are now within reach of the smallest Pentecostal gathering in some of the remotest places. Radio and television, quite simply, are no longer the only (or preferred) media for Pentecostalism.

At the same time, there continues to be a certain degree of public unease surrounding televangelists. Typically, especially in America, most are allied to right-wing political concerns and wedded to agendas and groups such as the Christian Coalition and other conservative or neotraditional moralistic crusades. Ironically, it is their courting of theological and political controversy, coupled to an extreme social conservatism, that continues to keep them in the public eye, and thereby maintains their solid if small support base.

MARTYN PERCY

See also Evangelism

Further Reading

Bruce, S. (1990). *Pray TV: Televangelism in America*. London: Routledge.

Coleman, S. (2000). *The globalization of Charismatic Christianity: Spreading the gospel of prosperity*. Cambridge, UK: Cambridge University Press.

Hadden, J., & Shupe, A. (1988). *Televangelism: Power and politics on God's frontier*. New York: Henry Holt.

Memphis Miracle

Memphis Miracle is the term popularly used to refer to the 1994 gathering in Memphis, Tennessee (from 17 through 19 October), of white and African-American Pentecostals. The dramatic series of events at the gathering was quickly dubbed a miracle because it represented to those in attendance a historic reconciliation between groups that for nearly a century had been separated along racial lines.

Historical Background

The explosive development of the modern Pentecostal movement is often traced to the Azusa Street Revival in Los Angeles in the first decade of the twentieth century. William Seymour, a black man, served as the pastor of the small church on Azusa Street where thousands came from 1906 to 1909 to receive the baptism in the Holy Spirit. One of the remarkable aspects of these meetings was that, in the words of one participant, "the color line has been washed away in the blood [of Christ]" (Bartleman 1980, xviii). At a time when American society was racially segregated, the sight of men and women of both races mingling at the altar was, depending on one's perspective, either inspiring or scandalous.

In their early stages Pentecostal movements in America were generally interracial; however, within a few years Pentecostals had adapted to the dominant social patterns and become segregated. For example, when a collaboration of Pentecostal groups formed the Pentecostal Fellowship of North America (PFNA) in 1948, black churches were not invited to participate. In 1992, however, the PFNA board, following the initiative of Bishop Bernard Underwood of the International Pentecostal Holiness Church, voted to "pursue the possibility of reconciliation with our African-American brethren." This decision, along with the cooperation of Bishop Ithiel Clemmons of the predominantly black Church of God in Christ (COGIC), led to a series of four meetings over the next two years at which leaders discussed the idea of racial reconciliation. By the last of these four meetings, in January of 1994, it was the intent of the representatives to replace the PFNA with a new, racially inclusive fellowship. Accordingly, a committee drafted a new constitution to be presented for consideration. The proposed name for the new organization was Pentecostal Churches of North America.

Memphis Gathering

Representatives from the various churches gathered in Memphis for a conference entitled "Pentecostal Partners: A Reconciliation Strategy for Twenty-First-Century Ministry." Morning sessions were devoted to the presentation of scholarly papers that candidly dealt with the racism and neglect of the past century. Evening sessions, open to the public, were typically Pentecostal in worship and sermonic delivery.

On the afternoon of 18 October, Bishop Charles Blake of the COGIC expressed with tears his commitment of love to the participants. Moments later, there was an utterance in tongues. Jack Hayford, pastor (and in 2004 elected president) of the International Church of the Foursquare Gospel, went to the microphone and gave the interpretation. He said the utterances spoke of two separate streams of the Spirit that had been muddied, but God was bringing the two streams together in a newly pure river of love that would satisfy multitudes of the thirsty. A white Assemblies of God (AG) pastor then came to the platform, explaining that God had called him to wash the feet of a black leader as a sign of repentance. Tearfully asking forgiveness for the sins of whites against their black brothers, he washed the feet of Bishop Clemmons. People began weeping throughout the auditorium. Bishop Blake then washed the feet of Thomas Trask, the general superintendent of the AG.

Hours later, the PFNA was dissolved. The next day, 19 October, the new body was proposed. It was to have an equal number of blacks and whites on its governing board. A last minute request to include "Charismatic" in the title of the organization was approved, and the Pentecostal and Charismatic Churches of North America (PCCNA) was created. The new fellowship unanimously approved a "Racial Reconciliation Manifesto" that confessed the sin of racism and condemned it for "having hindered the maturation of spiritual development and mutual sharing among Pentecostal-Charismatic believers for decades." Participants committed themselves to oppose all forms of personal and institutional racism, pray and work for genuine and visible manifestations of Christian unity, and appeal to their own constituencies to oppose racism. Bishop Clemmons was elected chairman and Bishop Underwood vice-chairman of the fellowship.

On that last day of the gathering, Paul Walker of the Church of God in Cleveland, Tennessee, coined the phrase "miracle in Memphis." Participants of the conference returned to their homes with a conviction that God's blessing was on these steps toward reconciliation. They had sensed the Holy Spirit in a powerful way, calling Pentecostals back to the heritage of racial unity established at Azusa Street.

Implications

The Memphis conference was significant in itself because it was a rare instance in which Pentecostal leaders publicly confronted their failings and submitted to blunt criticisms of them. At the start of the twenty-first century, however, signs of lasting change in the wake of Memphis are difficult to discern. Black Pentecostals note that their white brothers and sisters continue to reflect the larger civic agenda of political conservatism, which tends to be at odds with black concerns. They suspect, for example, that the white participants at Memphis would still vote against affirmative action measures giving preference to minorities in various circumstances, if such a measure were put to a vote.

Other historically marginalized groups within Pentecostalism are looking for signs of long-term change in the movement as well. Hispanic Pentecostals, who comprise the fastest growing segment of the church in North America, question whether prejudice against them will be addressed. Pentecostal women are asking whether the openness to their ministry characteristic of the early revival will be restored after many years of decreasing acceptance. Others wonder whether the principle of reconciliation will influence the attitudes of member congregations of the PCCNA toward Oneness Pentecostals, who deny the theology of the Trinity.

The long-term effects of the Memphis Miracle remain to be seen. All acknowledge that such a long history of separation and prejudice cannot be overcome by one event or even in the short term. Indeed, many white Pentecostals do not know how to take the next steps toward realizing the vision of Memphis. The symbolic actions of leaders in Memphis in 1994 were historic and memorable, but the "miracle" will be validated by the manner in which individual Pentecostals treat one another and by the extent to which local pastors demonstrate loving cooperation and foster increasing fellowship between and within Pentecostal congregations of every background.

ROBERT A. BERG

See also Black Pentecostalism; Hispanic Pentecostalism; Race Relations

Further Reading

Bartleman, F. (1980). *Azusa Street*. Plainfield, NJ: Logos International. (Original work published 1925)

Clemmons, I. (1996). What price reconciliation: Reflections on the "Memphis Dialogue." *Pneuma, 18*, 116–122.

Daniels, D. (2002). Charles Harrison Mason: The interracial impulse of early Pentecostalism. In J. R. Goff & G. Wacker (Eds.), *Portraits of a generation* (pp. 255–270). Fayetteville: University of Arkansas Press.

Hollenweger, W. J. (1997). *Pentecostalism: Origins and developments worldwide*. Peabody, MA: Hendrickson.

Macchia, F. D. (1995). From Azusa to Memphis: Evaluating the racial reconciliation dialogue among Pentecostals. *Pneuma, 17*(2), 203–218.

Poewe, K. (1988). Links and parallels between black and white charismatic churches in South Africa and the States: Potential for cultural transformation. *Pneuma, 10*(2), 141–158.

Robeck, C. M. (n.d.). *The past: Historical roots of racial unity and division in American Pentecostalism.* Retrieved from http://www.pctii.org/pccna/papers/robeck.html

Synan, V. (1998). Memphis 1994: Miracle and mandate. *Reconciliation, 1,* 14–18.

Messianic Jews

There is a growing movement of Messianic Jews in the world today, especially in Israel, the United States, parts of the former Soviet Union, and in Latin America. Messianic Jews consider themselves Jews who confess faith in Jesus (Yeshua) of Nazareth as the Messiah of Israel, the Savior of mankind, and the Son of God. As Jews believing in Jesus, they refuse to assimilate into Gentile Christianity, preferring to remain with their Jewish people. They claim that they have not changed their Jewish religion, but rather fulfilled its most inner meaning. They form Messianic Jewish congregations that enable them to express their identity as Jewish disciples of Yeshua within a distinctive lifestyle.

Terminology

Messianic Jews define their movement as a resurrection of the original Jewish *ekklesia*. For them the movement is the fulfillment of biblical prophecy concerning the End Times according to Romans 11:15 and Ezekiel 37: 11–14. They relate to the image of the olive tree in Romans 11:17–24 as it underlines the continuing centrality of the Jewish people in God's purposes after the Christ-event. The Messianic Jews believe they belong both to Israel and to the church, bridging the two.

Particularly in the United States, in order to affirm the relationship to the Jewish people, their faith and way of life, many prefer to use the designation "Messianic Judaism" to identify the movement as one type of Judaism (Kinzer 2001). In Israel, though, members of the movement dislike the term and prefer to speak of the "Messianic Jewish movement."

Beginnings

Although the origins of the Christian Church had been almost all Jewish until the third century, the new Gentile majority within the church began to neglect the Jewish heritage and systematically to destroy any distinctive Jewish witness to Jesus within the Christian fellowship. The church had replaced apostate Israel as the new covenant people because of Israel's rejection of the Messiah. The conclusion was that the Jews as a people had no further significance in salvation history. Converted Jews must join the church and give up all Jewishness as irrelevant. Church edicts threatened all members with excommunication, especially those with Jewish roots who observed any Jewish practice (e.g., the Second Council of Nicea, 787 CE). Despite its origins, it became impossible for a person to be both Christian and Jewish, at least in public (e.g., the lifestyle of the Moranos in the Spanish world).

The Protestant Reformation did not immediately change the inherited "replacement" theology. But the high valuing of Scriptures within Protestantism around 1620 led Calvinistic and Presbyterian scholars (e.g., Johann Alsted, Joseph Mede) to affirm the ongoing relevance of Old Testament prophecies concerning Israel.

Probably the first Christian leader to see the need for a restoration of a distinct Jewish witness within the church was Count Nikolaus von Zinzendorf (1700–1760), who started the first "Messianic Kehila" within the Jewish ghetto of Amsterdam.

Since the 1820s, an interest in the Jewish people began to reach a wider circle of Christians (e.g., Edward Irving, John Nelson Darby), as part of a new focus on the End Times provoked by the French Revolution and the Napoleonic wars. In 1840 the British and German governments established a joint Protestant bishopric in Jerusalem, of which the first bishop was a converted Jewish rabbi, Michael Solomon Alexander.

The Hebrew Christian Alliance was formed in Britain in 1867, in the United States in 1915, and as an International Alliance in 1925 to help Jewish believers to affirm in some way their Jewish identity within the church. Those Hebrew Christians remained in their churches, but developed growing structures for fellowship and some form of liturgy among themselves.

Especially in Eastern Europe, individual Jews came to faith in Jesus without any contact with Christians. Of these the best known is Joseph Rabinowicz who founded the congregation Israelites of the New Covenant in Kishinev, Moldova, at the end of the nineteenth century as an entity distinct from any Gentile church.

Around 1920 the Presbyterian Church in the United States founded the first Hebrew-speaking Jewish congregations following their evangelistic efforts among Jews.

Transformation from Hebrew Christianity

In Israel, only a few families of Jewish Yeshua-believers remained after the establishment of the state of Israel in

Messianic Jews and Yeshua

Below is the Union of Messianic Jewish Congregations' *Statement on the Identify of Yeshua* *[Jesus]*:

The Union of Messianic Jewish Congregations holds that the One GOD, the GOD of creation, the GOD of Israel, the GOD of our ancestors, of Whom our tradition speaks, reveals Himself uniquely, definitively, and decisively in the life, death, resurrection, and return of Yeshua the Messiah.

Yeshua is the incarnation of the Divine WORD through Whom the world was made, and of the Divine GLORY through Whom GOD revealed Himself to Israel and acted in their midst. He is the living Torah, expressing perfectly in His example and teaching the Divine purpose for human life. Yeshua is completely human and completely divine.

As the risen Messiah and the heavenly Kohen Gadol (High Priest), Yeshua continues to mediate GOD's relationship to His people Israel, to those of the nations who have joined the greater commonwealth of Israel in Him, and to all creation. GOD's plan of salvation and blessing for Israel, the nations, and the entire cosmos is fulfilled only in and through Yeshua, by virtue of His atoning death and bodily resurrection, and GOD's gift of life to both Jews and Gentiles, in this world and in the world to come, is bestowed and appropriated only in and through Him.

Source: Union of Messianic Jewish Congregations. (2003). *Statement on the identity of Yeshua.* Retrieved September 21, 2004, from http://www.umjc.org/net1/docs/yeshua_statement.aspx

1948. The few pioneers developed their own style of typical Israeli Messianic fellowships independent of the expatriate Evangelical missions.

The dynamic for the Messianic Jewish phenomenon came from the Jesus movement in California in 1967. Great numbers of young Jews had embraced faith in Yeshua but at the same time were experiencing a new fervor of Jewish identity as a response to the 1967 Six-Day War out of which they resisted all assimilation into the various forms of Gentile Christianity. This new fervor for Messianic congregations won a majority in the Hebrew Christian Alliance of America and led in 1975 to its being renamed the Messianic Jewish Alliance of America (MJAA). This Messianic Jewish identity had major implications for theological self-understanding and ecclesiology, and for worship and lifestyle.

The theology of the Messianic Jews until today has reflected the doctrinal positions of conservative Evangelical Protestantism, because it had been the conservative Evangelicals who supported the Hebrew Christian missions. But as the movement continues, there is often some tension between the need for an authentic Jewish expression and the Evangelical theological framework.

The Messianic Jewish movement in the United States also has a strong charismatic component. This is especially true for those independent congregations, which in 1979 formed the new Union of Messianic Jewish Congregations (UMJC). The charismatic style is also found in those Messianic Jewish congregations belonging to the Assemblies of God. There are quite a few non-charismatic Messianic congregations, almost hostile to the charismatic movement, such as those congregations set up by the Southern Baptists as part of their mission policy.

Current Extent

The estimated number of members and congregations are as follows:

- Israel: (according to published statistics for 1998) 3,560 adult members, 81 congregations/house groups, with 61 percent Jewish members. Currently: around 110 congregations, about 8,000 members.

- United States: MJAA—about 110 congregations, UMJC—73 congregations. Together with the independent congregations—about 300 congregations.

- Eastern Europe: rather rapid growth in the countries of the former Soviet Union. The largest

Messianic congregation in the world (over 1,000 members) is in Kiev, Ukraine.

- Western Europe: about 50 Messianic Jewish congregations.

- Latin America: a rapid growth among the descendants of Morano families, who join the movement as an answer to their double loyalty over centuries.

- South Africa: growing numbers of congregations founded by British and Dutch descendants with Jewish heritage.

- Worldwide estimate: around 300,000 Messianic Jews, many of them are not integrated in Messianic congregations.

Messianic Jewish Life

Shabbat observance is central for Messianic Jews. Virtually all congregations hold their weekly worship on the Shabbat (Friday evening or Saturday). For the opening of Shabbat in the family, Messianic Jews use traditional Jewish prayers adapted to indicate that Yeshua is the Lord of the Shabbat.

Messianic Jews commonly observe the biblical Jewish feasts: Passover, Shavuot, Sukkot, the Jewish New Year, and Yom Kippur. The Jewish feasts are presented as finding their fulfillment in Yeshua.

In the United States, most congregations use some elements from Jewish liturgy in their Shabbat worship. The strict use of the Siddur, the Jewish liturgical book, is practiced only by a small minority, particularly in Israel. Messianic Jewish worship is either influenced by traditional Evangelical elements or is highly charismatic. The charismatic sector has been prolific in new forms of music and is also marked by Israeli forms of dance. Many seek to combine a sensitivity to the Holy Spirit with a sensitivity to the Jewish heritage in free-flowing structure (e.g., the *Shema*, the Aaronic blessing, special festival prayers). The debate about whether Messianic Jews should or should not use the Siddur runs parallel to the debate about the value of rabbinic Jewish tradition and scholarship. Some messianic scholars point out that this estrangement of Messianic Judaism from Jewish (liturgical) tradition makes the movement vulnerable in the long run to the process of assimilation. They argue for adopting certain elements to Messianic faith.

Almost all Messianic congregations practice believers' baptism of adults by immersion and do not baptize infants. There is a wide variation in the practice, the theological understanding, and the liturgical form of The Lord's Supper.

In many ways the patterns for governmental, leadership, and theological training are closest to those in the nondenominational charismatic networks. Currently efforts are being made to provide more adequate theological formation (e.g., Caspari Center/Israel, King of Kings Bible College/Israel, Messianic Jewish Bible Institutes).

Torah in Messianic Jewish life

Messianic Jewish authors commonly argue that Gentile Christians have habitually misunderstood the Torah, reducing it to legislation. They would affirm that the Torah is the locus of Jewish practice and that the Torah is renewed through the new covenant, reaching its fulfillment in Yeshua (Matthew 5:17) as the Law fits to the new covenant order. There is a great tension though among them about seeing the Law as just "permissible as part of Christian liberty" or "mandatory" or "recommended." But all who assert the need for Messianic Jews to observe the Torah as fully as possible do not make this a requirement for salvation.

Rabbinic Jewish Heritage

The views on rabbinic Judaism range from total rejection as a human creation of the rabbis who had rejected Yeshua, through a spectrum of positions, to an acceptance of everything that is not explicitly forbidden in the New Testament. Those against the dismissal of rabbinic Judaism are arguing that the Messianic Jews are to represent "national Israel" within the multinational *ekklesia*. If the Messianic Jews do not participate actively in Israel's "national" life, which is mostly expressed by the *Halakhah*, they will eventually either assimilate to the Gentile majority in the *ekklesia*, as happened in the Pauline churches, or become an irrelevant sect, like the Nazarenes or Ebionites. As a practical consequence of this, many in the American movement argue for the need of a Messianic Jewish *Halakhah*. The opponents of a Messianic *Halakhah* are strongest in Israel, fearing that the movement will lose its freedom in the Messiah when coming under a Messianic *Halakhah* based on customs and decrees originating from Jews who where non-believers in Yeshua.

"One New Man"

The longer the Messianic Jewish movement has been in existence, the more important becomes its relationship to the whole church, despite the hurtful facts of church behavior towards the Jews throughout centuries. The task requires a new theology of Israel and the church. Almost all Messianic Jews today see themselves as the link between Israel and the church, because they belong to both. They constitute the Jesus-believing part of Israel and the Jewish part of the church. The goal is the common witness in the unity of the One New Man in the Messiah (Ephesians 2:15). Both the Jewish and the Gentile expression need each other as essential components of the One Body of the Messiah.

A practical question faces most Messianic Jewish congregations: the issue of Gentile membership. Is it possible for Messianic congregations to have a majority of Gentile members? What is required of Gentile candidates for full membership? The mainstream of the movement argues for distinctive congregations with a Messianic Jewish identity. For them, the "One New Man" is realized through fellowship between the Messianic congregations and the Gentile churches. For a minority, each local church is to manifest the "One New Man" by consisting of both Messianic Jews and Gentile believers.

Since 1996, the initiative Towards Jerusalem Council II (TJCII)—under the guidance of twelve international Messianic Jewish leaders and twelve Gentile representatives—fosters the reconciliation between Jew and Gentile. This can only be realized if there is understanding and repentance for the historic wrongdoing of the church against the Jews in general and against any Jewish expression of faith in Yeshua. Through diplomatic actions and spiritual initiatives, TJCII works on all levels for an ongoing recognition of the Messianic movement. The goal is something like a "Second Council of Jerusalem" (with a reversed starting point to Acts 15) for the full reconciliation between the Jewish and the Gentile part of the church.

JOHANNES FICHTENBAUER

See also Evangelism; Judaism, Relationship to

Further Reading

Ariel, Y. (2000). *Evangelizing the Chosen People: Missions to the Jews in America, 1880–2000.* Chapel Hill: University of North Carolina Press.

Berger, B., & Berger, R. (1993). *Israel und die Kirche: Endzeitliche Perspektiven.* Hombrechtikon, Switzerland: Echad-Verlag.

Cohn-Sherbok, D. (2000). *Messianic Judaism.* New York: Cassell.

Cohn-Sherbok, D. (Ed.). (2001). *Voices of Messianic Judaism.* Baltimore: Lederer Books.

Goldberg, L. (2003). *How Jewish is Christianity? 2 views on the Messianic movement.* Grand Rapids, MI: Zondervan.

Hocken, P. (2004). *Towards Jerusalem Council II. The vision and the story* (2nd ed.). Ventura, CA: TJCII.

Hocken, P., & Juster, D. (2004). *The Messianic Jewish movement.* Ventura, CA: TJCII.

Hornung, A. (1994). *Messianische Juden zwischen Kirche und Volk Israel. Entwicklung und Begründung ihres Selbstverständnisses.* Tübingen, Germany: TVG Brunnen.

Juster, D. (1995). *Jewish roots: A foundation of biblical theology.* Shippensburg, PA: Destiny Image Publishers.

Kinzer, M. (2001). *The nature of Messianic Judaism.* West Hartford, CT: Hashivenu Archives.

Kjaer-Hansen, K. (1995). *Joseph Rabinowicz and the Messianic movement.* Grand Rapids, MI: Eerdmans Publishing Co.

Liberman, P. (1977). *The fig tree blossoms.* Indianola, IA: Fountain Press.

Nerel, G. (1997). "Messianic Jews" in Eretz Israel (1917–1967), *Mishkan* 27.

Rausch, D. A. (1982). *Messianic Judaism: Its history, theology and polity.* New York: The Edwin Mellen Press.

Stern, D. (1991). *Messianic Jewish manifesto.* Clarksville, MD: Jewish New Testament Publications.

Wasserman, J. S. (2000). *Messianic Jewish congregations.* Lanham, MD: The University Press of America.

Mexico

See America, Latin; Hispanic Pentecostalism

Ministry

Ministry, in its basic sense, means service. In a biblical perspective, ministry entails the service rendered by Christians unto other persons for the glory of God, as well as ministry unto God primarily through the worship of the saints gathered in Jesus' name. An examination of ministry is crucial because ministry is among the most foundational elements of the church's structure and existence. Moreover, the specific contributions of a Pentecostal-Charismatic view of ministry will assist believers of other traditions to understand their charismatically inclined brothers and sisters, as well as introduce them to new ways of construing the church's mission for the twenty-first century.

One of the most important features of the biblical concept of ministry—especially as it is delineated in the New Testament—is the idea of diversity or variety.

New Testament ministry was variegated and all members of the church were involved in some way, because ministry was not yet institutionalized but anchored to spiritual giftedness. If one had a gift from the Spirit, then one had a ministry in which to engage. Central to Pentecostal ministry is the involvement of every believing member of the redeemed community. Pentecostals recognize that the Spirit is poured out upon every Christian empowering each for ministry. These affirmations are evident in the writings of classical Pentecostal ministers and scholars and echoed in the modern period.

Classical Views

In this section, we focus our attention on some representative voices of what may be called the classical Pentecostal view of ministry. Although Pentecostals have not devoted a great deal of scholarly attention to theology until recently, the classical writers do give us a significant albeit brief analysis of biblical ministry. Myer Pearlman, an early Assemblies of God minister, classified two types of New Testament ministry: the first is "general and prophetic," the second is "local and practical" (Pearlman 1937). Apostles and prophets occupy the first group and are defined by a broad ministerial reach while the second group—elders, deacons and deaconesses—were confined to a local assembly.

Pentecostal minister and scholar P. C. Nelson argued that Pentecostals affirm with the reformers that each believer is a priest unto God and thus no special mediation is required to gain access to God except that already provided in the atonement of Christ. The priesthood of all believers yields the truth that each believer is a minister responsible to render service that contributes to the achievement of God's redemptive goals for the world. Though every believer is a minister, God has ordained a structure of leadership for the church to facilitate order and unity in the fulfillment of gospel ministry. Specifically, God has ordained offices within the church: apostle, prophet, evangelist, pastor, teacher, and deacon. The first two offices are unique and these titles are not applied to believers today. For Nelson, though many Christians may function apostolically and prophetically, no individual believer may be designated as an apostle or prophet. The remaining four offices are for the church at all times. The evangelist is an itinerant minister primarily responsible for preaching to the unconverted. Pastors shepherd God's flock, teachers expound the word of God to local assemblies, and deacons (as well as deaconesses) minister to the material needs of God's people. Nelson notes that at least two of the first seven deacons were also preachers and concludes that New Testament ministry had more to do with function than title. He concludes that "there can be no rigid distinction between 'clergy' and 'laity'" (Nelson 1948).

E. S. Williams suggests that apostleship was the highest order of New Testament ministry and that apostleship may still continue in our modern day but only in the generic sense of "messenger." The second order of ministry—the prophet(s)—is "a permanent gift" to the church (Williams 1953). Other ministries still function in the church but the pastor has developed into the primary spiritual leader; pastors are to be accorded the respect due their office.

Pentecostal scholar Anthony Palma asserts that the Spirit and the church are inseparable, concluding that the Spirit sovereignly distributes gifts that enable members of the covenant community to function in ministry for God's glory. Every member—including women—function in these ministries.

Melvin Hodges' *A Theology of the Church and its Mission* represents the first attempt to substantially develop a Pentecostal theology of ministry as it relates to ecclesiology. Hodges notes that for Pentecostals, ministry is not merely post-Resurrection but, more important, post-Pentecost. The fundamental task of the church—the preaching of the Gospel to the unconverted—cannot be achieved through human effort. The Holy Spirit supplies the "inward impulse" necessary to accomplish this great commission. The Spirit distributes gifts to believers enabling them to accomplish redemptive tasks. Each gift of the Spirit is "closely related to ministry and the body of Christ" (Hodges 1977). Some have criticized Pentecostals for a perceived overemphasis on the Spirit overshadowing Christ's atoning work. Hodges carefully notes that the Spirit operates in congruity with the Trinitarian impulse to achieve God's overall cosmic purposes.

Zenas Bicket follows Hodges in closely associating an understanding of ministry with the church. He holds that the church is a living organism, the bride of Christ and the temple of God's presence. Each believer is a vital part of this organism and is united by a common faith in Christ. The main task of the church is to make humans aware of God's love and grace in the gospel of peace. This task, says Bicket, is accomplished most effectively when believers share the responsibility of proclaiming the Gospel.

Recent Developments

Reflecting a common feature of Pentecostal thinking about ministry, Guy Duffield and Nathaniel Van Cleve assert that the titles (i.e., "apostle," "prophet," etc.) "were more descriptive of [New Testament] ministries than of office and rank," and these titles "are probably different ways of describing the same function" (Duffield and Van Cleve 1983). Thus there is some overlap among the various roles or offices of the New Testament. This communicates the idea that each member—including women—is an important element in God's redemptive plan as it unfolds in the church.

Byron Klaus stands in continuity with the older Pentecostal scholars while advancing their thought. He states that the gifts of the Spirit, which when expressed as ministries serve as foundations of the church, are not objects that God distributes but rather are "manifestations of grace." He also claims that Pentecostal experience (i.e., ecstatic speech) "is a doorway to heightened awareness of Christ's ministry" in the church (Klaus 1989). Klaus notes that the transcendent realities that penetrate believers through the Spirit result in the Pentecostal community's being able to sing the "'old, old story of Jesus and His love'…in the present tense" (Klaus 1989). More recently, Klaus, following Hodges, suggests three essential aims of Pentecostal ministry: first, the church is to minister to God; second, the church is to minister to other believers in the community of faith; and third, the church is to minister to the world beyond the church, to the great unwashed. Each of these aims is conducted in and through the Holy Spirit.

Ken Gurley, in the tradition of Duffield and Van Cleve, claims that "The fivefold ministry [of Ephesians 4:11] is more functional than positional" (Gurley 1993). He adds that there are positional offices—bishop, elder, deacon—that are localized and essentially responsible for the maintenance of the church, that is, administrating and governing it. Gurley concludes, in a manner similar to E. S. Williams, that the pastor has become the "chief representative of the church in all of its affairs" (Gurley 1993).

Benny Aker suggests that spiritual gifts are really ministries and are associated with "one's being part of the temple of God" (Aker 2002). Gifts or ministries are determined by the needs of the community and follow Jesus' pattern of removing walls that separate believers. Specifically, the dissemination of gifts removes the wall consisting in the distinction between clergy and laity.

Summary

One can discern a number of common features of the classical Pentecostal view of ministry. First, it affirms the participation of every member of the believing community. Second, there is an egalitarian spirit among these assessments of ministry; that is, no one ministry is to be esteemed as more essential than or superior to another. An apostle is no more valued as an agent of the Spirit than is a deacon. Third, every member of the community is equally called and ordained for the ministry. To be sure, some giftings mean that a few will function in ways that allow for distinctions (see 1 Corinthians 12:28–30). Nevertheless, as people empowered by the Spirit, every believer is equipped and commissioned for service in the kingdom. Fourth, Pentecostals are nearly unanimous in their cautious embrace of an ongoing apostolic office today. Most affirm the weaker definition of apostle as messenger and say it is in this sense that apostles are still operating in the church.

These Pentecostal assertions about ministry are confirmed by others from different traditions. For example, Evangelical theologian Donald Bloesch connects the principle of the priesthood of all believers with a charismatic impulse: "The priesthood of believers, as the New Testament understands this, cannot be adequately understood apart from the gifts of the Holy Spirit" (Bloesch 1978). Every Christian is dependent on these gifts to exercise this priestly office for God's glory. Bloesch's work on this point parallels P. C. Nelson's.

More recently, Bloesch has clarified this point: "In the original or Pauline communities of the church, ministry and charism were closely related; there are indeed as many ministries as charisms" (Bloesch 2002). This fact yields the conclusion that the New Testament endorses "no definitive form or pattern of ministry" (Bloesch 2002). Catholic theologian Hans Küng affirms this ideal: "Anyone who is qualified for a particular ministry—as prophet, teacher, helper, superior, bishop or deacon, etc.—and who performs it properly, has received the call of God and the charism of the Spirit" (Kung 1968).

Interestingly, there is another parallel between Bloesch's recent work and that of P. C. Nelson; just as Nelson affirmed that believers may function apostolically, so Bloesch (2002) suggests that "every Christian has an apostolic vocation" bearing witness to the gospel even in secular tasks. Finally, Bloesch agrees with many Pentecostal and charismatic church leaders when he notes that "the deadly enemy of charismatic ministry in the church has always been centralization of power and the substitution of ecclesiastical authority for the authority of Word and Spirit" (Bloesch 2002). Bloesch is no Pentecostal but is still representative of the growing influence of the charismatic renewal on the broader Evangelical communities.

Implications

What does the Pentecostal view of ministry mean for other Christian traditions? First, non-charismatic believers need to rethink the idea of ministry from the ground up, particularly in relation to the so-called distinction between clergy and laity. The renewing efforts of the Holy Spirit seem to flatten our attempts to divide ourselves into groups. The Spirit enables *every* Christian equally even if some function in ways that are profoundly different. The offering of help and the exercise of administration is no less Spirit-inspired and Spirit-sustained than the working of miracles. A believer who offers exhortation is as ordained for ministry as the pastor who preaches and administers the sacraments regularly, or the exorcist who casts out demons in Jesus' name. The foundation for Christian ministry should be seen in the Spirit's extension of the kingdom in our midst and not in the perpetuation of some traditional practice of ordaining a special class for service.

What has been said here of the dissolution of the distinction between clergy and laity should also be applied to other stultifying distinctions, most notably, the gender distinctions that have been used as a wedge to divide and isolate gifted women from accessing ministry among the body of Christ. Pentecostals have a commendable history of inviting and including women in ministry though there is always room for growth.

Second, giftings for ministry should be acknowledged as being rooted in the needs of the community and the enablement of the Spirit rather than in intrinsic abilities that are offered to God and church. Inasmuch as Pentecostals affirm the divine origin of ministry, they recognize that ministry is ultimately not something believers do but something the Spirit does in and through Christians. Often, people are convinced that they are called into ministry because they are good public speakers or because they have a desire to preach the gospel. While these inclinations—and many others like them—are not unimportant, they do not constitute a sufficient ground for entering ministry. Only the work and agency of the Holy Spirit can sufficiently account for ministry in the body of Christ.

Third, the fact that the Spirit is the origin of the ministries in the covenant community confirms his sovereign deity. Paul declares that the Spirit distributes gifts according to his own prerogatives (1 Corinthians 12:11). The writer to the Hebrews concurs: The Holy Spirit is the sovereign Lord who allocates spiritual gifts in harmony with his own redemptive goals (Hebrew 2:4). There is always a danger of presuming on the presence of the Spirit. Karl Barth advises, "A foolish church presupposes [the Spirit's] presence and action in its own existence, in its offices and sacraments, ordinations, consecrations and absolutions" (Barth 1963). The church—any church and any tradition—must never carelessly presuppose the manifestation and work of the Spirit, but must always humbly acknowledge his presence and action as a gift of grace resulting from Christ's redemptive work on the cross. Pentecostal understandings of ministry must carefully avoid the danger of advocating an unstructured free-for-all while affirming that the Spirit's work can never be fully predicted or rigidly anticipated.

CHRISTOPHER C. EMERICK

See also Charismata; Gifts of the Spirit; Healing, Gifts of; Laity, Clergy

Further Reading

Aker, B. C. (2002). Charismata: Gifts, enablements, or ministries? *Journal of Pentecostal theology, 11*(1), 53–69.

Allen, R. (1960). *The ministry of the spirit* (D. M. Paton, Ed.). London: World Dominion Press.

Barth, K. (1963). *Evangelical theology: An introduction* (G. Foley, Trans.). Grand Rapids, MI: Eerdmans.

Bicket, Z. J. (1978). *We hold these truths*. Springfield, MO: Gospel Publishing House.

Bloesch, D. G. (1978). *Essentials of Evangelical theology* (Vol. 2). San Francisco: Harper & Row.

Bloesch, D. G. (2002). *The church*. Downers Grove, IL: Inter-Varsity.

Duffield, G. P., & Van Cleve, N. M. (1983). *Foundations of Pentecostal theology*. Los Angeles: L.I.F.E. Bible College.

Dunn, J. D. G. (1977). *Unity and diversity in the New Testament: An inquiry into the character of earliest Christianity*. London: SCM Press.

Dunn, J. D. G. (1985). Ministry and the Ministry: The Charismatic Renewal's challenge to traditional ecclesiology. In C. M. Robeck, Jr. (Ed.), *Charismatic experiences in history* (pp. 81–101). Peabody, MA: Hendrickson.

Dusing, M. L. (1995). The New Testament church. In S. M. Horton (Ed.), *Systematic theology* (rev ed.) (pp. 525–66). Springfield, MO: Logion Press.

Fee, G. D. (1994). *God's empowering presence*. Peabody, MA: Hendrickson.

Gurley, K. (1993). The Church. In J. L. Hall & D. K. Bernard (Eds.), *Doctrines of the Bible*. Hazelwood, MO: Word Aflame Press.

Hodges, M. L. (1977). *A theology of the church and its mission*. Springfield, MO: Gospel Publishing House.

Kärkkäinen, V-M. (2002). *Introduction to ecclesiology: Ecumenical, historical and global perspectives*. Downers Grove, IL: InterVarsity.

Klaus, B. D. (1989). A theology of ministry. *Paraclete 23*(3), 1–10.

Küng, H. (1968). *The church* (R. Ockenden & R. Ockenden, Trans.). London: Search Press.

Menzies, W. W. (1993). *Bible doctrines: A Pentecostal perspective*. Springfield, MO: Logion Press.

Nelson, P. C. (1948). *Bible doctrines*. Springfield, MO: Gospel Publishing House.

Palma, A. D. (1974). *The spirit—God in action*. Springfield, MO: Gospel Publishing House.

Pearlman, M. (1937). *Knowing the doctrines of the Bible*. Springfield, MO: Gospel Publishing House.

Volf, M. (1998). *After our likeness: The church as the image of the Trinity*. Grand Rapids, MI: Eerdmans.

Williams, E. S. (1953). *Systematic theology* (Vol. 3). Springfield, MO: Gospel Publishing House.

Miracles, Gifts of

This article examines the Pentecostal-Charismatic position on the gift of the working of miracles. This gift is listed by the apostle Paul as one Christ gives to the church by the Spirit for the edification and unity of the body. We shall identify the biblical foundation of the gift, then retrace the Pentecostal tradition's perspective on this spiritual gift, and conclude highlighting some of the strengths of the view. Before examining the classical Pentecostal position on the working of miracles, we must establish the biblical foundation of the doctrine.

Biblical Foundation

The chief texts for establishing the biblical basis of the doctrine of the gift of the working of miracles are 1 Corinthian 12:10 and 12:28–29. Because 12:28–29 add little to our understanding of the concept, our main concern is with 12:10. In 1 Corinthians 12, Paul is addressing the abuse of spiritual gifts in the Corinthian church and begins the chapter saying that he does not want them to be unaware of this important matter. The point of 12:1–3 is to set the stage for what follows: Whereas the Corinthians were once pagan idolaters, they now operate in and are infused with a different Spirit by which they are able to proclaim the Lordship of Jesus. In 12:4–11, Paul proclaims the diversity and divine origin of the gifts that the Spirit distributes among the Corinthian believers. Especially noteworthy is his use of the term *energōn* in verse 6 (and *energei* in verse 11), which emphatically anchors the operation of the gifts in the divine agency. That these diverse gifts come to believers "through the Spirit" (12:8) underscores the unity they engender among the body as well as confirming their divine origin.

The specific list of gifts includes utterances of wisdom and knowledge (verse 8), faith and gifts of healing (verse 9), working of miracles and prophecy (verse 10) along with others. Our attention is drawn to verse 10 and the "working of miracles" (*energēmata dynameōn*). *Energēmata* harkens back to verse 6 and recalls the divine source of the gift. *Dynameōn* is literally "powers" but is usually translated "miracles." Both terms are plural and this likely means that the gift was not a permanent enablement, but would address the needs of the community as they appeared and would be made manifest at the Spirit's discretion. That is, the gift did not necessarily reside in a particular individual but may have been apportioned to anyone in the community according to the Spirit's prerogative. What is the nature of this working of miracles? Though it may have included healing, it is much broader and probably involves exorcisms as well as so-called miracles of nature. With this very brief presentation of the biblical foundations of the doctrine in place, we turn now to examine how the Pentecostal and charismatic tradition has affirmed this important gift.

Classical Pentecostal and Charismatic Views

Myer Pearlman (1937) was among the earliest Pentecostal theologians to attempt to systematize the Pentecostal faith. Surprisingly, he devotes little attention to the spiritual gift of the working of miracles. He translates the phrase "works of power" and places the accent on power. He proposes that the "special miracles at Ephesus" (Acts 19:11–12) serve as an illustration of this gift in action. In discussing the related gift—gifts of healing—Pearlman notes that the dual plural indicates that God uses one supernaturally and not that a particular believer possesses the gift. Some maintain the notion that Pentecostals abuse the gifts, exercising them to excess and in ways that violate the boundaries set in Scripture. However, Pearlman recognizes that the gifts must be regulated and states that God sovereignly bestows gifts "without human intervention" or permission.

E. S. Williams (1953) follows Pearlman in citing the "special miracles" at Ephesus as examples of the working of miracles (1953). Williams seems to isolate healing as indicative of this gift; in addition to Acts 19, he cites the healing of the lame man in Act 3:1–8 and the healings resulting from the cast of Peter's shadow in Acts 5:15 as further examples.

Ralph Riggs holds Stephen (Acts 6:8; "full of grace and power" [*dynameōs*]) up as an instance of one to whom the working of miracles was given and in whose life and ministry it operated (1949). Like Pearlman and Williams he cites Acts 19:11–12 as a case of the working of miracles. However, he adds the healing of Aeneas in Acts 9:32–35 and the raising from the dead of Dorcas in 9:36–42 as well as several examples from the Old Testament. Finally, Riggs seems to identify some of the so-called miracles of nature; these include the transformation of Moses' rod into a serpent (Exodus 4:1–5), the rescue of Shadrach, Meshach, and Abednego from the fiery furnace (Daniel 3:24–30), Elijah's being fed by ravens (1 Kings 17:4), the earthquake that opened prison doors for Paul and Silas (Acts 16:25–26), and Philip's being carried away by the Spirit (Acts 8:39–40).

Donald Gee discusses the working of miracles (along with the gift of healing) as "divine advertising for the preaching of the gospel" (1936). Though the operation of these gifts was a constant companion of apostolic proclamation, the working of miracles is "incidental and secondary" to the ministry of the Word. Gee provocatively suggests two classes of miracles: the special miracles (cf. Acts 19:11) and the ordinary miracles. The latter were evidently a regular feature of early church gatherings, while the former were by definition sporadic and infrequent. Gee comments how odd it is that some want to make commonplace that which Scripture identifies as exceptional. Gee also recognizes that miracles are not necessarily redemptive only but may "even be punitive and destructive."

German lay minister Siegfried Grossman adopted a similar approach to the working of miracles, suggesting that the gift was concentrated primarily around presentations of the Gospel. He notes that many tend to "overrate the sensational miracles" that divert from the indispensable matters of the faith (1971). He concludes that the working of miracles is "no special gift for 'super-Christians', but rather part of the normal equipment for a Christian's everyday life."

Anthony Palma offers insights similar to Gee. For example, he cites both Acts 5:1–11 and 13:8–11 and says that the working of miracles results occasionally in "the reverse of healings" (1974). He says further that this gift is particularly prominent in Jesus' ministry. He presents the calming of the storm, the multiplication of the loaves and fishes, and the transforming of water into wine as examples. He concludes by suggesting that the gift of faith is usually a "prerequisite for the manifestation" of the working of miracles.

Stanley Horton (1976) states that the various manifestations of the working of miracles "are direct divine interventions in the world of man and nature." They include raising the dead, so-called nature miracles (almost exclusively in Jesus' ministry), and exorcism. Each miracle reveals that Jesus is victor.

Guy Duffield and Nathaniel Van Cleve (1983) recognize with others that the gift of working of miracles does not make "one a 'miracle worker.'" They underscore the idea that miracles are signs. God does not perform miracles simply to get press or boost the divine ego. No, miracles point to or teach something. In addition to the many texts others cite, Duffield and Van Cleve add Acts 28:3–5 where Paul shook off a poisonous viper.

Recent Perspectives

In the last two decades, there has been an increase of Pentecostal publications on spiritual gifts. In this brief section, we highlight some of the representative statements consistent with the traditional Pentecostal position. Siegfried Schatzmann's *A Pauline Theology of the Charismata* (1987) breaks no new ground but proclaims emphatically that the gift must contribute to the unity of the body: "Paul never intended [the working of miracles] to become the *raison d'être* of professional miracle workers and healing artists." David Lim, while affirming what others have also held, proposes that spiritual gifts are "incarnational." That is, the operation of the gift is fully divine and fully human; the Spirit uses human faculties to perform the gift among the people of God bringing results for which God alone is responsible. Craig Keener avers that those gifted to work miracles should bear in mind that miracles result from God's command or the request of one walking closely with the Lord (2001). One cannot flippantly exercise the gift or wield it in accord with self-seeking desires.

Peter Davids notes that for Paul, "true faith leads to…an experience of the Spirit that includes the working of miracles" (1993). For support, Davids cites Galatians 3:4–5: "Did you experience so much for nothing? —if it really was for nothing. Well then, does God supply you with the Spirit and work miracles (*energōn dynameis*) among you by your doing the works of the law, or by your believing what you heard?" This critical passage has figured prominently in recent literature. It is cited and discussed by Grudem, Deere, and Fee as indicative of the early Christian reality of ongoing or regular miracle activity. Inasmuch as one applies Galatians 3:1–5 to Christian existence today, one affirms that the working of miracles should be a regular part of Christian worship.

Going Forward

The Pentecostal and charismatic tradition maintains that the spiritual gift of the working of miracles was and should continue to be a regular element in the life of the church. It may accompany the proclamation of the Gospel or stand alone as a comfort for God's people. It includes healings of various kinds but also involves exorcism and miracles of nature.

This position has four strengths. First, the Pentecostal and charismatic view on the working of miracles affirms the sovereignty of the Spirit. The Spirit distributes the working of miracles (and indeed all the gifts) according to the divine will. That the gift is not something that believers possess further speaks of a commitment of ascribing sovereignty to the Spirit. While some abuse the gift, the majority of charismatically-inclined believers respect the sovereign rights of the Spirit to move in unexpected ways and operate through unexpected persons. The second strength follows from the first: Pentecostal and charismatic affirmations represent a careful balance that stresses both the redemptive and the punitive nature of miracles. Through human agency God may heal sicknesses and exorcize demons, or he may announce a curse or inflict a malady.

That no individual Christian owns the gift yields the observation that the gift is for the greater good and development of the body. This third strength asserts that there are no super-Christians who may exist without need or benefit of the giftings of others. Each receives a gift that contributes to the growth of the whole.

Pentecostals and charismatics eagerly and humbly anticipate the operation of miracles in their midst. This expectancy is the fourth strength of the position. There is an excitement in the moments of worship when one expects the Spirit to visit in the grace and power of the miraculous. Pentecostals and charismatics are careful though, to couch this expectancy in a humble acknowledgment that the Spirit may not demonstrate divine power in dramatic ways but often does so in less than spectacular fashion.

CHRISTOPHER C. EMERICK

See also Faith, Gift of; Gifts of the Spirit; Healing, Gifts of; Prophecy, Gift of

Further Reading

Carson, D. A. (1987). *Showing the spirit: A theological exposition of 1 Corinthians 12–14*. Grand Rapids, MI: Baker.

Collins, C. J. (2001). *The God of miracles: An exegetical examination of God's action in the world*. Wheaton, IL: Crossway.

Davids, P. H. (1993). A biblical view of the relationship of sin and the fruits of sin: Sickness, demonization, death, natural calamity. In G. S. Grieg & K. N. Springer (Eds.), *The Kingdom and the power* (pp. 111–132). Ventura, CA: Regal Books.

Deere, J. (1993). *Surprised by the power of the Spirit*. Grand Rapids, MI: Zondervan.

Duffield, G. P. & Van Cleve, N. M. (1983). *Foundations of Pentecostal theology*. Los Angeles: L.I.F.E. Bible College.

Dunn, J. D. G. (1975). *Jesus and the Spirit: A study of the religious and charismatic experience of Jesus and the first Christians as reflected in the New Testament*. London: SCM Press.

Fee, G. D. (1987). The first epistle to the Corinthians. *New international commentary on the New Testament*. Grand Rapids, MI: Eerdmans.

Fee, G. D. (1993). Gifts of the spirit. In G. F. Hawthorne & R. P. Martin (Eds.), *Dictionary of Paul and his letters* (pp. 339–347). Downers Grove, IL: InterVarsity Press.

Fee, G. D. (1994). *God's empowering presence*. Peabody, MA: Hendrickson.

Garland, D. E. (2003). 1 Corinthians. *Baker exegetical commentary on the New Testament*. Grand Rapids, MI: Baker.

Gee, D. (1936). *Spiritual gifts in the work of the ministry today*. Springfield, MO: Gospel Publishing House.

Grossman, S. (1971). *Charisma: The gifts of the spirit*. Wheaton, IL: Key Publishers.

Grudem, W. A. (1993). Should Christians expect miracles today? Objections and answers from the Bible. In G. S. Grieg & K. N. Springer (Eds.), *The kingdom and the power* (pp. 55–110). Ventura, CA: Regal Books.

Horton, S. M. (1976). *What the Bible says about the Holy Spirit*. Springfield, MO: Gospel Publishing House.

Keener, C. S. (2001). *Gift and giver: The Holy Spirit for today*. Grand Rapids, MI: Baker.

Lim, D. (1991). *Spiritual gifts: A fresh look*. Springfield, MO: Gospel Publishing House.

Lim, D. (1995). Spiritual gifts. In S. M. Horton (Ed.), *Systematic theology* (pp. 457–488, rev ed.). Springfield, MO: Logion Press.

Menzies, W. W., & Menzies, R. P. (2000). *Spirit and power: Foundations of Pentecostal experience*. Grand Rapids, MI: Zondervan.

Njiru, P. K. (2002). *Charisms and the Holy Spirit's activity in the body of Christ: An exegetical and theological study of 1 Corinthians 12:4–11 and Romans 12:6–8*. Rome: Editrice Pontificia Università Gregoriana.

Oss, D. A. (1996). A Pentecostal/Charismatic view. In W. A. Grudem (Ed.), *Are miraculous gifts for today? Four views* (pp. 239–283). Grand Rapids, MI: Zondervan.

Palma, A. D. (1974). *The Spirit—God in action*. Springfield, MO: Gospel Publishing House.

Pearlman, M. (1937). *Knowing the doctrines of the Bible*. Springfield, MO: Gospel Publishing House.

Riggs, R. M. (1949). *The Spirit himself*. Springfield, MO: Gospel Publishing House.

Schatzmann, S. (1987). *A Pauline theology of the charismata*. Peabody, MA: Hendrickson.

Thiselton, A. C. (2000). The first epistle to the Corinthians: A commentary on the Greek text. *New international Greek testament commentary*. Grand Rapids, MI: Eerdmans.

Twelftree, G. H. (1993). Signs, wonders, miracles. In G. F. Hawthorne & R. P. Martin, (Eds.), *Dictionary of Paul and his letters* (pp. 875–877). Downers Grove, IL: InterVarsity.

Twelftree, G. H. (1999). *Jesus the miracle worker*. Downers Grove, IL: InterVarsity Press.

Williams, D. (1993). Following Christ's example: A biblical view of discipleship. In G. S. Grieg & K. N. Springer (Eds.), *The kingdom and the power* (pp. 175–196). Ventura, CA: Regal Books.

Williams, E. S. (1953). *Systematic theology* (Vol. 3). Springfield, MO: Gospel Publishing House.

Music

Music has always been prominent in Pentecostal churches. Traditions established in the early twentieth century associated Pentecostals with exuberant, joyful, spirited singing. "Liberty" in the Spirit was emphasized. Music, like preaching and prayer, resisted a time schedule. Typically a large portion of each service (one-third or more) has been devoted to music. With its spiritual power and universal acceptance, music has been integrated into every aspect of Pentecostal and charismatic church ministry—congregational worship, evangelism, missions, and Christian education.

As in the New Testament church, Pentecostals placed little emphasis on ritual or form. Leaders encouraged reliance on the Holy Spirit's inspiration and anointing. Active congregational participation—including lusty singing—was desirable.

Pentecostal music has its roots in frontier camp meetings, early Holiness churches, various Baptist groups, and others emphasizing Evangelical outreach. While emotional, high-spirited singing, hand clapping, and even shouting and dancing were Pentecostal traditions, musical roots of the Pentecostals and charismatics are, in some measure, the same as other Christian churches. Distinctions result from doctrinal emphases and cultural differences. But much of the music stems from the same sources and influences of other groups.

From the beginning years, Pentecostals have sung songs about a loving heavenly Father; Jesus and salvation through His blood; the Holy Spirit, Comforter and Baptizer. Songs of testimony (personal experience), praise to God, divine healing, the Rapture of the church, and other subjects closely aligned with doctrinal issues, were favorites.

In recent decades, the Pentecostal church has gained recognition and significance. Adherents worldwide now exceed 200 million. While the "old-time religion" still attracts, some believers yearn for the new and fresh. In churches and homes, a deep joy finds expression in singing and instrumental music. A fine line sometimes divides worship and entertainment. Pentecostals sing in many styles, from the classic melodies of notable composers to almost every music style popular in each culture and region. Enthusiastic, sincere, and dedicated singing, as well as the playing of instruments of almost every kind, is being experienced all over the world in Pentecostal and charismatic churches. The music, guided by biblical traditions and a unique theology, is being sung on every continent and in almost every known language. Despite strong influences from the English-speaking West, Pentecostal music in other countries reflects, at least to some degree, the indigenous culture of the people.

Our Musical Heritage

Pentecostal and charismatic music has deep, strong roots that reach back through the centuries to biblical times. These roots, watered and nourished by early church influences, were kept alive and grew through the struggles of the Reformation and the powerful forces of inspired musicians and people of God. When modern Pentecostalism was born in the United States in 1901, the intention was to follow biblical examples of Christian living, worship, and communion. "These ideals have had great influence upon…Pentecostal music" (Alford 1967, 18).

Music in the Old Testament

The music of the early Hebrews (prior to 2000 BCE) was principally unison (unharmonized) chanting or singing. From about 2000 to 1000 BCE, the music of the Hebrews included instruments used for signaling, announcing military maneuvers, and calling assemblies.

From about 1000 to 500 BCE Jewish music centered largely on tabernacle and temple worship. King David set up a well-structured order for worship and music, with the Levites responsible for music administration and performance. A great example of music from this biblical period is recorded in 2 Chronicles 5:11–14. The occasion was a huge choir of prepared singers accompanied by instrumentalists using "cymbals, harps, and lyres" (NIV) and 120 players of the trumpet (*shophar*) at the dedication of Solomon's temple. The worship is a model suitable for Pentecostal and charismatic Christians today: The participants were consecrated. The musicians were prepared, rehearsed, and appropriately attired. The instrumentalists and the vocalists were unified as with one voice, and the music was praise and worship directed to the Lord.

Music in the New Testament

Fewer references to music are found in the New Testament. Nevertheless, music was important in worship and in the lives of believers. Matthew 26:30 and Mark 14:26 refer to Jesus and the disciples singing a hymn. At first there were daily services (Acts 2:46) mainly in homes. Worship was simple and informal. Psalms, hymns, and spiritual songs were the congregational repertoire (Ephesians 5:19, Colossians 3:16). God used the singing of Paul and Silas in prison (Acts 16:25) to break open the doors and win the jailer and his family to Christ. In the Book of James (5:13), the writer challenges, "Is anyone happy? Let him sing songs of praise." The apostle Paul in 1 Corinthians 14:26 teaches that, brought in an edifying manner, singing would benefit the church.

The Early Christian Church

Until 313 CE, when Emperor Constantine legalized Christianity in the Roman Empire, Christians were not allowed to openly profess their faith. Music, especially instrumental music, was limited to quiet house gatherings and often-secret meetings. In the following centuries, the church's music was guided and controlled by clergy. Monasteries and cathedrals became educational centers, musical conservatories, libraries, and museums. Bishop Ambrose of Milan (340–397 CE) encouraged congregational singing, but other influences gradually reduced the laity's role to spectator. There were two elements missing that would later prove to be vital characteristics of Pentecostal and charismatic music—spontaneity and Christian joy.

Reformation Influences

Reformers John Huss, Martin Luther, Ulrich Zwingli, John Calvin, and others believed music was a potent element capable of either positive or negative influences. Radical and uncompromising, they set out to correct abuses and establish new church-music patterns. The focus was on congregational involvement, but they prohibited instruments and song texts other than purely scriptural settings (mainly from the Psalms).

Seventeenth and Eighteenth Centuries

In seventeenth-century England, the Puritans were more extreme than John Calvin, whose teachings they followed. They wanted no church choirs and no organs.

"The Comforter Has Come" by Frank Bottome, 1890

O spread the tidings 'round, wherever man is found,
Wherever human hearts and human woes abound;
Let ev'ry Christian tongue proclaim the joyful sound:
The Comforter has come!

Refrain: The Comforter has come, the Comforter has come!
The Holy Ghost from Heav'n, the Father's promise giv'n;
O spread the tidings 'round, wherever man is found—
The Comforter has come!

The long, long night is past, the morning breaks at last,
And hushed the dreadful wail and fury of the blast,
As o'er the golden hills the day advances fast!
The Comforter has come!

Refrain

Lo, the great King of kings, with healing in His wings,
To ev'ry captive soul a full deliverance brings;
And through the vacant cells the song of triumph rings;
The Comforter has come!

Refrain

O boundless love divine! How shall this tongue of mine
To wond'ring mortals tell the matchless grace divine—
That I, a child of hell, should in His image shine!
The Comforter has come!

Refrain

They used only (unharmonized) metrical psalms for unison singing by the congregation.

Isaac Watts (1674–1748), an energetic and forceful Englishman, believed congregations needed updated Christian versions of scriptural texts, as well as other hymns and songs for expressing individual and corporate devotion to God. Songbooks and hymnals published in the twentieth century by Pentecostals often included hymns by Isaac Watts, including "Joy to the World," "We're Marching to Zion," "At the Cross," "When the Battle's Over," and "When I Survey."

The Wesleys

The Wesley brothers, John (1703–1791) and Charles (1707–1788), together sparked a great revival and religious reform in the eighteenth century. The Methodist Holiness movement was a direct precursor to the twentieth-century outpouring of the Holy Spirit in 1901. John was the "revival preacher," while Charles was "poet and songwriter." John, nevertheless, had considerable influence on Christian hymnody through his editing of songs, translations of Moravian hymns (from the German language), and his compilation of "A Collection of Psalms and Hymns for Anglican Congregations" (1737). Charles Wesley authored more than 6,000 song texts. His hymns are simple yet scriptural and poetic and more personal and intimate than those of Isaac Watts. Often included in twentieth-century Pentecostal hymnals are "Love Divine, All Love's Excelling," "O For a Thousand Tongues," "And Can It Be,"

"Hark! The Herald Angels Sing," "Rejoice, the Lord is King," and others.

Nineteenth Century

The Pentecostal outpouring was anticipated by a variety of religious preachers, composers, hymn writers, and songbook publishers appearing on the scene in the last half of the nineteenth century. American camp meetings began in the early nineteenth century. The music was simple, yet vibrant and enthusiastic. Thousands of songs were written and published with tunes and lyrics in the same book. Dwight L. Moody and his famous singer and musician, Ira D. Sankey (1840–1908) helped spread gospel music's popularity. Songs popular among Pentecostals included a large number of song texts to which he composed the music ("A Shelter in the Time of Storm," "Hiding in Thee," "Under His Wings," and "Faith is the Victory."

The prolific blind songwriter, Fanny J. Crosby (1820–1915), wrote the words for more than 8,000 songs. Many were translated and sung around the world. Her hymns loved by Pentecostals include "To God Be the Glory," "Blessed Assurance," "Redeemed," "Pass Me Not," "Near the Cross," "In the Twinkling of an Eye," and "My Savior First of All."

The Modern Pentecostal Revival

From roots reaching back through the centuries came the Pentecostals. Revival stirrings in Tennessee and North Carolina were followed by Agnes Ozman's Pentecostal baptism in Topeka, Kansas, in January of 1901. Then came the great outpouring in Los Angeles in 1906. These spontaneous and isolated events set off a worldwide revival and missionary movement. From the beginning years, involvement in music and singing (as well as the operation of spiritual gifts) was focused on the congregation. With no one specifically designated to direct or lead the music, a song might be started by anyone present, with others joining in. Occasionally a guitar, pump organ, or piano would be available to accompany the singing. These early Pentecostals were concerned with religious and social issues, and many of their songs spoke about struggles, a better life, and deliverance from "the sinful world."

African-American Contributions

Negro spirituals and black music made significant contributions to church music and laid the foundation for American black Pentecostal music that was to follow.

Black Pentecostals were identified with exciting instrumental music, stirring congregational singing, and, later, widely recognized soloists and choirs. They remained a vital movement all through the twentieth century.

According to black Pentecostal scholar James S. Tinney, different leadership styles, music preferences, and worship appear to have developed for blacks and whites. Yet the early years of Pentecost were strikingly interracial. The black preacher William Seymour led the famous Azusa Street Revival that "defined Pentecostalism nationally and globally," giving it its multicultural character (Synan 2001, 274). Bishop C. H. Mason was a black leader of the Church of God in Christ who ordained several white pastors that later joined the Assemblies of God. Early twentieth-century black Pentecostals created a number of gospel songs popular among both whites and blacks. These include the prolific hymn writer Garfield T. Haywood ("Jesus, the Son of God," "I See a Crimson Stream") and Thoro Harris ("All That Thrills My Soul," "He's Coming Soon," "More Abundantly," "Oh, How I Love Jesus," "Looking for That Blessed Hope," and "Pentecost in My Soul").

Black Pentecostals—both men and women—were influential in the development of black religious folk music related to West African and slave cultures. This music was characterized by improvisation, call and response, polyrhythms, and diatonic harmonies. Traveling musicians organized gospel choirs in black churches. In the 1920s and 1930s, black Pentecostal recording artists like Sallie Sanders, Ford McGee, and Arizona Dranes added new gospel songs to the repertoire, introducing new gospel compositions to thousands of homes. During the 1960s, black Pentecostals created music borrowed from "soul" and various pop idioms. Influences from this would evolve into "Contemporary Christian Music." In the 1980s, black Pentecostals such as Shirley Caesar, the Clark sisters, Andrae Crouch, Edwin Hawkins, Walter Hawkins, and the Winans governed the gospel music field. "By the 1990s black Pentecostals such as Ron Kenoly would shape the praise music movement with sounds drawn from the musical culture of black Pentecostalism and introduce the sounds of African-American music to Pentecostals across the races" (Synan 2001, 289).

Shape-Note Singing Schools

America's eighteenth-century singing schools, patterned after England's, created shape notes that enabled congregations to find a pitch through shapes without reading music. The first was a four-shape system (fa, so,

A Pentecostal orchestra in the 1920s.

la and mi). A seven-shape system (with each distinctive shape representing one note of the diatonic scale) soon was created, and it became the standard for sacred music. Singing conventions flourished among Pentecostals and others who would bring instruments and sing and play for hours and days at a time polyphonic melodies, folk tunes, and sacred songs. Shape-note books and singing schools declined in the last half of the twentieth century, but a few vigorous traditions remain.

Choirs and Orchestras

The first Pentecostal choirs were volunteers who went to the front and sang, often unrehearsed. Denominational Bible schools and training centers, however, began training musicians. By 1950, most churches had organized choirs singing three- and four-part arrangements, most with piano accompaniment, though some singing was a cappella.

Almost anyone who loved the Lord and could play an instrument was welcome to participate in orchestras ranging from two players to twenty or more. Male and female players, from young to old, played organ and/or piano, accordions, guitars, drums, and every other kind of band or orchestral instrument. Musicians played by ear or used notes from a songbook or something transposed or sketched by hand on staff paper.

By the 1950s, some church bands or orchestras were well organized and structured much like their secular counterparts with volunteer or hired directors. Gradually, sacred-music publishers produced orchestrations and transposed parts for every instrument. After 1960, elaborate musicals for choir, orchestra, and soloists (with narration and/or drama) became fash-

ionable for Christmas or Easter and special events. Publishers supplied taped sound tracks and/or printed music for orchestra.

Sunday School Songs and Graded Choirs

In the 1930s, Sunday school became an outreach and Christian-education method for children and their parents. Sunday school songs became a means of inculcating Scripture and doctrinal truth and were a huge success.

"Graded choirs" enhanced Pentecostal Christian education and Sunday-school efforts. Small churches sometimes struggled with a shortage of competent directors and accompanists, making it necessary to divide age groups differently. The choirs help children grow spiritually, musically, intellectually, and socially.

Missions Music and Indigenous Church Music

Much of the music used in Pentecostal and charismatic churches worldwide originated in the English-speaking countries of the Western world. The reasons for this are tied to patterns of missions evangelism, economic growth, religious development, and the general spread of Western popular music. In every part of the world Western pop music is played in cafes, restaurants, trade centers, and department stores. By contrast, Pentecostals today are placing increasing emphasis on indigenous church music, wanting to avoid any suggestion that Christianity is a Western religion. This is done by encouraging the use of indigenous instruments and the use of original songs composed by local Christians. The careful selection of folk songs or other local tunes, combined with Scripture or other strong gospel texts, also promotes this concept. The intention

The Voices of Children in Song

Many Pentecostal songs have been embraced as favorites for children. The following selections, compiled by Ruth and Stan Burgess, are from choruses sung by young people. (Gestures often have been used while singing many of these choruses.)

I
We're going to the mansion on the Happy-Day Express,
The letters on the engine are JESUS,
The guard calls out for heaven,
We gladly answer YES,
We're going to the mansion on the Happy-Day Express.

II
It's bubbling, it's bubbling, it's bubbling in my soul,
There's happy and singing since Jesus made me whole,
Some folks don't understand it, Nor can I keep it quiet,
It's bubbling, bubbling, bubbling, bubbling, bubbling day and night.

III
This little light of mine, I'm gonna let it shine,
This little light of mine, I'm gonna let it shine,
Let it shine, let it shine, let it shine.

Not gonna let Satan blow it out, I'm gonna let it shine,
Not gonna let Satan blow it out, I'm gonna let it shine,
Let it shine, let it shine, let it shine.

Let it shine till Jesus comes, I'm gonna let it shine,
Let it shine till Jesus comes, I'm gonna let it shine,
Let it shine, let it shine, let it shine.

---

is to provide songs with both words and music that are clearly a part of the culture of the people who are to sing them—songs with which the people can best express to the Lord their inner feelings and desires.

Music Publishing

Pentecostals R. E. Winsett and Seeley Kinney were among the first Pentecostal-music publishers. Their songbooks were published first as inexpensive paperbacks. Organized denominations began publishing Pentecostal hymnals in the 1920s and 1930s. While the earlier ones were weighted with camp meeting and revival songs, later publications included a wider variety, with choruses and traditional hymns as well as gospel songs.

Some of the more widely used books were *Songs of Pentecostal Fellowship* (1924, Assemblies of God), *Spiritual Songs* (1930, Assemblies of God), *Radiant Gems* (1931, Church of God), *Songs of Praise* (1935, Assemblies of God), *Assembly Songs* (1948, Assemblies of God), *Church Hymnal* (1951, Church of God), *The Foursquare Hymnal* (1957, International Church of the Foursquare Gospel), *Hymns of the Spirit* (1969, Church of God), *Hymns of Glorious Praise* (1969, Assemblies of God), *The Gospel Hymnal* (1973, Pentecostal Holiness Church) and *Sing His Praise* (1991, Assemblies of God). They are clearly repositories of *interdenominational* hymnody. Herbert Buffum was a Nazarene preacher and wrote many songs both before and after he embraced Pentecost ("I'm Going Through," "He Abides," "Lift Me Up Above the Shadows," and "In the City Where the Lamb is the Light"). Selections often chosen for inclusion in Pentecostal hymnals are compositions by Isaac Watts (1674–1748), Charles Wesley (1707–1788), Fannie Crosby (1820–1915), Frances R. Havergal (1836–1879), Philip P. Bliss (1838–1876), Elisha A. Hoffman (1839–1929), D. W. Whittle (1840–1901), Will L. Thompson (1847–1909), C. H. Gabriel (1856–1932), Lelia N. Morris (1862–1929), James Rowe (1865–1933), Thomas O. Chisholm (1866–1960), George Bennard (1873–1908), Haldor Lillenas (1885–1959), Margaret J. Harris (b. 1903), and B. E. Warren (twentieth century).

Pentecostal songwriters have contributed significantly to hymnbooks. These include F. A. Graves ("Honey in the Rock" and "He Was Nailed to the Cross for Me."), Cleavant Derricks ("When God Dips His Love in My Heart"), Vep Ellis ("Have Faith in God"), Jack Hayford ("Majesty" and "The Light Has Come"), Otis L. McCoy ("I'm on the Battlefield"), Ira Stanphill ("I've Got a Mansion," "I Know Who Holds Tomorrow," and "Room at the Cross"), and Andre Crouch ("My Tribute," "Bless the Lord, O My Soul," and "The Blood Will Never Lose Its Power"). Songs by these and other Pentecostal composers have also been featured at country-Western gospel concerts, and almost any place gospel is sung.

Unique Music

Pentecostal music has much in common with the music of non-Pentecostal Christians. There is music, however, that is distinct and unique to Pentecostals and charismatics. This includes hymns and songs with texts that clearly emphasize a Pentecostal theology as well as the phenomenon of "singing in the Spirit."

Singing in the Spirit emerged as a practice in the early twentieth-century Pentecostal church; it is simply singing in tongues. A main Pentecostal theological characteristic is the emphasis on the person and work of the Holy Spirit—including the exercise of tongues or glossolalia as the physical evidence of Spirit baptism (Acts 2:4). A natural outflow of this Pentecostal emphasis is singing in the Spirit. Biblical passages which seem to encourage singing in the Spirit include the apostle Paul's discourse in 1 Corinthians 14 concerning the use of tongues in corporate worship, with a specific reference (in verse 15) to singing with the Spirit. In Colossians 3:16 and Ephesians 5:19, Paul, under the inspiration of the Holy Spirit, urges believers to sing to one another using psalms, hymns, and *spiritual songs.* Logic tends to support Paul's teaching that public singing in tongues is subject to the same controls as public speaking in tongues (1 Corinthians 14).

A revival of emphasis on praise and worship in the early 1960s coincided with the Charismatic Renewal that impacted Episcopalians, Baptists, Methodists, Catholics, Presbyterians, and others. By the late 1960s and in the decade of the 1970s, this renewal was characterized by expanding traditional Pentecostal predilections for free worship, jubilant singing, and personal praise to God. It included dancing in the Spirit, singing in the Spirit (in tongues), and "praise singing" that sometimes mixed vernacular praise expressions ("I love you, Lord," or "hallelujah!") with tongues.

Glossolalia is spontaneous and has no written form. The same is true for singing in the Spirit. It is believed that the Holy Spirit orchestrates words and syllables, as well as the melody. A person in private prayer may speak or sing praise to God in tongues. It is more difficult to understand how a group, especially a large group, could be caught up in such a practice with each individual simultaneously improvising a unique melody and using his or her personal, Spirit-inspired tongue. But congregational glossolalic song has been evidenced many, many times, sometimes with small groups and at other times with congregations numbering in the thousands. The Spirit-prompted utterances are in ordinary speech rhythm with no prescribed beginnings or endings. The music is usually simple, yet the musical texture and counterpoint can be beautifully edifying. The practice of singing in the Spirit continues among a number of Pentecostals but is not as widespread as during the 1970s and early 1980s.

Outlook in the Twenty-first Century

Music and worship in Pentecostal and charismatic churches underwent considerable change during the latter part of the twentieth century. Improved communications media and the rise of megachurches and strong multicultural congregations brought a new sophistication. This compelled even the smallest of churches to evaluate the organization and function of their music and worship programs. Church-related universities are graduating professionals in the arts and sciences as well as prospective ministers of music and music teachers for local schools. These trained musicians, in turn, have brought fresh ideas and well-honed skills to the churches.

Twenty-first-century Pentecostal churches usually have a song leader with a small group of singers (a worship team) to lead congregational singing. A rhythm section (with drums, guitar(s), bass, and electronic keyboard) accompanies the congregation's singing. Many churches also use an orchestra.

In the last five decades, gifted Christians have had significant influences on church music. These include Chuck Smith and the Jesus movement in the 1960s, Bill and Gloria Gaither in the 1970s, Carol Cymbala and The Brooklyn Tabernacle in the 1980s, Lindell Cooley in the 1990s, and, more recently, Zschech and Hillsong. Pentecostal and charismatic churches have not escaped debate and controversy. There are many in congregations who resist the contemporary popular style of the newer music. Others, especially the younger generations, are eager to avoid what they view as out-of-date traditions in favor of music that is current to their own time period.

Pentecostal and charismatic congregations today use fewer gospel songs and hymns. Indeed, the majority of churches have largely abandoned hymnals in favor of choruses and songs projected on a screen. Texts tend to be vertically focused (praise to God) rather than experiential (testimony). Critics view this practice as a great loss for teaching Scripture and theological truth. Supporters argue that this allows for greater freedom and more personal expression in praise and worship. Despite controversy, there is today a rekindled freshness and spontaneity in many churches. There is a strong emphasis on congregational singing; importance is attached to the use of Scripture put to music; there is freedom of worship and praise. Many seek earnestly for a fresh outpouring of the Holy Spirit that marked so graphically the early days of the twentieth century and the revivals of the Charismatic Renewal.

JOSEPH M. NICHOLSON

See also Filled with the Spirit; Glossolalia; Praise; Worship

Further Reading

Alford, D. L. (1967). *Music in the Pentecostal church*. Cleveland, TN: Pathway Press.

Blumhofer, E. L. (1989). *The Assemblies of God: A chapter in the story of American Pentecostalism*. Springfield, MO: Gospel Publishing House.

Blumhofer, E. L. (1993). *Restoring the faith: The Assemblies of God, Pentecostalism, and American culture*. Urbana and Chicago: University of Illinois Press.

Conn, C. W. (1996). *Like a mighty army: A history of the Church of God*. Cleveland, TN: Pathway Press.

Goss, E. E. (1958). *The winds of God*. New York: Comet Press.

Johansson, C. M. (1993). *Music and ministry: A biblical counterpoint*. Peabody, MA: Hendrickson Publishers.

McDonald, T. (Ed.). (2003). *Empowered worship*. Springfield, MO: Gospel Publishing House.

Menzies, W. W. (1971). *Anointed to serve: The story of the Assemblies of God*. Springfield, MO: Gospel Publishing House.

Moriarty, M. G. (1992). *The new charismatics*. Grand Rapids, MI: Zondervan Publishing House.

Nicholson, J. M. (2003). Musical worship—A sacrifice of praise. *Enrichment*, 104–108.

Poloma, M. (1982). *The Charismatic movement: Is there a new Pentecost?* Boston: Twayne Publishers.

Rhoden, H. R. (2003). The essence of Pentecostal worship. *Enrichment*, 19–23.

Synan, V. (2001). *The century of the Holy Spirit: 100 years of Pentecostal and charismatic renewal, 1901–2001*. Nashville, TN: Thomas Nelson Publishers.

Tinney, James S. (1980). Black Pentecostals: The difference is more than color. *Logos*, 16–19

Zschech, D. (2002). *Extravagant worship*. Minneapolis, MN: Bethany House.

N

Nationalism

Nationalism is an ideology, which in the strictest sense of the word encompasses the concept that the citizen of a nation should hold the interests of that nation above the interests of other nations and, in the extreme, other allegiances. This definition of nationalism centers upon an understanding that a nation is a sovereign political entity in which the citizens enjoy a common culture, history, language, ethnicity, geographical region, or combination of features such as these and which acts as a unifying force in identifying the citizens of that nation as a distinct people. A key point in the understanding of the idea of nation is that a nation may not be associated with a state and a state may not consist of only one nation. Often the terms nationalism and civil religion are used in much the same way and even interchangeably. However, these two concepts should not be confused. Civil religion more closely describes the institutions that have arisen around nationalism such as rituals (e.g., the United States Pledge of Allegiance), icons (e.g., national flags), and national holidays or festivals that modern nations establish as unifying elements.

Nations and nationalism are realities of the modern world and interactions between Christianity and nationalism are inevitable. In order to appreciate the complexities of these interactions, an understanding of the academic theories that describe the origins of nationalism and the concept of nationalism as an ideology is required. Once these theories have been outlined, the history of interactions between nationalism and Christianity, and more specifically the Pentecostal and Charismatic movements, will be summarized. Finally, several examples from the modern era will be presented in which the Pentecostal and Charismatic movements are in differing stages of tension with nationalism.

Development of Nationalism

There are essentially two types of nationalism, one type arising from an existing ethnic identity and which excludes members of other ethnic groups, and another that arises as civic or political structures often with "artificially drawn boundaries" (Catherwood 1997, 27). Many of the African states are examples of where the underlying nationalist identity is based upon boundaries rather than ethnic identity, while the Balkan states provide a contrasting look at the development of national identities that are closely aligned to ethnic identity. To provide an understanding of the origins of these nationalisms and the concept of nationalism as an ideology, three of the more common views are examined.

Natural State of Human Organization

This view of the origins of nationalism has two essential subdivisions, the first is that nationalism is perennial, and the second is that nationalism is primordial. Although the differences between these two views are subtle, they are nevertheless significant. The concept that nationalism is perennial postulates that modern nationalism is a recurring and inevitable theme in history, as can be seen in antiquity, and that modernity and postmodernism will fade rather than nationalism. In order to support this position, some scholars have identified states in antiquity as examples of nation. Some, such as Conor Cruise O'Brien, would identify the origins of nationalism in the concept of the state of Israel, as presented in the writings of the Hebrew Bible/Old Testament. Others, such as Adrian Hastings, would identify the origins of nationalism as early as the fourteenth century in England. The second idea, that nationalism is primordial, is that nationalism results from environmental conditions such as religion, language, region, and race, and are so much a part of the human condition as to be fixed. Clifford Geertz and Harold Isaacs are two prominent scholars that hold to the primordial view. Both view nationalism as a natural state of human organization and assert that the factors that were essential in the formation of nations—economy, politics, and technology—are a weaker binding force upon human social and political structures than culture, language, ethnicity, and religion.

Product of Modernity

Probably the most widely held view of the origins of nationalism argues that nationalism is a wholly modern ideology that arose because of the economic, sociological, and technological changes that have occurred because of the Reformation, the Enlightenment, and the Industrial Revolution. Many of these social upheavals have caused the redefinition of traditional economical, political, and societal divisions. The nation, and therefore nationalism, in this view is not only required, but is essential in the stabilization of modern societies and will remain the primary means of organization of states in a modern world. An essential factor in this view of the rise of nationalism is that the factors that were essential in the formation of nations—economy, politics, and technology—have a stronger binding force upon human social and political structures than culture, language, ethnicity, and religion. In addition, under this view, nations generally arose in two stages. The first stage of nation building occurred primarily in the West and during the late eighteenth and early nineteenth centuries. The second stage of nation building happened after the general collapse and withdrawal of the colonial powers in the early twentieth century and then again in the latter half of the twentieth century. Some scholars, such as Benedict Anderson, argue that nations are imagined constructs with imagined borders, sovereignty, and community. Although imagined, nations are powerful entities, as long as the citizens of that nation believe in the nation. Still other scholars, such as Eric Hobsbawm and Ernest Gellner, state that nations are real, but created entities, which have arisen from the collapse of a cultural iden-

tification that has been redefined in light of new economical and scientific realities.

Both Ancient and Modern

The third view of the origins of nationalism, held by scholars such as Anthony Smith, postulates that the two forms of nationalism, civic and ethnic, developed independently from separate underlying principles. The modern nations, drawn from essentially arbitrary borders, such as the United States and many African states, are essentially civic in nature, and that economic, technological, and political factors were the more significant factors in their formation. The older nations, such as those in Europe, formed from an ethnic identity that is historical and preceded the nation, and in which factors of culture, language, ethnicity, and religion were more significant than the factors of economy, technology, or politics in the development of the nation.

Nationalism and Christianity

A tension has existed between nationalism and Christianity since Jesus said "Give therefore to the emperor the things that are the emperor's, and to God the things that are God's" (Matthew 22:21, NRSV), and St. Paul said "Let every person be subject to the governing authorities; for there is no authority except from God, and those authorities that exist have been instituted by God" (Romans 13:1). Notables of the Christian faith such as the Apostle Paul in the first century, Clement of Alexandria and the saints Polycarp and Irenaeus in the second century, and Tertullian and the saints Hippolytus and Cyprian in the third century have debated and expanded upon this theme for two millennia. However, it was not until the post-Reformation Church that nationalism and the debate between church and state expanded beyond this uneasy tension. The Puritans, arriving in the New World, believed that they were a chosen people going to a promised land. Two centuries later, the marriage of nationalism and Protestantism within the United States had solidified to the point that "The Battle Hymn of the Republic" had become a common Protestant hymn.

Nationalism and Pentecostal-Charismatic Churches

Rhetoric in the early years of the Pentecostal movement concerning patriotism and nationalism often centered upon the idea of pacifism and war. However, there were notable personages, particularly in the Assemblies of God, who commented beyond the bounds of whether a Christian should or should not take-up arms and addressed the underlying issues of allegiance to a nation. These statements, presented as they were by general superintendents and presidents of seminaries and published in the official publications of the movements, received a level of authority.

In 1915, Stanley Frodsham warned Christians that they should not embroil themselves in the conflicts of the world. Even though they were citizens of a nation, their real citizenship was in heaven and "national pride, like every other form of pride, is abomination in the sight of God" (Frodsham 1915, 3). Then in 1933, William Booth-Clibborn condemned the "fierce fanatical nationalism" that swept through the churches during the years of World War I and placed the blame for the empty pews of those days upon the church because it "prostituted itself to become the miserable mistress of Mars" (Booth-Clibborn 1933, 1). Myer Pearlman, in 1934, clarified the stance of the Church when he reaffirmed the statement by Jesus that what belonged to the government should be given to the government. Further, he stated that "the Christian conscience is God's private territory" (Pearlman 1934, 9) and that the Christian had a duty to defy the government only when the government violated God's law and the Christian conscious. By 1936, the General Superintendent of the Assemblies of God, Ernest Williams, shed further light on the distinction while writing in opposition to those who would prohibit saluting the flag and those who berated the leaders of the country during the previous election. Williams said that Christians are "also citizens of our native land and subject to its laws" (Williams 1936, 1). However, an undercurrent of nationalism began to appear in this same article when Williams wrote: "We are Americans. We are blessed with unbounded liberty."

For the next thirty years, rhetoric was mostly limited to exhortations to act as a responsible citizen of the nation, the world, and the kingdom of heaven while remembering that the law of man must be subservient to the law of God. Then, during the social unrest of the late 1960s, J. Robert Ashcroft again outlined the ideal for a Christian: to pay taxes, to pray for leaders, and to obey the government within the bounds of conscience. Once more, the tone subsided for several years until 1988 when George O. Wood affirmed what had been the established position of the Assemblies of God for more than fifty years: the Christian was required to be a good citizen, pay taxes, pray for leaders

of the country, and submit to the country within the bounds of individual conscience.

Today, Pentecostal churches such as the Assemblies of God and the Church of God, have refined their stance on the scriptural interpretation of duty and responsibility to the government only slightly and agree with the basic message that had been published for the last seventy years: that it is the responsibility of the Christian to provide loyalty and respect, and adhere to the laws of the nation, as long as individual conscience allows. Though this statement of doctrine declared by the church seems straightforward, in practice a tension exists between church and state, and respect and loyalty to nation often allow an underlying current of nationalistic fervor to surface. While the church officially speaks of citizenship in a heavenly realm, individual Christians and congregations at times exhibit nationalistic tendencies.

Africa

Some scholars, such as Paul Gifford and Rijk van Dijk, have argued that Pentecostalism within the African continent, or at least in many of the postcolonial nations of Africa, has globalized and become transnational in nature. However, despite the examples of globalized Pentecostalism found in Benin, Burkina Faso, Ghana, Malawi, and Nigeria, other nations, such as Zimbabwe, indicate that nationalism has a history in the Pentecostal tradition of some African countries. Since the attainment of political independence by the country of Zimbabwe, the Zimbabwe Assemblies of God, Africa (ZAOGA) have become increasingly involved with the ruling Zimbabwe African National Union Patriotic Front (ZANU/PF) in an effort to grow and legitimize the religious organization. In the mid-1990s, ZAOGA publicly endorsed the political positions of the ZANU/PF ruling party and sponsored a Benny Hinn Healing Crusade at ZANU/PF headquarters. An emphasis within the ZAOGA hierarchy upon the significance of the association of Ezekiel Guti, head of the ZAOGA, with President Robert Mugabe of the ZANU/PF further indicates the extent to which nationalism has penetrated the Pentecostal movement in Zimbabwe.

North America

While the United States provides for the separation of church and state, individuals within the church do not always choose to maintain that barrier. Every year near Independence Day, churches across the United States offer special services and events commemorating the founding of their nation. Many of these events such as the "I Love America" events at Westbank Cathedral Assembly of God in Marrero, Louisiana, and James River Assembly of God in Ozark, Missouri, draw large numbers of people, as many as ninety thousand in 2004. Other events in the United States, which have had significant coordination and organizational efforts by leading Pentecostals, include the "Washington for Jesus" rallies held in 1980, 1988, and 1996 that drew as many as 350,000 and at which the message and format had Pentecostal and nationalistic overtones. Special events are not the only examples of nationalism in the Pentecostal and Charismatic movements. Public leaders in the Pentecostal movement such as Pat Robertson have expressed the idea that the United States is a country with a special relationship with God. Much of this rhetoric is about morals in society and centers upon returning the United States to the Christian heritage from which it came.

Christian Zionism

Zionism is a specific form of nationalism whose objective is the establishment of an Israeli state in the land of Palestine and which first became a significant political topic in the late nineteenth century. Christian Zionism is Zionism within a Christian context and is closely related to a premillennial eschatological view. This view requires the establishment of the state of Israel as a fulfillment of End-Times prophecy and as a prerequisite to usher in the millennial kingdom of Christ. The premillennial view is the predominant eschatological view held by the Pentecostal and charismatic churches. Accordingly, the establishment and success of the state of Israel is often a key goal for Pentecostal and charismatic Christians such as the former president of Zambia, Frederick Chiluba. During the political campaign season of 1991 that resulted in the presidency of Chiluba, the Evangelical community stressed the need for diplomatic ties with Israel and tied the current economic and social conditions of the country to current foreign policy that had no ties to Israel. After his election, Chiluba declared that Zambia was a Christian nation and not only established ties with Israel, but also severed ties with Iraq and Iran. Christian Zionism also plays a significant role in politics in the United States where there are prominent Pentecostal advocates for the state of Israel such as Pat Robertson.

Future Trends

The Pentecostal-Charismatic movements have traditionally distanced themselves from government and taken an apolitical stance. However, as has been shown, there are times when the church courts nationalistic rhetoric. Sometimes the reason may be social such as the privatization of morals, in the case of the United States, at other times, as in the case of Zimbabwe, the reason may be a means of legitimizing the church, or the reason may be theological in nature, as in the case of Christian Zionism. While nationalism is likely to have little impact on the Pentecostal-Charismatic churches as a whole, it will most likely continue to have an impact on movements in localized regions.

JAMES W. BENNETT

See also Ethics (Social, Sexual); Globalization of Pentecostalism; Pacifism and Peace; Society, Pentecostal Attitudes toward

Further Reading

Anderson, B. R. (1991). *Imagined communities: Reflections on the origin and spread of nationalism* (Rev. and extended ed.). New York: Verso.

Ashcroft, J. R. (1968). God and government. *The Pentecostal Evangel*, 2838.

Booth-Clibborn, W. E. (1933). The miserable mistress of Mars. *The Latter Rain Evangel*, 26(1).

Catherwood, C. (1997). Nationalism, academia and modernity: A reply. *Transformation*, 14(4), 26–31.

Corten, A., & Marshall-Fratani, R. (2001). *Between Babel and Pentecost: Transnational Pentecostalism in Africa and Latin America*. Bloomington: Indiana University Press.

Frodsham, S. H. (1915). Our heavenly citizenship. *Word and Witness*, 12(10).

Geertz, C. (1973). *The interpretation of cultures; selected essays*. New York: Basic Books.

Gellner, E. (1983). *Nations and nationalism*. Ithaca, NY: Cornell University Press.

Gifford, P. (1993). *New dimensions in African Christianity*. Ibadan, Nigeria: Sefer.

Gushee, D. P. (2000). *Christians and politics beyond the culture wars: An agenda for engagement*. Grand Rapids, MI: Baker Books.

Hadden, J. K., & Shupe, A. D. (1988). *Televangelism, power, and politics on God's frontier* (1st ed.). New York: H. Holt.

Hastings, A. (1997). *The construction of nationhood: Ethnicity, religion, and nationalism*. Cambridge, UK: Cambridge University Press.

Hobsbawm, E. J. (1990). *Nations and nationalism since 1780: Programme, myth, reality*. Cambridge, UK: Cambridge University Press.

Isaacs, H. R. (1989). *Idols of the tribe: Group identity and political change*. Cambridge, MA: Harvard University Press.

Jewett, R., & Lawrence, J. S. (2003). *Captain America and the crusade against evil: The dilemma of zealous nationalism.* Grand Rapids, MI: W.B. Eerdmans.

Maxwell, D. (2000). Catch the cockerel before dawn: Pentecostalism and politics in post-colonial Zimbabwe. *Africa, 70*(2).

Motyl, A. J. (Ed.). (2001). *Encyclopedia of nationalism.* San Diego, CA: Academic Press.

O'Brien, C. C. (1988). *God land: Reflections on religion and nationalism.* Cambridge, MA: Harvard University Press.

Pearlman, M. (1934). Christianity and patriotism. *The Pentecostal Evangel,* 1047.

Smith, A. D. (1995). *Nations and nationalism in a global era.* Cambridge, UK: Polity Press.

Viviano, B. T. (1998). Nationalism and Christian faith. In W. R. Farmer, S. E. McEvenue, A. J. Levoratti & D. L. Dungan (Eds.), *The international Bible commentary: A Catholic and ecumenical commentary for the twenty-first century.* Collegeville, MN: Liturgical Press.

Williams, E. S. (1936). Our duty as Christian citizens. *The Pentecostal Evangel,* 1177.

Neocharismatic Movements

Any attempt to develop a classification system that encompasses all of Pentecostalism is fraught with great difficulties and requires continual rethinking and flexibility. In the 1980s such an attempt was made. Various groups in the Charismatic Renewal were categorized as belonging to the first wave (classical Pentecostals), the second wave (charismatics in the historic mainline churches), or the third wave (non-Pentecostals, noncharismatics, mainstream church renewal). The third wave was also referred to as the Neo-Pentecostals.

Problems surfaced soon afterwards. Several additional waves of renewal reached the Christian shore. In addition, historians of Pentecostalism began to recognize that many existing groups in Pentecostalism remained outside the triad described above. For example, David Barrett and others studying African Initiated Churches recognized charismatic-like beliefs, worship, and practices well before the dawning of classical Pentecostalism in America in 1901. We now are aware that other groups appeared in Finland, India, and elsewhere with glossolalic worship well before the twentieth century.

More recently an amazing array of independent and post/nondenominational groups were surfacing throughout the world, including what are called churches of the "New Apostolic Reformation."

In 1997 the eminent historian of Pentecostalism, Walter Hollenweger, called for a revision in the classification scheme. In 2000 David Barrett and Todd Johnson responded by introducing a new name and definition for what had been described as the "third wave." They selected the catchall term, *neocharismatics.* Included were 18,810 independent and indigenous churches and groups that cannot be classified as either Pentecostal or charismatic, but share a common emphasis on the Holy Spirit, spiritual gifts, Pentecostal-like experiences (*not* Pentecostal terminology), signs and wonders, and power encounters. In virtually every other way, however, they are as diverse as the world's cultures they represent.

The greatest neocharismatic concentrations of strength are in the prophetic African Independent Churches, in Asia—especially the house-church movement in China—and in Latin American countries, especially Brazil. Barrett and Johnson discovered that the neocharismatics actually outnumber all Pentecostals and charismatics combined. In January 2005, the total in Pentecostal-Charismatic Renewal was 588,502,000 (up from 523,916,000 in 2000). Approximately 60 percent were neocharismatics.

STANLEY BURGESS

See also African Initiated Churches; Charismatic Movement

Further Reading

Barrett, D, Johnson, T., & Crossing, P. (2005). Missiometrics 2005: A global survey of world mission. *International Bulletin of Missionary Research, 29*(1), 29.

Hollenweger, W. (1997). *Pentecostalism.* Peabody, MA: Hendrickson.

Neo-Pentacostals

See Neocharismatic Movements

Non-Pentecostal Christians, Relationship to

The extent and quality of relationships that Pentecostals and charismatics have with Christians who are neither Pentecostals nor charismatics can be charted on a continuum. If one end of the spectrum, A, is a total absence of any positive relationships and the other end, B, is the highest possible degree of positive relationships, Pentecostals are closest to A, charismatics are closest to B, and neocharismatics are somewhere in the middle. Of course, these are broad generalizations regarding a movement of great diversity. It also fails to reflect changes over time, such as the Pentecostal movement over the last century away from A and closer to the middle. Such a continuum, however, is a helpful starting point for our discussion.

Pentecostals

For decades after the initial outbreak of the modern Pentecostal revival at the beginning of the twentieth century, the participants in the movement were not considered a part of mainstream Christianity. The Pentecostals themselves believed that what they were involved in was the sovereign work of God in the Holy Spirit signaling the imminent return of Jesus Christ. They had been called out of the "world," including the godless denominational institutions.

Mainstream Christianity was just as willing to judge them outside the family. The Pentecostals, they said, were "holy rollers" (due to accounts of rolling on the ground in spiritual ecstasy) whose speaking in tongues reflected, depending on the theological perspective, either psychological illness or demon possession. The new churches were shunned and ridiculed.

American Pentecostals continued in virtual isolation until the 1940s, when representatives of a number of Pentecostal denominations were invited to become members of a new organization called the National Association of Evangelicals (NAE). This was a momentous step up to respectability. Pentecostals began at this point to assimilate into the larger conservative Christian milieu. In the years since, Pentecostals have served terms as president of the NAE and today make up the majority of the membership of the organization. Local practice varied widely; some Pentecostal pastors participated in ministerial fellowships at least with those of evangelical persuasion, while others never did so. Many others spent time with other local pastors only when Billy Graham came to the area for a crusade.

It is to be noted that it was the white Trinitarian Pentecostals who were invited to participate in the NAE. The experience of black Pentecostals reflected that of black Americans; much greater association occurred among blacks of various denominations than between black and white Pentecostals.

On our continuum, Oneness Pentecostalism has been and continues to be closest to A. The wall between Oneness and Trinitarian Pentecostals has been built and reinforced by both sides. Trinitarian Pentecostals, drawing on their orthodox roots, denounced Oneness members as being unbiblical. The Oneness churches, based on their belief that salvation necessarily involved being baptized using the formula often found in the Book of Acts, "in Jesus' name," pronounced unsaved all those baptized using a Trinitarian formula.

American Pentecostals have continued to maintain separation from what is considered the more liberal wing of Protestantism, most notably the World Council of Churches (WCC). The WCC, they felt, had abandoned biblical teaching essential to the Christian faith (e.g., inspiration of the Bible and the deity of Christ) and advocated social and political causes that were totally unacceptable (e.g., support of radical leftist groups).

The Charismatic movement that began about 1960 was initially rejected by Pentecostals, or at best was viewed with suspicion. When mainstream Christians claimed to have received the baptism of the Holy Spirit, yet failed to leave their "apostate" churches en masse and continued to exhibit worldly behavior (e.g., drinking alcohol, smoking, attending the theater), most Pentecostals refused to accept that God was at work. But some charismatics did find their way into Pentecostal congregations, and over time elements of the Charismatic movement, such as its music, began to infiltrate Pentecostal worship and practice. Pentecostals and charismatics mingled at large meetings associated with organizations such as the Full Gospel Businessmen's Fellowship International and with popular figures such as Kathryn Kuhlman.

By far the most earthshaking movement resulted from the Charismatic movement in the Roman Catholic Church. It is this development that has been most unbelievable for many Pentecostals. Even today, for many Pentecostals, Catholics are not Christians. They believe that the Vatican represents unbiblical teaching and superstition, and will develop into the one world church of the End Times. The only acceptable stance toward Rome, then, is condemnation. Roman Catholics, for their part, have even in recent years stigmatized Pentecostals under the category of "sect."

So it is noteworthy that at least some Pentecostals have joined the longstanding ecumenical dialogues occurring among Christians over the last century. Many Pentecostals continue to oppose such steps vehemently. Thus the beginning of a dialogue between Pentecostals and Roman Catholics was a remarkable development.

When David du Plessis felt God leading him to initiate contact with individuals in the WCC in New York, he did so with some trepidation. At the time he was the (first) Secretary of the Pentecostal World Conference, through which Pentecostals "learned about ecumenism on a worldwide scale" (Sandidge 1987, 28). But as he shared his testimony of the working of the Holy Spirit, he was, somewhat to his surprise, warmly received. His initial contacts have led to the dialogue now occurring.

In contrast to the formal dialogues in which representatives of the Roman Catholic Church meet with official representatives of other Christian denominations, the dialogue with Pentecostal representatives has not had the stated goal of leading toward eventual institutional unity. When the first session began in 1972, du Plessis and the others he invited to join him could speak only for themselves. The Assemblies of God received many complaints from their own ministers as well as their partners in the NAE about du Plessis' association with institutions and individuals whom they considered to be marginally Christian, at best.

There have been five rounds of what is described as "the Roman Catholic-Pentecostal dialogue" (Gros 2000, 713). For the third round (1985–1989), a few Pentecostal denominations for the first time sent official representatives. The most recent meetings have tackled the controversial issues of evangelization and proselytizing. Will Roman Catholics and Pentecostals recognize members of the other's church to be Christians? Past persecution and "sheep stealing" continue to affect relations today.

The stances taken by Pentecostal denominations toward ecumenical involvement vary widely. The Church of God in Christ, representing the largest number of Pentecostals in the United States, has been involved in WCC activities, probably reflecting the less conservative political views of black Pentecostals. A noteworthy example of ecumenical leadership among the white groups is the Church of God (Cleveland, Tennessee). It was among the few denominations that officially sanctioned a representative to the Roman Catholic dialogue in the 1980s. More recently, it has participated in and even hosted conferences sponsored by the WCC.

Many Pentecostal scholars refer to the breaking down of social barriers in the early years of the Azusa Street Revival (1906–1908) as a paradigm. The earliest Pentecostals believed that God was collecting and empowering people of all colors and classes before Christ's coming. The "unity" that Azusa Street spoke of, however, was of those who came into this Pentecostal experience. The Azusa Street newspaper, *The Apostolic Faith*, stated that congregations may "turn you out of church houses and the organizations of men, but not out of the one church" (Seymour 1997, 16). While the early Pentecostals spoke of the unity of God's church, they could not have foreseen the modern ecumenical movement any more than they could imagine a century passing without the return of Jesus.

Charismatics

On our continuum, charismatics are much further toward the B pole than are Pentecostals. In contrast to Pentecostals, who left existing churches to create new congregations and then denominations of their own, charismatics remained in their churches. Some members of mainline churches did join local Pentecostal congregations. But most found that personal renewal in the Spirit intensified their appreciation for their particular Christian tradition.

The story of the early Pentecostals was not that of the charismatics. Charismatics were as much a part of the cultural mainstream as were others in their churches. As a whole they were middle and upper middle class. Thus they escaped the nearly universal derision and rejection directed at the Pentecostals, who were mostly of the lower or working class. Their emotion and exuberance were more acceptable since these were people of standing in their communities. They also did not share the early Pentecostal conviction that Jesus' return was imminent and very few shared their predominantly Holiness backgrounds. Thus they were not characterized by the Pentecostal eschewing of anything not related to the winning of the lost. The Pentecostals' urgency to evangelize along with their relatively narrow view of what being "saved" entailed had been a cause for friction with other Christian churches; many in the mainline churches, given the Pentecostal worldview, were prospective converts. Most mainline congregations were angered by Pentecostal attempts to proselytize their members. In contrast, charismatics have not emphasized evangelism as much and thus have provoked less hostility from other Christian groups. In short, charismatics never made the break with mainstream Christianity that the Pentecostals did and so have not had to deal with repairing that breach. Rather, charismatics are much more ecumenical in perspective. Gatherings in settings ranging from church basements to football stadiums and the numerous conferences that were generated as the result of the renewal movement brought Christians of all sorts together as brothers and sisters in the Spirit.

This is not to say that the formation of charismatic groups within the mainline denominations has been uniformly smooth. At times, non-charismatic members of these churches have been hostile to the renewal movement. Most local congregations dealt with the renewal movement by developing services, prayer meetings, and ministries for the new sub-group. Some Roman Catholic parishes, for example, provided for masses that stylistically allowed for the more expressive worship style of charismatics. Other denominations resisted changes in the standard Sunday service but fostered mid-week prayer meetings and Bible studies where gifts of the Spirit were allowed within certain guidelines. Frequently the development of charismatic elements in mainline congregations resulted in tensions. If not monitored, a spiritual elitism could develop among the charismatic group. On the other hand, the non-charismatics at times were hostile to unfamiliar practices and what seemed to be emotionalism.

Most active opposition to charismatics within mainline denominations has died away, with a few exceptions (e.g., the Orthodox Church, Southern Baptists). Many have affirmed the positive aspects of the movement while rejecting unacceptable teaching.

Neocharismatics

This is the most diverse group from an international perspective and thus the most difficult to characterize. On the whole, however, they are situated on our continuum somewhere between the Pentecostals and the charismatics. They are not as separatist in orientation as the Pentecostals but are more separatist than the charismatics. This aligns with the working definition of neocharismatics as those who have formed separate churches and denominations rather than stay in mainline denominations as have the charismatics.

Neocharismatics, like charismatics, tend to be more comfortable, both economically and socially. In contrast to the asceticism often found among early Pentecostals, one observes a much more positive perspective of "secular" life in the present. Indeed, quite a number of scholars and church representatives have faulted neocharismatic teachers and pastors for espousing a "health and wealth" gospel, according to which God intends all believers to be prosperous physically and materially. Such teaching is often reflected in the preaching of popular figures on Christian mass media, such as the Trinity Broadcasting Network. For Pentecostals, identification and loyalty generally are tied to denomination affiliation, and for charismatics to ecclesiological tradition. Neocharismatics tend more to identify with a particular teacher or pastor, whose ministry has made a dynamic impact on their lives. Neocharismatics, then, will have less concern for denominational groupings or labels. This might lead one to expect that they would be more open to ecumenical efforts. On the other hand, those in what C. Peter Wagner (1998) calls the "new apostolic churches" that stress dynamic worship and demonstration of the supernatural are liable to the sort of elitism that has sometimes characterized Pentecostals.

While all Pentecostals and charismatics teach and practice the contemporary work of the Holy Spirit both in individual experience and in congregational worship, the neocharismatics particularly emphasize what are called "signs and wonders" as a demonstration of the divine presence and as a means of drawing unbelievers. This thrust, associated most closely with John Wimber and the development of the Vineyard Fellowship of congregations, reflects a focus on evangelism that has characterized Pentecostals more than charismatics. This inevitably brings with it the charges of proselytizing that have been leveled at Pentecostals.

Global Picture

Generalizations about global Pentecostal and charismatic Christianity are difficult for many reasons, including the bewildering diversity of the movement and the impossibility of placing many groups into clearly defined categories. Some of the groups tracing back to the early twentieth century reflect a European or North American mission effort, and some do not. The Charismatic movement around the world did lead at times to renewal within mainline denominations as room was allowed for it, but in many other cases, the renewal resulted in schisms and created new congregations and denominations. Much attention has been given to the widespread growth of independent Pentecostal-Charismatic churches, many of which have come to exercise considerable social and political power. This is especially true for Africa and Latin America, where the explosive growth of Christianity is largely due to the Pentecostal-Charismatic churches.

Many recent studies in Latin America have been done and provide intriguing results. Our three-fold distinction is nearly impossible to maintain, but certain observations can be made. Some of the Pentecostal churches, including those with the closest ties to North America, remain suspicious of anything ecumenical. Many others, however, have shown a surprising willingness to work with other Christian groups; the first Pentecostal churches to join the WCC were from Chile.

At times, Pentecostal churches join with other Christian organizations in harsh criticism of the doctrinal or behavioral aberrations of some of the rapidly growing independent congregations. The stereotype of Pentecostals as so "other-worldly minded" that they neglect difficult social, economic and political issues has been debunked. It is true that Pentecostals in past years have not been active politically, especially in contrast to the participants in the Roman Catholic "base communities." But this was more a product of social and economic forces than theology. In recent years, Pentecostal-Charismatics have assumed an important place in the political landscape of Latin American countries, and not uniformly as conservatives. Their politics, though, tends to be pragmatic and is driven by their overriding concern to preach the gospel.

Changes to the Continuum

Any Pentecostal-Charismatic Christianity true to its name will be vibrant and changing. Regarding relationships with other Christians, one can expect the following:

As a whole, Pentecostals will move further away from A, possibly bypassing the neocharismatics on the continuum, though the latter group is more difficult to predict. At the same time, new Pentecostal groups will form that tend to maintain attitudes of separation closer to A. Pentecostals, charismatics, and neocharismatics will continue more specifically to play a larger political role around the globe. They are more likely to be aligned with other Christian churches and denominations that hold to conservative positions on biblical authority and on moral issues, such as homosexuality and abortion. Such moral issues will be more important in interchurch alignments than will theological tradition. Though characteristics of Pentecostal Christianity (e.g., individual expression in worship) will continue to be adapted by other churches, trends suggest that some Pentecostals in turn will be increasingly drawn to more liturgical and sacramental congregations, and thus into fellowship with Christians of those congregations.

Robert A. Berg

See also Azusa Street Revival; Dialogues, Catholic and Pentecostal; Ecumenism and Ecumenical Movement

Further Reading

Blumhofer, E. L. (1993). *Restoring the faith: The Assemblies of God, Pentecostalism, and American culture*. Urbana: University of Illinois Press.

Cleary, E. L., & Stewart-Gambino, H. W. (Eds.). (1997). *Power, politics, and Pentecostals in Latin America*. Boulder, CO: Westview Press.

Corten, A., & Marshall-Fratani, R. (Eds.). (2001). *Between Babel and Pentecost: Transnational Pentecostalism in Africa and Latin America*. Bloomington: Indiana University Press.

Dempster, M. W., Klaus, B. D., & Petersen, D. (Eds.). (1999). *The globalization of Pentecostalism: A religion made to travel*. Oxford, UK: Regnum Press.

du Plessis, D. J. (1970). *The spirit bade me go*. Plainfield, NJ: Logos International.

Gros, J., Meyer, H., & Rusch, W. G. (Eds.). (2000). *Growth in agreement: Reports and agreed statements of ecumenical conversations on a world level, 1982–1998*. Geneva, Switzerland: WCC Publications.

Hocken, P. (1986). *Streams of renewal. The origins and early development of the Charismatic movement in Great Britain*. Exeter, UK: Paternoster.

Hollenweger, W. J. (1997). *Pentecostalism: Origins and developments worldwide*. Peabody, MA: Hendrickson.

Hunt, S., Hamilton, M., & Walter, T. (Eds.). (1997). *Charismatic Christianity: Sociological perspectives*. New York: St. Martin's Press.

Jackson, B. (1999). *The quest for the radical middle. A history of the vineyard*. Cape Town, South Africa: Vineyard International Publications.

Jenkins, P. (2002). *The next Christendom: The coming of global Christianity*. Oxford, UK: University Press.

McDonnell, K. (Ed.). (1980). *Presence, power, praise. Documents on the charismatic renewal* (3 Vols.). Collegeville, MN: Liturgical Press.

Petersen, D. (1996). *Not by might nor by power. A Pentecostal theology of social concern in Latin America*. Oxford, UK: Regnum.

Quebedeaux, R. (1983). *The new charismatics II*. San Francisco: Harper & Row.

Sandidge, J. L. (1987). *Roman Catholic/Pentecostal dialogue (1977–1982): A study in developing ecumenism* (Vol. 1). Frankfurt, Germany: Peter Lang.

Schaull R., & Cesar, W. (Eds.). (2000). *Pentecostalism and the future of the Christian churches. Promises, limitations, challenges*. Grand Rapids, MI: Eerdmans.

Seymour, W. J. (Ed.). (1997). *The Azusa Street papers. A Reprint of The Apostolic Faith Mission Publications. Los Angeles, CA (1906–1908)*. Foley, AR: Together in the Harvest Publications.

Synan, V. (1998). *Old time power. A centennial history of the international Pentecostal Holiness Church*. Franklin Springs, GA: Life Springs Resources.

Wacker, G. (2001). *Heaven below: Early Pentecostals and American culture*. Cambridge, MA: Harvard University Press.

Wagner, C. P. (1998). *The new apostolic churches*. Ventura, CA: Regal.

O

Oceania

In this article Oceania includes those islands normally identified collectively as Micronesia, Polynesia, Melanesia, Australia and New Zealand, and Indonesia. With the exception of Indonesia, Oceania is one of the most Christianized regions in the world.

The Fifth Evangelical Awakening

In respect to the renewal movements of the twentieth century, at the very dawn of the century there was an outburst of revivals that J. Edwin Orr has combined under the name Fifth Evangelical Awakening. Two of the better-known manifestations of this awakening are the great Welsh Revival and the Azusa Street Revival that gave birth to the Pentecostal movement. Less well known and documented, though, are the numerous outbreaks of Christianity that occurred throughout the Indonesian archipelago and the Pacific islands.

As a consequence of this fresh outbreak of spirituality in Oceania thousands of new believers entered the Christian faith, especially in areas that had either been unevangelized or previously resistant to the gospel. In many cases conversion to Christianity took the form of people-group movements or folk movements that embraced entire tribal groups. In this manner tribal people throughout Indonesia embraced Christianity, including such regions as the South Moluccas, Timor, Sulawesi among the Toradja, Borneo (now Kalimantan), Sumatra (among the Batak), and the island of Nias. In Dutch New Guinea (now the Indonesian province of Papua) the Dutch mission with only fifty or so believers exploded with inquiries incorporating thousands of believers into the church along the north coast, the Bird's Head region, and the surrounding islands. Similar interest and conversion movements also occurred in Papua and New Guinea (now Papua New Guinea) where tens of thousands of new believers were added to mission registers, and in the Marshall Islands (Nauru) a people-movement conversion resulted in more than half of the island's population identifying themselves with the Christian religion. In these, and in other areas as well, new converts were recorded as additions to existing mission and church activities, creating a new sense of hope and optimism for the Christian faith and for the West.

A second consequence of the Fifth Evangelical Awakening was the renewal of believers in mainline churches or preexisting denominations. For instance, at the Edinburgh World Missionary Conference in 1910, missionary representatives from Polynesia reported an unprecedented awakening of spiritual fervor throughout Oceania. Newly inspired missionary zeal among revived churches spurred new missionary interest in Micronesia and new missionary recruits from the American Board of Foreign Commissioners for Foreign Missions arrived in Guam. Simultaneously, in the nearby Micronesian islands of Truk, Palau, and Yap missionaries from the Liebenzell Mission in Germany assumed their duties with high expectations and positive responses from the Micronesian people.

Meanwhile, in Australia and New Zealand revival spread throughout the region fueled both by the new high levels of spiritual interest as well as by the organized campaigns of revival evangelists. During the first decade of the 1900s Baptists in New South Wales, Australia, increased by 50 percent, while the Australian

A young Toraja woman in Indonesia reads from the Bible at a Pentecostal church. *Courtesy of Douglas Hayward.*

Methodist Church grew by 60 percent during this same period. Under the impact of the ministry of revivalist campaigns led by such evangelists as Edgar Geil, Reuben Torrey, James Lyall, J. Wilbur Chapman, and others, Anglican, Congregational, and Presbyterian churches also reported new growth and renewed spiritual enthusiasm in their churches during this remarkable period of Evangelical growth.

The Birth of Pentecostalism

Typical of every Evangelical awakening, the new spiritual fervors inspired both theological and liturgical controversies. During this Fifth Awakening these controversies sparked the formation of numerous Pentecostal, Holiness, and independent churches as a third significant outcome of this period.

In Australia and New Zealand this resulted in the formation of dozens of Pentecostal churches including the Assemblies of God of Australia, the Foursquare Church, the United Pentecostal Church, the U.S.-based Assemblies of God, and many others.

In Indonesia the first Pentecostal missionaries arrived in Jakarta in 1921. They subsequently served in Bali, Surabaya, and other surrounding areas. The Pentecostal message quickly spread throughout the archipelago as enthusiastic new converts joined the fledgling missionary teams, and as new missionary recruits arrived to take up the task of training more local evangelists. One of the common criticisms lodged against the early Pentecostals during this period was that their adherents were from people groups that had already identified with the Christian faith so that much of this growth to Pentecostalism represented a renewal within Christianity rather than new conversions to Christianity.

This early Pentecostal endeavor in Indonesia officially registered with the government as the Gereja Pentekosta Di Indonesia in 1924, and in subsequent years splintered into forty other denominations as the movement spread into new geographical areas and people groups spawning new liturgical and theological challenges to their founding organizations. While these splinter denominations represent mostly the independent Pentecostal tradition, missionaries with ties to the Assemblies of God in the United States also began to come to Indonesia and by 1950 more than sixty Assemblies of God families from the United States, Australia, and the Netherlands were engaged in ministries in north Sulawesi, Kalimantan, and Java.

In Oceania the formation of Pentecostal churches began after the first Assemblies of God missionary arrived in Fiji in 1926. Once the Assemblies established their presence in Oceania the church experienced explosive growth, particularly during the latter two decades of the twentieth century.

The Charismatic Renewal

Beginning around 1963 the term "Charismatic movement" began to emerge as a way of designating a new renewal movement that was taking place within the older historic churches including the Roman Catholic Church. Believers not normally associated with the Pentecostal church tradition were experiencing a new outbreak of manifestations of spiritual gifts, including speaking in tongues, miracles, healing, and Spirit empowerment in ministry and worship. These new charismatics choose to be classified differently from the Pentecostals because while they share a common desire to experience the "fullness" of the Holy Spirit and accept the relevance of all of the gifts of the Holy Spirit for today, they have significant theological differences regarding the nature and function of the baptism of the Holy Spirit.

Measuring the impact of the Charismatic movement on Christians in Oceania presents its own special challenge inasmuch as renewed Christians have not always left their churches to form new denominations. For instance, more than one million members of the Anglican Church in Australia are designated as charismatics. Nevertheless the impact of the renewal movements can be established by noting the growing numbers of believers who choose to identify themselves as Pentecostals or charismatics in religious surveys (see tables below).

The Charismatic movement in Oceania resulted in three important developments for the Christian faith. First, it infused new excitement and enthusiasm into believers in areas where the Christian faith already existed, but in which believers had lost some of their original "love." The appearance of "new prophets," the excitement of miracles of healing, the practice of speaking in tongues, and the exuberant worship services inspired believers to seek the fullness of God in a new way, and to put God first in their lives. A second consequence is that the Charismatic movement gave further impetus to missions throughout Oceania, including Pentecostal missions. With the help of new missionary personnel numerous Bible schools and training institutes were established as channels for preparing enthusiastic converts to go throughout the region with their message of living in the fullness of the Holy Spirit. This resulted in an exponential growth of renewed Christians during this period of time throughout Oceania. Undoubtedly some of this growth can be attributed to the fact that as the gifts of the Spirit become more acceptable within mainstream Christian denominations, the newer Pentecostal and independent charismatic churches that were formed became more socially and theologically mainstream and less marginal to the Christian faith. A third consequence of the Charismatic movement was its emphasis on spiritual warfare and its aggressive confrontation with unbelief and other non-Christian religions. Missionaries and evangelists in the renewal tradition aggressively sought out unevangelized peoples or regions where a corrupt or folk version of Christianity prevailed, and, using miracles, boldness, and spiritual confrontations, they challenged local inhabitants to embrace a full-gospel form of Christianity. This had a particularly powerful impact on the conversion of people throughout Melanesia and Indonesia.

The Third Wave Movement

Peter Wagner coined the phrase "the Third Wave" in 1983 to designate still a third manifestation of spiritual renewal during the twentieth century. According to Wagner this movement is marked by believers who ac-

cept the need for and the role of the Spirit of God to empower Christians for daily living that includes the so called "sign gift" of the Spirit, but who nevertheless wish to retain their own denominational identities and do not want to be identified as Pentecostal or charismatic. In effect such people embrace the Pentecostal practices that emphasize the role of the Holy Spirit, speaking in tongues, ecstatic prayer, and singing and dancing during worship but they reject the labels that threaten church unity. This group is sometimes referred to as neocharismatics and their presence in Oceania is indicated in Table 3 on the following page.

As evidenced by Table 1, the entire Oceania region with the exception of Indonesia has become a highly Christianized area of the world. In Table 2 the growth of the influence of the three major renewal movements of the twentieth century on Oceania can be traced. In Table 3 Renewal Christians, including Pentecostals, charismatics, and neocharismatics, are identified as now representing some 17.7 percent of the total Christian population throughout the region (excluding Indonesia). This number ranges from a high of 47.2 percent in the Marshall Islands down to 2 percent in some of the smaller islands where strong social and family ties restrict the prospects of religious diversity.

Nature of Oceanic Renewal Christianity

As Renewal Christianity is the fastest growing branch of the Christian faith in Oceania, it is appropriate to ask why this form of Christianity appeals to the Oceanic populations. In full recognition that Pentecostalism is a global phenomenon that shares many similarities across regions of the world that are recognizably Pentecostal, nevertheless the Oceanic peoples have localized the Pentecostal experience in order to meet their own particular cultural configurations and their spiritual and community needs. The following three terms may best exemplify the regional character of Pentecostalism in Oceania: power, hope, and community.

Power is a universal theme in Pentecostalism but takes on a special importance in Oceanic cultures as God's provision for addressing the pervasive sense of systemic evil, witchcraft, and malevolent principalities and powers that continue to provoke fear even in the lives of believers from older denominations. Many traditional missionaries and church leaders appear to have come under the influence of Enlightenment theologies that deny the existence of magic and spirit beings and cannot address them. Spiritual warfare metaphors, power confrontations with demonic presences, and a

Table 1. Christian Population of Oceania Compared to Total Population

Region	Population in 2000	Christians	% of Population
Australia/N. Zealand	22,915,649	17,848,995	77.8%
Melanesia	6,482,345	5,824,069	89.8%
Micronesia	516,132	479,269	92.8%
Polynesia	606,421	558,219	92%
Indonesia	212,092,024	21,004,116	9.9%
Totals (exc. Indonesia)	30,520,547	24,710,552	80.9%

Source: D. Barrett (Ed.). (2001). *World Christian encyclopedia.* Oxford, UK: Oxford University Press.

Table 2. Number of Pentecostal and Charismatic Christians in Oceania by Year

Region	1900	1970	1990	2000
Polynesia	0	8,440	65,737	81,127
Micronesia	0	6,760	52,130	72,870
Melanesia	0	138,000	97,800	1,066,300
Australia/New Zealand	0	85,040	2,630,170	3,045,225
Indonesia	0	3,590,000	7,860,000	9,450,000

Source: D. Barrett (Ed.). (2001). *World Christian encyclopedia.* Oxford, UK: Oxford University Press.

Table 3. Number of Renewal Christians in Oceania by Category

Region	Charismatics	Neocharismatics	Pentecostals	Total Renewed	% of Christian Population
Australia/N. Zealand	2,156,331	669,059	226,725	3,052,115	13.3%
Melanesia	440,966	322,762	432,373	1,196,101	20.5%
Micronesia	24,479	5,213	41,295	70,987	14.8%
Polynesia	38,480	11,859	24,717	75,056	13.3%
Indonesia	1,137,702	6,875,909	1,504,390	9,450,000	44.9%
Totals (exc. Indonesia)				4,394,259	17.7%

Source: D. Barrett (Ed.). (2001). *World Christian encyclopedia.* Oxford, UK: Oxford University Press.

total commitment to God resulting in the enabling power of the Holy Spirit for victorious living, therefore, constitute a dynamic appeal for Oceanic peoples.

Hope is one of the promises of the gospel to its followers, but has relevance to the Oceanic peoples who struggle as entire people groups with issues of economic marginalization, unemployment, cultural disintegration, ethnic identities, rapid social change, even the powerful demands of traditional cultures that now place onerous or conflicting demands on their citizens. By participating in the shared objectives of a Pentecostal congregation believers are actively restructuring their lives to address the forces of chaos and stress in their lives and are able to create havens of resistance against the continuous waves of modernity that are sweeping in on them. During highly charged emotional services participants express their anxieties and

distress in an environment where the congregation gathers around them in support as the Holy Spirit brings healing and comfort to the afflicted. These struggles may be financial difficulties, illness, sorrow or loss, marital disharmony, rebellious children, personal moral failures, or emotional debilitation. In all cases, victory over them and over Satan is claimed, allowing the participants to experience a sense of shared strength and spiritual hope.

Community seems to be a strange outcome of a religious tradition that places so much emphasis on individualism, but the Pentecostal practice of embracing every inquirer, of walking with them through the rituals of transition and then incorporating them into the new community of believers in effect creates a whole new sense of a "community of the faithful." In the process of creating this new community, believers are often forced to renounce their old ways of life, their former religious convictions, even their own cultures in what one writer describes as a "scorched earth policy" toward culture. In spite of this high cost the dynamic appeal of the new community draws inquirers into the fold and is especially attractive to young people exploring the boundaries of their own worlds and willing to explore fresh options, or among individuals who are at the margins of their own world and desperate for new solutions.

Within the community of believers the weekly services function as rituals of solidarity and empowerment during which individuals affirm their personal identities and their commitment to the goals of the community and where they can function on behalf of other members of the community. In effect believers unite to form a transformational community in which they re-envision the world in which they want to live. Leadership in these meetings is almost always local and lay participation is encouraged. The Pentecostal emphasis on local autonomy for congregations means that each community has a maximum sense of "ownership" of their own branch. Leadership for these nascent congregations is provided by men who are trained in the more than forty-three Pentecostal Bible schools throughout Oceania that offer training programs. Some of these Bible schools require only a few months of training, while others require a full three years. Through these short-term and locally available training centers, leaders remain grounded in their communities while their education focuses primarily upon Bible study, preaching (often relying on a narrative style), and the search for godliness rather than on critical exegesis and erudite scholarship. They are in effect home-grown ministries addressing local spiritual concerns.

DOUGLAS HAYWARD

See also Asia, East; Philippines

Further Reading

Hayward, D. (1977). [Awakenings in Papua New Guinea; folk movements in Indonesia]. Unpublished research.
Orr, J. E. (1973). *The flaming tongue*. Chicago: Moody Press.
Orr, J. E. (1981). *Evangelical awakenings in greater Oceania*. Minneapolis, MN: Bethany House Publications.
Stewart, P., & Strathern, A. (2001). [Special issue]. *Journal of Ritual Studies on Charismatic and Pentecostal Christianity in Oceania, 15*(2).
Flannery, W. (1983). Religious movements in Melanesia today [Special issue]. *Point Magazine*.

Oil, Anointing with

We can define "anointing with oil" as the act of pouring oil (usually olive) onto a person or object, either for cosmetic purposes, to aid in healing, or as an act of dedication. Oil was widely used for medicinal purposes in the ancient world and the use of oil for anointing plays a role in the Bible and in the spiritual lives of Pentecostal and charismatic Christians. Although oil is still used for cosmetic purposes, Pentecostals and charismatics anoint with oil to enact God's healing power and as a public declaration of God's guidance, choice, or protection.

Use of Oil in the Hebrew Scriptures

The Hebrew Bible contains a number of references to the act of anointing, which is not surprising because in ancient Israel olive oil was used for cooking, medicine, cosmetics, lighting, and dedication. Anointing was usually performed with olive oil alone (plain or perfumed and spiced), but it sometimes included sacrificial blood (Exodus 29:19–21). Both objects and people were anointed. The Hebrew Bible records the anointing of sacred pillars (Genesis 28:18), altars (Exodus 29:36), priestly garments (Exodus 29:21), the Ark of the Covenant (Exodus 30:26), and the Tabernacle and its contents (Exodus 40:9–11). The purpose of the anointing was to set these objects apart for God—that is, to declare them "holy."

People were anointed to declare that they were set apart for special service. Priests were the earliest people to be anointed (1 Chronicles 29:22). The Hebrew Bible also describes the anointing of Israelite kings—for instance Saul (1 Samuel 10:1), David (1 Samuel 16:13), Solomon (1 Kings 1:39), and Jehu (2 Kings 9:6)—and even foreign kings—for instance Hazael of Syria and Aram (1 Kings 19:15). There is also an instance of someone being anointed as a prophet (1 Kings 19:15). Many kinds of people could do the anointing, including individuals (Genesis 31:13), priests (1 Kings 1:39; 2 Chronicles 23:11), prophets (1 Samuel 10:1; 1 Kings 1:45, 19:16), people of the land (2 Samuel 2:4; 2 Kings 23:30), and Israelite elders (2 Samuel 5:3; 2 Chronicles 11:3).

The anointing of a royal successor often superceded a previous anointing, as in the cases of David (1 Samuel 16:12–13) and Jehu (1 Kings 19:16; 2 Kings 9:3, 6, 12). There are two very different responses to anointing. For example, David refused to kill Saul because of Saul's status as God's anointed (1 Samuel 24:6, 10; 26:9–11), and David executed someone who claimed to have done so (2 Samuel 1:14, 16). Conversely, Jehu's anointing drove him to kill King Joram (2 Kings 9:24; 2 Chronicles 22:7) and King Ahaziah (2 Kings 9:27); both these kings would have been "God's anointed." A person did not have to be physically anointed to be considered God's "anointed." For example, Cyrus the Persian was called "My Anointed" (Isaiah 45:1) and after the exile, Zerubbabel was called Yahweh's "anointed" (Zechariah 4).

Cosmetic anointing occurs in both Testaments. In the Hebrew Bible it is often associated with gladness (Isaiah 61:3; Jeremiah 31:12; Hebrews 1:9) and fine living (Ezekiel 16:9; Amos 6:6). Ruth was told to anoint herself prior to her meeting with Boaz (Ruth 3:3). An absence of anointing was associated with mourning (2 Samuel 14:2) or judgment (Deuteronomy 28:40). The medical benefits of oil are described as both physical (Isaiah 1:6) and spiritual.

Use of Oil in the Christian Traditions

Although the New Testament does not mention the anointing of objects, oil retains its role as a mark of well-being, gladness, health, and even the presence of the Holy Spirit. On the level of hospitality, offering oil to a guest appears to have been expected (Luke 7:46), which resembles the use of oil in the Hebrew Bible. Again, the term "anointed" is not always used in a purely physical sense, as various believers are described as anointed (2 Corinthians 1:21; 1 John 2:20, 27). As a result of the Christian emphasis on "the Anointed One" (that is, the Christ), there is less emphasis on other anointed ones (2 Corinthians 1:21; 1 Joshua 2:20, 27) in the Christian writings. Although many Pentecostals and charismatics speak of "the anointing" in terms of a special preparation for service (such as preaching or ministering) granted by the Holy Spirit supernaturally to an individual, this should not be confused with the physical act of anointing with oil.

Two passages are likely to stand out for Pentecostals and charismatics regarding the use of oil in the healing process. The first passage occurs in Mark 6. After Jesus sends out his disciples, "they cast out many demons, and anointed with oil many who were sick and cured them" (7–11, 13, NRSV). Pentecostals and charismatics are likely to view all of Jesus' commands to his disciples as relevant to their experience and thus take seriously what they see as a mandate to heal the sick and preach the Gospel to the entire world. The second passage is the suggestion in James regarding the prayer for the sick, which is often invoked by Pentecostals and charismatics to validate the relevance of healing gifts. James states, "Are any among you sick? They should call for the elders of the church and have them pray over them, anointing them with oil in the name of the Lord. The prayer of faith will save the sick, and the Lord will raise them up" (5:14–16). Some assert that this anointing by elders should be viewed only in a spiritual sense (as dedicating someone's healing to God), while others see in James's command a call to use oil to enact or encourage the healing or faith of an individual.

Charismatic Catholics are familiar with the use of anointing oil through the sacrament of the "Anointing of the Sick" officially declared by the Council of Florence in 1439 CE and by the Council of Trent in the mid-sixteenth century. For Catholics, this sacrament is a sign and instrument of divine grace, and "the main object of the institution of the Sacrament is the infusion of sanctifying grace in order that the soul be purified from sin . . . In the Catholic Tradition, even when the major emphasis was placed on the physical cure as the primary and absolute effect of the Sacrament, the spiritual cure was never discarded" (Cuschieri 1993, 62–63). In addition to the oil specifically set apart for the anointing sacrament, Catholic tradition utilizes three other types of oils, namely, oil of catechumens, chrism, and oil that is blessed for the sick.

Although some Protestant groups have been more hesitant to accept the use of oil, many of them do use anointing with oil to consecrate leaders and missionaries for service or to pray for healing in certain circumstances.

Anointing Oil in Pentecostal and Charismatic Traditions

The use of anointing oil, especially in a healing context, flows out of the belief that spiritual gifts are still available for Christian believers. For charismatics and Pentecostals, divine healing acts a foreshadowing of the ultimate and true healing—that is, the resurrection of the dead and the reception of a new body at the coming of Christ (1 Corinthians 15:42–54). Although there has been no serious attempt to collect or explain beliefs and practices regarding the use of oil by Pentecostal and charismatics, it is possible to identify three key areas in which anointing oil is commonly employed.

Healing of the Sick

A common practice in Pentecostal churches involves a call (commonly called an "altar call") for those who are physically or emotionally sick to come forward and receive healing. Often this time of healing is initiated by a public reading of James 5, verses 14 and 15. The clause at the end of verse 15, that "anyone who has committed sins will be forgiven" has proved difficult for Pentecostals and Protestant charismatics to deal with, since most of them do not believe that the anointing process effects forgiveness. And for Catholics, even though the sacrament of Anointing of the Sick imparts divine grace, the anointing sacrament "can never, for any reason whatsoever, substitute for sacramental absolution" (Cuschieri 1993, 145).

Typically the pastor or a prayer leader gives the invitation for healing, inviting the elders to come forward and lay hands on the sick and anoint them. Often a small vessel of oil is kept behind the pulpit or even at the altar itself and it is then administered to the forehead, hands, feet, or any other relevant body part. (The pastor or church elders in a Protestant setting may or may not pray over the oil to consecrate it before using it in the service; whether or not church members see any special value in the presence of the oil itself depends on the particular community.)

Many Pentecostal and interdenominational or independent charismatic churches designate certain individuals as "prayer warriors" or have a "prayer team" (in addition to the elders) who are authorized to lay hands on congregants and anoint with oil. In many churches (especially with smaller congregations) it is more common to find that the church as a whole approves of any "Spirit-filled" individual operating a "healing ministry," and thus a wide variety of individuals can be found anointing with oil. In Catholic and Greek Orthodox settings the sacrament of anointing can only be given by the priest, although within the last decade some Catholics have claimed that there is no theological or scriptural barrier to a deacon or layperson administering the oil. Although the use of oil for healing by laypersons in the Catholic church is largely practiced outside the formal church setting, it is not entirely uncommon in Pentecostal and Protestant charismatic church services for an individual to claim that by a "word of knowledge" they have sensed the need for physical healing for someone in the congregation and proceed to call for individuals with sickness to come forward to receive the healing and be anointed with oil.

Consecration, Initiation, and Approval

Anointing with oil can serve as a physical symbol of the church's approval and blessing, reminding the recipient of God's call or purpose for their task. It is often used to bless individuals undertaking a missionary venture, special groups like mothers on Mother's Day,

A young church member is anointed with oil.
Courtesy of Amber Wachtl.

students embarking on a seminary education, or congregants leaving to begin new ministries.

Physical Protection

Sometimes oil is used to anoint church buildings, private homes, or even vehicles in order to ensure evangelistic power or physical protection. This particular use of anointing oil is often practiced by individuals who take the efficacy of oil itself very seriously. Although the anointing of a building or church vehicle is viewed as purely symbolic by many participants, others see the use of the oil as a physical token of the Holy Spirit that is necessary for ensuring healing, consecration, or protection. Charismatic and Pentecostal believers who are heavily immersed in what they perceive to be the reality of demon possession or demonic influences are likely to invest the oil itself with special significance and will often anoint "possessed" or "oppressed" individuals in hopes of attaining their deliverance.

BRIAN R. DOAK AND WILLIAM P. GRIFFIN

See also Anoint, Anointing; Healing, Gifts of

Further Reading

Baxter, J. S. (1979). *Divine healing of the body*. Grand Rapids, MI. Zondervan.

Bundrick, D. R. (1985). Hebrew bible background of anointing. *Paraclete, 19*(2), 13–17.

Bundrick, D. R. (1985). New Testament fulfillment of anointing. *Paraclete, 19*(3), 15–18.

Carlson, G. R. (1969). Anointing with oil. *Paraclete, 3*(2), 15–17.

Cuschieri, A. (1993). *Anointing of the sick: A theological and canonical study*. Lanham, MA. University Press of America.

Dudley, M., & Rowell, G. (1993). *The oil of gladness: Anointing in the Christian tradition*. London. Society for Promoting Christian Knowledge.

The General Council of the Assemblies of God. (1994). Divine healing: An integral part of the gospel. *Where we stand: The official position papers of the Assemblies of God*. Springfield, MO: Gospel Publishing House.

Hoy, A. L. (1974). The spirit as oil. *Paraclete*, 8(2), 17–21.

Menzies, W. W., & Horton, S. M. (1993). *Bible doctrines: A Pentecostal perspective*. Springfield, MO: Logion Press.

Parr, J. N. (1955). *Divine healing: An exhaustive series of Bible studies on this important subject*. Springfield, MO: Gospel Publishing House.

Thomas, J. C. (1993). The Devil, disease, and deliverance: James 5.14–16. *Journal of Pentecostal Theology*, April(2), 25–50.

Oneness Theology

Oneness theology, some form of which is held by an estimated one-fourth of Pentecostals worldwide, arose from the Trinitarian Pentecostal milieu of the early twentieth century. At a camp meeting in Arroyo Seco, California in 1913, Canadian evangelist R. E. McAlister (1880–1953) referred to the practice of baptism in the name of Jesus as seen in the book of Acts. He suggested that the first-century church baptized in the name of the Lord Jesus Christ to fulfill Christ's command to baptize in the name of the Father, Son, and Holy Spirit.

Frank Ewart (1876–1947), a former Baptist minister from Australia, spent the following year studying the implications of the baptismal formulas in Acts and discussing these ideas with his associate, Glenn A. Cook (1867–1948), McAlister, and others. He came to the conclusion not only that the baptismal formula should follow the Acts pattern, but also that the formula had theologically informative significance for the Godhead. Although God had three manifestations, God was not three persons. Moreover, Jesus is not one of three divine persons but the incarnation of the undivided Godhead.

On 15 April 1914, in Belvedere, California, near Los Angeles, Ewart preached his first sermon on Acts 2:38. He baptized Cook in the name of Jesus; Cook, in turn, baptized Ewart. In January 1915 Cook traveled east, proclaiming baptism in Jesus' name in St. Louis, Missouri, where Leanore O. Barnes (1854–1939) and the entire staff of her Mother Barnes's Faith Home were baptized, and to Indianapolis, where G. T. Haywood (1880–1931) and 475 church members were baptized in the name of Jesus. Haywood soon became an influential contributor to Oneness theology.

This nascent Oneness theology spread rapidly, so that by 1915 it had been embraced by a significant number of ministers in the Assemblies of God. A theological crisis developed between those who identified with Oneness theology and those who adhered to the historic doctrine of the Trinity, leading to the adoption of a Trinitarian affirmation at the fourth council of the Assemblies of God in 1916. As a result, 156 ministers who had accepted Oneness theology were expelled from the Assemblies of God, leaving 429 ministers who retained their Trinitarian convictions.

Christian Monotheism

The common emphases of Oneness theology are to read Scripture through the lens of its testimony to the unity of God and to identify God with the name of God. The Shema (Deuteronomy 6:4) is central. Jesus is the one God manifest in human existence (1 Timothy 3:16). The threefold revelation of God as Father, Son, and Holy Spirit is not denied, but Oneness theology sees this revelation as indicative not of three centers of consciousness within the one God, but as evidence of the full-orbed richness of the economy of salvation.

The emphasis on God's name is influenced by Hebrew theology of name, virtually equating God's name with God's person. To say that the Messiah's name will be Everlasting Father identifies him (Isaiah 9:6). The name by which God is known to Moses is Yahweh (Exodus 6:2–3). The name Jesus ("Yahweh is salvation") incorporates the name Yahweh, identifying the Messiah and describing him as the Savior (Matthew 1:21).

Because of its firm monotheism and emphasis on Jesus Christ as God, David Bernard, a prolific Oneness author, suggests for Oneness theology the term "Christian Monotheism" (Bernard 1983, 13).

A Developing Theology

Apart from these common themes, Oneness theology has developed over the past century as its adherents continued to study Scripture from this perspective and to participate in the exchange of ideas by means of printed publications and theological symposia. During the first half of the twentieth century, some proponents of Oneness theology embraced a variety of views that were largely discarded in the second half of the century. Oneness theology adherents continued to use the word "Trinity" to describe the Godhead, but with the word redefined. For example, the Pentecostal Church,

The first Pentecostal baptism in Jesus' name east of the Mississippi River.
Courtesy of Historical Center of the United Pentecostal Church International, Inc.

Inc. (PCI), which merged with the Pentecostal Assemblies of Jesus Christ (1925) in 1945 to form the largest Oneness Pentecostal denomination in North America, the United Pentecostal Church International (UPCI), included this statement in its preamble and constitution: "God is triune, a trinity. Three manifestations of one God, not three eternally distinct persons or Gods, as that is tritheism." Although Trinitarian terminology was not to endure in Oneness theology, the PCI statement revealed the chief concern of Oneness theology's adherents: They feared that Trinitarian language tended toward tritheism.

Although Oneness theology elevates Jesus Christ, emphasizing that the fullness of the Godhead dwells in him (Colossians 2:9), the Christology of some early proponents sacrificed or compromised the integrity of Christ's person, the hypostatic union of deity and humanity. This includes the idea that Jesus had a human body and soul, but not a human spirit. Instead, the divine Spirit replaced the human spirit. This was a form of Apollinarianism. Some taught that the divine nature withdrew from Jesus on the cross, leaving a mere human to die. Although this was not full-fledged Cerinthianism, which taught that the divine nature came on Jesus at some point after his birth (that is, at his baptism) and withdrew from him before his death, this view at least had a major point in common with Cerinthianism. Some taught that the Incarnation was not permanent, but that there will come a time when Jesus will divest himself of

his human existence and return to his preincarnate state of exclusive deity. Another line of thought was that there was a permanent manifestation of God before the Incarnation, the Word, which took on human existence in the person of Christ. Ewart referred to the Father, Son, and Holy Spirit as "dispensational manifestations" (Ewart n.d., 18), bordering, at least, on Sabellianism (in the sense of sequential modalism).

Some of these views faded in Oneness theology in the latter half of the twentieth century, but there is still a struggle to avoid and overcome the Nestorian tendencies of some perspectives. Some adherents still question the permanence of the Incarnation, and some wrestle with the integration of deity and humanity within the one person of Christ. Indeed, some want to identify the Son of God exclusively with the human nature of the Messiah, rather than seeing the Son as God as he is manifest in human existence.

Another aspect of Oneness theology still under development is the significance of the Logos texts (John 1:1–1, 14; 1 John 1:1–3) for Christology. Some read these texts from the perspective of Greek thought, but not embracing the Greek view that the Logos was merely reason as the controlling principle of the universe. From this perspective, the Logos was a thought or plan or idea in the mind of God from eternity, a plan that was incarnated in Jesus Christ. Others read the Logos texts from the perspective of Hebrew thought as developed in the Targums: the Logos is the *Memra*, God speaking or acting. Thus, the Logos is not the enfleshment of a plan, but of God.

Oneness theology has often been viewed as Sabellianism by its critics. In order to remove this misconception, the UPCI revised its articles of faith in 1995 to avoid a Sabellian interpretation. Although the Logos is identified as the Son only in the Incarnation, God is at once Father, Son, and Holy Spirit.

Commonalities with Trinitarianism

In common with Trinitarianism, Oneness theology agrees that there is only one God. Oneness theology holds that Jesus Christ is fully God and fully man, the God-man. It also affirms with Evangelicalism that Scripture is inspired of God; the Messiah's virgin birth; His substitutionary, atoning death; His bodily Resurrection; and His Second Coming. Oneness theology affirms salvation by grace through faith and not by works, although typically the normative pattern for the new birth is traced from Peter's Pentecostal pronouncement, involving repentance, baptism in the name of Jesus Christ for the remission of sins, and the experience of baptism with the Holy Spirit, evidenced as on Pentecost by speaking with tongues (Acts 2:38).

Distinctives

Oneness theology is distinct from Trinitarianism in a variety of ways. First, Trinitarian language—specifically the words "Trinity" and "persons"—are not typically used of God. The reason for this is that they are nonbiblical words; the concern of Oneness theology is that they impose meaning on Scripture not inherent in the text itself. Adherents of Oneness theology read "persons" as a reference to distinct and separate individuals on the basis of the current significance of the word. This would be tritheism. On the other hand, many—but not all—who hold Oneness theology embrace a variety of nonbiblical words to express their understanding of the terms "Father," "Son," and "Holy Spirit." It is common for these to be described as "roles," "modes," or "offices" of God. It is also common for Christ's ministry to be described as "Sonship." Like the word "persons," these words have the potential to introduce meaning not found in the biblical text.

Second, Oneness theology views communication between the Father and the Son as rooted in the Incarnation. Jesus' prayers arise from the genuineness and completeness of his humanity; like any human being, he needed to pray. With Trinitarianism, Oneness

theology agrees that the humanity of Christ was not overwhelmed or consumed by his deity, but Oneness theology emphasizes Christ's humanity as the basis of all references to the dependence of the Son on the Father and the superiority of the Father to the Son. In a very real sense, Oneness theology sees the Son as the human manifestation of the Father (Isaiah 9:6; John 14:7–9; 1 John 3:1–5).

Third, as it pertains to the Holy Spirit, Oneness theology does not see the Spirit as a distinct person within the Godhead. God is Spirit, and the Holy Spirit is the Spirit of Yahweh (Isaiah 11:2; 40:7). This same Spirit is also identified as the Spirit of the Son (Galatians 4:6; Philippians 1:19).

Oneness theology is willing to attribute personality to the Father, Son, and Holy Spirit, but it does not see this as indicative of distinct personalities. Evidence of distinction is due to the Incarnation.

Challenges for the Future

Although Oneness theology has developed significantly over the last century, it is still very much in process. David K. Bernard has assisted the movement in working past some of its former excesses and errors, but there is significant work left to be done. Within the broad sweep of the movement there are lingering traces of Sabellianism, Nestorianism, Apollinarianism, and Monophysitism. There is still some disagreement about the Son's preexistent identity as it pertains to the Logos.

On a practical level, the adherents of Oneness theology face the challenge of thoroughly investigating the historic doctrine of the Trinity so as to accurately understand and represent its views rather than succumbing to popular misconceptions and misrepresentations. Only by making the effort to understand a perspective with which they do not agree can they have meaningful interaction with those who hold an opposing view.

On the other hand, it is to be hoped that those who embrace Trinitarian theology will reciprocate by carefully examining the claims of mainstream Oneness theology, even as it continues to develop, rather than focusing on abandoned extremes to justify a quick dismissal of legitimacy.

If Trinitarian and Oneness theologians can refrain from drawing caricatures of opposing viewpoints, seeking understanding and doing theology in a spirit of godly reverence and mutual respect, they may discover diminishing differences and increasing agreement on essential points. Although the two views will doubtless never coalesce, God would be honored by a decrease in heated rhetoric and an increase in prayerful and thoughtful interaction.

DANIEL L. SEGRAVES

See also Baptism, Water; Trinitarianism

Further Reading

Bernard, D. K. (1983). *The oneness of God*. Hazelwood, MO: Word Aflame.

Clanton, A. L., & Clanton, C. (1995). *United we stand*. Hazelwood, MO: Pentecostal Publishing House.

Discipline (n.d.). Dallas, TX: The Pentecostal Church.

Ewart, F. J. (1947). *The name and the book*. Hazelwood, MO: Word Aflame.

Ewart, F. J. (n.d.). *The revelation of Jesus Christ*. Hazelwood, MO: Pentecostal Publishing House.

Graves, R. B. (2000). *The God of two Testaments* (Rev. ed.). Hazelwood, MO: Word Aflame.

Kärkkäinen, V.-M. (2000). Trinity as communion in the spirit: Koinonia, trinity, and filioque in the Roman Catholic–Pentecostal dialogue. *Pneuma: The Journal of the Society for Pentecostal Studies, 22*(2), 209–230.

Urshan, A. D. (1919). *The almighty God in the Lord Jesus Christ*. Portland, OR: Apostolic Book Corner.

Witherspoon, W. T. (2002, March). Who was Jesus Christ? *Pentecostal Herald*, 12–15.

Yong, A. (1997). Oneness and trinity: The theological and ecumenical implications of creation *ex nihilo* for an intra-Pentecostal dispute. *Pneuma: The Journal of the Society for Pentecostal Studies, 19*(1), 81–107.

Ordinances and Sacraments

Central ritual practices such as baptism in water and Holy Communion are understood either as *ordinances* or as *sacraments*, depending on which Pentecostal or charismatic group is using the term. Most classical Pentecostal denominations and others deriving from the Free Church tradition prefer the term *ordinance,* for the same reasons the Anabaptists and other Reformers did: it avoids certain implications communicated in the Roman Catholic view of the sacraments as imparting grace simply by their being performed (in Latin, *ex opere operato*, "from the work performed"). On the other hand, Catholic, Anglican, and other more liturgical charismatics continue to use the term *sacrament,* even as their understanding of the concept has continued to evolve.

Historical Perspectives

Sacrament derives from the Latin *sacramentum*, originally a translation of the Greek *mysterion*, or mystery. During the patristic period, the sacraments were understood to be outward, visible, and efficacious signs of Christ's miraculous and gracious power at work within the hearts and lives of those who participated in rites celebrating the basic Christian mysteries. Developments since the time of St. Augustine (354–430 CE) led to the dominant view during the medieval period that this inward or spiritual grace was not only wrought by the power of Christ through the Holy Spirit, but was also mediated by the priesthood. The Council of Trent (1545–1562) formally recognized and identified seven sacraments as these had come to be practiced by the medieval (both Latin and Eastern) Church: baptism, confirmation, Eucharist, penance, holy orders, matrimony, and anointing of the sick (also known as healing or the last rites in preparation for death).

Trent's formal definition was a specific response to various challenges posed by the Reformation. Magisterial Reformers like Martin Luther and John Calvin continued to use sacramental language, but most limited the sacraments to two: baptism and the Lord's Supper (Communion). These were the ceremonies instituted by Jesus himself, and the Reformers believed they ministered the grace of God only when faith was present in the celebrants. Reformers like Ulrich Zwingli and the Anabaptists dispensed with sacramental language altogether in favor of the term *ordinances* precisely because they rejected the idea that the Christian ceremonies communicated grace to the participants. Rather, they saw the ordinances as emblems, symbols, or expressions of the grace *already* imparted through Jesus by the Spirit.

While there is a wide spectrum of Pentecostal-Charismatic views on the ordinances or sacraments, most have been influenced by the traditions from which the founding Pentecostal leaders drew. Coming out of various Holiness, Methodist, and Baptist churches, classical Pentecostals questioned neither the language of ordinances nor their anti-Catholic bias. (The exception would have been the early Pentecostals in Europe, who were much more ecumenically oriented and therefore often accepted and used sacramental language.) Later Pentecostal alliances with Evangelicalism (since the 1940s) solidified Pentecostals' understanding of the ordinances as acts of confession that symbolized the obedient lives of Christian saints. Yet, whereas most Evangelicals regard the ordinances as merely symbolic and not effecting grace, most Pentecostals emphasize the various results of celebrating the ordinances, such as the experiences of revival, renewal, restoration, physical healing, Spirit baptism, and other such works of the Spirit. Finally, the Charismatic renewal movement that started in the late 1950s resulted in a situation in which many did not see any direct connection between their experience of the Spirit and their understanding of the sacraments (for those in liturgical or High Church Protestant denominations, or Catholic or Eastern Orthodox churches) or ordinances (for those in the Low Church and Free Church traditions).

Water Baptism

The significant differences between liturgical charismatic and classical Pentecostal perspectives on water baptism amount essentially to whether or not a sacramentalist understanding persists. The contrasts are most obvious in the administration, mode, and function of baptism. Sacramentalists (i.e., liturgical charismatics) insist on the importance of duly ordained ministers (bishops, priests, or pastors) performing the baptism, whereas nonsacramentalists are open to laity doing so (especially as some Pentecostal churches do not even have ordained clergy). Further, sacramentalists tend to baptize by sprinkling or pouring in contrast to those who come from Baptistic traditions and almost always baptize by immersion (except when such is not possible for the candidate). Finally, sacramentalists tend to understand the rite as effecting the salvific grace of God, regenerating the heart from original sin, and initiating the celebrant into Christian faith; nonsacramentalists, however, view it as a public confession of faith by the believer. The former see baptism as enacting the identification of the individual with Christ's death, burial, and resurrection (Romans 6:1–4), while the latter see it as simply signifying the identification that has already been accomplished by the Spirit.

Sacramentalists point to the baptism of entire households in the early Church (e.g., Acts 16:15, 33; 1 Corinthians 1:16) as support for this practice. The pre-Nicene churches disagreed on whether or not this should be done, but St. Augustine's argument eventually came to be accepted, that baptism accomplishes the regenerating work of the Holy Spirit, both removing the stain of original sin and effecting the forgiveness of actual sins (Titus 3:5; Acts 2:38–39). Nonsacramentalists insist on the New Testament criterion that only those who believe in their hearts and confess with their mouths can be saved (Romans 10:9–13). Hence, most classical Pentecostals believe that baptism should be limited to believers who have made such professions.

An exception to the general rule of Pentecostal nonsacramentalism is the Oneness Pentecostals, who deny that God exists in three persons because that compromises the monotheistic character of Christian faith. The Oneness view of salvation involves a distinctive perspective on water baptism in at least two ways: First, Oneness followers baptize not in the name of the Father, Son, and Holy Spirit (Matthew 28:19), but in the name of Jesus, according to the apostolic practice of the early Church; second, the Oneness understanding of salvation is that it occurs by water and Spirit (see John 3:5). This is why on the Day of Pentecost, Peter enjoins his listeners, "Repent, and be baptized…that your sins may be forgiven; and you will receive the gift of the Holy Spirit" (Acts 2:38, NRSV). In short, while Oneness Pentecostals do not use the language of sacramentality, they nevertheless understand baptism in Jesus' name to effect salvation, and their inclusion of the gift of the Holy Spirit as part of what it means to be saved parallels the sacramental understanding of first Eucharist and confirmation (usually during the early teenage years) as culminating the initiation into the Christian faith begun at infant baptism. The significant difference is that for most Oneness Pentecostals, the reception of the gift of the Holy Spirit is evidenced by speaking in other tongues.

The Lord's Supper (Eucharist)

Liturgical sacramental and classical Pentecostal perspectives on Communion also break down to sacramentalist and nonsacramentalist understandings. A primary issue concerns the question of the presence of Christ. Catholic charismatic perspectives have attempted to remain faithful to the doctrine of the Eucharist articulated at the Council of Trent. Some retain a fairly traditional notion of transubstantiation, whereby the Eucharist mediates the saving grace of God because the consecrated elements (usually unleavened bread and wine) are transformed into the body and blood of Christ, thereby reenacting the sacrifice of Christ for the sins of the world. This not only takes seriously the explicit teachings of Jesus—"This is my body….This is my blood," and "unless you eat the flesh of the Son of Man and drink his blood, you have no life in you" (John 6:53ff.)—but also is explicated using the Aristotelian metaphysics of accidents and substances. Other Catholic charismatics prefer a less literal interpretation whereby the Eucharist is considered to be the "Gospel enfleshed" by the Holy Spirit. In this view, the Eucharist becomes the chief means through which the Holy Spirit empowers, forms, and expresses the body of Christ on earth.

Classical Pentecostals, of course, talk about neither the Eucharist nor Mass, but about the Lord's Supper or Holy Communion. They interpret the language of Jesus figuratively and therefore reject the Catholic doctrine of transubstantiation (and usually its Lutheran variant, consubstantiation). Rather, they emphasize either the language of memorial reflected in the New Testament—e.g., "Do this is remembrance of me"—and retrieved by Zwingli and the Anabaptists, or the language of the "new covenant," in which Communion is a sign, like circumcision was a sign of the "old covenant." Further, reflecting also the dominant Holiness ethos of early modern Pentecostalism, most Pentecostals do not allow the "fruit of the vine" (Matthew 26:29) to become fermented. On the question of who can participate, Pentecostals differ from Catholic charismatics in at least two ways. First, in keeping with their understanding of believer's baptism, only adults and those children who have come to the point of being able to "examine themselves" (see 1 Corinthians 11:28–29) are allowed to partake. Second, unlike the Catholic view, which connects the Eucharist to baptism in such a way that only those baptized into the Church can partake, most Pentecostals practice an open Communion table, around which all believers are welcomed. Additionally, in contrast to the weekly Eucharist celebrations of Catholics and most charismatic sacramentalists, Pentecostal denominations and churches have no standard schedule of celebration.

Recent ecumenical developments, however, hold promise for those seeking a convergence of classical Pentecostal and Catholic charismatic understandings of rituals like Communion. Ecumenical documents like *Baptism, Eucharist and Ministry* (1982) emphasize the Holy Spirit's role in the Supper, beginning the ceremony with a prayer (*epiclesis*) inviting the Spirit's presence amidst the congregation gathered around the meal. The Spirit then helps congregants remember (*anamnesis*), not just all that Jesus said and did, but also all the ways believers can appropriate the life, death, and Resurrection of Christ in their daily lives. The fellowship around the table is thereby enlivened and edifying, transformed by the presence and activity of the Spirit. In these ways, the past is rendered present by the Spirit, in anticipation of the future return of Christ.

Other Ordinances/Sacraments

Pentecostals practice some of the traditional seven sacraments recognized by Catholic and Orthodox charismatics, while identifying them as ordinances; but some Pentecostals have a number of additional rites they also understand as ordinances. A few smaller classical Pentecostal groups include foot washing among the ordinances instituted by Christ, although most others regard this practice as merely an example set by Jesus regarding mutual Christian servitude. In today's social context, Pentecostals who practice foot washing consider it to be an important witness in overcoming racism, classism, and sexism. In addition to foot washing, various smaller groups of Pentecostals identify other traditional practices as ordinances through which the Holy Spirit works, such as the laying on of hands or anointing (especially the sick) with oil.

These smaller groups within Pentecostalism tend to believe, like sacramentalists, that the Holy Spirit heals in and through the ordinances (sacraments). Within the Pentecostal theological academy, there has also developed a recognition that, insofar as the traditional notion of sacramentality understands divine grace to be mediated through physical realities, Pentecostal experience too can be understood as sacramental, since the Holy Spirit is seen to be working through real human bodies and human congregations—in glossolalia, the dance, the shout, the clap, being slain in the Spirit, and other phenomena. In each of these ways, Pentecostal doctrines and practices exhibit dynamic fluidity.

Present and Future Issues

Undoubtedly, there will be an ongoing convergence of understanding regarding ordinances and sacraments as Pentecostals and liturgical charismatics continue their dialogues with one another. Just as some Pentecostals have begun to see the value of sacramental perspectives, so too have recent developments in Catholic sacramental theology emphasized Christ's humanity as the primordial or fundamental sacrament mediating the salvific grace of God, and, in turn, the church and its rites as secondary sacraments (as the body of Christ). While Pentecostals have come to value the communal aspect of the ordinances, sacramentalists are also emphasizing the need for personal faith alongside the faith of the community. Further, Pentecostals are also increasingly talking about the physical, psychological, and spiritual benefits experienced through the ordinances, while sacramentalists are acknowledging them also as acts of obedience. In these and other ways, future dialogue will clarify the respective contributions of classical Pentecostals and liturgical sacramentalists toward a more complete understanding of these central Christian mysteries.

AMOS YONG

See also Baptism, Water; Communion (Eucharist)

Further Reading

Baptism, eucharist and ministry (1982). Faith and Order Paper No. 111. Geneva, Switzerland: World Council of Churches.

Beall, J. L. (1974). *Rise, to newness of life: A look at water baptism*. Detroit, MI: Evangel.

Bernard, D. (1984). *The new birth*. Hazelwood, MO: Word Aflame.

Bicknell, R. (1998). The ordinances: The marginalised aspects of Pentecostalism. In K. Warrington (Ed.), *Pentecostal distinctives* (pp. 204–222). Carlisle, UK: Paternoster.

Gortner, J. N., Gee, D., & Pickering, H. (n.d.). *Water baptism and the Trinity*. Springfield, MO: Gospel Publishing House.

Gunstone, J. (1994). *Pentecost comes to church: Sacraments and spiritual gifts*. London: Darton, Longman and Todd.

Hocken, P. (2001). *Blazing the trail: Where is the Holy Spirit leading the church?* Stoke-on-Trent, UK: Bible Alive.

Kärkkäinen, V.-M. (2002). The spirit and the Lord's Supper. In A. Yong (Ed.), *Toward a pneumatological theology: Pentecostal and ecumenical perspectives on ecclesiology, soteriology, and theology of mission* (Ch. 10). New York: University Press of America.

Lancaster, J. (1976). The ordinances. In P. S. Brewster (Ed.), *Pentecostal doctrine* (pp. 79–92). Cheltenham, UK: Greenhurst Press.

Macchia, F. D. (1993). Tongues as a sign: Toward a sacramental understanding of Pentecostal experience. *Pneuma: The Journal of the Society for Pentecostal Studies, 15*(1), 61–76.

Macchia, F. D. (1997). Is foot washing the neglected sacrament? A theological response to John Christopher Thomas. *Pneuma: The Journal of the Society for Pentecostal Studies, 19*(2), 225–238.

Osborne, K. B. (1988). *Sacramental theology: A general introduction*. Mahwah, NJ: Paulist Press.

Tan, S. G. H. (2003). Reassessing believer's baptism in Pentecostal theology and practice. *Asia Journal of Pentecostal Studies, 6*(2), 219–234.

Yong, A. (2005). *The Spirit poured out on all flesh: World Pentecostalism and the reconstruction of Christian theology in the twenty-first century*. Grand Rapids, MI: Baker Academic.

Orthodoxy, Eastern

No portion of the contemporary Christian church has been more resistant to the modern Pentecostal and charismatic movements than Eastern Orthodoxy in its many forms. At the same time, no branch of Christianity has been more charismatic in both theology and practice during most of the first two millennia of the church's history than Orthodoxy. In large measure, Orthodox resistance to modern charismatic overtures seems to stem from their belief that they have long experienced and taught what the West is just now discovering.

Eastern fathers are known for their more balanced emphasis on the entire Trinity, together with the relationships between members of the Trinity. Basil of Caesarea, the famous fourth-century Cappadocian father, wrote what many consider the most seminal work on the Holy Spirit—considering the Spirit in Trinitarian context. Together with the other Cappadocian greats, Gregory of Nyssa and Gregory of Nazianzen, Basil added the insight that each hypostasis in the Godhead indwells and reciprocates with the other two. From this synthesis came the "three in one" concept that has remained the basis of Orthodoxy from the time of the Council of Constantinople (381). Basil's grasp of the full range of the Holy Spirit's work in the life of believers is perhaps the most exceptional in the ancient world. As the Spirit is the conductor of the symphony of creation, so he is also creator of the church—again a symphony operating in the harmony of the Spirit, which sanctifies all of creation through the work of the Spirit. The church is composed of individual members, each of whom is assigned a particular charisma by the Spirit. Life in the Spirit occurs when there is mutual cooperation by its members in the exercise and participation of the individual gifts.

Throughout the history of Eastern Orthodoxy, there are examples of mystics who insist with great emphasis upon the need for all baptized Christians to experience a direct and conscious awareness of the indwelling Holy Spirit. In a seminal paper (1997), Kallistos Ware, Bishop of Diokleia, describes the "Personal Experience of the Holy Spirit according to the Greek Fathers." He clearly demonstrates that the fourth-century ascetics Mark the Monk and pseudo-Macarius of Egypt, together with John Climacus, author of the seventh-century Ladder of Divine Ascent, place great importance on the indwelling presence of the divine Spirit and on gaining full awareness of the Spirit who dwells within from the time of baptism.

Pseudo-Macarius speaks of ecstatic experiences, while John Climacus describes the charisma of spiritual tears that accompanies the ascent of the Ladder. Symeon the New Theologian (949–1022) disagrees with Mark the Monk that one can possess the divine Spirit without knowing it. He insists that the greatest heresy of his time is the teaching that it was impossible to experience the Holy Spirit in the same measure as did the first-century church. Kallistos Ware attempts to demonstrate that Symeon's second baptism, that of the Spirit with the accompanying gift of tears and experience of God as light, is the full realization of sacramental baptism, not a new and different grace. George Maloney (1980) disagrees, recognizing Symeon's clear attempt to distinguish the two baptisms and directly likening his baptism in the Spirit to that of modern charismatics.

Three centuries after Symeon, another Byzantine monk, Gregory Palamas (1296–1359), faced the same issue of whether God can be fully and directly experienced. He argued against the teachings of the rationalist Barlaam the Calabrian, who rejected the claims by the Hesychasts (Byzantine mystics) of spiritual knowledge of God. Palamas argued that God cannot be known, communicated with, or participated in as he is in his essence. But he can be known, communicated with, and participated in as he is in his energies—the uncreated light that took on flesh in Jesus Christ and the deifying gift of the Holy Spirit. In his energies, God reveals himself positively to the spiritual senses, without losing anything of his transcendence. The saints become instruments of the Holy Spirit, having received the same energy as he has. As proof of this, Palamas cited such graces as the gifts of healing, miracles, foreknowledge, irrefutable wisdom, diverse tongues, interpretation of tongues, and the word of knowledge. He lays particular emphasis on the practice of "Paul's laying on of hands" for receiving such gifts. A person also may experience ecstasy, a condition in which human powers are elevated above their natural states, so that the individual receives a vision of divine light and is received into that light.

With Palamas the Eastern Christian tradition of experiencing God received its most accepted theoretical explanation. Numerous Eastern saints and mystics since the fourteenth century have experienced God as light, with gifts of tears and healing. One such was Seraphim of Sarov (1759–1833), a Russian Orthodox Charismatic leader, who experienced repeated healings and spiritual raptures as a boy and young adult. In 1831, Seraphim informed Nicholas Motovilov that the true end of the Christian life was the acquisition of the Holy Spirit. The evidence for the reception of the Spirit was a transfiguration experience, being transformed while still in the flesh into divine light. To the Eastern mystic, this is the process by which theosis, or deification, is achieved. With this Orthodox heritage, rich in both pneumatological definition and spiritual experi-

ence, the Pentecostal and Charismatic movements of the twentieth century should not have been perceived so negatively.

The case of Father Eusebius A. Stephanou (b. 1924) serves to illustrate the seeming dichotomy between contemporary Orthodoxy in doctrine and Orthodoxy in actual practice. Stephanou was ordained a priest in Greece in 1953 and pastored Greek Orthodox churches in Michigan, Massachusetts, Ohio, Illinois, and Indiana. From 1955–1962 he served on the faculty of Holy Cross Greek Orthodox Seminary as professor of theology. He later taught in the department of theology at Notre Dame University as visiting professor (1967–1968). In 1968 Stephanou founded the Logos Ministry for Orthodox Renewal and began publication of the Logos monthly periodical. He also embarked on an itinerant ministry of evangelism among Orthodox Christians in the United States and abroad, including such countries as Greece, Australia, Cyprus, and Kenya. In 1972 he received the baptism in the Holy Spirit, having been introduced to the Charismatic Renewal by fellow Orthodox priest, Athanasius Emmert. Thereafter he has been actively involved in the Holy Spirit renewal. He soon was recognized inside and outside his church as a leader in the Orthodox renewal. Between 1972 and 1978, and then again in 1986 and 1987, he sponsored the first five annual Orthodox Charismatic conferences. His communication center was located in Fort Wayne, Indiana, until 1988, when he relocated to Destin, Florida. His ministry of evangelism has stressed an End-Times message of salvation, healing, and deliverance. He has attempted to demonstrate to the worldwide Orthodox community that the Charismatic Renewal can find a natural home in the Orthodox church because it is the church par excellence that has been intrinsically charismatic for almost two millennia. Stephanou's outreach has met with misunderstanding and even the opposition of the official Orthodox church. He had been placed under suspension off and on since 1968. In 1986 he was notified that proceedings were in progress for the purpose of defrocking him. However, the petition of the Greek Orthodox Archdiocese of North and South America was turned down by the Ecumenical Patriarch of Constantinople. Reformers who demand change are often denigrated by their change-resistant peers. In this, Stephanou is similar to his spiritual ancestor, Symeon the New Theologian.

STANLEY M. BURGESS

See also Holy Spirit; Trinitarianism

Further Reading

Burgess, S. (1989). *The Holy Spirit: Eastern Christian traditions.* Peabody, MA: Hendrickson.

Burgess, S. (1991). Implications of eastern Christian pneumatology for western Pentecostal doctrine and practice. In Jan A. A. Jongeneel (Ed.), *Experiences of the Spirit, Studien zur interkultureen Geschichte des Christentums, 68,* 23–34.

Maloney, G. (1980). *Introduction to Symeon the New Theologian: The discourses.* New York: Paulist Press.

Meyendorff, J. (1974). *Byzantine Theology: Historical trends and doctrinal themes.* New York: Fordham University Press.

Ware, K (1997, September). *Personal experience of the Holy Spirit according to the Greek fathers.* Paper presented at the European Pentecostal/Charismatic Research Conference, Prague, Czech Republic.

Ware, T. (Kallistos). (1963). *The Orthodox Church.* New York: Penguin.

P

Pacifism and Peace

The majority of Pentecostal denominations formed between 1907 and 1934 (including the Church of God in Christ, Church of God [Cleveland, Tennessee], and the Assemblies of God) believed Christians should not, as the U.S. Assemblies of God (AG) stated in 1917, "conscientiously participate in war and armed resistance which involves the actual destruction of human life since this is contrary to our view of the clear teachings of the inspired Word of God, which is the sole basis of our faith" (Alexander 2000, 1). Pacifism within Pentecostalism was disproportionately higher than within the average population of America and Europe. Pentecostals believed the Holy Spirit was leading them to restore the apostolic faith of the New Testament and this included reclaiming the primitive church's commitment to peace. Although Pentecostals did not like the term "pacifism" because of its secular associations, they boldly declared that their commitment to Jesus Christ and evangelism precluded their involvement in killing people whom God had sent them to redeem. Though this conviction was not universal, denominational publications such as *The Pentecostal Evangel* (AG) presented scores of articles, tracts, and books by Pentecostal pacifists for the first few decades of the twentieth century. The American Pentecostal peace witness withered after World War II and several (though not all) denominations eventually changed their positions to reflect the fact that most of their constituents supported Christian participation in combat. However, various peace witnesses emerged in the charismatic and neocharismatic renewals in the second half of the twentieth century.

First Generation Pentecostal Pacifism

Pacifism fit well within the energetic countercultural nonconformist theology of many first generation Pentecostals. The roots grew from the black oral heritage, the Holiness movement, and the Evangelical and pietist traditions that influenced Pentecostalism. The Church of God in Christ (CGIC), founded by Bishop C. H. Mason (1863–1961) in 1907, declared that the "shedding of human blood or taking of human life [is] contrary to the teaching of our Lord and Savior, and as a body, we are adverse to war in all its various forms" (Kornweibel 1997, 61). During World War I many Pentecostals in Europe and America were "tarred and feathered," shot at, brought before firing squads, and imprisoned for their conscientious objection. The U.S. Bureau of Investigation opened cases on C. H. Mason and many other Pentecostals of various ethnicities. In 1918 CGIC congregations sacrificed to raise funds to pay the bails of their jailed leaders and members who had conscientiously opposed war. Charles Parham (1873–1929), an original proponent of tongues as the initial physical evidence of the baptism in the Holy Spirit, was an absolute pacifist for twenty years before World War I and he maintained that belief until his death.

European Pentecostals consistently opposed Christian participation in war and in 1917 the U.S. Assemblies of God claimed that:

From the very beginning the movement has been characterized by Quaker principles. The laws of the kingdom, laid down by our elder brother Jesus Christ, in his sermon on the mount, have been unqualifiedly adopted. . . . Every branch of the movement, whether in the United States, Canada, Great Britain, or Germany has held to this principle. (Beaman 1989, 33)

The pacifist witness was also cited as being in Holland, Russia, South Africa, and Switzerland. Donald Gee (1891–1966), eventual chairman of the British AG (1945–1948), was a conscientious objector and author of many articles that gave biblical and theological rationales for a peace witness from a Pentecostal perspective. Arthur Booth-Clibborn (1855–1939) of England and his son Samuel Booth-Clibborn wrote about and preached peacemaking and abstinence from war in numerous Pentecostal publications and meetings.

In 1924 J. W. Welch (1858–1939), general chairman of the U.S. Assemblies of God from 1915 to 1920 and from 1923 to 1925, warmly observed that its position against war was stronger than that of the Quakers. Between 1928 and 1935 they considered withdrawing their financial support from Russian Pentecostals because the Russians had been forced to change their position from pacifism to support of combatant participation.

Some leaders moderated the conscientious objector stance during World War I, even though it appeared that the majority of Pentecostals were pacifists. E. N. Bell (1866–1923), chairman of the U.S. Assemblies of God in 1914 and 1920–1923, recommended that Pentecostals become imbued with the spirit of Arthur Booth-Clibborn's "striking, realistic . . . [and] wonderful" pacifistic book, *Blood Against Blood*. However, he also believed that Pentecostalism "leaves [going to war] with the conscience of each man." Because Pentecostals were going to jail for antiwar preaching, Bell suggested tempering the rhetoric during wartime and taking a "strong stand for Loyalty to our Government and the President and the Flag" (Bell 1918, 4). A. A. Boddy, a leader of the Pentecostal Missionary Union in Britain, wrote articles for *Confidence* and the *Evangel* supporting Christian participation in combat during World War I. The Texan AG pacifist William Burton McCafferty (1889–1963), Frank Bartleman (1871–1935), and others rebutted his views in the following months, but Boddy and Bell reflected the dual citizenship struggle within Pentecostalism that contributed to the eventual decline of pacifism.

Theological Rationale

First generation Pentecostal theology was conducive to a peace witness. First, Pentecostals believed that the Pentecostal movement was God's plan to restore the church to her former glory in preparation for Christ's return. Therefore, the Pentecostals wanted to be as much as possible like the first century Christians. Pentecostals believed that the New Testament church did not kill its enemies but that Christians became increasingly militant after Constantine (c. 272–337 CE) co-opted Christianity for his own imperial ends. For Pentecostals pacifism was a "moral sign of a restored New Testament apostolic church" (Dempster 1997, 35). Frank Bartleman, Stanley Frodsham (1882–1969), and J. Roswell Flower (1888–1970) believed that the early church separated from nationalistic violence and so must the church of the End Times. Arthur Booth-Clibborn argued that, "wherever there is a revival of the spirit of Apostolic Christianity there also appears a revival of the conviction that war is anti-Christian" (Booth-Clibborn 1914, 146). The restoration of primitive Christianity necessarily included the restoration of a peace testimony in anticipation of the end of the world and the establishment by God of his peaceable kingdom.

Second, Pentecostals focused tremendous amounts of resources and energy on evangelism and missions. Pentecostal pacifists reasoned that, "converting men by the power of the Gospel, and later killing these same converts, across some imaginary boundary line is unthinkable" (Bartleman 1922). Evangelization and pacifism fit together well because Pentecostals hoped to convert sinners to the prince of peace rather than kill them for transient nations:

Christ gave himself for us. We give ourselves for humanity. We do exactly what the worldly soldiers do in their wars. We sacrifice our lives if need be; but we kill no one. All complications disappear once this point is made plain. It seems so simple that it appears childish to say it. In this it resembles the whole plan of salvation by grace (Booth-Clibborn 1914, 97).

Third, Pentecostals believed that only the power of the Holy Spirit made possible this radical restoration of the New Testament church and the evangelization of the world. Pentecostal theology and practice emphasized Holy Spirit empowerment, spiritual warfare, and miraculous healings. Sacrificially witnessing to the point of death or not killing one's enemies could be explained as possible because of the outpouring of

Pentecostal Peace Fellowship

Inspired by the Pentecostal and charismatic heritage of peacemaking, an Assemblies of God minister in July 2001 called for the formation of a Pentecostal Peace Fellowship (PPF). Following the initial proposal to the European Pentecostal Charismatic Research Association in Leuven, Belgium, an initial group of twenty people agreed that contact should be maintained among Pentecostals and charismatics who were concerned about engaging in dialogue and action regarding the emerging just-peacemaking theory, reconciliation, and social justice. They represented several countries and denominations (including Belgium, Canada, England, Germany, India, Nigeria, Norway, Switzerland, and the United States; Assemblies of God, Baptist, Catholic, and Pentecostal Holiness).

The PPF was also presented at the Society for Pentecostal Studies meeting in March 2002 in Lakeland, Florida, as the opportunity for evangelical, ecumenical, and Pentecostal integrity. About eighty more interested persons joined at that time. It then gradually developed into a transnational, multiethnic, and interdenominational association of students, laity, professors, pastors, teachers, full-time parents, missionaries, and many others.

The PPF believes that "Jesus Christ is relevant to all tensions, crises, and brokenness in the world and that addressing injustice and making peace as Christ did is theologically sound, biblically commanded, and realistically possible" (www.pentecostalpeace.org). The PPF has continued to grow as Pentecostals and charismatics from around the world work together to discover, appreciate, and further develop their heritage of peacemaking.

Paul Alexander

the Spirit of God in the lives of believers. Samuel Booth-Clibborn argued that "Spiritual power—not carnal brute force—is the weighty fact we must grasp" that empowered "a poor, humble, practically unknown man of the laboring class" to cleanse the temple, "it was simply God's Holy Ghost power" (Booth-Clibborn 1917, 5). Pentecostal pacifists believed the Spirit also empowered what Dempster calls the "unmasking of the reality of social evil" (Dempster 1997, 38). Pentecostals issued strong moral critiques of the social order, condemning the wealthy class's exploitation of the poor and the high loss of human life that results from war. They believed that their witness included reminding the nations that God would judge all military, economic, and political systems, even democracies. Spirit-empowered witness to Christ's redemption, prophetic critique of national and international injustice, and nonparticipation in war coalesced into a consistent peace testimony for the Pentecostal pacifists.

Fourth, Pentecostals attempted to take Scripture seriously. They appealed to Scripture for their doctrine and required biblical arguments from their opponents. The rationale for pacifism as a doctrine and way of life was based on Scripture as a whole being fulfilled in Jesus Christ. Pacifists such as Samuel H. Booth-Clibborn explained the use of the Old Covenant to justify Christians killing in warfare as:

> thick ignorance...resulting in this everlasting muddling up of O. T. and N. T. teaching....Find me in the New Testament where Christ ever sent His followers on such a mission? On the contrary He sent them out to save men—not to butcher them like cattle....No! as far as the Christian is concerned, the 'eye for an eye' system has given place to the 'Turn to him the other cheek also' of Matt. 5:39–44. (Alexander 2000, 109)

Fifth, pacifism served as "the certification of the universal value of human life" (Dempster 1997, 42). Pentecostal pacifists were more "pro-Christian" than antimilitaristic, their real war was for Christ and against sin and this precluded killing people. The difference

Two white doves, a symbol of peace.
Courtesy of istockphoto.com/crocus.

between killing and not killing was, for Arthur Booth-Clibborn, "an essential difference in...the means employed to remedy the evils in the world.... To the Christian it is spiritual power and gospel war, expressed in love and ending in life." They taught that Christians see above "the fogs of prejudice or party, of politics or nationality" and realize that "everything comes finally to a point, and that point is life—human life" (Dempster 1997, 45).

Decline of Pacifism

During World War II Ernest S. Williams (1885–1981), the general superintendent of the U.S. Assemblies of God from 1929–1949, recommended that its young men read the *Pacifist Handbook*, published by the Fellowship of Reconciliation, and that they enter the military as noncombatants. By so doing he reconciled duty to government with the belief that Christians should not kill. He also suggested the adoption of the statement from New York's Broadway Tabernacle, "I cannot reconcile the way of Christ with the way of war" (Wilson 2002, 954). But the instructions did not determine the course of action for the majority. Of the approximately fifty thousand American AG men who joined the military, "quite a large number" entered as noncombatants but a "far larger number" entered as combatants. Only a "minute company" of conscientious objectors went to

Civilian Public Service camps. Nevertheless, in 1947 the U.S. Assemblies of God affirmed their pacifist stance and did not change it until 1967. The AG had thirty-four military chaplains by 1944 and the chaplaincy department later pushed to change the military service statement to reflect the actual practice of the U.S. Assemblies of God, affirming "the right of each member to choose for himself whether to declare his position as a combatant, a noncombatant, or a conscientious objector." Only 131 of 11,950 American conscientious objectors during World War II were listed as Pentecostals.

Scholars suggest various reasons, both religious and cultural, for the decline of pacifism among Pentecostals. First, since pacifism was debated even in the first generation perhaps it was only a minority position that eroded before pacifists could cultivate a theologically informed tradition for later generations. Second, early prima facie biblicism did not develop into a solid ethical hermeneutic. Third, upward social mobility and participation in the mainstream led to a quest for prosperity, respectability, and the political establishment, rather than prophetic critiques of classism and violence. Fourth, the premillennial nonconformity of women in ministry, interracial worship, and nonviolence gave way to culturally approved structures of sexism, racism, and war. Fifth, evangelization of the military through chaplaincy was tacit approval of military service that led to justifying and promoting it. Sixth, perhaps Pentecostal denominations that joined the National Association of Evangelicals needed to mute their "pentecostal zeal" and pacifism in order to be accepted by a group whose president (Harold Ockenga) declared in his 1943 presidential address that "the United States of America has been assigned a destiny comparable to that of ancient Israel" (Blumhofer 1989, 30). This perhaps led the maturing Pentecostal denominations to realize that their earlier interpretations of Scripture in support of pacifism had been flawed.

Contemporary Peace Witness

The charismatic renewal in the 1960s and 1970s invigorated the peace witness in mainline denominations and in the two-thirds world even as the older Pentecostal denominations were moving away from it. In 1970 Dorothy Day herself (Catholic Worker Movement) wrote that a breakthrough had come through the "Catholic pentecostal movement" which "intensified growth in the non-violent movement...the fight against poverty and injustice...[and] Cesar Chavez' strike of the Farm Workers of California" (Day 1970, 8). The charismatic renewal among the Historic Peace Churches in the 1960s and 1970s brought Christian pacifism and an emphasis on the Holy Spirit together once again. In 1986, 10 to 15 percent of members and 25 to 30 percent of pastors in Mennonite Church congregations in North America identified themselves as charismatic. British Pentecostal and charismatic leaders have supported the banning of nuclear weapons and German charismatics and neocharismatics participated in the nonviolent protests in the 1980s that helped bring down the Berlin Wall. In the 1970s and 1980s in South Africa some Apostolic Faith Pentecostals challenged apartheid by integrating worship services and engaging in political discourse and then suffered at the hands of other Pentecostals who supported apartheid. The Church of God in Christ has maintained their doctrinal opposition to war though it is not taught as the normative stance of the church. However, the presiding bishops wrote a letter to President Bush of the United States opposing the invasion of Iraq in March 2003. The Pentecostal-Charismatic movement has had pacifists and a peace witness from the very beginning. It has changed locations and practically disappeared at times, but many still claim that the Spirit is guiding them in Jesus' path of peace.

PAUL NATHAN ALEXANDER

See also Nationalism; Society, Pentecostal Attitudes toward

Further Reading

Alexander, P. (2000). *An analysis of the emergence and decline of pacifism in the history of the Assemblies of God*. Unpublished doctoral dissertation, Baylor University, Waco, TX.

Alexander, P. (2002). Spirit empowered peacemaking: Toward a Pentecostal peace fellowship. *The Journal of the European Pentecostal Theological Association, XXII*, 78–102.

Bartleman, F. (1922). *Christian citizenship*. Los Angeles: Author.

Beaman, J. (1989). *Pentecostal pacifism*. Hillsboro, KS: Center for Mennonite Brethren Studies.

Blumhofer, E. (1989). *The Assemblies of God: A chapter in the story of American Pentecostalism* (Vols. 1 & 2). Springfield, MO: Gospel Publishing House.

Booth-Clibborn, A. (1914). *Blood against blood* (2nd ed.). New York: George H. Doran Company.

Booth-Clibborn, S. (1917, April). The Christian and war. Is it too late? *The Weekly Evangel, 28*, 4–5.

Day, D. (1970, March–April). On pilgrimage—March–April 1970. *The Catholic Worker, 2*, 8.

Dempster, M. (1990). Reassessing the moral rhetoric of early American Pentecostal pacifism. *Crux, 26*(1), 23–36.

Dempster, M. (1991). 'Crossing borders:' Arguments used by early American Pentecostals in support of the global character of pacifism. *The Journal of the European Pentecostal Theological Association, 10*(2), 63–80.

Dempster, M. (1997). Pacifism in Pentecostalism: The case of the Assemblies of God. In T. F. Schlabach & R. T. Hughes (Eds.), *Proclaim peace: Christian pacifism from unexpected quarters*. Chicago: University of Illinois Press.

Kauffman, J. H. (1996). Mennonite charismatics: Are they any different? *Mennonite Quarterly Review, 70*, 449–472.

Kornweibel, T., Jr. (1997). Race and conscientious objection in World War I: The story of the church of God in Christ. In T. F. Schlabach & R. T. Hughes (Eds.), *Proclaim peace: Christian pacifism from unexpected quarters*. Chicago: University of Illinois Press.

Schlabach, T. F. & Hughes, R. T. (Eds.). (1997). *Proclaim peace: Christian pacifism from unexpected quarters*. Chicago: University of Illinois Press.

Shuman, J. (1996). Pentecost and the end of patriotism: A call for the restoration of pacifism among Pentecostal Christians. *Journal of Pentecostal Theology, 9*, 70–96.

Wilson, D. J. (2002). Pacifism. In S. M. Burgess & E. M. van der Maas (Eds.), *New international dictionary of Pentecostal and Charismatic movements*. Grand Rapids, MI: Zondervan.

Pentecostal Theology

Pentecostalism is a rapidly growing global phenomenon, with its greatest increases registered over the past several decades in what is often called the "two-thirds world"—that is, Africa, Latin America, and Asia. The number of different Pentecostal churches and the diversity of their teachings make it difficult to form any general conclusions about the nature of global Pentecostalism today. However, some general observations can be made regarding its spirituality and theology, and common traits can be found in the areas of Spirit baptism, sanctification, healing, and divine revelation.

The Pentecostal movement is usually described as having risen out of the cradle of the 1906 Azusa Street Revival in Los Angeles and spreading from there to Europe and then to third-world countries. However, there are theories that support the view that similar revivals were birthed in other continents outside of and previous to the North American influence (for example, in South America, Asia, Africa, and Europe). Most Pentecostal scholars recognize the impetus the Azusa

Mission gave to this movement with the understanding that there were multiple origins around the globe. This movement of the Spirit, due to its varied origins, is able to use existing cultural religious practices, those with vestiges of pre-Christian beliefs, and to renew them by the purifying effects of the Spirit, the Word, and the Church.

Pentecostal theology is pneumatologically Christocentric, meaning that salvation is by faith in Christ, as believers confess through the enabling of the Spirit (*Abba Father*). The believer is re-created into a person of the Spirit who on the basis of love is able to act according to the fruit of the Spirit and to lead a life of holiness. This re-creation as an act and a process extends to the physical realm; it belongs within the work of the cross that provides physical healing and other forms of restoration by the power of the Spirit to those inflicted with diseases or who are living under oppressive circumstances. The Spirit of Love between Father and Son awakens within the believer a deeper level of love for the coming king. The new eschatological consciousness stimulates missionary zeal empowered by the baptism of the Holy Spirit, which is normally evidenced by speaking in tongues and the use of supernatural gifts.

Thus, Pentecostal theology is permeated with the concept of Christ as one who is "God with us," the Immanuel, Christ being present in the person of the Holy Spirit, and primarily being made manifest in and through the church as a visible sign before the world. The result is a theology that is affective-relational and oral-experiential, where the narrative of the lives of the community takes precedence over a rational development of written doctrine and a literal interpretation of Scripture.

Baptism in the Holy Spirit

The outpouring of the Spirit is a baptism of love and passion for the coming king. For Pentecostals, being infused with affection for Christ means the restoration of the faith and practices of the early church. Pentecostalism holds to an eschatological view of time, an overlapping of the "not yet" into the "yet." The global outpouring of the Holy Spirit signifies a Pentecost of worldwide dimensions that accelerates the fulfillment of the new age. They recontextualize the prophecies spoken in Acts 2:17 (NIV) and emphasize the nearness of the culmination of the "last days" event. For them, the reemergence of the global priestly community that is anointed to speak in tongues and perform signs and wonders, as in apostolic times, is proof that they are living in the eschatological era. The present has entered a period when the new creation in Christ through the Spirit is being established. Jesus as the *new Adam* is seen as the first among those who are the *last Adam* (*eschatos*), those who lead a life of the Spirit.

Most Pentecostals adhere to a dual experience of grace, and though at times it may be a simultaneous event upon conversion, it is often a gift of grace received subsequent to it. Upon conversion, the believer is regenerated; the fullness of this experience, nevertheless, can occur at a later time as the believer is immersed and baptized in the Holy Spirit. Though often misunderstood outside the circle of Spirit-filled believers, Spirit baptism is considered to be within the context of the salvation event, a necessary element for a Spirit-led life.

The baptism in the Holy Spirit is a promise (Luke 24:49; Acts 1:4), a gift (Acts 2:38, 5:32), and a command (Acts 5:32; Ephesians 5:18). Its purpose is to empower the believer for special service with miracles, anointed preaching and healing (Luke 4:18), and spiritual warfare (Ephesians 6:12). It is also for improving the ability to follow, love, and exalt, and the ability to exercise the spiritual gifts, to suffer, to live a holy life, and to work for God until Jesus comes. The baptism is for all who believe, have repented from sin, and have a definite experience of salvation, and for those who have demonstrated a measure of consecration.

According to religious historian Vinson Synan, in the beginnings of the Pentecostal movement a number of physical evidences would accompany the baptism of the Holy Ghost—for example, the holy dance, hallelujah earthquakes, shouting in drunken ecstasy, and speaking in tongues. However, the early twentieth-century preacher Charles Parham identified tongues as the only evidence in the reception of the Spirit baptism, and this doctrine was formalized at the Azusa Street Revival. Today the fundamentals of faith in most classical Pentecostal denominations, including Assemblies of God, Church of the Foursquare Gospel, Open Bible, and the Church of God in Christ, contain the statement that speaking in tongues is the initial physical evidence of the baptism of the Holy Spirit. This belief seems to be shared by Pentecostal churches worldwide. For example, in some African countries, while salvation by faith and the baptism of the Holy Spirit are aspects of spiritual rebirth, speaking in tongues is a sign of being born again, and thus an integral element of their Christian identity.

For many Pentecostals, speaking in tongues is also an important way in which God makes himself present in the Church. As the message in tongues comes forth in the congregation, the presence of Christ is embodied in the community of the Spirit in a sacramental or theophanic way. For these believers, tongues are the language of love, an outcome in their intimate conversation with God, the message of love that comes forth as a result of their mystical union with the Spirit. It is out of this level of intimacy that love is transformed into its outward mode, service to the Church and a witness to the world. Since it is but a foretaste of the unhindered human-divine communication, it becomes an eschatological sign of the soon-coming king.

Sanctified Life

Spirit-filled believers are holy and being made holy, a new creation constantly being renewed by the purifying power of the Spirit. In their identification with the Resurrection of Christ, as they are filled with the Resurrection and baptizing Spirit that re-creates within and turns the affections of the believers toward God, they view themselves as empowered to overcome sin and to become a community of and for righteousness. The filling of the Spirit produces a Christ-like character by grace through faith. The Spirit transforms the being and causes its human activity to be oriented toward its eschatological freedom from sin and its effects. Holiness becomes an eschatological mark of the Spirit, a stamp of holiness that bears the image of Christ.

The movement of history toward its fulfillment becomes an expression of the holy love that bears the burden and passion for justice in the world in the life of the believer. It stems out of the death of the old person and the life of the new. It is in this love unto death that the Law is fulfilled, all righteousness is met, and the demonstration toward God and neighbor is accomplished. Therefore the church is not only being sanctified, but it is also an instrument of sanctification in the world. Since God, Son, and Spirit were involved in the creative process of the cosmos, the death and Resurrection of Christ set in motion "an eschatological hope of a cosmic restoration" (Macchia 2001, 208). The groaning of the Spirit is related to the mission of the church toward victimized humanity, where the church is to be an agent of social liberation.

To non-Western people Pentecostals bring a relevant message that interprets oppression and poverty within a framework of empowering spirituality that grants the believing community access to a more exhaustive form of liberation and freedom. Theologian Allan Anderson describes it as contextual pneumatology, one in which life is seen in its totality with no separation between sacred and secular, where Christianity belongs in the daily lives of the people in the midst of

their problems and struggles. He sees this faith as the greatest contribution of third-world Pentecostals to the West. In Latin America, many churches are located in poor communities such as *barrios* and urban slums, giving them ready access to both indigenous and displaced city dwellers, and allowing them to become spiritual and material agents of restoration of the dignity that a renewed humanity has in Christ.

In Africa, on the other hand, Pentecostalism is defined more in terms of its power to liberate believers from an oppressive spiritual reality and to displace the guardian forces with true authority, bringing freedom in the person of Christ. Pentecostals believe that the name of Jesus, his blood, and the supernatural endowment of spiritual gifts can be used to reverse a curse brought upon Africans by the incantations of diviners. They hold spiritual deliverance services to attack what they see as spiritual forces responsible for agricultural and economic crises.

Healing

For Pentecostals healing was present in the atonement (Isaiah 53) in the same manner in which it was included in the Hebraic cleansing ceremonies (for instance, Leviticus 14:1–32). The Levitical atoning sacrifices have become "the types of the Sacrifice and provision made by Jesus Christ on the cross. The antitype must be true to the type, so it is suggestive of the fact that Jesus also made atonement when He was offered" (Duffield and Van Cleave 1987, 388). Methods of healing include individual and corporate prayer, and prayer administered through the anointing of oil and the laying on of hands (James 5:14, 16). Sometimes Pentecostals make use of anointed objects such as handkerchiefs and aprons in their healing practices (Acts 19:11, 12).

Since healing is an eschatological down payment on the salvation event, healing is an experience available to all believers through faith. It is a foretaste of what is to come and a benefit that can be at least partially experienced in the present, a constitutive element of the transformation of creation as fallen humanity is being restored. In salvation, there is a simultaneous provision of forgiveness of sins and healing, body and soul being renewed by the Spirit. Most Pentecostals, however, do not avoid doctors or view sickness as a sign of sin.

In third-world countries, healing has become a doorway to the reception and spread of the Gospel. In animistic cultures where healing is a common practice, Pentecostalism elevates believers by pointing them to the true Healer. The failure of the spirit world to ameliorate their condition, in the midst of the miraculous acts of divine healing, enables many to turn to Christ. Among many Pentecostal missions, preaching without healing is considered useless.

Revelation

The Pentecostal community of faith confers a position of authority on the Scriptures, not as a written text that stands alone, but as the proclaimed word. The word is heard and becomes an event of salvation as it affects the reality of its proclamation. As the living Word of God, the Scriptures take place within the services and life of the community. The Scripture is proclaimed so that humanity can reach its destiny, which is to be re-created in the image of God. It is in the Scriptures that the message of salvation is perpetuated, but it is only through their practical character that the Scriptures become reality and fulfill the purpose for which they were written.

Pentecostals exercise a biblical hermeneutic of praxis and experience in the Spirit, a dialogical hermeneutic that rests on the authority of the text as the word of God and the contemporary message of the Spirit. For Pentecostals the Gospel and their personal experience are interdependent, where the Word of God interprets the life of the community through the use of narratives and testimonials. The Scriptures become a witness of the transformation power of the Spirit, a witness of its new creation and mission of reconciliation to the world.

The direct revelation of God becomes primary in the use of Scripture; the believer expects to hear from God, but not through the text alone. Through the gifts of teaching, prophecy, tongues and interpretation, wisdom, and knowledge, the message of the text addresses the needs of the congregation. The message empowers and proves itself to be true as believers live out its statutes and receive the written promises of God. "Experiential interpretation of the Bible as it is prayed, sung, danced, prophesied and preached in the worship of Pentecostal churches implies an understanding of the Bible from the underside of society, where ordinary people can interpret the Bible from the perspective of their own experiences and struggles" (Anderson 2004, 13). It is a reflective theology where beliefs, actions, and affections work in connection with, but are not necessarily shaped by, Scripture.

Implications

Pentecostals maintain a pneumatologically Christocentric theology, where Jesus Christ is savior, sanctifier, healer, and coming king, in the Spirit. It is a theology in which Spirit baptism, sanctification, healing, and

modes of revelation become experiences that infuse the narrative and testimony of the believer, experiences where the Word is lived through the Spirit in the Church. These experiences of the Spirit have come to be the backbone of the present ecclesiastical renewal among Christians of all persuasions.

Today Pentecostals are no longer a marginalized minority but rather one of the largest Christian groups in the world. The renewed emphasis that they placed on the person and role of the Holy Spirit in the Church has permeated the life and worship of other Protestant churches and of Catholic churches too. Though aspects of this theology continue to be redefined, the common experience of a personal encounter with God through his Spirit will continue to transform the Church and the world as people are empowered to testify to the goodness of God through signs and wonders.

ELAINE PADILLA

See also Baptism in the Holy Spirit; Church, Theology of the; Doctrine, Development of; Faith, Gift of

Further Reading

Álvarez, C. (Ed.). (1992). *Pentecostalismo y liberación: Una experiencia Latinoamericana*. San José, Costa Rica: DEI.

Anderson, A. (2001). Stretching the definitions? Pneumatology and 'syncretism' in African Pentecostalism. *Journal of Pentecostal Theology, 10*(1), 98–119.

Anderson, A. (2004). Pentecostal and Charismatic theology. In D. F. Ford & R. Muers (Eds.), *The modern theologians: An introduction to Christian theology since 1918* (3rd ed.). Oxford, UK: Blackwell.

Bridges Johns, C. (1998). *Pentecostal formation: A pedagogy among the oppressed*. Sheffield, UK: Sheffield Academic Press.

Cox, H. (1995). *Fire from heaven*. Reading, MA: Addison-Wesley.

Dabney, D. L. (2001). Saul's armor: The problem and the promise of Pentecostal theology today. *Pneuma, 23*(1), 115–146.

Dayton, D. W. (2000). *Theological roots of Pentecostalism*. Metuchen, NJ: Scarecrow Press/Hendrickson.

Duffield, G. P., & Van Cleave, N. M. (1987). *Foundations of Pentecostal theology* (2nd ed.). Los Angeles: L.I.F.E. Bible College.

Faupel, D. W. (1996). *The everlasting gospel: The significance of eschatology in the development of Pentecostal thought*. Sheffield, UK: Sheffield Academic Press.

Gutiérrez, B., & Smith, D. A. (1996). *In the power of the spirit: The Pentecostal challenge to historic churches in Latin America*. Mexico: AIPRAL.

Kalu, O. U. (2002). Preserving a worldview: Pentecostalism in the African maps of the universe. *Pneuma, 24*(2), 110–137.

Kalu, O. U. (2003). *The embattled gods: Christianization of Igboland, 1841–1991.* Trenton, NJ, & Asmara, Eritrea: Africa World Press.

Kärkkäinen, V.-M. (2001). David's sling: The promise and the problem of Pentecostal theology today: A response to D. Lyle Dabney. *Pneuma, 23*(1), 147–152.

Land, S. J. (1997). *Pentecostal spirituality: A passion for the kingdom.* Sheffield, UK: Sheffield Academic Press.

Litonjua, M. D. (2000). Pentecostalism in Latin America: Scrutinizing a sign of the times. *Journal of Hispanic/Latino Theology, 7*(4), 26–49.

Ma, J. (2002). Manifestation of supernatural power in Luke-Acts and the Kankana-eys tribe of the Philippines. *The Spirit and Church, 4*(2), 109–128.

Ma, J. C. (2001). *When the spirit meets the spirits: Pentecostal ministry among the Kankana-ey tribe in the Philippines* (2nd rev. ed.). Frankfurt am Main, Germany: Peter Lang.

Macchia, F. (1993). Question of tongues as initial evidence. *Journal of Pentecostal Theology, 2,* 117–127.

Macchia, F. (1993). Tongues as a sign. *Pneuma, 15*(1), 61–76.

Macchia, F. (1998). Groans too deep for words. *Asian Journal of Pentecostal Studies, 1*(2), 149–173.

Macchia, F. (2001). Justification through new creation: The Holy Spirit and the doctrine by which the church stands or falls. *Theology Today, 58*(2), 202–217.

Sepúlveda, J. (1992). Reflections on the Pentecostal contribution to the mission of the church in Latin America. *Journal of Pentecostal Theology, 1,* 93–108.

Symposium on Oneness Pentecostalism 1988 and 1990. (1990). Hazelwood, MO: Word Aflame.

Synan, V. (1997). *The holiness Pentecostal tradition: Charismatic movements in the twentieth century* (2nd ed). Grand Rapids, MI: Eerdmans.

Young, A. (2002). The marks of the church: A Pentecostal re-reading. *Evangelical Review of Theology, 26*(1), 45–67.

Yong, A. (1998). "Tongues of fire" in the Pentecostal imagination: The truth of glossolalia in light of R. C. Neville's theory of religious symbolism. *Journal of Pentecostal Theology, 12,* 39–45.

Pentecostalism, Classical

The term "classical Pentecostalism" originated in the 1960s in the United States as a means to distinguish existing Pentecostal churches from the emerging charismatic renewal in mainline Protestant denominations and in the Roman Catholic Church. At the same time, scholars were beginning to take note of the theological pluralism and diverse historical roots within the burgeoning non-Western Pentecostal churches. Classical Pentecostalism came to denote churches and denominations that originated in the United States at the turn of the twentieth century.

Possible Origins

Historians of Pentecostalism generally regard two early twentieth-century revivals as central to the story of the movement's origins: Topeka, Kansas (1901) and Azusa Street, Los Angeles, California (1906–1909). In 1900, Kansas Holiness preacher Charles F. Parham became convinced that xenolalia (speaking in actual languages) was the biblical evidence of Spirit baptism. Tongue-speakers, he determined, could serve as instant missionaries who would prompt a worldwide revival and usher in Christ's premillennial return. Parham encouraged students at his short-lived Topeka Bible school to search for the scriptural evidence of Spirit baptism, directing them to Acts 2. One of his students (Agnes Ozman) spoke in tongues on 1 January 1901, and Parham and other students had similar experiences over the next few days. Parham's popularity peaked in about mid-1906, when he counted between eight thousand and ten thousand followers in Kansas, Missouri, eastern Oklahoma, and Texas.

It was not until revival erupted in April 1906 at the Apostolic Faith Mission at Azusa Street, led by William J. Seymour, that this restoration of the gift of tongues became widely known. Seymour, a black man and former student of Parham, soon became the central figure in a movement eclipsing that of his teacher. News of a modern-day Pentecost spread quickly through the Azusa Street mission's newspaper, *The Apostolic Faith,* and through existing networks of radical Evangelicals, many of whom accepted what they deemed to be a restoration of New Testament Christianity. Seymour's small black congregation had gained worldwide attention, and soon most in attendance were white. The congregation was fully integrated with both black and white leaders, and Hispanics and other ethnic minorities were regularly present.

Seymour adopted Parham's doctrine of evidentiary tongues, although believers began to understand them to be glossolalic (unknown languages) rather than xenolalic, after disappointed missionaries reported their inability to communicate using the gift of tongues. However, Seymour did not adopt other beliefs of Parham, such as his eschatology or his racist British-Israelism. By 1909, attendance at Azusa Street had

Acts 2:1–4 (King James Version)

[1]And when the day of Pentecost was fully come, they were all with one accord in one place.

[2]And suddenly there came a sound from heaven as of a rushing mighty wind, and it filled all the house where they were sitting.

[3]And there appeared unto them cloven tongues like as of fire, and it sat upon each of them.

[4]And they were filled with the Holy Ghost, and began to speak with other tongues, as the Spirit gave them utterance.

dropped off, followed by one last big surge in 1911. By 1912, Los Angeles Pentecostals had fractured into at least twelve congregations and, in 1915, Seymour's dwindling congregation numbered but a handful.

The Pentecostal movement spread quickly, often building upon established networks. Charles H. Mason, a gifted black preacher in the Mississippi Holiness movement, visited Azusa Street and spoke in tongues. Mason returned home and, with part of his old network, founded the Church of God in Christ, which he built into the largest black Pentecostal denomination in the United States. North Carolina Holiness evangelist Gaston B. Cashwell, after visiting Azusa Street in 1906, led the Fire-Baptized Holiness Church, the Pentecostal Holiness Church, the Free Will Baptist Church, and the Church of God (Cleveland, Tennessee) into the movement. Chicago, which rivaled Los Angeles as an early Pentecostal center, was home to William H. Durham's North Avenue Mission and William H. Piper's Stone Church, both of which published influential periodicals. Durham's congregation held some sway among the city's immigrants and participated in planting Pentecostalism in Brazil and Italy. On Chicago's South Side, Piper led many disenchanted followers of faith healer John Alexander Dowie into Pentecostalism. Numerous other Pentecostal powerhouses developed, including Robert and Marie Brown's Glad Tidings Tabernacle in New York City (formed 1907), James and Ellen Hebden's Queen Street Mission in Toronto (which became Pentecostal in 1907), and Andrew H. Argue's Calvary Temple in Winnipeg (formed 1907).

Division

Theological scuffles soon divided Pentecostals into three camps: "second work" (Holiness) Trinitarians, "finished work" (Baptistic) Trinitarians, and "finished work" (Baptistic) Oneness Pentecostals. Many Pente-

costals, particularly in the South, held to the Holiness teaching that the Christian experience contained three successive instantaneous experiences: justification, sanctification, and Spirit baptism. Several denominations started out as Holiness organizations before they embraced Pentecostalism, including the Pentecostal Holiness Church, the Church of God (Cleveland, Tennessee), and the Church of God in Christ.

Some Pentecostals came from non-Holiness backgrounds and were uncomfortable with an emphasis on a second instantaneous experience of sanctification. In 1910, Chicago pastor William H. Durham, a former Baptist, began articulating a "finished work" view of sanctification, claiming Christ's finished work on the cross accomplished both justification and sanctification. According to Durham, there were only two experiences: salvation and Spirit baptism. When Pentecostal denominations formed, they did so along Holiness and finished work lines. Pentecostals who taught a finished work view of sanctification initially existed in networks of independent congregations and later formed denominations such as the Assemblies of God (formed 1914), the Pentecostal Church of God (formed 1919), and the International Church of the Foursquare Gospel (incorporated 1927).

The third type of Pentecostalism, Oneness Pentecostalism, emerged among finished work Pentecostals who, in their quest to restore New Testament practices, determined that water baptism should be done in the name of Jesus, following the formula in Acts 2:38 rather than the triune formula in Matthew 28:19. Chicago pastor Andrew Urshan began advocating baptism in the name of Jesus as early as 1910. Additional Pentecostals began to rethink the doctrine of the Trinity and, at the 1913 Worldwide Camp Meeting at Arroyo Seco, near Los Angeles, California, debate erupted over the correct baptism formula and the nature of the Godhead. Terms used to describe the new movement were

"Oneness," "new issue," "new light," "Jesus only," and "Jesus name." Some of the more radical Oneness proponents denied the doctrine of the Trinity and claimed that full salvation required baptism in the name of Jesus and Spirit baptism evidenced by speaking in tongues. This debate raged for several years and resulted in networks of black and white Oneness churches. In 1916 approximately 35 percent of Assemblies of God ministers left that denomination when it adopted a Statement of Fundamental Truths that was Trinitarian. Many early Oneness believers joined the Pentecostal Assemblies of the World, an interracial denomination that may have been formed in 1908. White Oneness Pentecostals, many of whom split from the Pentecostal Assemblies of the World, gradually came together through a series of mergers to form the United Pentecostal Church in 1945.

Other issues that divided Pentecostals included racial and cultural differences, modern day apostles and prophets, worship styles, eschatology, church polity, and personality conflicts. A movement originating in 1948 in Canada, the New Order of the Latter Rain, sought to counter a perceived declension within Pentecostalism. Heralding the restoration of apostles and prophets and advocating extreme congregationalism, Latter Rain proponents quickly alienated other Pentecostals. Suffering numerous scandals and failing to bring a promised End-Times revival, the movement fell apart. Latter Rain leaders and themes became marginalized, existing at the periphery of Pentecostalism until emerging years later as some of the more radical elements within the Charismatic and Word of Faith movements.

Growth

Pentecostalism, pushed to prominence through the divine healing and deliverance crusades by Oral Roberts, Tommy Hicks, Jack Coe, and T. L. Osborn, experienced unprecedented worldwide growth following World War II. The 1940s also saw a change in attitudes among Pentecostals toward interdenominational cooperation. The National Association of Evangelicals, formed in 1942, included the Assemblies of God and the Church of God (Cleveland, Tennessee). Pentecostal leaders next formed their own cooperative agencies: the Pentecostal World Conference (founded 1947) and the Pentecostal Fellowship of North America (founded 1948). The latter group was dissolved in 1994 and replaced by the Pentecostal-Charismatic Churches of North America that, unlike its predecessor, included charismatics and black Pentecostal denominations.

At the grassroots level, Pentecostalism was introduced to new audiences through the Full Gospel Business Men's Fellowship International (founded 1951) and Women's Aglow (founded 1967), both of which attracted many members of non-Pentecostal churches. This interdenominational cooperation, combined with the high profile ministry of Pentecostal healing evangelists, helped to stir interest in Pentecostal themes among mainline church members, resulting in what came to be known as the Charismatic Renewal.

Classical Pentecostal churches, which claimed approximately 75 million followers worldwide in 2004, have grown to become the largest family within Protestantism. In recent decades, most of the growth in North American classical Pentecostal churches has occurred among ethnic minorities, particularly Hispanics and African-Americans. While classical Pentecostal churches generally lay claim to particular North American historical origins and theological distinctives, probably less than a tenth of their worldwide adherents reside in the United States and Canada. Notably, Yoido Full Gospel Church, an Assemblies of God congregation in Seoul, South Korea, is the world's largest local church, with over 700,000 members.

North American Pentecostalism, since its beginning, emphasized missions and evangelism. Despite Parham's belief in "missionary tongues," his group did not send the first Pentecostal missionary. The earliest known Pentecostal missionary from North America to venture overseas hailed from the Scandinavian Mission Society (Sällskapet), a small association of immigrant churches in Minnesota and North Dakota whose practice of tongues-speech in connection with Spirit baptism developed separately from Parham. Mary Johnson, along with Ida Andersson, who spoke in tongues several years later, set sail for South Africa in late 1904. The existence of these pre-Azusa Street missionaries underscores the movement's multiple origins and the complexities associated with using labels such as "classical Pentecostal." It was not until 1906, however, that the Pentecostal missionary enterprise began in earnest. Pilgrims to Azusa Street brought the "baptism" back to their own countries and, within two years, missionaries were sent to at least twenty-five nations. By 1920, North American classical Pentecostal denominations had become firmly established in Africa, Asia, Europe, and Latin America. Classical Pentecostal denominational histories tend to date Pentecostalism's introduction to a particular nation with the arrival of that denomination's first missionary. However, as historian Paul Shew demonstrated with the Assemblies of God in Japan, such denominations often built upon existing Pentecostal networks.

Acts 2: 17 (King James Version)

And it shall come to pass in the last days, saith God, I will pour out of my Spirit upon all flesh: and your sons and your daughters shall prophesy, and your young men shall see visions, and your old men shall dream dreams.

Debate Over Origins

Historians have hotly contested the question of Pentecostal origins. Most early Pentecostal historians were "participant-observers" who believed the movement to be of divine origin and who discounted human agency. They identified multiple movements with diverse theological and cultural backgrounds that coalesced to form Pentecostalism. Since the 1960s, academically trained historians have offered several new interpretive paradigms tracing the movement to a single source, arguing alternatively that Parham, Seymour, or both should be viewed as the movement's founder. Much attention has been paid to the interracial quality—albeit short-lived—of the Azusa Street mission. Historian Walter Hollenweger, among others, views Seymour as the movement's founder because he prefers Seymour's egalitarianism over Parham's racist views. Many also argue that Azusa Street is evidence of an intrinsic racial and gender equality at the core of the movement, despite evidence that most Pentecostals have reflected the racial attitudes common in their day.

Defining Pentecostalism

Most recently, scholars have wrestled with defining the contours of Pentecostalism in light of its rapidly-growing non-Western varieties. While most Pentecostals reside in non-Western nations, scholars lack enough up-to-date information to begin to form a comprehensive picture of the movement. Most scholarship, including this article, relies largely on Western (North American) sources. Not all Pentecostal outbursts can be traced to North America. Gary McGee showed that Pentecostalism in India predated Topeka by at least forty years, and Juan Sepúlveda argued that the sizable Pentecostal movement in Chile developed independently from events at Azusa Street. Allan Anderson eschewed reductionism that equates Pentecostalism with tongues-speech, noting that Pentecostals in England date the movement's beginning to the 1904–1905 Welsh revival. African historians Ogbu Kalu and Inus Daneel

suggested that many indigenous groups employ identity markers other than those associated with Western Pentecostal churches. The question of what constitutes a Pentecostal complicates the subject of Pentecostal origins. Many Western observers have labeled large segments of the emerging indigenous churches as Pentecostal, chiefly because their theology and practices are phenomenologically related to Western Pentecostalism. "Classical Pentecostalism"—despite the term's limitations and implicit paternalism—identifies significant elements of the movement emanating from North America.

Darrin J. Rodgers

See also Antecedents of Pentecostalism; Azusa Street Revival; Oneness Theology; Trinitarianism

Further Reading

Anderson, A. H. (2004). *An introduction to Pentecostalism.* Cambridge, UK: Cambridge University Press.

Anderson, R. M. (1979). *Vision of the disinherited: The making of American Pentecostalism.* New York: Oxford University Press.

Blumhofer, E. L. (1993). *Restoring the faith: The Assemblies of God, Pentecostalism, and American culture.* Urbana: University of Illinois Press.

Clemmons, I. C. (1996). *Bishop C. H. Mason and the roots of the Church of God in Christ.* Bakersfield, CA: Pneuma Life Publishing.

Conn, C. W. (1996). *Like a mighty army: A history of the Church of God.* Cleveland, TN: Pathway Press.

French, T. L. (1999). *Our God is one: The story of Oneness Pentecostals.* Indianapolis, IN: Voice and Vision.

Goff, J. R. (1988). *Fields white unto harvest: Charles F. Parham and the missionary origins of Pentecostalism.* Fayetteville: University of Arkansas Press.

Hollenweger, W. J. (1997). *Pentecostalism: Origins and development worldwide.* Peabody, MA: Hendrickson Publishers.

Jacobsen, D. (2003). *Thinking in the spirit: Theologies of the early Pentecostal movement.* Bloomington: Indiana University Press.

McGee, G. B. (2004). *People of the spirit: The Assemblies of God.* Springfield, MO: Gospel Publishing House.

Miller, T. W. (1994). *Canadian Pentecostals: A history of the Pentecostal Assemblies of Canada.* Mississauga, Canada: Full Gospel Publishing House.

Synan, V. (1997). *The Holiness-Pentecostal tradition: Charismatic movements in the twentieth century.* Grand Rapids, MI: Eerdmans.

Van Cleave, N. M. (1992). *The vine and the branches: A history of the international church of the Foursquare Gospel.* Los Angeles: International Church of the Foursquare Gospel.

Wacker, G. (2001). *Heaven below: Early Pentecostals and American culture.* Cambridge, MA: Harvard University Press.

Perfection and Perfectionism

Perfectionism is a doctrine, especially popular in the early years of the Pentecostal movement, which states that a Christian is capable of attaining a sinless state. Perfection was achieved in a moment when he or she experienced a move or act of the indwelling of the Holy Spirit, with the physical evidence of speaking in tongues, which rendered him or her perfect and able to live without sin.

Wesleyan Foundation

John Wesley's teaching largely influenced the idea and growth of perfectionism in American religious beliefs. His teaching about perfection, or the possibility of achieving sinlessness, was central to the Methodist religion. Wesley identified perfection as the inward death to the carnal self and the identification with the resurrection of Christ, with the full atonement of sin. Wesley wrote that he did not equate perfection with the complete absence of sin. Wesley's teaching suggested that sanctification was a process in the life of the converted Christian, and that perfection could only be achieved with continued dependence on Christ's love. His definition of "perfection" was the attainment, or obtainment, of perfect love, allowing the will to be steadily devoted to God. He shied away from identifying a single moment or instance when a Christian receives sanctification and achieves sinless perfection.

The Second Blessing and the Holiness Movement

The interest in perfectionism spiked among Methodist congregations in the 1820s and 1830s. A doctrine called the "second blessing" gained prominence among Methodist churches (then the largest denomination in the United States). The second blessing grew directly out of the doctrine of sanctification taught by Wesley. In 1835, a New York woman named Sarah Lankford received the "second blessing," and soon thereafter started prayer meetings in her home to help others attain perfection through the second blessing. The meetings were carried on by the woman's sister, Phoebe Palmer, every Tuesday night, and eventually became known as the Tuesday Meeting for the Promotion of Holiness. These meetings marked a significant change in the understanding of Wesley's doctrines. As opposed to a process of attaining sanctification over time through God's love, Phoebe Palmer began to put forth that it was an instantaneous act produced by the Spirit at a definite point of time. The second blessing was performed by the Holy Spirit directly upon the heart of an individual, occurring sometime after his or her initial conversion, and rendering him or her perfect and able to achieve a sinless life. This was also referred to as a "second work of grace," a necessary continuation of carrying out the Christian life.

With the growing influence of Palmer's views, the doctrine of the second blessing spread. Increasing numbers of leading pastors, bishops, and theologians in the Methodist Church began to teach the perfectionist doctrine of the second blessing. Soon came the idea of re-creating the camp meeting revivals that had been effective in the first half of the nineteenth century for spreading the gospel. Methodist leaders planned a camp meeting in Vineland, New Jersey, in July of 1867. The meeting was specifically to promote the work of "entire sanctification." Out of this camp meeting, the National Camp Meeting Association for the Promotion of Holiness was formed. The popularity of these meetings spread into other Protestant denominations, and by the late 1860s it was known as the "Holiness movement." Various Holiness publications sprang up around the country, and even spread abroad to Europe, where the Keswick Convention, another Holiness movement, was formed.

The concept of the Spirit-filled life became a key concept of the Holiness movement. Instead of focusing on just conversion, or "justification," the goal was to experience "sanctification," or true holiness and the attainment of a complete victory over sin, subsequent to conversion, through the second blessing. The Holiness groups were comprised of people who formerly belonged to other major denominations such as Methodists, Presbyterians, and Baptists. Those who participated disagreed with the growing wealth and materialism of mainstream churches. With these new concepts, a rift began to form between the Holiness groups and those who resisted the new ideas, claiming that the emphasis on the experience of the second blessing strayed from Wesley's original message of perfection. They still held that instantaneous sanctification strayed from the true doctrine of the progression of sanctification that would be complete only in heaven. This caused the Holiness movement to distance themselves even farther from denominational boundaries.

The Third Blessing and the Holy Spirit

As the Holiness movement expanded, there was increased stress on the outward evidences of sanctification, visible signs of separation from the world of sin. This external evidence differed from region to region, including anything from clothing styles and abstinence from certain foods or substances to involvement in certain activities. One group began to speak of a "baptism of fire." The Fire-Baptized Holiness Church was a church that originated in Iowa in 1895 and was led by Benjamin Irwin. The physical expression of this baptism would cause people to shout, scream, fall into trances, or speak in tongues. The result of the baptism of fire was believed to be the indwelling of the Holy Spirit, and they began to refer to this as the "third blessing." Other more conservative teachers of the Holiness movement refused to acknowledge this baptism as a "third" blessing, maintaining the belief that it was not a separate experience from the sanctification of the second blessing.

Charles Parham was involved in the fire baptism Holiness movement, but did not feel comfortable with the extreme emotionalism of the fire baptism meetings. He did, however, believe the theology of the "third experience" of a "baptism of the Holy Ghost and fire" with the evidence of speaking in tongues, or glossolalia. He felt that this experience would prepare Christians to usher in the new century. In order to train pastors to spread the teaching of the second blessing and Holy Spirit baptism, he set up a school in Topeka, Kansas.

On New Year's Eve, 1900, one of Parham's students, Agnes Ozman, requested prayer during the night's service so that she would receive the baptism of the Holy Spirit, with the evidence of speaking in tongues. The next day, she purportedly began speaking in Chinese, and for three days she was unable to converse in English. News of the "third experience" spread, and soon it was beginning to gain as much popularity as the "second grace" doctrine of sanctification. The reports of the event directly linked it to the original upper room Pentecost of the apostles as told in the book of Acts. The event in Topeka was described with imagery of the Holy Spirit descending into the room with fire and light. It was, in fact, referred to as the "second Pentecost."

Glossolalia began to be practiced increasingly among Holiness groups. Speaking in tongues was believed to be the universal evidence of the endowment of the Holy Spirit, and the sign that the life of the Christian was now sanctified and free of sin. This experience came to be seen as essential for a believer to fulfill his or her Christian mission. This power of perfection marked the central doctrine and the beginning of the Pentecostal movement. It was taught that the gift of tongues, as well as the gift of healing, was part of a revival of the apostolic church, and that it had occurred in order to unite the worldwide church and to perfect the believers by confirming the sanctifying indwelling of the Spirit. Many believed that it was a preparation for the second coming of Christ. The gift of languages was seen as a way to fulfill the Great Commission, by enabling believers to communicate the gospel to other nations, preparing them for Christ's return.

Pentecostal Perfectionism

Parham left the school in Topeka and went on the road to spread the doctrine of the "full gospel," with the third blessing, including healing as well as the gift of tongues as evidence of the Spirit's indwelling. With roots in both Wesleyan theology and the Holiness movement, Parham's theology contained a significant emphasis on perfectionism. Though he claimed that his beliefs were built only upon his personal study of the Bible, Parham was influenced not only by his experience in the Holiness movement, but also by his wife's family background. Her relatives were members of the Quaker religion. The doctrine of perfection was an integral part of the Quaker faith, identified as the death to self that results from experiencing the perfect love of God. Parham, after extensive Bible study, came to believe that the baptism of the Holy Spirit was not part of the second blessing sanctification, but that it was a separate endowment of the Spirit for the power of service. One man who heard and was influenced by Parham's message was William Seymour. He was a pastor who then moved to Los Angeles, and in April of 1906 was instrumental in the birth of the well-known Azusa Street Revival. The Azusa Street Revival lasted for three years and is considered to be the true launch of the Pentecostal movement.

During this revival, two radical Holiness papers in particular, the *Pentecostal Herald* (Louisville, Kentucky) and *God's Revivalist* (Cincinnati, Ohio), were particularly instrumental in the transition from Holiness to Pentecostal. These papers represented the growing Holiness movement in that they superseded geographic as well as social boundaries. The Pentecostal revival gained most of its followers in the locations where Holiness movements were already prospering. However, it attracted far more people from denominations other than Methodists than had the other Holiness groups. In addition to the belief in the baptism of the Holy Spirit, Pentecostalism recognized and prayed for divine healing and also demanded high standards of personal conduct that would reflect the perfect, sinless life.

The perfectionist doctrine caught on quickly within the Pentecostal movement. Pentecostal Holiness publications wrote of the commitment to perfectionism. The evangelist G. D. Watson from Virginia stated in his periodical *Living Words* (Pittsburgh, Pennsylvania) that anyone born of God no longer committed sin. Other Pentecostals believed that when they were entirely sanctified, they were freed from their "carnal mind" and cleansed of all sin. Some Pentecostal denominations, particularly those that grew out of the Azusa Street Revival, substantiated their claim that joy and rapture must indeed be prominent in the perfected Christian life. The joy and rapture was evident in the enthusiastic and emotional services as well as in the act of receiving the Holy Spirit and speaking in tongues. This belief contradicted Wesley's writings, which spoke of a progressive discovery of God's love that did not always reflect joyous or happy emotions.

Concerning the theology of perfectionism, there were differing positions between early Wesleyan congregations and members of the Holiness movement on whether perfection was an ongoing process within a growing Christian life or an instantaneous act. However, the emphasis on perfectionism remained basically the same between Holiness and Pentecostal groups. They both conceived sanctification as a separation from the world. While the non-Pentecostal Holiness churches continued to follow the doctrine of sanctification as a second grace, most Pentecostal denominations that began after 1911 incorporated the belief of a further, finished work in their statements of faith. This finished work was the visible sign of a believer receiving the Holy Spirit with the power to exercise one or more of the supernatural gifts.

Controversies and Perfectionism Today

In 1910 a group of Pentecostals emerged under the leadership of William Durham that rejected the doctrine of perfectionism. This group maintained that at the point of conversion, the believer became a new being and did not need an additional work of grace. This was referred to as the Finished Work doctrine, and it marked the first major split in the Pentecostal movement. This disagreement was never resolved, but has become less intense in recent years. The Pentecostal groups that continued to stress the definitive perfectionist experience of receiving the Holy Spirit have tended to reflect a more strict, defined set of expectations for the visible evidence of a Spirit-filled life. These groups are smaller and tend to be more radical. The Assemblies of God, one of the largest Pentecostal denominations, for the most part does not endorse perfectionism; however, there are members who continue to uphold the doctrine. For the most part, it is believed that perfectionism is accomplished in fractions, with the believer defeating or overcoming sin moment by moment. The pursuit of the communion with the Holy Spirit has contributed to the emphasis on separation from the world.

The Charismatic Renewal movement of the mid-twentieth century maintained the second blessing format, but began to move away from the strong perfectionist stance. Instead, baptism in the Holy Spirit was defined as a second work of grace by the Holy Spirit in the believer's life in order to empower him or her to witness and serve Christ in victorious Christian living. The Charismatic Renewal, therefore, draws on a long tradition of second-blessing teaching, but the concept of perfectionism has faded somewhat into the background in favor of emphasis on actively living out Christ's commands.

SHERRY L. THOMAS

See also Azusa Street Revival; Baptism in the Holy Spirit; Glossolalia; Sanctification; Second Work of Grace

Further Reading

Burgess, S. M. (Ed.). (1986). *Reaching beyond: Chapters in the history of perfectionism*. Peabody, MA: Hendrickson.

Hughes, R. T. (1986). Christian primitivism as perfectionism: From Anabaptists to Pentecostals. In S. M. Burgess (Ed.), *Reaching beyond: Chapters in the history of perfectionism* (pp. 213–255). Peabody, MA: Hendrickson.

Panning, A. J. (1980). *A look at Holiness and perfectionism theology*. Mequon: Wisconsin Lutheran Seminary. Retrieved August 28, 2004, from http://www.wls.wels.net/library/Essays/Authors/PQ/PanningPerfectionism/PanningPerfectionism.pdf

Pierard, R. V. (2001). American Holiness movement. In W. A. Elwell, (Ed.), *Evangelical dictionary of theology*. Grand Rapids, MI: Baker Academic. Retrieved August 28, 2004, from http://mb-soft.com/believe/text/holiness.htm

Protestant revivalism, Pentecostalism, and the drift back to Rome. *Present Truth, 5,* 20–28. Retrieved August 28, 2004, from www.presenttruthmag.com/archive/V/5-5.htm

Stephens, R. J. (2002). There is magic in print: The Holiness-Pentecostal press and the origins of southern Pentecostalism. *Journal of Southern Religion, 5.* Retrieved August 28, 2004, from http://jsr.fsu.edu/2002/Stephens.htm

Persecution and Martyrdom

Persecution and martyrdom has been a regular, albeit sporadic, feature of Christian history. Barrett and Johnson (2001) estimate that in twenty centuries some 70 million Christians have been killed for their faith. Half of those deaths were recorded in the twentieth century alone. One out of every 120 Christians is martyred. This number continues to grow in the new millennium, as over four hundred Christians are martyred every day.

History of Christian Persecution

When most Christians hear the words "persecution" or "martyrdom," their minds gravitate to the Roman persecution of the early Christians. Actually the history of Christian persecution and martyrdom extends back to the trial and execution of Jesus of Nazareth as a political subversive. Furthermore, the meaning of Christian martyrdom was derived from the exemplary courage of the prophets of the Hebrew Scriptures and the priestly freedom fighters of the Maccabean period. The writers of the Christian Scriptures urged their readers to stand fast in the thick of persecution, as did the ancient Hebrew prophets (Hebrews 10: 32–36; cf. John 15: 18–21; Philippians 1: 29–30; 2 Timothy 1: 8–10; 1 Peter 4: 12–19; Revelation 1: 9, NIV). All of the apostles suffered martyrdom, save one, John the Seer. The first martyr was Stephen (Acts 8: 54–60) and the next was James, who was one of the original twelve disciples of Jesus (Acts 12: 2). According to legend, Peter and Paul suffered martyrdom in Rome during the reign of Nero.

The term "martyr," derived from the Greek *martys* (literally "witness"), originally denoted the witness of a Christian. With the spread of persecution it took on the connotation of suffering voluntarily for one's faith. Later "martyr" became a technical term for those who had given up their lives for their faith, in contradistinction to a "confessor," one who survived the ordeal of interrogation and torture. Barrett and Johnson define martyrs as "believers who have lost their lives prematurely, in situations of witness, as a result of human hostility" (2001, 227).

The early martyrs included many women. Martyrs were venerated as those who had followed Christ's example literally. They were regarded as specially inspired by the Holy Spirit. Their utterances and relics were treasured and preserved. Beginning in the third century, it was common for churches to be built upon the tombs of martyrs. Such a church was called a "martyrium," and the bishop in charge was known as the "martyrarius." Early Christian calendars designated feast days for martyrs, recording their names and places of martyrdom. Persecution in the early church resulted in a new genre of literature, known later as the "acts of the martyrs." A further stage in the development of the literature of martyrdom was the emergence of martyrology, that is, collections of martyr stories. Martyrologies were heavily tinged with hagiography, as is evident in the works produced by Bede (c. 730), Florus of Lyons (c. 850), and George Fox (1559).

Roman persecution was due in part to Roman misunderstandings concerning early Christian practices, and in part to the firm stance of Christians. The Romans accused Christians of *flagita*, that is, gross sexual promiscuity, and atheism. To no avail, a number of Christian Apologists attempted to convince the Roman authorities that Christians were neither flagitious nor atheistic. In every imperial reign of any length there was persecution. However, it should be said that the Roman government made no comprehensive attempt to exterminate Christians. Persecution was sporadic and ineffectual. The first general enactment against the Christian faith was issued in 248 when Decius decreed that all subjects must sacrifice and obtain certificates of a loyalty oath, called the *sacramentum*. By this means Christians were identified and prosecuted. In 257, Valerian forbade Christian meetings and ordered the clergy to sacrifice. Those who refused were subjected to death. In 303 Diocletian issued a general edict that led to the demolition of churches and the burning of the Scriptures, the incarceration of clergy, and prohibition of Christian worship. A fearful wave of persecution swept across the empire and was not abated until Constantine's celebrated conversion in 312. After 312 Christianity was no longer a proscribed religion in the Roman Empire, but that did not mean the cessation of persecution and martyrdom. Some of the worst persecution occurred in the Persian Empire. Syrian Christians suffered terrible persecutions in the 340s, 420s, and 440s, usually during times of war with the Roman Empire. Isolated martyrdoms continued until the end of the Sasanian dynasty in 651. In Islamic lands Christians and Jews were allowed a modicum of religious freedom as "people of the Book," but their position was subordinate, as defined by the *dhimmi* system. The concept of *dhimmi* was derived from the voluntary contracts between the prophet Muhammad and the Jewish and Christian tribes in Arabia in the seventh century. After Muhammad's death the contracts became compulsory for Jews and Christians and entailed several repressive measures, such as limitations on places of residence and clothing, and onerous land and poll taxes. The *dhimmi* system produced waves of pragmatically motivated conversions to Islam.

Martyring Their Own

The sad fact is that Christians not only suffered persecution and martyrdom from outside rivals, but also at their own hands. Surprisingly, Christians themselves have been responsible for martyring 5,539,000 other Christians. The story of the in-house martyrdoms begins with the Donatists of North Africa, who took the position that those clergy who had recanted their faith and turned over the Scriptures to be burned in the heat of the Diocletian persecution should lose their ecclesiastical positions. Constantine opposed the Donatists and imposed severe measures against them in 317–321 and 346–348, confiscating churches and exiling their leaders. During the intense persecution a whole congregation was killed inside the basilica of Carthage. To say the least, the Donatists had many martyrs.

Another case of mortal conflict was the Iconoclasm Controversy of the Eastern Church. In two phases, 726–787 and 813–843, Byzantine emperors attempted to remove icons from places of worship. This policy was stiffly resisted by the clerics and monks. The rulers persecuted icon venerators and ordered the widespread destruction of icons. Some monks who were icon painters were executed and many were driven into exile. After prolonged destruction and suffering, the icons were restored in what came to be known as the Triumph of Orthodoxy. Martyrdom then became a prominent subject in iconography. The icons of martyrs show little concern with how a martyr might have died. As with catacomb art in Rome, Orthodox iconography focuses on the beatified state of the martyr. As Taylor says, "The drama of the represented situation is not so much the very moment of sacrifice as the internal spiritual state of the person, i.e. the state of prayer" (Taylor 1979, 54).

Whether in East or West, heretics paid a heavy price for their heterodox views. The notion that religious deviation was a threat to Christian society and should be punished with the civil sword reached its denouement in the Crusades. Along with Islamic people in Palestine, Eastern Christians perished at the hands of the Crusaders of the Western Church, most tragically in the sacking of Constantinople. In addition, the Albigenses in France and the Waldenses in Italy also died at the hands of Crusaders.

The most notable martyr of the medieval Western church was John Huss of Bohemia, who died for his proto-Protestant views. During the Reformation period, Protestants and Catholics persecuted each other, and there were numbers of martyrs on both sides. Some would say that the real martyr church of the Reformation was made up of the Anabaptists. Although Martin Luther (1483–1546) is reported to have averred, "The burning of heretics is against the will of the Holy Spirit," he nevertheless called on the civil authorities to execute Anabaptists (Oyer 1964, 126–129, 135–139). The grounds for the death penalty were neglect of public church attendance and confession, participation in unauthorized Mennonite services, adult baptism, communion in the "Mennonite manner," marriages not legally solemnized, and participation in conventicles (akin to the home Bible studies or house churches of today). Many Christians died in England during the reigns of Henry VIII and his daughter, Mary Tudor, who put to death Hugh Latimer, Nicholas Ridley, and Thomas Cranmer for their Protestant beliefs. The Catholic/Protestant carnage reached its horrific worst during the Thirty Years War in 1618–1648.

Of all the centuries of Christian history, the century of greatest persecution was the twentieth. Barrett and Johnson estimate that 45 million Christians have died, more than twice as many as in the previous nineteen centuries combined. The legacy of the Crusades has had a particularly deleterious effect on relations between Christians and Muslims in the Near East. Terrible persecution was inflicted by Muslims on Christians during the disastrous "year of the sword," 1915, when the Church of the East and the Syriac Orthodox Church suffered large scale massacres and forced flight. Worst of all, the genocide of Armenian Christians was carried out ruthlessly by the Ottoman Turks, resulting in up to 1 million deaths.

Of the waves of persecution in the twentieth century, none were more deadly than the purges of the Soviet Union. Many Orthodox clergy were arrested, tortured, exiled, and killed. When the KGB files were opened to full scrutiny during perestroika, the official secrets of the Soviet nightmare were unveiled, revealing that during the regime of Josef Stalin, 330,000 Christians were killed per year for the purpose of eliminating every social element that was deemed to be "religious and monarchist." During the administration of Nikita Khrushchev a five-year persecution was unleashed with the intent of liquidating religion. Between 1958 and 1964 the number of monasteries and convents dropped from sixty-nine to ten, with a handful of monks and nuns in each. In the same period the number of theological seminaries was reduced from eight to three, and the number of churches decreased from 22,000 to 11,500. Russian Pentecostals also endured a full share of the persecution. The Russian American Ivan E. Voronaev returned to his homeland from New York City to proclaim the Pentecostal message. Under the aegis of the Russian and Eastern European Mission, he began in Bulgaria and moved on to Russia, where he met with considerable success during the early Soviet period. However, during Stalin's reign of terror, he was arrested and died in a Siberian labor camp.

Pentecostal Persecution

Pentecostals can empathize with those who undergo persecution, because from the outset of the Azusa Street Revival in 1906 they were subjected to persecution, although of a milder variety. Hostile journalists caricatured first-generation Pentecostals as the lunatic fringe. Acerbic ridicule was heaped on the practice of speaking in tongues. Segregationists found the interracial composition of the early Pentecostals to be deeply threatening. People known to be Pentecostals sometimes faced employment discrimination. Church buildings were defaced and even burned. The prejudiced public image of Pentecostalism has only changed since the Charismatic movement in mainline denominations made speaking in tongues more respectable.

Most of the Pentecostals who have suffered outright physical persecution and martyrdom were missionaries. Along with other Christian missionaries, Pentecostals have suffered the repercussions of the intense resentment in developing countries toward the colonial policies of the West. The first Pentecostal missionary to die for his faith was Paul Bettex, an independent missionary to China early in the twentieth century. Others have come under the threat of death, such as the Swedish Pentecostal missionaries in the Belgian Congo (later Zaire) and Tanganyika (later Tanzania), when in the 1930s local tribespeople attempted to poison them, fearing that they had come to kill them. In addition, Lillian Trasher (1887–1961) dodged bullets to save two toddlers at her orphanage in Assiout, Egypt, when caught in crossfire between Egyptian and British troops. Others were not so fortunate. William

Ekvall Simpson, an Assemblies of God missionary, was killed by bandits in 1932 in southwestern China while transporting supplies for his mission station in Tibet. Along with many others, J. Elmore Morrison and his wife faced the threat of harm when the Japanese invaded China.

Perhaps the most famous Christian martyr of the twentieth century was the German Lutheran pastor Dietrich Bonhoeffer (1906–1945), who was imprisoned and executed for his role in an attempt to assassinate Hitler. The Nazis also severely persecuted Pentecostals, clamping down on them for practices that were deemed subversive, such as praying for healing. The Nazis accused Pentecostals of exploiting the masses with the intention to make them feeble-minded and for diverting from their theory of race. In short, the Nazis were deeply troubled by the Pentecostals' commitment to the Jews as the chosen people of God. All of this led to surveillance of meetings and the confiscation of literature. The most harrowing year for the Pentecostals in Germany was 1937, as they were faced with an order to disband. The Gestapo imprisoned Herman Lauster of the Church of God (Cleveland, Tennessee) on the grounds that his preaching was detrimental to national health. Because of good behavior, he was appointed supervisor to a group of Jews in a cell and ministered to them in secret with apparently favorable results. Later he was inducted into the German army. Another Pentecostal minister, G. Herbert Schmidt, who founded the Danzig Institute of the Bible, was detained by the Gestapo, but escaped and smuggled aboard a merchant ship leaving for Sweden. Only after the close of the war was he reunited with his family.

According to McGee, Pentecostal missionaries suffered most in the Far East. During World War II, several were imprisoned by the Japanese. Many were on the run, such as Warren Anderson of the Open Bible Standard Churches, who fled on foot along the Burma Trail. Others were not so fortunate. The W. H. Turners of the Pentecostal Holiness Church spent two years in prison. Alan Benson, a missionary to China with the Assemblies of God in Britain and Ireland, was brutally tortured in a prolonged and unsuccessful attempt to gain a confession of spying. Undaunted in his faith, he later recounted how he prayed for his captors:

> Once the police required of me that if I was a real Missionary and not a spy, then I must pray in their presence....I fell to my knees and offered up a prayer for the salvation of their souls. In my prayer I mentioned the fact that they were sinners and needed their sins forgiven, and asked the Lord to

bring them to a condition of heart in which they would be able to repent of their sins and turn unto the Lord Jesus for cleansing. (McGee 1992, 36)

The Baptist Press Service reported that Hossein Soodmand, an ordained minister of the Assemblies of God, was martyred in Iran on 2 December 2000, having been tortured during two months of imprisonment. Prior to his arrest on charges of spying, Soodmand, who once worked with the Iranian Bible Society and is one of a handful of Iranian pastors who converted from Islam, had been conducting private meetings in Gorgan, a city northeast of Tehran, since the closing of his church in Mashad in 1988. Although Christianity is one of the four religions officially recognized by the Islamic government of Iran, expatriate Iranian Christians say that recognition applies only to ethnic Armenians and Assyrians.

There are many current cases of the persecution of Pentecostals. For instance, in Romania where Pentecostals constitute one of the largest religious minorities and the Church of God alone claims 220,051 members, the Romanian Orthodox Church has collaborated with authorities to restrict evangelism, the performance of baptisms and burials, and acquisition of permits to build churches. Of a more serious nature, in July 2001 two priests of the Georgian Orthodox Church organized a three-day attack on a Russian-language Pentecostal church in Tblisi. When the raid began, some one hundred Pentecostals were in the sanctuary when the mob burst in and attacked the congregation, many of whom required hospitalization.

The most egregious persecution of Christians today is occurring in sub-Sahara Africa, where the Commission on International Freedom has documented the deadly struggle going on in the Sudan, which is a country with a population of 20.5 million people, 73 percent of whom are Muslims, mostly concentrated in the north. In the south 83 percent of the population is Christian. For the past seventeen years the Islamic government has been attacking the Christian population in an attempt to depopulate the region for oil exploration. About 2 million Christians have been martyred, which is more than all the victims in Kosovo, Bosnia, and Rwanda combined, and many more have been kidnapped, enslaved, tortured, and forced to flee as refugees.

One might wish that the problem of persecution and martyrdom would become less of a threat to the Christian church, but this is unlikely. The apostle Paul writes, "Indeed all who desire to live a godly life in Christ Jesus will be persecuted" (2 Timothy 3: 12). On the one hand, there will always be those who are hostile to the advance of the Christian faith. On the other hand, out of ultimate allegiance to Christ, there will always be Christians who voluntarily accept death rather than deny their faith. As the above history of persecution has demonstrated, persecution tends to rage in one region of the world for a time and then simmers down only to spring up elsewhere. We might hope that persecution and martyrdom would cease and desist, but this has never happened.

Results of Martyrdom

Martyrdom has served two important functions in Christian history. The first is Evangelical. In line with Tertullian's famous maxim that the blood of the martyrs is the seed of the church, there is a correlation between martyrdom and evangelization. In some countries we find that martyrdom was followed by church growth. A contemporary example is the church in the Peoples Republic of China. In 1949 there were only 1 million Christians. During fifty years of anti-religious Communist repression, there were some 1.2 million martyrs. In the same period the church has grown explosively to today's 90 million believers. Another example would be the church in Iran. It is estimated that there are twenty thousand to thirty thousand indigenous Evangelical and Pentecostal believers today, most from Muslim backgrounds. In June 2004, *Charisma* magazine quoted Lazarus Yeghnazar, an Iranian evangelist based in Great Britain: "In the last 20 years more Iranians have come to Christ compared to the last 14 centuries." Even though faced with arrest, torture, and martyrdom, the growth rate of Iran's Pentecostals is 7.5 percent, which makes Pentecostalism the fast growing religious movement in Iran.

The second function is ecumenical. Martyrdom has created a sense of communion transcending the visible disunity of Christian denominations. This was seen recently in 1998 with the dedication of ten statues in niches in front of Westminster Abbey in London, representing the Russian Orthodox, Roman Catholic, Anglican, Presbyterian, Lutheran, and Baptist (but not Pentecostal) churches. The statues, which are emblematic of the martyrs of the twentieth century, include Martin Luther King, Jr., Maximilian Kolbe, Dietrich Bonhoeffer, plus lesser-known figures such as Esther John, murdered in Pakistan, and the Anglican catechumen Manche Maemola, killed by her animist parents in South Africa in 1928. In the words of Pope John Paul II, "We Christians already have a common martyrology. This also includes the martyrs of this century, more numerous than one might think, and it shows how, at a profound level, God preserves communion among the baptized in the supreme sacrifice of life itself" (Cunningham 2002, 374–375).

ERIC N. NEWBERG

See also Africa, North (and the Middle East); Islam, Relationship to

Further Reading

Barrett, D. B., & Johnson, T. M. (2001). Martyrology: The demographics of Christian martyrdom, AD 33–AD 2001. In *World Christian Trends, AD 30–AD 2200: Interpreting the annual Christian megacensus*. Pasadena, CA: William Carey Library.

Bigham, S. (2001). Death and orthodox iconography. *St Vladimir's Theological Quarterly, 29*(4), 325–341.

Bourdeaux, M. (1970). *Patriarch and prophets: Persecution of the Russian Orthodox church today*. London: Mowbrays.

Conway, J. S. (1968). *The Nazi persecution of the churches, 1933–1945*. London: Winfeld & Nicolson.

Cuningham, L. (2002). On contemporary martyrs: Some recent literature. *Theological Studies, LXIII*, 374–381.

Frend, W. H. C. (1965). *Martyrdom and persecution in the early church: A study of a conflict from the Maccabees to Donatus*. Grand Rapids, MI: Baker Book House.

Hefley, J., & Hefley, M. (1979). *By their blood: Christian martyrs of the 20th century*. Milford, MI: Mott Media.

Kolb, R. (1995). God's gift of martyrdom: The early reformation understanding of dying for the faith. *Church History, 64*(3), 399–411.

McGee, G. (1992). Historical perspectives on Pentecostal missionaries in situations of conflict and violence. *Missiology: An International Review, XX*(1), 33–43.

Mursurillo, H. (1972). *The acts of the Christian martyrs*. London: Oxford University Press.

Oyer, J. S. (1964). *Lutheran reformers against the Anabaptists: Luther, Melancthon and Menius and the Anabaptists of central Germany*. The Hague, Netherlands: Marin us Nijhoff.

Schlossberg, H. (1991). *A fragrance of oppression: The church and its persecutors*. Wheaton, IL: Crossway Books.

Taylor, J. (1979). *Icon paintings*. New York: Mayflower Books.

Tilley, M. A. (1996). *Donatist martyr stories: The church in conflict in Roman North Africa*. Liverpool, UK: Liverpool University Press.

Philippines

The Republic of the Philippines is the only country in Asia with a Christian majority. It has a unique heritage of Malay, Chinese, Spanish, and North American cultures. Today, its cultural characteristics are in some ways more akin to those of the nations of Latin America than those of Southeast Asia. Spain ruled the Philippines for nearly 330 years until 1898 when it was ceded to the United States of America. It was not until 1946 that the Philippines achieved full political independence, following four years of occupation by Japanese armed forces during World War II.

The coming of the Americans in 1898 paved the way for Protestant mission. It is said that Protestantism arrived in the Philippines wearing an American soldier's uniform because the first Protestant minister came as an army chaplain. The succeeding years saw the coming of missionaries from various denominations: the Methodists, Episcopalians, and Baptists in 1900, United Brethren and Disciples of Christ in 1901, Congregationalists in 1902, and Christian and Missionary Alliance and Seventh-Day Adventists in 1905. The first Pentecostal missionaries arrived in 1918 from the Church of God, then the Assemblies of God in 1926 and 1937, and the International Church of the Foursquare Gospel in 1937.

Pentecostalism, like Protestantism in general, has always been associated with the United States. All major Pentecostal denominations in the United States, and some minor ones, have sent missionaries to the Philippines starting in the 1920s. Initially they went to places not yet reached by Roman Catholic priests or in remote areas where the Roman Catholic Church did not have a strong presence. As a minority group, many Pentecostal churches are located outside of the city or town centers. The Pentecostals' strong emphasis in miraculous and divine healing is a major reason why people are attracted to its faith and practice. Another reason is their tendency to be "member-oriented," which results in effective mobilization of lay leaders in recruitment activities (e.g., evangelism). In contrast, classical and more established churches tend to monopolize power in the hands of an elite clergy. Pentecostal churches are known to provide opportunities in empowering their members through the gifts of the Spirit. This means that any member in the congregation has equal opportunity to "move in the Spirit" such as prophesying, interpretation of tongues, healing, or discerning of spirits.

The Pentecostal movement in the Philippines can be categorized in various ways but for this survey, the writer has limited it into two, namely: "classical" and "independent." Classical Pentecostal churches are those that have strong links with their U.S. counterparts and are usually the oldest. The independent Pentecostals are those that either have informal links with churches abroad or indigenous characteristics. The word "independent" is chosen because of the difficulty with the term "indigenous." Various disciplines attribute different meanings to the term. For instance, it is widely accepted within missiological circles that self-government, self-support, and self-propagation define what an indigenous church is. In the social sciences, however, indigenization refers to a process whereby religions initiated by outsiders are transformed through contact with native religion and culture. Doctrinally, the basic tenets of faith of the independent churches are either similar to that of the classical groups or simply a derivative. In fact, many of them came into existence as a splinter group from the bigger and older Pentecostal denominations such as the Assemblies of God and the Foursquare Church. While it can be argued by some that these congregations are "self-propagating" and "self-generating," and therefore indigenous; their basic theological perspective is one that is merely inherited from North America. Pentecostalism is more globalized than localized as far as the Philippine situation in concerned. A case in point is the Assemblies of God, which merely adopts what its counterpart does in the United States. To date the Philippine Assemblies of God continue to maintain the 16 Fundamental Truths introduced by the first missionaries in 1926.

Classical Pentecostals

The arrival of the Americans in 1898 brought the first wave of the mainline denominations. Missionary work had already been in progress by the time the first Pentecostals came. Presently the Philippine Council of Evangelical Churches lists around eighteen Pentecostal groups. The following are some of the major denominations.

Assemblies of God

It was in September of 1926 when the first Assemblies of God (U.S.) missionary Benjamin H. Caudle arrived in the Philippines. Shortly thereafter, he and his wife established church work in various parts of Manila. However, due to Mrs. Caudle's illness, their developing ministry was cut short when they returned to the United States. For a period, the Assemblies of God work in the Philippines was suspended. Meanwhile the wave of Filipino laborers coming to the United States in the early 1920s paved the way for them to be exposed to Pentecostalism. Eventually many of them became missionaries to their own people and pursued the vision of developing Assemblies of God churches in the Philippines. The first who was involved in this endeavor was Cris Garsulao. He became a Pentecostal while studying at a university in the United States. His conversion led him to commit himself to full-time church ministry. After finishing his training at Glad Tidings Bible Institute, an Assemblies of God school in California, Garsulao returned to his hometown in the Philippines. Later, several other Filipinos with similar experiences became instrumental in starting Pentecostal churches in various parts of the country.

The coming of Leland E. Johnson and his family in December 1939 marked the beginning of the arrival of more Assemblies of God missionaries from the United States to the Philippines. The 1941 invasion of the country by the Japanese forces hindered the growing work but did not stop the preaching of the Gospel. Despite the difficulties, several American missionaries remained in the country, and as a result, inspired local converts to carry on with their newfound faith. After the war, the work of establishing new churches throughout the country continued with much better results. In the intervening time, a group of Filipino Assemblies of God preachers in the United States combined their efforts in organizing the Philippine Assemblies of God. Their initial action was to request a U.S. Assemblies of God–appointed missionary to the Philippines to help them achieve this goal. Because the Philippines was still under the United States protectorate, any church denomination was required to have a duly appointed missionary from the home body in the United States. For fourteen years, the work of the Assemblies of God in the Philippines was under the U.S. General Council. In 1953, the Philippines General Council of the Assemblies of God was formed with Rev. Rodrigo C. Esperanza as the first superintendent.

The remarkable growth of the Assemblies of God in the 1950s and 1960s was hampered by leadership conflict within the organization during the 1970s. Other contributing factors to the lower growth in the 1970s could be attributed to the nascent independent Pentecostal and charismatic groups (mainly Roman Catholic). However, twenty years later, a significant recovery of growth was reported in the Missions World Edition of the *Pentecostal Evangel* magazine, a U.S. Assemblies of God publication. In that account, the Assemblies of God in the Philippines grew from "1,230 churches with 198,000 members and adherents to 2,600 churches attended by 420,830 people making it the largest evangelical body in the country" (Kennedy 2000, 5). A more conservative estimate however, is given in the *World Churches Handbook* edited by Peter Brierley (1997), which only showed 94,000 total memberships.

Church of the Foursquare Gospel

In 1931 Vicente Defante, a U.S. Navy cook, became a convert and later worked with Aimee Semple McPherson. After attending L.I.F.E. Bible College in California, he went back to the Philippines as a missionary. He returned to his home in Iloilo City and helped erect the first Foursquare church building in 1937. By 1949, Foursquare churches had increased to thirteen, located in various parts of the country. There were eight in the Visayas region and four in Luzon. Later the work spread to Mindanao with U.S. missionaries assisting in breaking ground for a new Foursquare church there. By 1958, the denomination was organized into four districts: Northern Luzon, Luzon, Mindanao, and Visayas.

A Church Growth Report Golden Jubilee Convention in 1999 showed there were Church of the Foursquare Gospel in the Philippines (CFGP) churches in sixty-four of the seventy-seven provinces. There were 888 or 78.2 percent of CFGP churches in barrios, towns, or municipalities and 247 or 21.8 percent in populated areas such as provincial capitals, chartered cities and the National Capital Region.

Church of God (Cleveland, Tennessee)

The work of the COG began in 1921 through the pioneering efforts of Joseph Warnick from the United States. Warnick along with Filipino Teodorico Lastimosa and a missionary from the United Free Gospel and Missionary Society, Frank Porada, started the first church in San Nicolas, Ilocos Norte (north of Manila). By 1947, the Philippine Church of God became an official extension of the mission work of the COG, Cleveland, Tennessee. At present, the COG has 540 local churches, 65,354 members, 677 pastors and 8 training schools throughout the country. Of these three classical Pentecostal groups (Assemblies of God, Foursquare Church in the Philippines, and the Church of God in the Philippines), the Assemblies of God is the largest with 2,600 churches as of mid-2000.

Filipino Assemblies of the First Born

Filipinos who worked as laborers in Hawaii and California received the Pentecostal blessing and later formed the Filipino Assemblies of the First Born. Among those who were converted and baptized in the Holy Spirit was Rev. Julian Bernabe. He was instrumental in starting the denomination. The Filipinos felt they were not welcome in many of the churches they visited. This frustration led them to organize a Filipino Pentecostal community in California. After several failed attempts to link up with the local Pentecostal groups in the United States, the First Filipino Assemblies of the First Born was registered in 1933.

In 1935, Rev. Silvestre Taverner heeded the call of God to share his newfound faith to his people in the Philippines. He began his ministry with his relatives and friends in the northern part of the Philippines.

Independent Pentecostals

These groups are mainly those that do not have formal association with churches abroad. Although their doctrines and church structure are similar with those of established Pentecostal denominations in the U.S., the organization is totally administered by the nationals. Some of the major groups are as follows.

Jesus Is Lord Church (JIL)

Among the independent Pentecostal churches, the most prominent is the Jesus is Lord Church (JIL) headed by Bishop Eddie Villanueva, a former radical activist, communist, and atheist. The church started as Bible study groups in the various parts of the Polytechnic University of the Philippines (PUP) campus where Villanueva used to teach. His experience in leading people to protest against the evils of capitalism when he was an activist helped him find a vibrant group of young people willing to sacrifice their time and efforts to advance the Kingdom of God. Today JIL has grown into a worldwide multiministry network, establishing churches from Asia, Australia, Europe, Africa, the Middle East, Canada, and the United States of America mainly from Filipino immigrants. As of 1999, the JIL Church had 106 Sunday services in metro Manila, 25 in the province of Bulacan, 275 in other regions all over the Philippines, and 72 worldwide; a total of 478 Sunday services. The Church also owns a television station called ZOE Broadcasting Network that broadcasts JIL's services on a regular basis. JIL is perhaps the only Pentecostal group in the country that runs a multilevel school, which includes nursery, kindergarten, elementary (first to six grade), and secondary (high school). The church is also planning to build a Christian university out of the existing structure in the future.

Bread of Life Ministries

The church started in 1982 with twelve people led by its senior pastor Butch Conde. Initially they envisioned a halfway house for prostitutes but God showed them a bigger plan, which was to start a new church. The first venue for their services was held in a Roman Catholic school called Maryknoll College (now Miriam College). Butch Conde took this as a confirmation of God's will as they began to meet with 120 attendees during its Sunday fellowship. Two years later the congregation grew to twelve hundred in attendance and had to relocate to a bigger place in Celebrity Sports Plaza, Capitol Hills, Quezon City. In 1987 the church moved to Circle Theater to accommodate roughly eighteen hundred to two thousand people attending its five services. About ten years after, in November 1998, a church-owned property named Crossroad 77 was dedicated to God as the main worship facility for Bread of Life Ministries. Currently, there are five services held on Sundays with each averaging twenty-five hundred people.

Prayer and the importance of commitment to the Word of God and the experience of a new life in Christ have been the major reasons behind the remarkable expansion of the Bread of Life Ministries. As the church grew, discipleship-training programs were used to address the need of developing rising leaders for the ministry.

Jesus Christ Saves Global Outreach

Started in 1980 by Jonathan Sebastian as a Bible study group for couples, this ministry grew into 140 local congregations, 8 overseas churches, close to 5,000 workers (perhaps including volunteer workers) and 25,000 members. The primary focus of the Jesus Christ Saves Global Outreach is family but the church is now sending missionaries among overseas Filipino workers worldwide.

Love of Christ

Mel Gabriel, a medical doctor, founded this ministry after he left a large "cultic" indigenous Filipino church, Iglesia ni Cristo (Church of Christ). Although he was severely persecuted by his former church, this did not stop him from conducting aggressive Bible studies in his own clinic that later grew into a sizeable congregation. Emphasis on Pentecostal-type of worship and healing through their meetings and radio broadcast were contributing factors in the remarkable growth of the ministry. Presently there are forty local churches with seventy pastors.

JOSEPH SUICO

See also Globalization of Pentecostalism

Further Reading

Brierley, P. (Ed.). (1997). *World churches handbook*. London: Christian Research.

Gowing, P. G. (1967). *Islands under the cross: The story of the church in the Philippines*. Manila: National Council of Churches in the Philippines.

Kennedy, J. W. (2000). Embracing the challenge. *Pentecostal Evangel*.

Montgomery, J. (1972). *New Testament fire in the Philippines*. Manila: Church Growth Research in the Philippines.

Tuggy, A. (1971). *The Philippine church growth in changing society*. Grand Rapids, MI: Eerdmans.

Wourms, M. (1992). *J.I.L. love story*. El Cajon, CA: Christian Services Publishing.

Philosophy and Theology

The history of Christianity is well populated with scholars—Augustine, Boethius, and Thomas Aquinas, to name only three—who were both theologically sophisticated and conversant with the philosophical tradition. The same cannot be said of late nineteenth- and early twentieth-century leaders in the classical Pentecostal tradition. While some of them were educated, having come to Pentecostalism from mainline denominational churches that valued education, most of them, including evangelists, missionaries, and ministers in local churches, lacked formal university or seminary education. They may have had some classroom exposure to study of the Scriptures in a local Bible training school or regional Bible institute, but by and large they had little formal theological education and virtually no formal introduction to the Western philosophical tradition. The situation was hardly different for lay people, except that, in addition to having no philosophical background, they also generally had even less theological training than their church leaders. What explains these facts?

First, Pentecostal forms of worship and spirituality appealed initially and most powerfully to people in the lower socioeconomic strata of North American society: rural farming families, especially in the southern United States, and urban poor and working-class families. These people generally enjoyed fewer educational opportunities than urban middle- and upper-class people of the same period. They cannot be said to have consciously considered and then rejected theological and philosophical inquiry, because for the most part they had few, if any, educational opportunities to do so. Also, within the social world they inhabited, there were few models of this type of inquiry. The kind of intellectual activity exemplified by theologians and philosophers undoubtedly would have seemed abstract and remote, given the day-to-day economic exigencies they faced. In addition, they were attracted by a form of religious expression that offered a transforming spiritual experience, the promise of divine provision and healing, and an apocalyptic vision of the future. All of these seemed more hopeful and satisfying than what they endured in their daily routines and also more immediately appealing than anything the life of the mind might have had to offer. The long-term result has been mixed: Pentecostals reminded the Christian world that worship can legitimately incorporate a powerful experiential component, but they largely banished the intellect from their conception and practice of worship.

Perhaps more important, developing appreciation for theological and philosophical inquiry did not seem to integrate well with Pentecostals' understanding of the Scriptures. Deeply motivated to spread the Gospel, Pentecostals tended to interpret passages like Matthew 28:18–20, the so-called great commission, as saying that humankind's most fundamental call is to engage in evangelism. The practical upshot of this reading of the Bible was both good and bad: Pentecostalism became a leading force in missions work, and Pentecostal churches worldwide grew spectacularly during the twentieth century; but theology was relegated to the role of providing apologetics for church dogma, while education generally served only to provide vocational training for missions or parish work.

The emphasis on missions and evangelism, together with the apocalyptic orientation, brought dignity and prestige to ecclesiastical callings, but it also had certain negative effects. It encouraged church leaders and parishioners alike to adopt a pragmatic, problem-solving approach that was consistent with their sense of urgency for evangelism, but it tended to discount critical reflection on the long-term consequences of their decisions and actions. In addition, it implicitly demeaned all other callings—including those of the theologian and philosopher—by relegating them to second-class status. (If evangelism is our primary call, any other endeavor can at best be secondary.)

With respect to the disciplines of theology and philosophy, two contrasting trends emerged among Pentecostals in the second half of the twentieth century. First, the vast majority of those who came to occupy mid-level and senior leadership positions in Pentecostal churches arrived at their positions by completing a Bible institute training program (sometimes via correspondence) or completing a three- or four-year Bible school degree, and then proving themselves to be effective pastors or evangelists. This common pathway was not conducive to serious reflection on theological issues, and it included virtually no exposure to the history of ideas or to contemporary philosophical trends. Second, the emergence of liberal arts colleges and seminaries in Pentecostal denominations saw a rapid increase in the number of Pentecostal scholars in many disciplines, particularly theology and biblical studies (though much less so in philosophy). Scholarly theological discussions developed steadily, and several attempts were made in the 1960s and 1970s to publish scholarly journals, such as *Agora* and *Paraclete*.

In 1970 the Society for Pentecostal Studies (SPS) was formed, and in 1979, the first issue of *Pneuma: The Journal of the Society for Pentecostal Studies* was published. In 2001 one of the founding members of the SPS, Russell Spittler, an Assemblies of God Pentecostal who earned his Ph.D. in early Christian origins at Harvard University, reflected on the maturation of Pentecostal scholarship:

> If evangelicals battled a reputation for anti-intellectualism, Pentecostals a lot more so. 'When you preach to Pentecostals,' one of my patriarchal mentors advised (himself president of a Pentecostal college), 'you have to throw away your brains.' Things have changed. The ecclesial tradition that loathed liturgy and functioned orally and spontaneously, that still more easily speaks of 'Bible doctrine' than of 'systematic theology,' now features graduate theological seminaries along with colleges that began life as unaccredited Bible institutes but since have joined the recent evangelical tide toward self-designation as 'universities.' Increasingly, their presidents hold university doctorates. (Spittler 2001, 2–3)

Current Situation

In the first decade of the twenty-first century, the preponderance of Pentecostal pastors, missionaries, evangelists, and top administrators continue to be people with a Bible school educational background, which means that, while they may have a firm grasp of their own church doctrines, they are not particularly conversant with historical or systematic theology or with contemporary theological discussions. In general, they also continue to have little or no formal exposure to the history or contemporary discussion of philosophical ideas. Interesting exceptions to this general pattern appear among Pentecostal missionaries who have found themselves compelled to become conversant with the religious and philosophical worldviews of the people to whom they feel called to minister.

In contrast to the general trend among those involved in church ministry, missions, and evangelism, a growing number of scholars in Pentecostal colleges, universities, and seminaries are theologically and philosophically informed. The most promising trend has shown up in the emergence of a cadre of young theologians whose writings are being published by reputable presses and journals. The SPS has grown in numbers and diversity of views; its annual meetings now include several study groups devoted to inquiry in specific scholarly fields, among which are groups in theology and philosophy. In addition, *Pneuma* has come to be recognized in the academy as a mature scholarly journal.

While theological inquiry is flourishing among Pentecostals (and between Pentecostals and members of other denominations), there is little evidence that the reflections and writings of Pentecostal theologians are making a significant impact in Pentecostal churches. Pastors, evangelists, and guest speakers that frequent the pulpits of Pentecostal churches still largely represent a pattern that dates back to the beginning of the modern Pentecostal movement: speakers proclaiming a simple message in a popular way. Their messages often do not reflect either significant theological preparation or serious engagement with worldviews or philosophical ideas that underlie important global trends. Sustained exegetical preaching, informed by theological reflection, is much less common in Pentecostal churches than thematic sermons buttressed by proof texts from the Bible.

Pentecostal Educational Institutions

The narrow Pentecostal emphasis on calling became evident during the 1910s and 1920s in the rapid development of local church Bible training schools and later in the development of regional Bible institutes and their successors, the Bible colleges. Until the 1950s, most Pentecostal denominations neither owned nor endorsed anything resembling a Christian liberal arts college or university where subjects like philosophy were offered. The Church of God (COG) of Cleveland, Tennessee, authorized the establishment of a Bible training school in 1911, but this school did not evolve into an accredited college until many decades later. In 1957, an attempt was made to expand the school's junior college into a four-year liberal arts college, but this effort did not finally succeed until the mid-1960s, with regional accreditation being awarded in 1969. After several

decades of founding and supporting Bible training schools, the Assemblies of God (AG) at its 1953 General Council passed a resolution to establish a four-year liberal arts college. The action was controversial, and had the council not been held in Milwaukee, Wisconsin, a northern city not readily accessible to some of the most conservative southern representatives, the authorizing resolution probably would not have been approved. The college of arts and sciences, called Evangel College (later renamed Evangel University), opened its doors in 1955; however, the denomination's general superintendent, Ralph Riggs, is believed to have lost his position because of his support for it.

Today, the strongest segment of the curriculum in Pentecostal Bible schools is in the area of biblical studies. Numerous courses are offered in specific books of the Bible and in biblical themes. Theology offerings often represent a mixture of introductory surveys that tend to emphasize conversancy with church doctrine over teaching students how to think theologically, and topical or historical courses with more emphasis on challenging students' assumptions and forcing them to assess their own theological commitments. Bible schools, particularly unaccredited ones, offer few if any philosophy courses. Where philosophy courses are offered, they are seldom taught by people with advanced degrees in the field. Pentecostal Bible schools, whether accredited or not, rarely require students to take a philosophy course.

Almost all regionally accredited Pentecostal liberal arts colleges and universities offer at least some philosophy courses and a few offer a substantial number, though the more challenging upper-division courses tend to be taught on an infrequent rotation. Unlike Bible schools, liberal arts colleges and universities commonly offer philosophy courses as part of the general education curriculum. At these institutions it is not uncommon to have philosophy courses taught by a professor with at least some graduate training in the discipline, though there continue to be a scant few Pentecostals who hold a doctorate in philosophy. Although philosophy is rarely a requirement at Pentecostal colleges and universities, several require courses that have some philosophical content or that take a philosophical approach; e.g., discipline-specific courses in ethics and critical reasoning, and general education courses that deal with worldview formation or analysis. No Pentecostal liberal arts colleges or universities offer a major in philosophy; however, several offer a concentration or minor. The AG's denominational liberal arts institution, Evangel University, is unique among Pentecostal educational institutions in requiring its preseminary biblical studies majors to take nine semester hours of philosophy.

Comparing American Pentecostal liberal arts colleges and universities to other American Christian colleges and universities, certain trends are evident. Pentecostal schools offer about the same number and kind of philosophy courses as do other Protestant schools. Evangelical schools are more likely than Pentecostal schools to require students to take at least one philosophy course; however, they generally require substantially fewer courses in theology. But mainline Protestant colleges and universities are generally no more likely to have a philosophy requirement than Pentecostal schools. Roman Catholic colleges and universities, by contrast, generally do have a philosophy requirement. The most robust requirements (6–9 semester credits) are found at Catholic universities with student populations over 5,000, such as DePaul, St. Johns, Georgetown, Marquette, Notre Dame, and Boston College. Almost no Catholic undergraduate institutions require as many hours in theology as Pentecostal colleges and universities. The requirements in Catholic colleges and universities, with the mix of roughly equal components of philosophy and theology, probably reflect the Catholic Church's longstanding commitment to helping students develop a robust worldview and preparing them to engage both the popular culture and the intellectual tradition.

It is not clear what to make of the fact that Pentecostal schools generally require more theology but less philosophy than Catholic schools. It may indicate that Pentecostals have generally become more comfortable with and open to theological conversation; but it may also indicate a continuing attempt use theology apologetically, as an instrument to defend church doctrine. The minimal philosophy requirement at Pentecostal liberal arts institutions seems consistent with what is seen in other Protestant colleges and universities, except that no Pentecostal school offers a degree in philosophy; this may suggest continuing discomfort among Pentecostal leaders with the deliberative, self-reflective, analytical, and exploratory nature of philosophical thinking.

Among Pentecostal educational institutions in North America, seminaries represent the most robust commitment to theological exploration. Schools like Regent University's School of Divinity, the Church of God Theological Seminary, and the Assemblies of God Theological Seminary, all established in the 1970s, have developed credible masters and doctoral programs that include strong historical and thematic theological components. As a rule, their theology professors hold doctorates in the relevant fields. On the other hand, no North American Pentecostal seminary has a full-time faculty member who holds a Ph.D. in philosophy or any of its traditional subdisciplines like ethics, epistemology, or the history of philosophy. Moreover, no North American Pentecostal seminary requires its students to take courses in philosophy, though some of them offer elective courses in subjects like ethics.

In sum, relative to the strength of theological offerings in Pentecostal seminaries, philosophy seems underrepresented in the curriculum. What explains the apparently diminished role of philosophy in Pentecostal scholarship? There are probably at least three reasons. First, Pentecostal seminaries have taken as their primary task preparing people for professional ministry and leadership roles in the church (pastors, missionaries, chaplains), rather than for research and writing careers in academic fields. They have thus tended to give more attention to courses in spiritual formation and leadership training than graduate training in philosophical subjects. Second, Pentecostal seminaries have tended to assume, often wrongly, that students will come to the seminary with a broad undergraduate preparation that includes exposure to philosophical thinking. Third, although Pentecostal seminaries obviously devote scant attention to traditional philosophical subjects and offer few courses in the discipline, they have not ignored developing the mindset and key skills commonly associated with philosophical reasoning. Deliberation, analysis, synthesis, reflection, logical thinking are all commonly integrated into theological courses at the seminary level. In a certain respect then, in Pentecostal seminaries theology courses have replaced philosophy courses as the primary vehicle for developing the reflective, deliberative, and critical capacities of the mind.

Challenges and Implications

In the early twenty-first century, Pentecostals find themselves at a historical turning point both hopeful and precarious—hopeful because demographics and wider acceptance by the dominant culture have placed them in a strategic position both to challenge and to shape the surrounding culture, and precarious because for too long they have traded on the experiential aspects of faith and sold short the life of the mind. The precarious position of Pentecostals shows itself in two general ways. First, although they have long identified negative trends in popular culture, their lack of a robust intellectual tradition has left them vulnerable to being co-opted by these very trends they claim to disdain. Second,

Pentecostals' tradition of anti-intellectualism has left them with only limited intellectual resources for dealing with new cultural and intellectual issues. The strain is particularly evident in churches where pastors with only a Bible-school education are expected to address complicated social and moral issues such as poverty and racism, ethical questions related to fast-emerging biomedical developments, and issues related to globalization and technology.

Pentecostal liberal arts colleges and universities, and seminaries, have much to offer their constituencies. But for them to deliver it effectively, two things seem necessary. First, the churches themselves must come to grips with their longstanding ambivalence about their own educational institutions, which they would like to see function both as educational institutions and as places of indoctrination. Second, Pentecostal educational institutions (particularly the Bible colleges) will have to re-think both the content and approach of their course offerings in theology and philosophy. Theology courses will have to be designed to focus less on defending Pentecostal doctrines (and behavioral distinctions) and more on preparing students to engage in a more active conversation with both the church and the wider culture. Requiring students to complete more coursework in philosophy—particularly in moral theory, applied ethics, and worldview formation—will enhance students' capacity to make a difference in the conversation by strengthening their grasp of deeply embedded social problems. In the last analysis, whether Pentecostals come to value theological and philosophical education is a matter of both practical consequence and urgency, because how they finally come to live their lives will depend in large measure on the stewardship they exercise over the processes that shape their minds.

MICHAEL D. PALMER

See also Anti-intellectualism; Education

Further Reading

Blumhofer, E. L. (1993). *Restoring the faith: the Assemblies of God, Pentecostalism, and American culture.* Champaign: University of Illinois Press.

Blumhofer, E. L., Spittler, R. P., & Wacker, G. A. (Eds.). (1999). *Pentecostal currents in American Protestantism.* Urbana & Chicago: University of Illinois Press.

Borgmann, A. (2003). *Power failure: Christianity in the culture of technology.* Grand Rapids, MI: Brazos (Baker).

Cox, H. (1995). *Fire from heaven: The rise of Pentecostal spirituality and the reshaping of religion in the twenty-first century.* Cambridge, MA: Da Capo Press.

Dayton, D. (1987). *Theological roots of Pentecostalism.* Peabody, MA: Hendrickson.

Palmer, M. D. (Ed.). (1998). *Elements of a Christian worldview.* Springfield, MO: Logion Press.

Palmer, M. D. (2001). Orienting our lives: The importance of liberal education for Pentecostals in the 21st century. *Pneuma: The Journal of the Society for Pentecostal Studies, 23*(2), 197–216.

Palmer, M. D. (2004). Scripture study in the age of the new media. In C. Ess (Ed.), *Critical thinking and the Bible in the age of new media.* Lanham, MD: University Press of America.

Spittler, R. P. (2001). The dawning of the Pentecostal mind. In M. E. Roberts (Ed.), *Society for Pentecostal studies: commemorating thirty years of annual meetings 1971–2001* (pp. 2–3). Lexington, KY: Society for Pentecostal Studies.

Synan, V. (1971). *Holiness Pentecostal tradition: Charismatic movements in the twentieth century.* Grand Rapids, MI: Eerdmanns.

Wacker, G. (2000). *Religion in nineteenth century America.* New York: Oxford University Press.

Wacker, G. (2001). *Heaven below: Early Pentecostals and American culture.* Cambridge, MA: Harvard University Press.

Positive Confession Theology

In an age where science and technology were producing so many tangible benefits, Evangelicals increasingly sought to demonstrate that Christianity "worked." To this end, Evangelicals increasingly couched their teachings in "scientific" terms, offering laws and formulas for reaching the lost, receiving the fullness of the Holy Spirit, and so on. Calvinistic stress on the sovereignty of God was being displaced by an emphasis on the autonomous individual, as seen in Charles Finney's (1792–1875) declaration that a revival was "not a miracle or dependent on a miracle, in any sense...[but] purely a philosophical result of the right use of constituted means...." (Finney 1978, 4).

It was only a matter of time before the right use of means was applied to obtaining any and all of God's blessings. This is particularly evident in Phoebe Palmer's (1807–1874) presentation of entire sanctification. For Palmer, the right use of means for obtaining the "promise of the Father" was twofold—believe and confess (Romans 10:9–10). Accordingly, Palmer maintained that one must have naked faith in the naked Word of God. Such faith was not a wishful hope that someday God *might* grant the desired gift but the confident assurance that, one having met the conditions, God has *already* sent the blessing sought. Consequently, people were encouraged to testify to the experience of entire sanctification as soon as they had claimed the blessing by faith. They did not need any evidence that the promise had been granted—God's Word was evidence enough. In fact, it was frequently stressed that one should believe and confess *against all contrary evidence*. It was further claimed that failure to make a continual public confession of entire sanctification would result in one's losing "the blessing."

Although strongly opposed by many in the Holiness movement, Palmer's "shorter way" to sanctification soon became the template for obtaining any of God's blessings, and finding an appropriate "promise" in the scriptures that covered what one was seeking became a paramount concern. Since the promises were legally binding, Christians were to plead their case before the Judge armed with chapter and verse.

A dramatic example of the application of claiming and confessing scriptural "promises" was the emergence of the divine-healing movement under Charles Cullis (1833–1892), A. B. Simpson (1843–1919), A. J. Gordon (1836–1895), and others. As previously in church history, James 5:14–15 was a central text for nineteenth-century faith-healing practitioners. Eventually, however, the focus was placed on the "prayer of faith," to the practical exclusion of the elders and anointing oil. This shift was due to a broader interpretation of the atonement, wherein healing, and not just forgiveness of sins, was viewed as procured via Christ's death (Isaiah 53:4 and Matthew 8:16–17). As such, healing, like salvation and sanctification, must be procured by the same process—belief and confession. Once the prayer of faith had been offered, and/or the promises claimed, the patient was assured that he or she was *already* healed—based on the naked promises of the Bible—and, therefore, they were encouraged to confess healing and "act faith," citing Mark 11:24 as the biblical warrant. Symptoms that persisted were simply lies of the devil that the patient should ignore and/or *"temptations* to sickness," which only became an *actual* illness if one yielded to them.

1890s through 1948

At the turn of the nineteenth century, E. W. Kenyon (1867–1948) built on this tradition while expanding the role of confession, finding great significance in the past tense of the final clause in 1 Peter 2:24, "by whose stripes ye *were* healed." Reasoning that if we *were* healed then, we *are* healed now, Kenyon concluded that all one needed was "to recognize and accept that fact"

and then "thank the Father for our perfect deliverance." Like faith curists before him, Kenyon employed forensic and scientific language, declaring healing to be a "legal right" that can only be manifested by applying the spiritual laws governing confession.

Since Kenyon viewed "sense knowledge" as in conflict with "revelation knowledge," he held that symptoms were lies of the devil. Whether such false symptoms developed into real disease depended on the verbal confession of the Christian and whether his or her actions corresponded to the confession.

While Kenyon was highly critical of New Thought and Christian Science, his insistence on making positive confession and avoiding any hint of a negative confession (or even negative thoughts) is strikingly similar to theirs. In Kenyon's mind, the key distinction between his teachings and the "cults" was that his confessions are based on the Word of God—albeit the Word as *he* interprets it.

1920–1948

Although one of the hallmarks of the Holiness movement was its opposition to the accumulation and conspicuous display of wealth, it laid the groundwork for the same formula, claim and confess, to be applied to an ever-growing menu of "needs." The gentrification of the Holiness/Pentecostal traditions throughout the twentieth century, however, may explain why increasing numbers within that movement began to receive "fresh light" on the scriptures that convinced them that untold prosperity was their legal right as "King's kids."

Again, Kenyon was both emblematic and catalytic in this transition. His early ministry (particularly from 1896 through 1923) was patterned on the faith works of George Müller (1805–1898) and Charles Cullis. However, beginning in the 1920s Kenyon's teachings demonstrate a drift toward a materialistic mind-set that paralleled the wider American culture of the period. By the 1930s Kenyon increasingly emphasized the material benefits available to every believer, as seen in a series of radio addresses entitled *Sign-Posts on the Road to Success* (later published as a book).

1948–1966

Among Kenyon's many admirers, few were more important than Fred Francis Bosworth (1877–1958) and "Tommy" Lee Osborn (b. 1923). In the 1948 edition of his highly successful *Christ the Healer*, Bosworth includes a chapter entitled "Our Confession," drawn entirely from Kenyon (with permission). Bosworth's book became a textbook for scores of healing evangelists during the 1950s, further spreading Kenyon's influence and his teachings on positive confession. One of these healing evangelists, T. L. Osborn, focused his ministry on the two-thirds world. Unlike others, Osborne openly acknowledged his indebtedness to Kenyon, noting that his sermons were often readings from Kenyon's books. Similarly, Osborne's writings contain pages of direct quotes from Kenyon, "seeing that they were penned by a divinely inspired hand" (Osborne 1953, 130).

1966 to Present

In the modern era, no one has done more to expand the menu of items obtainable via confession than Kenneth Erwin Hagin (1917–2003). Although the substance of Hagin's teachings came directly from Kenyon, he maintained that his main teachings came directly from God through a series of dramatic visions. In one such vision, Jesus appeared to Hagin and admonished him to embrace his primary calling as a latter-day prophet. Jesus then explained the consequences for those who would not accept Hagin's prophetic position in the church, warning that churches would lose their power, while pastors might even lose their lives as judgment for not heeding Hagin. Jesus concluded their conversation by promising, "If my children will listen to me, I will make them wealthy" (Hagin 1972, 114–117).

Thus, Hagin gives this message a divine authority, reinforced with threats, beyond even Kenyon's grandiose claims. The addition of prophetic sanction to these teachings has had serious consequences throughout the Pentecostal and Charismatic movements but especially within the Word of Faith movement represented by Hagin and his disciples (e.g., Kenneth Copeland, Frederick K. C. Price, John Osteen, et al.). These ministers claim a special prophetic anointing, and they warn followers that positive confession is not enough; they must avoid all negative confessions and not entertain the slightest doubt, lest everything they have been claiming crumble like a house of cards.

In response to the growing health-and-wealth gospel, individual Pentecostal and charismatic theologians have published pointed critiques of the movement, while denominations such as the Assemblies of God have issued position papers opposing the excesses of positive confession theology. While agreeing that the individual believer can and should boldly confess what the Bible says, critics take issue with the way Scriptures are twisted and divorced from their biblical context by members of this movement. In addition, they note that the movement tends to embrace a form of realized eschatology that demands that virtually all of the Kingdom's blessings be manifested here and now, leaving little for the hereafter.

DALE H. SIMMONS

See also Healing, Gifts of; Prosperity Theology; Rich and Riches

Further Reading

Assemblies of God (2004). *Position paper: The believer and positive confession*. Springfield, MO: General Council of the Assemblies of God.

Bosworth, F. F. (1973). *Christ the healer.* Old Tappen, NJ: Fleming H. Revell.

Carter, R. K. (1884). *The atonement for sin and sickness: Or, a full salvation for soul and body.* Boston: Willard Tract Repository.

Carter, R. K. (1897). *"Faith healing" reviewed after twenty years.* Boston: The Christian Witness Company.

Copeland, G. (1978). *God's will is prosperity.* Tulsa, OK: Harrison House.

Farah, C. (1979). *From the pinnacle of the temple: Faith vs. presumption.* Plainfield, NJ: Logos International.

Fee, G. (1985). *The disease of the health and wealth gospels.* Vancouver, Canada: Regent College Publishing.

Finney, C. G. (1978). *Revivals of religion.* Virginia Beach, VA: CBN University Press.

Gossett, D., & Kenyon, E. W. (1977). *The power of the positive confession of God's word.* Tulsa, OK: Custom Graphics.

Hagin, K. E. (1966). *Right and wrong thinking.* Tulsa, OK: Faith Library Publications.

Hagin, K. E. (1972). *I believe in visions.* Old Tappan, NJ: Fleming H. Revell.

Hagin, K. E. (1979). *The ministry of a prophet.* Tulsa, OK: Faith Library Publications.

Hagin, K. E. (1979). *The name of Jesus.* Tulsa, OK: Faith Library Publications.

Hagin, K. E. (1979). *Plead your case.* Tulsa, OK: Faith Library Publications.

Hagin, K. E. (1979). *"You can have what you say!"* Tulsa, OK: Faith Library Publications.

Hagin, K. E. (1980). *How to write your own ticket with God.* Tulsa, OK: Faith Library Publications.

Hagin, K. E. (1980). *Words.* Tulsa, OK: Faith Library Publications.

Kenyon, E. W. (n.d.). *The Bible in the light of our redemption.* Lynnwood, WA: Kenyon's Gospel Publishing Society.

Kenyon, E. W. (1943). *Jesus the healer.* Seattle, WA: Kenyon's Gospel Publishing Society.

Kenyon, E. W. (1964). *The father and His family* (15th ed.). Lynnwood, WA: Kenyon's Gospel Publishing Society.

379

Kenyon, E. W. (1966). *Sign-posts on the road to success* (14th ed.). Lynnwood, WA: Kenyon's Gospel Publishing Society.

Kenyon, E. W. (1966). *The two kinds of knowledge* (18th ed.). Lynnwood, WA: Kenyon's Gospel Publishing Society.

Kenyon, E. W. (1969). *In His presence: A revelation of what we are in Christ* (21st ed.). Lynnwood, WA: Kenyon's Gospel Publishing Society.

Kenyon, E. W. (1969). *The two kinds of faith: Faith's secrets revealed* (11th ed.). Lynnwood, WA: Kenyon's Gospel Publishing Society.

Kenyon, E. W. (1970). *Advanced Bible course: Studies in the deeper life*. Seattle, WA: Kenyon's Gospel Publishing Society.

Kenyon, E. W. (1970). *The hidden man: An unveiling of the subconscious mind*. Lynnwood, WA: Kenyon's Gospel Publishing Society.

Lie, G. (2003). *E. W. Kenyon: Cult founder or evangelical minister?* Oslo, Norway: Refleks Publishing.

Montgomery, C. J. (1936). *"Under His wings"—The story of my life*. Oakland, CA: Office of Triumphs of Faith.

Osborne, T. L. (1953). *Healing the sick and casting out devils*. Tulsa, OK: Voice of Faith Ministry.

Palmer, P. (1856). *Incidental illustrations of the economy of salvation, its doctrines and duties*. Boston: Henry V. Degen.

Popoff, P. (1984). My Personal Word to You. *Faith Messenger*, 12, 2–5.

Simmons, D. H. (1997). *E.W. Kenyon and the postbellum pursuit of peace, power, and plenty*. Lanham, MD: Scarecrow Press.

Simpson, A. B. (1915). *The gospel of healing*. Harrisburg, PA: Christian Publications.

Torrey, R. A. (1897). *How to obtain fullness of power in Christian life and service*. New York: Fleming H. Revell.

Praise

Praise is a heartfelt and soulful expression of esteem for God and veneration of His holy nature. Praise glorifies God for who He is and for what He does. To praise God is to come into agreement with all that God has spoken about Himself in His word, the Bible. Praises may be audible or verbal or by physical demonstration. God deserves our praises because He is the only one who is worthy of our praise (Revelation 5:12, NASB). God created the world to praise Him (Isaiah 43:21). Praise is important because God dwells in the praises of His people (Psalm 34:1).

Types of Praise

Multiple words are used in Hebrew and Greek to convey the idea of praise, and the shades of meaning de-

pend upon the context. Praise of God for redemption through Jesus Christ is an important facet of Christian worship (Hebrews 13:15). Praise takes many forms when it is offered to God in response to His greatness, goodness, and power. Offering praise to the incomparable name of God is descriptive praise (Psalm 113). Praising God for His marvelous deeds forms declarative praise (Psalm 63). Praise offered to God regardless of the circumstances becomes a praise of gratitude (Habakkuk 3:17–18). Praise offered as loving gratitude flowing from a worshipper's innermost being becomes the voice of faith (Psalm 119: 17). God is also praised because He is the only one who is able to answer prayers.

Source

Praise is eternal: God is forever being praised (Romans 1:25). Praise does not have a beginning or an end. God dwells in the praises of His people. Engaging in an act of praising God is an eternal exercise. The apostle John had a vision of the throne room of God, saturated with the praises of angels, elders, and creatures who bowed down before the throne forever praising the attributes of God (Revelation 4, 5, 19). When we praise God on earth, we join with the heavenly host who continually praise God. The structure of praise begins with an inward emotion accompanied by gladness and rejoicing of the heart (Psalm 4:7; Psalm 33:21). Praise is the music of soul and spirit, which cannot be adequately expressed by any human language (Psalm 106:2; Psalm 103:1; Luke 1:46).

Purpose

Praise enhances and energizes believers, and empowers them to worship. It is a powerful weapon for spiritual warfare. The sprit of heaviness yields to praise (Isaiah 61:3). Praise destroys the strongholds. Praise is important because the Bible reveals God as the object of praise (Isaiah 6:3). When we praise God we fulfill His purpose (1 Corinthians 10:31), for He desires us to praise Him continually (Ephesians 1:13–14). God is praised not only for creating us but also for sustaining us with health, strength, wisdom, and new life (Psalm 23:6; Psalm 103:1–4). We are called to praise the Father for having blessed us, to praise the Son for His redemptive work, and to praise the Holy Spirit for sealing the believer (Ephesians 1:6, 12, 14).

Different Ways to Praise God

Praise was offered in the form of speech (Psalm 35:28), singing (Psalm 40: 3), shouting (Isaiah 12:6), clapping

(Psalm 47:1), dancing (Exodus 15:20), and lifting holy hands (Psalm 63:4), and through the use of musical instruments (Psalm 33:2). Praise can also take the form of a physical demonstration that may be an expression of joy following a healing or deliverance. The lame man praised God by walking and leaping (Acts 3:8).

Praise God Though Song and Dance

Ancient Hebrews took pleasure in musical poetry. Moses employed ballad singers who preserved historic moments in music (Numbers 21: 27). King David appointed priests who sang praises day and night until Solomon dedicated the temple (2 Chronicles 5:11–14). During the time of Ezra a great celebration followed the laying of the temple foundations: The priests wore new garments and blew their trumpets, and all the people gave a great shout, singing and praising God for his love and mercy toward Israel (Ezra 3:10–11). Israel celebrated the inauguration of the second temple foundation with responsive singing between two choirs (Ezra 3:11; Nehemiah 12:24, 31).

Praise God with Musical Instruments

In 1050 BCE, David appointed Levites to provide music for liturgical services (1 Chronicles 16:4–7). The Dead Sea scrolls record the instruments used during worship in David's time. Some of the instruments mentioned in the Bible are the lute, harp, timbrel, tambourine, drum, and tom-tom (Psalm 150; 2 Samuel 6:1–5; 1 Chronicles 13:1–8). Several of these instruments, though slightly different in form, are still used to praise God.

Praise in the Old Testament

In the Old Testament Israel praised God for its election as a nation (1 Chronicles 16:8–36; Psalm 57:9; Isaiah 42:10–12; 66:18). God was praised for His acts of creation, providence, and redemption. Victories in battles resulted from praise (Judges 5). Moses, Miriam, and the children of Israel sang, danced, and praised God for their deliverance (Exodus 15). When Jehoshaphat praised Him, God changed the situation into a celebration of victory (2 Chronicles 20:5–12). Praises went up as a thanksgiving for God's provision (Numbers 21:16–17). Praise is shown to remove reproach (1 Samuel 2:1–10).

Praise in the New Testament

When the Holy Spirit came upon the early Christians on the day of Pentecost, the Spirit moved them first to speak the praises of God (Acts 2:11). When the early believers praised God, the place where they gathered was shaken and they were filled with the Holy Ghost (Acts 2:2). They saw themselves as a holy priesthood called to offer up spiritual sacrifices acceptable to God through Jesus Christ (1 Peter 2: 5–9). Paul urges us to admonish one another with psalms and hymns and to sing before the Lord continually with a grateful heart (Colossians 3:16). When the lame man was healed he praised God by walking and leaping (Acts 3:8). When Peter and Paul praised God, even prison doors could not hold them captive (Acts 16: 25). Praising God set captives free.

Praise in the Early Church

Christian service was built upon the pattern of worship in temple ritual and synagogue liturgy. The Jewish pattern of synagogue worship consists of three elements: praise, prayer, and instruction. According to the Talmud, worship always began with corporate praise. The New Testament scholar Ralph Martin (1975) states that "the Christian church was born in song," and the writings of the ante-Nicene church fathers (before the Council of Nicea, 325 CE) confirm the tradition of singing in the early church. Clement of Alexandria, Origin, and Tertullian all attest to the fact that the singing of psalms and hymns was an integral part of worship. The liturgical sequence of scripture, sermons, and creeds led the way for the believing community to a Eucharistic prayer, which climaxed in praise.

The early Christian adaptation of the Jewish expression of praise in worship services appeared later in Orthodox, Roman Catholic, Anglican, and some Protestant liturgies and hymns. Great preachers such as St. Chrysostom, St. Augustine, and John Calvin, in their desire to bring others to praise God, ended their sermons with an acknowledgement of praise. Wesley's opening hymn for the collection of Methodist hymnals started by calling for universal praise for Jesus Christ. The style and method of praising God varied from church to church, but the history of Christian liturgy shows that praise was an integral part of the church.

Pentecostal Concept of Praise

The pattern of worship for the Pentecostal church is modeled on the New Testament church (1 Corinthians 14: 26). It focuses on Jesus as Baptizer, Healer, Savior, Redeemer, and soon-coming King, and sees speaking in tongues as the initial evidence for the Baptism of the Holy Spirit. During Pentecostal worship, believers sing, clap, shout, dance, and use musical instruments to praise God (Acts 4:24). Preaching is lively and powerful (Acts 2). Believers are encouraged to glorify God by using their spiritual gifts (1 Corinthians 12: 8–11). Speaking in tongues is one of the main expressions of praise because it communicates with God (1 Corinthians 14: 2). Praise released with faith may result in other powerful manifestations such as healing, deliverance, salvation, prophecy, and repentance. (Acts 4:31).

Areas of Growth

One of the criticisms of the way Pentecostals praise God is that they lack rational understanding during praise. Jesus warned against meaningless repetition (Matthew 6:7), and some early Pentecostal writers, like Gary Erickson and Donald Gee, warned believers that true praise was not a repetition of sacred words without understanding. Erickson found many powerful expressions of praise with meaning taken from the word of God; he asserted that worshippers would be guilty of vain babbling if true praise originated from the heart (Exodus 20:7). Gee also instructed Pentecostal believers against the dangers of repeating praise formulas mechanically.

Praise in Indian Pentecostal Churches

The Apostolic Christian Assembly (ACA) in Chennai, India, shows the high priority accorded to praise in Pentecostal churches in India. These Pentecostal believers witness to others through their simplicity and lifestyle. Their main teachings are focused upon Holiness. They grow in holiness not by conforming to the world but by being changed to the image and likeness of the Lord Jesus. In the ACA church, even though the morning service starts at nine, the preparation for the Sunday morning worship starts at six. Devout believers and intercessors—irrespective of caste, creed, or color—gather together early in the morning in the sanctuary to praise and worship God. They prepare their hearts to receive the word by singing, kneeling, walking, and praying in the sanctuary before the actual service.

Sam Sundaram, senior pastor of ACA church, which has a growing congregation of twenty thousand, believes that praise and worship are the main reasons for the tremendous growth of the church. He affirms that praising God increases grace and unites people from different backgrounds into one family. During worship, praising God creates an environment of expectancy from the Lord (Psalm 22:3). Hindu visitors are touched by the power of God, and physical healings and deliverances begin to take place (John 12:32). New converts find that praising God increases grace and breaks bondages, lending them the strength to endure persecution from their unsaved families (Acts 4:23–31). Praise also makes them bold enough to witness to unsaved families. Children in the ACA church are taught to praise God and testify from a very young age. During worship in the children's church, even the smallest children praise God by clapping, shouting, dancing, and jumping under the power of God.

Implications

In spite of opposition and criticism, Pentecostal and charismatic believers form the largest, fastest-growing Christian communities in the world. The contemporary style of worship has taken the act of praising God into a dynamic new phase in the unfolding history of Christianity. God is restoring praise globally to the body of Christ. All nations become one family when they praise the almighty God. Powerful manifestations are taking place around the world as a result of praise. Praising God is a wonderful incense with which to welcome the presence of the Spirit of God in our generation, as we seek with longing in our hearts to enter into the fullness of all that God has for us in the future.

EDITH DHANA PRAKASH

See also Music; Prayer; Worship

Further Reading

Alford, D. L. (1967). *Music in the Pentecostal church*. Cleveland, TN: Pathway.

Allen, R. B. (1980). *Praise! A matter of life and breath*. Nashville, TN: Nelson.

Brant, R. (1980). *Ministering to the Lord*. Tulsa, OK: Harrison House.

Canon, W. (1966). *Christian worship of God*. Mysore, India: Wesley.

Carothers, M. R. (1974). *Walking and leaping*. Escondido, CA: Carothers.

Cornwall, J. (1973). *Let us praise*. Plainfield, NJ: Logos International.

Duck, R., & Wilson-Kastner, P. (1999). *Praising God: Trinity in Christian worship*. Louisville, KY: Westminster John Knox.

Erickson, G. D. (1989). *Pentecostal worship*. Hazelwood, MO: Word Aflame.

Gee, D. (1969). *Pentecost*. Springfield, MO: Gospel Publishing.

Hill, A. E. (1996). *Enter His courts with praise*. Grand Rapids, MI: Baker.

Holmes, T. (1996). *The holiness and honor of praise*. South Plainfield, NJ: Bridge.

Hoon, P. W. (1971). *The integrity of worship.* Nashville, TN: Abingdon.

Jesupatham, J. R. (1999). *Christian worship and homiletics.* Chennaim, TN: Christian Literature Society.

Law, T. (1985). *The power of praise and worship.* Tulsa, OK: Victory House.

Martin, R. P. (1975). *Worship in the early church.* Grand Rapids, MI: Eerdmans.

Rees, P. S. (1960). *Stand up in praise to God.* Grand Rapids, MI: Eerdmans.

Segler, F. M. (1967). *Christian worship its theology and practice.* Nashville, TN: Broadman.

Taylor, J. R. (1983). *The hallelujah factor.* Nashville, TN: Broadman.

Wainwright, G. (1984). *Doxology: The praise of God in worship, doctrine and life: A systematic theology.* Oxford.

Westermann, C. (1965). *The praise of God in the Psalms.* Richmond, VA: John Knox.

Prayer

Simply stated, prayer is the act of communication between a man or a woman and his or her God. The practice of humanity conversing with a deity or deities is not unique to Christianity. Every known religion in the world engages in some form of prayer. Prayer defines a religious practice, and in most definitions of prayer, there is at least an implication of belief in a higher power who is in touch with human life. Prayer can take place in public or in private, can be formal or spontaneous, whispered or shouted. Whatever the form or posture, prayer shapes what one believes about one's God.

Prayer in the Bible

Numerous examples of prayer are contained in the Bible. The Book of Psalms is essentially a book of prayers written by a variety of individuals over a period of five hundred years. There are a great many Biblical passages other than Psalms that refer to the spontaneous prayers of men and women. (For examples see Genesis 17:18; Genesis 24:12; Genesis 28:20; 32:9–12; 1 Samuel 8: 6–18; 2 Samuel 7:18–29; 1 Kings 18; Jeremiah 20; Luke 2: 29–32; Matthew 6:9–15; Ephesians 3:14–21 and Colossians 1:9–23.) Turning to God in prayer is a natural response to pain, anxiety, and joy. Though intensely private, prayer is regarded as the most fundamental of all expressions of religion and is portrayed in a variety of forms, sometimes with extraordinary simplicity and other times with great complexity and formality.

The Hebrew Scriptures contain numerous examples of prayers but little to no instruction regarding prayer. The Old Testament man or woman prayed, but the reader is not given any specific details or instructions on how they prayed. However, the New Testament, while containing dramatically fewer examples of prayer, is specific on instructions regarding how to pray.

Forms of Prayer

The most common form of prayer found in the Bible is that of petition. When petitioning, one is directly confronting God in prayer asking for certain needs to be met. Biblical prayer moves back and forth between plea or petition and praise or thanksgiving. The fundamental aim of the prayer of petition is to seek help from God. Petitions are made for several reasons: to be heard by God (1 Kings 8), for physical healing (Jeremiah 7:14), for forgiveness (Exodus 32:31–32), for deliverance (2 Kings 19:19), to execute judgment against enemies (Jeremiah 11:20), for remembrance (2 Kings 20:3), to receive instruction and direction (1 Kings 3:9), and for blessings (I Chronicles 14:10).

When one has a favorable response to a petition or there is an unexpected blessing or a surge of faith assuring the one petitioning God that He has heard, then the second form of prayer is engaged: praise and thanksgiving. In prayers of thanksgiving, one encounters the basic elements of the prayers that God heard and delivered on, prayers of praise and trust. Psalm 18:46–48 is typical of a prayer of thanksgiving. This expression of gratitude implies reciprocity, a human way of saying "thank you" for the divine intervention.

The third form of prayer to be considered is that of confession or forgiveness. The fallen nature of humanity and the holiness of God makes the need for forgiveness a necessity. The one praying begins with a verbal confession of his or her infraction, then moves on to a renouncing of the deed, a declaration that they will not engage in the confessed sin again. The prayer then has a petition for mercy and cleansing as it recognizes the wrath and judgment of God. Psalm 51 is the classic example of a prayer for forgiveness.

The final form of prayer to be considered is that of intercession. Intercession is basically the act of mediating between God and humanity. The man or woman who is praying petitions God on behalf of an individual or community; typically, the petition will

Indigenous Papua New Guineans at an outdoor prayer service. *Courtesy of Douglas Hayward.*

be for forgiveness or deliverance. The most well-known prayers would be those of Abraham on behalf of Sodom and Gomorrah (Genesis 18:16–21), Moses on behalf of Israel (Numbers 14:13–23), and Jesus on behalf of all his disciples, past and present (John 17:1–26).

Posture of Prayer

While prayer is predominantly a verbal act, there are nonverbal elements indicated in the Biblical text and in present-day experience. David sat before the Lord as he prayed (2 Samuel 7:18), and there are examples of those who stood (Matthew 6:5), prostrated, knelt (Ephesians 3:14), and bowed their heads (Genesis 24:26). One of the most common postures associated with prayer is that of raising one's hands (Psalm 28:2). In both petition and praise, the uplifted hands convey a sense of the transcendent, that prayer is directed beyond oneself and this world to the God who is in heaven.

The Trinity in Prayer

In the Hebrew Scriptures, prayer is directed exclusively to God the Father. This changes in the New Testament by taking on a Trinitarian emphasis.

Christian prayer remains prayer to God the Father. Our starting point must be that the object of prayer is God, not Christ. When Jesus taught his disciples to pray, they were to pray to God the Father (Matthew 6:9). In the New Testament, prayer to God the Father is made possible because of Jesus Christ the Son. Paul's prayers are frequently addressed to "the Father of our Lord Jesus Christ" (Romans 1:7, 1 Corinthians 1:3, 2 Corinthians 1:2, Galatians 1:3, Ephesians 1:2, 2:18). This mode of address marks the Trinitarian character of Christian prayer because it arises out of the filial relation of Jesus of Nazareth to the God of Israel. The parental relationship between Jesus the Son and God the Father introduces the Trinitarian nature of prayer. Believers are made joint heirs with the Son (Romans

James 5:13–16 (New International Version)

¹³Is any one of you in trouble? He should pray. Is anyone happy? Let him sing songs of praise.

¹⁴Is any one of you sick? He should call the elders of the church to pray over him and anoint him with oil in the name of the Lord.

¹⁵And the prayer offered in faith will make the sick person well; the Lord will raise him up. If he has sinned, he will be forgiven.

¹⁶Therefore confess your sins to each other and pray for each other so that you may be healed. The prayer of a righteous man is powerful and effective.

8:14–17), and therefore children of the Father, invited to call upon Him as Father because of the Son.

The Christian is invited to bring his or her petitions to the Father because of the salvific work of the Son (Hebrews 4:14,16) and His present role as intercessor on behalf of those who are His (Romans 8:34). The Christian belief that Jesus stands before God the Father on our behalf is the source of great encouragement. The prayers of believers are heard because the Son is with the Father in heaven, and He can sympathize with our human weaknesses. In His earthly life He felt the reality of every trial and temptation; He is understanding of the needs and frailties of humanity. Therefore, the Christian prays to God the Father through Jesus Christ the Son.

The role of the Holy Spirit in prayer is multifaceted. Twice in the New Testament believers are mandated to "pray in the Spirit" (Ephesians 6:18 and Jude 1:20). The Spirit also helps us to pray (Romans 8:26a) and He intercedes on our behalf (Romans 8:26b). The Spirit intercedes on behalf of believers because of an ongoing communication between Himself and the Father (Romans 8:27). The Spirit retains a personhood of His own, somehow distinct from God's. God and the Spirit interact; they search each other out and always in a way that brings the person and work of Christ close to believers (John 14:15–23, 16:14). Believers are not left on their own to pray; they have one who assists. The Holy Spirit helps believers pray and even intercedes for the believer, through the believer. The Holy Spirit is present to help in weakness. Believers desire to do the will of God but often do not know how to pray as they should. The Spirit comes to their aid and makes intercession for them with unutterable groans.

Praying in the Spirit

The meaning of "praying in the Spirit" is a point of contention among scholars. The definitions range from "complete silence" to ecstatic utterance or glossolalia. The biblical materials give a solid witness to the pneumatological aspect of Christian prayer. Many who participate in the charismatic or Pentecostal traditions interpret "praying in the Spirit" as including glossolalia, deep groans and sighs, and even reverential silence. Praying in the Spirit is far more than an exercise in emotional utterances; it is a Spirit-empowered event that allows the believer to pray in perfect agreement with the will of the Father. Those who pray in the Spirit believe that they are able to communicate with God in an unhindered way.

Spiritual Warfare

Often one will find spiritual warfare in close connection with praying in the Spirit. Warfare prayers are found in three venues: 1) A request that the evil forces of Satan and his imps be bound and rendered helpless through the act of prayer (Matthew 26:41, Ephesians 6:17–19). All genuine efforts toward peace and personal righteousness are met with resistance by these unseen forces of the demonic realm; therefore, it is significant to engage in warfare prayer to circumvent any spiritual attacks. 2) Prayer for the deliverance from or exorcism of demons is another venue of warfare praying. The New Testament is filled with examples of Jesus and the disciples praying for people to be released from the control or oppression of demons (Acts 8:7, 16:16–18). 3) A third venue of warfare prayer is characterized by discernment and deployment. Ephesians 6:10–20 is an exposition on this type of prayer. Central importance is given to declaring the Gospel in the fray of the battle. Fighting demonic powers effectively requires a declaration of the Good News, which is empowered and directed by the Holy Spirit. It is not stated that believers are to directly address the demonic powers with the Word of God. Rather, as the Gospel of peace and grace is declared to one's neighbors, the demonic powers must take note and retreat, though never without a fight.

MARTHA S. KIMBRELL-WILLIAMS

See also Holy Spirit; Preaching; Trinitarianism; Worship

Further Reading

Brandt, R. L., & Bicket, Z. (1994). *The spirit helps us pray: A Biblical theology of prayer.* Springfield, MO: Gospel Publishing House.

Clements, R. E. (1985). *In spirit and truth: Insights from Biblical prayers.* Atlanta, GA: John Knox Press.

Horton, S. M. (1976). *What the Bible says about the Holy Spirit.* Springfield, MO: Gospel Publishing House.

Koenig, J. (1998). *Rediscovering New Testament prayer: Boldness and blessing in the name of Jesus.* Harrisburg, PA: Morehouse Publishing.

Miller, P. D. (1994). *They cried to the Lord: The form and theology of Biblical prayer.* Minneapolis, MN: Fortress Press.

Morris, J. W. (1983). The Charismatic movement: An orthodox evaluation. *Greek Orthodox Theological Review, 28*(2), 103–134.

Stendahl, K. (1980). Paul at prayer. *Interpretation, 34*(1), 240–249.

Westermann, C. (1981). *Praise and lament in the Psalms.* Atlanta, GA: John Knox Press.

Preaching

For Pentecostals and charismatics, the purpose of preaching is to facilitate God's intervention to deliver people from disease, death, and the demonic and into an experience of wholeness and healing. This perspective on preaching is informed by a high view of Scripture and eschatology and a feeling of being in spiritual continuity with the early Church.

Pentecostals and charismatics regard preaching as the proclamation of the Word of God. By far the majority of preaching happens within a congregation at set times, though it can occur in various venues by evangelists moving from one site to another—including, rarely, preaching on street corners. The regularly pre-

sented message is usually called the sermon and, because it is considered very important and is not assigned or delivered casually, it is usually delivered by the senior clergy person; however, it may be given by a guest preacher or a church member without any specific office. Most denominations require that preachers be licensed, and all traditions provide for their training. Though different groups may vary in their expectations as to the length and style of the sermon, all consider the preacher endowed with a great responsibility to speak a message of truth about God's will for His people that will both challenge and comfort them and provide wisdom about how to live a better life. All traditions regard the sermon as more than a speech, and believe that in some way God is involved. Martin Luther called the Church "God's Mouth House"—that is, a place where God speaks through the preacher.

History of Christian Preaching

Understood as one person speaking to a group about a divine power, preaching can be assumed to predate written history. In the Bible, Moses clearly functions as a preacher, and the activity of most of the prophetic figures such as Zechariah could be considered preaching. The Christian tradition knows John the Baptist as a preacher who proclaimed the need for a baptism of repentance. All four Gospel writers say Jesus came preaching that God's Kingdom was drawing near. A model for regular weekly preaching is shown in the fourth chapter of Luke, when at a set time Jesus acted as a guest preacher, reading from Scripture and following with an explanation and contemporary application of the text to the gathered listeners.

Models for preaching appear in Acts, as when Peter said the apostles need to be set aside to preach the word of God early in the life of the Christian community (Acts 6:4). Early Christian writings document regular preaching within gathered communities, as well as its continuance as a missionary activity. An enormous collection of early sermons from key figures such as John Chrysostom (347–407) and Augustine (354–430) are available in libraries and on the Internet. Preaching has remained a central activity of the Church, and large historical movements such as the Great Awakening have begun through preaching.

Revivalist Roots

Pentecostal and charismatic preaching is rooted in the eighteenth- and nineteenth-century revival movements on both sides of the Atlantic (the first and second Great

Awakenings). During the first Great Awakening, leaders like John Wesley (1703–1791), George Whitefield (1714–1770), and Jonathan Edwards (1703–1758) preached sermons whose themes can be heard today in Pentecostal and charismatic preaching. The Methodist movement spread through licensed "circuit riders" who traveled regular routes in rural areas preaching a need for repentance, conversion, and a "second blessing" or "sanctification." Using the words of John Fletcher (1729–1785), an associate of Wesley, revivalist and Holiness preachers proclaimed the need for "the baptism of the Holy Spirit." When a revival broke out at the frontier community of Cane Creek, Kentucky, at a joint communion service of mainly Presbyterians and Methodists in 1801, people loudly repented of their sins, professed a deeper experience of faith, and many experienced physical manifestations of the Holy Spirit, including fainting, shaking, etc. This second Great Awakening swept the nation in varying forms during the nineteenth century; but it is the post–Civil War camp meetings of what became known as the Holiness movement that gave birth to Pentecostalism, in which preaching was a central activity.

The beginning of the Pentecostal movement is usually dated from the Azusa Street Revival that began in Los Angeles in 1906. The locus of activity, which drew people from around the nation, was the Azusa Street mission, where worship services were held three times a day every day for three years, under the leadership of Pastor William J. Seymour (1870–1922). Many manifestations of the Spirit were evidenced, and Azusa Street became the springboard for the founding of new denominations and the departure of missionaries. Seymour's newspaper, the *Apostolic Faith Messenger*, provides a source for the authentic content of early Pentecostal preaching. Descriptions of the services and of Seymour's worship leadership illustrate what was distinctive about Pentecostal preaching.

Early Distinctive Aspects

The first distinctive aspect of early Pentecostalism was the freedom worshippers felt to reject many of the traditional features of worship and the sermon: there were no hymnbooks, programs, collection of an offering, set readings from the Scriptures, or subject for the sermon. At Azusa Street, Seymour often sat behind two wooden crates with his head buried there until he felt moved to say something. Behind this apparent lack of structure and an exaggerated physicality of worship lies a primary principle of Pentecostalism: freedom in the Spirit. Pentecostals believed then, as they do today, that it is

most important to seek God first in all things, including worship, and He will then lead the people by the Holy Spirit in singing, the order of worship, what Scripture to read, and what to say. This happens when the people stay deep in prayer, as Seymour modeled. Out of this sometimes trancelike prayer came spontaneous, charismatic (Spirit-induced) responses, including shouting, speaking in unknown languages, weeping, ejaculatory prayer, and verbal descriptions of images and messages from God.

Seymour's preaching happened within extended prayer and worship. It did not center on the manifestations of the Holy Spirit, but on the need to renounce sin and to accept Jesus Christ as Savior. Neither early Pentecostal preaching nor the movement's developing theology contained a great deal of explanation about the person and work of the Holy Spirit; the emphasis was on Jesus Christ. Central to any understanding of these distinctive beliefs and practices of the movement is an understanding of Pentecostalism's hermeneutics—the presuppositions that inform its approach to Scripture.

Rejection and Restoration

Pentecostals believed then, as they and charismatics believe still, that all the phenomena that characterized the original apostolic Church are still in effect for them. They believe the stories in the Acts of the Apostles are a description of how the Church should still be, not of how it was for a limited period of time in the past. In other words, Paul's description of the gifts of the Spirit in 1 Corinthians is prescriptive, not descriptive. Since the fourth century the Western Church had taught varying degrees of *cessationism*—that God had ceased giving gifts of the Spirit, either for the most part (Catholics) or almost totally (Protestants); but Pentecostals believed that the gifts were for anyone with apostolic faith, and they sought them until they received evidence of the baptism of the Holy Spirit.

Charismatic gifts were also proof for the first Pentecostals that they were participating in the last battle between the powers of evil and the heavenly powers. Jesus Christ was described as Savior, Sanctified, Healer, Baptizer, and the Coming King. Pentecostalism should be seen as an eschatological (concerned with the Last Days) missionary movement. Pentecostal eschatology emphasizes not just the Last Days, but also the entry of the Holy into this world, especially into the lives of those who have been baptized in the Holy Spirit. Through the events of Christ's life—His Incarnation, crucifixion, resurrection, and sending of His Spirit at Pentecost—God's people are called to actively participate in the final days, wielding spiritual power against demons. If people who experience Pentecostal preaching accept the invitation to come forward to pray and receive Christ into their heart, their place in front of the congregation is understood by those extending the invitation to be a spiritual battlefield, where demons are exorcised from some and others receive miraculous healing. Pentecostal preaching is thus both a message and a practice concerning freedom from spiritual oppression, however that is manifested.

Theological Aspects

Pentecostalism is known primarily by the practice of its worship, not by its dogma. In the second decade of the movement's existence, as it sought to train new leaders and gain credibility with other Christians, it embraced Fundamentalism, primarily because of Fundamentalists' high view of Scripture and rejection of the modern scientific worldview.

Although some acculturation began to be seen by mid-century, in specific ways Pentecostals and charismatics pursue a theology that they regard as being in historical continuity with the early Church. They believe in the literal truth of Scripture, and that the Christ of faith is the Jesus of history. While they generally accept the methodology of the historical-critical study of Scripture and welcome its contributions, they regard as suspect any interpretation that contradicts the uniformity of the apostolic witness. They believe their experience with the Holy Spirit, which gives them existential awareness of the miraculous in Scripture, is neither mythological nor only in the past, but is objectively real in the present. For Pentecostals and charismatics, the contemporary experience of divine healing, prophecy, miracles, tongues, and exorcism are evidence of an entry into the physical world of the Kingdom of God. Interaction with that reality affects Pentecostal hermeneutics and preaching decisively.

Methodology

Pentecostal preaching shares much with Evangelical preaching, which intends the hearer to make a decision for Christ to be his or her personal Savior; but Pentecostal preaching is distinctive in its assurance of the immediate presence of Christ and the Spirit to help the preacher accomplish God's work at that moment. While preachers in many other contemporary churches rely on argumentation to make an appeal to the intellect, a Pentecostal preacher appeals directly to the truth of salvation. More than proclaiming objective truth, the Pentecostal preacher makes him- or herself available as a vehicle for God to achieve what God wants at that moment.

Pentecostal preaching is therefore part of a worship activity that is an encounter with the Holy Spirit. Between periods of prayer and praise, the preacher's sermon is a time devoted to what God is declaring on that day for the gathered people. Therefore, it is the Pentecostal understanding of God's moment-to-moment involvement in history that is distinctive, not the preaching per se. The Pentecostal listener understands the preacher's message differently than the non-Pentecostal, since Pentecostals share a belief that neither God nor they are bound by physical laws. Pentecostals have an expectation of God's immediate presence during their worship and prayer, which is rare, if not unknown, in most other traditions in the West.

Pentecostal Influence

What was once unique to Pentecostal preaching has become more common since the spread of Pentecostalism. Because of the movement's dramatic growth in the twentieth century, the influence of Pentecostalism spread to the mainline denominations, especially in the 1960s and 1970s. Millions of mainline Christians either became charismatic members of their home congregations, switched congregations or denominations, or helped begin new congregations. However, the intensity, expectancy, and immediacy of Pentecostalism spread in some degree to all denominations. Pentecostal preaching has reached the mainstream culture as well, through television and radio ministries. The Pentecostal position that God is working today is received well by those with a primary desire for not what is objectively true, but what can only be subjectively verified.

To achieve this subjective verification, the affections—the deep religious feelings—of the preacher and the listeners are important. Affections are more than the target of a story the preacher introduces to evoke a certain emotion at a particular stage in the message; affections are part of the very religious being of the listener—not so much a place to seek out as a place where one lives, from whence activity springs. Steven Land proposes that religious affections are developed through worship—through the knowledge of the righteousness of God and through the experience of God's grace, goodness, and gifts. Cultivating religious affections gives the believer a love for God and a compassion for humanity, of the sort from which missionary activity springs. Hence, affections are more than emotions to which to appeal; they are an additional vehicle for God's plan for humanity.

ERIC SWENSSON

See also Evangelism

Further Reading

Ervin, H. (1979). Hermeneutics: A Pentecostal option. *Pneuma: The Journal of the Society for Pentecostal Studies,* 3(2), 11–25.

Hollenweger, W. (1997). *Pentecostalism: Origins and development worldwide.* Peabody, MA: Hendrickson.

Land, S. J. (1997). *Pentecostal spirituality: A passion for the Kingdom.* Sheffield, UK: Sheffield Academic Press.

Synan, V. (2001). *The century of the Holy Spirit.* Nashville, TN: Thomas Nelson.

Turner, W. C. (1995). Pentecostal preaching. In W. Willimon & R. Lischer (Eds.), *The concise encyclopedia of preaching.* Louisville, KY: John Knox Press.

Prophecy, Gift of

The Judeo-Christian tradition is replete with prophets, men and women who not only spoke God's revealed words, but also performed His mighty works. Ultimately, Jesus modeled for all believers this ideal: to be "a prophet mighty in deed and word"—miracle and prophecy (Luke 24:19, RSV). Romans 12:6 and 1 Corinthians 12:10 imply that all prophecy is a "gift" from God, and a survey of Old Testament archetypal prophets, upon whom the "gift of prophecy" in the New Testament was modeled, is included here. In the Old Testament, prophets are identified by a variety of terms including the Hebrew *nabi'* and Arabic *nabû* formerly called a *ro'eh,* which means "one who sees" a vision (1 Samuel 9:9), or a visionary (*hozeh*). A prophet is sometimes called "a man of God," implying experiences and special knowledge of the deity.

Old Testament Prophets and Prophecy

Throughout biblical times and even today, humans in virtually all cultures seem drawn to seek out those who offer revelations or "psychic hotlines" to see into the future. Most kings in the Ancient Near East consulted their "wise men" who were not "scientific" political analysts or members of "think tanks" as we have today, but rather "diviners" and "soothsayers" who consulted

their gods for advice (1 Samuel 6:2; Isaiah 44:25; Jeremiah 27:9; Daniel 4:7; 5:7–11). Indeed much of Ancient Near East history was originally structured on the theme of a king asking his god for advice on invading other kingdoms, with the god empowering the king to do so. Modern historians tend to ignore the centrality of seeking revelation and divine guidance in even the daily lives of the ancient world.

Against this background of pagan deities and their "prophets," Moses, the primal Israelite prophet, was called by God (Yahweh) to confront the Pharaoh (who was usually regarded as a deity by his subjects) and the gods of Egypt to gain release of Yahweh's people. "You are to say everything I command you.…But…when I multiply my miraculous signs and wonders in Egypt, he will not listen to you. Then I will lay my hand on Egypt and with mighty acts of judgment" (Exodus 7: 1–5). By prophetic revelation and empowerment, Moses predicted and unleashed each plague, which amounted to successive victories over each of the Egyptian gods. This theme is repeated in later prophets who pronounce God's miraculous promises and judgments to both Israel and the nations so that all will *know* Yahweh's holiness and uniqueness. This is a constant theme in Exodus and is frequently echoed in Ezekiel as well as other prophets (Isaiah 45:3; Jeremiah 16:20–21; Joel 3:17; Zechariah 2:11).

After Moses, the second primal prophetic figure in God's revelation to Israel is Elijah. Elijah was known not only for his verbal predictions, but for his healings and miracles as well (1 Kings 17:1, 16, 22; 18; 2 Kings 1, 2). Elijah's pattern of ministry stands as a positive example in the New Testament, in which John the Baptist (Luke 1:17; Matthew 17:12) and even Jesus (Mark 6:15; 8:28; Acts 3:22–26) are compared to him. The Epistle of James sees Elijah as a flawed but yet powerful example to its readers because of his intense and persistent prayer of faith (5:17–18). To a greater or lesser extent, the subsequent prophetic tradition followed this pattern: prophets received revelation of God's instructions to his people as well as his impending actions, whether of blessings or judgments.

Bizarre Prophetic Behavior

Sometimes prophets delivered their messages with an urgency, even desperation, that led to sometimes bizarre actions. For example, the highly articulate and dignified Isaiah walked the streets of Jerusalem naked for three years, demonstrating how Israel would enter captivity (Isaiah 20:3–5). Ezekiel lay on his side for 390 days and cooked his food over dung.

He shaved all the hair from his head, divided it into three parts and dispatched each by fire, wind, and sword, all as a prophetic warning of the captivity of Jerusalem (Ezekiel 4–5). Hosea was told by God to re-marry his sexually immoral ex-wife, in clear violation of divine law, as a prophetic sign of God's love for Israel. Sometimes a prophet was "called" for prophetic service in a dramatic way. For example, Elisha found the cloak of Elijah thrown upon him as a sign of initiation and confirmation (1 Kings 19:19; 2 Kings 2:13). In the prom-ise of Pentecost (Acts 1), the "cloaking/enduing" with power from on high carries many points of analogy with the Elijah/Elisha transfer of the prophetic Spirit.

Prophets were known for their shouting (Jeremiah 4:5), weeping (Isaiah 22:4; Jeremiah 9:1) and falling down under inspiration (1 Samuel 19:24; Ezekiel 1:24; Daniel 10:8–9) and often other more extreme actions than those for which modern Pentecostal preachers and worshippers have been criticized. Earlier scholars often saw this bizarre prophetic behavior as a sign of mental derangement. However, as in modern family systems theory, it is more likely that the prophets be-came the "identified patient" in the society—the only ones responding reasonably, insightfully, if urgently to Israel's pathological denial of evil.

Psychology of the Prophetic Experience

The prophetic subjective experience was often memo-rable, particularly as it was marked by a "call" into min-istry (Isaiah 6; Jeremiah 1–2; Ezekiel 2–3). Prophets seemed particularly aware of the impulse to prophesy. This was variously described as a palpable feeling: "the hand of the Lord was upon me" (Ezekiel 1:3; 3:14; 33:22), or "the burden" of the Lord (Isaiah 13:1; Jeremiah 23:33; Zechariah 9:1), or simply, in over one hundred cases, "the word of the Lord came" (Genesis 15:1). Sometimes the prophet had an "out-of-body" experience in which he could view things God was revealing (2 Kings 5:26; Ezekiel 3:12; 8:3; 11:1, 24). Jeremiah was conflicted about facing opposition to his prophecies (an occupational haz-ard), but felt nonetheless compelled to prophesy. "But if I say, 'I will not mention him or speak any more in his name,' his word is in my heart like a fire, a fire shut up in my bones. I am weary of holding it in" (Jeremiah 20:9). Many in the Pentecostal-Charismatic movement will res-onate with this experience of prophetic urgency.

Spirit and Prophecy

In the 128 or so references (some of the references fall into two or more of the categories below) to the Spirit

of God (ruach) in the Old Testament, the overwhelming percentage of contexts refers to His revelatory or mirac-ulous activity: prophetic revelation (76 cases), charis-matic leadership (17), bestowals of divine power for healing, miracles, special skills, and so on (15), and in a special miracle category, the creation, including the sus-tenance of life (17). The remaining eleven cases of ruach appear to be a metonymy for God. A study of the con-texts in the Old Testament shows that the Spirit is al-most exclusively associated with the revelatory and miraculous (i.e., prophetic) acts of God, and the New Testament repeats this Old Testament pattern of the Spirit with the prophetic.

In the New Testament, the Spirit is mentioned twice as many times as in the Old Testament, making the *fre-quency* of mention some six times greater. In the con-texts, the Spirit is most closely associated with prophetic revelation sixty-five times and Spirit-empowered utter-ances seventy-two times, involving as it does, a direct communication of God by the Spirit. The very Spirit of the exalted Jesus, says the writer of Revelation (19:10), is "the Spirit of prophecy."

The Spirit prophetically reveals and guides the course of the Christian mission, for example, the Spirit drives/leads Jesus into the wilderness (Matthew 4:1; Mark 1:10; Luke 4:1) and leads in various situations in the Book of Acts, 8:29; 10:19; 11:12; 16:6,7; 19:21; 20:22. In-deed, being "led" by the Spirit—the life of faith (hearing and obeying)—is the central characteristic of the Chris-tian experience (Romans 1:17; 8:14; Galatians 5:16, 18).

Prophecy and Other Spiritual Gifts

Prophetic revelation by the Spirit is an essential element of most of the gifts of the Spirit, as in "wisdom," "knowl-edge," "faith," "healing," "discerning of spirits," "prophecy," "tongues," and "interpretation of tongues" (1 Corinthians 12–14). Indeed, the whole concept of spir-itual gifts is incomprehensible without the revelation of the Spirit (1 Corinthians 2:14). To "have the Spirit of God" is virtually equated with a revelation of wisdom (1 Cor-inthians 7:40). The wisdom of God is only known be-cause, "God has revealed it to us by his Spirit. The Spirit searches all things, even the deep things of God" (1 Cor-inthians 2:10). Prophecy, then, in its varied manifestations, modeled on Old Testament patterns, is *the characteristic* expression of the Holy Spirit in the New Testament.

Spirit-Inspired Prayer

Spirit-inspired prayer characterizes normative proph-etic Christian communication with God in a way that similarly characterizes the communication and reception of the Gospel. The believer receives the Spirit of access (Ephesians 2:18) and adoption, which "bears witness" to that reality by "crying out, Abba, (Daddy)" (Romans 8:15, 16). The one praying "in the Spirit" is guided, via prophetic revelation, in prayer (Romans 8:26, 27) and worship (Philippians 3:3). Prophecy and revelation do not instantly happen just because one has previously expressed the "gift." Jeremiah had to pray for ten days (42:7), and Daniel (10:2) for twenty-one days before receiving a prophetic word.

Prophetic Miracles

Prophetic miracles are characteristic of the prophetic mission, which includes healings, raisings from the dead, and unspecified acts of divine power. These are associated with the Spirit of God and they occur frequently in contexts of the proclamation/demonstration of the Gospel (Luke 4:14,18; Acts 1:8; 6:5[8]; 8:39; 9:[15]17; 10:38; 13:[7]9; Romans 1:4; 15:19; 1 Corinthians 2:4; 6:6[7]; 1 Thessalonians 1:5; Hebrews 6:4; Revelation 11:11), or as part of the edifying activity of the Spirit within the Christian communities (1 Corinthians 12:9; Galatians 3:2, 3, 5, 15; Hebrews 2:4). We see that like the prophetic word of old, the Gospel was not simply proclaimed, but demonstrated in "word *and* deed."

Against this biblical portrayal of the tight association of Spirit with prophecy and power, later traditional theology of the Spirit concentrated on Greek notions of being, persons and essences (Trinity), the procession of the Spirit, ethics, and later, mostly limiting the Spirit's work within the Protestant *ordo salutis*: call, justification, regeneration, sanctification, and so on.

Prophecy and the New Covenant

The "New Covenant" in traditional theology focuses on the movement from animal sacrifices to the sacrifice of Christ (Hebrew 9–10). In the New Testament, the new covenant equally includes the promise of the Spirit of prophecy (Isaiah 59:20; Jeremiah 31:33–34; Joel 2:26–28). At the Last Supper, Jesus introduces the New Covenant in his body and blood, but throughout, as part of New Covenant, he also promises the Spirit, the Comforter (John 14:26). Here, the new covenant is fulfilled about the prophetic Spirit for all Israel (Numbers 11:29) because they would enter the new Messianic Age as it is ratified by the outpouring of the Spirit (Joel 2:26–28, Acts 2:16–18; 8; 9–10; 19:1–7). This theme is reaffirmed in St. Paul (2 Corinthians 3:12–18). All classes of people are included in the New Covenant of the Spirit (see

Acts 2:16–18, paraphrased as divine authority in Galatians 3:26–28). This explains the list of nations at Pentecost, the ratification of the Spirit covenant with successive ethnic groups (Acts 2, 8, 9–11, 19:1–7), and the fact that women are often mentioned as prophets (Luke 1:41–45, 46–55; 2:36; Acts 2:17; 21:9; Galatians 3:26–28) or even as an apostle (Romans 16:7).

Authority of Prophecy Today

Because prophecy is so closely associated with the creation of Scripture (Matthew 11:13; 2 Peter 1:12), some suggest that prophecy only existed until the completed Scripture was written. The argument is made that Ephesians 2:20 teaches that the church is founded on the apostles and prophets, and after that "foundational" generation died, those gifts would cease. Grudem compromises, suggesting that there are two levels of the gift of prophecy in the New Testament: inerrant Scripture-creating prophets and a somewhat flawed gift of prophecy for the rest of us. However, this attempt to preserve the gift of prophecy for today is artificial and reads back into the text theological issues that appear centuries later. The "foundational" gifts here are offered as a pattern to be copied in the church, not locked in the first century. Moreover, Pentecostal and charismatic leadership has always maintained that the true gift of prophecy today can neither add new doctrine to the Bible, nor contradict it. They would also agree with the widespread opinion of the early church fathers: that the prophetic gift both has and will "continue in all the Church until the final coming" (cited in Ruthven 1993, 27).

JON MARK RUTHVEN

See also Charismata; Covenant; Dispensationalism; Gifts of the Spirit; Visions and Dreams

Further Reading

Aune, D. E. (1983). *Prophecy in early Christianity and the ancient Mediterranean world.* Grand Rapids, MI: Eerdmans.

Blenkinsopp, J. (1996). *A history of prophecy in Israel.* Louisville, KY: Westminster John Knox.

Cartledge, M. J. (1994). Charismatic prophecy: A definition and description. *Journal of Pentecostal Theology, 5,* 79–120.

Ellis, E. E. (1993). *Prophecy and hermeneutic in early Christianity.* Grand Rapids, MI: Eerdmans.

Gitay, Y. (1997). *Prophecy and prophets: The diversity of contemporary issues in scholarship.* Atlanta, GA: Scholars Press.

Grudem, W. (1988). *The gift of prophecy in the New Testament and today.* Westchester, IL: Crossway Books.

Heschel, A. (1962). *The prophets: An introduction*. New York: Harper & Row.

Hill, D. (1979). *New testament prophecy*. Richmond, VA: John Knox.

Hui, A. (1999). The spirit of prophecy and pauline pneumatology. *Tyndale Bulletin*, 50, 93–115.

Kienzle, B. M., & Walker, P. J. (1998). *Women preachers and prophets through two millennia of Christianity*. Berkeley: University of California Press.

Kydd, R. (1984). *Charismatic gifts in the early church*. Peabody, MA: Hendrickson.

Lindblom, J (1963). *Prophecy in ancient Israel*. Philadelphia: Fortress.

Maudlin, M. (1991). Seers in the heartland: Hot on the trail of the Kansas City prophets. *Christianity Today*, 35, 18–22.

Merklein, H. (1992). Der theologe als prophet: zur funktion prophetischen redens im theologischen diskurs des paulus. *New Testament Studies*, 38, 402–429.

Milavec, A. (1994). Distinguishing true and false prophets: The protective wisdom of the didache. *Journal of Early Christian Studies*, 2, 117–136.

Neff, D. (1991). Testing the new prophets. *Christianity Today*, 35, 15.

Osiek, C. (1990). Christian prophecy: Once upon a time? *Currents in Theology and Mission*, 17, 291–297.

Robeck, C. M., Jr. (1992). *Prophecy in Carthage: Perpetua, tertullian, and cyprian*. Cleveland, OH: Pilgrim Press.

Ruthven, J. (1993). *On the cessation of the charismata*. New York: Continuum.

Ruthven, J. (2002). Ephesians 2:20 and the "foundational" gifts. *Journal of Pentecostal Theology*, 10, 28–43.

Shogren, G. (1997). Christian prophecy and canon in the second century: A response to B. B. Warfield. *Journal of the Evangelical Theological Society*, 40, 609–626.

Shogren, G. (1999). How did they suppose "the perfect" would come? 1 Corinthians 13.8-12 in patristic exegesis. *Journal of Pentecostal Theology*, 15, 99–121.

Sommer, B. (1996). Did prophecy cease? Evaluating a reevaluation. *Journal of Biblical Literature*, 115, 31–47.

Stronstad, R. (1999). *The prophethood of all believers: A study in Luke's charismatic theology*. Sheffield, UK: Sheffield University Academic Press.

Turner, M. (1992). The spirit of prophecy and the power of authoritative preaching in Luke–Acts: A question of origins. *New Testament Studies*, 38, 66–88.

Turner, M. (1998). *The Holy Spirit and spiritual gifts in the New Testament and today*. Peabody, MA: Hendrickson.

Ukpong, J. (1993). Jesus' prophetic ministry and its challenge to Christian ministry. *Africa Theological Journal*, 22, 176–185.

Witherington, B. (1999). *Jesus the seer: The progress of prophecy*. Peabody, MA: Hendrickson.

Yocum, B. (1993). *Prophecy: Exercising the prophetic gifts of the spirit in the church today*. Ann Arbor, MI: Servant.

Prosperity Theology

Prosperity theology is an immensely significant and highly controversial theological system that continues to influence large segments of the Christian church. This religio-philosophic worldview, labeled variously as "Word Faith," "Word of Life," "Faith Movement," and "Positive Confession," is particularly important because while it rightly issues a wake-up alarm for depressed, apathetic, disbelieving Christians, it nevertheless issues a challenge to orthodox doctrines held by the Christian church for nearly two millennia.

Appeal and Aversion

With its focus on the character of God as the divine Benefactor, prosperity theology offers an appealing array of doctrines. Paul reminded the Roman believers of both "the kindness and sternness of God" (Romans 11:22, NIV), but people naturally cling to the former and recoil from the latter. As C. S. Lewis observed, most people are not so much interested in a *Father* in Heaven. What they really want is a Heavenly *Grandfather*, "a senile benevolence...whose plan for the universe was simply that it might be truly said at the end of each day, 'a good time was had by all'" (Lewis 1940, 40).

For most proponents of prosperity theology, this "good time" notion accords well with the "chief end of man" as expressed in the Westminster Catechism: "to glorify God and enjoy Him forever." A healthy, wealthy, and happy life truly glorifies God and brings delight. On the contrary, pain, poverty, and grief dishonor God, stifle enjoyment, and are a poor draw card for evangelism.

Critics of prosperity theology see God's master plan differently. A "pleasurable ride," they argue, is hardly all God has in mind for His people. His primary concern is moral advancement, not unalloyed happiness. Consequently, pain and poverty are not inherently evil; instead, they are the sometimes-necessary means by which God sculpts His people into the image of His Son.

Thus, unlike traditional orthodox doctrines that have long held nearly universal acceptance, prosperity

The Premium of Financial Prosperity

To encourage people to become "partners" of the Christian Broadcasting Network (CBN), the network offers a special premium: *Secrets of Financial Prosperity*, a video by CBN Chairman Pat Robertson. The text below—from the CBN website—explains the advantages of the video.

God's intention is to bless His people. The very word "blessing" means to "confer well being and prosperity on someone."

In his latest teaching series, Pat Robertson reveals the secrets of living a life of Financial Prosperity.

Pat uncovers the 6 essential keys to the life God blesses as well as outlining over 100 tips and strategies that you can use to:

- Get out of debt

- Earn supplemental income

- Build a safe retirement

- Invest profitably

- Learn effective money-management

- Acquire wealth

- And develop an attitude toward wealth that will honor God.

The Bible speaks many times about money and its use. The worth of our lives is not founded on material possessions. But wealth and its proper use can enhance the work of the Kingdom of God and bless many people.

This series will allow you to gain the right amount of leisure, provide peace of mind, eliminate nagging worry and free you from the pressure of debt.

Source: Christian Broadcasting Network. (2004). *Secrets of financial prosperity.*
Retrieved September 21, 2004, from http://www.cbn.com/partners/secrets-prosperity/

---

theology has proved to be a sword of division within the ranks of Christendom.

Prosperity Theology Defined

Since prosperity theology is not a monolithic theological system, any attempt to describe it inevitably risks some degree of distortion and oversimplification. Nevertheless, identifying common threads and recurring premises among the preachers of prosperity is a necessary and profitable enterprise. Allowing for differences among various brands, the label "prosperity theology" typically refers to Christian worldviews that emphasize an earthly life of health, wealth, and happiness as the divine, inalienable right of all who have faith in God and live in obedience to His commands. Here we must distinguish prosperity theology, as such, from a "Biblical theology of prosperity." The former highlights the benefits of God's blessings and details how to obtain them; the latter stresses the responsibilities of God's blessings and outlines how to administrate them.

Roots of Prosperity Theology

The history of human ideas reveals the multiple debts that any philosophical system has to antecedent thinkers.

Prosperity theology is no exception. Though the current place of pride as the leading proponents of prosperity theology belongs to Kenneth (b. 1937) and Gloria Copeland (birth date unavailable), their spiritual mentor, Kenneth Erwin Hagin (1917–2003), is typically revered as the "father of the modern faith movement." Notwithstanding this acclaim, every major doctrine of Hagin's faith teaching echoes (frequently verbatim) the undeniably earlier writings of Essek William Kenyon (1867–1948). Heavily influenced by—though in some measure reacting against—a variety of Christian movements and non-Christian ideologies, Kenyon merged selected metaphysical concepts from New Thought, Unitarian, and Christian Science ideologies with outer-fringe distortions of Holiness, faith-healing and Pentecostal traditions and produced the hybrid theological well from which Hagin copiously drew. Thus, without diminishing the immensely impressive leadership role with which Hagin "forged the movement that has catapulted Kenyon's doctrines throughout the world" (McConnell 1988, 77), recognition for importing many of the tenets of prosperity theology from the metaphysical cults to the church must go to E.W. Kenyon.

Owing to the verbal artisanship of Kenneth Hagin, Kenyon's teachings fell on fertile soil and received abundant water from other ideologically similar streams. During the 1950s and 1960s, Carl Rogers (1902–1987) propounded a client-centered, non-directive psychotherapeutic approach, the goal of which was to assist counselees in becoming self-actualized. The Rogerian model stressed, on the one hand, the counselee's innate ability to determine what is best for him- or herself, and, on the other hand, the counselor's role to assist the counselee by encouraging and reinforcing positive thinking.

Along with this new wave in psychology, an ideological upheaval was beginning to shake the theological world out of its "business-as-usual" mode. In the late 1960s and early 1970s, Gustavo Gutiérrez (b. 1928), Juan Luis Segundo (1925–1996), and others launched a new way of "doing theology." Influenced on one hand by the post–World War II optimism reflected in European theologians, particularly Jürgen Moltmann (b. 1926), and by Marxist ideology on the other, liberation theology was born. Concern for the economically disadvantaged in the third world countries sounded a wake-up call for the theological establishment whose heavenly-minded perspective was squelching its earthly value. Liberation theologians argued that theology wrongly had distanced itself from the practical responsibilities of the church. To express concern for people's souls while ignoring their economic plight was deemed ludicrous. The proper task of theology is to deliver oppressed peoples from poverty to a legitimate level of prosperity, not just by proclamation but also by self-help programs, by financial support, and if necessary, by force. Thus, Rogerian psychology and the rise of liberation theologies created a favorable climate for cultivating Hagin's prosperity teaching.

Yet the roots of prosperity theology plunge deeper still—at least as far back as Gnosticism, a second-century philosophical threat to orthodox Christianity. While a direct historical connection from Gnosticism to the metaphysical cults may be difficult to prove, the parallels are striking indeed. Of particular importance are: (1) an epistemology that radically bifurcates reality into (a) knowledge accessible only through the physical senses and (b) knowledge accessible only through esoteric illumination; (2) a soteriology that ousts objective, historical revelation and enthrones subjective, personal enlightenment; and (3) an ecclesiology that stratifies adherents by a kind of unspoken ecclesiastical caste system. Unfortunately, these notions have emerged rebaptized in some quarters of the Word Faith movement.

Bones of Contention

For reasons of space, we must leave untreated such doctrinal flash points as "the born-again Jesus," "the atonement of the devil," and "the divine incarnation of all believers." Here we focus our discussion on the concept of faith, since, according to most champions of prosperity theology, faith is the key that opens the door to prosperity. The typical proof-text is Hebrews 11:1: "Now faith is being sure of what we hope for and certain of what we do not see" (NIV).

Hebrews 11:1 is a packed theological proposition. Both proponents and critics of prosperity theology have scrutinized nearly every word to support their position. Both deserve commendation for esteeming the Bible as the foundation for theology, but accuracy of interpretation is critical; for just as surely as sound exegesis fortifies a theological position; faulty exegesis undermines it. Legitimate application of sound hermeneutical principles is the quintessential adjudicating standard for each element of Hebrews 11:1.

Proponents of prosperity theology use Hebrews 11:1 to support an ontological understanding of faith. Following the King James Version's rendering of the Greek predicate nominative $u\rfloor povstasi$ as "substance," they find here a succinct job description of faith. Faith begins with desire and, by confessing it as already done, substantiates it. Hence, the label "Word of Faith."

The spoken word has power to bring desire into space-time existence, hence, the title of one Word-Faith teacher's booklet: *There is a Miracle in Your Mouth*. For many Prosperity teachers the actualizing power of Word-Faith is a spiritual law that functions independently from the Lawgiver's will and the practitioner's morality. That is to say, ungodly people can experience health, wealth, and happiness, if they (even inadvertently) follow this "spiritual" principle.

Critics deem this schema fanciful eisegesis and idiosyncratic theology. They charge that understanding *uJpovstasi* as literal substance imports a rare nuance that finds meager scholarly support and dubious contextual verification. Far more defensible is the interpretation that recognizes the coordinate predicate phrases as Hebrew parallelism stressing a single point: faith conquers all doubt. Indeed, nothing in this verse suggests that faith is a free-floating formula for success intended to be applied carte blanche. It simply asserts that faith brings an unflagging conviction that the "things hoped for" and the "things not seen" will indeed be actualized.

And my God will meet all your needs
according to his glorious riches in Christ Jesus.

Philippians 4:19 (New International Version)

In the first chapter of his booklet *What Faith Is*, Hagin unreservedly makes the assertion that faith is strictly present tense and hope is strictly future tense. To prove his point he quotes and comments on Hebrews 11:1 from the King James Version, "Notice what our text says: '*NOW faith is* . . .' That's present tense. If it's not now, it's not faith. Faith is present tense. Hope is future tense. Get in the right tense; get in the present tense [emphasis original]" (Hagin 1983, 5).

The word translated "now" in Hebrews 11:1 is not an adverb denoting the present moment (Greek, *nu`n*), but a mild conjunction (Greek, *deV*) that here means something like "having said all that" or "on the basis of what we have already said" or perhaps even "pay attention because what follows is important." The word "now" in this context has nothing whatever to do with the present tense. The truth is that faith is as grounded in the past and enduring into the future as active in the present, that is, we can trust God *now* and continue to trust Him in the *future* because He has proved Himself reliable in the *past*.

Thus, both proponents and critics of Prosperity theology agree that God has promised every believer health, wealth, and happiness. The former hold that this utopian lifestyle is a divine right attainable in the here and now by confession of faith; the latter, see it as a by-faith-only-partially-realized divine gift that awaits ultimate fulfillment in the age to come.

Benefits of Prosperity Theology

Proponents of prosperity theology are worthy of commendation for their emphasis on the goodness of God. Humans tend to take personal credit for good things in life and blame God for difficulties and hardships. They perceive moral boundaries as unwelcome restrictions on personal freedom. According to this darkened understanding, God views all enjoyment as sin and takes sadistic pleasure in raining on humanity's parade. Prosperity theology sees the parallel between earthly parent-child relationships and the relationship between God and humanity. If parents take pleasure in bringing enjoyment to their children, how much more must our Heavenly Father delight in blessing His children. Honorable parents take no pleasure in seeing their child hurt or sick. Although they recognize that sometimes short-term pain pays rich dividends of long-term gain, they do whatever they can to bring comfort. Surely, God shares and exceeds this desire to bless.

Another benefit of prosperity theology is that it guards the church from an "unrealized" eschatology. Some view earthly life as the necessarily miserable passageway to the bliss of heaven. For them, pain and difficulty are somehow more "spiritual" than health and ease. Prosperity theology teaches that while earthly life is indeed a shadow of our eternal abode, it is not entirely different from its heavenly counterpart. God created cosmic material for our enjoyment. Admittedly, this is not the ideal world, but it does bear some resemblance.

Prosperity theology also does the body of Christ an important service in keeping us from over-spiritualizing the promises of God. The gospel affects the mundane as well as the celestial. God wants to meet humanity's needs—and He is not partial. He calls the church to give attention to feeding the hungry, clothing the naked, and caring for widows and orphans.

Weaknesses of Prosperity Theology

Much like the swings of a pendulum, the history of foundational theological concepts is a history of dialectical movements between overemphasis and disregard, full acceptance and complete rejection. The church's constant theological task is retrospection and repair. While prosperity theology has succeeded in pulling the theological pendulum from some distorted extremes, it has failed to strike an appropriate balance.

Prosperity theology stresses God's promise to bless His people and notes that His blessings are not restricted to the heavenly realm, but it often allows the "material" aspect of blessing to overshadow the spiritual aspects. God sometimes allows pain, poverty, and sorrow to impact a person's life for didactic reasons, perhaps as chastisement, perhaps as discipline, perhaps to test the genuineness of one's faith. The desert of adversity forges character far better than the streams of comfort. As C. S. Lewis put it: "God whispers to us in our pleasures, speaks in our conscience, but shouts in our pains: it is his megaphone to rouse a deaf world" (Lewis 1940, 93).

Although prosperity theology stresses the beneficial character of creation, it frequently views the benefits of creation from a mundane perspective. Pleasure is not a product, but a by-product. True pleasure comes from a right relationship with God, not from run-amok materialism. Promoting programs for the poor is laudable, but sanctifying affluence is untenable.

Challenges for the Future

The quest for truth must move us to judiciously evaluate all interpretations, not to anxiously await the results of an opinion poll, nor to muster troops for battle. We must recognize that neither the proponents of prosperity theology nor its critics are the "enemy." Leaving aside charlatans, who claim virtually every denomination and theological stripe, the church has sincere, godly men and women on both sides of the Prosperity issue. Neither side is immune to distortion. The health of the church demands issue-driven dialogue, not scathing ad hominem attacks. A thoroughgoing repentance-baptism from all arrogant approaches and self-serving epistemologies is an important first step to reciprocal understanding.

Lamentably, many critics of prosperity theology ignore the biblically-faithful theological contributions this viewpoint offers. If these critics desire to bring prosperity theology into closer alignment with historic Christianity, they first must recognize and affirm the biblically-faithful contributions of the Prosperity preachers. Equally lamentable, however, is the fact that many propagators of prosperity doctrines seem to display little awareness or concern that some of their specific teachings have departed from historic Christianity. They typically fault the traditional church for holding people in bondage and write it off as sub-Christian at best. Thus, those proponents of prosperity

theology who do seek a rapprochement with historic Christianity face two additional obstacles that are largely the making of their own most vocal champions: first, an apparent unfamiliarity with biblical languages and culture; and second, a questionable use of hermeneutical principles and their application in exegesis. Apart from significant improvement in these areas on both sides of the prosperity table, the historic Christian community may discard the wheat of prosperity theology along with its chaff, and prosperity theology will continue to be a divisive force in the Christian church.

ROB STARNER

See also Liberation Theology; Positive Confession Theology; Rich and Riches

Further Reading

Barron, B. (1987). *The health and wealth gospel*. Downers Grove, IL: InterVarsity Press.

Bowman, R. M., Jr. (1992). *Orthodoxy and heresy: A biblical guide to doctrinal discernment*. Grand Rapids, MI: Baker.

Bowman, R. M., Jr. (2001). *The Word-Faith controversy: Understanding the health and wealth gospel*. Grand Rapids, MI: Baker.

Capps, C. (1987). *Faith and confession*. Tulsa, OK: Harrison House.

DeArteaga, W. L. (1996). *Quenching the spirit: Discover the REAL spirit behind the charismatic controversy*. Lake Mary, FL: Creation House.

Fee, G. D. (1979). *The disease of the health and wealth gospels*. Costa Mesa, CA: The Word for Today.

Fee, G. D. (1984). The gospel of prosperity—An alien gospel. *Reformation Today* (Nov.–Dec. 1984).

Geisler, N. (2002). *The roots of evil*. Eugene, OR: Wipf and Stock.

Hagin, K. (1979). *How to write your own ticket with God*. Tulsa, OK: K. Hagin Ministries.

Hagin, K. (1980). *Having faith in your faith*. Tulsa, OK: K. Hagin Ministries.

Hagin, K. (1980). *You can have what you say*. Tulsa, OK: K. Hagin Ministries.

Hagin, K. (1983). *What faith is* (2nd ed.). Tulsa, OK: Faith Library Publications.

Hanegraaff, H. (1993). *Christianity in crisis*. Eugene, OR: Harvest House.

Harder, G. (1975). uJpovstasi. In C. Brown (Ed.), *The new international dictionary of New Testament theology* (Vol. 1). Grand Rapids, MI: Zondervan Publishing House.

Horton, S. (Ed.). (1994). *Systematic theology: A Pentecostal perspective*. Springfield, MO: Gospel Publishing House.

Kenyon, E. W. (1964). *The father and his family: The story of man's redemption*. Lynnwood, WA: Kenyon's Gospel Publishing Society.

Kenyon, E. W. (1969). *What happened from the cross to the throne?* Lynnwood, WA: Kenyon's Gospel Publishing Society.

Köster, H. (1972). uJpovstasi. In G. Friedrich (Ed.), *Theological dictionary of the New Testament* (Vol. 8). Grand Rapids, MI: Wm. B. Eerdmans Publishing Company.

Lewis, C. S. (1940). *The problem of pain*. New York: Macmillan.

McConnell, D. R. (1988). *A different gospel*. Peabody, MA: Hendrickson.

Meyer, D. E. (1980). *The positive thinkers: Religion as pop psychology from Mary Baker Eddy to Oral Roberts*. New York: Pantheon Books.

Murray, A. (1982). *Divine healing*. Springdale, PA: Whitaker House.

Osteen, J. (1972). *There is a miracle in your mouth*. Humble, TX: J. H. Osteen.

Price, F. K. C. (1992). *Name it and claim it! The power of positive confession*. Tulsa, OK: Harrison House.

Simpson, A. B. (1915). *The gospel of healing*. Harrisburg, PA: Christian Publications.

Vreeland, D. (2002). Reconstructing Word of Faith theology: A defense, analysis and refinement of the theology of the Word of Faith Movement. *Refleks, 1–2*(2002), 51–68.

Wenham, J. W. (1985). *The enigma of evil*. Grand Rapids, MI: Zondervan.

Williams, J. R. (1988, 1990). *Renewal theology: Systematic theology from a charismatic perspective* (2 Vols.). Grand Rapids, MI: Zondervan.

Protestantism

Pentecostal and charismatic movements have maintained a somewhat tumultuous and multifaceted relationship with the larger body of Protestant Christians worldwide. Indeed, the question of whether or not Pentecostals and certain charismatics should even be included under the heading *Protestant* is a matter of debate with no easy or universally accepted conclusions. The last century has produced a variety of Pentecostal and Charismatic movements on a worldwide scale, and the connection of these groups to Protestant Christians remains a complex issue.

What is Protestantism?

Defining the term *Protestantism* is a slippery task, and one could argue that the term is so broad that it holds negligible value. Protestants often trace their roots to the movement initiated by Martin Luther in 1517 by the posting of his famous *Ninety-five Theses* (indicting the Catholic practice of "indulgences"), along with similar actions taken in Switzerland by Ulrich Zwingli in 1518. Initially, the term *Protestant* was first used in 1529 when a group of political supporters for Luther and Zwingli's reformation program issued a *protestatio* to establish their shared "reforming beliefs" and consolidate politico-religious power among various German princes and cities. The title *Protestant* was thus first used only in a very narrow sense, and "it is therefore problematic to use Protestant as a simple description for sympathizers with reform in the first half of the sixteenth century" or even for subsequent groups that choose to call themselves "Protestant" (MacCulloch 2003, xviii).

Some opt to define "Protestant" as "not Catholic," and this opposition retains at least some value since, in many parts of the world, Protestants have defined themselves primarily vis-à-vis their relationship to Catholics. Perhaps Protestantism can be defined as a Christian movement that primarily identifies itself with the "protests" of the sixteenth-century reformers and maintains some continuity or historical relationship to one of the three major churches spawned by the Reformation, namely the Lutheran, Reformed, and Anglican churches, or any of their thousands of denominational and independent branches (including Methodists, Baptists, Lutherans, Presbyterians, United Church of Christ, and numerous independent and "non-denominational" churches). Protestantism describes this historical tradition of church movements, continuing through the present day, and its multiplicity of doctrines and beliefs formulated partly in opposition to and partly in dialogue with the Catholic Church. Broadly speaking, Protestants have historically not embarked on a wholesale rejection of Catholic doctrine so much as they have rejected certain Catholic practices and spiritual emphases, choosing to move away from infant baptism, viewing communion/Eucharist in terms of "transubstantiation," and the veneration of Mary and the Saints. Yet Protestants have generally accepted a certain set of their own doctrinal affirmations, many of which can be dated back to Protestantism's earliest days and the teachings of Martin Luther. For example, most Protestants embrace some notion of "faith alone" or "saved by grace" theology that focuses on the "justification" of sinners by God's unmerited favor and their faith in the gospel. Protestants often speak of their biblical canon (which conspicuously omits the so-called "deutero-canonical" books such as the Maccabees, the Greek chapters of Daniel, Baruch, etc., accepted by the

Catholic and Orthodox churches) in terms of "inspiration" or "authority," while more "conservative" Protestants are likely to use the language of "inerrancy" or "infallibility" to describe the Bible. Other characteristic Protestant beliefs and emphases are the priesthood of all believers; one eternal God, existent in three eternal persons (Father, Son, Holy Spirit); the deity and virgin birth of Jesus, His sinless life, miracles, death, burial, Resurrection, and vicarious sacrifice for sin; the Second Coming of Christ and the resurrection of the dead. Incidentally, most Pentecostal Christians also affirm these doctrinal ideals in some form or another, although the identification of Pentecostals with Protestants is somewhat problematic.

Are Pentecostals Protestants?

Scholars of Christianity have tended to divide Christians into three broad camps: Catholics, Eastern Orthodox, and Protestants. Under these divisions, Pentecostals would be assumed under the label Protestant. Still others (Knoll 2004, 15–16), however, have recently suggested that Christianity be divided into four groups, namely Catholic, Eastern Orthodox, Protestant, *and* Pentecostals. We can therefore pose the question, "Are Pentecostals Protestants?" or "Do Pentecostals consider themselves to be Protestants?" These questions do not admit a univocal answer. A key facet of Pentecostal self-identity lies in its classification with various "renewal" or "restorationist" movements; as a renewal movement, Pentecostalism has historically been hesitant to identify itself with *any* other Christian group. Many of the earliest Pentecostal "organizations" refused to call themselves a "denomination" (such as the Assemblies of God) and feel that the "limitations" of structure, bureaucracy, and hierarchies impede the spread of their message.

On the other hand, various self-proclaimed Protestant groups (i.e., Lutherans, Methodists, Presbyterians, etc.) have historically regarded Pentecostals as deviant and unorthodox because of a) the highly conservative and/or Fundamentalist nature of Pentecostal practice and doctrinal emphasis, b) the Pentecostal emphasis on the "gifts of the Spirit" and glossolalia, and c) the "separatist" attitude of many Pentecostal churches. Consequently we must recognize that there has often been unwillingness on the part of Protestants to include Pentecostals as orthodox (or at least "traditional"), "Protestant" Christians.

Thus, one's view of whether or not Pentecostals should be classified as Protestants (or whether certain Pentecostals denominations or individuals choose to consider themselves Protestants) will determine if Pen-

tecostals are viewed in terms of acting *within* or *outside/against* the greater Protestant matrix. It is fair to assume that many Pentecostals have never considered whether or how their particular denomination or faith expression fits within the greater Christian community and do not particularly care whether or not they are identified with any overarching body of Protestants. For analytical purposes, however, we can be justified in describing Pentecostals under the heading *Protestant* so long as we recognize the difficulties involved with such identification and the fact that at least some Pentecostals and charismatics are not comfortable with the Protestant epithet.

Nevertheless, some Pentecostals are contented with the Protestant label and many Protestant charismatics see little or no discontinuity between their distinctively "charismatic" spirituality and the social or doctrinal demands of their local church body or greater denominational structure. (Obviously, charismatic Catholics would typically not call themselves Protestant, although they may view themselves as "reformers" and would thus posses a reform-minded "Protestant outlook.") Within existing Protestant denominational structures, charismatic believers are likely to hold to similar (if not identical) doctrinal stances on "key" issues in relation to non-charismatic members; the same is also true of several Pentecostal denominations. A notable exception occurs in the case of so-called "Oneness Pentecostals," who reject Trinitarian theology in favor of faith in Jesus alone. Believers in Oneness traditions are baptized in "Jesus' name" only (as opposed to other Pentecostal denominations who baptize in the name of the Father, Son, and Holy Spirit) and comprise approximately one percent of worldwide Pentecostalism (about 2–5 million members).

Pentecostalism: Protestant Roots and Reactions

As an example of the complicated and fluid relations between denominational Pentecostals and Protestant Christians at large, we will briefly survey some of the Pentecostal-Protestant interactions in the late nineteenth and twentieth centuries. These relations can be considered as somewhat of a continuum between a rejection of Pentecostal belief and experience by many Protestants (and an accompanying Pentecostal desire for distinctiveness and separation), and a Pentecostal yearning for cooperation with other Christians and acceptance in the greater Christian landscape.

Although many of the early Pentecostal leaders promoted some doctrinal views that would place them squarely in the Protestant camp (as discussed above), they still felt uncomfortable maintaining a formal affiliation with recognizably Protestant groups. Perhaps the most key element in early Pentecostal identity involves the birth of Pentecostalism in the midst of wider *restorationist* movements of the late nineteenth and early twentieth centuries. Central to restorationist ideology is the notion that the church has at some point become extremely corrupt and dysfunctional, and it is the job of a chosen few to "restore" apostolic ideals and "true" practice to the church. Obviously, this kind of mentality is inherent to the Protestant ethos, although many Pentecostals felt (and still feel) that the more popular Protestant churches themselves had grown impotent and needed substantial change.

The restoration mindset of the late nineteenth century held a natural attraction for those uncomfortable with ecclesiastical authority. Charles Parham (1873–1929), who is credited as the first to identify speaking in tongues as the normative evidence of the baptism in the Holy Spirit, was a Methodist lay minister who repudiated his denominational affiliation because of the "narrowness of sectarian churchism" (Blumhofer 1989, 71). When numbers of Protestants felt that denominational hierarchy had lost its authority to define what the church should be, preachers like Parham gained the opportunity to define a "truly restored church." This restorationist thrust was not accepted by everyone; opposition to Pentecostals grew through the publication of the *Scofield Reference Bible* (1909), a Bible whose notes espoused the view that tongues and other gifts found in the book of Acts were part of a "dispensation" that ceased at the end of the Apostolic period, providing a unified doctrinal basis for many Protestants to reject the Pentecostal experience. The uneasiness with Pentecostal experiences seemed to culminate at the Fundamentalist Convention of 1928 (held in Chicago), where members voted overwhelmingly in favor of a resolution against the Pentecostal movement.

Following the formal ostracism by the Fundamentalists, the great question about the relationship of Pentecostals to Protestantism during the next fifty years seemed to revolve around who was considered "the enemy." For extreme separatists, the fundamentalists were just one more enemy, and persecution is often interpreted as a sign of "authenticity." Therefore, the trappings of denominations were rejected and replaced with a sense of pride in what Pentecostals did not have, i.e., money, buildings, liturgy, formal education, and tradition. For much of their early history poverty has been a mark of dedication; at times this disenfranchisement has been married to the holiness tradition in such a way as to ascribe value

to a way of dress or an activity simply because doing so was socially unacceptable. Ironically, this rejection of tradition allowed them to quickly *adapt* worship styles or marketing techniques to changing social and cultural situations, sometimes with little thought to theological considerations.

However, the distance (and differences) between Pentecostals and Protestants began to blur toward the middle of the twentieth century. With the participation of the Church of God (Cleveland, Tennessee) and the Assemblies of God (AG) as founding members of the National Association of Evangelicals (NAE) in 1941 Pentecostals enjoyed broader acceptance on the Protestant scene.

Pentecostal identity took a new turn around 1960 as word spread of glossolalia occurring among non-Pentecostals in both Protestant and Catholic churches. Ironically, the initial response of the Pentecostal members of the NAE was to identify more with the separatist mindset of the NAE than the new charismatic experience of some Protestant church members. David du Plessis, an AG minister, was defrocked in 1962 because of his participation in the charismatic renewal and his subsequent "ecumenical" positions. In fact, the anti-ecumenical sentiment grew so strong that the same year a resolution was passed by the General Presbytery and later by the General Council of the AG identifying the ecumenical church as culminating in the religious Babylon of Revelation. This illustrates what some view as a tendency of Pentecostal denominations to identify more closely with conservative Protestants than with the distinctively Pentecostal practices, a tendency that is often not met with support among the independent Pentecostal constituencies.

By the 1970s, the Pentecostal denominations seemed to be opening their arms to embrace the Charismatic movement. This may have been brought about by the divergent pressures of classic Pentecostals involved with charismatic ministries and the increasing acceptance of the Charismatic movement by many Protestant churches. Perhaps the interaction of Pentecostals with the Charismatic movement has done more to shift the mindset of many Pentecostals away from the restorationist mentality and into a more "acceptable" position within Protestantism. The expansion of the Charismatic movement in Western civilization is paralleled by an unprecedented growth among Pentecostals in less developed areas of the world during this same time. The effect has not only been the acceptance of Pentecostals into "mainstream Protestantism," but to some extent, the acceptance of "mainstream Protestantism" by Pentecostals. Many Pentecostals have shed their differences with Protestant denominations in dress and practices, and have shifted the purpose of their educational institutions from "protection" and seclusion to innovation and influence. Pentecostals embraced certain elements of traditional worship that they once shunned, while a significant number of Protestant churches adopted the spontaneous and emotional elements formerly exclusive to Pentecostals.

Outlook for the Twenty-first Century

It remains to be seen how, in the long term, Pentecostal and charismatic groups will relate to each other and to the Protestant world; Pentecostal-Charismatic identities are constantly being formed and reformed in the context of explosive growth and missionary efforts, as these new groups have only recently become de facto leaders and spokespersons for Protestant Christianity. Despite their humble beginnings in relatively small revival meetings, denominational Pentecostals have arguably grown to what accounts for the largest Protestant group on the world scene in the twenty-first century. Pentecostal and charismatic missiologists are quick to assert that virtually all new Christian believers in the world today can be classified as either charismatic or Pentecostal, driving the worldwide number of Pentecostals and charismatics (in Protestant denominations) to over 500 million members.

BRIAN R. DOAK AND PHIL DUNCAN

See also Antecedents of Pentecostalism; Non-Pentecostal Christians, Relationship to

Further Reading

Ahlstrom, S. E. (1971). *A religious history of the United States.* New Haven, CT: Yale University Press.

Anderson, R. M. (1992) *Vision of the disinherited.* Peabody, MA: Hendrickson Publishers.

Blumhofer, E. L. (1989). *The Assemblies of God*, Vols. 1–2. Springfield, MO: Gospel Publishing House.

Blumhofer, E. L., Spittler, R. P., & Wacker, G. A. (Eds.). (1999). *Pentecostal currents in American Protestantism.* Urbana: University of Illinois Press.

Cox, H. (2001). *Fire from heaven: The rise of Pentecostal spirituality and the reshaping of religion in the 21st century.* New York: DaCapo Press.

Cross, T. L. (2002). A proposal to break the ice: What can Pentecostal theology offer Evangelical theology? *Journal of Pentecostal Theology, 10*(2), 44–73.

Dayton, D. W. (1991). *Theological roots of Pentecostalism.* Peabody, MA: Hendrickson.

Hempelmann, R. (1994). The Charismatic Movement in German Protestantism. *Pneuma: The Journal for the Society of Pentecostal Studies, 16*(2), 215–226.

Hollwenweger, W. J. (1997). *Pentecostalism: Origins and developments worldwide.* Peabody, MA: Hendrickson.

Knoll, M. (2004, March). *Is the Reformation over? An Evangelical Protestant assessment of Roman Catholicism in the era of Vatican II and Pope John Paul II.* Paper presented at Lewis University, Romeoville, IL.

MacCulloch, D. (2003). *The Reformation: A history.* New York: Viking.

McGee, G. B. (2004). *People of the Spirit: The Assemblies of God.* Springfield, MO: Gospel Publishing House.

Nichol, J. T. (1966). *The Pentecostals.* Plainfield, NJ: Logos International.

Synan, V. (1987). Pentecostalism: Varieties and contributions. *Pneuma: The Journal for the Society of Pentecostal Studies, 9*(1), 31–49.

Synan, V. (1997). *The Holiness-Pentecostal tradition: Charismatic movements in the twentieth century.* Grand Rapids, MI: William B. Eerdmans.

Synan, V. (2001). *The century of the Holy Spirit: 100 Years of Pentecostal and charismatic renewal.* Nashville, TN: Thomas Nelson Publishers.

Wacker, G. (2003). *Heaven below: Early Pentecostals and American culture.* Cambridge, MA: Harvard University Press.

R

Race Relations

Frank Bartleman, a participant in the famous Azusa Street Revival, declared in his memoirs that the color line had been "washed away in the blood [of Jesus]" (1980). Yet since its inception, the Pentecostal movement has been racially conflicted. The history of race relations within the Pentecostal movement in the United States runs parallel to the history of race relations within the larger American society. Though some of the earliest adherents felt that racial animosity could be overcome by the radical concept of Spirit empowerment and love that transcended barriers to Christian fellowship, several elements at the beginning of the movement set the tone for continued racial division.

One indication that the movement failed to overcome racial animosity is the ongoing controversy over the founding of the movement. Until the middle of the twentieth century, white historians regularly highlighted the leadership of Charles Fox Parham while relegating the contribution of African-American William J. Seymour and the Azusa Street Mission and Revival to little more than a footnote. In attempting to correct this oversight, many black scholars diminished the contribution of Charles Fox Parham and attacked his moral indiscretion in an attempt to discredit him. A more balanced picture of the movement's founding would recognize the valuable contributions of both men. Such an approach would credit Parham for developing the theological understanding of tongues that became the foundational doctrine of the movement. At the same time, it would credit Seymour for leading the revival that catapulted a local revival meeting of primarily black household servants and their families into worldwide notoriety.

Seymour himself endured the indignity of sitting outside the classroom in Parham's Houston Bible School to listen to Parham describe his theory that tongues provided a doctrine of initial evidence. Yet Seymour championed the cause of racial reconciliation, believing that a surer evidence of Holy Spirit baptism than tongues was unity among all races of Spirit-baptized believers. Following the radical egalitarian heritage of the Holiness movement out of which Pentecostalism sprang, Seymour presided over a dream of racial unity that proved to be short-lived.

Early Signs of Racial Tension

From the beginning, the interracial character of the Azusa Street meetings was both applauded and disdained. Within the revival, white women from various walks of life joined with black household servants to exercise their ministry gifts. One element that drew public attention, and a degree of derision from the secular press, was the regular sight of white men, many of them prominent members of the clergy or the community, kneeling before black women who prayed with them to receive prayer for Holy Spirit baptism. When Parham visited the Azusa Street mission at Seymour's invitation, his disgust for the racially mixed atmosphere of the meetings was obvious. He said the scene he observed "made me sick to my stomach...to see white people imitating unintelligent crude Negroisms ...and laying it on the Holy Ghost" (Synan 1971, 180).

Another sign of early tension along racial lines came with the decision of Florence Crawford, a white woman, to leave the Los Angeles Apostolic Faith Mission and establish a work of her own in the Northwest.

On first setting up a ministry in Oregon, she maintained close relations with Seymour. But when she later decided to sever ties with his organization over doctrinal issues, several white congregation members sided with her and broke with Seymour's group. In a later split over the oneness doctrine, many of the whites who had remained with Seymour left. By 1914, at the end of the first seven years of the revival, the interracial character of the movement had virtually ended, never to be fully recovered.

Racial Issues Among the Denominations

Most Pentecostal denominations, whether predominantly black or white or integrated, can trace their heritage directly back to the Azusa Street Revival meetings. One denomination whose ties are less evident is the Pentecostal Holiness Church, which was formed out of the merger of three existing holiness bodies and a racial split. Although the denomination had been interracial from its inception and African-Americans had been members, in 1907 black members left to form the Fire Baptized Holiness Church of God. Two years later the parent group changed its name to the Pentecostal Holiness Church, amending its statement of faith and adding a Pentecostal article to its statement of faith. In 1911 a second merger occurred when this parent group joined with the Holiness Church of North Carolina. A merger with the Tabernacle Pentecostal Church occurred in 1915, after which another contingent of African-Americans (some of whom had remained loyal during the first split) voted to separate to become the Negro Pentecostal Holiness Church.

One body that directly traces its Pentecostal roots to Azusa Street is the Church of God in Christ, arguably the largest Pentecostal body in the United States and the second largest African-American denomination in the country (National Baptist is the largest). It was co-founded about 1897 by two black preachers, Charles Harrison Mason and Charles Price Jones, as a black holiness denomination.

After his 1906 pilgrimage to the Azusa Street Revival, Mason embraced the Pentecostal message and formed a new body that retained the name Church of God in Christ and added a Pentecostal paragraph to its statement of faith. From 1907 to 1914, the Church of God in Christ was an interracial organization and the primary body providing ordination and ministerial credentials to hundreds of white ministers because it was the only legally incorporated Pentecostal body in the country. However, in 1914 several of the white ministers pulled out to form what is today the Assemblies of

God. Reportedly, the split was by mutual consent and relationships between the two bodies remained cordial. In the intervening years, these two groups have grown to be the largest Pentecostal bodies in the United States—one essentially white, the other essentially African-American.

Pentecostal Assemblies of the World (PAW) was the largest Pentecostal denomination to maintain a significant degree of racial diversity throughout the early years of Pentecostalism. But even those efforts met with only limited success, and the racial climate within the denomination was not always smooth. The prominent black preacher Garfield T. Haywood accepted the oneness message of PAW and brought a large number of African-Americans into the oneness movement and the PAW denomination. In 1915 he and 486 members of his congregation were rebaptized into the new movement. In 1925, when the organization reorganized from a congregational to an episcopal form of government, Haywood was elected to serve as the first presiding bishop. He held that post until his death in 1931.

However, in spite of Haywood's powerful influence and the multiracial dimension of the oneness movement, in 1924, racial tension in the South forced the group to split along racial lines. A large white contingent left to form its own body, although a number of whites stayed. From 1924 to 1936, the existing denomination was successful in pulling a number of independent congregations into its organization. In 1931 the denomination split again when many, but not all, of the remaining whites left.

The youngest of the major Pentecostal denominations and the largest oneness body, the United Pentecostal Church, came into being with the 1945 merger of two largely white bodies. The Pentecostal Church Incorporated pulled out of the Pentecostal Assemblies of the World to form a separate loose organization of oneness ministers and the Pentecostal Assemblies of Jesus Christ, which resulted from the merger of several smaller bodies over a protracted period. After the merger, it remained predominantly white.

Though predominantly white denominations continued to open the doors of membership to other races, in most instances they placed restriction on their participation. These restrictions included separate black enclaves, limited access to denominational leadership, and a demand that black church members tolerate the participation of white church members in racist organizations such as the Ku Klux Klan. In the southern states, blacks were often excluded from statewide meetings or forced to use separate facilities at such meetings.

In 1922, for example, the general board of the International Pentecostal Holiness Church agreed that anyone, regardless of race, should be accepted into the denomination. However, it set in place a number of restrictions, including that "the colored element shall always be confined to the Conference, or Conferences, north of the Mason and Dixon line," that "no colored person shall ever hold office in an Annual Conference," and that "no colored person shall ever be a delegate to a General Conference" (Minutes of the General Board, 1922).

Likewise, almost since its inception, restrictions were placed on the black constituency of the Church of God (Cleveland, Tennessee), which was made up primarily of immigrants from the Caribbean Islands and their families and descendents. By 1912 a separate overseer was appointed over the black churches in Florida, the state with the most blacks. Continued paternalistic attitudes, along with inadequate accommodations for blacks, forced Church of God African-American ministers to request the right to hold their own General Assembly. This practice continued until the mid-1960s.

During the period of segregation in America, Pentecostal bodies generally followed the leadership of the broader American society. White Pentecostal institutions of higher education, for example, refused to admit black students even if they were members of the denomination. Black bodies attempted to establish separate institutions to train their young, but these generally met with only limited success. It was not until the emergence of the civil rights movement that most of these institutions changed this practice.

Since most Pentecostal bodies have their roots in the South, denominational decisions often unintentionally increased the discomfort of black constituents. When denominations held national meetings in Southern states, blacks could not gain assess to the same accommodations as their white brothers and sisters and were sometimes locked out of meeting facilities entirely; sometimes they were subjected to such indignities as racial slurs or less than adequate service. In some cases, this treatment resulted in blacks not being able to attend national meetings where the important business of the denomination was carried out.

Outlook for the Future

As American society becomes more inclusive, there are some signs that the Pentecostal community is moving toward racial reconciliation. With the advent of the civil rights movement, several majority-white bodies, including, notably, the Church of God, the International Pente-

Pentecostal pioneers in the United States. *Courtesy of Isak Burger.*

Adams, F.F. Bosworth, Tom Hesmalhach, Daddy Seymour van Azussah en John G. Lake

costal Holiness Church, and the Assemblies of God have developed statements condemning racism and embracing racial inclusiveness. Since that time, these bodies have seen an increase in the number of black and interracial congregations and members. Unfortunately, however, the leadership of these denominations remains highly segregated, with the highest administrative and governing offices still held by whites.

The Pentecostal Fellowship of North America (PFNA), an exclusively white umbrella group, was formed by eight Pentecostal denominations in 1948 to foster fellowship and cooperative effort within the movement, and African-American groups were not invited to participate. However, in 1994, the heads of the major African-American and white Pentecostal bodies gathered in Memphis, Tennessee, to dissolve the PFNA. In its place, a new biracial organization, the Pentecostal and Charismatic Churches of North America, was created. Its first elected president, the late Bishop Ithiel Clemmons of the Church of God in Christ, was an African-American and its twelve-member leadership board included an African-American woman, Bishop Barbara Amos.

The emergence of the Charismatic movement signaled an advance in race relations within the realm of Spirit-filled believers, but despite these beginnings, the leadership of most major Pentecostal denominations remains segregated. Racial integration is more common in the larger congregations that populate the nation's more cosmopolitan metropolitan areas, and several large congregations have come into existence that have significantly greater racial inclusiveness in their congregation makeup and leadership than is generally found in more traditional Pentecostal bodies. These newer organizations and congregations are characterized by racially diverse leadership, both within the local congregations and at the institutional level.

The Pentecostal movement falls short of total inclusiveness of all races and has focused almost exclusively on healing wounds between blacks and whites. Hispanics and Asians, who have a relatively high proportional representation among Pentecostals, are rarely found within the leadership or on the faculties of Pentecostal institutions, and are almost entirely excluded from discussions of racial reconciliation, as are Native Americans, who have a proportionally smaller representation. Additionally, the attention of the Memphis racial-reconciliation conference was almost entirely on healing racial wounds among Pentecostals. The broader issue of the need for racial justice within the wider society remains largely untouched by Pentecostal leaders and scholars.

ESTRELDA Y. ALEXANDER

See also Azusa Street Revival; Memphis Miracle

Further Reading

Anderson, R. M. (1992). *Vision of the disinherited: The making of American Pentecostalism*. Peabody, MA: Hendrickson Publishers.

Bartleman, F. (1980). *Azusa Street*. Plainfield, NJ: Logos International.

MacRoberts, I. (1988). *The black roots and white racism of early Pentecostalism in the USA*. New York: St. Martin's Press.

Michel, D. ((2000). *Telling the story: Black Pentecostals in the Church of God*. Cleveland, TN: Pathway Press.

Minutes of the general board of the International Pentecostal Holiness Church. January 4, 1922.

Nelson, D. J. (1981). *For such a time as this: The story of Bishop William J. Seymour and the Azusa Street Revival: A search for Pentecostal/Charismatic roots*. Unpublished doctoral dissertation, University of Birmingham, UK.

Synan, V. (1971). *Holiness-Pentecostal Movement in the United States*. Grand Rapids, MI: Eerdmans.

Religious Life

From the Pentecostal-Charismatic perspective, "religious life" is a comprehensive concept that indicates a life marked by the experience of the presence of God expressed in a variety of forms that are inspired and nurtured by the Holy Spirit. This conception of a life in the Holy Spirit represents, to a certain extent, a shift in understanding religious life; it is modeled on the church of the early centuries and preserves Christian identity while meeting some religious-spiritual claims of the third millennium and responding to their multirational epistemic paradigms. The etymology of "religious" begins with "binding" and "holding together," expressing the idea of a relationship with God. The term "religion," which extends to a set of practices required for a consistent life according to that relationship, is also included in the Pentecostal-Charismatic concept of religious life.

Historical Framework

The easiest way to approach and understand the concept of religious life from the Pentecostal-Charismatic perspective is to start with some historical elements. Pentecostals, charismatics, and neocharismatics do not share the same history, though they do have in common the conviction that underpins the beginning of the Pentecostal movement—that is, an awareness of the central role of the Holy Spirit in the plan of salvation, in the mysteries of the life of Christ, and in the life of the Christian believer.

Pentecostalism has its roots in Pietism, which was preached in Germany by Johann Arndt (1555–1621) and Philipp Jakob Spener (1635–1705), and then spread outside Germany by Nikolaus Ludwig von Zinzendorf (1700–1760). Pietism arose as a reaction to the rationalistic approach that had characterized theology in Europe for centuries. The pietistic idea of a relationship with God as a bond of the heart, with an emphasis on the spiritual/devotional/emotional aspects of religious experience, was increasingly successful in the United States. This was mainly a consequence of the Civil Rights movement, which caused an upheaval of the lower classes and brought their importance to the attention of the Pietists, who found a way to introduce the Gospel to them in a simple way. The success of Pietism was also a consequence of the emphasis on the local/congregational rather than the universal/institutional matrix of the Second Revival in the United States (the shift from the "denominational" to the "network" concept of religious experience). In such a context the Pentecostal-Charismatic vision, which stressed the individual rather than the confessional family, easily spread and developed. This attitude also characterized the neocharismatic groups that developed in the last decades of the twentieth century.

The Charismatic movement had a different history, though it shared the same pneumatological focus. Sprung from a claim of renewal and developed since

1950 within the historical churches (Lutheran, Episcopalian, Catholic, Anglican, Orthodox, and so on), it framed the pneumatologically oriented religious life within the respective confessional theologies.

The Pentecostal-Charismatic experience, regardless of the specific historical streams, has an intrinsic geo-ethnical plasticity, because it can adapt to the culture and spirituality of any group in any country; this very circumstance is also considered an eschatological sign: no race barriers, no cognitive-emotional barriers, and so on.

Conceptual Focus

Pentecostals and charismatics make reference to a founding experience concerning the life of the believer, as witnessed in the Bible, which they hold to be possible for every Christian in all times. For this reason they tend to keep a distance from theoretical systematizations and to consider, on the contrary, the life of the believer as the place to encounter the Spirit and enjoy His power. In the very beginning of Pentecostal history and throughout the first decades of its existence, such an attitude was one of the consequences of believers being illiterate, a feature (in their perspective a valuable one). Although this has changed slightly in recent years, the importance of the oral tradition has been maintained.

Experience requires, in fact, some criteria able to qualify experience itself as valid or adequate (for instance, gifts and charisms, an experience of personal salvation, a confession of the person of Jesus, feelings of joy and peace, a sense of mission, or turning away from the world's values) and to help discernment (for instance, in dealing with some groups of the Third Wave Pentecostals). Such criteria—mainly singled out from the Gospel—make it possible to sketch a conceptual framework that explains the Pentecostal-Charismatic outlook on religious life.

The relationship between God and human beings and consistent moral behavior is a close one in the Pentecostal-Charismatic view, because it is the same Spirit filling a person and enabling him or her to manifest His presence to the world. At the core of the religious experience of the Spirit is an inner conversion, bearing the deep conviction that for those who belong to God, no separation is possible between what is proclaimed and what is lived out. Religious life reveals itself, then, as a personal journey undertaken by the believer and confirmed by baptism in the Holy Spirit.

Baptism in the Holy Spirit invests the whole person, as the biblical language expresses through terms such as "outpouring," "filling in," "falling," or "coming upon"; the emphasis is on conveying the idea of a power, an enablement, a strength encompassing and filling the person to the extent that the whole life, options, acts, and behaviors of those baptized in the Holy Spirit will witness to the world, for those baptized in the Holy Spirit are empowered for worship and apostolate in the world.

Baptism in the Holy Spirit is intrinsically a Christological confession for it is the same and only Holy Spirit who "swept over the face of the water" (Genesis 1:2) in Creation, who made possible the mystery of incarnation, and who sanctifies, thus making it possible for believers to become children of God. Recognizing and confessing Christ is decisive and works as a criterion of belonging to either the world or to God. The Prologue of the Gospel of St. John states this salvific truth in powerful language: "People who did not accept Him [are opposed to] all who received Him" (John 1:11–12) and they are generated by God, not by the blood and the flesh.

Religious experience is, according to the Pentecostal-Charismatic perspective, a personal journey of and in faith: The believer lives under the guidance of the Holy Spirit, aware of His presence and anointing and responsive to the signs and wonders outpoured for the well-being of the community of believers. These signs and wonders are manifestations of the glory of God, which calls for spreading the Gospel and hastening the Kingdom of God while nurturing the community and building up the Body of Christ. Signs and wonders—which in the Pentecostal view are manifestations of the fullness of Christian life and witness to the "full Gospel" of Jesus Christ—are acts of worship (in the sense of being situated in unceasing praise to the Lord) as well as moral acts (in the sense of being put at the service of others).

Such signs and wonders are, according to the New Testament, speaking in tongues (the primary evidence of baptism in the Spirit in classical Pentecostal theology) and healing; then all the charisms (exemplified rather than listed by St. Paul in chapter 12 of his First Letter to the Corinthians), including wisdom, knowledge, discernment of spirits, the gift of healing, working of miracles, various kinds of tongues, prophecy, and interpretation of tongues.

Aware of the importance and gravity of dealing with gifts from above, both Protestant and Catholic theology and Pentecostal and charismatic language have always been very cautious in describing or classifying these gifts. They are manifestations of divine endowment, signs from God freely given by the Spirit. For this reason it has always been very difficult to single out links, connections, and comparisons and to highlight similarities and differences among signs, wonders, gifts of healing, gifts of tongues, the charisms listed by St. Paul, graces freely given (*gratiae gratis datae*), gifts of the Spirit, fruits of the Spirit, talents given to the believers, and so forth, although the community of believers has tried to give some definitions—whether articulated in a structured theology or descriptive of a praxis—to make it easier to grasp God's unceasing care for human beings throughout history.

Spiritual Implications

From the Pentecostal-Charismatic perspective, religious life constitutes an old and yet new pattern of Christian understanding of the relationship with God. "Old" here is not used as a synonym for "traditional" or "old-fashioned" to describe this understanding (as it is described in the Acts of the Apostles). At the core of the Pentecostal-Charismatic vision is the idea that what has been experienced and witnessed by the first communities is possible today. The rediscovery of the old paradigm constitutes the newness of the Pentecostal-Charismatic proposal. "New" is not used here as a synonym for "unedited" but as opposed to "worn out" and as a synonym for "revival."

The novel Pentecostal-Charismatic pattern meets the spiritual claims of twenty-first century men and women in most postmodern contexts. What makes the Pentecostal-Charismatic universe so attractive to so many people (Pentecostal-Charismatic groups grow by twenty-five thousand units every day, which means roughly 9 million people per year) is its ability to harmonize the old Christian radical lifestyle with the new Christian need for a more direct and immediate relationship with God. It does this in two ways—first, as far as faith is concerned, for it is understood as an access to experience the power of the Spirit, the Almighty God, rather than to conceptualize His attributes; and second, as far as human skills and abilities are concerned, for the human potentialities of healing, prophesying, speaking in tongues, having visions, practicing the gifts and charisms, and so on, are appropriated to the free initiative of the Holy Spirit and oriented to the confession of Christ rather than to the ascetic effort of an individual (and not at the end of an esoteric initiation).

The specifically Pentecostal-Charismatic spirituality has been called "primal spirituality" by the theologian Harvey Cox and further distinguished into primal speech (speaking in tongues), primal piety (signs and wonders), and primal hope (eschatological orientations). However, while "primal spirituality" marks all the different streams of Pentecostal groups, among charismat-

ics peculiar ways of expressing and living their spirituality are found that constitute a specific tradition or form of religious life ("consecrated life" in the canonical sense). Such forms are said to be inspired by a specific charism (like assistance, teaching, or nursing), to bear an intrinsic and clear eschatological meaning, and to be witnesses to other Christians and signs of Christian perfection to the world. In this sense, a link can be established between the religious life so far surveyed and the religious life as consecration to God, which implies a refusal of worldly goods and a commitment to the vows of chastity, poverty, and obedience. This particular way of living the exigencies of the Gospel is present in many different Christian traditions, including the Lutheran and Anglican traditions, but especially in the Catholic and Orthodox traditions.

Social Aspects

The Pentecostal-Charismatic perspective can be traced back to the experience of the first Christian communities in what may be called a "catholic" experience—that is, not only in the sense of the universality of the message (the "katholon of the apostolic faith," as Jean Marie Tillard [1994] pointed out), but also in the original etymological sense of "kath'olou," meaning "according to each one, to the wholeness, to the integrity." The experience of the first Christians was according to the wholeness of faith, since each believer was called to manifest his or her own faith in fundamental options, in everyday life choices, and in individual and community prayers, and to address the Lord in spontaneous ways with all his or her faculties, abilities, and skills.

Such totality of life in the Spirit would seem to lead to an explicit social or political commitment, and in fact, this was the attitude of the Pentecostal groups at the very beginning of their history when they tried to reconcile conflicts in society (racial differences, social barriers, and so on) with differences in the Spirit (Galatians 3:28). In other words, they preached and acted against social injustice; later this involvement decreased but in recent years it has reappeared, varying according to geo-political areas (for instance, in Latin America Pentecostals-Charismatics are more active than in Europe). On the whole, Pentecostals and charismatics do not put forward any social-political ideas that have not already been stated by their local/institutional Church, which may share their difficulties in dealing with political dynamics, especially in public debates concerning moral matters. Nonetheless, some major streams of opinions in political life can be singled out according to the different attitudes of Pentecostals and charismatics in different countries.

At the beginning of the third millennium some scholars have been rather skeptical about the impact of Pentecostal-Charismatic evangelization despite its success in many areas, because they believe that Christians are not zealous enough in their witness to the Gospel.

Hermeneutical Hints

While the Pentecostal-Charismatic interpretation of the religious life demonstrated that the visible power of the Spirit is always at work in salvation (and not limited to the first centuries of the spread of Christianity), it also introduced a wide spectrum of complex questions about the relationship of the confession of Christ rendered possible by the Holy Spirit and the action of the same Spirit in other religions. And while the convergence of Pentecostals and charismatics is of particular interest from an ecumenical viewpoint because it creates a link that overcomes and unifies believers of different confessions, their lack of interest in the visible aspect of ecumenical dialogue is rather surprising.

Pentecostals and charismatics are a richness to the one Church of Christ and reveal a manifold heuristic potential as long as curiosity is turned into respect, difference into cooperation, and problems into challenges.

TERESA FRANCESCA ROSSI

See also Charismata; Experience, Theology of; Gifts of the Spirit

Further Reading

Bartleman, F. (1980). *Azusa Street: the roots of modern day Pentecost.* Los Angeles: Bridge Publishing.

Bloch-Hoell, N. (1964). *The Pentecostal movement. Its origin, development, and distinctive character.* Oslo, Norway: Universitetsforlaget.

Blumhofer, E. L. (1993). *Restoring the faith. The Assemblies of God, Pentecostalism and the American culture.* Urbana: University of Illinois Press.

Blumhofer, E. L., Spittler, R. P., & Wacker, G. A. (1999). *Pentecostal currents in American Protestantism.* Urbana: University of Illinois Press.

Clark, M. S., & Lederle, H. I. (1983). *What is distinctive about Pentecostal theology?* Pretoria: University of South Africa.

Cox, H. (1996). *Fire from heaven. The rise of Pentecostal spirituality and the re-shaping of religion in the 21st century.* London: Cassel Wellington House.

Crowe, T. R. (1993). *Pentecostal unity. Recurring frustration and enduring hopes.* Chicago: Loyola University Press.

Del Colle, R. (2003). Pentecostal/Catholic dialogue: Theological suggestions for consideration. *Pneuma, 25*(1), 93–96.

Ford, J. M. (1976). *Which way for Catholic Pentecostals?* New York: Harper & Row.

Horton, H. (1934). *The gifts of the spirit.* Springfield, IL: Gospel Publishing House.

Johns, C. B. (1997). From Babel to Pentecost: The renewal of theological education. In J. Pobee (Ed.), *Towards viable theological education. Ecumenical imperative: Catalyst of renewal* (pp. 132–146). Geneva, Switzerland: WCC Publications.

McDonnell, K. (1976). *Charismatic renewal and the churches.* New York: The Seabury Press.

McDonnell, K. (Ed.). (1993). *Toward a new Pentecost for a new evangelization. Malines document I.* Collegeville, MN: The Liturgical Press.

O'Connor, E. D. (1971). *The Pentecostal movement in the Catholic Church.* Notre Dame, IN: Ave Maria Press.

Robeck, C. M. (1993). Taking stock of Pentecostalism: The personal reflections of a retiring editor. *Pneuma, 15*(1), 35–60.

Tillard, J.-M. R. (1994). The future of faith and order. In T. F. Best & Gassmann, G. (Eds.), *On the way to fuller Koinonia. Official report of the fifth world conference on faith and order* (pp. 189–194). Geneva, Switzerland: WCC Publications.

Volf, M. (1996). *Exclusion and embrace. A theological exploration of identity, otherness, and reconciliation.* Nashville, TN: Abingdon Press.

Volf, M., & Bass, D. C. (Eds.). (2002). *Practicing theology. Beliefs and practices in Christian life.* Grand Rapids, MI: William B. Eerdmans.

Wogen, N. L. (Ed.). (1973). *Jesus, where are you taking us? Messages from the first international Lutheran conference on the Holy Spirit.* Carol Stream, IL: Creation House.

Renewal, Church

Renewal is a twentieth century religious movement that locates its meaning in Joel 2:23–32. The origin of its dating could be Topeka, Kansas, in January 1901 or more specifically in 1906 from Azusa Street in Los Angeles, California. Under the ministry of William J. Seymour and others, the Pentecostal baptism of the Holy Spirit with the evidence of "speaking in tongues" launched a movement of gigantic proportions around the world. As Steven J. Land (1993) writes, "The 'full gospel' for the fullness of times was needed for the filling of the saints so that they could fill the earth with the apostles' doctrine." Renewal is a divine moment when God invades a person's time and space by a conviction of sin and the offer of salvation. This action of God places a person in contact with the divine (baptism of the Holy Spirit) and opens their life to the operation of the spiritual gifts mentioned in 1 Corinthians 12:1–11 of words of wisdom, a word of knowledge, healing, miracles, prophecy, discernment of spirits, various tongues, and interpretation of tongues. Renewal has affected the church in the areas of theology and worship, missions, and denominational growth. Today the Renewal groups are Pentecostals, charismatics, and Third Wave (Neo-Pentecostals).

Theology and Worship

Pentecostal theology has a major characteristic of experience. Reformed theology has used the doctrines of God, Jesus Christ, and the Holy Spirit to establish proper guidelines for the study and understanding of Scripture. Correct theological interpretation is built on proper exegetical methods, yet experience poses a challenge to Reformed methodology in current theological constructs. Pentecostal theology introduces a relationship with God by a three-step formula of salvation, sanctification, and baptism of the Holy Spirit. Each event points to a subjective experience in the life of a believer. Douglas Jacobsen (2003) writes, "Theology and experience deeply influenced each other within the pentecostal movement." Another aspect of Pentecostal theology is that the relationship with God is communicated by narrative. Early Pentecostals comprised members at varying levels of literacy, and the key for presentation of material was the ability to write a sermon (narrative) in a manner understood by all readers. Telling the story properly is a means of placing the hearer in the stream of salvation history and Pentecostal believers act within this history.

The historical accounts of God's presence in the life of individuals, churches, and special events are influential in writing of Pentecostal theology. The experience of history offers the material for theology to answer and provide the proper understanding of experience in the life of an individual. A common statement found in letters to editors of early Pentecostal publications was "Thank God that I am still saved, sanctified, and filled with the Holy Ghost." Early Pentecostal publications such as *The Apostolic Faith, The Bridegroom's Messenger, The Pentecostal Holiness Advocate, The Evening Light and Church of God Evangel* and others, provide an insight into the lives of individuals, Bible teachings of early Pentecostal teachers, and major camp meetings around the country where the new Pentecostal outpouring was manifested.

Theological writings by Pentecostals have been produced since the early days of the movement. George Floyd Taylor published *The Spirit and the Bride* in 1907, which was the first major exposition of the gifts, work, and purpose of the Holy Spirit and an apologetic to the Holiness movement. J. H. King's *From Passover to Pentecost* and A. J. Tomlinson's *The Last Great Conflict* are examples of early theological exploration. J. Rodman Williams (*Renewal Theology: Systematic Theology from a Charismatic Perspective*), Steven Land (*Pentecostal Spirituality: A Passion for the Kingdom*), Max Turner (*The Holy Spirit and Spiritual Gifts in the New Testament Church*), Frank Macchia, Veli-Matti Kärkkäinen (*Pneumatology: The Holy Spirit in Ecumenical, International, and Contextual Perspective*), and others have produced modern theological writings. The goals of these publications are to advance previous theological positions with a pneumatological understanding. Renewal is a rereading of orthodox positions with a greater emphasis on the work of the Holy Spirit.

The latter part of the twentieth century opened the door for a renewal in music and worship for the Renewal movement. Music is the arena where heart and spirit develop into an experience with God as joy overcomes the soul, broken hearts are healed, and Scriptural truths are taught to the people. The development of worship in Renewal can be understood by the early hymns of Charles Wesley and the impact of hymnody upon the Wesleyan revival in England. Worship includes hymns, spontaneous choruses, praise choruses, and gospel music. The Charismatic movement has introduced many new forms of music such as praise choruses, Scripture songs, and worship dance and liturgy. Recording companies such as Marantha and Integrity Music have moved renewal music forms from the church walls into a larger arena of the world. Christian radio stations and television stations serve as an outlet to fill the airways with the new music.

Renewal theology and worship establish an eschatological vision and power to evangelize the world and advance preparation for the return of Jesus Christ.

Missions

The initial issue of *The Apostolic Faith* (1906) in Los Angeles, California, printed this message concerning the new Pentecostal outpouring and the call to the mission field of the new recipients:

Many are the prophecies in unknown tongues and many the visions that God is giving concerning His soon coming. The heathen must first receive the gospel. One prophecy given in an unknown tongue was interpreted, "The time is short, and I am going to send out a large number in the Spirit of God to preach the full gospel in the power of the Spirit."

This statement clearly points to the heart of missions in a renewal context. The heart of missions is reaching all persons with the Gospel of Jesus Christ prior to His Second Coming. Renewal missions is the move to respond to the commandment of Matthew 28:18–20.

Early Pentecostal missionaries believed that they received the call to the foreign fields and by faith they left in obedience to God. Many persons left with little or no support, yet they had faith in God for their provisions. Early Pentecostal newspapers carried many testimonies of foreign missionaries and their victories and trials. George Floyd Taylor of the Pentecostal Holiness Church established one of the first missions departments for new Pentecostal denominations. His vision was that a true church was a missions-oriented church. Other famous Pentecostal missionaries were A. G. Garr, Aimee Semple McPherson, Carrie Judd Montgomery, J. C. Lehman, and Lillian Trasher. These people went into all parts of the world, and today the growth of Renewal denominations is evident due to the explosive growth of Pentecostalism.

Denominational Growth

Renewal brought the birth of several new Pentecostal denominations, and the Charismatic movement of the 1960s created Renewal movements within established denominations. The theology, worship, missions, and new enthusiasm generated friction between the traditional thinking of denominations. Within new Pentecostal groups, the initial thought was to return to the church as found in Acts 2 in Jerusalem. This primitivist urge to recover the past eventually yielded to differences among interpretation of the Pentecostal blessing into camps of Full Gospel (Apostolic), Finished Work, Oneness Pentecostals, and other varieties.

In 1959, an Episcopalian priest, Dennis Bennett, reached the Baptism of the Holy Spirit. His congregation experienced this new outpouring of the Holy Spirit and one may date the birth of the Charismatic movement to this time. Kevin and Dorothy Ranaghan became early leaders in the Roman Catholic renewal. The United Methodist Church developed under the leadership of Ross Whetstone and Tommy Tuttle with the United Methodist Renewal Service. All major denominations experienced renewal and in 1977 at the Kansas City Charismatic Conference, they organized into denominational characteristics.

The latter part of the twentieth century has witnessed an explosive outpouring of renewal as Pentecost has invaded South and Central America, South Korea, and Africa. This renewal is due directly to the early missionary ventures into these areas to proclaim the full Gospel of Jesus Christ. At the close of the twentieth century, Renewal has seen a growth among Pentecostal, charismatic, and neocharismatic groups around the globe to total nearly 500 million members.

H. STANLEY YORK

See also Charismatic Movement; Catholic Charismatic Movement; Neocharismatic Movements

Further Reading

The Apostolic Faith. (1906). Los Angeles.

Cox, H. (1995). *Fire from heaven: The rise of Pentecostal spirituality and the reshaping of religion in the twenty-first century.* Reading, MA: Addison-Wesley.

Jacobsen, D. (2003). *Thinking in the spirit: theologies of the early pentecostal movement.* Bloomington: Indiana University Press.

Kärkkäinen, V-M. (2002). *Pneumatology: The Holy Spirit in ecumenical, international, and contextual perspective.* Grand Rapids, MI: Baker Academic.

Land, S. (1993). *Pentecostal spirituality: A passion for the kingdom.* Sheffield, UK: Sheffield Academic Press.

Stephens, R. J. (2003). *"The fire spreads": The origins of the southern Holiness and Pentecostal Movements.* Unpublished doctoral dissertation, University of Florida, Gainesville.

Synan, V. (1997). *The Holiness-Pentecostal tradition: Charismatic movements in the twentieth century* (2nd ed.). Grand Rapids, MI: Eerdmans.

Synan, V. (2001). *The century of the Holy Spirit: 100 years of Pentecostal and charismatic renewal.* Nashville, TN: Thomas Nelson Publishers.

Turner, M. (1999). *The Holy Spirit and spiritual gifts in the New Testament church.* Peabody, MA: Hendrickson Publishers.

Wacker, G. (2001). *Heaven below: Early Pentecostals and American culture.* Cambridge, MA: Harvard University Press.

Williams, J. R. (1996). *Renewal theology: Systematic theology from a charismatic perspective.* Grand Rapids, MI: Zondervan.

Woods, D. G. (1997). *Living in the presence of God: Enthusiasm, authority, and negotiation in the practice of Pentecostal Holiness.* Unpublished doctoral dissertation, University of Mississippi, Oxford.

York, H. S. (1997). *George Floyd Taylor and the formation of the Pentecostal Holiness Church's missionary endeavour.* Unpublished masters thesis, Duke University, Durham, North Carolina.

Revival and Revivalism

Writers use the terms "revival" and "revivalism" in various ways. *Webster's Third New International Dictionary* defines revival as "a period of religious awakening: renewed interest in religion" with "meetings often characterized by emotional excitement." Revivalism is "the spirit or kind of religion or the methods characteristic of religious revivals." Some authors, and especially Calvinists, define revival as an unplanned event that reflects God's initiative, and revivalism as a humanly orchestrated effort to stir up religious interest. Yet in practice it is often difficult to draw this distinction. What is common to all accounts of revivals is an *intensification* of spiritual experience. Participants in revivals speak of their vivid sense of spiritual things, great joy and faith, deep sorrow over sin, passionate desire to evangelize others, and heightened feelings of love for God and fellow humanity. A revival is a communal event, in which groups of people share these sorts of experiences.

Revival Phenomena

Revivals can best be understood through firsthand accounts, such as the following from Sixto Lopez, a participant in a 1949 Pentecostal revival in Detroit:

> I opened my heart to the Lord, and felt as though I was giving myself as an offering to Him. Every Scripture and every message took on a new meaning to me. The most outstanding thing I felt in those meetings was a desire to pray—just to stay before the Lord. I have always found it difficult to spend long periods in prayer, but there I felt a great desire to stay before the Lord in prayer. Many of the people there have lost their appetite for food and go days without food. I had a big appetite for food but came to the place that I did not care to eat. (Quoted in Riss 1988, 118–119)

Thousands of such accounts document the Pentecostal and charismatic revivals of the last century.

In times of revival, people often crowd into available buildings for religious services, and fill them beyond capacity. The services may last from morning until midnight or later. News of a revival usually travels rapidly, and sometimes the reports of revival—in person, print, or broadcast media—touch off new revivals in distant localities. During a revival, clergy and other Christian workers may receive many requests for their services, and find themselves harried by inquirers. Sometimes people openly confess their sins in public settings. Another mark of revivals is generosity—individuals willing to give their time, money, or resources to support the work of the revival. Revivals are usually controversial, with opponents and proponents who vehemently criticize one another. Often there are bodily manifestations as well, such as falling down, rolling on the ground, involuntary muscle movements, and spiritual dancing.

Many of the above phenomena appeared in Protestant Evangelical revivals prior to the birth of Pentecostalism around 1900. Yet a distinguishing feature of Pentecostal and charismatic revivals is a stress on the "gifts of the Holy Spirit," including speaking in tongues, visions and prophecies, the healing of the sick, and the casting out of demons.

Of all the gifts, speaking in tongues is the most characteristic feature of Pentecostal-Charismatic revivals in distinction from Evangelical revivals. Yet today the boundaries between Evangelicalism and the Pentecostal-Charismatic movement are probably blurrier than ever before. During the last two centuries, the gifts of the Spirit that first appeared in isolation have tended to flow together. In North America, a stress on divine healing first emerged in the mid-1800s, tongues-speaking began on a large scale just before and after 1900, and prophecy became increasingly important in the 1946–1950 revival and subsequently. Exorcism and spiritual warfare (with demons through prayer) is distinctive of the 1980s and 1990s. Twenty-first century Christians are heirs to all these preceding movements. Tongues-speaking, prophecy, healing, and exorcism occur in varied combinations today in Pentecostal, charismatic, and some Evangelical groups.

Revival Phases

Pentecostal and charismatic revivals in North America during the twentieth century were not evenly distributed across the decades, but clustered into three major phases and two minor periods. The years 1904–1909 witnessed the Welsh Revival of 1904–1905, which touched off revivals throughout the world in 1905, and played a role in the Azusa Street Revival of 1906–1909 in Los Angeles. After World War II, from 1946 to 1950, the Healing and Latter Rain movements burst forth, Evangelical revivals inundated Southern California, college revivals swept through dozens of institutions, and Billy Graham came into celebrity after his 1949 Los Angeles crusade. The third period dates from 1960 to about 1977 and includes the emergence of the Charismatic movement among mainline Protestants and Roman Catholics, and the Jesus movement that sprang from the 1960s counterculture. Sporadic revivals occurred in 1911 to 1916, when Pentecostalism experienced a second peak, and in the

1980s and 1990s, with John Wimber's Vineyard Church and powerful local revivals in the mid-1990s in Pensacola, Florida, and Toronto, Canada. These twentieth-century revivals were interrelated in complex ways. The Welsh Revival was not Pentecostal as such, yet much of the impetus for the Azusa Street Revival came from those who had visited Wales in 1905 and brought back soul-stirring reports of what they had seen there. The Charismatic movement and the Jesus movement also overlapped, though the former highlighted the gifts of the Spirit and the latter street evangelism.

Azusa Street Revival

The Azusa Street Revival of 1906–1909 was the granddaddy of all Pentecostal revivals, the leading point of dissemination for global Pentecostalism, and arguably the most influential localized revival of the twentieth century. The leader at Azusa Street was the African-American William J. Seymour, the son of former slaves in Louisiana, who was exposed to the teaching on the gift of tongues through the white Holiness teacher Charles Parham in Houston, Texas, in 1905. With Parham's blessing and money for rail fare, he journeyed to Los Angeles to pastor a black Holiness congregation, only to find himself locked out of the church because of his controversial teaching that tongues-speaking was the necessary evidence of the baptism of the Spirit. At this point Seymour himself had not yet spoken in tongues. Seymour went to a nearby home on Bonnie Brae Street, and joined with other seekers to pray and fast for several days, seeking the filling of the Holy Spirit. On 9 April 1906, the first person in this prayer meeting spoke in tongues, followed soon after by Seymour and a number of others. Soon the crowds in the home grew so large that the porch of the house collapsed (though no one was injured), and the fledgling group rented a facility for their meetings. On 14 April 1906, the revival settled into its new home on Azusa Street, from which it exerted an enduring and far-ranging influence in world Pentecostalism.

Charismatic Movement

The origins of the Charismatic movement stretch back to the late 1950s, when Harald Bredesen—an ordained Lutheran minister, baptized in the Holy Spirit in 1946—began work among mainline Protestants in a Dutch Reformed Church outside of New York City in 1957. The date usually assigned for the commencement of the Charismatic movement is 3 April 1960, when Dennis Bennett—an Episcopal priest in Van Nuys, California—

announced to his congregation that he had recently been baptized in the Holy Spirit and spoke in tongues. Some congregants called for his resignation, while hundreds of others joined in the charismatic experience. Reports in *Time* and *Newsweek* magazines created the sense that a new movement of the Spirit was taking shape. Bredesen received national publicity in 1963 because of his activities at Yale University, and in the same year he coined the term "charismatic renewal" to distinguish the emerging movement from Pentecostalism. The newly-christened charismatics belonged to denominations that did not include speaking in tongues as a part of their tradition. Theologically, they found common ground between older traditions and newer experiences. Practically, they accepted and appreciated fellow Christians who had not undergone Spirit baptism. Sociologically, they represented a different demographic group. First- and second-generation Pentecostals included few persons of wealth and influence, while charismatics often came from society's upper echelon.

The Charismatic movement in the Roman Catholic Church began soon after its Protestant counterpart. A group of lay Catholics at Duquesne University in Pittsburgh, Pennsylvania, had been praying for the revitalization of the church, and, having read about the baptism of the Spirit, they sought out a group of mainline Protestant charismatics, and themselves entered into the charismatic experience in 1967. The Catholic Charismatic Renewal spread quickly to Notre Dame, Michigan State University, and other campuses throughout the nation. Among its early leaders were Kevin and Dorothy Ranaghan, Ralph Martin, and Stephen Clark. On the international level, the Catholic primate of Belgium, Leon-Joseph Cardinal Suenens, provided crucial support, and the Vatican endorsed the movement during its formative phase and subsequently. The high water mark of the Charismatic movement in the United States was the Kansas City conference of 1977—a fully ecumenical occasion with fifty thousand Protestant and Catholic participants. More recently the Catholic Charismatic Renewal in the United States has become more parish-centered, and its public presence has diminished correspondingly. The greatest growth of the Catholic Charismatic Renewal during the last generation has been outside of the United States.

Revivals Today

Recent events in Toronto, Canada, and Pensacola, Florida, indicate the continuing relevance and power of Pentecostal revivals. The awakening that began at the Toronto Airport Christian Fellowship drew hundreds of thousands of visitors within a few years after its inception in January 1994. Planes from England, Europe, and other regions of the world were chartered to bring in those who sought a new and more powerful experience of God. A characteristic, though much-debated, feature of the Toronto revival was the practice of "holy laughter." Perceived abuses in this revival, such as worshipers who made animal sounds in the services, led the denominational Association of Vineyard Churches to sever its connection to the Toronto Fellowship. The revival at the Brownville Church (Assemblies of God) in June 1995 drew more than 2 million visitors in three years. A separate entrance into the church building was set up to accommodate international visitors and the press, and would-be worshipers have waited on the sidewalk at 4:00 a.m. to get a seat for the evening service. Some observers characterized the atmosphere at Pensacola as sober and penitential, in contrast to the more joyous and festive ethos in Toronto. An important feature of these recent revivals is their translocal and transnational character. Because of extensive media attention they received, and the newer technologies of e-mail and the Internet, these revivals had instantaneous effects all around the world, and it seems likely that twenty-first century revivals will continue to exert influence far from the localities where they emerge.

International Expansion

The story of Pentecostal and charismatic revivals begins in North America, but now stretches into every region of the globe. Less than a year after the start of the Azusa Street Revival, Pentecostalism spread to Europe. Beginning in Oslo, Norway, in 1906–1907, Thomas B. Barratt spread a Pentecostal message that took root in England, Germany, Sweden, and elsewhere in Europe. Pentecostalism began in Brazil with the arrival of two Swedish-American missionaries in 1910, experienced exponential growth in the period from the 1950s to the present, and now claims as many as one of every four Brazilians. Other parts of Latin America, including Chile, Argentina, and Guatemala, have been ripe soil for Pentecostalism. In sub-Saharan Africa, the African-initiated churches exhibited the gifts of the Spirit from the mid-1800s up to the present, and yet the Pentecostal and charismatic styles that first appeared in the United States have been adopted in certain regions, especially South Africa and Nigeria. During the 1980s and 1990s, the German-born charismatic evangelist Reinhard Bonnke has preached to African audiences of a million or more at a time. The Catholic Charismatic movement, which simultaneously began in Pittsburgh,

Pennsylvania, and Bogota, Colombia, in 1967, today includes as many as 100 million Latin American Catholics. While certain Protestant denominations, such as the various Baptist groups, were often hostile toward the Charismatic movement in the 1960s and 1970s, attitudes have changed in the last decade or so. A substantial percentage of Baptist pastors and an even larger segment of Baptist missionaries now report that they are charismatic. The Pentecostal-Charismatic movement has exercised little influence up to this point in the Orthodox churches of Russia, Europe, and North America, and in the ancient churches of the Middle East—Maronite, Coptic, Armenian, Nestorian, Chaldean, Assyrian, Jacobite, and Melkite.

One of the most significant recent developments has occurred in China. In the 1980s and early 1990s, the American-born, Hong Kong-based pastor Dennis Balcombe introduced tongues-speaking and charismatic practices into the Chinese house churches. The majority of these churches, comprising 80 to 100 million members, are now charismatic in theology and practice. House-church Christians today speak of a divine mandate for the Chinese to spread the Gospel to the Islamic, Hindu, and Buddhist nations, and thus, by traveling west, to take the Christian faith "back to Jerusalem" where it began. Should these charismatic Chinese Christians succeed in their evangelistic aims, one may expect a Pentecostal-Charismatic form of Christianity to grow throughout the Middle East, South Asia, and Southeast Asia.

MICHAEL J. MCCLYMOND

See also Azusa Street Revival; Catholic Charismatic Movement; Charismatic Movement

Further Reading

Bartleman, F. (1980). *Azusa Street*. South Plainfield, NJ: Bridge Publishing.

McClymond, M. J. (Ed.). (2004). *Embodying the spirit: New perspectives on North American revivalism*. Baltimore: Johns Hopkins University Press.

McClymond, M. J. (Ed.) (in press). *Encyclopedia of religious revivals in America* (2 Vols.). Westport, CT: Greenwood Press.

Riss, R. M. (1988). *A survey of 20th-century revival movements in North America*. Peabody, MA: Hendrickson Publishers.

Synan, V. (Ed.) (2001). *The century of the Holy Spirit: 100 years of Pentecostal and charismatic renewal, 1901–2001*. Nashville, TN: Thomas Nelson.

Synan, V. (Ed.). (1997). *The Holiness-Pentecostal tradition: Charismatic movements in the twentieth century* (2nd ed.). Grand Rapids, MI: Eerdmans.

Rich and Riches

Images of early twentieth-century U.S. Pentecostals depict impoverished and working-class men and women meeting in storefront churches. Today, however, members of U.S. Pentecostal megachurches come from a broad socioeconomic spectrum and include middle and upper-middle-class professionals. How did so many members of a religious movement that drew upon the impoverished and working classes for its early growth and that required Holiness practices of self-denial come to associate financial success with God's blessings?

The Social Contract

The social mobility of Pentecostals in the United States parallels the government-supported rise of the middle class after World War II. A labor-capital accord (1947–1972) led to stable, well-paid jobs in exchange for efficient, productive manufacturing. This social contract, overseen by the federal government, balanced the interests of the laborers with those of the capitalists. As a consequence of powerful labor unions and the GI Bill, which offered federal subsidies for higher education and guaranteed home mortgages for returning veterans, the working class advanced economically. The labor-capital accord together with the GI Bill resulted in the unprecedented growth of the middle class, and among those enjoying this period of social mobility were working-class Pentecostals.

These economic changes combined with longer lifespans led to a shift away from Puritan values of asceticism and toward an emphasis on consumption. Some observers attribute social mobility in the South to incomes that increased because men were inspired by religion to forgo sociability that involved public drinking. Social mobility was also promulgated by wealthy ministers, evangelists, prophets, and faith healers who appeared regularly on Christian broadcasting networks. In exchange for the promise of God's intervention in their daily lives, viewers were asked to send money to televangelists. Those with the least money were urged to contribute their remaining dollars to prove that they believed that God would meet their needs. According to the preachers, these dollars would be spent to expand the technology needed to bring the message of salvation to every individual on the planet.

Having been given the "opportunity" to participate in the work of evangelizing the planet and believing that the prosperity enjoyed by the preachers would eventually reach the faithful, individuals who had only a few dollars sent them willingly to the programs. In return, they were promised God's blessing and assured that their needs would be met. When the preachers reported back that the dollars have been used to buy more satellite dishes, they told donors that this is evidence of how God is blessing their financial contributions. However, the financial successes of the networks were not balanced by evidence that the message was effective for the lower classes who sent in their money. Without a government infusion of money into the economies of developing nations that would parallel that of the labor-capital accord, prospects for upward mobility among Pentecostals in developing countries remain uncertain.

Gospel of Prosperity

Members of the early North American Pentecostal movement came from both the middle and the working classes, and their ascetic work ethic allowed them to set aside worldly pleasures in order to achieve long-term gains. Deprivation theory, which holds that social movements develop among people who feel denied their rights, offers insights into the relationship between social mobility and prosperity. According to this theory, the separation of Pentecostals from the world freed them from tradition, structure, and fear of embarrassment, which permitted them to respond to cultural challenges in a practical and effective manner.

For the poor there was also the promise of rewards in an afterlife, and glossolalia provided relief from the hardships of everyday life. To explain why Pentecostalism appealed to members of the middle class after World War II, theorists modified the definition of deprivation to include emotional as well as economic deprivation. The social roots of Pentecostal belief in faith-based prosperity may lie in the upward mobility of second and third generation Pentecostals, combined with the success of the Full Gospel Business Men's Fellowship International and the Charismatic movement's reach into the upper-middle class.

Flexibility combined with faith in supernatural powers worked well in a capitalist economy. As the Assemblies of God became institutionalized, administrators entered the middle and upper classes, bringing the Pentecostal message to the elite. To professionals who saw the Bible as the literal word of God and longed for a return to the father-headed nuclear family, Pentecostalism offered affirmation, values, and truth; in return, it demanded that believers abandon their traditions and embrace profit-promoting capitalist values of productivity and consumption. With the shift to a service economy fed by mass consumption, spiritual power became associated with prosperity, which strongly suggests that Pentecostalism was successful because of its accommodation of modernity.

ELAINE R. CLEETON

See also Capitalism; Prosperity Theology

Further Reading

Anderson, R. (1979). *Vision of the disinherited: The making of American Pentecostalism*. New York: Oxford University Press.

Berger, P. (1967). *The social reality of religion*. London: Faber and Faber.

Freire, P. (2000). *Pedagogy of the oppressed*. New York: Continuum International.

Horn, J. (1989). *From rags to riches: An analysis of the faith movement and its relation to the classical Pentecostal movement*. Pretoria: University of South Africa.

Lehmann, D. (1996). *Struggle for the spirit: Religious transformation and popular culture in Brazil and Latin America*. Cambridge, MA: Blackwell.

Martin, D. (2002). *Pentecostalism: The world their parish*. Malden, MA: Blackwell.

Menzies, W. (1971). *Anointed to serve*. Springfield, MO: Gospel Publishing.

Wacker, G. (2001). *Heaven below: Early Pentecostals and American Culture*. Cambridge, MA: Harvard University Press.

Rituals

Many of the central practices of Pentecostal-Charismatic spirituality are shared with other streams of Christianity, including water baptism and the Lord's Supper. However, other practices observed more particularly, though not exclusively, by Pentecostals include anointing the sick with oil and foot washing.

Many Pentecostals would refrain from using the term *ritual* (because of the fear that it might be associated with merely a ceremony) or *sacrament* (because of the relationship of that word with the notion that a sacrament may contain self-inducing power) as a descriptor for these practices, preferring the term *ordinances*, though the one they have chosen has little semantic or biblical support. Charismatics have less of a problem with the terms *ritual* or *sacrament*, those of a Roman Catholic background also identifying *sacrament* with the concept of *mystery* (from the meaning of the Latin *sacramentum*), it representing a manifestation of God's grace to the church. A disadvantage of the Pentecostal stance is that the characteristic of mystery can often be lost, resulting in a minimalist approach to the events themselves.

Water Baptism

Most Pentecostal and charismatic believers undergo water baptism because of their desire to emulate the baptism of Jesus (Matthew 3:16); to obey the command of Jesus (Matthew 28:19), and to be aligned to the practice of the earliest believers as recorded in the book of Acts (9:18, 10:47, 16:33, 18:8). The background for such a practice may be traced back to Jewish beliefs that the ceremonial application of water represented cleansing from defilement and sin, the initiation of proselyte status, and the receiving of new life (1 Corinthians 10:2). Pentecostals do not accept that the water is charged with any supernatural properties.

Procedures

Most Pentecostals and charismatics practice baptism by full immersion, administered by one or two leaders, generally in specially built baptisteries. Increasingly, locations outside churches are being used, including swimming pools, rivers, lakes, and the sea, partly because of the lack of baptisteries among new churches and also due to a desire to provide a public opportunity for declaring the faith of those being baptized. The baptism itself occurs subsequent to an affirmation of personal faith in Jesus, the event often incorporated in a service to which unbelievers are invited. Immediately prior to the baptism of an individual, the trinitarian formula, recorded in Matthew 28:19, is pronounced, though this is amended amongst some Pentecostals by the substitution of the name of Jesus Christ (Acts 2:38, 10:48) or "the Lord Jesus" (Acts 8:16, 19:5) to follow the practice of the early church. It is not normal that believers are rebaptized in accordance with a particular declaration, as both are valid. Sprinkling is more popular among a minority of charismatics who are associated with sacramentally based traditions, as is the assumption that at baptism, the resources of the Spirit are experienced in a novel way. For Classical Pentecostals, and charismatics whose tradition is not associated with sacramental traditions, there is little acceptance that baptism in water and in the Spirit have any necessary relationship. This is mainly due to limited New Testament precedent, concern that the Spirit could be viewed as being dormant

John 13:12–15 (King James Version)

¹²So after he had washed their feet, and had taken his garments, and was set down again, he said unto them, Know ye what I have done to you?

¹³Ye call me Master and Lord: and ye say well; for so I am.

¹⁴If I then, your Lord and Master, have washed your feet; ye also ought to wash one another's feet.

¹⁵For I have given you an example, that ye should do as I have done to you.

in the life of a believer to be actualized at water baptism, and reaction to the suggestion that the act of water baptism confers a spiritual grace.

Significance

The act is viewed as an opportunity to publicly declare one's commitment to Christ. Thus, it occurs after a personal acknowledgment of one's salvation and thus may be identified as a sign of that salvation. This necessarily results in its being administered mainly to adults and/or young people and less so to children. The baptism of infants is rejected by most Pentecostals because the act would be devoid of personal faith on the part of the recipient. Though not viewed as necessary for salvation, it is nevertheless regarded as normative practice and therefore to be expected of all believers as a sign of obedience to the command of Jesus. Increasingly, it occurs after a (short) period of teaching concerning essential elements of the Christian life.

Another aspect of water baptism is that it is intended to more closely identify the candidate with Jesus in His death and Resurrection, evidence being drawn from Romans 6:3–4 and Colossians 2:12. Thus, as being immersed in the water symbolizes being associated with and being the beneficiary of His death, so also being raised up out of the water signifies partnership in the benefits that accrue to the believer as a result of His Resurrection. In particular, the act of baptism is intended to signify the integration of the believer and Christ (Galatians 3:27), though there is no suggestion that such a relationship is initiated during baptism, the latter being the public affirmation of a previous integration at salvation. At the same time, the initiation of the believer into the church (1 Corinthians 12:13, Ephesians 4:5) that occurred at salvation is also publicized at baptism, though the emphasis on the individual response to Christ of the baptized person sometimes obscures this corporate significance.

Finally, baptism is sometimes viewed as the Christian parallel to the Jewish Passover (Luke 22:7–8, 1 Corinthians 5:7), in which the death of Jesus replaces the death of the Passover lamb in providing not freedom from slavery but from sin and its consequences.

The Eucharist

The commendation of this practice by Jesus to his followers (Luke 22:14–20); his desire to share it with them (Luke 22:15); his invitation that they share it with him (Luke 22:8); his command, "Do this in remembrance of me" (Luke 22:19); and its reiteration by Paul (1 Corinthians 12:23–26) form significant reasons for the practice.

Procedures

More generally known as the Lord's Supper or Communion, it is observed regularly and often every Sunday (Acts 20:7) with simplicity of form, frequently under the supervision of the leader of the church, aided by others who distribute the emblems. It traditionally follows a time of reflection, thanksgiving, and worship, focusing on the death of Jesus, and the reading of one of the New Testament passages describing the event. Associated with it is an opportunity to consider one's own spiritual journey and, in particular, shortcomings therein. The anticipated consequence is that, where necessary, a time of repentance and forgiveness should follow, especially where relational discord amongst believers has been identified. The recommendation by Paul that participants examine themselves to ensure that they take part worthily and, in particular, that they do not dishonor "the body" of the Lord (1 Corinthians 12:29) has been the cause of confusion. Many have assumed this to be a recommendation that unbelievers should not participate because they may not fully appreciate the significance of the death of Jesus on the cross. However, although that may be appropriate, it is

Luke 22: 15–20

15And he said unto them, With desire I have desired to eat this passover with you before I suffer:

16For I say unto you, I will not any more eat thereof, until it be fulfilled in the kingdom of God.

17And he took the cup, and gave thanks, and said, Take this, and divide it among yourselves:

18For I say unto you, I will not drink of the fruit of the vine, until the kingdom of God shall come.

19And he took bread, and gave thanks, and break it, and gave unto them, saying, This is my body which is given for you: this do in remembrance of me.

20Likewise also the cup after supper, saying, This cup is the new testament in my blood, which is shed for you.

probable that Paul is reminding the readers that if they participate without honoring the body of believers who share in the act with them, their participation is inappropriate and even counterproductive, especially since the death of Jesus brought unity amongst people (1 Corinthians 17–22, 31–34). The warning of potential judgment, sickness, and death (1 Corinthians 12:29f) is taken seriously by Pentecostals, resulting in a call to confess any sins prior to partaking of the emblems; Williams notes that the issue "is not our worthiness but our coming in a worthy manner" (1992, 258). Some advocate excluding errant or unrepentant believers from the event on the basis of 1 Corinthians 5:2, 11, though this runs the risk of making Communion a test of personal sanctification, a feature not present in its institution by Jesus.

Most Classical Pentecostals use broken bread (sometimes unleavened) or a loaf to represent the body of Jesus, presented on plates by servers, that the congregation partake of while seated. As a substitute for the wine of the New Testament, most Pentecostals offer (black currant or grape) juice. Very few offer fermented wine, often due to historical practice or a stance of total abstinence. The juice is generally administered in small goblets that are passed around the congregation, though some have begun to use a common cup. It is the normal practice for the participants to partake of the bread and the juice, in that order. Afterwards, the bread and juice are discarded; they are not viewed as being special in themselves, retaining the same constituent elements before, during, and after the Communion. Unlike much of Pentecostal worship, this is often a quiet and even sober occasion, the concentration being on the cost to Jesus in terms of his passion. It is a personal and private event, albeit in the context of a congregational act, with the emphasis on reflection. However, increasingly, congregational worship has become a more significant feature, and introspection has been joined by corporate praise and the singing of worship songs. A more relaxed style of Communion is partly due to the fact that the act of Communion is not now restricted to a set Sunday service.

There has been limited experimentation with the form of the Lord's Supper; sometimes, congregants are invited to celebrate it in family or small groups in the church or invited to the front of the church to be received from those administering it. In general, all who acknowledge Jesus as their Savior are entitled to participate, whether they are members of the local church or not, the question of age being generally irrelevant.

Significance

Most Pentecostals view the occasion as one of remembrance of the significance of the death of Jesus and less of His Resurrection, the broken bread representing the body of Jesus on the cross, the cup representing his blood, the association with the forgiveness of sins being paramount (Matthew 26:28, Hebrews 9:22). Associated with this act of remembrance is the opportunity to express gratitude for salvation. Related to such thanksgiving is the notion that it should result in a commitment to personal transformation. The Communion is also viewed as a sign of the eschatological life to come, to be celebrated "until he comes" (Luke 22:16, 1 Corinthians 12: 26).

To a lesser degree, there has been an expectation, on the part of some, that the presence of Jesus during this time should be of a more intense nature, attention being drawn to the concept of participation in the blood and body of Christ (1 Corinthians 10:16–17), as well as the experience of the two disciples in Emmaus whose eyes were opened when Jesus broke bread with them (Luke 24:30–31). However, this view needs to be contextualized in the belief that the presence of Christ can be experienced at any time. As a result of the latter perspective, the Communion act is viewed by many as being more memorialistic than spiritually revitalizing.

There has always been a rebuttal of any suggestion that the body and/or blood of Jesus is present in the elements, texts including John 6:52–57 and 1 Corinthians 11:24 being interpreted symbolically. Rather than acknowledge the real presence of Jesus in the emblems, they celebrate his realized presence in the Communion. Consequently, the concept of an altar is not present in Pentecostal language, the term *table* being preferred as a sign of fellowship both with the Lord and each other. The event also provides a visible reminder of the place of the participant in the larger body of the church (1 Corinthians 10:17).

Traditionally, Pentecostals have not engaged in critical or evaluative discussion, particularly concerning Communion. As with baptism in water, the individualism often present removes the Communion act from the corporate setting as reflected in the New Testament, resulting in its communal significance being largely marginalized. Finally, the danger of the event becoming a formality because of its regular celebration is also to be borne in mind. A fresh appreciation of its significance as well as creativity in its celebration may result in its vitalizing impact not being lost.

Anointing the Sick with Oil

Pentecostals have adopted this practice on the basis of the recommendation in James 5:14, leaders of a church corporately anointing sick people with oil, often lightly on the forehead, in association with prayer, in the expectation that healing would occur.

Significance

The assumption by many has been that the oil represents the Spirit (1 Samuel 10:1, 6), though the symbolic properties relating to oil located in Jewish literature reveal more reasons why James included it. Oil was used to signify an infusion of the strength of God (Psalms 89:20–21), and anointing was associated with restoration, occurring when a person had been cured of leprosy (Leviticus 14:12, 16). Oil was also used to demonstrate that a new situation had come into being (the completion of a marriage or the legitimate emancipation of a

slave). It was also linked with friendship and love (Psalm 23:5), honor and affirmation (John 12:3) and was understood to be a gift of God (Jeremiah 31:12). Anointing with oil was thus probably intended to be commemorative of features that would result in the sufferer's feeling secure, knowing that she or he was in the presence of friends who cared and a God who restored. The Old Testament (Isaiah 1:6; Jeremiah 8:22) refers to the medicinal properties of oil, though there is no evidence that oil was administered in the context of prayer. Josephus (*The Jewish Wars* 1.657) records that doctors recommended that Herod, in his final illness, bathe in oil, and Philo (*De Somniis* 2. 58) recommends oil for the toning of muscles. It was also regarded as being a medicinal agent outside Judaism. Seneca (*Epistles* 53. 5) refers to the benefit of anointing for seasickness while Pliny (*Natural History* 15. 4, 7) recommends the medicinal application of oil in combating toothache. However, although the medical properties of oil were well known at that time, they were only ever expected to alleviate suffering in a limited range of illnesses. There are serious deficiencies in assigning this as the reason for the inclusion of anointing by James.

Pentecostals, unlike some charismatics with a sacramental tradition, reject any suggestion that the oil carries healing properties, either supernatural or natural, and view it as being a symbolic medium of supernatural power, discharged when the healing is part of the sovereign plan of God for the individual being anointed.

Foot washing

Based on the narrative in John in which Jesus washed the feet of his disciples and commanded that they do likewise, some Pentecostals have adopted a similar practice. Because John records this as taking place after the Last Supper, it is sometimes undertaken in association with this event. The purpose is to remind everyone present that service is at the heart of the Christian community and that equality and unity are paramount in the family of God.

Implications

Pentecostalism emphasizes visual as well as spiritual phenomena as part of its spirituality. The above events allow for the celebration of the latter in the practice of the former.

KEITH WARRINGTON

See also Anoint, Anointing; Baptism, Water; Communion (Eucharist); Ordinances and Sacraments

Further Reading

Albrecht, D. E. (1999). *Rites in the Spirit. A ritual approach to Pentecostal/Charismatic spirituality.* Sheffield, UK: Sheffield Academic Press.

Anderson, A. (2004). *Introduction to Pentecostalism.* Cambridge, UK: Cambridge University Press.

Arteaga, W. D. (2002). *Forgotten power: The significance of the Lord's Supper in revival.* Grand Rapids, MI: Zondervan Publishing House.

Bicknell, R. (1998). The ordinances: The marginalised aspects of Pentecostalism. In K. Warrington (Ed.), *Pentecostal Perspectives* (pp. 204–222). Carlisle, UK: Paternoster Press.

Hollenweger, W. (1997). *Pentecostalism. Origins and developments worldwide.* Peabody, MA: Hendrickson Publishers.

Kärkkäinen, V-M. (2002). *Toward a pneumatological theology.* Lanham, MD: University Press of America.

Kay, W. K., & Dyer, A. (2004). *Pentecostal and Charismatic studies: A reader.* London: SCM Press.

Krieder, E. (1988). *Given for you: A fresh look at Communion.* Leicester, UK: Inter-Varsity Press.

Lancaster, J. (1976). The Ordinances. In P. S. Brewster (Ed.), *Pentecostal Doctrine* (pp. 79–92). Cheltenham, UK: Elim Publishing.

Marshall, I. H. (1980). *Last Supper and Lord's Supper.* Carlisle, UK: Paternoster Press.

Thomas, J. C. (1991). *Footwashing in John 13 and the Johannine Community.* Sheffield, UK: Sheffield Academic Press.

Warrington, K. (1993). Anointing with oil and healing. *EPTA Bulletin,* 14.5–22.

Williams, J. R. (1992). Ordinances. In *Renewal theology. The church, the kingdom, and the last things* (Vol. 3, pp. 221–263). Grand Rapids, MI: Zondervan.

S

Saints

"To be a saint" is a gift and a call from the Pentecostal-Charismatic viewpoint—although with different shades of meaning according to the different streams within the movement—for a historical and theological reason. Historically speaking, the Pentecostal movement sprang up as a development of the nineteenth- and twentieth-century Revival Movements, called "perfectionist movements," whose focus was on how to reach Christian sanctification and perfection. Theologically speaking, the call "to be saints" stands at the core of the Pentecostal-Charismatic dynamism, at the very crossroads of their hermeneutic—taking as a normative criterion the narrative experience of the first Christians who called themselves "saints"—and flows from the awareness of the presence of the Holy Spirit, the Sanctifier, as a sign of the new life the believers have received in the Resurrection of Christ.

Historical Framework

The key question, how can salvation be obtained—addressed by Martin Luther (1483–1546) and later by Ulrich Zwingli (1484–1531) and John Calvin (1509–1564)—has found an answer in the basic Reformation principle "Grace alone, Faith alone, Scripture alone" (*Sola gratia, sola fides, sola Scriptura*) with a great, although not exclusive, emphasis on the work of God, since the believer is justified and made righteous by simply accepting His grace. Although the principle remains within Protestantism, a growing sense of human cooperation in the work of grace characterizes later revivals (First Revival, seventeenth to eighteenth century;

Second Revival, nineteenth century). The interest is not only on salvation received by grace but increasingly on the process of sanctification, also called "Christian perfection," especially within the Holiness movement, one of the mid-nineteenth-century revival streams that influenced the ideas of the future Pentecostal movement. Although Christian perfection is given at once instantaneously with faith—the Holiness movement held—there is a sanctifying continuing grace that enables the faithful to Christlikeness. The Holiness movement rose in the context of the "Tuesday Meetings for the promotion of Holiness," gathered in New York City by Sarah (1806–1896) and Phoebe (1807–1874) Palmer—the latter being the author of "Guide to Holiness," whose publication in 1858 is considered the movement's official beginning. It spread through the preaching of Asa Mahan and Charles Finney at Oberlin College, Ohio, and soon developed among many different denominations in New Jersey, Michigan, Illinois, California, Tennessee, Indiana, and Missouri, also establishing a link with Hampshire, Great Britain, through the Keswick Conventions, begun in 1875.

The message conveyed by the Holiness movement and later by the Pentecostals, was the encounter with the Lord and the proclamation of Jesus Christ as Savior, Baptizer in the Holy Spirit, Healer and Coming King (the "foursquare" or "full" Gospel).

This new awareness and empowerment are rooted in baptism in the Holy Spirit and constitute the essence of holiness; the same radical commitment which William Edwin Boardman (1810–1886) called "higher Christian life" within the Holiness movement was expressed in Pentecostal terminology as "empowerment for mission and ministry." A question was soon raised about the intrinsic meaning of such experience, and a variety of answers were given by Pentecostal circles and leaders, which led to an important theological debate.

Theological Debate

While working out a "method" to grow in holiness, John Wesley (1703–1791) brought about the concept of entire sanctification/Christian perfection: Although still debated as to whether the term was created by Wesley himself or his follower Joseph Fletcher (1729–1785), in Wesleyan teaching—marking the First Revival in the eighteenth century—conversion (recognition of sins, cleansing and acceptance of forgiveness, and regeneration) had to be followed by a second experience of sanctification, called "perfection." Between 1893 and 1990, a deep theological debate was carried on about the different ways of understanding the meaning and the implications of the concepts, provoking divisions within the movement: Twenty-three Holiness denominations were founded within just a few decades, forming a two-fold stream: the "two-stage salvation" (supported by Baptist Pentecostals, some Holiness movements and the Assemblies of God) and the "three-stage salvation" (supported by Methodist Pentecostals and the majority of the Holiness groups).

According to the two-stage teaching, the believer experiences first conversion/regeneration and then sanctification (the so-called "second blessing"), which is baptism in the Holy Spirit, the "finished work." In "three-stage" teaching the experience of conversion/regeneration is followed by the grace of perfection/sanctification and then by baptism in the Holy Spirit, which is a further enablement to live out and witness a full Christian life. The debate reveals a shift from "purity" to "holiness as power," which links sanctity to moral and spiritual empowerment received by the grace of the Holy Spirit.

The debate has lost some of its impact at the beginning of the third millennium; leaving aside the questions concerning the chronological/logical order of the sanctification stages, as well as the dynamics according to which a sinner is first regenerated and then entirely sanctified, interest is focused on how the believer is made holy by the Holy Spirit. While the Reformed theological principle in which the believer is "simultaneously righteous and yet sinner" (*simul justus et peccator*) seems to shift toward a "simultaneously holy and sinner" perspective (*simul sanctus et peccator*), a need for an

anthropological reflection emerges, and it is likely to be enriched by recent charismatic contributions.

Pentecostal Perspective

The concept of empowerment moves the reflection from the theoretical level (about the process of sanctification) to the existential reality (about the believer as saint). The idea that the believers are the community of saints is rooted in the imperative, "As he who called you is holy, be holy yourselves, in all your conduct for it is written: 'You shall be holy for I am holy'" (1 Peter, 1:15–16).

The Bible provides a large variety of contexts and meanings for the word "saint"; in the Old Testament, especially in the Pentateuch, the term defines what belongs to God and cannot be made profane or corrupted: places, times, objects and, above all, the people God has elected and established a Covenant with. The people of God are, therefore, holy and must grow in holiness, both in worship and in moral standards (see Leviticus, 19:2). The New Testament offers similar views, though with a Trinitarian and ecclesiological emphasis: God, in fact, is addressed as the Holy Father (see John, 17:11), His Son as the Holy One "par excellence" and the Holy Spirit as the Sanctifier, present in the life of both Jesus and the faithful. The most frequent addressee of the term "saint" is, nevertheless, the community of believers (see Acts, 9:13; 26:10; Romans, 15:25–26; 2 Corinthians, 1:1; 8:4; 9:1; Ephesians, 1:1; 3:18; 1 Peter, 1:15). They are saints because the holiness of the church is enriched by the new dimension of parental relationship with God (see Romans, 11:16; Ephesians, 1:4; Colossians, 1:22; 1 Peter, 2:9), and their vocation is to become saints, because the community is sanctified by the Holy Spirit (see 1 Corinthians, 1:2; 6:1; Ephesians. 2:21; 5:25–26).

Commonly used by the church to talk about itself, the word "saints" has been replaced, since the second century CE, by "Christians" (used for the first time in Acts, 11:26) and in the expression "community of the saints" (Augsburg Confession of 1530, n. 7) is received by the First and Second Revivals and—consequently, by the Pentecostal movement—in the encompassing meaning of conversion, sanctification, and baptism in the Holy Spirit. While the former two stand primarily for purity, the latter refers to empowerment, the newness brought about by Pentecostal perspectives.

Pentecostals share with other contemporary revival movements (for instance, the Salvation Army, Seventh Day Adventists, and the Quakers) the vision of purity as a call to an intense spiritual life (made up of prayer, repentance, fasting, and so on), as well as a call for personal high ethical standards (ranging from the traditional moral discipline of rejection of sexual disorders, euthanasia, abortion, and so forth to a very rigorous lifestyle, including rejection of smoking, drinking, etc.). The forbidding of practices such as dancing, going to movies, gambling, and using cosmetics and jewelry had been included in the classic Pentecostal set of prescriptions as a claim of "otherworldliness," a concept related to the Old Testament understanding of holiness as separation from what is not holy (according to the etymological root of the Hebrew word "qd": "separated").

Recent developments in the movement, especially among charismatics and neocharismatics, have underemphasized otherworldliness that could lead to a sort of elitarianism and pointed to "inworldliness" or, as Harvey Cox suggested, to a "this-worldliness" attitude. Indeed, it must be noted that Pentecostals have always shown openness toward many "worldly realities" (the importance of the bodily dimension in worship and spirituality, the use of mass media in spreading the good news, the involvement in social activities). The Gospel reminder to be "not of the world" although "in the world" (John, 17:11.14) is an indication that it not only concerns moral behavior but also moral attitudes and lifestyle, besides, of course, soteriological truths.

The concept of empowerment as a feature of holiness could be linked to the Old Testament idea of "visibility" and "sanctity" as well as to that of holiness as communicated through contact, which in the New Testament is expressed by the bodily dimension of gifts, charisms and ministries (for instance, the imposition of hands), and that transference in Pentecostal praxis (for instance, the "point of contact" in healings through radio or TV).

Finally, the saints are those who sense and manifest the victory by Jesus Christ over evil through the signs and wonders of the Holy Spirit and grow in the fruits of the Spirit: love, joy, peace, patience, kindness, generosity, faithfulness, gentleness, self-control (see Galatians, 5:22–23).

Charismatic Perspective

There is a diverse, although complementary, vision of the development of the concept of holiness within the Pentecostal and charismatic streams, due to the different approaches. In the first place, for charismatics holiness is situated in a more structured theological/ ecclesiological framework, in which it is considered both ontologically (as a consequence of being God's creatures) and morally (as an open-to-all possibility to grow toward Christlikeness), supported by the sacramental dimension alongside the charismatic one. In fact, in the Catholic perspective sacraments are a means to receive grace and are meant to help the faithful in every difficult time, thus making sanctification a cooperation with the grace of God.

In the second place, the call to holiness is a universal one—as reaffirmed in the Vatican II teaching of *Lumen Gentium*—but every believer answers this call in a personal way, according to his/her state of life (clergy/ religious/lay). During the earthly pilgrimage, there is no way to fully accomplish this vocation because of human sin, and what each person is meant to be will be revealed only in the eschatological times (see 1 John, 3:2). The church, then, is the earthly Jerusalem, the community of those who are saints because they have been baptized but have not reached perfection yet and are in communion with those who have already reached the heavenly Jerusalem, properly called "communion of saints." According to Catholic-Charismatic theology, they can intercede with God for the faithful.

In the third place and consequently, the believers can be encouraged and supported by the example of the life of the saints.

Pentecostals do not share the above-mentioned ecclesiological principles regarding saints, nor do they believe in the saints' intercessory power; nevertheless, they recognize—in the life of many saints—men and women who have witnessed God and Christ in a radical way in their particular historical and geopolitical context.

Emerging Trends

Pentecostals and charismatics affirmed in the *Report on Koinonia* (n. 101), published at the end of the Third Phase of theological dialogue that some Pentecostals and the Catholic Church have engaged in since 1972, to recognize in the expression "so great a cloud of witnesses" (Hebrews, 12:1), an evocative image of the saints. Biographies and reports of witnesses and saints clearly show that holiness can be lived out in a variety of contexts and styles: Pentecostal witnesses have been healers, prophets, apostles, and intercessors; likewise, charismatic saints have been hermits, cenobites, educators, healers, martyrs. Among groups of Pentecostals in some geographic areas, in the context of prayer, litanies are sung to saints known to the major traditions along with founders of religions, witnesses to human rights or human values, and contributors to human culture in order to show the multifaceted and creative effect of the action of the Spirit in the human community.

Finally, a widespread attitude of praying for vocations is becoming part of the Pentecostal-Charismatic initiatives as a request for a manifestation of the Spirit. Vocation is considered to be any call of the Spirit to the baptized to live in a particular state of life, able to witness to the message of the Gospel to other believers and to the world, which they call a "second conversion."

TERESA FRANCESCA ROSSI

See also Baptism in the Holy Spirit; Perfection and Perfectionism; Sanctification

Further Reading

Blumhofer, E. L., & Balmer R. (Eds.). (1993). *Modern Christian revivals*. Urbana-Chicago: University of Illinois Press.

Classic pentecostal/Roman Catholic official dialogue. (1990). Third report, 1985–1989. Perspectives on Koinonia. *Information Service, 75*(4), 179–191.

Classic pentecostal/Roman Catholic official dialogue. (1998). Fourth report 1990–1997. *Information Service, 97*(1–2), 37–61.

Cordes, P. J. (1997). *Call to holiness: Reflections on the Catholic charismatic renewal*. Collegeville, MN: The Liturgical Press.

Cox, H. G. (1993). Personal reflections on Pentecostalism. *Pneuma, 15*(1), 29–34.

Crowe, T. R. (1993). *Pentecostal unity: Recurring frustration and enduring hopes*. Chicago: Loyola University Press.

Dayton, D. W. (1987). *Theological roots of Pentecostalism*. Metuchen, NJ: Hendrickson Publishers.

du Plessis, D. (1986). *Simple & profound*. Orleans, MA: Paraclete Press.

Harrell, D. E., Jr. (1975). *All things are possible: The healing & charismatic revivals in modern America*. Bloomington-London: Indiana University Press.

Hocken, P. (1994). *The glory and the shame: Reflections on the 20th-century outpouring of the Holy Spirit*. Glasgow, UK: HarperCollins.

Hollenweger, W. J. (1997). *Pentecostalism: Origins and developments worldwide*. Peabody, MA: Hendrickson Publishers.

Hunter, H. D., & Hocken, P. D. (Eds.). (1993). *All together in one place. theological papers from the Brighton Conference on World Evangelization*. Sheffield, UK: Sheffield Academic Press.

Jones, C. D. (1974). *A guide to the study of the holiness movement*. Metuchen, NJ: The Scarecrow Press & The American Theological Library Association.

Land, S. J. (2001). *Pentecostal spirituality: A passion for the kingdom*. Sheffield, UK: Sheffield Academic Press.

McDonnell, K., & Montague, G. T. (1991). *Christian initiation and baptism in the Holy Spirit: Evidence from the first eight centuries*. Collegeville, MN: The Liturgical Press.

Moltmann, J., & Kuschel, K.-J. (Eds.) (1996). Pentecostal movements as an ecumenical challenge. *Concilium, 32*(3).

Ranaghan, K., & Ranaghan, D. (Eds.). (1971). *As the spirit leads us*. New York: Paulist Press.

Ranaghan, K., & Ranaghan, D. (1983). *Catholic pentecostals today*. South Bend, IN: Charismatic Renewal Services.

Robeck, C. M., Jr. (1999). When being a "martyr" is not enough: Catholics and Pentecostals. *Pneuma, 21*(1), 3–10.

Smith, T. L. (1963). *Called unto holiness*. Kansas City, MO: Nazarene Publishing House.

Synan, V. (1992). *The Spirit said "grow."* Monrovia, CA: MARC.

Synan, V. (2001). *The century of the Holy Spirit: 100 years of Pentecostal and charismatic renewal, 1901–2001*. Nashville, TN: Thomas Nelson.

Wainwright, G. (2003). The one hope of your calling? The ecumenical and pentecostal movements after a century. *Pneuma, 25*(1), 7–28.

Wood, L. W. (1999). Pentecostal sanctification in Wesley and early Methodism. *Pneuma, 21*(2), 251–287.

Sanctification

The biblical doctrine of sanctification has played a crucial role in the development of Pentecostalism, a movement with major roots in the Holiness movement of the nineteenth century. In the Bible, the Old Testament word *Qadosh* (the verb form meaning "he consecrated" or "he sanctified") is translated as the verb *hagiazen* in the New Testament. In both cases the essential meaning is "holiness" or "sanctification," which, although primarily ascribed to deity, can be also applied to persons or things that are purified and set apart for God's service. For persons, the word sanctification describes the provision of God wherein he sanctifies the people who are called followed by a process whereby one becomes holy and separated from sin—a process that will be consummated at the Parousia. The English word *sanctification* comes from the Latin root *sanctus*, while the word *holiness* derives from the Anglo-Saxon root *Halig*.

In most of the Scriptures, sanctification is something that God does on behalf of a believer. God is always the subject of the verbs in the New Testament. At times, though, individuals are admonished to sanctify ("consecrate") themselves, as in 1 Chronicles 15:12, where the Levites were told to "sanctify yourselves, you and your brethren"(KJV). This was to be a separation from all that defiles. In the New Testament, Jesus is the only one who is capable of self-sanctification "and for their sakes I sanctify myself, that they also may be sanctified by the truth" (John 17:19). Other New Testament passages assign the work of sanctification to the Holy Spirit, to Jesus, and to the Father, but especially through the blood of the new covenant.

In the New Testament, the call to holiness was clear and unmistakable. "Follow peace with all men and holiness without which no man shall see the Lord" (Hebrews 12:14). "Be holy as I am holy" (1 Peter 1:16). "This is God's will, even your sanctification" (1 Thessalonians 4:3). Some Scriptures speak of those who were sanctified: "forgiveness of sins and an inheritance among those who are sanctified" (Acts 26:18); "all those who are sanctified" (Acts 20:32); "to those who are sanctified, in Christ Jesus, called holy ones/saints" (1 Corinthians 1:2); "To those who are called, sanctified by God the Father, and preserved in Jesus Christ" (Jude 1). For the earliest Christians, the rites of initiation culminating in baptism meant complete freedom from sin and from sinning.

Western and Eastern Traditions

In the primitive church, therefore, it was assumed that all the baptized were living in a state of sanctification and were thus called "saints." As Clement pointed out, Christians were "called to be saints" (*1 Clement* 29:1). In the writing of the Shepherd of Hermas, Christians are called "holy" and therefore should "do all that belongs to sanctification" (*Vision* 3:1). Often good works were seen as evidence and the fruit of sanctification. And it was commonly understood that the state of holiness was not only for the few, but that the sanctified life was a universal requirement for all Christians.

Since Hebrews 6:4–5 stated the "impossibility" of those who were once enlightened and "fall away" to be "renewed again," many believed that if a Christian committed only one sin after baptism, he or she was lost forever with no hope of restoration. Because of this, some converts, such as the emperor Constantine, delayed their baptisms until shortly before death.

As time went on, the problem of Christians committing sin after baptism led to a major reassessment of the requirement of holiness in this life. Since so many baptized Christians continued to commit acts of sin, the church faced the dilemma of excommunicating huge numbers of people. This eventually led to the creation of a system of penance and forgiveness while on earth and a place after death called purgatory, where one could be perfected before entering into heaven. Also, in Roman Catholic theology, a system called the "treasury of merits" was created where the accumulated good works of the whole church could be called on to atone for the sins of an individual believer. Furthermore, for those who aspired to perfection, the church approved the monastic system, where monks and nuns could completely separate themselves from the world to pursue holiness. Others, who were called mystics, became fervent seekers after union with God through visions and trances. In time, sanctity was recognized through the process of beatification and canonization into sainthood. Thus the idea of "heroic holiness" was ascribed to the few saints of the church while the majority of Christians were not expected to live up to their more exalted standards.

In Eastern Orthodoxy, the quest for sanctification eventually took the form of "deification," where the seeker after holiness became more godlike in this life through good works and a mystical union with God. In its development after the schism with the Western Church, the Orthodox began more and more to think of sanctification in its ritual sense (that is, of priests, vestments, buildings, the elements of the Eucharist) while in the West sanctification carried more of a moral personal sense (that is, sexual abstinence, avoidance of venal or mortal sin).

Protestant Tradition

The Protestant Reformation led to new views of sanctification and holiness in the life of a believer. With Luther's doctrine of justification by faith, an attempt was made to dismantle the Catholic system of "works righteousness" by asserting that Christians were saved "by faith" and not "by works." The later works of Luther and Calvin centered on the doctrine of justification with little time spent on the possibility of sanctification in this life. To Luther, a Christian was *simul justus et peccator* (at the same time justified and a sinner). Furthermore, the Reformed doctrine of "total depravity" seemed to discourage the pursuit of holiness in the believer with entire sanctification seen as attainable only after death. In the meantime, the struggle with sin continued.

To harmonize the call to holiness in Scripture with the recognition of sin continuing to exist in the believer, most Reformation churches adopted the "positional view" of sanctification, that is, a believer while committing sin is seen as holy by God because of the atonement of Christ. "Positional holiness" would be followed by "infused holiness" and absolute angelic perfection after death.

John Wesley and Methodism

A major change in Protestant teaching on sanctification came with John Wesley in the eighteenth century. Rejecting the prevailing views of Calvinism, Wesley began to teach a version of Christian perfection whereby a person could be freed from the power of original sin through seeking and receiving what he called "entire sanctification," a "second blessing properly so called" (Wesley 1925). As he explained in his *Plain Account of Christian Perfection* (1739), justification gave forgiveness for "actual transgressions" while entire sanctification removed the sin principle, which was inherited from Adam.

According to Wesley, the sanctification process began at conversion, progressed to the point of a subsequent "second blessing" where the sin principle was conquered, gradual growth in grace, and final glorification in heaven. To Wesley, this teaching, which he variously called "perfect love" and "Christian Perfection," was the foundation of the Wesleyan societies in the Anglican Church, and later of the Methodist Church itself. Wesley was careful not to endorse "sinless perfection," since even the sanctified could fall from grace. While he could be "perfected in love," in a instant of consecration, a sanctified person would still be subject to the weaknesses of the flesh and imperfect judgment, but could avoid committing a "willful violation of a known law of God."

A variant teaching by Wesley's colleague John Fletcher held that the proper name for the entire sanctification experience was the "baptism in the Holy Ghost." Using texts from the book of Acts, Fletcher found it easier to make a case for the instant crisis experience as a "second blessing" and also to use the fire of Pentecost as the element of cleansing and purification. In future years, Fletcher's theology was to gain great popularity and influence in the Holiness movement of the nineteenth century.

Holiness Movement

Although Methodism began as a holiness church, by the end of the nineteenth century it had effectively dropped the teaching of an instantaneous second blessing and opted for a more gradual and progressive approach. This led to the creation of several Holiness denominations in the last decade of the century, a development that not only continued the Wesleyan tradition but offered an increasingly radical approach to sanctification. These churches, which included such churches as the Church of God (Anderson, Indiana), the Salvation Army, and the Church of the Nazarene, taught not only crisis sanctification, but also divine healing and the Second Coming Rapture of the church. Other Holiness churches added rules of behavior known as the "holiness code," which forbade worldly dress for men and women, use of tobacco and alcohol, and the use of jewelry and cosmetics. In some cases, these rules served as "evidence" that a person had been sanctified.

Some of these Holiness churches, including the Church of God (Cleveland, Tennessee), the Pentecostal Holiness Church, and the Church of God in Christ, later became part of the Pentecostal movement and carried their sanctification teachings with them. True to their Wesleyan heritage, these, the first Pentecostal churches in the world, emphasized sanctification as a "second blessing" but added baptism in the Holy Spirit evidenced by speaking in tongues as a "third blessing" poured out upon the sanctified believer.

Pentecostal Movement

Emphasis on the second blessing and third blessing was the position of Charles Fox Parham, the theological founder of Pentecostalism, and his disciple William J. Seymour, pastor of the Azusa Street Mission in Los Angeles. Seymour, who spread the movement around the world, was an ardent teacher of second blessing sanctification, holding that one could not receive the Pentecostal baptism in the Holy Spirit and speak in tongues without a prior cleansing experience of entire sanctification. The experience of sanctification was central to the Azusa Street testimony of being "saved, sanctified, and filled with the Holy Ghost." In fact, black Pentecostal churches, such as the Church of God in Christ, were referred to in American black communities as the "sanctified churches."

A major variation of the holiness teaching in Pentecostalism came with the advent of the "finished work" teaching by William H. Durham after 1910. Rejecting the Wesleyan idea of a "second blessing" of entire sanctification, he taught that the baptism in the Holy Spirit was the second blessing and that sanctification began at conversion and grew progressively until death. The Assemblies of God, which was organized in 1914, based its theology on Durham's teachings.

A further division in the Pentecostal movement came with the advent of the "Oneness" movement in 1911. This movement denied the Trinity and insisted that the only valid form of water baptism was in "Jesus' name." With this movement, there was no second or third blessing, since everything was received in the baptismal pool, including speaking in tongues. For Oneness Pentecostals, sanctification began in water baptism in Jesus' name followed by a life of continued growth, which led to a life of strict adherence to the holiness code that had been handed down from the Holiness movement.

In the end, the teaching on second blessing sanctification played a crucial role in the beginning of the Pentecostal movement. The idea of a subsequent "deeper" crisis experience after conversion became the essential criterion for all Pentecostals. Before 1901, the Holiness churches taught that the second blessing was a "cleansing" brought about by the "baptism in the Holy Spirit." The Pentecostals added the idea of glossolalia (speaking in tongues) as the "initial evidence," and separated sanctification from the baptism in the Holy Spirit. All Pentecostals, however, continued to value the importance of holiness and sanctification in the lifestyle of a Spirit-filled believer.

VINSON SYNAN

See also Azusa Street Revival; Baptism in the Holy Spirit; Glossolalia; Second Work of Grace

Further Reading

Alexander, D. (Ed.). (1988). *Spirituality: Five views of sanctification.* Downers Grove, IL: InterVarsity.

Fletcher, J. (1851). *Checks to antinomianism. The Works of The Reverend John Fletcher* (4 vols.). New York: Lane & Scott.

Horton, S. (1994). *Systematic theology: A Pentecostal perspective.* Springfield, MO: Gospel.

King, J. (2004). *From Passover to Pentecost.* Franklin Springs, GA: Lifesprings.

Land, S. (1993). *Pentecostal spirituality: A passion for the Kingdom.* Sheffield, UK: Sheffield Academic.

Synan, V. (1997). *The Holiness-Pentecostal tradition: Charismatic movements in the twentieth century.* Grand Rapids, MI: Eerdmans.

Wesley, J. (1925). *A plain account of Christian perfection as believed and taught by Rev. John Wesley from 1725 to 1777.* New York: Methodist Book Concern.

Scripture, Holy

THE BIBLE: This Book contains—the mind of God, the state of man, the way of salvation, doom of

sinners, the happiness of believers. Its doctrines are holy, its precepts are binding, its histories are true, and its decisions are immutable. (*Weekly Evangel*, 25 September 1915, p. 4)

Although Pentecostals have not taken part in the vigorous debate on "inerrancy," they can fully identify with Timothy George's description of Evangelicals as "gospel people and Bible people" (1995, 17). Pentecostal-Charismatic believers are an important part of the Evangelical tradition, defined by Pinnock as "those believers who…are committed to the gospel as it is biblically defined" (2002, xi). *The Apostolic Faith*, representing the first wave of the Pentecostal interpretation of Scripture, affirms, "We stand on Bible truth without compromise" (December 1906, p. 1). The October 1906 issue exclaims, "We have thrown all doubts to the winds and taken to our hearts the whole word of Jesus. Dear friends, do not let any man riddle your Bible for you or cut out any part of it. You need the whole. Hallelujah for the Word" (p. 3).

Article 2 of the Lausanne Covenant (1974) can be fully embraced by Pentecostal and charismatic believers:

We affirm the divine inspiration, truthfulness and authority of both Old and New Testament Scriptures in their entirety as the only written Word of God, without error in all that it affirms and the only infallible rule of faith and practice. We also affirm the power of God's Word to accomplish His purpose of salvation.

The twenty-first-century Pentecostal-Charismatic movement represents a section of Christianity that upholds the "Scripture principle," over and against forms of "neo-Christianity," without the controlling influence of the authority of Scripture (Pinnock 2002, xiv). Pentecostal-Charismatic Christians consider themselves as continuing a tradition stretching back to Old Testament times that honors Scripture as the infallible Word of God.

Perspicuity of Scripture

Under the title "A New Love for the Word," *The Apostolic Faith*, October 1906, p. 2, reports:

Several have been healed. But, best of all, *many are getting the light, and as the Bible opens to us, they rejoice for the precious truths that have been hidden from us* for so long by the "traditions of the elders." This is the greatest power I ever saw. Glory to God! I have wanted just this for years, but did not know how to get it. But, Hallelujah! After all, the great God opened my eyes and let me see the truth, and it liberated me from the bondage of ignorant teachings and the devil in general. *I see the Bible now as never before.* (Emphasis added)

The relationship between Scripture and the Pentecostal experience can be viewed from two sides: First, Scripture gives rise to Pentecostal experience. In December 1900, Charles Parham left his Bible school for a few weeks. Before leaving, he instructed his students to study their Bibles carefully, especially the book of Acts, in order to understand the biblical evidence regarding the baptism with the Holy Spirit. Upon his return he was astonished to learn that all the students agreed that "speaking with other tongues" was the chief evidence of this phenomenon. Although they had not had such an experience, Parham and his students were convinced that this was the biblical pattern. They conducted a watch night service on December 31, 1900. Shortly after midnight on the first day of the twentieth century, after Parham had laid hands on her head and had prayed for her to be baptized with the Holy Spirit, Agnes N. Ozman began "speaking in the Chinese language" while a "halo seemed to surround her head and face." From this perspective we may say that knowledge of Scripture preceded and precipitated the Pentecostal experience.

Second, Pentecostal experience gives rise to a new understanding of Scripture. As evidenced by the quotation from *The Apostolic Faith* introducing this section, believers have repeatedly testified that they received a new love for and understanding of Scripture after experiencing the baptism in the Spirit. Howard Ervin introduced the concept of "pneumatic epistemology" (1981, 22), which posits that a deepened perception into Scripture is the product of an experience with the Holy Spirit. Ervin affirms, "When one encounters the Holy Spirit in the same apostolic experience, with the same charismatic phenomenology accompanying it, one is then in a better position to come to terms with the apostolic witness in a truly existential manner....One then stands in 'pneumatic' continuity with the faith community that birthed the Scriptures" (1981, 22).

Pentecostal-Charismatic Christians have a high regard for Scripture because Scripture introduces them to a saving, transforming knowledge of Christ. They personally experienced the reality of 2 Timothy 3:15–17 (NIV):

> ... and how from infancy you have known the holy Scriptures, which are able to make you wise for salvation through faith in Christ Jesus. All Scripture is God-breathed and is useful for teaching, rebuking, correcting and training in righteousness, so that the

man of God may be thoroughly equipped for every good work.

The clarity of Scripture is primarily a *religious* clarity, conveying the meaning of faith, salvation, and true community with God. By hearing the Word, faith is birthed in the human heart. Through faith, believers experience Christ's presence where Scripture is read. This presence is a pneumatic reality; the Spirit creates faith in the human heart, and Christ is present through the Spirit (1 Corinthians 2:4–5).

Relationship with Fundamentalism

James Barr defines *fundamentalism* as follows:

> As generally used, the term "fundamentalism" designates a form of conservative evangelical Protestantism that, along with other traditional doctrines such as the Trinity, incarnation, deity of Christ, original sin, human depravity, and justification by faith, lays an exceptional stress on the inerrancy and infallibility of the Bible as the absolutely essential foundation and criterion of truth. Along with this emphasis goes the stress on personal faith, the sense of sin and need for salvation, and personal involvement and appropriation of the grace of God. (2001, 363)

Fundamentalism is defined here with very broad strokes—what Barr terms "fundamentalism" actually sounds more like traditional orthodox Christianity. Although Barr's criteria for Fundamentalists accurately define Pentecostals, Pentecostalism was never part of the Fundamentalist coalition. The World's Christian Fundamentals Association was formed in 1919. Pentecostalism soon became one of the targets of this group, as is evident from the following 1928 resolution:

> WHEREAS, the present wave of Modern Pentecostalism, often referred to as the "tongues movement," and the present wave of fanatical and unscriptural healing which is sweeping over the country today, has become a menace in many churches and a real injury to the sane testimony of fundamentalist Christians,

> BE IT RESOLVED, That this convention go on record as unreservedly opposed to Modern Pentecostalism, including the speaking in unknown tongues, and the fanatical healing known as general healing in the atonement, and the perpetuation of the miraculous sign-healing of Jesus and His apostles, wherein they claim the only reason the church cannot perform these miracles is because of unbelief.

The editorial of the August 18, 1928, *Pentecostal Evangel* reacted to this resolution: "…this action disfellowshipped a great company of us who believe in all the fundamentals of the faith as much as they themselves do." Pentecostals indeed uphold the key beliefs of Fundamentalists, including Christ's virgin birth and substitutionary atonement, the verbal inspiration of Scriptures, the Resurrection of the body, the ascension, and a strong belief in Christ's imminent return. In addition, however, they value the baptism in the Holy Spirit and consequent charismatic gifts. This adds a spiritual dimension to their theology that distinguishes them from Fundamentalists. Pentecostal theology is, indeed, "Spiritual theology" (Chan 1998). Spittler succinctly summarizes the difference between Pentecostals and Fundamentalists by pointing to their different agendas: "Fundamentalists sought to rectify theological deviation. Pentecostals urged enhancement of personal religious experience" (1994, 113).

The American Council of Christian Churches (ACCC), an organization of Fundamentalists organized in 1940 by Carl McIntire, rejected Pentecostalism. Pentecostals are, however, a substantial part of the National Association of Evangelicals (NAE), an association of Evangelical, Holiness, and Pentecostal churches formed in 1942 with a 1999 membership of 6.8 million (compared to the 2 million members of the ACCC).

Scripture and the Triune God

There is an intimate relationship between Scripture and our view of God. We read Scripture in order to know God, and our knowledge of God determines our approach to Scripture. This is a circular relationship in which our interpretation of Scripture is continually corrected as our understanding of the text deepens. Ultimately, we are accountable to the text.

The conviction arose in early Pentecostalism that in the Scriptures God is present in the midst of his people through the risen Christ and in the power of the Spirit. This presence is a "saving fellowship" (Webster 2003, 15).

The object and end of all the precious Scripture is that a definite work may be wrought out in our hearts by the Holy Ghost. God's design through the ages and through all His work with the children of men, has been to implant His own . . . love, in a fallen race. Oh how sweet to feel the tender thrills of that love, going through every part of our being. This is real Bible salvation—not a mere theory or contention over different passages of Scripture. (*The Apostolic Faith*, November 1906, p. 4)

In worship, Pentecostal and charismatic believers experience the eschatological power of Jesus Christ through the power of the Spirit. They view Scripture, themselves, and the world accordingly: "the resurrection of Jesus [is viewed] as their own resurrection, the first Pentecost as their own 'Pentecost,' the crucifixion of Jesus as their own crucifixion…" (Land 1993, 60–61).

Holy Scripture

From its earliest days the Pentecostal-Charismatic movement has had the highest respect for Scripture's power to save, to heal, and to encourage. *The Apostolic Faith*, November 1906, p. 1, reports:

As soon as it is announced that the altar is open for seekers for pardon, sanctification, the baptism with the Holy Ghost and healing of the body, the people rise and flock to the altar. There is no urging. What kind of preaching is it that brings them? Why, the simple declaring of the Word of God. There is such power in the preaching of the Word in the Spirit.

Because of this high regard for Holy Scripture, Pentecostals reacted strongly against the doubts raised by "higher criticism" regarding the nature of Scripture. Bert F. Webb commented in *The Pentecostal Evangel*, 24 August 1929, p. 7:

If those who are denying and trying to destroy the Scripture would humble themselves before the Lord and seek His face until He reveals Himself to them in saving power and until He could "open their understanding that they might understand the Scriptures," much controversy would be avoided and thousands of people would be re-established in the old-time faith of Jesus Christ.

Early Pentecostals were aware of the human authors and circumstances surrounding Bible authorship. In the 11 September 1926, edition of *The Pentecostal Evangel* (p. 6), Donald Gee points to the fact that the Bible consists of sixty-six books, written by about forty contributors "including kings, shepherds, fishermen, prisoners, and at least one physician." Gee mentions that a period of more than fifteen hundred years passed between the writing of the first and last books. Evangelist Watson Argue affirms that "the Bible was written by men from various walks of life; the highest and the lowest.…It was written in three different languages; the New Testament was written in Greek and the Old Testament in Hebrew, with the exception of some small parts which were written in the Aramaic language" (*The Latter Rain Evangel*, October 1936).

Still, Scripture is highly revered as *Holy* Scripture by Pentecostal and charismatic believers. They are firmly convinced that—although composed by human writers in different languages and over many years—Scripture embodies the Spirit-generated, redemptive communication of a loving God to his creatures. Elder D. W. Kerr comments in *The Weekly Evangel*, 16 December 1916, p. 3:

> The Bible is the only Book that fits into the need of man. For "man shall not live by bread alone, but by every word that comes out of the mouth of God." There are very many things we need to know for the sake of our own health and happiness, and for the sake of the creatures, and the good of the people with whom we live, and the powers which are over us, and for the glory of God.

Outlook in the Twenty-first Century

Pentecostals view themselves as part of the worldwide church of Jesus Christ. The global Pentecostal-Charismatic movement has become a key component of twenty-first century Christianity due to the movement's numerical growth with an estimated 620 million believers at present. The Pentecostal desire for unity among churches and believers is evidenced by the statement in *The Apostolic Faith* at the very beginning of the movement (September 1906): "'Love, Faith, Unity' are our watchwords."

The present challenge for Pentecostals and for the church at large is to interpret the Bible in a meaningful way in our increasingly secular postmodern cultural context. Within Christianity a great divide is emerging and becoming all the more prominent. This is not a divide between Roman Catholics and Protestants as in previous times but between Christians accepting the authority of Holy Scripture and those wanting to redefine this authority—"classical Christians of every kind and liberals who seem bent on shifting the church from her scriptural foundations" (Pinnock 2002, 223). Today Catholic and Pentecostal scholars are discovering new convergences in their views of Scripture on key issues such as Jesus Christ as the final revelation, the consummation of God's speaking to us, the basic affirmation of biblical inspiration by the Holy Spirit, the infallibility of Scripture, the necessity of the Holy Spirit in understanding and appropriating the Word of God, and the integral relationship between Spirit, Word, and *koinonia*/Communion.

Within a Christianity that accepts biblical authority, Pentecostal-Charismatic believers can make a unique contribution, strengthening the commitment to Holy Scripture. While affirming the convictions of conservative Evangelicals, Pentecostals, and charismatics emphasize the *relational dimension*, the importance of the Spirit, who has not only inspired Scripture but who also enlightens present-day readers and makes Christ present wherever the Bible is being read.

PETRUS J. GRÄBE

See also Doctrine, Development of; Fundamentalism

Further Reading

Barr, J. (2001). Fundamentalism (G. W. Bromiley, Trans.). In E. Fahlbusch, J. M. Lochman, J. Mbiti, J. Pelikan, L. Vischer & D. B. Barrett (Eds.), *The encyclopedia of Christianity* (Vol. 2, pp. 363–365). Grand Rapids, MI: William B. Eerdmans.

Chan, S. (1998). *Spiritual theology: A systematic study of the Christian life*. Downers Grove, IL: InterVarsity Press.

Clark, M. S. (1997). The nature and authority of scripture. In P. J. Grabe & W. J. Hattingh (Eds.), *The reality of the Holy Spirit in the church* (pp. 1–13). Hatfield, Pretoria, South Africa: J.L. van Schaik.

Ervin, H. M. (1981). Hermeneutics: A pentecostal option. *Pneuma, 3*(2), 11–25.

George, T. (1995, October 23). What we mean when we say it's true. *Christianity Today*, 17–21.

Gräbe, P. J. (1997). Hermeneutical reflections on the interpretation of the New Testament with special reference to the Holy Spirit and faith. In P. J. Gräbe & W. J. Hattingh (Eds.), *The reality of the Holy Spirit in the church* (pp. 14–26). Hatfield, Pretoria, South Africa: J.L. van Schaik.

Kärkkäinen, V.-M., & Yong, A. (2002). *Toward a pneumatological theology*. Lanham, MD: University Press of America, Inc.

Land, S. J. (1993). *Pentecostal spirituality: A passion for the kingdom* (Vol. 1). Sheffield, UK: Sheffield Academic Press.

Möller, F. P. (1998). *Understanding the greatest of truths* (Vol. 1). Hatfield, Pretoria, South Africa: J. L. van Schaik.

Pinnock, C. H. (1993a). The role of the spirit in interpretation. *Journal of the Evangelical Theological Society, 36*(4), 491–497.

Pinnock, C. H. (1993b). The work of the Holy Spirit in hermeneutics. *Journal of Pentecostal Theology*, (2), 3–23.

Pinnock, C. H. (2002). *The scripture principle* (2nd ed.). Vancouver, Canada: Regent College Publishing.

Rossouw, H. W. (1963). *Klaarheid en Interpretasie*. Amsterdam: Drukkerij en Uitgeverij Jacob van Campen N. V.

Söding, T. (1995). *Mehr als ein Buch: Die Bibel begreifen*. Freiburg, Germany: Herder.

Spittler, R. P. (1994). Are pentecostals and charismatics fundamentalists? In K. Poewe (Ed.), *Charismatic Christianity as a global culture* (pp. 103–116). Columbia: University of South Carolina Press.

Stronstad, R. (1992). Pentecostal experience and hermeneutics. *Paraclete, 26*, 14–30.

Vanhoozer, K. J. (2002). *First theology: God, scripture & hermeneutics*. Downers Grove, IL: InterVarsity Press.

Von Campenhausen, H. (1972). *The formation of the Christian Bible* (J. A. Baker, Trans. & Ed. English edition). Philadelphia: Fortress Press.

Webster, J. (2003). *Holy scripture: A dogmatic sketch*. Cambridge, UK: Cambridge University Press.

Second Work of Grace

The call to holiness, or sanctification, a constant theme in both the Old and New Testaments, has also been an important theme in the origins and development of the world Pentecostal movement. The pursuit of holiness as a crisis experience of "second blessing" sanctification led eventually to the Pentecostal understanding of "baptism in the Holy Spirit," with the "initial evidence" of speaking in tongues as a definite experience after conversion. The outbreak of tongues speech in Topeka, Kansas, in 1901, under former Methodist pastor Charles Fox Parham, was preceded by a century of ever-expanding teaching on the deeper life of sanctification as a subsequent work of grace.

Although the primitive church held sanctification in high regard, it was seen as beginning in the rites of initiation and progressing throughout the life of a believer. The entire rite consisted of evangelization from paganism, exorcism of the evil spirits and gods of the prior life, catechism, water baptism, chrismation, and first communion. After this, new converts were expected to live lives of ever-increasing holiness. The idea of a "second blessing" after initiation came centuries later, when the rite of baptism was separated from the ritual of confirmation and first communion, which came several years later. A theology developed that called for the bishop to lay hands on the confirmed, who was then "baptized in the Holy Spirit" and admitted to first communion. Thus the idea of a "second blessing" became part of the official and accepted public ritual of the church.

Though perfect sanctification was expected in the earliest days of the church, the problem of baptized Christians committing sins soon caused the church to institute a sacramental system of confession, penance, and forgiveness in what came to be called "ongoing conversion." Those who desired to enter higher realms of holiness could become ascetic hermits or monastics and pursue lives of holiness separated from the mainstream of everyday life. A few became mystics and sought union with God with the goal of Christian perfection.

After the separation of Eastern and Western Christianity in 1054, the Orthodox churches continued to have the one rite of initiation without the "second blessing" of confirmation. They did, however, develop a teaching on "deification," whereby serious seekers after holiness could experience unity with God subsequent to baptism.

The Protestant Reformation

The Protestant Reformation led to a radical redefinition of the Christian life that emphasized justification by faith, in contrast to the Catholic emphasis on good works. This led to a mentality that argued for the cessation of the miracles and the pursuit of holiness as valued in the Roman Catholic system. In both Luther and Calvin, the idea of the pursuit of perfection and full sanctification in this life was largely abandoned, with the ultimate teaching in Calvinism that Christians are doomed to lives of "total depravity." None of the Reformation churches taught a doctrine of a "second blessing" of sanctification that would free the believer from the effects of original sin.

John Wesley and Methodism

The first major dissent from the standard Reformation views on sanctification was offered by John Wesley (1703–1791) in eighteenth-century England. The son of an Anglican priest, Wesley rejected the strict Calvinism that had held sway in England since the days of the Puritan revolution of the 1600s. Although he agreed with the general Protestant views on justification, he was dissatisfied with the general reformed view of sanctification. This process began while Wesley was a student at Oxford University. There he and his brother Charles were challenged by the biblical call to holiness and went so far as to organized a "Holy Club" with fellow students, using a "method" of Bible reading, study, prayer, and communion to seek the kind of holiness "without which no man shall see the Lord." After his evangelical conversion at Aldersgate Street in 1738, Wesley began to develop a doctrine of sanctification that he felt was never fully completed in the reformation.

In summary, Wesley taught that in justification a Christian was forgiven for his "actual transgressions" but that a "residue" of original sin remained within that needed to be cleansed through the process of sanctification. This work of sanctification, which began initially at conversion, was a lifelong progressive work of grace that included a "second blessing properly so called" that instantly freed the seeker from the power and penalty of sin. Thereafter, one could live a life of "Christian perfection," which he also called "perfect love." This experience he called "entire sanctification," using the language of 1 Thessalonians 5:23: "May the God of peace sanctify you wholly [entirely]." This was in contrast to the incomplete holiness that he saw in many nominal Christians of his day. After the moment of cleansing, the sanctified believer would "grow in grace" until death, after which angelic and sinless perfection would be experienced in eternity. Wesley never taught what he called "sinless perfection," since the sanctified would be subject to the mistakes, errors, infirmities, and limitations of everyday life. Since he was an Arminian, Wesley believed that a sanctified person could still fall from grace and be lost, but the possibility remained for a life of victory over sin.

A key to Wesley's teaching was his definition of sin for which a person would be judged. Sin was, he said, "a willful, conscious transgression of a known law of God." Therefore, sins of ignorance would not be charged against the sanctified. Most of these ideas were distilled in Wesley's often-republished work, *A Plain Account of Christian Perfection* (1739–1777).

When he organized his Methodist Societies in the Church of England, Wesley admonished his followers to "groan after" sanctification, which he called "the grand depositum" of Methodism, for which "the Lord has raised us up." Although there was a great deal of dissatisfaction among Wesley's preachers over some aspects of his teaching, instantaneous, entire sanctification, became the distinguishing experience and teaching of the people called Methodists.

During his lifetime, Wesley's theological colleague, John Fletcher of Madeley (1729–1785) refocused the second-blessing teaching by calling it a "baptism of the Holy Ghost" as well as sanctification. This, he felt, gave a better scriptural rationale for the instantaneous teaching, since one could point to the texts in the book of Acts that depicted the baptism in the Holy Spirit as a crisis event. It seems that Wesley accepted Fletcher's suggestions, although he seldom used such Pentecostal language himself. Fletcher's views were written in his major work, *Checks to Antoniminism*, which was published in 1803. Later Holiness and Pentecostal people were to be greatly influenced by Fletcher's work.

When Wesley established Methodist churches in colonial America, he charged his leaders to "reform the continent and spread scriptural holiness over these lands." American leaders such as Thomas Coke and William Asbury took Wesley seriously and led thousands of American Methodists into the Holiness experience. By the 1830s, however, the teaching and experience of sanctification began to decline in the church, which led to attempts to revive the doctrine. In 1839 Timothy Merrit began publication of the *Guide to Holiness* in Boston, while Phoebe Palmer began Holiness meetings in her parlor in New York City. Palmer's "altar terminology," which called for a faith experience of sanctification after "placing all on the altar," became a popular approach in Holiness meetings.

Holiness Movement

In 1867, after the Civil War, John Inskip of New York City led in forming the "National Holiness Association," an interfaith organization that spread the second-blessing teaching to many outside Methodist circles. After a period of acceptance and growth, the Holiness movement was curtailed by the Southern Methodist Church in 1894 and eventually rejected by mainstream Methodism in America. Thereafter, a generation of new "holiness churches" were formed to continue the teaching and experience of sanctification. These churches were small clones of original Methodism, and in time some of them became the first Pentecostal churches in the world. In addition to second-blessing sanctification, these churches also added an emphasis on divine healing and the imminent Second Coming of Christ in the rapture. Also added were long lists of "sins" that were forbidden to the sanctified. These directives included plain dress, restriction on the use of tobacco and alcohol, and after the turn of the century, no movies. This "holiness code" constituted outward "evidences" of the sanctified life.

These churches also added a Pentecostal emphasis in the last years of the nineteenth century that could be called "Pentecostal sanctification." In this view, sanctification and cleansing were accomplished through the fires of the "baptism in the Holy Spirit." By 1875, with the beginning of the Keswick movement in England, a new emphasis on the second blessing as an "enduement of power for service" began to gain popularity among many evangelicals such as Dwight L. Moody.

Holiness Pentecostal Movements

By 1900 many persons were seeking a second blessing with manifestations such as "falling under the power," weeping, and/or other "physical thrills." This led a

Holiness teacher in Topeka, Kansas, Charles Fox Parham, to conclude that the "Bible evidence" of baptism in the Holy Spirit was speaking in tongues. This occurred in his Bethel Bible College in Topeka on January 1, 1901, when a young lady, Agnes Ozman, spoke in tongues while seeking the baptism in the Holy Spirit. This event is looked on as the beginning of the modern Pentecostal movement. Five years later in 1906, the movement spread around the world under the leadership of the black pastor William J. Seymour at Azusa Street Mission in Los Angeles, California.

Both Parham and Seymour maintained the second blessing of entire sanctification as before but simply separated the tongues-attested baptism in the Holy Spirit as a "third blessing" after the two "works of grace," justification and sanctification. This "five-fold gospel" of salvation, sanctification, baptism in the Holy Spirit with tongues as evidence, divine healing, and the Second-Coming Rapture became the universal teaching of the first Pentecostal churches. All of these were "Holiness" churches that had been founded before 1906. These included the Church of God in Christ, the Pentecostal Holiness Church, and the Church of God (Cleveland, Tennessee). All these taught that sanctification was the necessary preparation for the baptism in the Holy Spirit. This was the standard teaching of world Pentecostalism for the first decade of its history.

Finished-Work Pentecostals

A major change in the view of sanctification came with the "finished work of Calvary" teaching of William H. Durham, a disciple of Seymour. In 1910 he began to teach that there was no need of a separate experience of instant sanctification in order to receive the Pentecostal experience. His view was that sanctification began at conversion and was a gradual and progressive work of grace throughout the life of the believer. This view was rejected by the Holiness-oriented churches but spread rapidly among independent Pentecostals who came to the movement from non-Wesleyan backgrounds.

Durham's theology became the basis for the Assemblies of God Church, which was formed in 1914. Afterwards, most of the later Pentecostal churches around the world adopted the finished-work view. In America the Pentecostals on both sides of the Holiness question maintained fellowship throughout the century. The Charismatic movement, which began in the mainline churches after 1960, also agreed with the finished-work theology of sanctification.

In summary, the Wesleyan experience of a subsequent second-blessing crisis of sanctification was the crucial model of seeking and receiving the Holy Spirit that led to the beginning of the Pentecostal movement. Although Pentecostals changed the content and timing of the experience, it could be said that Pentecostalism was born in a Holiness cradle and that the goal of Holiness in the life of a Spirit-filled believer is still a central goal of the movement.

VINSON SYNAN

See also Baptism in the Holy Spirit; Sanctification

Further Reading

Dayton, D. (1987). *The theological roots of Pentecostalism.* Metuchen, NJ: Scarecrow Press.

Dieter, M. (1996). *The holiness movement of the nineteenth century* (2nd ed.). Metuchen, NJ: Scarecrow Press.

Jones, C. (1974). *The perfectionist persuasion.* Metuchen, NJ: Scarecrow Press.

Menzies, W. (1971). *Anointed to serve: The story of the Assemblies of God.* Springfield, MO: Gospel Publishing House.

Synan, V. (1997). *The Holiness-Pentecostal tradition: Charismatic movements in the twentieth century.* Grand Rapids, MI: William B. Eerdmans.

Shepherding and Discipleship Movement

An influential and controversial expression of the Charismatic Renewal in the 1970s and 1980s, the Shepherding movement, or the Discipleship movement as it was sometimes called, dramatically challenged the ecumenical character of Neo-Pentecostalism as heated controversy broke out in 1975 over the movement's teachings and practices. The debate focused on five popular Bible teachers: Don Basham (1926–1989), Ern Baxter (1914–1993), Bob Mumford (b. 1934), Derek Prince (1915–2003), and Charles Simpson (b. 1937). Each man was a regular on the charismatic conference and convention circuit in North America, and they were closely associated with Christian Growth Ministries based in Ft. Lauderdale, Florida, which published *New Wine Magazine,* the most widely circulated charismatic periodical at the time.

Mumford and the other men became the leaders of the first identifiable local church movement in the Charismatic Renewal. Three "Shepherds conferences" between 1973 and 1975 had helped birth an association of leaders and churches that was "submitted" to the five men. Critics believed the movement was trying to take over the large independent sector of the Charismatic Renewal, most of whom had left their denominational affiliations after experiencing Spirit baptism. Many charismatic leaders feared the movement was starting a "Charismatic denomination" led by Mumford and the other four men, a charge they always denied. Whether they intended it or not, the movement's five principle leaders were in charge of a large and growing network of churches by the mid-1970s.

Following the model of Jesus and the twelve disciples, the Shepherding movement emphasized the need for personal, one-on-one pastoral care for every Christian, including pastors. This pastoral relationship was central to the movement's concept of discipleship and pastoral care. Pastors in the movement, or "shepherds" as they termed them, were vested with significant authority in the lives of followers. This emphasis was intended to help produce mature Christians but brought allegations that the teachings led to domination by leaders. In all the controversy surrounding the movement's teaching, their distinctive ecclesiology was overlooked.

Those in the Shepherding movement believed the church was the agent of the kingdom of God and tasked with representing the Christ's rule and reign. They believed that society was falling apart and that the church was to be the light of the world in troubled times. All of this contributed to an emphasis on the importance of the leadership as outlined in Ephesians 4:11–12 that speaks of apostles, prophets, evangelists, pastors, and teachers. These leaders, given to the church by Christ according to Scripture, were central to mobilizing the church to full maturity and ministry in the midst of a declining culture. In their view the times they lived in supported their notions.

America was reeling at the time from the turmoil of the 1960s and the social changes that characterized that era. The Watergate scandal of the early 1970s only heightened public anxiety. The nominalism in so much of mainline Christianity had left many Christians hungering for renewal. This spiritual hunger began to be satisfied by the Charismatic Renewal as thousands experienced Spirit baptism. The Shepherding movement was a part of this religious revival that reshaped the religious landscape of America.

Mumford and the other four leaders were troubled as well by the extreme individualism and independence that was widespread in the Renewal. In addition, they observed a serious lack of ethics among some charismatic leaders and teachers. While each man had his own independent ministry, after a close associate experienced moral problems, Basham, Mumford, Prince, and Simpson decided to commit themselves to one an-

other in mutual submission and accountability. This association of the four men in 1970, later joined by Baxter in 1974, would prepare the way for the birth of the Shepherding movement. After the four decided to collaborate, they began teaching on the need for submission, spiritual authority, discipleship, and commitment between believers. With *New Wine Magazine* as a powerful spokes piece, and through books and audiotapes, their teaching themes spread throughout the Renewal.

The call for committed relationship and discipleship tapped into a leadership vacuum in the Charismatic Renewal. Young, untrained leaders, many out of the Jesus People movement, began to join the movement in large numbers. Other independent Pentecostals and some denominational charismatics joined and by 1975 thousands of leaders had submitted to the leadership of Mumford and the other four men. Church statistician David Barrett estimated that the Shepherding movement grew to as many as 100,000 adherents. While the movement never had a formal roster of churches, one leader claimed that at its height there were 500 churches in the movement.

The movement's churches were built around a cell group structure. Every ten to twelve households were under a pastor who led the cell group that met weekly. At least monthly all the cell groups came together for teaching and corporate worship. Deep and lasting commitments among fellow church members were a part of the movement's concept of "covenant relationship." In most cases Mumford and the other four men, or their designate, pastored translocally each church's lead pastor. One of the movement's most controversial teachings was the concept that church members gave tithes to their personal pastor who then tithed to his pastor and so on. Given what many saw as a kind of pyramidal structure of the Shepherding movement, some thoughts all tithes were going to the five men, a charge that was untrue.

During 1975 and 1976, three national meetings were held to try and settle what had become a serious division among charismatics. Bringing together the majority of the Renewal key leaders, such as televangelist Pat Robertson and charismatic patriarch Dennis Bennett, efforts were made to establish dialogue in hopes of bringing some resolution surrounding the bitter dispute. While the meetings quieted the controversy somewhat, in the end little was accomplished. In the years that followed, allegations continued to be raised over the authoritarian nature of the movement's pastoral relationships. Critics outside the movement and angry followers from within charged that many shepherds/pastors were controlling the lives of their people and abusing the privilege of spiritual authority. Mumford and the other four men spent much time traveling about the United States addressing serious problems in their movement. In subsequent years both Mumford and Simpson admitted serious mistakes and made public apologies.

Controversy over its teachings would be a continued hindrance to the movement's development, and it began to decline in size and influence beginning in 1982. In 1983, Prince quietly withdrew and in 1986 the remaining four men dissolved their formal association and decided to stop publishing *New Wine Magazine*. Today a number of smaller groups, led by Simpson and other leaders, carry on what they see as the movement's heritage in a more moderated form.

S. David Moore

See also Charismatic Movement; Renewal, Church

Further Reading

Burks, R. & Burks, V. (1992). *Damaged disciples: Casualties of authoritarian churches and the Shepherding movement.* Grand Rapids, MI: Zondervan Publishing.

Hadaway, C., Kirk, S., Wright, A., & DuBose, F. (1987). *Home cell groups and house churches.* Nashville, TN: Broadman.

Moore, S. D. (2003). *The shepherding movement: Controversy and charismatic ecclesiology.* London: T & T Clark.

Synan, V. (1997). *The Holiness-Pentecostal tradition.* Grand Rapids, MI: Eerdmans Publishing.

Synan, V. (2001). *Century of the Holy Spirit: 100 years of Pentecostal and charismatic Christianity.* Nashville, TN: Thomas Nelson Publishers.

Yeakly, F. (Ed.). (1988). *The discipling dilemma.* Nashville, TN: Gospel Advocate.

Slain (Resting) in the Spirit

See Ecstasy; Experience, Theology of; Laughter, Holy; Ordinances and Sacraments

Slavery

Slavery is the practice of involuntary servitude in which a person is held in bondage and must perform compulsory acts and services for the benefit of another. A slave is one who is the property of another, and thus is regarded as greatly socially inferior. Although Pentecostalism was born in the United States about forty years after the Civil War ended, the effects of U.S. slavery and racism were evident among the early Pentecostals. In 1948 the United Nations formally condemned the institution of slavery in Article 4 of the Universal Declaration of Human Rights and worldwide. Despite this declaration, the practice of slavery continues in countries like Sudan and Mauritania in the twenty-first century.

History

Slavery has been practiced for thousands of years and has been used and justified variously by countless groups. Evidence exists of slavery in ancient Mesopotamia, Egypt, the Indus River Valley, China, Crete, Rome, and many other civilizations. The Old Testament details the Hebrews' bondage in ancient Egypt, as well as the practice of slavery among the Hebrews themselves. Other known instances of ancient slavery occurred in the Babylonian and Assyrian empires, both of which frequently enslaved peoples they conquered in war. Situated on the eastern shores of the Mediterranean, the seafaring Phoenicians are among the earliest known slave traders; with their vessels, they took possession of people from other parts of the world to trade or sell to other civilizations they encountered.

The Hebrew Bible

The Hebrew Bible mostly mentions slavery in the context of Israelite law, especially in Exodus 21, Leviticus 25, and Deuteronomy 15. Much of the Old Testament occurs against the backdrop of the Hebrews' bondage under the Egyptian pharaoh. As slaves the Hebrews were forced to work making bricks. They were not able to make their own decisions and could not relocate of their own free will; at times they were restricted by law in the number of children they could have. According to the biblical narrative, the infant Moses was hidden in a basket by the edge of the Nile because of this restriction. Moses was then adopted and became an Egyptian prince, later freeing the Hebrews by leading them out of Egypt.

The Hebrews themselves practiced a type of slavery in which a Hebrew could sell himself or his family to another Hebrew or an outsider. However, as outlined in Exodus 21, the law concerning slaves stipulated that male slaves were to be set free every fifty years, on what was known as the Jubilee year. Other places that the Hebrew Bible mentions servitude or slavery include Jeremiah 2:14, Isaiah 24:2, and Job 3:19.

Ancient Greece and Rome

The Greeks and Romans, like most ancient peoples, considered slavery a normal part of life, not an immoral practice. Greek and Roman slaves were drawn from among conquered armies, criminals, children sold by their parents, or captives bought from pirates. Many Romans owned slaves, who performed jobs designated almost exclusively for them. Slaves did most of the manual labor for these societies, and their numbers were enormous; in Athens around 400 BCE, slaves made up a third of the total population, and Roman slaves were about as abundant.

The New Testament

According to one writer, "a typical Pauline congregation would include both slave owners and slaves" (Meeks 1983, 437). An important pericope in the New Testament concerning slavery is Paul's injunction in Ephesians 6:5 (NIV), "Slaves, obey your earthly masters with respect and fear, and with sincerity of heart, just as you would obey Christ." Although some see this verse as a troubling endorsement of slavery, Paul's injunction must be considered in its entirety; verse 9 reads, for example, "And masters, treat your slaves in the same way....He who is both their Master and yours is in heaven, and there is no favoritism with him." Considering how the zeitgeist in the ancient world was disposed toward slavery, this statement is revolutionary. Another key verse from the Pauline corpus related to slavery is Galatians 3:28: "There is neither Jew nor Greek, slave nor free, male nor female, for you are all one in Christ Jesus."

The British Empire

The British slave trade with East Africa began in the mid-sixteenth century and proved lucrative; slaves became known in the British trade system as "black gold" or "black ivory." Over a century later, Britain wrested a virtual monopoly of the trans-Atlantic slave trade from Spain and France in the 1713 Treaty of Utrecht. Parliament outlawed the trade in 1807, and in 1838 slavery was abolished throughout the British Empire.

The New World

Slavery began in the Americas in 1500 when the Portuguese started trading for slaves with the kingdom of Congo in Africa. In 1505, the Portuguese attacked several African ports to gain control of the slave trade, and it became a key part of the Portuguese economy. The labor-intensive sugar plantations of both Spanish and Portuguese colonies in the Americas became major slave buyers. In what is now the United States, the large tobacco plantations in the South had huge numbers of slaves from the colonial era up until the Civil War. The North had slaves as well, but slavery was less important to the northern economy, and the practice there died away relatively early.

The conditions under which most slaves in the Americas lived were horrific. Field slaves were normally treated harshly, often working from sunrise to sunset; they were subject to being whipped for infractions real or perceived, and they received minimal food and water. They were routinely housed like livestock, with many rows of people in one small room or shelter. House slaves usually received better treatment, working as they did in a domestic environment. They might sleep in the owner's house, work fewer hours, and be given more privileges; but they were nonetheless subject to the caprices of the owner's family.

Where voting rights existed in the Americas, slaves were certainly not entitled to them. While some slaves married, many were not allowed to marry, being considered mere chattel by their owners. Because of this abusive treatment, many slaves revolted or tried to run away; but revolts usually resulted in even more brutal treatment for all slaves. The issue of slavery in the United States proved intractable, and it was not resolved until the bloody Civil War, during which President Abraham Lincoln signed the Emancipation Proclamation, freeing all slaves effective January 1, 1863.

Arguments For and Against Slavery

Many religious leaders in the United States, notably starting in the nineteenth century, condemned the practice of slavery as infringing on God-given rights. One influential antislavery group was the American Anti-Slavery Society, founded in Philadelphia in 1833 by William Lloyd Garrison. Ardent advocates of abolishing slavery, like Garrison, came to be known as *abolitionists*, and as the debate over slavery became increasingly bitter and divisive, abolitionists were sometimes attacked by raging proslavery mobs. Most abolitionists were also Christians, and they opposed slavery on Christian grounds.

Many southern slave owners were Christians too, and they defended slavery through their interpretation of a number of biblical texts, including Leviticus

25:44–46, 1 Corinthians 7:20–24, and 1 Peter 2:18–21 But they relied most heavily on the "curse of Ham" that appears in Genesis. According to Genesis 9, Ham, the father of Canaan, walked into the tent of his father, Noah, and accidentally "saw his father's nakedness" (9:22). Unlike Ham, his brothers Shem and Japheth covered their father while not looking at him. When Noah awoke and learned that Ham had seen him naked, he cursed his grandson, Ham's son Canaan, in the following terms: "Cursed be Canaan! The lowest of slaves will he be to his brothers" (Genesis 9:25). This passage forms the basis of the biblical defense of slavery that became widespread among white, slave-owning southerners and clergy members who regarded Africans as the cursed descendents of Ham.

Wesleyan Revivals

John Wesley (1703–1791), the Methodist revival leader, and his brother Charles (1707–1788) were graduates from Oxford who desired to go to the Americas. They sailed to Georgia, and once there they started preaching and going to church, but they did not come into contact with slaves. In July of 1736, John went with his brother to Charleston, South Carolina, and encountered his first slaves. He was appalled at the practice of slavery and immediately started to gain converts. Wesley's mission trip lasted only two years, but he left the legacy of the Methodist Church. Methodists, like the Quakers before them, were strongly against the slave trade and slavery. The Holiness tradition of Wesley and others served as a precursor to the twentieth-century Pentecostal movement.

Early Pentecostalism and Racism

Though it developed after the end of slavery in the United States, early Pentecostalism was shaped in part by slavery's racist legacy. Charles F. Parham (1873–1929) and William J. Seymour (1870–1922) are commonly regarded as cofounders of the Pentecostal movement. Although both men were very important to the historical and theological beginnings of Pentecostalism, they had different understandings of what the Pentecost of the Bible meant. On one hand, Parham was a racist with connections to the Ku Klux Klan; he contended that a hierarchy of races existed, with Anglo-Saxons as the superior race. On the other hand, Seymour was an African-American whose parents were former slaves. Parham, Seymour's spiritual father, first gained widespread recognition in 1901 when one of his students, Agnes Ozman, spoke in tongues. Although Parham did

preach to interracial audiences, he did not allow African-Americans or other minorities into his classrooms. However, Seymour was permitted to sit outside Parham's classroom with the door partially open. The alliance between Parham and Seymour would be short lived. Upon acknowledging baptism in the Spirit, Seymour moved to Los Angeles to pastor a Holiness church at 312 Azusa Street.

The events that began at the Azusa Street Mission in 1906 were unheralded: under Seymour's leadership, what came to be known as the Azusa Street Revival became the cradle of Pentecostalism. The revival united a disparate group of believers from across the country, regardless of race or profession, gender or socioeconomic status, or clerical or lay status. The rediscovered phenomenon of speaking in tongues was interpreted as a sign that the Last Days and the imminent return of Jesus were at hand. But because of its mingling of various races—including whites, blacks, Hispanics, and Asians—and its "noisy spiritualism," Parham lashed out against the Azusa Street Revival. The elders at Azusa Street rebuked Parham, and his relationship with Seymour was permanently severed. After several rumors and a notorious scandal, Parham's ministry substantially declined, and he later died in relative obscurity.

Seymour too faded into obscurity starting in 1912, because of what some regarded as his own prejudice against whites, coupled with the fact that he recanted his position on glossolalia as the initial evidence of one's baptism in the Holy Spirit. Over 3,400 African-Americans were lynched during Seymour's lifetime, and many white Pentecostals viewed Pentecostalism's modest and interracial beginnings as a disgrace. Some, such as Parham's biographer James R. Goff, tried to deny Seymour's early impact on Pentecostalism, claiming Parham alone was the movement's founder. Despite Parham's popularity, many early white Pentecostals opposed racism.

Continuing Legacy

Early white Pentecostal leaders like Parham reflected much of the racist ideology of many of their southern constituents in the early twentieth century. Some have even remarked that the "original sin" of Pentecostalism is racism. Much of the separation still remains between black Pentecostals, such as those who formed the Church of God in Christ, and white Pentecostals, such as the founders of the Assemblies of God. However, important gestures of racial reconciliation have been made, including the watershed 1994 conference known as the "Memphis Miracle." Although many Pentecostals were critical of the second and third wave of charismatics from other denominations, many seek continuing racial reconciliation and are calling for a greater emphasis on an ecumenical theology such as Seymour promoted.

Although Pentecostalism surfaced in the United States after the time of slavery, slavery has remained a problem in the third world, where Pentecostalism has emerged as a major movement. It is difficult to calculate the number of people in slavery today; some experts estimate there are over 20 million around the world, including the victims of such phenomena as the slavery of boys and girls in the Southeast Asian sex market. Modern Pentecostals are opposed to all forms of slavery.

JOHN R. KENNEDY AND CRAIG MOORE

See also Azusa Street Revival; Memphis Miracle; Race Relations

Further Reading

Anderson, A. H., & Hollenweger, W. J. (1999). *Pentecostals after a century*. Sheffield, UK: Sheffield Academic Press.

Boles, J. B. (Ed.). (1988). *Masters and slaves in the house of the Lord: Race and religion in the American South, 1740–1870*. Lexington: University Press of Kentucky.

DuBois, W. E. B. (1903). *The souls of black folks*. Chicago: A.C. McClurg.

Hoffmann, R. J., & Larue, G. A. (Eds.). (1988). *Biblical versus secular ethics: The conflict*. Buffalo, NY: Prometheus Books.

Hollenweger, W. J. (1997). *Pentecostalism*. Peabody, MA: Hendrickson.

Johnson, P. (1987). *A history of Christianity*. New York: Atheneum.

McKivigan, J. R. (1984). *The war against proslavery religion: Abolitionism and the northern churches, 1830–1865*. Ithaca, NY: Cornell University Press.

Meeks, W. (1983). *The first urban Christians: The social world of the Apostle Paul*. New Haven, CT: Yale University Press.

Miers, S., & Roberts, R. (1988). *The end of slavery in Africa*. Madison: University of Wisconsin Press.

Peterson, T. V. (1978). *Ham and Japheth: The mystical world of whites in the antebellum South*. Metuchen, NJ: Scarecrow Press.

Smith, W. T. (1986). *John Wesley and slavery*. Nashville, TN: Abingdon Press.

Synan, V. (1997). *The Holiness-Pentecostal tradition* (2nd ed.). Grand Rapids, MI: Eerdmans.

Wacker, G. (2001). *Heaven below*. Cambridge, MA: Harvard University Press.

Webb, W. J. (2001). *Slaves, women, and homosexuals: Exploring the hermeneutics of cultural analysis*. Downers Grove, IL: Intervarsity Press.

Wiedemann, T. (1981). *Greek and Roman slavery*. Baltimore: Johns Hopkins University Press.

Social Taboos

The Old Testament nation of Israel was distinguished from other nations by the presence of God. The Jews were to be visibly different from their neighbors, and that difference (expressed, for example, in not having a king, and by the covenant sign of circumcision and their care for widows and orphans in their community) was to be their testimony.

Similarly, the New Testament teaches that Christians are to be distinguished by the indwelling presence of God's Holy Spirit, and that that spiritual reality should be evidenced by a lifestyle that distinguishes followers of Jesus from others. The Apostle Paul writes, "Live as children of light…and find out what pleases the Lord. Have nothing to do with the fruitless deeds of darkness" (Ephesians 5:8–10, NIV).

The Old Testament emphasizes Israel's complete separation from her idolatrous neighbors (intermarriage, for example, is specifically forbidden). The New Testament is nuanced, enjoining Christians to be *in the* world but not *of* the world, but the early church was characterized by moral and social standards so distinctive that its members were known as followers of "the Way" (Acts 9:2). It was their positive lifestyle, even in the face of severe persecution, that helped them Christianize the Roman Empire.

Lifestyle Challenge

How to live out the New Testament standard of holiness and unworldliness in a manner pleasing to the Lord has been the subject of debate in the church for two thousand years. Unfortunately social norms have sometimes been proclaimed with as much fervor as the Gospel message itself, leaving some people confused about what is essential for salvation.

Christian taboos or social norms may express moral standards that are beyond argument for those who accept basic biblical tenets as normative. For example, most Pentecostals and charismatics strongly oppose nontherapeutic abortions, are unsympathetic to the gay and lesbian agenda, and endorse traditional views on sex and marriage. And the Ten Commandments leave little room for debate about the sinful nature of murder and adultery. When Paul argues that those who are sexually immoral should be ostracized from the church (1 Corinthians 5:11), he does not need to provide a detailed catalog of behaviors that qualify as sexually immoral. He can assume that members of the Christian community understand what he means.

Post-Apostolic Social Norms

Once the original apostles passed from the scene, however, the church was left to develop appropriate responses to new social challenges. In the first chapter of his treatise *On Shows*, Tertullian (c. 160–c. 230), a prominent Carthaginian lawyer, theologian, and Christian apologist, addresses a contemporary social challenge in these words: "The pleasures of the public shows…are not consistent with true religion and true obedience to the true God." Tertullian acknowledges there is no specific scriptural injunction dealing with the sin of public entertainments and instead resorts to a version of the familiar slippery-slope argument—that is, he attempts to show a cause and effect connection between something that may not be wrong in itself but may lead to a sin. He applied immutable biblical principles to a challenging contemporary situation in order to discern appropriate behavioral norms for Christians. (A similar logic has led many Pentecostals to conclude that movies, dances, country fairs, and similar pleasures should be off-limits to Christians.)

The church in every age and culture since then has prescribed and proscribed the behavior of its adherents. Generally there is an earnest attempt to apply timeless scriptural principles to changing circumstances—in contemporary language, to ask "What would Jesus do?" But not all situations are reducible to unambiguous moral propositions. For example, while drunkenness is clearly condemned by Scripture, it is not clear that Christians must forgo alcohol entirely. Pentecostals generally call for total abstinence, basing their argument on 1 Corinthians 6:19 ("Your body is a temple of the Holy Spirit") and on Romans 14:21 ("It is better not to… drink wine or to do anything else that will cause your brother to fall"), and appealing to the harmful effects of alcohol abuse. Many charismatics, however, arrive at a somewhat different conclusion based on their understanding that abstinence is not mandated in Scripture, that Jesus (Luke 7:33) and Paul (1 Timothy 5:23) may have taken wine, and that Jesus' first recorded miracle was to replenish the failing wine supply at a community wedding (John 2). The argument in rebuttal that the "best wine" (John 2:10) was actually unfermented and therefore nonalcoholic is generally not supported by a closer look at the word *oinos*, the common Greek term used here and elsewhere for wine.

The New Testament Greek word *ekklēsia*, translated as "church," literally means "the called-out ones." Christians were to stand apart from contemporary society—their visible social distinctiveness would testify to their invisible standing as saved and Spirit-filled believers. Paul's letters frequently detail worldly behavior to be avoided by Christians (for example, Ephesians 4:25–5:18) and challenge Christians to separate themselves from those who habitually engage in such activities (2 Corinthians 6:14–18) on the principle that righteousness and wickedness (worldliness) have nothing in common.

Taboos Against Women

Social taboos across the ages seem to have paid disproportionate attention to placing restrictions on women in the church. Female clothing and personal adornment have been the subject of considerable social regulation. For instance, Paul makes some seemingly unequivocal statements about head coverings and hair length for women (1 Corinthians 11:3–16) (but many Western charismatics argue that they simply reflect Paul's own culture and values).

Paul also appears to restrict women's freedom to exercise certain ministries in the church (1 Timothy 2:12). This is the subject of considerable contemporary debate within some Christian circles, and traditional Roman Catholic, Orthodox, and Fundamentalist denominations are the most resistant to equal or expanded roles for women in the ministry. Mainline Protestant denominations have generally opened their ministerial ranks to women in recent years, but they still lag behind many Pentecostals and charismatics in this area. Historian Vinson Synan says, "Pentecostals by the middle of the twentieth century had more women preachers than any other branch of Christianity" (Synan 1997, 190).

This is due in part to the early influence of powerful Pentecostal preachers like Maria Woodworth-Etter and Aimee Semple McPherson. It is also due in large measure to the Pentecostal and charismatic belief that evidence of the Holy Spirit's gifting for ministry remains the primary qualification for ordination. The Azusa Street outpouring was notable for the unrestricted role accorded women preachers; and women such as Phoebe Palmer and Hannah Whitall Smith were prominent leaders and teachers in the nineteenth century Holiness antecedents to Pentecostalism. However, Synan also identifies two major Pentecostal churches that continue to restrict women's roles: the Church of God and the Church of God in Christ. And he notes further that there has been evidence of a declining trend in appointing women as senior pastors, in the Assemblies of God, for example.

Among non-Pentecostal charismatics, there is usually theological openness to women functioning equally in ministry. In practice, however, churches are frequently headed by pastoring couples, and it is usual for the husband to exercise the dominant role in this partnership. There are notable exceptions, though, and the general pattern is that recognized gifting or anointing, not gender, is the determining factor.

Taboos in Early Pentecostalism

Church historian Grant Wacker describes the wide variety of customs found in Pentecostal churches over the past century—many of which he categorizes as "culture-denying." He acknowledges "the standard evangelical taboos on dancing, gambling, cards, tobacco, alcohol, and immodest apparel. [Because there was no argument to be made in favor of such practices among committed Christians] believers focused their scorn...on a wide range of recreational activities that most evangelicals—not to mention most respectable men and women of the age—considered the innocent pleasures of God's creation" (Wacker 2001, 122). Wacker goes on to list specific taboos, beginning with forbidden foods and drinks. They included:

> [M]eat in general and shellfish and hog products in particular, soft drinks in general and Coca Cola in particular....taboos also included coffee, tea, ice cream, chewing gum and, of course, medicinal drugs. [Other taboos included] idle talk, foolish talk, jesting with friends, and telling tall tales.... [and] the reading of novels, newspapers, and comic books. (Wacker 2001, 122)

Modesty and plainness in clothing was enjoined for all Christians, and the meaning of these standards for women and girls was explained in detail.

Wacker points out that at one time or another there were specific Pentecostal proscriptions against:

> (in alphabetical order) bands, baseball, boating, bowling, circuses, fire-works, football, loitering, parades, skating, valentines, and zoos. They also denounced amusement parks, beach parties, big dinners, chatting on the telephone, Christmas trees, crossword puzzles, home movies, ice cream socials, kissing bees, scenic railroad trips, and visiting rela-

tives and going on automobile joyrides on Sundays. (Wacker 2001, 128)

Synan adds:

> [T]he Pentecostal Holiness Church held that it was sinful for a member to wear a necktie or attend a county fair. Most [Pentecostal] groups also denounced lodges, political parties, and labor unions as "instruments of Satan." Buying life insurance was frowned upon...[and] persons who took medicines or visited doctors were considered weak or even completely lost. (Synan 1997, 81)

The rejection of men's neckties, which were considered frivolous adornments, was also enthusiastically endorsed in the late 1890s by the Fire-Baptized Holiness Church. Its founder, B. H. Irwin, declared "that they would 'rather have a rattlesnake around their necks than a tie'" (Synan 1997, 58).

Since early Pentecostalism drew most of its followers from the social and economic fringes of society, there was a natural tendency to associate material poverty with spirituality and to be mistrustful of higher education (apart from basic Bible training). Healing evangelist Oral Roberts was a Pentecostal before his controversial decision in 1968 to leave the Pentecostal Holiness Church for Methodism. His father was a Pentecostal preacher and the family grew up poor. Typical of his day, Roberts "had been nurtured in a belief system that insisted 'you had to be poor to be a Christian'" (Harrell 1985, 66). And when as a young pastor Roberts decided to attend a university part time to improve his educational qualifications, he felt he had to do so "secretly at first, for fear his 'church board' would fire him" (Harrell 1985, 60). Indeed, "many of his pentecostal friends were distraught by his new interest in education—'they thought it would make me disbelieve the Bible or weaken my witness'" (Harrell 1985, 61).

"Instant" Sanctification

After nearly two centuries of debate in Wesleyan and Holiness circles about the nature of sanctification, Pentecostalism emerged to emphasize (at least initially) the immediate efficacy of the Spirit's work of sanctification (to be followed by the experience of Spirit-baptism). Because of the instantaneous nature of these encounters with the Spirit, a separate and identifiable lifestyle was expected to be the immediate result in a Spirit-filled Pentecostal believer. Thus, Pentecostals often identified lifestyle as the second physical evidence of Spirit-baptism (after tongues, the initial physical evidence). In reality, however, it was not always that straightforward. Many Pentecostals struggled in silence with moral and lifestyle issues, and many Pentecostal leaders have fallen in recent years (continuing a regrettable pattern of hypocrisy and moral failure stretching back to the earliest days of the movement—as caricatured, for example, in John Steinbeck's 1939 classic, *The Grapes of Wrath,* or James Baldwin's 1952 novel, *Go Tell It on the Mountain*).

Not Conformed…Transformed!

While it is true that both Pentecostals and charismatics practice "lifestyle evangelism," the witness of Pentecostals has historically emphasized separation from the world and challenged the faithful to "come out" (2 Corinthians 6:17). Charismatics, by contrast, have tended to emphasize engagement and attractiveness in lifestyle as their witness to the world, expressing their Christian distinctiveness more in terms of what Christians do differently than in terms of what they don't do. This created some points of social tension between the two major branches of what might otherwise be thought of as the Pentecostal-Charismatic continuum.

Today, however, there is general recognition that the church was pursuing a somewhat misplaced focus by devoting so much energy to identifying unacceptable practices. Contemporary Pentecostals and charismatics increasingly believe that Christians should be distinguished by the positive fruit of the Holy Spirit in their lives (Galatians 5:22)—especially by their love and unity—more than by what they avoid. Romans 12:2 is a call to "transformation," and personal and social transformation is increasingly seen as the fruit of an intentional application of the Great Commission's mandate to "make disciples" (Matthew 28:19). Toronto Blessing revival leader John Arnott notes that before the Spirit came in power to their church in 1994, it was "as though the devil was too big and the Lord was too small. Our solutions…centered around dealing with the darkness…instead of receiving more of the Holy Spirit's presence and power" (1995, 57).

Many Pentecostals and charismatics today agree that a distinctive Christian lifestyle should be a positive expression that consciously commends the Christ life to worldly onlookers. And at the same time, they are increasingly willing to amend a contradictory and negative history of vesting the relative and transient with the trappings of immutability in the realm of social and behavioral taboos.

DONALD R. KANTEL

See also Asceticism; Ethics (Social, Sexual); Society, Pentecostal Attitudes toward; Women

Further Reading

Arnott, J. (1995). *The Father's blessing.* Lake Mary, FL: Creation House.

Goff, J. R., Jr., & Wacker, G. (Eds.). (2002). *Portraits of a generation: Early Pentecostal leaders.* Fayetteville: University of Arkansas Press.

Harrell, D. E., Jr. (1985). *Oral Roberts: An American life.* Bloomington: Indiana University Press.

Latourette, K. S. (1953). *A history of Christianity.* New York: Harper & Row.

MacMullen, R. (1984). *Christianizing the Roman Empire (A.D. 100–400).* New Haven, CT: Yale University Press.

Poloma, M. M. (2003). *Main street mystics: The Toronto Blessing and reviving Pentecostalism.* Walnut Creek, CA: AltaMira Press.

Synan, V. (1997). *The Holiness-Pentecostal tradition: Charismatic movements in the twentieth century* (2nd ed.). Grand Rapids, MI: Eerdmans.

Wacker, G. (2001). *Heaven below: Pentecostals and American culture.* Cambridge, MA: Harvard University Press.

Social Transformation

Culture and social institutions are always changing, but the rate of change varies from place to place and time to time. The changes are sometimes intended and at other times unintended.

Traditional Societies

Social change began thousands of years ago with the domestication of plants and animals that transformed nomadic tribes to sedentary societies. In these early societies, extended families living in rural settings explained and managed life through religious beliefs and rituals. Childbearing rates were high and life expectancy was short. Education was informal, change was slow, and elders were revered for their knowledge of how to deal with daily life. Sociologists Ferdinand Toennies (1855–1936) and Emile Durkheim (1858–1917) defined traditional societies as groups of people held together by strong community ties and shared beliefs and values. Sociologist Max Weber (1864–1920) emphasized the extent to which traditional societies were driven by past practices.

Modern Societies

Societies shift from traditional to modern culture when manufacturing replaces agriculture as the primary form of income generation. Bureaucracies emerge in response to the capitalist need to manage production; laborers must be controlled to enhance efficiency, calculate costs, and predict profits. In England and the United States, the shift from agriculture to manufacturing saw traditional values replaced by secular-rationalist practices. Science replaced religion as the source of truth.

Toennies associated modernity with the loss of human community as industrialization and the rise of cities reduced the family to a nuclear unit comprised of mother, father, and children. Durkheim, however, argued that the loss of human connection through shared traditions and values was countered by a new human interdependence fostered by an increasingly specialized division of labor. Unlike Durkheim, Weber anticipated a dehumanized existence brought into being by the bureaucratic rules and regulations necessary to manage mass society.

Toennies, Durkheim, and Weber all viewed modern societies as industrial economies governed by bureaucracies, and most sociologist agree that modernization includes the decline of small cohesive communities, the growth of individual rights, a growth in the range of beliefs, and a shift from backward to forward thinking. Philosopher and historian Karl Marx (1818–1883) associated the growth of modern capitalist societies with persistent class inequality.

Social Movements

Pentecostalism is generally viewed as a reaction against the social changes associated with modernity. When social institutions fail to keep up with social changes, social movements often emerge to fill in the gaps of unmet social needs and to quell associated unrest. As a new social movement, Pentecostalism connects the everyday with the political; advanced satellite technology links structural struggles with challenges to identity and meaning. British sociologist Anthony Giddens (1990) identified a conflict between the transcendent aspects of tradition and the reflexivity of the end of the modern era. Pentecostalism addresses this conflict by holding the two in tension; it demands adherence to Biblical truth and offers recovery of the individual through accountability and worship.

Pentecostalism has been described as both anti-modern and pro-modern. Biblical inerrancy, the virgin birth, and the divinity of Jesus, all of which have been challenged by science since the Enlightenment, are vigorously defended by Pentecostals; the Pentecostal belief in baptism in the Holy Spirit mitigates the effects of the rationalization of modern life.

However, the passivity and the focus on evangelism over social action are more likely to leave military dictatorships in place than to promote political restructuring through citizen revolts. Interest in democratic practices may be subdued by religious orientation to authority. The four Asian tigers, Hong Kong, Taiwan, South Korea, and Singapore, noteworthy for the successes of capitalist modernization and Pentecostal growth, are reluctant to embrace democratic political structures. Among Pentecostals, evangelism has always taken precedence over social concerns. They claim that only the Second Coming of Christ can repair the fallen world, leaving believers to reach out to sinners.

Syncretism

Pentecostalism combines elements of traditional native beliefs and practices with Christian Evangelical theology. Debate continues over whether Pentecostalism, as a branch of Fundamentalism, is a reaction against modernity or whether it actually embraces social change, including the global shift to a capitalist economy. Pentecostal congregations join local religious practices with Western Protestant evangelical views of truth, good and evil, salvation, and healing. Spiritual gifts—healing and prophetic powers, supernaturally revealed knowledge of congregational and individual needs, faith, wisdom, miracles, spiritual discernment, and interpretation of tongues—are employed by believers to build congregations, restoring what Weber called "the enchantment of traditional society." Pentecostalism's lack of formal tradition, its resistance to formal theological education, its reliance on lay leadership, and its acknowledgement of the spirit world and the miraculous promote innovation at the local level.

Pentecostalism in the United States grew fastest during the first half of the twentieth century, which also saw the decline of the farming and laboring classes. Urbanization brought an increase in male violence associated with a rise in unemployment and a decrease in paternal authority. The Pentecostal family ethic, which emerged from similar circumstances in developing nations, attempted to stem this rise in male violence and to increase paternal authority. Current Latin American holiness constraints on appearance and activities resemble those that shaped early U.S. Pentecostalism: There are, for example, prohibitions against alcohol, tobacco, extramarital sex, contraception, and television.

In late capitalism, the loss of personal identity attributed to scientific objectivity is recognized and challenged. Recovering traditional belief in divine transcendence, Pentecostalism promotes submission to secular authority while recognizing individual identity and personal accountability through worship, prayer, testimony, and giving. Submitting to the authority of preachers and prophets prepares members for participation in bureaucratic capitalist structures, and emphasizing a personal relationship with Christ promotes the kind of individualism fundamental to developing a materialist society. The immediate gratification of glossolalia may promote participation in a marketplace that promises immediate gratification in exchange for money. In short, the authoritarianism of Pentecostalism encourages adherents to desire material success.

Pentecostalism increasingly functions as an international community, offering familiar forms of worship and prayer that can comfort migrants in a strange land. Religious symbols and not national flags mark the spaces where immigrants find security. A Pentecostal is first and foremost a member of the Kingdom of God, and afterward a citizen of one or more nations.

The imposition of capitalist interests on local life through instantaneous technological communication leaves the self fragile and fractured. Communicated through personal narrative, neighbor to neighbor, Pentecostalism promises resolution and not just survival of the social changes.

Postmodern Crises

In the United States, the end of modernity is marked by a widespread rejection of science's claim of objectivity. The emergence of multiple family structures, competing religious beliefs, and challenges to the objectivity claims of science indicates a period of transition. Members of culturally marginalized groups, including Pentecostals, have called for the recovery of the personal in a bureaucratized world.

Twentieth-century attempts to recover the individual in a rationalized world, even as capitalism increases its reliance on individual material consumption, include the civil rights movement of the 1960s that sought full citizenship for social minorities—women, blacks, and gays. The 1980s brought renewed opposition to these social movements, along with claims that the middle-class post–Industrial Revolution nuclear family was universal and timeless. The shift from manufacturing to service capitalism paralleled the longing of some professionals for supportive wives devoted to raising their children.

Early stages of Pentecostal movements saw women as preachers, evangelists, and healers. However, after groups institutionalized, they reasserted male authority over women, although they continued to recognize the value of women's much-needed gratis labor. The Latin American Pentecostal movement has been credited with drawing men away from drinking and partying, conserving their resources on behalf of supporting their families, and giving them in exchange supreme household authority. To professionals and other members of the middle class who rejected the liberal, secular view of education, family, and religion, Pentecostalism offered both a return to moral confidence and a renewal of gendered familial roles. The growth of Pentecostalism among American elites suggests that a malaise was addressed by the taking up of patriarchal family values. Even the contemporary North American Pentecostal movement recognizes the father as the authority and the mother as the nurturer, and cedes control of sexuality to the church.

The globalization of capitalism has broadened the gap between the bourgeoisie and the proletariat who are still suffering from the shift from agriculture to manufacturing and information technology. It is in the twentieth-century context of the challenges to modernity in the West, and the confluence of traditional, modern, and postmodern practices in the southern hemisphere, that Pentecostalism has experienced its extraordinary growth.

Social Activism

The emerging global culture is raising the tension between traditional and rational beliefs and practices. The highest rates of growth of both Pentecostalism and capitalism are in countries shifting from agrarian to manufacturing economies. For individuals forced to abandon home and religion, modernization produces substantial losses, and some observers argue that Pentecostalism grows out of loss. Pentecostal congregations cut their members off from urban society through a commitment to an ascetic lifestyle resulting in social passivity. Concurrently, emphasizing the equality of all believers and absent priests, conversion emphasizes personal responsibility and autonomy.

Pentecostalism also has liberating potential, as constant power struggles within and between Latin American congregations promote the development of leadership and social competence. Some point out that the ways in which Latin American Pentecostalism strikes a balance between fatalism and individual autonomy. Evil is personified as Satan, God works through the believer to overcome evil, and the brothers and sisters of the congregation constitute a social network able to meet the economic challenges of daily life.

Modernization dislocates the individual member of a traditional community because the emerging global culture now offers the resources necessary for survival. For those bereft of community and culture, a choice between passive acceptance and active rejection of the global culture looms large. To these, Pentecostalism brings the Western cultural values of work, education, and personal ethics along with a traditional belief in the presence of the divine in the everyday world. Traditional healers become preachers and evangelists. Dancing and drumming become the backdrop for speaking in tongues. Some have attributed the power of Pentecostalism to merge with indigenous practices to its recognition of evil personified in Satan.

Women comprise two-thirds of the membership of Pentecostalism in Latin America. Why do women help develop, promote, and maintain religious movements that advocate a return to patriarchal power and authority? One possible answer is that Pentecostal congregations offer women the hope of limiting their husbands' extracurricular activities, including sexual promiscuity and recreational drug use, because Pentecostals oppose extramarital sex and the use of alcohol, and advocate that fathers take up the roles of spiritual leader and financial supporter of their families. Offering clear distinctions between the forces of evil and good, Pentecostalism admonishes men to remain the final authority on all family matters; both men and women are encouraged to put family needs over their own personal desires.

As a movement energized by mobilizing the laity, Pentecostalism encourages women to assume substantial roles in building the congregation, especially through testimony, prayer, and evangelism. Because women comprise the majority of Pentecostals and the movement's growth rests on the efforts of the laity, it is not surprising that women have found substantial opportunities to participate. However, in nearly all the southern-hemisphere cultures, men fill the highest leadership position, that of pastor.

In effect, Pentecostalism serves the interests of the social status quo; it works to stymie social change through individual commitment to justice. However, while Pentecostal congregations appear to be apolitical, their efforts to build ties between neighboring and international congregations ultimately influence life in their communities.

While global modernization brings conditions of extreme poverty to developing nations, Pentecostalism offers hope for salvation in the afterlife. With the end of the world imminent (the return of Christ for believers, to be followed by the great Tribulation when sinners must endure Armageddon), each believer is challenged to bring family, friends, co-workers, and strangers into the fold through a salvation experience. However, the preeminence of salvation over social justice does not preclude efforts to address social inequalities. Generally congregations respond to the survival needs of their members and to their larger communities, and middle class Pentecostals, who are more likely to participate in government, have been drawing Pentecostals into efforts to bring about policy changes that will reflect Bible-based beliefs and values.

Elaine R. Cleeton

See also America, Latin; Capitalism; Race Relations; Society, Pentecostal Attitudes toward; Women

Further Reading

Berger, P. (1977). *Facing up to modernity: Excursions in society, politics, and religion.* New York: Basic Books.

Brouwer, S., Gifford, P., & Rose, S. (1996). *Exporting the American gospel: Global Christian fundamentalism.* New York: Routledge.

Burdick, J. (1993). *Looking for God in Brazil: The progressive Catholic Church in urban Brazil's religious arena.* Berkeley: University of California Press.

Corten, A. (1999). *Pentecostalism in Brazil: Emotion of the poor and theological romanticism.* New York: St. Martin's Press.

Cox, H. (1995). *Fire from heaven: The rise of Pentecostal spirituality and the reshaping of religion in the twenty-first century.* Boston: Addison-Wesley.

Durkheim, E. (1964). *The division of labor in society.* New York: Free Press. (Original work published 1893)

Giddens, A. (1990), *The consequences of modernity.* Cambridge, UK: Polity Press.

Kamsteeg, F. (1998). *Prophetic Pentecostalism in Chile: A case study on religion and development policy.* Lanham, MD: Scarecrow Press.

Lalive d'Epinay, C. (1969). *Haven of the masses: A study of the Pentecostal movement in Chile.* London: Lutterworth Press.

Lehmann, D. (1996). *Struggle for the spirit: Religious transformation and popular culture in Brazil and Latin America.* Cambridge, UK: Polity Press.

Levitt, P. (2003). "You know, Abraham was really the first immigrant": Religion and transnational migration. *International Migration Review, 37,* 847–874.

Mariz, C. (1994). *Coping with Poverty: Pentecostals and Christian base communities in Brazil.* Philadelphia: Temple University Press.

Marx, K. (1990). *Capital*. London: Penguin Classics. (Original work published 1867–1895)

Maxwell, O. (1999). Historicizing Christian independency: The southern African Pentecostal movement c. 1908–60. *The Journal of African History, 40*, 243–276.

Mellor, P. (1993). Reflexive traditions: Anthony Giddens, high modernity, and the contours of contemporary religiosity. *Religious Studies, 29*, 111–129.

Menzies, W. (1971). *Anointed to serve*. Springfield, MO: Gospel Publishing.

Riesebrodt, M., & Chong, K. (1999). Fundamentalisms and patriarchal gender politics. *Journal of Women's History, 10*, 55–79.

Smith, D. (1999). *Writing the social*. Toronto, Canada: University of Toronto Press.

Synan, V. (1971). *The Holiness-Pentecostal movement in the United States*. Grand Rapids, MI: Eerdmans.

Toennies, F. (1963). *Community and society (Gemeinschaft und gesellschaft)*. New York: Harper & Row. (Original work published 1877)

Vasquez, M. (1999). Toward a new agenda for the study of religion in the Americas. *Journal of Interamerican Studies and World Affairs, 41*, 1–26.

Weber, M. (1976). The Protestant ethic and the spirit of capitalism. New York: Scribner's. (Original work published 1905)

Willems, E. (1967). *Followers of the new faith: Culture, change, and the rise of Protestantism in Brazil and Chile*. Nashville, TN: Vanderbilt University Press.

Society, Pentecostal Attitudes toward

Pentecostalism began in the United States, but it quickly spread around the world and is truly a global movement, encompassing many different languages, cultures, nations, ethnic groups, and social classes. The greatest growth and the largest membership are in the so-called "two-thirds" or developing world. Because of this diversity, it is risky to generalize about the movement.

The theology of Pentecostalism comes from two sources. First, there are formal statements from the headquarters of denominations, largely produced by conservative, educated, middle-class Americans. Second, there are "grass-roots" interpretations of theology by congregations of people from many different cultures, with different worldviews, in many different social, economic, and political situations. Most but not all of these congregations are made up of poor to working-class people in the two-thirds world. There is bound to be a gap between the formal theology of denominations and the informal theology of practice.

"The World"

Pentecostals are very critical of society or "the world," which is said to be unjust and a place of sin and suffering. The Assemblies of God, for example, decry "declining morals and ethics" and identifies "unhealthy magazines, books, music, radio, television, cable programming, movies, videos, computer software, and the Internet" as "corrupting influences." Society is too materialistic and "obsessed with sex and permissiveness." This "depraved and evil world" is held to be controlled by Satan and his demons (http://ag.org/top/beliefs/christian_character/charctr_00_list.cfm).

The message of suffering can be very convincing to poor, uneducated, unskilled and therefore marginal and powerless people trying to survive on next to nothing in the slums of third-world cities, where crime, violence, hunger, death, disease, and drugs are ever present. Moreover, globalization may be increasing their poverty and marginalization at the same time as the well-off are prospering from it.

End Times

Pentecostal sermons routinely denounce the lax morals and corruption of the world, identified as signs of the End Times, the Last Days before the Rapture, the Reign of the Beast, the Tribulation, and the Second Coming of Christ.

The movement focuses on personal rather than social transformation. The mission of Pentecostalism is to prepare *individuals* for this Second Coming. The true "Christian" will be spared the Apocalypse. The first step towards salvation is to reject the world by abandoning sin: acknowledge sin, repent, resist worldly temptations, and lead a sin-free life. This sanctification will open the way to baptism in the Spirit, assuring that you will not be cast into eternal damnation in the Lake of Fire, as well as to gifts of the Spirit, such as speaking in tongues and healing. It should also bring many "blessings" into your life, hopefully health and well-being and possibly (and ironically) prosperity and worldly success.

Saints

Pentecostals draw sharp boundaries between the godly and ungodly or worldly, the saved and unsaved, saints and sinners. They are urged to separate from the world into communities of Christians, to denounce the world, and to define themselves in opposition to it.

The church offers shelter from the world. The congregation is often a close-knit, spiritual family, an alternative community, especially for women. Pentecostals set themselves apart from others in order to avoid sin and lead a life in accord with the Bible. In addition, the Assemblies of God states that Christians should "comfort one another" and "bear one another's burden."

The church is a temporary refuge, however. Pentecostals live and work in the world, but they try to live as Christians, every moment of every day. In addition, they are enjoined to go out into the world and bring others to Christ.

Godliness

Pentecostals not only set themselves apart from the world, they set themselves above it, and can act superior, elitist, and self-righteous. They are taught to live by a higher code than society, a strict code that requires considerable self-discipline. They sometimes consider themselves to be the only true Christians.

Pentecostals are expected to dress modestly so as to avoid calling attention to their body or person. They are often opposed to social dancing, considering it to be seductive and enticing. A woman should wear a simple dress and hairdo. Jewelry, perfume, and cosmetics are discouraged if not forbidden. Needless to say, Pentecostals are opposed to the current youth fashions of tattooing and body piercing.

Smoking, drinking, swearing, and gambling are of course proscribed, as are fornication, cohabitation, adultery, and homosexuality. The Assemblies of God also warns against horoscopes and astrology, the New Age Movement, yoga, and the martial arts, apparently because of their association with Eastern religions.

Christians are supposed to be hard working, responsible, disciplined, reliable, obedient, humble, honest, sober, simple, and thrifty. They should marry and live their life in faithful monogamy with the husband as provider and the wife as housekeeper and mother.

As Robert Mapes Anderson (1979, 239) has noted, Pentecostals are "ideal workers and citizens" for industrial capitalism, which is ironic, considering their ideological rejection of society. It is hard to say the extent to which these values lead to material progress, but it is logical to assume they can.

Attitudes toward Social Institutions

Pentecostals are very critical of society, but they also passively support it, being generally law-abiding and submissive to government authority. Although Pentecostal churches are generally apolitical, Pentecostals tend to support conservative politics and are almost always opposed to the left. Their chief concern is with moral issues, not social programs, and action is limited largely to taking a moral position. In Brazil and some other Latin American nations, Pentecostal churches have supported candidates, and Pentecostal leaders have been elected to office, but the main effect has been to enhance the respectability of their churches.

Pentecostals are mistrustful of social institutions. Often lacking in education, they may be anti-intellectual, placing their trust in the Spirit more than science and formal education. They are suspicious of wealth and corporations and opposed to unions, fraternal lodges, and political parties. One of the main targets of their criticism is other religions, particularly Christian denominations and, most of all, the Catholic Church, which are dismissed as "nominal churches" presumably lacking in true faith and morals.

Social Action

The majority of Pentecostals are on the margins of the industrial world and have a very small stake in it, being poor, uneducated, and unskilled. Not surprisingly, they are critical and rejecting of the status quo, but do nothing to change it. What could they do about it? The only power they have is spiritual, and that is what they rely on.

The future is already known to Pentecostals. The sad state of society is simply proof to them that we are indeed in the Last Days, and Jesus is coming soon to change the world. There will be much weeping and wailing, as well as rejoicing. In this worldview, it is hopeless and pointless to try and change society.

Pentecostal churches are opposed to the "social gospel" of good works and social reform practiced by so-called mainline Christians. They seek to save souls, one at a time, not society. Congregations limit themselves to activities that help their members and encourage others to join. This has been a very successful approach, in terms of attracting converts, more successful than the social gospel has been for mainline churches.

One area in which Pentecostals have made some social progress is in the empowerment of women. There is generally a greater percentage of women in Pentecostal churches than in other Christian churches. Indeed, it could be argued that it is a feminized (albeit not feminist) religion. The concerns of women are strongly voiced and women play many influential roles in a congregation. They testify, speak in tongues, prophesy, preach, and sometime serve as the head of Pentecostal churches, assuming more leadership roles than is generally the case in other Christian churches, but still defer to men.

Solving Problems

Pentecostal and neocharismatic Christianity is of considerable social importance in organizing poor and relatively powerless people into strong communities that offer a sense of order and direction, hope, enthusiasm, and social support. It can be crucial to individuals by providing a framework of meaning that can stabilize lives, bolster identity and self-respect, and give strength to face the very real struggles of getting through the week.

More specifically, Pentecostalism addresses many problems in living, including illness, drug and alcohol addiction, abusive relationships, desertion, raising children, unemployment, immigration, family and other interpersonal conflicts, lack of self-esteem, and depression. These problems are most prevalent among the poor and marginalized, who have fewer resources to deal with them. People come to Pentecostal churches in search of a miracle that will turn their lives around, and in many cases they find it.

This "palliative" benefit of Pentecostalism is widely acknowledged, but the movement is often criticized for failing to pursue a social agenda that would remedy the problems of the poor as a class. The problem is that the poor do not really control the conditions of their existence, and they do not have the means to change them. They are victims of a global political economy that is dislocating people from their homes, families, and livelihoods, and increasing the gap between rich and poor social classes and nation-states.

WILLIAM WEDENOJA

See also Ethics (Social, Sexual); Social Taboos

Further Reading

Anderson, R. M. (1979). The rejection of the world. In *Visions of the disinherited: The making of American Pentecostalism* (pp. 195–222). New York: Oxford University Press.

Assemblies of God. http://ag.org/top/beliefs

Chestnut, R. A. (1997). *Born again in Brazil: The Pentecostal boom and the pathogens of poverty*. New Brunswick, NJ: Rutgers University Press.

Robbins, J. (2004). The globalization of Pentecostal and charismatic Christianity. *Annual Review of Anthropology, 33*, 117–143.

Shaull, R. & Cesar, W. (2000). *Pentecostalism and the future of the Christian churches: Promises, limitations, challenges*. Grand Rapids, MI: William B. Eerdmans Publishing Company.

Toulis, N. R. (1997). *Believing identity: Pentecostalism and the mediation of Jamaican ethnicity and gender in England*. Oxford, UK: Berg.

Wedenoja, W. (1988). The origins of Revival, a Creole religion in Jamaica. In *Culture and Christianity: The dialectics of transformation* (pp. 91–116). New York: Greenwood.

Tears, Gift of

The "gift of tears" is not widely recognized among classical Pentecostals because it is not listed in any biblical gift list (e.g., Isaiah 11:2, Romans 5:1–5, 12:6–8; 1 Corinthians 12–14; Ephesians 4:8, 11–12, 2 Timothy 1:6–7). However, the gift of tears and compunction (remorse or contrition for sins) is highly regarded among peoples of the Spirit in both Eastern Christian traditions and in the Roman Catholic Church. Athanasius of Alexandria (c. 296–373) is among the first to describe tears as a divine gift (*Patrologiae Graecae* 28:272).

Eastern Christians frequently experienced a gift of tears. In the fourth century, Ephrem of Syria (c. 306–373) is said to have received from the Holy Spirit the gift of tears in such abundance that it was as natural for him to weep as it was for others to breathe. Evagrius Ponticus (d. 399) writes that "Before all else, pray to be given tears, that weeping may soften the savage hardness which is in your soul . . ." (*De Oratione*, Bamberger 1978, 6).

In his *Ladder of Divine Ascent,* John Climacus (c. 579–c. 649) indicates three levels of tears. The first, "contranatural tears," arise when our will is thwarted, leading to tears of anger, jealousy, or frustration. "Natural tears" arise in response to emotional and physical suffering, including tears of grief, pain, or compassion. Mystics speak of a third category, "supernatural" or spiritual tears, those that are commonly called "the gift of tears" (Climacus 1982, 139).

Spiritual tears are a renewal of baptism. Here tears express mourning for sins, but also joy at reconciliation with God. In this context, John Climacus is reminded of the prodigal son who sheds tears of sorrow for his sins—tears that turn to tears of joy at the love with which he is welcomed back home. The gift of tears is a charism conferred only upon some, whereas on others God bestows some different gift that takes its place.

John Climacus' younger contemporary, Isaac of Ninevah (seventh century), experienced an outpouring of tears frequently and in abundance. He reports that the sweetness of tears is such that, when deprived of them, the Christian realizes his deprived state and what has been taken from him. Tears of penitence and joy open the eyes so that they can perceive things supernaturally. Such tears mark the transition, the frontier between the present age and the age to come. Tears leading to ecstasy are beyond the reach of human language. Instead, Isaac offers examples of those who have received this elevated grace. In contrast to John Climacus, Isaac teaches that the gift of tears and the resulting ecstasy are available to all who seek them.

Of all Eastern Christians, Symeon the New Theologian (949–1022) placed the strongest emphasis on personally experiencing God. At about the age of twenty, Symeon described himself as a vain individual during the day, while at night he prostrated himself in prayer, pouring out tears in abundance as he prayed to God for mercy and spiritual vision. He received his first vision of God as light, his eyes were flooded with tears and his heart with inexpressible joy. Throughout his life, Symeon continued to experience visions of divine light, abundant tears, and an awareness of the indwelling Holy Spirit. For him, the greatest blasphemy was to deny that the Christian can experience God in his own day in just as great a measure as had the prophets and apostles of Bible times.

Based on his experiences, Symeon taught that a Christian must not only be baptized in water, but also with the Holy Spirit. This second spiritual baptism leads to a greater awareness of the Spirit's activity within, as well as a strong conscious awareness of living in Jesus Christ as Lord and Savior through the illumination of the Holy Spirit. No one receives this second baptism without the purification of many tears. Tears cleanse the heart and make it into a temple or resting place of the divine Spirit.

According to Symeon, those who come of age and receive the Spirit also receive a gift of tears, for tears initially shed in repentance ultimately give way to tears that flow in response to divine radiance. This gift is not given only to a few chosen persons, but to all who seriously enter into the spiritual battle of weeping for their sins.

Catherine of Siena (c. 1347–1380), among the most important Western Christian mystics, writes specifically on the gift of tears. In *The Dialogue* she attempts to convey all she has learned about the ways of God. Sections 88–92 deal with tears at various levels, leading eventually to "perfect tears," those of joy as the soul is united with God. She also writes of "tears of fire," tears wept by the Holy Spirit within each person who offers God the "fragrance of holy desire and constant humble prayer" (Karasig 1990).

Ignatius of Loyola is one of the most influential Roman Catholics who experienced a gift of tears. For Ignatius, tears signified the presence of the Holy Spirit. We are told that if he did not shed tears three times during Mass, he felt deprived. The first part of his *Spiritual Diary* mentions his tears about 175 times. In the second part, every single entry mentions tears. Often sobbing accompanied tears, with an intensity that frequently prevented him from speaking. Eventually, his doctor ordered him not to surrender to tears because it was destroying his eyesight and overall health.

In a letter (20 September 1548) addressed to Francis Borgia, who had been given to penitential excesses, Ignatius suggests that Francis seek God's greatest and "most holy gifts such as the gift of tears" (1991, 348). Five years later, in a letter to Father Nicholas Gaudano, Ignatius concedes that the gift of tears should not be asked for unconditionally, and that it is not a good gift for everyone.

While modern Pentecostals and charismatics have not emphasized the gift of tears, it is not unknown among individuals in modern renewal. For example, Michael Harper reports that David Wilkerson (of *The Cross and the Switchblade* fame) in the 1960s addressed ministers in London solely on the subject of the gift of tears, urging them to be prayed over to receive this gift. In June 2000, the well-known senior Kansas City prophet, Paul Cain, called for the same gifting, insisting that it is essential to spiritual renewal.

STANLEY M. BURGESS

See also Baptism in the Holy Spirit; Charismata; Gifts of the Spirit; Orthodoxy, Eastern

Further Reading

Bamberger, J. E. (Trans.). (1978). *Evagrius Ponticus: The traktikos. Chapters on prayer*. Kalamzoo, MI: Cistercian Publications.

Burgess, S. (1989). *The Holy Spirit: Eastern Christian traditions*. Peabody, MA: Hendrickson.

Cain, P. (2000, June). The gift of tears. *Revival Times Magazine Online*. Retrieved from http://www.revivaltimes.org/index.php/360.htm

Climacus, J. (1982). *The ladder of divine ascent*. New York: Paulist Press.

deCatanzaro, C. J. (Ed.). (1980). Symeon the new theologian: The discourses. *Classics of Western Spirituality*. New York: Paulist Press.

Divarkar, P. (Trans.). (1991). Ignatius of Loyola: Spiritual exercises and selected works. *Classics of Western Spirituality*. New York: Paulist Press.

Egan, H. (1987). *Ignatius Loyola the mystic*. Collegeville, MN: Liturgical Press.

Gillet, L. (1937). The gift of tears. *Sorbornost* n.s. 12:5–10.

Hausherr, P. I. (1944). Penthos. La doctrine de la compunction dans l'Orient chritien. *Orientalia Christiana Analecta* 13.

Ignatius of Loyola. (1991). *Spiritual exercises and selected works*. New York: Paulist Press.

Karasig, M. A. (1990). Affective self-transcendence in Catherine of Siena's beatitude of tears. *Review for Religious, 49*, 418–429.

Lot-Borodine, M. (1936). Le Mystere du "don des larmes" dans l'Orient chrétien. *Vie Spirituelle*, Vol. 18, Supplement: 65–110.

Noffke, S. (Trans.). (1990). Catherine of Siena: The dialogue. *Classics of Western Spirituality*. New York: Paulist Press.

Ware, K. (1980). The orthodox experience of repentance. *Sorbornost* ii: 26–28.

Wensinck, A. J. (1923). *Mystical treatises of Isaac of Nineveh*. Amsterdam: Verhandelingen der K. Akademies.

Third Wave

See Neocharismatic Movements

Trinitarianism

Trinitarianism (or the doctrine of the Holy Trinity) in many ways stands at the very center of theology for Pentecostals and charismatics, due to their distinctive interest in the formulation and articulation of a theology of the Holy Spirit (known more technically as pneumatology or a theology of the "third article").

Pentecostals and charismatics generally hold to the doctrine of the Trinity as passed down by Christian tradition and expressed in the Nicene and Athanasian Creeds of the fourth and fifth centuries, which affirms both unity (Greek: *homoousios*) and distinction within the Godhead, while "neither confounding the Persons: nor dividing the Substance" (Athanasian Creed). In short, there is one God who eternally exists in three distinct, yet coequal, persons: Father, Son, and Holy Spirit. These are not three modes or expressions of God, nor are they three gods. It is also important to note that the concept of *person* as completely individual does not fully carry over here, in light of the complete unity of God. However, the capacity for relationship, especially love, among the persons of the Godhead is affirmed. Creedal formulas notwithstanding, it is generally agreed that there remains an element of mystery that must be affirmed in order to maintain the biblical tension between God as one and three, without leaning too far to one side (i.e., modalism) or the other (i.e., three gods). This is seen as the mystery of the Holy Trinity.

A Balanced Trinitarianism

While Pentecostals and charismatics have often been depicted as emphasizing the Holy Spirit over the other members of the Holy Trinity, Pentecostal-Charismatic doctrine may actually be more Christocentric, as seen in the doctrinal statements of most Pentecostal denominations, including those of the Assemblies of God, Church of God (Cleveland, Tennessee), Church of God in Christ, and the International Pentecostal Holiness Church. At the foundation of the doctrine of the International Church of the Foursquare Gospel is an understanding of Jesus, the Son, as Savior, Holy Spirit Baptizer, Healer, and Soon-Coming King. Thus, Pentecostals have tended to integrate their distinctive understanding of the Holy Spirit with a robust Christology. During the 1980s and 1990s, a renewed interest in the Fatherhood of God emerged, perhaps in part as a response to the generation coming of age that experienced deep inner wounds as a result of the progressive disinte-gration of the traditional family in Western society observed since the 1960s and 1970s.

Pentecostal and Charismatic Trinitarian Scholarship

Historically, Pentecostals and charismatics have, by and large, doubted the value, truth, and validity of philosophical and intellectual argumentation. As a result, they chose to base most of their doctrines upon biblical proof-texts and the teachings of the specific traditions from which they came. Pentecostal and charismatic Trinitarianism is no exception to this practice. However, with the proliferation of Pentecostal and charismatic Bible colleges and seminaries, a new generation of scholars is coming of age that has sought to engage the theologies of other traditions. As a result, Pentecostal and charismatic scholars have developed an interest in articulating a "Renewal Theology" that truly reflects the distinctive contribution of the Pentecostal-Charismatic tradition to all facets of the Christian theological conversation. This is pushing Pentecostal and charismatic theologians to reexamine all areas of Christian doctrine, asking how the role of the Holy Spirit may have been neglected in their formation and how new studies in this area may inform these doctrines, not just those historically attributed to Pentecostals and charismatics (e.g., baptism in the Holy Spirit and the gift of tongues). They see their rediscovery of the importance of the Holy Spirit, in many ways, as a recovery of Trinitarian theology, which has the potential to contribute substantially to the revitalization of all theological categories. Also, the question of the relationship between the immanent Trinity (the eternal relationship within the Godhead) and the economic Trinity (the expression of that relationship as God interacts with creation) that has occupied the attention of theologians from other traditions has begun to capture the interest of Pentecostal and charismatic scholars as well, particularly as they seek to articulate pneumatological concerns. As it finds expression in other theological categories, Pentecostal-Charismatic Trinitarianism has taken on a profoundly relational character.

Trinitarian Christology

The emergence of Spirit-Christology is one example of how Pentecostal-Charismatic Trinitarianism is affecting other theological categories. In this area, the concern is the development of a Christology that recognizes the important contribution of the Holy Spirit to the life and mission of Jesus Christ, particularly in His humanity.

St. Augustine on the Holy Spirit

Lo, now the Trinity appears unto me in a glass darkly, which is Thou my God, because Thou, O Father, in Him Who is the Beginning of our wisdom, Which is Thy Wisdom, born of Thyself, equal unto Thee and coeternal, that is, in Thy Son, createdst heaven and earth. Much now have we said of the Heaven of heavens, and of the earth invisible and without form, and of the darksome deep, in reference to the wandering instability of its spiritual deformity, unless it had been converted unto Him, from Whom it had its then degree of life, and by His enlightening became a beauteous life, and the heaven of that heaven, which was afterwards set between water and water. And under the name of God, I now held the Father, who made these things, and under the name of Beginning, the Son, in whom He made these things; and believing, as I did, my God as the Trinity, I searched further in His holy words, and to, Thy Spirit moved upon the waters. Behold the Trinity, my God, Father, and Son, and Holy Ghost, Creator of all creation.

Source: St. Augustine. (n.d.) *The confessions* (E. B. Pusey, Trans.). Retrieved September 20, 2004, from http://etext.library.adelaide.edu.au/a/augustine/a92c/a92c.html

Some within this discussion advocate a replacement of the traditional word (*logos*) Christology of the West with a more pneumatological Christology, while others seek simply to enrich the current understanding of Christology with what is seen as a more Trinitarian perspective. This theological debate also includes many who are outside of the Pentecostal and charismatic stream, which is evidence of how Pentecostal-Charismatic Trinitarianism is both affecting and being influenced by the broader theological conversation. Further, a reopening of the discussion concerning the relationship between Christ and the Holy Spirit may hold promise for future progress in resolving the *filioque* debate—the question of whether the Holy Spirit proceeds from just the Father or from both the Father and the Son, which contributed to the Great Schism of 1054, the first major split in Christianity between the West (Rome) and the East (Constantinople).

Doctrine of Justification

Ecumenical discussions have necessitated a revisiting of the doctrine of justification, which has opened the door for discussion of how this doctrine may also be informed by Pentecostal-Charismatic Trinitarianism. More specifically, it has been proposed that the traditional Protestant forensic view of justification be expanded to include the work of the Holy Spirit in bringing about justice and righteousness through new creation. The work of the Spirit in the death and resurrection of Jesus is identified as the same power that produces rebirth and transformation in the believer and in the whole of creation. This transformed life is lived out by the believer now through the empowering of the Holy Spirit, producing a breaking in of the Kingdom of God manifested in deliverance of the oppressed and pointing to a future eschatological realization of redemptive justice for all creation by God. Such a view holds much in common with Eastern Orthodox soteriology (doctrine of salvation) and so, again, presents the possibility for Pentecostal-Charismatic Trinitarianism contributing to the increase of unity in the Church.

Trinitarian Ecclesiology

Scholars are also asking how the ecclesiology (doctrine of the church) may be enriched by consideration of the Pentecostal-Charismatic doctrine of the Trinity. While the church has traditionally been seen as the gathering of believers in Christ, it is now also being seen as the community of the Spirit. In this model, the Holy Spirit continues to manifest the liberating effects of the redemptive work of Christ by His ministry in and through the Christian community as it is active in the world. Thus, identification of the role of the Spirit in the formulation of a Trinitarian ecclesiology fosters a renewed sense of mission for the church and further strengthens its sense of connection to the life and mission of its Lord, Jesus Christ, the Son.

Oneness Pentecostals

The debate between Trinitarian Pentecostals and Oneness Pentecostals (those who deny the Trinity), which resulted in the departure of Oneness Pentecostals from the Assemblies of God in 1916 and the formation of several Oneness denominations, continues today. Efforts to promote unity have mainly consisted of proposals, albeit of varying complexity, to ignore differences rather than to actually resolve the theological tensions and so, have largely been unsuccessful. However, relational progress has been made as evidenced by increased openness to dialogue on both sides and fellowship in scholastic contexts.

Challenges for the Future

The future appears to hold many challenging opportunities for Pentecostal and charismatic Trinitarianism as the movement seeks to develop and define its distinctive theology in the quest to articulate its contributions to the broader Christian theological conversation and the Christian tradition. While exploring the many possibilities for applying a fully-orbed Trinitarian theology to traditional theological categories and enriching these with its own distinctive contributions, the next generation of scholars also needs to carefully guard the rich biblical theological heritage with which it has been entrusted by preceding generations. As it does so, the continued presence of the Oneness stream of Pentecostalism serves as a reminder to Trinitarian Pentecostals and charismatics not to neglect the unity of God while further exploring the implications of its Trinitarian theology.

DAVID J. MASSEY

See also Christology; Doctrine, Development of; Holy Spirit; Oneness Theology

Further Reading

Bernard, D. K. (1983). *The oneness of God.* Hazelwood, MO: Word Aflame Press.

Bradbury, R. (1999). To be worshipped in unity: Towards a Trinitarian confession of renewal. *Stimulus: The New Zealand Journal of Christian Thought and Practice, 7,* 27–30.

Clanton, A. L., & Clanton, C. (1995). *United we stand.* Hazelwood, MO: Pentecostal Publishing House.

Del Colle, R. (1993). Spirit-Christology: Dogmatic foundations for Pentecostal-Charismatic spirituality. *Journal of Pentecostal Theology, 3,* 91–112.

Del Colle, R. (1997). Oneness and trinity: A preliminary proposal for dialogue with Oneness Pentecostalism. *Journal of Pentecostal Theology, 10,* 85–110.

Dunn, J. D. G. (1982). Was Christianity a monotheistic faith from the beginning? *Scottish Journal of Theology, 35*(4), 303–336.

Kärkkäinen, V. (2001). David's sling: The promise and the problem of Pentecostal theology today; A response to D. Lyle Dabney. *Pneuma: The Journal of the Society for Pentecostal Studies, 23*(1), 147–152.

Kärkkäinen, V. (2000). Trinity as communion in the spirit: Koinonia, trinity, and filioque in the Roman Catholic-Pentecostal dialogue. *Pneuma: The Journal of the Society for Pentecostal Studies, 22*(2), 209–230.

Macchia, F. (2001). Justification through new creation: The Holy Spirit and the doctrine by which the church stands or falls. *Theology Today, 58,* 202–217.

Menzies, W. M. (1971). *Anointed to serve: The story of the Assemblies of God.* Springfield, MO: Gospel Publishing House.

Smail, Thomas (1980). *The forgotten father.* Grand Rapids, MI: Wm. B. Eerdmans Publishing Co.

Synan, V. (1997). *The Holiness-Pentecostal tradition: Charismatic movements in the twentieth century.* Grand Rapids, MI: Wm. B. Eerdmans Publishing Co.

Volf, M., & Lee, M. (2001). The spirit and the church. In B. E. Hinze & D. L. Dabney (Eds.), *Advents of the Spirit.* Milwaukee, WI: Marquette University Press.

Yong, A. (1997). Oneness and the trinity: The theological and ecumenical implications of creation *ex nihilo* for an intra-Pentecostal dispute. *Pneuma: The Journal of the Society for Pentecostal Studies, 19*(1), 81–107.

V

Visions and Dreams

On the Day of Pentecost, Peter preaches that Joel's prophecy is fulfilled—that "your young men shall see *visions* and your old men shall *dream dreams*" (Acts 2:17, author's translation; italics added). Since the Pentecostal and charismatic churches stand in the same stream of divine revelation, it is important to understand the biblical witness concerning dreams and visions to affirm the reality of such experiences and also to evaluate such modes of divine revelation that have characterized the sweep of church history.

Terms

Biblical revelation includes accounts of divine communication through the means of dreams and visions, which are sometimes called "visions of the night." The term for "dream" (*chalom*—Hebrew; *enupnion*—Greek) covers ordinary dreams when people fall asleep, that is, a sequence of thoughts, stories, images, and emotions occurring during sleep, and revelatory dreams in which God communicates certain information to people during their natural sleep. A special term for a "deep sleep" (*tardema*—Hebrew) occurs in contexts of a "revelatory sleep," which is God-induced and leads to a communication of the divine purpose (for example, Genesis 2:21—Adam; Genesis 15:12—Abraham). The term "vision" (*chazon*—Hebrew; *horama, optasia*—Greek) refers to "supernatural visions, whether the person in the vision be asleep or awake" (Bauer, Arndt, Danker and Gingrich 1957, 480). It is an event in which God permits a person to see an event or truth that normally is hidden from human beings. Other related expressions are used in such revelatory contexts, for example, "seer," "prophet," "see," "mystery," "the word of the Lord came to...," and "one able to interpret dreams." Taken as a whole, the different modes of revelation express the truth that God chooses to reveal things about Himself and His will, which are otherwise inaccessible to human beings.

Fluidity of Terms

There is a certain ambiguity and fluidity in the use of the terms related to dreams and visions. For example, the following texts express the parallelism between the related terms "seer" and "prophet" in an alternating manner:

> Formerly in Israel, when a man went to inquire of God, he said, "Come, let us go to the *seer*"; for he who is now called a *prophet* was formerly called a *seer* (1 Samuel 9:9).

> And when David arose in the morning, the word of the Lord came to the *prophet* Gad, David's *seer*, saying...(2 Samuel 24:11).

> Now the acts of King David, from first to last, are written in the Chronicles of Samuel the *seer*, and in the Chronicles of Nathan the *prophet*, and in the history of Gad the *seer* (1 Chronicles 29:29) (italics added).

These texts reflect an alternation of terms in which a person is recognized as both a prophet and seer. The terms "dream" and "vision" coalesce with other such expressions: "The words of Amos...which he saw..." (Amos 1:1); "The vision of Isaiah, which he saw..."

453

(Isaiah 1:1); "The Vision of Obadiah" (Obadiah 1:1). The formula "Thus says the Lord" can also refer to a vision that a prophet saw. When we encounter narratives of extraordinary forms of divine communication, there are elements of human subjectivity and variety, which are reflected in the fluidity of terms, which cannot be neatly classified. For example, a vision is usually regarded as a supernatural appearance that conveys a divine revelation, which usually affects only the recipient in a mystical form. However, the term can also include an objective appearance that affects people other than the immediate recipient, for example, the appearance of the risen Jesus to Paul on the Damascus road affects not only Paul but the travelers on the Damascus road. Similarly, on the Mount of Transfiguration there are three disciples who simultaneously witness Jesus' transfiguration along with the appearance of Moses and Elijah, the enveloping cloud, and the voice from the cloud.

Purposes of Visions and Dreams

There are at least five different purposes of visions and dreams in Scripture, which are described as follows.

To Announce Divine Promises

In Genesis, Abraham experiences a "deep sleep," in which God reaffirms His covenant-keeping role in the making of Abraham into a great nation as innumerable as the stars. This visionary promise is sealed by the unilateral passing of God ("a smoking firepot with a blazing torch," 15:17) between the halved pieces of the ram, goat, dove, and young pigeon (verse 9). In a later narrative, Abraham lies about his wife Sarah, who is then taken into Abimelech's harem and God speaks to Abimelech in a dream. In order to protect the divine promise, God tells him that he is a dead man. Included in the dialogue, within the dream, Abimelech argues for his ignorance and innocence. Ironically, although Abraham has put his wife, marriage, and divine promise into jeopardy, God still regards Abraham as a "prophet," gifted with effectual prayer for healing, "for he is a prophet, and he will pray for you, and you shall live" (20:7).

Abraham's grandson Jacob experiences a dream of a ladder that spans earth and heaven with angels ascending and descending on it (Genesis 28:11). The event contains the promise of land and innumerable descendents, the presence of God, a source of blessing for all the families of earth, and God's protection (28: 13–16). When Jacob awakes, he expresses fear, pours oil upon the rock, which had been his pillow, and makes a vow of loyalty to God, who has made these promises to

him and renames the city from Luz to Bethel ("house of God"). Later in the Jacob cycle of stories, he experiences a dream, by which he would be able to multiply his flocks through special divine knowledge as to whether the flocks would be striped, spotted, or mottled (31:11–13); it appears to be a divinely inspired means of building his flocks, since Laban has previously cheated Jacob. Later in his life, Jacob experiences another vision of the night (Genesis 46:2), in which God reassures him of the rightness of his planned trip to see his long-lost son Joseph and that he will return, with Joseph closing his eyes at death. The promise is reaffirmed that Jacob/Israel will become a great nation (46:3).

The Joseph cycle of stories is introduced by Joseph's dreams, which he proudly announces to his family, thereby creating a fearful jealousy among his brothers (Genesis 37:5–10). This initial dream prepares Joseph for the later series of dreams (baker and butler in Genesis 40) in Egypt, which allows Joseph to interpret Pharaoh's dreams (Genesis 41). This gift of interpreting dreams thus leads to Joseph's important role in Egypt and the rise of the Hebrew nation under his leadership. Dreams are the means by which the divine promises are realized and represent divine interventions against obstacles that stand in the way of their realization.

In the New Testament, dreams are critical in the infancy stories in Matthew's Gospel for the preservation of Jesus, the Son of Promise. Through dreams, Joseph is informed of the source of Mary's pregnancy (Matthew 1:20); the astrologers are warned to return to their homeland another way (2:12); Joseph is directed to Egypt to avoid Herod's wrath, warned about settling in Judea, and redirected to Galilee (2:13). The emphasis of the dreams is directly related to the protection of the Christ child from a premature death.

Special Revelations at Critical Moments

In Israel's history, different individuals experienced dreams or visions at critical points, which served to guide, encourage, and assist the people of God at a new juncture. Solomon, for example, receives a dream, which sets the course for divine affirmation of his kingship—at the time in which he is faced with the new challenge of kingship. When he is offered a divine "blank check," Solomon asks for "a heart to hear and to govern" God's people and to discern between good and evil (1 Kings 3:9). Since he has not asked for selfish things such as long life, riches, or the lives of his enemies, God promises that these things will be his as well (cf. 2 Chronicles 1:3–12). During the time of the postexilic rebuilding of the temple and the cult,

Zechariah is given a series of night visions (Zechariah 1:7–6:8), which directly speak to the priesthood, the civic leader Zerubbabel, and the workers engaged in the task of rebuilding the temple. In the New Testament, Jesus experiences a vision—the transfiguration, which prepares Him for the upcoming Passion ("exodus") in Jerusalem (Luke 9:31). Paul's vision, coupled with Ananias's vision and ministry to Paul (Acts 9:10), serves to launch the Gentile mission. This "vision" belongs to a series of ecstatic or visionary experiences, which further direct Paul in his mission; they serve an apologetic role for Paul in defending the Gentile mission (Acts 9:12; 16:9–10; 18:9–11; 22:17–21; 23:11; 27:23–24). Peter substantiates the gift of tongues with interpretation on the Day of Pentecost through Joel's prophecy, that "your young men shall see visions and your old men shall dream dreams" (Acts 2:28). With the advent of the outpoured Spirit, Joel's prophecy is fulfilled in the events of Pentecost (Acts 2:17). The coming of the Spirit on Pentecost marks the new era, the birthday of the church, in which God would communicate in new and fresh ways to the people of God.

Genre of the Prophetic Call

Many of the prophetic calls are expressed through the mode of a dream or vision and include such elements as God's self-revelation, human fear, announcement of mission, human objections, overcoming of human objections, and confirming signs (Moses in Exodus 3; Isaiah in Isaiah 6; Jeremiah in Jeremiah 1; Ezekiel in Ezekiel 1; Amos in Amos 1:1–2; 3:8; 7:10–14; Paul in Acts 9; Galatians 1:11–17; 1 Corinthians 15:1–11; 1 Timothy 1:12–17; John in Revelation 1:9–20). Some of these inaugural visions include word plays (puns), which are impossible to render into English, for example, Jeremiah 1:11–12: "And the word of the Lord came to me, saying, 'Jeremiah, what do you see?' And I said, 'I see a rod of almond' (*shaqedh*). Then the Lord said to me, 'You have seen well, for I am watching (*shoqedh*) over my word to perform it.'" One of the earliest prophetic calls occurs with the young Samuel in Eli's tent, who does not yet know God or the word of the Lord (1 Samuel 3:7) at a time when there was no "frequent vision" (1 Samuel 3:1), and his first words to the aged Eli are the announcement of judgment upon Eli and his sons for sins that he knew about and failed to correct.

Revealing the Future through Interpretation

There are occasions when God speaks of the future to a king through the mode of a dream, which also needs

one gifted with the interpretation of dreams (*pithron*—Hebrew), frequently used in the Joseph cycle of stories in Genesis 40–41. In Daniel 2–5, the prophet Daniel is used in numerous instances with several kings to interpret the significance of the dreams. In Daniel, the term "vision" is used thirty times; and Ezekiel frequently uses the term to refer to "an appearance of the likeness of the glory of Yahweh" (Ezekiel 1:28). The subject matter of the vision includes Israel's present idolatry in the Temple (Ezekiel 8:1–9:8), Israel's future (Ezekiel 9:9–10), the return after the exile (11:16–11), and an idealized picture of Israel's future reorganization (Ezekiel 40–48). The affirmation is made again that God is the author of the interpretation of dreams (Genesis 40:8; 41:16; Daniel 2:19–23, 28). A similar thought is present in the book of Revelation, which is an unveiling of the divine purposes within human history—"to his servant John, who testifies to everything he saw—that is, the word of God and the testimony of Jesus Christ" (Revelation 1:2). The coupling of dreams with a needed interpretation parallels the public use of tongues, which also need interpretation.

False and Misleading Visions and Dreams

In Israel, when prophecy had fallen into such disrepute, the genuine prophets castigated the false prophets and their lying visions and dreams. Jeremiah spoke strongly against those who "prophesy lying dreams...and who lead my people astray by their lies and their recklessness" (Jeremiah 23:32), and linked them with "prophets, diviners, dreamers, your soothsayers or your sorcerers" (Jeremiah 27:9). These are persons who lead the people of God away from undivided service to Yahweh. Zechariah's words are equally harsh: "For the teraphim [idols] utter nonsense, and the diviners see lies; the dreamers tell false dreams, and give empty consolations. Therefore the people wander like sheep; they are afflicted for want of a shepherd" (Zechariah 10:2). A similar warning is expressed in Deuteronomy 13:1–5.

Further Reflections

In both the Old Testament and New Testament, the mystery of the "vision" and "dream" is really the "mystery" of the Divine Word—the disclosure of God and His purposes, His interaction with humanity by way of encouragement, perspective, warning, insight, and undoing of a human choice that threatens His divine promise. He continues to communicate with people through prayer, worship, community events, personal experience, tragedy, and misfortune. In the

Pentecostal and charismatic tradition, the community is aware that God also communicates through extraordinary modes of revelation through dreams and visions that lie outside of normal human experience. Such experiences cannot be manufactured or forced. People can only position themselves in the state of readiness as with Samuel, "Speak Lord for thy servant hears" (1 Samuel 3:10).

J. LYLE STORY

See also Charismata; Covenant; Dispensationalism; Gifts of the Spirit; Prophecy

Further Reading

Balz, H. (1972). Hupnos. *Theological dictionary of the New Testament* (Vol. 5, pp. 545–556). Grand Rapids, MI: Eerdmans.

Bauer, W., Arndt, W.F., Danker, F., & Gingrich, F.W. (1957). Horama. *A Greek-English lexicon of the New Testament and other early Christian literature* (pp. 580–581). Chicago: University of Chicago Press.

Black, D. A. (1992). Dreams. *Dictionary of Jesus and the Gospels* (pp. 199–200). Downers Grove, IL: InterVarsity.

Budd, P. J. (1971). Dream. *New international dictionary of New Testament theology* (Vol. 1, pp. 511–513). Grand Rapids, MI: Zondervan.

Camery-Hogart, J. (1993). Visions, ecstatic experience. *Dictionary of Paul and his letters* (pp. 963–965). Downers Grove, IL: InterVarsity Press.

Mendelsohn, I. (1962). Dream. *The interpreter's dictionary of the Bible* (Vol. R–Z, p. 868). Nashville, TN: Abingdon.

Michaelis, W. (1970). Horama. *Theological dictionary of the New Testament* (Vol. 5, pp. 371–372). Grand Rapids, MI: Eerdmans.

Napier, B. D. (1962). Vision. *The interpreter's dictionary of the Bible* (Vol. R–Z, p. 791). Nashville, TN: Abingdon.

W

Wisdom, Word of

Since the Pentecostal and charismatic tradition believes in the present reality of the grace gifts of the Spirit, it is important to understand the "word of wisdom" (1 Corinthians 12:8). It is difficult to be certain as to its exact nature in that the gift is mentioned only once in the New Testament and then is not clearly defined.

Definition

The "word of wisdom" (*logos sophias*) is one of the gifts of the Holy Spirit, an utterance inspired by the Holy Spirit to articulate the hidden yet revealed wonder of the crucified and resurrected Lord Jesus. It appears first in Paul's list in 1 Corinthians 12: 8–10 and is coupled with the "word of knowledge" (*logos gnōseōs*), which is also a manifestation of the Spirit: "To one is given through the Spirit *the utterance of wisdom,* and to another the utterance of knowledge according to the same Spirit" (1 Corinthians 12:8, RSV, emphasis added throughout).

The gift is not the possession of wisdom per se but rather the verbal expression of wisdom in the Christian community engaged in corporate worship. The term "word" (*logos*) is parallel here to the term "utterance" or "oracle" (*logion*) in 1 Peter 4:10 as a "Spirit inspired utterance...spoken by the charismatic" (Kittel 1967, 139). Paul regards this manifestation of the Spirit, along with the other manifestations of the Holy Spirit, as a "gift of grace," "act of service," and "operation" (verses 4–6) for the "common good" (verse 7), the building up of the Church (1 Corinthians 14:3) and the exaltation of the Lordship of Jesus (1 Corinthians 12:3). The "utterance of wisdom" is a revelation of the Spirit's activity in the community setting and expresses both the unity and diversity of the Godhead (verses 4–6) and the sovereign and powerful distribution of the Holy Spirit (verse 11). The purpose of the gift is for the well-being of the community as a whole and not primarily for the benefit of an individual. The utterance of wisdom, as well as the utterance of knowledge are derived from the inexhaustible treasure chest of Christ, "in whom are hidden all the treasures of *wisdom* and knowledge" (Colossians 2:3).

Original Situation

We suggest that Paul lists "utterance of wisdom" and "utterance of knowledge" at the head of this unsystematic list because of the Corinthians' fascination with wisdom and knowledge. It is striking that in this same epistle, Paul's first letter to the Corinthians, he uses a form of "wisdom" ("wise," "wiser") twenty-six times in the first three chapters alone. It appears that these words were catchphrases at Corinth and reveal an incipient Gnosticism; i.e., emancipation through "wisdom and knowledge" from a supposed dualism between evil matter and the spirit. Presumably, the Corinthians prized the possession of such speculative wisdom and knowledge that had set them free from human weakness and suffering discipleship into the life of the Spirit.

To the Corinthians who claimed to have "arrived" at the "End," Paul can only counter their false triumphalism with biting sarcasm and irony (1 Corinthians 4:6–13). While they think of themselves as mature adults, gifted with "spiritual" wisdom and knowledge, Paul can only relate to them as immature infants (1 Corinthians 3:1–2).

Paul affirms the Corinthian grace giftedness, that they lack nothing in terms of spiritual gifts, knowledge, and confirmation of the Spirit's activity (1 Corinthians 4:4–9). As Paul reminds them of their early days of Christian experience and witness, he reflects upon their initial calling that not many of them were *"wise* according to human standards" (1:26). He underscores the marvelous wonder that because they are "in Christ" they thereby participate in the *"wisdom* from God, righteousness, sanctification and redemption" (1:30). Paul recalls that his initial preaching to them was good news (gospel) and did not come to them as *"words of human wisdom"* (1:17). Paul had preached "Christ crucified," which he equates with the *"wisdom* of God," the "power of God" (1:23–24) and the "mystery of God" (2:1, 7). Paul makes the case crystal clear that his determination was to preach nothing other than "Christ crucified" (2:1) with the purpose in view that the bedrock of their faith might not be grounded in human *wisdom* but the power of God (2:5).

While Paul affirms the Corinthians' position "in Christ," he nevertheless takes them to task for their speculative "wisdom" and pride that removes them from a saving wisdom. Due to the fact that they believe that they have been transposed into a spiritual sphere above earthly mortals, they also assume that they are satiated with their gifts including "wisdom" and there is no more to come. To be sure, they have been enriched, entered the kingdom of God, and experienced the Spirit of God as the eschatological guarantee; however, Paul argues that they have not experienced the End, the consummation, including the resurrection (1 Corinthians 15). There is more that is yet to come in terms of human history and the Christian experience of being united with Christ. Citing Isaiah's warning (Isaiah 29:14), Paul labels their "supposed wisdom" as a *"wisdom of this world,"* which God will destroy (1 Corinthians 1:19). Paul heaps up rhetorical terms to summon various disputants to deal with his argument, "Where is the *wise man*? Where is the scholar? Where is the philosopher of this age?" (1:20 NIV). He summons the debaters to realize that God has countered "human wisdom" with the "wisdom of God" (1:20–21). The world does not know God through human wisdom but through *a wisdom that can only find its origin in God* (1:21). The Greeks, including many of the Corinthians, *"seek wisdom"* (1:22) but cannot find it, since wisdom can only be found in "Christ crucified" (1:23); they can only conclude that Christ crucified is "foolishness." For people in the first century as well as the twenty-first century, human religious wisdom seeks to appease God by religious performance, human activity, and

atonement of one sort or another. Christianity is the only religion wherein God makes the ultimate and vulnerable self-sacrifice in *The Crucified God* (Moltmann 1993). Paul's response to the religiously "wise" is that God's "foolishness" in the message of the cross is *wiser* than human wisdom analogous to the way that God's weakness and vulnerability in the cross is stronger than human power (1:24–25).

The message that infected the Corinthians was characterized as "persuasive words of human wisdom," which is contrasted with demonstration of the Spirit and power (2:4). The false wisdom is similarly called the "wisdom of this age" (2:6). In some manner, the Corinthians have "bought into" a wisdom that substantially deviated from the simple but powerful message of the cross.

In 2:10–16, Paul uses the analogy of the human person to express the need for a receptive faculty to understand the depths of God, including the wisdom and knowledge of God and the mind of God. Paul says that humans possess a human spirit. Correspondingly, one human can know the thoughts of another human by virtue of possessing a human spirit (2:11); this is what occurs in human communication. The key for communication lies in the shared experience of the human spirit. Correspondingly, if one wishes to understand the depths of God, including wisdom and knowledge, the human person needs to possess the receptive faculty—the Spirit of God. The Spirit of God is the faculty, which can be shared both by God and a human being. Thus, a person and community can be enriched by an utterance of wisdom, which God wishes to communicate, through the receptive faculty of the Holy Spirit.

Other Suggestions

Some Pentecostal and charismatic interpreters have argued that the word of wisdom is a particular revelation given to a worshipping community in a situation of difficulty or adversity when a wise word needs to be given. For example, Bittlinger has understood the manifestation as the following: "In a difficult or dangerous situation a word of wisdom may be given which resolves the difficulty or silences the opponent. It is not innate wisdom as a personal possession which is described here, but rather a word of wisdom given to someone in a specific situation" (Bittlinger 1967, 28). Support is garnered from examples such as Solomon's wise word to the two women (1 Kings 3:16–28) or Jesus' reply when His opponents sought to impale Him on the horns of a dilemma as to the legitimacy of paying taxes to Caesar (Luke 20:20–26). Harold Horton argues, "The Word of Wisdom is therefore the revelation, by the Spirit, of Divine Purpose; the supernatural declaration of the Mind and Will of God; the supernatural unfolding of His plans and Purposes concerning things, places, people, individuals, communities, nations" (Horton 1934, 57).

Other commentators link the word of wisdom with "teaching" or a "practical discourse, consisting mainly of ethical instruction and exhortation," parallel to the practical character of wisdom in the Old Testament (Barrett 1968, 285); "'Word of wisdom' is particularly needed in the preaching ministry of the Church" (Williams 1992, 353). The problems inherent for such specific interpretation are due to the fact that this is the only occurrence of the specific "word of wisdom" in the New Testament, the lack of precise definition of the manifestation of the Spirit, and the high frequency of the "wisdom" vocabulary earlier in 1 Corinthians.

Implications for the Church

If Paul borrows the language from the Corinthian pneumatics ("so-called spiritual ones") and reshapes and reinterprets their language, he may well intend that the church encourage verbal expressions, which highlight the saving wonder of Jesus' person and activity in the divine "foolishness, weakness and vulnerability." In the earlier chapters of 1 Corinthians, Paul hammers away at the paradoxes of divine wisdom, which are reflected in the crucified Christ, the messengers, and the recipients of the message—all are characterized by paradoxes: foolishness/power of God; wisdom of the world/wisdom of God; stumbling block and foolishness/power and wisdom of God; foolishness of God/wiser than humans; weakness of God/stronger than humans; calling of God/not many wise; weakness, fear, trembling/persuasive words/demonstration of the Spirit and power; wisdom of this age/being nullified; words taught by human wisdom/words taught by the Spirit. In the light of the shared faculty of the Holy Spirit by human beings and God, an "utterance of wisdom" may be given to a person in the Christian community that will explain, explicate, and illuminate the Church as to the marvelous wonder of Jesus' life, death, Resurrection, and exaltation—all in the context of the paradoxical nature of the Christian life—in between the ages of the "already but not yet." The people of God, gathered in community and open to the fresh inspiration of the Spirit, may be led into fresh understanding of the wonder of the person of Jesus and meaning of the Jesus event. As opportunity is given for expression, the Spirit can illumine gifted persons to convey a reverential awe in the depths of God, which the Spirit communicates in the context of the gathered community.

J. Lyle Story

See also Charismata; Gifts of the Spirit; Preaching; Scripture, Holy

Further Reading

Barrett, C. K. (1968). *First epistle to the Corinthians*. New York: Harper & Row Publishers.

Bauer, W., Arndt, W. F., & Gingrich, F. W. (1969). *A Greek-English lexicon of the New Testament and other early Christian literature*. Chicago: The University of Chicago Press.

Bittlinger, A. (1967). *Gifts and graces*. Grand Rapids, MI: William B. Eerdmans Publishing Company.

Bittlinger, A. (1973). *Gifts and ministries*. Grand Rapids, MI: William B. Eerdmans Publishing Company.

Conzelmann, H. (1969). *1 Corinthian*. Philadelphia: Fortress Press.

Fee, G. (1987). *The first epistle to the Corinthians*. Grand Rapids, MI: William B. Eerdmans Publishing Company.

Fee, G. (1993). Gifts of the spirit. *Dictionary of Paul and his letters*. Downers Grove, IL: InterVarsity Press.

Fee, G. (1994). *God's empowering presence*. Peabody, MA: Hendrickson Publishers.

Gee, D. (1972). *Concerning spiritual gifts*. Springfield, MO: Gospel Publishing House.

Horton, H. (1934). *The gifts of the spirit*. Springfield, MO: Gospel Publishing House.

Kittel, G. (1967). "lovgion" (word, oracle). *Theological Dictionary of the New Testament* (Vol. IV, p. 139). Grand Rapids, MI: Wm. B. Eerdmans Publishing Co.

Koenig, J. (1978). *Charismata: God's gifts for God's people*. Philadelphia: The Westminster Press.

Martin, R. P. (1984). *The spirit and the congregation*. Grand Rapids, MI: William B. Eerdmans Publishing Company.

Moltman, J. (1993). *The crucified God*. Minneapolis, MN: Fortress Press.

Wilckens, U. (1971). Sophia. *Theological dictionary of the New Testament* (Vol. IV). Grand Rapids, MI: William B. Eerdmans Publishing Company.

Williams, J. R. (1992). *Renewal theology*, II. Grand Rapids, MI: Zondervan Publishing House.

Women

The early Pentecostal movement attracted women in large numbers because it held the promise of greater participation for women in ministry and leadership. In the early years, Pentecostal women pastored churches, served as missionaries and evangelists and had roles in governance and leadership. There appeared to be almost absolute freedom to pursue whatever direction they felt God was leading them. As time passed and the movement attempted to gain the respectability of middle-class denominations, the role of women was curtailed in most Pentecostal bodies. Women could still preach and exhort, but leadership and governing roles became limited and gender-stratified like the hierarchy Pentecostals once denounced in mainline bodies. Even where official dogma was egalitarian, unofficial tradition concerning "male-only" leadership was different. While written polity made all levels of ministry accessible to all qualified persons, unofficial custom held that only men could hold top positions and or be appointed as pastor of viable congregations.

Call to Minister

This original freedom resulted from several factors. Pentecostal eschatology supported the premillennial understanding that saw their revival as a fulfillment of the biblical prophecy of Joel 2:28. Early Pentecostals understood themselves as living in the last days, before the return of Christ to establish His millennial kingdom. They felt an urgency to recruit everyone in winning as many souls as possible. Women as well as men were enlisted to preach the gospel. They held that individuals were empowered through Holy Spirit baptism to do ministry as the Spirit willed. They believed God supernaturally anointed people, without regard to social constrictions or formal preparation. The proof of one's call lay in a testimony to such call and the fruit of Spirit-empowered ministry, rather than in formal ecclesiastical system. Those who could convincingly convey the Gospel message and displayed charismatic ministry gifts were enlisted into action. This understanding of ministry, coupled with general disdain for hierarchical structures and denominationalism, initially resulted in radical egalitarianism.

Competing theologies complicated women's status. Preaching women modeled themselves after their Holiness predecessors and held to a radical concept of equality of the sexes. However, restorationist elements sought to return the church to "New Testament simplicity." For some, an essential rudiment of this restoration was the following of Pauline restrictions on women's ministry. Pentecostals also sought to distance themselves from any association with modernity including ideas of the "new woman" coming into fashion as the movement took off. They saw the women's

movement as representing rebellion against God and threatening the God-ordained social order. By dress codes, social constraints, and rhetoric they ensured there was a distinction between the "unsaved" world and themselves.

Pentecostals tended to hold a conservative understanding of women's role in the family and society that deepened when the movement sought to align itself more closely with the broader Evangelical community. They believed the proper place for women was in the home. Married women were to be submissive to their husbands and support their work and ministry. Like other Evangelicals, they made a place for those few, exceptional women God might use in an extraordinary way.

In some Pentecostal denominations, women who sought pastoral places encountered an unofficial restriction. Women were free to "dig out" or plant congregations and nurture them to viability or to take on congregations at the point of failing and rebuild them. Once these congregations could sustain a full-time pastor and other financial obligations, leaders would replace her with a male pastor and send the woman to another community to dig out or repair another congregation. Over several decades, a woman might start or renew several congregations, but would never be allowed to take any of them past this point.

Charles Parham organized his Bible school in Topeka, Kansas, to "fit men and women to go to the ends of the earth to preach" (Robuck 1998, 39). He ordained women, as well as men, and commissioned them to ministry. Many of these women assisted Parham in his evangelistic campaigns throughout the country. Of the first group of workers who went to Houston to work with him, eight of the fifteen were women. Under Parham's leadership, a woman ushered in the movement shortly after midnight on 1 January 1901; Agnes Ozman became the first person to speak in tongues publicly with the understanding that it was the initial evidence of Holy Spirit baptism. After her Pentecostal experience, Ozman evangelized throughout the Midwest. She later married Philemon LaBerge, and the two conducted meetings in Kansas, Oklahoma, Washington, and Texas.

Azusa Street Revival

Women played prominent roles in the Azusa Street Revival. Lucy Farrow introduced William Seymour to the doctrine and the experience of tongues as evidence of Holy Spirit baptism. Farrow also introduced Seymour to Parham, beginning a relationship that bore fruit in the famous Azusa Street Revival. After Seymour went to Los Angeles, Farrow came to assist him at the revival. On leaving there, she was a regular speaker in Holiness conventions, established a church in Norfolk, Virginia, and then traveled as a missionary to Africa. Neely Terry met Seymour in Houston and on returning to Los Angeles, convinced her pastor to invite him to serve as associate pastor. Though he only preached one sermon before being locked out, it was this invitation that brought Seymour to that city.

Of the twelve elders initially appointed to handle administrative matters at the Azusa Street Mission, six were female and five were to play important roles in the upstart movement. Florence Crawford received the baptism of the Holy Spirit and was instantaneously healed from numerous ailments at the revival. Crawford was instrumental in distributing *The Apostolic Faith* newspaper that chronicled the revival's events to supporters. She was one of the first Azusa Street converts to take the Pentecostal message on the revival circuit, primarily moving through the Northwest, then going on to Minnesota and Canada. When she and Seymour disagreed about his decision to marry, Crawford moved to Portland, where she set up her own ministry, which she named the Apostolic Faith Church.

Clara Lum served as secretary and co-editor (along with Seymour) of *The Apostolic Faith* newsletter from 1906–1908. She, like Crawford, objected to Seymour's marriage to Jennie Moore, left the mission, and moved to Oregon. She is accused of corroborating with Crawford in stealing the national and international mailing lists. They later began republishing the newsletter.

Ophelia Wiley preached from time to time in the Azusa Street meetings and wrote articles for *The Apostolic Faith* newspaper. She also went out as part of evangelistic teams to spread the news of the revival in various cities throughout the northwestern United States.

Jennie Moore was one of the earliest adherents to experience the baptism of the Holy Spirit with tongues. She was an active leader in the revival and the church. She and Seymour later married and during his lifetime, she helped lead the congregation. Upon his death, she served as pastor of the then-dwindling mission.

Several women went out from Azusa Street as evangelists and missionaries. Ivey Campbell preached revivals throughout Ohio and Pennsylvania. Louisa Condit went first to Oakland, California, and then to Jerusalem. Lucy Leatherman conducted evangelistic meetings in Israel, Egypt, Palestine, Chile, and Argentina, where she helped establish the Church of God missions effort. Julia Hutchins had been the pastor whose church originally objected to Seymour's

A young Toraja woman in Indonesia prays at a Pentecostal church. *Courtesy of Douglas Hayward.*

identification of tongues with the baptism of the Holy Spirit and locked him out. She later participated in the Azusa Street Revival, then traveled as a missionary, preaching in several U.S. cities and in Liberia.

Women were actively involved in every aspect of the ministry of the couples who went out from Azusa Street as revivalists and missionaries. Abundio and Rosa Lopez worked the altars at the Azusa Street revivals and held street worship services in the Hispanic sections of Los Angeles. G.W. and Daisy Batman went as missionaries to Liberia. Holiness missionaries Samuel and Ardell Mead worked in Liberia for twenty years before the Azusa Street Revival. After having the experience of tongues, they returned to that country and helped spread the message.

Restricted Ministries

The Church of God in Christ came into being as Pentecostal body less than one year after the start of the

Azusa Street Revival. COGIC placed restrictions on the ministry of women from the outset. Drawing on his Baptist roots, COGIC founder, Charles Harrison Mason, saw women playing a "vital" but distinctive role from men. The organization preserved ordination, the office of pastor and title of preacher for men. Women expounding on Scripture were said to be teaching—not preaching—and were allowed to speak only from a secondary lectern, not from the pulpit. COGIC women are not ordained, but can be licensed as "evangelists" or "missionaries" to teach, primarily other women.

Many Pentecostal denominations granted women "limited ordination" or credentialing without governing authority. When the first General Council of the Assemblies of God met in 1914 to organize as a body, almost one-third of the delegates were women ministers. Despite the presence of such a large number of women, the body authorized their ordination only as evangelists and missionaries, explicitly denying them the right to serve in pastoral ministry or any position with authority over men. Later, women missionaries outside the United States were granted the right to perform funerals, marriages, baptisms, and the Lord's Supper, in an emergency and when a man was not available. Subsequently distinctions of ordination were dropped. However, women clergy in the United States were not given the right to perform the sacraments on an emergency basis until 1922. At various times the vote in the Council has been restricted to male ministers and then granted back to women. Yet, the practical limits on women's ministry were not lifted until 1935 when women were granted full ordination without restriction on serving or voting. Even this concession did not, however, materially improve the ministry of most women or reduce the predominance of male congregational and administrative leadership.

By the end of its second General Assembly of the Church of God (Cleveland, Tennessee), there were substantially more women adherents than men. Initially, women were frequent speakers and had full voting rights in the early General Assemblies, were encouraged to preach, teach, evangelize, and pastor, and were given the same rights and privileges as their male counterparts. However, increasingly restrictive measures went in place with every succeeding session. Within a few years, women's right to serve in leadership roles was reduced to a few highly prescribed functions. Women were precluded from taking part in Assembly business meetings and from performing marriages and taking part in the business and government of local congregations. Subsequently, the church developed different licenses for male and female evangelists. The male license granted authority to establish churches, baptize converts, administer the Lord's Supper, and foot washing; the female's to "do all the work that may devolve ...as a prophetess or *female minister...*" (*20th General Assembly Minutes* 1926, 109). The differentiation stopped late in the twentieth century. Women still only attain two of three ranks of ministry and are restricted from voting in the Assembly, governance in the local congregation, and holding regional and national offices.

Outstanding Leaders

The Pentecostal Holiness Church, which began in 1895, was among the first Pentecostal body to grant women full ordination. As late as 1935, the Open Standard Bible Churches, one of the bodies to be founded as an offshoot of Aimee McPherson's International Church of the Foursquare Gospel, also incorporated full ordination for women as part of its founding polity.

Faith healer Maria Woodworth Etter (1844–1924) was regarded by many Pentecostals as a powerful leader and speaker. Some of her largest revivals were held when she was nearly seventy years of age with attendance regularly running in the thousands. A staunch believer in faith healing, she was also a committed feminist who biblically defended women's right to preach. She organized congregations and conducted baptisms throughout her ministry, and in 1918, she founded the only church she ever pastored, the Woodworth-Etter Tabernacle in Indianapolis, Indiana.

At age twenty-two, three years after being miraculously healed from a debilitating illness, Carrie Judd Montgomery wrote her first book, *The Prayer of Faith*, which was translated into four languages. A year later, she began publishing *Triumphs of Faith: A Monthly Journal for the Promotion of Healing and Holiness* and continued to publish it until her death in 1946. Montgomery also established Faith Rest Cottage, in Buffalo, New York, and became involved in leading a network of faith homes in western New York. After moving to California, she established the House of Peace, a respite home for missionaries from more than one hundred mission boards and denominations; Beulah Chapel, where she held weekly worship services; Shalom Training School for Missionaries; and a children's home.

Marie Burgess began preaching in 1906 and by 1907 Parham sent her to New York City to evangelize and set up Glad Tidings Hall in the heart of Manhattan. Burgess subsequently married Robert Brown, and together they guided the church to becoming Glad Tidings Tabernacle, for a long time the most prominent Pentecostal Church in New York City.

Lillian Trasher served in North Africa for fifty-one years, until her death in 1961. Her ministry was largely to abused women and orphans. At one time, she housed fifty orphans in her home. She subsequently used donations from wealthy Coptic supporters to build and operate a home for orphans and women that by the time of her death had expanded to thirteen buildings including a church, a clinic and an elementary school.

Aimee Semple McPherson founded the International Church of the Foursquare Gospel, and her Angeles Temple in Los Angeles, California, regularly drew crowds in the thousands. She also established L.I.F.E. Bible College and became the first woman in the United States to own her own radio station and broadcast weekly religious services nationwide.

Two African-American women, Mary Magdalena Tate and Ida Robinson, established denominations that gave a prominent role to the leadership of women. Tale founded the Church of the Living God Pillar and Ground of the Truth in Tennessee in 1907; Robinson established the Mount Sinai Holy Church of America in Philadelphia in 1924.

Decline

Despite these accomplishments by outstanding women, since World War II the actual number of women who answer the call to public ministry and leadership or attempt to move beyond the limited roles prescribed for them continues to decline. Few Pentecostal women serve as senior pastors. Most who do lead smaller rural churches or urban storefront congregations. Pentecostal women enter seminary in markedly smaller numbers than do their mainline counterparts. As the ministry moved from a primarily voluntary vocation to a paid occupation, Pentecostal women were much more likely to be bi-vocational than male colleagues or other women clergy.

Among factors contributing to this decline is fading eschatological, premillennial hope of the imminent return of Christ. With the realization that Jesus had not yet returned came the need for organizational structure. Loose sects formed denominations with written polity that incorporated some restrictions on women's ministry and leadership from the beginning. Built into more pronounced structures, "professionalization" of ministry with differing criteria for credentialing men and women, and hierarchical ranks of ministry with dual gender-based tracks are among a variety of mechanisms for precluding women's full participation.

ESTRELDA ALEXANDER

See also Azusa Street Revival; Feminism; Ministry; Society, Pentecostal Attitudes toward

Further Reading

20th General Assembly Minutes (p. 109). (1926). Cleveland, TN: Church of God Publishing House.

Alexander, E. (2002). *Gender and leadership in the theology and practice of three Pentecostal women pioneers.* Unpublished doctoral dissertation, The Catholic University of America, Washington, DC.

Anderson, R. M. (1992). *Vision of the disinherited: The making of American Pentecostalism.* Peabody, MA: Hendrickson Publishers.

Barfoot, C. H., & Sheppard, G. T. (1980). Priestly vs. prophetic religion: The changing roles of women clergy in classical Pentecostal churches. *Review of Religious Resources, 22*(1), 2–17.

Blumhofer, E. (1991). Women in Evangelicalism and Pentecostalism. In M. May (Ed.), *Women and church: The challenge of ecumenical solidarity in an age of alienation* (p. 4). New York: William B. Eerdmans Publishing Co.

Clemmons, I. (1996). *Bishop C. H. Mason and the roots of the Church of God in Christ.* Bakersfield, CA: Pneuma Life Publishers.

Epstein, D. M. (1993). *Sister Aimee: The life of Amy Semple McPherson.* New York: Harcourt, Brace, Jovanovich.

Hyatt, S. C. (2001). Spirit filled women. In V. Synan, *The century of the Holy Spirit: 100 Years of Pentecostal and charismatic renewal.* Nashville, TN: Thomas Nelson Publishers.

Poloma, M. (1989). *The Assemblies of God at the crossroads.* Knoxville: University of Tennessee Press.

Robuck, D. (1998). Loose the Women. *Christian History, 58* 17:2, 39.

Scanzoni, L., & Setta, S. (1981). Women in evangelical, Holiness and Pentecostal Traditions. In R. Ruether & R. Keller (Eds.), *Women in Religion in America, Vol 3, 1900–1968* (pp. 223–235). Cambridge, MA: Harper and Row Publishers.

Tucker, R., & Liefield, W. (1987). *Daughters of the church: Women and ministry from New Testament times to the present.* Grand Rapids, MI: Zondervan Publishing House.

Worship

It has been said that the worship service is the heart of Pentecostalism, a statement that is borne out in the writings of early Pentecostals who paint, over and over again, a picture of a worshipping community experiencing the awe, wonder, and joy of the Holy Spirit.

As in the early church, worship of and service to God in Pentecostal-Charismatic Christianity are based on the experience of the inbreaking of a heavenly reality. Through the Holy Spirit, the presence of God is experienced in a tangible way.

> When we receive the baptism with the Holy Spirit, we may sing in tongues, because the Lord drops down sweet anthems from the paradise of God, electrifying every heart . . . the Lord simply touches us by His mighty Spirit and we have no need of organs or pianos, for the Holy Ghost plays the piano in all our hearts . . . It is so sweet. It is heaven below. (*The Apostolic Faith* 1906, 2)

Worshippers testify about sinners being saved, sicknesses healed, relationships restored. The distinctive aspect of the Pentecostal-Charismatic worship service is an anticipation of the divine movement of the Spirit to restore, heal, and forgive a broken humanity. The services are full of energy, hand-clapping, and enthusiastic singing. Although the buildings in which they gather do not contain much imagery, the bodily postures of believers are rich in symbolism: hands are raised (an ancient Christian posture), and others kneel and sometimes fall prostrate before a holy God. Worship involves mind, body, and soul.

In the encounter with the divine, earthly categories of time and space become relative. This has especially been the case in times of revival. It is reported that the meetings at Azusa Street continued "all day and into the night." People from all over the world visited the Azusa Street meetings, and the message of Pentecost soon spread to Scandinavia, Africa, and all over the world. People assembled in houses, halls, churches—wherever an appropriate venue could be found—to worship and seek God for the baptism in the Holy Spirit, the gift of power upon the sanctified life. Believers were willing to wait on God and to seek him earnestly for this precious experience.

Affirmation of Early Christian Worship

Pentecostal-Charismatic believers view their worship experience as a continuation of the way early Christians worshipped God and experienced the baptism in the Spirit. This is reflected in the first paragraph of the very first edition of *The Apostolic Faith* (the newspaper of the early Azusa Street Mission in Los Angeles): "Pentecost has surely come and with it the Bible evidences are following, many being converted and sanctified and filled with the Holy Ghost, speaking in tongues as they did on the day of Pentecost" (1906, 1).

It is clear that the supernatural gifts of the Spirit did not cease in early post–New Testament Christianity. In his writing *Against Heresies*, Irenaeus of Lyons stated the following around 180 CE:

> For this reason does the apostle declare, "We speak wisdom among them that are perfect," terming those persons "perfect" who have received the Spirit of God, and who through the Spirit of God do speak in all tongues, as he used himself also to speak. In like manner we do also hear many brethren in the Church, who possess prophetic gifts, and who through the Spirit speak all kinds of languages, and bring to light for the general benefit the hidden things of men, and declare the mysteries of God, whom also the apostle terms "spiritual," they being spiritual because they partake of the Spirit. (Roberts & Donaldson 1886, 531)

Elsewhere, Irenaeus details the various gifts of the Spirit that may be bestowed on believers, including the ability to "drive out devils" as well as "see visions, and utter prophetic expressions." Some may "heal the sick by laying their hands upon them," and "the dead even have been raised up" (Roberts & Donaldson 1886, 409).

At the start of the third century, Tertullian describes in his *Treatise on the Soul* how the gifts operated in the midst of a worship service:

> We have now amongst us a sister whose lot it has been to be favoured with sundry gifts of revelation, which she experiences in the Spirit by ecstatic vision amidst the sacred rites of the Lord's day in church: she converses with angels, and sometimes even with the Lord; she both sees and hears mysterious communications; some men's hearts she understands, and to them who are in need she distributes remedies. Whether it be in the reading of Scriptures, or in the chanting of psalms, or in the preaching of sermons, or in the offering up of prayers, in all these religious services matter and opportunity are afforded to her of seeing visions. (Roberts & Donaldson 1976, 188)

A study of the supernatural charisms in the worship of the early church reveals how positively the Church Fathers wrote about them. The early church vigorously debated many issues—for example, the Eucharist—but not the charismata. The gifts of the Spirit were uncontroversial, and when the presence of the charisms declined, the increasing sinfulness of believers was seen to be the cause. This insight is important in understanding Pentecostal-Charismatic worship. Pentecostals emphasize that the supernatural gifts of the Spirit—the distinctive feature of Pentecostal-Charismatic worship—are not foreign to worship, but have been an essential part of Christian spirituality from the time of the early church.

Transcultural and Transdenominational

Although the Pentecostal movement started with only a few people in 1901, it has grown to become the second largest Christian tradition, exceeded in numbers only by Roman Catholicism. Not only classical Pentecostals but also millions of Christians in mainline denominations and nondenominational churches actively affirm the charismatic dimensions of the work of the Holy Spirit.

One of the most significant developments of the twentieth century was the charismatic renewal in the Roman Catholic Church. The renewal started at Duquesne University in 1967, spread to the University of Notre Dame, and quickly grew in size and influence in the church. On Pentecost Monday, 1975, Pope Paul VI addressed ten thousand Catholic charismatics with these words: "How then could this spiritual renewal not be a 'chance' for the church and the world…it ought to reopen its closed lips to prayer and open its mouth to song, to joy, to hymns, and to witnessing" (Synan 1997, 252).

Today Pentecostal-Charismatic believers include worshippers from the farthest corners of the earth, representing the most divergent nationalities and ethnic groups. The Pentecostal-Charismatic movement has influenced the way almost all Christian traditions worship today. People worship in ways appropriate to their specific cultural settings, but despite any cultural differences, Pentecostal-Charismatic worship distinguishes itself by the vibrancy and immediacy of the worship experience. God is present in their midst and people are no longer relegated to commemorating the experiences of saints who met God in the past. Male and female, black and white, young and old, rich and poor—all experience and enjoy God's liberating and empowering presence in the here-and-now. Such worship is an earthly participation in a heavenly reality.

Freedom and Order

"What then shall we say, brothers and sisters? When you come together, everyone has a hymn, or a word of instruction, a revelation, a tongue or an interpretation. All of these must be done for the strengthening of the church" (1 Corinthians 14:26, TNIV). Pentecostal-Charismatic worship is undergirded by a deep desire for God's presence in the midst of the body of believers, functioning through the gifts of the Spirit. Pentecostal and charismatic believers from all cultures share the conviction that the Holy Spirit must be able to operate in a spontaneous way in every worship service.

But leaders soon became aware of the potential problems such freedom and liberty in worship services can create. To try to set an appropriate tone at the Whitsuntide Pentecostal Convention held each year in Sunderland, England, from 1908 to 1914, participants were asked to sign the following declaration:

> I declare that I am in full sympathy with those who are seeking "Pentecost" with the sign of tongues. I also undertake to accept the ruling of the chairman …
>
> Prayer and Praise should occupy at least one third of our meetings for the Conference.
>
> As to choruses it is suggested that, as far as possible, they shall be left to the leader to commence or control, and friends are asked to pray (silently) that he may be led aright. Confusion is not always edifying, though sometimes the Holy Spirit works so mightily that there is a Divine flood which rises above barriers. (Hudson 1998, 179–180)

This bit of guidance provided a sense of order and allowed the Spirit to operate in all its fullness.

Music and a Sense of Awe

Fervent, spiritual singing has always been an important part of worship in the Pentecostal-Charismatic tradition, as it was in those branches of Christianity that preceded the Pentecostal revivals and had an important influence on the movement. As an intimate expression of praise, adoration, and thanksgiving, worship music reflects the culture, language, and age of worshippers, and the value of contemporary music styles has always been recognized in this movement. But despite the wide variety of music used in Pentecostal-Charismatic services, certain songs are sung all over the world; inspired by the Holy Spirit, these songs have become a transcultural way of worshipping the living God who is believed to inhabit the praises of His people (see Psalm 22:3).

Music plays an important role in Pentecostal-Charismatic worship services in facilitating the use of spiritual gifts. Songs that typically have simple lyrics but great emotional intensity are sung as worshippers wait on the Spirit to move through the gifts of tongues and interpretation of tongues, prophecy, words of knowledge, and gifts of healing. The congregation may

Indigenous Papua New Guineans at a Pentecostal service. *Courtesy of Douglas Hayward.*

also start singing in tongues (see 1 Corinthians 14:15, where Paul affirms, "I will sing with my spirit, but I will also sing with my mind"). During these moments in which the congregation sings in perfect harmony an unlearned song in a "heavenly language," God's presence is sensed in a special way.

God is spirit, and his worshipers must worship in spirit and in truth.

John 4:24 (New International Version)

The Pentecostal-Charismatic experience of singing to God both in earthly languages and "with the voices of angels" (Ensley 1977, 13) comports with the experience of the early church. Basil, for example, wrote (*Epistulae* 2, 2; *The Fathers of the Church*, Vol. 13, 7), "What, then, is more blessed than to imitate on earth the choirs of angels...to glorify the Creator with hymns and songs." Similarly Chrysostom (*In Psalmos* 8, 1) affirmed: "For when we sing the angels blend their voices with ours and we blend our voices with theirs; for the angels of heaven don't have anything else to do but sing the praises of God eternally." This singing deeply moved people, as witnessed by Augustine when he told about the profound effect congregational singing had on him in the days following his conversion: "How abundantly did I weep to hear those hymns of thine, being touched to hear those hymns of

thine, being touched to the very core by thy sweet Church songs" (Ensley 1977, 13–14).

Pentecostals testify to holy moments when God's presence can be "seen" in a supernatural way. Howard Goss, for example, relates that on visiting William H. Durham's North Avenue Mission in Chicago, a "thick haze...filled the top third of the Auditorium," and people fell to the ground in awe. A similar phenomenon was reported by A. J. Tomlinson in August 1908 in Chattanooga and also in Cleveland, Tennessee. Tomlinson described his experience in Cleveland: "I seemed to see a kind of blue vapor, or mist, settle down on the congregation, and people turned pale" (Wacker 2001, 103).

Crumbling Social Barriers

Traditional social barriers fell away when those in the Pentecostal movement began to experience God's presence. Remarkable equality prevailed in worship services. Women played a prominent role, freely testifying and even preaching. A United Holy Church bishop, Henry L. Fisher, noted in his diary for Sunday, 23 April 1922: "Conducted services at Mt Zion Holy church all day Sisters Delk of Norfolk VA and Harper of Kinston NC did the preaching Had a very large crowd attending" (Wacker 2001, 104). In the early days of the Azusa Street Revival, black and white believers mixed freely and harmoniously. Children testified about their experiences of Spirit baptism and were even asked by adults to deliver the principal address at worship services. Pentecostal believers realized that all people can be chosen vessels through whom the Holy Spirit may choose to speak.

Looking back at the early days of Pentecostal worship, Wacker (2001, 111) succinctly observed: "Pentecostal worship was more than it seemed. Outsiders saw only fanaticism, but insiders saw more. They discerned order within disorder, reason within unreason." Today the Pentecostal-Charismatic movement remains a worshipping community. Communal worship is highly valued, not only as an opportunity to meet with brothers and sisters in the Lord, but as a chance to experience something of heaven itself through the presence and work of the Spirit.

PETRUS J. GRÄBE

See also Music; Praise; Prayer

Further Reading

Aghahowa, B. E. (1996). *Praising in black and white: Unity and diversity in Christian worship*. Cleveland, OH: United Church Press.

The Apostolic Faith. (1906, September).

Blumhofer, E. L., Spittler, R. P., & Wacker, G. (Eds.). (1999). *Pentecostal currents in American Protestantism*. Urbana/Chicago: University of Illinois Press.

Ensley, E. (1977). *Sounds of wonder: Speaking in tongues in the Catholic tradition*. New York: Paulist Press.

Horton, W. H. (1972). *Pentecost yesterday and today*. Cleveland, TN: Pathway Press.

Hudson, D. N. (1998). Worship: Singing a new song in a strange land. In K. Warrington (Ed.), *Pentecostal Perspectives* (pp. 177–203). Carlisle, UK: Paternoster Press.

Kydd, R. (1984). *Charismatic gifts in the early Church*. Peabody, MA: Hendrickson.

Roberts, A., & Donaldson, J. (Eds.). (1886). Irenaeus: Against heresies. In *The Ante-Nicene Fathers: Vol. 1. The Apostolic Fathers*. Grand Rapids, MI: Eerdmans.

Roberts, A., & Donaldson, J. (Eds.). (1976). Tertullian: A treatise on the soul. In *The Ante-Nicene Fathers: Vol. 3. Latin Christianity*. Grand Rapids, MI: Eerdmans.

Suurmond, J.-J. (1995). *Word and Spirit at play: Towards a Charismatic theology* (2nd ed.). Grand Rapids, MI: Eerdmans.

Swanson, R. N. (Ed.). (1999). *Continuity and change in Christian worship*. Suffolk, UK: Boydell Press/Ecclesiastical History Society.

Synan, V. (1997). *The Holiness-Pentecostal tradition* (2nd ed.). Grand Rapids, MI: Eerdmans.

Synan, V. (2001). *The century of the Holy Spirit: 100 years of Pentecostal and Charismatic renewal, 1901–2001*. Nashville, TN: Thomas Nelson.

Wacker, G. (2001). *Heaven below: Early Pentecostals and American culture*. Cambridge, MA: Harvard University Press.

List of Contributors

Adogame, Afe
University of Bayreuth
Africa, East

Aker, Benny C.
Assemblies of God Theological Seminary
Born Again

Akinade, Akintunde E.
High Point University
African Initiated Churches

Alexander, Estrelda Y.
Regent University School of Divinity
Race Relations
Women

Alexander, Paul Nathan
Southwestern Assemblies of God University
Pacifism and Peace

Ayegboyin, Deji Isaac
University of Ibadan
Asceticism

Bartlotti, Leonard N.
CAPITAA
Islam, Relationship to

Bennett, James
Southwest Missouri State University
Nationalism

Berg, Robert A.
Evangel University
Judaism, Relationship to
Memphis Miracle
Non-Pentecostal Christians, Relationship to

Bergunder, Michael
University of Heidelberg
India

Bryant, Hershel O.
Mt. Olive Road Church of God
Discernment, Spiritual
Filled with the Spirit

Burger, Isak
Apostolic Faith Mission of South Africa
Africa, South

Burgess, Ruth
Missouri State University
Enculturation
Feminism

Burgess, Stanley M.
Regent University
Antecedents of Pentecostalism
Holy Spirit
Neocharismatic Movements
Orthodoxy, Eastern
Tears, Gift of

Castleberry, Joseph L.
Assemblies of God Theological Seminary
Knowledge, Word of

Cleeton, Elaine R.
State University of New York, Geneseo
Capitalism
Rich and Riches
Social Transformation

Cole, David L.
Eugene Bible College
Dialogues, Catholic and Pentecostal
Ecumenism and Ecumenical Movement

Doak, Brian R.
Southwest Missouri State University
Liberation Theology
Marxism
Oil, Anointing with
Protestantism

Dooley, John E.
Apostles Lutheran Church
Anoint, Anointing

Duncan, C. Philip
King's Chapel Christian Center
Protestantism

Embree, David E.
Southwest Missouri State University
Contextualization

Emerick, Christopher C.
Regent University
Ministry
Miracles, Gifts of

Fichtenbauer, Johannes
Independent Scholar
Messianic Jews

Fox, Charles R., Jr.
Regent University
Interpretation of Tongues

Gräbe, Petrus J.
Regent University
Scripture, Holy
Worship

Griffin, William P.
Evangel University
Oil, Anointing with

Hayward, Douglas
Biola University
Oceania

Hedlund, Roger E.
Mylapore Institute For Indigenous Studies
Indigenous Churches

Henderson, James H.
Regent University
Deliverance
Exorcism

Hittenberger, Jeffrey S.
Vanguard University
Education

Hocken, Peter
Independent Scholar
Europe

Horton-Parker, H. S.
Regent University
Creation, Re-creation

Hudson, Neil
Regents Theological College
Art

Irvin, Dale T.
New York Theological Seminary
Fundamentalism

Johnston, Robin M.
Gateway College of Evangelism
Latter Rain

Jones, Robert P.
Southwest Missouri State University
Liberalism

Kagarise, Robby J.
Living Water Family Worship Center
Experience, Theology of

Kantel, Donald J.
Africa Conservancy
Laughter, Holy
Social Taboos

Kay, William K.
King's College, London
Europe

Kennedy, John R.
Southwest Missouri State University
Anti-intellectualism
Slavery

Kimbrell-Williams, Martha S.
Regent University
Prayer

Klaus, Byron D.
Assemblies of God Theological Seminary
Fruit of the Spirit

Kowalski, David
Assemblies of God
Ecstacy
Enthusiasm

Kuhns, Erin D.
Duke University
Dissent
Entrepreneurs, Religious

LaPointe, Jessica A.
Berkshire Publishing Group
Azusa Street Revival

Lewis, B. Scott
Regent University School of Divinity
Middleton, Ohio
Evil, Problem of

Lewis, Paul W.
Asia Pacific Theological Seminary
China
Church Growth
Evangelism

Logan, James H., Jr.
Kingdom Fellowship Christian Center
Black Pentecostalism

Ma, Julie
Asia Pacific Theological Seminary
Animism

Ma, Wonsuk
Asia Pacific Theological Seminary
Asia, East
Korea

Macchia, Frank D.
Vanguard University of Southern California
Baptism in the Holy Spirit
Binding and Loosing
Church, Theology of the
Doctrine, Development of
Glossolalia

Massey, David J.
Regent University
Baptism, Water
Trinitarianism

McClymond, Michael J.
Saint Louis University
Revival and Revivalism

Michaels, J. Ramsey
Southwest Missouri State University
Charismata
Gifts of the Spirit

Mittelstadt, Martin William
Evangel University
Christology

Moore, S. David
Regent University School of Divinity
Historiography
Shepherding and Discipleship Movement

Newberry, Warren
Assemblies of God Theological Seminary
Initiation Rites

Newberg, Eric N.,
Regent University
Charismatic Movement
Persecution and Martyrdom

Nicholson, Joseph
Evangel University
Music

Nolivos, Eloy H.
SEMISU/Seminario Sudamericano
Hispanic Pentecostalism

Padilla, Elaine
Regent University
Pentecostal Theology

Palmer, Michael D.
Evangel University
Ethics (Social, Sexual)
Philosophy and Theology

Percy, Martyn
Ripon College
Great Britain
Media (Television, Radio, Internet)

Phelps, Mark Anthony
Drury University
Africa, North (and the Middle East)

Phillips, Wade H.
Independent Scholar
Apostle, Apostolic

Prakash, Edith Dhana
Regent University
Praise

Prosser, Peter E.
Regent University
Dispensationalism
Eschatology

Railey, James H.
Assemblies of God Theological Seminary
Initial Evidence

Roamba, Jean-Baptiste
Regent University
Africa, West

Robinson, Benjamin I.
Independent Scholar
Laity, Clergy

Rodgers, Darrin J.
Fuller Theological Seminary
Pentecostalism, Classical

Rossi, Teresa Francesca
Pontifical University St. Thomas Aquinas, Rome
Communion (Eucharist)
Religious Life
Saints

Ruthven, Jon Mark
Regent University School of Divinity
Cessationism
Covenant
Faith, Gift of
Prophecy, Gift of

Satyavrata, Ivan Morris
Southern Asia Bible College
Globalization of Pentecostalism

Segraves, Daniel L.
Urshan Graduate School of Theology
Oneness Theology

Service, Steven R.
Regent University
Hands, Laying on of

Simmons, Dale H.
Judson College
Positive Confession Theology

Starner, Rob
Central Bible College
Prosperity Theology
Social

Story, J. Lyle
Regent University School of Divinity
Demon Possession, Casting out Demons
Visions and Dreams
Wisdom, Word of

Suico, Joseph
Asia Pacific Theological Seminary
Philippines

Swensson, Eric
Holy Trinity Lutheran Church
Preaching

Syler, Eleanor G.
Evangel University
Blessing

472

Synan, Vinson
Regent University School of Divinity
America, North
Sanctification
Second Work of Grace

Thomas, Sherry L.
Washington University
Perfection and Perfectionism

Warrington, Keith
Regents Theological College
Healing, Gifts of
Rituals

Wedenoja, William A.
Southwest Missouri State University
Anthropology (Theology of Humans)
Society, Pentecostal Attitudes toward

Whitehead, J. Charles
International Charismatic Consultation
Catholic Charismatic Movement

Wilson, Everett A.
Seminario Evangélico Español
America, Latin
Brazil

Yong, Amos
Bethel University
Ordinances and Sacraments

York, H. Stanley
Regent University
Renewal, Church

Index

Note: Main encyclopedia entries are indicated by **bold** type

Index